GREEK HISTORICAL INSCRIPTIONS 478–404 BC

GREEK HISTORICAL INSCRIPTIONS 478–404 BC

Edited
with introduction, translations, and commentaries
by

ROBIN OSBORNE
and
P. J. RHODES

OXFORD
UNIVERSITY PRESS

OXFORD
UNIVERSITY PRESS

Great Clarendon Street, Oxford, OX2 6DP,
United Kingdom

Oxford University Press is a department of the University of Oxford. It furthers the University's objective of excellence in research, scholarship, and education by publishing worldwide. Oxford is a registered trade mark of Oxford University Press in the UK and in certain other countries

First published 2017
First published in paperback 2020

Published in the United States of America by Oxford University Press
198 Madison Avenue, New York, NY 10016, United States of America

British Library Cataloguing in Publication Data
Data available

Library of Congress Cataloging in Publication Data
Data available

ISBN 978–0–19–957547–3 (Hbk.)
ISBN 978–0–19–885445–6 (Pbk.)

PREFACE

We have been encouraged by the responses to our *Greek Historical Inscriptions, 404–323 BC* (2003) to move backwards and create a successor of the same kind to *A Selection of Greek Historical Inscriptions to the End of the Fifth Century BC* by Russell Meiggs and David Lewis (1969, reissued with *addenda* 1988). The concision of their commentaries, and the amount of more recently discovered material which deserved to be included, has led us to contemplate two volumes, and we begin with inscriptions from the period 478–404. Since with a lack of foresight we began the numbering in our previous collection at 1, for this collection we have reversed the order of our names, and to foreshadow another volume, devoted to the archaic period, we have here started our numbering at 101.

It is, of course, important that readings and restorations should be checked and not passed on uncritically from one edition to another. We have provided the best texts that we can, but we have no reason to think that we should be more accurate and successful than our predecessors in reading difficult stones (indeed, some stones have deteriorated, so that it has to be accepted that letters could be read in the past which cannot be read now), and in most cases we have not examined the stones ourselves: the purpose of our collection is to make inscriptions available and intelligible to people who need to use them, not to re-edit the texts from scratch. Many of our texts have recently been the subject of expert and painstaking work by Dr A. P. Matthaiou, and we are extremely grateful to him for making the results of his work available to us and allowing us to use them.

We thank also all those who have helped us in deciding what texts to include, and on various matters concerning the texts which we do include: Mr F. G. G. Basso, Prof. J. H. Blok, Prof. M. H. Crawford, Dr C. V. Crowther, Dr A. Ellis-Evans, Prof. K. Hallof, Dr D. M. Lewis, Prof. R. C. T. Parker, Prof. L. Rubinstein, Dr R. J. E. Thompson and Dr H. R. Willey. We owe a particular debt to Dr S. D. Lambert for his constructive engagement throughout this project and for his extensive and valuable comments. We are indebted to those who have supplied and allowed us to reproduce photographs, who are indicated in the list of illustrations: particularly the Epigraphical Museum in Athens, from whose archives most of our photographs are derived, and among its staff Dr E. Choremi, Dr A. A. Themos and Mrs E. Zavvou; and Dr Matthaiou has helped us greatly in this respect too. And we are grateful to the Oxford University Press for waiting for us and for publishing this successor to its distinguished predecessors, and to the staff of the Press and the printers for the care which they have devoted to our book.

In ancient dates, 478–477 denotes a period spanning the two Julian years; 478/7 denotes a year beginning in 478 and ending in 477, and 47$\underline{8}$/7 and 478/$\underline{7}$ denote the earlier and the later part of such a year respectively.

Cambridge R. G. O.
Durham P. J. R.
March 2017

Changes in the 2020 paperback edition are limited to the correction of errors—so few that we fear that others still await detection.

R. G. O.
P. J. R.

CONTENTS

(Numbers in parentheses are those of the edition of Meiggs & Lewis)

PLATES

REFERENCES

ANCIENT TEXTS

Most abbreviations are those used in the fourth edition (2012) of the *Oxford Classical Dictionary*, and should cause no difficulty; but the following should be noticed:

Ar.	Aristophanes
Arist.	Aristotle
Ath. Pol.	[Aristotle], *Athenaion Politeia*

Where there is a choice between numbering systems, we use the following:

Aristotle, *Politics*	books in manuscript order (as in Oxford Text), then not chapters and sections but Berlin pages
Pausanias	sections within chapters as in M. H. Rocha-Pereira's Teubner text
Plutarch, *Lives*	sections within chapters as in Teubner and Budé texts (and not as in Loeb texts)
Strabo	Casaubon's pages followed by book, chapter and section numbers

MODERN WORKS

Numerals in **bold type** refer to the numbered items in this book.

Articles in periodicals are cited in sufficient detail for identification in the course of the book. In general we use the abbreviations of *L'Année philologique*, with the usual anglophone divergences (*AJP* for *AJPh*, etc.; also *BSA* for *ABSA*); but the publications of continental academies are abbreviated as *Abh. Berlin*, *Sb. Leipzig*, etc. (cf. *Ann. Pisa* of the Scuola Normale Superiore), the *Mitteilungen des Deutschen Archäologischen Instituts, Athenische Abteilung*, as *AM*, and the titles of Greek-language periodicals are given (abbreviated or in full) in the Greek alphabet.

Collections of inscriptions which we cite are listed in section 1 of the Bibliography, and other books which we cite in section 2, and except where we use shortened titles of a kind which will cause no difficulty we indicate in the Bibliography the abbreviations which we use.

INTRODUCTION

I

Nowadays inscriptions on stone or metal are used in two main contexts: on public buildings (to announce the identity of the building, or to record the laying of the foundation stone or the formal opening of the building), and on tombstones, war memorials, lists of officials or benefactors and the like. In the ancient world, with no printing or duplicating, or other modern means of communication, inscription was used not only for these purposes but for many others as well. Public announcements could not be made in newspapers or delivered to individual members of the public: either a proclamation had to be made at a meeting attended by large numbers of the citizens, or a text would be set up in the centre of the city in the expectation that members of the public would come and read it. Temporary notices—lists of candidates for office, proposals for new legislation and so on—were written on whitewashed boards, and have not survived for us to read; for permanent publication bronze or wood was sometimes used, but the normal medium was stone. For example, texts of a city's laws and decrees, of the religious calendars contained in its laws and of its alliances with other cities; schedules of work on a public building project, and accounts of public expenditure on the project; inventories of precious objects in the temple treasuries or of ships in the dockyards; epigrams commemorating a famous victory; honours voted to a native or foreign benefactor; lists of office-holders and benefactors—all these and comparable documents might be inscribed on stone for members of the public to see. However, by far the largest number of inscriptions are texts set up by private individuals—mostly dedications and funerary monuments—and these no less than public inscriptions provide information of importance for historians (in this collection we include only two truly private inscriptions, the gravestones **113** and **179**, but for inscriptions of individuals, albeit rulers, see **101**, **105**, **193**).

We have deliberately used the verb 'see' rather than 'read'. Though in theory the purpose of a published text is that it should be available to be read, some texts were published in such a way that they were not easy to read, and the purpose of a lengthy inventory of items received by one board of treasurers from its predecessors and transmitted to its successors may have been to serve as a symbolic demonstration that the board had done its duty as much as to furnish material for an investigator who wanted to check that none of the items had disappeared. Nevertheless, some other texts were laid out in ways designed to aid intelligibility (e.g. **135**. *B*); and we think it would be a mistake to make too much of the symbolic aspect of inscription and too little of the notion that texts were published so that they could be read.[1]

[1] On the symbolic aspects of publication see e.g. J. K. Davies and D. Harris in *Ritual, Finance, Politics ... D. Lewis*, 201–12 and 213–25; on this and on other aspects of publication see Rhodes, *G&R*^{2} xlviii 2001, 33–44, 136–53.

Expressions such as 'So that whoever wishes may know, the secretary shall write up this decree ... and place it ...' (τὸ δὲ φσέφισμα τόδε, ὅπος ἂν ἔ͂ι εἰδέναι τô[ι] βολομένοι, ἀναγράφσας ὁ γραμματεὺς ... καταθέτο ... : **167**. 26–7) are strictly compatible with either function.

Very large blocks of stone were sometimes used for extensive documents or series of documents (the first *stele* of the Athenian tribute quota lists, cf. **119** in this collection, measured about 3.583 × 1.105 × 0.385 m. = 11′ 9″ × 3′ 8″ × 1′ 3″, **160** measured about 1.39 × 0.61 × 0.145 m. = 4′ 7″ × 2′ 0″ × 5¾″), but Greek inscriptions were not necessarily 'monumental'. Very often the *stele* would be a slab of stone no larger than a modern tombstone (**120** measures 0.89 × 0.46 × 0.10 m. = 2′ 11″ × 1′ 6″ × 4″, **148** 0.64 × 0.31 × 0.12 m. = 2′ 1″ × 1′ 0″ × 4¾″), and both on these and on the larger *stelai* the text was usually inscribed in letters 0.005–0.01 m. = 0.2–0.4″ high.[2] Documents emanating from the public authorities were normally published at public expense; but sometimes a man who had been honoured would himself pay for the publication of his honours, and often an Athenian decree for another state would stipulate publication at that state's expense (e.g. **120**. 26–7; in **191**. 39–40 Athens pays for publication in Athens but the Samians are required to pay for publication in Samos). Publication was not cheap. In Athens costs are not specified in the fifth century, but in the fourth century it became common to specify in advance how much the state would spend on the *stele*: R&O 22, a large stone, cost 60 drachmas; 30 drachmas were allowed for the even larger R&O 64 and for the elaborate R&O 70, and also for the small R&O 77. The *stele* would be set up in a public place, commonly the acropolis (the rocky citadel, normally used for public inscriptions in Athens) or the agora (the main square) of the city. Sometimes texts would be inscribed not on a separate *stele* but, for example, on a building: e.g. **114**, at Selinus.

Although there had been earlier attempts on a small scale, the view that for Athens, with its unusually large body of texts, it should be possible to identify the work of particular stone-cutters from their particular idiosyncrasies was first seriously advanced by S. Dow, and has been followed up most thoroughly by S. V. Tracy. He has worked mostly on later texts, but he deals with fifth-century texts in *Studies Presented to S. Dow*, 277–82, in *Gestures ... A. L. Boegehold*, 351–63, and recently in his *Athenian Lettering of the Fifth Century* BC. In our collection see on **108**, and note the identification of the same hand in **181**, **185**, **190**, which offers some indication of the possible date of **190**. Identifications cannot always be certain, and Tracy himself remarks in one of his fourth-century studies that in that period 'many of these cutters inscribed letters which are very much alike'.[3] He claims to have been

[2] **114**, from a temple at Selinus, has lettering *c.*3 cm. = nearly 1¼″ high; Athens' 'Hecatompedon Inscription' of 485/4 (*IG* i[3] 4), on two reused metopes from a temple, has letters 2.0–2.5 cm. = ¾″–1″ high; larger letters would be used for headings, e.g. the first two lines of **191**. Some epigraphists use the Greek *stele* as the technical term for a comparatively thin slab and *cippus* (the Latin term for a marker, particularly of a grave or a boundary) as the technical term for a block which is more nearly square in cross-section, but the words were not used in antiquity in accordance with that distinction.

[3] Tracy, *Athenian Democracy in Transition: Attic Letter-Cutters of 340–290* BC, 2.

conservative in his assignments; some might still be challenged;[4] but he has pursued investigations of this kind more thoroughly and systematically than anybody else, and only a scholar who had been equally thorough and systematic could reject his assignments with confidence.[5]

Sometimes more than one copy of a text would be published—an alliance, naturally, would be published in each of the cities participating; **153** was published in two places within Athens, and **141** at Eleusis and on the acropolis in Athens—and where more than one copy of a text has been found it has become apparent that the Greeks lacked our notion of word-for-word accuracy: instead they seem to have had the potentially dangerous belief that, as long as the sense was correctly recorded, small differences in wording did not matter (see particularly **155** and **165** with commentary). In spite of that, however, it was the inscribed text rather than the original text in the archives which was in some sense the official text of a public document: thus the Thirty in Athens in 404 'took down from the Areopagus' the laws of Ephialtes and Archestratus (*Ath. Pol.* 35. ii), and some of the texts in our collection are reinscriptions of decrees which they had demolished (see **157**, **161**, **191**; and cf. **177**. *B*, which mentions the demolition of the original); the monetary agreement between Mytilene and Phocaea makes provision for changes on the *stele* (**195**); and, in the fourth century, in the prospectus of the Second Athenian League, Athens undertakes that if for cities which join 'there happen to be unfavourable *stelai* at Athens, the council currently in office shall have power to demolish them' (R&O 22. 31–5; cf. 39. 31–3).[6]

Some *stelai* have survived intact—unbroken and completely legible. Far more often, however, only part of the original *stele* survives, some letters even on the part that does survive are hard or impossible to read, and modern scholars have had to do their best to reconstruct the text. This is harder for the fifth century than later, because the repertoire of standard formulations is less than it became later, and until the later part of the twentieth century some scholars tended to be too adventurous in their restorations and too confident in their adventures. Where only a few letters on the edges of a *stele* are missing, restoration is easy, often inevitable; where large parts of the text are illegible and/or missing, reconstruction is far more difficult. If the historical context to which a document belongs can be identified, this may provide clues as to what the lost parts of the text should have contained. If a piece of standardised documentary language can be recognised, this can be reconstructed by comparison with other documents (though the Greeks could not retrieve a standard clause from a database, and variations tend to be found even within 'standard' formulaic expressions: compare, for instance, the different forms of the clause ordering the publication of an Athenian decree in **108**, **120**, **131**, **153**, **166**,

[4] Cf. the review of *Athenian Democracy in Transition* by M. B. Walbank, *Phoenix* li 1997, 79–81. For Walbank's own work on Athenian letter-cutters see e.g. *BSA* lxxxiv 1989, 395–405; lxxxv 1990, 435–47; cf. for the fifth century lxix 1974, 295 n. 3.

[5] S. V. Tracy & C. Papodysseus, *AJA*[2] cxiii 2009, 99–102, report promising results from the trial of a computer program to apply Tracy's criteria.

[6] Cf. Rhodes with Lewis, 3–4 with n. 4.

182, **184**, **185**, **186**, **187**, **188**, **191**). If two or three lines can be reliably restored, the approximate length of the lines is fixed, and this limits the possibilities of restoration in the rest of the document. In this period most Athenian decrees, and some decrees of other states, were inscribed in a style known as *stoichedon* (a genuine Greek word, though not used of inscriptions in any ancient text), with the letters regularly spaced on a grid, precisely the same number of letters in each line, and little or no punctuation: this, though it made the *stelai* more attractive as monuments, cannot have made for easy reading, but for us it has the advantage that very often a formulaic expression can be found which allows enough reconstruction at one point to reveal the exact number of letters to be restored in each line. With a few exceptions, where a text is fragmentary but of sufficient importance to deserve inclusion, we have limited ourselves in this collection to inscriptions where a substantial stretch of continuous text survives or can be securely reconstructed.

Beyond that, we have tried to choose texts which are both important in themselves and give an indication of the range available; and readers whose interests are thematic can use our texts and commentaries to study not only the main narrative thread of fifth-century history but such matters as political institutions and administrative organisation; religious cults and religious financing; coinage, building funds and regulations, trade agreements and other economic matters. Geographically, we have material from Athens and other states of the Greek mainland, from the Aegean islands and Crete, from Thrace, from western Asia Minor and from the Greek states of Sicily, though these and their Italian neighbours produced very few inscriptions at any date, and some of our texts with Sicilian and Italian origins were dedicated at Olympia (and we have Athenian texts concerned with Phaselis on the south coast of Asia Minor, Macedon, Sicily and Italy, and Carthage, and a Samian text concerned with Egypt). Many of our documents are inter-state treaties, or laws or decrees of single states (especially Athens, which in the fifth and fourth centuries inscribed public documents on a much larger scale than other states). However, our material includes texts from bodies within a state (demes, **107**, **134**, **159**; a gentilicial group, **108**) as well as from the state itself; from Athens we have financial documents issued by the *hellenotamiai* (**119**, **168**), by *epistatai* of public works (**135**, **145**, **181**), by boards of sacred treasurers (**134**, **138**, **148**, **169**, **170**, **174**, **180**); by a board of *logistai* (**160**) and by the *poletai* (**172**); and both from Athens and from elsewhere we have such items as commemorations of men who died in war (**109**, **111**, **129**; cf. celebrations of victory, **101**, **110**, **112**, **114**, **140**, **192**); religious regulations of various kinds (**106**, **107**, **108**, **115**, **141**, **143**, **146**, cf. the public imprecations in **102**); texts concerning trade **103**, **136**. From Athens we have the republication of Draco's homicide law (and other laws) at the end of the fifth century (**183**); rare though such texts are, we have two public inscriptions from Sparta (**128**, **151**); and we have the tomb monument of a Lycian dynast, which includes verses in Greek as well as texts in Lycian (**193**).

II

Since many of our texts are public documents of the Athenian state, and since other Greek states had constitutions which, whether democratic or oligarchic, were similar in their general pattern though different in their detail and their balance, some information on the mechanics of the fifth-century Athenian constitution will help to make the texts intelligible.

Since the reforms of Cleisthenes (508/7) the citizens of Athens had been organised in ten *phylai* ('tribes'). In what for some purposes was an official order,[7] these were:

I	Erechtheis	VI	Oeneis
II	Aegeis	VII	Cecropis
III	Pandionis	VIII	Hippothontis
IV	Leontis	IX	Aiantis
V	Acamantis	X	Antiochis

Each tribe consisted of three *trittyes* ('thirds'), in different parts of Attica; and the *trittyes* consisted of one or more *demoi* ('demes': local units), of which there were 139 altogether.[8] To be a citizen of Athens a man had to belong to a deme and to the *trittys* and the tribe of which that deme formed a part (membership of these units was hereditary, and by the end of the fifth century not all Athenians lived in the deme in which they were registered[9]). Demes and tribes, though perhaps not *trittyes*, acted as independent decision-making bodies, and sometimes published their decrees (**159**, and cf. **107**, **134**); bodies outside this structure, such as phratries and *gene*, at least in the fourth century (e.g. R&O 5), made and published their decisions in the same way). Beyond that, a good deal of Athens' governmental machinery was based on this structure.

The body with the ultimate right of decision in most matters was the *ekklesia* ('assembly'), open to all full (i.e. adult male) citizens, which probably by the time of the Peloponnesian War had forty regular meetings a year and could probably have extraordinary meetings in addition (*Ath. Pol.* 43. iii–vi):[10] for certain categories of business, affecting a named individual, a quorum of 6,000 was required. Since there are limits to what can be done by a large body meeting infrequently, day-to-day affairs were in the hands of the *boule* ('council') of five hundred. This body comprised fifty members from each tribe; within the tribe seats were allocated to demes approximately in proportion to their size, so that in the fourth century several small demes had one member each but the largest deme, Acharnae, had twenty-two (there

[7] First clearly attested in **129**, perhaps of 447: against the suggestion of A. E. Raubitschek that earlier there was a different order (*AJA*² lx 1956, 280–1 n. 4) see Pritchett, *Marathon*, 146–7.

[8] On demes generally see Whitehead *The Demes of Attica*.

[9] On mobility in general see Osborne, *OJA* x 1991, 231–52 = his *Athens and Athenian Democracy*, 139–67 ch. viii.

[10] See as the most recent items in a long debate E. M. Harris, *AJP* cxii 1991, 325–41 = his *Democracy and the Rule of Law in Classical Athens*, 103–18(–20) (in favour of the view given here); M. H. Hansen, *GRBS* xlvii 2007, 271–306 (with an alternative view).

is no good evidence on the assignment of members to demes in the fifth century, and some reason to think that fifth-century figures may have been different from fourth-century figures[11]). Appointment was made by lot from those who stood as candidates; service was for one year at a time, and no man could serve under the age of 30 or for more than two years in his life. Within the council, at any rate from the 450s the fifty members from each tribe in turn served as the *prytaneis* ('prytany': standing committee) for a tenth of the year, in an order fixed by lot; all business went to them in the first instance; each day one of their members was chosen, again by lot, to be *epistates* ('chairman'), and for twenty-four hours he and some of his colleagues were permanently on duty. In the fifth century one of the duties of the prytany and its chairman was to preside at meetings of the council and assembly.

In the fifth century all decisions of the Athenian state were made by the assembly, and could be regarded as *psephismata* ('decrees') if one thought of their mode of enactment, or in some cases as *nomoi* ('laws'), if one thought of what it was that had been enacted. (For the compilation of an up-to-date code of current *nomoi* at the end of the fifth century see **183**.) Every matter on which the assembly was to make up its mind was first discussed by the council, which drew up the assembly's agenda (if a new matter was first raised in the assembly, a proposal to be brought to a later assembly could be commissioned: e.g. **141**. 59–61). On each matter which it sent forward to the assembly the council issued its *probouleuma* ('preliminary deliberation'). Procedure becomes clearer in the fourth and later centuries, when what is stated in the published texts is more informative. Sometimes the *probouleuma* contained a positive recommendation, which the assembly might if it chose accept as it stood (e.g. R&O 24); on other occasions the council put a question to the assembly without making any recommendation of its own (e.g. R&O 91); sometimes the council made its own recommendation up to a point but left certain details open (e.g. R&O 2. 49–50, 60–1; cf. here **150**. 5–9, 29–32, where we do not know whether or not the motion was included in the *probouleuma*). The *probouleuma* was read out at the beginning of the debate in the assembly; then—whether it had contained a positive recommendation or not—members were free to propose alternative motions, to propose amendments to a motion already before the assembly (if an amendment was carried, it was published after the original motion which it modified, and sometimes but not always the text of the original motion was modified in the light of the amendment: see e.g. on **184**, **187**), or to amend a motion by taking it over and rewriting it (usually this can be reliably detected only in the rare cases where the original motion has been published with the final version, e.g. R&O 95).

When the assembly approved a recommendation of the council, in a 'probouleumatic decree', from the beginning of the 370s the council's probouleumatic formula, embodying the recommendation, was often left in the published version of the text (e.g. R&O 24), and the Athenians also continued using the formula recording the decree's enactment which was standard from the 450s to the end of the fifth century,

[11] See e.g. M. H. Hansen *et al.*, *Analecta Romana* xix 1990, 30; Osborne *Greece in the Making*², 285–7.

ἔδοξεν τῆι βουλῆι καὶ τῶι δήμωι, 'resolved by the council and the people'. In 'non-probouleumatic decrees', when the assembly did not approve a recommendation of the council (either because the council made a recommendation which it rejected or because the council made no recommendation) the Athenians in the fourth century took to using enactment formulae and motion formulae ('be it resolved by ...', in the body of the decree) which did not mention the council, such as ἔδοξεν τῶι δήμωι, 'resolved by the people' and δεδόχθαι τῶι δήμωι, 'be it resolved by the people' (cf. Rhodes, *Boule*, 66–78).

By the late fifth century the layout of an Athenian decree had become more or less standardised. Not every text contains every possible element, but in a complete text we should find the following:[12]

(i) The *stele* is often surmounted by a pediment or a horizontal moulding, and sometimes has a sculptured relief, often set in an architectural frame, above and/or below the text (**150** is the earliest instance here and no decree relief can certainly be dated earlier; it is likely that the practice began in the 420s). The style and detail of the sculpture can sometimes help to indicate the date of the inscription.[13]

(ii) **Invocation**: θεοί, 'Gods'—perhaps reflecting the prayer with which proceedings in the assembly began (e.g. **149**. *A*, *B*); and most Athenian decrees were published on the acropolis, under the eyes of the gods.[14] After those two instances, the four letters θ ε ο ι are regularly spread across the full width of the *stele* (e.g. **153**), and may (for instance) be inscribed on the moulding above the main inscribed surface. This can be found with documents other than decrees, e.g. **170**.

Some other states also mention (good) fortune in this position (e.g. R&O 14, 32). When the Athenians mention good fortune they do so in the main text of the decree (e.g. **131**. 40).[15]

(iii) **Heading**, in larger letters (for easy identification of text):[16]
secretary (e.g. **150**, **191**, in each case naming the secretary under whom it was decided to inscribe a *dossier* of decrees enacted at different times; **141**); or towards the end of the century secretary and archon (e.g. **182**, **183**).
subject of decree (e.g. **150**, **153**, **187**, **192**).

(iv) **Prescript** (formal details taken from the secretary's records):
enactment formula: for a decree of the assembly, from at any rate the 450s to the end of the century, 'resolved by the council and the people' (cf. above, pp. xx–xxi); for a decree of the council, 'resolved by the

[12] Cf. Rhodes, *Boule*, 64–5; Rhodes with Lewis, 4–5.
[13] On decree reliefs see Lawton, *Attic Document Reliefs*; Meyer, *Die griechischen Urkundenreliefs*.
[14] Prayer, cf. R. L. Pounder, in *Studies ... S. Dow*, 243–50; acropolis, cf. Osborne, in Goldhill & Osborne (edd.), *Performance Culture and Athenian Democracy*, 346–7, P. Liddel, *ZPE* cxliii 2003, 79–93.
[15] Cf. S. V. Tracy, *Hesperia* lxiii 1994, 241–4.
[16] For a study of varations in headings and prescripts see Henry, *Prescripts*.

council' (no instance in the fifth century; in the fourth century, e.g. R&O 91 §i);

prytany: the name of the tribe (for more precise dating its number in the year's sequence of ten prytanies can be added, as in financial documents such as **160**, but in the fifth century that information is not given in the prescripts of decrees);

secretary: in the fifth century he was a member of the council from a tribe other than the current prytany, serving for one prytany, and a year could be identified by naming the 'first secretary', i.e. the man who was secretary during the first prytany (e.g. **149**. *A*. 5–6; frequent in financial documents such as **160**);

chairman, who 'put to the vote';

archon: first found in the prescripts of **149**. *A* and *B* (433/2), where he is combined with the first secretary (cf. above), next in *IG* i³ 21 (426/5), then e.g. **166**, **182**, but not **186**;

proposer: almost always an individual, identified by name with no indication of his office if he currently held an office, with the verb *eipen* (literally 'spoke'); but we have four proposed by ad hoc drafting committees, *syngrapheis* (including **141**), two proposed by the generals (*IG* i³ 89. 55 sqq., 92), and **191** and the amendment to it proposed by the *prytaneis*.

(v) **Main text**:

sometimes beginning with an invocation of good fortune (cf. above);

191 is the earliest instance of what was later to become standard: first a motivation clause (but in **191** the motivation is coupled with a resolution to praise the honorands), followed by a motion formula, in **191** 'be it resolved by the council and the people';

and then the positive proposals, commonly ending with an invitation to the *prytaneion* (town hall) for envoys or the recipients of honours;

orders for the publication of the text.

(vi) **Amendments**:

were published after the original motion. They normally begin with:

proposer of amendment;

either 'in other respects in accordance with the council', when what is amended is a motion contained in the *probouleuma* (e.g. **153**. 51), or 'in other respects in accordance with [name of proposer]', when it is not (e.g. **152**. 26–7; **142**. 32–5 has a non-standard formulation); in **137**. 14 sqq. we have a proposer's name and what looks like an amendment. but with neither of those formulae.[17]

(A decree could also be amended by rewriting it (cf. p. xx, above); when the clauses of a decree are presented in an illogical order, that has led some scholars to suppose that the misplaced clauses are the result of

[17] Cf. Rhodes, *Boule*, 52–81, Rhodes with Lewis, 18–23.

'concealed amendments', and that is possible but unprovable, but it is also possible that the proposer simply failed to draft his decree as coherently as he might have done: for an example of incompletely coherent drafting see **137**.)

Athenian administration was based on the principle that any good citizen could and should play at least a modest part in the running of the state: large numbers of annual boards were set up (mostly of ten men, one picked by lot from the candidates in each tribe), and were given strictly limited jobs to do; all worked under the general supervision of the council, which also had judicial powers in matters concerned with the running of the state. The success of this method in ensuring that offices were spread around can be demonstrated by comparing the origins of those chosen by lot to the origins of those chosen by election.[18] (In the course of the fourth century there was a move away from the fifth-century democracy's principle of equal participation, towards entrusting greater powers to men of proved ability.)

The collection of taxes was not made by state officials, but was farmed out to contractors. The contract (like other state contracts, e.g. for rentals or public works) was auctioned to the highest bidder or syndicate of bidders, in the presence of the council, by the *poletai* ('sellers': *Ath. Pol.* 47. ii–iv; for documents published by the *poletai* see **172**, R&O 36); the record of the contract was kept by the council; and in due course the contractors had to pay the sum agreed (irrespective of the amount they had actually collected) to the *apodektai* ('receivers'), again in the presence of the council (*Ath. Pol.* 47. v–48. ii); if they defaulted they would be pursued by a board of *praktores* ('exacters': e.g. law *ap.* Andoc. I. *Myst.* 77–9; for an instance of default on a tax-collecting contract see *Agora* xix P 26. 462–98). In the fifth century all revenue was paid into a central treasury, and until that treasury was combined with the Delian League's treasury (see on **180**) all state payments were made from that treasury—by yet another board, the *kolakretai* ('ham-collectors': cf. **167**).[19] In the fourth century the *apodektai* made a *merismos* ('allocation') to various spending authorities (first attested in R&O 19, of 386).

Each Greek state had its own calendar. Years were not counted from any real or imagined fixed point (the Olympic records, counting from a supposed first festival in 776, could be used to correlate the systems of different states; but their four-yearly basis was inconvenient, and the system did not pass into everyday use), but were identified by reference to an eponymous official, usually an annual official who gave his name to the year in which he served.[20] In Athens the eponymous official was the archon (though there are no inscribed decrees dated by archon before 433/2, and it did not become standard practice to date them by the archon until *c.*420: cf. pp. xxi–xxii, above), and the year began with the first new moon after the summer solstice: thus the year which

[18] C. E. Taylor, *Hesperia* lxxvi 2007, 323–45.

[19] Rhodes, *Boule*, 102 with n. 5.

[20] Thuc. II. 2. i dates the beginning of the Peloponnesian War in the systems of Argos, Sparta and Athens, and V. 25. i dates the Peace of Nicias in the systems of Sparta and Athens; V. 20. ii–iii comments on the problems of dating by official years and justifies his own practice of dating by seasonal years divided into summers and winters.

we call 409/8 (*c.*July 409–June 408: the year in which **183** was enacted) was to the Athenians the year of Diocles' archonship. In Athens, as in most states, this year was not a solar year of *c.*365 days, but was based on lunar months, of twenty-nine or thirty days. In an 'ordinary' year of twelve months there were *c.*354 days; in an 'intercalary' year a thirteenth month was added and there were *c.*384 days (and because of this discrepancy interest was commonly reckoned by the month rather than by the year). Decisions as to how long particular months were to be, and how many months there were to be in a particular year, might be taken ad hoc, not in accordance with a fixed rule; and what was decided one way in Athens might be decided differently elsewhere.[21] Because of these irregularities it is rarely possible to give the exact equivalents in our calendar of dates in a Greek calendar. The names of the months at Athens were:

i	Hecatombaeon	vii	Gamelion
ii	Metageitnion	viii	Anthesterion
iii	Boedromion	ix	Elaphebolion
iv	Pyanopsion	x	Munychion
v	Maemacterion	xi	Thargelion
vi	Poseideon	xii	Scirophorion

Hecatombaeon corresponded roughly to our July, and so on. In an intercalary year the extra month was usually a second Poseideon, added after the first. Within the month the days were counted in three decades: after 'new moon' (νουμηνία) came the 'second of the rising (month)' (δευτέρα ἱσταμένου) and so on; in the middle decade 'eleventh' and 'twelfth' were followed by 'third on top of ten' (τρίτη ἐπὶ δέκα) and so on; and in the last decade there was a backward count from the 'tenth of the waning (month)' (δεκάτη φθίνοντος) until the last day, which was designated 'old and new' (ἕνη καὶ νέα).[22]

The council worked to a calendar of its own, in which (perhaps from Ephialtes' reforms in 462/1) the year was divided into ten prytanies, in each of which one of the tribal contingents in the council acted as standing committee. Probably by the time of the Peloponnesian War there were four regular assemblies, with their own items of business, prescribed for each prytany (cf. p. xx, above), but one of the four was designated *kyria ekklesia*, and that designation may be a survival from a time when there was only that one regular assembly in each prytany. Perhaps until the restoration of the democracy in 403, after the regime of the Thirty,[23] the council's year was a solar year of 365 or 366 days, independent of the archontic calendar

[21] According to Diod. Sic. xii. 36. ii–iii and others, in 433/2 the astronomer Meton devised a system of nineteen-year cycles with seven years in each cycle intercalary, which most Greek cities adopted and continued to use to his own time: for their possible use in Athens see p. xxv with n. 24 below.

[22] On the count of days in the last decade see Meritt, *The Athenian Year*, 38–51.

[23] It used to be concluded from *IG* i³ 377 that the council's year was brought into line with the archontic year from 407/6, but although in (probably) 407/6 the archon's year and the council's year began on the same day that was probably a coincidence; there is no certain evidence that the two years had been brought into line before the middle of the fourth century, but the state's new start in 403 is the likeliest occasion (cf. J. Morgan *ap.* S. D. Lambert, *Attic Inscriptions On-Line*, Papers 5 (July 2014), 3 n. 5, accessible from <www.atticinscriptions.com>).

(cf. on **160**), but after that the council used the archontic year as its year of office. *Ath. Pol.* 43. ii states for the later system that the first four prytanies of the year were each of thirty-six days and the remaining six of thirty-five (which can have been true only of an 'ordinary' twelve-month year of 354 days). There has been argument between B. D. Meritt and W. K. Pritchett, which has affected the reconstruction of several financial documents in our collection, over whether that was an invariable rule, and an analogous rule of longer prytanies at the beginning of the year is to be postulated for the earlier system (Pritchett), or these are just illustrations and the longer prytanies were not necessarily placed at the beginning of every year (Meritt). In the present state of our knowledge there is no certain exception to Pritchett's interpretation of the rules, and we can believe that what *Ath. Pol.* states for the later system and what Pritchett inferred for the earlier system is what the laws stated; but, when there were certainly irregularities in other respects in Athens' calendars, we think it would be unwise to insist that there can never have been an irregularity in this respect.

Yet another complication is introduced by the fact that some officials, certainly (we believe) the treasurers of Athena and of the Other Gods, and probably the *hellenotamiai*, served for a 'Panathenaic' year, tied to the archontic calendar but beginning not on 1 Hecatombaeon but on 27 or 28 Hecatombaeon (τρίτη φθίνοντος). However the problems are to be resolved, it is clear that in their financial records the Athenians had a tendency to overlook the differences between the different kinds of year.[24]

The same names were used in different states for units of money, but the values of the different currencies varied in accordance with the weights of precious metal (usually silver) to which the names were applied in each state. The scale used in Athens was:

6 obols	=	1 drachma
100 drachmas	=	1 mina
60 minas	=	1 talent

Sums of money were usually expressed in talents, drachmas and obols, without the use of a mina as an intermediate unit. The word 'stater' is often used to denote the standard coin of a state, irrespective of its value on a scale such as the above, although silver staters are commonly the equivalent of 2 drachmas. Athens did not use the word of its own coins, but its standard coin, a 4-drachma coin, weighing

[24] On the Athenian calendar see Samuel, *Greek and Roman Chronology*, 57–64. There has been much controversy over the regularity of 'intercalary' years, with a thirteenth month (cf. p. xxiv with n. 21, above), and of 'hollow' 29-day and 'full' 30-day months in the archontic calendar, and over the matters mentioned in the text here. For summaries with references see Rhodes, *Boule*, 224–9; *Comm. Ath. Pol.* 518–20; and commentaries on **138**, **139**, **144**, **160** and **180**. S. D. Lambert, in Φιλαθήναιος ... *M. J. Osborne*, 91–102, focuses on the period 352/1–322/1, and finds it credible that then Metonic cycles were used to determine which years should be intercalary and *Ath. Pol.*'s rule about the lengths of prytanies applied, but would not insist that there cannot ever have been exceptions. For the council's solar year some years were certainly of 366 days, but it is likely that to keep pace with the sun some others were of 365 days (cf. F. M. Dunn, *AJP* cxx 1999, 369–80, who argues that this solar year was introduced after and reflected Meton's achievement in 433/2; but the use of the council's first secretary to identify a year, e.g. in *IG* i³ 436–51, preserved in 440 of 443/2, points to a year of the council distinct from the archontic year earlier than then).

*c.*17.2 grammes (*c.*0.6 oz.), was worth approximately the same as the electrum *hektai*, the 'sixths' (of a stater) that were the standard coins of Phocaea and Mytilene (**195**), which weighed 2.8 grammes. For exchange rates used to convert sums in one currency to another, see R&O 45, 57; for measures of capacity, again different in different states, see R&O 45. See further on **155**, **195**.

In the second half of the fourth century, payments for attending meetings of public bodies in Athens (juries, the council, the assembly, etc.) varied between ½ drachma (for juries: not increased since the 420s) and 1½ drachmas a day (*Ath. Pol.* 62. ii). At this time an unskilled labourer could earn 1½ drachmas a day, a skilled 2 or 2½ drachmas.[25] A man was regarded as rich enough to be liable for such burdens as the trierarchy or a festival liturgy if his total property was worth 3–4 talents or more,[26] while liability for the property tax known as *eisphora* perhaps extended a little further down the scale (cf. commentary on **145**), and he would have been one of the richest Athenian citizens if his property was worth as much as 15 talents. In 341 Demosthenes claimed that in the past few years the annual revenue of Athens had increased from 130 talents to 400 talents (Dem. x. *Phil. iv.* 37–8), whereas in 431, at the beginning of the Peloponnesian War, her annual revenue was about 1,000 talents (Xen. *Anab.* VII. i. 27: Thuc. II. 13. iii claims 600 talents tribute from the Delian League, but the tribute lists suggest not more than 400 talents).

The Athenian system of numerals was acrophonic, the symbol being taken from the first letter of the word represented (e.g. 𐅃 = πέντε = 5, Η = hεκατόν = 100); some intermediate symbols were produced by combining 𐅃 as a multiplier with another symbol (e.g. 𐅄 = 50, 𐅅 = 500). Complex numerals were produced by aggregation, the largest appearing first (and without the Roman practice of counting backwards in such numerals as ix, xcix). The basic scheme was:

Ι	= 1	𐅄	= 50
ΙΙ	= 2	𐅄Δ𐅃Ι	= 66
ΙΙΙ	= 3	Η	= 100
ΙΙΙΙ	= 4	𐅅	= 500
𐅃	= 5	Χ	= 1,000
𐅃Ι	= 6	𐅆	= 5,000
Δ	= 10	Μ	= 10,000
ΔΔ𐅃Ι	= 26	𐅇	= 50,000

For money, the system given above was used to indicate sums between 5 and 5,999 drachmas. Sums of 6,000 drachmas and more were expressed in talents, using Τ on its own or in combination (𐅈, 𐅉, 𐅊, etc.). For sums below 5 drachmas the symbols used were ⊢ = 1 drachma (and ⊢⊢ = 2 drachmas, etc.), Ι = 1 obol, C = ½ obol, Ɔ = ¼ obol. Thus in **160**. 9 ΤΧ𐅅ΗΗΔ𐅃⊢⊢⊢⊢ΙΙ = 1 tal. 1,719 dr. 2 ob. For sums

[25] See M. M. Markle, III, in *Crux ... G. E. M. de Ste. Croix*, 293–7; and cf. the detailed collection and analysis of data in Loomis, *Wages, Welfare Costs and Inflation in Classical Athens*.

[26] See Davies, *APF*, pp. xx–xxiv.

of money in non-Athenian currencies Σ = stater was sometimes used on its own or in combination.

To end this section something must be said about alphabets and letter forms. The standard Greek alphabet learned by students today is the Ionic alphabet, which became the standard by the mid-fourth century, but before then different parts of Greece had their own alphabets, and their own ways of writing individual letters.[27]

Athens shows a movement towards the Ionic alphabet towards the end of the fifth century,[28] which was consolidated when the Ionic alphabet was officially adopted at the state's new start in 403 after the regime of the Thirty (Theop. *FGrH* 115 F 155 cf. F 154). Before then the Athenian alphabet:

had no *eta* (H, ē)	but used E for ε, η and the ει which is a form of εε (but EI for η)
had no *omega* (Ω, ō)	but used O for ο, ω and the ου which is a form of οο
had no *xi* (Ξ, x)	but used XΣ
had no *psi* (Ψ, ps)	but used ΦΣ
did have an aspirate	H, which we transcribe as h

We note some of the idiosyncrasies of other parts of Greece in our commentaries on some of the inscriptions in this collection.

There were also variations in the ways in which different letters were written. Some of the principal features of fifth-century Athenian letter forms are as follows.

Throughout the fifth century:

gamma	was written Λ
zeta	was written I
lambda	was written 𐌋
pi	was written Γ

In the course of the fifth century:

beta	changed from ᛒ to B
rho	changed from P or R to P
upsilon	changed from ϒ to Y
theta	changed from ⊕ to ⊙
phi	changed from Φ or ⊖ to Φ
chi	changed from + to X
sigma	changed from 𐌔 to Σ

To interpret inscriptions we need to locate them in their correct context, and to do that we need a date, precise if possible, otherwise at any rate approximate. Many incomplete texts and not a few complete texts do not have preserved in them any

[27] Surveys of early alphabets and letter forms in different parts of Greece are provioded by Jeffery, *LSAG*.
[28] See A. P. Matthaiou, in *Greek History and Epigraphy ... P. J. Rhodes*, 201–12.

material such as an archon's name which would give us a definite date, and for these other approaches to a date have to be attempted. In some cases the content points to a context: for instance, most scholars have thought it overwhelmingly likely that **131** and *IG* i³ 39 and 41, Athenian settlements with Chalcis, Eretria and Hestiaea in Euboea, should be linked with Thuc. I. 114 and dated 446/5. Other approaches have been based on formal aspects of the inscriptions: for instance, Athenian decrees from the earlier part of the fifth century do not include the archon in their prescripts, but decrees from 433/2 onwards increasingly do (cf. pp. xxi–xxii, xxiii, above); texts from the earlier part of the fifth century tend to use the long form of the first declension dative plural (-αισι), but texts from the later part tend to use the short form (-αις).

And there has been a tendency to argue from the forms of letters, particularly those whose changes during the century are noted above, and among them particularly *sigma*. That practice can be traced back to the first half of the nineteenth century; more recently it was maintained particularly strongly by the editors of *ATL* that, while both older and newer forms could be found around the middle of the century, texts with older forms ought not to be dated later than 446. In principle, when there is a sufficient body of dated material (and Athens' financial documents provide such a body), it is reasonable to assume that instances of a phenomenon found in undated material should belong to approximately the same period as instances of the same phenomenon found in dated material. But, as their orthodoxy was challenged over several decades by H. B. Mattingly,[29] the editors of *ATL* and their supporters defended their version of the doctrine with excessive rigidity. It now seems certain that Mattingly was right to maintain that texts with the older forms of lettering could continue at any rate to the early 410s (see **166** with commentary)—but the conclusion to be drawn is not that mid-century dates for inscriptions with the older forms are automatically wrong, but that they are not automatically right.[30] And it is to be hoped that excessive rigidity about letter forms will not be superseded by excessive rigidity about other formal matters.

III

The use of inscriptions as evidence by historians goes back to Herodotus (e.g. inscriptions at Thermopylae, VII. 228; inscriptions commemorating the conquests of the Egyptian king Sesostris, some of which Herodotus had seen, II. 102–6; the

[29] First in *Historia* x 1961, 148–88; many but by no means all of his articles on this theme are collected in his *AER*.

[30] Mattingly himself in some cases reverted to the earlier date for inscriptions for which he once proposed a later date. For an attempt to judge which inscriptions should be kept about the middle of the century and which should not see Rhodes, *CQ*² lviii 2008, 500–6, and for an attempt to assess what remains of 'Periclean imperialism' see Rhodes, in *Ἀθηναίων ἐπίσκοπος … H. B. Mattingly*, 39–49. S. V. Tracy, *ZPE* cxc 2014, 105–15, focuses on a number of inscriptions with three-bar *sigma* which display a 'late fine plain style'.

story of Nitocris' inscriptions in Babylon, I. 187).[31] Thucydides used inscriptions more nearly in the modern academic manner (e.g. Pausanias' arrogant inscription on the Serpent Column at Delphi, subsequently deleted and replaced by a list of Greek states which resisted the Persian invasion, I. 132. ii–iii; an inscription whose lettering he described as faint, and an inscription cited to show that Hippias was the eldest son of Pisistratus, VI. 54. vii–55. i). In the fourth century Theopompus argued that the inscription recording the alleged Peace of Callias between Athens and Persia was a forgery, because it used not Athens' local alphabet but the Ionic alphabet which Athens adopted at the end of the fifth century (*FGrH* 115 FF 153–5: for the question of Ionic letters in Athenian inscriptions see on **156**); he also rejected the authenticity of R&O 88 §ii. In the third century Craterus (*FGrH* 342) made a collection of Athenian decrees; in the second Polemon of Ilium collected epigraphic texts and was called a 'glutton for *stelai*' (*stelokopas*: Ath. VI. 234 D). The *Lindian Chronicle*, an inscribed list of dedications at the sanctuary of Athena at Lindos on Rhodes, which reconstructed the lost dedications from literary mention of them, suggests that those writing local histories and similar works made abundant use of the evidence of inscriptions.[32] On the use of inscriptions by Pausanias, the traveller of the second century AD, cf. **113**, **164**.[33]

In the modern world, inscriptions have long been found and recorded by explorers and archaeologists. Their value as evidence for historians was in the nineteenth century particularly appreciated in Germany and resisted (as inferior to the literary sources) in Britain.[34] The first work planned explicitly as a corpus of Greek inscriptions was A. Boeckh's *Corpus Inscriptionum Graecarum*, published between 1825 and 1877. Towards the end of the nineteenth century, responsibility for a corpus of Greek inscriptions from Europe was accepted by the Berlin Academy, which undertook and is still continuing publication of the work which came eventually to be known as *Inscriptiones Graecae*: the first part of that appeared in 1873; some parts have reached a second or third edition, others have yet to appear in a first edition, and in some cases planned volumes have been rendered unnecessary by volumes published under other auspices. Responsibility for Asia Minor was accepted by the Vienna Academy, which issued the first volume of the series *Tituli Asiae Minoris* in 1901. Other series devoted to Asia Minor are *Monumenta Asiae Minoris Antiquae*, begun in 1928; and *Inschriften griechischer Städte von Kleinasien*, begun in 1972 and proceeding rapidly. Many inscriptions are first published in classical and archaeological periodicals; and, when a large number of inscriptions are found on one site, often one or more volumes of the excavation report for the site are devoted to a corpus of the site's inscriptions.

Every year sees the discovery of new inscriptions, and the publication of new inscriptions, new fragments of inscriptions already known, and new contributions to

[31] See S. R. West, *CQ*^{2} xxxv 1985, 278–305. On the use of inscriptions by ancient writers in general see Rhodes, in Marincola (ed.), *A Companion to Greek and Roman Historiography*, 56–66.

[32] See Higbie, *The Lindian Chronicle and the Greek Creation of their Past.*

[33] And see Habicht, *Pausanias' Guide to Ancient Greece*, 64–94 ch. iii.

[34] See P. Liddel, in Ma *et al.* (edd.), *Interpreting the Athenian Empire*, 13–42.

the reading and interpretation of familiar texts. Keeping up to date with the stream of publications is rendered easier by chronicles of new work. An on-line concordance, CLAROS, enables one to enter a reference and find earlier and later publications of the same text (but is not complete). *Supplementum Epigraphicum Graecum* was founded by J. J. E. Hondius in 1923 with a survey of work published in 1922, continued by A. G. Woodhead, and, after an interruption, resumed by a team of editors who have produced annual surveys of work published since 1976–7: this commonly reprints new and revised texts if they have been published otherwise than in a major corpus. For each text in our collection, the references in our introductory rubric include publication in a major corpus and/or in *SEG*, which will enable treatments in *SEG* to be traced through its indexes.[35] The *Revue des Études Grecques* regularly includes a Bulletin épigraphique: between volumes li 1938 and xcvii 1984 this was the work of J. & L. Robert, who were renowned for their vast knowledge and ability to make connections, and for their trenchant opinions; from volume c 1987 this too has been continued by a team, with different members focusing on different themes or geographical areas.[36] An epigraphical bulletin on Greek religion is published in the periodical *Kernos* by A. Chaniotis. More general chronicles of classical work, which include Greek epigraphy, are *L'Année Philologique*, begun in France with a volume for 1924–6[37] and again now produced by an international team; and the Bibliographische Beilage published in the periodical *Gnomon* (from vol. i 1925). The periodical *Lustrum* is devoted to bibliographical surveys of work on particular classical topics (from vol. i 1956). An epigraphical bibliography is provided by F. Bérard *et al.*, *Guide de l'épigraphiste: Bibliographie choisie des épigraphies antiques et médiévales* (kept up to date on line at <http://www.antiquite.ens.fr/publications/guide_fr.htm>).

Information on individual Greeks may be found in the P. M. Fraser & E. Matthews (edd.), *Lexicon of Greek Personal Names* (regional volumes: names with collections of references). For Athens, what was known a century ago is presented, with source references and Latin text, in J. Kirchner, *Prosopographia Attica*; more recent, and with more discussion, but limited to those attested as rich and paying more attention to their wealth and their families than to their careers, is J. K. Davies, *Athenian Propertied Families, 600–300 BC*;[38] J. S. Traill, *Persons of Ancient Athens*, is an exhaustive collection of *testimonia* organised under short rubrics.[39] There is an updated and searchable version of *LGPN* on line at <www.lgpn.ox.ac.uk>; and the Athenian volume (ii) is kept up to date at <www.seangb.org>; for *Persons of Ancient Athens* the website <www.chass.utoronto.ca/attica> contains *addenda* and *corrigenda*. For

[35] Each volume of *SEG* has concordances covering the major collections; an index volume is now being produced for each decade.

[36] The plans for the continuation of the Bulletin were announced by P. Gauthier in *REG* xcix 1986, 117–18.

[37] Only the first part, Auteurs et textes, was published of a backward projection into *Dix Années de bibliographie classique (1914–1924)*.

[38] This too is now somewhat dated: a new edition is in preparation.

[39] For an account of the project and of the computer-searches which it allows see J. S. Traill & P. M. Wallace Matheson, *hόρος* vii 1989, 53–76.

Sparta, P. Poralla's *Prosopographie der Lakedaimonier*, of 1913, was reissued in 1985 with an appendix by A. S. Bradford.

The best general introduction in English to Greek inscriptions is A. G. Woodhead, *The Study of Greek Inscriptions*; B. F. Cook, *Greek Inscriptions*, is a short book written at a more popular level; on what can be learned from different kinds of inscription see J. Bodel (ed.), *Epigraphic Evidence: Ancient History from Inscriptions* (which makes more use of Roman than of Greek examples). Introductions in other European languages include L. Robert, in C. M. D. Samaran (ed.), *L'Histoire et ses méthodes*, 453–97, translated by H. Engelmann as *Die Epigraphik der klassischen Welt*; G. Klaffenbach, *Griechische Epigraphik*; and, on a much larger scale, M. Guarducci, *Epigrafia greca* (with abundant and excellent illustrations).

IV

The texts in this collection are arranged in approximate chronological order, but we have taken advantage of the fact that not all texts can be precisely dated to do some thematic grouping.

We have not fully re-edited the Greek texts; but our texts are our own, in that we have reconsidered the texts of our predecessors and have made changes wherever we have thought it necessary: we have tried to verify readings ourselves or had them verified by colleagues where we thought it would be profitable to do so, but not consistently. In the introductory rubric for each text we mark with an asterisk the edition whose text has served as the basis for ours: our critical apparatus is selective, and we have not felt bound to provide a full history of the text and attribute every reading or restoration to its originator, but the apparatus includes a note on any point at which our text differs from that of the asterisked edition. Where the sign = is used, the references before and after the sign are to editions of the same inscription, but not necessarily to editions printing exactly the same text.

We number every fifth line in the Greek texts, the line corresponding with the beginning of each of our paragraphs in the translations. Practice is different in some older editions, but like most more recent editions ours uses dots and brackets in the Greek texts in accordance with the 'Leiden system':

α̣β̣	letters which survive in part, but not sufficiently to exclude alternative readings
[αβ]	letters not now preserved which the editors believe to have been inscribed
{αβ}	letters inscribed in error by the cutter and deleted by the editors
<αβ>	letters supplied by the editors *either* because the cutter omitted them *or* because the cutter inscribed other letters in error
(αβ)	letters supplied by the editors to fill out an abbreviation in the inscribed text

[[αβγ̣δ̣[εζ]]]	a passage which has been erased and can [or cannot] now be read
[...], [——*c*.10——]	lost letters which cannot be restored, of the number indicated
v	one letter-space uninscribed
vacat	(remainder of) line uninscribed

Since readers can see in the Greek texts how much is preserved, in the translations we have not distinguished between what is preserved and what is not, except to attach question-marks to restorations about which we are seriously uncertain (including some which in the Greek we print only in the *apparatus criticus*). While in the translations we have not strayed unnecessarily from the word order of the Greek, we have not felt bound to keep to it when to do so would produce unnatural or obscure results. We have not thought it necessary invariably to use the same English word for the same Greek word and a different English word for a different Greek word, but we have done that except when there was good reason to do otherwise.

The rendering of Greek words and names in the roman alphabet has been a matter of controversy for a long time: rigid adherence either to latinised forms or to direct transliteration tends to produce some results which are widely regarded as unacceptable, and most scholars take refuge in an awkward compromise. We have tended, though not with complete consistency, to use English or Latinate forms for names of persons and places and familiar words which we print in roman letters (Thucydides, Diodorus; Athens, Corinth; drachmas, talents), transliteration for some names, including epithets of deities, and for words which we print in italic letters (Zeus Eleutherios; *bouleutai*, *prytaneis*, *pylaia*).

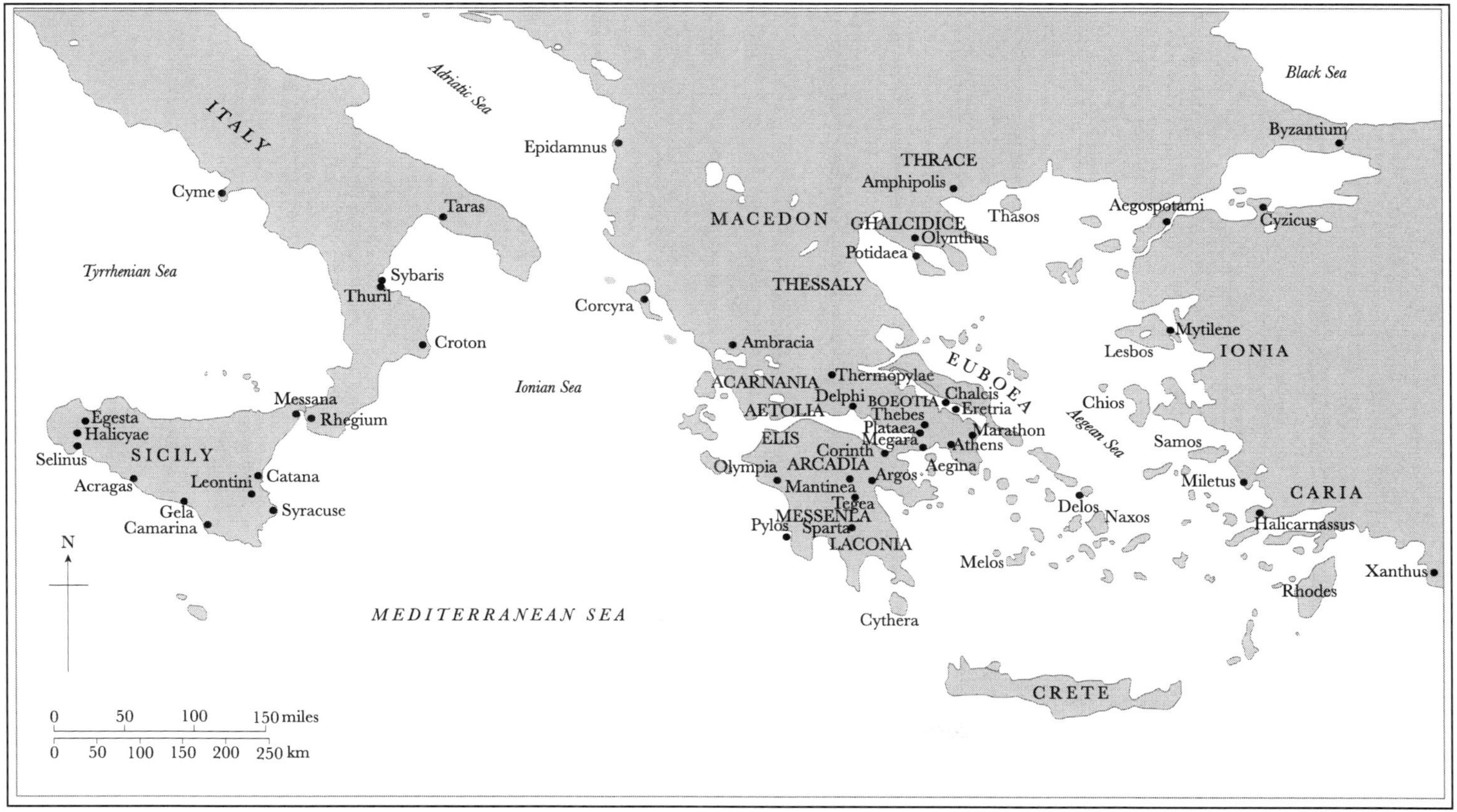

Map 1 The Greek world

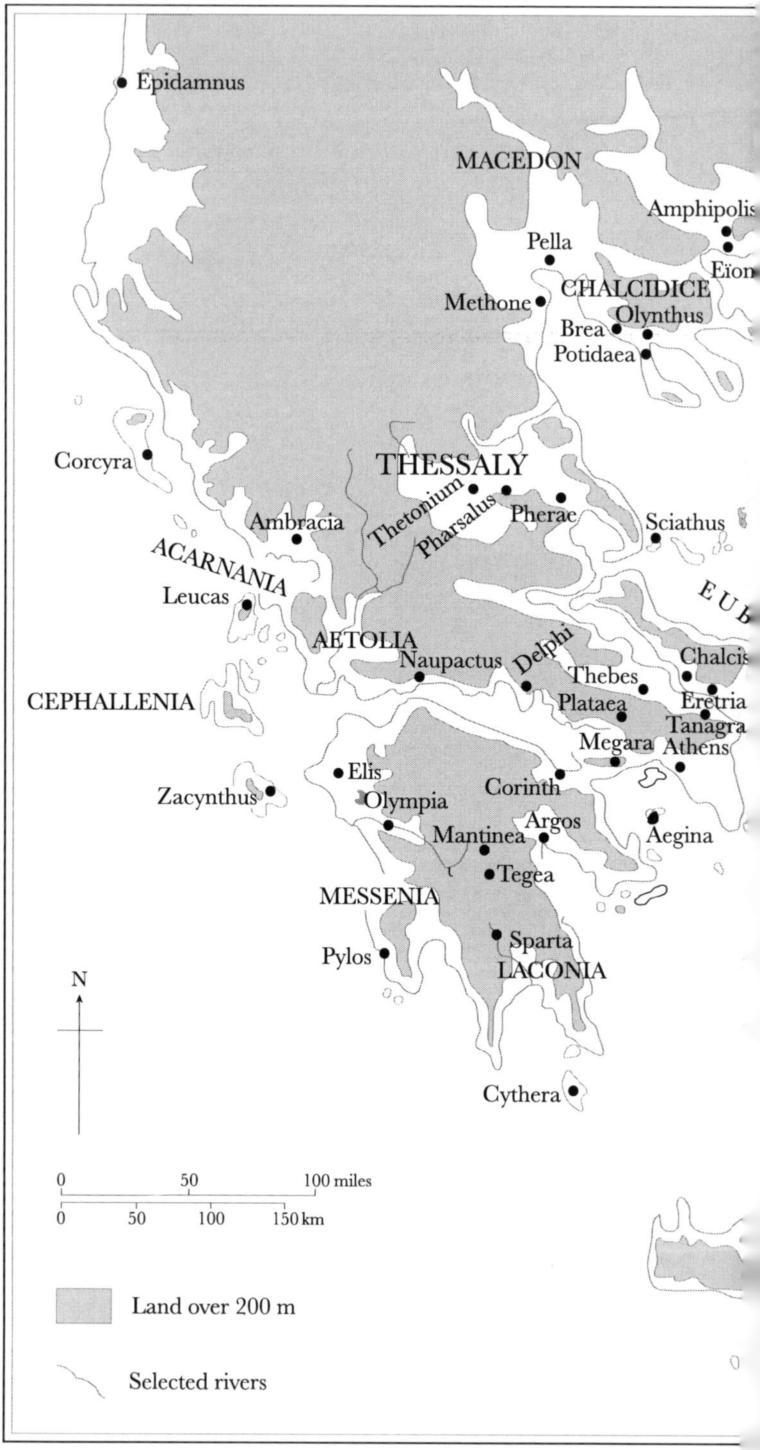

Map 2 Greece and the Aegean

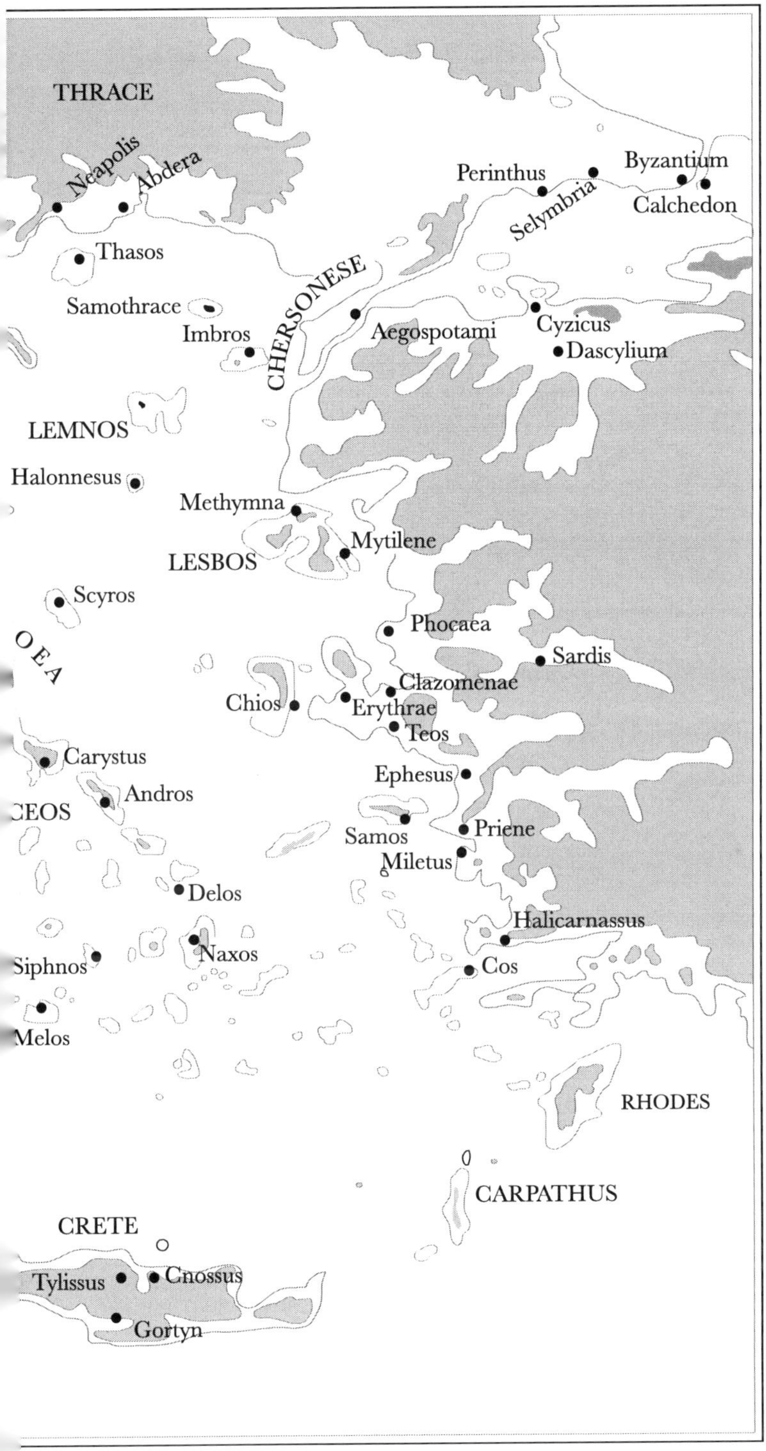
THRACE
Neapolis
Abdera
Thasos
Samothrace
Imbros
CHERSONESE
Perinthus
Selymbria
Byzantium
Calchedon
Aegospotami
Cyzicus
Dascylium
LEMNOS
Halonnesus
Methymna
Mytilene
LESBOS
Scyros
Phocaea
Sardis
OEA
Clazomenae
Chios
Erythrae
Teos
Carystus
Andros
CEOS
Ephesus
Samos
Priene
Miletus
Delos
Halicarnassus
Naxos
Siphnos
Cos
Melos
RHODES
CARPATHUS
CRETE
Tylissus
Cnossus
Gortyn

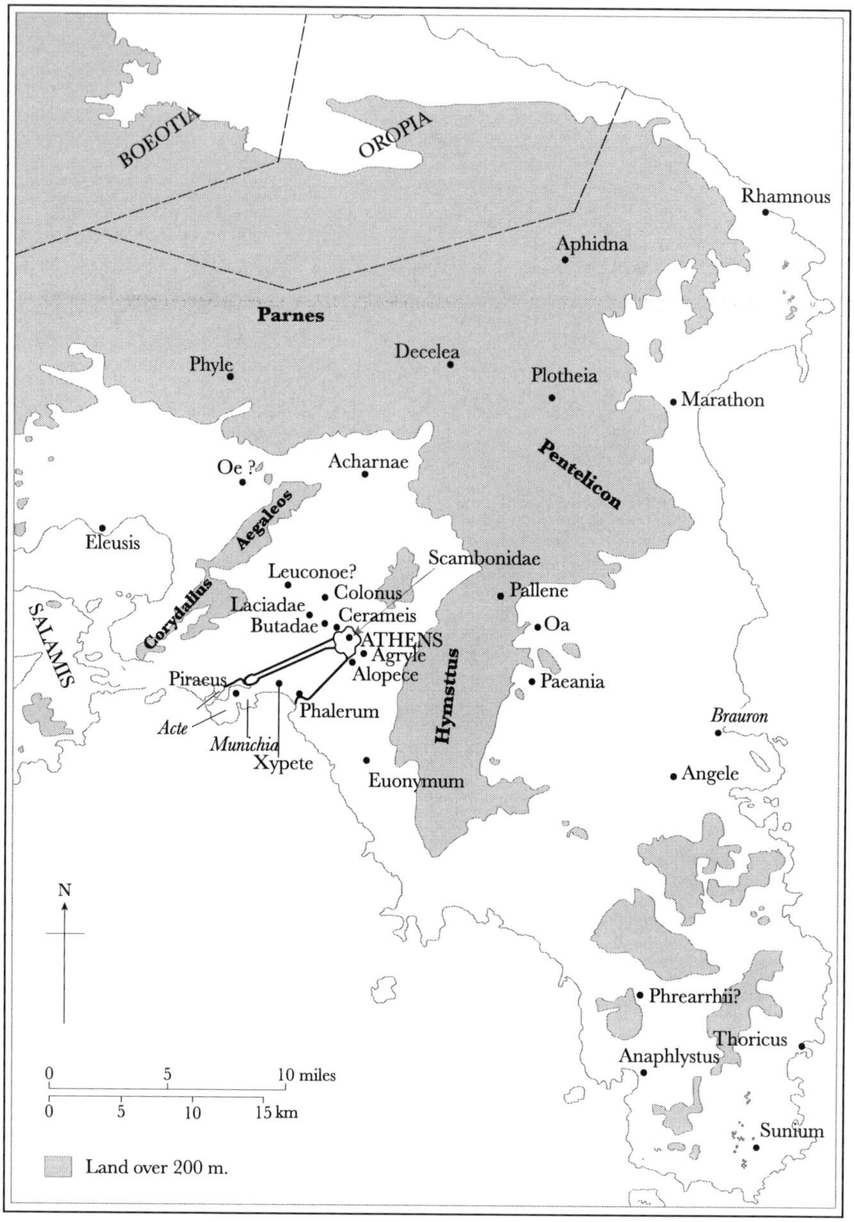

Map 3 Attica (Names of demes are in upright capital and lower case letters. Regional boundaries are purely schematic)

THE INSCRIPTIONS

101

Victory of Hieron of Syracuse at Cyme, *c.*474/3

Etruscan bronze helmet, discovered at Olympia in 1817, presented to the British Museum by King George IV in 1823. Phot. *LSAG*, pl. 51. 7.

Doric Greek, with Syracusan lettering: *LSAG*, pp. 266, 275, 410, no. 7.

I. Olympia 249; *SIG*³ 35. *B. a*; M&L 29*; Arena, *Iscrizioni greche arcaiche di Sicilia e Magna Grecia*, v. 67a (with facsimile). Trans. Fornara 64. A; Dillon & Garland³ 7. 46.

hιάρον ὁ Δεινομένεος
καὶ τοὶ Συρακόσιοι
τôι Δὶ Τυράν' ἀπὸ Κύμας.

Dedication of spoils of war as trophies in sanctuaries was common, but particularly so at Olympia, where a wide range of cities and individuals chose to commemorate and display their military victories (cf. **111**, and for Olympia **112**, **142**). The phenomenon is well discussed by A. H. Jackson in Hanson (ed.), *Hoplites*, 228–49; cf. *ThesCRA* i. 269–81 (R. Parker), 298–302 (J. Boardman). Among inscribed helmets at Olympia is one dedicated by Miltiades, the Athenian commander at Marathon (but perhaps dedicated at an earlier stage in his career).[1]

Gelon son of Dinomenes became tyrant of Gela, on the south coast of Sicily, *c.*491, and gained control of Syracuse, on the east coast, *c.*485. He died in 478/7; his brother Hieron ruled until his death in 467 (and had trouble with another brother, Polyzelus); Thrasybulus, the last brother, was driven out in 466. In 480 Gelon's enemies had invoked the support of Carthage, but Gelon defeated them at Himera, leaving the alliance of Syracuse and Acragas (on the south coast) dominant in Sicily. About 474/3 Cyme (Cumae), on the bay of Naples, asked for Hieron's help against an attack by the Etruscans, and they won a naval victory (Pind. *Pyth.* i. 71–5, Diod. Sic. xi. 51).

Two further helmets have been found at Olympia, with a different version of the last line: τôι/τῶι Δὶ Τυρρανôν/Τυραννῶν ἀπὸ Κύμας, 'dedicated this to Zeus: of the

[1] See in general Scott, *Delphi and Olympia: The Spatial Politics of Panhellenism in the Archaic and Classical Periods*, 151–2, 158, 224–5; Miltiades' helmet, Olympia Museum B 2600, with Kunze, *V Bericht über die Ausgrabungen in Olympia*, 69–74, cf. e.g. Yalouris, *Olympia: The Museum and Sanctuary*, 93.

Hieron son of Dinomenes
and the Syracusans
dedicated this to Zeus: Etruscan spoils from Cyme.

Etruscans, from Cyme' (*SEG* xxiii 253, trans. Fornara 64. B; *SEG* xxxiii 328). These further texts, with their different word order and orthography, argue against the old view that our text was deliberately metrical (two choriambic dimeters followed by a paroemiac), and against any pun on 'tyrant' in 'Tyrrhenian' (cf. *SEG* xl 385). Part of the base of a tripod which was part of a parallel act of dedication by Hieron at Delphi on the same occasion survives (*SIG*³ 35. *C* = Arena, 69, cf. *LSAG*, pp. 266, 275, no. 8); but an epigram ('Simonides' fr. lxxvi Page, *FGE*) suggests that other spoils destined for dedication at Delphi perished in a shipwreck.

Gelon and Hieron made a number of dedications in mainland Greek sanctuaries, and they regularly identified themselves by name, without any title. However, the dedication which commemorated a chariot victory at the Pythian games with the statue group to which the Delphic Charioteer belongs seems originally to have read [—— Γ]έλας ἀνέ[θ]εκεν ἀ[ν]άσσ[ον | huιὸς Δεινομένεος, τ]ὸν ἄεξ' εὐώνυμ' Ἄπολλ[ον], '—— lord of Gela dedicated this, | the son of Deinomenes, whom Apollo exalted as glorious', but the first line was erased and replaced by [νικάσας hίπποισι (?) Π]ολύζαλος μ' ἀνέθηκ[εν], 'Victorious with horses (?), Polyzelus dedicated me', so that the victory was perhaps originally attributed to Hieron as ruler of Gela (in 482 or 478) and subsequently reassigned to his brother Polyzelus (*SIG*³ 35. *D* = *F. Delphes* III. iv 452, cf. *LSAG*, pp. 266, 275, 410 no. 9; recent treatments *SEG* xl 427, xlv 495, lii 533).

Syracusan Doric has the aspirate but lacks *eta* and *omega*; note also τοί for οἱ in the article.

102

Public curses at Teos and Abdera, 480–450

One or two lost and one surviving *stelai*/blocks. *A* and *B*, fragments of the lost *stele* or *stelai*, were discovered in the early eighteenth century at Hereke, inland from ancient Teos, copied by William Sherard, British Consul in Smyrna, in 1709 and 1716, and by Samuel Lisle in 1716, and published by Edmund Chishull in *Antiquitates Asiaticae* (1728). *A* was rediscovered and copied by Le Bas in 1844 (Le Bas & Waddington iii. 59). *C*, of dark-veined grey limestone, inscribed on front (*a*), back (*b*) and sides (*c* and *d*), was found in 1976 at Sigacik (ancient Teos) and is in the Basmahane Museum at Izmir. Phot. (*C*) *Chiron* xi 1981, pls. 1–3.

Ionic Greek; cola are used to divide the text into separate words or words with conjunction and preposition (accentual units: see R. Wachter in *AION (filo)* xix 1997, 366); in *B*. 23 a letter form (Ͳ, *sampi*) found only in east Greek cities, and possibly derived from Phrygian or Carian, is used for double *sigma*. *A stoichedon* 20; *B* (probably) *stoichedon* 18; *C stoichedon* (*a*) 16, (*b*) 23, (*c* and *d*) 9.

A and *B*: *SIG*^{3} 37, 38; *DGE* 710; Buck 3; M&L 30*; *SEG* xxxi 984; Koerner 78; *Nomima* i. 104. *C*: P. Herrmann, *Chiron* xi 1981, 1–30*; *SEG* xxxi 985; R. Merkelbach, *ZPE* xlvi 1982, 212–13; Koerner 79; *Nomima* i. 105. Trans: *A* and *B*: Fornara 63; Dillon & Garland^3 1. 63; Ogden, *Magic, Witchcraft, and Ghosts in the Greek and Roman Worlds*, 278; Colvin 20. See also D. M. Lewis, in *Owls to Athens . . . Sir K. Dover*, 151–4; A. J. Graham, *JHS* cxi 1991, 176–8, *JHS* cxii 1992, 44–73 at 53–9.

A

ὅστις : φάρμακα : δηλητή-
ρια : ποιοῖ : ἐπὶ Τηίοισι-
ν : τὸ ξυνὸν : ἢ ἐπ' ἰδιώτηι, : κ-
ε͂νον : ἀπόλλυσθαι : καὶ α-
ὐτὸν : καὶ γένος : τὸ κένο :
ὅστις : ἐς γῆν : τὴν Τηίην : κ-
ωλύοι : σῖτον : ἐσάγεσθαι :
ἢ τέχνηι : ἢ μηχανῆι : ἢ κατ-
ὰ θάλασσαν : ἢ κατ' ἤπειρο-
ν : ἢ ἐσαχθέντα : ἀνωθεοίη, :
ἀπόλλυσθαι : καὶ αὐτ-
ὸν : καὶ γένος : τὸ κένο.

B

– – – απονοσ – – –
ξύοι : ἐν αὐτῶι – – –
ὅστις : Τηΐων: <τ>[ῶι ξ]υνῶι
ἢ αἰσυ[μ]νήτη<ν> : [ἱσταί]η: ἢ
ἐπανισταῖτο : <ἐπ'> αἰ[συμ]-
νήιηι : ἀπόλλυσθαι : καὶ
αὐτὸν : καὶ γένος : τὸ κείν-
ο : ὅστις : τὸ λοιπὸ : αἰσυμ-

1 ὄστις Buck: ὅστις M&L, and similarly throughout; we have restored consistent Ionic psilosis. 3–6 ὄστις: Τηΐων: <τ>[ῶι ξ]υνῶι | ἢ αἰσυ[μ]νήτη<ν>: [ἱσταί]η: ἢ | ἐπανισταῖτο: <ἐπ'> αἰ[συμ]|νήιηι: ἀπόλλυσθαι Herrmann: ὅστις Τηΐων ε[ὐθ]ύνωι | ἢ αἰσυ[μ]νήτηι:...ηι:ἢ | ἐπανισταῖτο: —6— | —5—: ἀπόλλυσθαι M&L.

A

Whoever makes harmful drugs (*or* spells) against the Teans as a community or against an individual, may he perish, both himself and his family.

6 Whoever prevents grain being imported to the Tean land by any craft or contrivance, either by sea or over land, or when it has been imported re-exports it (*or* 'pushes up the price'), may he perish, both himself and his family.

B

– – – Whoever sets himself up as *aisymnetes* for the community of the Teans, or leads an uprising to seize the post of *aisymnetes*, may he perish, both himself and his family.

8 Whoever in future holds the office of *aisymnetes* in Teos or the Tean

νῶ<ν> : ἐν Τέωι : ἢ γῆι τῆι Τη-
ίηι : . . . .οσαν : κ.σα. .τ-
ένει[3–4] αρον : να[– – – εἰδ]-
ὼς : προδο[ίη. . .] τὴ[ν] πό-
λ[ιν καὶ γῆν] τὴν Τηί-
ων : ἢ τὸ[ς] ἄνδρας[: ἐν ν]-
ήσωι : ἢ θα[λάσσηι :] τὸ
μετέ[πειτ' : ἢ τὸ] ἐν
Ἀρο[ί]ηι : περιπό[λιον : ἢ τô]
λοιπ̣ô : προδο[ίη : ἢ κιξα]-
λλεύοι : ἢ κιξάλλας : ὑπο-
δέχοιτο : ἢ ληίζοιτο : ἢ λ-
ηιστὰς : ὑποδέχοιτο : εἰ-
δὼς : ἐκ γῆς : τῆς Τηίης : ἢ [θ]-
αλάΤης : φέροντας : ἤ [τι κ]-
ακὸν : βολεύοι : περὶ Τ[ηί]-
ων : τô ξυνô : εἰδὼς : ἢ π[ρὸς]
Ἕλληνας : ἢ πρὸς βαρβάρο-
υς : ἀπόλλυσθαι : καὶ αὐ-
τὸν : καὶ γένος : τὸ κένο :
οἵτινες τιμοχέοντες :
τὴν ἐπαρὴν : μὴ ποιήσεα-
ν : ἐπὶ δυνάμει : καθημέν-
ο τὠγῶνος : Ἀνθεστηρίο-
ισιν : καὶ Ἡρακλέοισιν :
καὶ Δίοισιν : ἐν τὴπαρῆ-
ι : ἔχεσθαι : ὃς ἂν ταστήλ-
ας : ἐν ἧισιν ἠπαρὴ : γέγρ-
απται : ἢ κατάξει : ἢ φοιν-
ικήια : ἐκκόψε[ι :] ἢ ἀφανέ-
ας ποιήσει : κε̂νον ἀπόλ-
λυσθαι : καὶ αὐτὸν : καὶ γ-
ένος [τὸ κένο].

C

(*a*) [. . . . .]ΛΕ[. . . .]
[. . . .]ΟΣ̣ΙΗΝ: ποιόμε[ν]-
ος, τοῦ̣τογ̣: ἀπόλλυ[σθ]-
αι: καὶ αὐτὸν: καὶ γέ[ν]-
ος: τὸ [κ]ε̣νο: ὅς ἂν τιμὴ-
ν: ἔχων̣: [σ]ὺν θετοῖσιν

31 Δυνάμει M&L. Herrmann in text.

(*a*) 6–7 [σ]ὺν θετοῖσιν | [Τ]ηΐ[ο]ι[σ]ιν Herrmann in comentary: [.]ΥΝΘΕΤΟΙΣΙΝ | .HI.I.IN

land – – – knowingly betrays – – – the city and land of the Teans, or the men on the island or at sea thereafter, or the fort in Aroia, or in future commits treachery or commits theft or receives thieves or commits piracy or receives pirates knowingly, who takes goods from the land of Teos or the sea, or plots some bad thing concerning the community of the Teans, knowingly, in relation to Greeks or to foreigners, may he perish, himself and his family.

29 Whoever are *timouchoi* and do not make the curse to the best of their ability when the assembly is in session at the festival of the Anthesteria or at the festival of Heracles or Zeus, let them be subject to the curse.

35 Whoever either breaks the stelae on which the curses are written or erases the letters or makes them invisible, may he perish, himself and his family.

C

(*a*) – – – doing, may this man perish, himself and his family.

5 Whoever when holding office with the adopted

[Τ]ηΐ[ο]ι[σ]ιν : τὸμ π̣λ̣ησί-
[ο]ν: δολ[ῶ]ται: τοῦτον: ἀ-
[π]ό̣λ̣λ̣υσθαι: καὶ αὐτὸ-
[ν κα]ὶ γένος: τὸ κ̣ένο: ἐ-
πανά̣σ̣τα[σ]ιν: ο̣ὐ̣ βολε-
ύ̣σω: οὐδὲ π̣οιήσω: οὐδ-
ὲ λυ[ή]σ̣ω: ο[ὐ]δ̣ὲ̣ διώξω: ο-
[ὐ]δ̣ὲ [χρ]ή̣μ[α]τ̣α: δημιώσ-
[ω: οὐ]δε δήσω. οὐδὲ κατ̣-
[ακ]τ̣ε̣[ν]έ̣ω: ἂμ μ̣ὴ̣ σ[ὺ]ν δ̣ι̣-
[ακοσ]ί̣[ο]ι̣σιν : ἐν̣ Τ̣έωι
[ἢ] π̣λέ̣οσ[ι]ν: [κ]αὶ ἂμ̣ μ̣ὴ̣ ὑ̣-
π[ὸ] πόλεω[ς]: ν̣[ό]μ̣ο̣: κατα-
λαφθέν[τ]α̣: ἐν δὲ Ἀβδή-
[ρ]οισιν: [σ]ὺμ π̣ε̣ντακο̣-
[σ]ί̣οισιν : ἢ πλ[έο]σιν: α-
ἰσυμνήτην: οὐ στήσω̣
[ο]ὔτε· σὺμ πολλοῖσι[ν]

(*b*) [. . . . . Ἀβδ]ηρ̣ι̣τ̣έων: ἀ[π]α̣ι̣τ̣έο[ν]-
[τος τô ξ]υνô: μὴ ’π[ο]διδ[ο]ίη: κεῖ[ν]-
[ον ἀπ]όλλυσθαι: καὶ αὐτὸν: κ[αὶ]
[γ]ένος τὸ κένο

(*c*) IL
ΙΛ̣ΣΟΕ
\Ε. . .Ε.Ν
Μ̣
. . . : τοῦτον̣
[ἀ]πόλλυσθ̣α-
ι: ἐκ Τέω: κ[α]ὶ
Ἀβδήρ[ω]ν: [κ]α-
ὶ γῆς: [Τηΐ]η̣[ς]
καὶ α[ὐ]τὸν κ-
αὶ γένο[ς] τὸ
κείνο: . .Ν̣Τ
.ΠΑΡΑ.ΘΕ: .
.ΙΟ̣. . .Ι/.
.Α
.Η̣
(*6 lines*)

16–17 . . | [. . . .]Ι.Ι̣ΣΙΝ̣ Herrmann: δ̣ι̣|[ακοσ]ί̣[ο]ι̣σιν̣ Lewis. 21–2 [σ]ὺμ π̣ε̣ντακο̣|[σ]ί̣οισιν Gschnitzer: [σ]ύμπαντα κ̣ο̣|[ι]ν̣οῖσιν Herrmann.

Teans tricks (*or* enslaves) his neighbour, may this man perish, himself and his family.

I will not plot a revolt nor will I take part in one, nor will I cause civil strife, nor will I prosecute, nor will I confiscate property nor will I bind, nor will I execute unless with the consent of two hundred men or more in Teos and unless he is convicted by the law of the city, and in Abdera with five hundred men or more. I will not set up an *aisymnetes*, not even with many…

(*b*) if he fails to hand over when the community of the Abderites requests, may he perish, both himself and his family.

(*c*) may this man perish from Teos and from Abdera and from the land of Teos, both himself and his family.

. . .ON. . . Ͱ.
Ω.ΤΙ
ΕΙ.V. . .Ε.
ΙΟ.Ṭ. . . \ Ι

(*d*)
Ἀνθ[εστη]ϱ[ί]-
οισιν: καὶ Ἡ-
ρακλέοισι-
ν: καὶ {ι} Δίοι-
σιν: ἐν Ἀβδ[ή]-
ρο[ι]σιν: Ἀν[θ]-
εστηρίοι[σ]-
ιν: καὶ Ἡρα[κ]-
λέοισιν: κ[α]-
ὶ Ζηνὸς: ἑορ-
τῆι: ὅστις δ-
ὲ τιμοχέων
ἢ ταμιεύων
μὴ ʼναλέξεε-
ν: τὰ γεγραθ-
μένα: ἐν τῆι
[σ]τήληι: ἐπὶ
μνήμηι: καὶ
δυνάμει: ἢ [φ]-
οινικογρα-
φέων: κελευ-
[ό]ντων τιμό-
χων: κεῖνον

Curses are a feature of Greek writing from the earliest texts that we have. 'Nestor's cup' (M&L 1) promises the drinker the immediate attentions of Aphrodite in a formula which inverts a curse. In the *Iliad* Phoenix relates how he was cursed by his father (Hom. *Il.* IX. 447–57; cf. also IX. 567), and Oedipus' curses of his sons were related in the *Thebaid* that was part of the epic cycle (*Thebaid* fr. 11). There can be little doubt that curses were a regular feature of Greek life. Individuals and groups prayed for good things to happen to themselves and their friends, and in similar language asked for bad things to happen to those who act contrary to what they consider to be their reasonable expectations, as Chryses asks first for blessings on the Greeks if they give his daughter back and then for Apollo to punish them when they refuse (*Il.* I. 17–42).[1]

[1] On the difficulty of distinguishing the language of prayer and of curses see Pulleyn, *Prayer in Greek Religion*, ch. v. See also more generally R. L. Fowler, *ICS* xx 1995, 1–22 = Buxton (ed.), *Oxford Readings in Greek Religion*,

(*d*) – – – at the Anthesteria and the festivals of Heracles and of Zeus; and in Abdera at the Anthesteria and the Heracleia and the festival of Zeus. Whoever holds the office of *timouchos* or is a treasurer and does not read out what has been written on the *stele* according to his memory and to his best ability, or as scribe (does not read out) when the *timouchoi* order him, may he – – –

Like prayers, curses depended upon being heard by the gods to whom they were addressed. (It is unclear what the effect of being cursed was on a person's status in a human community, but the consequence of public cursing seems effectively to have been outlawry; this is effectively spelled out in *C. c.* 5 here; see further Parker, *Miasma*, 192–8). The greater moral force and urgency of curses, with their appeal for restorative justice, is perhaps reflected in their commonly being written on permanent physical objects (as is more rarely the case with prayers, for which cf. Manticlus' Apollo [*CEG* 326], and the physical recognition of prayer answered embodied in many dedications to the gods). In surviving epigraphy, curses written by individuals

317–43 at 318–22. On Greek oaths generally see Sommerstein & Bayliss, *Oath and State in Ancient Greece*, Sommerstein & Fletcher (edd.), *Horkos: The Oath in Greek Society*, and Sommerstein & Torrance, *Oaths and Swearing in Ancient Greece*. There remains much of interest in E. Ziebarth, *Hermes* xxx 1865, 57–70, and R. Vallois, *BCH* xxxviii 1914, 250–71.

are a feature of fifth-century and later texts.[2] The earliest epigraphic curses that we have are corporate. Although the prayers and curses which opened the business of the assembly at Athens were never recorded on stone (we know them from Dem. xxiii. *Aristocrates* 97 and the spectacular parody at Ar. *Thesm.* 295–351), the oath said to have been sworn by the people of Thera when the expedition to found Cyrene was launched, featuring an act of self-cursing backed up by the moulding of wax dolls, was recorded by the people of Cyrene in the fourth century (M&L 5. 40–51). But the earliest of all corporate epigraphic curses are these from Teos, where recording on stone goes together with the reading out of the oaths three times a year at major city festivals.

Although inscribed on different occasions and with different publics in mind, these stones clearly belong to a single context. This is apparent both in terms of their language—the texts involve very similar linguistic formulas—and in terms of formal epigraphic features (in particular the use of punctuation and the *stoichedon* arrangement). Dating the inscriptions depends on a combination of letter forms (which suggest a date after 500) and possible contexts.

Herodotus (i. 168; cf. also Strabo 644 / xiv. i. 30) tells us that when Harpagus took Teos by siege the Teans fled to Abdera in Thrace, and this is generally taken to have occurred around 540. In the Ionian Revolt (499–493) Teos was sufficiently recovered to contribute 17 ships to the Ionian fleet at the battle of Lade (Hdt. vi. 8. i). The refoundation of Teos from Abdera, after Teos had been destroyed by fire, is alluded to in Pindar's second *Paean*: whether that refoundation occurred in the later sixth century, and we should believe that Harpagus had burnt Teos, or after the Ionian Revolt, and that Teos had been one of many rebel cities burnt then by the Persians (Hdt. vi. 32), is unclear. But the inscriptions here strongly imply both that there had been serious political upheaval in which seizure of power as *aisymnetes* was involved, and that relations between Abdera and Teos were exceptionally close when these curses were inscribed. This perhaps points most strongly to a post-Ionian Revolt refoundation.

The text printed here as *A* is concerned with two sorts of threat: the threat of destruction by some lethal substance or spell and the threat of starvation by intervention in the grain supply. Grain supply was a regular headache for Greek cities because of the high inter-annual variability of rainfall (see generally Garnsey, *Famine and Food-Supply in the Graeco-Roman World*), and we have later evidence for such a concern at Teos (*SIG*[3] 344). Phanagoreia in the Black Sea identified herself as a colony of Teos, and this may have given the city privileged access to Black Sea grain. The Athenian assembly had grain supply as a standing agenda item in the main meeting of every prytany, and sought to prevent re-export and control prices of grain by legislation (Garnsey, 139–42). Embodying curses upon those manipulating the grain supply into a regularly performed ritual might be regarded as another means to the same effect. Poisoning was a less regular concern, though the Athenians

[2] On private 'binding curses' see Gager, *Curse Tablets and Binding Spells from Antiquity and the Ancient World*, and Eidinow, *Oracles, Curses and Risk among the Ancient Greeks*.

did wonder whether the plague in 430 was caused by enemy poisoning of wells (Thuc. II. 48. ii; cf. Paus. X. 37. vii). Poisoning of water would indeed affect a whole community, but since the word translated 'drugs' can also mean 'spells' it may be that it is not use of poisonous substances that is in mind but use of supernatural powers.

Text *B* is more directly concerned with political dangers, in the first place from someone who has become *aisymnetes*. Aristotle identifies the *aisymnetes* as an 'elected tyranny' (*Pol.* III. 1285 A 31)—i.e. a magistrate who is in, or gets into, a position to overrule others. The danger envisaged here is both of someone seizing the office of *aisymnetes*, and of someone causing unrest in an attempt to seize that office. The use of a curse is further used here to keep those who do hold the office of *aisymnetes* under control, reflecting the absence of effective sanctions to control those to whom power was ceded—a long-standing problem in the Greek city (cf. M&L 2). Here the list of prohibited actions reminds the chief magistrate of the areas in which his behaviour will be assessed, and the repetition of the curse three times a year at major festivals ensured that both magistrate and people were repeatedly reminded of the limits. On the basis of their appearance in a much later text (*SIG*³ 578. 60, of the second century) it seems likely that the *timouchoi* are the holders of a specific office of *timouchos* rather than just holders of any offices (*timai*).

The final clause of text *B* is indicative of the importance and role of writing. The stone constitutes both the record and the symbol of the public decision, and any breaking or defacement of the stone would constitute the subversion or annulment of the curses themselves. In text *C* we discover that it is an obligation upon the magistrates to read out what the inscription says and that the magistrates may order the scribe to do so. This responsible role for the scribe along with the formation of a name for a scribe from the basis of *phoinikeia* ('Phoenician letters' or 'purple letters', cf. Hdt. V. 58) is one also attested in other communities (most notably in the role of Spensitheus the Cretan *poinikastas*, *SEG* XXXV 993).[3]

The texts on block *C* further elucidate the political background and reveal an exceptionally close relationship between Teos and Abdera. Although the stone was found at Teos, it reckons to prescribe practice for Abdera as well, implying an identical magisterial structure and pattern of festival activity in Abdera as in Teos. This is particularly important because Abdera was not originally a Tean foundation (Herodotus claims that it was founded by Clazomenae). It appears that Abdera and Teos, finding themselves each in difficulty, voluntarily united for mutual assistance, cloning their institutions and issuing closely parallel coinage. They seem, however, to have kept themselves notionally distinct while sharing everything (Hdt. I. 168 talks of 'Teans in Abdera' and *C. a* talks of 'adopted Teans': see Graham, *JHS* CXI 1991). There seems to have been enough suspicion between the Abderans and the 'adopted Teans' to occasion a specific undertaking in magistrates not to side with the newcomers against the rump of Abderans (*C. a.* 5–10). In both communities power

³ See further R. Thomas, *BICS* XL 1995, 59–74 at 66–71 = Foxhall & Lewis (edd.), *Greek Law in its Political Setting*, 9–32 at 19–25.

is kept for the community rather than handed over to individuals. In clauses (*C. a.* 12–22) reminiscent of those by which the powers of the Athenian council of five hundred were limited (**183**. *B*), magistrates are made to agree not to participate in civil strife (λυ[ή]σω in *C. a.* 13 seems to be the verbal form derived from λύα, '(civil) strife') or to take drastic legal action without the consent of a larger body (of 200 in Teos and 500 in the larger and wealthier Abdera). Those who fail to conform to the strictures are expected to keep out of both cities (*C. c.* 5–12), and requests from Abdera seem to be equally binding in Teos (*C. b*). We may not here be

---

103

Thasian laws relating to wine, *c.*470/420

A

White marble block found in 1950, and now in Thasos Museum. Phot. Pouilloux pl. V. 3, Duchêne pl. XV. 1; our pl. 1.

Parian alphabet (*LSAG* 308 no. 71); *boustrophedon*.

Pouilloux, *Recherches sur l'histoire et les cultes de Thasos*, i, no. 7; *SEG* xviii 347; Duchêne, *La Stèle du port*, 119–20*; Koerner 66; *Nomima* ii. 96.

[– – – – – – – – – – – – – – – – –]Λ[– – – – – – – – – – – –]
[– – – – – – – – – – – – –]_ṬOM[— c.10 —]MH[– – –]
← [– – – – – – –]ον ποιέτω· ὅ τι ἄν τις τούτω[ν ποιῆι παρὰ τὰ]
→ [γεγραμμέν]α, τô οἴνο καὶ τô ὀχσέος στερέσ̣[θω ὑπὸ τô]
[κατειπ]όντος· καὶ ἕκτην κατ' ἀμφορέα ἔκα[στον ὀφελ]-
[έτω τῆι Ἀθ]ηναίηι τῆι Πολιόχωι καὶ τῶι Ἀπόλλω̣[νι τῶι Πυθί]-
[ωι κ]αὶ τῶι κατειπόντι ἑτέρην· ἀπενγυάτω ὁ [κατειπὼν]
[ἀπενγύην] παρὰ τριηκοσίοισιν κατάπερ τῶν βιαίων· [π]-
[ε]ρὶ τô οἴνο νηϊδίης οὐκ ἔστιν ὅρκος οὔτ[ε ἀστῶι οὔ]-
τε χσένωι.

2 O&R (see our pl.1): ṬOM – – – HM Pouilloux, Duchêne.

B

Orthostate of Thasian marble, found reused in Roman building at south-east of agora, and now in Thasos Museum. Part of §ii removed to write an inscription of the 2nd century AD. Phot. *BCH* l 1926, pl. XIII; *RA* 1948, fig. 1; Pouilloux pl. XII.

Ionic alphabet; §ii is *stoichedon* 45.

IG XII Supp. 347*; G. Daux, *RA* 1948, 241–51; Pleket, *Epigraphica*, i. 2 (I & II); Koerner 68–9. Trans. Fornara 169; Arnaoutoglou 36; Dillon & Garland[3] 1. 65.

dealing with anything that could be called a democracy in either place, but we are certainly dealing with constitutional government and a strong public display of magisterial subordination.

The inscription is written in Ionic letters and the Ionic dialect. Notable features are the contraction of ποιοῖ (*A.* 2), unusual outside Attic (contrast ἀνωθεοίη, *A.* 10); *A.* 3 ξυνόν (used adverbially here) for Attic κοινόν; *A.* 5, *C. a.* 5 etc. κένο for Attic ἐκείνου (but contrast *B.* 7–8 κείνο); *B.* 37 κατάξει is a short-vowel aorist subjunctive.

– – – he is to do. Whatever any of these people does contrary to what is written, he is to be deprived of the wine and the vinegar by the person who denounces him. And he is to owe one *hekte* per amphora to Athena Poliouchos and Apollo Pythios and another to the denouncer. The denouncer is to give a deposit to three hundred as in cases of violence.

8 There is no oath of ignorance in the case of wine either for a citizen or a stranger.

---

§i

γλεῦκος μηδὲ οἶνον τô καρπô τô ἐπὶ τῆις ἀμπέ[λοις ὠν]-
ἔσθαι πρὸ νεομηνίης Πλυντηριῶνος· ὃς δ' ἂν πα[ραβὰς]
πρίηται, ὀφείλεν στατῆρα παρὰ στατῆρα, τὸ μὲν [ἥμυσυ]
τῆι πόλι, τὸ δ' ἥμυσυ τῶι δικασαμένωι. δίκη δ' ἔστω κα[τά]-
περ τῶμ βιαίων. ὃς δ' ἂν ἐμ πίθοις οἶνον πρίηται, τὴν ὠν-
ὴν κυρίην ἶναι, ἂν τὸς πίθος σημήνηται.

§ii

[- - - αἱ δὲ]
θωιαὶ καὶ ἀπενγύαι ἔστων κατὰ ταὐτά· ἂν δὲ μηδὲς ἀπε[γγυ]-
ᾶι, οἱ πρὸς τὴν ἤπειρον ἐπιτετραμμένοι δικασάσθων· ὅτ[ε]
δ' ἂν νικήσωσι, τῆς πόλεως ἡ θωιὴ ἔστω πᾶσα· ἂν δὲ οἱ ἐπιτετ-
ραμμένοι μὴ δικάσωνται πυθόμενοι, αὐτοὶ τὴν θωιὴν διπ-
λησίην ὀφελόντων· δικασάσθω δὲ ὁ βολόμενος κατὰ ταὐτά,
καὶ τῆς θωιῆς τὸ ἥμυσυ ἰσχέτω, καὶ τὴν δίκην οἱ δημιοργο-
ὶ δόντ‹ων› κατὰ τῶν ἐπιτετραμμένων κα‹τὰ› ταὐτά· μηδὲ πλοῖον Θά-
σιον ξενικὸν οἶνον ἐσαγέτω ἔσω Ἄθ‹ω› καὶ Παχείης· εἰ δὲ μή,
τὰς αὐτὰς θωιὰς ὀφελέτω ἅσπερ παρὰ τὸν οἶνον ὕδωρ παρα-
χέων, καὶ ὁ κυβερνήτης τὴν αὐτὴν θωιὴν ὀφελέτω· αἱ δὲ δίκ-
αι καὶ αἱ ἀπενγύαι ἔστων κατὰ ταὐτά· μηδὲ ἐξ ἀμφορέων μη-
δὲ ἐκ πιθάκνης μηδ' ἐξ ψευδοπίθο κοτυλιζέτω μηδές. ὃς δ' ἂ-
ν πωλῆι, δίκαι καὶ ἀπεγγύαι καὶ θωιαὶ ἔστων κατὰ ταὐτὰ κ-
ατάπερ τô ὕδατος τῆς παραχύσιος.

§ii. 2–3 ἀπε[γγυ]ᾶι Daux: ἀπ[....|η]ι *IG*.

Thasos has left us a relatively rich epigraphic record (see also **104**, **176**, **177**; and generally Osborne in Mitchell & Rubinstein (edd.), *Greek History and Epigraphy . . . P. J. Rhodes*, 103–14. These three laws, which together span more or less the whole period covered by this volume, have economic and political as well as legal interest.

Thasos appears in our literary texts as a source of distinguished wine from the late fifth century on, first of all in Old Comedy (Hermippus fr. 82 K&A, Philyllius fr. 23, Ar. *Lys.* 195–8, *Eccl.* 1118–9, *Plut.* 1018–21, frs. 334, 364). At the end of the fifth century Critias' *Constitution of the Spartans* (Ath. XI. 463 E) referred to Thasian use of large cups, and the Hippocratic *Epidemics* to illness on Thasos following heavy drinking (*Epidemics* I Case 12, cf. Case 2; *Epidemics* III Cases 4 and 5). The sale of the property of those condemned for mutilating the Herms and profaning the Mysteries at Athens reveals two estates on Thasos owned by Adeimantus, so well equipped with *pithoi* and with amphoras of wine as to suggest that they were very large (**172**). Although Thasians began stamping their amphoras only from the beginning of the fourth century (Garlan, *Amphores et timbres amphoriques grecs*), distinctively shaped Thasian amphoras are attested from the early fifth century, and law *A* suggests that the

§i

Neither grape juice nor wine is to be bought from the fruit on the vines before the first of Plynterion. Whoever buys in contravention of this law is to be fined stater for stater, half to the city and half to the man who has brought him to justice. The case is to be heard as are cases of violence. Whoever buys wine in jars, the purchase is to be valid provided that he seals the jars.

§ii

The penalties and the deposits are to be made in the same way. But if no one offers a deposit, the officials who deal with the mainland are to bring a court action. Whenever they are successful, the whole penalty is the city's. And if the officials do not bring the case to court when they have learned about it, they are themselves to owe a double penalty. Anyone who is willing is to bring the case to court in the same way, and he is to have half the penalty and the *demiorgoi* are to give the verdict according to what has been laid down in the same way.

8 No Thasian boat is to bring in foreign wine between Cape Athos and Cape Paxi. If this law is breached, he is to owe the same penalties as someone pouring water into the wine, and the helmsman is to owe the same penalty. The court cases and the deposits are to be made in the same way. No one is to serve cups of wine from amphoras or jars or from false jars. If anyone does sell in this way, the court cases and the deposits and the penalties are to be in the same way as for the pouring of water.

Thasians were already peculiarly concerned about regulating the quality and sale of their wine at that date.

We do not know what the offence regulated in *A* was. The penalty involves giving wine to the two main Thasian civic sanctuaries and to the prosecutor, in both cases presumably for their use, and so the offence cannot have been to reduce the quality of the wine in some way. It must rather have been to sell wine and vinegar in some unauthorised way—implying that sales of wine and vinegar are strictly regulated. (The inclusion of vinegar in this law and of grape juice in *B* §i seems likely to be an attempt to prevent people trying to get round the law by claiming that their wine was really vinegar or really just grape juice. With this concern to prevent avoiding the law compare the express ruling-out of pleas of ignorance in *A*.)

The first law on the second stone relates not to selling but to buying wine. It is concerned to prevent purchase of wine when the grape crop is still on the vine until a date which is probably around June/July, at which time, presumably, it is thought that prediction of the size and quality of the crop is possible. The fine is made directly proportionate to the cost of the grape crop purchased, and those denouncing such transactions receive part of the penalty. What exactly is the concern here? Who or what stands to suffer from too early a purchase of grapes on the vine? One possible answer would be the growers. Early sale of the grape harvest offers them insurance against a bad harvest, but it also means that they do not profit from a good harvest. The risk is transferred to the purchaser, but so too the gain. But why should growers need protection? It is surely their choice whether or not to sell? A second possibility is that what suffers is quality. The purchaser will need to recoup his money whatever the crop turns out to be. If the crop is poor the purchaser will be tempted to maximise the quantity of wine produced, seeking to sell low-quality wine on the back of the reputation of Thasian wine. That quality might indeed be the issue which emerges from the second law on the stone.

B §i ends with a reassurance: this provision does not affect wine purchased in jars (*pithoi*), in which circumstances the purchase will be valid provided that the jars are sealed. What is referred to here has been much discussed. Do the seals/signs have reference to the stamping that we find on Thasian amphoras? The answer to this is surely no. Stamping of amphoras was a practice only just beginning at the end of the fifth century and does not seem to have extended to *pithoi*. And stamping happens before the manufacture of the amphora. Are the seals affixed by the seller, or by the purchaser? The structure of the sentence implies that the purchaser is the subject of the verb. Given that *pithoi* are large containers, moved only when empty, it would seem that what is at issue here is wine that is delivered to the purchaser in some portable container (e.g. wineskins?) and emptied into *pithoi*. The wine in a *pithos* become the property of the owner of the *pithos*, who is the purchaser, once he seals the *pithos*. What, in that case, is at issue here? It does not seem likely that those who poured wine into other people's *pithoi* would then think they could claim that they still owned the wine. Is this too a provision about quality: one can sell wine that one has in a *pithos* provided that at the point of sale a seal has to be breached? The seal guarantees the ownership, in the sense of the right to sell, because it guarantees that nothing has been done to the wine since the *pithos* was filled.

B §ii was partly obliterated to make way for another law more than half a millennium later. The text that we have opens with provisions to ensure that some unknown offence is prosecuted. The best clues to the content come from the rest of the law and from the magistrates to whom the ultimate duty to prosecute is given: those who have responsibility for the mainland. We can guess that the offence relates to movement of wine into or out of Thasos. The second provision is a prohibition on bringing non-Thasian wine anywhere near Thasos. The wide limits, which effectively exclude movement of non-Thasian wine in the sea immediately around Thasos, are presumably an attempt to ensure that all wine, from the mainland territory opposite Thasos as well as from the island itself, can be guaranteed entirely Thasian. This is unlikely to be protectionism (as is often suggested: see A. Bresson, in Bresson & Rouillard (edd.), *L'Emporion*, 203–4), not least because non-Thasian ships are not prevented from bringing non-Thasian wine into these waters; it is much more likely to be concern for quality: the authorities are making the best attempt they can to prevent non-Thasian being mixed up with Thasian wine. It is notable that the legal provisions in this law are repeatedly compared to those that apply to adding water to wine—very clearly a quality issue. A reputation for quality was a vital asset both in trade within the city and in the export trade (cf. **195**).

The final provision of this law concerns the vessels from which wine can be dispensed for sale in cups. Our understanding of this clause is hampered by our uncertainty about *pseudopithoi*, but we know that *pithaknai* were vessels larger than amphoras but smaller than *pithoi* (D. A. Amyx, *Hesperia* xxvii 1958, 170–4). The best guess is that these are all vessels that could be transported, and that this provision prevents some of the wine being sold out of such vessels and their then being sold on either with misleading quantities or having had their contents adulterated.

Together these three separate acts of legislation reveal the importance of commerce in wine for the Thasians and their determination to ensure that what is sold as Thasian wine is unadulterated and of the highest quality. They do this by regulating first producers (probably, in *A*), then purchasers (*B* §i) and traders (*B* §ii). The concern to control the sale and distribution of Thasian wine parallels the control which can be ascribed to amphora stamps (even though the precise nature of that control remains uncertain: see Garlan, *op. cit.* 154–71).

In legal terms the interest of these laws lies in their procedure and in the juridical structure which they imply. In *A*, with its language of 'denunciation', we have a procedure essentially similar to the procedure known as *phasis* in Athens (on which see D. M. MacDowell in *Symposion 1990* (*AGR* viii 1991), 187–98): individuals are encouraged to intervene to bring to court breaches of commercial regulations by being offered half the penalty (here measured in wine or vinegar). The prosecutors are similarly rewarded in *B* §i, although here the language is more neutral ('prosecutor' rather than 'denouncer') and the penalty that is shared is monetary. In *B* §ii the first of the offences is to be pursued by magistrates in the absence of any other prosecutor, and volunteer prosecutors, again rewarded with half the penalty, are invited to take action against the magistrates if they fail to act. The provision for prosecution by magistrates emphasises that the city is seen as the injured party. In all three legislative acts comparison is made with procedure in the case of another offence. In *A* and in *B* §i the comparison is with cases of violence for the court procedure. In *B* §ii comparison is twice with cases of watering wine. In the first case the comparison is for penalty alone, in the second case for court, deposits and penalties. The comparison of penalties is curious: carrying foreign wine seems a very different sort of offence from watering wine, and one might expect a different sort of penalty. So too, serving wine from amphoras seems a different sort of offence again. What penalty would suit all three offences? Confiscation of the wine, presumably with half the confiscated wine going to the prosecutor, seems most likely, though it is not clear that a prosecutor would want a quantity of watered wine.

The earliest law refers to making deposits before three hundred. Is this the name of a court? Or is it a quorum for the size of the court in these particular cases: deposits must be made before a court in which at least three hundred have gathered? The same figure is found in **176** and **177** (late fifth century). The invitation to volunteer prosecution points in the direction of general citizen involvement in the courts and it is most likely that three hundred is a quorum.

Two other bodies are mentioned in the latest law (*B* §ii): those in charge of the mainland and the *demiorgoi*. The former are presumably a board of officials charged with affairs relating to the mainland opposite (Thasian control of which was an issue throughout the fifth century and the occasion for the revolt of 465: Thuc. i. 100. i and see **187**). The latter are mentioned only here in Thasian epigraphy, though the same term is used for magistrates in various parts of the Greek world. Whether they are magistrates or a way of referring to (part of) the citizen body here is not clear. One possible context for this law would be the oligarchy in power from 411 to 407,

---

104

Thasian regulation of behaviour in the streets, 460s

Stele of grey Thasian marble, found in the harbour of Thasos in 1984 and now in the Thasos Museum. At some unknown date a head in an Athenian helmet was added below the text. Phot. Duchêne pls. 1–7

Parian letters, *boustrophedon*.

Duchêne, *La Stèle du port* (with French translation); *SEG* xlii 785*; *Nomima* ii. 95; Hellmann, *Choix d'inscriptions architecturales grecques*, 3. Trans: D. M. Lewis, *CR*[2] xliii 1993 402; Arnaoutoglou 85. See also A. J. Graham, *JHS* cxviii 1998, 22–40; *BSA* xcv 2000, 301–27; A. S. Henry, *BSA* xcvii 2002, 217–21; H. Duchêne, *Topoi* x 2000, 42–7.

→ ἀπὸ τῆς ὁδô τῆς ὄχθης ⁝ I[– – – – – – – – – – –]
← [– – – – – – – – – – –] τ̣ô Ἡρακλέος τô ἱρô ⁝ ἀπ-
ὸ τῆς ὁδô τô ἱρô Χαρίτων ⁝ ἐν τῆι ὁδῶι τ-
α̣ύ̣τηι ὁδὸν μ̣ὴ̣ ποιέτω ⁝ μηδὲ ὑδ[ρευ]-
έτω τῆι Ε[– – – – – – –]α̣ς̣ ⁝ μηδὲ φ[ρ]έ̣α̣-
τ̣α ἱ[σ]τάτ̣ω ⁝ μηδὲ [– – –] τιθέτω ⁝ μηδὲ [–]
[– – –]Α ποιέτω ⁝ ὃς ἄν τ̣ι τούτων ποιῆι πα-
ρὰ τὰ γεγραμμένα ⁝ ἑκατὸν στατῆρας
ὀφελέτω τῶι Ἀπόλλ[ω]νι τῶι Πυθίωι ⁝ κατ-
ὸν δὲ τῆι πόλι ⁝ πρ̣[ησσόντων δὲ οἱ ἀρχ-
οὶ ἐπ' ὧν ἂν ποιῆι ⁝ ἂν δὲ μή, αὐτοὶ ὀφελόν-
των ⁝ τὴν θωϊὴν διπλησίην τῶι θεῶι καὶ τῆι π-
όλι ⁝ καὶ εἴ τι̣ [μὴ] ἡ θωϊὴ γέγραπται τῶι πο-
[ι]ôντι, μὴ τ̣ε̣ι[σά]τω ὃς τάδε μὴ ἐποίησ-
εν, TO[.]O[– – – – – – – – – – –]δειχσάτ̣[ω]

5 φ[ρ]άγμα noted as also possible by Duchêne. 15 TO[.]O *SEG*; TO[Π]O Duchêne, *Nomima*.

which certainly attempted to gain control of Neapolis; this law would then be contemporary with the second law rewarding political informers, passed probably in 409 (**176**); a second possible context is after 407 or the 390s after Thasos and Neapolis have been reconciled (M. Brunet, in *Esclavage, guerre, économie . . . Y. Garlan*, 239–42; cf. below, **176**, **187**).

Ionic dialect features include psilosis (κατάπερ for καθάπερ) and the forms of nouns in -ις (πόλι, παραχύσιος). The dative plural τῆις in ἐπὶ τῆις ἀμπέ[λοις is a mark of Paro-Thasian dialect. ω is used for inherited ō, while ο is used for secondary close ō (= Attic ου) from contraction (τô οἴνο, δημιοργοί).

From the road of the quay – – – from the shrine of Heracles. From the road of the shrine of the Charites, in this road let him not make a threshold nor draw water for – – – nor establish a well nor place a – – – nor make – – – Whosoever does any of these things contrary to what is written is to owe a hundred staters to Apollo Pythios and a hundred to the *polis*. The magistrates in whose term he does this are to exact the fine. If not, they themselves are to be liable for double the penalty to the god and to the *polis*. If the penalty has not been recorded in writing for the offender, he is not to pay it. Who has not done this, – – – he

[.]ΔΕ[.]ΑΣΙΑΘ ⁄⁄⁄[– – – – – –]ịος ἔστω ⁝ ἐπὰ-
ṿ δὲ ἐς τωὐτọ̀ν [π]οιήσῃι, τότε χρήσθω τῶι
οἰκήματι. *vacat*
τὴν ὁδὸν καθαρὴν παρεχέτω ⁝ ὁ ἐνοικέων
κατὰ τô ἑαυτô ἕκαστος ⁝ ἂν δὲ μηδὲς ἐνοι-
κῆι, ὃἂν ἦι τοἴκημα ⁝ καὶ ẹ̓[πιστά]τ[αι] καθαι-
ρόντων ⁝ αὐτοὶ ἑκάστο μηνός ⁝ καὶ ἄν τι πέσ-
ηι, ποιόντων τῆς . ΑΓΛΙ Ι [-] μμένης ⁝ ἀπὸ δὲ
τộ Ἡṛακλέ[ος] ἱρô μέχρις θαλάσσης τὴν ὁδὸν
ταύτην ἐπιστάται καθαιρόντων ⁝ αἱρέτω δὲ τὰ
ἐκ τῶν κ̣α[τοικι]ῶṿ κ̣α̣[ὶ] τὰ ἐπ̣ὶ̣ τῆς ὁδô ἐπὰν οἱ
ἀρχοὶ κελεύωσιν · ὃς [ἄν] τ̣ι [τ]ούτων μὴ ποιῆι ⁝ [κ]-
ατὰ τὰ γεγραμμένα ⁝ ἕκτην ἑκάστης ἡμέρης
ὀφελέτω τῆι πόλι ⁝ πρησ[σ]όντων ἐπιστάται κα-
ὶ τὤμυσυ αὐτοὶ ἰσχόντων ⁝ ἐπὶ τô τέγεος τῶν
κατ̣ọι̣κ̣ιῶν τῶν δημοσίων τῶν ἐν τῆι ὁδῶι τ-
αύτηι ⁝ θῆς ἕνεκεν μηδὲς ἀναβαινέτω ⁝ μηδ-
ὲ γυνὴ δ' ἐ[κ] τῶν θυρίδων θήσθω · ὅ τι ἂν τούτ-
ων ποιῆι ⁝ στατῆρα κατ' ἕκαστον ὁ ἐνοικέων
ὀφελέτω τῆι πόλι ⁝ πρη[σ]σόντων ἐπιστάται κα-
ὶ τὤμυσυ αὐτοὶ ἰσχόντων ⁝ ἐκ τô προφ[ρ]άγμ-
ατο[ς] τô προέχοντος ⁝ ἐς τὴν ὁδὸν ταύτην
ὑδρορροίην μὴ ποιέτω ⁝ ἂν δὲ ποιῆι, ἡμίεκτ-
ον ἑκάστης ἡμέρης ὀφελέτω ⁝ τὤμυσυ τῆι πό-
λι τὸ δὲ ἥμυσυ ἐπιστάτῃσιν ⁝ πρησσόντων ἐπ-
ιστάται ⁝ ἀπὸ Χαρίτων ἱρô μέχρις τῶν οἰκ-
ημάτων ἔνθα τὸ ἀργυραμοιβήϊον ⁝ καὶ ἔν-
θα τὸ συμπόσιον ⁝ καὶ ὡς ἡ ὁδὸς παρὰ πρυτα-
νήϊον ⁝ ἐν τῶι μέσωι τούτων κόπρον μὴ ἐσβα-
λλέτω μηδὲ προϊστάσθω · ὃς δ' ἄν τι τούτων πο-
ιῆι, ἡμίεκτον κατ' ἕκαστον ὁσάκις ἂνν ποιῆι ὀ-
φελέτω τῆι πόλι, πρη[σ]σόντων ἐπιστάται καὶ τ-
ὤμυσυ αὐτοὶ ἰσχόντων ⁝ ἂν δὲ μή, διπλήσι-
ον ὀφελόντων τῆι Ἀρτ[έ]μιδι τῆι Ἑκάτηι.

23 τῆς.ΑΓΛΙ Ι P. Gauthier, *BE* 1993, no. 395: τῆς [-]ΑΡΛ Ι Ι Duchêne, *SEG*. 26 κ̣α[τοικι]ῶṿ Duchêne: κ̣α[πηλεί]ωṿ Gauthier.

The regulations on this *stele* are closely contemporary with the first of the wine laws (**103**. A), employing similar script, parallel language and directing fines in part to Apollo Pythios. These regulations, which are broadly parallel to the remit of the city magistrates (*astynomoi*) in Athens (*Ath. Pol.* 50. ii) and in second-century Pergamum (*OGIS* 483, *SEG* xiii 521), are divided into two sections. The first section (1–18) concerns

is to show – – – he is to be – – – But when he has restored it, then he is to use the building.

19 Each resident is to make sure the road up against his own property is clean. If no one is resident, the owner of the building is to do it; the *epistatai* are to clean it themselves each month. And if anything falls, let them make – – –. From the shrine of Heracles as far as the sea, this road the *epistatai* are to clean. He is to take up what comes from the buildings and what is on the road, when the magistrates request it. Anyone who does not do any of these things according to what is written, he is to owe a *hekte* for each day to the *polis*; the *epistatai* are to exact it and keep half themselves. No one is to go up onto the roof of the public buildings in this street to be seen, nor shall a woman look out of the windows. For whatever of these things he does, the person resident is to owe to the *polis* a stater for each offence; the *epistatai* are to exact it and keep half themselves. From the balcony which protrudes into this road, let him not pour water. If he does, he is to owe a *hemiekton* for each day, half to the *polis*, half to the *epistatai*; let the *epistatai* exact it. From the shrine of the Charites up to the buildings where the money-exchange is and where the *symposion* is and along the road by the *prytaneion*, between these let no one throw out rubbish and no one solicit as a prostitute. Whosoever does any of these things is to owe a *hemiekton* to the city on each occasion that s/he does so; the *epistatai* are to exact it and keep half themselves; if not, they are to owe double to Artemis Hecate.

---

what can be built or constructed in particular streets; the second section concerns keeping the streets generally clean and free, and behaviour in particular streets.

From a legal point of view what is most interesting in this case is the responsibility given to magistrates. Whereas offences to do with wine rely in the first instance upon individuals prosecuting, in this case it is magistrates—*arkhoi* (whatever magistrates are in office) and *epistatai* (well attested in other Thasian inscriptions from the fourth century onwards)—who are charged with seeing to prosecutions. They are required even to keep a written record of the penalties inflicted (13–14). Unlike in the regulations concerning wine, there is no further body enjoined to ensure that the officials do their duty.

The behaviour regulated is partly concerned with what can be built, partly with keeping the streets clean, and partly with behaviour. The prohibitions on building are not completely preserved, but seem to concern either building up or digging down in the street. The regulations of behaviour involve who is responsible for keeping the street clean but also the use of the roofs of public buildings, women looking from windows, water being poured from balconies (or possibly some other projecting structure), and the throwing out of rubbish. Not surprisingly, it is the prohibitions on climbing to the roof and on women looking from windows that have attracted most attention.

In the original publication Duchêne suggested that climbing to the roof and women looking from windows were prohibited in association with religious occasions. In the case of the roofs of public buildings, climbing there to see a religious procession or a funeral or a civic occasion was likely to cause damage. In the case of windows, women watching there was prohibited because women were not welcome participants at all religious occasions, and we know them specifically to have been prohibited from the cult of Heracles on Thasos (*IG* XII Supp. 414). Graham, however, supported by Henry, has championed the view rejected by Duchêne that the women at the windows are prostitutes, and the 'public buildings' onto whose roofs it is forbidden to climb in order to see, or be seen, are brothels. What is more, what is being 'put forth' (προϊστάσθω) in l. 45 is not rubbish: the reference is rather to women putting themselves forth—i.e. soliciting.

A variety of considerations argues in favour of Graham's view. Regulation of the prices charged by female musicians and of competition for their services was part of the job of the *astynomoi* at Athens, along with keeping the streets clean and free of

---

105

Micythus' dedications at Olympia, *c.*460

Identical inscription found on two (perhaps three) grey marble statue bases in the sanctuary of Zeus at Olympia between 1876 and 1879, between the temple of Zeus and the temple of Hera. Drawing: *I. Olympia* 267–9, *LSAG*, pl. 49. 8

Euboean letters, with characteristic rounded *sigma*. *Stoichedon* (in *I. Olympia* 267 and 269).

I. Olympia 267–9 (with drawings); *SGDI* 5276; E. Preuner, *JDAI* xxxv 1920, 59–62*; *DGE* 794; Eckstein, ἀναθήματα, 33–42, 112–6; C. Gallavotti, *BCAL* xxvi 1978, 23–6 (cf. *SEG* xxviii 431); Arena, *Iscrizioni greche*

obstruction. Aristophanes jokes about women attracting men by appearing at the window (*Thesm.* 797–9; *Eccl.* 693–8 cf. 878–82; cf. *Pax* 979–85). There is little doubt that scenes on south Italian pottery of women in a window are intended to be erotic (K. Schauenburg, *MDAI*[*R*] lxxix 1972, 1–15). Although the phrase τῶν κατ̣ο̣ι̣κ̣ιῶν τῶν δημοσίων, 'public buildings', is hard to parallel (see on **167**), it is not hard to understand as a reference to brothels, and the curious construction earlier with reference to (rubbish) from *katoikiai* (26), where no specific party is identified as having the duty to clear up, suggests that those buildings have an unusual status. In l. 45 the verb 'put forth' (προϊστάσθω) is simply redundant unless given the sort of meaning that Graham and Henry suggest.

We know the location of the Heracleum, which was in the west of the city and has been excavated, and of the quay (the best translation for ὄχθη), but we are less certain of the location of the other topographical indicators. Most interesting here is the final area delineated, which is described in terms of the location of the shrine of the Charites, the money-exchange, the *symposion* and the *prytaneion*. The money-exchange, *symposion* (= building with dining-rooms?) and *prytaneion* (civic dining-room) are all surely public facilities, but must be located outside the agora (otherwise we would expect reference to be made simply to the agora). This suggests the existence of another cluster of public facilities elsewhere (at Athens too the *prytaneion* was not in the classical agora). Although the word used for 'money-exchange' is unique, it seems to have been regular for cities to designate a place for exchange of money, presumably because of the desire to regulate money-changers (see R&O 25. 5 for Athens, *SIG*^{3} 218. 9–10 for Olbia).

The dialect is Ionic, with e.g. *upsilon* for *iota* in ἥμυσυ; contraction of Ionic θέη and the cognate verb into θῆς and θήσθω; *epsilon* and *omicron* for the ει and ου when these are spurious dipthongs (i.e. close–mid-long vowels, as in ποιόντων and μηδὲς), ει and ου when these are real dipthongs; psilosis, as, with crasis, in τὤμυσυ; dative plurals in -ηισι as in ἐπιστάτηισιν. The text is punctuated with sets of three points, but the usage of the punctuation follows no clear logic.

arcaiche di Sicilia e Magna Grecia, iii. 64. Löhr, *Griechische Familienweihungen*, no. 45; Dubois, *Inscriptions grecques dialectales de Grande Grèce*, i. 35; Muller-Dufeu, *La Sculpture grecque: sources littéraires et épigraphiques*, no. 478. See also *LSAG* 244–5.

[Μίκυθος hο Χοίρο Ῥεγῖνος καὶ Μεσσέ]νιος ϝοικέον ἐν Τεγέει
[τἀγάλματα τάδε θεοῖς ἀνέθεκε πᾶσι]ν καὶ θεαῖς πάσαις
[παιδὸς ἐκ νόσο φθινάδος σοθέντος κ]αὶ χρεμάτον hόσσα ϝοι πλεῖστα ἐγέν-
[ετο δεκάτεν ἀπερξάμεν, ἐς Ὀλυμπίεν] ἐλθόν, ἐπεὶ τὰ εὐξάμεν.

3–4(–5) [παιδὸς δὲ νόσον φθινάδα νοσέοντος κ]αὶ χρημάτων ὅσσα ϝοι πλεῖστα ἐγέν[ετο δυνατὸν] | [ἰητροῖς δαπανηθέντων, ἐς Ὀλυμπίην] ἐλθὼν, ἔπειτα εὐξάμεν | [ος . . . . ἀνέθηκεν] *I. Olympia*: [hυπὲρ παιδός] γ' ἐ[κφθίνοντος εὐχὲ]ṇ [κ]αὶ χρεμάτον, hόσσα ϝοι πλεῖστα ἐγέν | [ετο, ἀπαρχέν. ἐ]πε[τέλεσα δὲ τὰ τε͂]ịδ' ἐπ̣ελθόν, ἐπεὶ τὰ εὐξαμεν Gallavotti.

Herodotus (VII. 170), in the course of telling why the Cretans refused to get involved in the resistance to the Persian invasion, notes that the Tarantines made war on Hyria, that Micythus son of Choerus persuaded the citizens of Rhegium to help the Tarantines, and that the Rhegians then lost 3,000 men in battle. Herodotus then gives the briefest of biographies of Micythus: that he was a household servant (*oiketes*) of Anaxilas (previously introduced at VII. 165 as tyrant of Rhegium), that he had been left in charge (as *epitropos*) of Rhegium, that when expelled from Rhegium he took up residence at Tegea in Arcadia, and that he dedicated many statues at Olympia.

Micythus' story is filled out by later authors. Strabo (253 / VI. i. 1) adds the detail that Micythus ('archon of Messana') was responsible for populating Pyxous with new settlers. Diodorus (XI. 48, under 476/5, cf. Justin IV 2) records that when Anaxilas died he left his slave Micythus in charge until such time as his sons came of age, and then (XI. 66, under 467/6) says that Hieron summoned the sons of Anaxilas (here recorded as past tyrant of Zancle) and advised them to order Micythus to give an account. He gave so honest an account as to win general approbation, and Anaxilas' sons asked him to take back control. But Micythus refused and sailed off to Tegea to live out the rest of his life enjoying men's praise.

But the fullest account is given by Pausanias (V. 26. ii–v), writing in the middle of the second century AD. Pausanias notes Herodotus' account of Micythus and records that he found the dedications made by Micythus to be many and in no order, but that near the statue of Iphitus crowned by Truce, i.e. in the east colonnade of the temple of Zeus (V. 10. x), he found Amphitrite, Poseidon and Hestia, made by Glaucus of Argos; alongside the temple of Zeus he found Persephone, Aphrodite, Ganymede, Artemis, Homer, Hesiod, Asclepius, Health, Contest (*Agon*) with jumping weights, Dionysus, Orpheus and Zeus (a statue which Pausanias has already noted at V. 24. vi as being beardless), works of another Argive, Dionysius. He notes also that Nero was said to have carried off yet further dedications by Micythus. Pausanias then adds that the inscriptions give Micythus' father as Choerus and his origin as from Rhegium and Messana, and say that he dwelt in Tegea and made the offerings at Olympia in fulfilment of a vow made for the recovery of a son sick with a wasting

Micythus son of Choerus of Rhegium and Messana, living in Tegea, dedicated these statues to all the gods and all the goddesses after his son was saved from a respiratory disease, and he gave a tithe of the money, of all the great amount that he possessed, when he came to Olympia, since he vowed that.

---

disease (v. 26. v: εὐχήν τινα ἐκτελῶν ἐπι σωτηρίᾳ παιδὸς νοσήσαντος νόσον φθινάδα). On the basis of Diodorus' account these dedications must have been made after 467.

Two substantial and five small fragments have been identified by the distinctive information that the dedicant was 'living in Tegea', and by the Euboean script, as part of the dedicatory inscriptions on Micythus' statues. From where they were found they must have belonged to the second group of twelve statues seen by Pausanias on the north side of the temple of Zeus. The inscribed blocks from the statue base can be associated with further blocks, some of them reused and one bearing an inscription (by the people of Sparta) from the second century AD (*I. Olympia* 316). The most detailed study of the base, by Eckstein, concludes that it was almost 10 m. long and originally supported 20 to 22 figures, including all the Olympian gods (since the dedication was to all the gods and goddesses), before Nero removed some. It is easy to see the rationale for the addition of statues of Asclepius and Health to the Olympian gods, harder to see why the group also included Homer, Hesiod, Orpheus, Ganymede and a jumping Contest. There are some blocks of shelly limestone still in their original position north of the temple and incorporating building debris from the temple of Zeus which are probably the foundations for this dedication, and which further confirm a date for the dedication of *c.*460.

The marble blocks from the statue bases show where the feet of the statues were placed. These indicate that the statues were about three-quarters life-size, and had their feet more or less together; they were therefore standing still, rather than in motion, and not trailing a leg in the pose famous from Polyclitus' Doryphorus. This is in line with the date of around 460, which is generally taken to be the date of the (over-life-sized) Riace bronzes whose feet are similarly close together. Attempts to identify Roman copies of the gods and heroes featured here have yielded no definitive result.

The base certainly bore the same inscription twice, since much the same portion of the dedication survives from two blocks (*I. Olympia* 267 and 268). Although only 267 is *stoichedon*, the lines are very similarly aligned in 268. Whether five much smaller fragments (*I. Olympia* 269) belong to another repetition of the same dedication or to an inscription or inscriptions with different content is not clear. Preuner's restoration, given above, does not attempt to use these further fragments, but assumes that Pausanias got all his information from the dedicatory inscription, and that the inscription should therefore indicate the nature of the son's illness and the fact of his recovery. Pausanias' accuracy as a reader of inscriptions has been vindicated in recent years.[1]

The chief problem presented by the surviving remains is the change from third person to first person implied by the final verb ('he vowed', εὐξάμεν (= ηὐξάμην)). This difficulty caused the first editors to assume that the end of the fourth line was not the end of the inscription and that εὔξαμεν was part of the participle εὐξάμενος ('having vowed') which was followed with a third-person verb of dedication. However, the first two lines, which also finish short of the end of the block, end with a complete word, and there seems no reason for the scribe to break off in the middle of a word with plenty of room on the stone to complete the sense. It is a further difficulty that the article (τὰ) before the final verb has to be taken as the equivalent to the demonstrative (ταῦτα), a usage known from Homer, Pindar and some epigraphic texts, but not common.

The letter forms are Euboean, such as are common in Sicilian and south Italian communities tracing links with Euboea, with one exception: in the second version of

[1] See esp. Habicht, *Pausanias' Guide to Ancient Greece*, ch. iii, Zizza, *Le iscrizioni nella Periegesi di Pausania*; see also below **112**, **164**. An attempt to incorporate the fragments of 269 into the same text by Gallavotti is given in the apparatus; it has the weakness that Pausanias could not have derived his story from that text. The text in *I. Olympia* is further from Pausanias' text, has one too many letters in the first half of l. 3, and wrongly continues l. 3 beyond the preserved end of the stone.

106

Eleusinian regulations, before 460

White marble pillar, broken at top and bottom, inscribed on all four faces (*A*–*D*; we omit *D*, where only 2–3 letters are preserved and in only 10 lines). The break at the top is ancient and the stone seems to have been subsequently repaired. Found by the 'Theseum' (= Hephaesteum) at Athens but originally set up in the City Eleusinium, where further fragments have been found. Acquired by Elgin. Now in British Museum. Phot. *Hesperia* xiv 1945, 62–5 with xv 1946, 253; Clinton, pls. 5–6.

Attic letters. *Stoichedon* (*A* and *C* 23 except for *C*. 47–50, *B* and *D* 11).

*SIG*³ 42; *LSS* 3; *IG* i³ 6*; *I. Eleusis* 19. Trans: Fornara 75 (*B* and *C*), Dillon & Garland³ 3. 36–7 (*B* and *C*).

the inscription (*I. Olympia* 268) the λ of ἐλθόν takes a form common in Elis but not in Euboean script. The most ready explanation would seem to be that the inscriber was copying from a master version written by a Euboean hand, perhaps by Micythus himself, but at this point substituted the more familiar letter form for the form before him.

Historically the interest of these inscriptions lies in the confirmation that they give of the exceptional nature of Micythus' dedication. It was common enough to make dedications to mark recovery from illness, and the numerous votives in the form of body-parts are most plausibly taken to mark the recovery of the part dedicated. Dedications to mark recovery from illness are not, however, common at Olympia (they particularly concentrate in sanctuaries of gods associated with healing, such as Asclepius, though the massive expansion in such cult sites is a feature of the end of the fifth and the fourth century). But Micythus has not only chosen to commemorate the recovery of his son at a particularly prominent sanctuary, he has chosen sites for his dedications that were particularly prominent (in and beside the temple of Zeus, at that point either just finished or indeed under construction), and has dedicated a very large number of statues. His dedication will not only have put in the shade dedications by victorious athletes of single figures, it will also have put in the shade dedications by the tyrants of Sicilian cities (cf. **101**). The story told by Diodorus implies that Micythus himself had little to gain politically from this display, but his gesture can hardly have been politically innocent: if a dedication of this size could be made by a former slave who had held power for less than a decade, should we be impressed by the dedications made by those who were currently tyrants?

A

\- - - - - - - - - - - - - - - - -
[— 14 —] δραχμ̣ε̂ισ̣[ι]-
[— 13 —]τ̣ες τὸς ι̣ο̣[.]
[— 13 —]μενος δε̣μ̣ο̣[.]
[— 13 —] τ̣ο̂ν πόλεο[ν .]
[— 11 — δ]οκε̂ι ⁝ ἀνατιθ̣[.]-
[— 12 —]α̣ ⁝ ἐάν τι[ς] τ̣ο̂ν̣[.]
[— 14 —]ον ἒ ΗΟϟΑΛ̣[.]
[— 14 —]ο ἒ εν[.]ορ[. .]
[— 14 —]νας hίνα [. .]
[— 13 —]αντο[. .]ιν σ
[— 10 — το̂]ν πόλε[ον] ταυτ-
[— 12 —] χρε̣[— 8 —]
[— 11 —]μ̣εμ̣βολ[— 6 —]
[— 12 —]εχθεο[. . .]χε̣[.]
[— 11 —]ν δε[. .]ν̣[. . .]λ̣ο[.]
[— 10 — ἐ]ὰν δὲ μέ, [h]ε̣κασ[τ]-
[— 12 —]ο̣[. . . .]ε[.]σε[. .]
[— 12 —]α [. . .6. . .]ιν̣[. .]
[— 13 —]ιμ[. .]ιας πε[.]
[— 14 —]ετα[.]τεν[. .]
[— 16 —]ια̣[. .]ο[. .]
[— 12 —]Λ[. . .]π̣ο̣[— 5 —]
[— 8 —]σ̣ειαν̣ κ̣α̣[ὶ] λ̣αμ[. . . .]
[— 7 —]ολει κ̣α[ὶ] μ̣[ὲ] νεοτ̣ε̣[ρ .]-
[. . χρέσθ]ο το̂ι [hιε]ρ̣ο̂ι· [ἐ]ὰν δὲ [.]
[— 7 —]ι μὲ χ̣[ρέσ]θο· ἐ̣ὰ̣ν δὲ ἰ[.]
[— 5 — κ]ατὰ ταὐτὰ ταῦτα· ἐὰν [.]
[. . . πλε]ῖ̣στον κατὰ τὲν δύνα[μ]-
[ιν . . . . ·] πρᾶχσαι δ' ἔκπραχ<σι̣>[ν· ἐ]-
[ὰν δὲ μὲ] ἐγδο̂ι τὸν ὀφλόντα, μὲ
[χρέσθο] τ̣ο̂ι hιερο̂ι : ἐὰν ἀμφι[σ]-
[βετο̂σι] μὲ κλεθε̂ναι ἐμ πό[λει]-
[— 6 —]εν ἐλθο̂σαν ἀδικ[. . .]
[— 7 —] hύστερον hε̣ [β]ο̣[λ]ὲ α̣
[— 8 —]ι : τὸν Ἀθεναῖον μὲ [.]
[. .]ΕΣ [. . τ]ούτον το̂ν πόλεον μ[ε]-
δὲ hαμο̂[. .]ιᾶσθαι ἐὰν μὲ [δί]κ[ε]-

A We have throughout, following Clinton, *I. Eleusis* i, pp. 25–6, placed the text one *stoichos* further left on the stone than *IG*. *A*. 18 The first *epsilon* is Clinton's reading. *A*. 24 κ̣α̣[ὶ] Clinton: [.]Λ[.] *IG*. *A*. 37 [ἐκ γ]ε̂ς [πο τ]ούτον *IG*. *A*. 38 hαμο̂[ς β]ιᾶσθαι *IG*.

A

1 – – – drachmas – – – the people – – – the cities – – – decides, dedicate – – – if someone – – – of the cities this – – – if not, each – – –

26 – – – let him (not) use the sanctuary; but if – – – let him not use it; and if – – – this in the same way; and if – – – most according to its power – – – And to exact the fine; but if he does not turn in the debtor, let him not use the sanctuary. If they deny that they have been summoned on the acropolis – – – have come without justice – – – later the council. – – – the athenian is not – – – of these cities, in no way be – – –, unless he has been

ν̣ ὀφλόν[τα] ἐπιχορίαν ἒ ἐς πο[λ]-
εμίος λ[εφ]θ̣έντα· hέτις δ' ἂν τ[ô]-
μ πόλεον μὲ ἐθέλει, δ[ί]κας δ̣ι[δ]-
όναι καὶ δέχεσθαι Ἀθ̣εναί[οι]-
σιν ἀπὸ χσυ<μ>βολôν.
vacat

B

[— 9 —]ια̣ *d*
[— 8 —]ντο
[— 8 —]τοσ
lacuna
[— 10 — τ]-
[ὰ] μὲν hακόσι[α]
[h]απλêι, τὰ δὲ [h]-
[ε]κόσια διπλ[ê]-
[ι· σ]πονδὰς εἶν-
[αι] τοῖσι μύστ-
[εσιν] καὶ το[ῖς]
[ἐπ]όπτεισιν [κ]-
[αὶ τ]οῖς ἀκολ[ο]-
[ύθ]οισιν καὶ [χ]-
[ρέ]μασιν τôν [ὀ]-
[θ]νείον καὶ [Ἀθ]-
[ε]ν[α]ίοισιν [h]ά- *a*
πασιν· ἄρχε[ν] δ-
ὲ τὸν χρόνο[ν] τ-
ôν σπονδôν [τ]ô
Μεταγειτνιô-
νος μενὸς ἀπ[ὸ]
διχομενίας [κ]-
αὶ τὸν Βοεδρ[ο]-
μιôνα καὶ τô [Π]-
υανοφσιôνος
μέχρι δεκάτε-
ς hισταμένο· τ-
ὰς δὲ σπονδὰς
εἶναι ἐν τêισ-
ι πόλεσιν hό[σ]-
αι χρôνται τô-
ι hιερôι καὶ Ἀ-
θεναίοισιν ἐ-
κεῖ ἐν τêισιν
αὐτêσι πόλεσ-

convicted in a local court or captured among the enemy. Any city that is not willing is to give and receive court cases with the Athenians according to the existing conventions.

B

4 – – – in the case of involuntary acts there shall be a simple penalty, in the case of voluntary acts a double penalty.

8 There shall be a truce for the *mystai* and for the *epoptai*, and for the servants and property of foreigners and for all Athenians. The period of the truce is to begin during Metageitnion, from the full moon, during Boedromion and during Pyanopsion until the tenth. The truce is to apply to all the cities that use the sanctuary and to the Athenians there in the same cities.

ιν· τοῖσι δὲ ὀλ-
είζοσι μυστε-
ρίοισιν τὰς [σ]-
πονδὰς εἶνα[ι]
τô Γαμελιôνο-
ς μενὸς ἀπὸ δ[ι]-
[χ]ομενίας κα[ὶ]
τὸν Ἀνθεστε[ρ]-
[ι]ôνα καὶ τô Ἐλ-
αφεβολιôνος
μέχρι δεκάτε-
ς hισταμένο.
vacat

C

d [. . .]θ̣αι̣[—— 17 ——]
[.]α̣θεμ̣ι̣[—— 17 ——]
ν̣αι τ[—— 20 ——]
[.]σ̣τ̣[—— 20 ——]
lacuna
[—— 12 ——]ὀ̣βολ[ὸν παρὰ τ]-
[ô μύστο hεκάστ]ο : hιερ̣[οποιὸς]
[δὲ λαμβάνεν hε]μιοβέ̣[λιον . .]
[. . .]εραν [παρὰ τ]ô μύστο [hε]κ̣ά[σ]-
[το·] τ̣ὲν hιέρ[εα]ν τὲν Δέμ̣ε̣τρος
[λ]αμ[β]ά̣ν̣εν μυ̣[στ]ερίοις τ[ο]ῖς ὀ-
[λ]έζο̣σιν παρὰ̣ [τô μ]ύστο h[εκ]άσ-
[τ]ο ὀβολόν καὶ [τοῖς μ]είζ[οσιν]
[μ]υ̣στερίοις ὀ[βολὸν παρὰ τô μ]-
[ύσ]το hεκάστο̣· σ̣[ύμπαντας ὀβο]-
λὸς τοῖν θεο[ῖ]ν̣ [εἶναι πλὲν] hε-
χσακοσίον κα̣[ὶ χιλίον δρ]αχμ̣-
ôν· ἀπὸ δὲ τôν hε̣[χσακοσίο]ν κα-
ὶ χιλίον δραχμ[ôν τὲν hι]έρεα-
ν τἀναλόματα [δôναι καθ]άπερ
τέος ἀνέλοτο ⁝ Ε̣[ὐ]μ̣[ολπίδ]ας κα-
ὶ Κέρ[υ]κ̣α̣ς λαμβάν[εν παρὰ] τô μ-
ύστ[ο h]εκ̣άστο π̣έ̣ν̣[τε ὀβολὸς τ]-
ộν̣ [ἀρρ]ένον, θελειô[ν δὲ τρεῖς·]
[ἀτελε̂ μ]ύστεμ μὲ ἐν[εῖναι μυε̂]-
[ν μεδέ]να̣ π̣λὲν τô ἀφ' [ἑστίας μυ]-

C. 5–6 ὀ̣βολ[ὸν παρὰ τ|ô μύστο hεκάστ]ο Clinton (cf. *C.* 11–12): ὀ̣βολ[—— 7 ——]|[—— 12 ——]ο *IG*. *C.* 6 hιερ̣[οποιὸς] *IG*: hιερ̣[οφάντι|δε Clinton. *C.* 7–8 hε]μιοβέ̣[λιον κα|θ' ἑμ]έραν *IG*; hε]μιοβέ̣[λιον hε|κατ]έραν Clinton.

For the Lesser Mysteries the truce is to be during Gamelion from the full moon and during Anthesterion and during Elaphebolion until the tenth.

C

– – – an obol from each *mystes*. The *hieropoioi* are to take half an obol each from each *mystes*. At the Lesser Mysteries the priestess of Demeter is to take an obol from each *mystes* and at the Greater Mysteries an obol from each *mystes*. All the obols shall belong to the two Goddesses except for 1,600 drachmas. From the 1,600 drachmas the priestess is to give the expenses just as has been expended until now. The Eumolpidai and the Kerykes are to take from each *mystes* five obols from a man and three obols from a woman. An initiate who has not paid is not to enter any initiation except in the case

[ομέν]ο : Κέρυκας δὲ μυ[ε̂ν δίχα τ]
[ὸς] μύστας hέκαστον [καὶ Εὐμο]-
[λπίδ]ας [κ]ατὰ ταὐ]τα· ἐ[ὰν δὲ κατ]-
[ὰ] πλείος εὐθύνεσθα[ι χιλίασ]-
[ι] δρα[χ]με̂σι· μυε̂ν δὲ ḥ[οὶ ἂν hεβ]-
ο̂σι Κερύκον καὶ Εὐ[μολπιδο̂ν·]
το̂ δὲ hιερο̂ ἀργυρί[ο —7—]
[.]Eϟ K[....]ẹι̂ναι Ἀθεν[αίοισι χρ]-
[ε̂]σθαι ḥέος ἂν βόλο[νται καθά]-
περ το̂ τε̂ς Ἀθεναία[ς ἀργυρίο]
το̂ ἐμ πόλει· τὸ δὲ ἀρ[γύριον τὸ]-
ς hιεροποιὸς /// [.]το[—7— ἐ]-
[μ] πόλẹị ταμιεύεσθ[αι —6—]
[.]δ[....]χεν ἐν το̂ι ḥ[—8—]
[.]β[....]εν τοṇ [ὀ]ρφ[ανον —5—]
[.] τὸς ὀρφανὸς π̣α̣ι̂[δας καὶ τὸς]
[μ]ῦστας hεκαστομ. |⸗ [—8—]
[τ]ὸς μύστας τὸς Ἐλε[υσι̂νι ...]
[.]ẹνος ἐν τε̂ι αὐλε̂ι [ἐντὸς το̂ h]-
[ι]ερο̂, τὸς δὲ ἐν ἄστει [—7—]
[.] ἐν το̂ι Ἐλευσινίοι. [*va*c.]
[τ]ὸν ἐπὶ το̂ι βομο̂ι ἱερέα καὶ τ[ὸν —c.6—]
τὸν θεοῖν καὶ τὸν ἱερέα τὸ[ν —c.8—]
[λ]ανβάνεν ἕκαστον τότο[ν —c.8— παρὰ]
[το̂] μύστ[ο ἐ]κάστο I[- - -]

C. 26–7 μυ[ε̂ν δίχα τ|ὸς] Clinton; μυ[ε̂ν —5—]|[. .] *IG*. *C.* 28–9 ἐ[ὰν δὲ κατ|ὰ] πλείος Clinton: ἐ[—7—]|[.] πλείος *IG*. *C.* 32–3 ἀργυρί[ο τε̂ς ἀπαρ]|χ̣ε̂ς ẹχ̣[σ]ẹι̂ναι Clinton; ἀργυρί[ο —7—]|[.]Eϟ[....]ιναι *IG*; [.]ΕΣΚ[....] I. A. Pafford, *ZPE* clxxvii 2011, 75–8. *C.* 33–4 Ἀθεν[αίοισι χρ]|[ε̂]σθαι ḥọ́[τι] Clinton: Ἀθεν[αίοισι . .]|[.]σθαι ḥέος *IG*. *C.* 37–8 hιεροποιὸς /// [.]το[—7— ἐ]|[μ] *IG*; hιεροποιὸς τ̣[ὸ] το[ι̂ν Θεοι̂ν ἐ]|[μ] Clinton. *C.* 39 h Clinton: oblique stroke *IG*. *C.* 43–4 Ἐλε[υσι̂νι . . .]|[.]ẹνος *IG*; Ἐλε[υσι̂νι μυο]|[μ]ẹ́νος Clinton. *C.* 45–6 ἄστει [—7—]|[.] *IG*; ἄστει [μυομένο]|[ς] Clinton. *C.* 47–8 τ[ὸν φαιδυντὲν] | το<ι̂>ν θεοι̂ν καὶ τὸν ἱερέα τὸ[ν —c.12—] *IG*; τ[ὸν κέρυκα] |τὸν θεοι̂ν καὶ τὸν ἱερέα τὸ[ν παναγε̂ *vv*] Clinton. *C.* 49–50 τότο[ν —c.10— παρὰ]|[το̂] μύστ[ο ἐ]κάστο I - - - *IG*; τότο[ν ὀβολὸν παρὰ *vv*]|[το̂] μύστ[ο ἐ]κάστο ἱ[ερὸν τοι̂ν Θεοι̂ν *vvvv*] Clinton.

The laws on this stone, which are dated primarily from their letter forms, constitute the core regulation of the Eleusinian Mysteries in force for a century until superseded by *SEG* xxx 61 (= *Agora* xvi 56, *I. Eleusis* 138) *c.*360, though variously supplemented later in the fifth century (e.g. by the decree of 432 or later of which only the amendment survives, establishing *epistatai* to look after the finances of the two Goddesses, *IG* i³ 32 = *I. Eleusis* 30). They show the Athenians taking concern both for the way in which initiation is run and what the financial aspects might be, and for the international aspects of the festival.

of the person being initiated from the hearth. The Kerykes are to initiate the *mystai* separately, each one, and the Eumolpidai in the same way. If they initiate in larger groups they are to be fined a thousand drachmas at their scrutiny. Any of the Kerykes and Eumolpidai who has reached adulthood is to initiate. The Athenians may use the sacred money – – – as they wish, just as in the case of the money of Athena on the acropolis. The *hieropoioi* – – – are to look after the money on the acropolis. – – – of the orphans – – – the orphan children and the initiates each – – – the initiates who are – – – at Eleusis within the hall of the sanctuary, and those who are – – –in the city in the Eleusinion. The priest at the altar and the – – – of the two Goddesses and the priest who – – – are to take, each of these, – – – from each *mystes*, – – –

The early history of cult at Eleusis has been subject to much debate, not only over whether there was cult continuity from the Bronze Age but also over the date at which the ritual at Eleusis first involved 'Mysteries'. None of the archaeological or other indicators (e.g. the fact of widespread diffusion of Demeter Eleusinia in Ionia) either prove or disprove cult continuity from the Bronze Age.[1] Archaeological

[1] For discussion see Parker, *Athenian Religion: A History*, ch. ii, and Cosmopoulos (ed.), *Greek Mysteries*, chs. i and ii.

evidence for cult is certain from the eighth century, but clear archaeological and literary evidence for a major Mystery cult appears only in the sixth century with distinctive cult buildings, a possible mention of the Mysteries in the laws of Solon (Andoc. I. 111; cf. *Ath. Pol.* 57. i–ii), and the *Homeric Hymn to Demeter*.[2] As early as the first half of the seventh century there was a shrine on the south slope of the acropolis almost certainly already devoted to the Eleusinian deities (the 'City Eleusinion': see Miles, *The Athenian Agora*, xxxi. 16–23), and it is there that both the earliest regulations of the Eleusinian sanctuary (*IG* i³ 231 = *I. Eleusis* 7, dated to the end of the sixth century, very fragmentary but naming a number of cult officials and mentioning bushels of wheat) and this law were found.

Recognition that the cult of Demeter and Persephone (Kore) at Eleusis may be a phenomenon of the archaic period, rather than of the Bronze Age, has gone together with rejection of the traditional view that Eleusis was once independent of Athens and incorporated into Attica only after conflict. Evidence for such conflict is minimal (largely misinterpretation of Hdt. I. 30. v combined with the Athenian tradition about synoecism, Thuc. II. 15. i–ii). The more or less simultaneous appearance of the cult of Demeter in Eleusis and in Athens itself, the existence of an Eleusinion at Phaleron in the classical period, the close association with the Lesser Mysteries held at the sanctuary of the Mother at Agrae (just outside the town of Athens), and evidence for what is either further local Eleusinia in the demes or deme use of the city Eleusinion, instead indicate a cult embraced by the whole *polis* community from the beginning, with merely its centre in the fertile Thriasian plain.[3]

City regulation of the Eleusinian Mysteries is therefore little surprise. A significant part of the Solonian lawcode, like the lawcode that replaced it at the end of the fifth century, consisted of the calendar of Athenian religious festivals (including Eleusinian provisions); see S. D. Lambert, *BSA* xcvii 2002, 353–99. A number of early fifth-century Athenian decrees concern themselves with cult-related matters—games related to the cult of Heracles at Sunium (*IG* i³ 3), behaviour on the Athenian acropolis (*IG* i³ 4), the ritual programme at one of the Eleusinian festivals (*IG* i³ 5 = *I. Eleusis* 13); and see further **108**.

Nevertheless, this is a very revealing inscription. In the first place, it makes clear the status of the Eleusinian Mysteries as a panhellenic event. The Athenians talk of worshippers 'using the sanctuary' (repeatedly in *A*) in exactly the same language as that used of worshippers at Olympia (cf. Thuc. V. 50. i). They make the Mysteries—the Lesser Mysteries as well as the Greater Mysteries—the occasion for a truce not only for all who are participating, but for Athenians anywhere (for Athenian action in response to breaches of the Eleusinian truce see R&O 35), systematically laying out to whom the truce applies (*B*. 8–17), when the truce applies (*B*. 17–27), and where the truce applies (*B*. 27–36). Although the surviving inscription does not provide for

[2] On the *Homeric Hymn to Demeter* see Richardson, *The Homeric Hymn to Demeter*; Foley (ed.), *The Homeric 'Hymn to Demeter'*; Suter, *The Narcissus and the Pomegranate*.

[3] Cf. Parker, *Polytheism and Society at Athens*, 332–3, *Athenian Religion: A History*, 25; for the prominence of Eleusinian cult in the Tetrapolis calendar see S. D. Lambert in Blok *et al.* (edd.), *Feasting and Polis Institutions*.

the proclamation of this truce, advertisement will have been essential. Such advertisement will have made clear to Greeks that the Eleusinian Mysteries were as much the concern of them all as were the Olympic games, for which there was a comparable truce. The Greater Mysteries took place from 13 to 16 (or 17) and 19 to 22 Boedromion (approximately our September), the Lesser Mysteries around 20 Anthesterion (February). The truces therefore allow about three weeks for travel to and from Attica. Together the two truces allow all initiates and all Athenians four months a year when they can travel under truce. *A*. 36–40 insists that the only Athenians not covered by the truce are those who have been convicted in a local court or are prisoners of war. The political importance to the Athenians of asserting the truce cannot be underestimated.

Second, it shows that although the Eleusinian Mysteries were, exceptionally, open to participation from all over Greece, they were very much an Athenian civic event. Offences in relation to the use of the sanctuary are regarded as civic offences. Dealing with them may involve cult officials (the text of *A* is too fragmentary to be sure), but it certainly involves the Athenian council (*A*. 35; see further **141**). Andocides alleges that according to Solonian law the council met in the City Eleusinion on the first day after the Mysteries. The only other civic festival that we know to have attracted similar attention from the council was the Dionysia. The final clause of *A* (40–3), confirms the superiority of legal agreements between cities (for which see **120**) over particular arrangements made, as here, in regard to particular local offences.

These laws also regulate both the financial and ritual procedures during the festival. The Athenians lay down the fees to be collected. After the addition, in what is evidently an afterthought, of fees to the priest at the altar, some other officer of the two Goddesses, and a further priest, no fewer than 7 obols per person are here collected (apart from the further 3 obols paid by females and 5 by males to the Eumolpidai or Kerykes). The 7 obols are to be deposited in the funds of the Goddesses, and from these the sum of 1,600 dr. is allowed for the expenses of the festival, at the discretion of the priestess (an interesting example of the practical responsibility accorded to women by virtue of their priestly roles). Some further fees may be missing from the surviving fragments, but on the basis of a 7-obol fee, covering the expenses would require the participation of 1,372 individuals, giving some idea of the scale of the event. Since one is only initiated once, 1,372 initiands in any one year, of an average age (for the sake of argument) of 30 in an age structure where 30-year-olds constitute about 1.5 per cent of the population, imply a total population from which the initiated are drawn of over 80,000.[4]

Whether the city is also concerned with how the ritual is conducted has been subject to some discussion. On the text given here, the city, while leaving who is initiated entirely to the discretion of any adult member of the priestly families of the

[4] *C*. 34 has sometimes been restored to refer to income from the collection of firstfruits, but this reading is neither epigraphically plausible nor plausible in its immediate context: see I. A. Pafford, *ZPE* clxxvii 2011, 75–8.

Eumolpidai and Kerykes, expressly forbids initiation in groups and requires individual initiation. But the word for 'separately' is restored in *C.* 26, and it has been suggested that prohibition on 'more' in *C.* 29 might be a prohibition on exacting more money, rather than on initiation in larger groups (for the alternative case see R. M. Simms, *GRBS* xxxi 1990, 183–95). Nevertheless, alternative restorations of the text give a very forced sense to the Greek, and since the following clause is concerned with exactly who may initiate we should expect a transition in topic from finances to the act of initiation at this point in the text. What constitutes initiation here is never specified, and has again been disputed (see Clinton, *I. Eleusis*, ii. 8–11), but it can apparently happen in the city (*C.* 45) as well as at Eleusis (*C.* 43–4). The most plausible interpretation is that some ritual introduction was required before an individual could take part in the Mysteries. This preliminary initiation enabled participation in the rites at Eleusis as a *mystes*; the person initiated as a *mystes* one year could

---

107

Decree of the Athenian deme Scambonidae, *c.*460

A white marble *stele* inscribed on three sides, broken on the fourth side and at the bottom, discovered by R. Chandler in the floor of a house near the 'Theseum' (= Hephaesteum). Now in British Museum (presented by the Society of Dilettanti in 1781). Phot. (of *B*) Cook, *Greek Inscriptions*, 41; our pl. 2. *a*, *b* (*A*, *B*).

Attic letters; those of face *C* (especially β) have been thought earlier in form, and since there are other reasons for thinking that that is where the inscription begins we print that first. *Stoichedon* 14 (*C*), 15 (*A*), 7 (*B*).

LSCG 10; *IG* i³ 244*. Trans. Dillon & Garland³ 10. 20. See also Humphreys, *The Strangeness of Gods*, 145–6; Wijma, *Embracing the Immigrant*, 103–9.

C

[θέσ]μια : Σ̣[καμβονι]
[δ]ôν ⁝ τὸν δέ[μαρχον]
[κ]αὶ τὸς ⁝ hι[εροποι]-
ὸς ⁝ τôι Λεô[ι δρᾶν τ]-
[έ]λεον ⁝ λε̑χ[σιν . . .]
[ὀ]βολὸν : hε[κάστοι]
Σκαμβονι[δôν καὶ]
τ̣ὸς μετοίκ̣[ος λαχ]-
ε̑ν : ἐν ἀγορᾶ[ι τε̑ι Σ]-
[κ]αμβονιδô[ν . . . .]
[.]οισι̣ : δρᾶν [τέλεο]-
[ν] : νέμεν δὲ : ε[—5—]

C. 1–2 [θέσ]μια : Σ̣[καμβονιδ]ôν Humphreys: [. . .]μια : κ̣[—7—|.]ον *IG*.

return in the following year as an *epoptes* (*B.* 11) (K. Clinton, in Cosmopoulos (ed.), *Greek Mysteries*, 50–78, and in *I. Eleusis*, ii. 8–11). There was one special initiate: the 'child initiated from the hearth', who is here exempted from any fees (*C.* 25–6). This child may have been the only child initiated, and appears to have been in some way a representative of the city—'the hearth' in question is perhaps the hearth of the *prytaneion*. The fourth-century regulations appear to allow anyone who wishes to propose a candidate for the 'hearth-initiate' (*SEG* xxx 61. *A.* 41–2). For the provisions here for orphans cf. **178**.

Andocides, a member of the priestly family of the Kerykes who himself was responsible for initiations (1. 132), claims (1. 116) that a law displayed on a *stele* in the City Eleusinion forbade anyone laying a suppliant branch in the Eleusinion, with a penalty of 1,000 drachmas. It is possible that that law was originally somewhere on this *stele*, but it might have been a subsequent additional law.

C

Laws of Scambonidae. The demarch and the sacred officials are to make a sacrifice of a full-grown victim to Leos: distribution of — obols to each of the Scambonidae, and the metics are to take a share, in the agora of Scambonidae. – – – At the ?Cronia make a sacrifice of a full-grown victim and distribute – – – At the Synoikia,

[.]α[.]τα : τôι : σ[–5–]
[.]ο[. .]ειον : κα[. . . .]
[. . .]οντα : ἐπι[. . . .]
[. .]εν : Χσυνοι[κίοι]-
[ς] : ἐ[μ] πόλει : τέ[λεον]
[τ]ὰ [δ]ὲ κρέα : ἀπο[δόσ]-
θαι : ὀμά : Ἐπιζε[φύρ]-
[ο]ισι : ἐμ Πυθίο[ι . .]
[.]ον : τὰ <δ>ὲ κρέα [ἀπο]-
[δ]όσθαι : ὀμά : ⁝ [. . . .]
[.]οι[ς] κ̣ατὰ τ[αὐτά?]
– – – – – – – – – – –

A

[–11–]μεν : [.]
[–8–] τ̣[ὸ] τ̣έλος
[–7–]ε̣ν: νέμεν δ-
[ὲ τὰ κρέα] μέχρι hελ-
[ίο δυ. .]ο[.] : [ἐὰν] δὲ μὲ
[–7–]Ο⁄. . : [ε]ὐ̣θυ-
[ν–5–] : [.]ο[––5–]μα
[–13–]αι
[–6–] : [ἐ]ν̣ ἀ̣[γ]ορᾶι : ἀ-
[πο. .]σθ[αι] : [ἀπ]ο[μ]ισθ-
[ôσαι] : [–5–]τα : τάδε
[–5–] : [π]λὲν τô κομα
[. . .] Ο ⁝ τοδε : τô δεμά-
[ρχο] ε̣̂ν̣α̣ι τὸ δέρμα : δ-
[–5–]ος : hοποίαν δ’
[ἂν hαρμ]όττεσθαι δ-
[έει θυσ]ίαν : διδόνα-
[ι Διπολ]ιείοις : καὶ
[Παναθ]εναίοις : νέμ-
[εν ἐν] ἀ̣γορᾶι : τε̂ι Σκ-
[αμβο]νιδôν : hόσα δ̣ὲ̣
[. . . .]ΑϟΕϟ : hεμίχον̣
[–7–] ΡΕΝ̣ . ΟΜ̣ . Ο
– – – – – – – – – – – –

A. 12–13 κομά | [ρχο] Hicks, Wijma, 104.

on the acropolis, a full-grown victim, and sell the meat raw; at the Epizephyria in the Pythion a — and sell the meat raw; at the – – – in the same way – – –

A

– – – end – – – distribute the meat until sunset. If they do not – – – audit. – – – sell in the agora, rent out – – – these – – – except for – – – this, the skin is to belong to the demarch – – – whatever sort of sacrifice it is necessary to be appropriate, give at the Dipolieia and at the Panathenaea, distribute in the agora of Scambonidae all – – – a half *chous* – – –

B

[.] κερυχ[θ]-
ε̑ι : ἐπαγγ-
ελθε̑ι : κα-
ὶ τὰ κοιν-
[ὰ] τὰ Σκαμ-
βονιδο̑ν
σοο̑ : καὶ ἀ-
ποδόσο : π-
αρὰ τὸν ε-
ὔθυνον : τ-
ὸ καθε̑κο-
ν : ταυ̑τα ἐ-
πομνύνα̣-
ι̣ : τὸς τρε̑-
ς θεός : hó
τι ἂν το̑[ν]
κοινο̑ν : μ-
ὲ ἀποδιδ-
ο̑σιν : παρ-
ὰ τὸν εὔθ-
υνο[ν π]ρὸ
– – – – – –

Cleisthenes' reforms at the end of the sixth century in Athens had given formal political powers to local communities ('demes') in Attica, requiring them in particular to register citizens and to produce volunteers for allotment to the council of five hundred. This in turn required demes to have some administrative structure, including most particularly a 'demarch' (Whitehead, *The Demes of Attica*, 60–2). The inscriptional evidence suggests that demes rapidly acquired quite a strongly structured local life, with deme officials subject to audit and the deme taking responsibility for a wide range of local cult activity.

This is the best-preserved of a series of more or less fragmentary inscriptions with decrees that can be attributed to Athenian demes and that can be dated by letter forms to the decades immediately after the Persian War (cf. *IG* i^3 243 [Melite], 245 [Sypalettus], perhaps 246). In all cases the decrees relate to religious sacrifices and to financial responsibility for them, with frequent mention of audit of magistrates. If *C.* 1 is correctly restored, this decree is exceptional in declaring itself a law, using the archaic term *thesmion* (statute; see Ostwald, *Nomos and the Beginnings of the Athenian Democracy*, 12–19).

When Cleisthenes had given political status to the villages of Attica as demes he had dealt with the town by recognising distinct 'wards' as demes in the same way. As in the case of the countryside, where all or almost all demes were pre-existing

B

– – – let it be declared, let it be announced: I will also preserve the common funds of the people of Scambonidae and I will hand over what I ought before the auditor; and they are to swear this by the Three Gods. Whatsoever of the common funds they do not hand over before the auditor before – – –

---

settlements, so in the town Cleisthenes was almost certainly making formal existing divisions between residential areas. Five Cleisthenic demes were within the area fortified immediately after the Persian Wars with the so-called 'Themistoclean' wall. Of these two were among the larger demes and returned, in the fourth century, twelve (Cydathenaeum) and seven (Melite) representatives to the council; the other three, Coele, Collytus and Scambonidae, were small, each returning three men to the council. Scambonidae was the northernmost of these demes, and its focus was probably in the area now bounded to the north by Odhos Evripidou and to the south by Odhos Ermou. It was the deme to which the Cleinias–Alcibiades family belonged.

The interest of this inscription is threefold. It gives us an insight into the early organisation of a deme; it sheds light on the relationship of deme religious activities to the activities of the city as a whole; and it gives us what is almost certainly our first glimpse of metics.

The decree reveals three different administrative figures in the deme, the demarch, who is responsible for sacrifices (and rewarded with the skins as a priest might be, cf. **137**), other officials who share some of that responsibility at least (probably referred to as *hieropoioi* (sacred officials; cf. **134**. 33), and a *euthynos* (auditor) to whom some official or officials are obliged to swear that they will hand over what they ought (on cult personnel in the demes see Whitehead, 180–4, Parker, *Polytheism and Society at Athens*, 64–5). We are given in *B* the text of an oath to be sworn by each official individually (for the link of audit and oath see **146**. 12, R&O 63. 8–17), followed by a statement about who the oath is to be sworn by. Pollux (VIII. 142) claims that Solon had stated that oaths were to be sworn by three gods, *Hikesion*, *Katharsion*, and *Exakesterion*: all of these are cult titles used of Zeus—'of Suppliants', 'Purifier', and 'remedying evil'—but in fact oaths are regularly sworn by Zeus, Apollo and Demeter (see **121**. 16 and Sommerstein & Bayliss, *Oath and State in Ancient Greece*, 164). This decree shows that, from the very beginning, demes had, like the democratic city itself, devices both to maximise the chances that officials would do their duty and to check that the duty had been done. Athenian tradition held that audit of magistrates went back at least as far as Solon (Arist. *Pol.* II. 1274 A 15–18, III. 1281 B 32–4; *Ath. Pol.* 8 iv); it is uncertain who was responsible for the audit of magistrates in Athens before 462, and it has often been thought that this was a role of the Areopagus, but this passage may encourage the idea that appointment of auditors, as in the later fifth and fourth centuries (*Ath. Pol.* 48. iv–v), went back to before 462 (for audit in the demes see further **146**. 12).

At least five sacrifices were listed in *C*, and sacrifices on perhaps four occasions in *A*. The first sacrifice to be listed is to Leos, the tribal hero of the tribe Leontis to which Scambonidae belonged and the father of daughters worshipped at the Leokoreion, which may have been in the deme (see Kearns, *The Heroes of Attica*, 86, Wijma, 107). There follow sacrifices at the Synoikia, at the (otherwise unknown) Epizephyria, and at two festivals of uncertain identity. The sacrifices at the Synoikia and the Epizephyria happen away from the deme, on the acropolis and at the Pythion (which was near the Olympieion in the south-east of the city; cf. M&L 11). The sacrifices on side *A* include deme provision for the Panathenaea and the Dipolieia. The three festivals named that are otherwise known, Synoikia, Dipolieia and Panathenaea, were all festivals of some antiquity (the participation of the pre-Cleisthenic tribes and *phylobasileis* in the Synoikia is known from the calendar of the reinscribed Athenian lawcode at the end of the fifth century; Aristophanes makes fun of the old-fashioned Dipolieia (*Clouds* 984–5)). Deme involvement in the Panathenaea is known from the fourth century and, given the status of the Panathenaea as a 'national' festival, to be expected. So too since the Synoikia celebrated Theseus' unification of the villages of Attica into a single political unit (Plut. *Thes.* 24. iv, where the Synoikia is curiously referred to as the 'Metoikia', a name that puts the stress on movement of people rather than unity), deme involvement is unsurprising. The Dipolieia too was a festival of Zeus Polieus, and so linked to the city as a whole, but the focus of its concerns was with the justification of sacrifice (Porph. *Abst.* II. 28. iv–31. i, from Theophrastus). The curious nature of the aetiological myth attached to this festival has been much discussed (see especially Parker, *Polytheism and Society*, 187–91); the feature that is perhaps most relevant here is the insistence that the whole community is involved in the killing of the working ox: deme participation in the Dipolieia played that out for the new Cleisthenic political structure.

Whereas meat from the sacrifices at Dipolieia and Panathenaea is distributed (with the verb νέμειν), the meat in the cases of the Synoikia and Epizephyria is to be sold raw. The implication is that while it is important for the deme to sacrifice on the occasion of these city festivals, most demesmen would not be present (see M. H. Jameson, in Goldhill & Osborne (edd.), *Performance Culture and Athenian Democracy*, 321–40). Other variations in terminology may be less significant: it is uncertain why the distribution at the agora of Scambonidae after the sacrifice to Leos should be described uniquely as λε̂χ[σιν . . .][ὀ]βολο̂ν ('distribution of — obols'), when it is most plausible that what is being distributed is sacrificial meat on spits (with in this case obol = spit, rather than obol = ⅙ drachma). The general pattern here seems to be that if there is a distribution of meat to the demesmen it is specified that this happen in the 'agora of Scambonidae', and this includes distributions after sacrifices on the occasion of the city festivals of the Panathenaea and Dipolieia (*A*. 18–19).

With the exception of the sacrifice to the tribal hero, all the sacrifices whose occasion is preserved are sacrifices to mark city festivals: such sacrifices are found too in the Thoricus calendar (**146**), but the local sacrifices characteristic of that later calendar are notably absent here. To some extent that may mark the smaller part that sacrifices linked to agricultural fertility played in an urban deme, but the way in which this deme here re-enacts (only) the festivals of city and tribe is very marked. Just how often the deme sacrificed is unclear. Two of the three festivals named in *C* and *A* can be dated, one occurring in Hecatombaeon and the other in Scirophorion, but the way in which the festivals are listed does not suggest that it deals only with two months. It seems more plausible that the religious role of the deme in an urban setting, when access to city festivals was easy, was rather different from the religious role of a more isolated rural community.

The most unexpected element of this decree is its mention of metics and explicit inclusion of them in the distribution in the agora of Scambonidae after the sacrifice to the tribal hero. This is the earliest occurrence of the term 'metic' as a formal term for a status group in any Athenian inscription (the first use in a state decree comes with their inclusion in the Hephaestea in 421, *IG* i^3 82. 23). Scholars have debated whether the formal designation of resident foreigners as a special group should be attributed to Cleisthenes at the end of the sixth century or was a later development. Recent work favours the conclusion that metics were invented only in the 460s, perhaps as part of the Ephialtic reforms, or later, and that some of the issues around metic status were explored in the late 460s by Aeschylus in his *Suppliant Women* (G. W. Bakewell, *Cl. Ant.* xvi 1997, 209–28; J. Watson, *CCJ* lvi 2010, 259–78, arguing for formal metic status as a product of Pericles' citizenship law of 451/0). As in some other areas of Athenian life (cf. R&O 46 commentary), it is not implausible that the desire to distinguish between temporary visitors and non-Athenians resident long-term may have been more pressing for demes than for the city as a whole, and particularly for demes in Athens itself (cf. the five metics from Scambonidae who appear in the Erechtheum building inscriptions, **181**). It is notable that here, as in the later provision for the Hephaestea, metics are privileged as participants. One important reason for the Athenians to distinguish long-term resident foreigners was to impose various obligations on them, in particular to contribute military service to Athens, to perform some liturgies and to pay tax in a way that neither visitors nor Athenians were taxed (see Whitehead, *The Ideology of the Athenian Metic*), but these obligations went together with privileges, most particularly selective inclusion in Athenian religious life (see Wijma).

As well as the use of *lexis* noted above, there are two other linguistic curiosities in this inscription. The form σοô (σωῶ) for the future σώσω is not otherwise attested.

108

Athenian decree concerning the *genos* of the Praxiergidai, 450s to 420s

Three fragments from a Pentelic marble *stele* found on the Athenian acropolis, fragment *a* preserving the original top and fragment *b* the original left edge. Now in the Epigraphical Museum. Phot. *BSA* xlix 1954, pl. 3; Immerwahr, *Attic Script*, pl. 41.

Attic letters but with *omega* in ll. 8, 10 and 20. *Stoichedon* 40 (ll. 1–12); 32–3 (ll. 13–25).

LSCG 15; *IG* i³ 7*; Immerwahr, *Attic Script*, p. 108 no. 742; N. Robertson, *GRBS* xliv 2004, 107–61 (*SEG* liv 38). Trans. Garland, *Introducing New Gods*, 101; Davies, *Democracy and Classical Greece*², 57–8; Robertson, 114. See also Parker, *Athenian Religion: A History*, 307–8; Sourvinou-Inwood, *Athenian Myths and Festivals*, 145–51.

a [ἔδοχσεν τε͂]ι βο[λ]ε͂[ι καὶ τοῖ δέμοι· —6— ἐπρυτάνε]-
[υε, —6—]ς ἐγραμμ[άτευε, —7— ἐπεστάτε, —5—]
[. εἶπε· πε]ρ̣ὶ ὂν δέο[νται Πραχσιεργίδαι, τὲν μαντεί]-
[αν τô θ]εô καὶ τὰ πρ̣ό̣[τερον αὐτοῖς ἐφσεφισμένα ἀνα]-
[γράφσ]αντας ἐν στέ[λει λιθίνει καταθε͂ναι ἐμ πόλει̣]
[ὄπισ]θεν τô νεὸ τὸ ἀρχ[αίο· —20—]
[. . .]τον· ᵛ τὸ δὲ ἀργύριο[ν —18— ἀπὸ]
[τôν] τε͂ς θεῶ κατὰ τὰ πάτρι[α· —19—]
[hοι] κολακρέται διδόντον [αὐτοῖς τὸ ἀργύριον. *vacat*]
[τά]δε hο Ἀπόλλων ἔχρεσεν ἄ̣[μεινον Πραχσιεργίδαις]
[ἀμ]φιεννύοσιν τὸν πέπλον τ̣[ὲν θεὸν καὶ προθύοσιν]
[Μοί]ραις, Διὶ Μοιρ<α>γέτει, Γ[ε͂ι - - - - - - - - - - -]

vacat 0.035

[τάδε] πάτρια Πραχσ̣[ιεργίδαις· —9—]
[—8–9—]ιτο[—21—]

lacuna

7 τὸ δὲ ἀργύριο[ν ἐς τὲν ἀναγραφὲν ε͂ναι ἀπὸ] *IG*. 8 πάτρι[α· hοι δὲ ταμίαι τε͂ς θεô καὶ] *IG*: πάτρι[α· ὅταν δὲ hε hιέρεια θύει Robertson. 9 διδόντον [αὐτοῖς τὸ ἀργύριον. *vacat* *IG*: διδόντον [τὸ ἀργύριον. *vacat* Robertson. 10 ἄ̣[μεινον Πραχσιεργίδαις] Sokolowski: ν̣[όμιμα Πραχσιεργίδαις] *IG*.

The subjunctives κηρυχθῆι and ἐπαγγελθῆι in *B.* 1–3 appear to be jussive or voluntative, a usage seen in Dem. XIII. *Syntaxis* 6, Pl. *Leg.* VI. 761 C and in an inscription from hellenistic Elis (*I. Olympia* 39 = Buck 66. 30–2, 36–7), and perhaps in a fourth-century or later contract or lease from the agora (*Hesperia* lxi 1992, 375, ll. 1–2: see 377 n. 11) and which may represent a sub-literary usage (see Wackernagel, *Lectures on Syntax*, 297–8).

Resolved by the council and people.—— was the prytany. —— proposed: Concerning the request of the Praxiergidai, to write up the oracle of the god and the decisions formerly made about them on a stone *stele* and erect it on the acropolis behind the old temple. – – – The money – – – of the goddess, in the ancestral fashion – – – the *kolakretai* are to give them the money.

10 Apollo issued the following oracle: it is better for the Praxiergidai if they put the *peplos* on the goddess and make preliminary sacrifice to the Fates, to Zeus Leader of the Fates, to Ge – – –

13 These are the ancestral customs of the Praxiergidai – – –

lacuna

[—— 28-9 ——π]αρέ- *c*
[χεν —— 11-12 —— Πραχσιεργί]δ̣α̣ις vvvv
[—— 21-2 —— τὸ] δὲ κόιδιον
[—— 22-3 ——] ν̣αι κατὰ τὰ v
[πάτρια —— 15-16 —— π]αρέχεν vvvv
[—— 22-3 ——]ω δὲ Θαργελι̣-
b [ôν . . .]ε̣[—— 16 ——]ίτες διδόναι̣
[. .]ΑΣΕΜΕ[—— 12 —— τὸ]ν ἄρχοντα vvv
[v] κατὰ τὰ πάτρ̣[ια *vacat*] *vacat*
[v] Π̣[ρ]α̣χσιεργ̣ί̣[δας τὸν πέπλον] ἀμφιεννύ[ν]-
[αι· . .] Πραχσιε̣ρ̣[γίδ—— 8 ——]τ̣ίνεν vvvvv
[v μέ]δίμνον χρ̣[ιθôν.] *vacat*
vacat

18 διδό]ν̣αι *IG*. 20–6 Robertson is responsible for suggesting that fragment *b* fits one line lower than *IG* had assumed. We have adopted this suggestion, but not his detailed text: the inconsistent use or omission of the aspirate (h) required by Robertson's restorations is without parallel in a text of this period (the closest parallel would be **145**; see Threatte, *The Grammar of Attic Inscriptions*, i. 493–4). 20–5 [—— 5-6 ——]ε̣ [—— 14 ——]ι·[ν]ε̣ὼ δὲ Θαργελι̣- | [ôν]α σεμε[νάμενον ἄχρι τε̂ς τ]ρ̣ίτες διδόναι̣ | [v] κατὰ τὰ πάτρ̣[ια κλε̂ιδας τὸ]ν ἄρχοντα vvv | [v] Π̣[ρ]α̣χσιεργ̣ί̣[δαις·?*vacat*]*vacat* | [v τὸς] Πραχσιε̣ρ̣[γίδας τὸ hέδος] ἀμφιεννύ[ν | v αι] δίμνον χι[τôνα ἒ μνᾶν ἀπο]τ̣ίνεν*vacat* *IG*. 20–1 τ̣ῶ δὲ Θαργελι̣ | [ôνος μ]ε̣[νὸς φθίνοντος πρὸ τ]ρ̣ίτες Robertson. 22 [μι]ᾶς ἐμε[ρας σῖτον πάσι τὸ]ν ἄρχοντα vvv Robertson. 25–6 [αι· vv] Πραχσιε̣ρ̣[γίδας δὲ παρέ]χ̣ενvvvvv | [v μέ]δίμνον χρ̣[ιθôν.] *vacat* Robertson. 25 We have checked squeezes of this fragment and have no doubt that the last three letters of this line are νεν.

This very fragmentary inscription sheds a tantalising light upon Athenian ritual and on the relationship between the various groups involved. It also well illustrates the wide range of appearance and presentation of epigraphic documents and the problems of interpreting epigraphic language and of textual restoration.

We meet the *genos* of the Praxiergidai in literature only in Plut. *Alc.* 34, which tells that Alcibiades returned to Athens in 407 during the festival of the Plynteria, and explains: 'The Praxiergidai perform the secret rituals on 25 Thargelion, both removing the adornment and covering up the statue'; Plutarch goes on to claim that this made the Athenians consider this the most inauspicious day for business in Athens. A late lexicon explains Praxiergidai as 'those who clothe the ancient statue of Athena' (Hesychius π 3205 Latte *et al.*, using the same verb, ἀμφιέννυμι, as occurs in the inscription).

To this exiguous information we can add what we deduce from this fragmentary inscription and from later epigraphic allusions. A fourth-century inscribed altar to Heracles declares itself to belong to the Praxiergidai and another group (M. H. Jameson, in *Polis and Politics . . . M. H. Hansen*, 217–27; S. D. Lambert, *hόρος* xiv–xvi 2000–3, 79–82); an honorific inscription from the third century praises a priestess of Athena Polias for giving 100 dr. from her own money to the Praxiergidai for their ancestral sacrifice (*IG* ii^2 776. 18–20); and much later, in the second or third century AD, we have a mention of the Praxiergidai in the context of religious matters in connection with the priestess of Athena Polias (*IG* ii^2 3678).

15 provide – – – for the Praxiergidai – – – the fleece – – – according to – – – provide – – – Thargelion, – – – the archon is to give – – – in the ancestral manner.

23 The Praxiergidai are to put on the *peplos* and the Praxiergidai are to pay for a bushel of barley.

What is certain from this is that the Praxiergidai was the priestly family (*genos*) responsible for the rituals of the Plynteria involving the washing and the clothing of the statue of Athena Polias. Whether they claimed descent from one Praxiergus is unknown, though an Athenian archon of that name is recorded for 471/0; we might suspect Praxiergidai to be a speaking name for doers of (ritual) actions.

This inscription records a moment when something has caused the *genos* to make a request of the Athenian people. For some reason the *genos* feels it necessary to record on the acropolis, and in a specific location (by the 'old temple', i.e. the sixth-century temple of Athena Polias left in ruins after the Persian sack), the authoritative statement of Apollo at Delphi about its role in clothing the statue, along with a more general statement of what the *genos* does. The question is, what has occasioned this request?

Consultation of the Delphic oracle before making changes to ritual or to religious status seems to have been regular (cf. below, **141**, and R&O 97. 1; for Athenian consultations in the classical period see Bowden, *Classical Athens and the Delphic Oracle*, 122–30). Equally the citation of past oracular advice continued to be persuasive years after the event (cf. M&L 5). This inscription is not the record of a consultation, but the publication of advice from the oracle in the (possibly recent) past. As so often, we can reconstruct the question that the Delphic oracle was asked only from the answer received. In this case if the answer is coextensive with the question, the question must have been whether the Praxiergidai should clothe the statue of the goddess, and what sacrifices they should make, or perhaps, to echo a common form of oracular question (cf. Hdt. I. 67. ii, Xen. *An.* III. i. 6), 'What sacrifices should the Praxiergidai make when they clothe the statue of Athena?' But if that was the question, what had prompted it? Robertson has argued that the whole ceremony of clothing the statue is initiated at this point, but the oracle that is reported here certainly does not require that.

Although this inscription has been taken as evidence for tension between the *genos* and the city, the preserved text does not require such a conflict. Something has happened to make the Praxiergidai desire to have their practices inscribed and displayed on the acropolis, but in a context where, as we have already seen, the inscription of religious duties has become one of the major activities of corporate groups (**106**, **107**), any incident in which there was unclarity about responsibility for some aspect of the ritual involving the statue of Athena would be enough to justify that request. Lambert has suggested, in the light of a new text recording a role for a previously unknown *genos*, the Euenoridai, in the vestment rituals for Athena, that this decree may have been occasioned by a dispute between the Praxiergidai and Euenoridai (*ZPE* clxvii 2008, 26).

There is a tantalising inexact match between the information we have from literary texts about the Praxiergidai and their practices as emerge from this inscription. Plutarch tells us about the stripping and concealing of the statue, these regulations deal with its clothing. Plutarch gives a date of 25 Thargelion (late May) for the stripping, and here we have a date in Thargelion for its clothing. The Athenian Sacred Calendar records the gift of a cloak to Athena, accompanied by a sacrifice on 29 Thargelion (S. D. Lambert, *BSA* xcvii 2002, 363–4, 374, 392). We know of two festivals in Thargelion, the Plynteria and the Kallynteria, the former etymologically connected with washing, the latter with adornment, but whether the 29 Thargelion ritual was still part of the Plynteria or part of the Kallynteria is not clear; it makes sense for adornment to follow washing, and if the Plynteria was on 25 Thargelion the Kallynteria might be well placed on 29 Thargelion. We would not be surprised to discover that the Praxiergidai were responsible for the Kallynteria as well as the Plynteria. Whether they also had a role in the Panathenaea, when the statue of Athena was given a new *peplos*, is entirely uncertain, though some scholars have been keen to give them a role there (see especially M. Steinhart, *AA* 1997, 475–8; *contra* Sourvinou-Inwood, *Athenian Myths and Festivals*, esp. 22–3, 307–11).

One further element of ritual may be indicated by the surviving text. Since we have lost the text immediately before and afterwards we are left in ignorance of the role that the fleece played (κόιδιον, 17). Fleeces were an inevitable by-product of sacrificing sheep, and outside Attica we know of them being awarded as perquisites to priests or sold (*IG* IX. ii 287. *A*. 24, Delos; *LSA* 40. 6, Thebes by Mycale). But fleeces were also used in ritual contexts, both incubatory (Paus. I. 34. v) and purificatory (Polemon of Ilium frs. 87, 88 (*FHG* iii. 143–5)), and a fleece may have had some part in the ritual of the Plynteria.

In appearance this *stele* and its letter forms are unusual (see further Immerwahr, *Attic Script*, 95, 108, 166, 167). The stone was not of even thickness, but twice as thick in the middle as at the sides. The *stoichedon* grid is practically square, and the letters fill the grid, or even overrun their margins. In the lower part of the stone the cutter seems intermittently to have begun the line in the second letter space rather than the first. The letters, on which the dating of the *stele* is based, are not regular Attic letters, but include *omega*, used sporadically both for long *o* and for the diphthong *omicron upsilon*, and a four-bar *sigma* of very open shape. Parallels for the various letter forms point in slightly different chronological directions, with the backwards-leaning *lambda* suggesting the beginning of the fifth century. The same stonemason's hand has been identified in a dedication from the Athenian acropolis (*IG* i³ 838) and perhaps some accounts from Eleusis (*IG* i³ 384). The dedication is accompanied by a fragmentary relief of crude execution that would naturally be placed before the middle of the fifth century. The peculiarities of script seem best explained by the influence of writing in other media. *Omega* is not uncommon even at this date in private inscriptions, but this, along with one deme inscription (*IG* i³ 245), is likely to be the earliest public use. However, along with the peculiarities of letter form there is one peculiarity of language: the use of the dative plural in -αις, which is a regular feature of texts only after *c.*420 (but note the occurrence in **120**. 5; see generally Introduction, p. xxviii). We incline to a mid-fifth-century date, but a date *c.*420 cannot be excluded.

The fragmentary state of this inscription, along with the obvious interest of the surviving traces, has invited scholars to attempt to restore the text. There are a number of traces of phrases that are or become almost formulaic in Athenian epigraphy, but at this date the corpus of public inscriptions is too small to be sure of any regular patterns. The prescript here is restored along the lines of those of the Phaselis decree (**120**) and the alliance with the Amphictyony (**116**). The naming of the 'old temple' makes a publication provision very likely, but no publication provision quite like this is found elsewhere, and the suggestion of complex financial responsibility for the inscribing of the *stele* is unlikely, particularly in the light of the present tense of the instruction to the *kolakretai* in line 9, which ought to imply that the payment is for a regular rather than a one-off expenditure.[1]

The second part of the inscription relies on the survival of two small fragments which for part of the text give different parts of the same lines. Even with a rearrangement of the fragments, which we think plausible, it remains impossible to complete the evident date in Thargelion with a normal dating formula. At the end of the inscription some form of the verb to pay, (ἀπο)ṭίνειν, and the mention of a bushel of something seem secure. Much has been made (cf. most recently Sourvinou-Inwood, *Athenian Myths and Festivals*, 148–51) of features based on earlier restorations (the sealing of the temple, the giving of the key to the Praxiergidai, clothing the statue in a *chiton* rather than the usual *peplos*), but all of these depend on the imagination of modern scholars.

[1] So A. S. Henry, *ZPE* lxxviii 1989, 247–95 at 250.

109

Casualty-list of the Athenian tribe Erechtheis, 459

A marble *stele* (the 'Nointel Marble') found in Athens; now in the Louvre. Phot. *φόρος . . . B. D. Meritt*, pl. V. 1; *BCH* xcix 1995, 151–2; Clairmont, *Patrios Nomos*, ii, pls. 17, 18; *hόρος* ii 1984, 191, Arrington, *Ashes, Images and Memories*, 93.

Attic letters. Lines 62–70 are added in other hands. For the curious *theta* (made up of concentric circles) see Daux (below) and G. Németh, *ACD* xxviii 1992, 17–24 (*SEG* xlii 1734).

M&L 33; G. Daux, in *φόρος . . . B. D. Meritt*, 40–2; Daux, *BCH* xcix 1975, 150–6; Stupperich, *Staatsbegräbnis und Privatgrabmal im klassischen Athens*; *IG* i³ 1147*. See also D. W. Bradeen, *CQ*² xix 1969, 145–59; Clairmont, *Patrios Nomos*, i. 130–5 no. 20a. Trans. Fornara 78 (omitting most names); Dillon & Garland³ 12. 14 (omitting all but two names); Sage, *Warfare in Ancient Greece*, no. 143.

Ἐ ρ ε χ θ ε ΐ δ ο ς
ḥοίδε ⁝ ἐν τôι πολέμοι ⁝ ἀπέθανον ⁝ ἐν Κύπροι ⁝ ἐν Αἰγ[ύ]-
π̣τοι ⁝ ἐν Φοινίκει ⁝ ἐν Ἁλιεῦσιν ⁝ ἐν Αἰγίνει ⁝ Μεγαρο[ῖ]
τ ô α ὐ τ ô ἐ ν ι α υ τ ô

col. i	*col. ii*	*col. iii*
[σ]τ[ρα]τεγôν	Φάνυλλος	Ἄκρυπτος
Φ[. . . .]χος	Χ[σ]έ̣νιος	Τιμοκράτε[ς]
Π[αντ]αλέον	Ε[ὐ]γείτον	Ἀρχέλας
Πολύστρατος	Ἄλκ̣ιππος	Εὐθυκράτες
[Δρ]ακοντίδες	Λυσ̣ικλε̂ς	Πατροκλείδε[ς]
[. .]μόστ[ρ]ατος	Κέ[λ]ευσος	Ἀλκμεονίδες
[. .]μέας	Εὐ[θ]ύδεμος	Γλαύκον
[. .]κλείδες	Δίκαιος	Δεμόνικος
[. .]κράτες	Φιλ[ῖ]νος	Ἀναχσίδορος
[Χα]ιρέδεμος	Καλλικλε̂ς	Γλαύκον
[Κ]τ̣εσίας	Ναυσικλε̂ς	Προκλε̂ς
[. .]έσανδρος	Τ̣ιμεσίθεος	Ἀντιφôν
[Λυ]κόφρον	[Μ]νεσιγένες	Ἀναχσίλα[ς]
[Ἀ]πολλόδορος	Π[ο]λυκλε̂ς	Ἀρχέπολι[ς]
Ἀριστοτέλες	Ἀλ[ε]χσίας	Καλλέας
Π̣ροτίας	Ἀμύδριππος	Θαλίαρχο[ς]
Δράκαλος	Ἀπολλόδορος	Φιλόνιχο[ς]
Μεχανίον	Γοργίας	Εὐκλείδε[ς]
Φιλιστίδες	Νόθαρχος	Διόδορος

2 Punctuation between τôι and πολέμοι *IG*; denied by Daux (*BCH*). 3 Punctuation after Φοινίκει and Ἁλιεῦσιν printed *IG*, visible to Daux (*BCH*). Μεγαρο[ῖ] Daux (*BCH*): Μεγαροῖ *IG*. 6 Φ[. . . .]χος *IG*: Φ[ρύν]ι̣χος Daux (*BCH*). 72 Χ[σ]έ̣νιος Daux (*BCH*): Χ[. .]νιος *IG*.

Of the tribe Erechtheis, these died in the war, in Cyprus, in Egypt, in Phoenicia, in Halieis, in Aegina, at Megara, during the same year.

col. i

Of the generals:
Ph . . . . chus
Pantaleon
Polystratus
Dracontides
. . mostratus
. . meas
. . cleides
. . crates
Chaeredemus
Ctesias
. . esandrus
Lycophron
Apollodorus
Aristoteles
Protias
Dracalus
Mechanion
Philistides

col. ii

Phanyllus
Xenius
Eugeiton
Alcippus
Lysicles
Celeusus
Euthydemus
Dicaeus
Philinus
Callicles
Nausicles
Timesitheus
Mnesigenes
Polycles
Alexias
Amydrippus
Apollodorus
Gorgias
Notharchus

col. iii

Acryptus
Timocrates
Archelas
Euthycrates
Patrocleides
Alcmeonides
Glaucon
Demonicus
Anaxidorus
Glaucon
Procles
Antiphon
Anaxilas
Archepolis
Calleas
Thaliarchus
Philonichus
Eucleides
Diodorus

Τιμογένες
Χαρίσανδρος
[Μ]ενέκλες
[Μ]ελάνοπος
Κ̣λεόνβροτος
Ἀ̣ριστοκλείδες
Θ̣οκυδίδες
Εὐθύδεμος
[Κ]αλλικράτες
Ἀφσέφες
[Ἀ]ριστείδες
[Φ]ιλόδεμος
[Κ]εφισόδοτος
[Σ]όφιλος
[Ἀ]ντιμένες
[Ἐ]παίνετος
Ἐργαῖος
Διογένες
Φρῦνος
[Κ]τεσιάδες
[Κ]όροιβο̣ς
[Κ]ράτυλλος
[Σ]υνφέρμιος
Νικίας
Λυσικλείδες
Φρούραρχος
Χαρ̣ί̣σ̣ανδρος
Ὀ[λυμ]π̣ιάρατος
Σ[. . . .]ος
Μνε̣[σ]ίφιλος
Σοσίας
Ἀρχῖνος
Λυκῖνος
Καλλίας
Μνεσιγένες
Σίκον
Ἀμφικέδες
Χσένυλλος
Vacat

Παρμον[ί]δες
Βάκον
Πίθον
Λυσίας
Σόστρατος
Φιλῖνος
Φίλαιθος
Φιλέταιρος
Σοτέλες
Λυσίας
Ἀριστογένες
Φιλῖνος
Διότιμος
Καλλονίδες
Καλλίχσενος
Δεινίας
Σμίκυθος
Τιμόδεμος
Λῦσις
Ἀκεσίας
Ἐπιχάρες
hιερόνυμος
Ἀναχσίλας
Χαιρίας
hερακλείδες
Ἀγασικλε̑ς
Ἄλκας
Κεφισόδοτος
Καλλικλε̑ς
Κεφισόδορος
Νομένιος
Χσενόφιλος
hυπέρβιος
hάγνον
Πολύχσενος
Ἐρχσιμένες
Νίκον
vacat
vacat

Νίκαρχος
Ἐπιτέλες
Κύβον
Χ[α]ιρίας
Δεμέτριο[ς]
Ἀρκεσίλας
Εὔθοινος
Δεμέτριος
Γόργον
Στρά[το]ν
Ἀρισ[τ]οφάνες
Γλα[ύ]κ̣ον
Φυσ[ον]ίδες
hαγ[ν]όδεμος
Διο[κ]λε̑ς
Φανόστρατο[ς]
Εὐμένιος
Θε[ό]δορος
[Εὐρ]ύλεος
[Κέ]ρδον
[Ἐπ]ιχάρες
Ε[ὔ]δοχσος
Π[ο]λύζελος
Γ[λ]αυκίας
Ἐριγένες
Ἀντιχάρες
Φιλιστίδε[ς]
Ἀμφικλείδ[ες]
Φροῦρος
Τίτον
Εὔβιος
Καλλίβι̣[ος]
Σμῖκρο[ς]
Νεαῖος
Ἐργοτέ[λες]
Φοκίον
Ἄραιθ[ος]
vacat
vacat

53 Μνε̣[σ]ίφιλος Daux (*BCH*): Μν[εσ]ι̣φιλος *IG*.

Timogenes
Charisandrus
Menecles
Melanopus
Cleonbrotus
Aristocleides
Thucydides
Euthydemus
Callicrates
Aphsephes
Aristeides
Philodemus
Cephisodotus
Sophilus
Antimenes
Epaenetus
Ergaeus
Diogenes
Phrynus
Ctesiades
Coroebus
Cratyllus
Synphermius
Nicias
Lysicleides
Phrourarchus
Charisandrus
Olympiaratus
S . . . . us
Mnesiphilus
Sosias
Archinus
Lycinus
Callias
Mnesigenes
Sicon
Amphicedes
Xenyllus
vacat

Parmonides
Bacon
Pithon
Lysias
Sostratus
Philinus
Philaethus
Philetaerus
Soteles
Lysias
Aristogenes
Philinus
Diotimus
Callonides
Callixenus
Deinias
Smicythus
Timodemus
Lysis
Acesias
Epichares
Hieronymus
Anaxilas
Chaerias
Heracleides
Agasicles
Alcas
Cephisodotus
Callicles
Cephisodorus
Noumenius
Xenophilus
Hyperbius
Hagnon
Polyxenus
Erximenes
Nicon
vacat
vacat

Nicarchus
Epiteles
Cybon
Chaerias
Demetrius
Arcesilas
Euthoenus
Demetrius
Gorgon
Straton
Aristophanes
Glaucon
Physonides
Hagnodemus
Diocles
Phanostratus
Eumenius
Theodorus
Euryleos
Cerdon
Epichares
Eudoxus
Polyzelus
Glaucias
Erigenes
Antichares
Philistides
Amphicleides
Phrourus
Titon
Eubius
Callibius
Smicrus
Neaeus
Ergoteles
Phocion
Araethus
vacat

στρατεγός ⁝
Ηιπποδάμας
Εὐθύμαχος :
Εὔμελος :
Ἀνδροσθένες
τοχσόται ⁝ Φρῦνος
Ταῦρος
Θεόδορος
Ἀλεχσίμαχος

ἐν Αἰγύπτοι

Τελένικος
μάντις

The Athenians commemorated those who had died in war in various ways. Thucydides (II. 34) claims that it was their 'ancestral custom' to hold a public burial of the war dead, and describes the way in which ten coffins containing the bones of the dead from each tribe were taken in procession to the public burial place in the Ceramicus. *Ath. Pol.* 58. i adds that there were funeral games, organised by the polemarch (for the date in the year of all this see Rhodes, *Comm. Ath. Pol.*, *ad loc.*). Thucydides also mentions that a funeral oration was given by a man chosen by the city, and Diodorus (XI. 33. iii) says that the funeral oration and games were instituted in 479 to mark the deaths of those who had died in the Persian Wars. Pausanias (I. 29. iv), who records that in the cemetery on the road to the Academy (part of what is today referred to as the Ceramicus cemetery) there was a monument for all the Athenians who had died in war, except those who died at Marathon, and that there were *stelai* set up bearing their names, claims that the first who were buried were those who died at Drabescus in Thrace in conflict with the Edonians, a conflict datable to 465/4 (Thuc. I. 100. iii).

Scholars have struggled to reconcile these various pieces of information (see Gomme, *HCT* ii. 94–101). They have found it implausible that Thucydides could describe as 'ancestral' a custom instituted since the Persian Wars. They have worried about the inaccuracies of Thucydides, whose mention of the exceptional burial of the dead at Marathon on the battlefield 'for their outstanding valour' ignores the fact that the dead at the battle of Plataea were also buried on the battlefield to receive annual cult there with the other Greek dead (Hdt. IX. 85, Paus. IX. 2. v–vi), and of Pausanias, who goes on to record earlier monuments to war dead in the cemetery (from wars with Aegina and from the battle of the Eurymedon, II. 29. vii, xiv).

A composite account of Athenian behaviour is not, however, impossible to distil from these disparate testimonies. It may well have been ancestral custom for the Athenians to bury their war dead at Athens—albeit a custom with various exceptions (cf. Hdt. I. 30. iii–v; IX. 105)—although the full ceremony, with separate tribal coffins, must post-date the organisation of the army into the ten Cleisthenic tribes. But such burial does not demand an oration, and nothing prevents the oration being added in 479 (though one might still doubt whether the exceptional circumstances of 479 make it a very plausible occasion for the invention of a recurrent ceremony: see also

General:	In Egypt
Hippodamus	*vacat*
Euthymachus	Telenicus
Eumelus	seer
Androsthenes	
Archers: Phrynus	
Taurus	
Theodorus	
Aleximachus	

Loraux, *L'Invention d'Athènes*, 56–60). Nor does such burial demand that the names of the war dead are listed. Indeed the listing of war dead demands relatively sophisticated record-keeping, and it is easy to believe that the state had no such records in the sixth century or in the early days of democracy. It remains the case that we have no list of the Athenian war dead surviving that can be dated before 464: *IG* i³ 1144 records men who died at Eïon, at Sigeum and on Thasos, and almost certainly marks the year of the great defeat at Drabescus to which Pausanias refers. It requires only a little creative interpretation of Pausanias to interpret his statement about 'the first whom they buried' as meaning in fact 'the first whose names are listed in this way' (though Pausanias is mistaken in saying that the war dead were listed by name and deme; they are listed by name and tribe).

The Athenians knew that they were exceptional in having an oration over the war dead (Dem. xx. *Leptines* 141). They were unusual, too, in systematically bringing home the war dead, whose return was a moving moment, invoked by Aesch. *Ag.* 441–2. In other cities some of those who died in war were brought home for burial (cf. Paus. i. 43. iii, on the burial of Persian War dead in Megara, or Plut. *Lyc.* 27. iii, allowing only men who died in war epitaphs at Sparta, or, most notably, the *polyandrion* at Thespiae, *I. Thespies* 485), but the norm was burial on the battlefield (cf. Dem. xviii. *Crown* 285–8, Paus. ix. 40. x on Chaeronea; see in detail Pritchett, *The Greek State at War*, iv. 125–259: 243–6 on Sparta; 249–51 for summary). But the idea of having some epigraphic commemoration of the war dead was not unique to Athens (see P. A. Low, *World Archaeology* xxxv 2003, 98–111), and certainly in the later fifth century monuments very similar in form to those at Athens are known from Megara, Tanagra and Thespiae, even organising their lists by tribe (in Megara) and by personal name only, without patronymic (in Tanagra and Thespiae).

The 464 monument seems to have taken the form of a series of *stelai*, one for each tribe, and to have recorded for each tribe the dead under the location where they died. It also recorded at least some dead from the Athenian allies and some slaves (*therapontes*, *IG* i³ 1144. 139; for the use of the term see **190**). The surviving fragments from that monument record some 124 Athenian dead, with 46 from an unknown tribe and 68 from the tribe Oineis. Our stele may have been part of a similar monument, although the smooth sides of the *stele* indicate that it was not hard up against other *stelai* and it has a heading appropriate to just the one tribe. A more recently discovered *stele* with at least 51 names may record casualties from the tribe Aegeis during the same year, but neither the tribe nor the year are certain (*IG* i^3 1147 bis).

Subsequent lists of war dead are too poorly preserved for us to be sure of the extent to which there was a standard format, but a single *stele* listing the dead of all the tribes seems to have been normal (see **129**). By the time of the Peloponnesian War *stelai* appear to have featured a relief at the top, then an epigram, then an indication of the theatre of war and lists of the dead, with all the tribes on a single stone. Our list of the dead of Erechtheis is exceptional among surviving *stelai* for the independent way in which it treats the dead of one tribe, and for its insistence that they all died 'during the same year' (presumably the campaigning year rather than an archontic year).

The insistence that the deaths occurred in a single year has not prevented scholars disputing whether in fact deaths from two years might be grouped together here. This is because Thucydides records that, in a year likely to be 460, the Athenians, who were engaged with 200 ships in an expedition to Cyprus, heard about the revolt of Inaros in Egypt, and turned their attentions to Egypt (I. 104. ii). He records too (I. 105) that 'at this time' they fought the Corinthians and Epidaurians at Halieis, then fought the Peloponnesian fleet off Cecryphalea, and subsequently were engaged in a great battle at sea against the Aeginetans. Meanwhile, he says, the Corinthians invaded the Megarid, thinking that the Athenians were too occupied to assist Megara, but the Athenians left their army on Aegina and sent 'the oldest and youngest' to Megara. These two chapters of Thucydides account for all the theatres of war apart from Phoenicia (not hard to add to the Cypriot and Egyptian campaign), and suggest that the stone lists the places in chronological order for each of the two theatres. Casualties in Egypt will have occurred throughout the campaign there, so the campaign need not have started in this year, but Thucydides says that the Cypriot campaign was abandoned for the intervention in Egypt, so Cypriot casualties should relate to the start of the Egyptian campaign, usually reckoned to be 460 (cf. Thuc. I. 110. i)—though the return of the cremated remains of the dead to Athens from these distant theatres of war might itself take some time. Could all this military activity have been happening at the same time? Diodorus did not think so, and spreads the events over some seven years (464/3–458/7: XI. 70–9), but there is no serious reason to doubt the lapidary claim here if it is interpreted to mean that dead from these campaigns were all returned to Athens within a single twelve-month period. The most likely date for the *stele* itself is surely 459 (cf. Salmon, *La Politique égyptienne d'Athènes*, 112–8, 156–7).

Among the dead are listed two generals: they may have served together (double representation of a tribe being clearly attested later: see on **139**) or Hippodamas (63) succeeded Ph[....]chus either in the regular elections or in a special election occasioned by his death. That being a general was dangerous is not surprising; more surprising is that the dead should include a seer, the person who accompanied the army in order to interpret the omens by inspecting the liver of animals sacrificed before battle.[1] Neither cavalry at one end of the social scale, nor peltasts and rowers at the other, are distinguished from hoplites, but four archers are identified by their role (67–70). One of these names, Taurus (Mr Bull), is not otherwise attested for Athenians, but the other three are familiar Athenian names, and indeed two of them, Phrynus and Theodorus, occur elsewhere in this list. The Athenians certainly used non-citizen archers, but only their separate listing creates the suspicion that these may be non-citizens.

Repeated names are frequent in this inscription, with several names occurring twice or even three times (Glaucon in ll. 136, 139, 160). Not all the repeated names are names that are otherwise common (cf. e.g. Anaxilas in ll. 112 and 142), and given Greek naming patterns it is likely that those bearing such names may have been related (as e.g. cousins). There is scope for further work on the social significance of particular names at Athens, but it is likely that certain names implied a wealthy background or foreign links (so perhaps Arcesilas,154, a name common in Athens only at a later date but familiar in Spartan circles) and others suggested a poorer background (e.g. Sicon, 59, a name otherwise mainly attested on pottery; cf. also Pithon, 92, and note Bacon, 91, and Cybon, 151, both uniquely attested at Athens here; Ergaeus, 40, only otherwise met in another casualty list; or Mechanion, 22, otherwise found as a self-professed scribe in *IG* i³ 841).

Because the dead are recorded without patronymic or demotic it would be impossible for anyone reading the inscription to be sure which occurrence of a name referred to which individual (and for the same reason we are unable to associate any of these individuals with known families). Depriving the individual of his social context in this way has been seen as a democratic feature, but it is in fact shared by lists of war dead from Tanagra and (admittedly atticising) Thespiae. It is nevertheless striking that in death these Athenians are identified only with the tribe, a group which had limited social reality, bringing individuals together in any numbers only in a military context or the context of one or two festivals with tribal competitions, and not with the family, deme or indeed phratry with which the individual interacted on much more frequent basis. In the face of these commemorations which subsumed individuals into long lists, it is perhaps unsurprising that some Athenians came to have separate individual memorials (see R&O 7).

One effect of the absence of patronymics and demotics is to reduce the impact of this long list of names: had these lists been organised by deme, and so in this case divided up the 175 names among the 14 demes of Erechtheis, they would have revealed much more clearly the effect of these losses on (often very small) village communities. Particular tribal contingents might suffer particularly badly in an engagement (as the tribe Aiantis is said at Plut. *Arist.* 19. v–vi to have borne all the Athenian losses at the battle of Plataea), and so we cannot simply multiply the death

[1] On seers see J. Dillery, in Johnston & Struck (edd.), *Mantike*, 167–231; H. Bowden, in *Herodotus and his World . . . G. Forrest*, 256–74. For an (admittedly extreme) case of the importance of obtaining good omens before fighting see Xen. *An.* VI. iv. 12–v. 8. Sthorys of Thasos was honoured by Athens for his service as seer before the battle of Cnidus in 394: *IG* ii² 17 = Osborne, *Naturalization*, D 8.

toll in Erechtheis by ten to achieve the total losses for the year. Nevertheless, and particularly given the second tribal *stele* perhaps related to this year, there can be little

---

110

Samians fight in Egypt, *c*.460–454

A

A white marble block, apparently a statue base, found in the Heraeum at Samos and now in the museum there. Phot. *Klio* xxxii = [2]xiv 1939, 290; *LSAG*, pl. 63. 21.

Ionic lettering; non-*stoichedon*: *LSAG*, pp. 331, 342, 414, no. 21.

W. Peek, *Klio* xxxii = [2]xiv 1939, 289–306; M&L 34; *CEG* 421; Clairmont, *Patrios Nomos*, i. 156 no. 20A; *IG* x̣ii. vi. 1 279*. Trans. Fornara 77; Osborne, *The Athenian Empire*[4], 43.

[τôδ'] ἔργο πολλοὶ π̣ά̣ρ̣α̣ [μάρ]τ̣υ̣ρ̣ε̣[ς ‑ ⏑ ‑ ⏑ ⏓]
[Μέμ]φιος ἀμφ' ἐρατῆς νηυσὶν ἔθηκ̣[ε μάχην]
[θο]ῦ̣ρος Ἄρης Μήδων τε καὶ Ἑλλήν[ων, Σάμιοι δὲ]
[νῆ]ας Φοινίκων πέντε τε καὶ δ[έκ' ἕλον].
[-] Ἡγησαγ̣όρην Ζωΐ̈λο τô καὶ [⏑ ‑ ⏓]
‑ ‑ ‑ ‑ ‑ ‑ ‑ ‑ ‑ ‑ ‑ ‑ ‑ ‑ *traces* ‑ ‑ ‑ ‑ ‑ ‑ ‑

1 [τôδ'] ἔργο πολλοὶ π̣α̣ρ̣ὰ̣ [μάρ]τ̣υ̣ρ̣ε̣[ς, εὖτ' ἐπὶ Νείλωι] Peek: we translate this, bracketing the parts restored only by him. 2 ηκ̣ inscribed in an erasure: original letters εκ̣. 5 [ἀλλ'] Peek; Ζωΐ̈λο τô considered by Peek, adopted by Hallof (*IG*): Ζωϊλότο previous edd. (Ζωΐ̈λος is a frequent name, and including this there are twenty-one Samian instances of it in *LGPN*, but Ζωΐ̈λοτος and Ζωϊλότης have no entry in any volume of *LGPN*).

A monument had been set up to commemorate Samians who distinguished themselves in (probably) the battle of the River Eurymedon, *c*.469, with verses celebrating the achievements in that battle of a man called Maeandrius added *c*.300 (*IG* xii. vi 277–8, cf. *LSAG*, pp. 331, 342, no. 20). Here another Samian military achievement is celebrated, but there is no trace of comparable monuments in Samos after this. Samos had been subject to Persia in the late sixth and early fifth centuries, and at this stage was proud of its involvement in the Delian League; for the later history of Samos in this period see **138**, **139**, **152**. 20–1, **170**. 18–19, **180**. 20, 34–5, **191**. Peek supposed that the 'witnesses' of l. 1 were the spoils displayed on the monument ('Here are many witnesses . . . '), but we cannot be sure what stood on the base.

Memphis is the only possible restoration at the beginning of l. 2 which would make sense of this text, and the allusion must be to Athens' war in Egypt supporting Inaros against the Persians, *c*.460–454 (Thuc. 1. 104, 109–10, mentioning allied

doubt that Athenian losses in this year reached four figures—and that out of a total male citizen population at this date of the order of 40,000.

Of this deed many were witnesses, [when on the Nile] around lovely Memphis furious Ares set to battle ships of the Medes and Greeks, and the Samians captured fifteen ships of the Phoenicians. [But] Hegesagoras son of Zoïlus who also – – –

---

involvement at 104. ii and Memphis, slightly south of the apex of the Nile delta, at 104. ii, 109. iv; cf. **109**). Ctesias (*FGrH* 688 F 14. 36 [32]) mentions a victory 'at sea' in which twenty Persian ships (referred to in this text as Phoenician ships, since it was the Phoenicians who provided the Persian navy) were captured and thirty destroyed, and singles out an Athenian commander, Charitimides. The Samians seem to have picked out some act involving Hegesagoras, either on his own or along with others. Peek suggested that a statue of him stood on this base; but Clairmont remarks that the Athenians did not honour individuals with statues in the fifth century (though they did in the fourth, beginning with Conon in the 390s), and it appears from *IG* XII. vi 280 sqq. that the Samians did not do so until the end of the fourth century, so Peek's suggestion seems unlikely. Hegesagoras' name is in the accusative, and we do not know what the verb was; we have no reason to believe that he was a general.

B

Two fragments of a dark marble base: *a* (left) find-spot unknown, now in the Antikensammlung, Staatliche Museen zu Berlin—Preußischer Kulturbesitz; *b* (right) built into a wall of a later building in the Heraeum and now in the museum there. Phot. *AM* lxxxvii 1972, Taf. 60. 1–2.

Ionic lettering; non-*stoichedon*.

G. Dunst, *AM* lxxxvii 1972, 153–5; M&L 34 (1988 *addenda*); *IG* xii. i. 1 468*.

Ἰνάρως Ψαμμητίχ[ο ὁ τῆς Αἰγύπτ]ο βασιλεὺς
Λεωκρίτωι Ἰφι . [- - - τοῖς να]ύτηισιν
τῶν συμμάχων ἐπ̣[- - - ἀ]ριστήιον.

2 the character after Ιφι has been read as α̣ or μ̣. 2–3 Ἰφιά̣[δο Σαμίωι, τοῖς να]ύτηισιν | τῶν συμμάχων ἐπ̣[εστεῶτι *vacat* ἀ]ριστήιον Dunst, but the *vacat* is awkward: we translate this, bracketing the parts restored only by him.

In this second text the mention of Inaros is explicit (and he is described as king—'of Egypt' if the restoration is correct: Thuc. i. 104. i, 110. iii, calls him king of the Libyans), and he himself has awarded a prize to Leocritus. This is the only Samian

---

111

Casualty list of the Argives killed at Tanagra, 458 or 457

Fifteen fragments from a pedimental *stele* of Pentelic marble, two found on the Athenian acropolis, eight in the agora, two near the Library of Hadrian and one in the Ceramicus. We print below the provisional arrangement of the fragments suggested by Papazarkadas and Sourlas. All the fragments are in the Epigraphical Museum except fr. *c*, which is in the British Museum, and fr. *e*, once in the Karapanos Collection in Athens, current location unknown. Phot. *a–f, i, m, Kerameikos* iii, pls. 10–11; *c, f–l, Hesperia* xiv 1945, 139-43;

n [τοί]δ' ἔθ̣[ανον Ταν]άγραι Λακ[εδαιμο]- *d*

f Ἀ ρ γ ε [ί ο ν·]

[νίον hυπὸ χερσ]ί, πένθο[ς - - -]

col. i		*col. ii*	*col. iii*	*col. iv*	
hυλλεε͂ς	*a*	[Μ]ά̣τριος	[—7—]ος	Ἀντ[- - -]	
[Π]όλλιχος		[Ἀ]ριστίον	- - -	Θε[- - -]	
[Ἀλ]κ̣ισθένες		[Σ]φενδονίον	- - -	Ε[. .]λ[. .]ς	*c*
[—7—]ος		[Λ]υκῖνος	- - -	Φοῖνιξ	

2 πένθο[ς δ' ἔτλασαν | γᾶς πε]ρὶ μαρναμ[ένον] Meritt (cf. Pind. *Isthm.* vii. 51); πένθο[ς δ' hῖκε πά|τρας πε]ριμαρναμ[ένον προτὶ ϝάστυ] W. Peek, *ZPE* xxx 1978, 18–19; πένθο[ς δ' hῖκε πά|τραν εὖ πε]ρὶ μαρναμ[ένον] Peek, *GVI* 15. 5 [Ἀλ]κισθένες Meritt, Papazarkadas & Sourlas: [Σο]σισθένες Peek, *Kerameikos* iii, no. 29.

Inaros son of Psammetichus the king of Egypt awarded this to Leocritus [son of Iphiades the Samian, commander of] the sailors of the allies, as a prize.

---

instance of that name, and Iphiades (if that is correct) is the only Samian instance of that name. Dunst's restoration makes him commander not simply of the Samian contingent but of the whole allied element in the force.

---

n, *Hesperia* xxi 1952, pl. 89; all fragments except *e* in *Hesperia* lxxxi 2012, 585–619 figs. 1, 3–5, 7–15; facsimile of the upper part, *Hesperia* xxi 1952, 354 (= *LSAG*, pl. 29).

Early Argive letters, *stoichedon* (except for the epigram).

M&L 35; *Agora* xvii. 4; *CEG* 135 (epigram only); *SEG* xxviii 30, *IG* i³ 1149; N. Papazarkadas & D. Sourlas, *Hesperia* lxxxi 2012, 585–617*.

Of Argives, these died at Tanagra at the hands of the Lacedaemonians, and suffered grief fighting . . .

col. i	*col. ii*	*col. iii*	*col. iv*
HYLLEIS	Matrius	—us	Ant—
Pollichus	Aristion		The—
Alcisthenes	Sphendonion		E–l–s
—us	Lycinus		Phoenix

– – –
– – –
– – –
– – –
– – –
– – –
– – –
– – –
– – –
– – –
– – –
– – –
– – –
– – –
– – –
m [. . . .]μα[– – –]
[. . .]θισ[–?]
[hι]πποσ[θένες]
[Μ]ικέας
Ἀ̣ριστόβι[ος]
Τελέστας
Αἰθέρ
Φιλοκράτες
Στίλπον
Ἐπίτιμος
– – –
– – –
– – –
– – –
– – –
– – –
– – –
lacuna
– – –
– – –
– – –
– – –
– – –
– – –
– – –
– – –

Ϝ̣αναξίλας
[Δ]έρκετος
[Ἐχ]εμένες
[—5—]ις
– – –
– – –
– – –
– – –
b [. .]ΟΣ[–?]
[. .]ιος
[.]ύρος
[.]ιμοσ[–?]
[Ἆ]γις
Μ̣οσ̣[χ – – –]
– – –
– – –
– – –
– – –
– – –
– – –
– – –
– – –
– – –
– – –
– – –
– – –
– – –
– – –
– – –
– – –
– – –
– – –
lacuna
– – –
– – –
– – –
– – –
– – –
– – –
– – –
h Π̣οσ[– – –]

– – –
– – –
– – –
– – –
g [– – –]ος
– – –
– – –
[– – –]ς
– – –
– – –
– – –
– – –
– – –
k [. . . .]αι[– – –]
[. .]οκας
[Σ]πινθέρας
[Ἐπι]μένες
[Δαμ]άρετος
[—4–5—]
Σ̣τ̣ίλπ̣[ον]
o Λυσίμαχ[ος]
Δαμοφάν[ες]
Μικέας
Θαλλίας
Κάσσαβος
Ἐρίφαντ[ος]
Ε̣ὐνοστί[δας]
[Λ]ύ̣σιχος
[. .]ο̣ος
[. . .]ον
[. . . .]ιάδ[ας]
[—5—]υλ[– – –]
lacuna
e Αἰσ[– – –]
Δαμ[ά]hι[ππος]
Πανται[– – –]
Δορρ̣υ[λ– – –]
Μυσπε̣[– – –]
Ἀρχε[– – –]
Λυ[– – –]
– – –

[Φ]ιλέας
[Β]ράχας
Τελέσστας
Δαμοφάνες
Θυμάρες
Δαΐκλε͂ς
Σύλιχος
Δέρκετος
Λυϙοδόρκας
Κλέον
Κρατιάδας
[Α]ἰσχύλος
[Εὐ]α̣ρχί[δ]α̣ς
– – –
– – –
– – –
– – –
– – –
– – –
– – –
– – –
– – –
– – –
– – –
– – –
– – –
– – –
– – –
– – –
– – –
– – –
– – –
lacuna
– – –
– – –
– – –
– – –
– – –
– – –
– – –
j [– – –]ς

[– – – πε]ρὶ μαρνάμ[ενοι.]

10 [Μ]ικέας Papazarkadas & Sourlas (cf. l. 63); [Ν]ικέας Peek *Kerameikos* iii, no. 29.

. . . . ma—
. . . this–?
Hipposthenes
Miceas
Aristobius
Telestas
Aether
Philocrates
Stilpon
Epitimus

lacuna

Wanaxilas
Dercetus
Echemenes
—is

. . os–?
. . ius
. yras
. imos–?
Agis
Mosch—

lacuna

Pos—

—os

—s

. . . . ai—
. . ocas
Spintheras
Epimenes
Damaretas
———
Stilpon
Lysimachus
Damophanes
Miceas
Thallias
Cassabus
Èriphantus
Eunostidas
Lysichus
. . ous
. . . on
. . . . iadas
—yl—

lacuna

Aes—
Damahippus
Pantai—
Dorquyl—
Myspe—
Arche—
Ly—

Phileas
Brachas
Telesstas
Damophanes
Thymares
Daïcles
Sylichus
Dercetus
Lykodorchas
Cleon
Cratiadas
Aeschylus
Euarchidas

lacuna

—s

---	Εὐχ[- - -]	---	[- - -]ς
---	Λ̣εο[- - -]	---	[- - -]ας
---	---	---	[- - -]ς
---	*i* Ε[- - -]	---	[- - -]χος
---	Ἀλ[- - -]	---	[- - -]ν
---	Ἀρ[- - -]	---	[- - -]λ̣είδας
---	Λυ[- - -]	---	[- - -]μαχος
---	Τε[- - -]	---	[- - -]ος
---	Κα[- - -]	---	---
---	F[- - -]	---	---
---	Ῥ[- - -]	---	---
---	---	---	---
---	---	---	*vacat*
---	---	---	*l* Δα[- - -]
---	---	---	Με[- - -]
---	---	---	Δ[- - -]
---	---	---	*lacuna?*

In 458 or 457 the Spartans responded to a Phocian attack on Boeum, Cytinium and Erineum in Doris, the Dorian 'mother city', by sending an army of 1,500 Spartan hoplites and 10,000 allies (Thuc. I. 107. ii). This force compelled the Phocians to give up the city that they had taken, and then turned to march back to the Peloponnese. Thucydides tells us that Athenian naval presence in the Corinthian Gulf prevented their returning by ship and that the recent Athenian alliance with Megara meant that the attempt to return via Megara was risky also. He claims that while the Peloponnesian army was in Boeotia some Athenians secretly urged them to intervene in Attica to overthrow the democracy and prevent the building of the long walls. The Athenians summoned allies and received 1,000 Argive hoplites, Thessalian cavalry and other support. Battle ensued at Tanagra in Boeotia, and on Thucydides' account there was 'great slaughter on both sides' (I. 108. i). Diodorus, whose account of the whole campaign is very problematic, claims two successive days of fighting (XI. 80. i).

Pausanias, in noting the burial of the Argive allies in the Ceramicus, says that on the first day of the battle the Argives had the better of the battle against the Spartans, but that their success was not decisive at the point when night fell, and that on the following day the treachery of the Thessalians secured victory for the Spartans (Paus. I. 29. viii–ix). The Spartans took advantage of their victory to return to the Peloponnese via Megara without opposition, and set up a victory monument at Olympia (**112**). The Athenians, however, sixty-two days after the battle (Thuc. I. 108. ii) marched again into Boeotia, and at Oenophyta near Tanagra inflicted such a defeat on the Boeotians that they were able to take control of Boeotia and Phocis and take hostages from the Opuntian Locrians.

Euch——
Leo—
– – –
E—
Al—
Ar—
Ly—
Te—
Ca—
W—
Rh—

—s
—as
—s
—chus
—n
—leidas
—machus
—us

vacat
Da—
Me—
D—
lacuna?

This monument seems to have commemorated only the Argive dead. Pausanias tells us that the casualties from Cleonae, who had come to help with the Argives, were commemorated separately (Paus. I. 29. vii). Cities other than Athens inscribed casualty lists (including Argos itself, *SEG* xxix 361), but we know of none as early as this. Yet this stone does not simply mimic Athenian practice (cf. **109** above). The gable is unparalleled on Athenian monuments. But at the same time the curious layout of the heading and the epigram suggest that the Argive letter-cutter was not familiar with the task and did not initially expect to engrave an epigram. The presence at the top of the first column of the tribe name, Hylleis, suggests that the dead were recorded in four tribal groups, although separate columns were evidently not reserved for the separate tribes. More than one individual of the same name is recorded (Miceas, 10, 63; Stilpon, 15, 60), but as with Athenian lists no attempt is made to distinguish them by patronymic: individual performance of civic duty is thereby stressed. We cannot securely reconstruct the complete layout of the text, but 106 names survive, and the reconstruction by Papazarkadas & Sourlas, which we follow here, presupposes that at least 240 names were recorded—and there may have been significantly more. If this is correct it would confirm the literary record of unusually high casualties: it has been calculated that average casualty levels in hoplite battles were 14 per cent on the losing side (and 5 per cent on the winning), with greater than 20 per cent being rare (P. Krentz, *GRBS* xxvi 1985, 13–20).

As with Athenian dead, the dead Argive soldiers were cremated at the battle site and the bones then brought back to Athens. This raises the question of why neither Argive nor Cleonaean bones were taken back to their own city. The allusion to the Athenian alliance with Argos in Aesch. *Eum.* 773 (see Sommerstein, *Aeschylus,*

Eumenides, *ad loc.*), which was performed shortly before the battle, indicates something of the political importance of the new alliance, and the Athenians may have wanted to give their allies from the Argolid signal honour—and perhaps also to reduce the impact at Argos of a ceremony in which more than a quarter of her army was brought back dead.

The precise text of the epigram is disputed and we have not ventured a full restoration.

112

Thank-offering for the victory of Tanagra, 458 or 457

Three joining fragments of a marble *stele* found at Olympia; now in the Olympia Museum. Phot. *LSAG*, pl. 21. 38; Guarducci, *Epigrafia Greca*, i. 470 fig. 243.

Corinthian letters: *LSAG* 129–30, 132. 38 (but see C. Gallavotti, *BPEC* xxvi 1978, 4–11).

I. Olympia 253; M&L 36*; *CEG* 351. See also M. Guarducci, *RPAA* xii 1936, 125–32, *Epigrafia Greca*, i. 469–72; Zizza, *Le iscrizioni nella Periegesi di Pausania*, 158–66. Trans. Fornara 80; Dillon & Garland^{3} 6. 60; Sage, *Warfare in Ancient Greece*, 157.

[ναὸς μὲν φιάλαν χρυσέα]ν ἔχει, ἐγ δὲ [Τανάγρας]
[τοὶ Λακεδαιμόνιοι συμ]μαχία τ' ἀν[έθεν]
[δο̃ρον ἀπ' Ἀργείον καὶ Ἀθα]ναίον καὶ ['Ιάνον],
[τὰν δεκάταν νίκας hείν]εκα τοῦ πο[λέμου].
- - - - - - - - - - - - - - - - - - Κορ[ινθ]ι̣ - - - - - -
- - - - - - - - - - - - - - - - ρ - - - - - - - -

In the course of his description of the temple of Zeus at Olympia Pausanias (v. 10. iv) notes that the central acroterion takes the form of a Nike (cf. **164**), and that under this there is a golden shield bearing an image of the Gorgon Medusa and an epigram which declares who dedicated it and why. He then quotes, with minor textual variants, including the use of the Doric genitive ending in -ω, the first four lines of the inscription given above (for other inscriptions recorded or mentioned by Pausanias see **105** and **164**).

Scholars have puzzled over the discrepancy between what Pausanias records and the surviving fragments. They speculate that when he says that the epigram is ἐπὶ τῇ ἀσπίδι this means not 'on the shield' but 'concerning the shield', and that Pausanias was not copying the actual inscription but using a literary work which, for whatever reason, employed the Doric genitive (C. Clairmont, *ZPE* xlviii 1982, 79–85).

A mid-fifth-century tombstone for one Theotimus of Atrax who fought 'in the plain of Tanagra' has been found at Larisa in Thessaly (**117**. *B*). Some Thessalians seem not to have been ashamed of their behaviour in the battle. See also below on **112**.

The temple has a golden bowl: the Spartans and their alliance dedicated it from Tanagra, a gift from Argives, Athenians and Ionians, the tithe because of victory in the war – – – Corinthians – – –

Although such explanations cannot be ruled out, it seems more likely that there were two inscriptions, one actually on the shield, and consisting of just the four lines recorded by Pausanias, and one on a marble *stele* nearby that flagged up the particular part played by the Corinthians in this dedication.

This text sheds important light on the development and use of the sanctuary at Olympia. The decision to put a golden shield on the top of the pediment of the temple must indicate that the temple of Zeus was essentially complete (though the acroteria would follow only later: see **164**). This gives us our best dating for completion of the temple, which is likely to have been begun only after Elis established supremacy over the sanctuary (*c*.470). But this dedication in this position also shows how an Elis that set about constructing this temple to mark her own local success (Paus. v. 10. ii, cf. Hdt. IV. 148, Strabo 354–5 / VIII. ii. 30, 357–8 / VIII. ii. 33) was prepared to allow the temple to become a prominent advertisement for the success of the Spartan-led Peloponnesian League. Olympia had long been the place in which trophies were displayed celebrating the victory of one Greek city over another (cf. **101**), but by appropriating the enormous new temple to celebrate their victory at Tanagra the Spartans outclassed every other victory monument. The contrast between the way in which the epigram subsumes Sparta's allies into 'Spartans and alliance' but lists separately Argives, Athenians and Ionians, and in that order, is notable. Argos fought at Tanagra in accordance with a bilateral alliance concluded with Athens shortly before (Thuc. I. 102. iv; cf. **111**, above), the Ionians as members of the Delian League. This refusal to recognise others' alliances on the same footing as their own anticipates Spartan attitudes in the fourth century. It may have been their invisibility in the epigram that encouraged the Corinthians to replicate it on a *stele* in order to spell out exactly their own involvement in the alliance to which it referred.[1]

The use of 'offering bowl' (φιάλη) for 'shield' makes a visual pun which may already have been in play when Archilochus proclaimed himself unconcerned about throwing away his shield since he could get another (Archilochus 5 West). In Aristophon's *Philonides* (fr. 13 K&A) one character tells how his master brought him 'a well-rounded shield, overbrimming, mixed with equal parts' [wine and

[1] See generally Scott, *Delphi and Olympia*, 181–95.

113

An Athenian dead on Aegina, after *c*.457

A limestone *stele* found on Aegina, now in the Epigraphical Museum in Athens. Phot. *LSAG*, pl. 17; *IG* iv^{2} pl. 8; drawing in *IG* iv.

Aeginetan letters, written between incised lines.

IG iv 50; *IG* i^{3} 1503*; *CEG* 80; *IG* iv^{2} 906. See also C. Sourvinou-Inwood, *'Reading' Greek Death*, 211–12.

χαίρετε οἱ παριό-
ντες· ἐγὸ δὲ Ἀντιστά-
τες hυὸς Ἀτάρβο / κεῖμαι
τεῖδε θανόν, πατρίδα
γε͂ν προλιπόν. Ἀντιστάτες
Ἀθεναῖος.

3 The *h* seems to have been inserted after the other letters were inscribed. 5–6 Ἀντιστάτες Ἀθεναῖος is written in slightly smaller and more closely packed letters.

water]. Ath. x. 433 c quotes the phrase '*phiale* of Ares' from Antiphanes' *Kaineus*, and Aristotle in *Poet.* 1457 b (cf. *Rh.* iii. 1407 a 17) notes that the *phiale* could be called the 'shield of Dionysus' and the shield the '*phiale* of Ares'. But the use of *phiale* for shield in this inscription alludes more to the role of *phialai* in libations to the gods, and therefore as favoured items for dedication. It is *phialai* that the Caryatids of the Erechtheum carry in their hands, and *phialai* were dedicated in connection with the manumission of slaves on the Athenian acropolis in the fourth century.

The victory at Tanagra was marked also by a Thessalian dedication at Delphi of a bronze horse, on the base of which, in Phocian letters, was inscribed 'The Thessalians dedicated this horse to Apollo as a tithe (*dekate*) of the (spoils) from Tanagra (*or* from the Tanagraeans)', followed by the names of two polemarchs and five individuals (**117**. *A*). This is another reminder (cf. **111**) that the literary tradition of Thessalian treachery at the battle of Tanagra was not the only tradition in circulation. If the text did indeed read, as parallels (cf. **111**) suggest, 'from the Tanagraeans' then the Thessalians construed what they were doing in Boeotia as fighting against Tanagra: no doubt there were soldiers from Tanagra among the Spartan allies, but that would not justify singling them out for mention in a dedication.

Greetings passers-by! I,
Antistates son of Atarbus,
lie dead here, having
forsaken my homeland.
Antistates Athenian.

Aegina was one of the cities involved in the running of the sanctuary of Poseidon on the island of Calauria, off Troezen, known as the Calaurian amphictyony, and her early history seems to have been most closely bound up with Argos and Epidaurus, but Herodotus reports an 'old enmity' between Aegina and Athens, and at the end of the sixth century an Aeginetan raid on Attica led to a long war with Athens (Hdt. v. 81; Aeginetan history is usefully summarised in a chronological table by Figueira, *Excursions in Epichoric History*, 409–18). Aegina offered earth and water to envoys from the Persians before Marathon, but Cleomenes of Sparta took action to prevent Aegina becoming a useful Persian ally (Hdt. vi. 49. i, 73. ii). Among other hostilities in the years around 490 the Aeginetans captured an Athenian ship taking part in a festival at Sunium and Athens responded by supporting an Aeginetan exile, Nicodromus, who stirred up civil strife that became extremely bloody (Hdt. vi. 88–90).

In 481 the Aeginetans and Athenians put aside their differences and Aegina joined the Hellenic League against Persia. Aegina became a haven for Athenians evacuated from Attica, and Aeginetan ships distinguished themselves in the battle of Salamis (Hdt. vii. 145. i, viii. 41. i, 93 iii). But Aegina did not join the Delian League, and in the late 460s came under increasing Athenian pressure. The Erechtheid tribe records casualties on Aegina (**109**), and Thucydides records a sea battle in which the Athenians captured seventy ships and then besieged Aegina. After the battle of Tanagra (see **111**, **112**, **117**) the Aeginetans capitulated and agreed to demolish their walls, hand over their ships and pay tribute (Thuc. i. 105. ii, 108. iv). Diodorus records the campaign as having lasted nine months (xi. 78. iv). A fragmentary Athenian decree (*IG* i^3 38) making provision for a garrison in order to prevent harm to the Aeginetans or the Athenians seems to belong to the aftermath of 457 (Figueira, *Athens and Aigina*, 120–6). In 431 the Athenians expelled the Aeginetans and installed Athenian settlers (Thuc. ii. 27. i; cf. Hdt. vi. 91. i). A series of boundary-stones marks land taken over by the Athenians and given to various gods (*IG* iv 29–38 with J. P. Barron, *JHS* ciii 1983, 1–12, Figueira, *Athens and Aigina*, 115–20; but for the interpretation here see Parker, *Athenian Religion: A History*, 144–5, I. Polinskaya, *Hesperia* lxxviii 2009, 231–67) but these may post-date 431.

Where in all this does Antistates' gravestone belong? In terms of letter forms the inscription has been judged to belong between *c.*475 and 431 (*LSAG* 112, 113). Antistates could even, conceivably, be one of the Athenians evacuated to Aegina in 480. Most plausible, however, is the context of Athenian control of Aegina after 457 but before 431 (after that an Athenian settler would surely not present himself as a loner, and would be unlikely to use the ethnic). We get a rare glimpse here of what servicing Athenian imperial ambitions meant for individuals, removed from their homes and families for significant periods. The form of naming is eloquent here:

Antistates gives no demotic, since he is outside Attica, but it is only as an afterthought that he realises that he needs to give an ethnic, and 'Antistates, Athenian' is squeezed in at the end.

The epigram, a single elegiac couplet (but with an extra foot in the opening hexameter) followed by Antistates' name and ethnic, makes the deceased speak and address the passer-by. This is a not uncommon practice, and the phrase χαίρετε ... παριόντες can be precisely paralleled elsewhere, in a text from Eretria but for an Aeginetan, Mnesimachus, which is more or less contemporary with Antistates' memorial, and in three fourth-century gravestones, one from Thoricus, one from Crete and one from Piraeus (*CEG* 108, 487, 492, 677; see further Sourvinou-Inwood, *'Reading' Greek Death*, 211–12). All use the χαίρετε ... παριόντες phrase, followed as here by an emphatic contrast: ἐγὸ δὲ. The primary contrast is between the living passer-by and themselves, dead/ill-fated, but in three cases the deceased also draw attention to the fact that they had left their home—Mnesimachus (*CEG* 108) talks of himself as ξένος ἀπ' Αἰγίνες and Callimachus at Thoricus (*CEG* 492) as λιπὼν πατρίδα. There is a particular poignancy in addressing the passer-by, the traveller, when those who have died were themselves overtaken by death while not at home and their bodies have not been buried in an ancestral family plot. In this way Antistates presents himself as temporarily absent from his homeland, someone who happened to die abroad, rather than as someone who has settled in a new land.

We might ask whether there is any significance in there being two memorials, close in date and using closely parallel epigrammatic formulae, one of which was found on Aegina and the other for an Aeginetan on Eretria. The monument to Mnesimachus at Eretria declares itself to have been put up by his mother, Timarete. Had she commissioned an epigram from the local Aeginetan epigrammatist who had written (or would write) the epigram for Antistates? Or should we see both of these as essentially 'ready-made' epigrams into which a name is inserted? The extra foot in the opening hexameter here might encourage that view.

Neither Antistates nor Atarbus are common Athenian names. In the fifth century we meet an Atarbus among the war dead at various places in the north Aegean listed on a *stele* probably to be dated to 464 (*IG* i^3 1144. 41) and as the father of the secretary in 421/0 (*IG* i^3 80. 1), and an Antistates on a list of war dead of the tribe Aiantis from *c*.411 (*IG* i^3 1186. 125). In the fourth century no Antistates is recorded, but Atarbus of Thoricus is famous as a victorious *choregos* with *pyrrhichistai* at the Panathenaea (*IG* ii^2 3025). Despite the few occurrences, the names occur in at least three demes.

In the third line of the inscription 'h' seems to have been inserted afterwards by the letter-cutter. To be consistent he should also have inserted 'h' to aspirate οἱ in the first line (unless τοι was intended here as in Mnesimachus' epigram, *CEG* 108. 1).

114

A victory of Selinus, fifth century

A block of reddish limestone from Temple G at Selinus; now in the Museo Archeologico at Palermo; the base of the block was 2.4 m. above ground level, the letters are *c.*3 cm. high. Phot. Calder, *The Inscription* (below), pls.1, 3; our pl. 3.

Megarian/Western Greek, in the local alphabet; non-*stoichedon*: *LSAG*, pp. 271, 277, no. 39.

IG xiv 268; *SIG*[3] 1122; Buck 98; Calder, *The Inscription from Temple G at Selinus*; M&L 38*. Trans. Fornara 91. See also Calder, *GRBS* v 1964, 113–9; G. Manganaro, *Rendiconti Acc. Lincei*[9] vii 1996, 33–8 (cf. *SEG* xlvi 1271); A. Brugnone, in *Sicilia Epigraphica* . . . 15–18.*x*.1998, i. 129–39; G. Manganaro, in *Sicilia Epigraphica*, ii. 418 (cf. *SEG* xlix 1328).

[δι]ὰ τὸς θεὸς τό[σ]δε νικôντι̣ τοὶ Σελινόν̣[τιοι].
[δι]ὰ τὸν Δία νικôμες καὶ διὰ τὸν Φόβον̣ [καὶ]
δ[ιὰ] hερακλέα καὶ δι' Ἀπόλλονα καὶ διὰ Π[οτ]-
ε[ιδᾶ]να καὶ διὰ̣ Τυνδαρίδας καὶ δι' Ἀθ[α]-
ναίαν καὶ διὰ Μαλοφόρον καὶ διὰ Πασι̣[κ]-
ρά[τ]ειαν καὶ διὰ τὸς ἄλλος θεός, δ̣ιὰ δ[ὲ] Δία
μάλιστα̣. φιλία̣[ς] δὲ γενομένας ἐν χ[ρ]υσ-
έο[ι] ἐλά[σα]ντα[ς καὶ] ὀνύματα ταῦτα κολ-
άψαντ[ας εἰς] τ̣ὸ Ἀ[π]ολλ̣όνιον καθθέμε-
ν, τὸ Διὸ[ς ?προ]γρά[ψ]α̣ντες. τὸ δέ χρυσίον
ἑ̓ξ̣έκ[οντα τα]λάντον [ἔ]μεν.

7–8 ἐν χ[ρ]υσ|έο[ι] ἔλα[φο]ν, τὰ [μὲν] ὀνύματα Manganaro 1996. 10 [προ]γρά[ψ]α̣ντες Holm: space for 2 or 3 letters, [ἐν]γρά[ψ]α̣ντες Calder.

The massive temple G at Selinus (*c.*110 × 50 m.), in western Sicily, was under construction during the fifth century, and was still unfinished when the city was sacked by the Carthaginians in 409 (Diod. Sic. xiii. 54. vi–58). This text perhaps suggests that G was a temple of Apollo; but others think that the text did not accompany the shield and the temple it was set up in was that of Zeus (*SEG* lxvi 1100), and among the large number of temples at Selinus, the attribution of particular ones to particular gods is not clear (cf. e.g. V. Tusa, *Kokalos* xiii 1967, table on pp. 188–9).

This inscription marks an equally massive dedication: if the gold was of 60 talents weight, the only known victory which would justify such an expensive dedication would be the defeat of the Athenian forces in 413 (Calder); if it was to be what could be obtained for 60 talents of silver (J. Schubring, *Arch. Zeitung* xxx = [2]v 1873, 102–3), the possibilities are not limited to occasions we happen to know of: Selinus has been suggested as one of the actual parties to the war between 'Egesta and Lilybaeum' in

Because of these gods the Selinuntines are victorious.

2 Because of Zeus we were victorious and because of Phobos and because of Heracles and because of Apollo and because of Poseidon and because of the Tyndaridae and because of Athena and because of Malophorus and because of Pasicratea and because of the other gods, but because of Zeus particularly.

7 Now that friendship has been brought about, (the dedication) beaten out (?) in gold and these names engraved shall be set down in the Apollonium, writing the name of Zeus first (?). The gold is to be of sixty talents.

---

the manuscript text of Diod. Sic. xi. 86. ii under 454/3, and Jeffery in *LSAG* 271, 277, no. 39, thought 460–450 a suitable date for the lettering; A. M. Woodward in reviewing Calder favoured G. Ugdulena's suggestion of the victory over Egesta reported by Diod. Sic. xii. 82. iii–vi under 416/5, but not specifically mentioned by Thuc. vi. 6. ii (*JHS* lxxxxvi 1966, 296–7).

Calder regarded ll. 2–7 as a 'Zeus song' in choriambic dimeters, but that is probably to take the list more ingeniously than it deserves (P. A. Hansen does not include this text in *CEG*). Others have seen the formulaic wording as a reflection of an oracular answer to the question, 'Through which gods were we victorious?' (*SEG* lvi 1100). Phobos, 'Fear', is perhaps the war god of Selinus; the Tyndaridae are Castor and Pollux; Malophorus, probably 'Apple-Bearer' (cf. M. Perale, in Antonetti & De Vido (edd.), *Temi selinuntini*, 229–44), is Demeter (for the temple see Guido, *Sicily: An Archaeological Guide*, 96–9, and **115**; cf. Selinus' mother city, Megara: Paus. i. 44. iii, who there took it to mean 'Sheep-Bearer'); Pasicratea is probably Persephone (cf. *Hom. Hymn. Dem.* 365), but Manganaro suggests Artemis, to whom, with Apollo, deer were sacred (cf. below). Herodotus mentions an altar of Zeus Agoraios (VI. 46. ii) and our **115** orders sacrifices to Zeus Eumenes and Zeus Meilichios.

Lines 7–11 with their infinitives probably embody a decree of Selinus (M&L wondered about an oracle, and Brugnone thinks both parts are derived from an oracle; but an oracle would hardly have specified the amount of gold). Calder argued that ἐλαύνειν points to a shield as the dedication, but Manganaro's restoration of ἔλα[φο]ν, 'deer', has attracted support. If the syntax is taken seriously, this text orders the inscription of the list on the actual dedication, not on this stone

---

115

A sacred law from Selinus, 450s

A large lead tablet, given to the J. Paul Getty Museum in 1981; returned to Italy in 1992. No recorded provenance, but perhaps from the sanctuary of Zeus Meilichios on the Gaggera Hill at Selinunte. Phot. Jameson *et al.*, *A Lex Sacra*, frontispiece, pls. 1–5.

Selinuntine alphabet, including *qoppa* (only on *A*), *digamma* with practically no tail, *xi* in the form of a reversed E, and *beta* in the form of a reversed *nu* (*B.* 10: cf. *LSAG* 262). Three separate hands can be distinguished. The two columns are arranged so that whichever way up one has the lead tablet only the writing running right from the central margin formed of two vertical lines is the right way up; horizontal guidelines are given for the first 18 lines of col. *A*.

Jameson *et al.*, *A Lex Sacra from Selinous* (cf. *SEG* xliii 630)*; L. Dubois, *RPh* lxix 1995, 127–44, *AION* (filol.) xix 1997, 331–46; *NGSL* 27; Colvin 44 (*B.* 1–7 only). See also Robertson, *Religion and Reconciliation in Greek Cities*, 15–16. Trans. Jameson *et al.*, 15, 17; E. Curti & R. van Bremen, *Ostraka* viii 1999, 21–33; *NGSL* 27; Colvin 44 (*B.* 1–7 only); Robertson 16–18.

A

[— c.8 —].AN [— c.4 —]Ạ[- -]
[— c.6 —] . ΔΕΜΑ[.]Ạ[.]ΤΕ ΗẠḶΑΤẸΡΑ[.]ΚẠỊỌ [- - - - - - - - - - -]
[— c.4 —] . Ḅ[.]καταλ[ε]ịποντας, καṭhαιγίζẹν δὲ τὸς hομοσεπύος *vacat*
[[[— 8+ —]ΗỊ . [. c.2 .]ΤΑΣ[— 38 —]]]
[[Κ[— c.13 —]Χ[— 42 —]]]
[[Α[. c.3 .] . . . Η[— 7–8 —]Χ . [— 46 —]]]
τôν hιαρôν hα θυσία πρὸ ϙοτυτίον καὶ τᾶς ἐχεχερίας πένπ̣[τοι]
ϝέτει hôιπερ hόκα hα 'Ολυνπιὰς ποτείε· τôι Διὶ: τôι Εὐμενεῖ θύ[ε]ṿ [καὶ]
ταῖς : Εὐμενίδεσι : τέλεον, καὶ τôι Διὶ : τôι Μιλιχίοι τôι : ἐν Μύσϙο : τέλεον : τοῖς Τρ-
ιτοπατρεῦσι · τοῖς · μιαροῖς hόσπερ τοῖς hερόεσι, ϝοῖνον hυπολhεί-
ψας · δι' ὀρόφο · καὶ τᾶν μοιρᾶν · τᾶν ἐνάταν · κατακα-
ίεν · μίαν· θυόντο θῦμα : καὶ καταγιζόντο hοῖς hοσία · καὶ περιρά-

A. 4–6 Lupu in *NGSL*: Jameson *et al.* offer no readings.

(Dittenberger): κολάπτειν originally meant 'peck' (as done by birds), but it is used in several Sicilian inscriptions to mean 'inscribe', and here it does not necessarily mean 'prick out in dots' on the dedication. There is space in l. 10 either for [προ]γρά[ψ]α̣ντες or for [ἐν]γρά[ψ]α̣ντες; if we do not follow Calder on the 'Zeus song', the former, 'writing the name of Zeus first', gives the better sense.

Sicilian Doric has the aspirate but lacks *eta* and *omega*; notice also ο for the οο which in standard Greek becomes ου (e.g. τὸς θεὸς τό[σ]δε, 1); -μες for -μεν in first-person plural verbs; ὀνύματα for ὀνόματα, 8.

A

3 – – – leaving behind – – –, and the members of the same household are to ritually burn.

Three lines erased.

7 The sacrifice of the sacred things shall occur before the Kotytia and the truce in the fifth year, that is in whichever year the Olympiad takes place. Sacrifice to Zeus Eumenes and to the Eumenides a full-grown victim, and to Zeus Meilichios in (the plot of) Myscus a full-grown victim; to the polluted Tritopatores just as to heroes, with wine poured through the roof; and of the ninth parts burn one. Let those to whom it is permitted sacrifice a sacrifice and ritually burn, and when they

ναντες καταλινάντο : κἔπειτα : τοῖς κ<α>θαροῖς : τέλεον θυόντο : μελίκρατα hυπο-
λείβον · καὶ τράπεζαν καὶ κλίναν κἐνβαλέτο καθαρὸν hε͂μα καὶ στεφά-
νος ἐλαίας καὶ μελίκρατα ἐν καιναῖς ποτερίδẹ[σ]ι καὶ : πλάσματα καὶ κρᾶ κἀπ-
αρξάμενοι κατακαάντο καὶ καταλινάντο τ̣ὰς ποτερίδας ἐνθέντες·
θυόντο hόσπερ τοῖς θεοῖς τὰ πατρο͂ια : το͂ι ἐν Εὐθυδάμο : Μιλιχίοι : κριὸν θ̣[υ]-
όντο · ἔστο δὲ καὶ θῦμα πεδὰ ϝέτος θύεν · τὰ δὲ hιαρὰ τὰ δαμόσια ἐξh<α>ιρέτο καὶ τρά[πεζα]-
ν : προθέμεν καὶ φολέαν καὶ τἀπὸ τᾶς τραπέζας : ἀπάργματα καὶ τὀστέα κα[τα]-
κᾶαι · τὰ κρᾶ μἐχφερέτο · καλέτο [h]όντινα λε͂ι· ἔστο δὲ καὶ πεδὰ ϝέτ[ος ϝ]-
οίφοι θύεν : σφαζόντο δὲ : ΚΑΟΜ̣Τ̣ΕΟ[. . .]Ο ἀγαλμάτον [. . .]Δ̣ΕC[. .] . . [—c.6–7—]
Ο θῦμα hότι κα προχορε͂ι τὰ πατρο͂[ια.] . ΕΞΑΙ . [———c.24———]
Τ̣[. .] . ΙΤΟΙΑΠΤΟΧΟΙ τρίτοι ϝέτ̣[ει] Ẹ[- - - - - - - - - - - - - - - - - - -]
[—c.7–8—]Ẹ̣ΥΣΥΝΒ̣[- -]

vacat

B

[αἴ] ḳ' ἄṇθ̣ρ̣ο̣π̣ο̣ς [αὐτορέκ]τ̣α̣[ς ἐλ]αστẹ́ρον ἀ̣ποκα[θαίρεσθαι
[λεῖ], προειπὸν hόπο κα λε͂ι̣ κ̣αὶ τὸ ϝẹ́[τ]ẹος hόπο κα λε͂ι καὶ [το͂ μενὸς]
hοπείο κα λε͂ι καὶ <τᾶι> ἀμέραι hοπείαι κα λ<ε͂>ι, π{ο}ροειπὸν hόπυι κα λε͂ι, καθαιρέσθο̣, [—c.3–4?— hυ] -
ποδεκόμενος ἀπονίψασθαι δότο κἀκρατίξασθαι καὶ hάλα το͂ι αὐ[το͂ι]
[κ]αὶ θύσας το͂ι Δὶ χοῖρον ἐξ αὐτο͂ ἴτο καὶ περιστ{ι}ραφέσθο *vacat*
καὶ ποταγορέσθο καὶ σῖτον hαιρέσθο καὶ καθευδέτο hόπε ḳ-
α λε͂ι· αἴ τίς κα λε͂ι ξενικὸν ἒ πατρο͂ιον, ἒ 'πακουστὸν ἒ 'φορατὸν
ἒ καὶ χὄντινα καθαίρεσθαι, τὸν αὐτὸν τρόπο̣ν̣ ḳαθαιρέσθο
hόνπερ hοὐτορέκτας ἐπεί κ' ἐλαστέρο ἀποκαθάρεται· *vacat*
hιαρε͂ιον τέλεον ἐπὶ το͂ι βομο͂ι το͂ι δαμοσίοι θύσας καθαρὸ-
ς ἔστο· διορίξας hαλὶ καὶ χρυσο͂ι ἀπορανάμενος ἀπίτο·
hόκα το͂ι ἐλαστέροι χρέζει θύεν, θύεν hόσπερ τοῖς *vacat*
ἀθανάτοισι· σφαζέτο δ' ἐς γᾶν. *vacat*
ten lines blank

21 σφαζόντο δὲ : καὶ βο͂[ν πρ]ὸ ἀγαλμάτον [. . .]Δ̣ΕΣ[. .] . c.2–3 . [—c.6–7—] Lupu: σφαζόντο δὲ : κἄντερ[α πρ]ὸ ἀγαλμάτον [ἐκλ]ọἐσ[αντες καἀντο ἔστ-] Robertson. 22–4 τὰ πατρο͂[ια.]μ̣ἐξαιρ[έτο τὰ hιαρὰ τὰ δαμόσια. καὶ δό]|τ̣[ο τ]ρ̣ίτοια πτοχο͂ι τρίτοι ϝέτ̣[ει]. *vacat* | [ἔστο δὲ ε]ὐ̣σύνβ̣[ολα τὰ hιαρὰ. *vacat*] Robertson.

B. 1–2 [αἴ] ḳ' ἄṇθ̣ρ̣ο̣π̣ο̣ς [αὐτορέκ]τ̣α̣[ς ἐλ]αστẹ́ρον ἀ̣ποκα[θαίρεσθαι | λεῖ] Clinton; [. c.2–3 .] . . ἄṇθ̣ρ̣ο̣π̣ο̣ς [—c.6–7—] . . τ . [.(?) ἐλ]αστ̣ẹ́ρον ἀ̣ποκα[θαίρεσθ|αι] Jameson *et al.*: [. c.2–3 . α]ἴ̣ ḳ' ἄṇθ̣ρ̣ο̣π̣ο̣ς [αὐτορέκ]τ̣α̣[ς Lupu. 3 καθαιρέσθο̣, [hο δὲ hυ]- Lupu; [καὶ hυ]- Robertson. 4 το͂ι αὐ[τορέκται] Clinton, Lupu. 13 Full point Lupu.

have sprinkled around let them anoint and then let them sacrifice a full-grown victim to the pure, pouring out a libation of honey mix. And let him set out a table and bench and put upon it a pure cloth and olive wreaths and honey mix in new cups and cakes and meat, and once the preliminary offering has been made let them burn them and anoint after placing the cups. Let them sacrifice the ancestral sacrifices just as to the gods. To Meilichios in the plot of Euthydamus let them sacrifice a ram. Let it also be possible to sacrifice a victim after a year. Let him bring out the public sacred things and set a table in front and let him burn a thigh and the shares from the table and the bones. The meat is not to be taken away. Let him summon whoever he wants. Let it also be possible to sacrifice at home after a year. Let them slaughter – – – in front of the statues – – – whatever sacrifice the ancestral customs permit – – – in the third year.

B

If a person [who has killed another with his own hand] wishes to be purified from avenging spirits, having made a proclamation, wherever he wishes and whenever in the year he wishes and during whatever month he wishes and on whatever day he wishes, having made a proclamation in whatever direction he wishes, let him be purified. Let whoever receives him give water to wash with and something to eat and salt to him, and having sacrificed a piglet to Zeus let him go away from him and let him turn around. And let him be spoken to and let him take food and let him sleep wherever he wishes.

7 If anyone wishes to be purified with respect to the [avenging spirit of] a guest-friend or one of a relative on the father's side, one heard or one seen or anyone at all, let him be purified in the same way as the man who has killed with his own hand when he is purified of an avenging spirit Once he has sacrificed a full-grown sheep on the public altar let him be pure. Having marked the boundary with salt and performed aspersions from a golden vessel, let him depart. Whenever it is necessary to sacrifice to the avenging spirit, sacrifice as to the immortals. But let him kill [the animal so that the blood flows] into the earth.

This inscribed lead tablet, the largest yet found (0.6 × 0.23 m.), which can be dated only by its letter forms, carries what is conventionally termed a 'sacred law', i.e. a set of rules about customary practices with regard to the gods (cf. **106–8**, **146**).[1] The text is in two columns, which are (uniquely) arranged with one column upside down in relation to the other so that, however the tablet is rotated, at any one time only the right-hand column can be read. The separate columns contain regulations that are independent but related: both involve sacrifices and issues of purity and pollution. In both cases what have traditionally been described as 'chthonic' powers (the Eumenides, aspects of Zeus related to the dead, avenging spirits), as opposed to Olympian gods, are involved. Lead came to be regularly used in curse tablets, which themselves frequently invoke chthonic powers, and no fewer than twelve lead curse tablets, some dating as early as the sixth century, have been found in and around the sanctuary of Demeter Malophoros at Selinus, which is where this text is thought to have been found (Jameson *et al.*, 125–31, *SEG* lv 1018–28). Given the use of backward and scrambled writing in curse tablets it is hard to think that the peculiar arrangement on this tablet is independent of its chthonic connections.

In *A*, rules are laid down for regular sacrifices, sprinkling and anointing in the years of the Olympic games to gods and other supernatural powers involved with the dead. The sacrifices are timed to occur both before the Olympic truce and 'before the Kotytia', i.e. the festival of the goddess Kotyto, a goddess often thought, without good reason, to have particular Thracian connections. Robertson has made a case for the Kotytia being a summer-solstice festival. In *A*. 18, 20 and 23 provision is made for activity in the following year and the year after that. The group responsible for the sacrifice is identified in the fragmentary opening clause on *A* as those who have the same bread-basket (the *homosepuoi*, a term known from Arist. *Pol.* I. 1252 B 14), i.e. the family. In *A*. 12 the sacrificing group is referred to as 'those to whom it is permitted'.

As in the fourth-century purification law from Cyrene (R&O 97), a major role is played here by the Tritopatores (sometimes 'Tritopateres'), the embodiment of a group's collective ancestors. The main sacrifices take place at named locations, the land of Myscus and the land of Euthydamus (*A*. 9, 17). A late seventh-century gravestone of a Myscus is known from Selinus (Dubois 1989, no. 71), and the grave of a major figure from the first generation of the settlement is a possibility for the site of these rites.[2] It is even possible that Myscus was formally recognised as a hero, and that his grave had become, like the tombs of founders of settlements, a *heroon* (cf. Battus at Cyrene and his role in R&O 97. 22). But Myscus is a 'speaking name' (Hesychius' *Lexicon* glosses μύσκος (μ 1952 Latte) as μίασμα, pollution, and glosses εὐθύδημον (ε 6877 Latte), by contrast, as 'ordinary member of *demos*', ἁπλοῦν δημότην); given the association with the *im*pure Tritopatores the direction might be to offer sacrifice in polluted land. The sacrifices, sprinkling and anointing are

[1] See R. C. T. Parker, in Harris & Rubinstein (edd.), *Law and the Courts in Ancient Greece*, 57–70; Lupu, *GSL*, Part I.

[2] For an alternative view, see Curti & van Bremen.

designed both to celebrate the ritually satisfied dead (the pure Tritopatores) and to appease the ritually unsatisfied, restless, dead (polluted Tritopatores). Both receive burnt offerings (of a 'ninth part' in the case of the polluted Tritopateres), and anointing, but the sacrifices for the impure are 'as to heroes', those to the pure 'as for the gods', and the pure seem to be invited to come and share at the table—a ritual sometimes known as *theoxenia*, 'hospitality for the gods'—with wreaths of olive, cakes and meat laid out for their feast. But, significantly, whereas the 'polluted' Tritopatores get a direct infusion of unmixed wine, the pure Tritopatores are offered 'honey mix' rather than wine; wineless libations are characteristic offerings to supernatural powers associated with the dead, particularly the Eumenides (Paus. II. 11. iv; Soph. *O.C.* 481; cf. *LSS* 62, which is more or less contemporary with this text). For sprinkling and anointing in the context of purification following burial cf. **194**.

These laws have contributed significantly to the debate about the classification of gods and rituals: should we talk of 'chthonic' and 'Olympian', or should we rather divide between gods and heroes?[3] The close link here between Zeus and the Eumenides, and the presence of Zeus Meilichios between the Eumenides and the polluted Tritopatores in the list of sacrifices, does not encourage belief in a strong division between gods and other supernatural powers. The language used of sacrifice, here always employs the verb *thuein*, the verb for sacrifices to the gods (to sacrifice to heroes is *enagizein*), a usage which also suggests that the sacrifice of the pig at *B.* 5 is in celebration of purification rather than to achieve it (K. Clinton, in Hägg & Alroth (edd.), *Greek Sacrificial Ritual*, 174–6).

The epithet 'Eumenes' ('kindly') for Zeus is unique (the later use in areas ruled by kings of Pergamum, is clearly a different phenomenon[4]), but exactly parallel to 'Meilichios' ('gentle'). As in the case of the avenging Erinyes, made beneficent by being called 'kindly ones' ('Eumenides', cf. Aesch. *Eum.*; Soph. *O.C.* 43–4), who are always addressed as Eumenides in the context of cult, and called Erinyes only in the context of crime and punishment, so too calling Zeus 'kindly' or 'gentle' renders beneficent his potentially destructive powers (cf. A. L. Brown, *CQ*² xxxiv 1984, 260–81). Zeus Meilichios is a god closely associated with families and their prosperity, sometimes referred to as 'Zeus Meilichios of [some particular] family' (Μελίχιος τõν Κλευλιδᾶν, Dubois, *Inscriptions grecques dialectales de Sicile*, 45, cf. hο Μιλίχιος τᾶς πατριᾶς, 47), and, along with purification from bloodshed, is often closely linked to underworld powers.

Zeus Meilichios was sometimes represented in a way indistinguishable from other representations of Zeus—as a mature bearded man seated on a throne—but he was also represented with a cornucopia, as a snake, and at Selinus a number of stones without images ('aniconic images'), of various shapes, declare themselves to be Zeus Meilichios. Although in Sicily aniconic images of Olympian gods are known (Hera at Selinus, Heracles at Poggioreale), anthropomorphism was so fundamental a part

[3] S. Scullion, *ZPE* cxxxii 2000, 163–71; cf. more generally Scullion, *Cl. Ant.* xiii 1994, 75–119, R. C. T. Parker, in Hägg & Alroth (edd.), *Greek Sacrificial Ritual*, 37–45, and his *On Greek Religion*, 80–4 and Appendix 4.

[4] See *SIG*³ 985. 6–7 and L. Robert, *RPh*³ viii 1934, 287–91 = his *Opera Minora Selecta*, ii. 1186–90.

of Greek gods that these representations themselves suggest that Zeus Meilichios is being conceptualised in ways quite different from the ways in which the Olympian gods are normally conceptualised. If we locate the rituals described here in the sanctuary of Zeus Meilichios excavated in the Gaggera precinct in the Modione valley immediately west of the urban settlement at Selinus, then the images in front of which sacrifice is made in *A*. 21 would be the more than 200 *stelai*, variously aniconic and with one, two or even four heads, excavated in that sanctuary.[5]

The interpretation of *B* depends on the reading that one adopts in the first line. On the reconstruction which we print and translate here, the whole of *B* is specifically concerned with the ritual treatment of homicides, proceeding from simple homicide to peculiarly problematic homicides involving family or guest-friends. Such a move from less serious to more serious crime is paralleled in some homicide laws, notably Plato's provisions in *Leg.* IX. 865, 872–3. Those unconvinced by the restoration of 'killer' in l. 1 have wondered whether of the two different categories of individuals to be purified only the second group, or perhaps even neither group, is composed of killers (the murderer in l. 9 would be mentioned only by way of parallel). The more serious nature of the second category of offender seems to be indicated by the specification of a public sacrifice.

The sacrifices envisaged include a sacrifice not only to Zeus (here without epithet, 5; pigs are the regular victims in purificatory sacrifices, but see above for this being in celebration of purification) but also 'to the *elasteros*' (i.e. to the avenging spirits—*elasteroi* were like Erinyes: cf. Aesch. *Ag.* 1569), with the ritual specified to be 'as to the

[5] Robertson, 187–93; Fama & Tusa, *Le Stele del Meilichios di Selinunte*; Grotta, *Zeus Meilichios a Selinunte*; Gaifman, *Aniconomism in Greek Antiquity*, 197–206.

116

Athenian dealings with the Delphic Amphictyony, *c.*457

The upper right-hand part of a marble *stele*, found on the south slope of the Athenian acropolis, now in the Epigraphical Museum. Phot. *AJA*[2] lv 1951, pl. 37; Roux, *L'Amphictionie, Delphes et le temple d'Apollon au IVe siècle*, pl. I.

Attic, with some older-style letters, in particular three-bar *sigma*, v-shaped *upsilon*. *Stoichedon* 24.

Tod 39; *SdA* 142; *IG* i[3] 9*. Trans. Fornara 82. See also A. Wilhelm, *Mnem.*[4] ii 1949, 286–93; B. D. Meritt, *AJP* lxix 1948, 312–14 (*SEG* x 18), lxxv 1954, 369–73 (*SEG* xiii 3); Meiggs, *The Athenian Empire*, 418–20; M. Sordi, *RFIC* lxxxvi = [2]xxxvi 1958, 48–59; Bradeen & McGregor, *Studies in Fifth-Century Attic Epigraphy*, 116–17; Roux, *L'Amphictionie, Delphes et le temple d'Apollon au IVe siècle*, 44–5, 239–40; Lefèvre, *L'Amphictionie pyléo-delphique*, 219; Sánchez, *L'Amphictionie des Pyles et de Delphes*, 109–11.

immortals' but involving cutting the throat exactly as in heroic sacrifices (12–13; see further S. Scullion, *ZPE* cxxxii 2000, 163–71). This sacrifice to the avenging spirit as if the avenging spirit were an immortal can be compared to sacrifices elsewhere in the Greek world to Zeus Elasteros (cf. *LSS* 62 from Paros) or Zeus Alastoros (cf. two inscriptions from the Thesmophorion at Thasos, C. Rolley, *BCH* lxxxix 1965, 442–6, nos. 1 and 4; Pherecydes *FGrH* 3 F 175), where the god is both the agent for and the protector against the restless dead. The rituals prescribed here are comparable to those in the Cyrene purification law (R&O 97. 111–41) where sacrifices are made to appease supernatural visitants. In both places the concern for the public visibility of the purification is notable: it is important both that those seeking purification publicly acknowledge their need for purification and are seen by others to have been purified (see W. Burkert, in *Polis and Politics . . . M. H. Hansen*, 207–16).

Various linguistic features are notable. One of the three scribes inserts an extra vowel to divide consonant plus *rho*: *B*. 3 ποροειπόν for προειπόν, *B*. 5 περιστιραφέσθο for περιστραφέσθο. Aspiration is frequently marked, both at the beginning and within words (cf. esp. *A*. 10 hυποληείψας, *A*. 8 χôντινα for καὶ ὅντινα). In *B* as well as indefinite adverbs (hόπυι for ὅποι, hόπε for ὅπη, hόπο for ὁπόθεν) we find the indefinite adjective hoπεῖος for ὁποῖος. In *B*. 2 we find the West Greek verb λῶ (= θέλω), where λῆι is subjunctive. hόκ(κ)α in *A*. 8 can be paralleled by the Megarian in Ar. *Ach*. 762; ποτείε in the same line is subjunctive from προσιέναι (cf. R&O 97. 4 ἐπείηι). The verb καταλίνω in *A*. 8 had previously been known only from an entry in Hesychius' lexicon.

[ἔδοχσεν τε͂ι βο]λε͂ι καὶ το͂[ι δέμ]-
[οι· . . . ντὶς ἐπρ]υτάνευε, Αἰ[. . .]
[. . . . ἐγραμμάτ]ευε, Μένυλλ[ος ἐ]-
πεστάτε, —5—]ίες εἶπε· χσ[υνθ]-
έσθαι μὲν τὲν χ]συμμαχίαν [καθ]-
[άπερ hoι ἐκ τε͂ς] Πυλαίας ἀπ[αγγ]-
[έλλοσιν hάπασ]ι τοῖς Ἀμφι[κτί]-
[οσι hoῖσπερ μέ]τεστιν το͂ h[ιε]-
[ρο͂, ἐμμενε͂ν τε ὀ]μόσαντας ἐν [τε͂]-
[ι χσυνμαχίαι νὲ τ]ὸν Ἀπόλλο [κα]-
[ὶ τὲν Λετὸ καὶ τὲν] Ἄρτεμιν ἐ[χσ]-
[όλειάν τε καὶ hα]υτοῖς ἐπαρ[ομ]-
[ένος ἐὰν παραβαί]νομεν· φσε[φί]-
[——14—— πά]τριον π[. .]-
[———17———]ε͂ς Πυλ[αί]-
[———19———]φισ[. .]-

2 Αἰαντὶς or Λεοντὶς required by space. Last letter ι or π Bradeen & McGregor. 4 first letter at left of *stoichos*, so unfinished e.g. λ, κ or ρ Bradeen & McGregor. 13–end φσε[φί|ζεσθαι δὲ κατὰ τὸ πά]τριον π[ερ|ὶ hαπάντον hὰ hoι ἐκ τ]ε͂ς Πυλ[αί|ας ἀπαγγέλλοσιν hεφσε]φισ[μέ|να – – –] *IG*, after Meritt: we translate this, in brackets.

Our inclusion of this extremely fragmentary inscription is justified by the light that its very existence throws upon the obscure but important politics of central Greece in these years. Although restoration can only be speculative (what is printed here is due essentially to Wilhelm and Meritt), this text certainly involves an alliance connected with the Delphic Amphictyony (a πυλαία *sc.* ἀγορά was one of the regular biannual meetings of the Amphictyony), and an oath, presumably to abide by the alliance, sworn by the Delphic triad Apollo, Leto and Artemis (cf. e.g. *C. Delphes* i 10 = iv 1. 8).

In this restoration, the Athenians agree to form an alliance (ξυντιθέναι with ξυμμαχίαν is found in *IG* i³ 76. 13, 24–5) with all the Amphictyons, in accordance with a decision made at a *pylaia* (but [hoι ἐκ τε͂ς] Πυλαίας is unparalleled). Such a decision, that each member of the Amphictyony should join in an alliance with each of the others, is startling. Whether we think of it as a mark of desperation or of ambition will point to a different context. Sordi preferred 462–458, when Thessaly, which dominated the Amphictyony, was certainly in alliance with Athens (Thuc. 1. 102. iv, contr. 107. vii); that is possible (though it is by no means certain that Thessaly as a whole turned against Athens at Tanagra: cf. on **117**), but the sacred war which she built on that is not. Meritt dated the alliance after the battles of Tanagra and Oenophyta, *c*.457, when Athens was ambitious enough, and strong enough in central Greece, to be able to pursue a policy of that kind (cf. Thuc. 1. 108. iii). The view

Resolved by the council and the people; (Aiantis *or* Leontis) was the prytany; A— was the secretary; Menyllus was the chairman; —ies proposed:

4 Agree on the alliance as announced by the men from the Pylaea to all the Amphictyons who have a share in the sanctuary, swearing to abide by the alliance by Apollo and Leto and Artemis, invoking ruin on ourselves if we transgress.

13 [Make a decree in accordance with tradition concerning all the things which the men from the Pylaea announce as having been decreed - - -]

---

common to Meritt and Sordi, that 'the Amphictyons who have a share in the sanctuary' is not simply pleonastic but implies a distinction from a dissident body of Amphictyons who at the time did not have a share in the sanctuary, is unnecessary and seems unwarranted.

A date in the 450s (or the early 440s in connection with the Second Sacred War) provides the most likely context for this text, for it is at this point that, for the first time, the Amphictyony became an important player in southern Greek inter-state relations. Despite the back-dating of the Amphictyony's importance by classical and later writers, the Amphictyony had played little part even in the Persian Wars. It was, however, quickly brought into post-war inter-state relations, both in the debate about medisers and how to deal with them (Plut. *Them.* 20. iii–iv), and in the investigation of who had revealed the path which allowed the defenders of the pass at Thermopylae to be surrounded (Hdt. vii. 213–4). Manoeuvres with regard to the Amphictyony are likely to have been significant factors in the Spartan decision to send help to Doris (Thuc. i. 107. ii), and this decision may be either part of the causes or part of the consequences of that. In the following years, when Athens was powerful in central Greece, the Amphictyony will certainly not have been abolished, but Athens must in some sense have given control of Delphi to the surrounding people, the Phocians; in the Second Sacred War of the early 440s Sparta gave control to the *polis* of Delphi, but afterwards the Athenians gave it back to the

Phocians (Thuc. I. 112. v, Philoch. *FGrH* 328 F 34); but at the beginning of the Peloponnesian War the Delphic oracle responded to the Spartans that it would

---

117

Thessalian dedications after the battle of Tanagra, 458 or 457

A

A limestone base found in two pieces in the modern village of Delphi, now in the museum there. Phot. *BCH* lxxxii 1958, p. 331 figs. 1–2, pl. XXIII.

Delphian dialect; Phocian lettering with <-shaped *gamma*. Non-*stoichedon*.

G. Daux, *BCH* lxxxii 1958, 329–34; *SEG* xvii 243*. See also Sordi, *La lega tessala*, 344–7; J. A. O. Larsen, *CP* lv 1960, 241–2; B. Helly, *L'État thessalien*, 226–37.

Θεσσαλοὶ τὸν hίππον ἀνέθεν τὀπόλλονι δεκάταν τôν ἀ[π]ὸ Ταναγ[ραίον].
πολεμαρχεόντον τôνδε·

col. i	*col. ii*
Ἀμύντα	Μέννες
Ἀρχαγόρο	hυβρίλαος
καὶ {σ}	Πολυδάμας
Προτέας	
Εὐκρατίδας	

i. 5 and ii. 3 *sigma* later recarved in lunate form. i. 5 κἀι (= καὶ hοι) σ(τασίαρχοι) Helly.

The Thessalians made an alliance with Athens *c*.462/1 (Thuc. I. 102. iv); at the battle of Tanagra, in 458 or 457, a cavalry contingent came to support Athens, but defected to the Spartans (107. ii); Thessalians are not mentioned at the battle of Oenophyta, after which Tanagra had its walls demolished (108. ii–iii); *c*.454 an Athenian attempt to reinstate the exiled 'king of the Thessalians', Orestes, in Pharsalus was unsuccessful (111. i). At the beginning of the Peloponnesian War the Thessalians are not mentioned on either side in the list of allies in Thuc. II. 9, but in 431 Thessalian forces went to support Athens 'in accordance with the ancient alliance' (22. ii–iii).

Daux in first publishing the inscription assigned the lettering to the second quarter of the fifth century. The one occasion in that period when the Thessalians are known to have gone to Tanagra is for the battle of 458 or 457; he suggested that, having let

support them whether invited or not, and the Phocians were reckoned among Sparta's allies (Thuc. I. 118. iii, II. 9. ii).

The Thessalians dedicated the horse to Apollo as a tithe of their spoils from the Tanagraeans.

2 These being polemarchs:

col. i	*col. ii*
Amyntas	Mennes
Archagorus	Hybrilaus
5 and	Polydamas
Proteas	
Eucratidas	

---

down the Athenians in that battle, they returned to fight at Oenophyta and joined in a sack of Tanagra afterwards, and that that was the occasion commemorated with a horse or a mounted soldier here. Sordi saw the dedication as a consequence of the Thessalians' fighting on the Spartan side at Tanagra, and thought they remained anti-Athenian afterwards. The Athenian intervention on behalf of Orestes confirms that there were divisions among the Thessalians (cf. Larisa in Thuc. II. 22. iii; IV. 78. ii–v), and we find Daux's explanation of this text more likely than Sordi's.

The list of names is problematic, with two men named in the genitive as polemarchs (more likely after πολεμαρχεόντον than one with a patronymic; Sordi's attempt to see four in i. 3–4 and ii. 3–4 was mistaken), followed by 'and' with five further men named in the nominative with no indication of their standing (Helly's suggestion that they are *stasiarchoi*, commanders of military units called *staseis*, was based on a misunderstanding of *stasis* in Thuc. II. 22. iii). The polemarchs here must be officials of Thessaly as a whole, though the polemarchs attested in fourth-century inscriptions are city officials (as demonstrated by C. Habicht, *Hermes* cxxvii 1989, 254–6). It is commonly thought that at this time Thessaly consisted of four tetrads each with a polemarch: R. Bouchon & B. Helly, in Beck & Funke (edd.), *Federalism in*

B

A *stele* of white marble: on the face, a relief of a standing soldier with spear and shield; on the right-hand side four lines of text written from top to bottom; found at Larisa and now in the museum there. Phot.: none of the whole relief; of the right-hand side *ZPE* cxlviii 2004, 28.

Mixed Thessalian and Ionic–Attic linguistic forms; Thessalian alphabet. Non-*stoichedon*.

First published in Greek periodicals; G. Touchais, *BCH* cviii 1984, 790 (cf. *SEG* xxxiv 560); *CEG* 637; B. Helly, *ZPE* cxlviii 2004, 15–28 (cf. *SEG* liv 562). See also Helly, *L'État thessalien*, 227–8.

οὔ τι καταισχύ'νας πόλεος κλέος ἐνθάδε κεῖται
Ἄτραγος εὐρυχορο' Θεσσαλία' στέφανον
τεύχον, ὃ Θεότιμε, Μενύλλου παῖ, σὺν ἀριστο<ι>ς
ἀνδρ<ά>σιν Ἑλλένον ἐν Τανάγρας πεδίοι.

The four lines to be read beginning with that nearest to the face (though if the stone were placed horizontally that would appear to be the last) M. L. West *ap. CEG*. 1–2 ' used to indicate that the vowel which precedes is long Helly. 3 the stone has αριστος. 4 the stone has ανδρσιν.

The order of reading proposed by West yields two elegiac couplets (as opposed to pentameters followed by hexameters, for which there is no parallel until much later). Atrax was about 13 miles/22 km. south-west of Larisa in northern Thessaly, but the monument was set up at Larisa, perhaps by Theotimus' family but adjacent to a common Thessalian memorial (Helly 2004, 25–6). Here the allusion surely is to the battle of Tanagra, whatever role Theotimus may have played in it.

Given that the battle of Tanagra was a battle of Greeks against Greeks, the striking feature of this epigram is its failure to distinguish the two sides: the Thessalian dead lie with 'the best of the Greeks', not with the best of the Peloponnesians or the best of the Athenians. Helly sees the language and focalisation as Thessalian

Greek Antiquity, 234, suggest that 'two *polemarchoi* out of four, along with lower-ranked officers, were in command of a part of the Thessalian army'.[1]

Thessalian Aeolic has the aspirate but lacks *eta* and *omega*.

[1] For the four tetrads cf. earlier Larsen, *Greek Federal States*, 16. This is based on Harp. τετραρχία (τ 7 Keaney), citing Hellan. *FGrH* 4 F 52, Arist. fr. 497 (Rose, Teubner), Theop. *FGrH* 115 F 208, and on *SIG*³ 274, Dem. IX. *Phil. iii.* 26.

You have in no way disgraced the glory of the city to lie here, the glory of broad-landed Atrax, Theotimus son of Menyllus, together with the best men of the Greeks in the plain of Tanagra.

---

in the first couplet and panhellenic in the second, and interprets the text as rebutting the double charge of treachery to the Greek cause in the Persian Wars (Hdt. VII. 174) and to the Athenian cause at Tanagra, and asserting the position of Atrax and all the Thessalians among 'the best men of the Greeks'. There are echoes of Homer and other early poetry (καταισχυνεῖν e.g. *Od.* XXIV. 307–8, 512; εὐρυχόρος e.g. *Il.* IX. 478; τεύχειν e.g. *Il.* II. 101, στέφανον τεῦξαι Pind. *Ol.* viii. 32, but for a crown in this sense cf. Hyp. VI. *Epitaph.* 19; ἄριστοι e.g. *Il.* VI. 208–9, *Od.* XXIV. 507), and the *motifs* are found in Athenian funeral orations.

κεῖαι for κεῖσαι, *B.* 1, may be Thessalian (Helly: some scholars have printed κεῖ<σ>αι); but there is in any case a precedent in *Hom. Hymn. Hermes* 254, κατάκειαι.

118

Thetonium in Thessaly honours a Corinthian, *c.*450–425

A bronze tablet, found near Cierium in Thessaly, now in the National Museum in Athens. Phot. *LSAG*, pl. 11. 10; *Nomima* i, p. 142.

Thessalian; non-*stoichedon*: *LSAG*, pp. 98, 99, 402 no. 10.

IG ix. ii 257; *SIG*^{3} 55; Buck 35; *Nomima* i 33*; Colvin 9. Trans. Colvin 9. See also M. Sordi, *RFIC* lxxxvi = ^{2}xxxvi 1958, 59–65; J. T. Hooker, *ZPE* xl 1980, 272; Helly, *L'État thessalien*, 29, 148, 334.

ες hυλορέοντος Φιλονίκο hυῖος.

Θετόνιοι ἔδοκαν Σοταίροι τôι Κ-
ορινθίοι καὐτôι καὶ γένει καὶ ϝ-
οικιάταις καὶ χρέμασιν ἀσυλί-
αν κἀτέλειαν κεὐϝεργέταν ἐ-
ποίεσαν κἐν ταγᾶ κἐν ἀταγ-
ίαι. αἴ τις παρβαίνοι, τὸ-
ν ταγὸν τὸν ἐπεστάκοντα ἐ-
ξξανακάδεν. τὰ χρυσία καὶ τὰ
ἀργύρια τε͂ς Βελφαίο ἀπολ-
όμενα ἔσοσε. Ὀρέσταο Φερεκράτ-

Below l. 1 is a horizontal line, running from the margin and under the first three letters: the engraver ran out of space at the bottom of the tablet and finished the text at the top.

Inscriptions honouring individuals are at first rare in Greek epigraphic practice, but become commoner over time; and inscriptions for foreigners tend to be found earlier than inscriptions for members of the honouring community. *Asylia* ('immunity from seizure'), *ateleia* ('exemption from obligations' and especially from some or all taxes) and the title of *euergetes* ('benefactor') are benefits which states commonly conferred on foreigners whom they wished to honour.[1] Later they were commonly combined with the position of *proxenos*, originally a representative of the honouring state in their own state, but with the passage of time increasingly an honour detached from the original function; but in the fifth century the title regularly did imply the function, yet in this inscription the extension of the privileges to household servants and property suggests that Sotaerus was living in or near Thetonium and could not have functioned as its *proxenos* in Corinth. Thetonium was about 10 miles/16 km. west of

[1] Cf., in an Athenian context, for the variety of honours which might be conferred, Henry, *Honours and Privileges in Athenian Decrees*; and, for inscriptions for foreigners as earlier than inscriptions for Athenians, S. D. Lambert, *ZPE* cl 2004, 85–7 = his *Inscribed Athenian Laws and Decrees*, 352/1–322/1 BC, 3–6.

The Thetonians gave to Sotaerus the Corinthian, to himself and his descendants and his household servants and his property, immunity from seizure and exemption from taxation, and they made him a benefactor, both when there is a *tagos* and when there is no *tagos*. If anybody transgresses this, the *tagos* in office shall enforce it (?). He saved the gold and silver of the Belphaeus which was being lost.
11 Orestes son of Pherecrates son of Philonicus was forest warden.

Pharsalus, in southern Thessaly, and it is remarkable that this early instance of the *genre* comes from such an unprominent city.

The phrase in ll. 6–7 has commonly been translated, 'both when there is a *tagos* and when there is no *tagos*'. There were *tagoi* of Thessaly as a whole, whom we know best from the reinvention of the office by Jason of Pherae in the fourth century (Xen. *Hell.* VI. i. 8, 18), but these may have been appointed only in response to military emergencies. But *tagos* was used also as the title of local officials, and in ll. 7–8 'the *tagos* in office' will be an official of Thetonium. 'Both when there is a *tagos* and when there is no *tagos*' would then be a formula meaning 'at absolutely any time'. It has often been taken to mean 'in war and in peace' (e.g. Buck, Colvin; accepted by Helly, 148, 334); but as Helly himself has insisted it is not clear that the early Thessalian office of *tagos* was such as to make that a natural interpretation, and Hooker has argued that this passage also refers to the local officials and means what it literally says, that sometimes there was a *tagos* but sometimes there was not, and that we should not be worried by the illogicality that when there was no *tagos* the decree could not be enforced by the *tagos* (cf. Sordi, 59 n. 3, who thought that Thessaly was in a state of having no *tagos* after 457). Most recently, however, the *taga* has been identified as a unit of mobilisation, and the phrase in ll. 6–7 translated, 'in the ranks or out of the ranks', still with the underlying meaning 'in war and in peace', i.e. at any time (R. Bouchon & B. Helly, in Beck & Funke (edd.), *Federalism in Greek Antiquity*, 237–8). ἐξξανακάδεν in ll. 8–9 (= Attic ἐξαναγκάζειν: Colvin) is not found elsewhere.

It is usually thought that it was a local sanctuary of Delphic Apollo whose gold and silver was being lost, but Sordi argued for the sanctuary at Delphi itself (60–5). The collection of names which ends the text has caused difficulty. Some, including Sordi, have translated ἔσοσε Ὀρέσταο in l. 11 as 'saved from Orestes', and have seen here the Orestes whom the Athenians unsuccessfully tried to restore *c.*454 (cf. on **117**. *A*): that would be chronologically possible (in *LSAG* the lettering is dated

---

119

Athenian tribute quota lists, 454/3–432/1

One hundred and eighty-five fragments of the so-called Lapis Primus ('first stone'), found on the Athenian acropolis and nearby, from a marble *stele* which was originally more than 3.8 m. high, 1.1 m. wide and 0.39 m. thick. Upon this the Athenians recorded, in annual lists, from 454/3 to 440/39, the $\frac{1}{60}$ share of the tribute paid by their allies that was given to Athena. Most fragments are now in the Epigraphical Museum, some are in the Agora Museum and one in the British Museum.

Seventy-three fragments of the so-called Lapis Secundus ('second stone'), found on the Athenian acropolis and nearby, from a marble *stele* which was originally at least 2.2 m. high, 1.1 m. wide and 0.34 m. thick. Upon this the Athenians similarly recorded annual lists, from 439/8 to 432/1, of Athena's share of the tribute. Most fragments are now in the Epigraphical Museum, some are in the Agora Museum.

We here give extracts from the lists for (*A*) the first (454/3), (*B*) the 13th (442/1) and (*C*) the 21st (434/3) years.

A IG i³ 259 (at the top of the front of Lapis Primus). Heading ll. 1–4 and cols. v and vi of six, ll. 5–22 (this list was supplemented on the right-hand side of the stone); B. D. Meritt, *Hesperia* xli 1972, 403–17. Phot. *Hesperia* xli 1972, figs. 99, 100. Attic letters. *Stoichedon* 56 (heading). Trans. Fornara 85; Dillon & Garland 12. 28.

B IG i³ 270 (on the back of the Lapis Primus), supplemented by a new fragment, Matthaiou, 'Studies in Attic Inscriptions and the History of the Fifth Century BC', 133–6. Heading ll. 1–2 and cols. i and ii of five, ll. 3–38. Attic letters. *Stoichedon.*

C IG i³ 278 col. vi of six, ll. 3–37 (Lapis Secundus). Phot. *ATL* i, p.69. Attic letters. *Stoichedon.*

A

Year 1, 454/3

[ἀπαρχαὶ hαίδε χορὶς χ]σ̣ύμ̣[πασαι παρ]ὰ τôν hελλ[ενοτ]αμιôν h[οῖς ——7——]
[——7—— ἐγραμμάτευ]ε πρ[ô]τ[αι τοῖσι] τριάκο[ντα ἀπ]εφάνθεσαν [τêι θεôι]
[τô χσυμμαχικô φόρο ἐ]πὶ Ἀρίσ̣[τονος] ἄρχοντος Ἀ[θεν]αίοις μνᾶ ἀ[πὸ τô ταλ]-
[άντο.] *vacat*

c.450–425). Van Effenterre & Ruzé in *Nomima* see it as an ethnic identifying Pherecrates as of Orestia, but the only place known by a form of that name was far to the north, in the southern part of Upper Macedonia. Buck and Colvin both interpret as in our translation. For *hyloros* ('forest warden') as the title of an office cf. Arist. *Pol.* vi. 1321 b 30, vii. 1331 b 15: Thetonium was in or near the inland part of northern Greece characterised as having 'forest of Central European type' (Geographical Handbook Series, *Greece*, i (Naval Intelligence Division, 1944), 109 fig. 64).

In addition to the features noted under **117**, this text uses *digamma*, and has Βέλφαιον for Δέλφαιον. But 'a number of features anomalous in Thessalian [such as the Attic–Ionic χρέμασιν in l. 4] may point to an attempt to write the text in Ionic-influenced "chancellery" diction (perhaps by an Ionian secretary)' (Colvin).

A

Year 1, 454/3

All these first-fruits separately were first declared by the *hellenotamiai* to whom —— was secretary to the Thirty for the Goddess from the allied tribute in the archonship of Ariston at Athens, one *mna* from every talent.

col. v

hαβ[δερῖ]ται : ΧΗΗ𐅄ΔΔΔΓΙΙ
Ὀλύνθ[ιοι] : Σκα-
βλαῖο[ι : Ἀσ]σε-
ρῖται : Η[Η𐅄ΔΓ]𐅂ΙΙΙΙ
Σερμυλ[ιε͂ς] : 𐅅ΗΗ𐅄ΔΔ𐅂𐅂
Μεκυπερ[να]ῖοι *vacat*
Στόλιοι : Π[ολ]ι-
χνῖται : ΗΗΔ[Δ]Δ𐅂ΙΙ
Σίν<γ>ιοι : ΗΗ[. ? .]𐅂𐅂ΙΙ
Θάσιοι : ΗΗΗ
Μυσοί : ΔΔΔ𐅂[𐅂𐅂ΙΙ]
Πίκρες Συαν[γελεύς : 𐅄]
Κεδριε͂ται [: 𐅄]
Κεράμιοι : [Η𐅄]
Βουθειε͂ς [: – – –]
Κυλλάνδι[οι : ΗΗ]
Χῖοι : Κ̣[ᾶ]ρ̣[ες : ΔΔΔ𐅂𐅂𐅂ΙΙ]
– – – – – – – – – – –

col. vi

Ναρ[ι]σ[βαρε͂ς : ΔΓ𐅂ΙΙΙΙ]
Μυδ[ο]νε͂ς [: ΔΔΓ]
Κια[ν]οί : Δ[Γ𐅂ΙΙΙΙ]
Ἀρτακενο[ί : ΔΔΔ𐅂𐅂𐅂ΙΙ]
Νεάπολις
[ἐ]ν [Θ]ράικει : ΔΓ[𐅂ΙΙΙΙ]
Βερ[ύ]σιοι hυπὸ
τε͂ι Ἴδει : ΔΓ𐅂ΙΙΙΙ
Αὐλιᾶται Κᾶρες : Γ𐅂𐅂[𐅂ΙΙ]
Ἰᾶται : Η
Παριανοί : Η
[Δ]ασκύλειον
[ἐν] Προποντίδι : Γ𐅂𐅂𐅂ΙΙ
[Α]ἰγινε͂ται : ΧΧΧ
Μιλέσιοι
[ἐ]χς Λέρο : ΗΗΗ
[Μι]λέσιοι
[ἐκ Τ]ειχιόσσε[ς : – – –]

B

Year 13, 442/1

ἐπὶ τες τρίτες καὶ δεκάτε[ς] ἀρχες [hει Χαλ]κιδεὺς Μελιτεὺ[ς ἐγραμμάτευε, Δ]ο[ρ]ύφιλος Ἰκαριεὺς hελλενοταμίας ε͂ν, Σά[τυρος] Λευκονοιεὺς συνε[γραμμάτευε.] *vacat*

col. i

Ἰονικὸς φόρος	
Γ𐅂𐅂𐅂ΙΙ	Διοσιρῖται
𐅄	Θερμαῖοι ἐχς Ἰ
𐅄	Μαραθέσιοι
ΔΓ𐅂ΙΙΙΙ	Γρυνειε͂ς
ΔΔΔ𐅂𐅂𐅂ΙΙ	Νοτιε͂ς
Η	Νισύριοι
𐅄ΔΓ𐅂ΙΙΙΙ	Οἰναῖο[ι] Ἰκαρ
[Η]𐅄	Κολοφόνιοι
ΗΗ	Φοκαιε͂ς
Η	Αἰραιε͂ς
Η	Λεβέδιοι
Η	Μυριναῖοι παρὰ Κ
[𐅅]Η	Τέιοι
[𐅅Η]ΗΗΗ	Κυμαῖοι

col. ii

Η	Δα[ρ]δανε͂ς
Γ	hαρπαγιανοί
ΗΗ𐅄ΔΔΔΓ𐅂̣[𐅂]𐅂	Τε[ν]έδιοι
ΧΗΗ	Λαμφσακενοί
ΔΓ𐅂ΙΙΙΙ	Σιγειε͂ς
Η̣ΗΗΗ	Ἀβυδενοί
𐅅ΗΗΗΗ	Καλχεδό[νιοι]
Γ𐅂𐅂𐅂ΙΙ	Σέστιο[ι]
Γ𐅂𐅂𐅂ΙΙ	Λιμνα[ῖοι]
Γ𐅂𐅂𐅂ΙΙ	Μαδύ[τιοι]
Η	Χερ[ρονεσῖται]
ΔΓ𐅂ΙΙΙΙ	Ἀ[λοπεκοννέσιοι]
𐅄	[Ἐλαιόσιοι]
ΔΓ𐅂ΙΙΙΙ	Π̣[ερκότε]
ΔΔΔ[𐅂𐅂𐅂]ΙΙ	Παρ[ιανοί]

col. v

Abderites: 1285 dr 2 ob.
Olynthians, Sca-
blaiains, Asse-
rites: 266 dr. 4 ob.
Sermylians: 772 dr.
Mecypernians *vacat*
Stolians, Poli-
chnitans: 231 dr. 2 ob.
Singians: 2–2dr. 2 ob.
Thasians: 300
Mysians: 33 dr. 2 ob
Picres Syangelian: [50]
Cedrietans[: 50]
Ceramians: [150]
Butheians[: – – –]
Cyllandians[: 200]
Chians, Carians[: 33 dr. 2 ob.]
– – – – – – – – – – –

col. vi

Narisbareans[: 16 dr. 4 ob.
Mydones[: 25 dr.]
Cianians: 1[6 dr. 4 ob.]
Artacenians[: 33 dr. 2 ob.]
Neapolis
in Thrace: 1[6 dr. 4 ob.]
Berysians
under Ida: 16 dr. 4 ob.
Carian Auliatans: 8 dr. [2 ob.]
Iatans: 100 dr.
Parianians: 100 dr.
Dascyleum
in Propontis: 8 dr. 2 ob.
Aeginetans: 3000 dr.
Milesians
from Leros: 300 dr.
Milesians
from Teichioussa[: – – –]

B

Year 13, 442/1

Under the thirteenth board, in which Chalcideus of Melite was secretary, Doryphilus of Icaria was *hellenotamias*, Satyrus of Leuconoeum was co-secretary.

col. i

Ionian Tribute

8 dr. 2 ob.	Diosyritans
50 dr.	Thermaeans from I
50 dr.	Marathesians
16 dr. 4 ob.	Gryneians
33 dr. 2 ob.	Notians
100 dr.	Nisyrians
66 dr. 4 ob.	Oenaeans Icar
150 dr.	Colophonians
200 dr.	Phocaeans
100 dr.	Aeraeans
100 dr.	Lebedians
100 dr.	Myrinians from C
600 dr.	Teans
900 dr.	Cymaeans

col. ii

100 dr.	Dardanians
5 dr.	Harpagianians
288 dr.	Tenedians
1200 dr.	Lampsacenes
16 dr. 4 ob.	Sigieians
400 dr.	Abydenes
900 dr.	Calchedonians
8 dr. 2 ob.	Sestians
8 dr. 2 ob.	Limnaeans
8 dr. 2 ob.	Madytians
100 dr.	Chersonesitans
16 dr. 4 ob.	Alopeconnesians
50 dr.	[Elaeousians]
16 dr. 4 ob	[Percote]
33 dr. 2 ob.	Parianians

[ΔΓͰΙΙΙΙ]	Ἐλα[ιέα]	[ΗΗ]Η̣	Προκ[οννέσιοι]
[ΓͰͰͰΙΙ]	[Ἀστυρενοὶ Μυσοί]	𐅅ΗΗΗΗ	Κυζικ[ενοί]
[ΔΓͰΙΙΙΙ]	[Πιταναῖοι]	ΔΔΔͰͰͰΙΙ	Ἀρτακ[ενοί]
[Η]	[Πριανε͂ς]	Χ	Περίνθ[ιοι]
[𐅅ΗΗ]	[Ἐρυθραῖοι]	Χ𐅅𐅄ΔΔͰΙΙΙΙ	Βυζά[ντιοι]
[ͰΙΙΙΙ]	[Ἐλαιόσιοι]	ΔΓͰΙΙΙΙ	Κιαν[οί]
[𐅄ΔΓͰΙΙΙΙ]	[Πολιχνῖτ]αι	ΗΗ	Ἀρι[σβαῖοι]
[ͰΙΙΙΙ]	[Πτελεό]σιοι	Γ	Νεάπ[ολις]
[ΓͰͰͰΙΙ]	[Σιδόσι]οι	ΓͰΙΙ[ΙΙ]	Ἀζζε[ιοί]
[ΔΓͰΙΙΙΙ]	[Βούθε]ια	ΓͰͰͰ̣[ͰΙΙ]	Πρία[πος]
[Η]	[Μυέ]σσιοι	𐅅	Σελυ[μβριανοί]
[Η]	[Π]υγελε͂ς	Δ[ΔΔͰͰͰΙΙ]	Νεά[ν]δρ̣[εια]
[ΔΓͰΙΙΙΙ]	[Ἰ]σίνδιοι	*vacat*	
[𐅅]	Μιλέσιοι	ἐπ[ὶ Θράικες φόρος]	
[𐅅Η]	Ἐφέσιοι	ΔΓͰΙΙ[ΙΙ]	[Ν]εοπολιτ̣[αι]
[Η𐅄]	Κλαζομένιοι	ΔΓͰΙΙΙΙ	[Σ]κ̣α[φσαῖοι]
𐅄̣ΔΔΓͰͰΙΙΙΙ	Γαργαρε͂ς	ΔΔΓ	[Ἴκιοι]
hελλεσπόντιος φόρος		ΔΔΔͰͰͰΙΙ	[Ὀλοφύχσιοι]
ΔΓͰΙΙΙΙ	Δαυνιοτειχῖ(ται)	ΔΓͰΙΙΙΙ	[Σταγιρῖται]
ΔΓͰΙΙΙΙ	Διδυμοτειχῖ(ται)	Η	[Θύσσιοι]
ΔΓͰΙΙΙΙ	Λαμπονειε͂ς	Η	[Διε͂ς ἀπὸ τõ Ἄθο]
vacat		*vacat*	

ii. 29–33 Matthaiou, on the basis of a new fragment.

C

Year 21, 434/3

col. vi

Η	Στόλιοι
ΗΗ	Σίγγιοι
	πόλες αὐταὶ
	φόρον ταχσάμεναι
ΓͰͰͰΙΙ	Αἰολῖται
𐅄	Γαλαῖοι
𐅄	Μιλκό[ριοι]
Η	Ἀμ[όργιοι]
ΔΓͰΙΙΙΙ	Κ[άσιοι]
ΔΓͰΙΙΙΙ	Κα[λλιπολῖται]
ΔΔΓ	Σαρ[ταῖοι]
ΔΓͰΙΙΙΙ	Ἐτ[εοκαρπάθιοι]
ΓͰͰͰΙΙ	Φα[ρβέλιοι]
ΔΓͰΙΙΙΙ	[Χεδρόλιοι]

[16 dr. 4 ob.]	Elaeitans	300 dr.	Proconnesians
[8 dr. 2 ob.	Assyrenians Mysians]	900 dr.	Cyzicenes
[16 dr. 4 ob.	Pitanians]	33 dr. 2 ob.	Artacenes
[100 dr.	Prienians]	1000 dr.	Perinthians
[700 dr.	Erythraeans]	1576 dr. 4 ob.	Byzantines
[1 dr. 4 ob.	Elaeusians]	16 dr. 4 ob.	Cianians
[66 dr. 4 ob.	Polichnitans]	200 dr.	Arisbaeans
[1 dr. 4 ob.	Pteleosians]	5 dr.	Neapolis
[8 dr. 2 ob.	Sidosians]	6 dr. 4 ob.	Azzeians
[16 dr. 4 ob.	Butheia]	8 dr. 2 ob.	Priapus
[100 dr.]	Myessians	500 dr.	Selymbrians
[100 dr.]	Pygelans	[33 dr. 2 ob.]	Neandreia
[16 dr. 4 ob.]	Isindians		*vacat*
[500 dr.]	Milesians	THRACEWARD TRIBUTE	
[600 dr.]	Ephesians	16 dr. 4 ob.	Neopolitans
[150 dr.]	Clazomenians	16 dr. 4 ob.	Scapsaeans
77 dr. 4 ob.	Gargarians	25 dr.	[Icians]
HELLESPONTINE TRIBUTE		33 dr. 2 ob.	[Olophyxians]
16 dr. 4 ob.	Daunioteichitans	16 dr. 4 ob.	[Stagirites]
16 dr. 4 ob.	Didymoteichitans	100 dr.	[Thyssians]
16 dr. 4 ob	Lamponeians	100 dr.	[Dians from Athos]
	vacat		*vacat*

C

Year 21, 434/3

col. vi

100 dr.	Stolians
200 dr.	Singians
	CITIES WHICH ASSESSED THEMSELVES FOR TRIBUTE
8 dr. 2 ob.	Aeolitans
50 dr.	Galaeans
50 dr.	Milcorians
100 dr.	Amorgians
16 dr. 4 ob.	Casians
16 dr. 4 ob.	Callipolitans
25 dr.	Sartaeans
16 dr. 4 ob	Eteocarpathians
8 dr. 2 ob	Pharbelians
16 dr. 4 ob.	Chedrolians

ΔΓ⊢IIII	Πλευ[μες]
	πόλες hὰς h[οι]
	ἰδιôται ἐνέ[γ]ρα-
	φσαν φόρον
	φέρεν
Δ	Πίλορος
Γ⊢⊢⊢II	Κλεοναί
ΔΔΓ	Σίνος
	Διακρες
Δ⊢⊢⊢II	ἀπὸ Χαλκιδέο[ν]
Γ⊢⊢⊢II	Πίστασος
ΔΔΔ	Σύμε
	Τινδαῖοι
	Κίθας
𐅄	Σμίλλα
	Γίγονος
	hαῖσα
𐅄	Βύσβικος
Γ⊢⊢⊢II	Ὄθορος
	ἄτακτος πόλις
Γ	Κυστίριοι
vacat	

Thucydides tells us that as soon as the Athenians took over the leadership of the Greek allies against Persia in 478/7 'they made an assessment of which allied cities were to provide money for the war against the Persians and which were to provide ships' (I. 96. i). The assessment of what cities had to pay is attributed to Aristides by a later Athenian document recorded by Thucydides (V. 18. v) and by later writers (*Ath. Pol.* 23. iv, Diod. Sic. XI. 47, Plut. *Arist.* 24). The Athenians established *hellenotamiai* (Treasurers of the Greeks) to collect the tribute, and according to Thucydides 'the first tribute that was assessed amounted to 460 talents' (I. 96. ii), a figure repeated by Plutarch (*Arist.* 24. iv); Diod. Sic. has 560 talents (XI. 47. i). The money collected was deposited on Delos (cf. **147**).

The collection of the tribute on Delos has left no epigraphic trace (but it is likely that an offering was made from it to Apollo). But following the transfer of the treasury from Delos the Athenians began inscribing lists of the quota of one-sixtieth from each tribute payment that was given to Athena. These lists were begun on an extremely large stone (without any crowning relief: see C. Lawton, *Hesperia* lxi 1992, 244–6), known as the 'first stone' (*IG* i[3] 259–72), which ended up containing all the lists down to 440/39, after which the 'second stone' was brought into use, which in

16 dr. 4 ob.	Pleumians
	CITIES WHICH INDIVIDUALS SIGNED UP TO PAY TRIBUTE
10 dr.	Pilorus
8 dr. 2 ob.	Cleonae
25 dr.	Sinus
8 dr. 2 ob.	Diacres from the Chalcidians
8 dr. 2 ob.	Pistasus
30 dr.	Syme
	Tindaeans
	Cithas
50 dr.	Smilla
	Gigonus
	Haesa
50 dr.	Bysbicus
8 dr. 2 ob.	Othorus
	UNASSESSED CITY
5 dr.	Cystirians
vacat	

---

turn held the lists down to 432/1. One possible explanation for the extremely large stones is that they were blocks reused from building projects (in particular the Older Parthenon: see M. Miles, *Hesperia* lxxx 2011, 657–75); the choice of such stones points to the assumption, arguably implicit from the inception of the League (cf. *Ath. Pol.* 23. iv–v on sinking iron bars into the sea when oaths of alliance were originally taken), that the collection of tribute was going to continue for a long time. After 432/1 lists seem to have been inscribed on separate *stelai*.

The heading of the first list (*A.* 1–4) spells out the procedure: the *hellenotamiai* for 454/3 receive the tribute from the individual allies, they then pass over to a set of auditors (the Thirty) the one-sixtieth that was given as a 'firstfruit' to Athena, and the sum handed over was recorded on the stone. The list of cities follows, inscribed in six columns each of twenty-five lines (the two middle columns are perfectly preserved), with a sum inscribed after each city. The names of the cities are usually given in ethnic form ('Olynthians', *A.* v. 6) but sometimes we have simply the place-name ('Neapolis in Thrace', *A.* vi. 9–10), and sometimes the name of a ruler ('Picres Syangelian', *A.* v. 16). On the right-hand side of the stone a summary statement of the totals collected of gold and silver was inscribed (*IG* i^3 259 *postscriptum*).

The second year's list, which we do not reproduce, has a shorter introductory formula, restored as [ἐπὶ τε͂ς ἀρχε͂ς τε͂]ς δευτέρ[α]ς hε͂ι Λ[έον ἐγραμμάτευε: τοῖς τριάκοντα] ('Under the second board, to which Leon was secretary (the following was rendered) to the Thirty'). In this list the sums come before the names, and the names are listed in ten columns, seven on the front and three on the right-hand side of the stone. A similar arrangement follows for subsequent years except that the lists are all in five columns on the front of the stone only, and from the fourth list onwards mention of the Thirty is dropped. After six lists on the front of the stone, they turned to the remainder of the right-hand side and inscribed one list there in two long (110-line) columns (see Osborne, *The Athenian Empire*[4], p. 87); then they continued with five further lists on the back, starting, some way below the top, with the list labelled 'ninth', before fitting in two on the left-hand side. From 443/2 the heading gave the name and demotic of one of the *hellenotamiai*.[1]

The preservation of successive lists enables a history of tribute payment to be written. It becomes apparent, confirming [Xen.] *Ath. Pol.* iii. 5, that tribute was regularly reassessed in the years of the Great Panathenaea (changes are apparent in 450, 446, 434), but that in 443/2 (as again in 425/4, below **154**) there was an extraordinary tribute reassessment. It also becomes apparent that the rate of tribute payment for most cities was constant over long periods, but that there were variations both up and down for individual cities (in 446 payments from the islands remain constant but elsewhere there are many reductions and very few increases). More fundamentally, it is clear (though some, notably W. K. Pritchett, have argued otherwise, and see n. 3, below) that there is a whole year's list missing. The first five lists are numbered. The list below the fifth is not numbered, but headed simply

[ἐπ]ὶ τε͂ [ς ἀρχε͂ς h]ε͂ι Μενέτ[ιμο]ς ⁝ ἐγρα[μμάτ]ευε Λαμ[πτρευς.]

Under the board to which Menetimus of Lamptrae was secretary.

This list takes us to the bottom of the front of the stone. The list inscribed on the right-hand side of the stone includes some late payments from the unnumbered list, making it clear that it immediately follows Menetimus' list (e.g. Thasos pays [ΗΗΔΔΔ]ΔΓ𐅂, [24]6 dr., in Menetimus' list, and 𐅄𐅂𐅂𐅂𐅂, 54 dr., in the list on the right side, making up her usual quota payment of 300 dr.; [Δαρδ]ανε͂ς pay Δ[Δ]ΔΔΓ𐅂, 46 dr., in Menetimus' list, and 𐅄𐅂𐅂𐅂𐅂, 54 dr., in the list on the right side, making up their usual quota payment of 100 dr.). The list on the right-hand side had a number, but this is not preserved and can be restored as either 'seventh' or 'eighth'. The list numbered nine is at the top of the back of the *stele*, but with a vacant space above it.[2] It is almost certain that it is the list before Menetimus' list (i.e. the list for

[1] For further discussion, and division of the twenty-two lists on the Lapis Primus and Lapis Secundus between the hands of just six inscribers, see Tracy, *Athenian Lettering of the Fifth Century BC*, 41–53.

[2] Some have suggested that there might have been a short list at the top of the back of the *stele* (cf. e.g. M. Piérart, in *Stemmata . . . J. Labarbe*, 291–303). Such a list would have to be at most half the length of the next-shortest list, and to believe that we would need to believe that tribute was withheld by some ⅔ of the cities in the empire; subsequent tribute reductions (see below) might suggest some Athenian need to mollify allies, but 40 cities have their tribute reduced, not 140.

449/8) that is missing, and that it was because they knew that no list had been inscribed for that year that those who inscribed Menetimus' list (for 448/7) did not know how to number it (it was the sixth list, but the seventh year). Do the other lists contain any clue as to why no list was inscribed in 449/8?

From the number of lines in each we can work out more or less exactly how many cities paid in each year. The first four lists are shorter than subsequent lists, and the first list is shortest of all (with a maximum of 139 names; but the first eighteen names on the second list, written in a different hand from the rest of that list and all probably of Carian cities, seem to be late payments for the previous year, perhaps collected by an Athenian task-force to the area). But because of the irregular order and incomplete preservation of the names it is hard to answer the two questions that we most want to ask: which cities are paying, and how much is being collected?

If we take the second of those questions first, given that many cities pay very little tribute (1,000 dr. or under), but some pay very large sums (up to 30 talents—360 times the payments of those who pay least), the total collected depends very much on the identity of the cities paying. There is no way of securely restoring individual names in the early lists because the first eight lists have no clear geographical ordering, and cities may have been listed simply in the order in which they happened to pay. But from the middle of the 440s the good preservation of the lists and the new practice adopted in 443/2 of recording those who pay tribute in districts (five for five years, four subsequently), with explicit headings, makes restoration of names more secure and it becomes possible to have some confidence that the Athenians were collecting between 350 and 400 talents a year. This compares with the unique, but poorly preserved, separate figures for the total silver and total electrum collected in the first list (454/3), where the total for silver seems to be 383 or 333 talents of silver (*IG* i^3 259 postcript 9: 60 × 5 tal. 2,320 dr. or 60 × 6 tal. 2,320 dr.), with possibly 30 talents of electrum. These figures stand in contrast to the claims made in Thucydides that the first tribute assessed was 460 talents and that in 432 tribute payment amounted to 600 talents (Thuc. I. 96. ii, II. 13. iii). It has been suggested, on the parallel of the more explicit Propylaea accounts (M&L 60. 11–13), that the (restored) sum of 38,675 dr. given by the *hellenotamiai* for the building of the Parthenon in 444/3 (*IG* i^3 439. 73; cf. below, **145**), is Athena's one-sixtieth share of the (postulated) 376 tal. tribute for that year (for doubts about this see L. Kallet, *Cl. Ant.* viii 1989, 262–3).

Both this and the link between the building of the Parthenon and cessation of hostilities against Persia have suggested to some that the missing tribute quota list is absent because that year Athena's money, along with the rest of the tribute, was devoted to that project.[3] Building the Parthenon began in 447/6 (below, **135**), and planning must have begun rather earlier. From the beginning, the scale of the project will have indicated that it would cost well in excess of one year's tribute, and after

[3] The maximal case for the Parthenon as an anti-Persian monument is made by Castriota, *Myth, Ethos, and Actuality*. The case against is made by Osborne in Goldhill & Osborne, *Art and Text in Ancient Greek Culture*, 52–84, and Osborne, *Athens and Athenian Democracy*, 291–322.

thirty years of League activity against Persia using some League resources to celebrate the success of the enterprise would not be hard to justify. Nevertheless, this seems a poor explanation for the absent list: the tribute quota lists are about accounting for income, and one would expect Athena's share of tribute to be accounted for, even if the Athenians decided also to give the rest of that year's tribute towards the Parthenon project. If Athena's share of the tribute in 444/3 did go to fund the Propylaea, that did not prevent a normal tribute quota list being recorded in that year.

To return to the question of who did and who did not pay tribute, we can see the patterns even when we cannot know exactly how the gaps in the lists are to be filled. D. M. Lewis (*BSA* lxxxix 1994, 285–301) calculated that there was approximately a one in three chance that an individual state listed for the first time in the fourth list was actually present in earlier lists. He was able to show that list 3 most plausibly included almost all the cities listed in lists 1 and 2, but that some sixty-nine names mentioned in lists 1–3 do not appear in list 4. There are spaces for only forty-five names in the gaps on that list. Given this, it is highly unlikely that more than one of the nineteen new cities that appear for the first time in list 5 were present in list 4. We seem to have a pattern here where there were a significant number of absentees in list 4, and a significant influx of new tributary cities in list 5, immediately before the missing list.

These patterns of presence and absence demand interpretation. There might be a number of reasons why a city would fail to pay in any particular year (see further below, on **154**), but two have been thought particularly plausible in relation to these earliest lists. First, that that city was still contributing ships to the Delian League, rather than money payments. Lewis identified twenty cities, first listed in either list 4 (451/0) or list 5 (450/449), which both paid substantial amounts of tribute and were situated on the coast. These include Paros (which pays 16 tal. 3,000 dr.), Andros (which pays 12 tal.) and Teos (which pays 6 tal.). For these cities a change from ships to tribute at this point is an attractive explanation. Second, that a city was withholding payment because it was in dispute or in revolt. There are a number of cases in the early lists of small communities paying when their larger neighbours are absent (Butheia (*A*. v. 15; but NB *B*. i. 27 (restored), where Erythrae is restored in l. 22) in the absence of Erythrae: see **121**), or of groups of citizens from one state resident in another state paying separately (Milesians in Leros and Teichioussa (*A*. vi. 20–2)). These may indicate that the larger or home city was deliberately withholding payment.

The consistency of the first three lists, and the patterns of addition and absence in the fourth and fifth list, suggest that the League was generally at a moment of transition, when significant numbers of allies were reconsidering their position, perhaps in the wake of their own losses in the heavy Athenian defeat in Egypt or of Athenian negotiations with Persia.[4] The losses suffered in Egypt may have led allies

[4] For which cf. Hdt. VII 151. For the evidence for and against a Peace of Callias see Osborne, *The Athenian Empire*[4], pp. 30–2 with bibliography 132–3.

to wish to contribute money rather than ships, and any formal or informal agreement with Persia may have inclined allies to think that the League no longer had its original anti-Persian purpose and encouraged them to secede from the League altogether. There is separate evidence for the founding of cleruchies, settlements of Athenians on allied territory, during this period, and these too indicate that Athenian intervention had been needed to secure the loyalty of an ally.[5] Menetimus' list (for 448/7) is short (only *c.*150 entries), and has evidence for irregularity, notably in the payments made in two instalments but perhaps also with nine late payments (*IG* i³ 264. 30–9). The degree of disruption, however, is hardly sufficient to let us think that there could have been a mass boycott in 449/8, and some of it might be accounted for by purely mechanical problems in getting the tribute delivered on time (it is hard to think that withholding just 240 dr., as Sigeum seems to have done from its complementary quota payment of 4 dr., would constitute much of a protest). Such 'mechanical' problems, nevertheless, cannot account for the whole of the disruption, which seems great enough to make it less, rather than more, likely that the Athenians would have exempted everyone from payment for a year.[6] We should not exclude the possibility that there was an administrative problem at Athens, involving loss of the records made at the time that payments were handed over, from which the lists were then constructed. We know from Antiph. v. *Herodes* 69–71 that at some point in the 450s or 440s a whole board of *hellenotamiai* was executed after some money had disappeared and they were falsely blamed. Might that incident have disrupted the normal course of inscription?[7]

As well as potentially telling us a good deal about Athens' relations with her allies in general, the tribute quota lists also offer us potential insight into particular relations with individual allies through variations in individual tribute payments. When the record of an individual city is pursued across the tribute quota lists, striking changes in the level of tribute, or anomalously high or low payments, sometimes appear. On occasions this is plausibly the result of a cutter's error. Arguably, one example of this is the payment made by Argilus in Thrace in 454/3 (*IG* i³ 259. iv. 22). The number that appears there, 1050 dr. (XΓ), equates to a tribute of 10½ tal. The sum is itself somewhat irregular (but the earliest list does include more irregular sums than later lists), and contrasts with Argilus' payment in 446/5 and subsequent years of just 1 tal. In this case an inscription error may be suspected (XΓ for HΓ), and the tribute reckoned to have been 1½ talents.[8] But when in 433/2 (and then again in later lists) Argilus appears paying a tribute quota of 16 dr. 4 obols

[5] Cleruchy at Hestiaea: Thuc. I. 114. i, Theopomp. *FGH* 115 F 387, Plut. *Per.* 23. iv; at Chalcis: Ael. *V.H.* VI. 1; in Euboea more generally: Andoc. III. *Peace* 9, Diod. Sic. XI. 88. iii, XII. 22. ii, Paus. I. 27. iii; on Naxos: Andoc. III. *Peace* 9, Diod. Sic. XI. 88. iii, Plut. *Per.* 11. v, Paus. I. 27. iii; on Andros: Plut. *Per.* 11. v; Chersonesus: Andoc. III. *Peace* 9, Diod. Sic. XI. 88..iii, Plut. *Per.* 11. v; on Lemnos: cf. *IG* i³ 1164. See Figueira, *Athens and Aigina*, chs. 6 and 7, and esp. Table 4, pp. 217–25.

[6] Scholars used to think problems with tribute defaulters were further in evidence from Cleinias' decree (**154**), but we believe this to be a much later document.

[7] Cf. Samons, *Empire of the Owl*, 80 n. 246; S. V. Tracy, *CP* cix 2014, 1–10.

[8] So *ATL* iii. 5 (followed by *IG*); but see *contra* Hammond [& Griffith], *A History of Macedonia*, ii. 117–18; Isaac, *The Greek Settlements in Thrace*, 53–4.

(*IG* i³ 279. ii. 54, 281. ii. 24, 282. ii. 9, i.e. a tribute of 1,000 dr.), some different explanation of the drastic change is required. Since Argilus was absent from the 434/3 list and again from the 432/1 list explanation is not straightforward, but a connection with the Athenians having carved out territory from Argilus for their colony at Amphipolis in 437/6 may be suspected (for Argilians with citizenship in Amphipolis see Thuc. IV. 103. iv). As this example shows, changes in tribute quota can alert us to possible changes in political circumstances, but we rely on external evidence in coming to any interpretation. A good example of the way in which tribute changes may show up only our ignorance is the massive increase in tribute from Thasos from 3 tal. in 453–448/7 to 30 tal. from 443 onwards. Scholars guess that this marks in some way the end of particular sanctions imposed by Athens (Thuc. I. 101. iii) after the revolt of Thasos in 463 (the end of an indemnity, the return of Thasian possessions on the mainland, or similar: cf. C. Pébarthe, *ZPE* cxxvi 1999, 131–54); the truth is that we simply do not know the explanation.

In the tribute quota lists of the 430s some new types of entries appear. In 439 for the first time eight payments are labelled *epiphora*, a term most easily understood as 'additional payment'. These additional payments are small, varying in proportion from one-thirtieth to one-sixth of the usual tribute. They are best understood as penalty payments for late payment. Small numbers of such payments appear throughout the 430s (see further S. P. Eddy, *AJP* lxxxix 1968, 129–43). Then in the list of 434/3 and subsequent years, exemplified in *C*, new rubrics appear. These rubrics point to unassessed cities, cities that assessed themselves, cities where individuals paid on behalf of a city, and subsequently to 'cities for which the *taktai* for whom Cr—us was secretary made assessment' and 'cities for which the council and the court of 1,500 assessed tribute' (*IG* i³ 281. iii. 54–5, 61–2: see further F. A. Lepper, *JHS* lxxxii 1962, 25–55; W. Schuller, *ZPE* xlii 1981, 141–51). The 'unassessed city' in 434/3, the Cystirians, pays only 300 dr. in tribute, cannot be located and is never heard of again (except in Herodian). But of the eleven cities who assessed themselves in 434/3, ten reappear in the same category the following year, five in that category in the year after, and then some of these (Callipolitans, Sartaeans, Amorgians in both years, Casians, Aeolitans and Pleumeis in 282 only) make up the list of those assessed by the *taktai* in *IG* i³ 281 and 282, apparently paying exactly the same amounts (for the dating of later lists see on **153**). Of the thirteen cities registered for tribute by individuals in 434/3 at least five seem to have reappeared in the same category in the following year, and two in the year after that; four of these (Cleonaeans, Symaeans, Diacres from the Chalcidians and Bysbiceni) then appear in 281 as 'cities which the council and 1,500 assessed' and 282 as 'cities which the council with the court assessed'. Subsequently cities from both these groups appear listed regularly as part of a region.

These cities in special categories come from a number of different geographical regions, although the great majority are from Thrace, and they have different histories. The Chedrolians from Thrace (*C.* 16) had appeared in the lists for 448/7 and 447/6 (as Edrolians, *IG* i³ 264. iii. 3, 265. ii. 33) and then, probably as 'unassessed' in 435/4 (*IG* i³ 277. vi. 25) before assessing themselves, for double their previous payment, in 434/3. The Galaeans (from the city of Galepsus), Othorians and Pharbelians appear among Thracian cities in or down to the year 436/5 (*IG* i³ 276. v. 21, 26, 28) before moving into special categories in 434/3: the Pharbelians had paid 1,000 dr. from 454/3 onwards (259. i. 15), but assess themselves for only 500 dr.; the Othorians seem to have reassessed themselves from 700 dr. (*IG* i³ 269. iii. 27) to 500 dr.; by contrast the Galaeans increase their payments from 800 dr. to 3,000 dr. Various cities appear here first but then continue to appear through the 420s and sometimes beyond: the Casians (from the island of Casos near Carpathus), the Eteocarpathioi (see **136**), and the Sartaioi from Thrace, continue to appear down to *IG* i³ 290. i. 6, i. 23, iii. 11; the Diacrians from the Chalcidians in Euboea appear down to 289. i. 15–16, when they pay not the 800 dr. attested here but 3,000 dr., which compares with a 425/4 assessment of 2,000 dr.; the Callipolitans and the Bysbicenes, both from the Hellespontine region, appear down to 287. ii. 13, 29), and Sinus down to 285. iii. 9 (421/0), when it pays 800 dr., considerably down from the 1,500 here. But other names appear in these special lists alone: the Thracian cities of the Tindaeans, Cithas, Smilla, Gigonus and Haesa, which here all contribute a single sum, Pilorus, and the Pleumeis, and the Aegean islands of the Amorgians (a whole-island group: one would expect to see the cities of the island of Amorgus listed separately but they never are) and of Syme (listed by its island name initially, but then as Symaeans). Syme reappears in the 425/4 tribute reassessment, but on no later fragments of tribute lists—despite having produced two fragments of the Athenian standards decree (**155**).

There is clearly more than one thing going on in these special categories, but they are nonetheless of great interest, for they are some of our best evidence for cities being keen to join, or rejoin, the Athenian empire even in the 430s. It is possible that these are cities whose citizens suspect that they will be compelled to join and are choosing to anticipate that, negotiating for themselves a privileged status whereby they determine their own payment. That the categories are geographically diverse argues against any systematic Athenian pressure (but NB the Megarian decree, Thuc. 1. 139. i, by which the Athenians put pressure on their allies to exclude Megarians from their harbours, and Corinth's claim at Sparta in Thuc. 1. 120. ii that those not in the empire find their ability to import and export restricted). We should probably rather believe that either the city as a whole, or some group within it, thought that there was going to be a local, or wider, advantage, to joining Athens. The actions of these cities are clear testimony to the reach of Athenian power on the eve of the Peloponnesian War. That these cities in the Thracian area were deciding to join Athens at just the moment when Potidaea, other cities in the Chalcidice, and the Bottiaeans were deciding to leave (Thuc. 1. 58. ii) suggests something of the complexity of the political considerations behind attitudes to Athens.

The tribute quota lists are the richest source we have for the relative wealth of Greek cities. Although the tribute assessment can never have been based on a detailed scrutiny of a city's finances, what was demanded clearly had to bear some relationship to what could be provided, and a relationship that was not obviously out of line with what was demanded from other, particularly from neighbouring, cities.

We know that there were mechanisms for appealing against assessments; fragments survive of a speech by Antiphon 'On the tribute of the Samothracians', in which they argued that their island was small, high and rough, with little land suitable for agriculture, and the tribute quota lists enable us to trace the Samothracian tribute, which had been regularly 6 tal., being reduced to 2 tal. in *IG* i[3] 281. ii. 13, although then (probably) reassessed at 15 tal. in 425/4. There were no doubt anomalies, with some cities better at concealing their wealth than others, but generally we can be confident that cities paid tribute broadly in proportion to their resources (L. Nixon & S. R. F. Price, in Murray & Price (edd.), *The Greek City from Homer to Alexander*, 137–70).

What emerges from the tribute quota lists is a picture of marked inequality. Taking the tribute assessment of 442/1, the two biggest contributors of money, Thasos and Aegina, pay 30 tal., the smallest contributions are 1/1,800 of that—100 dr. (Pteleon and Elaeus in Ionia (for which see R&O 71), with Elaeus assessed at 100 dr. even in the 425/4 reassessment) or 1/600 of that—300 dr. (Rheneia, which had initially paid 1,000 dr., among the islands, and Neapolis and the Harpagion in the Hellespontine district). Even if we allow for the extraordinary mineral and commercial resources of Thasos and the peculiar place of Aegina in Mediterranean trade, and for the possibility of a lingering punitive element to payments in both these cases, we still have to reckon with contributions of 12 tal., 15 tal., 15 tal. 4,000 dr. and 18 tal. from Lampsacus, Abdera, Byzantium and Paros respectively. Pteleon and Elaeous are outliers, but some twenty-eight cities paid 500 dr., a twelfth of what

---

120

Athenian judicial relations with Phaselis, before *c.*450 (?)

A marble *stele* (complete, though the left-hand side is now illegible), once in the monastery of St John the Baptist on Mt Hymettus; now in the Epigraphical Museum. Phot. *Ἀρχ. Ἐφ.* 1922, 63; *hóρος* xiv–xvi 2000–3, pls. 3–4.

Attic Greek, but using Ionic writing. *Stoichedon* 22.

SdA 149; M&L 31; *IG* i[3] 10*; Cataldi, *Symbolai e relazioni tra le città greche nel V sec. a.C.*, 99–143 no. 5. Trans. Fornara 68; Osborne, *The Athenian Empire*[4], 234 (a different translation in earlier editions); Dillon & Garland[3] 12. 29. See also R. J. Hopper, *JHS* lxiii 1943, 39–45; Wade-Gery, *Essays in Greek History*, 180–92; G. E. M. de Ste. Croix, *CQ*[2] xi 1961, 100–8; Gauthier, *Symbola*, 158–61, 177–81, 184–6; H. B. Mattingly, *PACA* vii 1964, 37–9, *ZPE* lxxxiii 1990, 119 n. 40 = his *AER*, 514 n. 39; M. H. Jameson, *hóρος* xiv–xvi 2000–3, 23–9.

was paid by the twenty-nine cities paying 1 talent, and 1/120 of the 10-talent payments of Aenus, Perinthus and the Lycians.

Clearly part of what lies behind this inequality is difference in population. Some of these communities were tiny—and indeed, such a city as Pteleon was sometimes explicitly recognised as a dependency of Erythrae. But there is clearly much more to it than that. And the more that there is to it is in most cases unlikely to be agricultural. The role of minerals is most obvious with Thasos, but must surely be part of what lifts the tribute of Paros, which had major marble resources. The role of trade is most obvious with Aegina and Byzantium, but is surely responsible too for the prominence of Abdera, Lampsacus, Aenus and Perinthus, cities which contribute financially well beyond their prominence in the political history of the period.[9] Conversely it is notable that among cities with large territories (over 500 $km.^2$) Maroneia in Thrace pays only 1 tal. 3.000 dr., and in the Hellespontine area Parium pays only 2,000 dr., Cius only 1,000 dr. The full significance of these data for our understanding of the economy of classical Greece has yet to be realised.

[9] *Inventory* puts these cities into the following classes of size of territory (where 1 is the smallest, up to 25 $km.^2$), and 5 is the largest, over 500 $km.^2$): Thasos: 4; Paros: 3; Aegina: 2; Byzantium: 5; Abdera: 5; Lampsacus: 5; Aenus: 4 or 5; Perinthus: 5. This indicates that many of these cities did have large territories, but there are 61 cities in total in their largest size category, 66 in category 4, 71 in category 3 (out of a total of 635 cities for which a territorial estimate can be given).

[ἔδο]ξεν τῆι βολῆι καὶ τῶι δ[ή]-
[μωι, Ἀ]καμαντὶς [ἐ]πρυτάνευε,
[.]ν̣ά̣σιππος ἐγραμμάτευε, Νε-
ο̣[κ]λ̣έδης ἐπεστάτει, Λέω[ν ε]ἶ-
[πε· τοῖ]ς Φασηλίταις τὸ ψ[ήφ]ι-
[σμα ἀν]αγράψαι· ὅ τι ἂμ μὲ[ν] Ἀθ-
[ήνησι ξ]υ[μβ]όλαιον γένηται
[πρὸς Φ]ασηλιτ[ῶ]ν τινα, Ἀθή[ν]η-
[σι τὰς δ]ίκας γίγνεσθαι παρ-
[ὰ τῶι πο]λεμάρχωι, καθάπερ Χ-
[ίοις, καὶ] ἄλλοθι μηδὲ ἀμô· τῶ-
[ν δὲ ἄλλω]ν̣ ἀπὸ ξυμβολῶν κατ-
[ὰ τὰς ὅσας] ξυμβολὰς πρὸς Φα-
[σηλίτας] τὰς δίκας ἐ̑ν[α]ι· τὰς
[—7—]το[ς] ἀφελε̑ν. ἐὰν δέ τ-
[ις ἄλλη τῶ]ν̣ ἀρχῶν δέξηται δ-
[ίκην κατὰ] Φασηλιτῶν τινὸς
[—8—, ε]ἰ μὲν καταδικάσ-
[ει, ἡ καταδίκ]η ἄκυρος ἔστω. ἐ-
[ὰν δέ τις παραβ]α[ί]νηι τὰ ἐψη-
[φισμένα, ὀφ]ε[λέτ]ω μυρίας δ[ρ]-
[αχμὰς ἱερ]ὰς τῆι Ἀθηναίαι· τ-
[ὸ δὲ ψήφισ]μα τό[δε] ἀναγραψά-
[τω ὁ γραμμ]ατεὺς ὁ τῆς βολῆς
[ἐστήληι λιθί]νηι καὶ καταθ-
[έτω ἐμ πόλει τ]έλεσι τοῖς τῶ-
[ν Φασηλιτῶν.] *vacat*

Bradeen & McGregor, *Studies in Fifth-Century Attic Epigraphy*, 116, read more letters at some points and fewer at others, with no implications for the text to be restored except where noted below. 3 [Μ]ν̣ά̣σιππος or [Ὀ]ν̣ά̣σιππος. 3–4 Νε|ο̣[κ]λ̣έδης Jameson: Νε|[....]δης M&L, ἐγ[ραμ]μάτευεν, Ἐ|[πιμ]ήδης Bradeen & McGregor. 12 ἄλλοθι] Photiades, ἄλλοθ]ι Cataldi. 15 [δὲ ἐκκλή]το[ς] Dittenberger, *SIG*[2] 72. 18 [παρὰ τόδε, ε]ἰ Photiades more likely than [Ἀθήνησιν, ε]ἰ Wilhelm. 18–19 καταδικάσ|[εταί τι, ἡ δίκη W. W. Wyndham *ap.* Rhodes, *Boule*, 204 n. 1, [τούτο δ' ὀφε]ίλεν καταδικασ|[θῆι, ἡ μὲν δίκ]η Dittenberger, *SIG*[2] 72, cf. G. Thür, in *Law, Rhetoric and Comedy . . . D. M. MacDowell*, 38 (not discussing the beginning of 18).

Phaselis, on the south coast of Asia Minor in Lycia, was an important staging-point in trade between the Levant and Greece (Thuc. II. 69. i); Dem. XXXV. *Lacritus* 1–2 represents its traders as cunning and dishonest. At the time of the battle of the Eurymedon (perhaps 469) it joined the Delian League through the mediation of Chios, with whom it had a longstanding connection (Plut. *Cim.* 12. iii–iv), and Chios is cited as a precedent for the treatment which it is given in this decree.

Resolved by the council and people; Acamantis was the prytany; [.]nasippus was secretary; Neoclides was chairman; Leon proposed:

5 Write up the decree for the Phaselites. Whatever cause of action arises at Athens against any of the Phaselites, the trials are to be held at Athens before the polemarch, as for the Chians, and nowhere else; trials of other cases covered by convention shall be held in accordance with the existing convention with the Phaselites; the — shall be abolished. If any of the other officials accepts a case against any of the Phaselites contrary to this (?), if he condemns the condemnation shall be invalid. If any one contravenes what has been decreed, he shall owe ten thousand drachmas sacred to Athena.

22 This decree shall be written up by the secretary of the council on a stone *stele* and set down on the acropolis, at the expense of the Phaselites.

Two categories of lawsuit are dealt with. Cases arising at Athens (*xymbolaion* is not limited to cases arising from contracts, as early commentators thought, and Cataldi still thinks) against a Phaselite are to be tried before the polemarch. This treatment must be a privilege: it would be normal for a case arising in Athens to be tried in Athens, and the privilege will be trial in the court of the polemarch, who handled lawsuits for privileged foreigners (*Ath. Pol.* 58. ii); prestige apart, this perhaps guaranteed that Phaselite defendants would not be subjected to summary procedures

(Gauthier). Cases 'covered by convention' are those for which there is an inter-state agreement (originally signified by *symbola*, 'tokens': see Gauthier): there must have been a judicial agreement between Athens and Phaselis earlier than this decree. For *xymbolaia* and *dikai apo xymbolon* cf. **185**, **191**. 17–18; and for a different use of tokens see **154**. 11. Dittenberger's 'cases appealed (*sc.* to Athens)' is not convincing for what is abolished in ll. 14–15, but no better suggestion has yet been advanced. Ten thousand drachmas (21–2) is a very heavy fine, the heaviest attested in fifth-century inscriptions (cf. **153**).

The inscription is in Ionic writing, presumably because the Phaselites paid for it (for the significance of inscriptions paid for by the state or individual affected see P. Low, *JHS* cxxv 2005, 100–9): l. 5 has Φασηλίταις, whereas in Athens feminine dative plurals in -αις rather than -ασι or -ησι are rare before *c.*420 (Threatte, *The Grammar of Attic Inscriptions*, ii. 96–101), but an Ionic text should not be judged by this criterion. Most recent commentators have dated this text between Phaselis' entry into the League and *c.*450, and Mattingly, who once suggested 425/4, later accepted that. Jameson argued again for a later date, but rather half-heartedly. His identification of Neoclides as chairman does not help (a Neoclides was *bouleutes* probably in 424/3, but in that year the secretary for Acamantis was Phaenippus: **150** with Thuc. IV. 118. xi). For our text's secretary, the possible names are Mnasippus and Onasippus, but no Athenian Onasippus is known, and no Mnasippus before the hellenistic period. As for our proposer, Leon (*LGPN* ii *s.n.*, 1), there are several possible

---

121

Athenian regulations for Erythrae, late 450s

A marble *stele* copied by L. F. S. Fauvel on the Athenian acropolis, now lost. It has long been known only from the printed facsimile first published in *CIG* i, p. 891 (reproduced e.g. at *IG* i[3] 14); but the copy on which that was based, and a transcription by K. S. Pittakys of another copy by Fauvel, have been found in the archives of *IG*, and another copy by Fauvel, containing ll. 2–4 and part of 6 only, is in the Bibliothèque Nationale, Paris. These are studied by G. E. Malouchou, in *Ἀθηναίων ἐπίσκοπος . . . H. B. Mattingly*, 73–95.

Attic, with early lettering, including ΒΡϟΦ (to judge from the *CIG* copy: Pittakys' copy uses standard letter forms); perhaps *stoichedon* 47.

IG i[1] 9 (A. Kirchhoff, not retaining the fifth-century Attic orthography); *SIG*[3] 41; *IG* i[2] 10; *ATL* ii D 10; *SdA* 134; M&L 40; *IK Erythrai und Klazomenai* 4; IG i[3] 14; Malouchou (cf. above)*. Trans. Fornara 71 (two reconstructions); Osborne, *The Athenian Empire*[4], 216A (a different translation in earlier editions); Dillon & Garland[3] 12. 30. See also Highby, *The Erythrae Decree*; *ATL* iii. 252–7; Meiggs, *The Athenian Empire*, 112–18, 421–2; K.-W. Welwei, *Historia* xxxv 1986, 179–81; A. Moroo, in *Ἀθηναίων ἐπίσκοπος . . . H. B. Mattingly*, 97–119.

identifications so none can be certain: there was a Leon active in 421 (Thuc. v. 19. ii, 24. i: *LGPN* 4), who may be identical with the Leon active in and after 412 (Thuc. VIII. 23. i, etc.: *LGPN* 5); but there was a Leon who proposed the treaty with Hermione which may belong either *c.*450 or *c.*425 (*IG* i³ 31. 6: *LGPN* 3), and Λ[έον] is restored as secretary to the *hellenotamiai* in 453/2 (*IG* i³ 260. 1: *LGPN* 2). Jameson seems to have regarded the short dative as decisive, but we do not, and we think an early date provides a better context.

Wade-Gery argued that the language of ll. 9–10 and especially ll. 18–19 points to a personal jurisdiction exercised by the polemarch, that the personal jurisdiction of the archons was ended by Ephialtes in 462/1, and that the decree must be earlier than that (cf. Hignett, *A History of the Athenian Constitution to the End of the Fifth Century BC*, 397, not linking the change with Ephialtes but claiming that it cannot be much later—with which we agree). On the other hand, (*a*) the decree has a standard fifth-century prescript (cf. Introduction, pp. xxi–xxii), of which there is no certain instance before the 450s (cf. Hignett; and Rhodes has argued that the tribal contingents in the council did not function as prytanies before 462/1: *Boule*, 17–19); (*b*) it is not improbable that language reflecting personal jurisdiction should have continued for some time after personal jurisdiction was abolished; (*c*) it is possible to restore ll. 18–19 with a middle or passive form which would not imply personal jurisdiction (see *apparatus*). Our preference is therefore for a date in the 450s.

[ἔδοχσεν τε͂ι βολε͂ι καὶ το͂ι δέμοι. – – – – – ἐπρυτάνε̣υε· – – – – –]
[. . . .] ἐπεστάτε· Λ[. . .] Γ [– ἐγραμμάτευε· – – – – εἶπε· Ἐρ]-
[υθραί]ος ἀπάγε̣ν σ[ῖ]το[ν ἐ]ς Παναθέναια τὰ με̣γάλ̣α̣ ἄ̣[χσιον μὲ ὀλέ]-
[ζον]ος ἒ τριο͂ν μνο͂ν καὶ νέ̣με̣[ν] Ἐρυθραίον [τ]ο[ῖ]ς παρο͂σι|[. . . .]
[. . τ]ὸ{ι}ς hιε̣ροπο[ι]ὸς ΑΠΗΔΙΝΟΝΜΙΘΑΝΟΙ· ἐ̣ὰν δὲ̣ ἀπ̣αγ̣ . . . [. . . .]
[. . .]ν ἄχσια[.] ἒ ΤΙΠΟΣΜΝΕΟΚΑΙΑΤΑΣΕ . . ΕΝΗΑΠΡΙΣΘΑΙΒΙ [— c.4 —]
[. . .]ΣΗΒΛΚΕΑΤΜΟΝΗΟ . ΟΥΧΙΟΨΟΝΟΣΣΤΙΝΑΧΑΝΡΛΧ[— c.9 —]
[. . .]ΡΕΟΝΟΣ . ΟΑΣ[. . . .]λον το͂ι̣ β̣ολομένοι Ἐρυθραίον. . . [. . . .]
[. κ]υάμον βολὲ̣ν ΟΝΑΚ εἴ̣κοσ̣ι καὶ ḥεκατὸν ἄνδ̣ρας· τὸν δὲ κ̣[υαμ]-
[ε]υθ̣έντ̣α ΘΕ . ΘΕ . Θ̣Ν . ἐν τ̣ε͂ι [β]ολε͂ι καὶ ΕΝΟΣΕΟΟΝ ἒ̃ναι βολε[ύε]-
[ν μ]ὲ̣ ὄλεζ̣ον ἒ τρ̣ιάκοντα ἔ̣τ̣ε̣ γ̣εγονότα· δίοχ̣σιν δ’ ἒ̃ναι [το͂ . . .]
ΟΣΕΙΕΧΟΕΝΟΣ. βολεύεν δὲ μὲ ἐντὸ̣ς τεττάρον ἐ{ι}το͂ν [δίς. ἀπο]-
κυαμεῦσα̣[ι δ]ὲ καὶ καταστ̣ε͂σαι τ̣ὲ̣ν μὲν νῦ̣ν̣ βολὲν τός τ̣’ [ἐπισκ]-
ό̣π̣ος καὶ [τὸν] φρ[ό]ρ̣αρχον, τὸ δὲ λοιπὸν τὲ̣ν βολὲν καὶ τὸν [φρόρ]-
αρχον, μὲ̣ ὄλεζον ἒ τ̣ρ̣ιάκ̣οντα ἐ̣μ̣έ̣ρας π̣ρ̣[ὶ]ν ἐ̣χσιέναι [τὲν βολ]-
έν· ὀμνύναι [δὲ? Δ]ία κα[ὶ] Ἀπόλλο καὶ Δέμε[τρα] ἐ̣παρομ̣έ̣νο[ς ἐχσό]-
λ̣ειαν ἐφ[ιορκο͂ντι τε κ]αὶ παι[σ]ὶν ΕΧΣΟ[.]Ο[. .]ΝΔΕΠΟΝΟΝΟ[— 4–5 —]
[. .]ΚΑΙΑ[.]ΙΕΚΟΝ[— 2–3 —]ΕΙΣΟΝΝΟΕΓΟΝ δὲ βολὲν ΝΒΟL[.]Τ̣ΟΝΕΑΤΑ[— 1–2 —]
[.]ΟΝ|ΑΚΑΙΝΕΓΚΟΝ δὲ μὲ ἒ̃ναι ζ̣εμιο͂σαι [. .]ΛΕ[.]ΣΑΝΑΤ[— c.7 —]
ΟΑΝΕΟΔΕΜΟΕΟΝΝΣΟΕΝΟΝ δε͂μον κατακαίεν μὲ ὄλεζον·[— c.6 —]
ὀμν[ύ]να[ι δ]ὲ [τά]δε [τὲν] β̣ολέν· β̣ολεύσο hος ἂν [δύ]νομ̣α̣ι̣ ἄρ̣ι̣στ[α .]
[.]ΔΕΚΑ[. .]ΤΑ Ἐρυθραίον το͂ι πλέθει καὶ Ἀθεναίον καὶ το͂ν [χσυ]-
νμά[χ]ον· [κ]αὶ οὐκ [ἀποσ]τέσομαι Ἀθεναίον το͂ π[λ]έθος οὐδὲ [το͂ν]
χσυνμάχον το͂ν Ἀθεναίον οὔτ’ αὐτὸς ἐγὸ οὔτ’ ἄλ̣λ̣οι π̣ε[ί]σομ̣[αι]
ἀφ̣ι̣σ̣[τα]μ̣ένο̣[ι] οὔτ’ αὐτὸς ἐγὸ οὔτ’ ἄλλον [.]ΕΙ[— c.10 — οὐδὲ]

We follow Malouchou on the beginnings and ends of lines, and in placing dots under letters misread by Fauvel and using square brackets where letters have to be restored; she supplies a much fuller *apparatus criticus*. **C** denotes the *CIG* copy, **P** Pittakys' copy, **F** Fauvel's copy in Paris (ll. 2–4, 6 only).

2 Highby 7–11, H. B. Mattingly, *AJP* cv 1984, 345–6 (cf. *SEG* xxxiv 4): Λ[. . .] Γ **C**, **F**, Λ[– –] **P**, Λ[υσι]κ̣[ράτες ἔ̃ρχε· γνόμε το͂ν χσυγγραφέον] *ATL* (cf. **141**). 4 νέ̣με̣[ν] Boeckh: νομον **C**, νομο . **P**, **F**. 6 ἄχσι[ον] ἒ τρ̣ιο͂[ν] μν[ο͂]νκατ̣ὰ τὰ εἰ[ρη]μένα πρί<α>σθα̣ι σ̣ῖ[το|ν] Kirchhoff. 8–9 ἀπ[ὸ το͂ν | κ]υάμον Malouchou: ἀπ[ὸ | κ]υάμον Kirchhoff. 9 ΟΝΑΚ: hένα Boeckh, ἒ̃ναι Kirchhoff, preferred Malouchou. 10 ΘΕ . ΘΕ . Θ̣Ν **P**: ΘΕ . ΘΕ . ΟΝ **C**, ΘΕ . ΘΕ[σ]θ̣α̣ι̣ Malouchou, δο[κι]μά[ζ]ειν Kirchhoff, ἐ̣λ̣[έ]γχ̣ε̣ν *ATL*. 11–12 [το͂ μὲ | δ]οκ̣ι̣μ̣α̣σ̣θ̣έν[τ]ος Malouchou ([το͂ ἀπο|δ]οκ̣ι̣μ̣α̣σ̣θ̣έν[τ]ος Rhodes, but one letter too many), syntactically preferable to [κατὰ τ]ο͂ν ἐλε[γ]χο[μ]ένον Kirchhoff, [κατὰ τ]ο͂[ν] ἐλ̣εχθ̣έν[τ]ο[ν] *ATL*. 12–13 [δίς Malouchou, post *ATL*, ἀπο]|κυαμεῦσα̣[ι] Malouchou after Kirchhoff. 13 τ̣ὲ̣ν μὲν νῦ̣ν̣ Malouchou after *ATL*: ΛΙΝΜΕΝΝΟΣ **C**, ΛΙΜΕΝΝΟΣ **P**. 13–14 ἐ[πισκ]-ό̣π̣ος Kirchhoff: – – ΘΟΟΣ, restoration doubted by D. M. Lewis (*IG* i^{3}). 17 ἐ̣φ[ιορκο͂ντι τε κ]αὶ Malouchou: ἐ̣φ[ιορκο͂σι κ]αὶ *ATL*. 17–18 ἐχσο[ρ]κ̣[ο͂]ν δὲ τ̣ὸν φρ̣ό[ραρ|χο]ν? κατὰ [h]ιερ̣ο͂ν [τελ]εί{σ}ον Malouchou ([h]ιερ̣ο͂ν Dittenberger *ap.* *SIG*^{3}; [τελ]εί{σ}ον not impossible Lewis in *IG* i^{3}): ἐχσό[λ]-ε̣[ια]ν. [τὸ]ν δὲ ḥό[ρ̣]κ̣ον ὀ[μ|νύνα]ι̣ κατ̣ὰ [h]ιερ̣ο͂ν κα̣ιο̣μ̣ένο̣ν̣ *ATL* after Kirchhoff. 18–19 μ̣ὲ̣ ὄ̣λ̣[ε]ζον κ̣ατα[καί|ε̣ν ἒ β]ο͂ν τὰ ḥι̣ερ̣ε͂α̣· ἐὰν δὲ μέ, *ATL*, μ̣ὲ̣ ὄ̣λ̣[ε]ζον κ̣ατα[κα|ί]ε̣ν Malouchou. 20 [ι, καὶ h]ό[τ]αν ḥο δε͂μος ὀμ̣νύ̣ε̣ι̣ τ̣ὸν δε͂μον *ATL*, highly improbable Malouchou. 21–2 ἄ[ρ]ιστ[α καὶ] δικα[ιότα]τα Kirchhoff. 25 ἀφ̣ι̣σ̣[τα]μ̣ένο̣[ι] Malouchou: [οὔ]δ’ αὐτομολέ[σο] Kirchhoff. 25 οὔτ’ ἄλλον [π]εί[σο οὐδὲ hένα A. P. Matthaiou *ap.* Malouchou.

Resolved by the council and the people. —— was the prytany; —— was the chairman; —— was the secretary. —— proposed:

2 The Erythraeans shall bring grain (?) to the Great Panathenaea, to the value of not less than three minas, and shall distribute it to those of the Erythraeans who are present – – – *hieropoioi* – – – If they bring – – –

8 – – – whoever of the Erythraeans wishes. There shall be a council appointed by lot of a hundred and twenty men; the (man appointed shall be examined?) in the council, and – – – shall be a councillor or a man under thirty years old; there shall be prosecution of one who has not undergone examination. No one shall be a councillor twice within four years. The council now shall be allotted and installed by the *episkopoi* (?) and the garrison commander, and in future by the council and the garrison commander, not less than thirty days before the council's term of office ends.

16 They shall swear by Zeus and Apollo and Demeter, invoking ruin on one who breaks the oath and his children; the oath shall be administered by (the garrison commander over full-grown victims?). – – – the council (shall sacrifice as victims not less than a cow, or if not it shall?) be possible to punish – – – (And when the people swear?), the people shall burn no less.

21 The council shall swear as follows: 'I shall be a councillor as best and most justly I can for the mass of the Erythraeans and of the Athenians and of the allies; and I shall not defect from the mass of the Athenians or of the allies of the Athenians myself, nor shall I be persuaded by another who defects, or persuade any single other (?);

τôν φ[υγά]δον [κατ]αδέχσομαι οὐδ[ὲ] hένα ΟΥΤΟΠΟΙΚΑΙΝΑ[—5—]
ΙΠΕΙΣ[.]Θ[.]Α[—1–2— τôν ἐς] Μέδος φευ̣γό[ντο]ν ἄνευ τε̣̂[ς] βολ̣ε̣̂ς τ̣[ε̂ς Ἀθε]-
ναίον καὶ τô δέ̣μο· [ο]ὐδὲ τôν μενόντον ἐχσελô [ἄ]νε̣υ̣ τε̣̂ς βο̣[λε̂ς]
τ̣ε̂ς Ἀθεναίον καὶ τ̣[ô] δέ̣μο. ἐὰν δέ τις ἀποκτέ̣νει̣ [—10—]
ΕΟΣ hέτερον ΕΡΤΟΙ[—c.4—]ΟΝ, τεθ[ν]άτο ἐὰν [γν]οσθε̂ι· ἐ̣[ὰ]ν Δ[—6—]
[.] γ̣ν̣οσθε̂ι̣, φευγέτο ḥάπ̣ασα̣ν̣ τὲν̣ Ἀθεναίον χσυνμαχίδ̣[α, καὶ τ]-
ὰ χρέματα δεμόσ[ια ἔσ]τ̣ο Ἐρυθραίον. ἐὰν δέ̣ τ̣ις [.]ΒΟ[—8—]
ΟΣ[..] τὸς τυράννος ΤΕΜΝΑΝ[—1–2—]ΟΣ ἘρυθραΐΝ καὶ [αὐτ]ὸς [—c.6—]
ΧΑΠΙ τεθνάτο [κ]α̣[ὶ] π̣α̣ῖδες ḥοι ἐχς ἐ̣κ̣ένο̣ ΕΓ. ΝΕΟ[—10—]
ΕΙΟΘΕΜΙΛΕΘ[.]ΕΧΟΣ[—c.5—]παῖδες [h]οι ἐχς [ἐ]κέν[ο —c.10—]
Ἐρυθραίο[.] καὶ [...]ν Ἀθεναίον ΑΠΟΣΑΝΟΝ, τὰ δὲ χρέ̣ματα [αὐ]τô Τ?
traces of ten further lines, including
42 [—6—]ΝΑΜΕΝΕΙ[.]ΤΟΜ[.]ΟΡ[.]ΟΝ τ̣οχσό̣τ̣ας ΔΕΚΑΤΑ[.]ΟΙ[..]ΟΟΣΕΝ
45 [....]βολε[....]ΚΑΝΑ[—1–2—]ΟΑΣΙΕΡΑ ἐκ̣ τε̣̂ς φυλε̂ς hεκάστες Χ[—3–4—]

26–7 οὔτ' ἄ̣λ̣[λ]ον κατ̣α̣δ̣[έχεσθα]ι πείσο[μ]α[ι τôν ἐς] Μέδος φευ̣γό[ντο]ν Malouchou in commentary, ἄλλον ἐ[άσω οὐδὲ hένα] Boeckh, ἄλλο[ι π]εί]σομαι Kirchhoff. 29–30 – –]έως i.e. end of adverb Kirchhoff, [Ἐρυθραῖ]ος Wilamowitz *ap.* *IG* i². hέτερον Ἐρ[υθραῖ]ον Dittenberger *ap.* *SIG*³, but hέτερον curious with Ἐρυθραῖον Malouchou. 32–3 ἐὰν δέ τις [.]ΒΟ[—8—]ΟΣ[..] τὸς τυράννος τεχνά[ζει] ἐ̣ν̣ Ἐρυθραῖς or ἐ̣ς Ἐρυθρὰ{ς} Malouchou in commentary, ἐὰν δέ τις [ἁ]λῶ[ι προ|δι]δὸς το[ῖ]ς τυράννοις τὴμ πόλιν [τ]ôν Ἐρυθραί[ο]ν Kirchhoff, [τ]ὲν Ἐρυθραί[ο]ν Kirchner (*SIG*³), ΤΟΣ ΤΥΡΑΝΝΟΣ **P**, ΤΟΣ ΤΥΡΑΝΝΟΙΣ **C**.

In this text based on transcriptions of a lost original there are uncertainties due both to Fauvel's problems in reading the stone and to subsequent scholars' problems in making sense of what Fauvel read. The stone which bore our text is still lost, but the transcripts rediscovered by Malouchou take us nearer to the original than we have been for a long time.

Erythrae was on the mainland of Asia Minor opposite the island of Chios; it was an Ionian city in the narrow sense of that term (whereas in a broader sense the term could be applied to all the Asiatic Greeks), and is likely to have joined Athens' Delian League at an early stage. In addition to our text there exist from about the same date (i) four fragments from Athens, which are possibly all from the same *stele* and possibly from the same *stele* as this text (but they have tailless P: *IG* i³ 15; Moroo dissociates fr. *b* from the others, but thinks *IG* i³ 16 might belong with the other fragments), of which *a* certainly mentions Erythrae, *episkopoi* and a garrison commander, and *d* can be restored with references to Erythrae and a garrison commander, and an oath similar to the one in our text; (ii) a *stele* from Erythrae containing constitutional laws (**122**).

This decree begins with a requirement to send offerings to the Great Panathenaea in Athens: σ[ῖ]το[ν in l. 3 is problematic, since 3 minas' worth of grain would imply an improbably large number of Erythraeans attending the festival (M. H. Jameson, *AJP* xciii 1972, 477–8, reviewing M&L), but it is remarkable that the decree envisages attendance by Erythraeans and distribution of the offering among them, perhaps a sign that the view of Ionian Erythrae as a colony of Athens (Harp. ε 141 Keaney

nor shall I take back any single one of the exiles, nor shall I be persuaded to take back another, of those who have fled to the Medes, without the permission of the council and people of the Athenians; nor shall I exile any of those who remain, without the permission of the council and people of the Athenians.'

29 If any of the Erythraeans (?) kills another Erythraean, he shall be put to death if he is condemned; if – – – is condemned he shall be exiled from the whole alliance of the Athenians, and his property shall become public property of the Erythraeans.

32 If any one contrives – – – the tyrants in Erythrae, he – – – shall be put to death – – – sons born from him – – – the sons born from him – – – of the Erythraeans and – – – Athenians – – – the property – – –

42 – – –archers – – –

45 – – – from each tribe – – –

Ἐρυθραῖοι = Hellanicus *FGrH* 323a F 11) was taken seriously. Later Athens' colony at Brea was to send a cow and a panoply to the Great Panathenaea and a phallus to the Dionysia (**142**. 15–17); the decree demanding firstfruits for Eleusis from League members and inviting them from others we date *c*.435 or earlier (**141**); a requirement of a cow and a panoply at the Panathenaea from all League members makes its first appearance in Thudippus' assessment decree of 425/4 and is echoed in Cleinias' tribute decree of 425/4 or soon after (**153**. 55–7, **154**. 41–3).

Next Athens establishes for Erythrae a council resembling but not identical with the democratic council of Athens (in Athens the council was of five hundred, the minimum age was 30 as here, and the limit was two years in a man's life: *Ath. Pol.* 43. ii, 62. iii, Xen. *Mem.* I. ii. 35). (P. Liddel, *BICS* liii. 1 2010, 116–21, considers the possible impact of this document on Erythrae, notes that δίοχσιν ('prosecution': 11) is not a standard term in Athenian judicial procedure, and wonders whether the proposer was using language with which the Erythraeans would be familiar.) An Athenian garrison commander is to be involved both at first and subsequently, and at first also perhaps Athenian *episkopoi*, ad hoc commissioners sent to implement the new regime (Lewis in *IG* doubted [ἐπισκ|όπ]ος in ll. 13–14, but the word appears in *IG* i^3 15. 19, and is acceptably restored later in **155**. 7). The oath of allegiance is probably to be sworn annually by the council. The reference restored by *ATL* in l. 20 to an oath sworn by the people, perhaps on a single occasion, will be awkward if that is our text's only reference to an oath sworn by the people; fr. *d* of *IG* i^3 15 contains an oath which is restored but not unavoidably in *IG* as to be sworn by the people, and which includes an undertaking to obey Athens, stronger than anything in our text ([τε̂ι δὲ γνό|μ]ει τε̂[ι] Ἀθ[ε]ναίον πείσ[ομαι]: ll. 41–2, cf. πείσομαι τôι δέμοι τôι Ἀθ|εναίον in **131**. 31–2). The oath in our text is milder than some later oaths (see **131**, **139**), with allegiance to Athens and to the allies; *plethos*, 'mass', appears only here and (restored) in **139**. *c* . 6 and *IG* i³ 15. 40, and is probably used in order to emphasise the democratic nature of Athens and of the regime imposed on Erythrae (but contrast Welwei, who stresses that not all of the allies will have been democratic). The undertaking not to receive back without permission from Athens those who have fled to the Medes, i.e. to the Persians,[1] suggests that our text represents intervention by Athens when Erythrae had been recovered after defecting with Persian support, and the 'tyrants' of l. 33 are probably the leaders of that anti-Athenian regime.

Trials for homicide are not transferred to Athenian courts, as was to happen later (cf. **131**. 71–6), but Athens demands the death penalty and (presumably for those who escape before the sentence is passed) exile from the whole of what is here called the alliance of the Athenians.

[1] This need not refer to suppliants, as suggested by F. S. Naiden, *ZPE* clxxxviii 2014, 136–8.

122

Regulations from Erythrae, *c.* late 450s

Part of a trachyte *stele* from Erythrae, inscribed on three faces (*B* to the right of the broad face *A*, and *C* to the left), now in the museum at Chios. Phot. (*A*) *JŒAI* xiv 1911, Beiblatt 50; (*B* + *C*) *IK Erythrai und Klazomenai*, i, Tafel I; (all) Archontidou *et al.*, *Ἀρχαιολογικὸ Μουσεῖο Χίου*, 66 (reported by *SEG* xlix 1499).

Eastern Ionic, with *sampi* in *A*. 17. *Stoichedon*, *A* 16, *B* 6 but 5 letters ll. 20–2, *C* 6 but 5 letters ll. 17–18.

SGDI iv pp. 879–82 (Die neuen Inschriften 60); *DGE* 701; Hill rev. Meiggs & Andrewes, *Sources for Greek History between the Persian and Peloponnesian Wars*, B 116; *IK Erythrai und Klazomenai* 2*; *Nomima* i 106. Trans. Arnaoutoglou 69; Osborne, *The Athenian Empire*⁴, 217 (a different translation in earlier editions). See also A. Wilhelm, *JŒAI* xii 1909, 126–41 = his *Abhandlungen und Beiträge*, i. 348–63; *LSAG* 338, 344 no. 52; D. M. Lewis, in *Πρακτικά τού Η′ Διεθνούς Συνεδρίου . . . Ἐπιγραφικῆς*, i. 59 = his *Selected Papers in Greek and Near Eastern History*, 56–7.

When did this intervention occur? The imposition of a democratic constitution we should expect to be later than Ephialtes' reform in Athens in 462/1; if the copies can be trusted, the lettering was so old-fashioned as still to make a date *c.*450 more likely than a date *c.*425. This is accepted by Mattingly (*Epigraphica* xxxvi 1974, 33–56 at 39 n. 23 = his *AER* 361–85 at 367 n. 23); but Moroo argues that **139**, for Samos, is the earliest inscribed settlement with a recovered ally and dates this text 435/4 (shortly before the Great Panathenaea of 434). *ATL*'s restoration of l. 2 pointing to 453/2, Λ[υσι]κ̣[ράτες ἐ͂ρχε· γνόμε τôν χσυγγραφέον], is not acceptable, since no other decree with an archon's name in its prescript now seems datable this early, and no other decree attributed not to an individual proposer but to a board of *syngrapheis* now seems datable this early (*IG* i^3 21, with archon restored and *syngrapheis* preserved, is to be dated 426/5); there is no reason not to restore normal fifth-century formulae (for which see Introduction, pp. xxi–xxii). Nevertheless, the late 450s, after the failure *c.*454 of Athens' campaign in Egypt (Thuc. i. 109–10), provide a credible context for a revolt with Persian backing, and this can be supported from the tribute record: Erythrae is absent from the lists of 454/3 and 453/2, while its neighbour Butheia is present (*IG* i^3 259. v. 19, 260. x. 5), it is not certain what should be restored in the next two lists, but in 450/49 Erythrae and its neighbours are listed together, and Erythrae makes a substantial later payment (263. ii. 13–17, v. 3). Our text and *IG* i^3 15 may be two products of the same episode, or products of two episodes about this time; for **122** see below.

A

[— 12 —] μηδ[ὲ]
κύαμ[ον — 6 —] μηδὲ
τιμάς· ἢ̣ν [δ'] ἁμαρτάνη-
ι, ὀφελέτω δέκα στατ-
ῆρας· δίωξιν δ' ἒναι τ-
ῶι βολομένωι, καὶ τῶ-
ι καταλαβόντι τὥμι-
συ, τὸ δ' ἥμισυ τῆς πόλ-
εως. ἢν δ' ἐκχωρῆι ὁ δι-
ώξας, ὀφελέτω ὅπερ ο-
ἶ νικῶντι γίνεται, κ-
αὶ τούτο δίωξιν ἒνα-
ι κατὰ ταὐτά. δικάζε-
ν δὲ ἀπὸ τῶν φυλέων ἄ-
νδρας ἐννέα ἀπ' ἑκάσ-
της, οἶσίν ἐστιν μὴ ἐ-
λάΤονος ἄξια ἢ τριή-
κοντα στατήρων, ὀμό-
σαντας τὸν αὐτὸν ὅρ-
κον τῆι βολῆι δικᾶν
κατὰ νόμος καὶ ψηφί-
σματα. πληρôν δὲ τ[ὸ δ]-
ικαστήριον μὴ ẹλ̣ά̣[σ]-
σονας ἢ ἑξήκο[ντ]α̣ κ̣α̣-
ὶ ἕνα· δικάζεν [δὲ π]λη-
σίον τιθέντα̣ κ̣ατὰ τ-
ọν νόμον. ἐσάγεν δὲ τ-
[ὰ]ς δίκας καὶ συγγρ[ά]-
[φεν] πρυτάνεας, καὶ [γ]-
[ράφε]σθαι τὸν ὀφ[έλο]-
[ντα· ἢ]ν̣ δὲ μή, αὐτ[ὸς ὀφ]-
[έλεν. ἐ]γδικάζ[εσθαι]
[— 5 —]ην[— 9 —]

B

[. . . . ἀν]-
[αγράψα]-
[ι δὲ τόδ]-
[ε τὸ] ψήφ-
ι̣σμα ἐ[σ]-
τ̣ήληι [λ]-
ι̣θίνηι
καὶ ἐς [τ]-
ὸγ κύκλ-
ον στῆσ-
αι τô Ζη-
νὸς τὠγ-
οραίο τ-
ὴν δευτ-
έρην πρ-
υτανη[ί]-
ην. δίωξ-
ιν δ' ἒνα-
ι, ὅτις α-
ụτὸς ζώ̣-
ει μὴ κα-
τὰ νόμο-
ν τραφ-
ὲς ἢ ἐξ-
ελευθ-
έρο παῖ-
ς ἢ ξένο.
ὅτεο δὲ
π̣ατὴ[ρ] ἢ̣
παλαιό-
τερον τ̣-
ιμὰς ἴσ-
χεν ἢ κύ-
α̣μον ἐδ-
[έ]ξατο [.]
[. .]π̣ερ[.]
[. . .]λ̣[. .]

C

[. ἐπι]οπ-
[τεύ]εν. ἤ-
ν δ' ἀπὸ ν-
όθο ἦι, ἐ-
πιοπτε-
υέτω κα-
ὶ ὑποζυ-
γὴν ἒνα-
ι. τῶν δ' ἀ-
ληθῶν ὅ-
ς ἂμ μὴ ἔ-
λθηι ἐπ̣-
[α]γγελά-
ντων τῶ-
μ πρυτά-
νεων, ὀφ-
ελέτω
ἡμιστ-
άτηρον
(ἔστω δὲ
τῶμ πρυ-
τάνεων),
ἤν τι μὴ
τῶν ἀνα-
γκαίων
ἀπέρ[γη]-
ι. *vacat*
vacat

B. 33 τ W. G. Forrest *ap*. *IK*. *B*. 34 *vacat?* Forrest.

A

– – – neither allotment – – – nor offices.

3 If he offends, he shall owe ten staters: prosecution shall be open to whoever wishes, and if he obtains a conviction he shall receive half and half shall go to the city. But if the prosecutor abandons the case he shall owe what goes to a successful prosecutor, and prosecution of him shall be on the same basis. Judgment shall be given by nine men from each of the tribes, who have property worth not less than thirty staters, swearing the same oath as the council, to judge in accordance with the laws and decrees.

22 The court shall be convened by not fewer than sixty-one men: they shall judge having placed the law nearby, in accordance with the law. The *prytaneis* shall introduce the cases and draw up the indictment, and record those who owe penalties; if they do not, they themselves shall owe a penalty. The trial shall be completed – – –

B

– – – Write up this decree on a stone *stele* and place it in the circle of Zeus Agoraios during the second prytany. There may be prosecution by any one who himself has not been brought up in accordance with the law, or is the son of a freedman or foreigner.

25 Any one whose father either previously held office or received by lot – – –

C

– – – inspect. But if he is born from a bastard he shall be inspected and is to be enslaved. If any of the true (Erythraeans) does not come when the *prytaneis* proclaim, he shall owe half a stater (and it shall go to the *prytaneis*), unless he was prevented by necessity.

These regulations are generally dated about the middle of the fifth century, but unless various questions are begged it is not clear whether they belong before or after the Athenian intervention of **121**. H. Engelmann & R. Merkelbach in *IK*, while inclining to make this the earlier text, see in the references to allotment as contrasted with (elected) offices (*A*. 1–3, *B*. 28–32) membership of the allotted council of 120 in **121**, and in the sixty-one men in *A*. 22–5 a majority of the members of that council (first suggested by Wilhelm). We do not know how much the constitution was changed by Athens' intervention, but it is possible that there was already a council of 120 and that Athens imposed appointment by lot and perhaps a restriction to one year's service in four. In general, Lewis doubted whether the Athenians would have bothered with the finer details of local practice, and did not think a date before **121** was epigraphically attractive.

We do not know what offences lay behind *A*, but if they incurred a fine of 10 staters (= 20 drachmas?) they were not very grave. Rewards to encourage prosecutors were widespread in cases in which there was a 'public' interest: for Athens cf. [Dem.] LIII *Nicostratus* 2, and for the award of half of the total sum, in cases brought by *phasis*, [Dem.] LVIII. *Theocrines* 13 (see more generally Osborne, *JHS* cxv 1985, 40–58 = his *Athens and Athenian Democracy*, 171–200[–4]). Erythrae possibly had three tribes, but Paus. VII. 5. xii does not guarantee that (Lewis), and Jones thought Erythrae might at this time have had the six Attic–Ionic tribes (*Public Organization in Ancient Greece*, 303–6; see also J. A. O. Larsen, *Representative Government in Greek and Roman History*, 196–7). By the third century the *prytaneis* served for four months (e.g. *SIG*[3] 442 = *IK Erythrai und Klazomenai* 29), but again we do not know if this was so in the fifth century (Lewis). Prosecution was to be by 'whoever wishes', as in *graphai* in Athens (*Ath. Pol.* 9. i). In contrast to Athens, juries were small, and jurors had to satisfy a (low) property qualification. The jurors' oath was to judge in accordance with the laws and decrees (*A*. 20–2): we cannot tell whether at this date Erythrae made a formal distinction between the two, but there is no comparable mention of laws and decrees

---

123

Political expulsions from Miletus, *c.*450–440

A marble base on which a now-lost *stele* stood; found in the North Market at Miletus, now in the Antikensammlung, Staatliche Museen zu Berlin—Preußischer Kulturbesitz. Phot. *Milet* I. vi, p. 101 Abb. 98; *Milet* VI. i, Taf. 15. 1.

Ionic lettering. *Stoichedon*, with room for 44 letters on the face, but apparently more (on the right-hand side: overflow indicated by | below) or fewer used so that each line ends with the end of a word or of the preposition in a compound verb.

in Athens until the period in the fourth century in which the two categories were formally distinguished, when Andoc. i. *Mysteries* 86 refers in 400 to men who were vulnerable under the laws or previous decrees, and the version of the dicastic oath included in Dem. xxiv. *Timocrates* 149(–51) is comparable to what we have here; the two categories do not appear in Athenian inscriptions until the hellenistic period (e.g. *IG* ii^2 1299. 54–5). Placing the text of the law near the court (Wilhelm, comparing Diod. Sic. i. 75. vi; and we can now compare the placing of Athens' law of 337/6 against the Areopagus on the Areopagus, R&O 79. 24–6), if that is what *A*. 27 means, symbolises the rule of law in a striking way.

In what survives of *B* Engelmann & Merkelbach seem right to see prosecution even by non-citizens (cf. the construction in *A*. 5–6) of the major offenders dealt with before the text which survives (against Wilhelm, who saw here a new provision for dealing with men who wrongly claimed citizenship); and they interpret 'any one who himself has not been brought up in accordance with the law' as a man who had not been through an ephebic system for young citizens (cf. for Athens R&O 88. 1–20 with commentary), but it would be surprising to find such a system and requirement in Erythrae as early as this.

In *C* Engelmann & Merkelbach take 'inspect' to be a euphemism meaning 'arrest' after an unsatisfactory inspection (for the enslavement of men rejected cf. *Ath. Pol.* 42. i, but if ὑποζυγή here does denote slavery this will be a unique metaphorical use of a concept otherwise applied to beasts of burden), and assume that the *prytaneis*' proclamation would be issued in a major emergency.

Ionic features include ἤν for ἐάν e.g. in *A*. 3, ὀφέλω for ὀφείλω e.g. in *A*. 4, βολομένωι for βουλομένωι in *A*. 6 and βολῆι for βουλῆι in *A*. 20, ἦναι for εἶναι e.g. in *A*. 12–13 and infinitives in -εν e.g. in *A*. 13–14, γίνεται for γίγνεται in *A*. 11, uncontracted φυλέων in *A*. 14, masculine genitive singular in -ο e.g. in *B*. 8 and ὅτεο in *B*. 25, ἐπιοπτεύειν in *C*. 1–6. The inscription has ἐλάΤονος with *sampi* in *A*. 16–17 but ἐλάσσονας in *A*. 23–4.

SIG^3 58; *Milet* i. vi 187; M&L 43.* Trans. Fornara 66. *Milet* vi. i pp. 5–9 reproduces i. vi 187; p. 197 contains P. Herrmann's Nachtrag. See also (more recent studies, through which earlier ones can be found) M. Piérart, *AC* xxxvii 1969, 365–88; H.-J. Gehrke, *Historia* xxix 1980, 17–31; N. Robertson, *Phoenix* xli 1987, 356–98, esp. 378–84; Gorman, *Miletos: The Ornament of Ionia*, 215–36.

[—15—]σ[—5— τ]ο[. Ν]υμφαρήτο καὶ Ἄλκι[μον]
[καὶ Κ]ρεσφόντην [τὸ]<ς> Στρατώνακτος φεύγεν τὴν ἐπ᾽ αἵμ̣[ατ|ι]
[φυγὴν] καὶ αὐτὸς̣ [κα]ὶ ἐκγόνος, καὶ ὃς ἄν τινα τούτωγ κατ[α]-
[κτείνε]ι, ἑκατὸν [στ]ατῆρας αὐτῶι γενέσθαι ἀπὸ τῶν
[χρημά]τ̣ων τῶν Ν̣υμ[φαρή]το· τὸς δ̣᾽ ἐ̣πιμηνίος ἐπ᾽ ὧν ἂν ἔλθωσ|ιν̣
[οἱ κατα]κτείναντ̣ες ἀποδοῦναι τὸ ἀργύριον· ἢν δὲ μή, αὐτὸ|[ς]
[ὀφε]ί̣λεν. ἢν δὲ ἡ πόλι[ς ἐ]γκ̣ρ̣α̣τ<ὴ>ς γένηται, κατακ̣τε̂ναι
[αὐ]τὸς τὸς ἐπιμηνίος̣ [ἐ]π᾽ ὧν ἂν λαφθέωσιν· ἢν δὲ μὴ κατα-
[κτ]είνοσιν, ὀφείλεν ἕ[κ]α̣σ̣τον πεν̣τήκοντα στατῆρας·
τὸν δὲ ἐπιμήνιον, ἢν μὴ προθῆι, ἑκατὸν στατῆρας ὀφείλε[ν].
καὶ τὴν ἐσιôσαν ἐπιμηνίην αἰὶ ποιε̂ν κατὰ τὸ ψήφισμα·
ἢν δὲ μή, τὴν αὐτὴν θωιὴν ὀφείλεν. *vacat*
vacat

1 [τ]ὸ[ν] *or* [τ]ὸ[ς]. 2 the stone has [τὸ]ν. 7 the stone has [ἐ]γκ̣ρ̣α̣τὲς.

In this text, specified sons of Nympharetus and of Stratonax are exiled for 'blood guilt' (for ἐπ᾽ αἵμ̣[ατι] cf. Dem. XXI. *Midias* 105); but the publicity and relentless enforcement, and the extension of the exile to their descendants, suggest that this is the result of a political disturbance, not simply a family feud. What is more, there are reasons to believe that the sanctions against these men were part of a more extensive imposition of similar sanctions. Our text is inscribed on a base on which stood a *stele*, and there is not room on the base before the preserved text starts for a prescript; this suggests that our text began on the lower part of an existing *stele*, but if this is so then the *stele* must have been inscribed with related matters. The most likely story is that similar sanctions had been passed on an earlier occasion in relation to other individuals and inscribed upon the *stele*; when the sanctions were passed against these men the decision was taken to add them to the *stele*. But since there was not enough room on the *stele* itself the inscription was continued on to the base, which alone has survived. For series of documents generated by a political settlement cf. the inscription from Dicaea, *c.*364/3, published by E. Voutiras, *CRAI* clii 2008, 781–92 (*SEG* lvii 576).

We do not know enough about Milesian history to be certain about the context. Political violence and murder, which is the likely background to these sanctions, are not the exclusive preserve of either oligarchy or democracy, but the small number of men who seem to be exiled here, and the way in which a price is put on their heads, suggest *stasis* within the oligarchy rather than the expulsion of a whole class, as perhaps does the expectation that the bounties can be paid from one man's property. However, L. Rubinstein reminds us of the alternative possibility that the Milesians decided to proscribe only a few leading men when a larger number had been involved on their side (cf. the settlement in Athens in 403, Xen. *Hell.* II. iv. 38, Andoc. I. *Mysteries* 90, *Ath. Pol.* 39. vi; and a fourth-century *dossier* of 306–301 from

– – – son/s of Nympharetus, and Alcimus and Cresphontes the sons of Stratonax, shall be blood-guilt exiles, themselves and their descendants, and if any one kills any of these he shall receive a hundred staters from the property of Nympharetus. The *epimenioi* in whose term of office the killers come forward shall pay the money; if they do not, they shall owe it themselves.

7 If the city gets the exiles in its power, they shall be executed by the *epimenioi* in whose term of office they are caught; if they do not execute them, each of them shall owe fifty staters; if an *epimenios* does not pay, he shall owe a hundred staters. The succeeding board of *epimenioi* shall always exact this in accordance with the decree; if it does not do so, it shall owe the same penalty.

Telos in which specified individuals are punished, *IG* XII. iv 132). Epigraphically the second quarter of the fifth century cannot be ruled out, but Herrmann judged the 440s more likely.

Not later than 434/3 Miletus had a constitution modelled on the Athenian (**143**), but that constitution was not in force in 447/6 when the law of the Molpoi was enacted (*Milet* I. iii 133 = SIG^3 57 = *LSAM* 50; date Rhodes, as above). According to the Old Oligarch, at some time Athens supported an oligarchy in Miletus, but that led to an uprising and a massacre of the *demos* ([Xen.] *Ath. Pol.* iii. 11). Miletus' record in the tribute lists of the Delian League is hard to interpret (for up-to-date summaries see Robertson, 392–3, Gorman, 223–30), but would allow for a revolt *c.*450 and/or in the mid-440s, though the Athenian regulations in *IG* i^3 21 should be dated not 450/49 but 426/5 (e.g. Rhodes, CQ^2 lviii 2008, 501, 503). Miletus was presumably pro-Athenian when Athens supported it against Samos in 440–439 (Thuc. I. 115. ii–117).

G. Glotz (*CRAI* 1906, 511–29), identifying Alcimus and Cresphontes as Neleid names, compared Nic. Dam. *FGrH* 90 F 53 and suggested that the lost *stele* marked an expulsion of Neleids in the sixth century and our text another expulsion of Neleids *c.*450. That was tenuous; but J. P. Barron took it as a basis for arguing that Neleids were still in power in the mid-440s and that this expulsion is subsequent to that (*JHS* lxxxii 1962, 1–6).

Our interpretation of ll. 10–12 is based on L. Rubinstein, *Symposion* 2011 (*AGR* xxiii 2012), 335–42 with 337 n. 21, and we thank her for discussion in advance of publication and for further discussion of this text. τὸν ... ἐπιμήνιον (10) means not the chairman of the *epimenioi* ('monthly' officials: Barron suggested that this was a new title for *prytaneis* introduced under a new regime) but any *epimenios* who fails to pay the penalty stipulated in 9; προθῆι (10) means not 'bring forward for debate' in the council or assembly (most edd.), or 'bring to sentencing or punishment' (R. Koerner, *Klio* lxix 1987, 476–7), but 'pay' (cf. LSJ *s.v.*, I. 8) (doubling is a widespread penalty for unpaid dues); τὴν ἐσιôσαν ἐπιμηνίην (11) means not 'board after board' in general but specifically the board succeeding the one whose members have defaulted; ποιε̂ν (11) means not 'act' in general but 'exact' (LSJ *s.v.*, II. 2, is

---

124

Lead tablets from Camarina, *c*.450

Lead tablets from a deposit in the temple of Athena at Camarina. Phot. Cordano (below), pls. 1–10, Arena (below), pls. 35–7.

Sicilian Doric letters, close to those of archaic Gela.

SEG xli 778-95; *SEG* xlii 846; Cordano, *Le tessere pubbliche dal tempio di Atena a Camarina* (and *RAL* xliv 1991, 135–50, tav. 1–10);* Arena, *Iscrizioni greche arcaiche di Sicilia e Magna Grecia*, ii. 124–41 (with photographs of some of the texts, tav. 35–7). See also E. W. Robinson, in *Oikistes . . . A. J. Graham*, 67–78.

O&R	*SEG*	Cordano	Arena
124. *a*	xli 788	27	134
124. *b*	xlii 846	69	–
124. *c*	xlii 846	2	–
124. *d*	xli 784	17	130
124. *e*	xlii 846	109	–
124. *f*	xli 782	9a	128
124. *g*	xli 790	43	136
124. *h*	xlii 846	15	–
124. *i*	xli 779	1a	125
124. *j*	xlii 846	98	–
124. *k*	xlii 846	45	–
124. *l*	xli 785	23	131
124. *m*	xli 794	75	140
124. *n*	xlii 846	64	–
124. *o*	xlii 846	81	–

a	*recto:*	Νικόμαχος Σίμο hενδε|κάτα φράτρα πράτα τρια|κάς hεβ[δ]έμα hικάς
	verso:	traces of earlier use
b	*recto:*	Δίον Νεμοναίο | hενάτας φράτας
	reinscribed:	Δίον Μεμοναι̣ίο ἐν<ά>τας φ |άτ[ρ]ας τρ[ί]τας τριακάδος
	verso:	hενάτα φράτρα δέκα λίτραι.
c	*recto:*	[– – –]οσις Θράσυος
	verso:	hενάτα | [τ]ρίτα τριακάς

nearest; cf. πράσσω VI); and the decree referred to will be the one whose text we have.

Ionic Greek has no aspirate but does have *eta* and *omega*; this text uses ε for the εε which in standard Greek becomes ει, and ο for the οο which in standard Greek becomes ου (e.g. [τὸ]<ς> . . . φεύγεν, 2); notice also αἰὶ for ἀεὶ, 11.

---

a	*recto:*	Nicomachus son of Simos: 1 | 1th phratry, 1st *tria* | *kas*, 7th *hikas*
	verso:	*traces of earlier use*
b	*recto:*	Dion son of Nemonaeus | 9th phratry
	reinscribed:	Dion son of Memonaeus, 9th ph | ratry, 3rd *triakas*
	verso:	9th phratry, 10 *litrai.*
c	*recto:*	–osis son of Thrasys
	verso:	9th | 3rd *triakas*

d	*recto:*	Δαϊκράτες Λυκίσ|κο
	verso:	φράτρα πέμ|πτα̣
e	*recto:*	Παιδικὸς Θυ[- - -] | νεάτας φρά[τας]
	verso:	*vacat*
f	*recto:*	[h]ερακλείδας | [Κ]ρατίνō | [π]ένπτ̣ας
	verso:	[π]ένπτας
g	*recto:*	Πύρριχο[ς] | Νικοφάν[εος]
	verso:	∇ ὀγδόα
h	*recto:*	hενάτας | Ἀριστίον Δεινία | Τίμον Φ<ι>λίνο
	verso:	hενάτας *and illegible traces*
i	*recto:*	Αἰσχύλος : Ἀρίστιος
	verso:	τετάρτας ἐπὶ δέκα
j	*recto:*	Χρόμιος Γύγα
	verso:	τρίτας ἀπὸ νέτας
k	*recto:*	Θέον | Νίκιο̣[ς]
	verso:	τερτάτα{α} | ἀπὸ νέατας | τετάρτα | δεκάτ[α]
l	*recto:*	Σικανὸς | Ἀρχονίδα
	verso:	νέτας
m	*recto:*	Εὐαρχίδας Καλλ[ι]σ[θ]ένεος
	verso:	hυπάτα
n	*recto:*	Εὐκλε̂ς Ηερμαίο δεκάλιτ|ρον
	verso:	τετ[ά]ρτας ἐπὶ δέκα
o	*recto:*	[- - -]υς Εὐκλείδα | τέθνακε
	verso:	[τετ]άρ[τ]ας ἐπὶ δέκα

g recto 2 Νικοφάν[ος?] Arena. *k recto* 2 Νίκιο̣[ς]:*SEG*; Νίκιο̣[υ] Cordano. *m* On both sides traces of various uses; *recto* and *verso* were inscribed on different occasions; the final *sigma* of the patronymic is inscribed under the line.

This is a selection from the more than 150 lead tablets excavated under the temple of Apollo at Camarina on the south coast of Sicily in 1987. The tablets appear to have been stored, folded, in a wooden box, to judge by the bronze studs found with them. Inscribed with names, with patronymics on one side, and on the other an attribution to a phratry (sometimes spelled 'phatry') and occasionally to further civic subdivisions, they clearly constitute a set of public records. They can be dated to the middle of the fifth century by letter form, and so constitute the earliest cache of such public records. But what was their purpose? And what do they imply about the civic arrangements at Camarina?

We know a little about the history of Camarina in the fifth century, but relatively little about its civic structure. Thucydides (VI. 5. iii) records that Camarina had been founded by the Syracusans 135 years after Syracuse (implying 598), Dascon and Menecolus being the *oikistai*, but that Camarina revolted and the Syracusans removed the Camarinans (an event that can be dated to the middle of the sixth

d	*recto:*	Daïcrates son of Lycis|cus
	verso:	phratry: 5|th
e	*recto:*	Paedicus son of Thy— | newest phratry
	verso:	*vacat*
f	*recto:*	Heracleidas | son of Cratinus | 5th
	verso:	5th
g	*recto:*	Pyrrichus | son of Nicophanes
	verso:	*inverted delta* 8th
h	*recto:*	9th | Aristion son of Deinias | Timon son of Philinus
	verso:	9th *and illegible traces*
i	*recto:*	Aeschylus : son of Aristis
	verso:	14th
j	*recto:*	Chromius son of Gygas
	verso:	3rd from newest
k	*recto:*	Theon | son of Nicis
	verso:	4th | from newest | 4th | 10th
l	*recto:*	Sicanus | son of Archonidas
	verso:	Newest
m	*recto:*	Euarchidas son of Callisthenes
	verso:	Topmost
n	*recto:*	Eucles son of Hermaeus 10-*lit|ron*
	verso:	14th
o	*recto:*	—ys son of Eucleidas | has died
	verso:	14th

century). When in the early fifth century Hippocrates of Gela defeated Syracuse he acquired the territory of Camarina and refounded the city (Hdt. vii. 154. iii, Thuc. vi. 5. iii). However, Gelon then removed the Camarinans again (in 484, Hdt. vii. 156. ii). Camarina was then refounded by men from Gela in 461/0 (Diod. Sic. xi. 76. v, whose dates seem correct at this period), apparently following the same plan as the earlier city. There are some signs that regular urban divisions were exactly paralleled by rural divisions, implying a high degree of centralised control.

The lead tablets most plausibly belong to the refounded city of 461, and to soon after the refoundation. But their purpose must be deduced from their find-spot, nature and contents. The tablets are sufficiently uniform—in both form and content—to imply a single purpose for them all. But they are sufficiently varied to suggest that they are not the product of a single occasion. The main purpose of the record seems to be to identify men according to their phratry. Reference to other subdivisions is rare enough to suggest that it was used only when there might be a need to distinguish individuals with the same names. Reference to death on a number of tablets implies that it mattered whether a man was alive or not, but that death was not necessarily a reason for destroying or discarding the record. Reference to *litrai*, the denomination of silver coinage issued after the 461/0 refoundation (Westermark & Jenkins, *The Coinage of Kamarina*; a *dekalitron* was the equivalent of a Corinthian stater), and the presence of symbols plausibly linked to sums of money, imply that payment of sums of money might be relevant. But equally the absence of such signs from most records implies that recording payments was not the main purpose of these records.

Some light is shed on these tablets by comparison with similar surviving documents from elsewhere. Nothing comparable survives from the fifth century, but from fourth-century Athens we have a cache of 111 lead tablets recovered from a well and almost certainly originating from the office of the hipparch, which was at the north-west corner of the agora, and a further 570 similar tablets found in a well close to the Dipylon Gate (see J. H. Kroll, *Hesperia* xlvi 1977, 83–140; K. Braun, *AM* lxxxv 1970, 129–32, 198–269). These tablets, which are similar in size and were similarly folded, give a personal name on one side and repeat that name on the other (without patronymic or demotic), followed by a term appropriate to the colour of a horse, an identifying brand mark (or a record that there was none), and a number, which is the valuation of the horse in round 100 drachmas. These tablets enabled an up-to-date record to be kept of the cavalry, with the annual valuation of each cavalryman's horse. Their use was to attach the record of a particular horse to a particular cavalryman. Presumably a cavalryman who lost his horse and claimed compensation would come to the hipparch's office, and identify himself by his name. The hipparch would then sort through the tablets, looking for that man's name on the outside, which had the personal name only. When he found it, he would unfold the tablet and check that the right horse was being claimed for, and what the valuation was. A procedure like this shows why there was no need for patronymic or demotic.

A cache of almost 500 tablets, dated to the fifth century by letter form, was found in the nineteenth century at Styra in Euboea (*IG* XII. ix 56, O. Masson, *BCH* cxvi 1992, 61–72). These are slightly smaller than the Camarina tablets and carry just one name (although some have been reused several times). Written by a range of often poor hands, these too seem to have had some official function, but can have served for little more than the registration of individuals, whether as members of a group or in the context of voting.

The Camarina tablets fall between these two groups. Here it seems to be the phratry that is identified on the outside of the tablets, and when the tablet is unfolded the name of a member of that phratry is revealed. The fuller identification of the individual by patronymic, by comparison with either of the other caches of tablets (or the related clay tokens from Mantinea, *IG* v. ii 323) implies that the individual is not present but has to be found. However, there are a dozen examples where no phratry is indicated: in ten cases that side of the tablet is left blank (in some cases with some signs that writing has been obliterated) and in two the personal name is repeated on both sides. Despite their significant number, these anomalies seem best explained by forgetfulness on the part of the person writing. The writing is of high quality, with few errors and omissions and a clarity comparable to that shown by the Athenian cavalry tablets. Although a number of hands are involved, each of them is well practised in writing on lead. Presumably there was some registration process, involving an individual identifying themselves to a scribe. If there were one scribe per phratry this would explain the scribe forgetting on some occasions to turn the tablet over to record the phratry—or turning it over, forgetting what he had just done, and writing the personal name again. In the two most complete of the six possible cases where 'has died' is added, it is clear that this was written on a subsequent occasion—presumably at some point when the tablets were used to gather phratry members.

But what were the phratry members being gathered for? Of this the tablets give little clue. If the occasional indications of a sum of money represent a sum given by the person in question, that might be an indication that the tablets were used to assemble phratry members to perform some duty from which payment of money (or death) alone might exempt them. That the tablets were found in the temple of Athena might indicate performance of some religious duty, but given that Athena was the main *polis* deity at Camarina, storage of the tablets there is compatible with almost any civic duty. As Robinson (71) observes, the folding of the lead implies that it was not expected that the tablets would be consulted frequently. The important characteristic of the particular civic duty involved here is that it is performed by one phratry (or a group of phratries) at a time, or by equal numbers of representatives from all phratries. The archive is designed to enable the selection of individuals by phratry. It may be that there is prior selection of which phratry members are recorded on a tablet (these might all be wealthy men, all of hoplite status, or whatever), but when the archive is used the only information that differentiates men is their phratry membership.

Our understanding of what the tablets were useful for would be enhanced if we knew more about Camarina's constitution. Diod. Sic. xi. 76 implies that tyranny in Sicily was generally replaced by democracy, by which in any case he may mean no more than constitutional government, but we have no specific indication for Camarina. These tablets are, indeed, the best evidence we have for Camarina's constitution. What they suggest is division into fifteen or eighteen phratries, depending on the interpretation of tablet *k*: if this tablet indicates that phratry 14 was also the fourth from last, then there were eighteen; if, however, the tablet has been rewritten on one or more occasions then there is no reason to associate 'fourth from last' with the numbers that follow (L. Del Monaco, *Mediterraneo Antico* vii 2004, 597–613 = *SEG* liv 892). In favour of there being fifteen phratries is that in the event of their being eighteen, no tablets survive from either phratry 16 or phratry 17. Although no tablets survive from phratry 7 it seems implausible that chance would have picked out these two phratries not to be represented (otherwise there is one tablet from the first phratry, and just two from five or six phratries). It is a curiosity that some phratries are referred to both by their own number and by a number counting back from the end, but on any hypothesis this is true of some phratry since, in addition to *k*, one other tablet (Cordano 16) records itself as 'fourth from last'.[1]

Phratries at Camarina are also mentioned in a number of contracts in which the parties to the exchange are identified by both tribe and phratry, each indicated by a number (see *SEG* liv 872). The tribes are numbered 'first', 'second' and 'third', the phratries are numbered up to thirteen and then 'last'. Different people in the same number of phratry are in different tribes. It is perhaps most plausible that those who had belonged to a Doric tribe elsewhere remained in that tribe when they came to Camarina, but that distribution across phratries was new. However, the same contracts also suggest that phratries were active social units: men from the same phratry and tribe tend to be found as parties to and guarantors of the same contract.

In addition to phratries, two tablets indicate further subdivisions: the *triakas* and the *eikas*. However, there are some indications that division into *triakades* related to tribe, not phratry. At least, when *triakades* are also attested at Acrae (*IG* xiv 209, 211/2) there are nine *triakadarchoi*, which suggests three *triakades* for each of three tribes. The *triakas* and the *eikas* are also attested at Morgantina (*SEG* xxxviii 949 as interpreted at *SEG* xlii 871). Exactly how these 'Thirties' and 'Twenties' related to each other is unclear. If the *eikas* was a group of, at least notionally, twenty people, and if a *triakas* was made up of thirty *eikades*, then we would be dealing with 600 people in each *triakas*. Nine *triakades* would give a notional population of 5,400. As it happens this is close to the size of the ideal city of Plato's *Laws*, though lacking the mathematical properties of Plato's 5,040 (v. 737 E, 746 D). But we should not rule out the possibility that the Camarinans were organised into groups of thirty for some purposes and groups of twenty for others.

[1] The possibility that the same phratry might be referred to in two different ways makes it technically possible that the last phratry was also referred to in a different way: hence there could be just fourteen phratries. However, with three tribes and a likelihood of co-ordination between phratry and tribe structure (even though members of the same phratry can be in different tribes: see below), fifteen is much more likely.

125

Civil laws of Gortyn, *c*.450

Twelve columns engraved on the inner side of a circular wall which became the supporting wall for a Roman theatre. One fragment now in the Louvre, otherwise in Gortyn. Phot. *I. Creticae* iv 72, Willetts (below).

Archaic Cretan letters. *Boustrophedon*. The columns follow in sequence from right to left.

Tod 36 (i. 1–2. i only); Buck 117; *I. Creticae* iv 72 (with photos); Willetts, *The Law Code of Gortyn**; M&L 41 (iv. 23–vi. 1 only); Koerner 163–82; *Nomima* ii 30–6, 40, 45, 48–9, 51, 53–4, 66); Calero Secall, *Leyes de Gortina* [*non vidimus*]; Gagarin & Perlman, *The Laws of Ancient Crete*, G 72. Trans. Willetts; Fornara 88 (excerpts); Dillon and

Scholars have been much exercised over the political significance of these tablets.[2] The tablets themselves, along with the contracts, show a highly organised civic body, in which every individual was located by tribe, phratry, *triakas* and *eikas*.[3] The use of numbers for all these units, rather than names, points to their formal rather than affective importance for individuals; at Athens, where there is indeed an official ordering of the ten tribes (see Introduction, p. **xix**), documents use the tribe name but no number. But a highly formal and elaborate organisation does not necessarily mean a democratic organisation. The suggestion that Camarina may have been democratically organised is a product of the belief that when the city was refounded each of the settlers received equal urban and rural land. This is a suggestion for which the regular plan of the town, and perhaps of the countryside, gives some support, but which cannot be demonstrated (for archaeological traces at Camarina see *Inventory* no. 28, pp. 202–5 at 204).

The names on the tablets give some indication of the variety of origins of the residents of Camarina. Names like Sicanus suggest a native Sicilian origin, while names like Xenon seem to indicate recent arrivals (cf. esp. Xenon son of Corcyraeus, Cordano 79). Some names seem to have been local specialities: Theston (Cordano no. 42) is attested otherwise only at Halaesa, and Exacestidas (Cordano no. 133) suggests a Cretan connection; see further Cordano, in Poccetti (ed.), *L'onomastica dell'Italia antica*, 43–7.

The tablets reproduce various features of Doric Greek. These include *phratra* or *phrata* for *phratria*, *hikas* for *eikas*, *hebdema* for *hebdoma*, etc. The term *neta* corresponds to Attic *neata* and, with *hypata*, seems to belong originally to musical terminology, indicating the highest-pitch string. For the name Nemonaeus, which seems likely to be the correct form of the name (= child of the new moon), see O. Masson, *ZPE* cii 1994, 167–73.

[2] The problems with interpretations of the tablets as allotment plates and so intimately linked to democracy are well brought out by Robinson.

[3] For a particularly elaborate construction on this basis see B. Helly, *PP* lii 1997, 365–406; see more generally O. Murray, in Hansen (ed.), *The Polis as an Urban Centre and as a Political Community*, 493–504.

Garland[3] 4. 49 and 5. 27 (substantial excerpts). See also J. K. Davies in Foxhall & Lewis (edd.), *Greek Law in its Political Setting*, 33–56; Maffi, *Il diritto di famiglia nel Codice di Gortina*; E. Lévy in Lévy (ed.), *La Codification des lois dans l'antiquité*, 185–214; K. R. Kristensen, *Dike* vii 2004, 135–68; Greco & Lombardo (edd.), *La Grande Iscrizione di Gortyna*; J. K. Davies in Gagarin & Cohen (edd.), *The Cambridge Companion to Ancient Greek Law*, 305–27; Gagarin, *Writing Greek Law*, 122–75.

col. ii

αἴ κα τὸν ἐλεύθερον ἒ τὰν ἐλευθέραν κάρτει οἴπει, ἑκατὸν στατε̂ρανς καταστασεῖ· αἰ δέ κ' ἀπεταίρο, δέκα· αἰ δέ κ' ὁ δο̂λος τὸν ἐλεύθερον ἒ τὰν ἐλευθέραν, διπλεῖ καταστασεῖ· αἰ δέ κ' ἐλεύθερος ϝοικέα ἒ ϝοικέαν, πέντε δαρκνάνς· αἰ δέ κα ϝοικεὺς ϝοικέα ἒ ϝοικέαν, π[έν]τε στατε̂ρανς. *vac.* ἐνδοθιδίαν δόλαν αἰ κάρτει δαμάσαιτο, δύο στατε̂ρανς καταστασεῖ· αἰ δέ κα δεδαμ̣ν[α]μέναν, πεδ' ἀμέραṿ, [ὀ]δελόν, αἰ δέ κ' ἐν νυττί, δύ' ὀδελόνς· ὀρκιοτέραν δ' ἔμεν τὰν δόλαν. *vac.* αἴ κα τὰν ἐλευθέραν ἐπιπερε̂ται οἴπεν ἀκεύοντος καδεστα̂, δέκα στατε̂ρανς καταστασεῖ αἰ ἀποπονίοι μαῖτυς. *vac.* αἴ κα τὰν ἐλευθέραν μοικίον αἰλεθε̂ι ἐν πατρὸς ἒ ἐν ἀδελπιο̂ ἒ ἐν το̂ ἀνδρός, ἑκατὸν στατε̂ρανς καταστασεῖ· αἰ δέ κ' ἐν ἄλο, πεντέκοντα· αἰ δέ κα τὰν το̂ ἀπεταίρο, δέκα· αἰ δέ κ' ὁ δο̂λος τὰν ἐλευθέραν, διπλεῖ καταστασεῖ· *vac.* αἰ δέ κα δο̂λος δόλο, πέντε. προϝειπάτο δὲ ἀντὶ μαιτύρον τριο̂ν τοῖς καδεσταῖς το̂ ἐναιλεθέντος ἀλλύεθ̣θαι ἐν ταῖς πέντ' ἀμέραις· *vac.* το̂ δὲ δόλο το̂ι πάσται ἀντὶ μαιτύρον δυο̂ν. *vac.* αἰ δέ κα μὲ ἀλλύσεται, ἐπὶ τοῖς ἑλόνσι ἔμεν κρε̂θθαι ὄπαι κα λείοντι. *vac.* αἰ δέ κα πονε̂ι δολο̃σαθθαι, ὀμόσαι τὸν ἑλόντα το̂ πεντεκονταστατέρο καὶ πλίονος πέντον αὐτὸν ϝὶν αὐτο̂ι ϝέκαστον ἐπαριόμενον, το̂ δ' ἀπεταίρο̄ τρίτον α̣ὐ̣τὸν, το̂ δὲ ϝοικέος τὸν πάσταν ἄτερον αὐτ-

col. ii

If someone has sex by force with the free man or the free woman he shall pay one hundred staters; and if in the case of an *apetairos*, ten; but if the slave with the free man or the free woman, he shall pay double; but if a free man with a slave man or slave woman, five drachmas; and if a male slave with a male slave or a female slave, five staters.

11 If someone deflowers by force a household slave, he shall pay two staters; but if she has been deflowered one obol, during the day, and two obols during the night. The slave woman is to have the stronger oath.

16 If someone attempts to have sex with a free woman when a relative has charge of her, he shall pay ten staters if a witness testifies.

20 If someone is caught having extra-marital sex with a free woman in the house of her father or in that of her brother or in that of her husband, he shall pay one hundred staters. But if in anyone else's, fifty. And if the woman of an *apetairos*, ten. And if the slave with the free woman, he shall pay double. But if slave of slave, five. Let him proclaim before three witnesses to the relatives of the person caught that he is to be ransomed in five days (in the case of the slave to the master before two witnesses). If he is not ransomed, it is up to the captors to act in whatever way they wish. But if someone declares that he has been tricked, the person who has taken him is to swear, in a case involving fifty staters or more, along with four others, each swearing destruction to himself, and in the case of an *apetairos* with two others, and in the case of a slave the master and one other, that he did catch him

ὀν μοικίοντ' ἐλέν, δολόσαθθαι δὲ μέ. *vac.*αἴ κ' ἀνὲρ [κ]ạὶ γụνὰ διακρ[ί]νον[τ]αι, τὰ ϝὰ αὐτᾶς ἔκεν, ἅτι ἔκονσ' ἐ̃ιε πὰρ τὸν ἄνδρα, καὶ τô καρπô τἀννεμίναν, αἴ κ' ἐ̃ι ἐς τôν ϝôν αὐτᾶς κρεμάτον, κὄτι ḳ' ἐνυπᾴνει τὰν [ἐμίνα]ν ἅτι κ' ἐ̃ι, καὶ πέντε στατε̃ρανς, αἴ κ' ὀ ἀνὲρ αἴτιος ἐ̃ι τᾶς ḳẹ[ρ]εύσιος· α[ἰ] δ̣ὲ πονίοι ὀ ἀ̣ν̣ὲρ [αἴτι][ος μὲ ἔ]μεν, τὸν δικαστὰν

col. iii

ὀμνύντα κρίνεν. αἰ δέ τι ἄλλο πέροι τô ἀνδρός, πέντε στατε̃ρανς καταστασεῖ κὄτι κα πέρει αὐτόν, κὄτι κα παρέλει ἀποδότο αὐτόν. ὀ̃ν δέ κ' ἐκσαννέσεται δικάκσαι τὰν γυναῖκ' ἀπομόσαι τὰν Ἄρτεμιν πὰρ Ἀμυκλαῖον πὰρ τὰν Τοκσίαν. ὅτι δέ τίς κ' ἀπομοσάνσαι παρέλει, πέντε στατε̃ρανς καταστασεῖ καὶ τὸ κρέος αὐτόν. *vac.* αἰ δέ κ' ἀλλόττριος συνεσάδδει, δέκα στ[ατ]ε̃ρανς καταστασεῖ, τô δὲ κρέιος διπλεῖ ὅτι κ' ὀ δικαστὰς ὀμόσει συνεσσάκσαι. *vac.*

col. iv

τὸν πατέρα τôν τέκνον καὶ τôν κρεμάτον καρτερὸν ἔμεν τᾶδ δαίσιος καὶ τὰν ματέρα τôν ϝôν αὐτᾶς κρεμάτον. ἇς κα δόοντι, μὲ ἐπάνανκον ἔμεν δατέθθαι· αἰ δέ τις ἀταθείε, ἀποδάτταθθαι τôι ἀταμένοι ἇι ἔγρατται. ἐ̃ δέ κ' ἀποθάνει τις, (σ)τέγανς μὲν τὰνς ἐν πόλι κ' ἅτι κ' ἐν ταῖς (σ)τέγαις ἐνε̃ι, ἆι-

having extra-marital sex and did not trick him.

45 If a man and a woman divorce she is to have her own things, which she had when she came to her husband, and half the produce, if there is any from her own property, and half of what she wove, whatever that is, and five staters, if the man is the cause of the divorce. But if the man swears that he is not responsible, the judge

col. iii

is to take an oath and decide. But if she take anything else of the man, she shall pay five staters and whatever she takes, and whatever she takes from him let her give back. Whatever she denies, the judge shall decide that the woman take an oath of denial by Artemis at the Amyklaion by the Archeress. Whatever someone takes from a woman who has taken an oath of denial, he shall pay five staters and the thing itself.

12 If an unrelated man helps her take anything, he shall pay ten staters and double the value of whatever the judge swears that he has helped to take.

col. iv

23 The father shall have power over the division of the property among the children, and the mother over that of her property. As long as they live, there is no obligation to divide it; but if one is fined, a division shall be made for the one fined, in accordance with what is written. But if a man dies, the houses in the city and whatever is in the houses,

ς κα μὲ ϝοικεὺς ἐν ϝοικε͂ι ἐπ-
ὶ κόραι ϝοικίον, καὶ τὰ πρόβατα κα-
ὶ καρταί̣ποδα, ἃ κα μὲ ϝοικέος ἐ͂ι,
ἐπὶ τοῖς υἱάσι ἔμεν, τὰ δ' ἄλ-
λα κρέματα πάντα δατέθθα-
ι καλο͂ς καὶ λανκάνεν τὸς μ-
ὲν υἱύνς, ὀπόττοι κ' ἴοντι, δύ-
ο μοίρανς ϝέκαστον, τὰδ δ-
ὲ θυγατέρανς, ὀπότται κ' ἴον-
τι, μίαν μοῖραν ϝεκάσταν. δ̣-
ατέθ[θ]αι δὲ καὶ τὰ ματρο͂ια, ἐ͂-
κ' ἀποθά̣[νε]ι, ᾆιπερ̣ τὰ [πατρο͂]ι'
ἔγ[ρατ]τ̣αι. αἰ δὲ κρέματα μὲ εἴ-
ε, στέγα δέ, λακὲν τὰθ θ[υ]γ̣ατέ-
ρας ᾆι ἔγρατται. *vacat* αἰ δέ κα λε͂-
ι ὁ πατὲρ δοὸς ἰὸν δόμεν τᾶ-
ι ὀπυιομέναι, δότο κατὰ τ-
ὰ ἐγραμμένα, πλίονα δὲ μέ. *vacat*
ὀτείαι δὲ πρόθθ' ἔδοκε ἒ ἐπέσ-
πενσε, ταῦτ' ἔκεν, ἄλλα δὲ μὲ
ἔτι το̣͂ν̣ π[α]τρόι[ο]ν [κ]ρ̣έ[ματ']

col. v

ἀπολαν[κά]νεν. γυνὰ ὀ[τ]εία κ-
ρέματα μὲ ἔκει ἒ [πα]τρὸδ δό-
ντος ἒ ἀ̣[δ]ελπιο͂ ἒ ἐπισπέν-
σαντος ἒ ἀπολά[κ]ονσα ᾆ-
ι ὅκ' ὁ Αἰθ[α]λεὺς (σ)ταρτὸς ἐκόσ-
μιον οἱ σὺν Κύ[λ]λ̣οι, ταύτ-
ας μὲν ἀ̣π̣ολανκάνεν, ταῖ-
δ δὲ πρόθθα μὲ ἔ[ν]δικον ἔμεν.
leaf ἐ͂ κ' ἀποθάνει ἀνὲρ ἒ γυν-
ά, αἰ μέν κ' ἐ͂ι τέκ̣ν̣α ἒ ἐς τέ-
κνον τέκν̣α̣ ἒ ἐς τούτον τέ-
κνα, τούτος ἐκε[ν] τὰ κρέμα-
τα. *palm* αἰ δέ κα̣ μέτις ἐ͂ι τούτο-
ν, ἀ[[α]]δελπιοὶ δὲ το͂ ἀποθανόν-
τος κ' ἐκς ἀδε[λ]πιο͂ν τέκν-
α ἒ ἐς τούτον τέκνα, τούτ-
ος ἔκεν τὰ κρέματα. *palm* αἰ δέ κα
μέτις ἐ͂ι τούτον, ἀδευπιαὶ δ-
ὲ το͂ ἀποθανόντος κ' ἐς ταυτ-
ᾶν τέκνα ἒ ἐς το͂ν τέκνον τέ-

provided that a slave living on the land does not live in them, and the sheep and the cattle, provided that they do not belong to a slave, shall belong to the sons; the other property shall be divided well and the sons, as many as there are, shall take two shares each, and the daughters, as many as there are, one share each. The mother's property too, if she dies, shall be divided in the same way as is written for the father's property. But if there is no property but a house, the daughters shall take their share as is written.

48 If a father while alive wishes to make a gift to a daughter on marriage, let him give it, as is written, but no more.

52 To whatever woman a father formerly gave or promised, she shall keep it, but a further share of property from her father she shall not

col. v

take. Any woman who has no property, either by gift or by promise of a father or brother, or by inheritance, at the time when the *startos* of the Aethaleis, Cyllus and the others, were *kosmoi*, these shall take their share, but there shall be no proceedings against those (who received property) formerly.

10 If a man or woman dies, if there are children or children's children or their children, these shall have the property. But if there are none of these, but brothers of the dead or children of the brothers or their children, these shall have the property. But if there are none of these, but sisters of the dead or their children or their children's children, these shall

κνα, τούτος ἔκεν τὰ κρέμα-
τα. *palm* αἰ δέ κα μέτις ἐ͂ι τούτον,
οἷς κ' ἐπιβάλλει ὀπô κ' ἐ͂ι τὰ κρ-
έματα̣, τούτος ἀναιλέθθα-
ι. *palm* αἰ δὲ μὲ εἶεν ἐπιβάλλοντε-
ς τᾶς ϝοικίας, οἴτινές κ'
ἴοντι ὁ κλᾶρος τούτονς ἔ-
κεν τὰ κρέματα. *vacat* αἰ δέ κ' οἱ
ἐπιβάλλοντες οἱ μὲν λεί-
οντι δατέθθαι τὰ κρέματ-
α οἱ δὲ μέ, δικάκσαι τὸν δι-
καστὰν ἐπὶ τοῖλ λείονσι δ-
ατέθθαι ἔμεν τὰ κρέματα π-
άντα πρίν κα δάττονται. *vacat*
αἰ δέ κα δικάκσαντος τô δ-
ικαστᾶ κάρτει ἐνσείει ἒ ἄ-
γει ἒ πέρει, δέκα στατε͂ρανς
ς καταστασεῖ καὶ τὸ κρέι-
ος διπλεῖ. *vacat* τνατôν δὲ καὶ καρ-
πô καὶ ϝέμας κ' ἀνπιδέμας κ'
ἐπιπολαίον κρεμάτον αἴ κα μ-
ὲ λείοντι δατ̣έ̣θ̣[θαι, τὸ]ν̣ δ̣-
[ικαστ]ὰν ὀμνύντα κρίνα-
ι πορτὶ τὰ μολιόμενα. *vacat* [α]ὶ [δ]-
έ κα κρέματα δατιόμενοι
μὲ συνγιγνόσκοντι ἀν-
πὶ τὰν δαῖσιν, ὀνε͂ν τὰ κρέμ-
ατα κ' ὃς κα πλεῖστον διδ-
ôι ἀποδόμενοι, τᾶν τιμᾶν
δια[λ]ακόντον τὰν ἐπαβο-
λὰν ϝέκαστος. *palm* δατιομέ-
νοιδ δὲ κρέματα μαίτυρα-
νς παρέμεν δρομέανς ἐλε-
υθέρονς τρίινς ἒ πλίανς.

col. vi

θυγατρὶ ἐ͂ διδôι, κατὰ τὰ αὐτ-
ά.

Cretan cities were famous in antiquity for their laws. Herodotus records the Spartans' claim that Lycurgus got his famous constitution for Sparta from Crete (1. 65. iv), and Plato starts his *Laws* with the story of Minos bringing laws to the Cretan cities from

have the property. But if there are none of these, the next relations, from wherever the property descends, shall have the property. But if there are no relations of the family, those who are the *kleros*, they shall have the property.

28 If, of the heirs, some wish to divide the property and others do not, the judge shall rule that the property be managed by those who wish to divide until it is divided. If, after the judge has made his ruling, anyone enters the property by force or leads anything off or takes it, he shall pay ten staters and double the value of the object. And for living things, fruits, clothing, ornaments and furniture, if they do not want to divide them, the judge shall take an oath and judge the contentions advanced. And if in dividing property they do not agree about the division, they shall sell the property to whoever offers most to buy it and each one shall take the share of the price. When they are dividing property, there shall be present three or more adult and free witnesses.

col. vi

If a man makes a gift to his daughter, the same shall apply.

---

his father Zeus, before setting on Crete the imaginary city for which laws are devised in this dialogue. This ancient reputation is confirmed by surviving epigraphic material: laws constitute an extremely high proportion of archaic Cretan epigraphic material, both absolutely and by comparison to other parts of Greece (cf. J. Whitley, *AJA* ci 1997, 635–61). And of all Cretan cities Gortyn is the one from which the largest quantity of laws survives.

With the exception of one graffito hailing one Damagoras as beautiful (*I. Creticae* iv 50), all the earliest epigraphic texts from Gortyn, beginning in the seventh century, are legal texts (see Davies, in *Cambridge Companion*). From the late sixth century the Gortynians began to inscribe their laws onto the walls of public buildings, and the surviving texts include some of considerable length, in particular the so-called Little Code in eight columns (*I. Creticae* iv 41). Around the middle of the fifth century (although a slightly earlier date cannot be excluded) the so-called Great Code was inscribed in twelve columns. Further acts of legislation followed in the later fifth century (*I. Creticae* iv 73–140) and beyond (141–59).

It is clear that we are not dealing with a 'code' of law in any simple sense. That is, there was not a single moment when the Gortynians decided to settle all the rules under which they would live. Rather we are dealing with piecemeal legislation, adding to and, implicitly at least, amending what had been previously decided. This contrasts both with the traditions about lawgivers who designed lawcodes (going back to Lycurgus and beyond) and e.g. with the Athenian decision to republish/overhaul their whole lawcode in the late fifth century (below, **183**); but we do not know the story the Gortynians told themselves about the history of their legislation.[1] Individual legislative acts at Gortyn tend to be more or less coherent, but the relationship between the different laws is far from coherent (see Davies, in Foxhall & Lewis; Lévy; Gagarin, *Writing Greek Law*, 159–73). Each of these separate acts of legislation raises the question of why the Gortynians considered a new or amended law to be needed. It is not generally possible to tell what it is that the new law introduces or changes—though that has not prevented scholarly speculation. What the very fact of frequent additions to the corpus of law at Gortyn shows is a readiness to respond to particular new situations by revisiting the general problem. In this respect there is a striking contrast with the conservatism of both Sparta and Athens, where current law was at least attributed to a long-vanished lawgiver and where old legislation might be re-enacted verbatim.[2]

We present here two separate passages of the Great Code, illustrating both its subject-matter and its method of exposition. From columns ii–iii we present the provisions on rape and divorce. From columns iv–vi we present the provisions for inheritance of property. In both cases different provisions are separated off by small gaps in the text, but without anything that might count as a heading.[3] The section on rape and adultery has been described as 'really rather a mess' (Davies, in Foxhall & Lewis, 40, 43; note the jumbled use of *dolos* and *woikeus* for the same slave status in

[1] For lawgivers see A. Szegedy-Maszak, *GRBS* xix 1978, 199–209; for the question of whether archaic laws were merely isolated enactments or fuller sets of laws see Osborne in Mitchell & Rhodes (edd.), *The Development of the Polis in Archaic Greece*, 74–82, and Gagarin, *Writing Greek Law*, 74–5.

[2] On Spartan law see Xen. *Lac.* i. 1–2, 14; Plut. *Lyc.* 29. x–xi; on Athens see **183**.

[3] How systematically the text is divided by *vacats* has been debated: M. Gagarin, *GRBS* xxiii 1982, 129–46 at 138 sqq., makes the case for systematic use.

col. ii here: see S. Link, *Dike* iv 2001, 87–112, D. M. Lewis, *Historia* lxii 2013, 392–3), that on divorce and that on inheritance by contrast are impressively clear. Both show something of the methods and principles of the legislation, and illustrate the importance, among other things, of status.

The overall structure of the code into which these two sections fit is as follows. After an initial invocation of the gods, the first column treats disputes over the status and ownership of human beings (on the status groups see E. Lévy, in *Esclavage, guerre, économie . . . Y. Garlan*, 25–41, with corrections in Lewis, *Greek Slave Systems and their Eastern Neighbours*, ch. vii); the second and third columns treat rape, other sexual offences and divorce; the fourth and fifth columns concern rights over children, inheritance and gifts to women. The sixth column concerns sale of property and ransom of prisoners. The seventh and eighth columns concern marriage and heiresses, the ninth the property of heiresses and heirs and business contracts. The tenth column concerns gifts and adoption. The last column and a half largely contain amendments and clarification, ending (xii. 17–19) by stating the legal age of marriage for a woman (12 years old)—something that was frequently referred to in earlier sections without ever being stated.

As this brief summary reveals, the Great Code is dominated by issues of property and ownership. What it does not reveal is the way in which the form that the law takes is determined by its focus on telling plaintiffs and defendants on the one hand, and judges on the other, what they have to do.[4] Such an emphasis is normal in Greek law, but particularly interesting in this case is the way in which the whole law depends on the figure referred to as the judge (*dikastes*). There may be more than one judge at any one time, and one reference suggests that there may be specialised roles (vi. 25–31, cf. xii. 7, 11–12). The extent and elaboration of the laws should not blind us to the fact that we are dealing with a small community with a thin administrative structure.

The laws on rape and other sexual offences in column ii are interesting both in their own right and in comparison to those known elsewhere in Greece (see generally S. G. Cole, *CP* lxxix 1984, 97–113). Only at Gortyn is the legal and linguistic distinction between rape and *moicheia* (which covers extra-marital sex generally) clear. Whereas the Athenians lacked a clear term for rape and it is not certain that there was a single Athenian law on rape, the Gortynian 'have intercourse by force' is unambiguous. The scale of fines for rape depends upon status and can be tabulated (see table 1).

Three features are notable here. One is the curious term *apetairos*. This term appears only in relation to rape and adultery. It appears to be a subordinate free status (apparently a free person not belonging to a mess group) which it was important to distinguish only in the case of sexual offences which might lead to offspring.

[4] Cf. M. Gagarin, in Harris & Rubinstein (edd.), *Law and the Courts in Ancient Greece*, 173–83, and his *Writing Greek Law*, 154, 158–9 (contrasting the code of Hammurabi).

Table 1. Scale of fines for rape (obols)

Victim / Perpetrator	*Eleutheros*	*Apetairos*	*Dolos / Woikeus*	*Endothidion dolos*
Eleutheros	1,200	120	30	24 if virgin; otherwise 2 by night or 1 by day
Dolos / Woikeus	2,400	240	60	

The second notable feature is the variable treatment of rape of a household slave depending on whether she had previously had intercourse or not, and whether the act took place during the night or not. That the law should set a price on virginity (only) in the case of the household slave is striking: by implication the value of the household slave to her master depends upon his being able to be sure that if he has sex with her resulting children will be his own. Presumably the lesser fine during the day is because the possibilities of this happening by day without the owner's knowledge are less. The fines here are likely to be comparable to the lowest rates charged by prostitutes. But if the vast differential between the fines for rape of a free woman and of a household slave suggest that slaves were hardly rated as independent persons, we should note that when it comes to conflicting oaths as to what had happened the oath of the (female) slave is to take precedence (ll. 15–16). Later in the code we find this sort of evidentiary oath being required of a woman who denies taking the property of the husband whom she divorces. Use of the oath by women is familiar in Athens, also, where women did not appear in person in court but their statements under oath could be quoted (cf. Dem. xxxix. *Boeotus i.* 3–4, and L. Foxhall, in Foxhall & Lewis (edd.), *Greek Law in its Political Setting*, 143–4).

The third notable feature is the size of the fine imposed upon a slave rapist. It is not, of course, surprising that rape of a free woman by slave man should be treated as a serious offence—the general absence of anxiety about slave sexuality is in some ways the surprising thing about ancient Greek cities.[5] But since the slave, who has no property of his own, is given a large fine, the penalty falls in effect on the master. At Gortyn, as at Athens, masters were liable for the debts of their slaves (and conversely took the fines imposed on anyone who offended against their slaves: *I. Creticae* iv 47. 1–16 with K. Kristensen, *ZPE* cxlix 2004, 73–9): this large fine is a reminder to masters that they were responsible for keeping their slaves under control.

Adultery is effectively treated as like rape, except in as far as the sums of money stated appear to be paid not as fines but as ransom: they are the price of securing the release of the adulterer (see table 2). The difference between rape and adultery seems to be that adultery involves being caught in the act. Those who catch adulterers in the act seem obliged to offer the adulterer the opportunity to be ransomed, but if no ransom is forthcoming within the stated time period, they are free to exact any punishment they wish. In effect what is being stated here is the price of sexual

[5] S. C. Todd (forthcoming).

TABLE II. Scale of fines for adultery (obols)

Victim / Perpetrator	*Eleuthera* in father's/ brother's/husband's house	*Eleuthera* elsewhere	Wife of *Apetairos*	*Dolos*/ *Woikea*
Eleutheros	1,200	600	120	—
Dolos/*Woikeus*	2,400	1,200	240	60

intercourse in different circumstances. It is notable that this is the only section of the Gortyn code that lists crimes and punishments, and makes no mention of a judge, other than to arbitrate over property taken by a divorcing wife (a role elaborated in the additional clause on divorce at xi. 46–55).

Much of the thought-process involved in these Gortyn laws on rape and adultery is closely parallel to that involved in Athenian legislation. In particular, the right of the person who caught a man in adultery to punish him as he pleases, in the event of no ransom being paid, seems to parallel the powers of an Athenian in similar circumstances ([Dem.] LIX. *Neaera* 67). So too the way in which a woman's sexual status is affected by whether she is or is not in her father's/brother's/husband's house parallels the way in which the homicide of an adulterer caught with 'wife, mother, sister, daughter or concubine kept for procreation of free children' was regarded as justifiable at Athens (law at Dem. XXIII. *Aristocrates* 53; cf. Lys. I. *Eratosthenes* 31). But comparison is very difficult here. In Gortyn we are dealing with laws specifically about rape and adultery; at Athens, although we think that there was a law on adultery (*moicheia*), we do not know its terms: only how adultery affected justifications for homicide. At Gortyn the only possible references to homicide that we have come in two early and fragmentary laws (*I. Creticae* iv 8 and 9). This difference in the concerns of the surviving laws may be in part a product of the very different sources of our knowledge (primarily orators at Athens; entirely inscribed law at Gortyn), but this cannot be the whole story: after all the homicide law at Athens is well attested epigraphically, and forensic oratory dwells repeatedly on rape and adultery. What is more we do have some non-epigraphic evidence for penalties for adultery at Gortyn, in Ael. *V.H.* XII. 12, but even Aelian's longer list of penalties does not include allowing violence. It is not a matter of source material alone that shows that we are here a world away from the modern Mediterranean world of 'honour killings' which has sometimes been thought to be an appropriate parallel for the Athens of Lysias I.[6]

Between the laws on rape and those on adultery the Gortyn code includes, set off as a separate clause, a different short provision: ii. 16–20. This concerns not someone who has intercourse by force, nor someone who commits adultery, but someone who 'tries to have intercourse when the woman is under the care of a

[6] To reject the picture conjured up by Cohen, *Law, Sexuality and Society*, esp. ch. ii and ch. vi, is not, however, to embrace the non-violent world pictured by Herman, *Morality and Behaviour in Classical Athens*.

relative', i.e. someone who has a legal guardian. The penalty is 10 staters (120 obols). What differentiates this from rape and from extra-marital sex (*moicheia*) is that the attempt was unsuccessful. One circumstance in which a woman was under the care of a guardian was when she was an heiress, and later in the code the marital position of the heiress is described at length (vii. 15–ix. 24; xii. 6–19). Even unsuccessful seduction in such cases carries a fine equivalent to rape of or adultery with the wife of an *apetairos*.

The discussion of adultery is followed by discussion of divorce (ii. 45–iii. 16). Divorce is never stated as a requirement following adultery, as it seems to have been at Athens ([Dem.] LIX. *Neaera* 87), and it is not clear whether this section or the previous section is the first of a series on how marriages end (after this the code goes on to discuss the death of the husband (iii. 17–31), the death of the (childless) wife (iii. 31–7) and the separation of *woikeus* from *woikea*. The wife is given the property that she brought to the marriage, half of what it and half of what she has produced (women seem to be assumed only to produce textiles), plus a 5-stater penalty from a husband who is responsible for divorce, and a 5-stater penalty to pay if she takes more than she is allowed (with a 10-stater fine to anyone who helped her).

The second section of the law featured here is the provision for inheritance (see further K. Kristensen, in *Symposion* 2005, 89–100). Just as a wife on divorce can take away her property, so it is for her to divide it; only in the case of the need to pay a child's fine is division compelled during either a father or a mother's lifetime, an exception implying parental responsibility for a child's actions. But although neither husband nor wife are in other circumstances compelled to divide their property, the circumstances in which husband or wife can choose to alienate some of their property in life are highly restricted. The husband is envisaged giving gifts to his wife (iii. 20–2, 29–30, x. 15) or to his mother (x. 14–15) or daughter (iv. 46–54), but witnesses are required for the former transactions, and a limit placed. The inclusion at the beginning of column vi of the only date in all the Gortyn laws implies that this provision, at least, is new, and that previously greater freedom of gifts to women

---

126

Relations between Argos, Cnossus and Tylissus, *c*.450

(*A*) The most substantial, with top and bottom preserved, of five fragments of *poros* from the boundary wall of a *temenos* at Tylissus; now in the Herakleion Museum. (The other fragments, which we omit here, are very small.) Phot. *I. Creticae* I, p. 307. (*B*) Two joining fragments of a *stele* of greyish limestone found at Argos; now in the Argos Museum. Phot. *BCH* xxxvii 1913, pl. IV; Vollgraff (below), pls. I–II.

(*A*) Doric Greek, with Argive lettering. In columns, each *stoichedon* 22 (but 23 letters in l. 22). (*B*) Doric Greek, with Argive lettering (some later forms in ll. 43 sqq.). *Stoichedon* 37 (but irregularities in ll. 42 sqq., i.e. from slightly before the beginning of the amendment in 44).

(and of not giving to daughters) had occurred. The Gortyn law is repeatedly concerned to insist that individuals have power (only) over their own property, not over the property of parents or children (vi. 2–44).

The order of succession at Gortyn is straightforward, and more generous to daughters than succession at Athens. If there are children they inherit (unequally), if not, grandchildren or great-grandchildren; in their absence brothers/brothers' children/grandchildren, followed by sisters/sisters' children/grandchildren. After that, any relations inherit, and in their absence 'those who are the *klaros* ['lot']'. This is an extremely obscure phrase—not least because this is the only use of the word *klaros* in the Great Code.

At Gortyn sons receive houses, sheep and cattle and a double share of other property (where other property may include land); daughters receive a single share (except that if there is no other property daughters take a single share of any house). Special provision is made in the case of slaves living in the house and any cattle owned by the slaves. Neither the slaves nor their cattle are to be among the property for which sons have privileged inheritance. They are presumably therefore among the goods divided up between sons and daughters. (On these lines see Maffi, 64–70.)

It is worth noting that the main interest of this section of the lawcode seems to be to avoid dispute over inheritance. The law does not ensure that land stays in the family, since if the family do not agree about division then the whole property is to be sold and the proceeds divided. This provides a nice example of the usefulness of coinage: goods may be impossible to compare, but by being converted to money they are rendered comparable and hence divisible.

The Gortyn laws are our best source for the Cretan dialect, which is a form of Doric. As well as various peculiarities of phonology and inflection there are a number of dialect words, either not met with elsewhere or not used with these meanings. In this inscription the alphabet consists of only eighteen letters, including *digamma* but not *zeta*, *xi*, *phi*, *chi* and *psi*, *eta* and *omega* (see further Willetts, *Law Code of Gortyn*, 5–7).

(*A*) *I. Creticae* I xxx. 1. (*B*) *SIG*[3] 55; *I. Creticae* I viii. 4; Buck 85; Colvin 38 (ll. 3–17 only). (*A* + *B*) Vollgraff, *Le Décret d' Argos relatif à un pacte entre Knossos et Tylissos*; M&L 42*; *SdA* 147–8; Piccirilli, *Gli arbitrati interstatali greci*, 18–19; *Nomima* i. 54. Trans. Fornara 89; Colvin 38 (*B*. 3–17); Dillon & Garland[3] 1. 53 (*B*. 2–17). See also *LSAG* 165, 170; Graham, *Colony and Mother City in Ancient Greece*, 154–65, 235–44; Tomlinson, *Argos and the Argolid*, 134–6; W. P. Merrill, *CQ*[2] xli 1991, 16–25; S. Minon, in Hatzopoulos with Psilakakou (edd.), *Φωνής Χαρακτήρ Ἐθνικός*, 169–210; E. Kyriakides, *CCJ* lviii 2012, 115–44.

A

col. i [. . . . ἱαρὰ παρ]εχόντο τοὶ πα-
[ρὰ τôν Ἀργεί]ον, δέρματα δὲ φ-
[ερόσθο hοι Κν]όhιοι. πρὸ Ταυ-
[ροφονίον θύε]ν ἐν Τυλισôι ϝ-
[άρνα — 6 —, ἀμ]νὰν δὲ καὶ δι-
[— 11 —]. σπονδὰς νεοτ-
[έρας] μὲ τιθέσθαι μεδατέρο-
[νς, αἰ] μὲ συνδοκοῖ τôι πλέθε-
[ι, συνβ]άλλεσθαι δὲ τὰν τρίτ-
[αν αἶσ]αν τὸς Ἀργείος τᾶν ψά-
[φον. καἴ] τινας τôν εὐμενέον
col. ii δυσμενέας τιθείμεθα καὶ τ-
ôν δυσμενέον εὐμενέας, μὲ θ-
έσθαι, αἰ μὲ συνδοκοῖ τôι πλ-
έθει, συνβαλλεσθαι δὲ τὸνς
ἐκ Τυλισô τᾶν ψάφον τὰν τρί-
ταν αἶσαν. αἰ δὲ μάχα γένοιτ-
ο μὲ παρέντον τôν ἀτέρον, σπ-
ονδὰνς θέσθο ’ν τôι δεομένο-
ι πέντε ἀμέρανς. αἰ στρατήα
ἐνσ[ιείε] ἐνς τὰν γᾶν τὰν Κνο-
h̲ί̲αν, [Τυλισίονς] ὀφελêν παντ-
col. iii ι σθένει [— 10 — σῖτον]
παρεχόν[το hοι Κνόhιοι τοῖ]-
ς Ἀργείο[ις Κνοhοῖ, τοὶ δ’ Ἀργ]-
εῖοι τοῖ[ς ἐν Τυλισôι. — 5 —]
ιεν στρα[τήαν τριάκοντα ἀμ]-
ερᾶν. αἰ δ[ὲ — 14 —]
ίμεν τὰν [— 15 —]
ς κὲν Τυλ[ισôι — 11 —]
ε κα ϝαρθ[— 15 —]
πάγεσθα[ι — 14 —]
να. αἴ κ’ ἔνθ[— 14 —]
- - - - - - - - - - - - - -

A. 5–6 hερμᾶι, ἀμ]νὰν δὲ καὶ δί|[δομεν Δαίραι] Vollgraff, which we translate in brackets. 23 [κὰτ τὸ δύνατον] Vollgraff, which is two letters too long. 28 sqq. Vollgraff offered a speculative reconstruction.

A

– – – those from the Argives shall provide sacrifices, and the skins shall be received by the Cnossians. Before the Taurophonia they shall sacrifice at Tylissus a sheep [to Hermes], and also [give] a lamb [to Daera].

6 New treaties shall not be made by either party, unless it is agreed jointly by the majority (?); and the Argives shall cast a third part of the votes. And, if we make any of our friends enemies or any of our enemies friends, it shall not be done unless it is agreed jointly by the majority (?), and those from Tylissus shall cast a third part of the votes.

17 If there is a battle with either party not present, a truce shall be made for those who need it for five days.

20 If an army invades the land of Cnossus, the Tylissians shall help with all their strength – – –. Food shall be provided by the Cnossians for the Argives at Cnossus, and by the Argives for those at Tylissus – – – army for thirty days – – –

B

[——24——] νεσ [——10——]
[——23——] τὸν χô[ρον τô]ν Ἀ[χ]ạ-
[ρναίον τôι Τυλισίοι ἐξε̂μ]εν ξύλλεσθαι πλὰ[ν] τ-
[ὰ μέρε τὰ Κνοσίον συν]ṭέλλοντα ἐνς πόλιν. hó τ[ι]
[δέκα ἐκ δυσμενέ]ον hέλομες συνανφότεροι, δα[σ]-
[μôι τôν κὰτ γ]ᾶν τὸ τρίτον μέρος ἔχεν πάντον· τὰν δὲ [δ]-
[εκ]άταν τὸνς Κνοσίονς ἔχεν, hó τί χ' ἕλομες κοι[ν]-
[ᾶ]ι· τôν δὲ φαλύρον τὰ μὲν καλλ<ι>στεῖα Πυθόδε ἀπ[ά]-
γεν κοινᾶι ἀμφοτέρονς, τὰ δ' ἄλλα τôι ["Αρει Κνοσ]-
οî ἀντιθέμεν κοινᾶι ἀμφοτέρονς. ἐξ[αγογὰν δ' εἶ]-
μεν Κνοσόθεν ἐνς Τυλισὸν κἐκ Τυλι[σô Κνοσόνδ]-
ε· α[ἰ] δὲ πέρανδε ἐξάγοι, τελίτο hόσσα[περ hοι Κν]-
όσιοι· τὰδ' ἐκ Τυλισô ἐξαγέσθο hóπυ[ί κα χρεῖ. τô]-
ι Ποσειδᾶνι τôι ἐν 'Ιυτôι τὸν Κνοσίο[ν ἰαρέα θύ]-
εν. τᾶι hέραι ἐν Ἐραίοι θύεν βôν θέλει[αν ἀμφοτ]-
έρον[ς κ]οινᾶι, θύεν δὲ πρὸ Ϝακινθ[ίον ——8——]
[.]κο[...]κ[- - - - - - - - - - - - - - - - - -]

two lines lost

[——14——]ανοντο[——14——]πρ[α]-
τομενίαν ἄγεν κατὰ ταὐτ[ὰ κατὰ τὸ δόγμα] ṭὸ ἀμ[φ]-
οτέρον. χρέματα δὲ μὲ 'νπιπασκέσθο hο Κνόσιο[ς]
ἐν Τυλισôι, hο δὲ Τυλίσιος ἐν Κνοσôι hο χρέιζ[ο]-
ν. μὲ δὲ χόρας ἀποτάμνεσθαι μεδατέρονς μεδ' ἅ[π]-
ανσαν ἀφαιρῖσθαι. ὄ̑ροι τᾶς γᾶς· hυôν ὄρος καὶ Α-
ἰετοὶ κἀρταμίτιον καὶ τὸ τô Ἀρχô τέμενος κα[ὶ]
hο ποταμὸς κἐλ Λευκόπορον κἀγάθοια, hᾶι hύδο-
ρ ρεῖ τὄμβριον, καὶ Λᾶος. hî κα τôι Μαχανεῖ θύομ-
ες τὸνς ϝεξέκοντα τελέονς ὄϝινς, καὶ τᾶι h<έ>ραι
τὸ σκέλος ϝεκάστο διδόμεν τô θύματος. αἰ δὲ συ-
μπλέονες πόλιες ἐκ πολεμίον ἕλοιεν χρέματα,
hóπαι συνγνοῖεν hοι Κνόσιοι καὶ τοὶ Ἀργεῖοι,
hούτο ἔ̑μεν. τôι "Αρει καὶ τἀφροδίται τὸν Κνοσί-
ον ἰαρέα θύεν, φέρενδὲ τὸ σκέλος ϝεκάστο. τὸν Ἀ-
ρχὸν τὸ τέμενος ἔχεν τὸν Ἀχάρναι· τοῖς θύονσι
ξένια παρέχεν τὸνς Κνοσίονς, τὸνς δ' Ἀργείονς
τôι χόροι. ἐν Τυλισôιαἴ κα καλε̂ι hο Κνόσιος πρ-
εσγέαν, hέπεσθαι hóπυί κα δέεται,καἴ χὸ Τυλίσ-
ιος, τὸν Κνόσιον κατὰ ταὐτά· αἰ δὲ μὲ δοῖεν ξένι-
α, βολὰ ἐπαγέτο ῥύτιον δέκα στατέρον αὐτίκα ἐ-

B. 2 τôν χο[ρôν. 9 the stone has καλλστεια. 30 the stone has Ηραι, either omitting ε or using the first character to denote hε. 38 punctuation M&L: some editors punctuate after ἐν Τυλισôι rather than after τôι χόροι.

B

– – – The territory of the Acharnaeans (?) the Tylissians shall be permitted to plunder except for the parts belonging to the city of Cnossus. Whatever we take jointly from the enemy, in the division of things on land (the Tylissians) shall have a third part of everything, and of things at sea they shall have a half of all. The Cnossians shall have a tithe of what we take jointly: the finest of the spoils the two parties shall take jointly to Delphi, and the rest the two parties shall dedicate jointly to Ares at Cnossus.

11 There shall be export from Cnossus to Tylissus and from Tylissus to Cnossus; if (a Tylissian) exports beyond, he shall pay the same (taxes) as the Cnossians; goods fromTylissus shall be exported to wherever they wish.

14 To Poseidon at Iytus the Cnossian priest shall sacrifice; to Hera at the Heraeum the two parties shall sacrifice a female cow jointly; there shall be a sacrifice before the Hyacinthia – – –

21 – – – the first day of the month shall be observed in the same way in accordance with the decree of both parties.

23 A Cnossian shall not possess property in Tylissus but a Tylissian who wishes shall possess property in Cnossus. Neither party is to cut off land of the other or take all of it. Boundaries of the land: Swine's Mountain, Eagles, Artemisium, the precinct of Archus, the river towards Leucoporus and Agathoea, where the rainwater flows, and Laos.

29 When we sacrifice to Machaneus the sixty full-grown rams,we shall also give to Hera a leg of each victim.

31 If several cities together take property from the enemy, however the Cnossians and Argives decide together, thus it shall be done.

34 To Ares and Aphrodite the Cnossian priest shall sacrifice, and he shall receive a leg of each victim.

35 Archus shall keep the precinct at Acharna. For those who sacrifice the Cnossians shall provide hospitality, and the Argives shall provide it for the chorus.

38 If a Cnossian summons an embassy in Tylissus, it shall follow wherever he needs, and if a Tylissian summons one (in Cnossus) the Cnossians shall follow in the same way. If (the Cnossians who summon an embassy) do not provide hospitality, the council shall impose a fine of ten staters on the *kosmos*, and in the same way at

πὶ κόσμος, κἐν Τυλισδι κατὰταὐτὰ ho Κνόσιος. *v*
hα στάλα ἔσστα ἐπὶ Μελάντα βασιλέος. ἀϝρέτευ-
ε Λυκοστάδας hυλλεύς. *v* ἀλιαίαι ἔδοξε τᾶι τôν *v*
ἰαρôν· ἀ(ϝρέτευε) *v* βολᾶς *v* Ἀρχίστρατος Λυκοφρονίδας.
τοὶ Τυλίσιοι ποὶ τὰν στάλαν ποιγραψάνσθο τάδε·
αἴ τις ἀφικνοῖτο Τυλισίον ἐνς Ἄργος, κατὰ ταὐτά
σφιν ἔστο hᾶιπερ Κνοσίοις. *vacat*
vacat

Although *A* comes from Tylissus and *B* from Argos (but *A* is the more strongly Argive in language, with e.g. Κνόhιοι to *B*'s Κνόσιοι), the two appear from their lettering to be of about the same date, *c*.450, and if not parts of the same document (which Vollgraff argued insecurely from one of the small fragments not included here: see *LSAG* 165 n. 2) they ought at least to be part of the same series of documents.

Cnossus was about 4 miles/6 km. inland from the modern Heraklion, in the north of central Crete, Tylissus about 8 miles/12 km. west of Cnossus, and Acharna, restored at *B*. 2–3 and certainly mentioned at *B*. 36, probably at Arkhanes, about 5 miles/7 km. south of Cnossus. Iytus (*B*. 15) was perhaps Mt Iuktas, immediately west of Arkhanes. Here we have arrangements for cooperation between the larger Cnossus and the smaller Tylissus, which protect the rights of Tylissus and do not amount to the absorption of Tylissus into Cnossus, as in the early fourth century in Arcadia Helisson was absorbed into Mantinea but retained some of its individuality as a *kome* (R&O 14). There is a mixture of religious and of political-military provisions, presumably on points which had been disputed and which needed to be adjudicated. Kyriakides sees the boundaries of 'the land' in *B*. 26–9 as those of Tylissus, and discusses them; he considers Archus to be a human leader rather than a hero, and thinks Archus' two plots of land at *B*. 27 and 35–6 are different.

In *A*. 6–17 *plethos* (which we have translated 'majority') has often been interpreted as a joint meeting of a federal body, in which Cnossus, Tylissus and Argos have equal voting rights (an unbalanced federation, in which Cnossus and Tylissus would have no say in the affairs of Argos). However, Merrill insists that there is no parallel for that use of *plethos*: he takes *plethos* to refer to the Argive assembly; we doubt that, but otherwise accept his view that when Cnossus and Tylissus disagree there is to be reference to Argos and the decisions of Cnossus, Tylissus and Argos will then have equal weight so that the support of Argos will tip the balance in favour of one of the others (thus van Effenterre & Ruzé in *Nomima*). The text emphasises that Argos is to have an equal share in the voting on new treaties and (presumably to protect the interests of the small city) Tylissus on any departure from existing friendships and enmities. Likewise, in military activity, if the restorations are correct, Cnossus is to pay for Argive troops at Cnossus, but Argos for Argive troops at Tylissus (*A*. 23–6).

Tylissus for the Cnossian.

43 The *stele* was set up when Melantas was *basileus*; Lycotadas of the tribe Hylleis was chairman.

44 Resolved by the assembly for sacred business; the chairman of the council was Archistratus of the Lycophronid phratry. The Tylissians shall add to the *stele* the following: if any of the Tylissians comes to Argos, it shall be for him in the same way as for the Cnossians.

What is most remarkable is the involvement of Argos,[1] not simply as an arbitrator invoked for the occasion but with an ongoing interest in Cnossus and Tylissus: the sacrifices at the beginning of *A* may (but need not) be on a single occasion, but Argos is to have rights in decisions about treaties (*A*. 6–17: cf. above) and is envisaged as being involved in wars (*A*. 17 sqq.). In religious matters, while the sacrifice of bulls is not rare, a festival called Taurophonia (*A*. 3–4) is otherwise attested only on the island of Anaphe (*IG* XII. iii 249. 23) and at Carian Mylasa (*IK Mylasa* 201. 2: see commentary); the sacrifice 'to Hera at the Heraeum' (*B*. 16) is probably at the Argive Heraeum; Hyacinthus was a Dorian god or hero associated with Amyclae in Laconia, and his cult (*B*. 17) was widespread in Dorian cities; Machaneus, a 'saviour' who knows the *mechanai* which men need, is an epithet of Hera's husband Zeus, at Argos among other places (Paus. II. 22. ii), and Hera is to benefit from his sacrifices (*B*. 29–31); Ares and Aphrodite are linked (*B*. 34) often in Crete, but also at Argos (Paus. II. 25. i); and the Argives are involved in the sacrifices to Archus (*B*. 35–8). The original text is dated by an Argive *basileus* (by now an annual official) and chairman (*B*. 43–4); and the amendment (*B*. 44–8), with lettering of a slightly later style, has an Argive enactment formula and chairman (cf. Rhodes with Lewis, 70–1). For tribes and phratries (φάτραι) at Argos see M. Piérart in *Polis and Politics . . . M. H. Hansen*, 297–300; and p. 69 above.

Argos was regarded as a mother-city of these Dorian cities in Crete (cf. Vollgraff, 91–102), and probably they had appealed to it to settle their disputes and to act as a guarantor of the settlement (Graham, 158–9, compares Achaea and its colonies in southern Italy in the sixth or fifth century: Polyb. II. 39, but Polybius' stress is on the Achaeans' reputation rather than on the colonial tie). In the fifth century Crete scarcely appears in what we know of the mainstream of Greek history, but the Athenian squadron which in 429 took part in a war in Crete on its way to the Gulf of Corinth (Thuc. II. 85. v–vi, 92. vii) reminds us that Crete was not as far off the horizon as we may be tempted to think. If the occasion for this intervention was an appeal to Argos by Cnossus and Tylissus, there is no reason to suppose that to be

[1] The view of U. Kahrstedt, *Klio* xxxiv = [2]xvi 1941, 72–91, that this is a treaty between Cnossus and Argos in which Tylissus figures as a dependency of Argos which has broken away from it, created far more problems than it solved.

more likely in the ten years before 451 when Argos was an ally of Athens (Thuc. i. 102. iv: thus e.g. *LSAG* 165) than in the period after 451 when it had made peace with Sparta (Thuc. v. 14. iv).

Argive Doric has *digamma* and the aspirate but lacks *eta* and *omega*. On the language of these texts see Minon, who notes that Argive forms which might cause difficulty in Crete are avoided, so σ is normally used between vowels rather than h

---

127

Elis honours a Spartan and a Euboean, *c.*450

A bronze tablet in the shape of a flat ring, found at Olympia and now in the museum there. Phot. Kyrielis (ed.), *Olympia*, 1875–2000, p. 360 Abb. 1.

Elean lettering of the middle third of the century, in a spiral of four coils beginning at the outside. Non-*stoichedon*.

J. Taita, *Dike* iv 2001, 57–60, with Italian translation (*SEG* li 532); P. Siewert, in Kyrielis, 361–70, with German translation*. See also Perlman, *City and Sanctuary in Ancient Greece*, where pp. 63–4 cite our text as an unpublished inscription.

vacat τοὶ Ϝαλεῖοι Ἀθανάδαν καὶ Ϝρίνονα ἔθεαν κ' αὐτὸ κ' ἀπογένειαν Ϝαλείο· κ' ἐν φυλὰν
ἐνίμεν ὀποίαν λε̂ν, καὶ τᾶρ ἐπιϝοικίας τᾶρ ἐν Σπάρται κ' <ἐ>ν Εὐβοίαι κοιν-
ανε̂ν, καὶ τὰν θε<α>ρίαν δέκεσαι̣ ΤΑΡΑΕΟΙ . ΙΣΚΡΟΕΠΙΤΑΜΙΣΟΝ Ἀθ-
ανάδαν καὶ Κικυσια. ὀ δὲ πίνα̣ξ ἄ̣γαλμα τô Διός. *vacat*

2 the tablet has κπν. 3 the tablet has θεριαν; the unread letter could be Α, Λ or Ν.

This is one of a number of tablets of similar form and of similar date from this part of the Peloponnese: *SEG* xl 392 is a grant of citizenship by the Triphylians, in the area south of Elis proper but claimed by the Eleans, and *IG* v. ii 387 is a list of *proxenoi* from Lusi in Arcadia. Siewert suggests that the model for this kind of circular tablet was the 'discus of Iphitus' at Olympia (Plut. *Lyc.* 1. ii, Paus. v. 20. i).

The honorands receive not only citizenship but *theorodokia*, the right and duty to act as official host to sacred envoys (which presumably involved expenditure as well as help of other kinds)—in this case envoys from Olympia, announcing the Olympic truce and games. There are three later inscriptions which confer both citizenship and *theorodokia*: *I. Olympia* 39 = Buck 66, conferred by Elis on Damocrates of Tenedos, late third–early second century; also *ISE* 41, by Argos on Alexander of Sicyon, first half of third century; *IG* v. ii 394, by Lusi on Mnasilaus of Amphissa, *c.*200. Our

(for Κνόhιοι in *A* but Κνόσιοι in *B* cf. above), and in *B*. 30, 31, 35 ϝ is used rather than ϝh. Other features of this text include -ανς and -ονς for -ας and -ους accusative plural, and ἐνς for εἰς and ἐνσ[ιείε] for εἰσίῃ, *A*. 21; πόλιες for πόλεις, *B*. 32; εἶμεν for εἶναι; ποι for προσ and -γραψάνσθο for -γραψάντω, *B*. 46; κα for ἄν; hî for 'when', *B*. 29.

The Eleans made Athanadas and Rhinon Eleans, themselves and their descendants; and they shall enter whatever tribe they wish, and shall share in the *epoikia* in Sparta and Euboea, and shall receive the *theoria* – – – Athanadas (shall receive land in the region of?) Cicysium also.

4 The tablet is sacred to Zeus.

---

inscription is the earliest text to use the expression 'receive the *theoria*' (it recurs in *SEG* xxxvii 340 = R&O 14. 10, early fourth century); the earliest occurrence of the word *theorodokia* is in *I. Olympia* 36 = *SIG*[3] 171. 2, of 365–363. Pind. *Isthm.* ii. 23–4, perhaps of 470, refers to *spondophoroi*, 'truce-bearers'.

Earlier texts which might mention such grants are in any case rare, but it seems to be in the fifth century that we first encounter formal grants of citizenship to men from outside a community who are not the sons of citizens. In Athens Solon in the 590s is said to have allowed citizenship to exiles from elsewhere and to craftsmen (Plut. *Sol.* 24. iv), but this could have been done without formal grants, and Pericles' citizenship law of 451/0 (e.g. *Ath. Pol.* 26. iv) may have been the first formal definition of the qualification for Athenian citizenship. Early in the fifth century the seer Teisamenus of Elis and his brother are said to have been the only men ever made citizens by the Spartans (Hdt. IX. 33–5). As *poleis* became more institutionalised, they became more likely to have defined criteria for citizenship and formal procedures to confer it as an honour on men who did not satisfy those criteria.

The two honorands here are made Elean citizens although they do not reside in Elis. They are to be treated as if they were Elean *epoikoi* ('settlers', as opposed to *metoikoi* in Athens who might be long-term residents but were not necessarily so), who formed a distinct sub-community, in their own cities. These bodies will consist primarily of Elean seers living there (cf. Tisamenus and his brother in Sparta, above), who are probably citizens both of Elis and of the city in which they have settled, but these men, probably priests of Zeus Olympios, become additional members, as adopted citizens of Elis who presumably retain citizenship in their home cities. Over time citizenship was increasingly given as an honour to men who would not live in the honouring city and exercise their rights, but incorporation in a body of expatriate Eleans would give some substance to the honour. The Euboean city is not specified: Strabo 448 / x. i. 10 mentions Eleans who

---

128

Treaty between Sparta and the Erxadieis, *c*.450 (?)

The upper left-hand part (but the top left-hand corner is missing) of a *stele* of bluish-grey Taygetan marble, found on the acropolis at Sparta and now in the museum there. Facs. *Abh. Leipzig* LXV. iii 1974, 4, reproduced *LCM* i 1976, 87, and *ὅρος* xiv–xvi 2000–3, 460; *ὅρος* xiv–xvi 2000–3, 461; phot. *Abh. Leipzig* LXV. iii 1974, Taff. I (stone), II (squeeze), *ὅρος* xiv–xvi 2000–3, πιν. 100–1; our pl. 4.

Careless Spartan lettering of the fifth century; non-*stoichedon*.

W. Peek, *Abh. Leipzig* LXV. iii 1974; P. A. Cartledge, *LCM* i 1976, 87–92 (cf. *SEG* xxvi 461); Gschnitzer, *Ein neuer spartanischer Staatsvertrag und die Verfassung des Peloponnesischen Bundes* (cf. *SEG* xxviii 408); M&L (1988 reissue) 67 bis; *Nomima* i 55 (with Gschnitzer's text); G. A. Pikoulas, *ὅρος* xiv–xvi 2000–3, 455–67*. Trans. Dillon & Garland[3] 6. 61. See also D. H. Kelly, *LCM* iii 1978, 133–41; W. Luppe, *ZPE* xlix 1982, 23–4; U. Cozzoli, in *Xenia . . . P. Treves*, 67–76; Pistorius, *Hegemoniestreben und Autonomiesicherung in der griechischen Vertragspolitik klassischer und hellenistischer Zeit*, 87–93, 120–5; M. Sordi, *Aevum* lxv 1991, 35–8; Baltrusch, *Symmachie und Spondai*, 21–4; S. Bolmarcich, *GRBS* xlv 2005, 5–34; Matthaiou, "*καττάδε ἔδοξε τοῖς Λακεδαιμονίοις*", 8–10; Bolmarcich, *Historia* lvii 2008, 69–75.

[συνθε̑κ]αι Αἰτολοῖς. κ̣[αττάδε]
[?φιλία]ν̣ καὶ hιράναν ι̣[– – ποτ']
[Αἰτο]λ̣ὸς καὶ συνμαχ̣[ίαν ?ἀίδιον]

Restorations by Peek except where otherwise stated. 1 Ἐ̣[ρξαδιεῦhι·] Gschnitzer, but Pikoulas reports that Ε̣ is not possible. 2 [σπονδὰ]ς G. T. Griffith *ap.* Kelly. ε̑[μεν ποτ] Peek, ἴ[σχεν? ποτ'] Pikoulas & Matthaiou. 3–4 ἀίδιο|ν Pikoulas & Matthaiou (ἀίδιον | Matthaiou, personal communication, to match syllabic breaks at ends of other lines): unrestored Peek.

went as *epoikoi* to Eretria; but Chalcis is said originally to have been called Euboea (Hecat. *FGrH* 1 F 129), and probably here the reference is either to Chalcis or to the island as a whole.

Cicysium is said by Strabo 356–7 / VIII. iii. 31–2 to have been the greatest of the eight cities of Pisatis, the region around Olympia, which by this time formed part of the state of Elis (J. Roy, in Hansen (ed.), *The Polis as an Urban Centre and as a Political Community*, 298). However, until this text was published there was no evidence for its existence before the hellenistic period (J. Roy, in *Inventory*, 491 n. 2, not knowing this text). Normally only citizens could own land in a city's territory, so a grant of land there would give substance to Athanadas' status as citizen.

Elean has *digamma*, before *rho* as well as before vowels, and has the aspirate but lacks *eta* and *omega*; note also ἔθεαν for ἔθεσαν, 1; ἐν . . . ἐνίμεν for εἰς . . . εἰσιέναι, 1–2; λε̂ν for ἐθέλειν, 2; δέκεσαι for δέχεσθαι, 3; and in the article τᾶρ for the genitive feminine singular and τοί for the masculine nominative plural.

Alliance with the Aetolians.

1 On the following terms [friendship?] and peace [shall be?] made with the Aetolians, and alliance [for all time? – – –];

[- - -]ạνμονος μαν[- - hεπο]-
[μ]ẹνος hόπυι κα Λα[κεδαιμόνι]-
[ο]ι hαγίονται καὶ κạ[τὰ γᾶν]
ḳαὶ καθάλαθαν, τὸ[ν αὐτὸν]
φίλον καὶ τὸνν αὐτ[ὸν ἐχθρὸν]
ἔχοντες hὸν περ [καὶ Λακε]-
δαιμόνιοι. μεδὲ ḳ[ατάλυhιν]
ποιε͂θαι ἄνευ Λα[κεδαιμονίον]
μεδενί, ἀνhιέν[τας τὸν πόλεμον?]
ἐπὶ ταὐτὸν πόθ' ὄṿ [περ Λακεδαι]-
μονίος. φεύγον[τας δὲ μὲ δεκέθο]-
hαν κεκοινανεκ[ότας ?ἀδικε]-
μάτον. αἐ δέ τίς κα [ἐπὶ τὰν το͂ν]
['Ε]ρξαδιέον χόραν [στρατεύει]
ἐπὶ πολέμοι, ἐπι[κορε͂ν Λακεδαιμο]-
νίος παντὶ σθένε[ι ?κὰ τὸ δύνατον·]
αἰ δέ τίς κα ἐπὶ τὰ[ν το͂ν Λακεδαιμο]-
νίον χόραν στρạ[τεύει ἐπὶ πολέ]-
μοι, ἐπικορε͂ν 'Ε[ρξαδιε͂ς παντὶ]
[σθένει κὰ τὸ δύνατον? - - - - -]
- - - - - - - - - - - - - - - - - -

4 – –]νμονος μαν[τι – Peek, ?πλ]ạ̀ν μόνος Μαν[τινε͂ς? Gschnitzer (Mantinea is the only *polis* whose name begins thus in *Inventory*), ?πλ]ạ̀ν μόνος Μαν[– – Pikoulas & Matthaiou (thinking of another unknown subdivision or dependency of the Aetolians). 10 For κατάλυσις in this sense cf. e.g. Thuc. III. 18. ii, 37. vi; *IG* i³ 83. 11, 17, 105. 35 (cf. on **183**). 12 Pikoulas & Matthaiou: μεδενίαν hιέν[τας πρέσβες] Peek, μεδενί, ἀνhιέν[τας πολεμε͂ν?] Gschnitzer, μεδενί, ἀνhιέṃẹ[ν δὲ μαχομένος] Luppe. 15–16 ?ἀδικε] | μάτον considered but rejected by Peek; Gschnitzer. 17 Rhodes: 'Ερξαδιέον Peek, [.]ρξαδιέον Pikoulas & Matthaiou. 19 Lewis: κραττὸ δύνατον Peek, *c*.7–8 letters unrestored Pikoulas & Matthaiou. 20 Pikoulas & Matthaiou: τὰ[ν Λακεδαιμο]- Peek. 22–3 Lewis: καττὸ δύνατον Peek, Ε . . [– – and no further restoration Pikoulas & Matthaiou.

This is the earliest surviving inscribed treaty from Sparta, and establishes an unequal alliance between Sparta and the other party, followed by reciprocal clauses in which each party undertakes to join in the defence of the other against attackers. Surprisingly, if correctly restored it mentions friendship before peace.

Almost everybody has accepted, we think rightly, that the Aetolians mentioned here are those of north-western Greece, though a fragment of Androtion claims that there was a perioecic city called Aetolia in Laconia (*FGrH* 324 F 63), and that has been preferred by Gschnitzer and in *Nomima*.[1] What begins as a treaty made by

[1] More recently Gschnitzer has suggested that these Aetolians were an amphictyony centred on Olympia: *Symposion* 1993 (*AGR* x 1994) 34: cf. Pind. *Ol.* iii. 12, Bacchyl. viii. 29 Snell & Maehler, Strabo 354 / VIII. iii. 30, Tzetz. *Chil.* xii. 354–69, and P. Siewert in *Symposion* 1993, 403–4, J. Ebert & P. Siewert in *Olympia Bericht* xi 1977–81 (publ. 1999), 403–4.

4 following where the Spartans lead both by land and by sea, having the same friend and the same enemy as the Spartans.

10 Neither shall they make a settlement with any one without the Spartans, but giving up [the war?] against the same enemy (?) as the Spartans.

14 They shall not receive exiles who have taken part in [wrongdoing?].

16 If any one campaigns against the land of the Erxadieis for war, the Spartans shall support with all their strength [as far as possible?]; and if any one campaigns against the land of the Spartans for war, the [Erxadieis shall support with all their strength as far as possible?]. – – –

Sparta with the Aetolians becomes later a treaty with one particular subdivision or dependency of them. Even if the first letter of l. 17 cannot be read, the *epsilon* in l. 22 makes Erxadieis the likeliest name of this subdivision (as Pikoulas agrees, though he is not confident enough to print it in his text), but knowing the name does not help us, since there is no other attestation of this name or of a name which could be another form of it. Presumably the treaty was in fact made with this subdivision, which established a relationship with the Spartans when the other Aetolians did not, but referring to it as the 'Aetolians' at the beginning makes the treaty and the subdivision seem more important.

To interpret the text we need to know when this treaty was made, but that is very difficult to establish,[2] and suggested dates have ranged over almost the whole period of the Peloponnesian League's existence, from the late sixth century (*Nomima*) or 500–470(–450) (Peek), on the basis of the lettering, to *c*.388 (Kelly), on the grounds that Agesilaus' march through Aetolia then (Xen. *Hell.* IV. vi. 14, cf. *Ages.* ii. 20) provides an occasion when the Aetolians, or some of them, might have become friends of Sparta after previously being enemies. This is bound up with the question how we envisage Sparta's relationships with its allies as developing, and how early we can expect to find an unequal relationship which involves 'following where the Spartans lead both by land and by sea'. As the debate on the dating of Athenian inscriptions has made clear, we cannot rely heavily on the lettering; but scholars experienced in Spartan epigraphy agree that the lettering favours the fifth century rather than the fourth; Jeffery's opinion that it need not be earlier than the 420s was connected with her defence of a date in the 390s for **151**,[3] and the earlier date which now seems established for that might point to a date before the Peloponnesian War for this text. This argues against a dating *c*.400 (Sordi, Bolmarcich 2005, in connection with Aetolia's involvement in the war between Sparta and Elis *c*.402–400 (Diod. Sic. XIV. 17. ix–x), and the subsequent expulsion of the Messenians from Naupactus (below)), and the suggestion of Bolmarcich 2008 that the terms imposed on Athens in 404 are the first instance of the terms found here, newly arrived at by combining the Delian League's oath to have the same friends and enemies with an oath to follow a leader. In the absence of other evidence, it does not seem safe to assume that that must have been the first instance of a new obligation. The traditional view that the essentials of the Peloponnesian League's organisation were created between *c*.506 and *c*.504 (cf. Hdt. v. 74. i, 91–3; also what he believed about Cleomenes in VI. 74. i) has been questioned, and the formulation of the traditional view by

[2] For a fuller discussion see Rhodes, *A.A.Hung.* li 2011, 9–15.
[3] Johnston in the revision of *LSAG* 447–8 (**G**), suggested '*c.* 400 (?)'.

129

Athenian casualty list, *c*.447

A marble *stele* from an unknown location, now in the Epigraphical Museum. Phot. Conze, *Die attischen Grabreliefs*, 1427 pl. 293A.; Guarducci, *Epigrafia greca*, ii. 165–7 figs. 40a–c; Clairmont, *Patrios Nomos*, ii, pls. 45–6; our pl. 5.

Developed Attic letters. Lines 15, 18, 19, 35, 36, 67, 72 (Ἀρχέπολις), and perhaps the epigram (45–8) seem to be later additions for which space had been left (S. Dow, *HSCP* liii 1942, 97).

A. Kirchhoff, *Hermes* xvii 1882, 623–30 (with facsimile); Tod 48; Peek, *GVI* 18; M&L 48*; *IG* i[3] 1162; *CEG* 6. See also R. Meiggs, *HSCP* lxvii 1963, 17–18; Pfohl, *Geschichte und Epigramm*, 25–6 n. 28; Guarducci, *Epigrafia greca*, ii. 165–7 (with images); Clairmont, *Patrios Nomos*, i. 165–9 no. 32b.

G. E. M. de Ste. Croix was certainly too rigid;[4] but, while we should accept that the League developed and that problems were addressed as they arose, it does seem credible to us that Sparta might have made an unequal treaty of this kind at any time in the fifth century.

We have no knowledge of Sparta's being involved in this part of Greece before the 450s, and from the end of the Persian Wars until then Sparta had enough preoccupations nearer home to make that positively unlikely. If we are to look for an occasion in the fifth century, it is likely that the exiles about whom Sparta is concerned in ll. 14–16 are the Messenians settled by Athens at Naupactus, and that will limit us to the period between *c.*455, when they arrived there (Thuc. I. 103. i–iii with 108. v, cf. Diod. Sic. XI. 84. vi–viii), and afterwards captured but were driven out of Oeniadae (Paus. IV. 25), and *c.*400, when Sparta expelled them and they departed to fight in wars in Cyrene and the west (Diod. Sic. XIV. 34. ii–v, Paus. IV. 26. ii cf. X. 38. x). Cozzoli argued for a date *c.*450, soon after the arrival of the Messenians (for Sparta's willingness to act north of the Gulf of Corinth in the middle of the century cf. Thuc. I. 107–108. ii, 112. v), and that is preferred by Pikoulas and Matthaiou; Cartledge for *c.*426 (when Sparta joined the Aetolians in attacking Naupactus: Thuc. III. 100–2) or shortly after. On the basis of the lettering the earlier date seems the more likely, but we should not rule out the later.

In the language, aspirate for *sigma* as in κ[ατάλυhιν] (10) and [δεκέθο]|hαν (14–15), and *iota* for *epsilon* as in hαγίονται (6), were already-known features of the Spartan dialect. Additions to our knowledge are hόπυι for ὅποι (5); the remarkable θάλαθαν (7), with *theta* for *sigma* and single letter for double (cf. R. A. Bauslaugh, *Hesperia* lix 1990, 663–5); ποιε̃θαι for ποιεῖσθαι (11); Peek regarded τὸνν (8) as a simple mistake, and was puzzled by αἐ (16) when we have the expected αἰ in 20.

[4] Traditional view, de Ste. Croix, *The Origins of the Peloponnesian War*, 101–51, 333–41; doubts, G. L. Cawkwell, *CQ*[2] xliii 1993, 364–76; D. C. Yates, *CQ*[2] lv 2005, 65–76. J. E. Lendon, *GRBS* xxxv 1994, 159–77, argued that all the members had unequal alliances with Sparta and Sparta never had a formal obligation to consult them.

col. i

ἐγ Χερρονέσοι
Ἀθεναίον : hοίδε
ἀπέθανον·
Ἐπιτέλες : στρατεγός
Ἐρεχθεΐδος
Πυθόδορος
Ἀριστόδικος
Τέλεφος
Πυθόδορος

Αἰγεΐδος
Ἐπιχάρες
Μνεσίφιλος
Φαιδιμίδες
Λάχες
Νικόφιλος

Πανδιονίδος
Λυσικλε̑ς

Λεοντίδος
Χαιρε̑ς

Οἰνεΐδος
Ῥοδοκλε̑ς
Εὐρύβοτος
Πολίτες
Ἑροκλείδες

Κεκροπίδος
Ἀρίσταρχος
Καρυστόνικος
Θεόμνεστος
Ἀρίσταρχος
Εὐκράτες
Νικόμαχος

col. ii

ἐμ Βυζαντίοι
Ἀθεναίον : hοίδ[ε]
ἀπέθανον·

Ἐρεχθεΐδος
Νικόστρατος
Φιλόκομος

Αἰγεΐδος
Χίονις

Πανδιονίδος
Φιλιστίδες

Λεοντίδος
Λυσίμαχος

Ἀκαμαντίδος
Καλλισθένες

Οἰνεΐδος
Κάλλιππος

Κεκροπίδος
Κνίφον
Δεμοτέλες

Hιπποθοντίδος

Hαίσον

Αἰαντίδος
Νικόδεμος

col. i

In Chersonese,
of the Athenians these
died:
Epiteles, general.

Of Erechtheis:
Pythodorus
Aristodicus
Telephus
Pythodorus

Of Aegeis:
Epichares
Mnesiphilus
Phaedimides
Laches
Nicophilus

Of Pandionis:
Lysicles

Of Leontis:
Chacres

Of Oeneis:
Rhodocles
Eurybotus
Polites
Herocleides

Of Cecropis:
Aristarchus
Carystonicus
Theomnestus
Aristarchus
Eucrates
Nicomachus

col. ii

In Byzantium,
of the Athenians these
died:

Of Erechtheis:
Nicostratus
Philocomus

Of Aegeis:
Chionis

Of Pandionis
Philistides

Of Leontis
Lysimachus

Of Acamantis:
Callisthenes

Of Oeneis:
Callippus

Of Cecropis:
Cniphon
Demoteles

Of Hippothontis:

Haeson

Of Aiantis:
Nicodemus

Ἱπποθοντίδος
Σοτελίδες
Ποσείδιππος
Αἰαντίδος
Δίφιλος

Ἀντιοχίδος
Κράτον
Ἀντικράτες
Εὔδοχσος

hοίδε : ἐν τοῖς ἄλλοις
πολέμοις : ἀπεθανον

Ἐρεχθεΐδος
Λυσανίας

Ἀντιοχίδος
Φανίας

Πανδιονίδος
Σιμονίδες
Αἰσχύλος Ἀρχέπολις
Σμικρίον
Χαροπίδες
Ναχσιάδες
Λεοντίδος
Φίλον
Εὔδεμος
Ἀκαμαντίδος
Πρόταρχος
Κεκροπίδος
Χαιρίας
Ἀστυάναχς
Λυσίστρατος
Ἱπποθοντίδος
Τιμόνοθος
Ἀντιφάνες
Αἰαντίδος
Κλένοθος
Φίλιος
Καλλικλε̃ς
Ἐλευθερα̃θεν
Σεμιχίδες

hοίδε παρ' hελλέσποντον ἀπόλεσαν ἀγλαὸν hέβεν
βαρνάμενοι, σφετέραν δ' εὐκλέϊσαμ πατρίδα,
hόστ' ἐχθρὸς στενάχεμ πολέμο θέρος ἐκκομίσαντας,
αὐτοῖς δ' ἀθάνατον μνε̃μ' ἀρετε̃ς ἔθεσαν.

43–4 and 74–97 carved in more crowded letters.

Of Hippothontis:
Sotelides
Poseidippus
Of Aiantis:
Diphilus

Of Antiochis:
Craton
Anticrates
Eudoxus

These in the other wars died:

Of Erechtheis:
Lysanias

Of Antiochis:
Phanias

continuation from l. 44 follows:

Of Pandionis:
Simonides
Aeschylus Archepolis
Smicrion
Charopides
Naxiades
Of Leontis:
Philon
Eudemus
Of Acamantis:
Protarchus
Of Cecropis:
Chaerias
Astyanax
Lysistratus
Of Hippothontis:
Timonothus
Antiphanes
Of Aiantis:
Cleinothus
Philius
Callicles
From Eleutherae:
Semichides

These lost their glorious youth fighting by the Hellespont, and their fair-famed fatherland, so that their enemy groaned, reaping the harvest of war, and they placed an immortal memorial of excellence for themselves.

This casualty list takes the form that became normal in the fifth century: by contrast to **109**, the dead of all the tribes are listed on a single *stele*; as in several other cases, but not all, the list is divided both by tribe and by place of death. Division by tribe was required by the ceremony of the annual commemoration of the war dead (Thuc. II. 31); division by theatre of war may indicate that the lists were based on reports from individual generals (see G. Bakewell, in Cooper (ed.), *Politics of Orality*, 94–5). The *stele* bears physical signs that recording the war dead did not wait till the end of the year—perhaps because of a desire to have the *stele* inscribed by the time of the ceremony: various names seem to have been added subsequent to the original inscription, but spaces had been left to accommodate such additional names. Presumably these were either men who died from wounds received in warfare but not on the battlefield, or men who died in subsequent engagements in the war zone later in the year. What does not seem to have been fully foreseen was that the Athenians would be engaged in fatal combat in regions other than the Chersonese and Byzantium: the other regions are not only grouped together as 'in the other wars' but are written in a smaller script. The implication would seem to be that towards the end of the archon-year the Athenians embarked on warfare in new areas. The nineteen dead 'in the other wars' compare with twenty-eight dead in the Chersonese and twelve at Byzantium. The epigram explicitly commemorates those who died at the Hellespont, and must have been commissioned and written early in the year, rather than at its conclusion, although it appears to be inscribed by the same hand that inscribed ll. 41–4 and 74–97. At a stretch Byzantium could be considered to be covered by 'at the Hellespont', but hardly 'the other wars'.

There are various features of interest in this inscription, and one big question. The features of interest concern tribal order, the status of generals, naming patterns and the distribution of war casualties. The big question is about its date.

The ten Athenian tribes had an official order which determined not only how they were listed in catalogues like this but also the order in which tribes took it in turns to provide secretaries, etc. We cannot show that there was ever a time when the Cleisthenic tribes did not have an official order, but, on the basis of the date we opt for here, this is the earliest substantial positive evidence of that tribal order (see Introduction, p. xix with n. 7). Indirect evidence for the order may be provided by the heavy casualties suffered by Erechtheis (**109**), which are easiest to explain if, as tribe I, they had a vulnerable position on the end of a battle-line (but this will not straightforwardly explain why at Plataea all fifty-two Athenian casualties came from tribe IX, Aiantis (Plut. *Arist.* 19. v–vi, from Clidemus *FGrH* 323 F 22)).

The first name on the list is that of a general, Epiteles. He is not listed under a tribe. This may be because, although generals were basically chosen one from each tribe (see Rhodes, *Comm. Ath. Pol.* 265–6), all generals were thought of as serving all the Athenian forces, not commanding a tribal contingent. It is possible that this is Epiteles son of Soinautes from Pergase who made a dedication on the acropolis to Poseidon Erechtheus dated around 450 (*IG* i^3 873), in which case he would have belonged to Erechtheis and so be listed next to his own tribe; listing of a general at the head of his tribe is found elsewhere (**109**. 5–6, *IG* ii^2 5221, *Agora* xvii 25). The only other man not listed by tribe is the man from Eleutherae (96–7). His presence is a puzzle: although Eleutherae, on the south flank of Cithaeron in the far north-west of Attica, was not in the deme system, we should expect that if the man was a citizen he would have belonged to a tribe and a deme, while if he was not a citizen it is strange that he should be listed among the Athenian war dead.

Many names on this list are extremely common at Athens—indeed, in two tribes we find repetitions of the same name (cf. above on **109** and **111**), presumably because of family naming traditions (two men named Pythodorus in Erechtheis, two men named Aristarchus in Cecropis); but some names are distinctive. Two have provoked particular comment because they seem to be connected to earlier events: Carystonicus in l. 27 and Naxiades in l. 79 seem plausibly linked to events in the 470s: the Athenian compulsion upon Carystus to join the Delian League, and Athenian subjugation and 'enslavement' of Naxos (Thuc. i. 98. iii–iv). If those connections are real then the men bearing those names would have come of age in the 450s and we might expect to find them dying in war at any point from then until around 420.

There is a striking difference between the distribution of casualties in the Chersonese and in the other wars on the one hand, and at Byzantium on the other. The distribution of casualties across the tribes at Byzantium could not be more even: every tribe has one casualty, except for tribes I and VII which have two. By contrast, casualties in the Chersonese vary from none in tribe V (with one in tribes III, IV and IX) to five in tribe II (with four in tribes I, VI and VII). So too in the other wars, there are no casualties in tribes II, VI or X, but six in tribe III (and three in both tribes VII and IX). This may indicate rather different types of conflict in the different areas, with formal battle occurring in the Chersonese and 'in the other wars' and much more casual conflict at Byzantium.

Both the pattern of naming and the distribution of casualties give some evidence for the date of this inscription. Scholars have looked for occasions when Athenians are known to have been in conflict with Byzantium and at the Hellespont. There was plenty of conflict in this area in the last stage of the Peloponnesian War, but by that time someone born in the 470s would hardly be on active service. There was conflict at Byzantium in 440, but this was in connection with still more major conflict on Samos, and the failure to name Samos as a theatre of war points against that, as does the casual nature of the Byzantium casualties. What we are looking for is a conflict leading to battle in the Chersonese, minor conflict around Byzantium and some further formal conflict elsewhere. Conflict in the Chersonese is known from the year 447 (Plut. *Per.* 19. i in combination with evidence from the tribute lists) and 'other wars' are not implausible in that year, which is also compatible with the letter forms of the inscription.

It is a matter of curiosity that a fragment of a red-figure *loutrophoros* in Amsterdam (2455) pictures five *stelai*, evidently intended to represent lists of war dead, and that the two phrases that can be read are [ἐ]χς Ἐλευ<θερõν> and ἐν Βυζαν<τίοι>, i.e. phrases that occur on this *stele* (though they are shown occurring on different *stelai* in the picture): see Immerwahr, *Attic Script*, 100, no. 674, fig. 130; Arrington, *Ashes, Images and Memories*, 79–80, fig. 2. 6). This *loutrophoros* at least suggests that the lists of public war dead were read by Athenians, and perhaps that theatres of war with significant casualties and anomalous individuals, like the man from Eleutherae, attracted some public attention.

The epigram is a conventional one whose phrases can be paralleled in other inscriptions: 'glorious youth lost' is found in *CEG* 82 (of similar date, found on Lemnos but in Attic dialect); 'famous fatherland' is found in *CEG* 10, the epigram for those who died at Potidaea, perhaps in 432; 'memorial of excellence' occurs at

---

130

Athenian campaign in the Megarid, 446

A *stele* found among the graves near the Acharnian Gate (south of the modern Omonoia); subsequently defaced and reused in a modern building, and a fragment from the left-hand side broken off and rediscovered separately; now in the Epigraphical Museum. Phot. Clairmont, *Patrios Nomos*, ii. pl. 59.

Mixed Attic and Doric forms, in Ionic lettering. Non-*stoichedon*. The text comprises nine hexameters, the ends of which are marked with a vertical stroke in the Greek text below, followed by the note of the three tribes in prose.

IG ii^{1} 1675, with the transcription made by L. F. S. Fauvel before the stone was damaged; M&L 51; *CEG* 83; Clairmont, *Patrios Nomos*, i. 180–1 no. 32A; *IG* i^{3} 1353*. Trans. Fornara 101; Dillon & Garland^{3} 12. 23. See also Ferrario, *Historical Agency and the 'Great Man' in Classical Greece*, 49–51.

μνῆμα ṭ[όδ' ἐστ' ἐ]πὶ σάματι κείμενον ἀνδρὸς ἀρίστο. | Πυθίων
ἐγ Μεγάρω<ν> δαιώσας ἑπτὰ μ<ὲ>ν ἄνδρας, | ἑπτὰ δὲ ἀπορρήξας λ-
όγχας ἐνὶ σώματι ἐκείνων | εἵλετο τὰν ἀρετὰν πατέρα εὐκ-
λείζων ἐνὶ δήμωι. | οὗτος ἀνήρ, ὃς ἔ<σ>ωισεν Ἀθηναίων τρ-
ε̃ς φυλὰς | ἐκ Παγᾶν ἀγαγὼν διὰ Βοιωτῶν ἐς Ἀθήνας, | εὔκλ-
εισ' Ἀνδοκίδαν δισχίλοις ἀνδραπόδοισιν. | οὐδέ{δε}να
πημάνας ἐπιχθονίων ἀνθρώπων | ἐς Ἀΐδα κατέβα πᾶσιν μα-
καριστὸς ἰδέσθαι. | φυλαὶ αἵδ' εἰσίν· Πανδιονίς, Κεκρ-
οπίς, Ἀντιοχίς. *vacat*
vacat

2 the stone had Μεγαρω . . . μν. ἀπορρήξας *IG* i^{3}: -σας read by Fauvel. 4 the stone had εωισεν.

This stone was originally dated to the fourth century because of its Ionic lettering, but has long been regarded as belonging to the campaigns of 446. (A one-paragraph summary of an unpublished paper by C. N. Edmonson, *AJA*^{2} lxxiv 1970, 193, suggested without indicating the reason that the battle of Tanagra, 458 or 457, was more likely.) According to Thuc. I. 114. i–ii Euboea rose in revolt and Pericles took an army there;

Olympia on the dedication of Praxiteles, perhaps dated to the 470s (*CEG* 380), on the Parian monument to those who died at Eïon in the 470s (*CEG* 155), on the dedication of Ecphantus on the acropolis from the 460s (*CEG* 272) and on the *stele* of Sosinus the bronze-worker (*CEG* 96). The conceit that the dead 'died fighting' features also in the epigram on the Marathon casualty list (see Arrington, *Ashes, Images and Memories*, 108, cf. 99).

This is the memorial lying on the tomb of an excellent man, Pythion from Megara, who slew seven men and broke off seven spears in their bodies: he chose virtue and brought honour to his father among the people.

4 This man, who saved three tribes of Athenians, bringing them from Pegae through Boeotia to Athens, brought honour to Andocides with two thousand captives (*or* slaves?).

6 He harmed none of the men on earth, and went down to Hades blessed for all to see.

8 These are the tribes: Pandionis, Cecropis, Antiochis.

---

but then Megara revolted, the Peloponnesians prepared to invade Attica and most of Megara's Athenian garrison was killed; Pericles returned from Euboea, and the Peloponnesians under Plistoanax invaded Attica but withdrew after going no further than Eleusis and Thria. Diod. Sic. xii. 5. ii adds an Athenian expedition into the Megarid, which ravaged the territory, defeated the Megarians in a battle and drove them back into their city; and the three tribes of Athenians commanded by Andocides will be the force used in that expedition.

Pegae was Megara's harbour on the Gulf of Corinth, gained by Athens when Megara became an ally *c.*461 (Thuc. I. 103. iv); Pythion will have guided the Athenians by the roundabout and awkward route via Aegosthena and Creusis identified by N. G. L. Hammond, *BSA* xlix 1954, 113 with 106 fig. 1 = his *Studies in Greek History*, 433–4 with 421 fig. 18, in order to avoid Plistoanax' force. Pegae (and Nisaea, the harbour on the Saronic Gulf) remained in Athens' hands until the Thirty Years' Peace, when they were among the mainland possessions which Athens gave up (Thuc. I. 115. i, cf. IV. 21. iii).

Pythion is one of seven men of that name from the Megarid in *LGPN*, but none of the others is earlier than the second half of the fourth century. We do not know when he died: the lettering would suit a date 446–*c.*425. Andocides, grandfather of the orator, was one of the Athenians involved in making the Thirty Years' Peace (Hellan. *FGrH* 323a F 24, Andoc. III. *Peace* 6, Aeschin. II. *Embassy* 174), and one of the generals in the war against Samos in 440–439 (Andr. *FGrH* 324 F 38), but his mention in Thuc. I. 51. iv as one of the generals commanding the second squadron sent to Corcyra in 433 is probably a mistake (cf. on **148**). The tribes Pandionis, Cecropis and Antiochis were respectively III, VII and X in the order in which the tribes were

131

Athenian relations with Chalcis, 446/5 or 424/3

A marble *stele* found built into the south wall of the acropolis, formerly in the Epigraphical Museum and now displayed in the Acropolis Museum. This was originally joined to a second stone on the left, and both were surmounted by a further stone (see below). Phot. *ATL* ii, pl. 10.

Attic letters (but with H = η in l. 77). *Stoichedon* 32, except ll.1–2 and 80.

SIG^3 64; Tod 42; M&L 52*; Balcer, *The Athenian Regulations for Chalkis*, 27–9; *IG* i^3 40. Trans. Fornara 103, Osborne, *The Athenian Empire*^{4}, 78 (a different translation in earlier editions); Dillon & Garland^3 13. 19. See also M. Ostwald, *JHS* cxxii 2002, 134–43 = his *Language and History in Ancient Greek Culture*, ch. xii.

ἔδοχσεν τε͂[ι β]ολε͂ι καὶ το͂ι δέμοι. Ἀντιοχὶς ἐ[πρυτ]-
άνευε· Δρακ[ον]τίδες ἐπεστάτε. Διόγνετος εἶπε·
κατὰ τάδε τὸν hόρκον ὀμόσαι Ἀθεναίον τ-
ὲν βολὲν καὶ τὸς δικαστάς· οὐκ ἐχσελο͂ Χα-
λκιδέας ἐχ Χαλκίδος οὐδὲ τὲν πόλιν ἀνά-
στατον ποέσο οὐδὲ ἰδιότεν οὐδένα ἀτιμ-
όσο οὐδὲ φυγε͂ι ζεμιόσο οὐδὲ χσυλλέφσο-
μαι οὐδὲ ἀποκτενο͂ οὐδὲ χρέματα ἀφαιρέ-

regularly listed (cf. Introduction, p. xix): the use of just three tribes for this campaign is the kind of deployment which could result in heavy casualties in some tribes but none in others (cf. **129**).

K. J. Dover, *Greek Popular Morality*, 280, remarks on the incongruity of the claim that a man who 'slew seven men' had 'harmed none of the men on earth', which presumably meant in fact that he had harmed no Athenians.

Private gravestones with epigrams are rare in fifth-century Attica before *c.*430, so this stone—not for an Athenian but for a foreigner—with its nine hexameters is exceptional. There is poetic vocabulary in much of the epigram (δαιώσας, εὐκλεΐζων, πημάνας, ἐπιχθονίων), though the factual account in ll. 4–5 is jarringly prosaic. Although μάκαρ is found from Homer onwards, ll. 7–8 provide possibly the earliest instance of the form μακαριστός (Hdt. vii. 18. iii might be earlier): for the use of the word with reference to the blessedness of the afterlife cf. the Orphic gold leaf *IG* xiv 641 (1) = *Vorsokr.* i b 18. 10. Ionic lettering appeared gradually in Athenian inscriptions during the fifth century, but more slowly in documents of the Athenian *polis* than in other texts, before being officially adopted in 403/2 (Theopompus *FGrH* 115 FF 153–5, cf. Introduction, p. xxvii). For its use in funerary epigrams cf. *IG* i^3 1154 (mid-5th century), 1178 (433/2).

Resolved by the council and people. Antiochis was the prytany; Dracontides was the chairman. Diognetus proposed:

3 The Athenian council and jurors shall swear an oath on the following terms: 'I shall not expel Chalcidians from Chalcis, nor shall I uproot their city; I shall deprive no individual of civic rights nor punish any with exile nor take any prisoner, nor execute any, nor

σομαι ἀκρίτο οὐδενὸς ἄνευ τô δέμο τô Ἀθ-
εναίον, οὐδ' ἐπιφσεφιô κατὰ ἀπροσκλέτο
οὔτε κατὰ τô κοινô οὔτε κατὰ ἰδιότο οὐδ-
ὲ ἑνός, καὶ πρεσβείαν ἐλθôσαν προσάχσο
πρὸς βολὲν καὶ δêμον δέκα ἑμερôν hόταν
πρυτανεύο κατὰ τὸ δυνατόν. ταῦτα δὲ ἐμπ̣-
[ε]δόσο Χαλκιδεῦσιν πειθομένοις τôι δέ-
[μ]οι τôι Ἀθεναίον. hορκôσαι δὲ πρεσβεία-
[ν] ἐλθôσαν ἐχ Χαλκίδος μετὰ τôν hορκοτô-
ν Ἀθεναίος καὶ ἀπογράφσαι τὸς ὀμόσαντ-
ας. hόπος δ' ἂν [ὀ]μόσοσιν hάπαντες, ἐπιμελ-
όσθον hοι στ[ρ]ατεγοί. *vacat*
κατὰ τάδε Χαλκιδέας ὀμόσαι· οὐκ ἀπο[σ]τέ-
σομαι ἀπὸ τô [δ]έμο τô Ἀθεναίον οὔτε τέ[χ]ν-
ει οὔτε μεχανêι οὐδεμιᾶι οὐδ' ἔπει οὐδὲ
ἔργοι οὐδὲ τôι ἀφισταμένοι πείσομαι, κ-
αὶ ἐὰν ἀφιστêι τις κατερô Ἀθεναίοισι, κ-
αὶ τὸν φόρον hυποτελô Ἀθεναίοισιν, hὸν
ἂν πείθο Ἀθεναίος, καὶ χσύμμαχος ἔσομα-
ι hοῖος ἂν δύνομαι ἄριστος καὶ δικαιότ-
ατος καὶ τôι δέμοι τôι Ἀθεναίον βοεθέσ-
ο καὶ ἀμυνô, ἐάν τις ἀδικêι τὸν δêμον τὸν
Ἀθεναίον, καὶ πείσομαι τôι δέμοι τôι Ἀθ-
εναίον. ὀμόσαι δὲ Χαλκιδέον τὸς hεβôντ-
ας hάπαντας· hὸς δ' ἂμ μὲ ὀμόσει, ἄτιμον αὐτ-
ὸν ἐ͂ναι καὶ τὰ χρέματα αὐτô δεμόσια καὶ
τô Διὸς τô Ὀλυμπίο τὸ ἐπιδέκατον hιερὸ-
ν ἔστο τôν χρεμάτον. hορκôσαι δὲ πρεσβε-
ίαν Ἀθεναίον ἐλθôσαν ἐς Χαλκίδα μετὰ τ-
ôν hορκοτôν τôν ἐν Χαλκίδι καὶ ἀπογράφ-
σαι τὸς ὀμόσαντας Χαλκιδέον.
vacat
Ἀντικλε͂ς εἶπε· ἀγαθêι τύχει τêι Ἀθεναί-
ον ποε͂σθαι τὸν hόρκον Ἀθεναίος καὶ Χαλ-
κιδέας, καθάπερ Ἐρετριεῦσι ἐφσεφίσατ-
ο hο δε͂μος hο Ἀθεναίον· hόπος δ' ἂν τάχιστ-
α γίγνεται, ἐπιμελόσθον hοι στρατεγοί.
hοίτινες δὲ ἐχσορκόσοσι ἀφικόμενοι ἐ-
ς Χαλκίδα, ἑλέσθαι τὸν δε͂μον πέντε ἄνδρ-
ας αὐτίκα μάλα. περὶ δὲ τôν hομέρον ἀποκ-
ρίνασθαι Χαλκιδεῦσιν, hότι νῦμ μὲν Ἀθε-
ναίοις δοκεῖ ἐᾶν κατὰ τὰ ἐφσεφισμένα· h-
όταν δὲ δοκêι βολευσάμενοι ποέσοσι τὲ-
ν διαλλα[γ]έν, καθότι ἂν δοκêι ἐπιτέδ̣ειο-

confiscate the money of anyone not condemned in court without the authority of the Athenian people; whenever I am a *prytanis* I shall not put anything prejudicial to the interests of an individual or the community to the vote without due notice, and any embassy that is sent I shall bring before the council and people within ten days, as far as I can; I shall maintain this while the Chalcidians obey the Athenian people.' An embassy is to come from Chalcis with the commissioners for oaths and administer the oath to the Athenians and list the names of those who have sworn; the generals having responsibility to see that all take the oath.

21 The Chalcidians shall swear an oath on the following terms: 'I shall not revolt from the people of Athens by any means or device whatsoever, neither in word nor in deed, nor shall I obey anyone who does revolt, and if anyone revolts I shall denounce him to the Athenians, and I shall pay to the Athenians whatever tribute I persuade them to agree, and I shall be the best and fairest ally I am able to be and shall help and defend the Athenian people, in the event of anyone wronging the Athenian people, and I shall obey the Athenian people.' All the Chalcidians of military age and above shall swear. If anyone does not swear he is to be deprived of his civic rights and his property is to be confiscated and a tithe of it dedicated to Zeus Olympios. An embassy shall go from Athens to Chalcis with the commissioners for oaths and administer the oath in Chalcis and list those of the Chalcidians who have sworn.

40 Anticles proposed: For good fortune for the Athenians: the Athenians and Chalcidians shall make the oath just as the Athenian people voted for the people of Eretria, and the generals shall have responsibility to see that that happens as quickly as possible.

45 The people as soon as possible shall choose five men to go to Chalcis to exact the oaths. And on the matter of hostages, they shall reply to the Chalcidians that for the moment the Athenians have decided to leave matters as decreed.

50 But whenever they decide they will deliberate and draw up an agreement [*or* 'exchange'] on conditions which seem suitable for the Athenians and the Chalcidians.

ν ἒναι Ἀθεναίοις καὶ Χαλκιδεῦσιν. τὸς δ-
ὲ χσένος τὸς ἐν Χαλκίδι, hόσοι οἰκôντες
μὲ τελôσιν Ἀθέναζε, καὶ εἴ τοι δέδοται h-
υπὸ τô δέμο τô Ἀθεναίον ἀτέλεια, τὸς δὲ ἄ-
λλος τελêν ἐς Χαλκίδα, καθάπερ hοι ἄλλο-
ι Χαλκιδέες. τὸ δὲ φσέφισμα τόδε καὶ τὸν
hόρκον ἀναγράφσαι, Ἀθένεσι μὲν τὸν γρα-
μμ[α]τέα τêς βολêς ἐστέλει λιθίνει καὶ κ-
αταθêναι ἐς πόλιν τέλεσι τοῖς Χαλκιδέ-
ον, ἐν δὲ Χαλκίδι ἐν τôι hιερôι τôι Διὸς τô
Ὀλυμπίο hε βολὲ Χαλκιδέον ἀναγράφσασ-
α καταθέτο. ταῦτα μὲν φσεφίσασθαι Χαλκ̣-
ιδεῦσιν. *vvvv* τὰ δὲ hιερὰ τὰ ἐκ τôν χρεσμ-
ôν hυπὲρ Εὐβοίας θῦσαι ὀς τάχιστα μετὰ
hιεροκλέος τρêς ἄνδρας, hὸς ἂν ἕλεται ḥ-
ε βολὲ σφôν αὐτôν· hόπος δ' ἂν τάχιστα τυθ-
êι, hοι στρατεγοὶ συνεπιμελόσθον καὶ τ-
ὸ ἀργύριον ἐς ταῦτα [π]αρεχόντον. *vacat*
Ἀρχέστρατο[ς] εἶπε· τὰ μὲν ἄλλα καθάπερ Ἀ-
ντικλêς· τὰς δὲ εὐθύνας Χαλκιδεῦσι κατ-
ὰ σφôν αὐτôν ἒναι ἐν Χαλκίδι καθάπερ Ἀθ-
ένεσιν Ἀθεναίοις πλὲν φυγêς καὶ θανάτ-
ο καὶ ἀτιμίας· περὶ δὲ τούτον ἔφεσιν ἒνα-
ι Ἀθέναζε ἐς τὲν ἑλιαίαν τὲν τôν θεσμοθ-
ετôν κατὰ τὸ φσέφισμα τô δέμο· περὶ δὲ φυ-
λακêς Εὐβοίας τὸς στρατηγὸς ἐπιμέλεσ-
θαι hος ἂν δύνονται ἄριστα, hόπος ἂν ἔχε-
ι hος βέλτιστα Ἀθεναίοις.
hόρκος.

This is an important document for the way in which the Athenians governed their allies in the Athenian empire, but its precise significance depends upon its uncertain date. What we have is one of a sequence of decisions about Chalcis, with reference made to earlier decrees (49) as well as to an embassy from Chalcis, and so we see something of the process of Athens' deliberation about its allies, as well as its decisions.

The inscription that we have is substantially complete. The left side of the stone is finished in such a way as to make clear that it abutted tightly to something else, but there is no trace of any clamp, so it is unlikely that a further *stele* was fixed there. The top of the stone has a shallow cutting, but this appears to be to insert a tenon of an object that did not fit tightly to the top and did not cover the whole top surface: most plausibly this was a low, heavy finial (C. Lawton, *Hesperia* lxi 1992, 248–50).

The foreigners who live in Chalcis—except as many as pay no taxes to Athens, and if someone has been given tax exemption by the Athenian people—the rest shall pay taxes in Chalcis, just like the other Chalcidians.

57 The secretary of the council shall write up this decree and oath at Athens on a stone *stele* and set it up on the acropolis at the expense of the Chalcidians, and let the council of the Chalcidians write it up and deposit it in the sanctuary of Zeus Olympios at Chalcis. This is the decree about the Chalcidians.

64 Three men, chosen by the council from their own number, shall go with Hierocles to carry out the sacrifices required by the oracles about Euboea as quickly as possible. So that this happens as quickly as possible the generals shall take joint responsibility and provide the money for it.

70 Archestratus proposed. In other respects as Anticles had proposed, but *euthynai* (audits) are to be in the hands of the Chalcidians by themselves in Chalcis, just as of the Athenians at Athens except in cases involving exile, execution or loss of civic rights. On these matters there shall be appeal to Athens to the court of the *thesmothetai* in accordance with the decree of the people. As to guarding Euboea, the generals shall take responsibility for doing that as best they can in the best interests of the Athenians.

80 Oath.

We should therefore treat the text that we have as complete, despite the unusual omission of any mention of the secretary in the prescript.

The stone records three proposals: the proposal of Diognetus (2) for the terms of the oaths that the Athenians and Chalcidians are to swear; the proposal of Anticles (40) that the same oath should be sworn in relation to Chalcis as was sworn in relation to Eretria, and that no immediate change be made to the decision about hostages, about who should pay taxes at Chalcis and about the making of sacrifices ordered by the oracle; and the rider moved by Archestratus (70) determining which court cases involving people of Chalcis should be tried at Athens and which at Chalcis. Of these three proposals, that by Archestratus is explicitly an addition to Anticles' decree; but what of Diognetus' decree (Rhodes, *Boule*, 71 n. 2)? The opening of Anticles' decree is redundant if Diognetus' decree has been passed specifically in relation to Chalcis, since Diognetus' decree specifies the content of the oath and specifies who is to oversee it and who to swear it. Either, therefore, Diognetus' proposal simply spells out the oath that Anticles had proposed, or Diognetus was the proposer of the oath administered in the case of Eretria, and what he had proposed in that case is repeated here, with 'Eretria' changed to 'Chalcis'. The second alternative is perhaps more plausible: the text of an earlier decree has been silently adapted but its proposer preserved. If this is the case, then unless the two decrees were passed on the same day, Dracontides will have been president on the day when Anticles made his proposal, but not when Diognetus made his. Part of the oath used in the case of Eretria seems to be preserved (*IG* i^3 39) and can be restored to have identical wording (though written in Ionic rather than Attic letters).

Diognetus' proposal has the oath sworn by the Athenian council and by the jurors—the appropriate swearers given the content of the oath which concerns matters over which courts and council have control (though some clauses are relevant only to councillors, some only to jurors). Council and court worked together to set tribute (*IG* i^3 282. ii. 43–4; **119** above, p. 106), but this arrangement for the oath is unusual. It was the generals and others who swore at Samos (**139**), the archons who swore at Miletus in 426/5 (*IG* i^3 21), and the council and the 'magistrates at home' who swore to the treaty with Argos, Mantinea and Elis in 420/19 (Thuc. v. 47. ix, not preserved in **165**). Although some restorations of the Egesta alliance (**166**) also have the jurors swear, there are more plausible restorations of the lines in question. An oath involving the jurors is remarkable because of the number of people involved: 6,000 (*Ath. Pol.* 24. iii). Those 6,000 had to come together annually to take the 'dicastic oath' (Isoc. xv. *Antid.* 21), but otherwise they would only exceptionally gather as a single group (for a trial with 6,000 jurors see Andoc. i. *Mysteries* 17). An oath administered to 500 councillors and 6,000 jurors would have required a major public gathering. This certainly underlines the importance of this agreement and the seriousness with which the Athenians regarded it.[1] At Chalcis the oath is sworn by all adult males. We do not know the citizen population of Chalcis, but it is not implausible that it was in the region of 6,500.[2]

The terms of the Athenian oath may bind them to behave differently in the future from the way they have behaved in the past. Aelian (*V.H.* vi. 1) claims that the Athenians, when they subdued the people of Chalcis, divided the land known as the 'land of the *hippobotai*' into 2,000 lots, dedicated some to Athena and leased out the rest, with the leases being listed in the Stoa Basileios in the Athenian agora. Plut. *Per.* 23. iv, plausibly referring to the same occasion, talks of the expulsion of the *hippobotai*. Thuc. i. 114. iii does not refer explicitly to Chalcis but implies that the Athenians reduced Euboea to agreement in 446 without taking over the land except

[1] International oaths are discussed by S. Bolmarcich, the dikastic oath by D. C. Mirhady, and one particularly striking example of mass oath-taking by J. L. Shear, in Sommerstein & Fletcher (edd.), *Horkos*, 26–38, 48–59, and 148–60 respectively.

[2] M. H. Hansen, *The Shotgun Method*, includes Chalcis in those city-states of 5 km.^{2} or over to which he assigns a total population of 27,300, remarking (33 n. 99) that this is probably the right order of magnitude in the case of Chalcis.

at Hestiaea. Despite some terminology used by Aelian, we are unlikely to be dealing with a cleruchy here (Figueira, *Athens and Aigina in the Age of Imperial Colonization*, 258–60), and the oath would be undertaking not to do to Chalcis (or Eretria) what Athens had done to Hestiaea (Athens had already on an earlier occasion taken over the land of Chalcis: Hdt. v. 77. ii). Similarly, the promise not to take any prisoner without due legal process would be a promise not again to keep prisoners in chains, as Aelian claims had been done.

Two details of the Athenian oath are worth noting. One is the use of 'the people of the Athenians' as a term to describe the Athenian courts. The issue of the equivalence of the courts and the assembly has been much discussed; here, if 'without the *demos*' is, as it seems to us that in practical terms it must be, an explanatory gloss on 'untried', the courts are explicitly identified as the Athenian people.[3] The second is the undertaking to bring matters raised by any embassy from Chalcis to the Athenian assembly within ten days. In the fourth century the assembly certainly met four times each prytany (*Ath. Pol.* 43. iii), which, with ten prytanies a year, meant every nine or ten days. This undertaking implies that regular meetings were already occurring in the middle of the fifth century, and also that the council would bring to the notice of the assembly on the following day matters that came to its attention on the day before a scheduled assembly meeting. Getting a hearing in Athens was a well-known problem ([Xen.] *Ath. Pol.* iii. 1), so this was a valuable promise.

The oath that citizens of Chalcis swear gains interest from comparison with the oath required of the council at Erythrae (**121**). We notice the absence here of mention of Athens' allies: it is revolt from Athens alone that is at issue, to Athens that tribute is considered to be paid, and alliance with Athens alone that is mentioned. Since 'revolt' is a political matter, involving political groups, not an individual matter, Athens' other allies are tacitly present when the Chalcidians swear to denounce anyone who revolts. But we should not overdo the emphasis on Athens' strong arm: that it is the gods who oversee the oath is made clear by the way in which a tithe of the property confiscated from any defaulter goes to Zeus Olympios, in whose sanctuary at Chalcis the other copy of the *stele* was erected. More significantly still, at Erythrae the oath is given in the context of new political arrangements on which the Athenians have insisted. Beyond making all adult (male) Chalcidians responsible for this agreement, Athens imposes no political conditions. All references are to 'the Chalcidians' or 'those at Chalcis', not even, as at Athens, to the *demos*.

Anticles' proposal comes in the wake of an embassy from Chalcis, and represents the Athenian council's response (though the order of clauses, with the publication clause before the final substantive clause, does not suggest the best of drafting). The embassy seems largely to have made the council think that they should act quickly. On the matter of hostages, where the request seems to have been to change

[3] The champion of the view that *demos* is not used to refer to the courts but only to the assembly is M. H. Hansen. See Hansen, *The Athenian Ecclesia*, 139–58, *The Athenian Ecclesia II*, 213–18, and most recently *GRBS* l 2010, 499–536. The debate is usefully reviewed by A. J. L. Blanshard, *Phoenix* lviii 2004, 28–48, though at 31–2 he takes a different view of this passage.

who is kept as a hostage, the Athenians agree only that such an exchange might happen in future. The Athenians do, however, clarify what they expect the financial arrangements at Chalcis to be.

Who exactly is at question in the clause about finance has been much debated. Taxes identical to those paid by the citizens of Chalcis are to be paid by the *xenoi* resident at Chalcis, except those who pay taxes to Athens (or perhaps, better, 'owe duty', even 'are registered in the Solonian system of *tele*') or those who have been given tax exemption by the Athenians (see S. R. Slings, *ZPE* xxv 1977, 277–9; A. S. Henry, *ZPE* xxxv 1979, 287–91). But who are these *xenoi*?[4] Scholars have repeatedly suggested that they are Athenian cleruchs, but, even if there were Athenian cleruchs at Chalcis (see above), reference to them as *xenoi* would be very strange, and there is no reason why any of them would have exemption from Athenian taxes. It is likely to be the case, as Ostwald has insisted, that the Athenians are reflecting back the terms of the Chalcidians' question: 'Are foreigners to pay taxes in Chalcis?', and that for the Chalcidians the Athenians were indeed foreigners, but that even the Chalcidians would talk of 'foreigners' rather than 'Athenians' only if they had in mind a group that significantly included non-Athenians (Ostwald, 140). Though our evidence for grants of tax exemption is much better for the fourth than for the fifth century, our earliest evidence for such a grant dates to *c.*450 (*IG* i^3 24; cf. 73 in an amendment proposed by one Archestratus: cf. **118**); Athens conceded tax exemptions in return for services rendered, and in particular services related to the import of grain (cf. esp. Dem. xx. *Lept.*). The community of 'foreigners' whom Chalcis is to be permitted to tax is thus likely to be a normal temporary or semi-permanent community of those engaged in trade, and Athens is insisting both that Athenians among them, and those whose favour the Athenians have particularly courted, should be exempt and that the others pay no more tax than the Chalcidians themselves.[5] Far from making a concession here, the Athenians are insisting on special tax-free status at Chalcis for all those who have obligations or exemption from obligations at Athens (= Athenian citizens and metics, including, it is true, any citizens of Chalcis who were metics at Athens), and equal tax status for other foreigners.[6] The awkwardness of the Greek is perhaps a reflection of some attempt to conceal this.

The third substantive item in Anticles' proposal concerns sacrifices. Here what is most interesting is what must have gone on before. The council clearly knows of particular oracles 'about Euboea' (this phrase may reflect the oracular question, although it would also be possible to construe the sentence as 'sacrifice on behalf

[4] The most important of the many discussions of this question are P. Gauthier, *REG* lxxxiv 1971, 44–79 at 65–76, and A. Giovannini, *ZPE* cxxxiii 2000, 61–74.

[5] Athenian interest in Euboean trade and in the taxing of that trade emerges also from the long but fragmentary decree concerning Hestiaea (*IG* i^3 41) which is plausibly contemporary with the Chalcis decree.

[6] Ostwald, 143, puts the clause into a more positive light by stressing that what is at issue is not simply paying tax but performance of civic obligations, so that this clause stresses the right of Chalcis to impose civic obligations on foreign residents; but this underplays the central part of paying special taxes in the normal obligations of non-citizens to their city of residence.

of Euboea').[7] The oracles mentioned sacrifices (presumably to a particular god), and carrying them out 'as quickly as possible' is entrusted to a group of three men with one Hierocles, helped and funded by the generals. It is notable that it is matters that involve the gods (the oath, the sacrifices) that make the council anxious and call for rapid action. Hierocles is to be identified with a *chresmologos* who is also referred to in Athenian comedy (Ar. *Pax* 1047; Eupolis fr. 231 KA) and who came to be associated with Euboean Hestiaea. It is tempting to think that Hierocles has himself come to the council with these oracles—perhaps oracles suggesting that the Athenians would not fare well in matters concerning Euboea unless they offered particular sacrifices—and that following his performance of those sacrifices, and Athenian success, he was rewarded with land at Hestiaea (cf. Flower, *The Seer in Ancient Greece*, 62). The way the Athenians worked with oracles is both noted by historians (Thuc. II. 21. iii, III. 104, VIII. 1. i; Diod. Sic. XII. 58. vi) and documented in **141** and R&O 158 (see further Bowden, *Classical Athens and the Delphic Oracle*).

Archestratus' amendment imposes a limit on the judicial independence of Chalcis. But the extent of the limitation has been disputed (see M&L, p.143). If we understand εὐθύναι ('audit') in the sense in which it is generally used in Athenian inscriptions, with reference to the audit of magistrates at the end of their term of office, then the limitation will be simply upon punishing officials found guilty of malpractice with death, exile or loss of civic rights. Such cases would have to be heard again (this is the implication of ἔφεσις) in the Athenian court of the *thesmothetai*. If εὐθύναι is understood to mean simply 'punishment' (as at Pl. *Prt.* 326 D), and as recent commentators including M&L and Balcer have preferred, all cases at Chalcis where the punishment involved exile, execution or loss of civic rights would be referred to Athens. Which interpretation is correct? Antiphon v. *Herodes* 47 implies that by the date of that speech (*c.*420) Athens insisted that all cases among the allies in which a penalty of death was called for had to be heard again in Athens. That Athens is making special provision here shows that that rule did not yet apply. Did the Athenians initially apply it to only some cases? We would have to believe that initially Athens was particularly concerned about the audit being used to condemn officials (presumably because those officials had done Athens' bidding) and only later extended her concern to political use of trials more generally. Given the tasks which the Athenians imposed upon magistrates (*archontes*) in the cities (cf. **155**), this is not implausible (cf. their special measures to protect *proxenoi*: **157**, **184**), and we believe that *euthynai* should be understood here in the otherwise invariable epigraphic sense of 'audits of magistrates'.

Attempts to date this decree have been based on arguments from historical and epigraphic context. In terms of historical context we must find a time when there has been both some major disruption in relations between Athens and Chalcis, and a recent and similar disruption in relations between Athens and Eretria. This needs to be within the active lifetime of the oracle-monger Hierocles (Aristophanes' *Peace*

[7] For hυπὲρ Εὐβοίας as 'the oracles concerning Euboea' see e.g. Flower, *The Seer in Ancient Greece*, 62; for hυπὲρ Εὐβοίας as 'sacrifices for Euboea' see e.g. Parker, in *Crux* . . . *G. E. M. de Ste. Croix*, 307.

dates to 421, Eupolis' *Poleis* around the same time). Thucydides (I. 113–4) records that after the Athenians had been defeated at Coronea in spring 446 by Boeotian exiles from Orchomenus, Locrians, and Euboean exiles, and had withdrawn from Boeotia, Euboea revolted. Pericles led an army to deal with Euboea, and having briefly had to withdraw to deal with trouble elsewhere, returned and subdued the whole island, reaching agreement with other cities but removing the population from Hestiaea and settling the land with Athenians. These events provide the conditions presupposed by this inscription, although this implies a long lifetime of activity by Hierocles (25 years; cf. the 30-year career of the seer Lampon, below **141**). Thucydides records no further Athenian military action in Euboea until 412/1, but a scholiast to Ar. *Vesp.* 718 quotes Philochorus (*FGH* 328 F 130) saying that in the archonship of Isarchus (424/3) 'they campaigned against Euboea'.

Although we know nothing further about this campaign, and Thucydides' failure to mention it might suggest it was minor, H. B. Mattingly has made the case for dating this decree to 424/3 (*JHS* lxxxi 1961, 124–32 = his *AER* 53–67; *CQ*^{2} lii 2002 377–9). The case rests largely on epigraphic parallels for the layout of Anticles' decree (which he takes to be an amendment) and a three-man commission with

---

132

Halicarnassian law concerning disputed property, *c*.450

A marble *stele* first seen and copied at Bodrum (Halicarnassus) in 1749 by the Earl of Charlemont; later recovered by Charles Newton, and now in British Museum. Photo: Thompson *et al.*, *Facsimiles of Ancient Manuscripts, etc.: Second Series*, pl. 62; Virgilio, *Epigrafia e storiografia*, pl. 9. Facsimile: Roehl, *Imagines Inscriptonum Graecarum Antiquissmarum*, 23. 14; Virgilio, *op. cit.*, pl. 8; facsimile of Charlemont's copy *GIBM* iv, p. 50.

Ionic letters, with *sampi* (T) used in ll. 2, 6, [7] and 16, but not in 41 (cf. **102**. *B*. 23). Dotted *omicron* (and dotted *omega* in 41–5) hard to distinguish now from *theta*.

SIG^3 45; *DGE* 744; Buck 2; Tod 25; M&L 32*; Maffi, *L'iscrizione di Ligdamis*; Koerner 84; *Nomima* i 19. Trans. Fornara 70; Carawan (below) 163–4. See also Hornblower, *Mausolos*, 85–8; E. Carawan in Mackay (ed.), *Orality, Literacy, Memory in the Ancient Greek and Roman World*, 163–84.

τάδε ὁ σύλλο[γ]ος ἐβολεύσατο
ὁ Ἁλικαρναΐέ[ω]ν καὶ Σαλμακι-
τέων καὶ Λύγδαμις ἐν τῆι ἱερῆ[ι]
ἀγορῆι, μῆνος Ἑρμαιῶνος πέμ-
πτηι ἱσταμένο, ἐπὶ Λέοντος πρυ-
ταν[εύον]τος τõ Ὀαΐατιος κα-

the first Athena Nike decree, which he dates to 425/4 (but which we consider to belong to the 430s: see below **137**), and for mention of 'good fortune', for putting a clause identifying what chosen people are to do before the verb of choice (here 45–7), and for mentioning further action after the instruction to vote on the proposal (here 63–5), all belonging in the later 420s. These parallels, and in particular the appearance of 'good fortune', are not trivial, but the Philochorus reference which does not mention Chalcis remains a thin thread on which to hang a major Athenian intervention (cf. Rhodes, *CQ*[2] lviii 2008, 504–5).

Mattingly has sought further support from the individuals mentioned in the decree, but apart from Hierocles it is not possible securely to identify any of those named. A Dracontides (son of Leogoras of Thorae) was politically active, opposing Pericles, in the 430s (Plut. *Per.* 32. iii–iv), general in 433/2 (Thuc. 1. 51. iv; below, **148**. 20–1), and being prosecuted at the time of Aristophanes' *Wasps* (157, cf. 438), but the 'president' was appointed by lot from the current *prytaneis*, and the position might be held at any stage of a man's career. Diognetus and Anticles are relatively common names, and identification with an otherwise-known individual depends on the date assumed.

The meeting of the Halicarnassians and the Salmacians along with Lygdamis took the following decision in the sacred agora on the fifth of the month Hermaion, when Leon son of Oassassis was *prytanis* and Sarussolus son of Thecuïlus *neopoios*, with regard

[ὶ] Σα[ρυΤ]ώλλο τô Θεκυΐλω νε-
[ωπ]οί[ο, πρ]ὸς μνήμονας· μὴ παρ[α]-
δίδο[σθαι] μήτε γῆν μήτε οἰκ[ί]-
[α] τοῖς μνήμοσιν ἐπὶ Ἀπολλω-
νίδεω τô Λυγδάμιος μνημονε-
ύοντος καὶ Παναμύω τô Κασβώ-
λλιος καὶ Σαλμακιτέων μνη-
μονευόντων Μεγαβάτεω τô Ἀ-
φυάσιος καὶ Φορμίωνος τô Π[α]-
νυάΤιος. ἢν δέ τις θέλῃι δικάζε-
σθαι περὶ γῆς ἢ οἰκίων, ἐπικαλ[έ]-
τω ἐν ὀκτωκαίδεκα μησὶν ἀπ' ὅτ[ε]
ὁ ἅδος ἐγένετο· νόμωι δὲ κατάπ[ε]-
ρ νῦν ὁρκῶ{ι}σ<α>ι τὸς δικαστάς· ὅ τ[ι]
ἂν οἱ μνήμονες εἰδέωσιν, τοῦτο
καρτερὸν ἖ναι. ἢν δέ τις ὕστερον
ἐπικαλῆι τούτο τô χρόνο τῶν
ὀκτωκαίδεκα μηνῶν, ὅρκον ἖ναι τ-
ῶι νεμομένωι τὴν γῆν ἢ τὰ οἰκ-
[ί]α, ὁρκôν δὲ τὸς δικαστὰς ἡμί-
[ε]κτον δεξαμένος· τὸν δὲ ὅρκον εἶ-
[ν]αι παρεόντος τô ἐνεστηκότος. κ-
αρτερὸς δ' εἶναι γῆς καὶ οἰκίων οἵτινες
τότ' εἶχον ὅτε Ἀπολλωνίδης καὶ Πανα-
μύης ἐμνημόνευον, εἰ μὴ ὕστερο-
ν ἀπεπέρασαν. τὸν νόμον τοῦτον
ἤν τις θέλῃι συγχέαι ἢ προθῆτα-
[ι] ψῆφον ὥστε μὴ εἶναι τὸν νόμο-
ν τοῦτον, τὰ ἔοντα αὐτô πεπρήσθω
καὶ τὠπόλλωνος εἶναι ἱερὰ καὶ α-
ὐτὸν φεύγεν αἰεί· ἢν δὲ μὴ ἦι αὐτ-
ῶι ἄξια δέκα στατήρων, αὐτὸν [π]-
επρῆσθαι ἐπ' ἐξαγωγῆι καὶ μη[δ]-
αμὰ κάθοδον εἶναι ἐς Ἁλικαρν-
ησσόν. Ἁλικαρνασσέων δὲ τῶς σ-
υμπάντων τούτωι ἐλεύθερον ε[ἶ]-
ναι, ὃς ἂν ταῦτα μὴ παραβαίνῃι κατό-
περ τὰ ὅρκια ἔταμον καὶ ὡς γέγραπτ-
αι ἐν τῶι Ἀπολλω[νί]ωι, ἐπικαλ῀εν.

8–9 μὴ παρ[α] | δίδο[ναι] Virgilio, Maffi, with earlier editors: it is unclear whether the space requires 2 or 3 letters in l. 8, 3 or 4 letters in l. 9 (Charlemont marks three spaces in 8 between οι and ος but only one in 9 between ο and ι).

to the *mnemones*:

8 Neither land nor houses are to be handed over to the *mnemones* when Apollonides son of Lygdamis is *mnemon* along with Panamys son of Casbollis and when of the Salmacians Megabates son of Aphyasis and Phormio son of Panyassis are *mnemones*. If anyone wishes to bring a court case concerning land or houses, let him make the summons in eighteen months from when this decision was made. And by this law as it is now the *dikastai* are to administer an oath; whatever the *mnemones* know, this is binding. And if anyone makes a summons later than this time of eighteen months, there is to be an oath from the person in possession of the property, the *dikastai* receiving half a *hekteus* per oath. The oath to be taken in the presence of the claimant. He is to get charge over land and houses who possessed them at the time when Apollonides and Panamys were *mnemones*, unless they sold them later.

32 If anyone wishes to annul this law or bring a vote that this law should not exist, his property is to be sold and be sacred to Apollo and he himself shall go into exile for life. And if he does not have property worth ten staters he himself is to be sold abroad and in no way is there ever to be return for him to Halicarnassus.

41 There is liberty to whoever of all the Halicarnassians does not transgress the oaths as they have been sworn and as it has been written in the sanctuary of Apollo, to prefer claims.

This inscription initially attracted attention because it seemed possible to link it with known historical figures and circumstances. Whether or not that is the case, this stone provides a fascinating glimpse into a city dealing with the aftermath of a political crisis, and casts some light on relations between Greeks and non-Greeks on the edge of the Greek world that are all the more fascinating given that Halicarnassus was the birthplace of Herodotus.

Political upheavals that brought about exile had significant consequences for property ownership (well illustrated by the provisions required at Tegea when Alexander revoked exile, R&O 101; see also **133** and R&O 54). Here we see the people of Halicarnassus and Salmacis attempting to avoid problems by providing a period in the immediate future (the *mnemones* named must be already in office or about to come into office) when the magistrates' view will necessarily prevail, and then setting up provision to secure the ownership of the current owners. Ferocious penalties, including being sold into slavery, are then instituted for anyone proposing to change or abolish this law.

While we do not know the full background to this law, we can work out part of the picture. Halicarnassus traced its origins back to Troezen (Hdt. vii. 99. iii), but its date of foundation and history in the archaic period are obscure other than its participation in the settlement at Naucratis in Egypt (Hdt. ii. 178. ii). As this inscription shows, by the fifth century Halicarnassus, although regarded as a Doric settlement, was using both Ionic alphabet and dialect. Herodotus (vii. 99) tells us that at the time of the Persian War Artemisia daughter of Lygdamis was tyrant of Halicarnassus; she had taken up power after the death of her husband because her son was still only a young man. She commanded not only the ships provided by Halicarnassus to the Persian fleet but also those from Cos, Nisyrus and Calynda, and she put up a famously impressive showing at the battle of Salamis (Hdt. viii. 87).

Signs of conflict over tyranny appear in the traditions about Herodotus. The *Suda* (η 536 Adler Ἡρόδοτος) says that Herodotus left Halicarnassus because Lygdamis became tyrant, Lygdamis being son of Pisindelis who was the son of Artemisia. It also claims that Herodotus returned to Halicarnassus and expelled the tyrant, but then found himself disliked by the Halicarnassians and so joined those who were founding Thurii. In the entry on Panyassis (π 248 Adler Πανύασις), Herodotus' uncle and a significant poet, the *Suda* says that Panyassis was killed by Lygdamis, the third tyrant of Halicarnassus. The *Suda* records various variant traditions as to the parentage of Herodotus and his relationship with Panyassis, as well as about the age of Panyassis, and we should not assume that every detail related is correct (it is not clear whether we should think of Lygdamis as son or grandson of Artemisia, for instance). However, there is enough consistency in the theme of hostility to the tyrant Lygdamis to make anti-tyrant unrest likely both at Lygdamis' accession and later in order to remove him. It is such unrest, and accompanying exile or voluntary departure from Halicarnassus, that is the background to this law. Given Lygdamis' continued presence it looks as if it is the opponents of Lygdamis who have fled, and that this law governs their attempts to regain their property.

The law—variously referred to as *bouleuma* (i.e. decision made after counsel), *hados* (i.e. what had pleased the parties), and *nomos*—is decided upon by a meeting of Halicarnassians and Salmacians and by Lygdamis. The implication is that the people are exercising some form of sovereignty under, and in support of, a tyrant, who is certainly ruling Halicarnassus and probably Salmacis too.

Salmacis was a community very close to Halicarnassus; by *c.*400 it figured in Halicarnassian property sales only as a toponym (*SIG*[3] 46. 11, 13, 19), and in the fourth century it was incorporated into Halicarnassus. Later in antiquity it was famous particularly for its fountain, the quality of the water of which was held to have been responsible for good relations between Greeks and Carians (Vitr. *Arch.* II. viii. 12, cf. Strabo 656/XIV ii. 16, Arr. *Anab.* I. 23. iii; for the building remains at the Salmacis fountain see Isager & Pedersen (edd.), *The Salmakis Inscription and Hellenistic Halikarnassos*, 15–42). Here it has its independent magistrates, though clearly very closely linked to Halicarnassus: the phrase 'all the Halicarnassians' in ll. 41–2 ought to include the Salmacians.

Although there are also officials known as the *prytanis* and the *neopoios* ('temple-curator') the major roles are given in the law to the *mnemones* and to the judges/jurors (*dikastai*). The role of the *mnemones* has been much discussed, partly because the correct restoration of ll. 8–9 is uncertain. What we appear to have is a ban on property exchange in relation to the mnemonship of Apollonides and the other named *mnemones*, and the inauguration of a period of eighteen months when claims about property ownership must be made in court; once this period is over, the presumptive claim to land lies with those holding it during the time when Apollonides and colleagues were *mnemones*. Claims made in court during the eighteen-month period are decided by the knowledge of the *mnemones*.

Two issues are controversial. How does the period of mnemonship of Apollonides *et al.* relate to the time of the decree? And what do the *mnemones* know? On the second question, Arist. *Pol.* VI. 1321 B 34–40 talks of *mnemones* as registrars, in charge of an archive, but the name means 'remembrancer' and originally their job was to remember matters that were crucial to the community (see R. Thomas, in Foxhall & Lewis (edd.), *Greek Law in its Political Setting*, 19–25; Carawan). Carawan has argued that in this case what they were to remember was people: they were to recognise the people who claimed to have owned the properties in dispute. As to when Apollonides *et al.* were *mnemones*, the tenses used in ll. 28–32 strongly imply that this was in the past, but banning the transfer of property to *mnemones* who are no longer in office seems strange. We can make sense of it if we reckon that past *mnemones* were involved in transactions to recognise or deny the title of the seller. If the mnemonship of Apollonides *et al.* had been a time of political strife leading to exile, it would be those *mnemones* who were being called upon to deal with claims by returning exiles. What this law does is to insist that such claims had to be made in court, not simply via the *mnemones*.

Oaths play a crucial role in the legal procedure here. The *dikastai* take an oath, and in the event of a claim being brought later than the eighteen-month time-limit, the person in possession of the property is able to decide the case by taking an oath.[1]

Scholars have sometimes been surprised that there is not more explicit reference in this inscription to political crisis. But that is surely no accident. This is a law trying to prevent future property disputes. It is not in the interests of those who pass this law, and try to prevent it ever being modified, to draw attention to the fact that it was, as it were, written in warm blood.

This inscription is not easy to date. If Artemisia's son was still a 'young man' in 480 and Lygdamis is her grandson, then we must be looking at a date not much before 450 at the earliest. If the story of Herodotus playing a part in removing Lygdamis and then finding himself disliked by the Halicarnassians and so joining the founding of Thurii (*c.*444/3) is to be believed, then Lygdamis cannot have been removed after *c.*445. The *Suda* may be wrong in thinking Lygdamis was grandson (rather than son), and may have made Herodotus part of the foundation of Thurii just because he moved there at some point, so neither of these limits is fixed, but they are not implausible. Halicarnassus appears regularly on the Delian League's tribute quota lists from 454/3 to 429/8, paying (generally) 1 tal. 4,000 dr. But such payments provide no case for dating this before 454 since they are quite compatible with rule by a tyrant: the Carian tyrants Tymnes and Picres are regularly named in the tribute quota lists (e.g. *IG* i^3 259. v. 16, 271. i. 84, 280. i. 66). The *mnemon* Apollonides at Halicarnassus was the son of a Lygdamis, but that name was common enough for

[1] The role of the oath in early Greek law has been much discussed. See G. Thür, in Foxhall & Lewis (edd.), *Greek Law in its Political Setting*, 57–72; M. Gagarin, in *Symposion* 1995, 125–34; and more generally A. H. Sommerstein in Sommerstein & Bayliss, *Oath and State in Ancient Greece*, ch. v.

133

Land confiscation and its consequences on Chios, *c.*479–450

A marble *stele* inscribed on all four sides, broken at the top, discovered in the region of Bounaki west of the fortress in Chios town. Now in Chios Museum. Phot. Matthaiou, *τὰ ἐν στήλῃ γεγραμμένα*, pls. 1, 3 (sides *A*, *B* and *D*).

Ionic letters. *Stoichedon* sides *B*, *C* and *D* (*B* 10, *C* 20, *D* 10). The letter forms on side *A* differ slightly from those on the other sides.

Buck 4; Koerner 62 (A, B and *C*. 1–9 only); M. Faraguna, *Dike* viii 2005, 89–99; Matthaiou, *τὰ ἐν τῆι στήληι γεγραμμένα*, 13–34*. Trans. Buck 4.

this individual not necessarily to be son of the tyrant. The *prytanis* Leon and another *mnemon* Phormio also have fathers with Carian names. Another son of a father with a Carian name (Aphyasis), the Salmacian *mnemon* Megabates, himself bears a Persian name: as Hornblower observes, this is equally interesting whether it indicates patterns of intermarriage or changing political fashions (Hornblower, *Mausolos*, 26 n. 155, noting that *SIG*[3] 46. 36 records one Letodorus son of Megabates—Greek-name son of Persian-name). The other Salmacian *mnemon* is the son of a Panyassis, but again this is too common a Halicarnassian name to identify the man as Herodotus' cousin.

A community that claimed Dorian origin but had been expelled from the Doric hexapolis (Hdt. I. 144), Halicarnassus supplied mercenaries to Egypt (Hdt. III. 4. i), fought against the Greeks in the Persian Wars, incorporated Carians in its population, had a calendar that mixed Ionian and non-Ionian months, may have been an early producer of electrum coinage, and in the early fourth century minted silver coins on the Rhodian standard (see generally P. Flensted-Jensen, in *Inventory*, 1115–16). In the hellenistic period it erected an inscription at the Salmacis fountain enumerating the divine connections of which it was proud, along with a catalogue of Halicarnassian authors (S. Isager, *ZPE* cxxiii 1998, 1–23; Isager & Pedersen, *The Salmakis Inscription*; R. Gagné, *Cl. Ant.* xxv 2006, 1–33). In the end it wrote tyranny—not just the fifth-century tyrants, but even Mausolus (for whom see R&O 54–5)—out of its history, and whatever his role in its fifth-century political history it was Herodotus, and his openness to cultural difference, who came to represent what Halicarnassus was.

The assimilation of ν to ς in τῶς σ|υμπάντων (41–2) is a feature of Ionic; cf. in Attic ἐς Σάμοι (for ἐν Σάμωι) in **180**. 35.

A

[.]ος · ἀπὸ̣ τ̣οῦ̣το μέχρ̣ι̣ [τῆς]
τριόδο, ἧς Ἑρμώνοσσαν̣ [φ]-
έρει, τρε͂ς · ἀπὸ τῆς τριόδο ἄ[χ]-
ρι Ἑρμωνόσσης ἐς τὴν τρίοδ-
ον ἕξς · ἀπὸ τούτο μέχρι τô
Δηλίο τρε͂ς · σύμ̣παντες ὅρ̣-
οι ἐβδομήκοντα πέντε.
ὅση τῶν ὅρων τούτων ἔ-
σω, πᾶσα Δοφῖτις. ᵛ ἤν τίς τ-
ινα τῶν ὅρων τούτων
ἢ ἐξέληι ἢ μεθέληι ἢ ἀ-
φανέα ποιήσει ἐπ' ἀδικί-
ηι τῆς πόλεως, ἑκατὸν σ-
τατῆρας ὀφειλέτω κἄτι-
μος ἔστω, πρηξάντων δ' ὀ-
ροφύλακες · ἢν δὲ μὴ πρὴ-
ξοισιν, αὐτοὶ ὀφειλόντω
ν, πρηξάντων δ' οἱ πεντε-
καίδεκα τὸς ὀροφύλακας ·
ἢν δὲ μὴ πρήξοισιν, ἐν ἐπ̣-
αρῆι ἔστων.
vacat

B

[—⁷— οἱ π]-
[εν]τ̣εκα̣[ίδεκ]-
α ἐς βολὴ[ν ἐν]-
εικάντων [ἐν]
πέντ' ἡμέρη[ι]-
σιν · τὸς δὲ κή-
ρυκας διαπέ-
μψαντες ἐς τ-
ὰς χώρας κη[ρ]-
υσσόντων κα-
ὶ διὰ τῆς πόλ-
εως ἀδηνέως
γεγωνέοντε-
ς, ἀποδεκνύν-
τες τὴν ἡμέρ-
ην, ἣν ἂν λάβω-
ισιν, καὶ τὸ π̣-

A. 9 Λοφῖτις A. Fontrier.

A

From this point until the junction which leads to Hermonassa, three; from the junction as far as Hermonassa, to the crossroads, six; from this point until the Delium, three. All the boundary-stones: seventy-five. As much land as is within these boundary-stones, all of it is Dophitis. If anyone takes away any of these boundary-stones, or moves them or makes them invisible to the detriment of the city, he is to owe 100 staters and be without civic rights, and the boundary-guards are to exact the penalty. If they do not exact it, let them themselves be liable, and the Fifteen are to exact the penalty from the boundary-guards, and if they do not do this, they are to be under a curse.

B

Let the Fifteen bring it to the council within five days. They are to send the heralds to the lands and have them make a public announcement and throughout the city calling out plainly, indicating the day which they have chosen, and let them announce

ρῆχμα προσκ-
ηρυσσόντων,
ὅτι ἂμ μέλλη-
ι πρήξεσθαι·
κἀγδικασάν-
των τριηκοσ-
ίων μὴ λάσσο-
νες ἀνηρίθε-
υτοι ἐόντες.

vacat

C

[. .] ḤΔỊỊ[—— 14 ——]
[.]ιομένος ἡ π[ό]λις δεξαμ[έ]-
[ν]η δικαζέσθω κἂν ὄφληι, [ὑ]-
περαποδότω· τῶι δὲ πρια[μ]-
ένωι πρῆχμα ἔστω μηδέν. [ὃ]-
ς ἂν τὰς πρήσις ἀκρατέα[ς]
ποιῆι, ἐπαράσθω κατ' αὐτ[ô]-
ὁ βασιλεός, ἐπὴν τὰς νομ[α]-
ίας ἐπαρὰς ποιῆται.

vacat

τὰς γέας καὶ τὰς οἰκιέα[ς]
ẹπρίαντο· τῶν Ἀννικῶ παί-
δων Ἰκέσιος Ἡγεπόλιος π-
εντακισχειλίων τριηκ[ο]-
σίων τεσσαρακόντων, Ἀθ[η]-
ναγ[ό]ρης Ἡ[ρ]οδότο χειλί[ω]-
ν ἑπτακοσίων· [τ]'Αγγελέο[ς]
Τι[μ]οκλῆς Ζηνοδότο τὰν [Ε]-
ὐάδησιν δι[σ]χειλίων ἑ[π]-
τακοσίων, [Θ]εόπρọπος κο[ί]-
ν[ο]πίδης τὰγ Καμινήηι χ[ε]-
ιλίων καὶ [ὀ]κτακοσίων [. .]
ΤΑ Κήφιος τὰ ἐμ Μελαίνη[ι]
Ἀκτῆι τρισχελίων ἑπτακ-
οσίων ἐνενηκόντων Βία[ς]
Ἀσιῶ.

vacat

C. 1–2 [ἢν δέ τι|ς τὸς πριαμένος ἀποκληί|ηι] ἢ δικά[ζεται τὸς ἀποκλ|η]ιομένος F. Blass, in *Satura Philologica H. Sauppio*, 127–30. *C.* 16 [τ]'Αγγελέο[ς] Matthaiou commentary: [.]ΑΓΓελέο[ς] Matthaiou text.

the matter that is going to be dealt with. Let no fewer than three hundred men who are disinterested try the case.

C

– – – the city is to receive those who – – – and hear the case, and if the case is lost, pay on their behalf. Let there be no case against the person who has bought. Anyone who makes the sales invalid, let the *basileus* deliver a curse against him when he makes the customary curses. The following bought the plots of land and the houses: from the sons of Annices, Hicesus son of Hegepolis for 5,340; Athenagores son of Herodotus for 1,700; from Angeleus, Timocles son of Zenodotus, the lands in Euadae, for 2,700; Theopropus and Oenopides the lands in Camine, for 1,800; – – – from Cephis, the lands on the Black Shore, for 3,790, Bias son of Asies.

D

[. .]ιοπ̣[—5—]
[χ]ειλίων ἐνα-
κοσίων · Λεύκ-
ιππος Πυθῶ τ-
ὴν οἰκίην τ[ὴ]-
ν Ἀνδρέος π[ε]-
ντακοσίων π-
εντηκόντων
δυῶν ⁝ Ἄσμιος
Θεόπομπος Ἀ-
γυαίο τὰν Οἴ-
ωι χειλίων τ-
ριηκοσίων δ-
έκων δυῶν ⁝ Ἰ-
κ̣εσίο το Φίλ-
ωνος Στράτ[.]-
[.]ς Λυσῶ τοἰκ-
[ό]πεδον διηκ-
[ο]σίων ἑνός.
vacat

All the provisions on this *stele*, which must record an official decision by the *polis* of Chios, concern land. Side *A* describes the boundaries of a piece of land called 'Dophitis'; side *B* describes the appropriate legal procedure for dealing with some particular type of legal case where it is necessary to make announcements in the countryside; side *C* continues from *B* and determines the role of the state in cases arising from the purchasing of land. It begins a list of purchasers of land that continues on side *D*. But what lies behind these provisions? The text beginning on side *B* must be closely related to *A*, since no substantively new text would begin on a narrow side, but how exactly are *B–D* related to *A*? And why did the Chians feel the need at this point to define land boundaries and establish special conditions for the sale of land and houses?

The lost text at the top of the *stele* has been describing the boundaries of the territory known as 'Dophitis'. Some scholars have restored the name as 'Lophitis' ('hillock'), since the only known parallel for the name Dophitis is the satyr Dophius on a sixth-century Attic black-figure *aryballos* in New York (Metropolitan Museum 26. 49), and although the name suits him (δέφομαι means 'to masturbate'), it is hard to make sense of it as the name of a piece of land. Of the seventy-five boundary-stones that mark it, the location of just twelve is recorded in the first six lines of the inscription. We might therefore expect up to around thirty lines of inscription to have been lost. None of the features used to mark the boundary can be located (we know of no 'Delium' (*A*. 6), i.e. sanctuary of Apollo Delios on Chios). The only

D

– – – ?,900; Leucippus son of Pythees, the house of Andrees, for 552; from Asmis, Theopompus son of Agyaeus, the land in Oion, 1,312; from Hicesius son of Philon, Strat–s son of Lysees, a house plot, 201.

---

local identification that might tentatively be made is between the 'black shore' (*C.* 22) and the black beach just south of Emborio on the south-east of the island (on the topography of Chios see E. Yalouris, in Boardman & Vaphopoulou-Richardson (edd.), *Chios*, 141–68).

Inscribed descriptions of boundaries of territories are not uncommon, and normally are the consequence of dispute and adjudication (on frontiers and their delimitation see Daverio Rocchi, *Frontiera e confini nella Grecia antica*; D. Rousset, *CCG* v 1994, 97–126). But what is the dispute here? There is no sign that this is a dispute between communities, rather the temptation to move, remove or wipe out the boundary-stones seems to be one to which individuals are liable (see Pl. *Leg.* VIII. 842–3). And although it is not uncommon for one set of officials to be set to act if designated officials do not (cf. *SEG* XXX 380, from seventh-century Tiryns), the severity of the penalties involved here perhaps points to expectations that individuals will not only move the boundary-stones but also attempt to bribe the officials not to notice. Overall, this looks like a situation where the land that is bounded off here has been taken out of private and into public ownership. This would be even more clearly the case if the *orophylakes* responsible here are 'boundary-guards' as opposed to 'mountain-guards', since that would imply an office set up specifically to police the boundaries of land in the expectation of disputes (cf. Arist. *Pol.* VI. 1321 B 18–30). In Ionic the two words are indistinguishable, and although there is a strong case for 'mountain-guards' elsewhere (J. & L. Robert, *Fouilles d'Amyzon*, i. 101–4), the central concern with boundaries here encourages the thought that boundary-guards are at issue.

Belief that the background here is in civil dispute and land confiscation is encouraged by the very high number of boundary-stones involved (which suggests a plot with rather complex boundaries) and by the text on the sides and the back of the *stele*. This text is written by a different engraver, but seems essentially similar in date. Side *B* is concerned with the conduct of (land) sales. The same magistrates who oversee the boundary-guards on side *A* here bring (a list?) to the council, and heralds are sent to announce the sale in both country and town, indicating both the day and the substance. Such provision might occur in a number of circumstances, but that the circumstances here involve dispute is clear from the final clause, which foresees legal claims and sets up a special board of 300 'uncorrupt' individuals to hear them. At issue here is surely not choosing judges who will not be bribed, but choosing judges who are not themselves interested parties.

Further discussion of the nature of possible legal disputes, and how to deal with them, presumably occupied the top part of the back of the *stele* (*C*). By the point where the *stele* survives the discussion is about situations where men have bought land and find themselves being excluded from it. Here, unusually, the state (*polis*) is committed to stepping in and if necessary providing compensation, so that no liability falls on any purchaser. By contrast, those who try to invalidate, and presumably overturn, the sales are publicly cursed.

All of this implies a situation where land is being sold that some people think should not be sold, and where the force of the state is required to give potential purchasers the security that they can buy without reprisals or future loss. Such reluctance to purchase confiscated property is found in accounts of confiscation elsewhere: Herodotus (VI. 121. ii) claims that Callias was the only Athenian willing to purchase property confiscated from Pisistratus, and the Aristotelian *Oeconomica* (II. 1346 B 7–13) claims that Lygdamis found no buyers for land he had confiscated from those he exiled and had to sell it back to the exiles themselves. Here, it looks as if, following civil strife, some Chiots have been deprived of their land, which has been turned into public land (side *A*, cf. esp. ll. 12–13), and that that land (or the land of some others) is now being sold off to other citizens (sides *B*–*D*). The scholarly debate about whether the land sold in *C* and *D* should be located within the Dophitis cannot be resolved: see, on different sides, Faraguna, 97–8, and Matthaiou, 28–9.

The list of sales starts at *C*. 10 with a heading about sale of lands and houses. The sales were perhaps listed in this order, since the last sales recorded (on *D*) are of a house and a house-plot. The high price of the plots of land sold is notable, indicating sizeable estates. This further encourages the view that it is the whole of a person's property that is sold off: sometimes in more than one lot, as with the first and second examples. In the opening example the former owner has in fact already died—in the civil strife, one wonders?

Confiscation of property from defeated political opponents who have been exiled or otherwise deprived of civic rights was common across the Greek world (see **132** and **172**), and the provisions made by the Chians are not out of line with what we find elsewhere. If the whole inscription had survived we might have learnt a lot about the political geography and spatial distribution of wealth in Chios. As importantly, this inscription tells us something about the political history of Chios.

Herodotus (I. 27. v, VI. 31. i–ii, IV. 138. ii, VIII. 132. ii) provides quite rich information about the political history of late archaic Chios, which from 513 to 479 was ruled by a tyrant, Strattis (see L. Rubinstein, in *Inventory*, 1064–9). But the political history of classical Chios is much less clear. Chios joined the Delian League at the beginning (Hdt. XI. 106. iv) and remained a ship-providing ally until revolting in 412. In the context of Spartan intervention at Chios we are told that a narrow oligarchic regime was installed (Thuc. VIII. 38. iii–iv), and are told about (the restoration of) exiles (Diod. Sic. XIII. 65. iii–iv, on 409/8); some have been tempted to try to link this inscription to those events (Gehrke, *Stasis*, 45 n. 20). However, the letter forms of the script, and the complete absence of Attic influence from the language, argue strongly against so late a date. Some have suggested that this inscription dates to the 470s and the immediate aftermath of Strattis' tyranny, but it is far from implausible that beneath Chios' ongoing provision of ships to the Delian League there were significant political arguments (cf. neighbouring Erythrae, **121**).

This inscription provides the best evidence that we have for the constitution of Chios in these years, with a council (cf. Thuc. VIII. 14. i–ii; note the implication of M&L 8 that in the archaic period Chios had a more and a less populist council), a remarkably small executive body of Fifteen, a *basileus* with at least a prominent ritual role (for his customary curses cf. **102**; for plural *basileis* with a judicial role on Chios see *LSS* 116. 5–8, 26–7; *ὅρος* iii 1985, 105–11), and—the clearest indication that this was not a narrow oligarchy—the possibility of mustering a judicial body of 300 disinterested persons (for the number cf. Thasos, **103**, **176**, **177**; for the constitution of Chios see J. L. O'Neill, *Talanta* x–xi 1978–9, 66–73).

In this inscription (cf. **103**) ου represents the real diphthong, but the 'spurious diphthong' of Attic (close–mid long *o* from contraction and compensatory lengthening) is rendered ο (cf. l. 1 etc.: τούτο for genitive τούτου); similarly ω represents the inherited, open long o. The form of πρήξοισιν (l. 16) reveals influence from neighbouring Lesbos: the Lesbian short-vowel subjunctive ending -οισι is used together with Ionic stem πρηξ- and a final Ionic moveable ν.

134

Accounts of Nemesis of Rhamnous, *c.*450–440

A marble *stele* from the Sanctuary of Nemesis at Rhamnous, found in an antiques shop at Nea Palatia (Skala Oropou); now in the Epigraphical Museum. Phot.: *Ἀρχ. Ἐφ.* 1934/5, 128; *I. Rhamnous*, p. 148; our pl. 6.

Attic letters, whose forms vary between sections of the inscription. Ionic Η and Ω in §§ii, iv and v. *Stoichedon* ll. 1–14 and 15–18.

Pouilloux, *La Forteresse de Rhamnonte*, pp. 147–50 no. 35; M&L 53; *IG* i³ 248; *I. Rhamnous* 182*; Trans. Fornara 90. B; Davies (below), 117–18; J. H. Blok, *Mnemosyne*⁴ lxiii 2010, 69–70. See also J. K. Davies, in Meadows & Shipton (edd.), *Money and its Uses in the Ancient Greek World*, 117–28.

§i

ἐπ' Αὐτοκλείδ-
ο δεμαρχôντο-
ς: τô τêς Νεμέσ-
εος ἀργυρίο: κ-
εφάλαιον: τô π-
αρὰ τοῖσι τὰς
διακοσίας δρ-
αχμὰς ὀφέλοσι
ΜΜΜ𐅆:ΧΧ: τô δὲ ἄ-
λλο ἀργυρίο: τ-
ô τêς Νεμέσεο-
ς: κεφάλαι{:}ον: Μ
ΧΧ𐅅ΗΗΔΔΓ⊢⊢⊢
⊢ΙΙΙ.

§ii

ἐπὶ Μνησιπτολέμ-
ο ἄρχοντος κεφάλ-
αιον παντὸς τô ἱε-
ρô ἀργυρίο ⁝ 𐅇ΧΗ
ΗΗ𐅄ΔΔΔΓ⊢⊢ΙΙΙΙΙ.

§iii

ἐπὶ Ναυσιμένος ἄρχον-
τος κεφάλαιον τô ἱ-
ερô ἀργυρίο τô πα-
ρὰ τοῖς τὰς διακοσί-
ας ἔχοσι ⁝ ΜΜΜ𐅆ΧΧ
τô δ' ἄλλο ⁝ ΜΧ𐅅ΗΗΔΔ⊢⊢⊢
ΙΙ.

§i

Under Autocleides serving as demarch: the total of the money of Nemesis: money with those owing the two hundred drachmas: 37,000 dr.; total of the rest of the money of Nemesis, 12,729 dr., 3 obols.

§ii

In the term of office of Mnesiptolemus, total of all the sacred money: 51,397 dr., 5 obols.

§iii

In the term of office of Nausimenes, total of the sacred money with those having the two hundred drachmas: 37,000 dr. Of the rest: 11,723 dr. 2 obols.

§iv

ἐπ' Εὐαινέτο ἄρχον-
τος κεφάλαιον τρι-
ακοσιοδράχμων
ΜΧΧΧ𐅅 ⁝ παντὸς δὲ
𐅇𐅆𐅅ΗΗΔͰͰ.

§v

ἐπὶ Δημοφάνος δημάρ-
χο παρὰ ἱεροποιοῖς κε-
φάλαιον: 𐅆ΗΗ𐅃ͰIIII
τριακοσιοδράχμων
ΜΧΧΧΧΗΗΗΗ: διακοσι-
οδράχμων: ΜΜΜ𐅆ΧΧ
παντός: 𐅇𐅆Χ𐅅Η𐅃ͰIIII.

Rhamnous is one of the best known of Athenian demes. Situated at the very north-east corner of Attica, and bypassed by post-antique history, it was rediscovered in the 1670s by French and English travellers, led there by Pausanias (i. 33). The site was visited by Martin Leake in 1806 (Leake, *Travels in Northern Greece*, ii. 433–5), and first seriously investigated by John Peter Gandy for the Society of Dilettanti (W. Gell *et al.*, *The Unedited Antiquities of Attica*, chs. vi–vii). Some excavation was done by Ernst Ziller in the 1860s, but extensive (if rapid) archaeological work began with Valerios Stais in 1890. Thorough investigation of the fortress was made by Jean Pouilloux and the French School in the 1940s and early 1950s, and the architecture of the temple of Nemesis explored in detail first by Hugh Plommer and then by Margaret Miles (W. H. Plommer, *BSA* xlv 1950, 66–112; M. M. Miles, *Hesperia* lviii 1989, 137–249). Further extensive archaeological work was undertaken by Vasilis Petrakos in the 1980s and 1990s, and the whole site and its inscriptions have now been published in detail by him (Petrakos, *ο δήμος τού Ραμνούντος* (vol. ii cited as *I. Rhamnous*); on the deme generally see Osborne, in *Sociable Man . . . N. Fisher*, 25–43).

Finds of pottery and roof tiles indicate that the sanctuary of Nemesis dates back at least to the early sixth century. A second temple was constructed in the late sixth century and a third, which survives and is characterised by its polygonal masonry, in the second quarter of the fifth century. In the later part of the fifth century the *temenos* was much extended and the great classical hexastyle temple known today was built (Petrakos, i. 187–246).

This inscription not only sheds light on the financial background to building in the sanctuary, but together with **159** is our best evidence for the financial circumstances and financial management of fifth-century Athenian demes (cf. **107** and **146** for deme 'audit' culture, R&O 63 for the fourth century). One earlier financial document survives from the sanctuary, a lead tablet dated by letter forms

§iv

27 In the term of office of Euaenetus, total of three hundred drachmas: 13,500 dr.; of the whole: 55,712 dr. 1 obol.

§v

32 Under Demophanes, demarch, total with the *hieropoioi*: 5,206 dr. 4 obols; of three hundred drachmas: 14,400 dr.; of two hundred drachmas: 37,000 dr.; of the whole: 56,606 dr. 4 obols.

---

to around 500 (*IG* i^3 247 *bis* p. 957 = *I. Rhamnous* 181). It mentions *epistatai* and records money given to the *hieropoioi*, with sums of 162, 161, 100 and 152 dr. against four separate individual names. Two of those four names then recur in a list of three people whose money is kept by the sanctuary. The overall significance of this record is, however, quite obscure.

The handsome stone *stele* (pl. 6) recording five years' accounts, presumably but not certainly consecutive, and written up by a number of different hands using slightly different sized script, letter forms and language (so τοῖσι in §i, τοῖς in §iii), is the only other financial record from the sanctuary. Why for a brief period, which seems to be around 450–440 on the uncertain basis of the letter forms, these summary records were written on stone, and how the officials of this deme sanctuary otherwise kept track of what was clearly a very large number of financial transactions, is not at all obvious. The importance of these records lies both in the size of the financial operation that they record and in the nature of the records themselves.

One notable feature of the accounts is that they have no uniform format. The demarch is identified in three different ways (the verb δημαρχεῖν, the verb ἄρχειν and the noun δήμαρχος), the sacred officials (*hieropoioi*), who presumably had some actual responsibility, are mentioned only in the last year, the 200-drachma loans are referred to in three of the five years and in three different ways, the 300-drachma loans in only two years, the total written out in three years, but not in the other two, and in one year no breakdown at all is given. The question of whether inscribed accounts enabled accountability in Greek cities has been debated (see generally J. K. Davies, in *Ritual, Finance, Politics . . . D. Lewis*, 201–12); in this case, by contrast to the earlier lead tablet, the detail given is insufficient to establish more than the broadest accountability. Rather like the summary accounts shown to shareholders, these accounts offer simply an overview of how the sanctuary's finances are faring. It is notable that all fifth-century Athenian inscribed accounts have a strong religious aspect (cf. **119**, where it is Athena's quota of tribute, not the main payment, that is written up on stone), and we should think of accountability to the gods themselves as an important matter.

The second notable feature is the way in which the money is lent. The reference to 'those owing [or 'having'] the two hundred drachmas' and the use of the compounds 'two hundred drachmas' and 'three hundred drachmas' suggests that the temple monies were loaned in standard sums. Indeed the unchanging total of money loaned in 200-dr. loans implies a decision to commit a fixed amount of money in this way. This will have made accounting much simpler—just as recording sums in drachmas only, and not in talents, also made accounting simpler. We should probably presume that an individual could take more than one of these standard loans, although in that case it is unclear why the sanctuary thought it needed two different standard loans both of the same order of magnitude. If we are dealing with 200-dr. loans, then 185 such loans would be at issue, with an additional forty-five and then forty-eight loans of 300 dr. Rhamnous itself was quite a large deme, returning eight members to the council of five hundred in the fourth century, so proportionately if Athens' citizen population was 50,000 in the 440s, as it might have been, Rhamnous would have 800 citizens. The loans do not, of course, have to be restricted to demesmen of Rhamnous, but rather than dismiss 233 debtors as a 'fantastic' and impossible number, as Finley did, we should acknowledge the enormous part that lending and borrowing played in this society (Finley, *Studies in Land and Credit in Ancient Athens*, 285 n. 43; for the larger issue see Davies, in Meadows & Shipton (edd.); Millett, *Lending and Borrowing in Ancient Athens*, discussing Rhamnous at 175–6; and below, **159**).

The third feature is the amount of money that Nemesis has available to lend, and the rate at which it accumulates. Although the accounts are dated by deme official, rather than sanctuary official, and it is likely that the deme appointed the *hieropoioi* who held the money (l. 33; cf. the responsibility of the *hieropoioi* for the inscription and setting up of an honorific decree in the sanctuary, *SEG* xxii 120. 7–9), the money is explicitly identified as 'sacred' (ll. 17–18, 21–2). That is, this is money belonging to the god and for spending on sanctuary activities, but available on loan to others for

135

Accounts of Pheidias' statue of Athena, 447–438

A: Portions of two marble *stelai*, found on the Athenian acropolis. Formerly in the Epigraphical Museum, but §ii now displayed in the Acropolis Museum. Both are the same width and depth, but §i was abandoned at the point where figures would have to be inscribed, perhaps because the stone-cutter had not left room for figures.

any purpose they might choose (cf. **148**, **160**). In the course of these five years the total amount increases by almost 14 per cent, from just over 8 to just over 9 talents.[1] We do not know what interest, if any, was paid on the loans (but we certainly cannot assume them to have been interest-free),[2] or what other sources of income the temple had, but a lease of land of Nemesis by the demesmen survives from Rhamnous from 339/8 (*IG* ii^2 2493 = *I. Rhamnous* 180).[3] Although there is a dip in the total in year 3 (should we think of a quadrennial festival?), it is clear that generally income significantly exceeded outgoings. This is a prospering sanctuary (cf. **159**), a situation which makes sense of the decision, perhaps in the 430s (Miles, 227), to build a new and substantially larger and more elaborate temple—though the costs of that temple (Miles, 234, estimates 30 talents; cf. **145**) will have far exceeded the resources here.

All the officials involved in this inscription are deme officials, and it was the deme that leased out land at Rhamnous in 339/8 (*IG* ii^2 2493 + 2494 = *I. Rhamnous* 180), yet the Nemeseia festival was clearly of more than local importance (in the Lycurgan period ephebes were involved: *I. Rhamnous* 98), and it is possible that the new temple could be afforded because this, like the cult of Apollo at Cape Zoster (R&O 46), was a state cult run by a deme (see S. D. Lambert, *Historia* lix 2010, 164–9). However, although in 434/3 the Athenians decided to account for all the monies from Athenian state cults centrally (**144** *A*. 18–22), no money or other item from Rhamnous appears in inventories and other documents relating to the 'other gods' compiled during the war (*IG* i^3 369, 383; cf. **160**).

[1] Davies, in Meadows & Shipton (edd.), records the sum in ll. 12–14 as 2,728 dr. 3 ob. instead of 12,727 dr. 3 ob., and so miscalculates the total resources of the temple in this year and hence the increase in temple resources over five years (and is followed by von Reden, *Money in Classical Antiquity*, 168–9).

[2] Blok's attempt (70–1) to reconstruct interest rates from the changes from year to year only reveals the impossibility of doing so; see Millett, *Lending and Borrowing in Ancient Athens*, 175–6, for the possibility that the loans were interest-free.

[3] E. Stafford, in Ogden (ed.), *Companion to Greek Religion*, 76–7, deduces an increase in sanctuary wealth from comparison between the earlier financial document and this, and attributes it to the role Nemesis is supposed to have played in defeating the Persians (but we cannot assume that the earlier document records the distribution of the whole money of the sanctuary).

The two fragments of §ii (ll. 1–22 and 24–32) do not join. Phot. Cavaignac, *Études sur l'histoire financière d'Athènes*, xlix fig. 12; Austin, *The Stoichedon Style*, pl. 8; *BCH* xci 1967, 69, 72

Attic letters. §i non-*stoichedon*; §ii *stoichedon* (13 ll. 1–22, 14 ll. 24–32).

G. Donnay, *BCH* xci 1967, 50–86 at 68–71; M&L 54; *IG* i³ 459, 458*; Shear, *Trophies of Victory*, 421. Trans. Fornara 114. See also Shear, *Trophies of Victory*, 69–78.

B: Two joining fragments from the left side and the top half of a marble *stele*, once part of the Byzantine church in the Parthenon; formerly in the Epigraphical Museum but now displayed in the Acropolis Museum. Phot. *BCH* xci 1967, 72; Guarducci, *Epigrafia greca*, ii. 194 fig. 46; our pl. 7.

Attic letters. *Stoichedon*, with the numerals except in l. 7 in larger characters, each taking the horizontal space of two letters of text.

G. Donnay, *BCH* xci 1967, 50–86 at 71–5; M&L 54; *IG* i³ 460*; Shear, *Trophies of Victory*, 422. Trans. Fornara 114.

A

§i θεοί ⁝ Ἀθενᾶ ⁝ Τύχε
Κιχέσιππος ⁝ ἐγραμμά-
τευε ⁝ ἀγάλματος ⁝ ἐπι-
στάτεσι ⁝ Μυρρινόσιος
λε̑μμα ⁝ παρὰ *vacat*
vacat

§ii *a* Κιχέσιππος ἐγ[ρ]-
αμμάτευε: ἀγάλ[μ]-
ατος: ἐπιστάτε[σ]-
ι: Μυρρινόσιος: λ-
ε̑μμα: παρὰ ταμιο̑-
ꟷ ν: hοῖς Δεμόστρα-
τος: ἐγραμμάτευ-
ε: Χσυπεταόν: ταμ-
ίαι: Κτεσίον: Στ[ρ]-
οσίας: Ἀντιφάτ[ε]-
ς: Μένανδρος: Θ[υμ]-
οχάρες: Σμόκορ[δ]-
ος: Φειδελείδ[ες.]
vacat
𐅄ΔΔΔ χρυσίον: ἐονέθ-
𐅈ΤΤΧ ε, σταθμὸν: 𐅈ΤΧ𐅅Ḥ
ΧΧΧ𐅅 τιμὲ τούτο ΔΓ⊢⊢⊢Ι
Η𐅄⊢⊢ ΙΙΙΙΙ *vacat*
vacat
ΤΤ𐅅Η ἐλέφας ἐονέθε
ΗΔΔΔ *vacat*
Δ⊢⊢⊢ *vacat*
- - - - - - - - - - - - - - - - - -
vacat
b ἀναλόμ[ατα ᵛ χρυσ]-
[. .]𐅉Τ ίον : ἐον[έθε *vacat*]
[. . .]ΗΔ χρυσίο[ν ἄσεμον, σ]-
[Δ]ΔΔΓ ταθμόν [: – – –]

A

§i Gods. Athena. Fortune.

2 Cichesippus of Myrrhinous was secretary to the overseers of the statue.

5 Received from *vacat*

§ii

		Cichesippus of Myrrhinous was secretary to the overseers of the statue.
4	100 tal.	Received from the treasurers to whom Demostratos Xypete was secretary, Ctesion, Strosias, Antiphates, Menander, Thymochares, Smocordus, Pheideleides.
		vacat
15	87 tal.	Gold was bought, weight: 6 tal. 1,618 dr. 1 ob.
	4,652 dr. 5 ob.	Price of this *vacat*
		vacat
20	2 tal. 743 dr.	Ivory was bought.
		– – – – – – – – –
		vacat
24	31+ tal. 147+ dr. 1 ob.	Expenses: gold was bought: uncoined gold, weight 41+ dr.; Croiseid staters 110+.

[Ͱ]Ͱ	ΔΔΔͰ – – –
	Κροίσ[ειοι στατε͂]-
	ρες : Η̣Δ̣ – – –
	τιμὲ τ[ούτοιν ἀμφ]-
	οτέ[ροιν *vacat*]
[.]ΤΧΧ	*vacat*
[..]..	– – – – – – – – – – –

B

ἐπιστά[ται– – – – – –]
τάδε ἔλ[αβον – – – ἀργ]-
ύριον *vacat* [*vacat*]
𐅅ΗΗ̣[– – – – – –]
𐅄ΔΔ[– – – – – –]
——
χρυσι[ο – – – – – –]
ετο ⁝ ΗΗ – – – – – –
Κάλλα[ισχρος ------- ἀνέ]-
θεκεν – – – – – –
——
ἀναλό[ματα – – – – – –]
[.] Η̣ – – – – – –
𐅄ΔΔ – – – – – –
——
ἀπεργα[σία – – – – – –]
𐅅ΗΗ𐅄ΔΔ – – – – – –
——
κατάβλ[εμα – – – – – –]
Δ̣Δ̣Δ̣ – – – – – –
ΗΗΗ – – – – – –
——
χρυσιο [– – – – – –ἀγά]-
[λ]ματι π[– – – – – –]

The long-established rituals served by the Praxiergidai (**108**) centred upon the wooden cult statue of Athena, housed in the temple of Athena Polias. This cult statue seems to have been unharmed by the Persian sack of the acropolis. However, in the middle of the fifth century a bronze statue of Athena by Pheidias, said, impossibly, to be so tall it could be seen from Sunium (Paus. I. 28. ii), was set up as a trophy of Athenian bravery against the Persians (Dem. XIX. *Embassy* 272); and in the wake of that the Athenians decided to ask Pheidias to create a new colossal gold-and-ivory cult statue. The needs of that statue determined the unusual form of the

31 Price of both of these

2+ tal.

2000+ dr

B

Overseers – – – received these – – – money *vacat*

4 700+ tal.

5 520+ dr.

6 Gold – – – 200+ dr. – – – Callaeschrus – – –

dedicated – – –

10 Expenses – – – 100+ tal. – – – 70+ dr. – – –

13 Finishing – – – 770+ dr. – – –

15 Structure – – – 30+ tal. – – – 300+ dr. – – –

18 Gold – – – for the statue – – –

---

temple we know as the Parthenon—its width, (eight rather than the standard six columns across the façade) maximising space and allowing the statue to be set against an interior colonnade which returned behind the statue, and its shallow porches (prostyle rather than *in antis*), central placement of the statue, and windows in the east wall of the cella maximising the amount of light reflecting from the gold.

Separate accounts survive for the building of the Parthenon (see below, **145**, where we discuss the building project more generally) and for the cult statue (*agalma*). The two earliest of the seven fragments of the accounts for the statue (*IG* i^3 453–4) are inscribed on broader *stelai*; one is firmly dated by the name of the secretary of the treasurers to 446/5, the other may date to 447/6 or 445/4. In their most complete form, the accounts name the secretary to the overseers (*epistatai*, for whom see Marginesu, *Gli Epistati dell'Acropoli*), state what the overseers were given by the treasurers of Athena, who are listed by name with their secretary, and then say what weight of gold was bought, and for how much, and the price of the ivory.

We give here both *A*, the most complete single account, of uncertain date (but not 440/39, the date given by *IG*, because we now think that the secretary of the treasurers in that year was —poleus: see **138**), and *B*, the final summary account which should date from 438/7, the year in which Philochorus says that the statue was installed (*FGrH* 328 F 121, emending the archon's name from Pythodorus to Theodorus).

It appears that the stone-cutter had to make two attempts to carve *A*, having initially misjudged the spacing needed. The rejected stone remained on the acropolis, perhaps because it was upturned and another inscription written on the other end (now lost). The accounts inscribed list only seven of the board of ten treasurers; we do not know why this would be the case, but fewer than ten are listed in other years too: was it not always possible to recruit ten (only the rich were eligible), or did they record only those actually present when the money was handed over (cf. R&O p. 178 on underweight boards of *poletai*)? The particular value of *A* is that it preserves both the weight and the cost of the gold, indicating a gold : silver ratio of 14 : 1 (the same ratio is found when surplus gold is sold off at **145**. 21–3; see further D. M. Lewis, in *Essays in Greek Coinage . . . S. Robinson*, 105–10).

A scholiast on Ar. *Pax* 605 quotes Philochorus (*FGrH* 328 F 121) as saying that 'the gold cult statue' weighed in at 44 talents. Thucydides' figure of 40 talents (Thuc. II. 13. v) and Diodorus' figure of 50 talents (Diod. Sic. XII. 39) are close to this. Acquiring so large a sum of gold will not have been easy: *A* §ii. 29 records the acquisition of coins, including Croiseid staters, as a source of gold. At a gold : silver ratio of 14 : 1 this indicates that the gold cost 616 talents. Five of the seven surviving annual accounts (out of probably nine originally) preserve figures, ranging from 26 tal. in 442/1 to 160 tal. (probably in 443/2 or 441/0), and these add up to almost 354 tal. In the summative accounts the detailed figure is not preserved (l. 4), but is in excess of 700 tal. and less than 1,000 tal. The cost of the ivory and of other work on the statue will relatively easily account for the difference between 616 and over 700 tal., and so the various figures seem to tie up neatly.

Almost all these accounts are relatively well preserved, which has suggested to scholars that they were displayed within the Parthenon. The summative account is a notable, and monumental, document, quite different in appearance from the others (see pl. 7). The writing itself is extremely fine, and the surface of the stone carefully polished. It was clearly meant to put on display to the world, and no doubt also to Athena, the vast amount of money that the Athenians had spent. The total of money given (ll. 1–5) and spent (ll. 10–12) is written in extremely large characters (4.3 cm. for the talents, 3.5 cm. for the drachmas, as against 1.6 cm. for the standard script above and below, and each of the figures occupies two letter spaces in the *stoichedon* grid). The entry on ll. 6–9 most plausibly records a dedication of gold by Callaeschrus—a name too common to allow identification—which was additional to the gold bought by the *epistatai* and the value of which was probably added to the figure in ll. 3–4 to give the total expenses in 10–12. The expenditure here is broken down into various categories, including two not included in the other accounts, which limit themselves to gold and ivory (although the difference between the 100 tal. which the treasurers give in *A* and the sums spent on gold and ivory recorded there (just under 90 tal.) was presumably spent on other works relevant to the statue). Scholars have debated what exactly is meant by the terms *apergasia* ('finishing') and *katablema* ('structure') in *B.* 13 and 15, but there is no way of being certain. The small sum for *apergasia* could easily have been entirely labour costs, but since a sum of at least 30 tal. would purchase at least *c.*200,000 man-days of labour the expenses covered by *katablema* must include some material costs.

The statue is here referred to simply as the *agalma*. Elsewhere in inscriptions it is referred to as 'the (gold) statue in the *hekatompedon*' (e.g. *IG* ii² 1410. 7–8). In literary texts it appears as 'Athena' or 'the (gold) statue of Athena' (e.g. [Pl.] *Hp. Mai.* 290 B, Isoc. XV. *Antid.* 2, Philochorus, cited above). That the name 'Parthenos' was used for the statue from the beginning is indicated, however, by reference at Ar. *Av.* 670 to Procne wearing a lot of gold 'like Parthenos', and in the new comic poet Philippides objecting to Demetrius Poliorcetes 'introducing prostitutes to the Parthenos' (fr. 25. 3 KA). For the use of the name 'Parthenon' see below, **169**.

Our knowledge of the appearance of the statue is dependent on later copies (*LIMC* Athena 212–33). Although the tradition of making cult statues of gold and ivory goes back to the archaic period (Lapatin, *Chryselephantine Statuary in the Ancient Mediterranean World*), Pheidias' Athena Parthenos was the first colossal chryselephantine statue, setting a new model of what a divinity might look like and causing Olympia to commission Pheidias to produce a similarly colossal seated chryselephantine Zeus for the temple there.[1]

[1] On the theological consequences see Osborne, *The History Written on the Classical Greek Body*, ch. v, and Platt, *Facing the Gods*, 84–91, 105–14.

136

Cypress from Carpathus, 445–430

The upper part of one side of an opisthographic marble *stele* seen on Carpathus in the 1880s and 1890s, and said to have been found at Pini. Now lost (a squeeze survives in Berlin). Phot. Ma (below), 138–9.

Ionic letters with two different forms of Α and Σ. *Stoichedon* 22. The same stone-cutter on both sides.

P. Foucart, *BCH* xii 1888, 153–61; *IG* xii. i 977; *SIG*³ 129; Tod 110; *IG* i³ 1454*. Trans. *A.* Ma (below), 129. See also Low, *Interstate Relations in Classical Greece*, 215–17, 248–50; J. Ma, in Ma *et al.* (edd.), *Interpreting the Athenian Empire*, 125–48.

A

[ἔδοξεν τῆι βο]λῆι καὶ τῶι δή-
[μωι. . . .ηὶς ἐπ]ρυτάνευε· Τει-
[σίας ἐγραμμά]τευε· Ἀθηνόδω-
[ρος ἐπεστάτ]ε. Κτησίας εἶπε·
[— 8 — τὸ]γ Καρπάθιον κα-
[ὶ τὸς παῖδας] ḳαὶ τὸ Ἐτεοκαρ-
[παθίων κοιν]ὸν γράψαι εὐερ-
[γέτας Ἀθην]α̣[ί]ων, ὅτι ἔδοσα[ν]
[τὴν κυπάριτ]τον ἐπὶ τὸν νε[ὼ]-
[ν τῆς Ἀθηναί]α̣ς τῆς Ἀθηνῶμ μ-
[εδεόσης, καὶ] ἐᾶν τὸ Ἐτεοκαρ-
[παθίων κοινὸ]ν̣ [α]ὐ̣τ̣ονόμος ḳ-
[αὶ — 15 —]ο̣ς καὶ
[— 10 —]τα[— 8 —]ικ
[— 9 —]Λιασ[— 5 —]εσθα-
[ι — 8 —]ε[.] τῆι σφετέρα[ι]
[αὐτῶν καθά]περ πρ̣ὶν δôναι [.]
[. . . ὅσοι δὲ] νῦγ καθελήφασ̣[ι]
[τῶν στρατι]ω̣τ̣ῶν ἐξιέναι ἐ[κ]
[τῆς ἀκροπόλ]ε̣ως. ἐὰν δέ τις [.]
[— 11 —] Ἐτεοκαρπαθ[ί]-
[— 10 —] ἢ ἀ̣φαιρῆται ἢ λ-
[— 10 —] Λ///Ν[— 6 —]ων, ὀ-
[φέλεν πεντ]ήκοντα τάλαντα
[Ἀθηναίοις κ]αὶ τὀπιδέκα[το]-
[ν τῆς θεô εἶνα]ι· δίκην δὲ ἒνα-

5 τὸ]γ Καρπάθιον *IG* i³: [. . . . τὸν Ἐτεο]καρπάθιον Wilhelm *ap.* *SIG*³. 17 καθά]περ Wilhelm: see Ma, 142 n. 7.: [αὐτῶν — 5 —]ε[.] πρ̣ὶν *IG* i³. 20 [– – –]ΣΕΩΣ Ma. 20–3 ἐὰν δέ τίς [. |— 10 —]ν Ἐτεοκαρπαθί|[ων τὸ κοινὸν ἢ] ἀφαίρηται ἢ ἀ[δικῆι Foucart; ἐὰν δέ τίς [τ|ι Ἀγήσαρχον ἢ] Ἐτεοκαρπαθί|[ων τὸ κοινὸν ἢ] ἀφαιρῆται ἢ α|[ἴρηι τὴν στή]λην Hiller von Gaertringen (*IG* xii. i); ἐὰν δέ τις [.|. . . . ἀδικῆι ἢ] Wilhelm. 24 [ὄ|φλεν τὸν ἀδι]κôντα Foucart. 25 [τῶι κοινῶι] Hiller.

A

Resolved by the council and the people. — was the prytany; Teisias was the secretary; Athenodorus was the chairman. Ctesias proposed: To record — the Carpathian and his sons and the community of the Eteocarpathians as benefactors of the Athenians, because they gave the cypress wood for the temple of Athena who rules at Athens; and to allow the community of the Eteocar[pathians] to be autonomous – – –

[*Lines* 13–16 *cannot be satisfactorily restored*]

– – – their own – – – just as before. Those of the soldiers who now occupy it are to depart from the acropolis. If anyone – – – the Eteocarpathian – – – either takes away or – – – he is to owe fifty talents to the Athenians and a tenth of it is to belong to the goddess. The case

[ι πρὸς τὸς θεσμο]θέτας ΕΝΑ[.]
[—11— ἐὰ]ν̣ δὲ Ἐτεοκα-
[ρπάθιοι ἄλλο τ]ι δέωνται, Κω-
[ίος καὶ Κνι]δίος καὶ Ῥοδίος
[καὶ ξυμμάχ]ων οἵτινες ἂν δ[υ]-
[νατοὶ ὦσιν] περὶ ταῦτα τὰ χ[ω]-
[ρία ὠφελε͂]ν ὅ τι ἂν δύνωνται.
[γράψαι δὲ τ]αῦτα ἐν στήληι [λ]-
[ιθίνηι ἐμ] π̣όληι καὶ ἐγ Καρ[π]-
[άθωι ἐν τῶι] ἱερῶι τõ Ἀπόλλ[ω]-
[νος ὅθεν] ἐ̣τμήθη ἡ κυπάρι[ττ]-
[ος· Ἀγήσα]ρ̣χ̣ον δὲ τ̣ὸν Λίνδ[ιο]-
[ν —7—]τησ[..] Ἀθηναίο[..]
[—7—]ναι τὴγ κυπάριτ[το]-
[ν *vacant* 6] *vacat*

vacat 0.23

B

[.]Ψ[—20—]
ΗΚ[—19— ξ]-
υμπα[—18—]
Ο.ΙΟΙΝΕΝ[—11— πρέ]-
σβε δὲ δύο ἑλέ[σθαι καὶ ....]
εν ταῦτα Καρπα̣[θίοις .... τ]-
ὴ̣ν̣ στήλην κατα[—10—]
[.]ῃ̣τηρε ἒναι τω[—9— Ἀ]-
[γ]ησ̣άρχο καὶ το[—10—]
[...] τὴν πόλιν ε[—10—]
[..]όντων· ἐὰν δὲ [—10—]
[..]ε π̣ολεμιος π[—10—]
[.. Ἀθ]η̣ναίων ἀπο[—9—]
\ δὲ οἱ ἐπιμελητ[αὶ εἴκοσι ἡ]-
μερῶν μετὰ τὴν [—10—]
τ̣ὼ πρέ[σβ]ε τάδ̣ε [—10—]
[.]κοτα̣ ἐν τῶ̣ν̣ χω[ρίων —6—]
[.] παρέχων τ[.]ν ΓΓ[—9—]
[.]οι χρησθα[—13—]
ὅταν δέωνται [—11—]

vacat 0.54

30 Κνι]δίος Wilamowitz *ap.* *IG* xii. i: Λιν]δίος Foucart. 32 περὶ ταῦτα τὰ [..] Ma. 38 [ος· Ἀγήσα]ρ̣χ̣ον Hiller, Wilhelm, Jameson *ap.* Ma, 143 n. 10: [ος· —5—]ρχον *IG* i³. 38–40 Λίνδ[ιο]ν, ὥσπερ ἤι]τησεν Ἀθηναίο[ις | καθιστά]ναι Tod after Wilhelm. 49–50 [Ἀ]|γησ̣άρχο P. M. Fraser, *LGPN* i. 8: τω[—10—]|[.]ι[.]άρχο *IG*; [Ἀ]|[γ]ησ̣άρχο Hiller.

is to be tried [before the *thesmo*]*thetai* in A[thens.]

28 If the Eteocarpathians are in need of anything else, the Co[ans and the Cni]dians and the Rhodians [and] all [the allies] who [are able] around these regions are to provide whatever they can.

34 This shall be written on a stone *stele* on the Acropolis, and at Carpathus in the sanctuary of Apollo, from which the cypress was cut. Hagesarchus the Lindian – – – is to deliver the cypress to the Athenians.

B

45 – – – choose two ambassadors – – – these to the Carpathians – – – the *stele* according – – – shall be – – – Hagesarchus and – – – the *polis* – – – But if – – – hostile – – – of the Athenians from – – – the *epimeletai* within twenty days after the – – – the two ambassadors these things – – – have –ed in any of the places – – – providing – – – use – – – whenever they need – – –

The small island of Carpathus (300 km.^{2}) appears in the *Iliad* in the Catalogue of Ships (II. 676) as Crapathus, and a Carpathian makes an appearance in Archilochus (fr. 248 West). From some point in the fourth century it became subject to Rhodes, but in the fifth century it seems to have housed up to four separate independent political units, the cities of Arcaseia, Brycous, and Carpathus, and the community (*koinon*) of the Eteocarpathians. In the Athenian tribute quota lists Arcaseia appears from 450/49 onwards, paying 1,000 dr., Carpathus from 445/5 onwards, paying 1,000 dr., and Brycous from 448/7 onwards, paying 500 dr. The Eteocarpathians appear only in 434/3, and from then until 432/1 they are listed among 'the cities who assessed themselves for tribute' (i.e. who paid voluntarily). In later lists they appear as regular tribute-payers (cf. G. Reger, in *Inventory*, 745–7; and see above, **119** p. 107). The supposed find-spot of this inscription is the best evidence for the location of the Eteocarpathians, but no convincing identification of their acropolis or of the temple of Apollo has been made (for the archaeology of the area in question see R. Hope Simpson and J. Lazenby, *BSA* lvii 1962, 163–5).

This inscription is the only other evidence for the Eteocarpathians (cf. Eteocretans already in *Odyssey* XIX. 176, and compare 'Old Sciathus' in **184**), and reveals a fascinating picture of how communities within the Aegean might react to Athenian imperialism.

Chronologically, the story starts in l. 18, at the point when the text begins to become readable again after several lines where too little remains to yield clear sense. Here we meet soldiers who have been stationed on the acropolis (within the territory of the Eteocarpathians) and who are now required to leave without doing any damage, on pain of a massive 50-talent fine (restored here as payable to the Athenians).[1] Why the troops were there, and indeed whose troops they are, is not clear. The way in which the assistance of Cos, Cnidus and Rhodes is commanded to help the Eteocarpathians if they need anything suggests that the threat to them comes not from the Athenians themselves but from the other cities on Carpathus.

The occupation of the acropolis by troops should be seen as a reaction to local community formation but also as the occasion that enabled that newly formed community to achieve independent status by entering a relationship with the Athenians. They effectively buy the departure of the troops by offering the Athenians a cypress tree—presumably a particularly fine and long specimen. One particular member of their community, and his sons, were evidently sent to Athens, to promise the tree and to request that Athens grant the community of the Eteocarpathians autonomy. The Athenians were sufficiently impressed or flattered by the gift that they honoured as benefactors the individual involved and the Eteocarpathians, and agreed to grant autonomy and to see to the removal of the garrison—so effectively

[1] Ma has doubts about the restoration of 'acropolis' in l. 20, believing that he can see traces of a *sigma* rather than a *lambda* four letters from the end of the word. The reading and restoration of the text at this point is very fragile, but if 'soldiers' are restored correctly in l. 19 changing 'acropolis' to some other location (a name ending in -sis) would not significantly change the story.

making the community of the Eteocarpathians a legal entity (for a parallel see *IG* i³ 29).

The cypress is said to be destined for the temple of 'Athena who rules Athens', a naming formula which is familiar from a number of inscriptions from the Athenian empire, particularly boundary-stones (cf. **113**). Although in the past these have been interpreted as cults of Athena imposed by the Athenians, it is more likely that we have to do with land that the Athenians have taken and (part of) which has been leased out to yield revenue for the Athenian cult of Athena (cf. Smarczyk, *Untersuchungen zur Religionspolitik und politischen Propaganda Athens im Delisch-Attischen Seebund*, 58–70; Parker, *Athenian Religion: A History*, 144–5). The phrase here is a case of the Athenians using, in a document which is to be set up on Carpathus as well as at Athens, the language of their allies when they identify Athenian Athena.[2]

The question of exactly which Athenian building the cypress was destined for depends upon the precise date of the inscription. Lewis suggested that, notwithstanding the use of Ionic letters, the stone had been cut by an Athenian stonemason and that the letter forms implied a date 'probably in the 430s' (D. M. Lewis, in Carradice (ed.), *Coinage and Administration in the Athenian and Persian Empires*, 58 = his *Selected Papers in Greek and Near Eastern History*, 123). Early enough in that period it would be possible, as Meiggs suggested, that the cypress was offered to be the ridge-pole of the Parthenon (cf. **145**); we also know that the doors of the Parthenon were of cypress-wood (R. Meiggs, *Trees and Timber in the Ancient Mediterranean World*, 200–1; *IG* i³ 461. 35, perhaps of 438). But it would make sense for the Eteocarpathians to appear in the tribute lists from shortly after the date of this inscription, so if their first appearance was indeed 434/3 this inscription might reasonably be dated to 435 or 434—by which time it is just possible that the Erechtheum (for which see below, **181**), which housed the old statue of Athena Polias, was already being contemplated.

The reverse of the *stele* is unfortunately too poorly preserved to yield detailed sense. It is clear that the sending of two ambassadors is involved along with reaction to hostile persons, but exactly what Athens is promising and what the circumstances are remains obscure. The Lindian who is involved in getting the cypress to Athens at *A*. 38–41 is also mentioned at *B*. 50. The combination of a reference to Rhodians with reference to a man from Lindos is notable, and parallel to the use of 'Carpathian' (*A*. 5) to identify the spokesman of the Eteocarpathians: in neither case (cf. Thuc. VI. 43) does use of the island ethnic imply political unity (which came to Rhodes only in 408).

For reference to the *thesmothetai* at Athens cf. **131**. 75; it was the six *thesmothetai* who presided over the whole system of popular courts in Athens (see *Ath. Pol.* 59).

[2] There is no reason to think that a temple of 'Athena who rules Athens' on Carpathus is at issue. On the repeated arguments of A. Tonini see *SEG* xlv 25, xlix 54, and Ma, 130–1.

137

Athens' appointment of a priestess and building of a temple to Athena Nike, 438–435 or 450–445

A marble *stele* found in 1897 in a dump of inscriptions on the north slope of the acropolis. **156** is inscribed on the back. Formerly in the Epigraphical Museum, but now displayed in the Acropolis Museum. Phot. Kern, *Inscriptiones Graecae*, 14, Guarducci, *Epigrafia Greca*, i. 141, Blok (below), 100, 121; Tracy (below), 93; our pl. 8.

Attic letters (see below). *Stoichedon* 29. Tracy, *Athenian Lettering of the Fifth Century* BC, 93–6.

M&L 44*; *IG* i³ 35; Mark (below), 104; Hellmann, *Choix d'inscriptions architecturales grecques*, 4; J. H. Blok, *Kernos* xxvii 2014, 520; Shear, *Trophies of Victory*, 27. Trans. Fornara 93; Mark (below), 104–5; Price, *Religions of the Ancient Greeks*, no. 4; Dillon & Garland³ 3. 65; Kearns, *Ancient Greek Religion*, 249; Shear, *Trophies of Victory*, 27. See also Meiggs, *The Athenian Empire*, 497–503, Mark, *The Sanctuary of Athena Nike in Athens*; J. H. Blok, *Kernos* xxvii 2014, 99–126; Shear, *Trophies of Victory*, 27–35, 341–58.

ἔδοχσεν τε͂ι βολε͂ι καὶ τô]ι̣ [δέ]μ̣ο̣[ι. . . .]
[— 17 —]α̣ι̣κος εἶπε· [τε͂ι]
[Ἀθεναίαι τε͂ι Νί]κ̣ει hιέρεαν hὲ ἄγ[. .]
[— 11 —]ι ἐχς Ἀθεναίον hαπα[σô]-
[ν καθίστα]σθαι, καὶ τὸ hιερὸν θυρôσα-
ι καθότι ἂν Καλλικράτες χσυγγράφσ-
ει· ἀπομισθôσαι δὲ τὸς πολετὰς ἐπὶ τ-
ε͂ς Λεοντίδος πρυτανείας· φέρεν δὲ τ-
ὲν hιέρεαν πεντέκοντα δραχμὰς καὶ
τὰ σκέλε καὶ τὰ δέρματα φέρεν τôν δε-
μοσίον· νεὸν δὲ οἰκοδομε͂σαι καθότι
ἂν Καλλικράτες χσυγγράφσει καὶ βο-
μὸν λίθινον.
hεστιαῖος εἶπε· τρε͂ς ἄνδρας hελέσθ-
αι ἐγ βολε͂ς· τούτος δὲ μετ[ὰ] Καλλικρά-
[το]ς χσυγγράφσαντας ἐπ[ιδεῖχσαι τε͂]-
[ι βολ]ε͂ι καθότι ἀπομ[ισθοθέσεται . .]
[— 6 —]ει τοσ[-------------------]

IG inserts Λεοντὶς ἐπρυτάνευε before line 1, hypothetically on the separate stone joined to the top of this *stele*. 1 *IG*: [— 18 — τô]ι̣ [δέ]μ̣ο̣[ι . . .] M&L. 2]α̣ι̣κος M&L *apparatus*: Γλ]α̣ῦ̣κος *IG*. 3–4 [. . . |— 12 —] ἐχς M&L; κλ|ερομένε λάχε]ι *IG*.

This inscription raises complex epigraphical, historical, and archaeological problems. The archaeological issue concerns how the 'temple' whose building is decreed in l. 11 relates to the temple of Athene Nike, constructed in the second half of the fifth century, whose recently reconstructed presence impresses itself today upon every visitor to the Athenian acropolis. The historical issue concerns the date at which this decree was passed and its relationship to the decree on the

Resolved by the council and people. – – – —aecus proposed: To establish as priestess for Athena Nike whoever – – – from all Athenian women, and put doors on the sanctuary according to the specifications Callicrates draws up. The *poletai* are to put this to tender in the prytany of Leontis. The priestess is to take fifty drachmas and to take the legs and skins of the public sacrifices. And build a shrine according to the specifications Callicrates draws up, and a stone altar.

14 Hestiaeus proposed: choose three men from the council; these men are to draw up the specifications for the tender with Callicrates and show them to the council – – –

---

other side of this stone. The epigraphical issues concern the relationship between the script used for this decree and the script used for the decree on the reverse, but also the layout of this decree on this stone. The top of this stone is cut at an angle, sloping away to the back, and the upper surface is prepared for joining to another stone above, with mortice holes: but what sort of a stone was placed above?

The inscription on the reverse (**156**) is quite firmly dated to 424/3. Script, placing on the stone and content all indicate that this text is earlier than that, but how much earlier? There are some epigraphic indicators, in particular the form of the letters. These are of the developed Attic form except for the *sigma*, which is formed from just three strokes. Although (see Introduction, pp. xxvii–xxviii, and on **166**) the three-bar *sigma* is no firm indicator of a date before 445, as was once argued, it certainly allows a date in the 440s. Tracy ascribes to this letter-cutter nine other inscriptions, eight of them tribute quota lists dating from 440/39 to 432/1, which use 4-bar *sigma*, and the other an undatable fragment using a 3-bar *sigma*. A date in the 430s is particularly plausible, but nothing epigraphic excludes a date in the early 420s.

The content of the inscription suggests that there should be a firm *terminus ante quem*. The decree decides to 'put doors/gates on the *hieron*' and to build a *naos* (Attic *neos*) and a stone altar. All of those features we would expect to be visible in the archaeology, but none can be identified unambiguously. What exactly is referred to by *to hieron* and what exactly by *ho neos* is not clear. Either term can be used with reference to a temple, but given the contrast with *neos* here, *hieron* more plausibly means 'sanctuary', in which case we are probably looking for gates, not doors. But *neos*, although it might mean a temple, might equally refer to a less grand shrine, a *naiskos*. That in the end there was a temple with doors in the sanctuary of Athena Nike in the fifth century does not mean that that temple and those doors are what is referred to here.

We have a self-declared altar of Athena Nike found east of the classical temple in 1937 (*DAA* 329 = *IG* i^3 596), but that dates to the middle of the sixth century. We then have a rectangular altar and a square block, plausibly interpreted as another altar, which belong to what has come to be known as Stage III of the sanctuary. In this stage, perhaps dated between the Cimonian south wall of the acropolis, constructed in the 460s (a block from which project was found in the foundations), and the start of the building of the Propylaea in 437, belong a small shrine, of simple *pi*-shaped plan, measuring 3.65 × 2.47 m., and both the rectangular altar and the square block, all of Aeginetan *poros* stone (on the archaeological history of the sanctuary see Mark; I. M. Shear, *JHS* cxix 1999, 86–127 at 120–5; and T. L. Shear, *Trophies of Victory*, 32, 393–4), suggest an earlier date for Stage III.

The subsequent history of the sanctuary sees first a mud-brick extension to the rectangular altar, increasing it to 2.88 × 1.13 m., and then an entire reworking of the sanctuary from the ground up. The bastion was reshaped, with straight walls of ashlar blocks of limestone, crowned by a low course of Pentelic marble, sheathing the irregular outline of the old bastion; the level was raised by more than a metre; the small shrine was replaced by the temple we see today (measuring 8.17 × 5.4 m. at the stylobate); the enlarged rectangular altar was replaced by a monumental altar almost 4 m. long; and the whole sanctuary was paved with Pentelic marble slabs. All these changes post-date the inception of the Propylaea building project, but that project, and most particularly the treatment of the west face of the south-west wing of the Propylaea as an entrance to the Nike sanctuary, presupposes that the Nike bastion will be raised to this level. Indeed there is some evidence that the exact level of the Nike sanctuary was initially planned to be higher than executed, and that the Propylaea south-west wing design had to be altered subsequent to its foundations being laid. The alterations made imply that plans, at least, for the Nike sanctuary must have been under discussion well before the completion of the Propylaea in 432—and equally that after that date the Nike sanctuary reconstruction had to fit in with the Propylaea.[1]

If the refurbishment of the Nike sanctuary must have been planned by 432, the date at which the temple was actually built remains unclear, and depends upon the view taken of how the style of its architectural details relate to the architecture of Propylaea and Erechtheum and how the style of the sculpted frieze and parapet relate to other late fifth-century sculpture (the parapet can be shown archaeologically to be necessarily contemporary with the rest of the refurbishment). Architecturally the Nike temple has been judged closer to the Erechtheum, the uncertain date of the inception of which was perhaps *c.*420 (see on **181**), than to the Propylaea. Sculpturally the frieze of the Nike temple and the Nike parapet seem to belong immediately before the sculpture (including Caryatids) of the Erechtheum (see P. Schultz, in Palagia (ed.), *Art in Athens during the Peloponnesian War*, 147–52). None of these stylistic dates are firm, but they all point in the same direction: architecture and sculpture alike would be surprising before 430 or after 404, and seem to belong most comfortably just before or after 420. *IG* i³ 64 seems to be (fragmentary) accounts relating to the replacing of the old shrine and the building of the new temple, but provides no further clear dating evidence.

The archaeological evidence makes it necessary that if this decree dates to before 440 then the references to a *naos* and altar there are either to a project never carried out in the form planned or to the rectangular altar and small cella of Stage III. But it also makes it certain that some sort of plan for refurbishing the bastion must have been formulated in the 430s, so that if this decree refers to the classical temple it would have to be dated to the early or middle 430s.

Assuming that what is laid out in the decree eventually happened, the archaeology therefore allows two possible stories. One is that the decree was passed shortly after 450, perhaps at the end of regular warfare against Persia, and resulted in the rectangular altar and the small cella of Stage III. The other is that it was passed in *c.*438 or shortly afterwards and inaugurated Stage IV, though Stage IV then took almost two decades to complete, with the building of the temple itself beginning only in the 420s. Distinguishing between these stories depends upon a judgment of the historical context and returns us to epigraphic questions.

This decree is notable for its placing, form and content. Although we do not know for certain where the *stele* was erected it is extremely plausible that it belongs in the socket of exactly the right size next to and at right-angles with the double *anta* that

[1] See now Shear, *Trophies of Victory*, 342–7; however, Shear, 27–35, continues to maintain a date of *c.*450 for the inscription, even though he thinks that it refers to a temple and not to the constructions of Stage III.

ends the south-west wing of the Propylaea (Shear, *Trophies of Victory*, 33–5). With the *stele* erected in this position, the inscriptions on both sides could be read—which strongly suggests that the *naos* whose construction the decree orders was regarded as the *naos* that was constructed.

In terms of content what is remarkable is the selection of the priestess 'from all Athenian women'. Although the use of lot to select priests was common (cf. Pl. *Leg.* 759 B), and may have been employed within Athenian priestly families already in the archaic period (see J. H. Blok & S. D. Lambert, *ZPE* clxix 2009, 95–121), we know of no earlier priesthood filled 'from all Athenian women (or men)' in this manner, though some later parallels are likely (S. D. Lambert, *Historia* lix 2010, 153–6, 158–60). Selection by lot was standard Athenian selection practice for officials not required to have any special individual competence (lot is not used for generals or in the fourth century for top financial officials), but the decision that any Athenian woman should be eligible makes this strikingly democratic, and Blok has suggested a link with new guarantee of pure descent for women offered by Pericles' citizenship law. That such a process of selection was a noted innovation is further suggested by the wording of the gravestone of Myrrhine (**179**).

What is remarkable about the form is the way in which the decree moves from the appointment of the priestess to the putting doors on the sanctuary to the perquisites of the priestess and then the building of a *naos* and a stone altar. This not only mixes topics, it mixes arrangements for all time (which after 403 in Athens would have required the passing of a law) with one-off decisions. That the decree was not well thought out seems to have been apparent to some at the time: Hestiaeus' amendment, appointing a committee of the council to oversee the project, makes up for one glaring weakness in the original proposal.

Does the form of the decree suggest that it was only part of a rather longer decision? Meritt and Wade-Gery thought that the stone joined to the top of the *stele* carried a decree about the whole replanning of the western approach to the acropolis and that the extant decree was simply an amendment to that (B. D. Meritt & H. T. Wade-Gery *JHS* lxxxiii 1963, 109–11). In that case the three letters dubiously read in l. 1 would not belong to 'the people' in the clause 'Resolved by the council and people' but to some other word or words at the end of the decree. More recently Blok has proposed that this decree was supplementary to a decree passed earlier in the same prytany inaugurating civic sacrifices to Athena Nike. But we lack a precedent for such a continuation where the stone did not allow space (most decrees do not fill the stone chosen), or for a mason choosing a stone of insufficient size to carry what he is inscribing (but see **136**. *A*). If this decree is an amendment then we would expect it, like Hestiaeus' amendment, to start on a new line (particularly given that it lacks the regular amendment formula 'otherwise as X proposed'); if it is an independent decree one would expect it to be inscribed as such on a separate stone (or the reverse of the earlier stone).

Undoubtedly something was added to the top of the stone, but what? The very unusual scarf joint, apparently adopted so as to secure an uninterrupted run of text, argues against a relief (and the earliest certain decree relief dates to the 420s: see

Introduction, p. xxi), but it argues too against merely a crowning element. On the other hand, the placing of the decree on the reverse well below the top of this stone argues against there being a substantial stone above. It may be that for a unique stone we have to imagine unique circumstances: did a stone which had been elaborately prepared with a crowning element then break? The parallel for a stone being added on top of a decree that is otherwise effectively complete, provided by **131**, which plausibly dates to the 440s, is close epigraphically (that decree, like this one —if we restore 'Resolved by the council and people.' in l. 1—exceptionally omits a standard element from the introductory rubric: in that case the secretary is omitted, in this case the prytany and either the secretary or the president), but not physically (see C. Lawton, *Hesperia* lxi 1992, 239–51 at 247–8).

However we explain the oddly abbreviated heading, it is difficult to explain the structure of the decree. There is, however, some logic to the order. —aecus first proposes the appointment of a priestess, then thinks about the sanctuary in which she will operate, then about the finances required for the work on the sanctuary and for the priestess herself. Thought about like this, what remains most curious is the tagging on to the end of the decision to have a *naos* and a stone altar. One might have thought an altar and a *naos* not something to be added as an afterthought.

One further element may help here. Harpocration (ν 17 Keaney Νίκη Ἀθηνᾶ) quotes from 'Heliodorus the periegete' the claim that the Athenians worshipped a *xoanon* of Athena Nike that was wingless and held a pomegranate in one hand and a helmet in the other. Paus. III. 15. vii mentions this archaic wooden statue, which must have survived the Persian sack and will have needed some sort of shelter, and there may be reference to it in the accounts of *IG* i³ 64. 21–2 (τὸ ἀρχαῖον ἄγαλμα [——15—— Νι]|κε͂ς hος κάλλιστα, 'the ancient cult statue – – – of Nike as beautifully as possible'). The Stage III shrine provides a possible shelter, and has buried within it what appears to be the archaic cult statue base. If we take this statue into account, then the thought-process that moves from a designated priestess to a more suitable altar, and then sees an opportunity to provide the cult statue with a more appropriate home, a temple rather than a *naiskos*, would seem very possible.

Callicrates, the architect named, is known in a number of other contexts. Epigraphically he appears, in an inscription that cannot be closely dated, working on the walls of the acropolis, specifying the best and cheapest ways of keeping out runaway slaves and clothes-thieves (*IG* i³ 45). In Plutarch's *Pericles* he appears undertaking work on the Long (middle) wall (16. v) in the 440s and, more controversially, as joint architect of the Parthenon with Ictinus (13. iv). The latter is controversial because other sources list Ictinus alone or with Carpion, and R. Carpenter famously invented a Cimonian Parthenon for which Callicrates was responsible before Pericles and Ictinus took the project over (Carpenter, *The Architects of the Parthenon*).

Much remains uncertain in the interpretation of the decree and its relationship to the archaeology, but the following sequence of events seems plausible. First, in the course of planning the rebuilding of the acropolis attention turned to the west entrance and the issue of what to do about Athena Nike was raised. In the light of the military activities involved in Athenian imperialism, the need for systematic sacrifice to Athena Nike was pressed. Second, once further thought was given to this it became clear that the whole bastion needed to be rebuilt. Our decree, creating a

---

138

Payments for Athens' Samian war, 440 and 439

Three fragments of a marble *stele* from the acropolis, now in the Epigraphical Museum; on *a* the left-hand margin is preserved. Phot. (*a*) Meritt, *AFD*, p. 43 fig. 4; (*a* + *b* + *c*) Marginesu & Themos (below), 176, 183–4 figs. 1–3.

Attic, with developed lettering. *Stoichedon c.*80 (apart from the lines with numerals).

(*a*) *IG* i^2 293; Meritt, *AFD*, 42–8. (*b*) *IG* i^1 Supp. 560; Meritt, *AJA*^{2} xxxviii 1934, 69 no. 5. (*a*+*b*) Meritt, *AJP* lv 1934, 365–6, cf. *SEG* x 221; M&L 55; *IG* i^3 363. (*c*) *IG* i^2 360; *IG* i^3 454 (found in 1972 to join *b*, but the join was overlooked in *IG* i^3); G. Marginesu & A. A. Themos, in *Ἀθηναίων ἐπίσκοπος ... H. B. Mattingly*, 171–84*. Trans. (*a*+*b*) Fornara 113. See also C. W. Fornara, *JHS* xcix 1979, 9–14 (cf. *SEG* xxix 18); Shipley, *A History of Samos, 800–188* BC, 113–22; Osborne, *The Athenian Empire*^{4}, 90.

[—5—]εκ[- -]
[. . . .]ε̣σε[- -]
[. . .]σοσι[- -]
[. . .]Φρεά[ρριος? -]
𐅋𐅉𐅉𐅈ΤΤΤ[- - - *vacat*].
Ἀθεναῖοι ἀ[νέλοσαν ἐπὶ Μορυχίδο ἄρχοντος, ἐπὶ τε̂ς —7?— πρυτανείας πρότες πρυτανευόσες ἐς τὸν]
πρὸς Σαμίο[ς πόλεμον τάδε. παρέδοσ]α̣[ν στρατεγοῖσιν τοῖς ἐκπλέοσιν ταμίαι τôν] ἱερôν χρεμάτον τε̂ς]
Ἀθεναίας Π[—19—]ονε[—c.38— καὶ χσυνάρχοντε]-
ς, hοῖς Φυρό[μαχος —14—]ο̣ς ἐ[γραμμάτευε, ἐπὶ τε̂ς βολε̂ς hε̂ι —c.13— πρôτος ἐγραμμά]-
τευε· ταμία[ι —17—]Ε̣[ὐ]βο[—c.49— ἐ]-
χς Οἴο, Ναυσ[ι—16—]ρινο[—c.51—]

The placing of *b* (the letters in the middle of ll. 7–10) was due to H. T. Wade-Gery, and its horizontal alignment is confirmed by the vacant spaces in ll. 12, 17; *c* joins *b*, and contributes the ε before βο in l. 10 and the letters in the middle of ll. 11–19. The restorations printed in M&L and *IG* i^3, based on those of Meritt, and made without *c*, are open to objections (cf. below). 5, 19 The numerals in these lines are carved in erasures, suggesting that there was previously a wrong entry in 5 which entailed a wrong total in 19. 9 Φυρό[μαχος] is the only attested Athenian name which begins thus: he is restored as secretary to the treasurers of Athena for 441/0 in *IG* i^3 442. 177 on the basis of this text. 9, 14 πρôτος not restored in 9 by Marginesu & Themos but seems necessary; for identification of the year by the secretary of the council in the first prytany cf. **150**. 5–6. 10–11 A Eubulides of Oion who could be this man appears in [Dem.] XLIII. *Macartatus* 19, etc.

priesthood and refurbishing the sanctuary, might have been passed at either of these two stages. But though the arrival of war in 431 put a temporary halt to building plans, some progress was made and in 424/3 it became possible to actualise the plans made during the 430s. **156** marks the next stage of this story.

– – – of Phrearrhii (?) – – – 128[?+] talents.

6 The Athenians [spent in the archonship of Murychides (440/39), in the prytany of ——, the first prytany, for the war] against the Samians [the following. To the generals sailing out there was handed over by the treasurers of the monies of] Athena P[— son of —— of —— and his colleagues, to whom Phyro[machus son of —— of ——was secretary, under the council for which —— was first secre]tary; treasurers – – – Eubu [— – – –] from Oion, Naus[— – – –]:

𐅋𐅋𐅋𐅊𐅉𐅈TTT[- - -]. *vacat*
παρὰ ταμιô[ν ἐκ πόλεος hoῖς . . .]όλεος [—16–18— ἐγραμμάτευε καὶ ἐπὶ τε̂ς βολε̂ς hε̂ι ?'Επιχαρ]-
ῖνος Περαι[εὺς πρôτος ἐγραμμά]τευε, τά[δε παρεδόθε τοῖς ἐς Σάμον —11— hύστ]-
ερον· hοίδε [ταμίαι —5— ἐκ Κερα]μέον, Λ[—40–5—]
Ἀφιδναῖος [—16— Π]ρ̣ασιε̣[ύς, —40–3—]
𐅌𐅋𐅋𐅋𐅋𐅈TTT[- - -]. *vacat*
χσύμπαντο[ς κεφάλαιον - - -] *vacat*
𐅍𐅋[𐅋]𐅋𐅋[- -]¦[- - - - - - -].

13–14 ['Επιχαρ]|ῖνος Περαι[εὺς is not attested elsewhere (if Epicharinus is to be restored in the near-contemporary *IG* i³ 455. 22 and 462. 6, that is a different man, not from Piraeus). 14–15 [—11— hύστ]|ερον cf. Thuc. i. 116. ii, 117. ii, A. P. Matthaiou, *γραμματεῖον* iv 2015, 67–71 (www.grammateion.gr): ?ἐκπλέοσιν τὸ δεύτ]|ερον Marginesu & Themos.

Very little of this inscription survives, but we have agreed with our predecessors that its potential importance earns it a place in our collection. What is certain is that it concerns payments from the treasury of Athena towards Athens' war against Samos—a war which was prompted by Samos' defection from the Delian League when Athens supported Miletus against it in a dispute over territory, and which ended with Athens' regaining control but only after a major effort (Thuc. i. 115. ii–117; cf. **139**)—and that it lists four sums of money of which the last is the total of the previous three (the first item and the total having been corrected: see above).

The reconstruction of Meritt, which has been widely used, was based on an attempt to reconcile the total, 1,400(+?) talents, with the 1,200 talents given as the cost of the war by Nep. xiii. *Timotheus* i. ii (and obtainable by emendation in Isoc. xv. *Antid.* 111 and Diod. Sic. xii. 28. iii), by assuming that the first item concerns expenditure against Byzantium, which is mentioned with no information beyond the bare fact of its joining Samos in Thuc. i. 115. v, 117. iii, and that the other items concern Samos. However, we agree with Fornara that the literary texts are likely to have reported the total cost of the war rather than the cost of fighting against Samos on its own (in which case they do not give the correct amount), and consider Meritt's interpretation unjustified.

Thucydides dates the beginning of the war to 441/0, the sixth year from the Thirty Years' Peace of 446/5, and Samos' capitulation to the ninth month of the siege (i. 115. ii, 117. iii). Fornara suggested that the figures are totals for three successive years, which he presumed to be 442/1, 441/0 and 440/39 (for the generals of 441/0, 440/39 and 439/8 cf. **139**), followed by the final total. M&L suggested an alternative possibility which fits Thucydides and reduces this record to two years: that the first item belonged to 441/0, the second to year 440/39 of the council, but still to year

368[?+] talents.

13 From the treasurers [from the acropolis to whom —]poleus [son of —— of —— was secretary, and under the council for which ?Epichar]inus of Pirae[us was first secre]tary, the following [was given to those – – –] to Samos later. These [treasurers: —— of Cera]meis, L[– – –] of Aphidna [– – –] of Prasiae [– – –]: 908(?+) talents.

18 [Total] of the whole [– – –]

19 1,400(?+) talents. [– – –]

441/0 of the treasurers, whose year began at the Panathenaea on 28 Hecatombaeon (i) (cf. **144**), and the third to 440/39 after 28 Hecatombaeon. Lewis in *CAH*^{2} v. 502, and more recently Marginesu & Themos, accepted that, which if correct would limit the expenditure to 441/0 and 440/39, and in terms of our years to 440 and 439.[1]

However the chronological problem is to be resolved, it remains important that the treasury of Athena provided substantial sums of money for this war, as it and the treasury of the Other Gods were to do later for the Peloponnesian War (cf. **148**, **160**); and it may be that the 3,000 talents whose payment to Athena is mentioned in **144**. *A*. 3–4 represent the repayment of this and other sums borrowed from Athena. Fourteen hundred talents is a very substantial sum (later the siege of Potidaea cost 2,000 talents: Thuc. II. 70. ii). Whether there were further sums provided towards this war from Athens' secular funds and the funds of the Delian League is uncertain (see, against, *ATL* iii. 337; for, Gomme, *HCT* ii. 31–2). After the war Samos lost its status as a ship-providing member of the League, but instead of being assessed for tribute was required to pay reparations (Thuc. I. 117. iii; VII. 57. iv is carelessly expressed). *ATL* iii. 334–5 envisaged regular payments continuing to to *IG* i^3 371. 16, of 414/3; but W. S. Ferguson earlier and Gomme later maintained that payment could have been completed within a few years (*The Treasurers of Athena*, 154–5; *HCT* ii. 33)—and if that is correct, as we think more likely, subsequent payments by Samos must have been justified under some other rubric (cf. **152**. 20–1).

[1] If this is right, **135**. *A*, with a different secretary to the treasurers in §ii. 6–8, cannot belong to 440/39, the year to which it has been assigned in previous editions.

139

Athenian treaty with Samos, 439

Four fragments (which we designate as in *IG* i^3; some other editions designate them differently) of a marble *stele* from the acropolis, now in the Epigraphical Museum; parts of the right edge of *c* and *a*, and of the left edge of *d*, are preserved. Phot. *ATL* ii, pl. xi; *JHS* xcix 1979, pl. i; (*c* and *a*) *JHS* c 1980, pl. iv, Matthaiou (below) 164–9 figs. 1–6.

Attic, with developed lettering. *Stoichedon*, 37 in the text printed here, but earlier reconstructions used different line-lengths.

IG i^2 50; Meritt, *AFD* 48–56; *ATL* ii, D 18; *SdA* 159; M&L 56; *IG* i^3 48 (Meritt & McGregor); B. D. Meritt, *PAPS* cxxviii 1984, 123–33 (cf. *SEG* xxxiv 16); A. P. Matthaiou, in *Ἀθηναίων ἐπίσκοπος . . . H. B. Mattingly*, 141–69.* Trans. Fornara 115. See also Bradeen & McGregor, *Studies in Fifth-Century Attic Epigraphy*, 120–1; C. W. Fornara. *JHS* xcix 1979, 14–18 (with D. M. Lewis, 18–19) (cf. *SEG* xxix 9); A. P. Bridges, *JHS* c 1980, 185–8 (cf. *SEG* xxx 6); J. Breslin, *AncW* iii 1980, 104–6 (cf. *SEG* xxxi 10); Shipley, *A History of Samos, 800–188 BC*, 113–22; S. Bolmarcich, *Chiron* xxxix 2009, 45–64.

b

— — — ο̣ — — —
— — — απι̣ — — —
— — — Σαμίος δὲ ο]ἰκε͡ν̣ [αὐτονόμος *or* τὲν πόλιν τὲν hεαυτôν ? — — —
— — — Λε̂μνο[ν — — — *or* — — — ἐν] Λέμνο[ι — — —
— — — ι̣ καθαπ̣[ερ — — —
— — — οι κατασ̣ — — —
— — — ?καὶ τôν λοι]πôν νέσ[ον — — —
— — — δὲ ἐν τε̂[ι — — —
— — — σ̣οι δὲ κα[θελε̂ν — — —
— — — τô λοιπô] χ̣ρόνο ὑπάρ[χεν? — — —
— — — παραδôναι δ' α]ὐτὸς Ἀθεν̣[αί]-
[οισι τὰς ναῦς ἐς τὸν ἐσιόντα ἐνια]υ̣τὸν : hόσ[α δ' Ἀ]-
[θεναῖοι χρέματα ἐΣάμοι ἀνέλοσα]ν ἀποδ[ôναι Σ]-
[αμίος ἐς τὸν εἰρεμένον χρόνον· ἄνδρα]ς [δὲ ?hομέ]-
[ρος (*e.g.* hεκατὸν) δôναι αὐτὸς Ἀθεναίοις —]
lacuna

c

[—^{8}— κατὰ τάδε Σαμίος ὀμόσαι· δράσο καὶ ἐ]-
[ρô καὶ βουλεύσο hó τι ἂν δύνομ]αι ἀγαθὸ̣ν, [καὶ οὐ]-
[κ ἀποστέσομαι ἀπὸ τô δέμο τô Ἀ]θεναίον οὔ̣τε λ[ό]-
[γοι οὔτ' ἔργοι ?οὐδενὶ οὐδὲ τôν] χσυμμάχον τôν Ἀ-
[θεναίον, βοεθέσο δὲ καὶ ἀμυνô τ]ôι δέμοι τôι Ἀθ-
[εναίον. τάδ' ὀμόσαι Ἀθεναίος · δρ]άσο καὶ ἐρô καὶ

The four fragments were combined by H. T. Wade-Gery, *CP* xxvi 1931, 309–13, after A. Wilhelm. For the history of attempts at reconstruction see Matthaiou: he accepts (what some have doubted) that the four fragments are from the same inscription, agrees with Bridges that there were three lines between the last of fr. *c* and the first of fr. *a*, and (whereas others had suggested different alignments) aligns *d* with *c* and *a* as in the text printed above.

Restorations by Matthaiou except where otherwise indicated. *b* 5 *ATL*. 7 previous editors followed Pittakys in restoring Πελο]ποννεσ[—. *cda* 0–1 *init.* *IG* i^2.

b – – – the Samians shall live in independence *or* in their own city (?) – – – Lemnos – – – and the other islanders (?) – – – apply for the time to come (?) – – – they shall hand over the ships to the Athenians for the coming year. The monies which the Athenians spent on Samos the Samians shall repay by the time stated. They shall give (e.g. a hundred) men as hostages to the Athenians (?) – – –

lacuna

cda The Samians shall swear as follows: 'I shall act and speak and counsel what good I can, and I shall not defect from the people of Athens either by word or by any (?) deed, and I shall help and defend the people of Athens.'

The Athenians shall swear as follows: 'I shall act and speak and counsel

[βολεύσο ἀγαθὸν τôι πλέθει τôι] Σ̣αμίον hó τι ἂν
[δύνομαι ἀδόλος ποιόντον τôν Σα]μίον κατὰ hὰ χ]-
[συνέθεντο τοῖς στρατεγοῖς τοῖς] Ἀθεναίον. [. .]
[——29——]κράτε[. . . .]
d [στ]ρ̣ατεγο̣[ὶ Ἀθεναίον hοίδε ὄμοσαν· . .] | [. . . Ἐρε]-
χθεΐδος ⁝ Δεμ̣[—5— Αἰγεΐδος ⁝ ?Ἅγνον ⁝ Φορμίον Πα]-
νδιονίδος ⁝ Χ[αρισανδρίδες Λεοντίδος ⁝ Περικλ]-
ε͂ς ⁝ Γλαύκον Ἀ[καμαντίδος ⁝ ——17——]
a [. .]ίδος ⁝ Χ̣σ̣[——16—— ?hο]ί̣δ̣[ε ταχσίαρχ]-
[οι ——16—— ?Ἀντικλ]ε̣ς ⁝ Τλεμπ̣[όλεμος]
[——24——]ς ⁝ βολὲ ἔ͂ρχε Ι̣Ο̣[. .]
[——18—— πρôτ]ος ἐγραμμάτευε Ῥα-
[μνόσιος. *vacat*] *vacat*
vacat

12 Χ[αρισανδρίδες Λεοντίδος only possible restoration of this length, but the name is otherwise attested only in Hippothontis (*LGPN* ii 476 *s.n.*). 14–15 other possibilities hο]ί̣δ̣[ε τριέραρχοι, ταχσ]ί̣α̣[ρχοι hοίδε. 15–16 names of seven men if there are no names of tribes; for Anticles, Tlempolemus cf. Thuc. I. 117. ii (Tlepolemus MSS, but Tlem- is the normal form of the name). 16 βολὲ ἔ͂ρχε is on the stone but the formulation is unparalleled. 17–18 *IG* i².

For Athens' war of 440–439 against Samos cf. **138**. After the initial fighting, it culminated in a nine-month siege, at the end of which the Samians came to terms, agreeing to demolish their city wall, give hostages and pay reparations over time (Thuc. I. 117. iii: for the reparations cf. on **138**).

This inscription remains highly problematic: what is certain is that it involves one or two oaths sworn between the Athenians and the Samians, followed by a list of Athenian generals and perhaps others who were presumably involved in the oath-taking (cf. Thuc. V. 19. ii, 24, and from the fourth century R&O 48). The text which we print is based on suggestions by Matthaiou, but like earlier reconstructions it is speculative. The first secretary restored in *cda* 17–18 will be different from that in **138**. 13–14, so it has been thought that this treaty was delayed until 439/8 (cf. Meritt, *AFD* 52–3). Matthaiou considers as a possible refinement (since the council's year and the archon's year did not coincide: see Introduction, pp. xxiv–xxv) that this treaty was made at the beginning of the council's year 439/8 but still at the end of the archon's year 440/39 (cf. the suggestion that in **138** the second payment belongs to the council's year 440/39 but to the end of the treasurers' year 441/0, bounded by the Panathenaea). In that case the generals listed, compatible with Thuc. I. 116. i, 117. ii if Anticles and Tlempolemus were serving in another capacity, but not matching the list for 441/0 in Androtion *FGrH* 324 F 38, will be those of 440/39. However, we do not know when the council's new year fell in 439, and we should leave open the possibility that this treaty belongs to both the archontic and the bouleutic year 439/8 and that Anticles and Tlempolemus though not generals in the

what good I can for the mass of the Samians, as long as the Samians act without deceit in accordance with what they agreed with the Athenian generals.' – – –

10 These Athenian generals swore: —— of Erechtheis, Dem— of Aegeis, (?) Hagnon, Phormio of Pandionis, Charisandrides of Leontis, Pericles, Glaucon of Acamantis, (three other generals, from two other tribes).

14 The following taxiarchs *or* trierarchs (?): *perhaps seven names, with* Anticles (?) *and* Tlempolemus *third and fourth.*

16 The council in office – – – —— of Rhamnous was first secretary (?).

---

list here had been generals in 440/39 (their tribes are not certain). There is no evidence beyond Thucydides' narrative and this inscription for the generals of 440/39 and of 439/8.

Fr. *b* has been linked with the others because of its physical characteristics, and because the Athenians originally deposited hostages on Lemnos though the Samians later recovered them (Thuc. I. 115. iii, v), and the Peloponnesians considered supporting Samos against Athens (Thuc. I. 40. v—but Matthaiou abandons the restoration of the Peloponnesians in *b* 7); but Lemnos can be relevant to the final settlement only if the hostages of Thuc. I. 117. iii were at least originally sent there.

At the beginning of this episode Athens imposed a democracy on Samos (Thuc. I. 115. iii); but in 412 there was an 'uprising of the people against the powerful men' (Thuc. VIII. 21). The constitutional state of Samos between 439 and 412 has been disputed. Diod. Sic. XII. 28. iv says that the Athenians imposed a democracy in 439. That has been accepted e.g. by R. P. Legon, *Historia* xxi 1972, 145–58, in which case some time in or before 412 the oligarchs regained power (e.g. Barron, *The Silver Coins of Samos*, 81, 100) or else they threatened to do so (Legon) or a clique gained control of what was still technically a democracy (Hornblower, *Comm. Thuc.*, i. 192–3, iii. 808–9). Athens did not systematically impose democracies, and some have thought that it did not do so in the final settlement with Samos (e.g. E. Will, *REA* lxxi 1969, 305–19); but in view of the earlier attempt we should expect it now. In *cda* 6 *plethos*, if that is the correct restoration, might have been chosen as a more emphatic word than *demos*.

The preserved first-person future verbs in *cda* 5 point strongly to an oath. We can be certain of some features; and the oaths of *cda* 1–8 have been reconstructed by comparison with each other and with other oaths. As with Erythrae (**121**) but not Chalcis (**131**) there is mention of the allies as well as of Athens.

The Athenian swearers on this occasion (*cda* 10–16) included generals (10), and on Matthaiou's reconstruction (following the earlier suggestion of Bolmarcich, but the seventeen who swore to the Peace of Nicias in 421 (Thuc. v. 19. ii), which she cites, were probably determined by factors particular to that occasion) up to seven other men including Anticles and Tlempolemus, who are mentioned by Thucydides as bringing a contingent of twenty ships. Athenian practice on who should swear to treaties was variable, but the generals were often involved (cf. Rhodes, *Boule*, 43–4).

Athens' ten generals were appointed originally one from each tribe, but by the 330s/320s irrespective of tribe (*Ath. Pol.* 22. ii, 61. i). In at any rate the second half of the fifth century and the first half of the fourth, one per tribe remained the norm, but it was possible for at any rate one tribe to supply two generals and one other to

140

Victory of Taras over Thurii, *c.*443–433

A bronze spear-butt found at Olympia, now in the Antikensammlung, Staatliche Museen zu Berlin—Preußischer Kulturbesitz (displayed in the Altes Museum); two others with the same text are in the museum at Olympia (*I. Olympia* 255–6). Phot. our pl. 9; of *I. Olympia* 256, *Olympische Forschungen*, i, Taf. 63 (b). Facsimile *LSAG*, pl. 53. 10.

Laconian–Tarantine writing, avoiding curved strokes (cf. *LSAG* 279–80).

I. Olympia 254 (cf. 255–6); *SIG*[3] 61; M&L 57*. Trans. Fornara 112. See also P. Meloni, *RAL*[8] v 1950, 574–98; *LSAG* 284, 411; *Inventory*, 293–4.

σκῦλα ἀπὸ Θουρίον Ταραν-
τῖνοι ἀνέθεκαν Διὶ Ὀλυ-
μπίοι δεκάταν.

Taras and Thurii were both on the coast running from the 'heel' to the 'toe' of Italy. Taras was allegedly the one colony of Sparta, founded at the end of the eighth century to house men who for some reason had not qualified for a share of land conquered in Messenia (Arist. *Pol.* v. 1306 B 27–31, Theopomp. *FGrH* 115 F 171, Strabo 277–80 / VI. iii. 1–3); but for doubts about the Spartanness of Taras see Osborne, *Greece in the Making*[2], 168–9). Further west Sybaris was destroyed by its

supply none: the earliest certain instance is 441/0, for which Androtion *FGrH* 324 F 38 claims to name the ten generals, in fact seems to name eleven, and certainly has Pericles and Glaucon (on whom see Davies, *A.P.F.*, 91, and **148**) from the same tribe, Acamantis (V). It is plausible, though not certain, that Phormio (general several times until 429/8) as well as Hagnon was from Pandionis (III) (cf. Paus. I. 29. x), and on the reconstruction which we print there was one other pair of men from the same tribe and three of the tribes VI–X supplied no general. The phenomenon of double representation was first remarked on, in connection with 441/0, by F. W. Lenz, *TAPA* lxxii 1941, 226–32; it was demonstrated, against earlier interpretations, by K. J. Dover, *JHS* lxxx 1960, 61–77 = his *The Greeks and Their Legacy*, 159–80, that the purpose was not to elevate one of the ten above his colleagues. It has been suggested that the purpose was rather to provide for circumstances in which one tribe did not have a strong candidate, perhaps by allowing such a tribe to adopt a member of another tribe as its own candidate, by M. Piérart, *BCH* xcviii 1974, 125–46, refined by L. G. Mitchell, *Klio* lxxxii 2000, 344–60. It will be remarkable, but we think not impossible, if in this year there were three pairs and three unrepresented tribes.

Spoils from Thurii
dedicated by the Tarantines to Zeus Olympios
as a tithe.

---

neighbour Croton (both Achaean) in 510, and the last of a series of attempts to refound it, under Athenian auspices and with a change of name to Thurii, was perhaps in 444/3 (Diod. Sic. XII. 9–11[–18], cf. Arist. *Pol.* V. 1303 a 31–3, Strabo 263 / VI. i 13). Taras came into conflict with Thurii over a settlement at Siris, about halfway between the two, which they both claimed; Taras was victorious after a war lasting about ten years, and moved the city to a new site with the name Heraclea

(Diod. Sic. xii. 23. ii [444/3], 36. iv [433/2], Strabo 264 / vi. i. 14 = Antiochus of Syracuse *FGrH* 555 F 11, cf. for Siris' earlier history Strabo 264–5 / vi. i. 15 = F 12, discussed in *Inventory*).

Meloni argues that Athens' foundation of Thurii prompted Taras to take pre-emptive action, and that Thurii's holding out for ten years implies that it received substantial support from Athens. A bronze herald's wand, dedicated jointly by Thurii and Brentesium (*IG* xiv 672) and perhaps of this period, points to friendly contact between these cities.

For the practice of dedicating inscribed spoils of war at Olympia see **101** and **111**, and compare **126**. *B*. 9–11. This dedication could have been made at the end of the

---

141

Athenian decree regulating the offering of firstfruits at Eleusis, *c.*435 or earlier

A marble *stele* found at Eleusis, now in the Epigraphical Museum. (A fragment of a second copy of the same decree, covering ll. 15–22, found in the Plaka at Athens, is also in the Epigraphical Museum.) Phot. *I. Eleusis* (below), pl. 911; Tracy, *Athenian Lettering of the Fifth Century BC*, 117 fig.5, 118 fig. 6 (details).

Attic letters; *stoichedon* 50.

M&L 73; *IG* i^3 78; *I. Eleusis* 28a.* Trans. Fornara 140; Bowden, *Classical Athens and the Delphic Oracle*, 126–8 (ll. 1–46 only); Dillon & Garland^3 3. 38. See also Smarczyk, *Untersuchungen zur Religionspolitik und politischen Propaganda Athens im Delischen-Attischen Seebund*, 167–298; Cavanaugh, *Eleusis and Athens*, 29–95.

[Τιμο]τ̣έλ̣[ε]ς Ἀχαρνεὺ̣ς̣ ἐγραμμάτευε.
[ἔδοχσ]εν τε̑ι βολε̑ι καὶ το̑ι δέμοι, Κεκροπὶς ἐπρυτάνευε, Τιμοτέ-
[λες ἐ]γραμμάτευε, Κ̣υκνέας ἐπεστάτε̣· τάδε οἱ χσυγγραφε̑ς χσυνέ-
[γρ]α̣φσαν· ἀπάρχεσθαι τοῖν Θεοῖν το̑ καρπο̑ κατὰ τὰ πάτρια καὶ τὲ̣-
ν̣ μ̣α̣ντείαν τὲν ἐγ Δελφο̑ν Ἀθεναίος ἀπὸ το̑ν hεκατὸν μεδίμνο̣ν̣ [κ]-
ριθο̑ν μὲ ἔλαττον ε̑ ḥεκτέα, πυρο̑ν δὲ ἀπὸ το̑ν ḥε̣κ̣α̣τὸν μεδίμν̣ο̣ν̣ μ̣-
ὲ ἔ̣λαττον hεμιέκτεον· ἐὰν δέ τις πλείο καρπὸν ποιε̑ι ε̑ τοσο[ῦ]το-
ν ε̑ ὀλείζο, κατὰ τὸν αὐτὸν λό̣γο̣ν ἀ̣π̣άρχεσθαι. ἐγλέγεν δὲ τὸ̣ς̣ δεμ-
άρχος κατὰ τὸς δέμος καὶ παραδ̣ι̣δό̣ναι το̣ῖ̣ς hιεροποιοῖς τοῖ̣ς̣
Ἐλευσινόθεν Ἐλευσῖνάδε. οἰκο̣δομε̑σα̣ι̣ δὲ σιρὸς τρε̑ς Ἐλευσῖ̣ν-
ι̣ κ̣ατὰ τὰ πάτρια hόπο ἂν δοκε̑ι τοῖς ḥιεροποιοῖς καὶ το̑ι ἀ̣ρχιτ-
έκτονι ἐπιτέδειον ε̑ναι ἀπὸ το̑ ἀργυρί̣ο το̑ τοῖν Θεο̣ῖν. τ̣ὸν δ̣ὲ κ̣α-
ρπὸν ἐνθαυθοῖ ἐμβάλλεν ḥὸν ἂν παραλάβοσι παρ̣ὰ̣ τ̣ο̑ν δεμάρ[χ]ο̣ν̣,
ἀ̣πάρχεσθαι δὲ καὶ τὸς χσυμμάχος κατὰ ταὐτά. τὰς δὲ π̣ό̣λες ἐγλ[ο]-
γέας hελέσθαι το̑ καρπο̑, καθ̣ότι ἂν δοκε̑ι αὐτε̑σι ἄ̣ριστα ὁ καρπὸ̣-
[ς] ἐγλεγέσεσθαι· ἐπειδὰν δὲ ἐγλεχθε̑ι̣, ἀποπεμφσάντον Ἀθ̣ένα̣ζε·

war or after some success during the war.[1] It is one of the latest dedications at Olympia by Greeks of arms and armour taken from Greeks, and this pattern of decline in such dedications is also reflected elsewhere, although it occurs slightly later at Delphi (cf. Thuc. IV. 134 for an example from 423): see A. H. Jackson in Hanson (ed.), *Hoplites*, 246.

This text has ο in Θουρίον and ε in ἀνέθεκαν, and -αν rather than -ην in δεκάταν.

[1] The conflicts in Italy at this time are discussed by J. W. Wonder, *CA*^{2} xxxi 2012, 128–51.

Timoteles of Acharnae was secretary. Resolved by the council and the people. Cecropis was the prytany; Timoteles was the secretary; Cycneas was the chairman. The draftsmen (*syngrapheis*) drafted the following:

4 The Athenians shall give firstfruits of the harvest to the two Goddesses according to the ancestral practice and the oracle from Delphi, at the rate of not less than a *hekteus* per hundred *medimnoi* of barley [= $^1/_{600}$] and not less than half a *hekteus* per hundred *medimnoi* of wheat [= $^1/_{1200}$]. If someone produces a greater harvest than this, or a smaller, he shall give firstfruits at the same ratio.

8 The demarchs shall collect firstfruits by demes and hand them over to the sacred officials from Eleusis at Eleusis. They shall build three granaries at Eleusis, according to ancestral custom, wherever seems to the sacred officials (*hieropoioi*) and the architect to be suitable, from the funds of the two Goddesses.

12 The sacred officials shall deposit here the harvest that they receive from the demarchs, and the allies are to contribute firstfruits in the same way. The cities shall choose collectors of the harvest in whatever way it seems to them that the harvest will be best collected. When it has been collected let them send it to

τὸς δὲ ἀγαγόντας παραδιδόναι τοῖς hιεροποιοῖς τοῖς Ἐλευσι-
νόθεν Ἐλευσῖνάδε. ἐ[ὰ]ν δὲ μὲ παραδέχσονται πέντε ἐμερο͂ν [ν]ννν
ἐπειδὰν ἐπαγγελε͂ι, παραδιδόντον το͂ν ἐκ τε͂ς πόλεος hό̣θ̣εν ἂν ε͂-
[ι] ὁ κα̣ρ̣π̣ός, εὐθυνόσθον hοι ḥι̣ε̣ροποιοὶ χιλίαισιν *ν* δραχμ̣ε͂σι [h]-
έ[κα]στος· καὶ παρὰ το͂ν δεμάρχον κ̣ατὰ ταὐ̣τὰ παραδέχεσθαι. [κ]έρυ-
[κα]ς δὲ hελομένε hε βολὲ πεμφσάτο ἐς τὰς πόλες ἀ[γ]γέλλον[τ]ας *ν* [*ν*]
τ̣[αδ'] hεφσεφισμένα το͂ι δέμοι, τὸ μὲν νῦν ε͂ναι hος τάχιστα, τὸ δ̣ὲ λ-
οιπὸν hόταν δοκε͂ι αὐτε͂ι. κελευέτο δὲ καὶ ho hιεροφάντες κα̣ὶ [ὁ]
δαιδο͂χος μυστερίοις ἀπάρχεσθαι τὸς hέλλενας το͂ καρπο͂ κα̣τ̣ὰ̣
τὰ πάτρια καὶ τὲν μαντε̣ίαν τὲν ἐγ Δελφο͂ν. ἀναγράφσαντες δὲ ἐ̣μ̣
πινακίοι τὸ μέτρον το͂ καρπο͂ το͂ τε παρὰ το͂ν δεμάρχον κατὰ τὸ[ν δ]-
[ε͂]μον hέκαστον καὶ το͂ παρὰ το͂ν πόλεον κατὰ τὲν πόλιν hεκάστ̣ε̣[ν]
[κ]αταθέντον ἔν τε το͂ι Ἐλευσινίοι Ἐλευσ̣ῖνι καὶ ἐν το͂ι β̣ο̣λ̣ε̣υ̣[τ]ε-
ρίοι. ἐπαγγέλλεν δὲ τὲν βολὲν καὶ τε͂σι ἄλλεσι πόλεσιν τε͂[σι hε]-
[λ]λενικε͂σιν ἁπάσεσι, hόποι ἂν δοκε͂ι αὐτε͂ι δυνατὸν ε͂ναι, λέ̣γο̣ν-
τας μὲν κατὰ hὰ Ἀθεναῖοι ἀπάρχονται καὶ οἱ χσύμμαχοι, ἐκέ[ν]ο̣[ι]-
[ς] δὲ μὲ ἐπιτάττοντας, κελεύοντας δὲ ἀπάρχεσθαι, ἐὰν βόλοντα̣ι̣,
κ̣ατὰ τὰ πάτρια καὶ τὲν μαντείαν τὲν ἐγ Δελφο͂ν. παραδέχεσθα̣ι δ-
ὲ καὶ παρὰ τούτον το͂ν πόλεον ἐάν τις ἀπάγει τὸς hιεροποιὸς [κα]-
τ[ὰ] τ̣α̣ὐτά. θύεν δὲ ἀπὸ μὲν το͂ πελανο͂ καθότι ἂν Εὐμολπίδαι ἐσχ[hε]-
[γο͂]ν̣τα̣ι, τρίττοιαν δὲ βόαρχον χρυσόκερον τοῖν θεοῖν hεκατ̣[έρ]-
[αι ἀ]πὸ το͂ν κριθο͂ν καὶ το͂ν πυρο͂ν καὶ το͂ι Τριπτολέμοι καὶ το͂ι Θ̣ε̣-
ο͂ι καὶ τε͂ι Θεᾶι καὶ το͂ι Εὐβόλοι hιερεῖον hεκάστοι τέλεον κα̣ὶ
τε͂ι Ἀθενα̣ί̣α̣ι βο͂ν χρυσόκερον· τὰς δὲ ἄλλας κριθὰς καὶ πυρὸς ἀπ-
οδομένο̣ς τὸς hιεροποιὸς μετὰ τε͂ς βολε͂ς ἀναθέματα ἀνατιθέν-
αι τοῖν Θεοῖν, ποιεσαμένος hάττ' ἂν το͂ι δέμοι το͂ι Ἀθεναίον δοκε͂-
ι, καὶ ἐπιγράφεν τοῖς ἀναθέμασιν, hότι ἀπὸ το͂ καρπο τε͂ς ἀπαρχε͂-
ς ἀνεθέθε, καὶ hελλένον τὸν ἀπαρχόμενον· τοῖς δὲ ταῦτα ποιο͂σι
πολλὰ ἀγαθὰ ε͂ναι καὶ εὐκαρπίαν καὶ πολυκαρπίαν, hο̣ίτινες ἂν
μὲ ἀδικο͂σι Ἀθεναίος μεδὲ τὲν πόλιν τὲν Ἀθεναίον μεδὲ τὸ Θεό. *ν*
Λάμπον εἶπε· τὰ μὲν ἄλλα καθάπερ αἱ χσυγγραφαὶ τε͂ς ἀπαρχε͂ς τ̣ο͂
[κ]αρπο͂ τοῖν Θεοῖν· τὰς δὲ χσυνγραφὰς καὶ τὸ φσέφισμα τόδε ἀναγ-
ραφσάτο ho γραμματεὺς ho τε͂ς βολε͂ς ἐν στέλαιν δυοῖν λιθίναι-
ν καὶ καταθέτο τὲν μὲν Ἐλευσῖνι ἐν το͂ι hιερο͂ι, τὲν δὲ hετέραν ἐ-
μ πόλει· hοι δὲ πολεταὶ ἀπομισθοσάντον τ̣ὸ στέλα· hοι δὲ κολα̣[κρ]-
έται δόντον τὸ ἀργύριον. ταῦτα μὲν περὶ τε͂ς ἀπαρχε͂ς το͂ καρπο͂ τ̣-
οῖν Θεοῖν ἀναγράφσαι ἐς τὸ στέλα, με͂να δὲ ⁝⁝⁝ ἐμβ̣ά̣λλεν hεκατονβ̣-
αιο͂να τὸν νέον ἄρχοντα. τὸν δὲ βασ[ι]λέα hορίσαι τὰ hιερὰ τὰ ἐν τ[ο͂]-
ι Πελαργικο͂ι, καὶ τὸ λοιπὸν μὲ ἐνhιδρύεσθαι βομὸς ἐν το͂ι Πελα̣-
ργικο͂ι ἄνευ τε͂ς βολε͂ς καὶ το͂ δέμο, μεδὲ τὸς λίθος τέμνεν ἐκ το͂ [Π]-

18 the reason for the four spaces is not clear: there is no trace of erasure and the Athenian copy does not seem to have had these four extra letter spaces (cf. ll. 22, 46, 57 for *vacats* at the end of lines so that a new word can start on a new line). 53, 58 punctuation probably covers erasures.

Athens. Those who bring it shall hand it over to the sacred officials from Eleusis at Eleusis. If they do not accept it within five days from when it has been announced, although the men from the city from which the harvest comes are handing it over, let them be fined 1,000 drachmas each at their audit (*euthynai*). And they shall receive it from the demarchs in the same way.

21 Let the council choose heralds and send them to the cities announcing what has been voted by the people, as soon as possible on the current occasion and in future whenever the council decides. Let the hierophant and the dadouch at the Mysteries order the Greeks to give firstfruits of the harvest according to the ancestral practice and the oracle from Delphi.

26 When they have written up on a board the amount of harvest from the demarchs by deme and from the cities by city, let them deposit the record in the Eleusinion at Eleusis and in the council chamber.

30 The council shall have it announced to all the other Greek cities, wherever it seems possible, explaining the conditions on which the Athenians and the allies give firstfruits, and not instructing them but encouraging them, if they wish, to give firstfruits according to ancestral practice and the oracle from Delphi. The sacred officials shall accept harvest from these cities in the same way if any city brings it.

36 They shall sacrifice from the cake just as the Eumolpids advise, and a triple sacrifice, a bull with gilt horns to each of the two Goddesses from the barley and the wheat, and to Triptolemus and to the god and to the goddess and to Euboulus, a full-grown victim to each, and an ox with gilt horns to Athena.

40 The sacred officials in conjunction with the council shall sell the rest of the barley and wheat and dedicate dedications to the two Goddesses, doing whatever the people of the Athenians resolves, and shall write on the dedications that these dedications were made from the firstfruits of the grain, and that the Greeks were offering firstfruits. To those who do this may much good come, and good and plentiful harvests, as long as they do no wrong to Athenians or to the city of the Athenians, or to the two Goddesses.

47 Lampon proposed: in other respects in accordance with the drafts of the firstfruits of the two Goddesses; but let the secretary of the council write up the draft and this decree on two stone *stelai*, and let him place one at Eleusis in the sanctuary and the other on the acropolis. Let the sellers (*poletai*) put the two *stelai* out to tender; let the *kolakretai* give the money.

52 They shall write up these things about the firstfruits of the harvest for the two Goddesses on the two *stelai*, but the new archon shall insert a month of Hecatombaeon. The *basileus* shall define the boundaries of the sanctuaries in the Pelargikon, and for the future no altar shall be set up in the Pelargikon without permission of the council and people, nor shall anyone cut stones from the

ελαργικõ, μεδὲ γε̃ν ἐχσάγεν μεδὲ λίθος. ἐὰν δέ τις παραβαίνει ν
τ ⁝ ⁝ ⁝ οὔτον τι, ἀποτινέτο πεντακοσίας δραχμάς, ἐσα̣γγελλέτο δὲ h-
ο̣ βασιλεὺς ἐς τὲν βολέν. περὶ δὲ το ἐλαίο τε̃ς ἀπαρχε̃ς χσυγγράφ-
σας Λάμπον ἐπιδειχσάτο τε̃ι βολε̃ι ἐπὶ τε̃ς ἐνάτες πρυτανείας·
hε δὲ βολὲ ἐς τὸν δε̃μον ἐχσενενκέτο ἐπάναγκες.

The question of the involvement of the assembly in sacred affairs is nowhere so abundantly illustrated as in the evidence for Athenian actions in relation to the sanctuary of Demeter and Kore (Persephone) at Eleusis (cf. above, **106**). This decree making provision for the offering of firstfruits by the Athenian demes, Athens' allies and other Greek cities provides a particularly striking instance of the intertwining of the religious and the political. But its precise significance depends upon its date, which has been much debated. The debate has partly been over the weight to accord purely epigraphic factors (scholars have argued that the omission of the aspirate in ll. 3, 15, 18, 20, 24, 31, 32, 47 points to a date in the 420s or later), partly because the relationship between this and other documents has been obscured by the probable misdating of those documents. These arguments have been further complicated by the need to place this in a year in which an extra month was intercalated.

Epigraphic arguments make it probable that this inscription dates after 440 and before 421 (for further discussion see Cavanaugh, 19–27, 73–95). Absence of aspiration is attested before 433/2 (see **149**. *B*), while archons' names are first found in the new prescripts of **149**. *A* and *B*, and normally given in Athenian decrees from *c.*421 onwards (but not invariably, **186** being a certain exception: see Introduction, pp. xxi–xxii). The strongest argument for the date of this decree comes from the administrative arrangements that it presupposes. Mention is made of a number of officials, both civic and sacred, but the main agents in executing the proposal are to be the 'sacred officials (*hieropoioi*) from Eleusis at Eleusis'. They are the persons to whom the grain is handed over and who have responsibility for deciding on location of granaries, along with the architect (for this term see on **181**), for accepting the grain, storing it, making sacrifices, selling it and making dedications, and it is they who are punished if they fail to accept the grain within five days of its arrival. This is precisely the same situation that prevails in **106**. There is no mention here of any *epistatai*, although in the accounts for the previous four years written up at Eleusis in 419/8 (*IG* i³ 391) the *hieropoioi* are there recorded as handing over annually the money from the firstfruits to the *epistatai*. What has changed the arrangements seems to be the decision recorded in *IG* i³ 32 to create a board of five men to be *epistatai* at Eleusis and look after the financial affairs of the Eleusinian sanctuary on the model of the *epistatai* created to look after the works on the acropolis and the Parthenon and its cult statue. The date of this decree has been disputed also, since the use of the three-barred *sigma* once encouraged the view that it dated before 445. But the mention of the *epistatai* on the acropolis as a thing of the past (the imperfect tense is used of their

Pelargikon nor take away earth or stone. And if anyone transgresses any of these rules, let him pay 500 drachmas, and let the *basileus* announce it to the council. On the matter of the firstfruits of oil, let Lampon make a draft and show it to the council in the ninth prytany; let the council obligatorily bring it before the people.

---

activities) implies a date not earlier than the late 430s (the last board of *epistatai* for the acropolis works dates to 433/2; cf. the mention of working with the acropolis *epistatai* in **144** and our commentary there). It is, however, unlikely to be later than the end of the 430s, since it imagines building activity at Eleusis, not easily thinkable once Attica was subject to annual invasions. The firstfruits decree should therefore date before *IG* i³ 32 and so before 430. Exactly how much before is less clear; a date in the 440s cannot be excluded, but a date in the 430s seems overall rather more likely, perhaps, as Clinton suggested (K. Clinton, in *Φίλια ἔπη* . . . *Γ. Ε. Μυλωνᾶν*, ii. 254–62) as part of the improvement of facilities at Eleusis seen in the construction of the new Telesterion. Tracy (*Athenian Lettering of the Fifth Century* BC, 115–16) has ascribed this decree to the hand of a letter-cutter whose hand can be detected in inscriptions from *c.*440 to after 410, including our **179**.

The importance of establishing the date of this decree lies in its relevance to Athenian imperialism as well as to Athenian religious history (see further Smarczyk). That this proposal comes from a board of 'draftsmen' (*syngrapheis*) indicates that the assembly or council have been convinced that there is a complicated matter that needs careful thought. We otherwise first meet 'draftsmen' proposing the long and complex decree concerning Miletus (*IG* i³ 21, to be dated to 426/5; cf. above on **123**) and then find them brought in to devise what the Athenians should do to their constitution in 411 (Thuc. VIII. 67); for a different use of the word *syngraphai* see **167**. The question here might be as straightforward as 'What are we to do about offering firstfruits to Eleusis?', but may have involved from the outset a question about provision of firstfruits by non-Athenians also. The oracle at Delphi has been consulted (cf. R&O 58; for Athenian consultations of Delphi generally see Bowden, with a concordance of Athenian consultations in Appendix 2), and the terms in which the response is described (32–4) suggest that Delphi had been asked whether it was better 'to instruct or to call on' the other Greeks to give firstfruits (the near-synonyms used in the question being a way of maximising the chance that the Athenians got an acceptable answer). It is notable that despite stemming from a specially convened group of draftsmen, the order of clauses in this decree is not always logical.

Three groups of people are asked in this decree to bring firstfruits of their harvest to Eleusis: Athenians, whose firstfruits are to be collected for each deme by its demarch; Athens' allies, who are allowed to choose collectors in whichever way they wish; and all other Greeks. Whether any of these groups had previously contributed 'according to ancestral custom' is not clear, but certainly that new storage chambers will be needed is anticipated (l. 10; *siroi* usually means underground storage chambers, and their use at Eleusis has been linked to the founding myth of Persephone spending half the year in the underworld). The decree assumes that Athenians and allies will simply respond to the summons, but acknowledges that other Greeks may or may not want to. The way in which the insistence on the sacred officials accepting the grain within five days, or being subject to a substantial fine, is attached to the delivery of grain by the allies, and only in an afterthought also applied to grain brought by demarchs, implies concern that allies will have an excuse for claiming to have come, waited, but never been received (compare perhaps [Xen.] *Ath. Pol.* iii. 1). The oracular response received prior to this decree enables the Athenians to present the practice of offering firstfruits as traditional and ordained by Apollo for everyone, and draws gentle attention to Athens' priority in the development of agriculture and the special favour Demeter had bestowed upon her.

The expectation of Athenian allies that they bring firstfruits to Eleusis is parallel to the expectation that allies contribute materially to Athenian festivals, first recorded in the Erythrae decree from the 450s (**121**. 3: grain for the Panathenaea) but spelled out most clearly in the Brea decree (**142**: ox and panoply for the Panathenaea, phallus for the Dionysia) and Cleinias' decree (**154**: ox and panoply) from the 430s and 420s. There was, by contrast, no expectation that other Greeks would contribute to those festivals, but Plut. *Per.* 17 records a supposedly Periclean initiative to assemble all Greeks to discuss rebuilding temples, and if such a 'congress decree' was ever passed it would provide some parallels to this initiative.

To what extent the allies responded positively to being asked for firstfruits, and whether any other Greeks ever sent anything, is unclear (although Isoc. IV. *Paneg.* 31 implies that they did). The accounts from 422 to 418 (*IG* i^3 391) reveal rather small sums of money from the sale of grain—6 dr. in 420, 31 dr. in 419—tiny amounts even if the sacrificial victims have already been paid for from the proceeds. By the time we meet quantities of Eleusinian firstfruits again, in 329/8 (*IG* ii^2 1672), the precise arrangements have been changed and the quantities, now delivered by Athenian tribes rather than by demes individually, are much larger (see further K. Clinton, in Coulson *et al.* (edd.), *The Archaeology of Athens and Attica under the Democracy*, 161–72). Scholars have indeed made much of these fourth-century totals in calculating the yield of grain of Attica (the most sophisticated of these remains P. D. A. Garnsey, in *Crux . . . G. E. M. de Ste. Croix*, 62–75 = his *Cities, Peasants and Food in Classical Antiquity*, 183–95, with Addendum by W. Scheidel, 195–200), although methodologically this is an extremely suspect thing to do (see Johnstone, *A History of Trust in Ancient Greece*).

Was this decree motivated by a desire to oblige other Greeks and to make a monetary profit from the sale, or was there also a desire to increase the grain supply to Athens? Even those who are most optimistic about the grain production of Attica acknowledge that Athens had a massive need for imported grain by the end of the fifth century (see Garnsey, *op. cit.*) and the Athenian law of 374/3 collecting tax in grain from Lemnos, Imbros and Scyros seems at least in part motivated by grain-supply considerations. The acquisition of potentially significant quantities of grain from elsewhere which could be resold in Attica is unlikely to have been irrelevant to the attractions of this proposal.

The draftsmen's decree ends with the order to the sacred officials to sacrifice and make dedications. The sacrifice includes part of the *pelanos*, a form of cake made from the wheat and barley, the details of this to be determined by the exegesis of the Eumolpidae—and this seems to be exegesis by the whole *genos* (cf. Lys. VI. *Andocides* 10, Clinton, *The Sacred Officials of the Eleusinian Mysteries*, 89–91); the other *genos* involved at Eleusis, the Kerykes, did not give exegesis: Andoc. I. *Myst.* 110–6). The accounts of 328 (*IG* ii² 1672. 409–14) indicate that a very large *pelanos* was made, using almost 16 *medimnoi* of barley and 10 of wheat, the part not sacrificed being presumably consumed by worshippers, providing a significant amount of food (elsewhere priests' perquisites sometimes include a share of the *pelanos*: cf. **158**. *A*. 25–6). The sacrifice continues with a 'triple sacrifice starting with an ox'. We first meet such a sacrifice in the law of *c.*500 giving commands to the sacred officials at Eleusis about the Eleusinia (*IG* i³ 5). That sacrifice reveals the variety of deities to whom sacrifice might be made at Eleusis, besides Demeter and Kore. 'The god and the goddess' listed here appear in a number of Eleusinian dedications (e.g. *IG* ii² 4683), and should probably be identified as Hades and Persephone in their underworld guises: the names 'Hades' and 'Persephone' themselves are never used at Eleusis, only their upper-world names, Pluto and Kore (see Clinton, *Myth and Cult*, Appendix 4); sacrifice has just been made to 'the two Goddesses', but Demeter and Kore are treated as different from Hades and Persephone. It is notable that the instructions concerning the dedications, on which it appears that all the surplus money is to be spent (cf. *IG* ii² 1672. 427), stress both that the dedication should indicate that it was from the offering of firstfruits and that it was Greeks, not Athenians, who offered them. By contrast, the final invocation of a blessing on those doing this stresses the desire for good and plentiful harvests for those who do not harm the Athenians or the two Goddesses.

The rider which follows is very informative about assembly procedure and about religion and politics at Athens. It is moved by a man about whom we are rather well informed (see J. Dillery, in Johnston & Struck (edd.), *Mantikê*, 195–7; H. Bowden, in *Herodotus and his World . . . G. Forrest*, 269–70). Lampon had been involved as seer (*mantis*) in the settlement at Thurii (above, **140**) and gained a reputation for being a Thurii bore (schol. Ar. *Nub.* 332, Photius (θ 203 Theodoridis) and *Suda* (θ 418 Adler) Θουριομάντεις, Diod. Sic. XII. 10. iii–iv). Although ridiculed by comic poets as late as 414 (Ar. *Av.* 332, 987–8, Cratinus fr. 66 KA, Eupolis fr. 297 KA), he was taken seriously enough to be a signatory to the Peace of Nicias (Thuc. V. 19. ii, 24. i). This rider gives us our most vivid picture of the man. For here Lampon trades on his own religious expertise to attach to this decree some entirely alien concerns. The original decree had made provision for 'archive copies' in the council chamber and at Eleusis (cf. Sickinger, *Public Records and Archives in Classical Athens*, 73–83); Lampon insists on full publication at Eleusis and on the acropolis (we might have expected the city Eleusinion). He then orders an intercalary month and makes provision for tidying up the Pelargikon, the area around the western end of the acropolis on which the

Delphic oracle had forbidden building and insisted that the land be left idle (Thuc. II. 17. i), before proposing that he himself should draft provision for firstfruits of olive oil for consideration by a future assembly.

No reason for the provision of an intercalary Hecatombaeon is given in the inscribed text (on intercalary months see Introduction, pp. xxiv–xxv). The instruction to Lampon to bring proposals to the council in the ninth prytany suggests that this decree was passed in the eighth prytany, and so late in the year. The council has to choose and send out heralds and the cities have to decide on a collection mechanism and put it into operation. This would have taken time. Lampon may have been trying to give enough time for the firstfruits to come in before the sacrifices ordered in the decree, which seem to have happened in early Hecatombaeon (Clinton, in *I. Eleusis,* ii, p. 50); if so the proposal would be closely connected with the content of the decree. But since intercalary months followed the 'real' month, it is not clear that an intercalary Hecatombaeon would help with that, though it would give an extra month before the Mysteries in Boedromion.

The proposal about the Pelargikon seems entirely unconnected with Eleusis. Lampon attempts to prevent the exploitation of the Pelargikon for building materials and other resources (cf. Poll. VIII. 101, Lucian *Pisc.* 47), and also to prevent the proliferation of altars there. Foucart ingeniously suggested that the oracle about the Pelargikon referred to by Thucydides was linked to the oracle about the firstfruits exploited in the body of this inscription, and this would provide some justification for Lampon's proposal here. But if we are right about the date of this

142

Athenian colony at Brea, 430s (?)

Two fragments of a marble *stele* from the Erechtheum, now in the Epigraphical Museum, and a small fragment from the agora, now in the Agora Museum. The stone was cut in half in the Byzantine period to be reused for column bases: on the large upper fragment (*b*) the original text (*c.*30–5 lines) was deleted but an amendment to the original decree survives on the right-hand side (with its right-hand margin preserved); the large lower fragment (*a*) contains the end of the original decree; the agora fragment (*c*), with left-hand margin preserved, belongs between *a* and *b* but does not join either. Phot. (squeezes of *c* and the top left of *a* combined in a manner which was subsequently withdrawn) *Hesp.* xiv 1945, 87.

Attic, with developed lettering apart from *rho* (rounded, but with a tail). *Stoichedon*, *A* 35 (with the points in l. 30 occupying a single *stoichos*), *B* 17.

decree, then it precedes the occupation of the Pelargikon during the war by those coming in from the countryside, upon which Thucydides remarks. This proposal could hardly not have alluded to such occupation had it occurred before the decree was passed.

The assembly evidently heard Lampon patiently: the speech in which he laid out his motivation for these proposals cannot have been short. We must suspect that it did so because his status as a seer and expounder of matters religious gave him authority. Whereas the main body of this decree reveals a committee of draftsmen intervening to enforce religious behaviour and determine the activities of the sacred officials at Eleusis, this rider has a man whose standing depends on his claim to religious expertise attempt to add a range of religious concerns. On the one hand, then, no distinction is made between religious and civil: satisfactory relations with the gods, and responding to communications from them, is as much a political matter as are satisfactory relations with other cities and responding to communications from them. On the other hand, matters to do with the gods are different, and they are an area in which claims to expertise cannot be ignored (cf. the exegesis of the Eumolpidae discussed above). Not that the extent of Lampon's influence should be exaggerated: the assembly concedes an intercalary month and stricter regulation of a problematic area of sacred land, but on the matter of firstfruits of olive oil he gets only a guarantee that the next council meeting will take his draft forward. No offering of firstfruits of oil ever appears in our sources: Athenian self-interest seems here to have quashed Lampon's religious initiative.

(*a* and *b*) *SIG*^{3} 67; *IG* i^{2} 45; M&L 49. (*c*) *Hesp.* xiv 1945, 86–7 no. 5 (cf. *SEG* x 34); xxi 1952, 380 (cf. *SEG* xii 15). (all) *IG* i^{3} 46*; *Agora* xvi 7. Trans. (*a* and *b*) Fornara 100; Osborne, *The Athenian Empire*^{4}, 232 (a different translation in earlier editions); Dillon & Garland^{3} 12. 31. See also A. Wilhelm, *Sb. Wien* CCXVII. v 1939, 11–17 = his *Akademieschriften*, i. 531–7; B. D. Meritt, *Hesp.* x 1941, 317–9; *ATL* iii (1950), 284–9; A. G. Woodhead, *CQ*^{2} ii 1952, 57–62; Graham, *Colony and Mother City in Ancient Greece*; D. Asheri, *AJP* xc 1969, 337–40; H. B. Mattingly, *Epigraphica* xxxvi 1974, 53–6 = his *AER* 381–5; Th. Pazaras, *AEMT* XA 1996, 313–32, after excavation reports in previous volumes, cf. *AR* xliv 1997/8, 79; S. Psoma, *REG* cxxii 2009, 263–80.

A

\- -

(*c*) νε[———33———]
ελι[———32———]
αρχ[———32———]
νλ̣[———33———]

\- -

(*a*) [———18———]ε π̣ρ̣ὸς hὲν ἂν φα[ίνει ἒ]
[γράφεται, ἐσ]αγέτο. ἐὰν δὲ ἐσάγει ἐνεχ[—5—]
[—7—] ho φένας ἒ ho γραφσάμενος. πο[—5—]
[—6—]ν αὐτοῖς παρασχόντον hοι ἀπ[οικιστ]-
[αὶ καλλ]ιερε̂σαι hυπὲρ τε̂ς ἀποικίας. [hοπόσα]
[ἂν αὐτο]ῖς δοκε̂ι. γεονόμος δὲ hελέσθ[αι δέκα]
[ἄνδρας,] ἕνα ἐχ φυλε̂ς· hοῦτοι δὲ νεμάντ[ον τὲν]
[γε̂ν. Δεμ]οκλείδεν δὲ καταστε̂σαι τὲν ἀ[ποικί]-
[αν αὐτο]κράτορα, καθότι ἂν δύνεται ἄ[ριστα. τ]-
[ὰ δὲ τεμ]ένε τὰ ἐχσειρεμένα ἐᾶν καθά[περ ἐστ]-
[ί, καὶ ἄλ]λα μὲ τεμενίζεν. βοῦν δὲ καὶ π̣[ανhοπλ]-
[ίαν ἀπά]γεν ἐς Παναθέναια τὰ μεγάλ[α καὶ ἐς Δ]-
[ιονύσι]α φαλλόν. ἐὰν δέ τις ἐπιστρα[τεύει ἐπ]-
[ὶ τὲν γε̂]ν τὲν τо̂ν ἀποίκον, βοεθε̂ν τὰ[ς πόλες h]-
[ος ὀχσύ]τατα κατὰ τὰς χσυγγραφὰς hα̣[ὶ ἐπὶ . .]
[—6—]το γραμματεύοντος ἐγένον[το περὶ τ]-
ο̂ν πόλε]ον τо̂ν ἐπὶ Θράικες. γράφσαι δ[ὲ ταῦτα]
[ἐν στέλ]ει καὶ καταθε̂ναι ἐμ πόλει· πα[ρασχόν]-
[τον δὲ τ]ὲν στέλεν hοι ἄποικοι σφо̂ν α[ὐτо̂ν τέ]-
[λεσιν. ἐ]ὰν δέ τις ἐπιφσεφίζει παρὰ τὲ[ν στέλ]-
[εν ἒ ῥρέ]τορ ἀγορεύει ἒ προσκαλε̂σθα[ι ἐγχερ]-
[ε̂ι ἀφαι]ρε̂σθαι ἒ λύεν τι τо̂ν hεφσεφι[σμένον,]
[ἄτιμον] ε̂̓ναι αὐτὸν καὶ παῖδας τὸς ἐχς [ἐκένο,]
[καὶ τὰ χ]ρέματα δεμόσια ε̂̓ναι καὶ τε̂ς [θεо̂ τὸ ἐ]-
[πιδέκα]τον, ἐὰμ μέ τι αὐτοὶ hοι ἄποικ[οι . . . .]
[. . . . δέ]ονται ⁝ hόσοι δ' ἂν γράφσοντα[ι ἐποικ]-
[έσεν τо̂]ν στρατιοτо̂ν, ἐπειδὰν hέκοσ[ι Ἀθένα]-
[ζε, τριά]κοντα ἑμερо̂ν ἐμ Βρέαι ε̂̓ναι ἐπ̣[οικέσ]-
[οντας. ἐ]χσάγεν δὲ τὲν ἀποικίαν τριάκ̣[οντα ἑ]-
[μερо̂ν. Α]ἰσχίνεν δὲ ἀκολούθοντα ἀπο[διδόνα]-
[ι τὰ χρέ]ματα. *vacat*

vacat

4 ναε Meritt (*Hesp.* 1945), νλ̣ [D. M. Lewis (*IG*), νδ̣ε̣ A. G. Woodhead (*Agora*). 5 hε δὲ ἀρχ]ὲ Wilhelm. 6–7 ἐνεχ[υραζέ|το αὐτόν] J. Kirchner (*SIG*), ἐνέχ[υρα ἄχ|σια θέτο] Wilhelm. 7–8 π<ρ>ό[βατα ἐ|ς θυσία]ν Wilhelm, πό[ρον δ' ἐ|ς θυσία]ν Meritt. 19–20 Νι|κοστρά]το H. B. Mattingly, *Historia* xii 1963, 265 = *AER* 96, when arguing for 426/5 (cf. *SEG* xxi 29). 29–30 περὶ σφо̂ν δέ]ονται A. Boeckh, ?hεαυ|τοῖς δέ]ονται M&L.

A

5 – – – – – to which he makes a *phasis* ['demonstration'] or prosecutes, he shall introduce; if he introduces, the demonstrator or prosecutor (shall provide security?).

7 The *apoikistai* ['colonisers'] shall make provision for them to seek good omens for the colony, as much as they see fit.

10 Ten men shall be elected as *geonomoi* ['land-distributors'], one from each tribe: these shall distribute the land.

12 Democlides shall establish the colony, with full power, as best he can.

13 The *temene* ['precincts'] which have been set aside they shall leave as they are, and they shall not create others.

15 They shall bring a cow and a panoply to the Great Panathenaea, and a phallus to the Dionysia.

17 If any one campaigns against the land of the colonists, the cities shall come in support as quickly as possible, in accordance with the schedule drawn up for the Thraceward cities when —— was secretary.

21 This shall be written on a *stele* and placed on the acropolis; the *stele* shall be provided by the colonists at their own expense.

24 If any one puts a motion to the vote contrary to the *stele* or any speaker proposes or tries to issue a summons detracting from or annulling any of what has been decreed, he shall be *atimos* ['without rights'], himself and the sons born from him, and his property shall be confiscated and the tithe given to the Goddess, unless the colonists themselves make a request (for themselves?).

30 Those of the soldiers who are enlisted to go in addition to the colony shall go in addition as colonists to Brea within thirty days after they have arrived in Athens. The colony shall be led out within thirty days. Aeschines shall accompany them and disburse the funds.

B

(*b*) [Φ]αντοκλε̃ς εἶπε· περὶ
[μ]ὲν τε̃ς ἐς Βρέαν ἀποι-
[κ]ίας καθάπερ Δεμοκλ-
[ε]ίδες εἶπε· Φαντοκλέ-
[α] δὲ προσαγαγε̃ν τὲν Ἐ-
[ρ]εχθεΐδα πρυτανεία-
[ν] πρὸς τὲν βολὲν ἐν τε̃-
[ι] πρότει hέδραι· ἐς δὲ
[Β]ρέαν ἐχ θετο̂ν καὶ ζε-
[υ]γιτο̂ν ἰέναι τὸς ἀπο-
[ί]κος. *vacat*
vacat

36–41 and part of 42 now lost.

We read in the literary sources of a number of settlements founded by Athens from the middle of the fifth century onwards (see in particular Diod. Sic. XI. 88. iii; Plut. *Per.* 11. v, cf. 19. i; Hestiaea in 446/5, Thuc. I. 114. iii and later texts including Plut. *Per.* 23. iv; Amphipolis in 437/6, Thuc. IV. 102. iii, Diod. Sic. XII. 32. iii, schol. Aeschin. II. *Embassy* 31 (67 Dilts)). The mainland to the north of the Aegean was attractive to Athens for its mines and for timber suitable for shipbuilding, and the colony founded at Amphipolis was the culmination of a series of Athenian attempts beginning when Athens captured Eïon, on the coast nearby, *c.*476 (Thuc. I. 98. i, 100. 2, IV. 102, cf. schol. Aeschin. II. *Embassy* 31 (67a Dilts)). Further west Athens had an uneasy relationship with Perdiccas II of Macedon (Thuc. I. 56–7), and may have demanded increased tribute from Potidaea in the early 430s (*IG* i^3 277. vi. 5–6, 279. ii. 70, with Meiggs, *The Athenian Empire*, 528–9).

Brea except in this inscription is mentioned only by Cratinus fr. 426 KA, Theopomp. *FGrH* 115 F 145 and late writers (for Thucydides see below), and where Brea was and when the colony was founded have been much debated. Most commonly Brea has been linked with Athens' colony in Thrace founded jointly with the Bisaltae, to the west of the Strymon (Plut. *Per.* 11. v), has been dated to the 440s, and (to explain the fact that we hear no more of it) it has sometimes been thought that it was abandoned when Amphipolis was finally settled in 437/6. However, an alternative location has been sought by Woodhead and Asheri, on the coast north-west of Potidaea: this will allow us to make sense of Thuc. I. 61. iv by emending Βέροιαν, which produces a nonsensical route for the Athenians, to Βρέαν (Woodhead, arguing for 439/8 from the soldiers of ll. 30–3), and will place Brea in an area where Theopompus is more likely to have mentioned it in book XXIII of his *Philippic History* (Asheri). Within that region, the excavator of Verghia (near Nea Syllata) suggests that that is the site and that its modern name is derived

B

36 Phantocles proposed: Concerning the colony to Brea, in accordance with the proposal of Democlides; but the prytany of Erechtheis shall bring Phantocles before the council at its next meeting; and the colonists to go to Brea shall be from the *thetes* and *zeugitai*.

---

from Brea.[1] This has been accepted by E. N. Borza in map 50 of the *Barrington Atlas*, and recently championed by Psoma (placing the foundation in the context of Athens' deteriorating relations with Potidaea and its neighbours and with Perdiccas of Macedon, and suggesting 434–432).[2] This seems to us a more likely location, and on that basis we prefer a date not long before 432 (though perhaps not as late as 434). Like Amphipolis, Brea as a colony does not appear in the tribute lists. Mattingly, while not committing himself on the location, has argued for the 430s on prosopographical grounds.

A substantial amount has been lost from the beginning of the original decree. Fr. *a* begins with judicial matters, involving *phasis* (used in cases involving trade: D. M. MacDowell and M. H. Hansen, *Symposion* 1990 (*AGR* viii 1991), 187–98 and 199–201; cf. R&O 14. 22 and commentary) and *graphe* (an ordinary public prosecution); 'introduce' is used of the official who brought a case before a court.

For the *apoikistai* ('colonisers', a word not found elsewhere: perhaps deputies of the *oikistes*) M&L following M. N. Tod compare the ten *Thouriomanteis* ('Thurian seers') sent to Thurii when that was colonised (schol. Ar. *Nub.* 332); *geonomai* (*sic*: 'land-distributors') are noted in Phrynichus, *Praep. Soph.* 57 de Borries. Democlides is the *oikistes*, the formal leader of the colonists, and appears from ll. 38–9 to have been the proposer of the original decree; the same name is perhaps to be restored in **139**. 28 among the men swearing to Athens' treaty with Samos in 439/8, but it is not a rare name so the man will not necessarily be the same. The Athenians had a tendency to

[1] Earlier S. Pelekides, *Ἐπετηρίς Φιλοσοφικῆς Σχολῆς*, vi 1950, 481 sqq., esp. 488–90 (which we have been unable to see), had suggested that Verghia was another Beroea.

[2] In *ZPE* cxix 2016, 55–7, she suggests more precisely that the decision was made in 433, and that the soldiers of 30–1 were men who had been sent to support Corcyra (cf. **148**).

make men *autokratores*, 'with full powers', in connection with particular appointments, without specifying in what ways or to what extent their powers were made greater than they would have been otherwise; but the body conferring this status did not thereby renounce its right to disown what the men had done and punish them if it was later dissatisfied.

The *temene* ('precincts') which had been set aside, either for the construction of sanctuaries or to be rented out to yield money to pay for religious rites, may have been Greek precincts created in Brea in its former state, before the foundation of the colony (I. Malkin, *Chiron* xiv 1984, 43–8), or sites already chosen in connection with this foundation (M&L). For offerings at Athenian festivals cf. on **121**, **141**; that a cow and not a bull was sent to the Panathenaea is indicated by **154**. 41–3.

The schedule for the Thraceward cities was presumably some special arrangement for security in the region: the word *syngraphai* sometimes reflects drafting by an ad hoc board of *syngrapheis*, and the word can also be used of a detailed prescription (cf. on **141**). For the use of a secretary for dating cf. **149** and Introduction, pp. xxi–xxii.

Cities and individuals often in the fifth century pay for the inscription of decrees concerning them (cf. **120**. 22–7), but it is more surprising to find a colony which does not yet exist paying for its foundation document, and this like the already-existing precincts may indicate that there is already an Athenian presence in Brea. In ll. 24–30 there is an entrenchment clause, intended to protect the measure against modification or annulment: on these see D. M. Lewis, in *Φόρος . . . B. D. Meritt*, 81–9 = his *Selected Papers in Greek and Near Eastern History*, 136–49; Rhodes with Lewis, 16–17, 521–6, 552; they might prove ineffective when put to the test (cf. Thuc. II. 24. i with VIII. 15. i; VIII. 67. ii). *Rhetor* is a standard word for a speaker (and particularly a politician who was a regular speaker) in the assembly; *proskaleisthai* seems here to be used in its judicial sense ('issue a summons'), and to envisage an attempt to undermine a decree by means of a lawsuit. The Goddess, without further specification, is in Athens Athena, for whose treasury see on **144**. The paragraph ends by allowing an exception to the entrenchment clause, that the colonists may themselves ask for a modification of the decree.

The decree refers to this settlement as an *apoikia* ('colony'). A distinction can be made between colonies, whose members became citizens of a new, more or less independent, *polis*, and cleruchies (*klerouchiai*), bodies of allotment-holders, who received land outside Athens but did not to the same extent constitute a self-standing community; but Athens could still regard even men sent to a colony as Athenian citizens if circumstances made it appropriate (see the discussion by P. A. Brunt, in *Ancient Society and Institutions . . . V. Ehrenberg*, 71–92 = his *Studies in Greek History and Thought*, 112–34 + 134–6). The soldiers (not necessarily recently returned from a major campaign, as often supposed) enlisted to join the colony are described as *epoikoi*, men who were to go as reinforcements after the original expedition. The status of Aeschines and the funds available to him were presumably made clear in the original part of the decree.

On the right-hand side (fr. *b*) is an amendment proposed by Phantocles, presumably the Phantocles who appears as secretary in *IG* i³ 59. 1, since no other bearer of the name is known in Athens. Since what he is amending is a proposal attributed to Democlides, not a proposal attributed to the council (e.g. **157**. 12–13; his own formulation is not that which was to become standard in such cases), Democlides' proposal must have been non-probouleumatic, i.e. not incorporated in the *probouleuma* which the council sent to the assembly (cf. Rhodes, *Boule*, 52–81, Rhodes with Lewis, 18–23, and Introduction, pp. xx–xxi, xxii): in this case the most likely explanation is that Democlides, the man most enthusiastic for the colony, was not currently a member of the council but persuaded the council to refer him and his detailed proposal to the assembly. Phantocles calls on the assembly to refer him to the next meeting of the council (the order of prytanies was determined not in advance for the whole year but one prytany at a time, so this decree and its amendment were enacted almost certainly during the prytany of Erechtheis, though in theory it might have been enacted at the end of a prytany when it was known that Erechtheis would be next)—presumably in connection with the colony, but we can only guess. And he ends by specifying that the colonists are to be from the *thetes* and the *zeugitai*, the fourth and third of the Solonian property classes (cf. *Ath. Pol.* 7. iii–iv): in the fourth century the classes still existed in theory but were not taken seriously (*Ath. Pol.* 8. i, 47. i: see Rhodes, *Comm. Ath. Pol.*, *ad locc.*), but evidently at this time they were still taken seriously and it was known which men belonged to which class (the two higher classes are mentioned in 428: Thuc. III. 16. i). It is not obvious what the original proposal had stated in this respect: it may not have specified the classes of the colonists, or else it may have excluded the *thetes*; but, despite de Ste. Croix, *Athenian Democratic Origins and Other Essays*, 11, and others, it cannot have excluded the *zeugitai*, since the soldiers who were to go as *epoikoi* are likely to have belonged to that class).

143

Religious decree of Miletus, 434/3

A marble *stele*, damaged at the edges and on the face, found at Miletus in the heroum by the West Agora, now in the museum there. Phot. *Klio* lii 1970, 165.

Ionic writing; (3 sqq.) *stoichedon* 23.

P. Herrmann, *Klio* lii 1970, 163–73; *Milet* vi. iii 1218*. See also P. J. Rhodes, *ZPE* clviii 206, 116.

[— 10 —] / [— 12 —]
[— 9 — Ε]ὐδήμ̣ο· Λεω̣ντ̣[ὶς ἐ]-
[πρυτά]ν̣ε̣υεν· Τήλαγ[ρ]ος ἐγρα̣[μ]-
[μάτευ]εν· Τήμεν[ος] ἐ̣[πεστ]άτε. [.]-
[— 5 —]ς εἶπεν·[— 8 —]ΘΙΕ[.]
[ἐν τῶι] ἱ̣ερῶι τ[ô] Π̣ο̣[σε]ι̣[δέω]νος [τ]-
[ô Ἑλικ]ωνίο μή̣[τε — 10 —]
[— 5 —]κα μήτ̣[ε — 13 —]
[— 5 —]ν̣ μηδε[— 13 —]
[— 5 —]εος θιλ̣[— 12 —]
[— 6 —]νηι γ[— 13 —]
[— 6 —]ΝΕΛΙ[— 13 —]
[. . . . ἡ]μίεκτο̣ν [— 11 —]
[— 5 —]α̣ς τῶι τ̣[— 12 —]
[. . . .]ΔΟΛΕ[— 14 —]
[. . . .]ΗΓ̣ΑΣΠΕ[— 13 —]
[. . . τ]ούτων [— 13 —]
[. . . .]ς τὸν ο[— 14 —]
[. . . .]ιος δε[— 14 —]
[— 5 —]Ρ[.] ΜΕΝ[— 13 —]
[— 6 —]νοι π[— 13 —]
[— 6 —]δὲ πρὸς τὸν ἰέρε[ω τô]
[Ποσει]δ̣έωνος τόν [τ]ε̣ ἰέρ[εω τô]
[— 6 —]εν̣ . . ο . . . [τὸς] δὲ [. . . .]
[— 6 —]ΕΚ[— 8 —]ΟΝΤ[. . . .]
[. ἀποδô]ναι τοῖς νεωποί[ησι]-

5 Perhaps ἐσ]θίεν. 6 Restored on the assumption that there were two *iotas* in the fifth space. 10 Perhaps θία[σον. 12 The traces would not permit Ἑλι[κώνιος. 15 Perhaps δε]δομε[ν-. 16 π: ιι *Milet* vi. iii, apparently a slip. 25 Perhaps a sum of money, e.g. -κ]οντ[α μνᾶς].

– – – (the *stephanephoros* being?) Eudemus; Leontis was the prytany; Telagrus was the secretary; Temenus was the chairman. —— proposed:

– – – in the sanctuary of Poseidon Heliconius neither – – – neither – – –

22 – – – to the priest of Poseidon and the priest of – – –

26 – – – repay to the *neopoiai*,

[ν, ἢν] δ̣[ὲ] μή, αὐτὸς ὀφείλε̣ν. [ταῦτ]-
[α] δ̣ὲ ἢ̣ν δόξει τῶι δήμωι [ἀναγρ]-
[άψαι] ἐστήλην τὸς νεωπ[οίας ἕ]-
[ως] τῆς νεομηνίης τô μην̣[ὸς τô]
[Τ]α̣υρεῶνος, καὶ θεῖναι [τô τεμ]-
[έ]νεος ἵν' ἂν δοκῆι τοῖς [νεωπο]-
[ί]ηισιν· ἢν δὲ μὴ ἀναγρά̣[ψωισι]-
[ν] καὶ θέωισιν τὴν στή[λην . . .]
[. . .]Ο̣[—8—]Ρ̣Λ̣[—9—]

The text can be reconstructed only at the beginning and the end, but the beginning is of an importance which justifies the inclusion of this inscription in our collection. A Milesian decree of 379/8 (*LSAM* 45 = *Milet* VI. iii 1220)[1] has long been known whose prescript supplies, in a manner matching the Athenian, the eponymous *stephanephoros*, month, prytany (with the same name as an Athenian tribe), chairman, 'resolved by the council and the people', proposer; and the substance begins with τὰ μὲν ἄλλα καθότι ἐν τῆι στήληι γέγραπται ('in other respects as has been written on the *stele*'), an Athenian-like formula for amending a previous enactment (cf. *IG* ii^2 140. 8–10, of 353/2). Our decree, found in 1957, shows Miletus using a prescript of Athenian type, probably to be dated to the stephanephorate of Eudemus in 434/3,[2] and it helps us to reconstruct the history of Miletus as a member of the Delian League: by this date Miletus had a constitution modelled on the Athenian, and it was presumably already pro-Athenian when Athens supported it against Samos in 440–439 (cf. on **123**). This echoing of Athens was discussed by D. M. Lewis, in *Πρακτικὰ τοῦ Η΄ Διεθνοῦς Συνεδρίου . . . Ἐπιγραφικῆς*, 1982, i. 55–61 = his *Selected Papers in Greek and Near Eastern History*, 51–9.

[1] Milesian dates given here are those obtained by correcting the dates which A. Rehm inferred from *Milet* I. iii 122 in accordance with the better interpretation of E. Cavaignac, *REH* xc 1924, 311–14: see Rhodes.

[2] The other theoretical possibilities would be Hegemon son of Eudemus (407/6), and Eudemus son of Hegemon (401/0): in 407/6 Miletus was still democratic (oligarchic revolution 405; Diod. Sic. XIII. 104. v, Plut. *Lys.* 8), but we should have to make room for an opening formula giving both name and patronymic; the Athenian-type democracy attested again in *LSAM* 45 is not likely to have been restored by 401/0.

or if not they themselves shall owe it.

27 This if it is approved by the people the *neopoiai* shall inscribe on a *stele* before the first day of the month Taureon and place it in the sanctuary where the *neopoiai* decide; if they do not inscribe and place the *stele*—

Poseidon Heliconius was believed to be so named from Helice in Achaea (Hom. *Il.* VIII. 200–4, XX. 404 with schol.); but *Hom. Hymn.* xxii. 1–3 and epigram vi. 1–2 in [Hdt.] *Vit. Hom.* 17 (pp. 374–5 West) associate him with Mt Helicon in Boeotia, and that was preferred by Aristarchus (*ap. E.M.* 547. 15–19) and has been preferred by some modern scholars (e.g. U. von Wilamowitz-Moellendorff, *Sb. Berlin* 1906, 46; T. W. Allen *et al.*, *The Homeric Hymns*², 413–14). The Ionians' Panionium on Cape Mycale was dedicated to him (Hdt. I. 148. i; cf. I. 145 for Helice); Paus. VII. 24. v mentions Helice as the source and an altar of Poseidon Heliconius at Miletus. *Neopoies* (literally 'temple-builder') is a title found in various eastern Greek cities, sometimes for an office with responsibilities not limited to temples (e.g. Halicarnassus, **132**. 7–8; *SIG*³ 46. 6, perhaps late fifth century; Iasus, *IK Iasos* 48. 10–12, third quarter fourth century; Halasarna on Cos, *SIG*³ 569. 2, *c.*204–201); in Miletus they are otherwise mentioned, in religious contexts as here, in *I. Didyma* 444. 11, and their *neopoieion* in *I. Didyma* 39. 57, 40. 9. Later the Milesian year began in the spring and Taureon was its first month: Rehm was led by his interpretation of the Milesian *stephanephoroi* to suppose that before the late fourth century the year began in the autumn, but it is more likely that in the classical period as later it began with Taureon (Bilabel, *Die ionische Kolonisation*, 68–75, accepted by N. Ehrhardt in *Milet* VI. iii, p. 129).

The accusative ἱέρεω (22, 23) is a Milesian feature (cf. B. Bondesson *De Sonis et Formis Titulorum Milesiorum Didymaeorumque* (Diss. Lund 1946), 150–1); for the restored ἀναγρά̣[ψωισι | ν] (33–4) and preserved θέωισιν (34) Herrmann compares λάβωισιν in **133**, from Chios (Buck, p. 143 §184, regards this as an Aeolic feature, with ισ derived from νσ).

144

Athenian financial decrees, 434/3

A marble *stele*, of which a portion at the foot has been cut away, used as an altar in the Attic village Charvati, now in the Louvre, Paris; face *A* is well preserved but *B* (particularly ll. 1–16) seriously damaged. Phot. *JHS* li 1931, pls. 1–2 (with facsimile of *B* pl. 3), *ATL* i, pp. 210–1 figs. 185–6, *CSCA* iv 1971, pls. 1–4.

Developed Attic writing (same cutter for both faces asserted by A. Kirchhoff, *IG* i^{1} 32, then often denied, but considered possible by Pritchett, certain by Bradeen, accepted *IG* i^{3} and supported by S. V. Tracy [personal communication]); both faces inconsistent in the use of *h*; dative plurals -αις *A* but -ασι *B*. *Stoichedon*, *A* 54, *B* 51.

SIG^{3} 91; *IG* i^{2} 91, 92; Tod 51; *ATL* i, ii D1, 2; M&L 58; *IG* i^{3} 52* (Meritt & McGregor). Trans. Fornara 119; Dillon & Garland^{3} 13. 7. See also Kolbe, *Thukydides im Lichte der Urkunden*, 50–91 (reprinted from *Sb. Berlin* 1927

A

[ἔδ]οχσεν τε̑ι βολε̑ι καὶ το̑ι δέμοι. Κεκροπὶς ἐπρυτάνευε· Μνεσίθεος ἐ-
[γ]ραμμάτευε· Εὐπείθες ἐπεστάτε. Καλλίας εἶπε· ἀποδο̑ναι τοῖς θεοῖς
[τ]ὰ χρέματα τὰ ὀφελόμενα, ἐπειδὲ τε̑ι Ἀθεναίαι τὰ τρισχίλια τάλαντ-
[α] ἀνενένεγκται ἐς πόλιν hὰ ἐφσέφιστο, νομίσματος hεμεδαπο̑. ἀποδι-
[δ]όναι δὲ ἀπὸ το̑ν χρεμάτον ἃ ἐς ἀπόδοσίν ἐστιν τοῖς θεοῖς ἐφσεφισμ-
[έ]να, τά τε παρὰ τοῖς ἑλλενοταμίαις ὄντα νῦν καὶ τἆλλα ἅ ἐστι τούτον
[το̑]ν χρεμάτον, καὶ τὰ ἐκ τε̑ς δεκάτες ἐπειδὰν πραθε̑ι. λογισάσθον δὲ h-
[οι λ]ογισταὶ hοι τριάκοντα hοίπερ νῦν τὰ ὀφελόμενα τοῖς θεοῖς ἀκρ-
[ιβο̑]ς, συναγογε̑ς δὲ το̑λ λογιστο̑ν ἐ βολὲ αὐτοκράτορ ἔστο. ἀποδόντον
[δὲ τ]ὰ χρέματα hοι πρυτάνες μετὰ τε̑ς βολε̑ς καὶ ἐχσαλειφόντον ἐπει-
[δὰν] ἀποδο̑σιν, ζετέσαντες τά τε πινάκια καὶ τὰ γραμματεῖα καὶ ἐάμ π-
[ο ἄλ]λοθι ε̑ι γεγραμμένα. ἀποφαινόντον δὲ τὰ γεγραμμένα hοί τε hιερ-
[ε̑ς κ]αὶ hοι hιεροποιοὶ καὶ εἴ τις ἄλλος οἶδεν. ταμίας δὲ ἀποκυαμεύε-
[ν το]ύτον το̑ν χρεμάτον hόταμπερ τὰς ἄλλας ἀρχάς, καθάπερ τὸς το̑ν hι-
[ερο̑]ν το̑ν τε̑ς Ἀθεναίας. hοῦτοι δὲ ταμιευόντον ἐμ πόλει ἐν το̑ι Ὀπισθ-
[οδό]μοι τὰ το̑ν θεο̑ν χρέματα hόσα δυνατὸν καὶ ὅσιον, καὶ συνανοιγόν-
τον καὶ συγκλειόντον τὰς θύρας το̑ Ὀπισθοδόμο καὶ συσσεμαινόσθο-
ν τοῖς το̑ν τε̑ς Ἀθεναίας ταμίαις. παρὰ δὲ το̑ν νῦν ταμιο̑ν καὶ το̑ν ἐπισ-
τατο̑ν καὶ το̑ν hιεροποιο̑ν το̑ν ἐν τοῖς hιεροῖς, hοὶ νῦν διαχερίζο[σι]-
ν, ἀπαριθμεσάσθον καὶ ἀποστεσάσθον τὰ χρέματα ἐναντίον τε̑ς βολ[ε̑]-
ς ἐμ πόλει, καὶ παραδεχσάσθον hοι ταμίαι hοι λαχόντες παρὰ το̑ν νῦ[ν]
ἀρχόντον, καὶ ἐν στέλει ἀναγραφσάντον μιᾶι ἅπαντα καθ' ἕκαστόν τε
το̑ν θεο̑ν τὰ χρέματα hοπόσα ἐστὶν ἑκάστοι καὶ συμπάντον κεφάλαιο-
ν, χορὶς τό τε ἀργύριον καὶ τὸ χρυσίον. καὶ τὸ λοιπὸν ἀναγραφόντον h-
οι αἰεὶ ταμίαι ἐς στέλεν καὶ λόγον διδόντον, το̑ν τε ὄντον χρεμάτον
καὶ το̑ν προσιόντον τοῖς θεοῖς καὶ ἐάν τι ἀ[π]αναλίσκεται κατὰ τὸν ἐ-
νιαυτόν, πρὸς τὸς λογιστάς, καὶ εὐθύνας διδόντον. καὶ ἐκ Παναθεναί-
ον ἐς Παναθέναια τὸλ λόγον διδόντον, καθάπερ hοι τὰ τε̑ς Ἀθεναίας τ-

and 1929); H. T. Wade-Gery, *JHS* li 1931, 57–85; A. Wilhelm, *JHS* lxviii 1948, 124–9; H. B. Mattingly, *PACA* vii 1964, 35–55; *BSA* lxii 1967, 14–17 = his *AER* 208–13; Meiggs, *The Athenian Empire*, 519–23; D. W. Bradeen, *GRBS* xii 1971, 469–83; W. K. Pritchett, *CSCA* iv 1971, 219–25; H. B. Mattingly, *GRBS* xvi 1975, 15–22 = his *AER* 353–60; Linders, *The Treasurers of the Other Gods in Athens*, esp. 38–57; C. Triebel-Schubert, *QC* vi 1984, 355–75, cf. *SEG* xxxiv 17; L. Kallet-Marx, *CQ*^{2} xxxix 1989, 94–113; H. B. Mattingly, *ZPE* lxxxiii 1990, 110–22 = his *AER* 505–17; Fornara & Samons, *Athens from Cleisthenes to Pericles*, 176–8; H. B. Mattingly, *GRBS* xxxviii 1997, 113–26; Samons, *Empire of the Owl*, 113–63, 212–48.

A

Resolved by the council and the people. Cecropis was the prytany; Mnesitheus was the secretary; Eupeithes was the chairman. Callias proposed:

2 Repay to the gods the monies which are due, since the three thousand talents which were voted for Athena have been brought up to the acropolis, in local currency. Make the repayment from the monies which have been voted for repayment to the gods, that which is now in the hands of the *hellenotamiai* and the rest which is part of these monies, and the proceeds of the ten per cent when (the collection of that) is sold. The thirty *logistai* ['accountants'] now in office shall reckon accurately what is due to the gods, and the council shall have full power for the convening of the *logistai*. The *prytaneis* together with the council shall repay the monies, and shall delete (the records) when they have repaid them, seeking out the tablets and the notes and anything that may be written anywhere else. The priests and the *hieropoioi* and anybody else who knows shall reveal what is written.

13 Appoint by lot treasurers of these treasures when the other officials are appointed, as with those of the sacred (treasures) of Athena. These shall keep the treasures of the gods on the acropolis in the *opisthodomos* as far as is possible and righteous, and they shall join in opening and closing the doors of the *opisthodomos* and in sealing with the treasurers of (the treasures) of Athena.

18 From the current treasurers and *epistatai* and *hieropoioi* in the sanctuaries, who now handle the treasures, they shall measure out and weigh out the treasures in the presence of the council on the acropolis, and the treasurers appointed by lot shall take them over from the current officials and shall write everything on a single *stele* — according to each of the gods, how much treasure belongs to each, and the total of the whole, silver and gold separately.

24 And for the future the treasurers at any time shall write up on a *stele* and shall give account of the treasures in hand and the income of the gods and anything expended during the year, to the *logistai*, and they shall undergo *euthynai*.

27 And they shall give account from Panathenaea to Panathenaea, in the same way as the treasurers of (the treasures) of Athena.

[α]μιεύοντες. τὰς δὲ στέλας ἐν αἷς ἂν ἀναγράφσοσι τὰ χρέματα τὰ hιερ-
[ά θέ]ντον ἐμ πόλει hοι ταμίαι. ἐπειδὰν δὲ ἀποδεδομένα ἔι τοῖς θεοῖς
[τὰ χρ]έματα, ἐς τὸ νεόριον καὶ τὰ τείχε τοῖς περιôσι χρε͂σθαι χρέμασ-
[ιν ——— 52 ———]
- -

B

[ἔδοχσεν τε͂ι βολε͂ι καὶ τôι δέμοι. - - - - - ἐπρυτάνευε· - - - - -]
[- ἐγραμμάτευε· - - - - ἐπεστάτε. - - -] ẹị̂π̣[ε· —— 11 ——]
[—— 5 —— τὰ λί]θ̣ινα καὶ τὰς Νί[κας τὰς χ]ρ̣υσᾶς καὶ τὰ Προ[πύλαια· . . . .]
[—— 9 ——]εθε͂ι παντελôς [—— 7 ——]σει χρε͂σθαι ἀπ[—— 11 ——]
[—— 9 ——] κατὰ τὰ ἐφσεφι[σμένα], καὶ τὲν ἀκρόπολιν [—— 10 ——]
[—— 9 ——]ρ̣γμένα καὶ ἐπι[σκευά]ζεν, δέκα τάλαντα ἀ[ναλίσκοντα]-
[ς τô ἐνιαυτ]ô hεκάστο hέος [ἂν . . . .]θε͂ι, καὶ ἐπισκευα̣[σθε͂ι hος κάλ]-
[λιστα. συνε]πιστατόντ[ο]ν δ̣[ὲ τôι ἔρ]γ[ο]ι [ο]ἱ ταμίαι καὶ [οἱ ἐπιστάτα]-
[ι· τὸ δὲ γράμ]μα τὸν ἀρχιτέκ[τονα ποι]ε͂ν [ὅ]σπερ τôμ̣ Προ[πυλαίον· hoῦ]-
[τος δὲ ἐπιμ]ε̣λέσ[θο] μετὰ τô[ν ἐπιστ]α̣τôν hόπος ἄριστ̣[α καὶ εὐτελέ]-
[στατα —— 5 ——]έσεται hε ἀκρ[όπολις] καὶ ἐπισκευασθέ[σεται τὰ δεό]-
[μενα. τοῖς δ]ὲ ἄλλοις χρέμα[σιν τοῖ]ς τε͂ς Ἀθεναίας το[ῖς τε νῦν ὄσι]-
[ν ἐμ πόλει κ]αὶ hάττ' ἂν τ[ὸ] λο[ιπὸν ἀν]αφέρεται μὲ χρε͂σ[θ]α[ι μεδὲ ἀπα]-
[ναλίσκεν ἀ]π' αὐτôν ἐ[ς] ἄλλο μ̣[εδὲν ἒ] ἐς ταῦτα hυπὲρ μυ[ρ]ί[ας δραχμὰ]-
[ς ἒ ἐς ἐπισκ]ευὲν ἐάν τι δέε[ι. ἐς ἄλλ]ο δὲ μεδὲν χρε͂σ[θ]α[ι τοῖς χρέμα]-
[σιν ἐὰμ μὲ τ]ὲν ἄδειαν φσεφ[ίσεται] ὁ δε͂μος καθάπερ ἐ[ὰμ φσεφίσετ]-
[αι περὶ ἐσφ]ορᾶς· ἐὰν δέ τις [εἴπει ἒ] ἐπιφσεφ̣ί[σ]ει μὲ ἐ[φσεφισμένε]-
[ς πο τε͂ς ἀδεί]ας χρε͂σθαι το[ῖς χρέμ]ασιν τοῖ[ς] τε͂ς Ἀθε[ναίας, ἐνεχέ]-
[σθο τοῖς α]ὐ̣τοῖς hοῖσπερ ἐά[ν τι ἐσ]φέρεν εἴπει ἒ ἐπιφ[σεφίσει. θε]-
[οῖς δὲ πᾶσ]ι̣ν̣ κατατιθέναι κ[ατὰ τὸ]ν ἐνιαυτὸν τὰ hεκά[στοι ὀφελό]-
[μενα παρὰ τ]ο̣ῖς ταμίασι τôν [τε͂ς Ἀθ]εναίας τὸς ἑλλενο[ταμίας. ἐπε]-
[ιδὰν δ' ἀπὸ] τ̣[ô]ν διακοσίον τα[λάντο]ν hὰ ἐς ἀπόδοσιν ἐφ[σεφίσατο h]-
[ο δε͂μος τοῖ]ς ἄλλοις θεοῖς ἀ[ποδοθ]ε͂ι τὰ ὀφελόμενα, τα[μιευέσθο τ]-
[ὰ μὲν τε͂ς Ἀθ]ε̣ναίας χρέματα [ἐν τôι] ἐπὶ δεχσιὰ τô Ὀπισ[θοδόμο, τὰ δ]-

B. 1–2 [ἔδοχσεν τε͂ι βολε͂ι καὶ τôι δέμοι. Κεκροπὶς ἐπρυτάνευε· Μνεσίθε|ος ἐγραμμάτευε· Ε]ὐ̣π̣[ε]ί̣θ̣ε̣ς [ἐπεστάτε. Κ]α̣λλίας εἶπ̣[ε, as in *A.* 1–2, Wade-Gery: restoration not impossible but too speculative Pritchett, Εὐπείθες impossible (υ and θ wrong, only last ε certain) but Καλλίας possible Kallet-Marx, Καλλίας not supported by Berlin squeeze C. W. Fornara at conference at Sunium, July 2006. 2–3 ἐκποιε͂ν τἀγά|λματα τὰ λί]-θ̣ινα *ATL* ii. 3 Νί[κας —5—]ε[ι] δ̣ὲ καὶ Pritchett, *BCH* ci 1977, 9–10 n. 5. 3 Προ[πύλαια, 9 Προ[πυλαίον *IG* i², credible in 9, acceptable in 3. 3–4 καὶ ἐ|πειδὰν ποι]εθε͂ι *IG* i², [hόπο|ς δ' ἂν ἐκποι]-εθε͂ι *ATL* i, Wilhelm, [hέος | δὲ ἂν ἐκποι]εθε͂ι *ATL* ii.. 4–5 [ἀπαναλό]σει χρε͂σθαι ἀπ[ὸ τôν χρεμάτο|ν Ἀθεναίας] *ATL* ii, [διασκέφ]σει χρε͂σθαι ἀπ[αναλίσκοντα|ς ἐς τὸ δέον] Wilhelm. 5–6 [νέμεν πλὲν ε|ἰ μὲ τὰ ἐχσε]ρ̣γμένα *ATL* i–ii, [hε͂ρχσαι hόσ|α μέ ἐστι hε]ρ̣γμένα Wilhelm. 7 hέος [ἂν νεμε]θε͂ι *ATL* i ii, hέος [ἂν hερχ]θε͂ι Wilhelm. 10–11 εὐτελέ|στατα νεμεθ]έσεται *ATL* i–ii, ἀσφαλέ|στατα hερχθ]έσεται Wilhelm. 13–14 ἀπα|ναλίσκεν: δαν|είζεσθαι D. M. Lewis, private communication.

29 The *stelai* on which they write up the sacred treasures the treasurers shall place on the acropolis.

30 When the monies have been repaid to the gods, use the remaining monies for the dockyard and the walls – – –

B

Resolved by the council and the people. —— was the prytany; —— was the secretary; —— was the chairman. —— proposed:

2 – – – the stone – – – and the gold (?) Victories and the Propylaea – – – entirely – – – use – – – in accordance with what has been decreed; and the acropolis – – – and make good, spending ten talents each year until – – – and it is made good as finely as possible. The work shall be supervised jointly by the treasurers and (the *epistatai*; the plan?) is to be made by the architect of the Propylaea. He shall take care with the (*epistatai*?) that the acropolis is – – – in the best and (cheapest?) way and that (what is necessary?) is made good.

12 The other monies of Athena, what is now on the acropolis and whatever may be brought up in future, are not to be used or to have expenditure (?) made from them for any purpose other than these above ten thousand drachmas or for making good if any is needed. The monies are not to be used for anything else unless the people vote immunity as when they vote about *eisphora*: if anybody proposes or puts to the vote when immunity has not been voted that the monies of Athena shall be used, he shall be liable to the same penalties as when somebody proposes or puts to the vote that there shall be an *eisphora*.

19 Payment to (all?) the gods each year of what is due to each is to be made to the treasurers of Athena by the *hellenotamiai*.

21 When what is due to the other gods has been repaid from the two hundred talents which the people voted for repayment, the treasures of Athena shall be kept on the right in the *opisthodomos* and those of the other gods on the left.

[ἐ τôν ἄλλον θ]εôν ἐν τôι ἐπ' ἀρ[ιστερ]ά. *vacat*
[hοπόσα δὲ τô]ν χρεμάτον τôν [hιερô]ν ἄστατά ἐστιν ἒ ἀν[αρίθμετα, h]-
[οι ταμίαι] ḥ[ο]ι νῦν μετὰ τôν τẹ[ττάρο]ν ἀρχôν hαὶ ἐδίδο[σαν τὸν λόγ]-
[ον τὸν ἐκ Πα]ṇαθεναίον ἐς Παṇ[αθένα]ια hοπόσα μὲγ χρυ[σᾶ ἐστιν αὐ]-
[τôν ἒ ἀργυρᾶ] ἒ ὑπ̣ά̣ρ̣γ̣υ̣ρ̣α̣ στε[σάντον, τὰ δ]ẹ̀ ἄ̣λ̣λ̣[α ἀριθμεσάντον . . .]
- -

27 τẹ[ττάρο]ν *IG* i².
We translate χρέματα as 'monies' or as 'treasures', according to the context.

These decrees order the payment of sums due to the Other Gods, after sums due to Athena have already been paid, and the consolidation of separate sacred funds in a single treasury of the Other Gods, and they authorise some further building work on the acropolis but otherwise restrict expenditure from the treasury of Athena. The relationship between the two decrees, and their date(s), have been much disputed.

The view that the two decrees had the same prescript and were therefore enacted on the same day is unjustified, and it may even be that the proposer of the second decree was not Callias. Callias may be, but is not necessarily, the proposer named in the revised prescripts of **149**. *A* and *B*, and/or the Callias who was a general sent against Potidaea in 432 (Thuc. I. 61. i). If the proposers of *A* and *B* here are different, this will help to explain the differences between the two decrees, in particular the forms of the first-declension dative plural (above), 'the gods' in *A* but 'the other gods' in *B*, *polis* in *A* but *akropolis* in *B*. However, it is likely that the two were inscribed by the same cutter, and (more importantly) the connections between them are such (despite the doubts of Kallet-Marx and Samons) that the two must be close in time, though not enacted on the same day or proposed by the same man.

A. 2–13 orders the repayment of what is due to the gods (the Other Gods, in fact, since payment to Athena has been completed) from the monies which have been voted; and *B*. 21–5 makes arrangements for what is to be done when what is due to the Other Gods has been paid from the 200 talents voted. *A*. 13–24 creates a board of treasurers of the (Other) Gods and makes arrangements for them to share the *opisthodomos* with the treasurers of Athens and to take over the treasures for which they will be responsible from the various officials who currently have them (Linders stresses that the new treasury of the Other Gods contained monies of the Other Gods but not all their treasures); and *B*. 23–5 specifies how the *opisthodomos* is to be divided between the treasuries of Athena and of the Other Gods. *A*. 30 sqq. stipulates that any remaining monies are to be spent on the dockyard and the walls; and *B*. 2–12 perhaps makes arrangements for winding up the acropolis building programme (though the details are uncertain), after which 12–19 prescribes that there is to be no further expenditure from the treasury of Athena apart from small sums for the maintenance of the buildings without a special vote of *adeia* ('immunity' from prosecution for breaking the prescription). *B* reads naturally as a supplement to

26 As for those of the sacred treasures which are unweighed or uncounted, the current treasurers with the four boards which gave account from Panathenaea to Panathenaea shall weigh those of them which are gold, silver or gilded silver and count the rest – – –

A, enacted not long after it, and we think it likely rather than unlikely that they were enacted within the same year.

Which year? *B* is later than the beginning of the Propylaea in 437/6 (credibly restored in 3, 9), and the combination of 'the current treasurers with the four boards which gave account [imperfect] from Panathenaea to Panathenaea' (restored in *B*. 26–8) suggests that we are in a year of the Great Panathenaea. That has been generally accepted, but 434/3, 422/1 and 418/7 have all had their champions (434/3, Kolbe, Tod; 422/1, Wade-Gery, but in *JHS* lii 1933, 135, he accepted 434/3 and that date then became canonical; 422/1 reasserted Mattingly; 418/7, Beloch, *GG*^{2} II. ii. 344–56, on grounds not supported by other texts now available). Despite the continuing debate, we find the case for 434/3 compelling[1] (and do not think it is undermined by the reference to 'the monies from the other sanctuaries' in 431, in Thuc. II. 13. v, a formulation which need not mean that the monies were still there at that time). *A*. 13–24 seems to us to order the creation of the treasury of the Other Gods, and therefore to be earlier than their earliest attested existence, in 430/29 (in *IG* i^3 383 the treasurers of 429/8—only five men are named—record what they took over from their predecessors, and champions of a later date suppose that *A* was reorganising an existing board); *B*. 26 sqq. orders a full inventory of the treasures (of, or at any rate including those of, Athena), with reference to the four boards of the previous Panathenaic quadrennium, and the inscribed records of the treasurers of Athena are based on Panathenaic quadrennia and begin in 434/3 (*IG* i^3 292, 317, 343); it is a further indication that 433 marks a new beginning that the accounts of loans to the state from the sacred treasuries (**160**), while concerned primarily with 426/5–423/2, review previous loans from 433/2 onwards. *B*. 2–19 is the most uncertain part of the text, but it perhaps orders the winding-up of the acropolis building programme and more certainly strictly limits expenditure on buildings for the future, and the accounts both for the Parthenon and for the Propylaea seem to end in 433/2 (*IG* i^3 450, 466).[2] Recently A. P. Matthaiou has suggested that

[1] The case is argued more fully by Rhodes, in ἄξων . . . *R. S. Stroud*, i. 29–37.

[2] Triebel-Schubert thinks that the treasurers of the Other Gods should have been elected in time to serve for the whole quadrennium 434–430, and that their year of office was not 'from Panathenaea to Panathenaea' but the archontic year or the council's year (she does not distinguish the two), and that *A* was enacted in the

the need for repairs was a result of the earthquake of 426 mentioned by Thuc. III. 89;[3] but *episkeuazein* need not denote the repair of what was damaged, and if there had been earthquakes in the mid-430s Thucydides would not necessarily have mentioned them.

We then have to explain the completed payment of 3,000 tal. to Athena and the repayment due to the Other Gods in 434/3. There have been various suggestions (against that of *ATL* iii. 279–81, 326–32, that there had been a series of annual transfers, see L. Kallet-Marx, *Cl. Ant.* viii = *CSCA* xx 1989, 252–66). Rhodes, noting that Athena paid for the war of 440–439 against Samos (cf. **138**), has argued that then, as from 433 onwards (cf. **148**, **160**), the sacred treasuries had lent money to the state for military purposes, and that by 434/3, helped by the reparations from Samos, the state had repaid what was due to Athena and was then able to repay what was due to the Other Gods (e.g. *A History of the Classical Greek World, 478–323 BC*[2], 98).

What these decrees represent is a process of getting Athens' finances into good shape with a view to military needs (cf. the dockyard and walls, *A*. 31): outstanding loans from the sacred treasuries are repaid, the various smaller sacred treasuries are consolidated in a single treasury of the Other Gods (and this should be seen in that light, cf. Humphreys, *The Strangeness of Gods*, 137–9, rather than as the removal of these treasuries to the acropolis for greater safety, as suggested in *ATL*)—and a new series of loans begins with the expeditions to Corcyra in 433 (**148**). Thucydides remarked that the Athenians decided to make their alliance with Corcyra because 'it really did seem that the war against the Peloponnesians would come upon them' (I. 44. ii cf. 33. iii, 42. ii): the decisions recorded here, taken about the same time or slightly earlier, suggest that he was not over-influenced by hindsight but was right (cf. also **149**).

The *dekate* of *A*. 7 is a 10 per cent tax (for the auction of tax-collecting contracts cf. *Ath. Pol.* 47. ii–iv). The only other mention of an Athenian *dekate* in the fifth century is that imposed by Alcibiades in 410 on ships leaving the Black Sea (Xen. *Hell.* I. i. 22, Diod. Sic. XIII. 64. ii, for the first time according to Polyb. IV. 44. iv); for possible interpretations of this *dekate* see P. Fawcett, *Hesperia* lxxxv 2016, 153–99 at 160–1. The thirty *logistai* ('accountants') are attested only in *A*. 7–9, and are presumably a special

first half of 435/4; and C. Marcaccini, *Hesperia* lxxxiv 2015, 515–32, with a date of 433/2 for *A*, argues that *A* marks a change from use of the Panathenaic year (as in **148**) to the council's year. For the treasurers' year of office see further on **160**.

[3] At a conference in memory of D. M. Lewis, May 2014.

board, to be distinguished from those in *A.* 27, who were involved in the financial *logos* and general *euthynai* which all officials had to undergo on leaving office (cf. *Ath. Pol.* 48. iv–v, 54. ii). For the deletion of financial records when payments due are made (*A.* 10–11) cf. *Ath. Pol.* 47. v–48. i.

Military officers were elected 'in the first prytany after the sixth in whose term of office there are good omens' (*Ath. Pol.* 44. iv); we do not know when civilian appointments were made. It is presumably because of Athena that the treasurers' year of office began not with the archon's year on 1 Hecatombaeon (i) or the council's year (variable in terms of the archon's year: cf. Introduction, pp. xxiv–xxv) but with the principal day of the Panathenaea, 28 Hecatombaeon (*A.* 27–9).

The identity of the *opisthodomos* (*A.* 15–18, *B.* 23–5) has been disputed, between the rear (west) chamber of the Parthenon and a rebuilt western part of the 'old temple of Athena' (Travlos, *Pictorial Dictionary of Ancient Athens*, 143), which had stood on a site between those of the Parthenon and the Erechtheum from the 520s to the Persian sack in 480. Most recently Linders has argued for the latter until that was destroyed by fire in 406/5 (Xen. *Hell.* I. vi. 1), after which the name *opisthodomos* was transferred to the west chamber of the Parthenon, which had previously been called *parthenon* (*AJA*[2] cxi 2007, 777–82). For the handing over of the treasures of the Other Gods to the new treasurers in the presence of the council (*A.* 18–22), cf. the council's involvement in the making of contracts and receiving of revenue (*Ath. Pol.* 47. ii–48. ii), and in the receiving of tribute from the Delian League (**154**. 16–17). For non-monetary treasures cf. **169**.

The golden Nikai (statues of Victory, *B.* 3) were standard statues (in fact, gold-plated) derived from the Nike on the hand of Pheidias' gold-and-ivory statue of Athena, weighing 2 talents each: see D. B. Thompson, *Hesp.* xiii 1944, 173–209; Harris, *The Treasures of the Parthenon and Erechtheion*, 272–5. This is the earliest mention of them; for the cult, temple and priestess of Athena Nike cf. **137**, **156**.

For the entrenchment clause safeguarding the decree against breaches (*B.* 15–19) cf. **142**. 20–6. *Eisphora* was a tax on the property of those who admitted to owning more than a certain amount, levied not regularly but when the assembly decided; in winter 428/7 the Athenians 'first' levied an *eisphora* of 200 talents (Thuc. III. 19. i), but it is not clear what Thucydides means by 'first' in that context (cf. J. G. Griffith, *AJAH* ii 1977, 3–7), and there is no reason why the possibility of an *eisphora* should not have been provided before 434/3. On *eisphora* in general see Fawcett, *op. cit.*, 156–9; and for suggestions as to how fifth-century may have differed from fourth-century practice see M. R. Christ, *CQ*[2] lvii 2007, 53–69.

145

Building accounts of the Parthenon, 434/3

Four fragments from the right-hand side of a marble *stele* of which 25 fragments survive. Originally set up on the acropolis; now in the Epigraphical Museum (some other fragments now displayed in the Acropolis Museum). Phot. ll. 369–78 (squeeze), Cavaignac, *Études sur l'histoire financière d'Athènes au Ve siècle*, lv, fig. 18; Vlachopoulos (ed.), *Archaeology: Euboea and Central Greece*, 113 fig. 174.

Attic letters. Slightly irregular *stoichedon*: Austin, *The Stoichedon Style*, 61–2.

W. B. Dinsmoor, *AJA* xvii 1913, 53–80, xxv 1921, 233–45; M&L 59; *IG* i³ 449 (col. vii of 436–51)*; Shear, *Trophies of Victory*, 417; Trans. Fornara 120; Davison with Lundgreen, *Pheidias*, ii. 1132–3. See also R. S. Stanier, *JHS* lxxiii 1953, 68–76; A. Burford in Hooker (ed.), *Parthenos and Parthenon*, 23–35; Davison with Lundgreen, *Pheidias*, ii. 1134–45; Shear, *Trophies of Victory*, 44–69.

	τοῖς ἐπιστάτεσι hοῖς
	Ἀντικλε͂ς ἐγραμμάτευ[ε]·
	ἐπὶ τε͂ς τετάρτες καὶ δε-
	κάτες βολε͂ς hε͂ι Μετα-
	γένες προ͂τος ἐγραμμ-
	άτευε, ἐπὶ Κράτετος ἄρχ-
	οντος Ἀθεναίοισιν.
	λέμματα το͂ ἐνιαυτο͂
	τούτο τάδε·
ΧΗΗΗ	περιγενόμενομ
Η𐅄ΔΔ	μὲν ἐκ το͂ προτέρο
	__ἐνιαυτο͂
𐅄̣Δ̣Δ̣	χρυσο͂ στατε͂ρες
[ΣΣΣΣ]	[Λαμφσ]ακενοί
Δ̣Δ̣ΓΣΣ	[χρυσο͂] στατε͂ρες
hέκτε ⁝	__Κ[υζικεν]οί
	πα[ρὰ ταμι]ο͂ν [hοὶ τὰ]
ΜΜ𐅆 ⁝	τε͂ς θεο͂ [ἐτ]αμίευ[ον]
	hοῖς Κράτες ἐγρ[α]-
	__μμάτευε Λαμπτρε[ύς]
ΧΗΗΗ	χρυσίο πραθέ[ντος]
𐅄ΔΔ⊢⊢	σταθμὸν 𐅄ΔΔΔ[Δ]Γ̣[⊢⊢⊢]
	__τιμὲ τούτο
ΧΗΗΗ	ἐλέφαντος [πρα]θ[έν]-
ΓΙΙΙΙ	τος σταθμὸ[ν Τ]ΤΤ
	__𐅄Δ: τιμὲ τ[ούτο]

Restorations are largely secured by parallel entries in other lists; the sums of Lampsacene and Cyzicene staters remain unchanged throughout the lists, never being spent. Where numerals and words are not in alignment, we number lines of words. 389–90 The numerals are carved slightly lower than the words with which they are aligned in our text.

For the *epistatai* to whom Anticles was secretary; under the fourteenth council, to which Metagenes was first secretary, under Crates as archon for the Athenians. The following are the receipts for this year:

1,470 dr.	REMAINING FROM THE PREVIOUS YEAR:
74	Gold staters of Lampsacus;
$27\frac{1}{6}$	Gold staters of Cyzicus.
	From the treasurers who
25,000 dr.	were treasurers of the Goddess's property for whom Crates of Lamptrae was secretary;
1,372 dr.	from the sale of gold, weight 98 dr.: the price of this;
1,305 dr. 4 ob.	from the sale of ivory, weight 3 talents 60 dr.: the price of this.

	ἀ ν α λ ό μ α [τ] α
[. . .]ΗΗ:	
- - ⊢⊢Ι:	_ὀνεμάτο[ν]
	_μισθομ[άτον]
Χ𐅅̣[ΗΗ]	[h]υπορ[γοῖς Πεντελε͂]-
ΗΗΔ[Δ]	[σι καὶ λίθος ἀνατιθ]-
Γ⊢ΙΙ	___ε̣͂[σι ἐπὶ τὰ κύκλα]
Μ𐅆ΧΗΗ	ἀγ[αλματοπο]ιοῖς
Η𐅄ΔΔΔ	ἐνα[ιετίον μι]σθός
Δ⊢⊢	__
[Χ]𐅅ΗΗΗ	καταμ[ενίο]ις
[. .]Δ⊢̣Ι̣Ι̣	
- - -	[περ]ιε[γέν]ετο
- - -	[τὸ ἐνιαυτ]ὸ τού[το]
[𐅄ΔΔ]	[χρυσο͂ στατε͂ρες]
[ΣΣΣΣ]	[Λαμφσακενοί]
[ΔΔ𐅃ΣΣ]	[χρυσο͂ στατε͂ρες]
[hέκτε ⁝]	[Κυζικενοί]

After 395 the two lines of numerals are carved higher and lower than the word ὀνεμάτο[ν]. 401–2 three lines of numerals occupy the same vertical space as two lines of words. 404 The numerals are carved higher than the word καταμ[ενίο]ις.

A number of accounts relating to public works of a religious character survive from Athens from the middle of the fifth century onwards (*IG* i[3] 433–97; cf. above, **135**, for the accounts of the statue of Athena Parthenos; below, **181**, for the Erechtheum accounts), and these develop a standard form. Each project was assigned an annually changing board of overseers (*epistatai*), chosen by lot, with a secretary (see Marginesu, *Gli Epistati dell'Acropoli*). The board was given a sum of money by the treasurers of Athena or of the other gods, sometimes with supplementary sources of income, and accounted for expenditure both on raw materials and on wages. The accounts were inscribed and put on display on the acropolis, and will have been subject to examination at the audit of the magistrates when they demitted office.

The earliest accounts (*IG* i[3] 433), for an unidentified project that lasted eight years, incorporate the numbers into the text (like the first tribute quota list: cf. above, **119**), but from *IG* i[3] 435 onwards (accounts normally attributed to the statue of Athena Promachos, but for doubts see Stroud, *The Athenian Empire on Stone*, 26–32) the figures are given in a column to the left of the text. The Parthenon accounts were laid out on a large *stele*, 1.6 m. high and 1.8 m. wide. A prescript in large letters ran across the top of the stone and the first six years' entries, from 447/6 to 442/1, were then laid out below in three columns. The next seven years' accounts were inscribed on the back, and years 14 and 15 were inscribed on the two narrow (0.2 m.) faces of the

Expenses:	
904 dr. 1 ob.+	for purchases;
	for wages:
1,926 dr. 2 ob.	to workers at Pentele:
	they also place stones
	on the wheels;
16,392 dr.	to the sculptors
	of the pediment sculptures, wages;
≥1,831 dr. 2 ob.	for monthly wages.
– – –	Surplus
	for this year
74	Gold staters
	of Lampsacus
$27\frac{1}{6}$	Gold staters
	of Cyzicus

---

stele (causing the entries for large numbers to be split over two or three lines). The Athenian masons had anticipated that this would be a very extensive project, but perhaps not quite how extensive it was. In the preserved fragments the building is never named; from other mentions it appears that it was referred to as the *hekatompedon* ('Hundred-footer': cf. below, **169**). Separate accounts were kept not only for the chryselephantine statue of Athena (**135**) but also for the doors of the temple (*IG* i³ 461 with Theophr. *Hist. Pl.* III. 14. i, v. 3. v, v. 4. ii).

The Parthenon accounts give no indication of whose idea the building programme was (it is ascribed to Pericles by Lycurgus, fr. IX. 2 Conomis, and later authors), but they allow us to follow the course of the building (see further Burford, 27–34; Davison, 1142–4; J. B. Salmon, in Mattingly & Salmon (edd.), *Economies beyond Agriculture in the Classical World*, 198–201; and for illustration of the quarrying and transport Korres, *From Pentelicon to the Parthenon*). In 447/6 preserved payments are for cutting and transporting the stone and work on the road from the Pentelicon quarries. In 444/3 when expenditure is next preserved it includes purchase of pine; in 442/1 payment is made for work on the columns and something wooden; in 440/39 for work on doors; in 439/8 ivory is purchased, as is woodwork, and payment made for more marble to be quarried and transported, but also to a goldsmith and for work in silver; in 438/7 there is more quarrying but also work explicitly on the pediments and payment to sculptors working on pedimental sculpture, and similar payments are then made down to these accounts for 434/3. What appears to be the final year of accounts, for 433/2, preserves no detail of expenditure.

The accounts given here, for the fourteenth year (hence 'fourteenth council' in ll. 371–2), 434/3, are the best-preserved. The secretary, Anticles, first occurs in the accounts in 443/2, when he is under-secretary, and he took over as secretary, without any assistant, in 436/5, continuing to the end of the project. It was the secretaries who did the serious work of keeping account of what was going on, and the need for two secretaries in the late 440s and early 430s gives an indication of the level of activity. Anticles may have been himself politically active, if he is to be identified with the proposer of the Chalcis decree (**131**), but the name is common.[1] It is a curiosity of these accounts that they specify (ll. 374–5) that the archon named was archon 'for the Athenians', as if expecting to be read by a non-Athenian.

Few of the earlier accounts have well-preserved figures, but in 447/6 and 442/1 certainly the overseers handed on more than 200,000 dr. (33 tal.) to their successors (*IG* i³ 436. 30, 437. 40, 441. 165, 442. 173). Where had this money come from? The board of 444/3 seems to have recorded income of over 95,000 dr. from the treasurers of Athena, perhaps 37,000 dr. from the *hellenotamiai*, at least 19,000 dr. from the *xenodikai*,[2] and at least 90,000 dr. from the *trieropoioi* (officials responsible for building triremes), making a total income of over 40 tal. (*IG* i³ 439. 70–6). In the following year there is money from the *teichopoioi* (officials responsible for the walls of Athens, 440. 127): presumably both they and the *trieropoioi* contribute their surplus. Although other years record other sources of income including 'the treasurers of the Hephaestic fund from Laurium', who also contribute to the Propylaea, and named individuals, it is clear that contributions are generally listed in order of decreasing size and that the largest contributions come every year, sometimes in more than one instalment, from the treasurers of Athena (L. Kallet-Marx, *Cl. Ant.* viii 1989, 262). The largest share of the money is therefore likely to have come from Athena's quota of tribute, with some additional support from the rest of the tribute. In 434/3 the board receives just 1,470 dr. from the previous board (plus the Lampsacene and Cyzicene staters), and has income of just 25,000 dr. from the treasurers of Athena. The structure of the building was by this stage complete and the project winding down, as shown by the fact that the major expenditure in this year is to sculptors

[1] It is possible that Anticles was under-secretary from the start of the project, in which case a succession of conjectures will allow us to restore his demotic, 'of Oenoe': Shear, *Trophies of Victory*, 47–8.

[2] *Xenodikai* are mentioned only here and in the following year's accounts in all Athenian sources. Presumably they got their income from fines imposed on non-Athenians, but whether that included the *graphe xenias* is disputed. The *xenodikai* of *IG* ii² 46 are plausibly Troezenian officials (Gauthier, *Symbola*, 167, 192) which makes it possible that A. Körte (*Hermes* lxviii 1933, 238–40) was correct in thinking that the *xenodikai* at Athens were replaced by *nautodikai*.

working on pedimental sculptures (the last part of the sculptural programme to be put in place apart from the acroteria).

One of the sources of income in this year is the sale of gold and ivory. Given that there was a separate board of overseers for the chryselephantine statue (**135**), this must have been gold and ivory used in some other context, although it is not clear what. The sale of gold reveals a ratio of gold to silver of 14 : 1 (see above on **135**); the weight of ivory in l. 393 could be restored as either 7 tal. 60 dr. or (as in our text) 3 tal. 60 dr. Even the lower figure is a great deal of ivory, and gives a price for ivory that is three times cheaper than that found in Delphi in the fourth century (*F. Delphes* III. v 25. 5), perhaps because this is scrap.

We would like to know both the total cost of the Parthenon and the level of wages for those who worked on the project. Unfortunately too few figures are preserved for this text to offer much help. Although we are told how much is paid to the sculptors of the pedimental figures for a year's work we know neither the number of sculptors involved nor the length of the working year, and we cannot therefore compute a daily rate (see Loomis, *Wages, Welfare Costs and Inflation in Classical Athens*, 89, 116–17). On the cost of the Parthenon building as a whole, all that these accounts enable us to see is that, given the large sums passed on by some boards and the large annual income in at least some years, the building is unlikely to have cost less than 500 talents (compare Stanier's estimate of 470 talents). Plutarch's talk of 'thousand-talent temples' may not be completely wild (*Per.* 12. ii). Thucydides II. 13. iii has Pericles claim that at the start of the Peloponnesian War there were 6,000 tal. of reserves on the acropolis.

Harpocration (π 101 Keaney Προπύλαια ταῦτα) reports from Heliodorus that the cost of the Propylaea was 2,012 tal. (emended to 2,000 Keaney). The Propylaea accounts (M&L 60, *IG* i³ 462–6) are closely similar to those for the Parthenon (although regularly headed 'Gods, Athena, Fortune', drawing the attention of divinities in general, and particularly Athena and Fortune, for which see S. V. Tracy, *Hesperia* lxiii 1994, 241–4, to the work being undertaken to glorify them). They preserve no fully intact figures either for income or expenditure. But they include figures of greater than 20,000 dr. handed over from one board to the next, and a figure of 65,000 dr. of either income from a single source or (less plausibly) payment for a single category. They also reveal new sources of income, including 'from the *hellenotamiai* from the army', from the rent of a sacred house and from sale of wood and of leather. The Propylaea was notoriously magnificent for a building that was not a temple—Thucydides has Pericles single out the expense on it (and on the siege of Poteidaea) in II. 13. iii and Demetrius of Phalerum criticised Pericles for its extravagance (Cic. *Off.* II. 60; cf. also Dem. XIII. *Syntaxis* 28, Aeschin. II. *Embassy* 105)—but Heliodorus' figure cannot be correct for the Propylaea alone.

146

Calendar of sacrifices from the Athenian deme of Thoricus, *c*.430

A marble *stele*, from which the top left corner has been cut. First seen at Keratea in 1960. Acquired by the J. Paul Getty Museum in 1979 and returned to Greece in 2012. Now in the Epigraphical Museum in Athens. Phot. Daux (1983), pls. I and II; (*GMusJ*) fig. 1; Whitehead, *The Demes of Attica*, 195; *NGSL* figs. 3–7.

Ionic letters. Main face, *stoichedon* 30 (but the cutter regularly inscribes two contiguous *iotas* in a single *stoichos* and also so combines *tau* and *iota* in 57); sides not *stoichedon*.

G. Daux, *AC* lii 1983, 150–74, with corrections in *BCH* cviii 1984, 399–400 (= *SEG* xxxiii 147); Daux, *GMusJ* xii 1984, 145–52; *NGSL* 1*. Trans. Parker (below), 144–5; *NGSL* pp. 121–3; Kearns, *Ancient Greek Religion*, 224–5 (ll. 1–57). See also R. C. T. Parker, in Linders & Nordquist (edd.), *Gifts for the Gods*, 139–47; *IG* i³ 256 bis (without text); Rosivach, *The System of Public Sacrifice in Fourth-Century Athens*, 22–9; M. H. Jameson, in Goldhill & Osborne (edd.), *Performance Culture and Athenian Democracy*, 328–31.

[—— 19 —— Ἑκ]ạτομβαιῶν-
[ος —— 19 ——]ΑΚΙ καὶ τοῖ-
[ς —— 18 —— ἄ]ριστομ παρέ-
[χεν —— 14 —— δρα]χμὴν ἑκατερ-
[ο —— 19 ——] ΑΙ τὴν πρηρο[σ]-
[ίαν —— 14 —— Δελ]φίνιον αἶγ[α]
[—— 20 ——]ΕΑΙ Ἑκάτηι [.]
[—— 22 ——]ΗΝΟΣΑΤΗ [.]
[—— 18 ——] τέλεομ πρατό[ν].
[Μεταγειτνιῶνος, Διὶ Κατ]αιβάτῃι ẹ̓ṇ ṭ-
[ῶι σηκῶι π̣[αρ]ὰ τὸ [Δελφίνι]ọṇ ṭέλεον πρ-
ατόν : ὁρκωμόσιον π̣ạ[ρέ]χεν ἐς εὐθύνας.
Βοηδρομιῶνος, Πρηρόσια : Διὶ Πολιεῖ κρ-
ιτὸν οἶν : χοῖρον κριτόν, ἐπ' Αὐτομένας,
χοῖρον ὠνητὸν ὁλόκαυτον, τῶι ἀκολου-
θõντι ἄριστομ παρέχεν τὸν ἱερέα· : Κεφ-
άλωι οἶν κριτόν, : Πρόκριδι τράπεζαν· *v*
Θορίκωι κριτὸν οἶν : Ἡρωΐνησι Θορίκο
τράπεζαν : ἐπὶ Σούνιον Ποσειδῶνι ἀμν-
ὸν κριτόν : Ἀπόλλωνι χίμαρον κριτόν, Κ-
ουροτρόφωι χοῖρον κριτήν : Δήμητρι τέλ[εο]-
[ν], Διῒ Ἑρκείωι τέλεον, Κοροτρόφωι χοῖρ[ον],
[[Ἀθηναίαι οἶν πρατόν]] ἐφ' ἁλῆι Ποσ[ειδῶνι]
ṭέλεον, Ἀπόλλωνι χοῖρον. *vacat*

1 [τάδε θύεται Θορικίοις. Ἑκα]τομβαιῶν|ος Vanderpool. 10 Strictly we cannot be certain that the month name did not appear earlier, at the start of ll. 7, 8 or 9: cf. Humphreys, *The Strangeness of Gods*, 158 n. 70. 14, 47 ΕΠΑΥΤΟΜΕΝΑΣ *NGSL*, ἐπ' αὐτõ μένας (= ἐπ' αὐτοῦ μείνας), 'remaining on the spot/within the sanctuary' S. Scullion, *ZPE* cxxi 1998, 116–19.

– – – During Hecatombaeon – – – to — and to the – – – provide lunch – – (*from right side at ll.* 4–6 <at Mykenos – – – a full-grown victim – – – sacrifice a sheep at the Panathenaea, sold>); – – – a drachma each – – – the Prerosia – – – at the Delphinium, a she-goat – – – for Hecate – – – a full-grown victim, sold.

10 During Metageitnion: for Zeus Kataibates in the enclosure at the Delphinium a full-grown victim, sold; (*from left side at l.* 12) <for Phoenix, a full-grown victim>; provide an oath-victim at the audit.

13 During Boedromion: the Prerosia: for Zeus Polieus a choice sheep, a choice piglet; at Automenae a piglet, bought, to be burnt whole, the priest to provide lunch for the acolyte; for Cephalus a choice sheep; for Procris an offering-table; for Thoricus a choice sheep; for the Heroines of Thoricus an offering table; at Sunium for Poseidon a choice lamb; for Apollo a choice one-year-old goat; for Kourotrophos a choice female piglet; for Demeter a full-grown victim; for Zeus Herkeios a full-grown victim; for Kourotrophos a piglet; for Athena a sheep, to be sold; at the Salt Pan for Poseidon a full-grown victim; for Apollo a piglet.

Πυανοψιῶνος, Διῒ Καταιβάτηι ἐμ [Φιλομ]-
η<λ>ιδῶν τέλεον πρατόν, ἕκτηι ἐ[πὶ δέκα]
Νεανίαι τέλεον, Πυανοψίοις, Π[— 6 —]
Μαιμακτηριῶνος, Θορίκωι βοῦ[ν μῆλατ]-
τον ἤ τετταράκοντα δραχμῶν [μέχρι πε]-
ντήκοντα, Ἡρωΐνησι Θορίκο τ[ράπεζαν].
Ποσιδειῶνος, Διονύσια. *vacat*
Γαμηλιῶνος, Ἥραι, Ἱερῶι Γάμωι [— 7 —]
Ἀνθεστηριῶνος, Διονύσωι, δω[δεκάτηι],
αἶγα λειπεγνώμονα πυρρὸν ἢ [μέλανα, Δ]-
ιασίοις, Διὶ Μιλιχίωι οἶν πρα[τόν. *vac.*]
Ἐλαφηβολιῶνος, Ἡρακλείδα[ις τέλεον],
Ἀλκμήνηι τέλεον, Ἀνάκοιν τ[έλεον, Ἑλέ]-
νηι τέλεον, Δήμητρι, τὴν χλο[ῖαν, οἶν κρ]-
ιτὴν κυōσαν, Δὶ ἄρνα κριτόν. *vacat*
Μουνυχιῶνος, Ἀρτέμιδι Μουνυχ[ίαι τέλε]-
{ε}ον, ἐς Πυθίο Ἀπόλλωνος τρίτ[τοαν, κορ]-
οτρόφωι χοῖρον, Λητοῖ αἶγα, Ἀ[ρτέμιδι]
αἶγα, Ἀπόλλωνι αἶγα λειπογνώ[μονα, Δή]-
μητρι : οἶν κυōσαν ἄνθειαν, Φιλ[ωνίδι τρ]-
άπεζαν, Διονύσωι, ἐπὶ Μυκηνον, [τράγον]
πυρρὸν ἢ μέλανα. *vacat*
Θαργηλιῶνος, Διῒ ἐπ' Αὐτομένας, [κριτὸν]
ἄρνα, Ὑπερπεδίωι οἶν, Ἡρωΐνησι̣[ν Ὑπερ]-
πεδίο τράπεζαν, Νίσωι οἶν, Θρασ[— 5 —]
οἶν, Σωσινέωι οἶν, Ῥογίωι οἶν, Πυ[λόχωι]
χοῖρον, Ἡρωΐνησι Πυλοχίσι τρά[πεζαν].
Σκιροφοριῶνος, ὁρκωμόσιον <π>αρ[έχεν, Π]-
λυντηρίοις Ἀθηναίαι οἶν κρι[τόν, Ἀγλ]-
αύρωι οἶν, Ἀθηναίαι ἄρνα κριτ[όν, Κεφά]-
λωι βοῦν μηλάττονος ἢ τεττα[ράκοντα]
δραχμῶν μέχρι πεντήκοντα, Π[ρόκριδι]
οἶΔν : τόν δ'εὔθυνον ὀμόσαι καὶ τ[ὸς παρέδ]-
ρος εὐθυνῶ τὴν ἀρχὴν ἣν ἔλαχ[ον εὐθύν]-
εν κατὰ τὰ ψηφίσματα ἐφ'οἷς ἐ[γκαθέστ]-
η̣κ̣εν ἡ ἀρχή, ὀμνύναι Δία, Ἀπόλλ̣[ω, Δήμητρ]-
α ἐξώλειαν ἐπαρώμενον, καὶ [τὸς παρέδ]-
ρος κατὰ ταὐτά, ἀναγρά{ι}ψαι [δὲ τὸν ὅρκ]-
[ο]ν ἐστήληι καὶ καταθεῖναι π[αρὰ τὸ Δελ<φί>]-
[ν]ιον, ὅσαι δ' ἂν ἀρχαὶ αἱρεθῶ- [*vacat*]
σιν ὑπευθύνος ἓναι ἁπάσα[ς. *vacat*]

27 Π[οσειδῶ] (i.e. Π[οσειδῶ]<νι>), Daux, π[ρατόν] Parker, π[ύανα] Jameson. 57 two small *deltas* were inscribed after the *iota* in the second letter-space to indicate the price of the victim, 20 drachmas.

25 During Pyanopsion: for Zeus Kataibates in Philomelidae, a full-grown victim, to be sold; on the sixteenth a full-grown victim for Young Man; at the Pyanopsia – – – (*from left side at ll.* 30–2) <for Apollo, a full-grown victim at the Pyanopsia>.

28 During Maemacterion: for Thoricus a cow worth not less than 40–50 drachmas; for the Heroines of Thoricus an offering-table.

31 During Poseideon: the Dionysia.

32 During Gamelion: for Hera at the Sacred Marriage – – –

33 During Anthesterion: for Dionysus, on the twelfth, a she-goat lacking full-grown teeth, tawny or black; at the Diasia, to Zeus Meilichios a sheep, to be sold.

36 During Elaphebolion: for the children of Heracles, a full-grown victim; for Alcmene a full-grown victim; for the two Anakes [= Dioscuri], a full-grown victim; for Helen, a full-grown victim; for Demeter, the *chloia* offering, a choice pregnant ewe; for Zeus a choice lamb.

40 During Munychion: for Artemis Munychia a full-grown victim; at the sanctuary of Pythian Apollo a triple-victim; for Kourotrophos a piglet; for Leto a she-goat; for Artemis a she-goat; for Apollo a she-goat lacking full-grown teeth; for Demeter a pregnant ewe, the *antheia* offering; for Philonis an offering-table; (*from left side at l.* 42/*right side at l.* 44) <for Zeus Herkeios, a sheep>; for Dionysus at Mykenos a tawny or black he-goat.

47 During Thargelion: for Zeus at Automenae a choice lamb; for Hyperpedius a sheep; for the Heroines of Hyperpedius an offering-table; for Nisus a sheep; for Thras— a sheep; for Sosineus a sheep; for Rhogius a sheep; for Pylochus a piglet; for the Heroines of Pylochus an offering-table.

52 During Scirophorion: provide an oath-sacrifice; at the Plynteria for Athena a choice sheep; for Aglauros a sheep; for Athena a choice lamb; for Cephalos a cow worth not less than 40–50 drachmas; for Procris a sheep 10/10; (*from left side at l.*58) < for the heroines of Coroneia, a sheep.>

57 The auditor (*euthynos*) and his assistants are to swear 'I will hold the audit (*euthynein*) of the magistracy which I have been allotted to audit according to the decree by which the magistracy is established'. To swear by Zeus, Apollo, Demeter, cursing destruction on himself, and the assistants in the same way. And to write up the oath on the *stele* and stand it at the Delphinium. All magistracies are to be subject to audit, as many so ever are elected.

Additions to the text inscribed on the sides of the *stele*.

Left side:
At the level of l. 31 and the interspace between ll. 31–2 (Daux conjectures that this is a supplement to l. 27):

[Ἀπόλ]-
λωνι τέλεον Πυ-
ανοψίοις

At the level of l. 42 (cf. right side at l. 44)

-ι Ἑρκείωι ⁝ οἶν

At the level of l. 58:

-ωΐνησιν Κορωνέων ⁝ οἶν

Right side:
At the level of ll. 4–6:

Μυκηνω[ι] τέ[λεον – – –]
[– –]/αν οἶν Παναθ[ηναί]-
οις θύεν πρατ[όν]

At the level of l. 12:

Φοίνικι τέλ[εον]

At the level of l. 44 (cf. left side at l. 42):

[Διὶ Ἑ]ρκείωι ⁝ ọị̂ν

This offering would be in place in l. 44 before that to Philonis. Daux suggests that on the left side this same correction was made, but, since it was improperly placed, it was repeated on the right side.

Left side at 31 [Ἀπόλ] | λωνι Parker, Jameson: ωνι Daux, *NGSL*. Right side at 4–6 Jameson, 330 n. 32: Ị Μυκηνọ[ν – – – | .]Ạ N οἶν [:]N[– – –] | ΙΣỌ[– – –] Daux, *NGSL*.

Sacrificing together was fundamental for all groups of Greeks, from the family up, and from collections of states in amphictyonies and leagues down. Sacrifices were made both to commemorate particular events (cf. R&O 1; for sacrifice before battle see M. H. Jameson, in Hanson (ed.), *Hoplites*, 197–227) and on a regular schedule which required a calendar. We know a calendar of sacrifices to have been part of Solon's laws passed in the early sixth century, and when Solon's laws were republished in the late fifth century (see on **183**) a prosecutor tried to make a case against one of those responsible on the grounds that they had abolished some sacrifices to which the gods were accustomed and invented others (Lys. xxx. *Nicomachus*, with S. C. Todd, in Foxhall & Lewis (edd.), *Greek Law in its Political Setting*, 101–31; for remains of the late-fifth-century sacred calendar see S. D. Lambert, *BSA* xcvii 2002, 353–99).

Various fragments of sacrificial calendars survive from fifth-century Athens, the earliest known being that found on the Athenian acropolis and recording sacrifices both on the acropolis itself and at the sanctuary of Zeus Meilichios and Meter in Agrae (*IG* i^3 234), which dates to shortly after the Persian Wars. That calendar may relate to the city as a whole, but other fragmentary fifth-century inscriptions relate to subgroups of the city (e.g. *IG* i^3 246, 255), including demes (e.g. Paeania, *IG* i^3 250; cf. also **107**).

The calendar here is the best-preserved of fifth-century calendars. The fifth-century date rests both on letter forms (which are close to those of **144**) and on the form of the dative in Ἡρωΐνησι (ll. 18, 30, 48, 51, and left side at 58: on this as a dating criterion see Introduction, p. xxviii). The combination of calendar with regulations for the audit of officials marks this as belonging to a deme (cf. R&O 63 from the nearby deme of Hagnous, and above **107**) and the find-spot and repeated mention of the hero Thoricus and heroines of Thoricus (18, 28–30) identify the deme as Thoricus.

Thoricus was a deme modest in size, returning five men (= 1 per cent) to the council annually in the fourth century, which suggests a deme population of 300–500 adult male citizens in the fifth century, but of great antiquity, being reputed to be one of the original twelve towns of Attica (Strabo 397 / IX. i. 20). The settlement, which clusters round a conical hill on the north side of a relatively sheltered bay, is well known archaeologically and has yielded substantial late Bronze Age tholos tombs, which may have been associated with some of the heroes mentioned in the calendar, as well as cemetery, industrial workings (washeries), residential and religious buildings.[1] It lies towards the northern end of the silver-mining area, and there is evidence of mining on the site of the town itself; members of the deme of Thoricus are recorded in the fourth-century *poletai* records both as lessees of mines and as owners of the land on which mines stood (cf. R&O 36).

The calendar seems to have begun with a short heading (perhaps something like 'These sacrifices are made by the Thoriciots') and then the name of the first month of the Attic year, Hecatombaeon (July). The calendar does not provide dates during the month for the sacrifices, nor does it identify who in particular is responsible for them. Twice, or possibly three times, it provides prices for the victims, but, in contrast to the fourth-century deme calendar from Erchia (*SEG* xxi 541) it does not do so systematically. What then is its purpose?

The notable feature of this calendar is its concern with the audit of magistrates. The entries for Metageitnion (August) and Scirophorion (June), the second and last months of the Athenian year, include provision of an oath-victim for the audit, and the text ends with the oath taken by the auditor. That oath is a general-purpose oath, relating to the audit of any magistrate, but it is reasonable to think that the link between the oath and the rest of the inscription is that this inscription lays down what the magistrates will be expected to have done when it comes to their audit. If that is the case then one would expect the magistrates responsible for these sacrifices to be the demarch and the deme's financial officials, who provide money for purchase of victims and receive income from such victims as are sold. Although priests were also subject to audit (cf. R&O 46), the range of cults here cannot have been the responsibility of a single priest. What we have in this calendar is a list of those sacrifices that the deme as a whole insisted should be made; we would expect those sacrifices to be open to all members of the deme, and although we cannot know how many went on any particular occasion the size of the animals involved (a single sheep or a goat will yield around 20 kg. of meat, see Rosivach 157, and so feed perhaps just over 100 people) suggests substantial numbers.

Some of the sacrifices listed here seem to be independent, but others are on the occasion of festivals (the Panathenaea, the Prerosia, the Pyanopsia, the Dionysia, the Gamelia, the Anthesteria, the Diasia, the Mounychia, the Plynteria; for all these

[1] H. F. Mussche, *Fouilles de Thorikos*, ii. *A Mining Town in Attica* for the archaeology; J. Labarbe, *Fouilles de Thorikos*, i. *Les Testimonia* for the literary evidence; J. Bingen, *Pages d'épigraphie grecque, Attique–Égypte (1952–82)*, 27–39. For a general discussion of Thoricus see Osborne, in *Sociable Man . . . N. Fisher*, 28–38; for the remarkable double stoa (once thought to be a temple of Demeter) see M. M. Miles, in Miles (ed.), *Autopsy in Athens: Recent Archaeological Research on Athens and Attica*, 163–80.

festivals see the checklist in Parker, *Polytheism and Society*, 456–87). In the case of the (rural) Dionysia in Poseideon (December), the name of the festival alone seems to substitute for a list of sacrificial activity—perhaps because this festival did not fall to the demarch to organise. Thoricus is the Athenian deme with the oldest extant theatre, with epigraphic evidence of dramatic activity (P. J. Wilson *The Athenian Institution of the Khoregia*, 382 n. 42), and it seems likely that the rural Dionysia was a major event there, as it was in some other demes such as Aexone (Whitehead, 212–22).

For festivals other than the Dionysia, specific sacrifices are prescribed. So for the Prerosia in August, an ancient festival that anticipates the ploughing season, sacrifices are made to Zeus Polieus (as at Hagnous, R&O 63. 32–3, where the demarch is explicitly responsible) although elsewhere this festival is associated with Demeter. For the Pyanopsia (in Pyanopsion, October), in an addition on the left side of the stone, sacrifices are made to Apollo (Harpocration π 120 Keaney Πυανόψια says that almost all writers on Athenian festivals said that the Pyanopsia was celebrated for Apollo). For the Sacred Marriage (*Hieros Gamos*) that was the centre of the Theogamia or Gamelia after which the month Gamelion was named, sacrifices are made to Hera, whose marriage with Zeus was celebrated (parallel to those made by the deme Erchia in the fourth century, *SEG* xxi 541. *B*. 32–9, *C*. 38–41, and cf. the sacrifice to Zeus Heraios in the fifth-century sacred calendar from the acropolis, *IG* i^3 234. 20–1). At the Plynteria, centrally celebrated in Thargelion (May) but here (and probably in Erchia, *SEG* xxi 541. *A*. 57–65, *B*. 55–9, *C*. 59–64, *D*. 56–60: see N. Robertson, *HSCP* lxxxvii 1983, 281) in Scirophorion (June), the month that the Parians and Thasians called Plynterion (**103**. *B*. I. 2; Trümpy, *Untersuchungen zu den altgriechischen Monatsnamen und Monatsfolgen*, 71–2), sacrifice is made to Athena and Aglaurus (cf. Hesychius *s.v. Plynteria*).

The festivals celebrated, or at least marked by sacrifices, in this deme are festivals of long standing, and their celebration here may be of great antiquity (as e.g the differences in date of celebration of the Plynteria might suggest). The Thoriciots celebrate Poseidon outside the deme at Sunium, but whether the other sacrifices 'by the Delphinium', 'at the Salt Pan', 'at Automenai', 'in Philomelidai' involve leaving the deme is not clear. For the sacrifice to Apollo in Munychion the direction 'to the sanctuary of Pythian Apollo' occurs, but whether this sanctuary is the Pythion in Athens, at Daphni, or at Thoricus itself is not apparent. One festival that seems likely to be celebrated in Athens itself is the Panathenaea (where, at least in the fourth century, the meat from the publicly sacrificed cows was distributed to the people by demes, see R&O 82. *B*. 24–7). While the other festivals may have had a history in the deme as long as their history in the town, the Panathenaea, like the procedure of audit, would be an aspect of central Athenian life taken up by the demes (Scambonidae as well as here, see **107**; cf. Parker, *Polytheism*, 75–8). Parker (in *Gifts to the Gods*, 142) suggests that the sacrifice at the Diasia took place at Agrae rather than at Thoricus because this is a festival for which Erchians go to town (*LSCG* 18. *A*. 37–43, cf. Jameson, *BCH* lxxxix 1965, 159–67) and Thucydides (I. 126. i) says that the festival is celebrated by the whole people. We should beware of imposing uniform practice, however, and there is no sign here of an out-of-deme sacrifice. It is even more doubtful that the sacrifice of a goat to Dionysus on the main day of the Anthesteria took place in the city (as A. Henrichs, in *Cabinet of the Muses . . . T. G. Rosenmeyer*, 260–4, suggests). In the absence of precise dates we do not know whether the deme celebration was exactly coincident with the central festival–except in as far as we know that the Thoriciot celebration of the Plynteria was in a different month. It may be that demesmen could sometimes celebrate both centrally and locally at slightly different moments.

Apparently outside the context of festivals are the various sacrifices to Demeter, who receives three sacrifices in the course of the year (ll. 21 in Boedromion (September), 38 in Elaphebolion (March), and 43–4 in Munychion (April)). The two spring sacrifices are called 'green shoot' and 'flowery' sacrifices, both of them pregnant ewes, emphasising the links with the agricultural year (see generally Brumfield, *The Attic Festivals of Demeter and their Relation to the Agricultural Year*). Thoricus features in the *Homeric Hymn to Demeter* (l. 126), which may imply her cultic importance from an early date.

One striking feature of this calendar, as of some other local calendars such as that of the Tetrapolis (S. D. Lambert, in J. Blok, F. van den Eijnde and R. Strootman, forthcoming), is the part played by heroes and heroines (Parker, in *Gifts to the Gods*; Kearns, *The Heroes of Attica*; Larson, *Greek Heroine Cults*, 27–34; Ekroth, *The Sacrificial Rituals of Greek Hero Cults*, 150–69). There are twenty-eight sacrifices to gods, twenty-three to heroes or heroines. Sacrifice to heroes and/or heroines occurs in nine of the eleven months for which entries are complete. We find individual male heroes, pairs of hero and heroine or heroines, a group of heroes, and perhaps some independent heroines. Among the individual male heroes, Neanias ('Young Man') is known at Marathon (*ZPE* cxxx 2000, 43–70, ii. 21) and elsewhere in Attica (*Agora* xix, L6. 141), but Phoenix only here. Among the pairs of heroes and heroines we can find some clear local connections: Cephalus and Procris are localised at Thoricus in literature (Apollodorus II. 4. vii); Helen is supposed to have stayed on the island of Helene (Makronisi) just off the coast of Thoricus on her way back from Troy (Paus. I. 35. ii), though she is worshipped here with her brothers the Anakes (Dioscuri) who appear in Attica at an earlier stage in Helen's life to rescue her from Theseus (a story not otherwise connected to Thoricus). But we know of no connection to Thoricus (as opposed to Attica more generally) for the children of Heracles and their mother Alcmene, nor for Nisus. The groups of hero plus related heroines (Thoricus and the heroines of Thoricus, Hyperpedius and the heroines of Hyperpedius, Pylochus and the Pylochian heroines) are all unique to Thoricus. Most demes seem to have worshipped an eponymous hero (cf. Erchius at Erchia, Marathon/Marathus at Marathon; Kearns, *The Heroes of Attica*, 101–2) but the closest parallel for linked heroes and heroines is in the Tetrapolis calendar where some heroes seem linked to nameless heroines. Both Pylochus ('Gate-Holder') and Hyperpedius ('Above the Plain') are speaking names with plausible topographical associations, and it is attractive to see these as guardians of the deme in general and of particular places within it (Parker, in *Gifts to the Gods*). Among the individual heroes/heroines Philonis, who is said to have been seduced by both Apollo and Hermes, is a figure already localised at Thoricus by literary sources (Conon *FGrH* 26 F 1. 7), but Thras—, Sosineus and Rogius are unknown and the 'heroines of the Coroneans' are a mystery (Boeotian Coronea seems too far away to be relevant).

The heroes and heroines in this calendar are very much not second-class citizens to the gods, although heroines are subordinate to heroes. Procris (once), Philonis and the heroines closely associated with a hero receive only offering tables, but the other heroes and heroines receive significant victims: Thoricus a sheep and then a cow; Cephalus a sheep and then a cow; the Heracleidae, Hyperpedius, Nisus, Thras—, Sosineus, Rogius, Procris (on the second occasion) and the Heroines of the Coroneians sheep; Pylochus a sucking-pig; Neanias, Alcmene, the Anakes and Helen full-grown victims. The cluster of sacrifices in Boedromion to Thoricus and the heroines of Thoricus and to Procris and Cephalus may mark the celebration of the festival of the dead, the Genesia; Procris' father, Erechtheus, received sacrifices in the city Genesia (see S. D. Lambert, *ZPE* cxxxix 2002, 81).

This calendar gives fewer details of cult practice than we find in the Erchia calendar, but we have at least one holocaust sacrifice (15; and presumably another in l. 3, where again the servant has to have lunch provided since the sacrifice does not leave anything to eat). The calendar does regularly describe the victim as full-grown, insist that it be choice or declare it 'bought' or 'sold'. Whether there is a difference between the ἀμνὸν κριτόν of ll. 19–20 and the ἄρνα κριτόν of ll. 39, 47–8 and 54, both translated above as 'choice lamb', is not clear. It is specified that the piglet for holocaust sacrifice should be bought, which raises the question of how the other victims are acquired (purchase is implied elsewhere when a lower limit is placed on the cost of a cow; for costs of sacrificial victims compare R&O 37. 85–94, 81. 16–25). Although Rosivach (23 n. 40) wondered whether 'bought' and 'sold' might actually mean the same thing ('bought by' or 'sold to' the deme) it seems more likely that 'sold' indicates what is to be done with the victim once the god's and priest's share has been taken since explicit provision for sale of the victim is made only (given the erasure in l. 23) when the occasion includes only a single sacrifice and has been made at a specified, perhaps remote, location: these appear to be sacrifices which, like holocaust sacrifices, involve no feasting (Jameson, in *Performance Culture*, 329–31). Provision for sale of victims is otherwise rare, but paralleled in **107**.

147

Accounts of the Delian temples, 434–432

A fragment of a marble *stele*, the left side preserved, found in Athens, now lost.

Ionic letters: the numerals are slightly larger than the remaining letters. Only ll. 1–6 *stoichedon*.

M&L 62; *I. Délos* 89; *IG* i³ 402; Chankowski, *Athènes et Délos à l'époque classique*, no. 1*. Trans. Fornara 141. See also Chankowski, 127–34, 311–12.

– – – A – – –
Διοφ – – –
Ξανθῆς
Βολακλῆς
Δημοθάλης
Ἀναξίδημος
[– – – – – – – – – παρ]ὰ Δηλίων ὀφελόντ[ων – – – – – – – – – – – – – – – – –]
[– – – – – – – – – – – –]εγένετο καὶ αἱ παρα[– – – – – – – – – – – – – – – – – –]
[.... κεφάλαιον – – –] ϛύμπαν 𐅇𐅆ΗΗΗΗΔ[– – – – – – – – – – – – – – – – – – – –]
[— c.16 —]σιον τὸ βαλανεῖον ὥρισαν, Τ[– – – – – – – – – – – – – – –]
[— c.7 —ωικοδ]όμησαν, τὴν Ῥήνειαν ὥρισαν. ἀν[αλόματος κεφάλαιον — c.6 —]
[. . ἀργύριον] ἐδάνειϛαν 𐅈ΤΤΤΤΔΔ ⁝ ἐπιδε[κάτοις τόκοις πέντε ἔτη, ὥστε ἀπο]-
[διδόναι τὸ]ς δανεισαμένος 𐅉ΤΤΤΧΧΧΔ[ΔΔ ⁝ τό τε ἀρχαῖον καὶ τὸς τόκος ὧν]
[ἐδα]νείσαντο· χρόνος ἄρχει Μεταγειτνιὼν μὴν Ἀθήν[ησιν ἄρχοντος – – –],
[ἐν] Δήλωι δὲ Βουφονιὼν μὴν ἄρχοντος Εὐπτέρος. [τὴν γῆν τὴν ἐν Δήλωι τὴν]
[ἱ]ερὰν ἐμίσθωσαν καὶ τὸς κήπος καὶ τὰς οἰκίας καὶ [. . . . δέκα ἔτη (?)· χρόνος ἄρ]-
[χ]ει Ποσιδηιὼν μὴν Ἀθήνησι ἄρχοντος Κράτητος, ἐ[ν Δήλωι δὲ – – – μ]-
[ὴ]ν ἄρχοντος Εὐπτέρος· ὥστε ἀποδιδόναι τὴμ μίσθωσ[ιν ἁπάντων τούτων τὸς με]-
[μ]ισθωμένος κατὰ τὰς ξυγγραφάς· μισθώσεως κεφ[άλαιον τὸ μὲν πρώτο ἔτος]
𐅅ΗΗΔ𐅃⊢ ⁝ τῶν δὲ ἄλλων ἐτῶν ⁝ 𐅅ΗΗΗ[— c.7 —]τὴν γῆν τὴν ἐν Ῥηνεί]-
αι τὴν ἱερὰν ἐμίσθωσαν δέκα ἔτη· χρόνος [ἄρχει Ἀθήνησι – – – – – – – – – – –]
μὴν ἄρχοντος Ἀψεύδος, ἐν Δήλωι Ἱερὸς [μὴν ἄρχοντος – – – – – – – – – – – –]
ρο· ὥστε ἀποδιδόναι τὸμ μεμισθωμέ[νον τὸ ἔτος ἑκάστο τὴν μίσθ]-
ωσιν ⁝ ΤΧΗΔ ⁝ τὴν θάλατταν τὴν πο[– – – – – – – – – – – – – – – – – – – –]
[. . . .] τὴν ἐν Ῥηνείαι ἐμίσθωσαν δέκα [ἔτη –].

10 [τὰ κεραμεῖα ? οἷς πλη?]σιον Chankowski. 24–5 τὴν πο[ρφυρευτικὴν? – – –] Chankowski, comparing *I. Délos* 95. 10–12 with *I. Délos* 102. 14–16 τὴν πο[λύκολπον περὶ Ῥηνείας καὶ τὴν λί|μνην] τὴν ἐν Ῥηνείαι O. Hansen, *Eranos* lxxxv 1987, 100 (*SEG* xxxvii 32).

The decision in 478, when Athens took over the leadership of the campaign against Persia, that the treasury of the alliance of Greek states involved should be at Delos (above, **119**) was highly symbolic. Delos had long been seen as central to the

1 —A—, Dioph—, Xanthes, Boulacles, Demothales, Anaxidemus.

7 – – – from the Delians who owe – – – as with those from – – – Total 55,410+ dr.

10 – – – they drew up the boundaries for the – – – bath – – – they built, they drew up the boundaries for Rheneia – – – they loaned 9 tal. 20 dr. at 10 per cent interest for five years, so that those who borrowed are to give back, capital and interest on the money they borrowed, 13 tal. 3,030 dr. The period begins with the month Metageitnion at Athens, when Apseudes is archon, and on Delos the month Bouphonion, when Eupteres is archon.

15 They rented out the sacred land on Delos along with the gardens and the buildings and – – – for ten years. The period begins in the month Poseideon at Athens, when Crates is archon, and on Delos in the month Lenaeon when Eupteres is archon, so that the lessees pay the rent of all these according to the contracts. Total of the rent of the first year, 716 dr.; and for the other years 800+ dr.

20 They rented out the sacred land on Rheneia for ten years. The period begins – – – when Apseudes is archon, on Delos in the month Hieros when —— is archon – – – so that the lessee pays for each year the rent 1 tal. 1,110 dr.

24 The sea – – – the one in Rheneia, they rented out for ten years – – –

Cyclades (cf. Strabo 485 / x. v. 1) and the cult of Delian Apollo already extended beyond Delos itself, but that 'Athens and its allies', which seems to be the only ancient way of referring to the 'Delian League', should make its formal centre a place other than Athens was striking. The Athenians had already laid claim to the island and purified it in the sixth century, and they must have been confident that they continued to have it under control. The formal position of Delos during the period when the League treasury remained at Delos is explicit in none of our documentation, but scholars generally believe that the later arrangment of a sixtieth being offered to Athena (**119**) was anticipated by a share of allied tribute being given to Apollo (e.g. Chankowski, 39–40). This document, the earliest of what will be an extensive set of Delian accounts, found both at Athens and on Delos (cf. R&O 28), provides our best evidence for the relationship between Athens and Delos in the middle of the fifth century after the League treasury had moved to Athens.

The document has lost its heading, but begins with a series of names, two of which are unattested at Athens and which are unlikely all to be names of Athenians (Demothales is a name attested only on Delos; Anaxidemus is a name known in the Aegean but not in Athens). This could be a Delian board, a joint Athenian and Delian board, or the board of a Delian amphictyony made up of Athenians, Delians and others from the Cyclades. The name *amphiktyones* (spelled with *upsilon* by the Athenians where the Delphians use *iota*) for the Delian sanctuary administrators is first attested in 410/09 (*I. Délos* 93 = *IG* i^3 1460, found on Delos), when four Athenians are listed as in charge; whether the officials in our inscription were called *amphiktyones* or whether the Athenians invented that name, which certainly does not seem to have existed in the archaic period, only after the purification of 426 and subsequent reorganisation of the Delian festival calendar (Thuc. III. 104), or after the expulsion of Delians in 422 and their return in 421 (Thuc. V. 1, 32. i), is not clear. The double dating system, along with the find-spot at Athens, indicates that the Delian accounts are under Athenian oversight, though the presence of a Delian archon indicates that some form of independent administration continued on Delos.

This document is not a detailed listing of the financial activities of the officials, but a summary of what they have done. Rather than individual properties, separate categories of income are listed: income from debtors, new monetary loans, property rented on Delos, property rented on Rheneia, and probably fishing rights on Rheneia (for which compare the 'great income' from two sacred lakes near Ephesus, Strabo 642 / XIV. i. 26). The categories are not listed in the order in which the financial activities occurred; because the Athenian archon year ran from midsummer to midsummer and the Delian archon year from midwinter to midwinter, we can work out that the properties on Delos (ll. 15–20) were rented from the first half of 433 (Athenian month Poseideon, Delian month Lenaeon), the loans (ll. 12–15) ran from the second half of 433 (Athenian month Metageitnion, here Delian month Bouphonion: normally Delian Bouphonion corresponded with

Athenian Boedromion but in this year the Delian calendar appears to have been running ahead of the Athenian) and the properties on Rheneia (ll. 20–4) from the first half of 432 (Delian month Hieros; it is not possible to restore the Athenian month since it is not clear whether 432 was an intercalary year at Athens). It looks here as if the properties are rented according to the Delian year (of which Lenaeon was the first month; in 432 they were a month late starting, perhaps because of the prior definition of boundaries as recorded in ll. 10–11), but the loans were made according to the Athenian year (of which Metageitnion is the second month, but these magistrates seem to have been appointed according to the Panathenaic year, which began only on 28 Hecatombaeon: cf. on **144**). The Athenian officials have taken full responsibility for the loans, while the rental of properties, which demanded a presence 'on the ground', has been left with the Delian officials (Chankowski, 130–1) although conducted, as at Athens, in accordance with the terms of a general master document or contract (*syngraphe*) (ll. 18–19, cf. **167**. 6–7 and Papazarkadas, *Sacred and Public Land*, 82 n. 284). In the fourth century Athenians are prominent taking leases (along with Delians and occasionally men from Rheneia and Tenos), and we should not exclude the possibility of their presence in this case too.

This document, by contrast to the accounts from Rhamnous (**134**), is explicit about the interest rate for the loans: 10 per cent (l. 12), a rate maintained by Delos in the fourth century (cf. R&O 28). The picture given by this document is clearly incomplete, but if the new loans here of just over 9 tal. and their term of five years are typical we would appear to have a rather lower level of activity than in the 370s, when several cities borrow 3 tal. or more and Paros borrows 48 tal. (R&O, p. 144; see further Chankowski, 311–4), though something like five times as great as in the Athenian deme of Rhamnous. More striking than the sum of money loaned is the high rate of return on loans and the high rent for properties on Rheneia—apparently 1 tal. 1,110 dr. is paid by a single lessee in rent for property on this larger island neighbour of Delos, an island which probably paid only 300 dr. tribute at this point (300 dr. in 450/49, *IG* i³ 263. iv. 29; but in 425/4 it would be assessed for 1,000 dr.: *IG* i³ 71. i. 82). The Rheneia properties were rented for between 1 tal. 2 dr. and 1 tal. 992 dr. in 410/09 (*I. Délos* 93. 21 = *IG* i³ 1460. 21), and for sums of 1 tal. 610 dr. and just under 1 tal. 400 dr. in the 370s (R&O 28. 26–8, 64–5, and p. 145); by the end of the fourth century their rent has increased by around 25 per cent (but rents on Delos itself by more than 200 per cent: Chankowski, 288). There seem to have been eleven separate farms (later ten) leased on Rheneia from the 360s onwards, all on the southern part of the island, but these farms remained larger than those on Delos, and arguably beyond the means of many, reducing the competition to rent them (Chankowski, 283–4, 287–92; note also J. Kent, *Hesperia* xvii 1948, 243–338) from which wealthy Athenians benefited.

148

Payments for Athens' expeditions to Corcyra, 433/2

Part of a marble *stele*, with the right-hand and bottom margins preserved, found on the Athenian acropolis, now in the Epigraphical Museum. Phot. *AJA*^{2} xxxiii 1929, 399 fig. 1; Meritt, *AFD*, 70 fig. 10; facs. Meritt, 71 fig. 11.

Developed Attic writing, using h except with ἑμέραι (ll. 11, 22). *Stoichedon* 33–5, ending the line with the end of a syllable (Johnson).

IG i^2 295; M&L 61; *IG* i^3 364*. Trans. Fornara 126. See also J. Johnson, *AJA*^{2} xxxiii 1929, 398–400; Meritt, *AFD*, 68–71; C. Triebel-Schubert, *QC* vi 1984, 355–75 (*SEG* xxxiv 32).

[Ἀθεναῖοι ἀνέλ]οσαν ἐς Κόρκυρα[ν τάδε. ἐπὶ Ἀ]-
[φσεύδος ἄρχο]ντος καὶ ἐπὶ τε̃ς βολε̃ς hε̃ι Κρ[ι]-
[τιάδες Φαένο] Τειθράσιος προ̃τος ἐγραμμά-
[τευε, ταμίαι h]ιερο̃ν χρεμάτον τε̃ς Ἀθεναία[ς]
[—⁶— ἐκΚερ]αμέον καὶ χσυνάρχοντες, hοῖς
[Κράτες Ναύ]πονος Λαμπτρεὺς ἐγραμμάτευε,
[παρέδοσα]ν στρατεγοῖς ἐς Κορκύραν τοῖς
[πρότοις ἐκ]πλέοσι Λακεδαιμονίοι Λακιά-
[δει, Προτέαι] Αἰχσονεῖ, Διοτίμοι Εὐονυμεῖ,
[ἐπὶ τε̃ς Αἰαν]τίδος πρυτανείας πρότες πρυ-
[τανευόσες, τ]ρε̃ς καὶ δέκα ἑμέραι ἐσελελυ-
[θυίαι ἐ̃σαν, 𐅉𐅉]𐅈Τ. *vacat*
[ἐπὶ Ἀφσεύδος] ἄρχοντος καὶ ἐπὶ τε̃ς βολε̃ς
[hε̃ι Κριτιάδες] Φαένο Τειθράσιος προ̃τος ἐ-
[γραμμάτευε, τα]μίαι hιερο̃ν χρεμάτον τε̃ς Ἀ-
[θεναίας Προνάπ]ες Ἐρχιεὺς καὶ χσυνάρχον-
[τες, hοῖς Εὐθίας Αἴ]σχρονος Ἀναφλύστιος
[ἐγραμμάτευε, παρέ]δοσαν στρατεγοῖς ἐς Κόρ-
[κυραν τοῖς δευτέρ]οις ἐκπλέοσι Γλαύκονι
[ἐκ Κεραμέον, Μεταγ]ένει Κοιλεῖ, Δρακοντί-
[δει Θοραιεῖ, ἐπὶ τε̃ς] Αἰαντίδος πρυτανείας
[πρότες πρυτανευόσε]ς, τε̃ι τελευτ[αίαι ἑμέ]-
[ραι τε̃ς πρυτανείας, 𐅊]. *vacat*
vacat

The restored names of officials other than generals, on whom see below, are guaranteed by their appearance in other inscriptions. 8 [βοεθοῖς, 19 hυστέρ]οις A. P. Matthaiou, *γραμματεῖον* iv 2015, 70–1, which is possible but not necessarily preferable to the usual restoration. 10, 21–2 It would be possible to restore Λεον]τίδος πρυτανείας πρότες, Αἰαντίδος πρυτανείας | [τρίτες (or even [ὀγδόες or [ἐνάτες), but two and a half (or more) prytanies between the two expeditions would conflict with Thucydides' narrative. 12, 23 It would be possible to restore 𐅊𐅉]𐅈Τ, 𐅋] (66, 100 talents)—or indeed still higher figures—for expeditions of ten and twenty ships respectively, but the lower figures given above are much more likely.

The Athenians spent the following on Corcyra.

1 In the archonship of Apseudes and the council for which Critiades son of Phaeinus of Teithras was first secretary, the treasurers of the sacred monies of Athena, —— of Cerameis and his colleagues, to whom Crates son of Naupon of Lamptrai was secretary, handed over to the generals sailing out first to Corcyra, Lacedaemonius of Laciadae, Proteas of Aexone and Diotimus of Euonymum, in the first prytany, that of Aiantis, when thirteen days of the prytany had elapsed, 26 talents.

13 In the archonship of Apseudes and the council for which Critiades son of Phaeinus of Teithras was first secretary, the treasurers of the sacred monies of Athena, Pronapes of Erchia and his colleagues, to whom Euthias son of Aeschron of Anaphlystus was secretary, handed over to the generals sailing out secondly to Corcyra, Glaucon of Cerameis, Metagenes of Coele and Dracontides of Thorae, in the first prytany, that of Aiantis, on the last day of the prytany, 50 talents.

The first of Thucydides' *aitiai* ('grievances') leading to the Peloponnesian War was a quarrel between Corinth and its colony Corcyra, in which in 433 the Athenians made a defensive alliance with Corcyra and sent first ten ships and subsequently a further twenty to fight in defence of Corcyra. In the battle of Sybota, between the southern end of Corcyra and the mainland, the Corinthians were successful against Corcyra and the first Athenian squadron, but withdrew after the arrival of the second squadron (Thuc. I. 24–55). This inscription allows us to date the battle early in the second prytany of 433/2, about late August.

This *stele* is devoted simply to payments from the treasury of Athena for this campaign: presumably they were intended to cover the whole cost (cf. the payment for the Samian war of 440–439, **138**); if Athena paid for any other campaigning this year that must have been recorded elsewhere. Since the first expedition is described as such, the decision to set up this *stele* must have been made after the campaign had ended. It looks as if from time to time the Athenians decided that the expense of particular expeditions should be accounted for publicly, presumably because of the degree of public interest, and perhaps controversy, that the decision to undertake them had occasioned. These are therefore in some ways comparable to, though not as splendid as, **135**. There are different boards of treasurers for the two payments because their year of office began on 28 Hecatombaeon (i) (cf. **144**, **160**); the naming of one member of each board does not mean that he ranked officially above his colleagues (K. J. Dover, *JHS* lxxx 1960, 61–77 = his *The Greeks and Their Legacy*, 159–80). Triebel-Schubert, who does not believe that the treasurers' year of office was the Panathenaic year (cf. on **144**), argues that the alliance with Corcyra and the first Athenian expedition belong to the summer of 434/3, but this is hard to reconcile with Thucydides, and the first secretary of that year, Metagenes (*IG* i[3] 449, 372–4, 465. 115–16) cannot be restored in 2–3 here.

The names of the generals are given also by Thucydides (supplying patronymics rather than demotics). For the first expedition Thuc. I. 45. ii and the inscription agree. Lacedaemonius (Davies, *APF*, 305–6) was the son of Pericles' mid-century rival Cimon: Plut. *Per.* 29. i thought that appointing him to so small and unambitious an expedition was a move by Pericles to humiliate him; but we do not know whether that is derived from an early source or from later speculation. More probably either Lacedaemonius (like his relative, the historian Thucydides) had abandoned Cimon's political stance and was a supporter of Pericles or, more likely still (since generals were not always supporters of campaigns which they were appointed to command: cf. Nicias' appointment to Sicily in 415), after a close decision to make the alliance (Thuc. I. 44. i) Pericles' opponents were still strong enough in the assembly to have one of their men appointed. He is otherwise attested only as a hipparch in *IG* i^3 511. 2 and as a member of an ad hoc board in *IG* i^3 48 bis. 12; J. D. Morgan interprets *IG* i^3 30 (which mentions in l. 5 a Theran, in l. 6 a shortage of grain and in l. 7 Sparta or Spartans) as reflecting a sequel to his bringing Thera into the Delian League early in the Peloponnesian War (*AJA*^{2} cv 2001, 260–1; page reference given wrongly at *SEG* li 28). Proteas served as general several times in the 430s. Diotimus was from a family prominent over several generations (Davies, *APF* 161–5); he is said to have gone to Neapolis as *nauarchos* (Timaeus *FGrH* 566 F 98: for Athens' involvement there see S. Cataldi, *RFIC* cxvii 1989, 129–80, dating that campaign 433/2, and cf. on **150**) and to Susa as an envoy (Strabo 47 / I. iii. I).

For the second expedition the inscription again names three generals, but Thuc. I. 51. iv names only two, Glaucon and Andocides (cf. [Plut.] *X Or.* 834 C). Some scholars have attempted explanations to save Thucydides' reputation (e.g. Jacoby, commenting on Hellanicus *FGrH* 323a F 24), but it is overwhelmingly likely that Thucydides has made a mistake, perhaps misled by the fact that Andocides (grandfather of the orator, and a general in 441/0: Androtion *FGrH* 324 F 38) and the inscription's Dracontides both had fathers called Leogoras. Glaucon, from the same tribe as Pericles, had served as general on a number of occasions from 441/0 onwards (cf. **141**). Metagenes was restored by Müller-Strübing, *Aristophanes und die historische Kritik*, 600 n. **, seeing him as the Metagenes who had been first secretary in 434/3 (cf. above: named without demotic), and has been regularly accepted; regardless of that identification, if the name is rightly restored here, his son appears in *IG* ii^2 1635. 9, and his grandson in *SEG* xxxvii 124. Dracontides is probably to be identified with the man who was chairman in **131**. 2 and with the man who attacked Pericles in 438/7 (Plut. *Per.* 32. iii).

149

Reaffirmed Athenian alliances with Rhegium and Leontini, 433/2

A (Rhegium)

Part of a marble *stele*, with the top and right-hand margins preserved, now in the British Museum. Phot. Austin, *The Stoichedon Style in Greek Inscriptions*, pl. 6.

Developed Attic writing, with ll. 1–8 inscribed in an erasure. *Stoichedon* (1–8) 34, (9 sqq.) 33.

SIG^3 71; *IG* i^2 51; *SdA* 162; M&L 63; *IG* i^3 53* (Meritt & McGregor). Trans. Fornara 124; Dillon & Garland^3 12. 32. See also B. D. Meritt, *CQ* xl 1946, 85–91; H. B. Mattingly, *Historia* xii 1963, 272 = his *AER* 105; id., *AIIN* xii–xiv Supp. 1969, 207–9 = his *AER* 266–8; E. Ruschenbusch, *ZPE* xix 1975, 225–32; D. M. Lewis, *ZPE* xxii 1976, 223–5.

[θεοί. πρέσβες ἐκ Ῥεγίο h]οὶ τὲν χσυμμαχίαν
[ἐποέσαντο καὶ τὸν hόρκ]ον· Κλέανδρος Χσεν-
[———19———]τίνο, Σιλενὸς Φόκο,
[———15———. ἐπ' Ἀφ]σεύδος ἄρχοντος κ-
[αὶ τε͂ς βολε͂ς hε͂ι Κριτιά]δες προ͂τος ἐγραμμ-
[άτευε. vv ἔδοχσεν τε͂ι βο]λε͂ι καὶ το͂ι δέμοι. Ἀ-
[καμαντὶς ἐπρυτάνευε· Χ]αρίας ἐγραμμάτευ-
[ε· Τιμοχσενος ἐπέστάτ]ε. Καλλί- *vacant* 10
[ας εἶπε· χσυμμαχίαν εἶν]αι Ἀθεναίοις καὶ
[Ῥεγίνοις. τὸν δὲ hόρκο]ν ὀμοσάντον Ἀθενα-
[ῖοι hίνα ἐ͂ι hάπαντα πι]στὰ καὶ ἄδολα καὶ h-
[απλᾶ παρ' Ἀθεναίον ἐς ἀΐ]διον Ῥεγίνοις, κα-
[τὰ τάδε ὀμνύντες· χσύμ]μαχοι ἐσόμεθα πισ-
[τοὶ καὶ δίκαιοι καὶ ἰσ]χυροὶ καὶ ἀβλαβε͂ς
[ἐς ἀΐδιον Ῥεγίνοις, καὶ] ὀφελέσομεν ἐ[άν τ]-
[ο δέονται - - - - - - - - - - - - - - - - - - -]
- -

The original prescript has been replaced with a new one, with (at least: Lewis) one additional line, and one additional letter in each line, which can be restored by comparison with *B*: probably the cutter omitted γραμματεύς from l. 4 and that explains the ten empty spaces in l. 8 (doubted by Lewis); the two empty spaces in l. 6 will have been left so that l. 8 at the end of the replacement text should run on to l. 9 at the beginning of the original.   4 ἐπὶ M&L, but contrast *B*.   10–16 revised by Meritt.

B (Leontini)

The upper part of a marble *stele*, and a small further fragment from the bottom, found on the south slope of the Athenian acropolis between the odeum of Herodes Atticus and the theatre of Dionysus, now in the Epigraphical Museum. Phot. Bradeen & McGregor, *Studies in Fifth-Century Attic Epigraphy*, pl. xx (ll. 1–32); our pl. 10 (ll. 1–33).

(1–15) Developed Attic writing, inscribed in an erasure; (16 sqq.) careless and older Attic writing, especially *nu* and *upsilon*, but four-bar *sigma* and no h. *Stoichedon*, (1–15) 18, (16 sqq.) 17, but (to correct original omissions:

Gods.

1 Envoys from Rhegium who made the alliance and the oath: Cleandrus son of Xen—, —— son of —tinus, Silenus son of Phocus; (<secretary> —— son of ——).

4 In the archonship of Apseudes and the council for which Critiades was first secretary. Resolved by the council and the people. Acamantis was the prytany; Charias was the secretary; Timoxenus was the chairman. Callias proposed:

9 There shall be an alliance between the Athenians and the Rhegians. The oath shall be sworn by the Athenians, so that everything may be faithful and without deceit and straightforward on the part of the Athenians for all time towards the Rhegians, swearing as follows: 'We shall be faithful allies, just, strong and unharmful for all time to the Rhegians, and we shall help if they need anything – – –'

Meritt) with a letter inserted between two *stoichoi* in 16, 17 and 18, and to be restored in 21, 25 and 26 (here printed with underlining; which letter was so inserted in 21 can only be guessed).

SIG^3 70; *IG* i^2 52; *SdA* 163; M&L 64; *IG* i^3 54* (Meritt & McGregor). Trans. Fornara 125. See also B. D. Meritt, *CQ* xl 1946, 85–91; H. B. Mattingly, *Historia* xii 1963, 272 = his *AER* 105; id., *AIIN* Supp. xii–xiv 1969, 208–9 = *AER* 266–7; Bradeen & McGregor, *Studies in Fifth-Century Attic Epigraphy*, 121; E. Ruschenbusch, *ZPE* xix 1975, 225–32; D. M. Lewis, *ZPE* xxii 1976, 223–5; M. J. Osborne, *CR*^{2} xxxii 1982, 257.

[θ]εοί : πρέσβες ἐγ Λεον[τ]-
ίνον hοὶ τὲγ χσυμμαχί-
αν ἐποέσαντο καὶ τὸν h-
όρκον· Τιμένορ Ἀγαθοκ-
λέος, Σôσις Γλαυκίο, Γέ-
λον Ἐξσεκέστο, γραμμα-
τεὺς Θεότιμος Ταυρίσ-
κο. ἐπ' Ἀφσεύδος ἄρχοντ-
ος καὶ τε̂ς βολε̂ς hε̂ι Κρ-
ιτιάδες ἐγραμμάτευε.
ἔδοχσεν τε̂ι βολε̂ι καὶ
τôι δέμοι. Ἀκαμαντὶς ἐ-
πρυτάνευε· Χαρίας ἐγρ-
αμμάτευε· Τιμόχσενος
ἐπεστάτε. Καλλίας ε- vv
ἶπε· τὲμ μὲν χσυμμαχία-
ν εἶναι Ἀθεναίοις καὶ
Λεοντίνοις καὶ τὸν ὅρ̣-
κον δôναι καὶ δέχσασ-
[θαι. ὀμόσ]αι δὲ Ἀθεναί-
[ος τάδε·σύ]νμα[χ]οι ἐσόμ-
[εθα Λεοντ]ίν[οις ἀΐ]δ̣ιο-
[ι ἀδόλος κ]αὶ [ἀβλα]βôς.
[Λεοντίνο]ς ὁ[μôς ὀ]μόσ-
[αι· σύνμαχοι ἐσόμ]εθα
[Ἀθεναίοις ἀΐδιοι] ἀδό-
[λος καὶ ἀβλαβôς. π]ερὶ
[– – – 14 – – –]μπο
[– – – 14 – – –]ενα
[– – – 14 – – –]δεε
[– – – 15 – – –]σθ
[– – – 15 – – –]οπ

lacuna

[- - - - -]ι[- - - -]
[- - - -]εαθ[- - - -]
[- - - -]ιοι v[- - -]

vacat

The original prescript has been replaced with a new one, with (at least: Lewis) one additional line, and one additional letter in each line: the cutter omitted πρôτος from l. 10, perhaps in order to save space; the two empty spaces in l. 15 were left so that l. 15 at the end of the replacement text should run on to l. 16 at the beginning of the original. 1 [[θε]] οἱ [[:]], i.e. the cutter originally inscribed θεοί : πρέσβες, then imperfectly deleted θε and : to produce οἱ πρέσβες (Bradeen & McGregor), but contr. Lewis, Osborne. 22 sqq. read and restored by Meritt.

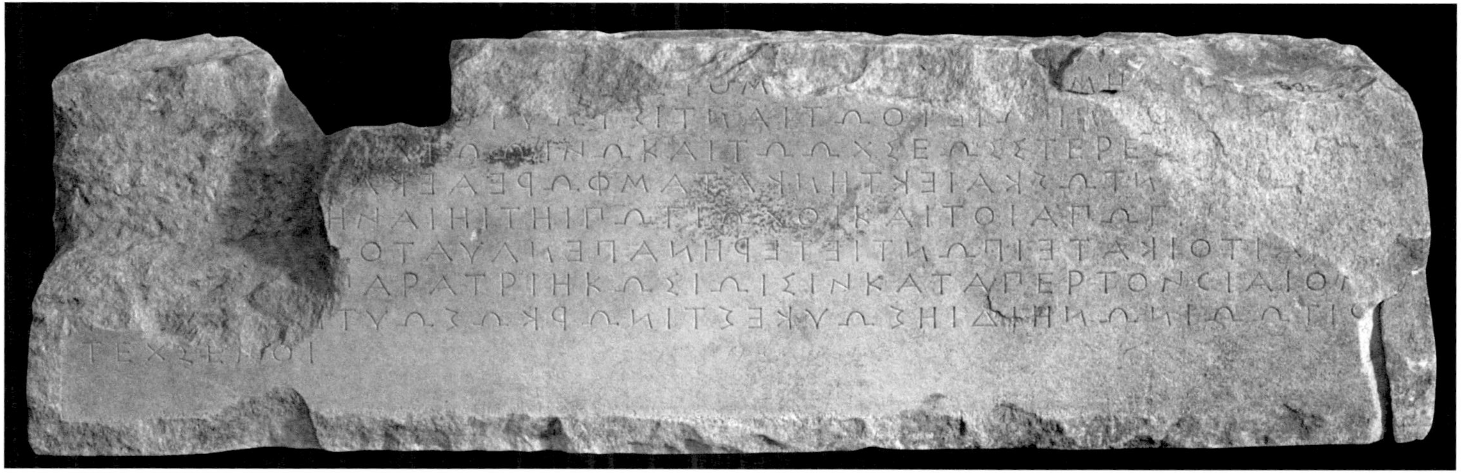

I. 103

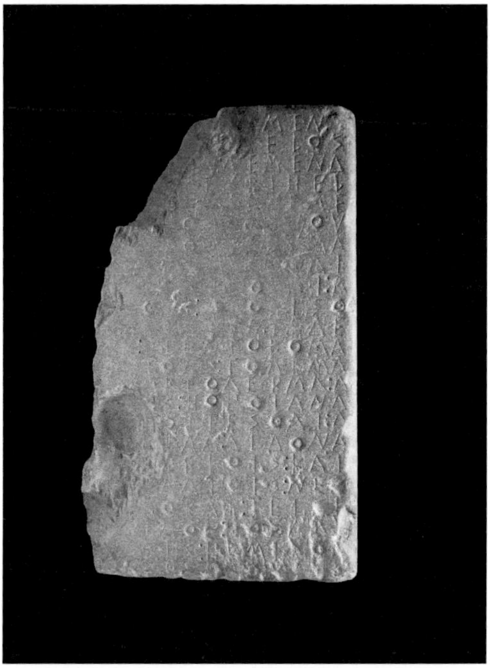

2 (*a*). **107**, Face *A*

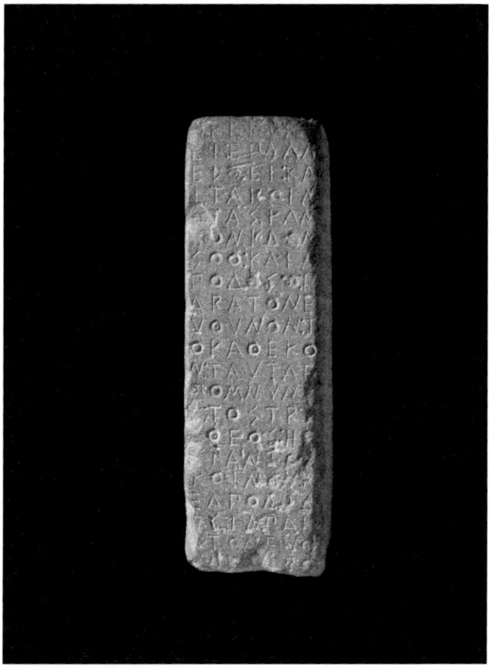

2 (*b*) **107**, Face *B*

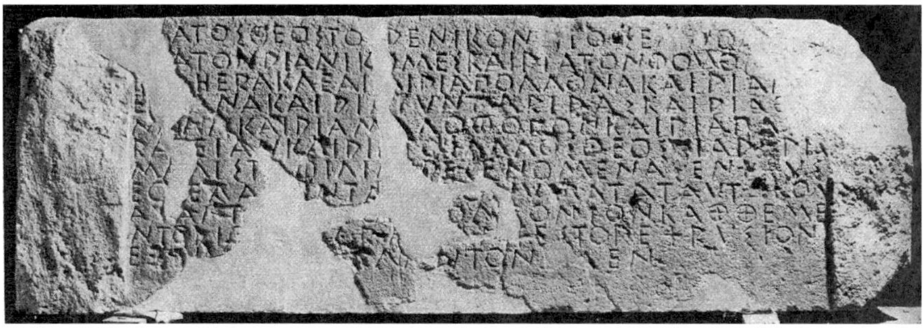

3. **114**

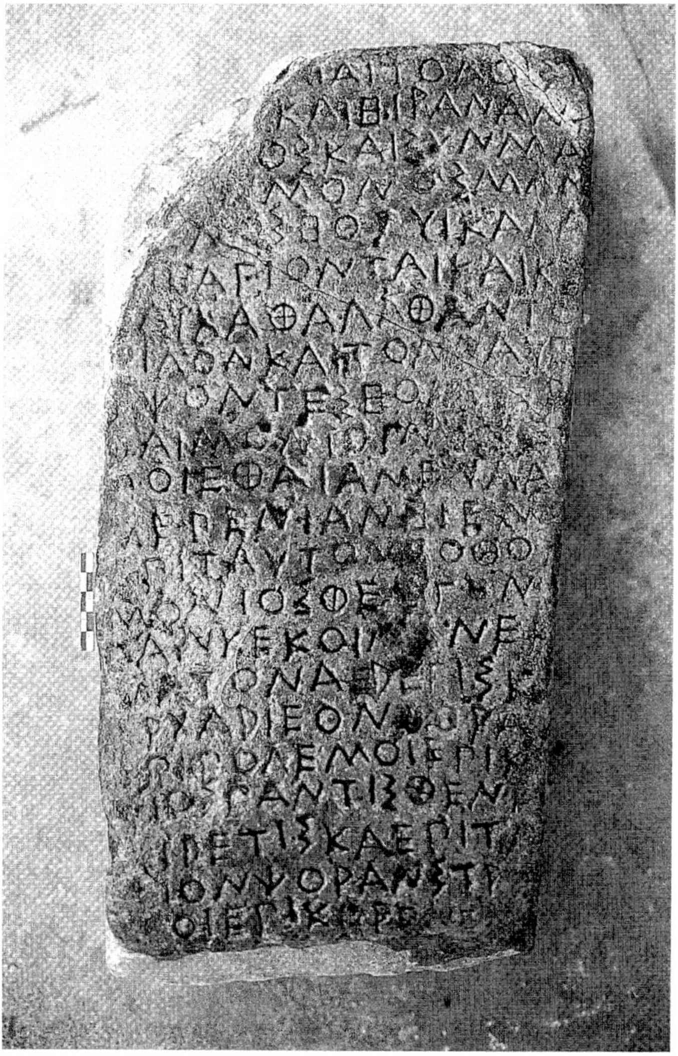

4. **128**

5. **129**

6. **134**

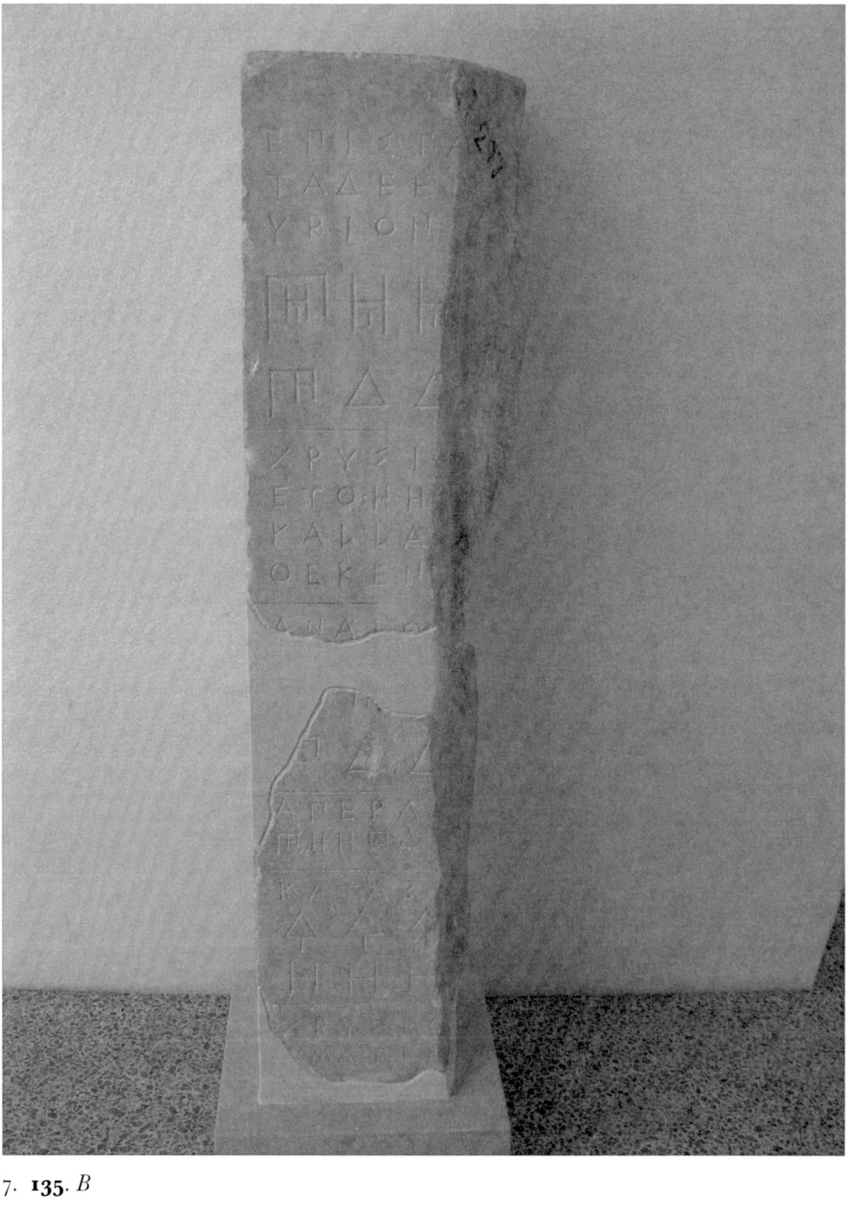

7. **135**. *B*

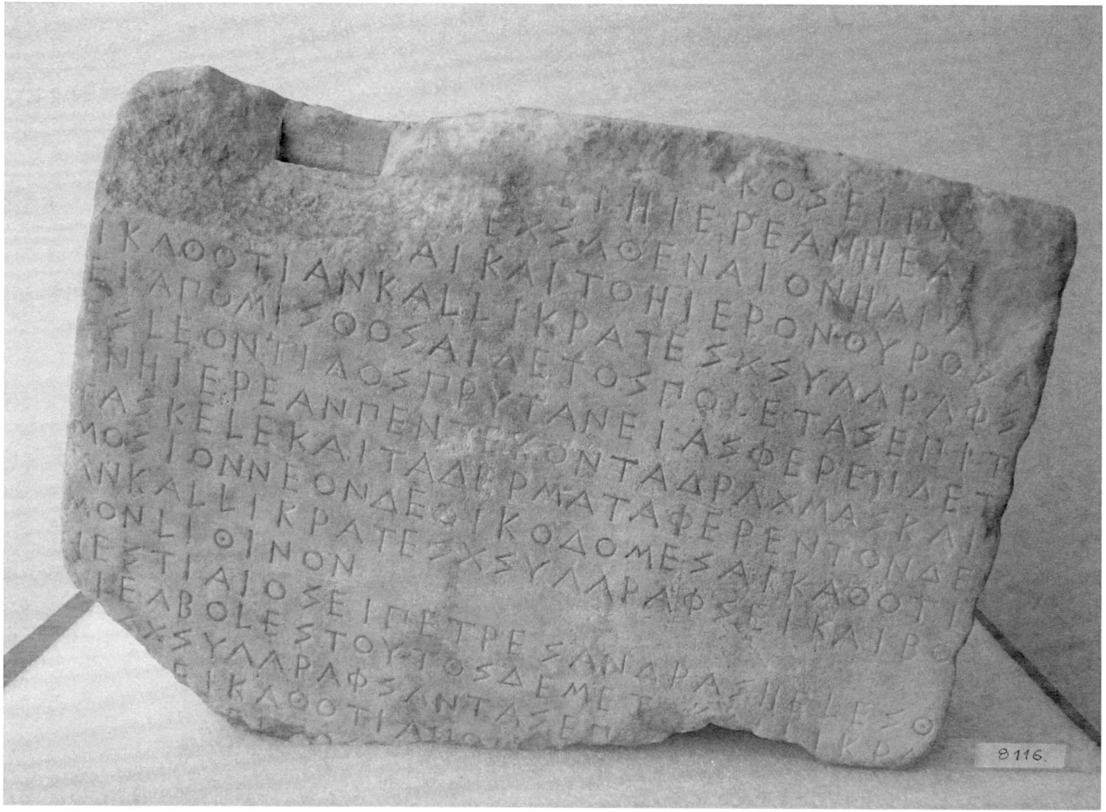

8. **137**

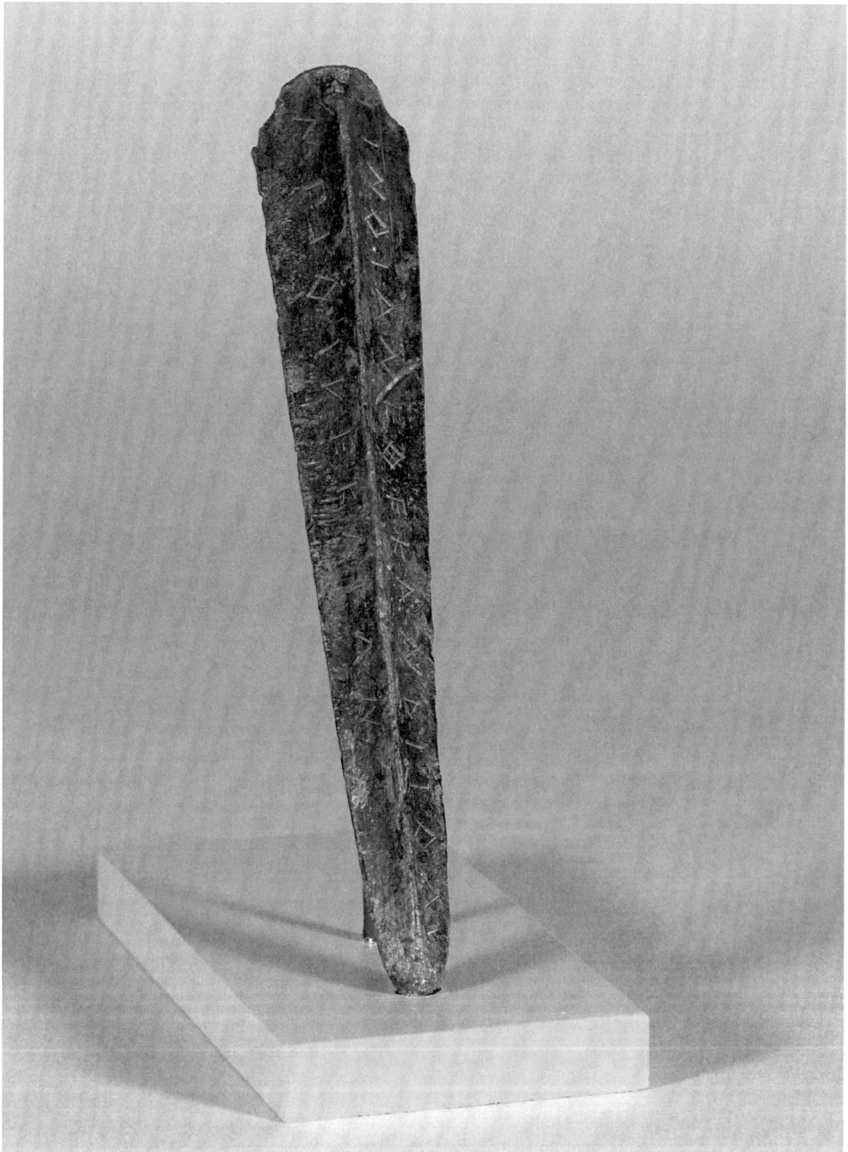

9. **140**

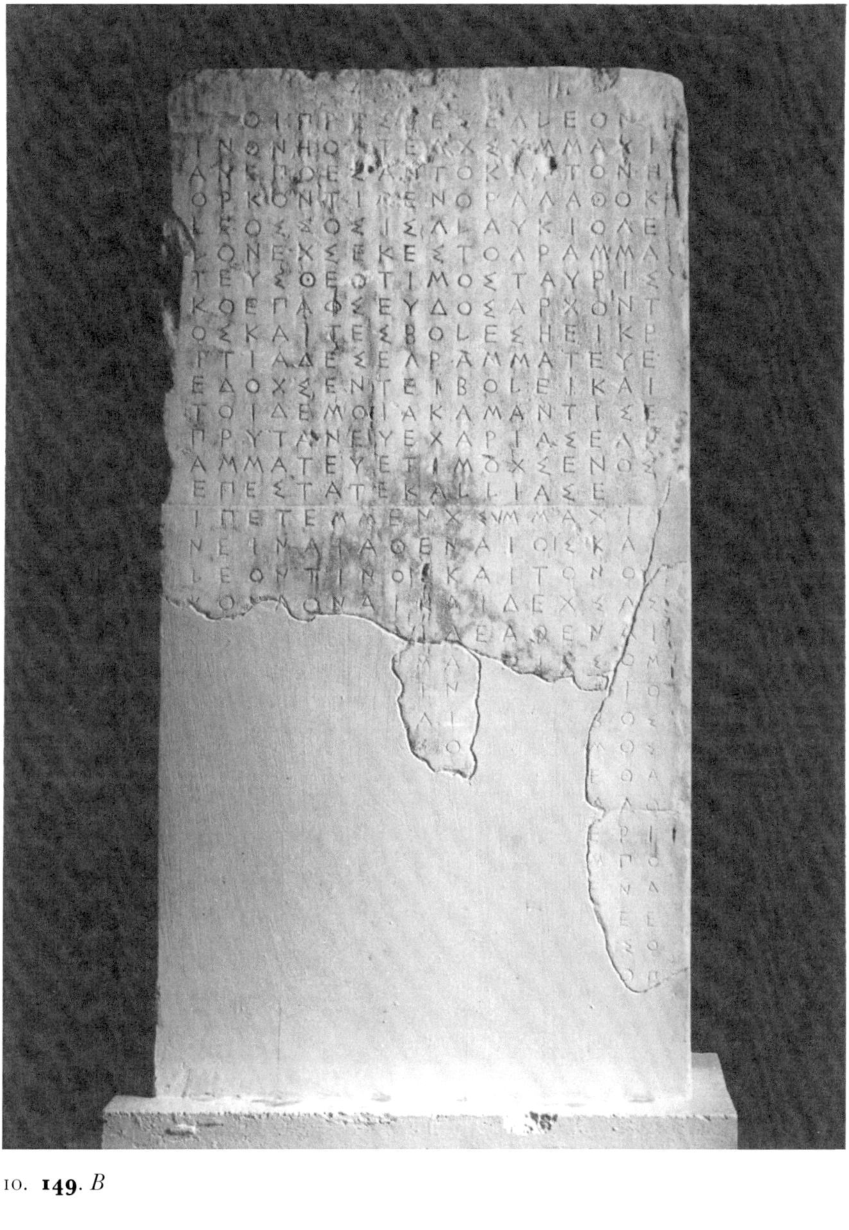

10. **149**. *B*

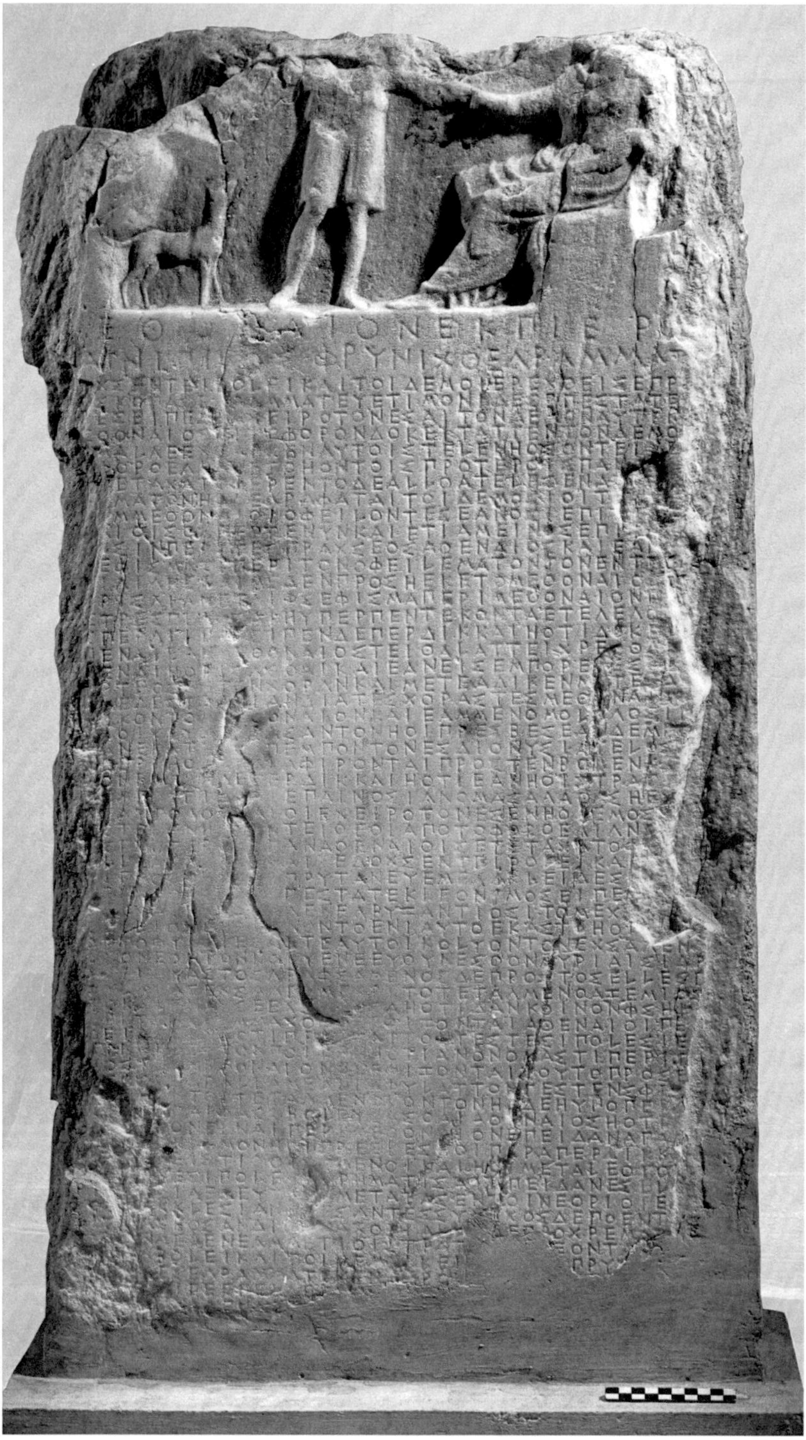

II. 150

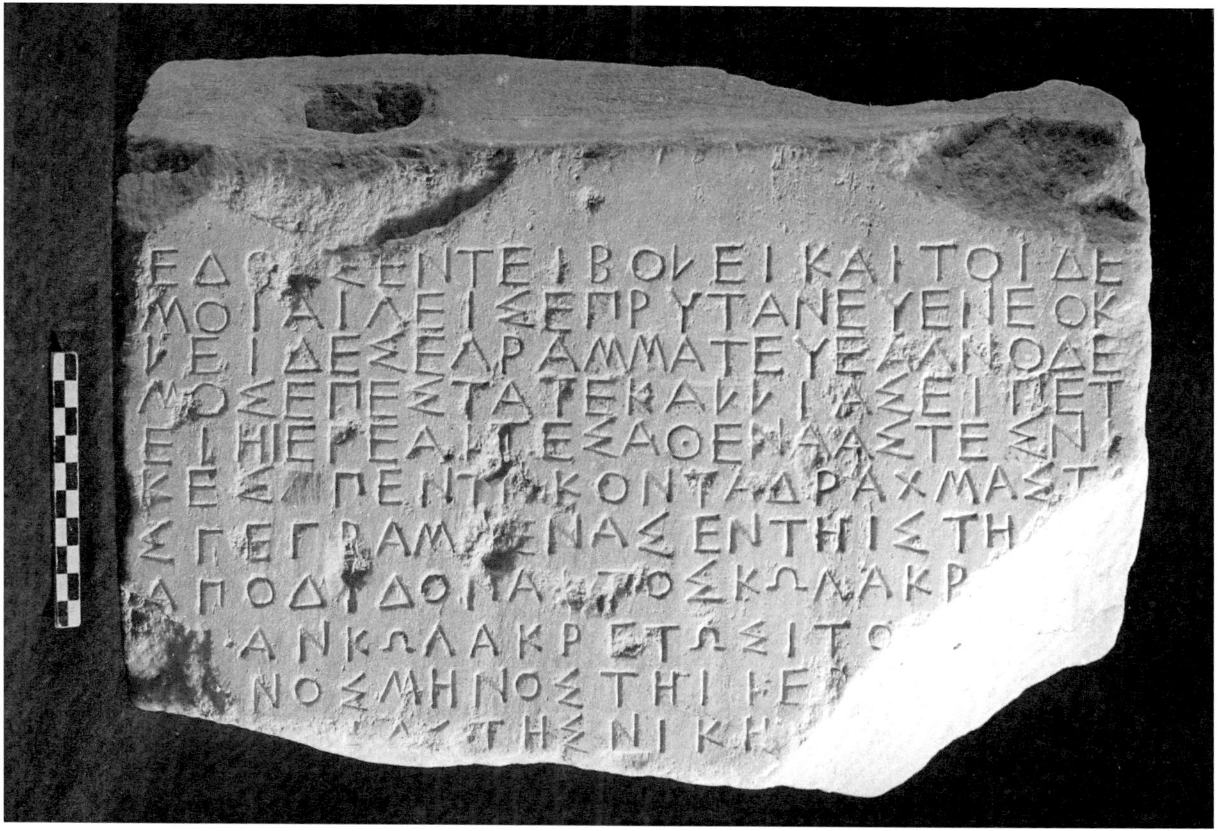

12. **156**

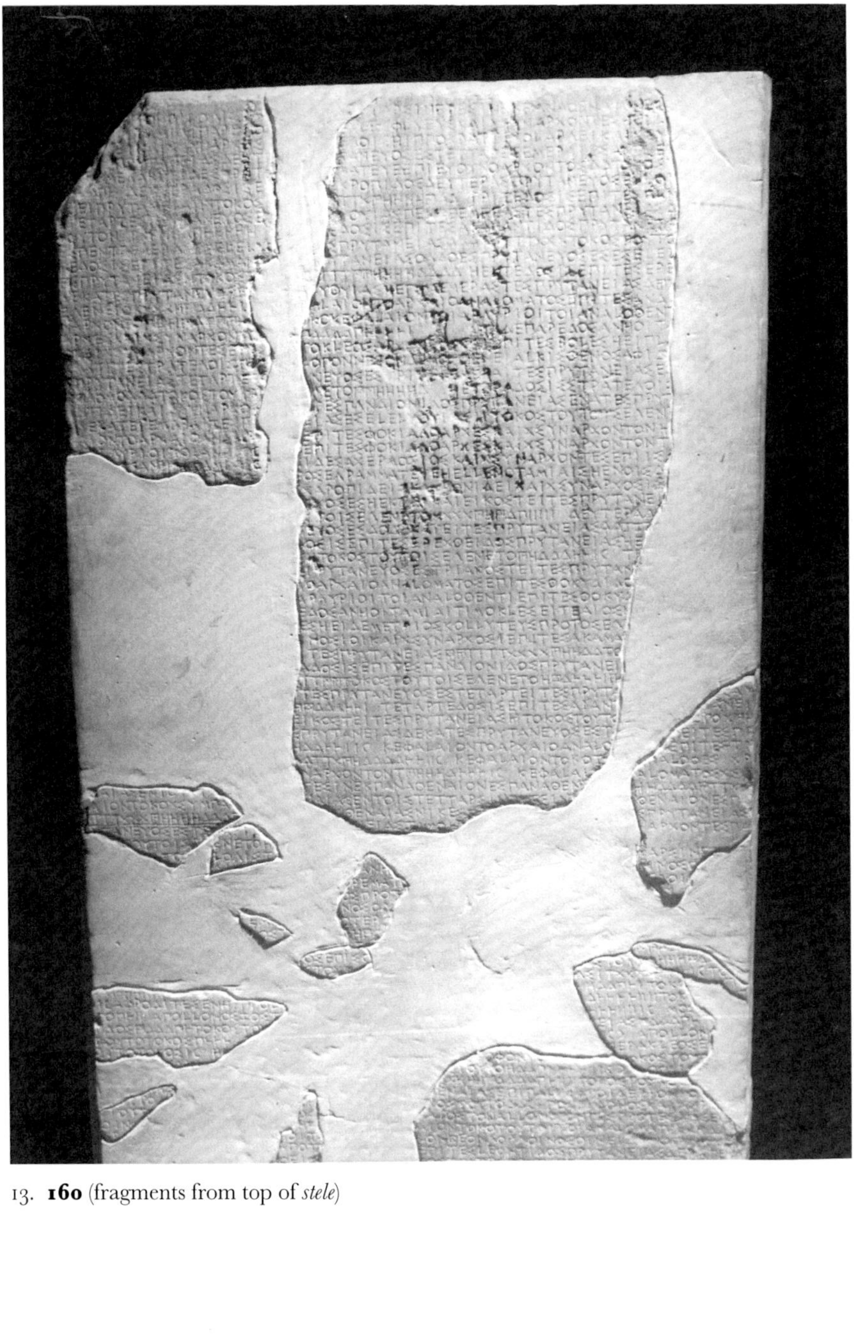

13. **160** (fragments from top of *stele*)

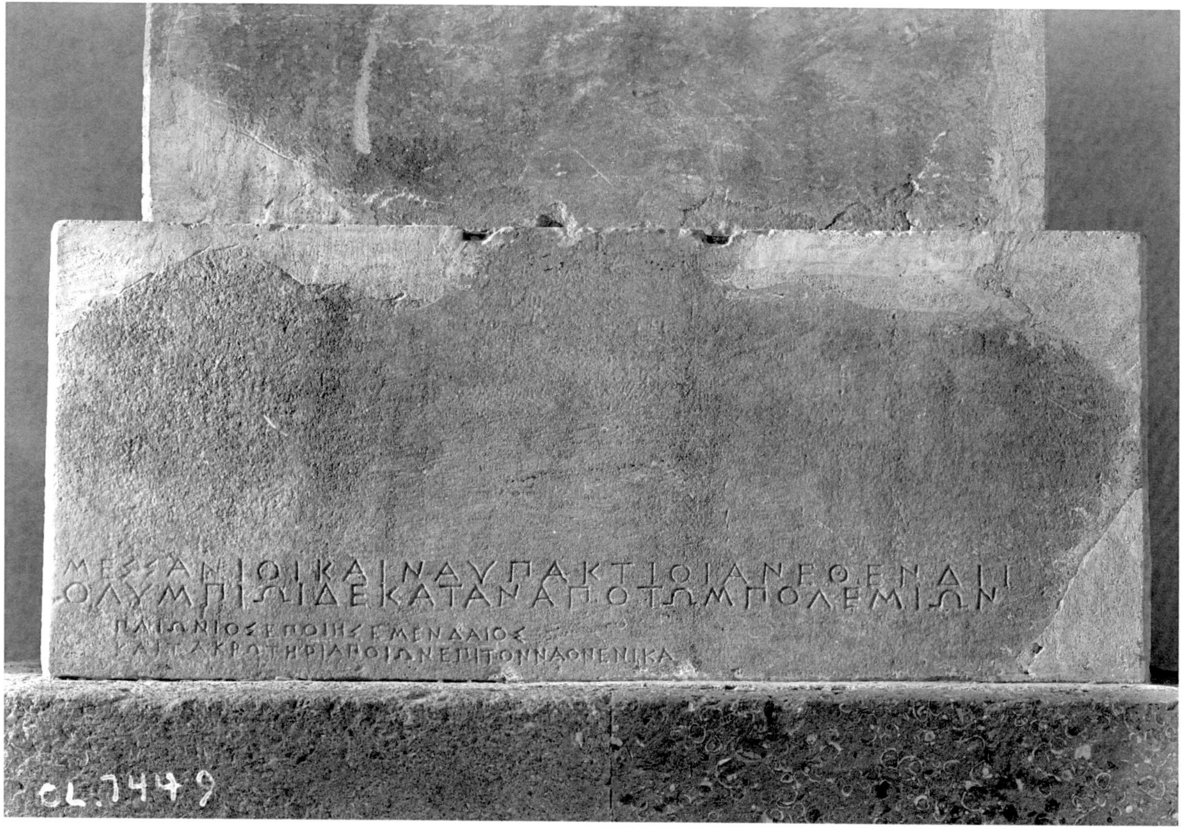
ΜΕΣΣΑΝΙΟΙ ΚΑΙ ΝΑΥΠΑΚΤΙΟΙ ΑΝΕΘΕΝ ΔΙΙ
ΟΛΥΜΠΙΩΙ ΔΕΚΑΤΑΝ ΑΠΟ ΤΩΜ ΠΟΛΕΜΙΩΝ
ΠΑΙΩΝΙΟΣ ΕΠΟΙΗΣΕ ΜΕΝΔΑΙΟΣ
ΚΑΙ ΤΑΚΡΩΤΗΡΙΑ ΠΟΙΩΝ ΕΠΙ ΤΟΝ ΝΑΟΝ ΕΝΙΚΑ
CL.7449

14. **164**

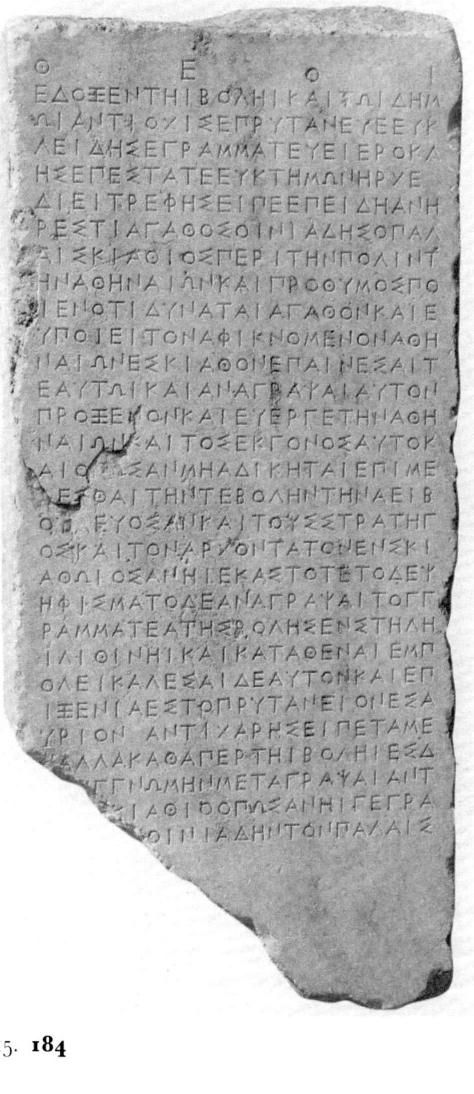

15. **184**

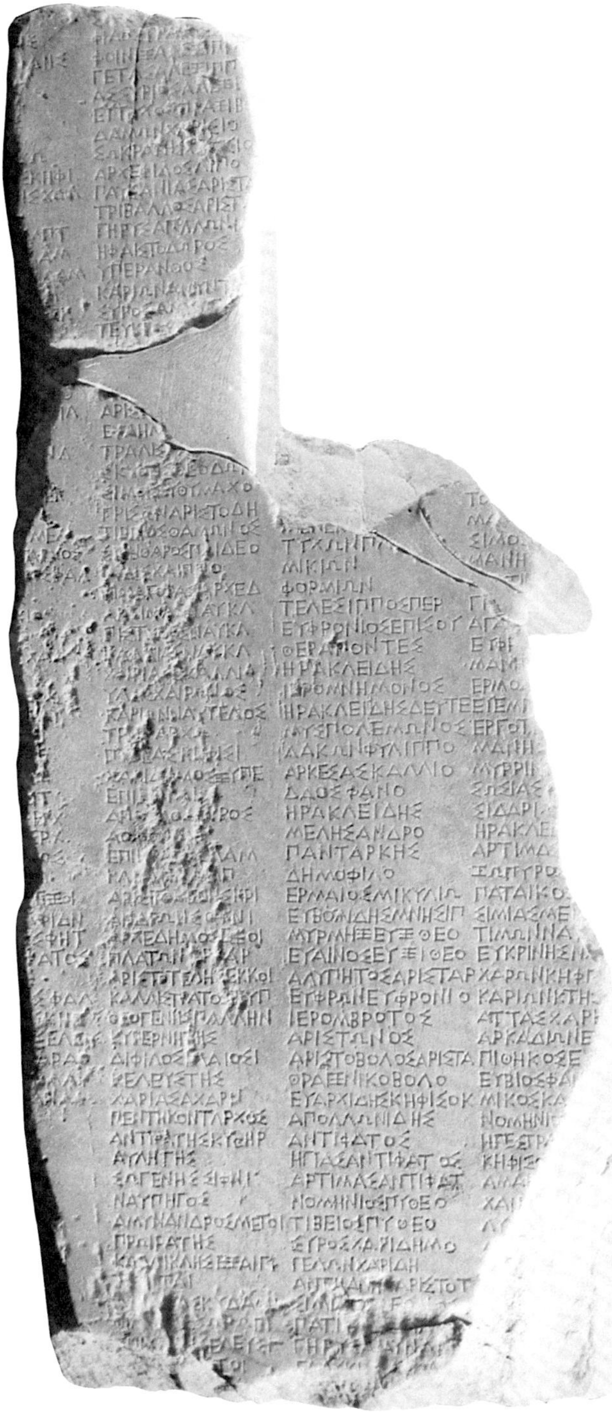

16. **190** (frs. *c*+*f*+*j*)

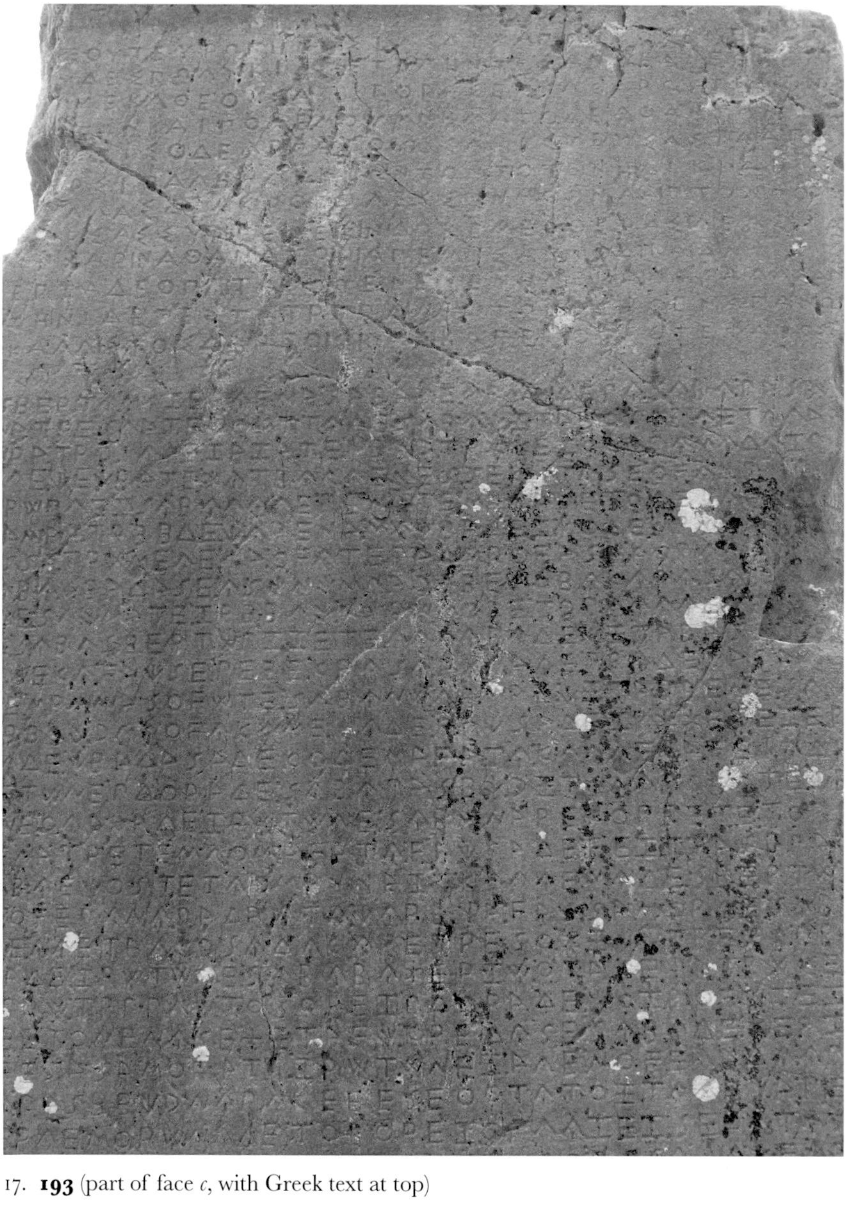

17. **193** (part of face *c*, with Greek text at top)

Gods.

1 The envoys from Leontini who made the alliance and the oath: Timenor son of Agathocles, Sosis son of Glaucias, Gelon son of Execestus; secretary Theotimus son of Tauriscus.

8 In the archonship of Apseudes and the council for which Critiades was secretary. Resolved by the council and the people. Acamantis was the prytany; Charias was the secretary; Timoxenus was the chairman. Callias proposed:

16 There shall be the alliance between the Athenians and the Leontinians, and they shall give and receive the oath. The Athenians shall swear as follows: 'We shall be allies of the Leontinians for all time, without deceit and unharmfully.' The Leontinians shall swear likewise: 'We shall be allies of the Athenians for all time, without deceit and unharmfully.'

27 Concerning – – –

These decrees each have a new prescript, longer than the deleted original, and identifying the same day in 433/2 (later than the first prytany, since the secretary named after the prytany is not the 'first secretary' who identifies the year); Callias, as proposer of both decrees and included in the new prescripts, should belong to this occasion, not to the original enactments (D. M. Lewis, *JHS* lxxxi 1961, 118 n. 8), and, while the name is common, it is possible that he is the Callias of **144**. The original decrees are not exactly parallel, and *A* invokes an unusual number of virtues; in *A* the two hands are similar, but in *B* the original hand is more old-fashioned than the replacement (which could be the same in both inscriptions). The new prescripts begin with the invocation of the gods, θεοί, perhaps reflecting the prayer with which the proceedings in the assembly began,[1] and are the earliest dated instances of the phenomenon (it appears also in *IG* i³ 50, perhaps of the mid-430s; except in these new prescripts the word is spread across a whole line); note also its appearance, with Athena and Tyche, at the head of the Propylaea accounts, perhaps from 437/6 onwards: *IG* i³ 462, 465.

It is usually, and we believe rightly, thought that in 433/2 the alliances were reaffirmed, having been made 'for all time' earlier. Mattingly and others, because the archon's name was not normally used in prescripts before *c.*421, suggested that the alliances were first made in 433/2 and reaffirmed later. In 427 Leontini appealed to Athens for support 'in accordance with their old (παλαιὰν) alliance' (Thuc. III. 86. iii): the use of that word does not guarantee that the reference is to a time earlier than 433/2, but it is hard to see why, if they were first made in 433/2, fuller prescripts

[1] Cf. R. L. Pounder, in *Studies . . . S. Dow*, 243–50.

150

Athenian decrees for Methone, 430/29–424/3

A marble *stele*, broken at the top and bottom, and with the left- and right-hand margins damaged, found in the theatre of Dionysus, previously in the Epigraphical Museum, but now displayed in the Acropolis Museum. At the top is a relief showing Athena seated, reaching out her hand to a standing figure behind whom stands a hound. Phot. *ATL* ii, pl. i; our pl. 11. Relief Meyer, *Die griechischen Urkundenreliefs*, 265 A4 with Taf. 4. 1; Lawton, *Attic Document Reliefs*, 81–2 A2 with pl. 1 no. 2.

Developed Attic writing, but εἶναι in ll. 35, 49, *eta* 41, 52, and Ionic *gamma* 51; aspirate frequently omitted. (1–2) larger letters; (3 sqq.) *stoichedon* 41.

*SIG*³ 75; *IG* i² 57; *ATL* D 3–6; M&L 65; *IG* i³ 61* (Meritt & McGregor). Trans. Fornara 128; Osborne, *The Athenian Empire*⁴, 121 (different translation in earlier editions). See also M. Hatzopoulos *et al.*, *BCH* cxiv 1990, 639–68 (on the location); *ATL* iii. 133–7; H. B. Mattingly, *CQ*² xi 1961, 154–65, xxviii 1978, 83–5 = his *AER* 427–30; N. G. L. Hammond [& G. T. Griffith], *A History of Macedonia*, ii, 124–7; M. Piérart, in *Comptes et inventaires dans la cité grecque . . . J. Tréheux*, 313–20.

of that year should have been inserted in these texts to mark their reaffirmation later. The archon's name is credibly restored in the prescript of *IG* i^3 21, of 426/5.

There is now no evidence that Athens had dealings with the west before 450 (see **166** with commentary); but Athens was involved in the last refoundation of Sybaris and its new foundation as Thurii, perhaps in 446/5 and 444/3 (Diod. Sic. XII. 9–11 [–18], cf. Arist. *Pol.* V. 1303 A 31–3, Strabo 263 / VI. i. 13: see **140**), and it was possibly about the same time that Athens was involved in a refoundation of Neapolis (Timaeus *FGrH* 566 F 98 with commentary on **148**; Strabo 246 / V. iv. 7, Lycoph. 732–7 with schol.). If Athens' presence in southern Italy is a necessary condition for south Italian and Sicilian cities' thinking that it would be a helpful ally, it was by no means a sufficient condition. We might guess that Leontini was always on the lookout for friends that might protect her against her mighty near-neighbour Syracuse, but the motivation for Rhegium's alliance is harder to guess. A date about the 440s would suit these alliances: possibly Leontini in Sicily earlier than Rhegium on the toe of Italy, but of course more and less old-fashioned cutters could have been working at the same time.

The reaffirmations should be seen in the context of Athens' alliance of 433 with Corcyra (cf. **148**): Thucydides comments on the island's convenient position for voyages to and from the west (I. 44. iii cf. 36. ii), and we should accept that the Athenians were already looking ahead not simply to the Peloponnesian War (cf. **144**) but to a war in which they expected the west to be involved.

One of Rhegium's envoys, Silenus, died and was buried at Athens, and his epitaph survives, describing him as a 'very just man' (φῶτα δι[κ]αιότατον: *IG* ii^2 5220 = *CEG* 12).

Μεθοναίον ἐκ Πιερ[ίας].
[Φ]αίνιππος Φρυνίχο ἐγραμμάτ[ευε].

§i

[ἔδ]οχσεν τε̑ι βολε̑ι καὶ το̑ι δέμοι. Ἐρεχθεΐς ἐπρ[υτάν]-
[ευε]· Σκόπας ἐγραμμάτευε· Τιμονίδες ἐπεστάτε. Δ̣[?ιοπ]-
[εί]θες εἶπε· δι[α]χειροτονε̑σαι τὸν δε̑μον αὐτίκ[α πρὸ]-
[ς Μ]εθοναίος εἴτε φόρον δοκεῖ τάττεν τὸν δε̑μο[ν αὐτ]-
[ίκ]α μάλα ἒ εχ[σ]αρκε̑ν αὐτοῖς τελε̑ν hόσον τε̑ι θε[ο̑ι.ἀπ]-
[ὸ τ]ο̑ φόρο ἐγίγνετο hὸν τοῖς προτέροις Παν[αθ]ε[ναίο]-
[ις] ἐτετάχατο φέρεν, το̑ δὲ ἄλλο ἀτελε̑ς ε̑̓να[ι. το̑ν δὲ ὀφ]-
[ει]λεμάτον hὰ γεγράφαται το̑ι δεμοσίοι τ[ο̑ι το̑ν Ἀθε]-
[να]<ί>ομ Μεθοναῖοι ὀφείλοντες, ἐὰν ο̑̓σι ἐπιτ[έδειοι Ἀ]-
[θε]ναίοις ὅσπερ τε νυ̑ν καὶ ἔτι ἀμείνος, ἐπι[— 7 —]
[. τ]αχσιν περὶ τε̑ς πράχσεος Ἀθεναῖος· καὶ ἐὰν̣ [κοινὸ]-
[ν] φσέφισμά τι περὶ το̑ν ὀφειλεμάτον το̑ν ἐν τε̑[ισι σα]-
[νί]σι γίγνεται, μεδὲν προσhεκέτο Μεθοναίο[ις ἐὰμ μ]-
[ὲ χ]ορὶς γίγνεται φσέφισμα περὶ Μεθοναίον. π[ρέσβε]-
[ς δ]ὲ τρε̑ς πέμφσαι hυπὲρ πεντέκοντα ἔτε γεγον[ότας]
[ho]ς Περδίκκα[ν]· εἰπε̑ν δὲ Περδίκκαι hότι δοκε[ῖ δίκα]-
[ιο]ν ε̑̓ναι ἐα̑ν Μεθοναίος τε̑ι θαλάττει χρε̑σθα[ι, καὶ μ]-
εδὲ] ε̑̓ναι hορίσασθαι, καὶ ἐα̑ν εἰσεμπορεύεσθ[αι καθ]-
[άπε]ρ τέος ἐ[ς] τ̣ὲν χόραν, καὶ μέτε ἀδικε̑ν μ[έ]τε [ἀ]δ[ικε̑σ]-
[θαι] μεδὲ στρα[τ]ιὰν διὰ τε̑ς χόρας τε̑ς Μεθ[ο]ναίον [διά]-
[γεν ἀ]κόντομ [Με]θοναίον. καὶ ἐὰμ μὲν ὁμολ[ο]γο̑σιν [hεκ]-
[άτερ]οι χσυ[μβι]βασάντον hοι πρέσβες, ἐὰν δὲ μέ, [πρεσ]-
[βεί]αν ἐκάτ[ερ]ο[ι] πεμπόντον ἐς Διονύσια, τέλος [ἔχον]-
[τας] περὶ hο̑[ν] ἂν διαφ<έ>ρονται, πρὸς τὲν βολὲν κα[ὶ τὸν]
[δε̑μ]ον. ε[ἰ]π̣ε̑ν δὲ [Π]ερδίκκαι hότι ἐὰν hοι στρατι[ο̑ται]
[hοι] ἐμ Ποτειδ[ά]αι ἐπαινο̑σι γνόμας ἀγαθὰς hε[χσοσι]
[περὶ] αὐτο̑ Ἀθε[ν]αῖοι. ἐχειροτόνεσεν hο δε̑μος [Μεθον]-
[αίο]ς τελε̑ν h[όσο]ν τε̑ι θεο̑ι ἀπὸ το̑ φορο ἐγίγνε[το hὸν]
[τοῖ]ς προτέρο[ις] Παναθεναίοις ἐτετάχατο φ[έρεν, το̑
[δὲ ἄ]λλο ἀτε[λε̑ς ε̑̓]ναι. ᵛ

§ii

ἔδοχσεν τε̑ι βολε̑ι καὶ [το̑ι δέμ]-
[οι. h]ιπποθο[ντὶς ἐ]πρυτάνευε· Μεγακλείδες [ἐγραμμά]-
[τευ]ε· Νι[κ]ο[— 5 — ἐ]πεστάτε. Κλεόνυμος εἶπε· Μ[εθοναί]-

4 Δ̣: only faint trace of left-hand diagonal visible S. D. Lambert *ap.* Parker, *Polytheism and Society at Athens*, 92 n. 11 (cf. *SEG* lv 53). 10–11 H reported by early edd.: text above Boeckh and other edd., M&L; τ[ο̑ν ἀπειτε|μέ]νομ *ATL*, *IG* i³. 12–13 ἐπι[τρέπεν τ|ε τ]άχσιν earlier edd., ἐπι[χορε̑ν ἀπ|ότ]αχσιν *ATL* iii. 137, but that does not suit the context (noted by A. P. Matthaiou). 14–15 *ATL* iii. 14–15. 19–20 A. S. Henry, *JHS* xcvii 1977, 155–6: χρε̑σθα[ι, μεδὲ] [ἔχσ]ε̑ναι edd. 26 The stone has I.

Of the Methonaeans from Pieria.

2 Phaenippus son of Phrynichus was the secretary.

§i

3 Resolved by the council and the people. Erechtheis was the prytany; Scopas was the secretary; Timonides was the chairman. Diopithes (?) proposed:

5 The people shall vote immediately with regard to the Methonaeans whether it seems right that the people should assess their tribute immediately or it should be sufficient for them to pay as much to the Goddess as resulted from the tribute which they were assessed at the previous Panathenaea to pay, and to be exempt from the remainder.

9 Of the debts which the Methonaeans have been recorded as owing to the Athenian (?) public treasury, if they are amenable to the Athenians as now and even better, the Athenians shall (allow an assessment?) concerning the exaction; and if there is any general decree about the debts (recorded) in the tablets, nothing shall apply to the Methonaeans unless there is a separate decree about the Methonaeans.

16 Send three envoys over fifty years old to Perdiccas, and say to Perdiccas that it seems right to allow the Methonaeans to use the sea and that they should not be limited, and that he should allow them to enter his territory and trade as before, and that he should not wrong them or be wronged by them, nor send a military force through the territory of the Methonaeans against the will of the Methonaeans. And if the two parties agree the envoys shall bring them to terms; if they do not, each should send a delegation to the Dionysia, with authority about the matters in dispute, to the council and the people.

27 Say to Perdiccas that if the soldiers in Potidaea praise him the Athenians will hold a good opinion of him.

29 The people voted that the Methonaeans should pay as much to the Goddess as resulted from the tribute which they were assessed at the previous Panathenaea to pay, and be exempt from the remainder.

§ii

32 Resolved by the council and the people. Hippothontis was the prytany; Megaclides was the secretary; Nico— was the chairman. Cleonymus proposed:

[οις] εἶν[αι ἐχ]σα[γο]γὲν ἐγ Βυζαντίο σίτο μέχ[ρι . . . . α]-
[κισχ]ιλίον μεδίμνον τô ἐνιαυτô ἑκάστο, hοι [δὲ ἑλλε]-
[σπ]οντοφύλακες μέτε αὐτοὶ κολυόντον ἐχσάγεν μ[έτ]-
[ε ἄλ]λον ἐόντον κολύεν, ἒ εὐθυνέσθον μυρίαισι δρ[αχ]-
[με̂ισ]ιν ἕκαστος· γραφσαμένος δὲ πρὸς τὸς ἑλλεσπ[ον]-
[το]φύλακας ἐχσάγε[ν] μεχρὶ τô τεταγμένο· ἀζέμιος [δὲ]
[ἔσ]το καὶ ἑ ναῦς ἑ ἐξσάγοσα. hό τι δ' ἂν κοινὸν φσέφ[ισμ]-
[α π]ερὶ τôν χσυμμάχο[ν] φσεφίζονται Ἀθεναῖοι πε[ρὶ β]-
[οε]θείας ἒ ἄ[λ]λο τι προ[σ]τάττο[ν]τες τε̂σι πόλεσι ἒ [περ]-
[ὶ σ]φôν [ἒ] περὶ τôν πόλεον, hό τι ἂν ὀνομαστὶ περὶ τ[ε̂ς π]-
[όλε]ος τε̂[ς] Μεθοναίον φσεφίζονται τοῦτο προσέ[κεν]
[αὐτῖ]ς, τ[ὰ] δὲ ἄλλα μέ· ἀλλὰ φυλάττοντες τὲν σφετ[έρα]-
[ν αὐτôν ἐ]ν τôι τεταγμένοι ὄντον. hὰ δὲ hυπὸ Περδ[ίκκ]-
[ο ἀδικε̂σ]θαί φασι, βουλεύσασθαι Ἀθεναίος hó τι ἂ[ν δο]-
[κ]ε̂ι [ἀγαθ]ὸν εἶναι περὶ Μεθοναίον ἐπειδὰν ἀπαν[τέσ]-
[ο]σ̣ι ἐ[ς τὸ]ν δε̂μον hοι πρέσβες [h]οι παρὰ Περδίκκο [οἵ τ]-
ε μετ[ὰ Πλ]ειστίο οἰ[χ]όμενοι καὶ hοι μετὰ Λεογό[ρο. τε̂]-
[σ]ι δὲ [ἄλλ]εσι πόλε[σι χ]ρηματίσαι ἐπειδὰν ἐσέλ[θει ἑ]
[π]ρυ[ταν]εία ἑ δευτ[έρα] μετὰ τὰς έν τôι νεορίοι ἕ[δρας]
[ε]ὐ̣θ[ὺς] ἐκκλεσίαν [πο]έσαντες· συν[ε]χôς δὲ ποε̂ν τ[ὰς ἐκ]-
[κ]λ̣ε[σία]ς ἕος ἂν δι[απρ]αχθε̂ι, ἄλλο δὲ προχρεμα[τίσαι]
[το]ύ̣[το]ν μεδὲν ἐὰμ μέ τι οἱ στρατε[γ]οὶ δέονται. ᵛ

§iii

ἔδοχ]-
[σεν τε̂ι] βολε̂ι καὶ τôι δέμοι. Κεκροπὶς ἐπρυ[τάνευε· .]
[—⁶—]ες ἐγραμμάτε[υ]ε· h[ι]εροκλείδες ἐ[πεστάτε. . .
[—⁶—] εἶπε· ἐπειδὲ ε[—²⁴—]
[—⁶— Ἀθ]εναι[—²⁹—]

§iv

[ἔδοχσεν τε̂ι βολε̂ι καὶ τôι δέμοι. Ἀκαμαντὶς ἐπρυτά]-
νευε· Φαίνιππος ἐγραμματευε· - - - - - - - - - - - -]

39 μεῖσ]ιν *ATL* iii. 16 n. 44, cf. τε̂[ισι in l. 14: μâισ]ιν previous edd. 54–5 τ[ὰς ἐκ|κ]λ̣ε[σία]ς earliest editors, Mattingly, *Acta of the Fifth International Congress of Greek and Latin Epigraphy* . . . 1967, 28 with 32 n. 7 = *AER* 316–17 with n. 7, confirmed by A. P. Matthaiou, 'Studies in Attic Inscriptions and the History of the Fifth Century BC', 39 with n. 141: τ[ὰς ἐκ|ε]ῖ ἕ[δρα]ς Leonardos *ap. IG* i². 57–8 Τ|ιμοτέλ]ες Mattingly, *BCH* xcii 1968, cf. **143**. 1–3. 59–60 ἐπειδὲ ἔ[ταχσαν hοι τάκται τε̂σι πόλεσ|ι hοπόσα]ι Ἀ̣θ̣εναί[οις φόρον φέροσι *IG* i³. 61–2 Fourth decree ordering publication of *dossier* necessary to explain secretary of l. 2: Ἀκαμαντὶς cf. *IG* i³ 73. 21–2 with 27.

Methone was an Eretrian colony (Plut. *Quaest. Graec.* 293 A–B) on the west coast of the Thermaic Gulf, on the edge of Macedon (for its location see Hatzopoulos *et al.*);

34 The Methonaeans shall be permitted the export of corn from Byzantium up to —— thousand *medimnoi* each year, and the *hellespontophylakes* [guardians of the Hellespont] shall not themselves prevent them from exporting or allow anybody else to prevent them, or else they shall be fined ten thousand drachmas each. The Methonaeans shall write to the *hellespontophylakes* and export up to the limit fixed; and the ship exporting shall be exempt also.

41 Whatever general decree about the allies the Athenians enact concerning going to support, or giving any other instruction to the cities either about (the Athenians) themselves or about the cities, whatever they enact mentioning the city of the Methonaeans shall apply to them, but otherwise not; but if they guard their own territory they shall be doing their duty.

47 As for the wrongs they say they have suffered from Perdiccas, the Athenians shall consider what may seem good to them concerning the Methonaeans when there appear before the people the envoys from Perdiccas, those who went with Pleistias and those with Leogoras.

51 Deal with the other cities' business when the second prytany has entered office, holding an assembly immediately after the sessions [of the council] in the dockyard: Hold the assemblies continually until the business is completed, and do not give precedence over this to any other business unless the generals ask for something.

§iii

56 Resolved by the council and the people. Cecropis was the prytany; —es was the secretary; Hieroclides was the chairman. —— proposed:

59 Since – – – Athen— – –

§iv

61 Resolved by the council and the people. Acamantis was the prytany; Phaenippus was the secretary; – – –

---

it first appears in the tribute lists perhaps in 432/1 (*IG* i^3 280. ii. 67, restored—and rejected by Piérart). For Athens' growing involvement in this region in the 430s cf. **139**. Athens' relations with the Macedonian king Perdiccas II (*c*.454–413) fluctuated. It was therefore important to Athens to keep Methone loyal, and in this dossier of decrees we see a series of attempts to do so during the 420s. §ii belongs to the first prytany (cf. 52–3) of 426/5, and §iv and the publication of the whole dossier to the eighth prytany of 424/3; §iii presumably belongs between §§ii and iv (and 426/5 can be ruled out); the date of §i has been disputed.

The Dionysia (25) was held in Elaphebolion (ix), approximately March, and was the occasion when the member states of the Delian League paid their tribute (**153**. 12–13, **154**. 18–22): this decree was probably enacted during the winter, i.e. some time, but not a very long time, before then. In more recent work three datings have been canvassed. In *ATL* it is assumed that assessment 'at the previous Panathenaea' (7–9) refers to the Great Panathenaea, with which regular assessments of tribute coincided (cf. **153**), and implies that the next Great Panathenaea and assessment are approaching; that *IG* i^3 281 and 282, in which Methone and some other states are recorded as paying Athena's share only (281. ii. 31–5, restored; 282. ii. 51–6, preserved), are the quota lists of 430/29 and 429/8; and that 'the soldiers in Potidaea' (27–8) are those besieging Potidaea, which capitulated to Athens in winter 430/29 (Thuc. II. 70). That leads to the conclusion that Methone joined the League in time to be assessed in 434, and that §i is to be dated (not in the winter but) shortly before the Panathenaea of summer 430. Mattingly accepts *ATL*'s argument that the Great Panathenaea and an assessment are approaching, but he finds a long lapse of time between §i and §ii awkward, believes that the soldiers are the garrison of the Athenian colony established after the capitulation of Potidaea (for such garrisons cf. Thuc. IV. 7), and argues (from the order in which the districts are mentioned in the lists) that *IG* i^3 282 belongs to 427/6 and 281 to 426/5. His date for §i is therefore 427/6. Hammond argues that Methone was not yet in the League when Athens atttacked Pydna in early summer 432 (Thuc. I. 61. ii–iii) but joined in 432/1; that 'the previous Panathenaea' is that of 430 and could have been referred to as such at any time between 430 and 426 (while the assessment contemplated in 6–7 could be an ad hoc reassessment for Methone only); and that the soldiers are the garrison of the Athenian colony. He therefore dates §i to 429/8, with 429/8 (*IG* i^3 282, dated as in *ATL*) the first year in which Methone paid Athena's share only; and the interpretation of Piérart is similar (with *IG* i^3 282 dated 429/8 or 427/6 and 281 between 430/29 and 427/6).

Perdiccas was hostile to Athens in 432 (Thuc. I. 57; a short-lived reconciliation 61–2); he rejoined the Athenians in 431 (II. 29. vi) but secretly supported Ambracia in 429 (II. 80. vii); the Athenians were expected, but failed, to support Sitalces' campaign against him in winter 429/8 (II. 95, 101. i); by summer 424 he was worried about Athens and his encouragement of Brasidas led Athens to declare war on him (IV. 79. ii, 82); suggested dates for Athens' inscribed treaty with Perdiccas (*IG* i^3 89) range from the 430s to the 410s: this record would not rule out any of the suggested dates for a decree in which the Athenians are encouraging him to be friendly, though it tells somewhat against 429/8. The dates of the quota lists from the 420s remain uncertain (cf. on **153**), and of course the earliest year in which Methone is attested as paying Athena's share only need not be the earliest year in which it did pay Athena's share only. We agree with Hammond and Piérart that §i is not necessarily to be dated shortly before a new assessment, and that 'the previous Panathenaea' is probably that of 430 and 'the soldiers in Potidaea' are probably the garrison of the colony established in 430/29. §i is to be dated after that, and perhaps not in 429/8, but before the summer of 426, and before *IG* i^3 281 (where the restoration is plausible) and 282; but without secure dates for those quota lists greater precision is impossible.

In §i Diopithes (4–5), possibly but not certainly the proposer, was a man interested in oracles, and religion generally, credited with a decree aimed at Pericles' associate Anaxagoras which provided for prosecution of the religiously unorthodox (Plut. *Per.* 32. ii), and mocked in comedy (e.g. Ar. *Eq.* 1084–5, *Vesp.* 380, *Av.* 988). In 5–9 we have an instance of a fairly common phenomenon, by which the proposer invites the assembly to choose immediately (i.e. immediately after the enactment of his proposal) between two options, and the choice is recorded at the end of the decree (29–32). Methone has presumably pleaded difficulty in paying its tribute, the assembly is invited to choose between making an ad hoc reassessment and requiring only Athena's $\frac{1}{60}$ of the current assessment, and chooses the latter. Money owed to the state treasury (9–11) is presumably something other than unpaid tribute, and for this Methone is promised special treatment as long as it behaves well (and we learn incidentally that Athens has enacted or may enact general decrees about such debts).

Perdiccas is to be asked (16–27) not to interfere with Methone's trade, and not to take military forces through Methone's territory without Methone's permission (a practice about which there seems to have been increasing anxiety during the Peloponnesian War: see on **165**). Athens' envoys are to be men over 50 (17): 30 was the normal age requirement for office-holding, but higher ages were required on some occasions, and the word *presbys* suggests that older men were thought likely to command more respect as envoys.

The proposer of §ii is Cleonymus (34), who probably in this same year 426/5 proposed **152** and *IG* i^3 69, and may well have been a member of the council. He is frequently mocked by Aristophanes as a glutton and a coward (e.g. *Eq.* 956–8, 1369–72), and seems to have confirmed his reputation for cowardice by running away at the battle of Delium in winter 424/3 (*Nub.* 353 and later allusions). Here Methone is given special permission to import corn from Byzantium (34–41): we see that Athens appointed *hellespontophylakes* to control the trade between the Black Sea and the Aegean, and can infer that stocks of corn were held at Byzantium and that other states could not draw on these without special permission from Athens (see Garnsey, *Famine and Food Supply in the Graeco-Roman World*, 121–3). Similar permission was granted to Aphytis, south of Potidaea on the western prong of the Chalcidic peninsula (*IG* i^3 62, referring to Methone: dated 428/7 by Meritt on the basis of his speculative restoration of ll. 16–17, but more probably shortly after §ii of our inscription: cf. Mattingly, e.g. *BSA* lxv 1970, 134–5 = his *AER* 289–90). As in §i Methone was exempted from general decrees about debts, here (41–7) it is exempted from other general decrees, particularly any concerning military support (for ἐ]ν τôι τεταγμένοι ὄντον in 47 as 'they shall be doing their duty' cf. R&O 44. 48).

Relations with Perdiccas remain precarious (47–51): we know nothing about the two embassies mentioned; since the name is rare in Athens it is likely that Pleistias is the man restored as first secretary in 425/4 (**153**. 56, **160**. 17), and it is possible that Leogoras is from the family of Andocides or from the family of Dracontides (cf. on **148**). The continual sessions in the dockyard (53–5) are presumably sessions of the council before the dispatch of an expedition (cf. R&O 100. 247–51), perhaps that mentioned in Thuc. III. 105. iii. In 55–6 we have one of the few texts (cf. **162**), probably all from the period of the Peloponnesian War, which indicate that the

---

151

Contributions to a Spartan war fund, *c.*427–412

Two joining fragments of a bluish-grey Taygetan marble *stele*, one built into a church south of Sparta, the other identified in 1987 in a monastery to the south-west of that church, now joined and in the museum at Sparta. Phot. *ὅρος* vii 1989, πιν. 12–23; Loomis, *The Spartan War Fund*, pls. 1–16.

Spartan lettering. Non-*stoichedon*.

IG v. i 1; *SIG*³ 84; Tod 62; M&L 67 (right-hand fragment only); A. P. Matthaiou & G. A. Pikoulas, *ὅρος* vii 1989 (publ. 1991), 77–124; Loomis, *The Spartan War Fund*; Matthaiou, *τὰ ἐν τῆι στήληι γεγραμμένα*, 35–43*. Trans. Fornara 132 (right-hand fragment only); Loomis, 13 (both fragments). See also *LSAG* 197, 201, no. 55; B. Bleckmann, *ZPE* xcvi 1993, 297–308; M. Piérart, *BCH* cxix 1995, 252–82; M. G. Seaman, *Historia* xlvi 1997, 391–402; B. Smarczyk, *Klio* lxxxi 1999, 45–67; B. Bleckmann, *Ktema* xxvii 2002, 35–8.

front

[ἔ]δ̣ον τ̣ο̣ὶ Ι̣ Φ̣Ι̣[.]ιο̣ι [—c.3–4—]Ο̣[—c.3–5— τοὶ Λα]κ̣ε̣δ̣α̣ι̣μ̣ο̣ν̣ί̣ο̣[ν φί]λ̣ο̣[ι]
[π]ο̣τὸν π̣ό̣λ̣εμον τ̣ε̣τρακατῖο̣ς δαρ̣ι̣χ̣ὸ̣ς Ε̣Φ̣Ε̣Ι̣Σ[.]α λ̣[ό]χοι̣.
ἔ̣δ̣ον τοὶ Αἰγινᾶται τοῖς Λ̣ακεδα̣ι̣μ̣ον̣ί̣οι̣ς π̣ο̣τὸ̣ν
[π]ό̣λεμ̣[ον τέτορε]ς καὶ δέκ̣α μνᾶς κα̣ὶ̣ δ̣έκα στατε̂ρας.
[ἔδο]ν̣ [τ]ο̣ὶ̣ [—c.4–5—]οι τοῖς Λ̣ακ̣εδα̣ιμονίοις ΛΥΡΕΙ δα<ρ>ιχό̣ς.
vacat
[ἔ]δ̣ο̣ν̣ Σ̣Ο̣Μ̣[—c.2–3—]ο̣φον Ἀχα̣ῖος Ὀλέ̣ν̣[ι]ος ẖΟ̣Δ̣[—c.6–7—]ΤΟΛ̣[—c.6–7—]
το̣ῖς Λ̣α[κεδ]α̣ιμονίοις π̣οττὸν π̣όλ̣ε̣μ̣ον τριέρεΓ . ΧΜ . .Ο̣[c.1–2]

The stone has deteriorated badly: letters underlined were read by earlier editors but not by Matthaiou & Pikoulas or by Loomis. From the width of the stone we should expect a substantial further amount from the bottom to have been lost (Matthaiou).

front 1 τ̣ο̣ὶ Ἐ̣φέσ̣ιο̣ι̣ or Ἐ̣φέσιο̣ν̣ [φεύγ]ο[ντες (?) Matthaiou: Τ̣ έ̣{ο̣}ιο̣ι̣ φεύγοντες τοὶ (?) Matthaiou & Pikoulas, [– – – τοὶ τôν Loomis. 2 Matthaiou: δα̣ρ̣ι<χ>ὸς Loomis. 5 Θ̣[ά]σ[ι]οι (?) Matthaiou & Pikoulas, [– – –]οι Loomis. δα<ρι>χό̣ς Matthaiou & Pikoulas, δα<ρι>χ{ι}ό̣ς Loomis. 6 ẖο̣δ̣[—c.4–5— Αἰ]-τολ̣[ός] (?) Matthaiou & Pikoulas, [καὶ —c.7—]ο̣[– – –] Loomis. 7 τριέρεẖ[ι]<ν> μ[ισ]θ̣[όν] (?) Matthaiou & Pikoulas, τριέρεΓ . Ξ Μ . . Loomis.

generals had a privileged position with regard to the council and assembly (see Rhodes, *Boule*, 43–6).

For Methone these decrees are favourable; but in ways which imply a contrast with Athens' treatment of its other allies. There may be general decrees about debts (13–16), and about military support and other matters (41–7), from which Methone is exempted; and the Athenian *hellespontophylakes* control the transport of corn to destinations other than Athens (34–41). This suggests that in general in the 420s Athens was controlling the allies firmly, as Pericles had recommended (Thuc. II. 13. ii, 63).

---

front

The Ephesian exiles (?) who are friends of the Spartans gave towards the war four hundred darics – – –

3 The Aeginetans gave to the Spartans towards the war fourteen minas and ten staters.

5 The —— gave to the Spartans – – – darics.

6 Som—ophon of Olenus in Achaea and Hod— of Aetolia (?) gave to the Spartans for the war pay

[— c.5–6 —] μ̣ν̣ᾶν καὶ ἀ̣ργυρί̣ο μνᾶ̣ς δύ̣ε̣ κα̣ὶ̣ τριάκο̣ν̣τ̣α̣.
ἔ̣δ̣[ον] τ̣οὶ φεύγοντες τôν Χίον τοὶ φίλ̣ο̣ι τοὶ τ̣ộν
[Λακ]ε̣[δα]ι̣μονίον χελίος στατε̣̄ρας Αἰ̣γιναί̣ο̣ς.
vacat
[ἔδοκε? — c.5–8 —]ον το[ῖ]ς Λακεδαιμονίοις π̣οττὸν
[πόλεμον — c.4–7 —]Ν̣Π̣[— c.2–3 —] τ̣<ε>τρακιν<χε>λίος καὶ ἄλλος
[— c.19–21 —]ακινχελίος καὶ ἀστα<φ>ίδος
[— c.15–17 — τάλ]α̣ν̣τ̣α̣.
[ἔδον *or* ἔδοκε — c.14–16 —]Η . . ΙΟΣΣ/ . . ΚΕΤ
[— c.18–20 —] πολλὰ καὶ <δ>αρικὸς ὀκτακατ<ί>-
[ος καὶ — c.16–18 —]ΝΔΙΟΤΙΤΑ τάλαντα.
[ἔδον *or* ἔδοκε — c.15 —]ΕΙ . . Ν ποττὸν πόλεμον
[— c.18 —]ΝΙΟΝ τριάκοντα μνᾶς
[— c.10–13 —]|Ε̣ . Ο̣ [– –]ισχελίος μεδίμνος καὶ
[— c.16 — κ]οντα καὶ ΑΙΜΥΡΙ . . ϝεξέ-
[κοντα –]
– –

written up right-hand margin of front

[ἔδον τ]οὶ Ἐφέσιοι τοῖς Λακεδαιμ[ονίοις]
[ποττὸ]ν πόλεμον χ<ε>λίο{υ}ς δ̣αρ[ικός].

right-hand side
beginning level with front l. 6

ἔδον τοὶ Μ̣ά̣-
λ̣ιοι τοῖ̣ς
Λακεδαί̣-
μονίοις
ἀργυρίο
ϝ<ί>κατι
μνᾶς.

ἔδοκε Μό[— c.3 —]
Λοκρὸς τοῖς
Λακεδαιμο-
νίοις τάλαν-
τ<ον?> ἀργυρίο.

8 [χρυσίο] μ̣ν̣ᾶν (?) Matthaiou & Pikoulas, [— c.8 —]ΑΝ Loomis. 15 τ̣ο<ῖ>ς{ς} Λ[α]κε<δ>[αιμονίοις] (?) Matthaiou & Pikoulas, Η . ΙΟΣΣ/ . ΚΕΤ Loomis. 20 [— c.10–13 —]Ι Ε̣ . Ο̣ . [– –] Matthaiou & Pikoulas, [καὶ – – –] Loomis. 22–4 Matthaiou & Pikoulas: [κοντα. ἔδον τ]οὶ Ἐφέσιοι τοῖς Λακεδαιμ[ο|νίοις πὸτ τὸ]ν πόλεμον χ<ε>λίο{υ}ς δ̣αρ[ικός]. | – – – Loomis. *side* There are horizontal lines between the entries. 8–9 Μό[λον?] | Λοκρὸς Matthaiou & Pikoulas, Μό|λοκρος Loomis: see commentary.

for triremes (?) and thirty-two minas of silver.

9 The exiles of the Chians who are friends of the Spartans gave a thousand Aeginetan staters.

11 —on gave to the Spartans towards the war – – – four thousand and other – – – —— thousand and raisins – – – talents.

15 – – – to the Spartans (?) – – – many and eight hundred darics and – – – talents.

18 – – – towards the war – – – thirty minas – – – —— thousand *medimnoi* and – – – – —ty and sixty.

– – – – – – – – –

written up right-hand margin of front

23 The Ephesians gave to the Spartans towards the war a thousand darics.

right-hand side

vacant space at top

The Melians gave to the Spartans twenty minas of silver.

8 Mo— the Locrian (?) gave to the Spartans a talent of silver.

ἔ̣δον τοὶ
Μάλιοι
τοῖς
[Λ]ακεδαι-
[μ]ονίο[ις]
. . . . Λ
– – – – – –

The new fragment has given us the previously missing upper left-hand part of the *stele*, but has not resolved disagreements about the date. We have a list of contributions to Sparta 'for the war', by communities and individuals, all outside the Peloponnesian League; some contributors, including the Ephesians, pay not in Greek coinage but in Persian darics; there are also raisins (13) and *medimnoi*, presumably of grain (20). The width of the stone suggests that a substantial amount has been lost from the bottom of the *stele*.

Almost everybody has agreed that the war was the Peloponnesian War, but Lewis *ap.* M&L and some others favoured the 390s, and P. A. Cartledge, *CR*[2] xliii 1993, 403–4, was still inclined to that dating. The arrangement of the text (in particular, the gaps on the front of the *stele* and the insertion of the Ephesian entry in the right-hand margin, and the insertion of another entry between the two for Melos) suggests that it was inscribed in instalments as contributions were received. Loomis, 56–60, surveys the older interpretations. Since the publication of the new fragment Smarczyk has suggested the period of enthusiasm for Sparta at the beginning of the war (cf. Thuc. II. 8. iv–v); but there have been two main schools of thought: a list beginning *c.*427, perhaps in conjunction with Sparta's venture into the Aegean under Alcidas (Thuc. III. 26. i, 29. i–34. i), and inscribed over more than ten years (Matthaiou & Pikoulas) or completed in a short period (Loomis); or a list compiled *c.*409 (Bleckmann, Piérart; the text on the side slightly later, Seaman). The entry for the Ephesians at *front* 23–4 appears in Fourmont's transcription at the bottom right, running up the page, and requires shorter lines than the other entries: Matthaiou & Pikoulas argue that the text cannot have begun at the left-hand margin but was added running up the right-hand margin of the stone as the last addition to the text on the front, as in Fourmont's transcription, after the entries on the side of the stone;[1] Loomis suggests that Fourmont simply ran out of space on his page. We review the individual entries.

At *front* 1–2 Matthaiou & Pikoulas had suggested restoring the Teans, Loomis had not restored, Matthaiou now sees traces which allow restoration of Ephesian exiles (to be contrasted with the Ephesian state at *front* 23–4). Teans, if that were right, might have included friends of Sparta either *c.*427 or *c.*409 (cf. Thuc. III. 32. i; VIII.

[1] For additions in this style cf. the Athenian casualty lists *IG* i³ 1144. 39–40, 128–9, 1147 *bis*, 50–1.

13 The Melians gave to the Spartans – – –
– – – – – – – – – –

16–20, Xen. *Hell.* i. v. 15 [Τέων for Ἠΐονα Schneider]); a payment by Ephesian exiles can plausibly be dated at the time of Alcidas' voyage, in 427, and contrasted with a later payment by the *polis* of Ephesus. The Aeginetans (3–4) were expelled by the Athenians in 431, and occupied Thyrea until that was taken by the Athenians in 424 (Thuc. II. 27, IV. 56. ii –57); the Spartans could well have regarded the community in Thyrea, or even a remnant elsewhere after 424 (cf. Xen. *Hell.* II. ii. 9) as the true Aeginetans, but Matthaiou argues that a fragment of the original citizen body should be identified as such. Thasos (possibly to be read in 5—but we should not expect it to be contributing darics) is not known to have been disloyal to Athens in the 420s, unless Thucydides' presence there in 424/3 (IV. 104. iv–105. i) is a sign of trouble; it defected from Athens in 411 (Thuc. VIII. 64. iii–iv), and was recovered possibly in 410 (Xen. *Hell.* I. i. 32, but Ἰασῷ for Θάσῳ Kahrstedt), more probably in 407 (I. iv. 9). For Olenus in Achaea (6–9) see *Inventory*, 483; individual Achaeans and Aetolians might have made contributions early or late, but pay for a trireme would not be likely between 425 and 412. Exiled Chians who are friends of Sparta (9–10) exclude the period from at any rate 408 to 394, when after the Spartan Cratesippidas' restoration of exiles there will not have been any Chians fitting that description (Diod. Sic. XIII. 65. iii–iv, XIV. 84. iii): supporters of the early date point to Athens' suspicions of Chios in 425/4 (Thuc. IV. 51), supporters of the late take the exiles to be those whom Cratesippidas restored in 409/8. The Ephesians (23–4) are not qualified as exiles or dissidents, so this contribution from them should have come from the *polis*: it is not known to have wavered in the 420s, though it was visited by Alcidas in 427 (Thuc. III. 32. ii–33. i) and he might have elicited a contribution; it appears as a tribute-payer in *IG* i^3 290, but that is not necessarily to be dated 415/4; it is not necessarily to be restored under 415/4 in **170**. 78–9; in 412 a Chian ship escaped to it, in 411 Tissaphernes sacrificed to Artemis there, in 409 Thrasyllus failed to recover it for Athens, and in 407/6 it was Lysander's base in the Aegean (Thuc. VIII. 19. iii, 109, Xen. *Hell.* I. ii. 7–13, v. 1–vi. 2, cf. Diod. Sic. XIII. 64. i, 70–1, 76. iii).

Melos (*side* 1–7, 13 sqq.) was attacked by Athens in 426 but did not succumb; it was assessed for tribute in 425 but we have no reason to think that it paid (**153**. i. 65); it was captured by Athens in 416/5 (Thuc. v. 116. iii–iv), but there were some survivors (cf. Xen. *Hell.* II. ii. 9), and as in the case of Aegina Sparta could have regarded these as the Melians. The individual between the two Melian entries (15–19) is better seen as a Locrian, since despite the attractions of Molo<b>rus (on the later dating a son of the Epitadas of Thuc. iv. 8. ix), we should be surprised to find a Spartan figuring here.

No single solution is obviously the best for all the entries, and the decision is difficult; but on balance the distinction between Ephesian exiles in *front* 1–2 and the *polis* of Ephesus in *front* 23–4, and the failure to characterise the Aeginetans in *front* 3–4 and the Melians on the side as fragments of the citizen bodies, favour the view of Matthaiou & Pikoulas that the list was begun *c*.427, and had the Melians added to it before 416/5 but the Ephesians in *front* 23–4 not earlier than *c*.412.

Loomis notes that the total of the preserved figures is equivalent to 13 tal. 274 dr. in Athenian currency, perhaps enough to support four triremes or 800 soldiers for three months—but if as Matthaiou argues material has been lost from the bottom of the *stele* the overall total will have been higher. Financially sums of this order

---

152

Athenian decree proposed by Cleonymus about Delian League tribute, 426/5 (?)

Thirteen fragments of a marble *stele*, found on or near the Athenian acropolis, now in the Epigraphical Museum. Phot. *ATL* i, 123–6 figs. 178–84 (frs. 1–11 = *a*–*k*), *ATL* ii, pl. V (fr. 12 = *l*), *AJP* lxxxviii 1967, pl. I (fr. 13 = *m*); *AJP* lxxxviii 1967, pl. II (the *stele* reconstructed). At the top (a little preserved on fr. 2) was a relief showing jars and sacks in which the tribute was carried, and l. 1 was carved on the moulding between that and the main surface. Relief Meyer, *Die griechischen Urkundenreliefs*, 265 A3; Lawton, *Attic Document Reliefs*, 81 A1 with pl. 1. 1.

Developed Attic writing, using h frequently but not invariably. Lines 3–57 *stoichedon* 36.

IG i^{2} 65; Meritt, *Documents on Athenian Tribute*, 3–42; *ATL* D 8; Meritt, *AJP* lxxxviii 1967, 29–32 (adding fr. 13 = *m*); M&L 68; *IG* i^{3} 68 (Meritt & McGregor); our text is based, by permission, on a re-editing by Dr A. P. Matthaiou (cf. his 'Studies in Attic Inscriptions and the History of the Fifth Century BC', 89–107). Trans. Fornara 133; Osborne, *The Athenian Empire*^{4}, 136 (different translation in earlier editions); Dillon & Garland^{3} 13. 15.

[- - - - -]ẹμạ[- - - - - - - - - -]ις *vacat*
φόρ[ο].

§i

ἔδοχσεν τε̑ι βολε̑ι καὶ τ[ο̑ι δέμοι]. Κεκροπὶς ἐπ-
ρυτάνε[υ]ε· Πολέμαρχος [ἐγραμμά]τευε·Ὄνασος ἐ-
πεστάτ[ε. Κ]λεόνυμ[ος εἶπε· hοπόσ]αι πόλες φόρο-
ν φέροσ[ι Ἀθ]ενα[ίοις hαιρέσθον] ἐν ἑκάστει τε̑-
[ι] πόλει [φόρο ἐγλογέας hόπος ἂν] hεκασταχόθε-

would not have made a great difference to Sparta, but contributions from outside the Peloponnesian League would have been important for Sparta's image, and that will explain why, despite the great rarity of public inscriptions from classical Sparta, this list was inscribed. *IG* v. i 219 seems to be a fragment from a comparable list, by another cutter on a different stone.

How did Sparta obtain these contributions from outside its own alliance, and how willingly were they paid? According to Thucydides (e.g. i. 75–7, ii. 8. iv), Athens' power was already widely resented at the beginning of the war; and Sparta's attempt to support Mytilene in 427, though ill-managed and ineffective (iii. 25–33), did at least show that it was willing to venture beyond the Greek mainland, and may have encouraged opponents of Athens. If Melos made contributions after the Peace of Nicias, that may help to explain why Athens attacked it in 416.

– – –

2 Of tribute.

§i

3 Resolved by the council and the people. Cecropis was the prytany; Polemarchus was the secretary; Onasus was the chairman. Cleonymus proposed:

5 As many cities as pay tribute to the Athenians shall elect in each city collectors [*eklogeis*] of tribute, so that all the tribute may be collected (?) for the

[ν Ἀθε]·[αίοις —— 15 ——] ho [φόρος] ἒ hυπ-
- -

lacuna

[. . τοῖς δὲ ἑλλενοταμίαις ἐκκλεσίαν ποεῖν] ἐπ-
[άναγκες(?) —— 13 —— τὲν πρυτανεία]ṿ hέτ-
[ις ἂν πρυτα]ṿεύε[ι —— 12 —— μετὰ] Διονύσ-
[ια· ἐς δὲ κοι]νον ἀ[—— 14 —— πό]λες hαιτ-
[ινες ἂν ἀπο]δôσι τ[ὸν φόρον καὶ αἴτιν]ες μὲ ἀπο-
[δôσιν καὶ h]αίτιν[ες —— 10 ——. ἐ]πὶ δὲ τὰς ὀφ-
[ελόσας πέ]μπεν πέ[ντε ἄνδρας hίνα] ἐσπράχσον-
[ται τὸμ φ]όρον. ἀναγ[ραφόντον δὲ hοι ἑλ]λενοτα̣-
[μί]αι ἐς σανίδι τὰς [πόλες τὰς —6—]σας τô φό-
[ρ]ο και τôν ἀπαγόντ[ον τὰ ὀνόματα κ]αὶ τιθέναι
[h]εκάστοτε πρόσθε[—— 10 —— ἔ]στο δὲ καὶ Σα-
μίοις καὶ Θεραίοι[ς —— 8 ——]ΣΛ̣|[.]Σ̣[..]|[.]|[..]
ον χρεμάτον ον τεχ̣[—— 8 ——]εν τε̂ς αἱρέσεος
[τ]ôν ἀνδρôν, καὶ εἴ τ[ις ἄλλ]ε πόλ[ι]ς ἐτάχσατο χρ-
[έ]μ̣ατα ἀπάγεν Ἀθέν[αζε. τ]ὸ δὲ φσέφισμα τόδε ἐσ-
[τέ]λει hε Κεκροπὶ[ς πρυτα]νεία θέτο ἐμ πόλει ⁝ Π-
[. . .]κριτος εἶπε· τ̣[ὰ μὲν ἄλ]λα καθάπερ Κλεόνυμ-
[ος· h]όπος δὲ ἄρι[στα καὶ ῥᾶ]ιστα οἴσοσι Ἀθενα-
[îοι τ]ὸν πόλεμ[ον, γνόμεν ἐς] τὸν δε̂μον ἐχφέρεν
[ἐκκλε]σίαṿ [ποέσοντας hε]οθινέν ⁝

§ii

ἔδοχσεν τε̂ι
[βόλει καὶ τôι δέμοι. Κεκρ]όπις ἐπρυτάνευε· Πο-
[λέμαρχος ἐγραμμάτευε· h]υγιαίνον ἐπέστατε.
[—— 9 —— εἶπε· τὰ μὲν ἄλλ]α κατὰ τὸ πρότερο[ν]
[φσέφισμα —— 14 ——]ματα ἐς τὸν [. . . .]

lacuna

We omit fr. 11, which contains a total of eight letters from three lines and has not been placed in relation to the others. We number the lines as in *ATL* and M&L; *Documents on Athenian Tribute* has a restored l. 10 and *IG* i³ an unrestored l. 10 after the first *lacuna*, after which our ll. 10 sqq. are numbered 11 sqq. Where there is no doubt about the words, we have not marked letters which were seen by earlier editors but not at all or only as 'dotted' letters by Matthaiou.

Except where otherwise stated, restorations are those of Meritt in *Documents on Athenian Tribute* (in some cases repeated from an earlier editor). 8 σύμπας ἐγλέγεται Meritt. 8–9 hυπ||[εύθυνοι ὂσι hοι ἐγλογε̂ς Meritt, ὄντον *IG* i³. 10–11 . . τοῖς δὲ ἑλλενοταμίαις ἐκκλεσίαν ποιε̂ν] ἐπ||[άναγκες(?) περὶ τôν πόλεον Meritt. 12 δέκα ἑμερôν μετὰ τὰ Meritt, perhaps χρεματίζεν or ἐς τὸν δε̂μον μετὰ τὰ M&L, εἰκοσι ἑμερôν μετὰ Meritt 1967. 13 ἀ[ποφαινόσθον hαι πό]λες Meritt, καὶ ἀναγ]νôνα[ι ἐν τôι δέμοι τὰς πό]λες M&L, ἀ[ποδεικνύναι τὰς (?) πό]λες Matthaiou. 15 ἂν κατὰ μέρε Meritt, ἂν ἐλλίποσι (?) Matthaiou (cf. **154**. 21–2). 18 ἐλλιπό]σας Meritt. 19 A. Wilhelm. 20 τô βέματος *ATL* ii cf. iii. 16, τôν hερόον *ATL* iv. ix–x, but there is no parallel for either. 21–2 π̣ε̣ρ̣[ὶ τ]||ôν Meritt 1967, π̣[ε]ρ̣[ὶ τ]||ôν (?) Matthaiou. 22 ὂντεχ[ρὲποε̂νπλ]ὲνMeritt1967,ὂντεχ[νάζοσιπλ]ὲν(?)Matthaiou. 25–6 Π||[ολύ]κριτος or Π||[υθό]κριτος. 32 Κλεόνυμος (Meritt 1967) is the right length, but so too are many other names.

Athenians from each place, or the collectors shall be accountable (?) – – –

lacuna

10 – – –an assembly shall be held obligatorily for the *hellenotamiai* (?) – – – by the prytany which is in office within twenty days (?) after the Dionysia, and they shall reveal (?) in public the cities which have paid the tribute and the cities which have not paid and the cities which have fallen short (?). To those which are in debt five men shall be sent to exact the tribute. The *hellenotamiai* shall write up on a tablet the cities which have fallen short with their tribute and the names of those who have brought it – – – and place it on each occasion in front of – – –

20 And there shall be for the Samians and Theraeans – – – the monies which – – – apart (?) from the election of the men, and if any other city has been assessed to bring monies to Athens.

24 The prytany of Cecropis shall place this decree on a *stele* on the acropolis.

25 [Polycritus *or* Pythocritus] proposed:

26 In other respects in accordance with Cleonymus; but, so that the Athenians may wage the war most well and easily, a proposal shall be brought to the people at an assembly to be held in the morning.

§ii

29 Resolved by the council and the people. Cecropis was the prytany; Polemarchus was the secretary; Hygiaenon was the chairman. —— proposed:

32 In other respects in accordance with the previous decree – – –

lacuna

[—12—]Ẹ[—23—]
[—12—]θα[—23—]
[.]\[—9—]ανε[—21—]δ-
εειΕΟ..Λ..|πλερ[—16— ἐπ]ιμελ-
ετὰς αἱρêσθαι τô[ν —17—] τôν Ἀ-
θεναίον χρεμάτον κα[τὰ τὸ —9— φ]σέφισ-
μα καὶ τôν στρατεγôν [—14—]ζεσθα-
ι hόταν περί τινος τôν [—18—]
ι. ἐὰν δέ τις κακοτεχνêι [hόπος μὲ κύριον ἔστα]-
ι τὸ φσέφισμα τὸ τô φόρο [ȇ hόπος μὲ ἀπαχθέσετ]-
αι hο φόρος Ἀθέναζε, γρά[φεσθαι —11—]
τον τον ἐκ ταύτες τêς πό[λεος τὸν βολόμενον π]-
ρὸς τὸς ἐπιμελέτας· hο[ι δὲ ἐπιμελεταὶ ἐσαγό]-
ντον ἔμμενα ἐς τὸ δ[ικαστέριον ἐπειδὰν hοι κ]-
λετêρες ἔκοσι· δι[πλε]ῖ δὲ [ὄντον hοι κλετêρες]
ȇ κατὰ hôν γράφεσθαί τις β[όλοιτο. ἐὰν δέ το κα]-
ταγνôι τὸ [δικ]αστέριον, τιμ̣[âν ὅ τι χρὲ αὐτὸν π]-
αθêν ȇ ἀ̣[π]ο̣τε̣ῖσαι. τὸς δὲ κέ[ρυκας —10—]
ες [.]σ[.]ος ἂν hοι πρυτάνες με[—10— hέλο]-
[ντα]ι πέμφσαι ἐς τὰς πόλες ἐ[πὶ τêς —9—]-
[ς πρ]υτανείας hόπος ἂν αἱρε[θôσι —9— h]-
[οι] τὸν φόρον ἐγλέχσοντες, κ[αὶ ἀναγραφôσι ἐν]
[τô]ι βολευτερί[ο]ι. τὲν δὲ στέλ[εν hοι πολεταὶ ἀ]-
[πο]μισθοσάντον. *vacat*
[φ]όρο ἐγλο[γêς τô]
[πα]ρὰ τôν πό[λεον].
vacat

38 τô[ν ἄλλον δικôν τôν περὶ] Meritt, τô[ν μὲ ἐσπραχθέντον ὑπὸ] (?) Matthaiou. 39 γενόμενον Wilhelm: πρότερον and Κλεονύμο are each one letter too short. 40–1 [hένα τάττεν παρέ]ζεσθα|ι Meritt (ḥ[in *IG* i[3]), [ἕνα ἀεὶ χσυγκαθέ]ζεσθα|ι (?) Matthaiou. 41–2 [πόλεον δίκε δικάζετα]|ι Meritt, [ὀφελοσôν χρεματίζοσ]|ι (?) Matthaiou. 44–5 προδοσίας αὐ]|τὸν τôν Meritt, κατὰ τôν πρατ]-|τόντον (?) Matthaiou. 48 Matthaiou: διπλô]ι Meritt. 51–2 h[όσοι ἄν τιν]|ες [ὃ]σι ὃς ἂν Meritt. 52 με[τὰ τές βολêς Meritt. 53–4 ἐ[πὶ τêς Κεκροπίδο|ς Meritt. 54 hοι ἄνδρες Meritt, hος τάχιστα (?) Matthaiou.

In the early years of the Peloponnesian War Athens spent money heavily and it seems confidently, but in the winter of 428/7 Thuc. III. 19 reports financial anxiety, and after that the drain on Athens' reserves was greatly reduced (cf. **160**). More money was raised from the citizens, through the property tax known as *eisphora* (cf. **144**. *B*. 16–17), and more money was raised also from the member states of the Delian League. Thucydides mentions ships sent to collect money (perhaps in addition to the regular tribute) in 430/29, 428/7 and 425/4 (II. 69. i, III. 19, IV. 50. i), and we have a series of three inscriptions from the mid-420s concerned with

37 – – – elect overseers [*epimeletai*] of the monies not exacted (?) by the Athenians in accordance with the – – – decree, and one of the generals shall always sit with them (?) when they deal with the business of any of the cities in debt (?). If any one contrives wickedly that the decree about the tribute shall not be valid or that the tribute shall not be brought to Athens, there shall be prosecution of those who do this (?) by whoever wishes from this city, before the overseers, and the overseers shall bring the case to the court monthly when the summons-witnesses [*kleteres*] have come; the witnesses shall be double the number (?) of those whom any one wishes to prosecute. If the court condemns, there shall be an assessment of what the man should suffer or pay.

51 The heralds – – – the *prytaneis* – – – shall elect and send to the cities in the prytany of ——, so that the men to collect the tribute shall be elected as quickly (?) as possible, and write them up in the council house.

56 The *poletai* shall make the contract for the *stele*.

58 Collectors of the tribute from the cities.

---

increasing the amount of tribute which reached Athens; on the need to raise more money to pay for the war, note here ll. 27–8.

Here we have (§i) a decree proposed by one Cleonymus, and (in accordance with the amendment which ends it) a supplementary decree (§ii), the proposer of which had a name of nine letters (so could have been the proposer of the amendment or Cleonymus or neither), enacted in the same prytany (Cecropis, secretary Polemarchus), and presumably on the day after §i as stipulated in the amendment. A Cleonymus proposed **150** §ii in the first prytany of 426/5; Cecropis held the second prytany in that year (**160**. 6), and a Cleonymus proposed *IG* i^3 69 on the same day as the supplementary decree (§ii) here. It is an attractive possibility that the well-known Cleonymus (see discussion of him on **150**) was a member of the council in 426/5 and proposed **150** §ii, *IG* i^3 69 and §i here, and perhaps also §ii here, in that year. However, the formula introducing the amendment, with reference not to the council but to him, suggests that his proposal here was not incorporated in the council's *probouleuma* for the assembly (cf. **142**. 32–5, and see Introduction, pp. xx, xxii): some have thought that suggests a year when he was not a member of the council; and Matthaiou argues that the *sanides* prescribed in ll. 17–19 here are those alluded to in **150**. 13–15, for which he accepts Mattingly's date of 427/6, and so thinks this decree ought to be earlier than that.[1]

We accept the date of 426/5 for this decree as probable but not certain. If assessments of tribute had been made regularly in the years of the Great Panathenaea, there will have been one in 430 and another in 426, shortly before the enactment of this decree: on the question whether that is what had happened, see **153** with commentary. If there had been an assessment in the spring of 426, with significant increases, that could have provoked opposition and Cleonymus' decree could be a reaction to that opposition; on the scenario of *ATL*, which we think less likely, there had been an assessment in 428, in 426 the regular assessment was not held but Cleonymus' decree was enacted, and this was followed by the assessment of 425.

Polemarchus is the only known fifth-century Athenian of this name, attested here and in *IG* i^3 69 (the Polemarchus of Plato's *Republic* was a metic, brother of the orator Lysias: I. 328 B 4–6); an Onasus is mentioned in the fragmentary *IG* i^3 109. 6 (410–407?). No Polycritus or Pythocritus (the two possibilities for the proposer of the amendment) is known in Athens from the second half of the fifth century. A Hygiaenon is named as *kalos* on vases of the 440s by the Achilles Painter (Beazley, *ARV*^{2}, p. 1586 with 997), and a Hygiaenon is said to have been involved in a lawsuit with Euripides (Arist. *Rh.* III. 1416 A 28–35).

To improve the receipt of the tribute by Athens, Cleonymus' decree introduces two requirements. First, the member states of the League are to appoint as 'collectors' individual citizens of their own, who are to be personally responsible for the collection and payment of their state's tribute (cf. Antiph. fr. 52 Blass & Thalheim = A. 2. 4 Maidment, and the collectors responsible for collecting firstfruits for Eleusis in **141**. 14–21); their duties were probably laid out in the lacuna between the first and second fragments. Secondly, lists are to be published each year of states which have paid, which have not paid and (probably) which have paid incompletely, and men are to be sent to exact payment from defaulters. Samos (20–1) did not pay tribute,

[1] Samons, *Empire of the Owl*, 188–9 with n. 84; Matthaiou, 'Studies', 105–7.

but if its payment of reparations after the war of 440–439 was by now complete it must have been making payments under some other rubric (cf. on **138**). Thera (21) was outside the League at the beginning of the war (Thuc. II. 9. iv), but included in the assessment of 425 (**153**. i. 68): its presence as a tribute-payer has been assumed in *IG* i[3] 281. ii 54 and restored in 282. iii. 23 (lists of the early 420s), and Meritt and colleagues supposed that it made payments under another rubric also, but Mattingly and Piérart argue that this decree makes better sense if at this time Thera like Samos did not pay tribute. (Piérart sugests that Thera gave in to Athenian pressure when Melos did not, in 426 (Thuc. III. 91. i–ii), but did not immediately become a tribute-payer.)

The use of an amendment to get a matter discussed further is not uncommon (cf. **141**, **142**), but is notable and surely indicative here of the seriousness of the issue. In the judicial arrangements of the second decree, the *epimeletai* ('overseers') appear to be special officials appointed to deal with the collection of tribute and to preside over trials in connection with it. 'Monthly' probably means that prosecutions may be brought in any month rather than that verdicts must be given within a month (Cohen, *Ancient Athenian Maritime Courts*, 9–59, cf. Rhodes, *Comm. Ath. Pol.* 583). On *kleteres* as witnesses to a summons by a volunteer prosecutor see Harrison, *The Law of Athens*, ii. 85–6, MacDowell, *The Law in Classical Athens*, 238–9; Aristophanes' plays of the 420s mention a single *kleter* (*Nub.* 1218, *Vesp.* 1408, 1416), but two are attested in the fourth century in [Dem.] XL. *Boeotus ii.* 28, LIII. *Nicostratus* 14. For offences for which the law did not prescribe a penalty, the court after deciding on guilt had to make 'an assessment of what the man should suffer [in his person] or pay', choosing between the proposals of the prosecutor and the defendant (cf. Harrison, 80–2, 168–9, MacDowell, 253–4). The heralds, who are to be dispatched either within the prytany in which the decree is enacted or in the following prytany, are presumably sent to the cities to announce the Athenian decision and to order them to act on it (cf. **155**).

Several fifth-century decrees specify that the *poletai* ('sellers' of public contracts: cf. *Ath. Pol.* 47. ii–v) are to make the contract for inscribing the text (cf. **153**. 25, **182**. 34–5, **183**. 8), and no doubt that was regular practice though it is not always stated. Although this *stele* has a heading, the second line of which specifies 'Of tribute', it ends with a postscript stating the subject more fully (cf. **157**. 24–6).

This is one of the earliest surviving Athenian decree inscriptions with a sculptured relief (**150** was not inscribed until 424/3): Lawton, 19–21 with 112–14, notes that no other decree with a relief need be earlier than the 420s: *IG* i[3] 21 (her B63) is best dated 426/5 and 28 (B64) to the late 420s (cf. Rhodes, *CQ*[2] lviii 2008, 503–4), 65 (B65) after 427 and 148 (B66) to the 420s; cf. also the likelihood that **154** had a painted illustration. Although not much survives of this relief, the pile of moneybags which can be clearly identified suggests that the image was not subtle.

153

Athenian decree proposed by Thudippus for the reassessment of Delian League tribute, 425/4

Forty-five fragments of a marble *stele*, found on or near the Athenian acropolis, now in the Epigraphical Museum (but one has been lost: see *apparatus*). Phot. Meritt & West, *The Athenian Assessment of* 425 BC; *ATL* i, 107–17 figs. 146–70.

Developed Attic writing, regularly using h. Lines 3–60 *stoichedon* 70.

IG i^2 63; Meritt & West; *ATL* A 9; M&L 69; *IG* i^3 71 (Meritt & McGregor); our text of ll. 1–60 is based, by permission, on a re-editing by Dr A. P. Matthaiou, who adds a further fragment in the middle of ll. 48–55 (cf. his 'Studies in Attic Inscriptions and the History of the Fifth Century BC', 18–68); after l. 60 we have followed *IG* i^3. Trans. Fornara 136; Osborne, *The Athenian Empire*^{4}, 138 (different translation in earlier editions); Dillon & Garland^3 13. 16. See also Y. Béquignon & E. Will, *RA*^{6} xxxv 1950, 5–34; Gomme, *HCT*, iii. 500–5; Meiggs, *The Athenian Empire*, 324–32; Kallet-Marx, *Money, Expense and Naval Power in Thucydides' History*, 160–70; C. Constantakopoulou, in Chrysostomides *et al.* (edd.), *The Greek Islands and the Sea*, 26–8, cf. her *The Dance of the Islands*, 220–1; M. B. Wallace with T. J. Figueira, *ZPE* clxxii 2010, 65–9.

θ[εοί].

τά[χσι]ς [φ]ό[ρο].

§i

ἔδοχσεν τε͂[ι βολε͂ι καὶ τοῖ δέμοι. —5—ις] ἐπρ[υτάνευε· —5—]ον ἐγρ[αμμάτευε· —6— ἐπε]-

στάτε. Θόδι[ππος εἶπε· πέμφσαι κέρυκας] ẹ̓κ τôṿ [—8— hòς] ἂν χερο[τονέσει hε βολὲ ἐς τὰς]

πόλες, δύο [μὲν ἐπ' Ἰονίαν καὶ Καρίαν], δ̣ύο δὲ ἐ[πὶ Θράικες, δύο δ]ὲ ἐπὶ Ν[έσος, δύο δὲ ἐφ' Ἑλλέσπ]-

οντον· hoῦ[τοι δὲ —12— τôι] κοινôι h[εκάστες τε͂ς πόλ]ẹος πα[ρε͂ναι πρέσβες τô Μαι]-

μακτεριôν[ος μενός —12— ἐ]σαγογέα[ς —9— τούτ]ος δὲ [—11— γραμμα]-

τέα καὶ χσυ[—19—]ον. hε δὲ β[ολὲ τάκτας —6—]σ̣θο [—10— δέκα ἄνδ]-

ρας· hoῦτοι [δὲ —13— ἑμερ]ôν ἀφ' ἓς ἂ[ν —32— ἒ τ]-

ε͂ς ἑμέρας h[εκάστες —13—] hέκαστ[ος —21— hορκοσάντον h]-

Except where otherwise stated, restorations are those of Meritt & West. Restorations attributed to Matthaiou 2010 are in Matthaiou 2009 also, but are more accessible in the later work.

3 Λεοντὶς (*ATL* ii) or Αἰαντὶς: see commentary. 4 παρόντον hὸς] ἂν (?) Matthaiou, better than βολευτôν Meritt & West or μισθοτôν *ATL* ii. 5 Matthaiou 2010: Θράικεν Meritt & West. 6 ἀνειπόντον ἐν Meritt & West, ἐπαγγελάντον (?) Matthaiou. 7–8 [προσελέσθαι γραμμα]|τέα (?) Matthaiou. 9 τὰς τάχσες δέκα ἑμερ]ôν ἀφ' ἓς ἂ[ν hαιρεθôσι ἀπογραφσάντον τε͂σι πόλεσι ἒ (?) Matthaiou. 10 hέκαστ[ος εὐθυνέσθον (?) Matthaiou. τὸς δὲ τάκτας hορκοσάντον Meritt & West.

Gods.

2 Assessment of tribute.

§i

3 Resolved by the council and the people. Aiantis *or* Leontis was the prytany; —on was the secretary; —— was the chairman. Thudippus proposed:

4 Send heralds from those present (?) whom the council shall choose to the cities, two to Ionia and Caria, two towards Thrace, two to the islands, two to the Hellespont. These shall announce (?) to the common body of each city that envoys are to be present in the month Maemacterion [v] – – – *eisagogeis* [presiding officials who 'introduce' cases to lawcourts]; these shall also choose (?) a secretary and a co-secretary (?) – – –

8 The council shall – – – *taktai* [assessors] – – – ten men. These shall write down the assessments for the cities within ten days from when they are appointed (?), or each of them shall be penalised (?) – – – for each day. The *taktai* (?) shall be

οι hορκοτα[ὶ —— 21 ——] τυγχ̣[άνοσιν
—— 27 —— τὲ]-
ν αὐτὲν ζεμ[ίαν —— 16 —— hοι] ẹ̀σ[α]γ[ογε͂ς ἐπ]ιμẹ[λ
—— 20 —— ἂν φσε]-
φίσεται hο [δε͂μος —— 9 —— hο . .]χογ κα[ὶ h]ο πολέμαρ̣[χος
—— 22 —— τ]-
ε͂ι ἐλιαίαι [—— 20 ——]λας τȏ[ν ἐ]λιαστο͂ν. ẹ[
—— 22 —— τε͂σι]
πόλεσ[ι] κατ[ὰ τὰς δ]ια[δικασίας, εὐθυνέσθο μ[υ]ριάσι δραχ[με͂σι
—— 12 —— hέκαστος αὐ]-
το͂ν. hοι δὲ [θεσμο]θ̣έτα[ι δικαστέριον] νέον κα[θ]ιστάντον χ̣[ιλίος —— 8 ——.
τȏ δὲ φόρο ἐπειδ]-
ὲ ὀλέζον ἐγ[ένε]το τὰς [. . . τάχσες χσ]ὺν [τε͂ι βολε͂ι χσυντα
[—— 26 ——]
αιας ἀρχ̣ε͂ς [. . . .] μέρο[ς hαπάσας τȏ Π]οσ̣[ι]δε[ιȏ]νος μενός.
χ[ρεματιζ—— 19 ——]
ἀπὸ νομενίας κα]τὰ τ[αῦτα hίνα ταχθ]ε͂[ι] ḥο φό[ρ]ος ἐν τȏι Πο[σιδειο͂νι μενί.
hε δὲ βολὲ —— 6 ——]
[.] χ̣ρεματι[ζέτο κ]αὶ χ[—— 7 —— hίνα τ]ạ[χσ]ες γ[έ]νονται ἐὰμ
[—— 24 ——]ς. τ̣-
[ὸ]ṿ δὲ φόρο[ν ὀλέζ]ο μὲ . [—— 14 ——]ον μ[ε]δεμιᾶι ἒ
hο[—— 23 ——]ọντ̣-
[ες] ἐὰμ μὲ τ[—— 6 ——]ετα[—— 14 ——]ες τ[ε͂]ς χόρας
ἀδυ[νατο—— 18 ——] ΔΕỊ[.]
[. .]νομεν[—— 20 —— τὸμ φ]όρο[ν] hος ἂν ταχθ[ε͂ι
—— 16 —— ανα]γρά[φσ]-
[ας] hο γρ[αμματεὺς τε͂ς βολε͂ς ἐν δυαῖν στ]έλα[ι]ṿ λ̣ιθίνα̣ιṿ [καταθέτο, τὲμ
μὲν ἐν τȏι βο]λευ[τε]-
[ρ]ίοι, τὲ[ν δὲ ἐμ πόλει· ἀπομισθοσάντον δὲ] hο[ι] π̣ολετ̣αί, τ[ὸ δὲ ἀργύριον
—— 11 ——] hοι κ[ο]-
λακρέτ[αι. —— 19 —— τε͂σι π]ọλ̣[εσ]ι περὶ τȏ φ[όρο . . . το͂μ
Παναθεναίον τ]ο͂μ μεγ̣-

11–16 The underlined letters were on the lost fragment. 13–14 διαδικαζόντον τὰς τάχσες τ]|ε͂ι (?) Matthaiou 2010. 14 διαφεσφιζομένον κατὰ φυ]λὰς (?) Matthaiọu 2010. 16 [θεσμο]θ̣έτα[ι Wade-Gery, *CR* xlix 1935, 186, one letter too long but more likely than [νομο]θ̣έτα[ι Meritt & West. 17–18 τὰς [μὲν τάχσες χσ]ὺν τ̣ε͂ι̣ [βο]λε͂ι ξσυντα[ττόντον μέζονας το͂ν τε͂ς τελευτ]|αίας ἀρχε͂ς (?) Matthaiou 2010. 18 [πρὸς] μέρο[ς Meritt & West, [κατὰ (?)] μέρο[ς Matthaiou. 19 Πο[σιδειο͂νι μενί Meritt & West. 21–2 μὲ π̣[όλει νῦν ταχσάντ]ον μ[ε]δεμιᾶι ἒ hο[πόσον πρὸ τȏ ἐτύγχανον ἀπαγ]οντ̣|[ες] Meritt & West, μὲ [γενέσθαι το͂μ πόλε]ον μ[ε]δεμιᾶι ἒ hο[σομπερ πρὸ τȏ ἐτύγχανον φέρ]ọντ̣|[ες] (?) Matthaiou, since [νῦν τάττεν το͂μ πόλε]ον would be one letter too long. 22 τ[ις φαίν]ετα[ι ἀπορία hόστε ὅσ]ες τ[ε͂]ς χόρας ἀδυ[νάτο μὲ πλείο ἀπάγεν Meritt & West, τ[οι γίγν]ετα[ι ἀφορία ἀργȏ δ' ὅσ]ες τ[ε͂]ς χόρας ἀδύ[νατον ε͂ι πλείονα φέρεν (?) Matthaiou. 22–3 τένδε] δὲ τ[ὲ|ν γ]νόμεν [καὶ τὸ φσέ]φ[ισμα τόδε καὶ τὸμ φ]όρο[ν] Meritt & West, τὰς] δ' ἐπ̣[ι|γε]νομέν[ας τάχσες] κ̣[αὶ τὸν χσύμπαντα φ]όρο[ν] (?) Matthaiou. 23–4 τε͂ι πόλει hεκάστει ἀνα]γρά[φσ|ας] Meritt & West, καὶ τὸ φσέφισμα τόδ' ἀνα]γρά[φσ|ας] (?) Matthaiou. 25 τ[ὸ δὲ ἀργύριον παρασχόντον Meritt & West, τ[ὸ δ' ἀργύριον αὐτοῖς δόντον] (?) Matthaiou. 26 τὸ δὲ λοιπὸν ἀποφαίνεν τε͂σι π]όλ[ε]σι Meritt & West, διαπέμπεν (?) Matthaiou. πρὸ το͂μ Meritt & West.

made to swear by the *horkotai* [oath-administrators] – – – happen – – – the same penalty.

12 The *eisagogeis* shall take care – – – the people shall vote – – – the man allotted from the *eisagogeis* (?) and the polemarch shall adjudicate about them in the *eliaia*, with the *eliastai* voting about them by tribes. – – – for the cities in accordance with the adjudications, each of them shall be penalised by ten thousand drachmas. The *thesmothetai* shall establish a new court of a thousand – – –

16 Since the tribute has become too little, they shall together with the council make the assessments greater than those of the last term of office (?), in proportion, all in the month Poseideon [vi]. Deal with the business (?) – – – from the beginning of the month in the same way, so that the tribute shall be assessed in the month Poseideon (?). The council – – – shall deal with the business and – – – so that the assessments shall be made if – – – There shall not be a lesser tribute for any of the cities than the amount which they were paying previously, unless for any one there is a problem that the land is unproductive so that it is impossible to pay more (?).

23 The assessments which are made and the total (?) tribute as it is assessed and this decree (?) shall be written up by the secretary of the council on two stone *stelai*, and placed one in the council house and one on the acropolis: the contract shall be made by the *poletai* and the money provided (?) by the *kolakretai*.

26 For the future, send (?) to the cities about the tribute before (?) the Great Panathenaea – – – the prytany

άλον εχ̣[- - - δὲ - - - πρυτανεία - - - ἂν] τυ[γ]χάνει πρυτ[ανεύοσα — 14 — Π]αναθ[έ]-
ναια· [ἐὰν δὲ hοι πρυτάνες μὲ — 9 —]σι ἐ[ς] τὸν δε̂μον κ[αὶ — 19 —]εριο̣ν
περὶ τ̣ο̣ [φόρο — 20 — ἐ]πὶ σ[φ]ο̂ν αὐτο̂ν, ὀφ[έλεν hεκατὸν δραχμὰς hιε]ρ̣ὰ̣ς τε̂-
[ι Ἀ]θ̣ε̣να[ίαι hέκαστον το̂μ π]ρ[υτάνεον κ]α̣ὶ το̂[ι] δεμοσίοι h[εκατὸν, καὶ εὐθύνεσθαι χιλί]ασι
[δρα]χμε̂[σι hέκαστον το̂μ πρ]υ̣τ̣ά̣[νεον. κα]ὶ ἐάν τις ἄλλος δι[— 11 —]σ̣ι [— 6 — μ]ὲ ε̂ναι τ-
[ὰς] τάχσ[ες κατὰ Π]α̣[ναθένα]ια τὰ μ̣[εγάλα] ἐπὶ τ̣ε̂ς πρυτανεί[ας hέτις ἂν πρ]ότε̣ [πρυτα]νεύει, ἄτ-
[ι]μος ἔσ[το καὶ] τὰ χ[ρέματα] αὐτο̂ δ[εμόσια ἔσ[τ]ο καὶ τε̂ς θεο̂ [τὸ ἐπιδέκατ]ο̣ν. ἐχ[σενε]γκέτο δὲ τ-
αῦτα ἐς [τὸν] δε̂μον [— 6 —]ὶς π[ρ]υτα̣[νεί]α ἐπά̣ν̣αγκες ἐπει[δὰν — 6 — ε] στρα[τιὰ] ἐς τρίτεν ἐ-
μέραν [προ̂τ]ον μετ[ὰ τὰ hιε]ρά· ἐ[ὰν] δ̣ὲ [μὲ δ]ιαπ[ρ]αχθε̂ι ἐν ταύ[τει, χρεματί]ζεν πε̣[ρ]ὶ τούτο προ̂[τ]-
ον τε̂ι [hυσ]τεραία[ι χσυνε]χο̂ς [hέ]ος [ἂν δ]ια̣π[ρ]αχθε̂ι ἐπὶ τε̂[ς — 8 —]ς πρυτανείας. ἐὰν δ[ὲ μ]-
ὲ ἐχσε[νέγ]κ̣οσι ἐς [τὸν δε̂μ]ον ε̣̂ [μὲ] δι[απρά]χσ[ο]σι ἐπὶ σφο̂ν α[ὐτο̂ν, εὐθυν]έσθο μ̣υ̣ρίασι δρ[αχμε̂]-
σιν hέκαστος το̂μ [πρυτάν]ε̣ο̣ν [. .]ρο[. . . .] διακολεύον ἐπιδ[— 8 —]ς στρα[τι]άς. τὸς δ[ὲ. . . .]
κας πρ[οσκε]κλεμέ[νος. . .]ε̂να̣[ι h]υπ[ὸ το̂ν δεμοσίον κλετέ[ρον hίνα h]ε βολ̣[ὲ. . . .]σ̣ε[ι αὐτὸς ἐ]-
ὰμ μὲ ὀ[ρθο̂ς] δοκο̂σ[ι — 5 —]νε[ν. τὰ]ς δ[ὲ πορ]είας τοῖς κέρυχ[σι — 23 — τ]-
ὸν hόρ[κον τὸς τάκ[τας hέο]ς τ[ο̂ πο]ρε[υθέσ]ο̣ν̣[τα]ι hίνα μὲ αὐ[— 26 —]
τὰς τά[χσ]ες τε̂σι π[όλεσι . .]σ̣[. . .]κ̣α[— 5 —]ο[. hό]πο ἂν δοκε̂[ι — 17 — hότι δὲ πε]-
ρὶ το̂ν [τ]άχσεον κα[ὶ το̂ φσεφίσμα]τ̣ο[ς τε̂σι] π[όλεσι] χρὲ λεγ[— 14 — τὸν δε̂μον φσε]φ-
ίζεσθ[α]ι καὶ ἐάν τ[— 12 —] h[— 10 — πε]ρ̣ὶ το̂ δ[— 6 — hόπος δ' ἂν τὸμ φόρον] ἀπά-

28 μὲ τότε ἐσάγο]σι ἐ[ς] τὸν δε̂μον κ[αὶ τὲμ βολὲν καὶ τὸ δικαστ]έριον Meritt & West, κ[αὶ μὲ ἐσίοσιν ἐς τὸ βολευτ]έριον (?) Matthaiou. 29 μεδὲ εὐθὺς χρεματίζοσι Meritt & West, μεδὲ hε βολὲ χρεματίζει (?) Matthaiou. 30 hέκαστον το̂μ π]ρ[υτάνεον *ATL* ii. 31 δι[ακολύει τι τε̂]σ̣ι (?) Matthaiou 2010. 34 hε Οἰνε]ὶς Meritt & West: see commentary. hέκει hε] στρα[τιὰ] Meritt & West. 36 τε̂[ς εἰρεμένε]ς Meritt & West, τε̂[ς Λεοντίδο]ς (or Αἰαντίδο]ς would be possible) M&L, τε̂[ς ἐνεστώσε]ς (?) Matthaiou. 38 [φό]ρο[ν hος] δια̣κολύον ἐπιδ[ο̂ναι ἐς τὰ]ς Meritt & West, [πό]ρο[ς (?) Matthaiou. 39 παρ]ε̂να̣[ι *IG* i², Matthaiou. κολά]σε[ι αὐτὸς (?) Matthaiou. 41 αὐτόβολοι ἀπίοσιν (?) Matthaiou. 43 λέγ[εσθαι περὶ τούτο τὸν δε̂μον Meritt & West, λέγ[εν καὶ περὶ τούτο τὸν δε̂μον (?) Matthaiou.

which is in office – – – Panathenaea. If the *prytaneis* do not – – – to the people and do not enter into the council house (?) concerning the tribute and do not deal with the business (?) in their own term of office, each of the *prytaneis* shall owe a hundred drachmas sacred to Athena and a hundred to the state treasury, and each of the *prytaneis* shall be penalised by a thousand drachmas. And if any one else in any way prevents the making of the assessments for the cities (?) at the time of the Great Panathenaea in the prytany which holds office first, he shall be deprived of his rights and his property shall be confiscated with a tithe for the Goddess.

33 This shall be brought before the people by the prytany of Oeneis (?) obligatorily when the force has come (?), on the third day, first after the sacred business. If the business is not completed on that day, they shall deal with this business first on the next day, and continuously until it is completed in the current (?) prytany. If they do not bring it before the people or do not complete it in their own term of office, each of the *prytaneis* shall be penalised by ten thousand drachmas for preventing the provision of funds (?) for the forces. The men summoned – – – to be present by the public summoners so that the council may punish them if they are judged not to – – – rightly.

40 The routes for the heralds – – – the oath, the *taktai*, how far they shall travel, so that they shall not depart on their own initiative (?). – – – What must be said to the cities concerning the assessments and the decree, concerning this the people also (?) shall decree, and if

[γ]οσιν [h]αι πόλες [—27—]ς hότ[αν
—16— τ]ὲν τάχσι-
[ν τô] φọ́[ρ]ο hίνα ει[—25— τὸμ] π̣όλ[εμον.
τὸς δὲ στρατεγὸς] χρε̂σθαι π-
[ερὶ τô φ]όρο κατα[—18—] | | [—10—]Λ̣
[—15—]ι θάλατταν πρ-
[—7—]α δεῖ ἒ ε[—7—]α[—9—]εγο[—23— τ]ε̂ς
βολε̂ς τε̂ι πρό-
[τει περὶ] τ[ο]ύτο Λ̣[—6—]α̣σ[—9—]χοσ[—14—τ]ôν
ἄλλον δικαστερίον ἐὰμ μ-
[—9—]προ[—7—]ṣα[—6— ἐπι]τεδε[ιο . . . . τôι] δέμ[οι]. τοῖς δὲ κέρυχσι
τοῖς ἰôσι τ-
[ὸμ μισθὸν] ἀ̣ποδ[όντον hο]ι κ̣[ολακρέται. Σ]οκρα[τίδες εἶπ]ε̣· τὰ μ̣ὲ̣[ν] ἄλλα
καθάπερ τε̂ι βολε̂ι· τὰς
[δὲ τάχσεις] hόσαι̣[—5—]Λ̣Π[—10—]Α̣Ν δε̂ṭ[αι τὸς πρ]υτάνε[ς]
hοι ἂν τότε τυγχάνοσι πρυτ-
[ανεύοντ]ες καὶ τὸ[γ γρα]μμ[ατέα τε̂ς βολ]ε̣̂ς. τε[—7— τ]ὸ δικαστέριον
hόταν περὶ τôν τάχσ-
[εον ε̂ι h]όπος ἂν α[—5—]νọ[—10—]Λ̣ΔΕ^{I}[—7—]ι. *v*

§ii

ἔδοχσ[εν] τε̂ι βολε̂ι καὶ τôι δέμοι. Α-
[ἰγεὶς ἐ]πρυτάνευ[ε· Φίλ]ιπ[πος ἐγραμμά]ṭε[υε· —7—]ορος ἐπεσ[τάτε.]
Θόδιππος εἶπε· hοπόσ-
[εσι πό]λεσι φόρος [ἐτάχ]θ̣[ε ἐπὶ τ]ε̂ς [βολε̂ς hε̂ι Πλειστί]ας πρôτος
[ἐγρα]μμάτευε ἐπὶ Στρατοκ-
[λέος ἄ][ρχοντος βộ[ν καὶ πανhοπ]λ[ίαν ἀπάγεν ἐς Παναθ]έναια τὰ
μ̣ε̣[γάλα] hαπάσας· πεμπόντον
δ[ὲ ἐν] τε̂ι πομπε̂ι [—11—]κ[. . . .

§iii

κατὰ ταῦτα ἔτα]χσεν τὸμ φό[ρον τε̂]σι πόλεσιν hε βολ[ὲ]
hε̂ι [Πλ]ẹιστίας π[ρôτος ἐγραμμ]ά[τευε —11— ἐ]πὶ Στρατοκλ[έος
ἄ]ρχοντος ἐπὶ [τô]ν [ἐσ]-
αγογ[έο]ν hοῖς Κα[—8— ἐγρ]α̣[μμάτευε —9—]ς. *vacat*
vacat

45 hότ[αν χσυντάχσει hε βολὲ Matthaiou. 46 ε̂ι [τôι δέμοι ἀργύριον hικανὸν ἐς τὸμ] Meritt & West, ε̂ι [τôι δέμοι χρέματα ἑτοῖμα πρὸς τὸν] (?) Matthaiou. 47 κατα[σκέφσει καθ' ἕκαστον ἐνιαυτὸν ἐχσετ]ά̣[σαντας κατὰ Meritt & West, κατὰ [ἔτος διασκέφσει . . . .] | | | [—5— εἰ ἐπι]δ̣[ôναι ἐς τὰ ἐς γε̂ν κα]ὶ Matthaiou. 47–8 πρ| [αττόμενα δεῖ, ἒ ἐ[ς ἄλλο ἀγ]α[θὸν hο ἂν ἐσ]εγô[νται περὶ αὐτô ἐν τε̂ι hέδραι τ]ε̂ς (?) Matthaiou. 49 περὶ τ[ο]ύτο δ̣[ὲ ἀεὶ δι]α̣σ[κοπε̂ν or συνδι]α̣σ[κοπε̂ν συνε]χôς [τὲν ἐλιαίαν ἄνευ or μετὰ τ]ôν (?) Matthaiou (ἐλιαίαν). 49–50 ἐὰμ μ| [ὲ τὲν βολὲν] προ[χρεματί]ṣα[ι δοκε̂ι ἐπι]τεδε[ιότατα τôι] (?) Matthaiou. 51 Σ]οκρα[τίδες (?) Matthaiou 2010. 52 hόσαι̣[σι κατ]ὰ̣ π[όλιν ἐπιτιμ]α̣̂ν δε̂ṭ[αι (?) Matthaiou 2010. 53 τε[ρε̂ν πρὸς (?) Matthaiou 2010. 58 [καθάπερ ἄποι]κ[οι. *vvv* κατὰ τάδε ἔτα]χσεν Meritt & West, *vv* κατὰ ταῦτα ἔτα]χσεν (?) Matthaiou. 59–60 demotics to be supplied Meritt & West, but 59 καὶ hε ἐλιαία ἐ]πὶ Béquignon & Will (ἐ).

– – – how the cities are to bring the tribute – – – when the council makes (?) the assessment of the tribute, so that the people shall have money available (?) for the war.

47 The generals shall make about the tribute each year an enquiry (?) if there is need for a contribution towards actions on land or at sea (?) or for any other good purpose which they may propose for the people (?) at the first session of the council.

49 Concerning this the *eliaia* shall – – – consider thoroughly with (?) / without (?) the other courts, unless it is judged most advantageous for the people that the council shall deal with the business first (?).

50 The payment for the heralds who are going shall be provided by the *kolakretai*.

51 Socratides (?) proposed: In other respects in accordance with the council; but with regard to the assessments which must be evaluated for cities (?) the *prytaneis* who happen to be in office and the secretary of the council shall keep (the documents) for (?) the court when there is a case about the assessments, so that – – –

§ii

54 Resolved by the council and the people. Aegeis was the prytany; Philippus was the secretary; —orus was the chairman. Thudippus proposed:

56 Those cities for which tribute was assessed under the council for which Pleistias was first secretary, in the archonship of Stratocles (425/4), shall all bring a cow and panoply to the Great Panathenaea; they shall take part in the procession like colonists (?).

§iii

58 In this way the tribute was assessed for the cities by the council for which Pleistias of —— was first secretary, in the archonship of Stratocles, under the *eisagogeis* for whom Ca— was secretary.

There follows a list of assessments in four columns, from which we give the upper part of the first column; the lettering is stoichedon, *with the names beginning in the sixth* stoichos:

Νεσιοτικὸς φόρο[ς]	
ΔΔΔ	Πάρι[οι]
Δ𐅃	Νάχσ[ιο]ι
Δ𐅃	Ἄνδρ[ιοι]
Δ𐅃	Μέλιọ[ι]
𐅃ΤΤΤΤ	Σίφνι[οι]
Δ𐅃	Ἐρετρι[ε͂ς]
𐅃	Θεραῖ[οι]
Δ	Κεῖọ[ι]
𐅃	Καρύσ[τιοι]
Δ	Χαλκι[δε͂ς]
𐅃Τ	Κύθνι[οι]
Δ	Τέν[ι]ο[ι]
ΤΤ	Στ[υ]ρε͂ς
[ΤΤ]	Μ̣[υ]κ̣όνι[οι]
[ΤΤ]	[Σ]ε̣ρίφιọ[ι]
[Τ]	Ἰέται
[Τ]*vac*	Διε͂ς
Τ	Ἀθενῖται
Τ	Σύριοι
ΧΧ	Γρυγχε͂ς
Χ	Ῥεναιε͂ς
ΧΧ	Διακρε͂ς ἀπ[ὸ] Χαλκιδέον
Χ	Ἀναφαῖοι
vac	Κερία ΔΙΙΙ
ΧΧ	Φολέγανδρος
ΗΗΗ	Βέλβινα
Χ	Κίμολος
Χ	Σικινε͂ται
Η	Ποσίδειον ἐν Εὐβοίαι
ΤΧΧ	Διά[κρ]ιοι ἐν Ε[ὐβ]οία[ι]
vac	[h]εφ[αισ]τ̣ι̣[ε͂ς]
ΤΤΤΤ	[h]ο[ι ἐν Λέμνοι]
[*vac*]	[Μυριναῖοι]
[Τ]	[Ἴμβριοι]
[Νεσιοτικο͂ φόρο]	
[κεφάλαιον]	

In the part of the list which follows we have followed M&L in adding in brackets on the right the rate at which each city paid tribute in the 430s.

Island tribute

30 tal.	Parians		[18 tal.]
15 tal.	Naxians		[6 tal. 4,000 dr.]
15 tal.	Andrians		[6 tal.]
15 tal.	Melians		[—]
9 tal.	Siphnians		[3 tal.]
15 tal.	Eretrians		[3 tal.]
5 tal.	Theraeans		[—]
10 tal.	Ceans		[4 tal.]
5 tal.	Carystians		[5 tal.]
10 tal.	Chalcidians		[3 tal.]
6 tal.	Cythnians		[3 tal.]
10 tal.	Tenians		[2 tal.]
2 tal.	Styrians		[1 tal.]
2 tal. (?)	Myconians		[1 tal.]
2 tal. (?)	Seriphians		[1 tal.]
1 tal. (?)	Ietians		[3,000 dr.]
1 tal. (?)	Dians		[2,000 dr.]
1 tal.	Athenitians		[2,000 dr.]
1 tal.	Syrians		[1,500 dr.]
2,000 dr.	Grynchians		[1,000 dr.]
1,000 dr.	Rhenaeans		[300 dr.]
2,000 dr.	Diacres from the Chalcidians		[800 dr.]
1,000 dr.	Anaphaeans		[—]
	Ceria	10 dr. 3 ob.	[—]
2,000 dr.	Pholegandrus		[—]
300 dr.	Belbina		[—]
1,000 dr.	Cimolus		[—]
1,000 dr.	Sicinetans		[—]
100 dr.	Posideum in Euboea		[—]
1 tal. 2,000 dr.	Diacrii in Euboea		[—]
4 tal.	Hephaestians in Lemnos (?)		[3 tal.]
	combined with Myrinaeans (?)		[1 tal. 3,000 dr.]
1 tal. (?)	Imbrians (?)		[1 tal.]

Island tribute:
total:

[Ͱ𐅄𐅉TTTHHHHΔIII]
below the four columns, vacat
181 [κεφάλα]ιον [τ]ô χσύμπαντος: [𐅍]ͰͰͰͰ<𐅄>𐅉[– – –]
below that, vacat

181 [𐅍]: [𐅄] C. Flament, *Une économie monétarisée* (Leuven: Peeters, 2007), 98–101, cf. *SEG* lvii 61; <𐅄>: the stone has 𐅄.

For tribute lists 1–23 (454/3–432/1), inscribed on two large blocks of stone, and regular assessments in the years of the Great Panathenaea, see **119**. After that a separate *stele* was used each year, and most cannot be securely dated: in the reconstruction of *ATL* (cf. Meiggs, *The Athenian Empire*, 531–7) we have the fragmentary *IG* i³ 281–4 (25 = 430/29 – 28 or 29 = 427/6 or 426/5), none of them in fact securely dated, and then nothing until 285 (34 = 421/0), the one later list which is securely dated. In this reconstruction there was an extraordinary assessment in 428, already involving some significant increases on the assessment of 430; in 426 there was not another assessment but **152** was enacted to improve the collection of tribute. Alternative schemes, both assuming a regular assessment in 426, have been proposed by H. B. Mattingly, *CQ*² xxviii 1978, 85–8 = his *AER* 431–4, and by M. Piérart, *BCH* cviii 1984, 161–76, and in *Comptes et inventaires dans la cité grecque . . . J. Tréheux*, 313–20. In addition, L. Kallet, *Hesperia* lxxiii 2004, 465–96, has suggested that some of the fragments assigned to 420/19–415/4 may in fact belong to 425/4–422/1 (see further on **168**).

We think it likely that the assessment of 430 was used for four years as usual, there was then another regular assessment in 426 (it possibly, but not necessarily, included some increases which provoked resistance), and that was followed by **152**. In either case, this extraordinary assessment was made in 425/4, with significant increases, on the grounds that the tribute was too little (16–17) and ordering that states' assessments should not be reduced (20–1), and for the future ordering a return to regular assessment in the years of the Great Panathenaea (26–7, 31–2).

In this inscription we have a decree with amendment (§i) and a supplementary decree (§ii), enacted in 425/4, which was not a year of the Great Panathenaea, ordering an extraordinary assessment of the tribute of the Delian League, and followed by the schedule of the resulting assessment (§iii). Not all of the details in the decrees can be reconstructed, and §i was less than ideally systematic and coherent, but the assessment procedures involved the council and assembly and a board of ten *taktai* ('assessors'), and a court of 1,000 jurors for which the introducing and presiding officials were *eisagogeis* ('introducers'), used at any rate for cases in which a city challenged its assessment (and Béquignon & Will, 14–27, thought that in addition the complete schedule had to be approved by the court). At every stage men who failed to do what was required of them were threatened with penalties.

The cities were to send representatives to Athens in the fifth month of the year, Maemacterion (6–7), and the assessments were to be made in the sixth month,

163 tal. 410 dr. 3 ob. (?)
and at the end
181 total of the whole: 1,460 tal. +

Poseideon (18–19). In terms of the council's year, which at this time did not coincide exactly with the archon's year (cf. Introduction, pp. xxiv–xxv), if the cutter kept strictly to *stoichedon* order §i was enacted under a seven-letter prytany, Aiantis or Leontis, but l. 34 seems to expect the proposal to be ratified under a six-letter prytany, Oeneis (Aegeis was the prytany when §ii was enacted: 54–5); and that has led to various attempts to reconstruct the chronology of the year.[1]

This reassessment will in any case have been ordered soon after but not immediately after Cleon's success at Pylos: there is no evidence of a direct link between the two (stressed by Gomme), but the tone of the decree fits the hard line which Cleon was encouraging, and it has been suggested that Thudippus, the proposer of the decree, was a son-in law of Cleon[2] (Wade-Gery & Meritt, *AJP* lvii 1936, 392 with n. 36; Davies, *APF*, 228–9; but doubted by F. Bourriot, *Historia* xxxi 1982, 409–18); the amendment formula in l. 51 indicates that Thudippus was a member of the council this year (cf. Introduction, p. xxii). Mattingly in particular has associated a harsher imperialism in the 420s with Cleon (e.g. *Historia* x 1961, 187–8 = his *AER* 51–2). We tend to think of the 420s as the decade of Cleon, and his role in the punishment of Mytilene after its revolt (Thuc. III. 36–50) shows that he was hard on the allies; but of the four documents of the mid-420s (**152**, this text, **154**, **155**) in which Athens increased its pressure on the allies only this, and this only if Thudippus was Cleon's son-in-law, can be linked with him. He shared his harshness with many others; and this text and **155**, from different proposers, are similar in their tendency to threaten penalties at every stage.

The tribute quota lists show that the members of the League came to be regularly listed in districts: originally five, from 443/2 (*IG* i^3 269), and later four, with the Carian district absorbed into the Ionian, from 438/7 (*IG* i^3 274) (see *ATL* iii. 68); normally the order in which districts were listed remained constant through an assessment period. Here (5) and in **154**. 25–8 and **155** §7 these districts form the basis for the routes to be taken by the messengers sent out from Athens.

Four assessments are recorded in *IG* i^3 282. i. 43–9 cf. 281. ii. 60–5 as having been made by the council with a court (*dikasterion*) of 1,500 jurors. This inscription uses

[1] See e.g. *ATL* iv, p. xi; Gomme, *HCT* iii. 478, 719; M&L, who thought it more likely that there was an irregularity in the carving of l. 3 or l. 34.

[2] In the fourth century there was a Cleon son of Thudippus of Araphen (Isae. IX. *Astyphilus* 17), and if this suggestion is right that Cleon will have been a grandson of the well-known Cleon and named after him.

eliaia (14, restored 49—and the inscription confirms that the word was not aspirated in Athens) and *dikasterion* (49 and 53, restored 16). Whatever the name and nature of Solon's appeal court was (*Ath. Pol.* 9. i and Plut. *Sol.* 18. iii both use *dikasterion*), it is clear that the word *eliaia* was in use in classical Athens (cf. **131**. 75): A. L. Boegehold judges that the two words 'are in most senses synonymous' (*The Athenian Agora*, xxviii. 3–5; see also M. H. Hansen, *C&M* xxxiii 1981–2, 9–47). *Diadikasia*, restored in ll. 13–15, is used particularly of adjudicating between rival claims (Harrison, *The Law of Athens*, ii. 79–80), and that term would appropriately be used of adjudication between an assessment proposed by the *taktai* and a lower assessment proposed by a city.

In l. 16, though [νομο]θ̣έτα[ι fits the number of spaces and [θεσμο]θ̣έτα[ι does not, the latter is to be preferred, since the *thesmothetai* had a general responsibility for Athens' lawcourts (*Ath. Pol.* 59. i), while there is no other evidence of *nomothetai* in Athens before the late fifth century.

It seems to have been standard fifth-century practice that the *poletai*, the 'sellers', responsible for making contracts (*Ath. Pol.* 47. ii–v), should make a contract when a text was inscribed at public expense, and the *kolakretai*, the paying officers of the state treasury (mentioned *Ath. Pol.* 7. iii), should provide the money: for other instances of both provisions see **141**. 51–2, **166**. 12–14; in **183**. 8–9 the *hellenotamiai* have replaced the *kolakretai* as paying officers.

In ll. 29–31 the combination of small fines payable to Athena and to the state treasury with a substantial fine is puzzling: Meritt & West take εὐθύνεσθαι to refer specifically to the end-of-year *euthynai* (cf. *Ath. Pol.* 48. iv–v), which might imply that the small fines were payable immediately, but they do not discuss the matter. In 31–3 earlier editors restored an entrenchment, formally protecting the decree against modification or annulment (cf. **142**. 24–30), but Matthaiou suggests a reference simply to preventing the implementation of this decree.

The passage in ll. 46–50 was thought by Meritt & West to allow the generals to propose changes before the next regular assessment, but the role which they assigned to the generals was over-speculative. But there does seem to be some sense that the generals were expected to forecast their needs.

§ii is best seen as imposing for the first time on all the member states of the League an obligation to send a cow and panoply to the Great Panathenaea, as earlier the strictly Ionian Erythrae had been required to send grain (**121**. 3) and the colony at Brea had been required to send a cow and panoply (**142**. 11–12): cf. on **154**. 41–3.

In the schedule of assessments Meritt & West postulated substantial gaps between the district lists, and still obtained a total of *c*.380 cities, significantly more than are otherwise attested as paying at any time and twice as many as are known to have paid in any one year; and if it is better not to postulate such gaps (S. Dow, *TAPA* lxxii 1941, 70–84; M&L) then the number of cities assessed will have been even greater. This list was clearly an optimistic list: for instance, at i. 65 it has Melos, which resisted Athenian pressure in 426 (Thuc. III. 91. i–iii) and remained outside the Athenian orbit until it was captured in 416/5; it also includes for the first time Euxine cities (iv. 126–72), and the Actaean cities taken over from Lesbos after the defeat of

Mytilene in 427 (iii. 124 sqq., cf. Thuc. III. 52. iii). It was also much higher in its demands than the pre-war assessments. The Islands were assessed probably for 163 tal. 410 dr. 3 ob., when before the war they paid *c.*90 tal. (then including 30 tal. from Aegina, taken over by Athens in 431); the Hellespont was assessed for over 250 tal. (𐅋𐅋𐅊[– – – , ii. 121–3), when before the war it had paid not more than 85 tal.; the Thracian district was assessed for over 310 tal. (𐅋𐅋𐅋𐅉[– – – , iii. 124–5), when before the war it paid *c.*130 tal. This makes it overwhelmingly likely that the overall total in l. 181 is to be restored as [𐅍]𐅋𐅋𐅋𐅋<𐅊>𐅉[– – –], over 1,460 tal., rather than [𐅌]𐅋𐅋𐅋𐅋<𐅊>𐅉[– – –], over 960 tal., in contrast to the 600 tal. claimed in 431 in Thuc. II. 13. iii (itself perhaps derived from an optimistic assessment) and to the actual pre-war receipts shown by quota lists of the 430s to be not more than 400 tal. a year (cf. **119**).

Within the Island district Thera, which by this time had joined the Athenians but probably had not yet paid tribute (cf. on **152**. 21), was now assessed (i. 67). The Diacres from the Chalcidians (i. 83–4) and the Diacrii in Euboea (i. 93–4) were probably in the mountains of central Euboea; Posideum in Euboea (i. 91–2) perhaps near the Artemisium at the north end of Euboea (*ATL* i. 480–1, 541–2). Constantakopoulou suggests that Ceria (i. 86), with its very small assessment given, unusually, after the name, was perhaps grouped with Anaphe, and some other small islands grouped silently with neighbours: she follows others in thinking that this Ceria was an island south-east of Naxos, but Anaphe would not be a natural island for it to be attached to.

Cities are listed largely but not entirely in descending order of assessment, and Wallace with Figueira suggests that the anomalies may be due partly to differences in the level of change from the previous assessment and partly to the results of appeals; he suggests also that cities which in the past had not provoked the Athenians and had been treated comparatively lightly, such as Siphnos, now lost their privileged status and suffered proportionally greater increases.

Gomme and Kallet-Marx have stressed that there is no sign of this reassessment in Thucydides or Aristophanes, though there are echoes of it in the references to increased tribute in Andoc. III. *Peace* 9 and Aeschin. II. *Embassy* 175 (1,200 talents), Plut. *Arist.* 24. iii–v (1,300 talents after Pericles' death), [Andoc.] IV. *Alcibiades* 11–12 (Alcibiades one of the assessors who doubled the tribute). To explain this, Gomme suggested that the increase was not an exceptional measure, and Kallet-Marx, that it perhaps had no great effect on Athens' finances. This seems to be trying too hard to save Thucydides' reputation. It is indeed highly unlikely that Athens came near to achieving total compliance, but it does seem likely that this extraordinary reassessment represented a significant increase on previous demands and resulted in a significant increase in the tribute actually received. Kallet-Marx has shown that Thucydides was not as blind to financial matters as has sometimes been alleged, but his omission of Athens' attention to the tribute in the mid-420s is still serious.

We should expect the next assessment to have been made at the time of the Panathenaea of 422, as §i prescribes (cf. M&L, p. 226). Fragments exist of an assessment list which has been attributed to that assessment, *IG* i^3 77 (*ATL* A 10): in

ATL that was dated 421 (cf. West & Meritt, *AJA*[2] xxix 1925, 59–69), but in *IG* i[3] Meritt & McGregor accepted the argument for 422. Not many comparisons between our list and *IG* i[3] 77 are possible (and *IG* i[3] 285, the quota list for 421/0̲, does not help). The Hellespontine total was 250 tal. + in 425 (cf. above), + 95 tal. 5,400 dr. + in 77. iv. 11–13 ([. .]𐅄ΔΔΔΔΓ𐅆ΗΗΗΗ̣[– – –, where each of the spaces before 𐅄 could either have contained the 100-talent sign 𐅉 or have been left empty to provide an

---

154

Athenian decree proposed by Cleinias about Delian League tribute, 425/4 or slightly later (?)

Four fragments of a marble *stele*, found on the Athenian acropolis, three now in the Epigraphical Museum and one (3 = *c*, the end of the decree) in the British Museum. Phot. *ATL* i, 121–2 figs. 175–7 (frs. 1–3 = *a–c*), *ATL* ii, pl. II (frs. 4 & 1 = *d* & *a*: these do not quite meet, but preserve the top and both sides). Lines 1–14 are shorter than the remainder, and A. M. Woodward saw traces of a painting in the vacant space to the right (*JHS* lviii 1938, 108–9).

Developed Attic writing apart from curved *upsilon*, regularly using h (and see *apparatus* for 36); using σ for χσ in 16. Lines 2–14 *stoichedon* 23, 15 sqq. *stoichedon* 40.

IG i[2] 66; Meritt, *Documents on Athenian Tribute*, 43–60; *ATL* i, D7; B. H. Hill & B. D. Meritt, *Hesperia* xiii 1944, 1–15 (adding fr. 4 = c); *ATL* ii, D7; M&L 46; *IG* i[3] 34 (Meritt & McGregor); our text is based, by permission, on a re-editing by Dr A. P. Matthaiou (cf. his 'Studies in Attic Inscriptions and the History of the Fifth Century BC', 69–88, and his *The Athenian Empire on Stone Revisited*, 24–8). Trans. Fornara 98; Dillon & Garland[3] 13. 17. See also H. B. Mattingly, *Historia* x 1961, 150–8 = his *AER* 8–16; Mattingly, *BSA* lxv 1970, 129–33 = his *AER* 281–7; Fornara & Samons, *Athens from Cleisthenes to Pericles*, 179–81.

θεοί.
ἔδοχσεν τε͂ι βολ[ε͂ι καὶ το͂ι] δέ-
μοι. Οἰνεὶς ἐπρυ̣[τάνευε· Σπ]ου-
δίας ἐγραμμάτε[υε· —6—]ον
ἐπεστάτε. Κλεινί[ας εἶπε· τὲ]μ β-
ολὲν καὶ τὸς ἄρχ[οντας ἐν] τε͂σ-
ι πόλεσι καὶ τὸς [ἐπισκό]π̣ος ἐ-
πιμελέσθαι hόπ[ος ἂν χσ]υλλέ-
γεται hο φόρος κ[ατὰ τὸ ἔ]τος h-
έκαστον καὶ ἀπά[γεται] Ἀ̣θενα-
ζε. χσύμβολα δὲ π[οιέσα]σθαι π-
ρος τὰς πόλες hό[πος ἂ]μ μὲ ἐχσ-
ε͂ι ἀδικε͂ν τοῖς ἀ[πάγο]σι τὸμ φ-
όρον· γράφσασα δ[ὲ hε] πόλις ἐς
γραμματεῖον τὸ[μ φό]ρ̣ον hόντινα ἀποπέμπει, σεμε-
ναμένε το͂ι συμβ[όλο]ι ἀποπεμπέτο Ἀθέναζε· τὸς δὲ ἀ-

indent: see on **168**); the tribute for Antandrus was 15 tal. in 425 (71. iii. 125: [𐅊]𐅉), restored as 8 tal. but could be higher in 77. iv. 15 ([𐅈T]); six Thracian cities have the same tribute in each list (71. iv. 108–13 [city names restored], 77. v. 21–6). In the summer of 422 peace was not evidently approaching, and we should not expect a significant relaxation.

Gods.

2 Resolved by the council and the people. Oeneis was the prytany; Spudias was the secretary; —on was the chairman. Cleinias proposed:

5 The council and the officials in the cities and the *episkopoi* ('inspectors') shall take care that the tribute is collected each year and brought to Athens.

11 Tokens shall be made for the cities so that it shall not be possible for those bringing the tribute to Athens to do wrong. The city shall write on a tablet the tribute which it is sending, and shall seal it with the token and send it to Athens; those

πάγοντας ἀποδô[ναι] τὸ γραμματεῖον ἐν τêι βολêι ἀ-
ναγνôναι hόταμ[πε]ρ τὸν φόρον ἀποδιδôσι. hοι δὲ πρ-
υτάνες μετὰ Διο[νύ]σια ἐκκλεσίαν ποιεσάντον τοῖ-
ς hελλενοταμία[σι ἀ]ποδεῖχσαι Ἀθεναίοις τôμ πόλ-
εον τὰς ἀποδόσα[ς τὸμ] φ̣ό̣ρ̣ο̣[ν] ἐ̣ντελê καὶ τὰς ἐλλιπό-
σας χορίς, hόσαι [ἂν ——9—— Ἀθ]εμαίος δὲ hελομέ-
νος ἄνδρας τέττ[αρας ἀποστέλλεν ἐς] τὰς πόλες ἀντ-
ιγραφσομένος τ[ὸμ φόρον τὸν ἀποδοθέντα κα]ὶ̣ ἀπαι-
τέσοντας τὸμ μὲ̣ [ἀποδοθέντα· τôν δὲ hαιρεθέντ]ο̣ν τ-
ὸ μὲν δύο πλêν ἐπ̣' [Ἰονίαν καὶ Καρίαν καὶ Νέσος ἐπὶ] τ-
ριέρος ταχείας, [τὸ δὲ hετέρο ἐπὶ hελλέσποντον κα]-
ὶ ἐπὶ Θράικες. ε[——25—— τὲμ]
βολὲν καὶ ἐς τὸ[ν δêμον ——20—— βο]-
λεύεσθαι περὶ τ[ούτον χσυνεχôς hέος ἂν διαπραχθ]-
εῖ. ἐὰν δέ τις Ἀθ[εναῖος ἒ χσύμμαχος ἀδικêι περὶ τὸ]-
ν φόρον hὸν δεῖ [τὰς πόλες γράφσασας ἐς γραμματεῖ]-
ον τοῖς ἀπάγοσ̣[ιν ἀποπέμπεν Ἀθέναζε, ——9—— γ]-
ράφεσθαι πρὸς [τὸς πρυτάνες το . β]ολομενο[. Ἀθενα]-
ίον καὶ τôν χσ[υμμάχον· hοι δὲ πρυτ]άνες ἐσαγ̣[όντον]
ἐς τὲμ βολὲν [——14——]ς̣ ἂγ̣ γράφσετα[ι ἒ εὐθ]-
υνέσθο δόρο[ν μυρίαισι δραχμ]ε̣̂σ[ι h]έκαστος· [hô δ' ἂν]
καταγνôι h[ε βολὲ, ——7—— αὐτ]ộι κ̣υ̣ρία ἔστο [. . . εκ]-
φερέτο ἐς τ[——13——]τ̣ο̣· [.]αν δὲ δόχσει [ἀδικê]-
ν, γνόμας πο[ιέσθον hοι πρυ]τ̣ά̣νες hό τι ἂν δοκ[êι αὐτ]-
ὸμ παθêν ἒ ἀ[ποτεῖσαι. καὶ ἐ]άν τις περὶ τὲν ἀπα̣[γογὲ]-
ν τêς βοὸς ἒ [τêς πανhοπλία]ς̣ ἀδικêι, τὰς γραφὰ̣[ς ἒνα]-
ι κατ' αὐτὸ κ̣[αὶ τὲν ζεμίαν κ]α̣τὰ ταὐτά. τὸς δὲ [hελλεν]-
ο[ταμίας ἀναγράφσοντας ἐ]ς πινάκιον λελ̣[ευκομεν]-
[ον ——20——]ν τô φόρο καὶ [——8——]
[——23——]ι ἀποΛ̣[——13——]

Except where otherwise stated, restorations are those of Hill & Meritt. 22 [ἄν τινες ὂσιν Hill & Meritt, [ἂν ἐλλιπôσιν R. G. Thomas *ap.* M&L, [ἂμ μὲ ἀποδôσι (?) Matthaiou (alternative rejected by Hill & Meritt). 23–7 Matthaiou 2010, 25–6: 23 ἀποπέμπεν ἐπὶ] Hill & Meritt; 24 τὸν ἀποδοθέντα A. Griffin *ap.* M&L: τêσι ἀποδοσêσι Hill & Meritt; 25–7 παρὰ τôν ἐλλιποσ]ôν, τ|ὸ μὲν δύο πλêν ἐπ̣[ὶ τὰς ἐπὶ Νέσον καὶ ἐπ' Ἰονίας ἐπὶ] τ̣|ριέρος ταχείας, [τὸ δὲ δύο ἐπὶ τὰς ἐφ' Ἑλλεσπόντο Hill & Meritt. 28 ἐ[σάγεν δὲ ταῦτα τὸς πρυτάνες ἐς τὲμ] Hill & Meritt, ἐ[χσενεγκêν δὲ ταῦτα ἐπάναγκες τὲμ] (?) Matthaiou. 29 εὐθὺς μετὰ Διονύσια καὶ βο]- Hill & Meritt, either that or αὐτίκα μάλα· τὸν δὲ δêμον βο]- (?) Matthaiou. 33–4 ἔστο αὐτὸν γ]|ράφεσθαι Hill & Meritt, κατὰ τούτο γ]|ράφεσθαι (?) Matthaiou. 34 τôι β]ολομένο[ι Hill & Meritt, τὸν β]ολόμενο[ν (?) Matthaiou. 36 [τὲν γραφὲν hέν τι]ς Hill & Meritt, [πέντε or τριôν ἐμερôν ἀφ' ἐ̂]ς (?) Matthaiou, but elsewhere this text uses h: δέκα hεμερôν? 37 μυρίαισι Hill & Meritt (cf. e.g. **154**. 15, 37), χιλίαισι M&L (cf. e.g. **154**. 30–1, but there 1,000 is more credible as ten times the 100 due to Athena). 38 Matthaiou 2010, 26–7: ἐς] Hill & Meritt. 39 τ[ὲν ἐλιαίαν εὐθύ]ς· ὅ̣τ̣αν Hill & Meritt (ἐ), τ[ὸν δêμον περὶ αὐ]τ̣ộ· [ἐ]ὰν (?) Matthaiou 2010, 26–7. 40 πο[ιέσθον Rhodes *ap.* M&L (cf. Thuc. III. 36. ii): πο[ιόντον Hill & Meritt. 45–6 ἀποφαίνεν καὶ τὲν τάχσι]ν τô φόρο καὶ̣ [τὰς πόλες | hόσαι ἂν ἀποδôσιν ἐντελê κα]ὶ ἀπογ̇[ράφεν Hill & Meritt, τὰς ἐλλιπόσας τôν πόλεο]ν τô φόρο καὶ̣ [τὸς ἀπάγο|ντας τιθέναι ——12——]ι ἀποΛ̣[——13——] (?) Matthaiou.

bringing the tribute shall hand over the tablet in the council to be read when they hand over the tribute. After the Dionysia the *prytaneis* shall hold an assembly for the *hellenotamiai* to reveal to the Athenians those of the cities which have handed over the tribute complete and, separately, those which have fallen short, which have not handed it over (?).

22 The Athenians shall elect four men and send them to the cities, to give receipts for the tribute which has been handed over and to demand what has not been handed over: of those elected, two shall sail to Ionia, Caria and the Islands in a fast trireme, and the others to the Hellespont and towards Thrace (?).

28 This shall be introduced obligatorily (?) to the council and the people immediately (?); and the people shall deliberate about this continuously until it is completed.

31 If any Athenian or ally does wrong concerning the tribute which the cities must write on a tablet for those bringing it and send to Athens, against him it shall be permitted to whoever wishes of the Athenians and the allies to write an accusation to the *prytaneis*; the *prytaneis* shall introduce it into the council within three *or* five days from when (?) the accusation is made, or they shall be penalised for bribery by ten thousand drachmas each. When a man is condemned by the council – – – have final power over him but shall bring out to the people about him (?); if he is judged to be in the wrong, the *prytaneis* shall institute a debate to judge what he should suffer [in his person] or pay.

41 And if any one does wrong with regard to the bringing of the cow and panoply, the accusations against him and the punishment shall be in the same way.

43 The *hellenotamiai* shall write up on a whitened board those of the cities which have fallen short in the tribute and those which have brought it, and place it (?) – – –

lacuna of c.10 lines

[— 24 — τὲμ] βολὲν τὲν ἐσι[ôσ]-
[αν, — 24 —. h]όσοι δὲ τôν ἀπα[γ]-
[όντον — 19 — ἀν]αγεγράφαται ὀφέ-
[λοντες — 18 — ἐπ]ιδεῖχσαι τôι δέμ-
[οι — 20 —. ἐὰν δ]έ τις τôμ πόλεον ἀ-
[μφισβετêι περὶ τô φόρο τε̂ς ἀποδ]όσεος, φάσκοσα ἀπ-
[οδεδοκέναι — 16 —]θαι τὸ κοινὸν τε̂ς
[πόλεος — 20 —]ας τὰς πόλες καὶ τ-
[— 26 —]θαι δὲ μὲ ἐχσε̂ναι
[— 26 —]τος ὀφελέτο ho γρ-
[— 26 —] τὲν δὲ γραφὲν ε̂να-
[ι— 25 —]λιôνι. ἐὰν δέ τις α-
[— 26 —]κλέσες he βολὲ βο-
[λευσα — 21 —]. ἐσαγόντον δὲ hoι
[— 23 — Ἀθε]ναίοις τὸμ φόρον
[— 19 — τὸν πίνα]κα τε̂ς μενύσεος ε-
[— 26 —] φόρο καὶ τô περυσ-
[ινô — 17 — βολὲν π]ροβολεύσασαν ἐχ-
[σενεγκε̂ν — 18 —] περὶ τε̂ι hυστερα-
ίαι ἐς τὸν δε̂μον — 12 — τ]ε̂ς hαιρέσεος χρε-
[ματι - - - - - - - - - - - - -] *vacat*

vacat

47 sqq. We do not list all of Hill & Meritt's speculative fuller restorations. 48–51 h]όσοι δὲ τôν ἀπα[γ|όντον Ἀθέναζε ἐς τὸ πινάκιον ἀν]αγεγράφαται ὀφέ|[λοντες ἐν τε̂ι βολε̂ι, τὲμ βολὲν ἐπ]ιδεῖχσαι Hill & Meritt, h[όσοι δὲ τôν ἀπα[γ|όντον τὸμ φόρον τôι δεμοσίοι ἀν]αγεγράφαται ὀφέ|[λοντες, τὲμ βολὲν τὲν ἐσιôσαν ἐπ]ιδεῖχσαι (?) Matthaiou. 51 κατὰ τὲν πόλιν hεκάστεν Hill & Meritt, ἐν τε̂ι πρότει ἐκκλεσίαι (?) Matthaiou. 53–4 Ἀθέναζε προσκαλε̂σ]θαι τὸ κοινὸν τε̂ς | [πόλεος ταύτες (?) Matthaiou. 61–2 [ἐσαγογε̂ς ἐς τὲν ἐλιαίαν τὸς Ἀθε]ναίοις τὸμ φόρον | [ὀφέλοντας hεχσε̂ς κατὰ τὸμ πίνα]κα Hill & Meritt (ἐ), [πρυτάνες hὸς ἂν μὲ ἀπάγοσιν Ἀθε]ναίοις τὸμ φόρον | [ἐς τὲν βολὲν εὐθὺς κατὰ τὸν πίνα]κα (?) Matthaiou.

This decree is concerned particularly with incomplete payments of a city's tribute. Originally it was dated in the 420s, shortly before **153** (e.g. Meritt, 59–60). An earlier date was suggested on account of the lettering by A. M. Woodward, *JHS* lviii 1938, 108, and A. E. Raubitschek, *AJP* lxi 1940, 477–9; and Hill & Meritt, in publishing the fragment which names the proposer as Cleinias, identified him with the father of Alcibiades, killed at Coronea in 447/6 (Thuc. I. 113. ii with Isoc. XVI. *Chariot Team* 28) and dated the decree 448/7; incomplete payment of tribute is a phenomenon attested in the early 440s (cf. **119**), but of course it occurred later too (cf. the concession to Methone, **150**). M&L were not confident in the identification of Cleinias, and thought the lettering would permit the 430s but not the 420s. It has

lacuna

47 – – – the in-coming council – – –. Those bringing the tribute who have been written up in public as being in debt the incoming council shall indicate to the people at the first assembly. (?)

51 If any of the cities disputes about the handing over of the tribute, claiming that it has handed it over, the *koinon* of this city shall be summoned to Athens (?) – – – the cities and – – – shall not be possible – – – shall owe – – – the accusation shall be – – –. If any one – – – the council shall deliberate – – – .

60 The *prytaneis* (?) shall introduce those who have not brought the tribute to the Athenians (?) into the council immediately (?) in accordance with the board of the denunciation – – – tribute and last year's – – – the council shall deliberate in advance and bring – – – for the next day before the people – – – of the election to deal – – –.

---

been widely thought that this decree and **155** display a similar temper and should be close in time.

Mattingly first argued in 1961 that the reference to 'the cow and panoply' in 41–3 (τε̃ς here makes it clear that a cow was demanded, not an ox) is best seen as referring to the imposition of that as a general demand in **153**. 55–8, and that the best chronological sequence is **152**–**153**–**154**. As M&L acknowledged, it is credible that there should have been incomplete payments of tribute in the 420s, and such partial payments may be alluded to in **152**. 15. In 1970 Mattingly saw the identifying of couriers in this decree as dependent on **152**. 17–19. We find his general arguments convincing. He places this decree in 425/4. However, this decree was enacted in the prytany of Oeneis, and if Oeneis is correctly restored as the prytany in **153**. 34 (which is by no means certain), this will be earlier than the prytany of Aegeis, in which Thudippus imposed the general requirement of cow and panoply—but there is no reason why this decree should not belong to a slightly later year.

In 5–7, while the council and the *episkopoi* (cf. **121**. 13–14, and for the notoriety of the *episkopoi*, 'inspectors', Ar. *Birds* 1021–34) are Athenian, the 'officials in the cities', often likewise regarded as Athenian, are better seen as local officials, as in **155** (H. Leppin, *Historia* xli 1992, 257–71, accepted by Rhodes, *The Athenian Empire*, 48, and in *Ἀθηναίων ἐπίσκοπος . . . H. B. Mattingly*, 43–4). *Symbola* (11–16) are tokens for recognition, originally the two halves of a single object separated by a unique jigsaw cut (Gauthier, *Symbola*, 65–76). Here Mattingly saw the *symbola* as seals, which 'would most naturally in most cases carry the very coin types which Athens had just prohibited [in **155**]. It would appear a quite unnecessary affront' (in I. Carradice (ed.), *Coinage and Administration in the Athenian and Persian Empires*, 71 = his *AER* 486; cf. Figueira, *The Power of Money*, 253–4). For Athens' messengers and the districts of the League cf. **153**, **155**.

155

Athenian decree enforcing the use of Athenian coins, weights and measures, *c*.425–415

Nine fragments: two of local limestone from Syme (now lost), two of marble from Aphytis (in museum at Thessalonica), and one each of marble from Cos (in Cos museum), Gülpinar (ancient Hamaxitus), Olbia (now lost) and Siphnos. A further marble copy was seen and copied at Smyrna but is now lost. The first Syme fragment probably has text of clauses 1–2, the Hamaxitus fragment has clauses 1–2, the Cos fragment has clauses 1–5, the two Aphytis fragments have clauses 2–10, the second Syme fragment has clauses 6–10, the Siphnos fragment clauses 7–10, the Olbia fragment clauses 8–10, and the fragment seen in Smyrna clauses 8–12. Phot. *ATL* ii, pls. 5–7; *BCH* lxxxix 1965, 438–9 (Cos fragment); *ὅρος* xiv–xvi 2000–3, pls. 5–8 (Aphytis fragments).

Cos fragment: Attic letters, *stoichedon*. Other fragments: Ionic letters; Aphytis and Olbia fragments only, *stoichedon*.

M&L 45 (composite text); *IG* i³ 1453 (texts of 7 fragments plus composite text); M. B. Hatzopoulos, *ὅρος* xiv–xvi 2000–3, 31–43 (full Aphytis text) (*SEG* li 55)*; H. B. Mattingly, *Klio* lxxv 1993, 99–102 (Hamaxitus fragment). Trans. Fornara 97; Osborne, *The Athenian Empire*⁴, 198 (a different translation in earlier editions); Dillon & Garland³ 13. 13. See also Carradice (ed.), *Coinage and Administration in the Athenian and Persian Empires*; Kallet, *Money and the Corrosion of Power in Thucydides*, 205–26; E. Crespo, *Incontri Linguistici* xxix 2006, 91–101; J. H. Kroll, in Ma *et al.* (edd.), *Interpreting the Athenian Empire*, 195–209.

If the *prytaneis* fail in their duty they are to be penalised for bribery (35–7): in *Ath. Pol.* 54. ii that, along with embezzlement (*klope*), is the most serious financial offence which an official can commit, attracting a penalty of ten times the sum taken; here it is perhaps assumed that the *prytaneis* would not offend in this respect unless bribed to do so. For the trial procedure (37–41) Hill & Meritt restored reference to a court, citing *Ath. Pol.* 45. i; Matthaiou suggests reference to the assembly, which makes better sense of the *prytaneis*' instituting a debate on the penalty.

It is impossible to make continuous sense of the later part of the decree, but references to the incoming council (47–8) and to the previous year's tribute (63–4) indicate that the pursuit of defaulters is expected to continue into the following year. Lines 51 sqq. make provision for a city to challenge Athens' claim that it has not paid in full; if Matthaiou's suggestion for 53–4 is right, *koinon* there must refer not to the community of a city as a whole but to the authorities of that community. The 'election' in l. 66 is perhaps that of the generals.

We print a composite text in Ionic letters, and we therefore divide, following *IG*, by clauses, rather than lines.

1 - - -αι τὰ γ[——— 32 ———π]όλεσι ἢ αρ[——— 27 ———]

2 οἱ δὲ ἑλληνοταμ[ίαι ——— ±16 ——— ἄρχ]οντε[ς ἀ]ναγραφόντων· ἐὰν δέ τις ἀμ̣[——— ±18 ——— π]όλεόν τινος, ἐσα[γ ——— ±11 ——— ἑ]λληνο[ταμίαι ἐς τ]ὴν ἡλιαίαν τὴν τῶ[ν θεσμοθετῶν κατὰ τὸν νόμον· ὁ]ι δὲ θεσμοθέ[τ]αι πε[——— 9 ———]αντον [——— 12 ———]ασι ἕκαστον.

3 ἐὰν δέ [τις τῶν ἄλλ]ων ἀρχόν[των ἐν τ]αῖσι πόλεσι μὴ ποιῆι κα[τὰ τὰ ἐψηφισ]μένα ἢ τῶν [πολι]τῶν ἢ τῶν ξένων, [ἄτ]ιμ[ος ἔστω καὶ τὰ χρή]ματα δημόσια [ἔσ]τω καὶ τῆς θεοῦ τ[ὸ ἐπιδέκατον].

4 [καὶ εἰ μ]ή εἰσι ἄρχοντες Ἀθηναίων, ἐ[πι ——— 13 ——— ἐν τῶι] ψηφίσματι οἱ ἄρχοντε[ς οἱ ἑκάστης τῆς πόλεως· καὶ] ἐὰμ μὴ ποιῶσι κατὰ τ[ὰ ἐψηφισμένα, ——— 14 ———όντων τούτων πέρι ἀτι̣[——— 17 ———].

5 [ἐν δὲ τῶ]ι ἀργυροκοπίωι τὸ ἀργύ[ριον ——— 20 ——— μὴ ἔλ]αττον ἢ ἥμυσυ καὶ α̣[——— 29 ———]ι αἱ πόλεις πραττο̣[——— 27 ———] δραχμὰς ἀπὸ τῆς μν[ᾶς ——— 23 ——— κατ]αλλάττεν ἢ ἐνόχο[υς εἶναι κατὰ τὸν νόμον·]

6 [ὃ δὲ ἂν περι]γ̣ίγνηται ἀργυρίο[——— 28 ———]σθαι ἢ τοῖς στρατ[ηγοῖς ἢ ——— 19 ——— ἐπε]ι̣δὰν δὲ ἀποδοθῆι, [——— 21 ——— τῆι Ἀθην]ᾱ̣ι καὶ τῶι Ἡφαίσ[τωι ——— 11 ——— καὶ ἐάν τ]ις εἴπ[ηι ἢ] ἐπιψηφίσηι περ[ὶ τούτων ——— 15 ——— ἐς ἄλλο] τι χρῆσθαι ἢ δανε[ίζεσθαι, ἀπαγέσθω αὐτίκα μάλα πρὸς] τοὺς ἕνδεκα· οἱ δ[ὲ ἕνδεκα θαν]άτωι ζ[ημιωσάντων· ἐὰν] δὲ ἀμφισβητῆι, ἐσ[αγαγόντων ἐς τὸ δικαστήρ]ιον.

7 κήρυκας δὲ ἑλέσθαι τὸ[ν δῆμον ἀπαγγελοῦντας τὰ ἐψηφισμ]ένα, ἕνα μὲν ἐπὶ Νή[σους, ἕνα δὲ ἐπὶ Ἰωνίαν, ἕνα δὲ ἐφ' Ἑλλήσπο]ντον, ἕν[α] δ̣ὲ̣ ἐ̣[πὶ τὰ ἐπ]ὶ Θράικης· το[ύτοις δὲ τὴν πορείαν ἑκάστωι συγγράψαντες οἱ στρατηγοὶ ἀπ]οστελάντ[ω]ν· ἐὰν δ̣[ὲ μή, εὐθυ]νόσθω μυ̣ρ̣ία[ισι δραχμῆσι].

8 [ἀναγ]ράψαι δὲ τὸ ψήφισμα τ[όδε τὸς ἄ]ρχοντα[ς ἐ]ν ταῖσι πόλεσιν [κ]α̣θ̣' ἕ̣να ἕκασ[τον· θεῖναι δὲ ἐν στή]ληι λιθίνηι ἐν τῆι ἀγορᾶι τέλεσι [ἑκάσ]τη[ς πό]λεως καὶ τὸς ἐπιστ[άτας ἔμπ]ροσθεν τô ἀργυροκοπίο· ταῦτα δὲ ἐπ̣[ιτελὲν συμμα]χίαν, ἐὰμ μὴ αὐτοὶ βόλωνται.

9 δεηθῆναι δὲ αὐτῶ[ν] τὸγ κήρυκα τὸν ἰόντα̣ ὅσα [κ]ε̣λεύο[σιν] Ἀθηναῖοι.

We have marked with an underdot letters that occur in only one copy and cannot certainly be read.

1 and 2 until ho]ι δὲ θεσμοθέ[τ]αι *IG*: Hatzopoulos offers no restoration before the start of the first Aphytis fragment). 2 οἱ δὲ ἑλληνοταμ[ίαι ——— ±16 ——— ἄρχ]οντε[ς ἀ]ναγραφόντων· ἐὰν δὲ τις ἀμ̣[——— ±18 ——— π]όλεόν τινος, ἐσα[γ ——— ±11 ——— ἑ]λληνο[ταμίαι ἐς τ]ὲν ἑλιαίαν O&R, restoring ἄρχοντες and ἑ]λληνο[ταμίαι on the basis of the first Syme fragment which preserves ολε from πόλεσι in 1, οντε from ἄρχοντες and λληνο̣ from ἑλληνοταμίαι in 2 at the appropriate spacing (to judge by the line length of the second Syme fragment), and restoring ἐὰν δὲ τις ἀμ̣[on the basis of the Hamaxitus fragment (perhaps ἐὰν δὲ τις ἀμφισβητῆι, cf. 6 below): [hοι] δὲ hελλενοταμ[ίαι ——— 24 ——— ἀ]ναγραφόντον· ἐᾱ̣[ν δὲ μὲ ὀρθôς ἀναγράφοσι τὸ τôν π]όλεόν τινος, ἐσα[γ ——— 23 ——— ἐς τ]ὲν ἑλιαίαν *IG*. 3 ἐὰν δέ [τις τῶν ἄλλ]ων ἀρχόν[των O&R on the basis of the Hamaxitus fragment: ἐᾱ̣[ν δὲ μὴ ὀρθôς ἀναγράφοσι τὸ τôν π]όλεόν τινος *IG*: ἐᾱ̣[ν δὲ μὴ - - - - - π]όλεών τινος M&L. 4 πόλεως· καὶ] ἐὰμ μὴ *IG*: πόλεως·] ἐὰν δὲ μὴ Hatzopoulos. 7 τὸ[ν δῆμον καὶ πέμψαι ἀπαγγελοῦντας *IG*: τὸ[ν δῆμον ἀπαγγελοῦντας Hatzopoulos. 8 βόλωνται *IG*: βούλωνται Hatzopoulos. 10 τὸν γραμματέα τῆς βολῆς κ[αὶ τοῦ δήμου Hatzopoulos: τὸν γραμματέα τὸν τῆς [βολῆς ——— c.10 ——— τα]δί *IG* (composite), τὸν γραμμα[τέα τὸν τῆς βολῆς ταδί] *IG* (Syme, cf. Olbia). ἐάν τις κόπτηι νόμισμα ἀργυρίο ἐν τῆσι πό[λεσι] καὶ μὴ χρῆται νομ[ίσμασιν τοῖς] Ἀθη[να]ίων ἢ σταθμοῖς ἢ μέτ[ροις ἀλλὰ ξενικοῖς νομίσμασι]ν καὶ σταθμοῖς καὶ [μ]έτροις *IG*; ἐάν τις κόπτηι νόμισμα ἀργυρίο ἐν ταῖσι πόλεσι [ἢ] χρῆται νομ[ίσμ]α̣τι ἄλλωι ἤ τῶι Ἀθηνα[ίων ἢ] σταθμοῖς καὶ μέτροις [ἄλ]λ̣οις ἢ τοῖς Ἀθηναίων κ[αὶ τιμωρήσομαι κα]ὶ ζ[ημιώσω] Aphytis (Hatzopoulos). See commentary.

– – – in the cities, or (?) magistrates – – –

2 The *hellenotamiai* are to – – – magistrates are to write up. If anyone ?disputes? – – – of any of the cities – – – the *hellenotamiai* ?are to bring them? to the court of the *thesmothetai* according to the law. The *thesmothetai* are to – – – each.

3 If any other of the magistrates in the cities does not act in accordance with the decrees, whether citizens or foreigners, let him lose his civic rights and let his property be confiscated and a tenth of it given to the goddess.

4 And if there are no Athenian magistrates – – – the magistrates of each city are to do as it says in the decree. If they do not act in accordance with the decrees – – – these concerning ?loss of civic rights – – –

5 In the mint, the silver – – – not less than half, and – – – the cities act – – – drachmas per mina – – – exchange, or be liable according to the law.

6 Whatever silver is over – – – either to the generals or – – – Whenever it is handed over – – – to Athena and to Hephaestus. – – – And if anyone makes or puts to the vote a proposal about these things – – – to use or loan for some other purpose, let him straightway be hauled off to the Eleven. The Eleven are to punish him with death. If he disputes the charge let them bring him to the court.

7 The people are to choose heralds to announce what has been decreed, one to the Islands, one to Ionia, one to the Hellespont, one to the Thraceward region. The generals are to dispatch them after they have prescribed the route for each. If they do not, they are to be fined 10,000 dr. at their audit.

8 The magistrates are to write up this decree in each of the cities individually. They are to place it on a stone *stele* in the agora at the expense of each city, and the *epistatai* are to place it in front of the mint. The alliance is to carry this out if the magistrates themselves are not willing.

9 The herald who goes to them is to ask them to do all that the Athenians order.

10 προσγράψαι δὲ καὶ πρὸς τὸν ὅρκον [τ]ὸν τῆς βολῆς τὸν γραμματέα τῆς βολῆς κ[αὶ τοῦ δήμου τα]δί· "ἐάν τις κόπτηι νόμισμα ἀργυρίο ἐν τῆσι πό[λεσι] καὶ μὴ χρῆται νομ[ίσμασιν τοῖς] Ἀθη[να]ίων ἢ σταθμοῖς ἢ μέτ[ροις ἀλλὰ ξενικοῖς νομίσμασι]ν καὶ σταθμοῖς καὶ [μ]έτροις, [— c.12? —]"

11 [..τ — c.6 — κατὰ τὸ πρότε]ρον ψήφισμα ὃ Κλέαρχ[ος εἶπεν — c.26 —]αι τὸ ξενικὸν ἀργύριον [— c.30 — ὅ]ταμ βόληται· τὴν δὲ πό[λιν — c.28 —]ΑΥΤΟΝ δὲ τὰ [ἑ]αυτô ἕκαστ[ον — c.23 — τὸ ἀργυ]ροκόπιον.

12 ο[ἱ δ'] ἐπιστάτ[αι — c.31 — ἀναγ]ράψαντες κατα[θέντων — c.12 — ἔμπροσθεν τô ἀργυροκο]πίο σκοπε̂ν τῶι βο[λομένωι· ἀναγραψάντων δὲ καὶ ξύμπαν τὸ ἀργύριον τὸ] ξενικόν, χω[ρὶς — c.41 —]ν ἀργύρι[ον ‒ ‒ ‒].

11–12 *IG* (here set out differently at the start of 11): Hatzopoulos prints no text of these clauses since they were not in the Aphytis copy).

In Aristophanes' frightening fantasy about imperial power, *Birds*, which won second prize at the City Dionysia in 414, one of the unwanted visitors who plague the new city of Cloudcuckooland is a decree-seller, come to sell the birds new laws. The law that he offers is: 'That the people of Cloudcuckooland use the same measures and weights and decrees as the Olophyxians' (χρῆσθαι Νεφελοκοκκυγιᾶς τοῖσδε τοῖς μέτροισι | καὶ σταθμοῖσι καὶ ψηφίσμασι καθάπερ Ὀλοφύξιοι: *Av.* 1040–1). He is told that he will soon use the same as the Ototyxians (the people who cry '*ototoi*' when hit), and to take his laws away. Aristophanes has inserted 'decrees' in place of 'coins' but there can be no doubt that he is parodying the decree recorded in this inscription, and doing so in a remarkable way, as he substitutes for the imperial city of Athens the name of an allied city on the Athos peninsula, Olophyxus (regular tribute 2,000 dr., **119**. *B*. ii. 35). Aristophanes expected his Athenian audience to recognise that their attempt to insist that their allies use Athenian measures, weights and coins was both unpopular with the allies, and faintly absurd.[1]

This decree is a rare example of an inscribed text which is referred to in contemporary literature, and where that literature offers significant assistance in its interpretation. Nevertheless it poses unusual and severe epigraphic problems that are closely related to its historical significance.

It is clear that we have lost the core of the decree. When our text starts it appears to be concerned with publication (at Athens?) and with sanctions against those not putting the decree into operation (§§2, 3 and 4). It then deals with the consequences of the decree for the mint, regulating mint behaviour (§§5–6). Getting the message out to the allies is the subject of §7 and publication in allied cities and securing their obedience the subjects of §§8 and 9. §10 then deals with an addition to the oath taken by the council, and §§11 and 12 reiterate an earlier ruling proposed by Clearchus (see further below), with an early example of a disclosure formula (see on **167**).

[1] U. von Wilamowitz-Moellendorff in 1880 hypothesised the existence of a standards decree on the basis of the *Birds* passage, not knowing of any epigraphic finds (*Aus Kydathen*, 30–1).

10 The secretary of the council and people is to add the following to the oath of the council: 'If anyone strikes silver coinage in the cities and does not use the coins of the Athenians or their weights or measures, but foreign coins and weights and measures – – –'

11 According to the former decree which Clearchus proposed – – – the foreign silver – – – whenever he wants. – – – the city – – – each his own – – – the mint.

12 The *epistatai* – – – when they have written up, are to deposit – – – in front of the mint for anyone who wishes to scrutinise. They are to write up the total of foreign silver, not counting – – – silver.

Although other Athenian decrees have been found in cities of the empire (cf. **136**), this is the only case where we can have some confidence that a decree was sent out to and inscribed in every allied state. (Note that §4 seems to consider it likely rather than unlikely that there will be Athenian magistrates in the various cities.) Since all surviving copies are fragmentary, the text has to be pieced together from overlapping fragments—no small problem when the text is inscribed once in Attic and elsewhere in Ionic letters (although the language remains basically Attic: see Crespo), and where textual variations are not all minor. Scholars have recently wondered whether we should think not of a single decree on this topic but of two or more slightly different decrees (see Stroud, *The Athenian Empire on Stone*; cf. Figueira, *The Power of Money*), but that it has been possible to find homes for recently discovered fragments within the text as previously restored encourages us to continue to think that we are dealing essentially with a single text.

Belief in a single text demands giving an account of how the differences have arisen between the texts that we have. Some variations are trivial: the Syme copy plausibly records the decision to choose heralds and to send them to announce, the Aphytis copy merely to choose heralds to announce; similarly the Smyrna, Syme and Aphytis copies record that the addition to the bouleutic oath (§10) should be written in by 'the secretary of the council and the people' where the Siphnos and Olbia copies record merely 'the secretary of the council'. Such variations are not hard to explain. Sending a copy of this text to every Athenian ally was a very major task: although it is possible to think that the heralds sent to each of the four regions listed in §7 (evidently also to the Black Sea) took just one copy each and oversaw the inscription from that one copy, it seems more practicable for them to take a separate copy for each ally, and this would involve more than 200 copies. That the Cos copy is inscribed in Attic script raises the issue of whether the copy taken by the heralds was in Attic or Ionic letters. Omissions that made no difference to the sense would be easy to make in so extensive and elaborate a copying process, and to go unnoticed or not be worried about.

But it is now apparent that there were two more substantial differences. One was in the wording of the council oath. The copy from Olbia certainly, and those from Syme and Smyrna plausibly, recorded the oath in the form we have given in our main text: 'If anyone strikes silver coinage in the cities and does not use the coins of the Athenians or their weights or measures, but foreign coins and weights and measures'. But the recent fragment from Aphytis certainly has an alternative form (which we give in the apparatus): 'If anyone strikes silver coinage in the cities or uses coinage other than the coinage of the Athenians or weights and measures other than those of the Athenians'. Figueira has wondered whether the former formulation might allow the offence to be understood as the combination of minting silver and not using Athenian silver, so that it allowed cities to continue to mint as long as they *also* used Athenian coins, and has therefore seen the Aphytis formula as more severe in excluding any coin use except use of Athenian coins.[2] This is implausible both as an understanding of the Greek and in historical terms (cf. Kallet, *Money and the Corrosion of Power*, 214–15). The Athenian decree is not simply about coins, but about weights and measures. The thought that the Athenians were licensing some double use (you can weigh/measure in non-Athenian measures as long as you also give the Athenian equivalent) is hard to entertain. The two forms of oath have no difference in substance, but the difference in wording seems unlikely to have arisen simply from copyists' error.

The second variation is yet more substantial. The recent Aphytis fragment definitely ends after the council's oath, allowing, indeed, very little space for the description of what the council is actually undertaking to do (the twenty-four letters available here contrast with the fifty-five letters taken to describe the punishment of those who disobey the decree in §3 but are comparable to the twenty-five letters describing the punishment of generals in §7 and the eighteen-letter description of the death penalty in §6). The Smyrna fragment continued for at least another ten lines, with a section beginning with the problematic phrase which begins, 'According to the former decree which Clearchus proposed'.

Two things need explaining. What exactly is recorded in the last ten lines of the Smyrna fragment? And why did this clause not get inscribed at Aphytis? It seems unlikely that 'the former decree which Clearchus proposed' would be a possible way of referring to the decree inscribed on the stone to this point, and this is not a standard amendment formula. So it appears that cross-reference is to another decree of Clearchus, probably with the implication that Clearchus was also the proposer of this decree. But what was the purpose of the cross-reference? That it was a cross-reference with regard to the nature of the punishment that the members of the council swear to deploy seems to be ruled out by the fact that the Aphytis copy did not include it; this needs to be a new clause. Unfortunately little could be read of the Smyrna text (the earliest to be published, and now lost), but it is clear that this clause relates to foreign silver, the mint and displaying something in front of the mint. The

[2] So A. P. Matthaiou, 'Studies in Attic Inscriptions and the History of the Fifth Century BC', 174–5, building on Figueira, *The Power of Money* (a book whose basic thesis is rendered increasingly unlikely by the newer fragments), 394; cf. also T. J. Figueira, *Annali* (Instituto Italiano di Numismatica) lii 2006, 9–44.

best guess is that this is about re-minting non-Athenian coins into Athenian coins and carefully recording the quantities of coin brought for re-minting and the quantities of Athenian coin then issued. One possibility is that in some earlier decree Clearchus had made it possible for allies to convert their own coin to Athenian coin by bringing their own coin to the Athenian mint. This clause would, in that case, merely repeat that provision in the now more urgent circumstances that the allies were obliged to stop using their own coinage.

But why was this additional clause not in the Aphytis copy? Those who believe that several versions of the decree were issued successively see here merely the most substantial of additions to a previous decree (cf. Kroll, 207 n. 27). But alternatively one might think about the role of these inscribed texts in giving information to the Athenian allies. Losses of text at earlier points mean that we do not know exactly what was said, and it does appear that §5 made some provision for the re-coining of non-Athenian coin into Athenian coin, but that clause may well not have answered all the questions that the allies had about what they should do. It seems conceivable that quotation at Smyrna of another earlier decree was in response to a question about exactly what should happen—and very conceivable that Athenian provision for the possibility of allies converting non-Athenian coinage into Athenian coinage (in a decree moved by Clearchus) preceded a separate decision to compel allies to do that.

None of the surviving fragments includes the beginning of the decree, and what survives gives no explicit indication of the decree's date. The Attic letters of the Cos fragment include a three-barred *sigma*, and when this was regarded as a strong dating indicator the decree was often dated to the 440s. No other letter forms on the Cos fragment look early, and it is now clear that three-barred sigma continued to be used into the 410s (see Introduction, pp. xxii–xxiii, and on **166**). Copies of the standards decree from Hamaxitus (on the Asiatic mainland north of Lesbos) and from Olbia (near the north coast of the Black Sea; the provenance is secure: see D. Braund, in Braund (ed.), *Scythians and Greeks*, 85), indicate that the decree was being sent to Athens' allies after 425: Hamaxitus only became an independent member of the Athenian empire after Mytilene's revolt (it is found in the tribute assessments of 425/4, our **153**, and later, *IG* i³ 77. iv. 18); and a Pontic panel of tribute-paying cities first appears in 425/4 (with Olbia itself perhaps listed, with tribute of 1 tal., and Olbia's neighbour Niconia there assessed at ½ tal. (**154** and *IG* i³ 71. iv. 162, 167).

It would be possible to believe that this decree was unique and notorious, and that as a result the Athenians sent copies to all new members even when the decree itself had been passed at an earlier date. But we would need good reason for not adopting the simpler hypothesis that the reason why Aristophanes parodies this decree in 414, and why allies who joined the empire only in the middle of the 420s received copies, is that the decree itself was passed shortly before 414. Just how shortly before will depend upon the historical context that we reconstruct for this decree.

By the decree the Athenians imposed on their allies an obligation which required them to change some of their basic behaviour. The Athenians had from the beginning imposed on allies one universal requirement—to contribute either ships or tribute—but the number of universal impositions known is otherwise few. We hear of the provision of a cow and a full set of armour for the Panathenaea (**154**. 41–2) and probably a phallus for the Dionysia (unless that was only for colonies: **142**. 11–13; cf. also **121**. 3–4), and we know that all allies were obliged to exclude Megarians from their harbours in the 430s. But those impositions can have had nothing like the impact of this requirement, which changed the coins people used and their measures. What can have occasioned such an alteration of Athenian policy? If we place this decree in the 420s then what occasioned this policy was the financial pressure Athens was under because of the Peloponnesian War, and the new style of Athenian politics that emerged in the face of the tensions caused by that war. This decree would belong with the extraordinary tribute reassessment decree of 425/4 and the tightening up of tribute-payment procedures in the decrees moved by Cleonymus and Cleinias (**153–5**). But there is an alternative context. Kallet has observed that the point at which unified coins, weights and measures were most useful to Athens is in 413, when she decided to change from demanding tribute payment to collecting a 5 per cent tax (*eikoste*) on all import and export trade within the empire (Thuc. vii. 28. iv; see Kallet, *Money and the Corrosion of Power in Thucydides*, 205–25, T. J. Figueira, *Incid. Antico* iii 2005, 83–133). Such a tax could be collected regardless of the measures and coins being used locally, but uniformity of units would certainly simplify matters. This argument is stronger, however, in establishing a very plausible date before which the standards decree had been enacted than in establishing the actual date at which it was passed.

Changes in what weights and measures were used may not be possible to detect (but note a quarter-mina weight dating to the second half of the fifth century, found in the Black Sea region and bearing both the Athenian owl and the Cyzicene tunny: H.-C. Meyer & A. Moreno, *OJA* xxiii 2004, 209–16). But for some cities, in particular Thasos, Abdera, Maronea, Aenus, Acanthus and Mende, which had access to local silver mines, prohibition on minting would seriously disrupt the way in which they exploited local resources. Both the increase in Athenian silver production needed to enable Athenian coins to replace all other silver coins in the empire and the cessation of minting of silver in any city across the Athenian empire (minting of electrum, as in Cyzicus, Lampsacus, Mytilene and Phocaea, seems not to be prohibited: cf. **195**) should be apparent (on both issues see further Kroll). There is indeed a massive increase in the production of Athenian 'owl' tetradrachms in the fifth century, but that increase seems to date to the middle of the century (and may be linked simply with the move of the Delian League's treasury to Athens in 454). It is likely that the very availability and convenience of Athenian coinage itself encouraged its widespread use. This is supported by the gradual decline of minting among Athens' allies during the Delian League: thirty-four of the seventy-nine cities that coined at some point after 478 had certainly ceased minting by 420, and among the other cities a number minted only low-value coinages that provided local small change (cf. Mytilene, **195**). Unfortunately the chronology of late fifth-century coinage is insufficiently well established to enable us to see whether there is any particular horizon at which all cities in the empire ceased to mint. Although the evidence is tenuous, some numismatists would argue for minting of at least low-denomination silver after 424 by at least some cities (cf. J. Kagan, *AJN*[2] xxvi 2014, 16–23). The later the date of this decree (and so the briefer its period of application) the easier it would be to understand why numismatic trace is hard to find.

The question of the purpose of the coinage decree relates closely to its date. Placed in the context of the imposition of the 5 per cent tax on imports and exports throughout the empire, the decree would become largely an instrument of the change in imperial policy, facilitating a move from direct to indirect taxation of the allies. Placed a decade earlier, the decree would become an independent instrument of imperial rule, imposing on the allies an obligation which hits hard at local pride and independence without bringing any significant economic advantage either to the allies or the Athenians. The Athenians do seem to expect some sort of profit from the decree, since §6 seems to refer to contributions to the funds of Athena and Hephaestus and to prohibit changes to the destination of the funds involved. Such profits would most reasonably come from re-minting charges (perhaps 5 per cent); this initial loss on the part of the allies might be partly recouped by saving on money-changers' fees, and it would be money-changers who would be the biggest losers (converting weights and measures requires only some straightforward mathematics and would bring no significant financial costs or gains, so demanding that is worthwhile only either for symbolic effect or to facilitate tax-collection).

From the 430s on (cf. **139** and the Megarian decree), Athens increased the gratuitous demands it made on its allies, and the coinage decree could sit happily in that context. Particularly striking in the decree are the penalties imposed: the entrenchment clause in §6, protecting the decree against annulment or modification, makes proposing or putting to the vote any other proposal on the destination of the funds involved a capital offence, while failure by the generals to support the heralds brings a 10,000 dr. fine (and in §4 recalcitrant officials may be threatened with *atimia*). Entrenchment clauses regularly have very harsh penalties attached (most often *atimia*, loss of citizen rights, and property confiscation (cf. **142**. 24–30 with commentary; also **153**. 31–3 with commentary), but the only parallel for the death penalty is that set in 431 for those proposing alternative uses for the 1,000-talent reserve set aside to be used only if Athens were attacked by a fleet (Thuc. II. 24. i). What is more, this is the only time an entrenchment clause is applied to allied officials, rather than to Athenian citizens. These excessive penalties seem at home with the excessive tribute demands made in the 425/4 assessment. Ironically, the parody in *Birds*, rather than supporting a late date, presents the decree as an independent instrument of allied oppression, not as preparatory to a major rethinking of how allies related to Athens. Overall, we consider either a date in the 420s or a date closer to 415 possible.

156

Athenian decree concerning the priestess of Athena Nike, 424/3

On the reverse of the *stele* which bears **137**; previously in the Epigraphical Museum but now displayed in the Acropolis Museum. Phot. Kern, *Inscriptiones Graecae*, 14; Blok (below), 101, 123; our pl. 12.

Attic letters in ll. 1–6 (up to the *vacat*), Ionic letters from there on. *Stoichedon* 23, with different letter grids in the Attic and the Ionic sections.

SIG^3 63. *b*; M&L 71; *IG* i^3 36*; Mark, *The Sanctuary of Athena Nike in Athens*, 107; J. H. Blok, *Kernos* xxvii 2014, 122; Shear, *Trophies of Victory*, 28. Trans. Fornara 139; Mark, 108, Blok, 123, Dillon & Garland^3 3. 66; Kearns, *Ancient Greek Religion*, 249; Shear, *Trophies of Victory*, 28. See also J. H. Blok, *Kernos* xxvii 2014, 99–126.

ἔδοχσεν τε̑ι βολε̑ι καὶ το̑ι δέ-
μοι· Αἰγεὶς ἐπρυτάνευε, Νεοκ-
λείδες ἐγραμμάτευε, Ἁγνόδε-
μος ἐπεστάτε, Καλλίας εἶπε· τ-
ε̑ι hιερέαι τε̑ς Ἀθενάας τε̑ς Νί-
κες ^{v} πεντήκοντα δραχμὰς τὰ-
ς γεγραμμένας ἐν τῆι στήλ[ηι]
ἀποδιδόναι τὸς κωλακρ[έτας],
οἳ ἂν κωλακρετῶσι το̑ Θ̣[αργηλ]-
[ιῶ]νος μηνός, τῆι ἱερ[έαι τῆς Ἀ]-
[θην]αίας τῆς Νίκη[ς —— 8 ——]

6 the first hand inscribed first an *alpha* (starting ἀποδιδόναι) and then a *pi*: these were then erased and the second hand left one letter space vacant before starting: see pl. 12. The ΠΑ of M&L is certainly wrong.

Unlike the decree on the other side of this stone (**137**), this decree can be dated with some confidence. The perfectly preserved opening rubrics reveal the prytany to have been Aegeis and the secretary Neocleides. Neocleides' name as secretary (with Aegeis plausibly restored as prytany) recurs in a treaty between Athens and Halieis (*IG* i^3 75) which belongs between Athenian ravaging of the land of Halieis in 425/4 (Thuc. iv. 45. ii) and the Peace of Nicias, and is extremely likely to be contemporary with the treaty with Troezen, mentioned at Thuc. iv. 118. iv, which will place it before spring 423. Aegeis held the fourth prytany of the year in 425/4 but the sixth in 424/3, and this must be the date when Neocleides was secretary.[1]

[1] B. D. Meritt & G. R. Davidson, *AJP* lvi 1935, 65–71 at 65–7; cf. Jameson, Runnels & van Andel, *A Greek Countryside*, 78. Technically the same Neocleides need not be involved in both cases, and the prytany of the Halieis decree could be Leontis, but given that these two decrees cannot in any case be many years apart identification of them as belonging to the same secretary seems highly plausible.

Resolved by the council and the people. Aegeis was the prytany; Neocleides was the secretary; Hagnodemus was the chairman. Callias proposed: For the priestess of Athena Nike the *kolakretai* who are serving as *kolakretai* during the month Thargelion are to pay the fifty drachmas stated on the *stele*, to the priestess of Athena Nike – – –

Callias is too common a name for us to be able to identify the Callias who proposed the decree.

Two things hang upon the date of this decree. The first is its relation to **137** on the obverse. That decree (see on **137**) must be before *c*.437, and a gap of at least twelve years between these two explicitly related decrees is certain. The second is its relation to Athenian success in war. Why was Athena Nike particularly in mind in 424/3? Three possibilities can be canvassed. One is that Athena Nike is in mind because the Athenians had just made an agreement with the Persians on the accession of Darius: the references back to the Persian Wars in the friezes of the Nike temple might support this association (see E. Harrison, *AJA*[2] lxxvi 1972, 353–78), but it seems that that treaty cannot be earlier than 423/2 (cf. **157** with commentary). The second is that Athena Nike is in mind because the bastion had just been used to display spoils from the Athenian victory at Pylos. There are ninety-nine cuttings on the faces of the Nike bastion that were plausibly used to attach shields that had been captured, and on the basis of a passage of Aristophanes' *Knights* (843–59) it has been argued that most plausibly these were ninety-nine of the 120 shields captured at Pylos in 425 (M. Lippman, D. Scahill & P. Schultz, *AJA*^{2} cx 2006 551–63). The third is that the Athenians had just dedicated a new cult statue of Athena Nike. In the 330s the Athenians passed a decree (*IG* ii^3 444) to repair a statue of Athena Nike that the Athenians had dedicated from the spoils from victories over the Ambraciots at Olpae (Thuc. III. 106–14), the revolting Corcyreans (Thuc. IV. 46–8) and the Anactorians (Thuc. IV. 49). All these victories fall in 426 or 425, and the concern of the Athenians a hundred years later to repair the statue may imply that this was not just any dedication to Athena Nike but a statue with a central place in the cult, and presumptively in her temple (Lippman, Scahill & Schultz, 559–60).

What, however, is this decree about? Although the *stele* is broken off and the text incomplete, it is unlikely, given that the decree on the other side has already reached the recording of an amendment, that much has been lost at the end; the main substance of the decree must be contained in what survives. Since, as the decree itself acknowledges, the decision to pay the priestess of Athena Nike 50 drachmas had already been taken, either that decision had not been implemented (which is possible if the earlier decree dates from *c*.437, in which case its decision about building the temple had not yet been implemented), or the issue concerns who pays the money or when the money is paid, neither of which were specified in the earlier decree. The *kolakretai*, who were the paying officers of the state treasury, served

---

157

Athens honours Heracleides of Clazomenae, 423 or later

Two joining fragments from the bottom of a marble *stele*, both found on the acropolis, now in the Epigraphical Museum. Phot. (*a*) Pečírka, *The Formula for the Grant of Enktesis in Attic Inscriptions*, pl. 1; Walbank, *Athenian Proxenies*, pl. 27; (*a* + *b*) Culasso Gastaldi, *Le prossenie ateniesi del IV secolo a.C.*, 36.

Ionic lettering of the early fourth century. Lines 1–23 *stoichedon* 31; ll. 24–6 non-*stoichedon*.

§i

[—— 19 —— ψήφισμα τόδε κ]-
[αὶ τὸ πρότερον γενόμενον Ἡρακλείδηι]
ἀναγράψαι τὸγ [γραμματέα τῆς βολῆς κα]-
ὶ θε͂ναι ἐν πόλει. *vacat*

vacat

only for one prytany,[2] so that specification of time of year is necessary, but the decision to indicate the month Thargelion (the eleventh month of the Athenian year, more or less corresponding to May), rather than a particular prytany, may be connected to the festival year, but we do not know enough of the duties of the priestess to be sure.

For the first priestess of Athena Nike see **137**, **179**. For use of the funds of Athena Nike by the Athenians see **160**, **174**, **180**; for the continued importance of the cult see R&O 81. *B*. 20–2.

In l. 6 there is a change in mid-sentence from Attic to Ionic script, and from one mason to another. At the point of change a space is left where first one letter and then another had been inscribed. The combination of Attic and Ionic letters in the same inscription is uncommon; it can be paralleled in a casualty list from 426, but even there the change does not happen in mid-sentence.[3] Something odd has clearly occurred in the course of inscribing this decree. It appears that one mason left off in the middle, and another resumed the text after some interval and had to mark up the *stoichedon* grid again.

[2] Cf. *IG* i[3] 73. 25–9; and see A. Wilhelm, *Sb. Wien* CCXVII. v 1939, 52–72 = his *Akademieschriften*, i. 572–92.

[3] Parlama & Stampolidis, *Athens: The City beneath the City*, 396–9 no. 452, the *stele* recording cavalry casualties from perhaps 429 and/or 426. The use of Ionic script in Athenian public inscriptions is reviewed by A. P. Matthaiou, in *Greek History and Epigraphy . . . P. J. Rhodes*, 201–12 (discussing this inscription at 203–4).

(*a*) *IG* ii[2] 8; *SIG*[3] 118; *SdA* 123; M&L 70; Walbank 47; *IG* i[3] 227. Trans. Fornara 138. (*b*) *IG* ii[2] 65; combined with (*a*) by Walbank, *ZPE* xlviii 1982, 261–3, li 1983, 183–4 (*SEG* xxxii 10); (*a* + *b*) M&L *addenda* 1988, p. 313; *IG* i[3] *addenda*, p. 955; Culasso Gastaldi, 35–55. See also A. B. West, *AJP* lvi 1935, 72–6; H. T. Wade-Gery, *HSCP* Supp. i 1940, 127–32 = his *Essays in Greek History* (Blackwell, 1958), 207–11; A. Andrewes, *Historia* x 1961, 1–5; D. Whitehead, *ZPE* lvii 1984, 145–6; E. M. Harris, *ZPE* cxxvi 1999, 123–8.

§i

– – – (this decree and the one previously made for Heracleides?) shall be written up by the secretary of the council and placed on the acropolis.

§ii

ἔδοξεν τῆι βολῆι κ̣[αὶ τῶι δήμωι· —6—]-
[.]ὶς ἐπρυτάνευεν· Σ[.... ἐγραμμάτευεν]·
[.]εοκλείδης ἐπεστ[άτει. —12—]
[εἶ]πεν· Ἡρακλείδην [τὸγ Κλαζομένιον ἀν]-
[αγρ]άψαι τὸγ γραμμ[ατέα τῆς βολῆς πρόξ]-
[ενο]ν καὶ εὐεργέτη[ν καθότι ἂν τῶι δήμω]-
[ι δο]κῆι καὶ θε͂ναι ἐ[ν πόλει ἐπειδὴ εὖ ἐπ]-
[όησ]εν τὰς Ἀθηναίω[ν πρεσβείας καὶ τὰ ἄ]-
[λλα ἀ]νήρ ἐστι ἀγαθ[ὸς εἰς τὸν δῆμον τὸν]
[Ἀθη]ν̣αίων. Θοκυδίδη̣[ς εἶπε· τὰ μὲν ἄλλα κ]-
[αθά]περ τῆι βολῆι· ἐπ̣[ειδὴ δὲ οἱ πρέσβες]
[οἱ π]α̣ρ<ὰ> βασιλέως ἥκ[οντες ἀγγέλλοσι Ἡ]-
[ρακ]λείδην συμπράτ[τεν ἑαυτοῖς προθύ]-
[μως] ἔ̣ς τε τὰσπονδὰς [τὰς γενομένας καὶ]
[εἰς ἄ]λλο ὅ τι ἐπαγγέ[λειαν, ε͂ναι Ἡρακλε]-
[ίδηι] γῆς ἔγκτησιν κα[ὶ οἰκίας Ἀθήνησι]-
[ν καὶ ἀ]τέλειαν καθάπ[ερ τοῖς ἄλλοις πρ]-
[οξένο]ις· καὶ ἐάμ πο βια̣[ίωι θανάτωι ἀπο]-
[θάνηι, ε͂ναι π]ερὶ αὐτô τ[ιμωρίαν καθάπε]-
[ρ ἐάν τις Ἀ]θηναί̣ω̣ν ἀπ[οθάνηι, καὶ τάδε τ]-
[οῖς ἐκγόν]οις τοῖς Ἡ̣[ρακλείδο. *vacat*

vacat

[Ἡρακλ]είδο Γ[—c.8—]
[προξέ]νο καὶ [εὐεργέτο]
[Κλαζο]μενίο. *vacat*

vacat

3–4 [Ἀκαμαν|τ]ὶς or [Πανδιο|ν]ὶς. 4 Σ[ίμων] West. 5 [Θ]εοκλείδης or [Ν]εοκλείδης. 10–11 [τὰ ἄ|λλα] Culasso Gastaldi: [ἐν π|ᾶσι] Köhler, other edd. 14 the stone has Λ. 16–17 [τὰς γενομένας καὶ | είς ἄ]λλο Wilamowitz, cf. below: [τὰς πρὸς βασιλέα ἔ|ς τε ἄ]λλο Köhler, other edd.; [τὰς πρὸς τὴν πόλιν | καὶ ἄ]λλο Culasso Gastaldi. 18–19 [Ἀθήνησι|ν καὶ] most edd.: [καὶ μετο|ικίο] Whitehead, which may be correct. 21 τ[ιμωρίαν] Whitehead: τ[ὴν τιμὴν] Walbank. 24–6 letters not on a regular grid, but with 5 letters to be restored in 24–5 [Κλαζο]μενίο in 26 is overwhelmingly likely.

The lettering is characteristic of the early fourth century, and each fragment was originally published as a fourth-century text. However, the decree which survives in ll. 3–23 (§ii) is preceded by the end of another decree (§i), and it is plausibly assumed that §ii was inscribed earlier but destroyed on the orders of the Thirty in 404–403, that §i was a later decree for the same honorand, in or after 403/2, and that §i ordered the publication of itself and together with it the republication of §ii (cf. e.g. **177**. *B*, *IG* ii^2 52; also **162**, **191**).

The last line of the inscription makes it virtually certain that Heracleides was Heracleides of Clazomenae, who was nicknamed *basileus*, was made an Athenian

§ii

3 Resolved by the council and the people; (Acamantis *or* Pandionis) was the prytany; S— was the secretary; (Theocleides *or* Neocleides) was the chairman. —— proposed:

6 Heracleides the Clazomenian shall be written up by the secretary of the council as *proxenos* and benefactor as the people shall decide, and this shall be placed on the acropolis, because he acted well by the Athenian embassies and in other respects is a good man towards the people of Athens.

12 Thucydides proposed: In other respects in accordance with the council. Since the envoys who have come from the King report that Heracleides has cooperated with them enthusiastically with regard to the treaty which has been made (?) and any other business which they proposed(?), Heracleides shall have the right to possess land and a house at Athens, and immunity (*or* and a house, and immunity from the metic tax), as for the other *proxenoi*; and if he is killed anywhere by a violent form of death there shall be the same punishment in his case as if any of the Athenians is killed; and this shall be extended to the descendants of Heracleides.

24 Heracleides son of G— the Clazomenian, *proxenos* and benefactor.

---

citizen in time to propose the increase in assembly pay from 1 obol to 2 obols *c.*400–395,[1] and at some time served as general (Plat. *Ion* 541 D 1–4, Ath. XI. 560 A, Ael. *V.H.* XIV. 5). The natural interpretation is that the lost decree was that which made him a citizen, and so we need an occasion earlier than *c.*400–395 when for the good offices mentioned in the surviving decree he was made *proxenos* and benefactor but not yet citizen. As a development of private *xenia* ('guest-friendship'), a *proxenos*

[1] The 1-obol payment was introduced after the democratic restoration of 403, and there was a further increase, to 3 obols, before Aristophanes' *Ecclesiazusae*, of the late 390s: *Ath. Pol.* 41. iii cf. Ar. *Eccl.* 289–311, 392.

was usually a citizen of the state in which he lived, appointed to look after the interests of, and visitors from, the state which appointed him; though over time such appointments became increasingly honorific. Heracleides' good offices, as mentioned in an amendment which indicates more precisely than the original decree the reasons for honouring him (cf. R&O 19, and on such unusual precision see Osborne, in Goldhill & Osborne (edd.), *Performance Culture and Athenian Democracy*, 351–2 = his *Athens and Athenian Democracy*, 74–5), involved the King (presumably the Persian King) and a treaty, and probably gave rise to his nickname.

Three possible occasions have been suggested. (*a*) While Thucydides says nothing further after mentioning an Athenian embassy to Persia which turned back on hearing of the death of Artaxerxes I (Thuc. IV. 50. iii), Andoc. III. *Peace* 29 mentions a treaty made through Andocides' uncle Epilycus, which the Athenians later abandoned to support the rebel Amorges (a rebellion which ended with Amorges' capture in 412: Thuc. VIII. 5. v, 19. ii, 28, 54. iii).[2] (*b*) From 412/11 (Thuc. VIII. 46–9) until 407/6 (Xen. *Hell.* I. v. 8–9) Alcibiades encouraged the Athenians to hope that Persian support could be diverted from Sparta to Athens, but that was never achieved, no treaty was made, and the only Athenian embassy known to have set out to see the King did not reach him (Xen. *Hell.* I. iii. 8–9, 14, iv. 1–7). (*c*) In 400 the Spartans began fighting against the Persians on behalf of the Asiatic Greeks (Xen. *Hell.* III. i. 3–4, Diod. Sic. XIV. 35. vi–36), while the Athenian Conon raised a fleet for the satrap Pharnabazus (Diod. Sic. XIV. 39. i–iv cf. Xen. *Hell.* IV. iii. 11), and at some point Timocrates of Rhodes was sent with Persian money to encourage Sparta's enemies in Greece,[3] but nothing in our evidence for this period suggests that a treaty between Athens and Persia was ever in prospect.

That the occasion was the Peace of Epilycus was first suggested by U. Köhler, *Hermes* xxvi 1892, 68–78, and has been widely though not universally accepted, particularly since the union of the fragments confirmed the identification of Heracleides; but Culasso Gastaldi has argued that details in the text do not suit so early a date and that (*b*) is possible but (*c*) most likely.[4] We believe that her details

[2] Whether what is stated in Andoc. III. 29 is true and whether the text is an authentic speech of Andocides are in principle independent questions: the authenticity of the speech has been challenged by E. M. Harris, in *Polis and Politics . . . M. H. Hansen*, 479–505.

[3] Probably by Pharnabazus in 397, as in *Hell. Oxy.* 10. ii, v Chambers, Polyaen. I. 48. iii, rather than by Tithraustes in 395, as in Xen. *Hell.* III. v. 1, Plut. *Artox.* 20. iv, Paus. III. 9. viii.

[4] What follows is argued in more detail by Rhodes, *ZPE* cc 2016, 177–86.

(e.g. 9–10 [εὖ ἐπ|όησ]εν, 18 γῆς ἔγκτησιν κα[ὶ οἰκίας], 19 [ἀ]τέλειαν) do not rule out a date as early as the 420s. She was right to object to Wade-Gery's attempt to fix the decree in 424/3: a Neocleides was *bouleutes* in 424/3 (*IG* i^3 36 = **156**, cf. 74, 75), but there are possible chairmen for our decree known in Acamantis but none in Pandionis, and the secretary for Acamantis in 424/3 was not S . . . . but Phaenippus (cf. Thuc. IV. 118. xi, and *IG* i^3 61, 73); an Epilycus can be restored as a *bouleutes* in 424/3 (*IG* i^3 369. 26), but we should not expect a *bouleutes* to serve on an embassy to Persia; there are several possible identifications for the Thucydides who proposed the amendment. However, Artaxerxes did not die until winter 424/3, and Darius had to deal with rival claimants, so a treaty as early as 424/3 is in any case unlikely (see Andrewes, believing in 424/3 but admitting the difficulty).

Culasso Gastaldi thinks (*b*) 412/1–407/6 possible but (*c*) after 400 more likely. However, (*c*) after *c.*400 there is very little time for Heracleides to earn the honours of our decree, then to become an Athenian citizen and then to propose the increase in assembly pay, and there is no good reason to think that anybody would have contemplated a treaty with the King. We should also then expect this decree to be published immediately, not combined with the decree granting him citizenship. (*b*) Between 412/1 and 407/6 there were times when some Athenians hoped for a treaty with the King, but none was obtained. This cannot be ruled out as an occasion for Heracleides' good offices, but we still think (*a*) the Peace of Epilycus the most likely occasion.

Harris has shown that in ll. 13–14 the envoys [οἱ π]α̣ρ<ὰ> βασιλέως ἥκ[οντες] ought to be Persian envoys to Athens, not returning Athenian envoys. In ll. 16–17 Wilamowitz' restoration is the most convincing if one believes that the reference is to a treaty actually made, i.e. the Peace of Epilycus; otherwise Köhler's [τὰς πρὸς βασιλέα ἔ|ς τε ἄ]λλο is, as Culasso Gastaldi points out, strictly illogical when the envoys of 13–14 are Persian, but it is an illogicality of which an Athenian proposer would have been capable, and is the best of the restorations which do not require a treaty to have been made. The text ends with a three-line 'heading' advertising Heracleides' status as *proxenos* and benefactor: there is a parallel from the 420s in the ending of **152**, though here the placing of this at the end may be due to the republication of the 390s and not to the original publication; it is in any case strange that the text should end in this way if the lost upper decree granted Heracleides the greater honour of citizenship.

158

Regulations on the duties of envoys sent to Delphi by Andros, inscribed at Delphi, *c.*425

Two fragments from a block of grey limestone inscribed on two adjacent faces, found between the south-east corner of the temple of Apollo and the Treasury of the Corinthians. *a* and *b* are the two faces from the upper part of the block, *aa* is from the lower part of face *a*. Phot. *Hesperia* xviii 1949, pl. 1; *C. Delphes* i, pl. 3 (squeeze).

Transitional Delphic letters. *Stoichedon* (with irregularities).

G. Daux, *Hesperia* xviii 1949, 58–72 and *BCH* lxxiii 1949, 293; Buck 7; *LSS* 38; *C. Delphes* i 7*; Rutherford, *State Pilgrims and Sacred Observers in Ancient Greece*, Appendix B 3. Trans. Rutherford. See also G. Rougemont, in *Études Delphiques*, 37–47; I. Rutherford, in J. Chrysostomides *et al.* (edd.), *The Greek Islands and the Sea*, 59–75; Rutherford, *State Pilgrims*, 198–201, 211, 369–72.

In *a*. 1–5 and *aa* the letters printed here do not accurately represent the letter forms of the inscription.

a

[——11——]Ε[. . . .]Θ[.]
[——10——]ΛΑΧΘ[.]ΑΝ[.]
..''''Ι...Θ...^ΛΘ...ι.
[.]ντον αἱ τ[ρ]ε̑ς οἰκίαι [.]
[..]Ο̣Ε̣.Α.ΖΕ. πρὸς τὸς [ἀ]-
[ρχ]εθεάρος. τόσδε σι̑τ[ο]-
[ν μ]ὲ τιθέναι μεδὲ φρ[υκ]-
τός· ἀρχεθεάρος τρε̑ς, μ̣-
άντιν, ἄρχοντα, κέρυκα,
αὐλετήν, κυβερνήτεν, κ[ε]-
λευστήν, π[ρ]οιρέτεν. δ̣έ[ρ]-
μα δὲ φερέτω κη̑ρυ[ξ], αὐλε-
τής, κελευστὴς ἕκαστος
τω̑ν δημοσίον ἱερέων. σι̑-
τον παρεχόντων τε̑ι πρό̣-
τει μα̑ζαν, κρέα, οἶνον ὁ-
πόσ̣[ον] βόλονται, καὶ τα̑[λ]-
λα ἁρμόδια· τὰς δὲ δύο ἡμ̣-
έρας καὶ [ἐ]κ̣τὸς τô σίτο τ-
ιθέτω ἕκασ<τ>ος καὶ παῖς κ̣-
α̣ὶ ἀνὲρ ὀβολὸν Α<ἰ>γιναῖον
τη̑ς ἡμέρης ἑκάστης· οἱ δ-
ὲ̣ ἀρχεθέαροι καθιερευ-
όντον ὑπὲρ ἔμισυ ἐνί. ὑπ-
α̣ρχέτο δὲ τὰ ἐξαίρετα· π[ε]-

a. 21 α<ἰ>γιναῖον; αγιναιον on stone.

a

– – – the three houses – – – to the leaders of the *theoria*.

6 The following are not to contribute food or firewood: the three leaders of the *theoria*, the seer, the archon, the herald, the helmsman, the boatswain, the prowman. And let each of the following take the skin of the public victims: herald, *auletes*, boatswain. Let them provide food for the first day: barley bread, meat, as much wine as anyone wants, and the other things that are suitable. For the two days, besides the food, let each person, child and man, contribute an Aeginetan obol for each day. Let the leaders of the *theoria* consecrate half on top of one.

24 The exemptions are: four

[λ]ανὸς τέσσαρας, μεταξέ[ν]-
[ι]α δύο, ἱερεῖ' ἓξ ἀπὸ τῆς ἐ[κ]-
[ατ]όμβης ἑκάστ[η]ς. ὁ δὲ ἰδι-
[ώτη]ς φερέτω τῶν δερμάτ-
[ων ὧ]ν ἂν θύσει τὸ τρίτομ μ̣έ-
[ρος, π]λὲν χρεστερίων καὶ κ-
[αθαρσ]ίων, καὶ ὅσοι σὺν τῶ-
[ι . . . .]λεῖ θεαρέοσιν
[—6—] δεμοσιον ΕΠΙΘΥΤΘ
[—8—]ʿ''.Θ.Ε̣[— — — — —]

aa

[—14—]ı[—5—]
[—13—]\̣ΝΙ/[....]
[—13—]ΤΑΙΚ[...]
[—13—]ΣΑΔΕΑΝ̣Α
[—13—]¯ΡΙΑ ἐστ
[—14—] Ἄνδριο
[- - - - - - - - - - - - -]

b

[—10—]ΟΝΤ
[—5—] Ἀρχιάδαν
[κα]θάπερ οἱ προγ-
ε̣ν̣ε͂ς. βολὲ δὲ τôν
πλεόντον ἐς Δελ-
φὸ̣[ς] hελέσθο πέν-
τ' ἄνδρας καὶ ὁρκο-
σάτο. σῖτον δὲ μὲ φ-
ερόντο ταύτες ὅν-
εκα τε͂ς ἀρχῆς. οἱ δ-
ὲ κύριοι ἔστων ζε-
μιῶσαι τὸν ἀκοσμ-
έοντα μέχρι πέν-
τε δραχ[μέ]ον ἑκάσ-
τες ἑμέρες· ὃν δ' ἂν
[ζ]ημιόσοσι ἀπογ<ρ>-
αψάντον ἐν βολε͂ι.
vacat

a. 33 βασι]λεῖ Daux; βασι?]λεῖ *C. Delphes*; ἐν τέ]λει *LSS*.

consultation-taxes, two *metaxenia*, six priestly services, from each hecatomb.

28 A private individual is to take the third part of the skins which he sacrifices, except for victims connected to oracular consultation and purification, and all those who go on *theoria* with the – – – public.

aa

– – – Andrian – – –

b

– – – Archiadas, just as the ancestors.

5 Let the council choose five men of those who sail to Delphi and exact an oath. Let them not bring food because of this office. Let them be authorised to punish those who are disorderly up to five drachmas a day. Let them record whomsoever they punish in the council.

To take part in a festival or sacrifice was to confirm that one belonged to the community whose festival or sacrifice it was (cf. **107**, **146**; and cf., from Delphi, R&O 1). To have a wide range of participants in a festival or a sacrifice was to indicate that what one did belonged, in some sense, to a wider community. From as early as we can talk of distinct political communities in archaic Greece there were also festivals at which those communities came together—notably the Olympic games. By the fifth century the participation of political communities in the festivals at Olympia, Delphi, the Isthmus and Nemea seems to have been organised. Not only do we meet participants in the competitive events who identify themselves with their city (cf. the public chariot of the Argives, victorious at Olympia in 472, *FGrH* 415 F 1, l. 31), but cities designated individuals to represent them. Such individuals were known as *theoroi* (cf. **127**): it is uncertain whether this term derives from *thea* ('sight', cf. *theatron*) or *theos* (god), so *theoroi* are either 'sight-seers' or 'god-seers' (see Rutherford, *State Pilgrims*, 5).

This inscription, displayed at Delphi but written in the Ionic script of Andros, is one of four surviving inscriptions which record the conditions on which delegates from a particular city take part in religious activity at Delphi (cf. *C. Delphes* i 1, 8, 13). Although it is primarily a regulation by the Andrians for the Andrians, the Delphians are implicated, since various privileges here, particularly with regard to sacrificial animals, impinge on what the Delphians themselves would normally receive. This inscription indeed nicely demonstrates the potential complexity resulting from the involvement at a sanctuary of delegates from other cities, a complexity increased when they came to the sanctuary as a group rather than as individuals.

The fragmentary opening, with its reference to 'three houses', most probably lays down the provision of accommodation for the Andrians (note the existence of three 'leaders of the *theoroi*'). What follows outlines the privileges that the *theoroi* enjoy (the leaders of the *theoroi* and the most important members of the crew of the ship are exempted from contributing a share of food or firewood, and those whose official roles are indispensable (herald, *aulos*-player and boatswain) are rewarded with the skins of the sacrificial animals (cf. **137**). What others are to provide by way of food is then laid down for the first day, and a payment required additionally for the two subsequent days—with a larger payment by the leaders of the *theoroi* (paralleled by the much larger tax for public consultations than private in the agreement with Phaselis, *C. Delphes* i 8).

The passage that follows has puzzled commentators, partly because the sense of *exaireta* is not clear. Scholars have often treated this as meaning 'prerogatives' (which works well with 'for the priest' on the parallel of *Etym. Magn.* ἱερωσύνη but is hard to understand with *pelanos*, for the normal sense of which cf. **141**, or *metaxenia*), but in this case they are perhaps 'exemptions' won per hecatomb of sacrifices: exemptions from the *pelanos*, which seems to be a tax on oracular consultations (already mentioned in *C. Delphes* i 1), from a mysterious *metaxenia* ('foreigners' share?') found only here, and from giving shares to the priest. What exactly a hecatomb (literally a hundred oxen) implies here is unclear: there are certainly some hecatombs that involve nothing like a hundred victims (e.g. *LSAM* 50. 19), but in other instances the term appears to have its full numerical force (e.g. *LSCG* 145. 16, a fine of a hecatomb, and cf. Hermesandrus of Cyrene marking the sacrifice of 120 cows, *ASAA* xxxix–xl 1961–2, 312–3).

The preserved text on face *a* concludes with a regulation about the right of private individuals to skins from sacrifices, granting them a third share except in the case of sacrifices connected with oracular consultation or purification—presumably because in these cases the sacrificial victim was given over to the Delphic priests. The mention of purificatory sacrifices implies that Delphi remained, as in myth (cf. Aesch. *Eum.* 280–3), a place to which those responsible for homicide would go for purification (*contra* R. R. Dyer, *JHS* lxxxix 1969, 38–56). These private individuals are an indication that we are not dealing here with a token delegation of officials, but with a large group some of whom are pursuing individual interests. The further regulations preserved from face *b* establish a group of five from those sailing, and give them authority to impose small fines upon the disorderly, reporting their action back to the council in Andros.

Scholars have found the close link between Andros and Delphi surprising given that Andros was part of the Delian League, in receipt of an Athenian cleruchy and in the fourth century a member of the Second Athenian League. But the sending of delegates to a panhellenic sanctuary was not a sign of any high degree of political independence (cf. R&O 14. 8). Although this inscription is dated only on the basis of letter forms, dates before 480 or after 408, in order to associate these regulations with a fully independent Andros, are both unnecessary and implausible.

There are various other pieces of ancient evidence which indicate strong Andrian interest in Delphi: Simonides wrote a paean 'For the Andrians for Delphi' (*PMG* 519 fr. 35. 11–12), the fourth-century *naopoioi* lists for the rebuilding of the temple of Apollo at Delphi record contributions of a single drachma each by large numbers of Andrians (*C. Delphes* ii 22 and 23), and Pausanias records a statue at Delphi of the eponymous hero of Andros, Andreus (Paus. x .13. iv).

Although this is in Ionic alphabet and dialect there is some use of E for H and of O for Ω, and H once = the aspirate (hελέσθō, *b.* 6): E is consistently used for the original η (μέ, μεδέ, ἀνέρ, ἔμισυ, etc.), but H and E are variously used for η from α; similarly O is consistently used for the secondary ο, but O and Ω are variously used for original ω. Two forms are remarkable, and may reflect the native Phocian dialect of the letter-cutter: θεαρός for Attic–Ionic θεωρός (*a.* 6, 8, 23); and φερόντο for the third-person imperative in *b.* 9, where elsewhere (e.g. *b.* 16–17) the normal Ionic form appears.

159

Decree of the Athenian deme Plotheia, *c*.420

A *stele* broken at the bottom and recut on the right side, now in the Louvre, Paris.

Ionic letters; *stoichedon* (28, ll. 11–40).

IG ii[2] 1172; *IG* i[3] 258; Koerner 21 (ll. 11–40 only). Trans. Dillon & Garland[3] 10. 19. See also Whitehead, *The Demes of Attica*, 165–9, J. H. Blok, *Mnemosyne*[4] lxiii 2010, 72–7.

[κεφ]άλαια *vacat*
[δη]μάρχωι Χ *vacat*
[τα]μίαιν ἐς τὰ δι' ἔτος ἱερὰ 𐅇 *vv*
[ἐ]ς τὸ Ἡρακλεῖον 𐅇ΧΧ
[ἐ]ς Ἀφροδίσια ΧΗΗ
[ἐ]ς Ἀνάκια ΧΗΗ
[ἐ]ς τὴν ἀτέλειαν 𐅇
[ἐ]ς Ἀπολλώνια ΧΗ
[ἐ]ς Πάνδια 𐅅Η
[μ]ισθώσεων ΗΔΔΔ⊢⊢⊢ΙΙϹ *vacat*
[ἔδ]οξεν Πλωθειεῦσι· Ἀριστότιμος [ε]-
[ἶπ]ε· τὸς μὲν ἄρχοντας τô ἀργυρίο ἀ[ξ]-
[ιό]χρεως κυαμεύεν ὅσο ἑκάστη ἡ ἀρ[χ]-
[ὴ ἄ]ρχει, τούτος δὲ τὸ ἀργύριον σῶν [π]-
[αρ]έχεν Πλωθεῦσι· περὶ μὲν ὅτο ἐστ[ὶ]
[ψ]ήφισμα δανεισμô ἢ τόκος τεταγ[μέ]-
ν̣ος κατὰ τὸ ψήφισμα δανείζοντα[ς κ]-
[α]ὶ ἐσπράττοντας, ὅσον̣ δὲ κατ' ἐν[ιαυ]-
[τ]ὸν δανείζεται δανείζοντας ὅ[στι]-
ς ἂν πλεῖστον τόκον διδῶι, ὃς ἂν [πεί]-
[θ]ηι τὸς δανείζοντας ἄρχοντα[ς τιμ]-
ήματι ἢ ἐγγυητῆι. ἀπὸ δὲ τô τόκο [τε κ]-
αὶ τῶμ μισθώσεων ἀντὶ ὅτο ἂν τ[ῶν κε]-
φαλαίων ὠνήματα ἦι μί[σ]θωσιν φ[έρο]-
ν̣τα, θύεν τὰ ἱερὰ τά τε ἐς Πλωθει[ᾶς κ]-
οινὰ καὶ τὰ ἐς Ἀθηναίος ὑπὲρ Πλ[ωθέ]-
[ω]ν τô κοινô καὶ τὰ ἐς τὰς πεντετ[ηρί]-
[δ]ας· καὶ ἐς τἄλλα ἱερά, ὅποι ἂν δέ[ηι Π]-
λωθέας ἅπαντας τελε͂ν ἀργύριο[ν ἐς]
[ἱ]ερά, ἢ ἐς Πλωθέας ἢ ἐς Ἐπακρέα[ς ἢ ἐς]
[Ἀ]θηναίος, ἐκ τô κοινô τὸς ἄρχο[ντας],
[ο]ἳ ἂν ἄρχωσι τô ἀργυρίο τô ἐς τὴ[ν ἀτ]-
[έ]λειαν, τελε͂ν ὑπὲρ τῶν δημοτῶν· [καὶ]

TOTALS:
for the demarch, 1,000 dr.
for the two treasurers for the sacred rites through the year, 5,000 dr.
to the Heracleion, 7,000 dr.
5 to the Aphrodisia, 1,200 dr.
to the Anakia, 1,200 dr.
to tax exemption, 5,000 dr.
to the Apollonia, 1,100 dr.
to the Pandia, 600 dr.
10 from rents, 134 dr 2 ½ ob.

11 Resolved by the Plotheians. Aristotimus proposed: to allot the officers, worthy of the money that each office controls. These are to provide the money securely for the Plotheians. Concerning whatever decree there is about the loan or setting the interest, loaning it and exacting interest according to the decree, and loaning as much as is loaned annually to whoever gives the greatest interest, whoever persuades the officers doing the loaning by their assessed wealth or guarantor.

22 From the interest and the rents, in place of whatever of the totals there may be purchases bearing rent, they are to sacrifice the rites, both the common rites for Plotheia and for the Athenians on behalf of the community of the Plotheians, and those for the quadrennial festivals. And for the other rites, for which all the Plotheians are to pay money for rites, whether to the Plotheians or to the Epakreis or to the Athenians, the officers from the community, who are in charge of the money for the exemption, are to pay on behalf of the demesmen. And for

[ἐ]ς τὰ ἱερὰ τὰ κοινὰ ἐν ὅσοισιν ἑσ[τι]-
[ῶ]ν̣ται Πλωθῆς οἶνον παρέχεν ἡδὺ[ν ἐ]-
[κ τô] κοινô, ἐς μὲν τὰ ἄλλα ἱερὰ μέχρ[ι]
[ἡμίχο ἑ]καστωι τοῖς παρôσι Πλωθέ[ω]-
[ν, —7— δὲ τῶ]ι διδασκάλωι κάδ̣ο̣[ν]
[—13— ἀ]ποκαίοντι κ[....]
[—16—] δημιοργ[—5—]
- - - - - - - - - - - - - - - - - - -

The Rhamnous accounts (**134**) give us insight into the amounts of money a deme with a prominent sanctuary might have at its disposal and the sort of income that might be achieved. The calendar from Thoricus (**146**) gives us insight into the volume of religious activity in a deme that might require funding. This document, from the very small deme of Plotheia in north-east Attica (south of modern Stamata), which returned only one representative to the council annually in the fourth century, gives us our best insight into how a deme might manage that funding.

This inscription, complete at the top but lacking any heading or other indication of its subject-matter or date, sets out the total monetary resources available to the deme, divided into separate funds. The demarch and two treasurers, who were probably the only deme officials in a deme of this size, have separate funds at their disposal to meet the expenses of their duties. There are then six other funds, five named in relation to gods or festivals, and the sixth named the 'exemption fund' (*ateleia*). Income from rents is listed separately from these funds.

A decree of the deme follows. It is awkwardly phrased throughout, even by comparison with other deme decrees, as the deme seeks to describe succinctly the administrative procedures to be followed. The selection of demarch by lot was normal (cf. *Hesperia* viii 1939, 178 l. 7), but here all deme officials are allotted but with a stipulation to ensure that they are 'worthy' of the amount of money they will control. This parallels the way in which central Athenian officials with financial responsibility were drawn only from those who were wealthy (*Ath. Pol.* 8. i, 47. i). Whether the officers referred to here are only the demarch and treasurers is not clear: in a number of other demes it is the demarch who has responsibility for seeing that the sacrifices listed in the calendar are carried out, and the existence of funds separate from those of the demarch himself does not mean that there were separate officials in charge of each fund (cf. **146**, which may list the demarch's sacrificial responsibilities).

The decree goes on to specify that the officers are to be responsible for the fund, lending the money out to whoever both offers the most interest and convinces the officers by the security offered by his wealth-status or by a guarantor, unless there is some arrangement for lending already agreed by decree. This makes it clear that rates of interest are not fixed, and that the officers are expected to assess the credit rating of those who will potentially borrow money. A complicated clause follows, all the community rites in which the Plotheians feast, to provide sweet wine from the common fund: for other rites up to half a *chous* for each Plotheian present, and for the *didaskalos* a *kados* – – – burning – – –

---

which seems to imply that part of the money of some of the funds has been invested in property from which there will be rental income.

The uses of the income from the funds are spelled out: they are to cover local sacrifices and festivals, Athenian festivals in which the Plotheians take part and festivals and sacrifices of the Epakreis—i.e. sacrifices and festivals that are for the deme alone, central city festivals in which deme participation was expected, and sacrifices and festivals celebrated by the local cult group to which Plotheia belonged.

As N. Papazarkadas has shown, the Epakreis here are the same as the *trittys* of the Epakreis, a pre-Cleisthenic *trittys* (*CQ*^{2} lvii 2007, 22–32). This *trittys* under the name Epakria appears in Philochorus' list of the twelve original *poleis* of Attica, a list in which major classical cult sites are prominent (it also includes Eleusis, Tetrapolis, Brauron and Thoricus: *FGrH* 328 F 94), and is known to have leased out land in the fourth century. Epakria is located next to Tetrapolis (Marathon, Tricorynthus, Oenoe and Rhamnous) by Photius (ε 1333 Theodoridis Ἐπακρία χώρα), and another fragment of Philochorus (328 F 206) shows that the small deme of Semachidae was also part of the Epakreis. If *trittys* is used in its original sense here of 'group of three', then the question arises of who the third member was; but it is possible that it had already come to mean just 'a third of a tribe' and that just Plotheia and Semachidae, without either Anacaea or Hecale, made up this *trittys*.

The decree divides the sacrifices and festivals on which the officers are to spend the funds first into three categories: sacrifices and festivals in which the whole deme of Plotheia shares, sacrifices and festivals of the Athenians in which participation is on behalf of the Plotheians, and the penteteric festivals. Then the festivals are redescribed in two categories, 'the other rites' which all Plotheians are obliged to spend money on, whether they are for the Plotheians, for the Athenians or for the Epacrians, and 'the community rites', the ones at which all Plotheians feast. Expenses for the former are to come from the large 'exemption' fund. The name of that fund (*ateleia*) usually refers to tax exemption, but we take it here simply to mean 'a fund to exempt people from having to pay'. This makes it seem as if there are some festivals which are provided and funded by corporate bodies, and others to which all Plotheians would be entitled to go but for which they would normally be expected to make individual monetary contributions. The exemption fund covers these contributions. For the second category of 'community rites' feasting is involved, and the officers are also to pay for the wine, at a rate of half a *chous* per person (it is an interesting question whether this decree simply assumed that 'each of the Plotheians present' will be male, or that though there will be women no one would ever think of giving them wine, or actually distributes wine regardless of gender or age).

Two questions arise. How do the expenses dictated in the decree relate to the funds identified above? And how much money was there in fact to spend?

Apart from the 'exemption' fund, none of the other funds obviously align directly with any category in the decree. Notable, for instance, is the absence of any fund to support the participation in the penteteric festivals which is explicitly mentioned in the decree. One possible way of aligning funds and decree would be to think that for each of the named funds there was a separately appointed officer. That officer would be responsible for managing the fund and for spending it on the particular festival or festivals to which it was devoted. But although the Pandia and Anakia are plausibly festivals, that seems less likely for Apollonia and Aphrodisia (which are otherwise unknown as festival names in Attica), which look more like funds that might support a number of sacrifices to Apollo and to Aphrodite during the year. But if these gods are singled out, why are no other gods? It would be surprising if Athena did not figure at all in the local cult calendar (though note her minimal

160

Loans to the Athenian state from the sacred treasuries, 426/5–423/2

Eighteen fragments (two uninscribed) of a marble *stele*, found on the Athenian acropolis, now in the Epigraphical Museum (but one has been lost: see *apparatus*); the left-hand and right-hand margins are nowhere preserved. Phot. Peppas-Delmousou, *The Institution of Public Accountants in Ancient Greece*, pl. II (which we have not seen); our pl. 13 (fragments from top of *stele*); references to photographs of individual fragments are given in *IG* i³. Facsimile Meritt, *The Athenian Calendar in the Fifth Century*, pl. I; *AFD*, pl. XII.

Developed Attic writing, using h except in ἅπασι (restored), ἕκαστος, ἐμέρα and ἕνδεκα. *Stoichedon*, *c*.75, with irregularities in numerals and at the ends of lines (the text below is based on the assumption of 75 in ll. 1–73, 74 in ll. 74–110).

IG i² 324 (and 306); Meritt, *The Athenian Calendar*; Meritt, *AFD*, 128–51; M. L. Lang & B. D. Meritt, *CQ*² xviii 1968, 84–94; M&L 72; *IG* i³ 369*. Extracts trans. Fornara 134. See also (from among a long list of studies) Pritchett & Neugebauer, *The Calendars of Athens*, 94–105; Meritt, *The Athenian Year*, 60–71; Pritchett, *Ancient Athenian Calendars on Stone*, 270–3, 290–312; M. L. Lang, *Hesperia* xxxiii 1964, 140–67, xxxiv 1965, 224–47; Pritchett, *Hesperia* xxxiv 1965, 131–47; Pritchett, *The Choiseul Marble*, 98–103; Meritt, *PAPS* cxv 1971, 101–13; Pritchett, *Athenian Calendars and Ecclesias*, 163–9.

presence at Thoricus, **146**). In the case of the fund for 'the Heracleion', scholars have wondered whether this might be supporting building activity, rather than just sacrifices and festival events. It is perhaps preferable to think that the demarch and the treasurers deal with all the expenditure on festivals and sacrifices, taking it from an appropriate fund if there is one, but otherwise paying out of their own funds. But the separation of the funds of demarch and treasurers implies that there must have been some scheme as to which officer was responsible for what. The lost lower part of the *stele* may have clarified matters.

Although the decree itself makes it clear that the interest from loans would be variable, scholars have attempted to work out the sort of income this small deme might have to spend every year (see Blok). The total of the funds is 22,100 dr., and although some have reckoned income at 12 per cent of this, calculation on the basis of the sorts of income Rhamnous appears to have achieved seems more reasonable and would indicate an income of perhaps 500 dr. per year (to which the 134 dr. of rent needs to be added). If we imagine that Plotheia constituted $^1/_{500}$ of an Athenian citizen population of 50,000, then there will have been in the region of 100 adult male Plotheians and the support offered by the deme will have amounted to something of the order of 3 obols per adult male per month.

[τάδε ἐλογίσαν]το hοι λογιστα[ὶ ἐν τοῖς τέτ]ταρσιν ἔτεσιν ἐκ Παναθεναίον ἐς [Παναθέναια ὀφελ]-
[όμενα. τάδε hο]ι ταμίαι παρέδοσ[αν Ἀνδρο]κλε͂ς Φλυεὺς καὶ χσυνάρχοντες hελλ[ενοταμίαις . . . .]
[——10——]εῖ καὶ χσυνάρχοσι[ν στρατ]εγοῖς hιπποκράτει Χολαργεῖ καὶ χσυ[νάρχοσιν ἐπὶ τε͂ς]
[Κεκροπίδο]ς πρυτανείας δευτέ[ρας πρυ]τανευόσες, τέτταρες ἑμέραι ἐ͂σαν ἐσελ[ελυθυίαι, ἐπὶ τε͂]-
[ς βολε͂ς hε͂ι] Μεγακλείδες πρôτο[ς ἐγραμ]μάτευε, ἐπὶ Εὐθύνο ἄρχοντος, Δ̣Δ̣· τόκος τ[ούτοις ἐγένετο]
[𐅆𐅅H𐅄ΔΔ]ΔΔΓ<u>⊢</u>⁝ *v* δευτέρα δόσις, ἐπ[ὶ τε͂ς Κ]εκροπίδος δευτέρας πρυτανευόσες, λοι[παὶ ἐ͂σαν hεπτὰ ἑ]-
[μέραι] τε͂ι πρυτανείαι, 𐅄· τόκος τ[ούτον *v*] ΤΤΧ𐅅HHHH𐅄ΔΔ. *v* τρίτε δόσις, ἐπὶ τε͂ς Παν[διονίδος πρυτα]-
[νείας] τετάρτες πρυ[τ]ανευόσες, [ἐσελελ]υθυίας πέντε ἑμέρας τε͂ς πρυτανείας, Δ̣[Δ̣ΓΤΤΤ𐅆𐅅HΔ<u>III</u>Ϲ· τ]-
[όκος τ]ούτον *v* ΤΧ𐅅HHΔΓ⊢⊢⊢⊢I. *v* τ[ετάρτ]ε δόσις, ἐπὶ τε͂ς Ἀκαμαντίδος πρυτανεία[ς ὀγδόες πρυταν]-
[ευόσ]ες, πέντε ἑμέρας ἐσελελυθ[ύας τε͂]ς πρυτανείας, Δ̣Δ̣Δ̣Δ̣[Τ]ΤΤΤΧΧΧ· τόκος τούτο[ν *v* ΤΧΧΧΧ𐅅HHI. *vv*]
[πέμπ]τε δόσις, ἐπὶ τε͂ς Ἀκαμαν[τίδος πρ]υτανείας ὀγδόες πρυτανευόσες, ἐσελελ]υθυίας δέκα ἑμε]-
[ρας τ]ε͂ς πρυτανείας, Ⱨ· τόκος τ[ούτον *v*] ΤΤΤ𐅆𐅅HHHHΔΔΔΔ. *v* hέκτε δόσις, ἐπὶ τε͂ς Ἐρε[χθείδος πρυταν]-
[είας] δεκάτες πρυτανευόσε[ς, ἐσελελ]υθυίας hεπτὰ ἑμέρας τε͂ς πρυτανείας, Δ̣ΓΤ[ΤΤΧΧΧ· τόκος τού]-
[τοις] ἐγένετο ΧΧΧΧH𐅄ΔΔ⊢⊢<⊢>[<u>IIII</u>. *v* κεφ]άλαιον τô ἀρχαίο ἀναλόματος ἐπὶ τε͂ς Ἀνδρ[οκλέος ἀρχε͂ς κα]-
[ὶ χσυ]ναρχόντον <u>ⱧⱧ𐅄Δ̣</u>Τ𐅆𐅅H[ΔIII<u>Ϲ</u>. *v* τ]όκο κεφάλαιον τôι ἀργύριοι τôι ἀναλοθέντ[ι ἐπὶ τε͂ς Ἀνδροκ]-
[λέος] ἀρχε͂ς καὶ χσυναρχόντο[ν Δ̣ΤH]𐅄ΔΔΔΔΓ⊢⊢⊢⊢. *va*$\frac{c.6}{}$ τάδε παρέδοσαν hοι τα[μίαι Φοκιάδες ἐ]-
[χς Οἴ]ο καὶ χσυνάρχοντες, ἐπὶ Σ[τρα]τοκλέος ἄρχοντος καὶ ἐπὶ τε͂ς βολε͂ς hε͂ι Πλ[ειστίας πρôτος *v*]
[ἐγραμμ]άτευε, στρατεγοῖς περ[ὶ Πε]λοπόννεσον Δε[μ]οσθένει Ἀλκισθένος Ἀφιδ[ναίοι, ἐπὶ τε͂ς Οἰν]-

Characters joined by an underline are compressed or spread so as not to occupy one *stoichos* per character (for details see *IG* i^3); the double underline in l. 51 denotes a (single) underline on the stone.

Dates and sums of money are interconnected in various restorations: the reconstruction of Meritt, *The Athenian Calendar*, is fundamental; we give a very short *apparatus criticus* here, not chronicling alternative suggestions for dates and sums of money, and fuller *apparatus* can be found in M&L and in *IG* i^3.

2–3 Διον|υσίοι Ἀχαρν]εῖ H. B. Mattingly, *BSA* lxv 1970, 138 = his *AER* 296–7, dating *IG* i^3 281 to this year. 8 this restoration matches 15 and 49, but the interest suggests 28 tal. 3,610 dr. 3½ ob. rather than 28 tal. 5,610 dr. 3½ ob. 10 or ἐσελελυθ[<u>υί</u>ας M&L. 14 the stone has I. 18 στρατεγôι{ς}? *IG* i^3.

These are the debts reckoned by the *logistai* ('accountants') in the four years from Panathenaea to Panathenaea.

2 This was handed over by the treasurers Androcles of Phlya and his colleagues to the *hellenotamiai* —— of —— and his colleagues for the generals Hippocrates of Cholargus and his colleagues in the prytany of Cecropis, the second prytany, four days from its entry, under the council for which Megacleides was first secretary, in the archonship of Euthynus [426/5], 20 tal.; the interest on this was 5,696 dr.

6 Second grant, in the prytany of Cecropis, the second prytany, seven days were left of the prytany, 50 tal.; interest on this 2 tal. 1,970 dr.

7 Third grant, in the prytany of Pandionis, the fourth prytany, five days from the prytany's entry, 28 tal. 5,610 dr. 3½ob.; interest on this 1 tal. 1,719 dr. 2 ob.

9 Fourth grant, in the prytany of Acamantis, the eighth prytany, five days from the entry of the prytany, 44 tal. 3,000 dr.; interest on this 1 tal. 4,700 dr. 1 ob.

11 Fifth grant, in the prytany of Acamantis, the eighth prytany, ten days from the entry of the prytany, 100 tal.; interest on this 3 tal. 5,940 dr.

12 Sixth grant, in the prytany of Erechtheis, the tenth prytany, seven days from the entry of the prytany, 18 tal. 3,000 dr.; the interest on this was 4,173 dr. 4 ob.

14 Total of the original expenditure in the office of Androcles and his colleagues 261 tal. 5,610 dr. 3½ob. Total of the interest on the money spent in the office of Androcles and his colleagues 11 tal. 199 dr. 1 ob.

16 This was handed over by the treasurers Phociades from Oeum and his colleagues, in the archonship of Stratocles [425/4] and under the council for which Pleistias was first secretary, for the general{s} around the Peloponnese Demosthenes son of Alcisthenes of Aphidna, in the prytany of

[είδος] πρυτανείας τετ<ά>ρτες [πρυτα]νευόσες, τρίτει ἑ[μέ]ραι τε̑ς πρυτανείας ἐσ[ελελυθυίας, ἐχς]
[Ὀπισθ]οδόμο, Δ̣Δ̣Δ̣· τόκος τούτο[ις ἐγέ]νετο 𐅆𐅅ΗΗΗΗΔ. *vv* hετέρα δόσις, στρατεγοῖς [Νικίαι Νικεράτ]-
[ο Κυδα]ντίδει καὶ χσυνάρχο[σιν, ἐπὶ] τε̑ς Π<α>νδιονίδος πρυτανείας ἐνάτες πρυτ[ανευόσες, πέμπτ]-
[ει καὶ δεκάτει ἑμέραι τε̑ς π[ρυταν]είας ἐσελελυθυίας, Ḥ̲· τόκος τούτοις ἐγένε[το ΤΤΧΧΧ𐅅ΗΗΗ. *vv*]
[κεφάλ]αιον τõ ἀρχαίο ἀναλόμ[ατος] ἐπὶ τε̑ς Φοκιάδο ἀρχε̑ς καὶ χσυναρχόντον Ḥ[Δ̣Δ̣Δ̣. *v* τόκο κεφάλα]-
[ιον τõι ἀ]ργυρίοι τõι ἀναλοθ[έντι] ἐπὶ τε̑ς Φοκιάδο ἀρχε̑ς καὶ χσυναρχόντον Τ[ΤΤΧΧΧ𐅅ΗΗΔ. *vac*.—c.5—]
[τάδε παρέδ]οσαν hoι ταμίαι Θ[οκυ]δίδες Ἀχερδόσιος καὶ χσυνάρχοντες, ἐπὶ Ἰσ[άρχο ἄρχοντος κα]-
[ὶ ἐπὶ τε̑ς βολε̑ς] ḥ[ε̑ι Ἐπί]λ[υ]κος [πρõ]τος ἐγραμμάτευε, hελλενοταμίαις hένοις Δ[—14—]
[—6— καὶ χσυνάρχοσι καὶ νέοις] Χαροπίδει Σκα[μβ]ονίδει καὶ χσυνάρχοσιν, [ἐπὶ τε̑ς hιπποθον]-
[τίδος πρυτανείας πρότες πρυταν]ευόσες, hέκτει καὶ εἰκοστε̑ι τε̑ς πρ[υτανείας, —12—]
[..Δ̣Δ̣Δ̣ΤΤ𐅆𐅅ΗΗΗΗ𐅄ΔΔΔ⊢⊢⊢· τόκος το]ύτοις ἐγένετο ΧΧΧΧ𐅅Η𐅄ΔΙΙΙΙΙ. *v* δευτέρα δόσις, ἐπὶ τε̑ς —5—]
[—21— πρυταν]ευόσες, δοδεκάτει τε̑ς πρυτανείας, Δ̣Δ̣ΤΤΤ[—15—]
[—21— τρίτε δ]όσις, ἐπὶ τε̑ς Ἐρεχθείδος πρυτανείας hε[—16—]
[—26—]Ḥ̣Η· τόκος τούτοις ἐγένετο 𐅅ΗΔΔΔ⊢⊢C. *v* τε[τάρτε δόσις, ἐπὶ τε̑ς]
[Ἀκαμαντίδος πρυτανείας ὀγδόες] <π>ρυτανευόσες, τριακοστε̑ι τε̑ς πρυταν[είας, Ḥ· τόκος —7—]
[—17— κεφάλαιον] τõ ἀρχαίο ἀναλόματος ἐπὶ τε̑ς Θοκυδ[ίδο ἀρχε̑ς καὶ χσυναρχόν]-
[τον Ḥ𐅄Δ̣ΤΤΤ. *v* κεφάλαιον τόκο τõι] ἀργυρίοι τõι ἀναλοθέντι ἐπὶ τε̑ς Θοκυδίδο ἀρχε̑ς καὶ χσυναρ]-
[χόντον ΤΤ𐅅ΗΗΔ —9—. τάδε παρ]έδοσαν hoι ταμίαι Τιμοκλε̑ς Εἰτεαῖος κ[αὶ χσυνάρχοντες, ἐπὶ]
[Ἀμενίο ἄρχοντος καὶ ἐπὶ τε̑ς βολ]ε̑ς hε̑ι Δεμέτριος Κολλυτεὺς πρõτος ἐγρ[αμμάτευε, —9—]
[—22— Μυρρ]ινοσίοι καὶ χσυνάρχοσι, ἐπὶ τε̑ς Ἀκαμα[ντίδος πρυτανείας *vv*]

19 the stone has Λ. 21 the stone has Λ. 30 τρίτες or τετάρτες. 31 hέ[κτες or hε[βδόμες. 32 𐅆ΧΧΧΧ𐅅Η̲]Ḥ̣Η Lang & Meritt. 33 the stone has ΙΙ. 33–4 τούτοι ἐ|γένετο ΤΧΧ𐅅ΗΗΗΗ𐅄Δ. *v* Lang & Meritt.

Oeneis, the fourth prytany, on the third day from the prytany's entry, from the Opisthodomos, 30 tal.; the interest on this was 5,910 dr.

20 The other grant, to the generals Nicias son of Niceratus of Cydantidae and his colleagues, in the prytany of Pandionis, the ninth prytany, on the fifteenth day from the prytany's entry, 100 tal.; the interest on this was 2 tal. 3,800 dr.

23 Total of the original expenditure in the office of Phociades and his colleagues 130 tal. Total of the interest on the money spent in the office of Phociades and his colleagues 3 tal. 3,710 dr.

25 This was handed over by the treasurers Thucydides of Acherdous and his colleagues, in the archonship of Isarchus [424/3] and under the council for which Epilycus was first secretary, to the old *hellenotamiai* —— of —— and his colleagues and the new Charopides of Scambonidae and his colleagues, in the prytany of Hippothontis, the first prytany, on the twenty-sixth of the prytany, – – – 32 tal. 5,983 dr.; the interest on this was 4,660 dr. 5 ob.

29 Second grant, in the prytany of ——, the —— prytany, on the twelfth of the prytany, 23 tal. + – – –

31 Third grant, in the prytany of Erechtheis, – – – [5 tal. 4,800 dr.?]; the interest on this was 632 dr. 1 ½ ob.

32 Fourth grant, in the prytany of Acamantis, the eighth prytany, on the thirtieth of the prytany, 100 tal.; the interest [on this was 1 tal. 2960 dr.?].

34 Total of the original expenditure in the office of Thucydides and his colleagues 163 tal. Total of the interest on the money spent in the office of Thucydides and his colleagues 2 tal. 5,210 dr. +.

36 This was handed over by the treasurers Timocles of Eitea and his colleagues, in the archonship of Ameinias [423/2] and under the council for which Demetrius of Collytus was first secretary, – – – of Myrrhinous and his colleagues, in the

[πρότες πρυτανευόσες, δοδεκάτε]ι τε̑ς πρυτανείας, 𐅊𐅈ΤΤΤΤΧΧΧΧ𐅅ΗΗΔΔ· τό[κος τούτοις ἐγένετο *v*]
[ΧΧΧΧΗΗΔΔΔΔ𐅂𐅂𐅂𐅂IIIII. *v* δευτέρ]α δόσις, ἐπὶ τε̑ς Πανδιονίδος πρυτανεί[ας τρίτες πρυτανευ *vv*]-
[όσες, δοδεκάτει τε̑ς πρυτανείας], ΤΤ𐅆𐅅· τόκος τούτοις ἐγένετο Η𐅄Δ𐅂𐅂𐅂IIII[I. *v* τρίτε δόσι]ς, [ἐπὶ τε̑ *v*]-
[ς —6—ίδος πρυτανείας τετά]ρτες πρυτανευόσες, τετάρτει τε̑ς πρυτανείας, παρὰ] Σαμ[ίον, 𐅉Τ *v*]-
[ΧΧΧΗΗΗ· τόκος τούτοις ἐγένετο] 𐅅𐅄ΔΔΔ𐅂𐅂. *v* τετάρτε δόσις, ἐπὶ τε̑ς Αἰαντ[ίδος πρυτ]ανεί[ας ὀγδό]-
[ες πρυτανευόσες, τετάρτει καὶ] εἰκοστε̑ι τε̑ς πρυτανείας, 𐅋· τόκος τούτο[ις ἐγέν]ετο Χ𐅅Η[Η. *vvvv*]
[πέμπτε δόσις, ἐπὶ τε̑ς Λεοντίδο]ς πρυτανείας δεκάτες πρυτανευόσες, τ[ε̑ι τρίτ]ει τε̑ς πρ[υτανεί]-
[ας, 𐅉𐅈ΤΤΤΗΔΔ𐅂𐅂IIC· τόκος τούτον] ΗΔΔ𐅂𐅂IC. *v* κεφάλαιον τô ἀρχαίο ἀναλό[ματος] ἐπὶ τε̑ς Τι[μοκλέο]-
[ς ἀρχε̑ς καὶ χσυναρχόντον 𐅋Η𐅄𐅉𐅉]𐅉𐅉ΤΤΧ𐅅ΗΔΔΔΔ𐅂𐅂IIC. *v* κεφάλαιον τόκο τ[οῖς ἀ]ναλοθε̑σι χρ[έμασι *v*]
[ἐπὶ τε̑ς Τιμοκλέος ἀρχε̑ς καὶ χσυ]ναρχόντον Τ𐅅ΗΗΗΔ𐅂𐅂𐅂IC. *v* κεφάλαι[ον ἀν]αλόματος χσύ[μπαντ *v*]-
[ος Ἀθεν]αίας ἐν τοῖ[ς] τέ[τταρσιν ἔ]τεσιν ἐκ Παναθεναίον ἐς Παναθέν[αια 𐅅]𐅋𐅋𐅉𐅉𐅉𐅈ΤΤΧ[ΗΗ𐅄𐅂𐅂𐅂. *v*]
[κεφά]λαιον τόκο χσύμπαν[τος Ἀθε]ναίας ἐν τοῖς τέτταρσιν ἔτεσιν ἐ[κ Παν]αθεναίον ἐς Πα[ναθέν *v*]-
[αια 𐅉]𐅈ΤΤΤΧΧΧ𐅅ΗΗΗΗΔΔΔ𐅃[—5—. τάδε] Ἀθεναίας Νίκες, ἐ[πὶ τε̑ς —7—ίδο]ς πρυτανείας [—6—]
[. . . πρ]υτανευόσες, τετάρτε[ι τε̑ς πρυτα]νείας, Τιμοκ[λε̑ς Εἰτεαῖος καὶ χσυ]νάρχοντες πα[ρέδοσα]-
[ν 𐅈Τ· τόκος] τούτοις ἐ[γ]ένετο Η[– – –.] *vacat*
[τάδε ἐλογίσα]ντο [hοι] λογιστ[αὶ ὀφελόμ]ẹν[α τοῖς ἄλλοις θεοῖς ἐν τοῖς τέττ]αρσιν ἔτ[εσιν ἐκ Παν]-
[αθεναίον ἐς Παναθέν]α̣ι̣α̣. [τάδε παρέδοσ]αν h[οι ταμίαι τôν ἄλλον θεôν Γόργο]ινος Ο[ἰνείδο Ἰκαρι]-
[εὺς καὶ χσυνάρχοντες ἐκ τôν ἑκάστο χ]ρεμάτο[ν, ἐπὶ Ἀμενίο ἄρχοντος, στρατ]εγοῖ[ς —11—]
[—8—, ἐπὶ τε̑ς βολε̑ς hε̑ι Δεμέτρι]ος πρôτ[ος ἐγραμμάτευε, ἐπὶ τε̑ς Ἀκαμαντ]ίδ[ος πρυτανείας]
[πρότες πρυτανευόσες, hεκατομβαιô]νος ὀγ[δόει φθίνοντος, πέμπτει καὶ εἰκοστε̑ι τε̑ς πρυτανε]-

42 Ἀντιοχίδος or Ἐρεχθεΐδος or Κεκροπίδος (but τε̑ς | —7—ίδος ruled out because Acamantis and Pandionis already accounted for). 42 πρὸς] Σαμ[ίος G. F. Unger. 51 Ἀκαμαντίδος or Πανδιονίδος. 58 hεκατομβαιô]νος doubted by Pritchett, *AJP* lxxxv 1964, 40–50.

prytany of Acamantis, the first prytany, on the twelfth of the prytany, 64 tal. 4,720 dr.; the interest on this was 4,244 dr. 5 ob.

40 Second grant, in the prytany of Pandionis, the third prytany, on the twelfth of the prytany, 2 tal. 5,500 dr.; the interest on this was 163 dr. 5 ob.

41 Third grant, in the prytany of ——, the fourth prytany, on the fourth of the prytany, from the Samians (?), 11 tal. 3,300 dr.; the interest on this was 582 dr. 1 ob.

43 Fourth grant, in the prytany of Aiantis, the eighth prytany, on the twenty-fourth of the prytany, 100 tal.; the interest on this was 1,700 dr.

45 Fifth grant, in the prytany of Leontis, the tenth prytany, on the third of the prytany, 18 tal. 122 dr. 2 ½ ob.; interest on this 122 dr. 2 ½ ob.

47 Total of the original expenditure in the office of Timocles and his colleagues 192 tal. 1,642 dr. 2 ½ ob. Total of the interest on the money spent in the office of Timocles and his colleagues 1 tal. 813 dr. 1 ½ ob.

48 Total of the whole expenditure of Athena in the four years from Panathenaea to Panathenaea 747 tal. 1,253 dr. Total of the whole interest of Athena in the four years from Panathenaea to Panathenaea 18 tal. 3,935 dr. +

51 Of Athena Nike, in the prytany of ——, the —— prytany, on the fourth of the prytany, Timocles of Eitea and his colleagues handed over 6 tal.; the interest on this was 100 dr. +.

54 This was reckoned by the *logistai* as due to the Other Gods in the four years from Panathenaea to Panathenaea.

55 This was handed over by the treasurers of the Other Gods Gorgonides son of Oeneïdes of Icaria and his colleagues from the monies of each, in the archonship of Ameinias [423/2], to the generals – – –, under the council for which Demetrius was first secretary, in the prytany of Acamantis, the first prytany, on the eighth of the waning of Hecatombaeon [22. i or 23. i], on the twenty-fifth of the prytany, from the

[ίας, ἐχσ Ὀπισθοδόμο. *v* Ἀρ]τέμι[δος Ἀγρ]οτέρα[ς,
— 40 —]
[— 18 —· τό]κος τ[ούτο ΗΗ]Η𐅄Δ
[— 42 —]
[— 29 —]Ḥ· τό[κος τούτο
— 18 —]𐅆Η𐅄ΔΔ[— 12 —]
[— 17 —. Ποσειδôν]ος ἐπὶ Σο[υνίοι, ΓΧΧ— 10 —· τόκ]ος
τοῦ̣τ̣ο̣ ΗḤΗ𐅄ΔΔ[— 9 —]
[— 21 —· τόκο]ς τούτο [— 6 —. Ἀρτέμιδος Μονιχί]<α>σι,
ΤΧΧΧΧ̣𐅅𐅄⊢ΙC· τό[κος τούτο]
[— 52 —]ΗΗΔΔΓ⊢Ι·
τόκο[ς το]ύτ[ο — 6 —]
[. . . .]ο Χ𐅅ΗΗΗΗ𐅄ΔΔΓ⊢ΙΙ[— 36 —]
Δ⊢⊢⊢⊢ΙΙΙΙ· τόκο[ς το]ύ̣τ[ο — 5 —]
[. . . .]I̲I̲C. Ἀφροδίτες ἐν hιππολυ[τείοι, — 24 —]⊢⊢⊢ΙΙΙΙΙC. *v*
Μοσ[ôν, 𐅅 . . . . · τόκο]-
[ς τού]το Γ⊢ΙΙ. *v* Ἀπόλλονος Ζοστε͂[ρος, — 21 —. Ἀδρασ]τείας,
𐅄ΔΔΔΓ⊢· τ[όκος τούτο ⊢.]
[Βενδ]ῖδος, 𐅄ΔΔΔΓ⊢· τόκος τού[το ⊢. — 29 —]ΙΟ. *v*
Ἀπόλλο[νος — 8 —]
[. . . .]· τούτο τόκος Γ⊢⊢⊢. *v* [— 36 —].
hερακλέος ἐν [Κυνοσάργε]-
[ι, ΔΔ· τ]ούτο τόκος ΙC. *v* hε[— 22 — Δεμ]οφôντος,
[— 6 —]· τόκος τούτ[ο — 9 —].
[Ἀθενα]ί[ας ἐπὶ] Παλλ[ενίδι, Τ𐅆ΗΗ— 11 —· τόκο]ς τούτο
ΗΔΔΓ⊢⊢⊢⊢ΙΙΙΟ. *v* Ἀπόλλο[νος — 8 —]
[— 20 —. Ἀρτέμιδος Βραυρονίας, ΧΗΗΗ𐅄ΔΔΔΔΓ⊢ΙΙΙΙ·
τόκος τούτο Δ[Γ⊢— 9 —]
[— 9 —]ΧΗΔ[— 24 —. Ἀθ]εναίας ἐπὶ Παλλαδίοι
Δεριονέ̣οι, [𐅅ΗΗΗ𐅄— 5 —.]
[τόκος το]ύτο ΔḤ[— 11 —Χ]𐅅Η[Η— 8 —· τό]κος τούτο ΔΔC. *v*
Ποσειδôνος Καλαυρε[άτο, — 5 —·]
[τόκος τούτο [— 4 —. κεφάλαιον τ]ô ἀ[ρχαίο ἀναλό]ματος τôν ἄλλον θεôν
τε͂ς πρότες [δ]όσεο[ς τε͂ς ἐπὶ]
[Γοργ]οίνο [ἄρχοντος Δ̣Δ̣Δ̣𐅆𐅅ΗΗ]ḤΗ[𐅄ΔΔΔΔ· *v* κεφάλ]αιον τόκο
τούτοι τôι ἀναλόματι ΧΧΗΔΔ[— 7 —.]
[δευτ]έρ[αν δόσιν παρέδοσαν] hοι τα[μίαι τôν ἄλ]λον θεôν Γόργοινος
Οἰνείδο Ἰκαριεὺς [καὶ χσυν]-
[άρχοντες καθ' ἕκαστον θεὸν] ἀπὸ τô[ν χρεμάτον] ἐπὶ τε͂ς Λεοντίδος πρυτανείας
δεκάτε[ς πρυταν]-
[ευόσες, Σκιροφοριôνος ὀγ]δ̣όει φθ[ίνοντος, εἰ]κοστε͂ι τε͂ς πρυτανείας. *v*
Ἀρτέμιδος Ἀγρ[οτέρας,]

63 the stone has Λ. 78 hελλενοταμίαις] ἀπὸ Mattingly, *opp. citt.*, 138 n. 62 = 296 n. 61. 79 [Σκιροφοριôνος] date doubted by Pritchett.

Opisthodomos. Artemis Agrotera – – – interest on this 360 dr. +. – – – interest on this – – –. – – – Poseidon at Sunium 5 tal. 2,000 dr. +; interest on this 370 dr. +. – – – Artemis at Munichia 1 tal. 4,551 dr. 1 ½ ob.; interest on this – – – 1,976 dr. 2 ob. + – – – + 14 dr. 4 ob.; interest on this + 2 ½ ob.; Aphrodite at the Hippolyteum – – – + 3 dr. 5 ½ ob.; the Muses 500 dr. +; interest on this 6 dr. 2 ob. Apollo Zoster – – – Adrastea 86 dr.; interest on this 1 dr. Bendis 86 dr.; interest on this 1 dr.– – – Apollo – – – interest on this 8 dr. – – – Heracles at Cynosarges 20 dr.; interest on this 1 ½ ob. – – – Demophon – – – interest on this – – – Athena at Pallenis 1 tal 5,200 dr. +; interest on this 129 dr. 3¾ob. Apollo – – – Artemis Brauronia 1,396 dr. 4 ob.; interest on this 16 dr. +. – – – Athena at the Derionean Palladium 850 dr. +; interest on this 11 dr. +. – – – interest on this 20 dr. ½ ob. Poseidon Calaureatis – – – interest on this – – – Total of the original expenditure of the Other Gods in the first grant in the office of Gorgoenus 30 tal. 5,990 dr.; total of the interest on this expenditure 2,120 dr. +.

77 The second grant was handed over by the treasurers of the Other Gods Gorgoenus son of Oeneïdes of Icaria and his colleagues according to individual gods from the monies, in the prytany of Leontis, the tenth prytany, on the eighth of the waning of Scirophorion [22. xii or 23. xii], on the twentieth of the prytany. Artemis

[TTTTX𐅅HHHH𐅈· τόκος τούτο] ΔͰͰͰΙΙ[ΙΙC. *v* Ἀφροδί]τες ἐν Κέποις,
TT𐅈H𐅅ΔΔΓΙ· τόκος τούτο ΓͰ[ͰͰͰIIIIC.]
[——16—— XX𐅅H]HHΔΔΔ[—5—· τούτο] τόκος ͰIIIO. *v*
Διονύσο, HHH𐅅ΓͰ· τόκος το[ύτο IC. *v*]
[——19——· τ]όκος το[ύτο . . *v* Ποσε]ιδôνος ἐπὶ Σουνίοι,
TTTTX𐅅ΔΔΓͰͰIIIIC· τό[κος τού]-
[το ΔͰͰͰIIO. *v* —5—XX]ẊX𐅅HHΔΔ[ΔΔΓͰͰͰͰIIII· τ]όκος τούτο
ͰͰIIIIC. *v* Ἀρτέμιδος Μονιχίασ[ι, —6—]
[——17——]ͰII. *v* Θεσέο[ς, 𐅅HHHΓͰͰͰI[IIIC· τόκος τούτο IIO. *v*
hιλισô, HHHHͰͰI· τόκ[ος τούτο]
[IC. ——14—— *v* τ]όκος τού[το . *v* hεφαίσ]το, TX𐅅HHΔΔΔΔΓͰͰ·
τόκος τούτο ͰͰͰͰIIC. Ἀφ[ροδίτε]-
[ς ἐν hιππολυτείοι, . .]ͰΙ· τόκο[ς τούτο —5—.] *v* Μοσôν, 𐅅ΔΔͰ·
τόκος τούτο IO. *v* θεô χσενικô, [—5—]
[——13——· τόκος τούτ[ο . . . *v* hερακλέ]ος ἐν Κυνοσάργει, 𐅅ΔΔΔ·
τόκος τούτο C. *v* Δεμο[φôντο]-
[ς, ——17——.] *v* Ἀθε[ναίας ἐπὶ Παλλ]ενίδι, XXXHHHHΔΓͰͰͰI·
τόκος τούτο ͰIIIIIC. *v* Ἀ[πόλλο]-
[νος ——15—— τ]όκο[ς —6—. *v* Ἀρτέ]μιδος Βραυρονίας, HHH𐅅ͰͰͰIIC·
τόκος τούτο I[C. *v* . . .]
[——34——]Ↄ. *v* Ἀθεναίας ἐπὶ Παλλαδίοι,
ͰͰIC· τόκος τούṭ[ο . . . .]
[——30——HΔΔΔ]ΔͰͰͰIII· τόκος τούτο C. *v*
Μετρὸς ἐν Ἄγρας, HH[—6—]
[——35——]ͰͰ· τούτο τόκος C. *v* Ἀθεναίας Ζοστερίας,
H[—7—]
[——30—— HHHH]ΔΔΓͰͰ· τόκος τούτο IC. *vvv*
κεφάλαιον τô ἀρχ[αίο ἀνα]-
[λόματος τôν ἄλλον θεôν τêς δευ]τέρ[ας δόσε]ος ἐπὶ Γοργοίνο ἄρχοντος *v*
ΔẠTTT𐅈𐅅HHHH[𐅅ΔΔΔΔ]
[ΓͰͰͰ· *vvvv* κεφάλαιον τόκο τού]τοι [τôι ἀργ]υρίοι 𐅅ΔΔΔͰͰ. *vv*
κεφάλαιον ἀναλόματος τô ἀ[ρχαίο]
[ἐπὶ Γοργοίνο ἄρχοντος *v* 𐅈TT]TT𐅈[𐅅HHHH]𐅅ΔΔΔΓͰͰͰ· *vvv*
κεφάλαιον τόκο χσύμπαντος το[ύτοι]
[τôι ἀργυρίοι XXHH – – –.] *vacat*
[τάδε ἐλογίσαντο hοι λογιστ]αὶ ἐν τ[οῖς τέτ]ṭạρσιν ἔτεσιν τόκον τοῖς τêς θεô
hὰ hοι πρό[τεροι]
[λογισταὶ λελογισμένα παρέ]δοσαν [ἐν τοῖς hε]πτὰ ἔτεσιν τόκον
τετρακισχιλίοις ταλά[ντοις]
[ταλάντοι τετρακισχιλίαι]ς πεντα[κοσίαις εἴ]κοσι δυοῖν δραχμαῖν·
τούτοις τόκος ἐγέ[νετο]
[Ͱ𐅈ΔΔΔΔΓX𐅅HHΔͰͰͰII.] *vacat*

91, 93 figures for principal from Pritchett, *Ancient Athenian Calendars on Stone*, 306–7.

Agrotera 4 tal. 1,950 dr.; interest on this 14 dr. 4½ ob. Aphrodite in the Gardens 2 tal. 5,175 dr. 1 ob.; interest on this 9 dr. 4½ ob. – – – 2,840 dr. +; interest on this 1 dr. 3¾ ob. Dionysus, 356 dr. 1 ob.; interest on this 1½ ob. – – – interest on this – – – Poseidon at Sunium 4 tal. 1,527 dr. 4½ ob.; interest on this 14 dr. 2¾ ob. – – – 4,749 dr. 4 ob.; interest on this 2 dr. 4½ ob. Artemis at Munichia – – – Theseus 808 dr. 4½ ob.; interest on this 2¾ ob. Hilisus 402 dr. 1 ob.; interest on this 1½ ob. – – – interest on this – – – Hephaestus 1 tal. 1,748 dr.; interest on this 4 dr. 2½ ob. Aphrodite at the Hippolyteum + 1 dr. 2 ob.; interest on this – – – Muses 521 dr.; interest on this 1¾ ob. The God of Strangers – – – interest on this – – – Heracles at Cynosarges 80 dr.; interest on this ½ ob. Demophon – – – Athena at Pallenis 3,418 dr. 1 ob.; interest on this 1 dr. 5½ ob. Apollo – – – interest – – – Artemis Brauronia 353 dr. 2½ ob.; interest on this 1½ ob. – – – Athena at the Palladium 2 dr. 1½ ob.; interest on this – – – 144 dr. 3 ob.; interest on this ½ ob. The Mother at Agrae 200 dr. +; – – – interest on this ½ ob. Athena Zosteria 100 dr. + – – – 427 dr.; interest on this 1½ ob. Total of the original expenditure of the Other Gods in the second grant in the office of Gorgoenus 23 tal. 5,998 dr.; total interest on this money 82 dr.

96 Total of the original expenditure [*sc.* of the Other Gods] in the office of Gorgoenus 54 tal. 5,988 dr. Total of all the interest on this money 2,200 dr. +.

98 This was reckoned by the *logistai* in the four years as interest on the monies of the Goddess for which the previous *logistai* reckoned and handed over the interest in the seven years on four thousand and one talents four thousand five hundred and twenty-two drachmas: the interest on this was 195 tal. 1,713 dr. 3 ob.

[τόκον ἐλογίσαντο τοῖς ἄλ]λοις θεο[ῖς ἐν τοῖς τέ]τ̲τ̲α̲ρσιν ἔτεσιν hὰ hοι πρότεροι λογι[σταὶ]
[λελογισμένα παρέδοσαν ἐ]ν τοῖς hεπ̣[τὰ ἔτεσιν πε]ντακοσίοις ταλάντοις διακοσίοις τ[αλάντ]-
[οις hεχσέκοντα ταλάντοι]ς hεχς ταλ[άντοις χιλί]αις ἐνενέκοντα δραχμαῖς πέντε δραχ[μαῖς]
[τέτταρσι δραχμαῖς ἐν τοῖ]ς τέτταρσ[ιν ἔτεσιν 𐅉]𐅉𐅉𐅈TTXXHHHΔΔΓͰͰͰIC. *vacat*
[τόκον ἐλογίσαντο καὶ τοῖ]ς Ἀθεναία[ς τε̂ς Νίκες ἐ]ν τοῖς τέτταρσιν ἔτεσιν hὰ hοι <π>ρότ[εροι *vv*]
[λογισταὶ λελογισμένα π]αρέδοσαν ἐ[ν τοῖς hεπτὰ] ἔτεσιν εἴκοσι ταλάντοις δυοῖν ταλ̣[άντο *vv*]-
[ιν τρισχιλίαις ἐνενέκον]τα δραχμ[αῖς] ὀκτὸ [δραχ]μαῖς δυοῖν ὀβολοῖν *v* T𐅅𐅄ΔΔΔͰͰII[III. *vacat*]
[τόκον ἐλογίσαντο τοῖς τô] ḥẹρμô ἐν τοῖς τέτ[ταρσι]ν ἔτεσιν hὰ hοι πρότεροι λογισταὶ λ[ελογι]-
[σμένα παρέδοσαν ἐν τοῖς hε]π̣[τὰ ἔ]τ̣[εσι]ν ταλάν[τοι τ]ετρακοσίαις ἐνενέκοντα δραχμαῖς [—5—]
[– – – HHHΔΓͰ – – –.] *vacat*
[Ἀθεναίας Νίκες ἀρχαῖον ὀφέλοσιν ἐν] ἔνδεκα ἔτεσιν ⁝ <𐅉𐅉>𐅈TTTXXX𐅅ΔΔΔΔΓͰͰͰII· *vacat*
[Ἀθεναίας Νίκες τόκος ἐγένετο 𐅈 . . .] ΔΔΔͰIC. *vacat*
[Ἀθεναίας Πολιάδος ἐν ἔνδεκα ἔτεσιν] τὸ ἀρχαῖον [ὀ]φέλοσιν | 𐅍𐅍𐅍𐅍𐅌𐅋𐅋𐅉𐅉𐅉𐅉𐅈TTT𐅆̣𐅅H[H𐅄ΔΔΓ.]
[Ἀθεναίας Πολιάδος τόκος ἐγένετο ἐν] ἔνδεκα ἔτεσ[ιν ⁝] 𐅍𐅋𐅋𐅉𐅉𐅉TTTXXX𐅅HHḤͰ̣ͰͰ. *vacat*
[ἐν ἔνδεκα ἔτεσιν Ἀθεναίας Νίκες καὶ] Πολιάδος ⁝ [𐅍𐅍𐅍𐅍]𐅌𐅋𐅋𐅊<𐅉>𐅉𐅈TTXXXHH[HΔΔ̣ͰͰͰII·]
[ἐν ἔνδεκα ἔτεσιν κεφάλαιον τô Πολιά]δος καὶ Νίκ[ες τόκ]ο ⁝ 𐅍𐅋𐅋𐅉𐅉𐅉𐅉𐅈TTT[– – –.]
[– – – *vacat*] *vacat*
[τοῖς ἄλλοις θεοῖς ἀναλόματος τô ἀρχ]αίο ἐν ἔνδεκα [ἔτεσιν κεφάλαιον ⁝ 𐅌𐅋𐅋𐅋𐅉𐅉TX𐅄ΔΔΔΓͰͰ·]
[τοῖς ἄλλοις θεοῖς τόκο χσύμπαντος ἐ]ν ἔνδεκα ἔτεσ[ιν κεφάλαιον ⁝ – – –.]
[– – – *vacat*] *vacat*
[ἀρχαῖον χσύμπαν ἐν ἔνδεκα ἔτεσιν ἅπ]ασι τοῖς θε[οῖς ⁝ 𐅎̣𐅌𐅊𐅉𐅉𐅉𐅉𐅈TTTTXXXX𐅅HHHH – – –.]
[τόκο χσύμπαντος ἅπασι τοῖς θεοῖς ἐν] ἔνδεκα ἔτεσ[ιν κεφάλαιον ⁝ – – –]
[– – –] *vacat*

108–23 fr. *h*, containing ὀκτὸ in the middle of 108 and letters below it in subsequent lines, has been lost. 112 the stone has ΔΔ. 𐅌 seems to be a mathematical error for 𐅊, carried forward to the totals in 116 and (presumably) 122 (Meritt, *The Athenian Calendar*, 49–50). 113 (fr. *h*) we print the text read by W. Gell: E.Dodwell read ΔΔΔΓIIC. 116 the stone has Δ.

102 They reckoned as interest for the Other Gods in the four years on what the previous *logistai* reckoned and handed over in the seven years, seven hundred and sixty-six talents one thousand and ninety-nine drachmas, in the four years 37 tal. 2,338 dr. 2½ ob.

106 Also they reckoned interest for the monies of Athena Nike in the four years which the previous *logistai* reckoned and handed over in the seven years, twenty-two talents three thousand and ninety-eight drachmas two obols, 1 tal. 592 dr. 5 ob.

109 They reckoned as interest on the monies of Hermes in the four years, which the previous *logistai* reckoned and handed over in the seven years, one talent four hundred and ninety drachmas +, 316 dr. +.

112 Of Athena Nike, original sum due in eleven years 28 tal. 3,548 dr. 2 ob.; of Athena Nike, the interest was [5 tal. 191 dr. 2½ ob. minimum, 6 tal. 1,131 dr. 2½ ob. maximum].

114 Of Athena Polias, in eleven years, the original sum due 4,748 tal. 5,775 dr.; of Athena Polias, the interest in eleven years was 1,243 tal. 3,804 dr.

116 In eleven years of Athena Nike and Polias 4,777 tal.3,323 dr. 2 ob.; in eleven years the total interest of Polias and Nike 1,248 tal. + [1,248 tal. 3,995 dr. 2½ ob. minimum, 1,249 tal. 4,935 dr. 2½ ob. maximum].

119 For the Other Gods, total of the original expenditure in eleven years 821 tal. 1,087 dr.; for the Other Gods, total of the whole interest in eleven years – – –

122 Whole original sum in eleven years for all the gods 5,599 tal. 4,900 dr. +; total of the whole interest in eleven years for all the gods – – –

144 attests to the repayment of outstanding debts to the sacred treasuries, completed in (we believe) 434/3. **148** shows the treasury of Athena paying for the expeditions to Corcyra in 433, and Thuc. II. 13. iii–v reports Pericles as remarking that Athens could draw on its sacred treasuries for the Peloponnesian War. This inscription gives a detailed account of money taken from the sacred treasuries in 426/5–423/2, with a summary for 433/2–427/6 and the overall totals to 422, which shows that Athens did draw on the sacred treasuries for the Peloponnesian War. The payments were regarded as loans, and interest on them was calculated: for 426/5–423/2 at 1 drachma per day for 5 talents = ¼ obol for 1,250 drachmas (about 1.2 per cent p.a.), before that probably at 1 drachma per day for 1 talent = ¼ obol for 250 drachmas (about 6 per cent p.a.). Lang showed how the calculations could have been made with an abacus. Whether the original rate and the reduced rate were simply decided by the assembly, in accordance with its right to decide religious matters as it decided secular, or steps were taken to secure divine approval, for instance by consulting the Delphic oracle, we do not know.

This inscription is important for the reconstruction of Athens' calendars in the late fifth century. It is clear from Antiph. VI. *Choreutes* 44–5 and *Ath. Pol.* 32. i that at this time the archon's year and the council's year did not coincide. From this inscription it has been calculated that the council's four years 426/5–423/2 had a total of 1,464 days, and Pritchett argued and Meritt eventually accepted that this should be seen as four solar years of 366 days each. For further discussion of the calendars see Introduction, pp. xxiii–xxv.

Reconstruction of this text depends on the interrelationship of dates, sums borrowed and interest calculated. It is complicated by (*a*) variations in the precise forms of words for various repeated expressions;[1] (*b*) irregularities in the *stoichedon* order, certainly for numerals and it seems at the ends of lines; (*c*) uncertainty over how approximations of interest were arrived at when a precise figure could not be expressed in obols and quarters; (*d*) the certainty that there are some erroneous figures in the document, and the possibility that there may be others; (*e*) ongoing disagreement over Athens' calendars. We have not made calculations and speculations of our own, but have reproduced the text of *IG* i³, itself based largely on the 1968 text of Lang & Meritt, which we believe to be correct in outline though still uncertain in various details.

This inscription begins by referring to 'the four years from Panathenaea to Panathenaea', i.e. years beginning on 28 Hecatombaeon (i) (1, cf. 49–50, 54–5: for this as the treasurers' year of office cf. **144**); but the individual entries are dated by prytany and day within the (solar) year of the council (4–5, etc.); they twice give the equivalent in the calendar of the archon's year (58, 79, for the two loans in 423/2 from the Other Gods: seen as 'a concession to rural conservatism' by J. A. Notopoulos, *AJP* lxvi 1945, 411–4), and they regularly identify the year by the archon as well as by

[1] In l. 4 ἐσελελυθυίαι is feminine dative singular, with τε̂ι πρυτανείαι understood: A. Oguse, *BCH* lix 1935, 416–20.

the council's first secretary (5, etc.). Around the summer solstice there will have been days which did not fall in the same year for officials serving from the Panathenaea, the archon and the council, but no allowance has been made for that in connection with items which fall on such days: the council's year seems to be primary for these records (Meritt, *The Athenian Calendar*, 11–16), and there will be some entries which have been wrongly classified in terms of the other years, so that a payment made shortly before the Panathenaea by the outgoing treasurers will have been recorded as if made by the treasurers who entered office at the Panathenaea (*The Athenian Calendar*, 16–19, cf. M&L; but Pritchett believed that the financial years of this document are Panathenaic years and that no payments were made between the beginning of the council's year and the Panathenaea: e.g. *The Choiseul Marble*, 99). There is one sign of awkwardness in ll. 26–7, a payment on the 26th day of the first prytany of 424/3 to 'the old *hellenotamiai* and the new': on Meritt's reconstruction that date will have fallen before the Panathenaea (according to his 1971 article it will have been 12 Hecatombaeon), and he inferred from this passage and from the problematic *IG* i^3 377 (*AFD*, 126) that the *hellenotamiai* also entered office at the Panathenaea. (Pritchett supposed that they served for a normal archontic year and, uniquely, in 424/3 the previous year's *hellenotamiai* remained in service alongside the new board: e.g. *Ancient Athenian Calendars on Stone*, 114; *Historia* xxvi 1977, 295–306; cf. Samons, *Empire of the Owl*, 300–4.)

Each payment is made from a particular treasury to the *hellenotamiai*, and the two from the Other Gods are distributed in a series of small amounts among a list of individual deities (in the same order each time: cf. W. E. Thompson, *C&M* xxviii 1967, 226–31): though physically amalgamated as a result of **144**, the individual treasuries remained notionally distinct. Athena Nike (cf. **137**, **156**) is treated separately, and so in the summary for earlier years is Hermes (109–11: *IG* i^3 376. 13, 71, suggests that his funds were administered by the treasurers of Athena, but we do not know why). In a few cases the purpose of a payment is specified, e.g. ll. 3–6, for Hippocrates in the second prytany of 426/5, perhaps for the invasion of the Megarid in Thuc. IV. 66–74; ll. 18–20, for Demosthenes 'around the Peloponnese' in the fourth prytany of 425/4, probably to consolidate the Athenian success at Pylos (cf. on **154**). Occasionally other information is given: 19–20, and restored in 59, a payment from the Opisthodomos; 42, from the Samians (?). There is a payment of 100 talents at the beginning of each campaigning season (11–12, 20–2, 32–4, 43–4), though since that was about the time when the allies' tribute was received the need for extra money then should not have been urgent.

For *logistai* ('accountants': 1, etc.) cf. **144**: those mentioned here may have been a special board. For the Opisthodomos (19–20, 59) cf. again **144**. For payments by the Samians, if that is the correct restoration (42), cf. **139**, **150**.

The deities among whom the loans from the Other Gods are divided offer a check-list of the major cults over which the city exercised some sort of central control, but there are some very minor cults here also. Most of these cults can be located, and the bulk have sanctuaries within or not far outside the Themistoclean city walls (Artemis Agrotera, Aphrodite in the Gardens, Dionysus, Theseus, Hilisus

(= the river god Ilissus: the name appears unaspirated in *IG* i[3] 383. 141), Hephaestus, the Muses, Heracles at Cynosarges, Demophon, The Mother at Agrae, Poseidon of Calauria, and probably (depending on which cult of Apollo is in question) Apollo. But there are also here cults scattered across the whole of Attica. Poseidon at Sunium (cf. **146**. 19) and Athena Pallenis had received new temples in the previous twenty years (the Athena Pallenis temple was moved from Pallene to the Athenian agora by Augustus), and Artemis Brauronia a new stoa. By contrast the fifth century seems to have been a period of relative neglect at the sanctuary on Cape Zoster (between Piraeus and Sunium: the modern Vouliagmene) shared by Apollo, Artemis, Leto and Athena (Paus. I. 31. i, cf. R&O 46), where Athena Zosteria seems to have been very much the minor deity. The celebration of the cult of Bendis is well known, not least because a new, or newly elaborated, Bendis festival features at the start of Plato's *Republic*, but the mention here in 429 is the first evidence that the Athenians had adopted this cult (Parker, *Athenian Religion*, 170–5); the Bendideum was close to the sanctuary of Artemis Munichia in the Piraeus. We have seen that Artemis at Munichia was important enough to be worshipped also in at least some Attic demes (**146**). Demophon was an important figure in Eleusinian myth, but his independent cult comes as something of a surprise here; he was held to have washed in the sea the image of Athena known as the Palladium and there may therefore be a link with the cult of Athena at the Palladium also mentioned here and which, with its associated lawcourt, can be located west of the Olympieum (Travlos, *Pictorial Dictionary of Ancient Athens*, 412–6). The Hippolyteum was the tomb of Hippolytus, on the south slope of the acropolis, and the cult of Aphrodite there, to which Hippolytus' myth lends some irony, is alluded to in Eur. *Hipp.* 31–2. We cannot locate the sanctuary of the river god Ilissus, and know nothing of the cult of Adrastea (a figure associated with Phrygia), or of the god who appears simply as the 'God of Strangers'.

Why it is that precisely these gods appear rather than others that we know as well or better from other sources remains a mystery. The very large sums of money which some gods have to lend is notable, though all other cults are simply dwarfed by Athena Polias, but so too are the small sums in other cases; that Athenian officials bothered to ascribe a loan of as little as 2 dr. 1½ obols (l. 91) and then, apparently, calculate the interest on this, is a matter of wonder. See further Parker, *Athenian Religion*, and for Aphrodite in the Gardens (80) see Garland, *Introducing New Gods*, 166–7; see also studies by N. Robertson noted in *SEG* liii 63, 153, lv 31, 60, and S. D. Lambert, *Historia* lix 2010, 144–7.

This document may be summarised as shown in table 1 (items in italics were not included in the document; the three entries marked with an asterisk at the end seem to have been too high by 450 dr. as a result of the misreading at some point of 𐅄 as 𐅅).

There are too many unknowns to justify an attempt to work out how much money remained in the sacred treasuries at particular times (cf. Kallet-Marx, *Money, Expense and Naval Power in Thucydides' History*, 194–8). It is certain that the 1,000 tal. set aside as an ultimate reserve were not touched until 412 (Thuc. II. 24. i, VIII. 15. i);

TABLE 1. Loans to the Athenian state from the sacred treasuries, 433/2–423/2

		Principal	Interest
1–2	HEADING		
	ATHENA POLIAS		
2–16	426/5	261 tal. 5,610 dr. 3½ ob.	11 tal. 119 dr. 1 ob.
16–24	425/4	130 tal.	3 tal. 3,710 dr.
25–36	424/3	163 tal.	2 tal. 5,210 dr. +
36–48	423/2	192 tal. 1,642 dr. 2½ ob.	1 tal. 813 dr. 1½ ob.
	426/5–423/2	747 tal. 1,293 dr.	18 tal. 3,935 dr. +
	ATHENA NIKE		
51–3	423/2	6 tal.	1 tal. +
	OTHER GODS		
54–97	423/2	54 tal. 5,988 dr.	2,200 dr. +
	INTEREST ON 433/2–427/6		
98–101	Athena Polias	4,001 tal. 4,522.dr.	195 tal. 1,713 dr. 3 ob.
102–5	Other Gods	766 tal. 1,099 dr.	37 tal. 2,338 dr. 2½ ob.
106–8	Athena Nike	22 tal. 3,098 dr. 2 ob.	1 tal. 592 dr. 5 ob.
109–10	Hermes	1 tal. 490 dr. +	316 dr. +
	INTEREST BROUGHT FORWARD FROM 433/2–427/6		
	Athena Nike		*2 tal. 5,598 dr. 3½ ob. +*
	Athena Polias		*1,029 tal. 4,155 dr. 3 ob.*
	Hermes		*?*
	Other Gods		*?*
	TOTALS FOR 433/2–423/2		
112–13	Athena Nike	28 tal. 3,548 dr. 2 ob.*	5 tal. 191 dr. 2½ ob. +
114–15	Athena Polias	4,748 tal. 5,775 dr.	1,243 tal. 3,804 dr.
116–18	Athena Nike + Polias	4,777 tal. 3,323 dr. 2 ob.*	1,248 tal. 3,995 dr. 2½ ob. +
	Hermes	*1 tal. 490 dr. +*	*316 dr. +*
119–21	Other Gods	821 tal. 1,087 dr.	?
122–4	GRAND TOTAL	5,599 tal. 4,900 dr. +*	?

we believe that the 6,000 tal. 'on the acropolis' of Thuc. II. 13. iii were monies in the treasury of Athena in 431 only, to which the monies of the Other Gods (§v) must be added. In table 2 we give, on the basis of a table in *ATL* iii. 342–4, an estimate of how much money was taken from the sacred treasuries in each of the eleven years.

Athens was using up its reserves at an unsustainable rate until *c.*428, but to a much lesser extent thereafter. We may note that Pericles, whose financial confidence

Table 2. Money taken from sacred treasuries, 433/2–423/2

433/2	76 tal. (cf. **148**)	427/6	100 tal.
432/1	1,145 tal. (cf. *IG* i³ 365)	426/5	261 tal.
431/0	1,370 tal. (cf. *IG* i³ 366)	425/4	130 tal.
430/29	1,300 tal.	424/3	163 tal.
429/8	600 tal.	423/2	253 tal.
428/7	200 tal.		

is reported in Thuc. ii. 13 and elsewhere, died in the autumn of 429 (cf. Thuc. ii. 65. vi), and that Thucydides refers to the Athenians' financial anxiety in the winter of 428/7 (iii. 19).

161

Athens honours Polypeithes of Siphnos, 422/1

Part of a marble *stele* found in a house north-east of the Athenian acropolis, now in the storerooms of the former First Ephorate. Phot. Matthaiou (below), 240.

Ionic writing. *Stoichedon* 40 (except ll. 3–4).

IG i³ Addenda 227 bis (ll. 3–7 only) (*SEG* xli 9); A. P. Matthaiou, in *Πρακτικά Ά Διεθνούς Σιφναϊκού Συμποσίου*, 239–48 (*SEG* l 45)*.

§i

\- -
[— 14 —] τὴν στήλην [— 17 —]
[— 5 — τῶι γρ]ạμματεῖ εἴκοσι δραχμ̣ά[ς. *vacat*]
vacat

§ii

[ἐπὶ] Ἀ̣λκαίο ἄρχοντος·
[ἐ]νάτηι καὶ δεκάτηι τῆς πρυτανείας.
ἔδοξεν τῆι βολῆι καὶ τῶι δήμωι. Ἀκαμαντὶς ἐπρυτά-
νευεν· Ἀρχικλῆς Ἁ̣λ̣αιẹὺ̣ς̣ [ἐγρ]αμμάτευεν· Διδυμίας
ἐπεστάτε. Ἀλκιβιάδης εἶπε· ἐπαινέσαι Πολυπείθη-
ṿ τὸν Σίφνιον, ὅτι ἀνήρ ἐστιν ἀγαθὸς ἐς τὸν δῆμον τ-
[ὸ]ṿ Ἀθηναίων καὶ αὐτὸς καὶ οἱ [π]ρόγονοι αὐτọ̉ Κάλλα-

1 ἐς τὴν αὐ]τὴν στήλην (?) Matthaiou.

This document takes us to the summer of 422; and we may assume that, apart from another nine months' interest (*c*.50 tal.) the situation will not have been greatly different when the Peace of Nicias was made in spring 421: the total debt to the sacred treasuries will have been *c*.5,600 tal. principal + over 1,300 tal. interest = over 6,900 tal. According to Andoc. iii. *Peace* 8, Aeschin. ii. *Embassy* 175, after the Peace of Nicias the Athenians deposited 7,000 tal. on the acropolis: that probably represents a decision to repay the sums due—which was perhaps carried out to a considerable extent but not completely. Samons, *Empire of the Owl*, 215, notes that this text cannot have been inscribed until 422/1, and suggests that it was not inscribed until peace seemed likely and repayment could be envisaged. D. Peppas-Delmousou, in *Comptes et inventaires dans la cité grecque . . . J. Tréheux*, 330–6, notes that an unpublished inscription records repayment to the treasurers of the Other Gods for Artemis Brauronia in three instalments.

---

§i

– – – on the same *stele* (?) – – – to the secretary twenty drachmas.

§ii

3 In the archonship of Alcaeus [422/1].

4 On the nineteenth of the prytany.

5 Resolved by the council and the people. Acamantis was the prytany; Archicles of Halae was the secretary; Didymias was the chairman. Alcibiades proposed:

7 Praise Polypeithes of Siphnos, because he is a good man towards the people of Athens, both himself and his forebears Callaeschrus and

[ισ]χ̣ρος καὶ [Σ]τησιλε̣[ί]δ̣ης. ἀποκρίνασ̣θαι δὲ αὐτῶι ὅ-
[τι Κά]λλ[α]ι̣σ̣[χρος —16—]ι ἀνθ’ ὧν εὖ ἐ̣π̣ο-
[ίει Ἀ]θηναίο̣ς̣ [κ]α̣[ὶ —6—]υ̣ δ̣ήμ̣[ο —5—]ναίων̣ [—5—]
[. . . .] ἅπαντα [. . . .]Π[—5—]υ καὶ Α[.]Γ̣[—13—]
[. . . .]ΟΙΠ[—33—]
[—5—]Π̣ΟΙΣ[—31—]
- -

11–13 Κα]λλ[α]ι̣σ̣[χρος ἐτετίμητο τῶι δήμω]ι ἀνθ’ ὧν εὖ ἐ̣π̣ο | [ίει Ἀ]θηναίο̣ς̣, [κ]α̣[ὶ ὑπὲρ το]ῦ̣ δ̣ήμ̣[ο τô Ἀθη]-ναίων̣ [ἔπρατ | τε ἐς] ἅπαντα [τὰ τô] π[ολέμο]υ (?) Matthaiou.

This inscription appears to contain the end of a later decree (§i: presumably of 403/2 or later) which ordered the republication of §ii, the decree which begins in l. 3 (cf. **157**).

Unless we can believe the statement of [Andoc.] IV. *Alcibiades* 11 that Alcibiades was one of the assessors of tribute—apparently in 425 (cf. **153**), but he will then have been under 30 (born 451/0: cf. Davies, *APF* 18) and not eligible for office—this decree gives us his earliest attested appearance in public life. We do not know of any connection between Alcibiades and Siphnos or this family which would explain why he proposed it; but, particularly if Matthaiou is correct in suggesting that we should restore l. 13 to say that Polypeithes had ‘acted with regard to all the matters of war’, we can perhaps get a glimpse here of an aspiring politician’s displaying his knowledge of Athens’ foreign affairs by taking the lead in responding to a prominent friend of Athens with a message that showed off both knowledge of past relations (the mention of Polypeithes’ forebears) and knowledge of what recent actions had and had not made a difference to Athens. The contrast between the expansiveness of this inscription and the brevity of **162** is notable.

The connection of Polypeithes’ family with Athens was substantial. Probably Stesileides was Polypeithes’ father and Callaeschrus his grandfather, and Callaeschrus may have been involved in Siphnos’ contributing one trireme to the Greek fleet in 480 (Hdt. VIII. 46–8). Siphnos was a tribute-paying member of the Delian League, and one fragment of **155** was found there, but otherwise the only epigraphic reference to Siphnos in the fifth century is *IG* i^3 1032. 162–3 (cf. **190**), where in a list of crews of ships probably late in the Peloponnesian War one ship has a Siphnian as its *aulos*-player; it is not mentioned at all by our literary sources for the Peloponnesian War, and we do not know what Polypeithes had done to earn his honours.

But the Athenian connection continued into the fourth century (cf. Davies, *APF* 590–2 [C 12]). Exceptionally for non-citizens, one Callaeschrus of Siphnos was a trierarch, mine-lessee and landowner in the middle of the century, and is perhaps to

Stesileides; and reply to him that Callaeschrus was honoured by the people in return for the good that he did to the Athenians, and on behalf of the people of Athens he acted with regard to all the matters of war (?) – – –

---

be identified with the Callaeschrus mentioned as the rich *hegemon* of an *eisphora* symmory in Dem. XXI. *Meidias* 157; his son Stesileides was a trierarch in the 330s; and one of the debts which he left at his death was paid by his son, another Callaeschrus, in 330/29. Whitehead claimed that these men must have been non-residents, imported as trierarchs in their capacity as allies (*The Ideology of the Athenian Metic*, 81 with 103 n. 86), but it seems better to accept the view that by the mid-fourth century they had been given not citizenship but *isoteleia* (equality with the citizens in respect of financial and other obligations) and had taken up residence at Athens (cf. R. J. Hopper, *BSA* xlviii 1953, 246; Gabrielsen, *Financing the Athenian Fleet*, 240–1 n. 25; B. Jordan, *AHB* xv 2001, 131–4).

Remarkably, l. 4 gives the date within the prytany (but we are not given the number of the prytany within the year). The earliest instance known to Henry (*The Prescripts of Athenian Decrees*, 27) of that in a decree prescript was *IG* ii^2 105 + 523 = R&O 34, of 368/7. In *Studies in Greek Epigraphy and History . . . S. V. Tracy*, 73–4, Matthaiou has attributed our inscription to S. V. Tracy's 'cutter of *IG* ii^2 17',[1] known to have been active 409/8–386/5; so not only is it interesting that this information was recorded in connection with a decree of 422/1 even though it was not the custom at that time to publish it, since this suggests that texts in the archives included information which was omitted from inscribed copies, but the publication of the information in this reinscription is one of the earliest attested instances of the inclusion of this detail in an inscribed decree prescript. Coincidentally, another instance earlier than R&O 34 is a treaty between Athens and Siphnos, carved by the same cutter and dated by Matthaiou 410/09–388/7.[2]

[1] Cf. Tracy, in *Gestures . . . A. L. Boegehold*, 351–63.

[2] *SdA* 294 = *Agora* xvi 50, with Tracy, *op. cit.*, 354 with n. 9, Matthaiou, in *Φιλαθήναιος . . . M. J. Osborne*, 45–54.

162

Athens honours Callippus of Thessaly, 422/1

The upper part of a marble *stele* with a three-pointed pediment found on the Athenian acropolis, now in the Epigraphical Museum. Phot. Kirchner rev. Klaffenbach, *Imagines Inscriptionum Atticarum*, Taf. 22 Nr. 39.

Ionic writing. Lines 2 sqq. *stoichedon* 25.

IG ii^2 27; *SIG*^{3} 132; *IG* i^3 92*; Walbank, *Athenian Proxenies*, 65. See also A. Wilhelm, *Hermes* xxiv 1889, 113 n. 2; B. D. Meritt, *Hesperia* viii 1939, 65–9.

Καλλίππο Θετταλô.
vacat 20 cm. (with no sign of carving or painting)
ἔδοξεν τῆι βολῆι καὶ τῶι δήμωι.
Ἀκαμαντὶς ἐπρυτάνευε· Ἀρχικλ-
ῆς ἐγραμμάτευε· Ἀντικράτης ἐπ-
εστάτε. γνώμη στρατηγῶν· Κάλλι-
ππον τὸν Θετταλὸν τὸγ Γυρτώνι-
ον ἐπαινέσαι, ὅτι δοκεῖ εἶναι ἀν-
ὴρ ἀγαθὸς περὶ τὴμ πόλιν τὴν Ἀθ-
ηναίων. καὶ ἀναγράψαι αὐτὸν ἐσ-
τήληι λιθίνηι πρόξενογ καὶ εὐ-
εργέτην Ἀθηναίων αὐτὸγ καὶ τὸ-
[ς] παῖδας τὸς Καλλίππο, καὶ κατα-
[θεῖναι ἐμ πόλει]. Εὐκρατίδας, Ἱππ-
- - - - - - - - - - - - - - - - - -

12–13 the letters underlined can no longer be read. 13 restored Wilhelm. 14 Walbank reports a horizontal top stroke in the last *stoichos*.

This decree was originally assigned to the fourth century; Meritt assigned it and another honorific decree, from the same prytany and secretary (and probably the same chairman, so enacted on the same day), to 416/5 (the other is *IG* i^3 91 = Walbank 64 = *Agora* xvi 20); **161** now shows that the correct year is 422/1—a date which was at one stage suggested by Mattingly (*PACA* vii 1964, 53–4), though he later preferred a slightly earlier year.

An 'opinion of the generals' (γνώμη στρατηγῶν) rather than a proposal attributed to a named individual is found only here and in *IG* i^3 89. 55 (not firmly dated, but concerning a treaty with Macedon): for other indications that the generals may have had an enhanced position with regard to the council and assembly during the

Of Callippus the Thessalian.

2 Resolved by tbe council and the people, Acamantis was the prytany; Archicles was the secretary; Anticrates was the chairman. Opinion of the generals:

5 Praise Callippus the Thessalian from Gyrton, because he is judged to be a good man with regard to the city of Athens.

9 And write up on a stone *stele* that he is a *proxenos* and benefactor of the Athenians, himself and the sons of Callippus, and place it on the acropolis.

Eucratidas, Hipp—, – – –

Peloponnesian War cf. on **150**. 55–6. This is one of the most bland of Athens' honorific decrees, giving as the only justification 'because he is judged to be a good man with regard to the city of Athens'; yet the fact that it was, unusually, proposed by the generals suggests that a much more specific justification might have been given.

Gyrton was in northern Thessaly, inland from the pass of Tempe (cf. J.-C. Decourt *et al.*, in *Inventory*, 693 no. 397): it is one of the Thessalian cities mentioned as sending forces to support Athens in 431 (Thuc. II. 22. iii); and when Mattingly dated this inscription 422/1 he linked it with the Spartans' being prevented from passing through Thessaly in that winter (Thuc. V. 13. i).

163

Naupactians and Messenians, *c.*420s

The left part of a limestone *stele* broken on the top and bottom; found outside the upper acropolis of Naupactus. Now in the storeroom of the Patras Ephoreia. Phot. *ὅρος* xiv–xvi 2000–3, pl. 96.

Ionic letters, without Ω, for which O is used, and with E frequently used for long *e*. *Stoichedon* (34?).

SEG li 642*, after A. P. Matthaiou & E. Mastrokostas, *ὅρος* xiv–xvi 2000–3, 433–54; see also Pritchett, *Thucydides' Pentekontaetia and Other Essays*, 69–71; Matthaiou, *τὰ ἐν τῆι στήληι γεγραμμένα*, 45–55.

[- -]
[— c.8 —]ΟΣΛ[— 17 — καὶ πᾶσ?]-
ας [τὰ]ς γυναῖκας τοὶ Ναυ[πάκτιοι τὸς δὲ Ναυ]-
πακτίοις τοὶ Μεσάνιοι· α[— 14 — κ]-
αὶ γυναῖκας καταβιβάσ[σκεν ποτὶ τὸ ἱερὸν]
τᾶς Ἀθάνας τᾶς Πολιάδο[ς·ὀμνύεν δὲ πάντας]
τὸν ὅρκον ἐνπεδήσεν-ὅσ[τις — 8 — τὸν ὅ]-
ρκον ἐναγὲς ἔστο τᾶς Ἀ[θάνας τᾶς Πολιάδος]
καὶ τὰ χρέματα ἱερὰ ἔσ[το αὐτο͂ τᾶς Ἀθάνας τ]-
ᾶς Πολιάδος καὶ ὅσσο κ[— 16 —]
ς σφυρηλάτος ἀνδριάν[τας — 13 —]
ο τᾶι θεο͂ι· ὀμνύεν δὲ κ[αὶ - - - τὸς - - -]
ατίδας καὶ καταβιβά[σσκεν ποτὶ τὸ ἱερὸν κ]-
ὰ<τ> ταὐτά· ὅστις δὲ κα Λ[— 17 —]
μος μὲ ὀμόσε͂ι, ἀποτε[ισάτο͂ — 10 — στα]-
τε͂ρας ἱαρὸς τᾶς Ἀθ[άνας — 13 — το]-
ὶ ιδῦοι ἐν δυνατο͂ι ἐό[ντες — 15 —]
αὐτοὶ ὀφελόντο͂ν τ[— 14 —·αἰ δέ κ]-
α ἀδύνατον ε͂ι τρι[— 20 —]
τοῖς ὁρκιστήροι[ς — 19 —]
ν ὅς κα δοκῆι τοῖ[ς — 14 — ·αἰ δέ κα]
δοκεῖ Μεσσανίο[ις — 19 —]
εστο͂ ποε͂ν· ΑΝΑΝ[— 22 —]
αδι ἑκάστει Ε[— 23 —]
ασοντι ΑΠΟΤ[— 21 — παν?]-
δημὶ τὸ δάμ[ο — 24 —]
ο· ὅσατις κα[— 25 —]
ι τὰν πόλι[ν? — 25 —]
α τοῖς π[— 28 —]
ΚΟ[.]ΓΕΙ[— 28 —]
[- -]

– – – the Naupactians – – – all the women, and the Messenians for the Naupactians. The women are to go down to the sanctuary of Athena Polias. All are to swear that they will ratify the oath.

6 Whoever – – – the oath is to be accursed of Athena Polias and his property is to become sacred to Athena Polias and however much – – – a bronze statue – – – to the goddess.

11 The —atidae are to swear – – – and to go down to the sanctuary in the same way. Whoever – – – does not swear, is to pay —— staters sacred of Athena – – –

15 The *widuoi* who are in power are to – – – or themselves owe – – –. If it is impossible – – – to the administrators of the oath – – – whoever seems to the – – –

20 If the Messenians resolve – – – to do. – – – on each – – – the whole people together – – – Whoever – – – the city – – – and to the – – –

In *c*.455, after ten years of being besieged on Ithome, the Messenians agreed with the Lacedaemonians to depart under truce and never to set foot in the Peloponnese again, under peril of enslavement if caught. The Athenians received the Messenians, men, women and children, and settled them at Naupactus which they had taken from the Ozolian Locrians (for whose occupation see M&L 20). So Thuc. I. 103. i–iii. This inscription, found outside the upper acropolis at Naupactus, clearly relates to this settlement.

This text records the conditions on which the whole community of the Messenians, women as well as men, and the whole community of Naupactians enter into an agreement which they bind with oaths. A group (a phratry?), only part of whose name survives, the —atidae, also join in the oath, which is taken by all parties in the sanctuary of Athena Polias, which they evidently share. Severe punishments are laid down for those who alter or break the oath (the closest parallel for the dedication of statues by offenders is the Zanes, statues of Zeus required by offenders at Olympia: Paus. V. 21. i), and if the magistrates do not enforce the oath they themselves are fined (probably double, given parallels elsewhere).

Unfortunately, because the beginning of the decree is lost, we do not know what sort of agreement this oath supports. The inclusion of women in the oath is extremely unusual (the only real parallel is M&L 5, the oath which the Therans claim that they made when they sent out a group to settle at Cyrene in the late seventh century); it certainly suggests that this is an oath whose importance was such that the whole community needed to be implicated, and might suggest that this is an agreement

---

164

Thank-offering of the Messenians and Naupactians, *c*.423

One block of a tall triangular base discovered in 1875 near the south-east corner of the temple of Zeus at Olympia; now in the museum there. Phot. *I. Olympia* p. 379 (cast); Berve, *Das neue Bild der Antike*, Fig. 5, facing p. 97; Harder, *Kleine Schriften*, Abb. 56; our pl. 14.

Ionic letters: ll. 3–4 are much smaller than ll. 1–2. Lines 1–2 in Doric dialect, ll. 3–4 largely Attic–Ionic.

I. Olympia 259; *IG* v. i 1568; *SIG*^{3} 80; *DGE* 65; *IG* IX. i^2 656; M&L 74*. Trans. Fornara 135. See further K. Herrmann, *JDAI* lxxxvii 1972 232–57.

Μεσσάνιοι καὶ Ναυπάκτιοι ἀνέθεν Διὶ
Ὀλυμπίωι δεκάταν ἀπὸ τῶμ πολεμίων.
Παιώνιος ἐποίησε Μενδαῖος
καὶ τἀκρωτήρια ποιῶν ἐπὶ τὸν ναὸν ἐνίκα.

---

that covers more than simply narrowly political rights (cf. J. Fletcher, in Sommerstein & Torrance (edd.), *Oaths and Swearing in Ancient Greece*, 163).

The inscription shows that what happened at Naupactus was not that the earlier inhabitants were expelled but that the Messenians joined the community that was there already (see further **164**), while keeping their own separate political status and their own magistrates (the *widuos* is known to be the magistrate who collects fines at Messene later: *IG* v. i 1498. 7–12). What else the inscription shows depends on its date.

One obvious possible context for this inscription is the moment at which the Messenians arrived at Naupactus in the 450s. But the inscription is not written in the letters used either by the Messenians or the Locrians, but in Ionic letter forms that, along with the various notable linguistic features, are closest to later fifth-century inscriptions (for the letters cf. especially *C. Delphes* 8, and our **158**). We might expect, in any case, an agreement of this sort to have required that relations between the Messenians and the Naupactians, onto whom they were foisted, settle down. With Matthaiou (and against Luraghi, *The Ancient Messenians*, 193) we believe that a date in the 420s is the most attractive context for both letter forms and content: the Ozolian Locrians were fighting in these years alongside the Athenians against the Aetolians, and thus had settled any disagreements that had arisen over the settlement of the Messenians (cf. Thuc. III. 95. ii–iii).

More of the nature of the relationship between Messenians and Naupactians emerges from **164**. The Messenians were expelled from Naupactus in 401/0 (Diod. Sic. XIV. 34. ii).

Use of α for η in τᾶς, and δάμο is characteristic of all dialects except Attic–Ionic.

The Messenians and Naupactians dedicated to
Zeus Olympios a tithe from the enemy.
3 Paeonius of Mende made this, and was victorious
in making the *akroteria* for the temple.

The Messenians settled at Naupactus in the 450s not only retained their separate political identity within the joint community there (**163**), but seem to have been keen to remind the other Greeks of their existence (T. J. Figueira, in Hodkinson & Powell (edd.), *Sparta: New Perspectives*, 214–15). We know of two spear-butts dedicated at Olympia and the sanctuary of Apollo Korythos near Corone and inscribed, respectively, 'Messenians from the Lacedaemonians' (Μεθάνιοι ἀπὸ Λακεδαιμονίον: *I. Olympia* 247) and (probably) 'Messenians dedicated from the spoils of the Athenians' (Μεθάν[ιοι] ἀνέθε[ν ἀπ'] Ἀθαναί[ον] λαίδος: *SEG* xl 362 with xlii 342). R. A. Bauslaugh made a plausible case for associating these with the Messenians in the aftermath of their 465 revolt (*Hesperia* lix 1990, 661–8, with Luraghi, *The Ancient Messenians*, 186–7). We also know of two monuments at Delphi, one a base dedicated by Messenians ([Μεσ]σάνιοι: *LSAG* 205–6 no. 8), and the other a triangular monument 8.25 m. high, bearing shields upon it and surmounted by a bronze tripod and statue, perhaps of Nike, inscribed 'Messenians and Naupactians dedicated a tithe to Apollo from the Calydonians ([Μ]εσσάνιο[ι καὶ Ναυπάκτιοι] ἀνέθ[εσαν | ἀ]πὸ Καλ[υδωνίων δεκάταν τ]ῶι Ἀπ[όλωνι]: *SEG* xxxii 550).

This inscription belongs to a monument that was designed to make its mark and to annoy. Situated close to the east end of the temple of Zeus, on which the Spartans advertised their success in war (**112**), neither the pillar, over 8 m. high, nor the sculpture that it supported, of Nike (Victory) landing on the back of the eagle of Zeus, could be missed. Leaving the enemy unnamed will hardly have softened the blow: identifying the enemy of the Messenians at Naupactus was hardly difficult—though it has to be admitted that Pausanias (v. 26. i) entertained, in the face of Messenian tradition that this marked the victory at Pylos, the view that it rather marked Messenian victory at Oeniadae (Pausanias himself, iv. 25, is our only source for this victory achieved in *c*.455 but soon reversed). Pausanias records the Messenians as saying that the enemy were left anonymous because of fear, an explanation that has been questioned because references to anonymous enemies are not uncommon in dedications, but the fact that it occurs elsewhere (e.g. six times at Delphi, and cf. Paus. v. 24. vii) does not mean that it is not a loaded practice (cf. Jacquemin, *Offrandes monumentales à Delphes*, 92–4).

The sculptor involved, Paeonius of Mende, is known only for this Nike, but the sculpture reveals his immense skill: the conception, composition, and execution of the life-sized winged figure, her drapery blown back against her body, coming in to land, are all unusually fine, and a step on from the figures of the Parthenon pediments (see further Stewart, *Greek Sculpture: An Exploration*, 89–92). Scholars have been tempted to see Paeonius' hand elsewhere (e.g. in the balustrade of the temple of Athena Nike at Athens: cf. **156**), but such identifications are merely speculative.

The *akroteria* for which Paeonius won the competition must be those of the temple of Zeus: there was a bronze-gilt Nike crowning the pediment and basins at the corners (Paus. v. 10. iv). The *akroteria* were presumably added in the 420s, perhaps in the wake of the addition of the new gold-and-ivory cult statue by Pheidias, which will have required various modifications to the temple. Fifth-century sculptural competitions are mentioned in various literary sources, notably the competition between Polyclitus, Pheidias, Cresilas, Cydon and Phradmon to sculpt Amazons for the sanctuary of Artemis at Ephesus (Plin, *H.N.* XXXIV. 53; but for problems with this see B. Ridgway, *AJA*[2] lxxviii 1974, 1–2) and the competition between Agoracritus and Alcamenes to sculpt Aphrodite (Pliny *H.N.* XXXVI. 17).

Pausanias seems to have misunderstood the reference to the *akroteria* and taken it to mean that Paeonius was responsible for the pedimental sculpture (v. 10. viii), something which is chronologically and stylistically impossible (for Pausanias as epigraphist see also **105**, **111**). This is perhaps the root also of his suggestion that the battle celebrated by the Victory was Oeniadae not Pylos: Oeniadae supplied a battle close in time to Tanagra, the commemoration of which (**112**) indicated the date of the pedimental sculptures. Putting together the Tanagra memorial with the pedimental figures and finding a battle that the Messenians might celebrate in the 450s gave Pausanias a tight chronological context for Paeonius' work at Olympia—but a wrong one.

The most plausible context for this statue is in the wake of the Spartan defeat at Pylos. We know the Athenians both to have put shields captured from Spartans at Pylos on display and themselves to have erected a statue of Nike on the Athenian acropolis in celebration (Paus. IV. 36. vi). Whether the monument could have been erected before the Peace of Nicias in 421 is less clear.

ἀνέθεν (for Attic–Ionic ἀνέθεσαν) in l. 1 is a Doric form. The use of the Ionic dialect for the signature inscription has led scholars to associate Paeonius with a Mende inland of Aenus referred to only by Pausanias (v. 27. xii) rather than the well-known Mende on the Pallene prong of the Chalcidian peninsula. But there is no other evidence for a second Mende near Aenus, and the use of Ionic letters at Chalcidian Mende seems unproblematic (*LSAG*[2] 365 and 480).

165

Alliance of Athens, Argos, Mantinea and Elis, 420

The upper right-hand part (two small fragments, now joined) of a marble *stele* found near the theatre of Dionysus in Athens, now in the Epigraphical Museum. Facsimile *Hermes* xii 1877, 370; Hornblower, *Comm. Thuc.* iii. 110 fig. 1.

Developed Attic writing, using h usually but not invariably. Lines 2 sqq. *stoichedon* 77.

A. Kirchhoff, *Hermes* xii 1877, 368–81; *IG* i^{2} 86; Tod 72; *SdA* 193; *IG* i^{3} 83*. See also Gomme, Andrewes & Dover, *HCT* iv. 54–63; Maurer, *Interpolation in Thucydides*, 44–8; K.-W. Welwei, *ZPE* cxi 1996, 88–92; M. Clark, in *Text and Tradition . . . M. Chambers*, 115–34; Hornblower, *Comm. Thuc.* iii. 109–20.

[Ἀργείον. Μαντινέον. Ἐλ]ε[ί]ον.
[σπονδὰς ἐποιέσαντο hεκατὸν Ἀθεναῖοι ἔτε καὶ Ἀργεῖοι καὶ Μαντινε̃ς καὶ Ἐλεῖο]ι πρὸς ἀλλέλος h-
[υπὲρ σφο̃ν αὐτο̃ν καὶ το̃ν χσυμμάχον hо̃ν ἄρχοσι hεκάτεροι ἀδόλος καὶ ἀβλαβε̃ς καὶ] κατὰ γε̃ν καὶ κα-
[τὰ θάλατταν. hόπλα δὲ μὲ ἐχσεῖναι ἐπιφέρεν ἐπὶ πεμονε̃ι μέτε Ἀργείος καὶ Ἐλείο]ς καὶ Μαντινέας
[καὶ τὸς χσυμμάχος ἐπὶ Ἀθεναίος καὶ τὸς χσυμμάχος hо̃ν ἄρχοσι Ἀθεναῖοι, μέτε Ἀθε]ναίος καὶ τὸς χ-
[συμμάχος hо̃ν ἄρχοσι Ἀθεναῖοι ἐπὶ Ἀργείος καὶ Ἐλείος καὶ Μαντινέας καὶ τὸς χσυ]νμάχος, τέχνει
[μεδὲ μεχανε̃ι μεδεμιᾶι. *vv* κατὰ τάδε χσυμμάχος ε̃ναι Ἀθεναίος καὶ Ἀργείος καὶ Μα]ντινέας καὶ Ἐλ-
[είος hεκατὸν ἔτε. ἐὰν πολέμιοι ἴοσι ἐπὶ τὲν γε̃ν τὲν Ἀθεναίον, βοεθε̃ν Ἀργείος καὶ] Μαντινέας καὶ
[Ἐλείος Ἀθέναζε, καθότι ἂν ἐπαγγέλλοσι Ἀθεναῖοι, τρόποι ὅτοι ἂν δύνονται ἰσχυρ]οτάτοι κατὰ τὸ
[δύνατον. ἐὰν δὲ δειόσαντες οἴχονται, πολεμίαν εἶναι ταύτεν τὲν πόλιν Ἀργείοις] καὶ Μαντινεῦσ-
[ιν καὶ Ἐλείοις καὶ Ἀθεναίοις, καὶ κακо̃ς πάσχεν hυπὸ hαπασо̃ν το̃ν πόλεον τούτον· κ]αταλύεν δὲ μὲ ἐ-
[χσε̃ναι τὸν πόλεμον πρὸς ταύτεν τὲν πόλιν μεδεμιᾶι το̃ν πολεον ἐὰν μὲ hαπάσαις] δοκ[ε̃]ι. βοεθε̃ν δὲ
[καὶ Ἀθεναίος ἐς Ἄργος καὶ ἐς Μαντίνειαν καὶ ἐς Ἔλιν ἐὰν πολέμιοι ἴοσι ἐπὶ τὲν γε̃]ν τὲν Ἀργείον ε̃

This text is quoted by Thuc. v. 47, which in §§viii–xii continues with further clauses not preserved in the inscribed text. In what follows, 'Thuc.' denotes the manuscript text of Thuc.; we do not note purely orthographical differences between that text and the inscribed text. 1 absent from Thuc. 2 restored from Thuc.: [σπονδὰς ε̃ναι hεκατὸν Ἀθεναίοις ἔτε καὶ Ἀργείοις καὶ Ἐλείοις καὶ Μαντινεῦσι]ν Cohen, noting that ἐποιέσαντο is not found in other inscribed treaties. πρὸς ἀλλέλος absent from Thuc. 4 ἐξέστω Thuc. 6 hо̃ν ἄρχοσι Ἀθεναῖοι absent from Thuc. 7–8 and 8–9 Ἠλείους καὶ Μαντινέας Thuc. 8 ἐς τὴν γῆν Thuc. 9 ὅτοι: ὁποίῳ Thuc. 11 πασῶν Thuc. 13 καὶ Μαντινέαν καὶ Ἦλιν Thuc. 13–14 Ἠλείων . . . Μαντινέων . . . Ἀργείων Thuc.

Of the Argives, Mantineans, Eleans.

2 A treaty was made for a hundred years by the Athenians and by the Argives, Mantineans and Eleans with one another, on behalf of themselves and the allies whom they rule on each side, without deceit or damage, by land and by sea.

4 It shall not be permitted to bear arms for hurt, either to the Argives, Eleans and Mantineans and their allies against the Athenians and the allies whom the Athenians rule, or to the Athenians and the allies whom the Athenians rule against the Argives, Eleans and Mantineans and their allies, by any craft or contrivance.

7 On these terms the Athenians and Argives and Mantineans and Eleans shall be allies for a hundred years.

8 If enemies go against the land of the Athenians, the Argives and Mantineans and Elans shall go to Athens in support, as summoned by the Athenians, in the strongest way they can as they are able. If they ravage and depart, this city shall be an enemy of the Argives and Mantineans and Eleans and Athenians, and shall suffer harm at the hands of all these cities. It shall not be permitted to put an end to the war against this city unless decided by all.

12 Also the Athenians shall go in support to Argos and Mantinea and Elis if enemies go against the land of the

[τὲν Μαντινέον ἒ τὲν Ἐλείον, καθότι ἂν ἐπαγγέλλοσι hαι πόλες hαῦται, τρόποι hοποί]οι ἂν δύνοντα-
[ι ἰσχυροτάτοι κατὰ τὸ δύνατον. ἐὰν δὲ δειόσαντες οἴχονται, πολεμίαν εἶναι ταύτεν] τὲν πόλιν Ἀθ-
[εναίοις καὶ Ἀργείοις καὶ Μαντινεῦσιν καὶ Ἐλείοις, καὶ κακôς πάσχεν hυπὸ hαπασôν το]ύτον τôν π-
[όλεον· καταλύεν δὲ μὲ ἐχσεῖναι τὸν πόλεμον πρὸς ταύτεν τὲν πόλιν μεδεμιᾶι τôν πόλεο]ν ἐὰν μὲ hαπ-
[άσαις δοκεῖ. hόπλα δὲ μὲ ἐᾶν ἔχοντας διιέναι ἐπὶ πολέμοι διὰ τε̂ς γε̂ς τε̂ς τε σφετέρας α]ὐτôν καὶ τ-
[ôν χσυμμάχον hôν ἄρχοσι ἕκαστοι, μεδὲ κατὰ θάλατταν, ἐὰν μὲ φσεφισαμένον τôν πόλεον] hαπασôν τ-
[ὲν δίοδον ἒναι, Ἀθεναίον καὶ Ἀργείον καὶ Μαντινέον καὶ Ἐλείον. *vv* τοῖς δὲ βοεθôσιν hε] πόλ[ις] hε π-
[έμποσα παρεχέτο μέχρι μὲν τριάκοντα ἑμερôν σῖτον, ἐπειδὰν ἔλθοσι ἐς τὲν πόλιν τὲν ἐπαγ]γέλασ-
[αν βοεθε̂ν, καὶ ἀπιôσιν κατὰ τὰ αὐτά. ἐὰν δὲ πλέονα βόλεται χρόνον τε̂ι στρατιᾶι χρε̂σθαι h]ε πόλις
[hε μεταπεμφσαμένε, διδότο σῖτον τôι μὲν hοπλίτει καὶ φσιλôι καὶ τοχσότει τρεῖς ὀβολ]ὸς Αἰγιν-
[αίος τε̂ς ἑμέρας hεκάστες, τôι δὲ hιππεῖ δραχμὲν Αἰγιναίαν. hε δὲ πόλις hε μεταπεμφσαμέ]νε τε̂ι σ-
[τρατιᾶι τὲν hεγεμονίαν ἐχέτο hόταν ἐν τε̂ι αὐτε̂ς hο πόλεμος ε̂ι. ἐὰν δέ ποι δόχσει hαπάσα]ις ταῖς
[πόλεσιν κοινε̂ι στρατεύεσθαι, τὸ ἴσον τε̂ς hεγεμονίας μετε̂ναι hαπάσαις ταῖς πόλεσιν. ὀμ]όσαι δ-
[ὲ τὰς σπονδὰς Ἀθεναίος μὲν hυπέρ τε σφôν αὐτôν καὶ τôν χσυμμάχον, Ἀργεῖοι δὲ καὶ Μαντινε̂ς καὶ Ἐ]-
[λεῖοι καὶ hοι χσύμμαχοι τούτον κατὰ πόλες ὀμνύντον.]

16 πασῶν Thuc. 17 μηδεμίᾳ τῶν πόλεων absent from Thuc. except recc. (doubted *IG* i³, but confirmed in the ed. of G. B. Alberti). 18 δοκῇ ταῖς πόλεσιν Thuc. τε absent from Thuc. 21 ἐπὴν ἔλθῃ Thuc., but *intraverint* Valla 22 βούλωνται Thuc., but *velit* Valla. 24–5 τε̂ι σ|[τρατιᾶι absent from Thuc., but *super exercitum* Valla. 25 τὲν hεγεμονίαν ἐχέτο cf. Thuc.: χρέσθο hεγεμονεύοσα Kirchhoff. hαπάσα]ις absent from Thuc., but *universis civitatibus* Valla. αὐτῆς Duker: αὐτῇ Thuc.

For the context see Thuc. v. 17. ii–46. In 421 Athens and Sparta made the Peace of Nicias and an alliance, but not all of Sparta's allies joined in the peace; Corinth, Elis and Mantinea made an alliance with Argos, which had been neutral until 421. After that, an attempt to add Boeotia to that alliance and to align it with Sparta misfired; Corinth increasingly inclined to Sparta; and Sparta angered Athens by making a treaty with Boeotia without consulting Athens. In the summer of 420 the Spartans sent envoys to Athens to try to repair the damage, but they were tricked by Alcibiades, who did not want the Peace of Nicias to be rescued, and an embassy of Nicias to

Argives or Mantineans or Eleans, as summoned by these cities, in the strongest way they can as they are able. If they ravage and depart, this city shall be an enemy of the Athenians and Argives and Mantineans and Eleans, and shall suffer harm at the hands of all these cities. It shall not be pernitted to put an end to the war against this city to any of the cities unless decided by all.

18 They shall not allow men bearing arms to pass for war through their own land and the land of the allies whom each rule, nor by sea, unless all the cities vote that there shall be passage, the Athenians and Argives and Mantineans and Eleans.

20 For those who go in support the sending city shall provide food for up to thirty days, after their arrival at the city which summoned them to support, and on the same terms when they go back. If the city which invited it wishes to use the army for a longer time, it shall provide food: for a hoplite, a light-armed soldier or an archer three Aeginetan obols for each day, and for a cavalryman an Aeginetan drachma.

24 The inviting city shall have the command of the army when the war is in its own territory. If all the cities decide in common to make a campaign, each of the cities shall have an equal share in the command.

26 The treaty shall be sworn to by the Athenians on behalf of themselves and their allies; the Argives and Mantineans and Elans and the allies of these shall swear by cities.

– – –

Sparta achieved nothing substantial. Alcibiades was then able to secure the making of this treaty, which offered Athens the prospect of an alliance which could fight against Sparta on land in the Peloponnese. Corinth refused to join this alliance (Thuc. v. 48); the alliance did proceed to fight in the Peloponnese in the years which followed, but in the battle of Mantinea in 418 the Spartans were victorious although they had been caught by surprise, and that enabled them to reassert their dominant position in the Peloponnese.

Thucydides quotes documents directly in IV. 118–V and VIII as he does not elsewhere, and this is one of the documents which he quotes: there are some discrepancies between his text and the inscription, though the 1452 translation of L. Valla suggests that in several of these cases Thucydides' own text did match the inscription but has been corrupted by copyists (Ferlauto, *Il testo di Tucidide in traduzione latina di Lorenzo Valla*, 20, 47, with D. M. Lewis, *CR*[2] xxx 1980, 277; cf. Maurer, Hornblower). Verbal differences tend to be found even between inscribed copies of the same text (cf. on **155**), and it may be that Thucydides was entirely correct in reproducing the text which he saw—but which text was that? He quotes a text in Attic Greek, though he quoted some other texts in other dialects; and it has sometimes been thought that he used the copy published at Olympia (e.g. Gomme in *HCT* iv. 55; Clark, noting that where Thucydides and the inscription mention the allies in a different order Thucydides tends to mention the Eleans earlier), but Hornblower thinks it more likely that he somehow saw the text published in Athens or a copy made from that (109–11). Athens and the other cities may well have had an archived copy as well as an inscribed text.

It has been disputed whether Athens made an alliance with the already-existing bloc of Argos, Mantinea and Elis, treating that as a single entity, or with the three states individually (cf. *HCT* iv. 55; Hornblower, 112); the treaty uses hεκάτεροι in l. 3 but hέκαστοι in l. 19 (both restored from Thucydides); part of the treaty favours the first view (ll. 2–17), but it is clear that Argos, Mantinea and Elis remain individual cities, bound individually by the treaty (and each claiming an equal share in the command of expeditions: 25–6). Hornblower's last word is that 'we should not . . . treat the Athenians like tidy-minded Romans'.

hέκατον Ἀθεναίοις ἔτε (2, restored) is a strange word order, for which there is no obvious explanation; for another hundred-year treaty involving Elis cf. M&L 17. It is suggested in l. 3 (restored) that Athens is not the only participant which has allies which it 'rules' (stressed by Welwei). In the case of Athens, by this time such language was being used in inscriptions (cf. P. Low, *JHS* cxxv 2005, 95–6 n. 9), but here the formulation was a convenient way of distinguishing between members of the Delian League and other allies such as the parties to this alliance. For Argos, the reference may be to lesser cities in the Argolid; for Mantinea, to cities in Maenalia, to the west of Mantinea (cf. Thuc. v. 29. i, 33, 67. ii, 81. i, R&O 14, and Nielsen, *Arkadia and Its*

Poleis, 367–72; for Elis, to the perioecic cities east and south of 'hollow Elis' (cf. J. Roy, in Hansen (ed.), *The Polis as an Urban Centre and as a Political Community*, 282–320).

For the matter of allowing an army to pass through territory (18–20) cf. **150**. 22–3 and Thuc. IV. 78. ii: Gomme, *HCT* iii. 542 *ad loc.*, thought it was normal to ask for consent; J. A. O. Larsen, *CP* liii 1958, 124–5, thought free passage was normal but was coming to be less tolerated; D. J. Mosley, *RIDA*^{3} xx 1973, 161–9, thought free passage was common practice, but was likely to arouse fear so asking for consent was desirable. Passage by sea became an issue in 419/8 when Argos complained that Athens had not prevented Sparta from sending a garrison by sea into Epidaurus (Thuc. v. 56. i–iii).

The state sending support troops must provide food for the outward and return journeys, and for thirty days at the city supported (20–2 with Andrewes in *HCT* iv. 56). For a longer stay hoplites, light-armed soldiers and archers are all to receive the same subsistence grant, 3 Aeginetan obols (*c.*4.3 Athenian obols), whereas in other circumstances a hoplite had an additional allowance for his servant (Thuc. III. 17.iv, IV. 16. ii): cf. Xen. *Hell.* v. ii. 21 for the Peloponnesian League in the early fourth century; D. M. Lewis interprets this as a standard Peloponnesian allowance (*CAH* v^2. 105). For commanding in one's own territory cf. Xen. *Hell.* VII. v. 3, R&O 41. 24–35 (the latter another alliance between Athens and Peloponnesian states); for equality of command cf. Xen. *Hell.* VII. i. 14, where command was to alternate between Athens and Sparta every five days.

Athens is to swear for itself and its allies, but the other states swear individually (26–8): cf. the Peace of Nicias, to which Athens swore for itself and its allies but Sparta's allies were called on to swear individually and some refused (Thuc. v. 18. ix with 17. ii, 22. i–ii). Here κατὰ πόλεις means that Argos, Mantinea and Elis are each to swear (cf. Thuc. v. 47. ix, not preserved in the inscription) but not their subordinate allies (cf. Gomme in *HCT* iv. 57).

Whereas the work of most identifiable cutters is spread over a number of years, this inscription is one of three which Tracy assigns to his 'cutter of *IG* i^3 80', the others both of 421/0 (*IG* i^3 80, 81).[1]

[1] Tracy, *Athenian Lettering of the Fifth Century* BC, 145–8.

166

Athenian Treaties with Egesta and Halicyae, 418/7–416/5

§§i–ii (Egesta): three fragments of a marble *stele* found on the Athenian acropolis, now in the Epigraphical Museum. Phot. (*a*) *Hesperia* xvii 1948, pl. 24; Bradeen & McGregor, *Studies in Fifth-Century Athenian Epigraphy*, pl. VIII; *ZPE* lxxxiii 1990, pl. I. 1; *Ἀττικαὶ Ἐπιγραφαί . . . εἰς μνήμην A. Wilhelm*, 101 πιν.1; drawing by M. Korres, *Ἀττικαὶ Ἐπιγραφαί*, 110 πιν.4; (among enlargements showing l. 3) *AJA*^{2} lix 1955, pl. 33. A–B; *ZPE* lxxxiii 1990, pls. I–III and colour plates A–B; drawings *Ἀττικαὶ Ἐπιγραφαί*, 112; (*b*) *TAPA* lxxv 1944, 10–14 pl. I (squeeze), Bradeen & McGregor, pl. IX; *Ἀττικαὶ Ἐπιγραφαί*, 102 πιν. 2. Matthaiou, *τὰ ἐν τῆι στήληι γεγραμμένα*, 67–70, publishes an additional small fragment (*c*) from the First Ephorate of Antiquities, probably from the lost upper part of the *stele*; phot. his pl. 11. 2–3

Developed Attic writing, but with tailed *rho* and three-bar *sigma*. Line 1 is carved in larger letters; ll. 2–20 *stoichedon* 48.

§i

(*c*)

\- - - - - - - - - -
\- - -]ΙΛ̣[- - -
\- - -]ΝΑ[- - -
\- - -]ΟΑΡ[- - -
\- - - Ἀ]θεν[αιο- - -
\- - -]ε Ἐγεσ[ται- - -
\- - -]ΣΑΝΤ[- - -
\- - -]ΑΤΕΣΙ̣[- - -
\- - -]ΣΘΕΟ̣Σ[- - -
\- - -]Σ[- - -
\- - - - - - - - - -

§ii

(*a*)

[—c.9— hόρ]κ̣ο̣[.].Ἀ̣[θ]ε̣ν̣α̣[ίον κα]ὶ Ἐγεσταί[ον].
[ἔδοχσεν τε̑ι βολε̑ι καὶ τ]ο̑ι [δέμοι. —6—ὶς] ἐπρυτάνευε· [. . . .]
[- - - ἐγραμμάτευε· - - -]Ο[—5—]Ι[—5— Ἀν]τ̣ιφο̑ν ε̑̓ρχε. Ἀρ[. .]Λ̣[.]
[- - εἶπε· - - -]ΙΟ[. . .]Ν[. .]Ρ̣[—8— δ]ο̑ν[α]ι αὐτὸ[ῖς . .]

§i, with 4 Ἀ]θεν[αιο—, 5 Ἐγεσ[ται—: tentative suggestions of Matthaiou include 3 ἐπὶ Εὐθύν]ο ἄρ[χοντος. 6 ὀμο]σαντ[- - 8 τὸς αὐτὸ]ς θεο̣ός.

§ii: the readings of Matthaiou 2011, given above, coincide very largely with those of Bradeen & McGregor. 1 χσυμμαχίας hόρ]κ̣ο[ς] or hόρ]κ̣ο[ι] Osborne: συμμαχία Ἀ]θ[εναίον κα]ὶ Ἐγεσταί[ον] *IG* i^2; [φιλία καὶ χσυνμαχία Ἀθεναίον καὶ] Ἐγεσταί[ον] Woodhead 1948; [χσυμμαχία καὶ hόρκ̣ο[ς] Ἀ̣[θ]ε̣ν̣α̣[ίον κα]ὶ Ἐγεσταί[ον] Bradeen & McGregor. 2 Ἀντιοχὶς or Ἐρεχθεὶς or Κεκροπὶς. 3 ἐ]π̣[εστάτε Bradeen & McGregor. Ἀν]τ̣ιφο̑ν Matthaiou 2011: Ἀρίστ]ον *IG* i^2, hά]β̣ρον Raubitschek, Ἀντ]ι̣φο̑ν Mattingly, Ἀν]τ̣ι̣φο̑ν Matthaiou & Korres. 3–4 Ἀρ[- - Bradeen & McGregor: Ἀρ[χέ]δ̣ε||[μος Lolling, Ἀρ[χί]α̣ς | *IG* i^3. 4 εἶπεν· περὶ Ἐγεστα]ίο[ν τὸ]ν [hό]ρ̣[κον εὐθὺς Bradeen & McGregor, εἶπεν· περὶ μὲν Ἐγεστα]ίο[ν τὸ]ν [hό]ρ̣[κον *IG* i^3.

IG i^{2} 19 + 20. 1–2; A. G. Woodhead, *Hesperia* xvii 1948, 58–60; *SdA* 139; M&L 37; Bradeen & McGregor, 71–81; *IG* i^{3} 11 (Woodhead); Matthaiou (2011), 55–68*. Trans. Fornara 81; Dillon & Garland^{3} 13. 22. See also A. E. Raubitschek, *TAPA* lxxv 1944, 10–14; W. K. Pritchett, *AJA*^{2} lix 1955, 58–9; H. B. Mattingly, *Historia* xii 1963, 267–9 = his *AER* 99–101; M. Chambers *et al.*, *ZPE* lxxxiii 1990, 38–57; A. S.Henry, *ZPE* xci 1992, 137–46; Matthaiou (2004), 99–122.

§iii (Halicyae): the lower part of fr. *b*. Phot. Matthaiou (2011), pl. 11. 1.

Developed Attic writing. *Stoichedon* 54 (?).

IG i^{2} 20. 4–9; A. G. Woodhead, *Hesperia* xvii 1948, 58–60; M. T. Manni Piraino, *Κώκαλος* vi 1960, 58–70 (*SEG* xxi 36); *SdA* 174; *IG* i^{3} 12*; H. B. Mattingly, *ZPE* ccxvi 1999, 118–19 (*SEG* xlix 50). See also J. D. Smart, *JHS* xcii 1972, 128–46, T. E. Wick *JHS* xcv 1975, 190 n. 32.

§ii

Oath/s of the alliance (?) of the Athenians and Egestaeans.

2 Resolved by the council and the people. —— was the prytany; —— was the secretary; —— was the chairman (?); Antiphon (418/7) was the archon. Ar— proposed:

4 – – – give to them – – –

[— 20 —]ΟΣΑ̣[— 16 —]Δ[. .]Ε[— 5 —]
[— 21 —]Σ[.]Ι[— 12 —]αι τὸς δι̣[— 5 —]
[— 19 —]ΕΡ[. . . .]Θ̣[. . . . .]Ν̣[.]α̣ [h]ι̣ερ̣ὰ [h]όσομπ̣[ε]ρ̣ ε[.]
[— 18 — τ]ὸν hό[ρκ]ο̣ν̣ ὀ̣[μνύν]α̣[ι. hόπ]ος δ' ἂν ὀμό[σοσ]-
[ιν hάπαντες, hοι στρατ]εγοὶ ἐπ̣ιμελεθέν[τον . . .]αγγ[ε]λτο̣[. . .]
[— 18 — τ]ο̂ν hορκοτο̂ν hόπ[ος — 5 —] Ἐγ[εσταιο .]
[— 11 — τὸ δὲ φσέ]φισμα τόδε κα̣ὶ τὸν [hόρκ]ο[ν] ἀνα[γρ]ά̣[φσα]-
[ι ἐστέλει λιθίνει ἐμ π]όλει τὸν γραμματέα τε̂ς βολε̂ς· [hοι δὲ π]-
[ολεταὶ ἀπομισθοσάντ]ον· hο[ι] δὲ κολακρέται δό[ν]το[ν τὸ ἀργύρ]-
[ιον. καλέσαι δὲ καὶ ἐπ]ὶ χσένια τὲν πρεσβείαν το̂ν Ἐγ[εσταίον]
[ἐς πρυτανεῖον ἐς τὸν] νομιζόμενον χρόνον. *v* Εὔφεμ̣[ος εἶπε· τὰ]
[μὲν ἄλλα καθάπερ τε̂ι β]ολε̂ι· τὸ δὲ λοιπὸν ἐπειδὰν π̣[ρέσβες Ἐγ]-
[εσταίον ἀφικνο̂νται hο κ]ε̂ρυχς προσαγ[έτο — 14 —]
[— 23 — τὸ]ς π[— 21 —]

lacuna

(*b*) [πρέσβες] Ἐγεσταί[ον — 32 —]
[— 7 —]ικίνο Ἀπ[— 34 —]

vacat

§iii

[ἔδοχσε]ν τε̂ι βολε̂ι [καὶ το̂ι δέμοι. — c.9 — ἐπρυτάνευε· — c.9 —]
[. . ἐγραμ]μάτευε· Ἀρ[— c.7 — ἐπεστάτε· — c.11 — εἶπε· Ἀθεναίοις]
[καὶ hαλι]κυαίοις Ἐλ[ύμοις (?) φιλίαν καί χσυμμαχίαν εἶναι κατὰ τὰ χσυ]-
[γκείμεν]α τὰ πρὸς Ἀθ[εναίος hὰ Ἐγεσταίοις ἐστίν· ταῦτα δὲ τὸγ γραμ]-
[ματέα τε̂ς β]ολε̂ς ἀναγ[ράφσαι ἐμ πόλει ἐν τε̂ι αὐτε̂ι στελει ἐν hε̂ι ἀναγ]-
[έγραπται κα]ὶ περὶ Ἐ[γεσταίον τὰ ἐφσεφισμένα το̂ι δέμοι. *vacat?*]

vacat?

5–7 [hοίτινες | ἐχσορκόσι ἀφικόμενοι ἐς Ἔγεσταν hελέσθα]ι τὸ[ν] δ[ε̂μον δέ|κα ἄνδρας αὐτίκα μάλα. π]ερ[ὶ δὲ τ]ο R. von Scala. 8–9 *IG* i². 10–11 hόπ[ος ἂν τὸς] Ἐγ[εσταίος | ἐχσορκόσοσι] Bradeen & McGregor, hόπ[ος εὐθὺς] Ἐγ[εσταίος | ἐχσορκόσοσι] (?) Matthaiou 2011. 16–17 Bradeen & McGregor noted that previous editors placed the surviving letters of this line one *stoichos* too far to the left: π[ρέσβες ἔλ|θοσιν ἀπ' Ἐγεσταίον A. M. Woodward *ap.* Woodhead 1948.

§iii: 22–4 Ἀρ[ίμνεστος (416/5) ε̂ρχε Wick; Ἀρ[— ἐπεστάτε· — ε̂ρχε. — εἶπε· τὸν ὅρ|κον hαλι]κυαίοις Mattingly. 24 Ἐλ[ύμοις doubted Manni Piraino, Smart.

Egesta (Segesta in its native form, but regularly represented as Egesta in Greek) was an Elymian but hellenised city in the north-west of Sicily; an appeal from it for support against Selinus in the south-west prompted Athens' Sicilian expedition of 415–413 (Thuc. vi. 6. ii).

The stone is badly worn, and the date of decree §ii has become highly controversial. The prescript included the name of the archon (3), but the only undisputed letters of the name were the last two, ON, and eleven archons in the period covered by this volume had names ending with those letters. The forms of *rho* and *sigma* were

7 – – – victims as many – – – swear the oath. So that all shall swear the generals shall take care – – – the men administering the oath so that they shall immediately administer the oath to the Egestaeans (?).

11 This decree and the oath shall be written up on a stone *stele* on the acropolis by the secretary of the council: the *poletai* shall make the contract; the *kolakretai* shall pay the money.

14 Also invite the Egestaean embassy to hospitality in the *prytaneion* at the customary time.

15 Euphemus proposed: in other respects in accordance with the council; but in future when envoys come from Egesta (?) the herald shall bring them forward – – –

lacuna

19 These envoys from Egesta – – – son of —icinus, Ap— – – –

§iii

Resolved by the council and the people. —— was the prytany; —— was the secretary; Ar— was the chairman. —— proposed:

23 That for the Athenians and the Elymian (?) Halicyaeans there should be friendship and alliance in accordance with the agreement which the Egestaeans have with the Athenians. This shall be written up on the acropolis on the same *stele* on which is written up also what was decreed by the people about the Egestaeans.

---

thought to point to an early date (already in the first publication, by U. Köhler, *Hermes* ii 1867, 16–36 at 17), and until the mid-twentieth century the preferred date was 454/3 (Ariston), on the weak grounds that Diod. Sic. XI. 86. ii mentions under that year a war in which Egesta was involved. In 1944 Raubitschek read [hά]βρον (458/7: 10 n. 3), and that was welcomed since a date in the early 450s when Athens was energetically expansive made better sense than a date in the later 450s when Athens' expansion had come to an end. Pritchett thought that no letters before ON could be recovered; but Mattingly in his campaign against the assignment of mid-century dates on the basis of letter forms read [Ἀντ]ịφο̑ν, the archon of 418/7. Chambers and colleagues applied modern technology in an attempt to reveal more of the text, supporting [Ἀντ]ịφο̑ν and making this inscription the linchpin of the debate on letter forms; Henry remained unconvinced; finally Cataldi read [Ἀντ]ιφο̑ν on the stone, Matthaiou and Korres read [Ἀν]τ̣ιφο̑ν—and we accept that, though Rhodes after studying photographs and the stone finds only the vertical which is read as *iota* clear. S. V. Tracy, *ZPE* cxc 2014, 106–7 = his *Athenian Lettering of the Fifth Century BC*, 219, includes this among the texts inscribed in his 'late fine plain style'.

If we reconsider other texts which had been dated early because of their lettering, we now have no good reason to date any decree with an archon in its prescript earlier than *IG* i^3 21 (426/5: cf. Rhodes, *CQ*^{2} lviii 2008, 504; an archon is not to be restored in **121**. 2).

Defenders of an early date for the decree objected that it would have been very perverse of Thucydides not to mention an alliance made so short a time before Egesta's appeal to Athens (e.g. M&L). However, there is very little space between the end of the prescript and the beginning of the arrangements for swearing the oath, and Matthaiou has plausibly argued that this decree did not make a new alliance but provided for oaths to reaffirm an existing alliance.

According to Thuc. VI. 6. ii the Egestaeans reminded the Athenians of τὴν γενομένην ἐπὶ Λάχητος καὶ τοῦ προτέρου πολέμου Λεοντίνων . . . ξυμμαχίαν, which refers to the war in which Athens was involved from 427 (cf. III. 86). That passage has been found problematic, and interpretations of it are reviewed by Chambers *et al.*, 58–60, and by Hornblower, *Comm. Thuc.*, iii. 303–7. Valla, followed by many early editors, took the reference to be to an alliance between Athens and Egesta: *itaque Egestani repetita memoria societatis sibi cum Lachete inite et superioris belli Leontinorum obsecrabant Athenienses* ('and so the Egestans, recalling the memory of the alliance they had entered with Laches and of the earlier war of the Leontinians, besought the Athenians'). V. Winsemis in 1580 understood Λεοντίνων not with πολέμου but with ξυμμαχίαν, as referring to the alliance between Athens and Leontini, and that has had the support of many more recent editors including, forcefully, Dover (*PCPS*^{2} iii 1954/5, 4–5, *HCT* iv. 221)—but Athens' alliance with Leontini was not made at the time of Laches' war but was reaffirmed in 433/2 after having been made earlier than that (**149**. *B*).[1] The first interpretation gives the

[1] A third line of interpretation, initiated by E. F. Poppo in 1838, saw a reference to an alliance between Egesta and Leontini, and some have accepted that. J. Classen in 1876 deleted Λεοντίνων, to obtain a reference to a more general alliance, and that too has had its supporters.

meaning which is by far the most appropriate in the context, that the Egestaeans 'reminded the Athenians of their alliance' made 'in the time of Laches and the previous war of the Leontinians'—as long as the Greek can bear that meaning, and, since it was the Leontinians who brought the Athenians under Laches into Sicily, we believe in spite of Dover's pronouncements that Thucydides could have meant 'war of the Leontinians', i.e. 'war fought by, or involving, the Leontinians' (cf. D. W. Madsen & M. F. McGregor, *Phoenix* xxxiii 1979, 233–8, dating the decree 458/7; S. Alessandrì, in *Giornate Internazionali di Studi sull' area Elima*, i. 43–4; Matthaiou). For Thucydides' mentioning only when it becomes relevant an alliance made earlier, compare Thuc. vi. 75. iii, where the Athenians go to Camarina κατὰ τὴν ἐπὶ Λάχητος γενομένην ξυμμαχίαν, and 82. i, where Euphemus (who could be the proposer of the amendment in l. 15: Matthaiou, cf. earlier Kirchner at *PA* 6035) says that they have gone there to renew the existing alliance, though that alliance is not mentioned at any earlier point.

Thucydides mentions the appeal from Egesta to Athens under winter 416/5, but does not indicate how long Egesta's dispute with Selinus had been running: it is not impossible that a stage had been reached in 418/7 at which, after the Athenians' rebuffs in Sicily in the 420s (Thuc. iv. 65, v. 4–5), the Egestaeans thought it desirable to assure themselves of Athenian support (cf. Smart, 136); and Thucydides' omission to mention the renewal of an alliance made in the 420s will be less shocking than his omission of an alliance newly made in 418/7 would have been.

It was regular practice to invite foreign envoys to 'hospitality' (*xenia*) in the *prytaneion* (14–15); later, when invitations were extended to Athenians, since they were not *xenoi* they could not be invited to *xenia* and the word used in their case was 'dinner' (*deipnon*) (cf. Rhodes, *ZPE* lvii 1984, 193–9). Commonly such invitations are ἐς αὔριον, 'for tomorrow' (e.g. *IG* i³ 57. 12–13, 63. 7–9; restored in **185**. 45–7); 'at the customary time' appears instead here and in *IG* i³ 165 (for variations in the formula see Henry, *Honours and Privileges in Athenian Decrees*, 262–71).

The lower part of fr. *b* gives us (as §iii) a fragment of an Athenian decree making with Halicyae (south of Egesta, mentioned in Thuc. vii. 32. i) what can be tentatively restored as an alliance on the same terms as that with Egesta. In Woodhead's restoration in *IG* i³ Halicyae is described as Elymian, like Egesta, but the truth of that has been doubted, and Thucydides seems to have regarded it as Sicel. As Hornblower notes in *Comm. Thuc.*, neither Egesta nor Halicyae is listed at all, even as a 'non-*polis* settlement', in *Inventory*. Mattingly suggested that this alliance should be dated 418/7 or 417/6, but it is more likely to have been made in 416/5, when Athens committed itself to campaigning in Sicily in support of Egesta (Smart, Wick).

167

Athenian decree about the sanctuary of Neleus, Basile and Codrus, 418/7

A marble *stele* found in the foundations of a house south-east of the Athenian acropolis, and now in the Epigraphical Museum. The decree is surmounted by a damaged relief (Meyer, *Die Griechischen Urkundenreliefs*, A 7; Lawton, no. 4). Phot. Meyer, pl. 6. 1; Lawton, pl. 2 (relief).

Attic letters with some irregularities (two occurrences of Λ for λ, three of H for η, and one use of Ψ. the aspirate H is used with hιερόν. *Stoichedon* 52 (with irregularities).

SIG^3 93; *LSCG* 14, *IG* i^3 84*. See also R. E. Wycherley, *BSA* lv 1960, 60–6; Behrend, *Attische Pachturkunden*, 55–61; H. A. Shapiro, *ZPE* lxiii 1986, 134–6.

θεοί.
[ἔ]δοχσεν τε̑ι βολε̑ι καὶ το̑ι δέμοι. Πανδιονὶς ἐπρυτάνευε· Ἀριστόχ-
[σ]ενος ἐγραμμάτευε· Ἀντιοχίδες ἐπεστάτει· Ἀντιφο̑ν ε̑̓ρχε. Ἀδόσιο-
[ς ε]ἶπε· ε̑̓ρχσαι τὸ hιερὸν το̑ Κόδρο καὶ το̑ Νελέος καὶ τε̑ς Βασίλες κ[α]-
ὶ μισθο̑σαι τὸ τέμενος κατὰ τὰς συνγραφάς. οἱ δὲ πολεταὶ τὲν ε̑̓ρχσ[ι]-
ṿ ἀπομισθοσάντον. τὸ δὲ τέμενος ὁ βασιλεὺς ἀπομισθοσάτο κατὰ [τ]-
ὰς χσυνγραφὰς, καὶ τὸς ὁριστὰς ἐπιπέμφσαι ὁρίσαι τὰ hιερὰ ταῦτα,
ὅπος ἂν ἔχει ὁς βέλτιστα καὶ εὐσεβέστατ<α>. τὸ δὲ ἀργύριον ἐς τὲν ε̑̓ρχ-
σιν ἀπὸ το̑ τεμένος εἶναι. πρᾶχσαι δὲ ταῦτα πρὶν ἒ̑ ἐχσιέναι τένδε
τὲν βολέν, ἒ̑ εὐθύνεσθαι χιλίασι δραχμε̑σι ἕκαστον κατὰ τὰ εἰρε-
μένα. ^{v} Ἀδόσιος εἶπε· τὰ μὲν ἄλλα καθάπερ τε̑ι βολε̑ι, ὁ δὲ βασιλεὺς μ-
[ι]σθοσάτο καὶ οἱ πολεταὶ τὸ τέμενος το̑ Νελέος καὶ τε̑ς Βασίλες κα-
[τ]ὰ τὰς χσυνγραφὰς εἴκοσι ἔτε· τὸν δὲ μισθοσάμενον ε̑̓ρχσαι τὸ hιε-
[ρ]ὸν το̑ Κόδρο καὶ το̑ Νελέος καὶ τε̑ς Βασίλες τοῖς ἑαυτο̑ τέλεσιν· ὁπ-
[ό]σεν δ' ἂν ἄλφει μίσ[θ]οσιν τὸ τέμενος κατὰ τὸν ἐνιαυτὸν ἕκαστον, κ-
αταβαλλέτο τὸ ἀργύριον ἐπὶ τε̑ς ἐνάτες πρυτανείας τοῖς ἀποδέκ-
ται[ς], οἱ δὲ ἀποδέκται τοῖς ταμίαισι το̑ν ἄλλον θεο̑ν παραδιδόντον
[κ]ατὰ τὸν νόμον· ὁ δὲ βασιλεὺς ἐὰν μὲ ποιέσει τὰ ἐφσεφισμένα ἒ ἄλλ-
ος τις οἷς προτέτακται περὶ τούτον ἐπὶ τε̑ς Αἰγεΐδος πρυτανεί-
ας, εὐθυνέσθω μυρίεσι δραχμε̑σιν. τὸν δὲ ἑονεμένον τὲν ἰλὺν ἐκκο-
μίσασθαι ἐκ τε̑ς τάφρο ἐπὶ τε̑σδε τε̑ς βολε̑ς ἀποδόντα τὸ ἀργύριον
το̑ι Νελεῖ ὅσο ἐπρίατο· ὁ δὲ βασιλεὺς ἐχσαλειψάτο τὸν πριάμενον τ-
ὴν ἰλύν, ἐπειδὰν ἀποδο̑ι τὲμ μίσθοσιν· τὸν δὲ μισθοσάμενον τὸ τέμ-
ενος καὶ ὁπόσο ἂν μισθόσεται ἀντενγραφσάτο ὁ βασιλεὺς ἐς τὸν τ-
οῖχον καὶ τὸς ἐγγυετὰς κατὰ τὸν νόμον ὅσπερ κεῖται το̑ν τεμενο̑ν.
τὸ δὲ φσέφισμα τόδε, ὅπος ἂν ε̑̓ι εἰδέναι το̑[ι] βολομένοι, ἀναγράφσα-
ς ὁ γραμματεὺς ὁ τε̑ς βολε̑ς ἐν στέλει λιθίνει καταθέτο ἐν το̑ι Νελεί-
οι παρὰ τὰ ἴκρια· οἱ δὲ κολακρέται δόντον τὸ ἀργύριον ἐς ταῦτα. ^{vv}
μισθο̑ν δὲ βασιλέα τὸ τέμενος το̑ Νελέος καὶ τε̑ς Βασίλες κατὰ

8 The stone reads εὐσεβέστατο.

Gods.

2 Resolved by the council and people. Pandionis was the prytany; Aristoxenus was secretary; Antiochides was chairman, Antiphon was archon. Adousius proposed:

4 Fence the sanctuary of Codrus and Neleus and Basile and lease the *temenos* (enclosure) according to the schedule. The *poletai* are to put the fencing out to tender. The *basileus* is to lease out the *temenos* according to the schedule, and dispatch the *horistai* to define the boundaries of these sanctuaries, in order that things may be as good and as respectful of the gods as possible. The money for the fencing is to come from leasing the *temenos*. This council is to deal with this before the end of its term of office, or each councillor shall be liable at his *euthynai* (audit) to a fine of one thousand drachmas according to what has been stated.

11 Adousius proposed: In other respects as the council proposes, but the *basileus* and the *poletai* are to lease the *temenos* of Neleus and Basile according to the schedule for twenty years. The man who takes up the lease is to fence the sanctuary of Codrus, Neleus and Basile at his own expense. However much rent the *temenos* brings in each year, the money is to be deposited with the *apodektai* in the ninth prytany and the *apodektai* are to hand it over to the treasurers of the Other Gods according to the law. If the *basileus*, or anyone else to whom instructions have been given on these matters, does not do what has been decreed in the prytany of Aigeis, he is to be fined ten thousand drachmas at his *euthynai* (audit).

20 The man who buys the mud is to remove it from the ditch during this council, after paying Neleus the price he agreed. The *basileus* is to delete the name of the purchaser of the mud whenever he pays the rent. The *basileus* is to record the name of the man who leases the *temenos* and how much he leases it for on the wall along with the sureties in accordance with the law that has been made about *temene*.

26 In order that anyone who wishes may know, the secretary of the council is to write this decree up on a stone *stele* and deposit it in the Neleion by the wooden seats. The *kolakretai* are to give the money for this.

29 The *basileus* is to lease out the *temenos* of Neleus and Basile on the following conditions:

τάδε· τὸν μισθοσάμενον ἒρχσαι μὲν τὸ hιερὸν τô Κόδρο καὶ τô Νελέ-
ος καὶ τε̑ς Βασίλες κατὰ τὰς χσυνγραφὰς ἐπὶ τε̑ς βολε̑ς τε̑ς εἰσιόσ-
ες, τὸ δὲ τ[έ]μενο[ς] τô Νελέος καὶ τε̑ς Βασίλες κατὰ τάδε ἐργάζεσθαι·
φυτεῦσαι φυτευτέρια ἐλαôν μὲ ὄλεζον ἒ διακόσια, πλέονα δὲ ἐὰν β-
όλεται, καὶ τε̑ς τάφρο καὶ τô ὕδατος κρατε̑ν τô ἐγ Διὸς τὸν μισθοσά-
μενον, ὁπόσον ἐντὸς ῥεῖ τô Διονυσίο καὶ τôν πυλôν ἒ<ι> ἄλαδε ἐ[χ]σελα-
ύνοσιν οἱ μύσται καὶ ὁπόσον ἐντὸς τε̑ς οἰκίας τε̑ς δεμοσίας καὶ τ-
ôν πυλôν αἳ ἐπὶ τὸ Ἰσθμονίκο βαλανεῖον ἐκφέροσι· μισθôν δὲ κατὰ
εἴκοσι ἐτôν.

35 The stone has ε ἄλαδε.

This perfectly preserved *stele* sheds light on Athenian political procedure and gives our best illustration of Athens' own practices in leasing sacred land in the fifth century (cf. **147** for leasing of sacred property on Delos). It also introduces us to a set of little-known Athenian heroes and deities.

Procedurally there are two interesting features of this inscription. The first is that the amendment is introduced by the speaker to whom the substantive proposal is also attributed. There is one further case of this known in the fifth century, **191** (note also **153** with a second decree perhaps from the same proposer as the first, and for the fourth century see R&O 70). In **191** both decree and amendment are put forward by the whole body of *prytaneis*, signalling their unanimity, and the amendment picks up a detail which they had not thought of in the initial decree. But this case is different. It takes up the whole subject of the initial decree and expands on the detail involved. The proposer, Adousius, is otherwise unknown (and is the only Athenian we know of with that name). It is tempting to think that we have a case here of an inexperienced council member who only realised after persuading the council to bring this proposal that he needed rather more detail to make it work.

The other peculiar feature is the way in which the terms of the lease are appended. It is not entirely clear whether ll. 29–38 are part of the main decree or part of the amendment. They set out the conditions of the lease, carefully repeating as little as possible of what has been said already. Most remarkably, only now is there mention for the first time of the obligation of the lessee to plant the land leased with olives.

The formula 'In order that anyone who wishes may know' (l. 26) is almost unique in Athenian epigraphy (there is a parallel a century later in *IG* ii^2 463. 29–31, where it is the names of those involved in rebuilding the city walls that is at issue). 'Formulae of disclosure', as they are sometimes called, are more generally motivated by a desire to advertise an item to those who might be interested than by an abstract concern for freedom of information (cf. **155** §12; see J. P. Sickinger, in *Greek History and Epigraphy . . . P. J. Rhodes*, 92–3). Here the inscription is put up by the *ikria* (wooden seats, presumably erected so that people could watch the religious ceremonies held

the lessee is to fence the sanctuary of Codrus and Neleus and Basile according to the contracts during the incoming council, and to cultivate the *temenos* of Neleus and Basile according to the following conditions: the lessee is to plant no fewer than two hundred young olive trees, more if he wants, and to control the ditch and the rainwater from Zeus, as much as flows within the area between the Dionysion and the gates where the initiates exit to the sea and as much as flows within the area between the public building and the gates which lead to the Isthmonic bath. He is to rent it for twenty years.

---

here, or perhaps railings), and the issue seems to be merely letting those who use the sanctuary know who has leased the *temenos*.

The land here is leased broadly according to the procedures described in *Ath. Pol.* 47. iv for leases of sacred land, except that this lease is for twenty rather than ten years (see Papazarkadas, *Sacred and Public Land in Ancient Athens*, 52–6). The leasing is done by the *basileus* (l. 6); whether the statement in ll. 11–12 that the *poletai* are involved also is because they shared responsibility for the leasing or because they too have actions specified in this decree is disputed (M. K. Langdon, in *Agora* xix. 64–5, Papazarkadas, 53–4, against; M. B. Walbank, in *Agora* xix. 149–51, 154–5, 166–7, and Rhodes, *G&R*[2] lx 2013, 211–2 in favour). The tendering that they are ordered to perform in the initial decree is here superseded by the transfer of responsibility for the fencing to the lessee. The rent seems to be decided by auction, rather than fixed in advance (ll. 14–15, using a verb (ἀλφάνω, aorist ἦλφον) otherwise hardly attested outside Homer and poetry), and the lessee is obliged to have more than one guarantor (ll. 24–6). Payment is to be made in the ninth prytany of the year, as became the legally enforced norm for all such leases in the fourth century. This is the first appearance of the *apodektai* in an Athenian inscription. Androtion apparently claimed (*FGrH* 324 F 5 from Harp. α 184 Keaney ἀποδέκται) that Cleisthenes instituted the office of *apodektai*, but their late appearance casts doubts over this. Their fourth-century duties, of receiving public revenues and distributing public funds, are described at *Ath. Pol.* 48. i–ii. Immediately after the appearance of the *apodektai* the financial officials known as *kolakretai* (Introduction, p. xxiii) disappear, and it is likely that these two facts are linked. The *apodektai* handled both sacred and non-sacred funds, and in the requirement here to hand on the money received in this case to the treasurers of the Other Gods 'according to the law' we have, as Papazarkadas has noted (84–5), an anticipation of the fourth-century division of funds between budget headings, with certain sources of income devoted to certain sorts of expense.

The wall on which the lease is written up (ll. 24–5) seems likely to be the wall of the Royal Stoa, which was the base of the *basileus* and which Aelian tells us held the lease records (*V.H.* vi. 1; Papazarkadas, 72–3). The schedule (*syngraphai*) referred to here may have specified what the money was to be used for, that is the sacrifices for which it paid (cf. Lys. xxx. *Nicomachus* 17 with Papazarkadas, 82); and cf. **147**. 19.

Agriculturally two features are notable. This is the earliest lease we know of where the lessee is obliged to adopt a particular regime of planting (a so-called emphyteutic clause). For such clauses in the fourth century see R&O 59, *IG* ii^2 2499, 2501, and *I. Rhamnous* 180. The point of specifying the planting of olives must be to increase the value of the land, and so raise a higher rent in future. The twenty-year lease period allows for planting and a return on the investment (and the ground between the olives can be used for other crops while the olives mature). The second notable feature is the independent value of the mud and the water. It appears that the mud (from the bottom of drainage channels?) is sold (presumably for use as topsoil or for making mud bricks), as part of an agreement already in place (cf. *IG* ii^2 2498. 9), before the lessee of the *temenos* takes the land over. The lessee of the land is explicitly identified as the person with rights to rainwater and the water in the ditches. The sanctuary, probably close to the sanctuary of Dionysus 'in the marshes', is likely to have had relatively abundant water, but what exactly the lessee would do with the water is not clear. Whether the driving motivation was to increase the income from sacred land or to make available more agricultural land we cannot tell.

The location of the sanctuary of Codrus, Neleus and Basile and of the *temenos* (enclosure) of Neleus and Basile (we should probably think of the sanctuary as being at one corner of the *temenos*) are broadly indicated by the description in the text of the lessee as having water-rights over land between a Dionysion and the Phalerum gate (defined by its role in the Eleusinian Mysteries' procession to the sea) and between the gate leading to the Isthmonic baths (= Itonian gate) and a 'public house'. A. J. Graham has suggested that here, as in **104**, 'public house' means brothel, though generally in Attic Greek (contrast Polyb. XXXVI. I. xii) *demosios* means 'belonging to' rather than 'used by' the public.

Scholars have disputed whether to place the sanctuary and *temenos* inside or outside the walls, and have sometimes assumed that it coincided with the place where Codrus was killed, which seems to be situated by Paus. I. 19. vi on the north bank of the Ilissus but which others in antiquity identified as outside the gate or in front of the wall. The size of the *temenos*, large enough for more than 200 olive trees and therefore likely to be at least 5 acres (= 2 ha.) in area (cf. Foxhall, *Olive Cultivation in Ancient Greece*, 116, citing Solon's law at Plut. *Sol.* 23. vi on olives being at least 9 feet (= 2.7 m.) apart), might suggest a location outside the walls, as might Plato's comment (*Chrm.* 153 A) that the *palaistra* of Taureas was opposite the sanctuary of Basile (emending the βασιλικῆς of most MSS). But the find-spot for this *stele* seems to have been just inside the walls, at the north-east corner of the junction of Makrigianni and Chatzichristou streets, and a fifth-century stone inscribed 'boundary of the sanctuary' (*IG* i³ 1076) was found *in situ* in 1962 at the junction of Chatzichristou and Syngrou, which seems most plausibly to relate to this sanctuary. If so, the sanctuary was indeed between the Phalerum and Itonian gates, but inside the walls, and the Dionysion is likely to be the sanctuary of Dionysus in the Marshes, thought to be just south of Chatzichristou on the west side of Makrigianni (Travlos, *Pictorial Dictionary of Ancient Athens*, 332–4).

A figure named Basile appears on a late fifth-century Athenian pot with Cecrops, first king of Athens (Shapiro, 134–5). Her appearance in this decree with Codrus, the last king of Athens, who gave up his life to save the city from the Dorians (N. Robertson, *GRBS* xxix 1988, 224–5), suggests that she was a figure with generalised queenly qualities who might be associated with any Attic king. In the fourth century she was worshipped in the Attic demes at Erchia (*SEG* xxi 541. *B.* 16–20) in the Mesogeia, and at Eitea, probably near Rhamnous, where an honorific decree put up in her sanctuary shows her crowning the honorand (*IG* ii³ 1025, Lawton, no. 43, pl. 22), and possibly at Phalerum, if the figure being abducted by Echelus in a votive relief (O. Walter, *Ἀρχ. Ἐφ.* 1937, 112–13; B. D. Meritt, *Hesperia* xi 1942, 284–6), who is named Iasile, is an alternative form of Basile. Part of the attraction of that identification is that it would make Basile's rape by Echelus parallel to Persephone's rape by Pluto, and this would fit the way in which at Erchia Basile receives a holocaust sacrifice of a white female lamb followed by a wineless libation at a date which associates it with the Genesia festival of the dead (see further S. D. Lambert, *ZPE* cxxxix 2002, 80–1). This generalised worship implies that the cult might be of some antiquity. The first, and only, appearances of Codrus in Attic iconography come in the Marathon dedication at Delphi (Paus. x. 10. i–ii) of the mid-fifth century, and on the name vase of the Codrus Painter (Beazley, *ARV*² 1268. 1). Neleus is a more complicated figure since myth-history knew two Neleis: Neleus the king of Pylos, son of Poseidon and Tyro, and Neleus the father of Codrus. The Pylian king appears just once in Attic iconography, on a pot of *c.*400 (*Agora* xii 205), despite Herodotus telling us that Pisistratus had claimed a connection with him (Hdt. v. 65). Codrus' father appears not at all.

We know nothing of the history of this sanctuary and *temenos* before this date. Scholars have sometimes suspected that the *temenos* is being restored to agricultural use after having been used as a place for those coming in from Attica to 'squat' during the Spartan invasions of the Archidamian War, but that is pure speculation. Apart from its use as a geographical locator in Plato's *Charmides* we also know nothing of its subsequent history.

168

Athenian tribute quota list, 418/7 (?)

Five fragments of a marble *stele*, one complete at the top and three joining at the back. Found on the south slope of the acropolis and in the agora. Now in the Epigraphical Museum. Phot. frs. 1 and 3: *Hesperia* viii 1939, 54; fr. 2: *ATL* i. p. 100 fig. 133; fr. 4: *Hesperia* xvii 1948, pl. 8, and *ATL* ii. p. 37 fig. 3; frg. 1,2, 3 and 5: *Hesperia* lxxiii 2004, 476 fig. 2, 478 figs. 3–6.

Developed Attic letters; in two of four instances the aspirate is dropped. *Stoichedon* 50 (prescript).

ATL i, list 33; *ATL* ii, list 33; *ATL* iii (1950) 357; M&L 75; B. D. Meritt, *Hesperia* xli 1972, 418–21; *IG* i³ 287*. See also L. Kallet, *Hesperia* lxxiii 2004, 465–96.

[ἐπὶ τε͂ς βολε͂ς ἒ͂ι —7— Ἀ]φιδναῖος προ͂ṭ[ος ἐγραμμάτευε, ἒ͂ρχε v]
[δὲ Ἀθεναίοις Ἀντιφο͂ν Σκ]ạμβονίδες ἐπὶ τε͂[ς hεβδόμες καὶ τρια v]-
[κοστε͂ς ἀρχε͂ς ἑλλενοταμί]αι ἒ͂σαν hοῖς Ἀντ[—17—]
[—16— Περγ]ασε͂θεν Μνεσίθεο[ς Ἀραφένιος —7—]
[—16— Εὐπυ]ρίδες Αἰσχίνες Π[εριθοίδες —8—]
[Θυμαιτ]άδε[ς Ἐργοκλε͂ς Βεσ]αιεύς *vacat*
[πόλες h]αίδε [ἀπέδοσαν ἀπα]ρχὲν τε͂ι θεο͂ι μνᾶ[ν ἀπ]ὸ το͂ ταλάντ[ο vvv]

i		ii	
Νεσιοτ[ικός]		hελλε[σ]πόντιο[ς]	
[—5—]vv	Ἀναφ[αῖοι]	H	Σι[γε]ιε͂ς
[—5—]vv	Θερα[ῖοι]	XX	Κυ[ζι]κενοί
[—5—]vv	Σερίφ[ιοι]	𐅄̣Δ̣[Γ⊢IIII]	[Ἀρτα]κενοί
[—5—]vv	Ἰε͂τα[ι]	[ΔΓ⊢IIIIv]v	Κια[ν]οί
[. . . .]vvv	Τένιο[ι]	[—5—]vv	[Βυσβ]ικενοί
[. . . .]vvv	Σίφνιο[ι]	[HHHvv]vv	[Προκ]οννέσιοι
[. . . .]vvv	Ἄνδριο[ι]	[. . . .]⊢IIII	[Παρια]νοί
[Γ⊢⊢⊢]IIvv	Σικινε͂[ται]	[𐅅Hvv]vvv	[Χαλχεδ]όνι[οι]
[—5—]vv	Κύθνι[οι]	[. . . .]vvv	Σελυ[μβριανοί]
		[. . . .]vvv	Σερι[οτειχῖται]
		[HHvv]vvv	Διδυ[μοτειχῖται]
		[HHvv]vvv	Δαυνι[οτειχῖται]
lacuna		[𐅄ΔΓ]⊢IIIIv	Σομβία
		[. . .]ΔΓ⊢⊢⊢II	Περίνθ[ιοι]
		[. . .]⊢IIIIv	Βρυλλ[ιανοί]
		[XHH]vvvv	Λανφσακ[ενοί]
		– – – – –	[Ἀβυ]δενο[ί]
		lacuna	
		– – – – –	[.]ε[– – –]

i. 23 *IG* inserts [HHHH Κύθερα] on the basis of Thuc. iv. 57. iv.

During the council for which —— of Aphidna was the first secretary, and Antiphon of Scambonidae was archon for the Athenians, under the thirty-seventh board, the *hellenotamiai* for whom Ant— was secretary were —— of Pergase, Mnesitheus of Araphen, —— of Eupyridae, Aeschines of Perithoidae, —— of Thymaetadae, Ergocles of Besa.

These cities paid firstfruits to the goddess of one mina in the talent:

i		ii	
ISLAND AREA		HELLESPONTIAN AREA	
– – –	Anaphaeans	100 dr.	Sigeans
– – –	Theraeans	2,000 dr.	Cyzicenes
– – –	Seriphians	66 dr. 4 ob.	Artacenes
– – –	Ietians	16 dr. 4 ob.	Cianians
– – –	Tenians	– – –	Bysbicenes
– – –	Siphnians	300 dr.	Proconnesians
– – –	Andrians	at least 94 ob.	Parians
8 dr. 2 ob.	Sicinetians	600 dr.	Calchedonians
– – –	Cythnians	– – –	Selymbrians
		– – –	Serioteichitans
		200 dr.	Didymoteichitans
		200 dr.	Daunioteichitans
lacuna		66 dr. 4 ob.	Sombia
		at least 48 dr. 2 ob.	Perinthians
		at least 4 dr. 4 ob.	Brylleians
		1,200 dr.	Lampsacenes
		– – –	Abydenes
		lacuna	
		– – –	–e—

[HΡΔΓΗΙΙ]ΙΙ	Χε[ρρονεσῖται]
	ἀπ' ['Αγορᾶς]
[—5—]vv	Κ[αλλιπολῖται]
	- - -

The assessment of 425 (**154**) had demanded massively increased tribute from Athens' allies. What happened next? The exceptional assessment of 425 had threatened severe penalties (**154**. 26–33) if a Great Panathenaea passed without tribute reassessment. Part of a reassessment decree survives (*IG* i³ 77) which must be from a reassessment subsequent to 425 (the Actaean panel of cities, one of whose assessments is recorded in what survives, had first appeared in 425). The surviving figures in this decree relate to Hellespontine and Thracian cities and to Antandrus from the Acte. The total for the Hellespont is partially preserved. Unfortunately where figures and names are both preserved in this assessment they do not survive in the 425 assessment, with the partial exception of Antandrus and the Hellespontine total. In 425 Antandrus was assessed at 15 tal.; in the later assessment the figure could be anything from 4 tal. to 17 tal. Meritt & McGregor in *IG* i³ favour 8 tal.; 13 tal. would also be possible. The Hellespontine total in 425 was in excess of 250 tal.; in the later assessment the figure of 96 tal. is preserved (and interpreted as such by Meritt & McGregor), but this figure is preceded by space for two letters: indenting totals by one letter is the pattern in 425, and if that pattern were followed here then the total would be 196 tal. (the figure favoured by M&L, p. 226); if there was no indenting the figure might have been 296 tal. There is also a run of figures for cities in the Thraceward region in the 425 assessment where the names of the cities are not preserved, but which matches exactly the run of figures for Heracleum, the Singians, the Mecybernians, the Galaeans, Traïlus and Bormiscus in the later list. If these figures in 425 are indeed the figures for those cities then their tribute was unchanged in the later assessment.

The gaps in these surviving assessment lists are frustrating. We do not know whether *IG* i³ 77 is from 422 or 418, and we do not know whether the assessment was largely as in 425 but with some more or less slight reductions (e.g. 15 to 13 tal. for Andandrus, 25 per cent for the Hellespontine total) or even some increases (Antandrus to 17 tal., the Hellespont to 296 tal.), or whether it saw sweeping reductions (Antandros from 15 to 4 tal., the Hellespont from 250+ to 96 tal.). *ATL* believed in large reductions, suggesting that the 422 assessment anticipated the return to the 'tribute of Aristides' which revolting allies returned to Athenian control in 421 were made to pay (Thuc. v. 18. v).

166 dr. 4 ob.	Chersonites
	from Agora
– – –	Callipolitans
	– – –

The tribute quota list which we print here is made up from five fragments, three of which Meritt found to join at the back. Kallet has questioned whether the fragments all join together, on the grounds that the shape of the letter *nu* seems to vary, but she herself admits that there is variation within a single fragment and also both sees those on frs. 2 and 3 as 'distinctly different' and those on fr. 1 as 'roughly similar' to frs. 2 and 3 (479). The evidence seems more to point to a slightly inconsistent letter-cutter than to the fragments belonging to different lists. In any case, most of the deductions made below arise simply on the basis of the joining fragments.

This tribute quota list seems to reflect demands that are hard to square with a general return to the 'tribute of Aristides', if what that signified was low levels of tribute, since they are significantly higher than the tribute demanded before 425. So Sombia can be restored here as paying a $^1/_{60}$ quota of 66 dr. 4 ob., representing a tribute of 4,000 dr., exactly the sum preserved in *IG* i^3 77. iv. 3; Cyzicus pays 2,000 dr. of quota (= 20 tal. tribute), when in the 430s she had paid 9 tal. tribute; Sigeum moves from a 430s tribute level of 1,000 dr. to 1 tal. (quota 100 dr.).

This tribute quota list requires an archon from the deme of Scambonidae whose name has seven letters. Either Alcaeus, the archon of 422/1, or Antiphon, the archon of 418/7 (see **166**), neither of whose demes is otherwise known, would be possible. The year 418 is preferable, since a perfect fit for the last *hellenotamias* named in this list (whom we would otherwise presume to be from tribe X, Antiochis) is provided by the *hellenotamias* for 418/7, Ergocles of Besa (see **170**. 10), and the first secretary of the council in 418/7 (*IG* i^3 472. 16) comes from the same deme as the first secretary here and the space for the name (lost in both cases) can be reconstructed to be identical.

What a date of 418/7 for this list tells us is that neither the 422 nor the 418 assessment (regardless of which assessment is represented by *IG* i^3 77) did more than, at most, slightly moderate the 425 assessment. The Peace of Nicias, on this basis, had little effect on the demands made by the Athenians of their allies. What is more, this list, unlike the assessment lists, shows that even seven years after the 425 reassessment significant numbers of Athens' allies were paying their increased tribute.

169

Inventory of the treasures in the *hekatompedon* at Athens, 418/7

A marble *stele*, found on the acropolis in two pieces; one is now in the British Museum, the other in the Bibliothèque Nationale (Cabinet des Médailles) in Paris. Inscribed on both sides, containing lists for 422/1–419/8 on one side, lists for 418/7–415/4 on the other. Phot. (Paris fragment): Robert, *Collection Froehner*, i, pl. xlviii.

Developed Attic writing; each list laid out on a separate stoichedon grid.

M&L 76; *IG* i[3] 329*. See also Harris, *The Treasures of the Parthenon and Erechtheion*.

τάδε παρέδοσαν hαι τέτταρες ἀρχαί, hα[ὶ ἐδίδοσαν τὸν λόγον ἐκ Παναθεναίον ἐς Πανα]θ[ένα]-
ια, τοῖς ταμίαις Πυθοδόροι hαλαιεῖ [καὶ συνάρχοσι, hοῖς Φορμίον Ἀριστίονος Κ]υδαθενα[ι]-
εὺς ἐγραμμάτευε· hοι δὲ ταμίαι, hοῖς Φο[ρμίο]ν Ἀ[ριστίονος Κυδαθεναιεὺς ἐγραμμάτε]υε, π[α]-
ρέδοσαν τοῖς ταμίαις Ἀναχσικράτει Λα[μπ]τρε[ῖ καὶ συνάρχοσι, hοῖς Εὔχσενος Εὐφάνο]ς Προσ-
π̣άλτιος ἐγραμμάτευεν, ἐν τôι νεὸι τôι [Ἑκατ]ομπέδ[οι· φιάλαι χρυσαῖ ΙΙΙ, σταθμὸν τούτ]ον ΧΧ𐅅̣
ΔΔΔ⊦⊦⊦⊦· κόρε χρυσê ἐπὶ στέλες, ἄσταθ̣[μος· ἀπορραντέριον ἀργυρôν, ἄσταθμον· στεφά]νο χρυ-
σὸ Ι[Ι], σταθμὸν τούτοιν 𐅄ΔΔΔ· [στ]έφανος χρ[υσôς, h]ὸ[ν hε Νίκε ἔχει, σταθμὸν τούτο 𐅄Δ· φιάλ]αι ἀρ[γ]-
υραῖ ΓΙΙΙ, σταθμὸν τούτον 𐅅ΗΗ[Η]· καρχέσιο[ν ἀργυρôν, σταθμὸν τούτο ΗΗ· καρχέσιον ἀργυ]ρôν Δ[ι]-
ὸς Πολιôς, σταθμὸν τούτο ΗΗ· στέφανος [χρυσôς, σταθμὸν τούτο . . . ⊦⊦⊦ΙΙ· στεφά]νε χ[ρυ]σê, σταθ-
μὸν ταύτες 𐅄Δ⊦⊦⊦· στέφανοι χρυσοῖ Ι[Ι]ΙΙ, σ[ταθμὸν τούτον ΗΔΔΔΓΙΙ· στέφανος χρυσ]ôς, σταθμὸν τ-
ούτο ΔΓ⊦⊦⊦ΙΙΙ· χρυσίδε ΙΙ, σταθμὸν τούτοι[ν ΗΗ𐅄ΔΔΔΔ⊦⊦⊦ΙΙΙ· χρυσίς, σταθμὸν] τ̣αύ[τε]ς ΗΔΔΔΓ⊦⊦⊦Ι[Ι]·
χρυσίς, σταθμὸν ταύτες ΗΔΓ⊦⊦⊦⊦· στέφ[ανος χρυσôς, σταθ]μ[ὸν τούτο ΔΔΓ⊦ΙΙΙ]· ἀργυρίς, σταθμὸν
ταύτες Η𐅄ΔΔΔΔ⊦⊦· θυμιατέριον ἀργυ[ρôν, σταθμὸν τούτο Χ. ἐπέτεια ἐπεγέν]ετο· [στ]έ[φα]νος χ[ρ]-
υσôς, σταθμὸν τούτο ΧΗΗ𐅄· στέφανος χρ[υσôς, σταθμὸν τούτο . . ⊦· στέφανος] χρυσôς, σταθμὸν τ-
[ο]ύ̣το ΔΔΔΓ. *vacat*

The following were handed over by the four boards who gave their accounts from Panathenaea to Panathenaea, to the treasurers Pythodorus of Halae and his fellow officers, to whom Phormio son of Aristion of Cydathenaeum was secretary: the treasurers to whom Phormio son of Aristion of Cydathenaeum was secretary handed over to the treasurers Anaxicrates of Lamptrae and his fellow officers, to whom Euxenus son of Euphanes of Prospalta was secretary.

5 In the *hekatompedon* temple: 3 gold bowls, weight of these 2,544 dr.; a golden maiden on a *stele*, not weighed; a silver holy-water sprinkler, not weighed; 2 gold wreaths, weight of these 80 dr.; a gold wreath which Victory has, weight of this 60 dr.; 8 silver bowls; weight of these 800 dr.; silver goblet, weight of this 200 dr.; silver goblet of Zeus Polieus, weight of this 200 dr.; golden wreath, weight of this [–]3 dr. 2 ob.; gold circlet, weight of this 63 dr.; 4 gold wreaths, weight of these 135 dr. 2 ob.; gold wreath, weight of this 18 dr. 3 ob.; two gold pieces, weight of these 293 dr. 3 ob.; gold piece, weight of this 138 dr. 2 ob.; gold piece, weight of this 119 dr.; gold wreath, weight of this 26 dr. 3 ob.; silver piece, weight of this 192 dr.; silver incense-burner, weight of this 1,000 dr.

13 Additions that occurred during the year: gold wreath, weight of this 1,250 dr.; gold wreath, weight of this [–]1 dr.; gold wreath, weight of this 35 dr.

The second of the financial decrees of 434/3 (**144**. *B*. 25 sqq.) ordered the treasurers of Athena to weigh and count all the sacred treasures that had not been weighed (if of precious metal) and counted. The resulting records survive not just for the rest of the fifth century but for the whole of the fourth century, although the form that they take varied over time. The treasurers, appointed annually from Panathenaea to Panathenaea, inventoried separately the three parts of the Parthenon in which treasures were stored, the cella in which the chryselephantine statue of Athena stood (known as the *hekatompedon*—'the one hundred-foot building', a term that can also be used for the whole building, cf. Plut, *Per.* 13. iv, ἑκατόμπεδον Παρθενῶνα) (*IG* i³ 317–42), the western chamber, known as the *parthenon* (*IG* i³ 343–62), and the east porch (*pronaos*, *IG* i³ 292–316). From 405/4 the contents of the east porch—by that time reduced to a single object, a gold wreath weighing 33 dr. 3 ob.—were no longer listed. Scholars have debated whether the *opisthodomos*, whose contents were regularly inventoried down to 405/4, but irregularly thereafter, was the rear porch of the Parthenon or a separate building (see on **144**).

Our earliest surviving list for the *hekatompedon* dates from 434/3: a first stone carried lists for every year from 434/3 to 427/6 (two Panathenaic cycles) on its front, and probably from 426/5 to 423/2 (one Panathenaic cycle) on its back. The second stone, on which this list is inscribed, carried lists for the cycle 422/1 to 419/8 on its front and lists for the cycle 418/7 to 415/4 on its back (that is, one Panathenaic cycle on the front, one on the back). A third stone similarly had the records for 414/3 to 411/0 on the front, and those from 410/09 to 407/6 on its back. Two further stones probably had records for the single years 406/5 and 405/4.

The annual lists are recorded in very spare form in the fifth century. They give a minimal description of the objects together with their weight if they are made of precious metal. These are descriptions for accounting purposes, and to allow the assessment of the potential wealth contained in the dedications (cf. Thuc. II. 13. iv) ready for the eventuality that they might need to be melted down so that, when the cash resources of the temples had been loaned out (cf. **160**), the resources tied up in these dedications could be lent to the city for use—as occurred in 407 (Philoch. *FGrH* 328 F 141). Detail was needed only in order to identify the object in question, but it was important that the lists were complete, and, despite some scholarly doubts, we should assume that they were.

Occasionally, even in the fifth century, there is more detailed description or indication of the origin of the object; so the objects in the *parthenon* include, added in 427/6, a gilded ivory *aulos*-case from Methymna, a shield from Lesbos with a shield device, an Illyrian helmet from Lesbos and three Lesbian cups of silver (*IG* i³ 350. 81–4), objects which must all have been the result of the Athenian action to put down the Mytilene revolt. From the very end of the fifth century the name of the person who dedicated an object begins to be given on some occasions; one of the earliest of these is 'Thrasyllus of Euonymon: a gold half-obol and two Aeginetan staters' (first recorded in 398/7: *IG* ii² 1388. 69–70), but we also get dedications by major non-Athenians: a gold wreath which Lysander son of Aristocritus, Lacedaemonian, dedicated appears in the accounts for 401/0 (*IG* ii² 1386. 2–4: one would like to know whether this was a wreath which he had been awarded by the Athenians), a garment dedicated by the Persian satrap Pharnabazus appears in 382/1 (*IG* ii^2 1412. 11), and a gold *rhyton* and gold necklaces dedicated by Roxane the wife of Alexander the Great appear in 305/4 (*IG* ii^2 1492. 51–7). Scholars have wondered if this indicates that private dedications were simply not recorded in the fifth century, but that seems unlikely since once dedicated the status of the object was identical whoever the dedicator had been.

In the fifth century the treasures recorded in the *hekatompedon* and in the *pronaos* were entirely of precious metal, whereas those in the *parthenon* included arms and armour, couches, chairs and tables, and lyres. The furniture and musical instruments there were present in the earliest list and not added to thereafter, the additional offerings being of precious metal. This may indicate that the furniture and musical instruments were equipment used in festivals, and owned by the goddess in that sense rather than being dedications. At the end of the fifth century there was clearly a reorganisation, and in the fourth century the range of items in the *hekatompedon* becomes much greater, including items of furniture, musical instruments, items of clothing and footwear, and arms and armour, and whether any of these items was used is not clear.

The lists allow us to see not simply what got dedicated in the Parthenon but how treasures accumulated over time. In these early lists the additions each year are identified separately. The earliest inventory for the *hekatompedon* has only two of the three golden bowls listed here, the golden maiden on a *stele* and the silver holy-water sprinkler, and everything else listed here has accumulated in the course of the sixteen years since 434/3. This includes 'the gold wreath which Victory has', i.e. the wreath worn by the Victory who stood on the hand of the chryselephantine statue of Athena Parthenos: it is hard to know whether this was added to the statue in 428/7, when it first appears, or was simply first listed then by some particularly diligent treasurers. When pairs or small groups of similar items are listed together this seems to have been because they were given as a group.

The number of gifts a year recorded in the *hekatompedon* ranges between zero and four, the number of individual items between zero and eleven. The level of accretion in the accounts of the *pronaos* (which started empty in 434/3) and *parthenon* are similar. But these precious items were only a fraction of the total dedications made to Athena. The acropolis excavations revealed a great deal of ceramic material, from both before and after the Persian sack (Graef & Langlotz, *Die antiken Vasen von der Akropolis zu Athen*), and Pausanias (I. 22. viii–28. ii) gives a powerful impression of the forest of sculptures on the acropolis (with a number of the fifth-century bases he mentions identifiable among the remains: see *DAA* 459–60; Keesling, *The Votive Statues of the Athenian Acropolis*, 12–16).

The weights of some items correspond to round numbers with suspicious frequency. In particular silver bowls (*phialai*) regularly weigh 100 dr. each, but we also find here two goblets (*karchesia*) weighing 200 dr. each, and a silver incense-burner weighing 1,000 dr. It is hard to think that these had not been made to order to a particular weight, and perhaps specifically for the purpose of dedication.

Occasionally an item stands out because its weight is rather different from that of other items similarly described. One example is the gold wreath found here, added to the *hekatompedon* in this year and weighing 1,250 dr. (i.e. worth almost 3 tal.). This compares with other gold wreaths weighing 18 dr. 3 ob., 26 dr. 3 ob. or 35 dr. There is clearly something special about this wreath. In the fragmentary list for 409/8, in the place in the list in which we would expect this item to occur, there is a mention of 'cleruchs dedicated' (*IG* i^{3} 339. 13), and since it is not

---

170

Payments from the treasury of Athena, 418/7–415/4

Seven fragments of a marble *stele*, found on the Athenian acropolis, six now in the Epigraphical Museum and one (*d* = the left-hand side of ll. 63–81) in the British Museum. Phot. (without *g*) *AJA*^{2} xxxiv 1930, 126–32 figs. 1–4, and facsimile pl. I; Meritt, *AFD*, 164–9 figs. 20–4, and facsimile pl. XIII.

Developed Attic writing, inconsistent in the use of h and sometimes omitting the initial χ of χσυνάρχοντες. Lines 2–58 *stoichedon* 85 (?); 61–79 *stoichedon* 96 (?).

IG i^{2} 302 (frs. *a–e*); Meritt, *AJA*^{2} xxxiv 1930, 125–32 (adding fr. *f* = ll. 46–9 near left-hand margin); Meritt, *AFD*, 159–74; M&L 77; *IG* i^{3} 370*; *IG* i^{3} Addenda (p. 962); A. P. Matthaiou, 'Studies in Attic Inscriptions and the History of the Fifth Century BC', 188–95* (fr. *g* = ll. 18–23 at left-hand margin; there is also text on the left-hand side, which we do not reproduce here). Lines 1–33 trans. Fornara 144. See also works cited in the commentary, below.

[θεο]ί.
[Ἀθεναῖοι ἀνέλοσαν ἐπὶ Ἀντιφôντος ἄρχοντος καὶ ἐπὶ τε̑ς βολε̑ς hε̑ι —7—
πρôτος ἐγραμμαετευε. τ]αμίαι h-
[ιερôν χρεμάτον τε̑ς Ἀθεναίας Πυθόδορος Ἁλαιεὺς καὶ συνάρχοντες, hοῖς Φορμίον
Ἀριστίονος Κ]υδαθεναιε-
[ὺς ἐγραμμάτευε, παρέδομεν hελλενοταμίαις Ἐργοκλεῖ Ἀριστείδο Βεσαιεῖ καὶ
συ]νάρχοσι καὶ παρέδροις h-
[ιεροκλεῖ Ἀρχεστράτο Ἀθμονεῖ καὶ συνάρχοσι, ἐπὶ τε̑ς —6—ίδος πρότες
πρυτα]νευόσες, καὶ hεμέραι δευτ-
[έραι ——————60——————]ος τοῖς μετὰ Δεμοσθένος. ἔ-
[δοχσεν τôι δέμοι κατὰ τὸ —6—]ί̣ο̣ [φσέφισμα τὸ ἀργύριον τὸ παραδοθὲν ἀποδôναι
τὸς hελλενοταμίας καὶ [τ]-

Characters joined by an underline are compressed so that two occupy one *stoichos*. The extent of the *lacuna* after l. 38 is unknown, as is the relationship of fr. *f* to what follows, but we retain the numbering and collocation of *AFD*, which have become standard. We follow M&L and *IG* i^{3} in omitting Meritt's more speculative restorations.

5 Ἀντιοχίδος or Ἐρεχθείδος or Κεκροπίδος. 6 ἐπὶ Ἐϊόν]ος A. Boeckh, *Die Staatshaushaltung der Athener*^{3}, ii. 24–5 (and ἐπὶ Ἐϊό]νος in 15), ἐς Ἄργος Dittenberger (*SIG*^{1} 36), ἐπὶ Ἄργος Tod. 7 M&L: καὶ τôι δέμοι. .]ι̣ο̣[—9— εἶπε Meritt.

uncommon for descriptions of items to be amplified in later listings it is tempting it identify this wreath with what the cleruchs dedicated, and to see in it a sign of the windfall which the award of property in a cleruchy represented for Athenians and of the profits that accrued to individuals from the Athenian empire (cf. **172**). On a ratio of gold: silver of 14:1 (see **135**, **145**) the value of the items listed here was *c.*12 tal., of which almost three-quarters had accumulated since 434.

Gods.

2 The Athenians expended in the archonship of Antiphon [418/7] and under the council for which ——was first secretary:

2 We, the treasurers of the sacred monies of Athena Pythodorus of Halae and his colleagues, for whom Phormion son of Ariston of Cydathenaeum was secretary, handed over to the *hellenotamiai* Ergocles son of Aristides of Besa and his colleagues, and to their *paredroi* Hierocles son of Archestratus of Athmonum and his colleagues, in the prytany of ——, the first prytany, and on the – -second day – – – with Demosthenes.

6 It was resolved by the people in accordance with the decree of —— that the money handed over should be given back by (?) the *hellenotamiai* and

[ὸς παρέδρος τοῖς ταμίαις τε̑ς] θεȏ Πυθ[οδόροι Ἁλαιεῖ καὶ χσυνάρχοσι, καὶ τὸς τα]μίας τε̑ς θεȏ πάλιν παραδȏ[ν]-
[αι τοῖς hελλενοταμίαις κ]αὶ τοῖς παρέδ[ροις, τούτος δὲ δȏναι στρατεγοῖς ἐπὶ Θ]ράϊκες Εὐθυδέμοι Εὐδέμο [*v*]
[—— max. 21 ——] *vacat*
[ἐπὶ τε̑ς — 6 —ίδος πρυτα]νείας δευτέρας [πρυτανευόσες hελλενοταμίαις Ἐρ]γοκλεῖ Ἀριστείδο Βεσαιεῖ [*v*]
[—— 17 —— Αἰχ]σονεῖ καὶ συνάρχο[σι καὶ παρέδροις hιεροκλεῖ Ἀρχε[στράτο Ἀθμονεῖ καὶ συν[ά]ρχ[ο]-
[σι —— 13 ——κοστε̑]ι τε̑ς πρυτανείας, π[αρέδομεν —— 14 —— χρυσί]ο Κυζικενȏ στατε̑ρας Χ̣Χ̣Χ̣Χ̣[..]
[—— 21 ——]· ἀργύριον τούτον [γίγνεται —— 20 ——]ΙΙ. τοῦτο τὸ χρυσίον παρέδομ[ε]-
[ν τοῖς τριεράρχοις ἐπὶ Ἄ]ργος τοῖς μετὰ Δεμ[οσθένος, φσεφισαμένο τȏ δέμο τὲν] ἄδειαν. *vacat*
[ἐπὶ τε̑ς —— 14 ——]ες πρυτανευόσες, ὀ[γδόει εἰκοστε̑ι hεμέραι τε̑ς πρυ]τ̣ανείας, στρατεγοῖς παρέδομ-
[εν —— 18 ——]δει, Αὐτοκλεῖ Ἀναφλ[υστίοι —— max. 20 ——] *vacat*
ἐπὶ τ[ε̑ς Πανδιονίδος ἐνά]τες πρυτανευόσες, τ[ρίτει καὶ δεκάτει hεμέραι τε̑ς π]ρυτανείας, παρέδομεν τȏ ἐχσ-
άμο ἀργ[υρίο —— 9 ——]ν ἐλθόντος hελλενοτ[αμίαις Ἐργοκλεῖ Ἀριστείδο Βεσ]αιεῖ καὶ χσυνάρχοσι καὶ παρ-
έδροι̲ς̲ h[ελ̲λ̲]ενο[ταμιȏν hι]εροκλεῖ Ἀρχεστράτο [Ἀθμονεῖ καὶ χσυνάρχοσι καὶ στρ]ατ{ρατ}εγοῖς Νικίαι Νικεράτ-
ο Κυδαν[τ]ίδει, Κ̣α̣λ̣[λιστρ]άτοι Ἐμπέδο hοε̑θεν, Κ[—— max. 26 ——] *vacat*
κεφάλα[ι]ον ἀναλ[όματος τȏ] ἐπὶ τε̑ς
ἀρχε̑ς 𐅈𐅈Τ̣Χ̣𐅅ΗΗΗ̣[— 8 —]ΙΙ. *vacat*
Ἀθεναῖοι ἀνέλοσαν ἐ[πὶ Εὐφέμο ἄρ]χοντος καὶ [ἐπὶ τε̑ς βολε̑ς hε̑ι — 9 — πρ]ȏτος ἐγραμμάτευε. ταμίαι hιε-
ρȏν χρεμάτον τε̑ς Ἀ[θεναίας Ἀναχσίκρατες Λαμπτρεὺς καὶ χσυνάρχοντες, hοῖς] Εὔχσενος Εὐφάνος Προσπάλτ-
ιος ἐγραμμάτευε, π[αρέδομεν —— 28 —— στρατεγοῖς ἐς] τὰ ἐπὶ Θράϊκες κα[ὶ] Ῥίνονι Χ-
αρικλέος Παιανιε[ῖ, ἐπὶ τε̑ς . . . είδος — 6 — πρυτανευόσες, καὶ hεμέραι δευτέ]ραι καὶ εἰκοστε̑ι τε̑ς πρυτα-
νείας, [φ]σεφισαμέν[ο τȏ δέμο τὲν ἄδειαν, —— max. 32 ——] *vacat*
ἐπὶ τε̑ς Αἰαντίδο[ς — 6 — πρυτανευόσες παρέδομεν στρατεγοῖς ἐς Με̑λον Τεισί]αι Τεισιμάχο Κεφαλε̑θεν, *v*

11 Ἀντιοχίδος or Ἐρεχθεΐδος or Κεκροπίδος. 17 Ἀλκιβιάδει Σκαμβονί]δει Meritt, but there are other possibilities. 19 κατὰ τάχσιν] (?) *IG*, ἐς τὲν πόλι]ν (?) Matthaiou. 20 Matthaiou: [Ἀθμονεῖ . . ·hοῦτοι δὲ ἔδοσαν *IG*. 21 Κ[λεομέδει Λυκομέδος Φλυεῖ the only known general who could be restored here M&L. 26 <προέδροι>? Tod. 27 Αἰγεΐδος or Οἰνεΐδος, πρότες or τρίτες. 29 ὀγδόες or ἐνάτες.

their *paredroi* to the treasurers of the Goddess Pythodorus of Halae and his colleagues, and that the treasurers of the Goddess should hand it over again to the *hellenotamiai* and their *paredroi*, and that they should give it to the generals to Thrace Euthydemus son of Eudemus – – –

11 In the prytany of ——, the second prytany, we handed over to the *hellenotamiai* Ergocles son of Aristides of Besa, – – – of Aexone and his colleagues and to their *paredroi* Hierocles son of Archestratus of Athmonum and his colleagues, on the —— of the prytany, – – – in Cyzicene gold 4,000 + staters – – – the silver from this was – – – + 2 ob. This gold we handed over to the trierarchs to Argos with Demosthenes, the people having voted the immunity.

16 In the prytany of ——, the —— prytany, on the twenty-eighth day of the prytany, we handed over to the generals —— of ——, Autocles of Anaphlystus, – – –

18 In the prytany of Pandionis, the ninth prytany, on the thirteenth day of the prytany, we handed over the money which came from Samos to the city (?) to the *hellenotamiai* Ergocles son of Aristides of Besa and his colleagues and to the *paredroi* of the *hellenotamiai* Hierocles son of Archestratus of Athmonum and his colleagues and to the generals Nicias son of Niceratus of Cydantidae, Callistratus son of Empedus of Oe, Cleomedes son of Lycomedes of Phlya (?).

22 Total expenditure in the office 16 tal. 1,800 dr. +.

24 The Athenians expended in the archonship of Euphemus [417/6] and under the council for which —— was first secretary:

24 We the treasurers of the sacred monies of Athena Anaxicrates of Lamptrae and his colleagues, for whom Euxenus son of Euphanes of Prospalta was secretary, handed over – – – to the generals to the Thraceward region and (the *paredros*?) Rhinon son of Charicles of Paeania, in the prytany of ——, the —— prytany, and on the twenty-second day of the prytany, the people having voted the immunity, – – –

29 In the prytany of Aiantis, the —— prytany, we handed over to the generals to Melos Teisias son

Κλεομέδει Λυκο[μέδος Φλυεῖ, —— 18 —— τε̑ς πρυτανείας, φσεφισαμέν]ο
τὸ δέμο τὲν ἄδειαν, Δ. *vvvv*
ἐπὶ τε̑ς Ἀντιοχί[δος -2/3-άτες πρυτανευόσες hελλενοταμίαις παρέδομεν —8/7—]οι
Α[ὐρ]ίδει, Τιμάρχοι Παλ-
λενεῖ καὶ στρα[τεγοῖς ἐς Με̑λον Τεισίαι Τεισιμάχο Κεφαλε̑θεν, Κλεομέδει
Λυκομέδ]ος Φλυεῖ, τρίτει καὶ δεκ-
άτ̣ε̣[ι τε̑]ς [πρυτανείας, φσεφισαμένο τὸ δέμο τὲν ἄδειαν, —— max. 22 ——] *vacat*
[κεφάλαιον ἀναλόματος τὸ ἐ]πὶ τε̑ς
[ἀρχε̑ς - - - - - - - - - - - - - - - - -] *vacat*
[Ἀθεναῖοι ἀνέλοσαν ἐπὶ Ἀριμνέστο ἄρχοντος καὶ ἐπὶ τε̑ς βολε̑ς hε̑ι Ἀρ—6— προ̑τος]
ἐγραμμάτευε· ταμίαι [h]-
[ιερο̂ν χρεμάτον τε̑ς Ἀθεναίας Δεχσίθεος . . . άσιος καὶ χσυνάρχοντες, hοῖς
Λυσικλε̑ς Δ]ρακοντίδο Βατε̑θ[εν]
[ἐγραμμάτευε —— 61 ——] Παλλενεῖ [—5—]

lacuna of unknown length

[—— 13 ——]ΔΔ. *v* [- -]
[ἐπὶ τε̑ς Κεκρο]πίδος [—— 69 ——]
[—— 11 ——]ονει[—— 45 ——]οι [- - - - - - - - - - - - -]
[ἐπὶ τε̑ς Κεκροπ]ίδος [—— 37 —— hεμέραι] τε̑ς
πρυτανεία[ς, στρατε]γο[ῖς Ἀλ]-
[κβιάδει Κλειν]ί[ο Σκαμβονίδει, Λαμάχοι Χσενοφάνος hοε̑θεν, Νικίαι Ν]ικεράτο
Κυδαντίδει καὶ παρέδρο[ις]
[—— 55 ——]ΗΗΗ. *vacat*
[ἐπὶ τε̑ς —— 36 —— hεμέραι, στρ]ατεγοῖς ἐς Σικελίαν
Ἀλκιβιάδει, Λαμάχο[ι],
[Νικίαι καὶ —— 38 —— Ἀντ]ιμάχοι hερμείοι Δ[Δ]Δ.
vacat
[ἐπὶ τε̑ς —— 36 —— hεμέρα]ι, στρατεγοῖς ἐς Σικελ[ί]αν
Ἀλκιβιάδει, Λαμάχοι,
[Νικίαι καὶ —— 38 ——] Ἀντιμάχοι hερμείοι
ΔΤΤΤΤΧ[.]ΗΗΗ. *vacat*
[ἐπὶ τε̑ς —— 36 —— hεμέρ]αι, στρατεγοῖς ἐς Σικελίαν
Ἀλκιβιάδει, Λαμάχο[ι],
[Νικίαι καὶ —— 38 ——] Ἀντιμάχοι hερμείοι χρυσίο
Κυ[ζ]ικενο̂ στατε̑ρ-
[ας —— 44 ——]ΗΗΗIIIC. *vacat*
[κεφάλαιον ἀναλόμα]τος τὸ ἐπὶ τε̑ς

31 ἐνάτες or δεκάτες. 37 Φυλάσιος (Meritt, M&L) or Θριάσιος.

of Teisimachus of Cephale, Cleomedes son of Lycomedes of Phlya, on the – – – of the prytany, the people having voted the immunity, 10 tal.

31 In the prytany of Antiochis, the —— prytany, we handed over to the *hellenotamiai* —— of Auridae, Timarchus of Pallene, and to (*or* for) the generals to Melos Teisias son of Teisimachus of Cephale, Cleomedes son of Lycomedes of Phlya, on the thirteenth of the prytany, the people having voted the immunity, – – –

34 Total expenditure in the office – – –

36 The Athenians expended in the archonship of Arimnestus [416/5] and under the council for which Ar— was first secretary:

36 We the treasurers of the sacred monies of Athena Dexitheus of (Phlya *or* Thria) and his colleagues, for whom Lysicles son of Dracontides of Bate was secretary – – – of Pallene – – –

lacuna

46 + 20 dr. – – – in the prytany of Cecropis – – –

49 In the prytany of Cecropis – – – day of the prytany, to the generals Alcibiades son of Cleinias of Scambonidae, Lamachus son of Xenophanes of Oe, Nicias son of Niceratus of Cydantidae and the *paredroi* – – – + 3 dr. 1 ob.

52 In the – – – day, to the generals to Sicily Alcibiades, Lamachus, Nicias and – – – Antimachus of Hermus 30 tal.

54 In the – – – day, to the generals to Sicily Alcibiades, Lamachus, Nicias and – – – Antimachus of Hermus 14 tal. 1,400 dr. *minimum*/2,300 dr. *maximum.*

56 In the – – – day, to the generals to Sicily Alcibiades, Lamachus, Nicias and – – – Antimachus of Hermus, in Cyzicene gold – – – staters – – – + 3 dr. 3½ ob.

59 Total expenditure in the office – – – + 16 dr. 4 ob.

[ἀρχε͂ς —— 11 ——]ΔΓ⊢IIII. *vacat*
[Ἀθεναῖοι ἀνέλοσαν ἐπὶ Χαρίο ἄρχοντος καὶ ἐπὶ τε͂ς βολε͂ς hε͂ι —5—]ίδες προ͂τος ἐγραμμάτευε. ταμίαι hιερο͂ν χρεμάτον *v*
[τε͂ς Ἀθεναίας Λεοχάρες Ἀλοπεκειεὺς καὶ χσυνάρχοντες, hοῖς Τελέα]ς Τελενίκο Περγασε͂θεν ἐγραμμάτευε, παρέδοσαν στρ-
[α]τεγοῖς Τελεφόνοι [—5— καὶ συνάρχοσι καὶ hελλενοταμίαι καὶ] παρέδροι Φερεκλείδει Πειραιεῖ, φσεφισάμενο το͂ δέμ-
[ο] τὲν ἄδειαν, ἐπὶ τε͂ς Αἰαντίδος τρί[τες πρυτανευόσες, —6— hεμ]έραι τε͂ς πρυτανείας, Δ̣ΤΧΧΧ𐅆[Η]Η𐅄ΔΔΔΓ⊢⊢I̲I̲I̲I̲Ϲ τε, καὶ χρυσίο
Κυζικενο͂ ΗΗΔ̣Δ̣Δ̣Δ̣ΓΣΣΣ· τιμὲ τούτον γίγν[εται —— max. 16 ——] *vacat*
hελλενοταμίαις καὶ παρέδροις ἐδανεισά[μεν —— 15 ——] Ἀριστοκράτει Εὐονυμεῖ καὶ χσυνάρχοσι 𐅈ΤΤΤΤ· οὗτοι δ-
ὲ ἔδοσαν ἀθλοθέταις ἐς Παναθέναια Ἀμέμπτο[ι —— 11 —— καὶ] χσυνάρχοσι, ἐπὶ τε͂ς Ἐρεχθείδος δευτέρας πρυτανευόσε-
ς, εἰκοστε͂ι hεμέραι τε͂ς πρυτανείας. *vacat*
ἐπὶ τε͂ς Κεκροπίδος τετάρτες πρυτανευόσες, hέ[κτει hεμέραι τ]ε͂ς πρυτανείας, hελλενοταμίαις καὶ παρέδροις Ἀριστοκρ-
άτει Εὐονυμεῖ καὶ χσυνάρχοσι στρατιόταις ἐ[μ Μελοι —7—]ΔΔ. *vacat*
ἐπὶ τε͂ς Ἀντιοχίδος ὀγδόες πρυτανευόσες, δεκ[άτει hεμέραι τε͂ς] πρυτανείας, hελλενοταμίαις καὶ παρέδροις Ἀριστοκρ[ά]-
τει Εὐονυμεῖ καὶ χσυνάρχοσι στρατιόταις ἐμ Μ[ελοι —9—] 𐅄̣Δ̣. *vacat*
ἐπὶ τε͂ς Ἀντιοχίδος ὀγδόες πρυτανευόσες, τρίτε[ι hεμέραι τε͂ς πρυ]τανείας, hελλενοταμίαις καὶ παρέδροις Ἀριστοκρ[άτ]-
ει Εὐονυμεῖ καὶ χσυνάρχοσι ΗΗΗΗ· οὗτοι δ’ ἔδοσαν [τε͂ι ἐν Σικελίαι σ]τρατίαι. *vacat*
ἐπὶ τε͂ς Ἀντιοχίδος ὀγδόες πρυτανευόσες, εἰκοσ[τε͂ι hεμέραι τε͂ς πρ]υτανείας, hελλενοταμίαις καὶ παρέδροις Ἀριστοκρ[ά]-
τει Εὐονυμεῖ καὶ χσυνάρχοσι ἐς τὰ<ς> ναῦς τὰς ἐς Σι[κελίαν διακομιόσα]ς τὰ χρέματα ΤΤΤΤΧΧ.
ἐπὶ τε͂ς Ἀντιοχίδος ὀγδόες πρυτανευόσες, δευτέ[ραι hεμέραι τε͂ς πρυτα]νεία[ς], hελλενοταμίαις καὶ παρέδροι Φιλομέ[λοι Μ]-
αραθονίοι καὶ στρατεγο͂ι ἐν τo͂ι Θερμαίοι κόλπο[ι —— 18 ——, καὶ τ]ε͂ι αὐτε͂ι hεμέραι hελλενοταμίαι κ[αὶ παρέ]-
δροι Φιλομέλοι Μαραθονίοι καὶ στρατεγο͂ι ἐν Ἐφ[—— max. 27 ——] *vacat*
κεφάλαιον ανα[λόματος τ]ο͂ ἐπὶ τ[ε͂ς]
ἀρχε͂ς ΗΗΗ𐅈ΤΤΤ[- -]

76 the stone omits σ. διακομιόσας Kirchhoff, cf. Dover, *HCT* iv. 266: ἐσκομισάσας (supposing that the ships had returned) Meritt, M&L. 78 hελλενοταμίαι<ς>? Rhodes. 79 Ἐφ[έσοι Meritt, *Hesp.* v 1936, 382, Ἐφ[αιστίαι A. P. Matthaiou, *hόρος* vii 1989, 122–3 (*SEG* xxxix 22), the only other city in *Inventory* beginning Εφ- is Ephyra, in Epirus.

61 The Athenians expended in the archonship of Charias [415/4] and under the council for which —ides was first secretary:

62 The treasurers of the sacred monies of Athena Leochares of Alopece and his colleagues, for whom Teleas son of Telenicus of Pergase was secretary, gave to the generals Telephonus – – – and his colleagues and to the *hellenotamiai* and their *paredros* Pherecleides of Piraeus, the people having voted the immunity, in the prytany of Aiantis, the third prytany, on the —— day of the prytany, 11 tal. 3,787 dr. 4½ ob., and in Cyzicene gold 248 staters: the value of this is – – –

66 We lent to the *hellenotamiai* and their *paredroi* – – – Aristocrates of Euonymum and his colleagues 9 tal.: they gave it to the *athlothetai* for the Panathenaea – – – and his colleagues, in the prytany of Erechtheis, the second prytany, on the twentieth day of the prytany.

69 In the prytany of Cecropis, the fourth prytany, on the sixth day of the prytany, to the *hellenotamiai* and their *paredroi* Aristocrates of Euonymum and his colleagues for the soldiers in Melos – – – + 20 dr.

71 In the prytany of Antiochis, the eighth prytany, on the tenth day of the prytany, to the *hellenotamiai* and their *paredroi* Aristocrates of Euonymum and his colleagues for the soldiers in Melos – – – + 60 dr.

73 In the prytany of Antiochis, the eighth prytany, on the third day of the prytany, to the *hellenotamiai* and their *paredroi* Aristocrates of Euonymum and his colleagues 300 tal. They gave it to the force in Sicily.

75 In the prytany of Antiochis, the eighth prytany, on the twentieth day of the prytany, to the *hellenotamiai* and their *paredroi* Aristocrates of Euonymum and his colleagues for the ships to take (?) the money to Sicily 4 tal. 2,000 dr.

77 In the prytany of Antiochis, the eighth prytany, on the second day of the prytany, to the *hellenotamiai* and their *paredros* Philomelus of Marathon and the general in the Thermaic Gulf – – –

78 and on the same day to the *hellenotamiai*(*s*?) and the *paredros* Philomelus of Marathon and the general in Eph— – – –

80 Total expenditure in the office 353 tal. +.

Whereas **160** was an account of all loans from the sacred treasuries and the interest due on them, this and other documents (cf. in this collection **174**, **180**; also **148**) list simply payments from the treasury of Athena, without mentioning interest, and if payments continued to be made from the treasury of the Other Gods no record of them has survived. Although the verb 'lend' is used only once here (ἐδανείσα[μεν, 66), and not at all in the other records of payments from the sacred treasuries, it is likely that as before the Peace of Nicias all these payments were technically loans. The exceptional case is a payment for the Panathenaea (66–8), and the fact that this is a loan indicates that the ultimate responsibility for funding Athena's festival lay not with Athena's treasury but with the state treasury (cf. D. M. Lewis, *Hesperia* xviii 1959, 246 = his *Selected Papers in Greek and Near Eastern History*, 261). There have been attempts to explain why this payment uniquely is specified as a loan, but we are inclined to agree with E. Meyer that this is merely a verbal difference (*Forschungen zur alten Geschichte*, ii . 135 n. 1).[1] *Ath. Pol.* 60. i mentions the *athlothetai* as quadrennial officials, concerned with the Great Panathenaea (cf. Rhodes, *Comm. Ath. Pol.*, 669–70, but see also on **180**), so J. A. Davison saw this as an advance payment for the next Great Panathenaea (*JHS* lviii 1958, 31–3, cf. R. Develin, *ZPE* lvii 1984, 136–7). There are further such payments in the second prytany of 4<u>10</u>/09 ('handed over for the Great Panathenaea', **180**. 5–6) and apparently in Elaphebolion [ix] or Munychion [x] of a later year (in the fragmentary *IG* i^3 378. 14). Meritt thought the payments were before the festival of the year in question (lastly *PAPS* cxxii 1978, 200–2), while Pritchett thought they were after the festival of the year in question, to make good a deficit (*Historia* xxvi 1977, 298–302). We think that Davison could be right to see the payments as advance payments for the next Great Panathenaea; in any case we do not think this entry can be exploited to yield conclusions about the calendar.

This is the only document which includes in some entries a reference to a vote of *adeia* (immunity: 15, 28, 30, [33], 63–4), which was required for expenditure over 10,000 dr. by **144**. *B.* 12–19: we do not know why it appears here but not elsewhere; **160** is a different kind of document, and of the others earlier than this **148** is the only one of which we can be confident that it is absent; we do not believe that it justifies a late date for **144**.

Except at l. 50 here, in this and later accounts the *paredroi* (assistants: cf. other officials' *paredroi* in *Ath. Pol.* 48. iv, 56. i) seem regularly to be attached to the *hellenotamiai*. This document is inconsistent in its listing of *hellenotamiai*, *paredroi* and the ultimate recipients of the money, and it is possible that in 50 the text is over-condensed and should have mentioned the *hellenotamiai* and their *paredroi*; but cf. 26, where Tod thought that Rhinon was a *paredros*.

Some of the payments appear to be for campaigns not mentioned by Thucydides. The first payment mentioned (2–10) was originally intended for Demosthenes, but was transferred to Euthydemus for operations in the north. The punctilious

[1] Lewis, *loc. cit.*., suggested that it was because there was no precedent for this payment; W. E. Thompson, *A. Class.* xxii 1979, 150–1, that it was a matter of formal correctness, the money having to be 'lent' because a vote of immunity had not been obtained.

observance of correct procedure, in that the money was not transferred directly but returned to the *hellenotamiai* and reissued, is notable (Thompson, *A. Class.* xxii 1979, 149). For Cyzicene 'gold' staters, are in fact electrum (13–14, 64–5), cf. **145**. In 17 Alcibiades is a possible but by no means a necessary restoration, so the inference that he was elected general at a by-election in 418/7 (Wade-Gery, *CQ* xxiv 1930, 34 n. 2) is insecure. The payment to Nicias and colleagues (18–21) was presumably for his campaign in the north (Thuc. v. 83. iv); for payments from Samos cf. **138**, **152** (and on the spelling ἐχσάμο see M. N. Tod, *AJP* lxvii 1946, 329–33, and cf. **180**. 20, 34, and **192**. *c.* 5). The account for 417/6 includes two payments for the campaign against Melos (29–33: cf. Thuc. v. 84).

The poorly preserved account for 416/5 included four payments for the Sicilian expedition (49–58), and may but need not have included more: none of them can be dated within the year (so they do not help us to establish dates for events in Athens); the two payments for which the figures are almost complete were small, and the other two, of very un-round sums, are likely to have been very small. In 415/4, when large sums will have been needed for Sicily, the amount provided by Athena was 304$^1/_3$ talents (73–6). Clearly most of the money spent on the expedition was provided in other ways (see **171**; and cf. Ferguson, *The Treasurers of Athena*, 159–62, and more recently Samons, *Empire of the Owl*, 236–40, Kallet, *Money and the Corrosion of Power in Thucydides*, 193–5).

Under 415/4 the record departs from chronological order to group payments by recipient. For the payment for the Panathenaea (66–8) cf. above. Two payments are credibly restored as intended for soldiers (still) in Melos, captured in Thucydides' winter 416/5, in the fourth and the eighth prytanies. Also in the eighth prytany, 300 tal. were provided for Sicily, and seventeen days later 4 tal. 2,000 dr. for the ships to take the money there (73–6). The payment for the Thermaic Gulf (77–8) may have been for the force which attacked Amphipolis (Thuc. vii. 9). For the last payment (78–9) Meritt restored Ephesus, and A. Andrewes linked this with Athens' support for the Persian rebels Pissuthnes and Amorges (*Historia* x 1961, 5); Matthaiou urges that Hephaestia on Lemnos is a likelier restoration; we see no way of deciding between the two.

How much of the debt accumulated by the Peace of Nicias had been repaid we do not know (cf. on **160**); in this account the sums preserved are modest, but it does not appear either that all Athens' campaigning expenses were funded in this way or that the sacred treasuries were used only as a last resort. References to Sicily in l. 10 and to Demosthenes in 12–13 allow *IG* i^3 371 to be identified as the account for 414/3 (cf. introductory rubric of **175**): no figures are preserved, but 120 tal., the probable figure in Thuc. vii. 16. ii for the amount sent from Athens to Sicily at the winter solstice, is restored in l. 8.

The fact that fr. *g* has text on the left-hand side also will require a reconsideration of the distribution across *stelai* of these financial records (cf. Matthaiou, 'Studies in Attic Inscriptions and the History of the Fifth Century BC', 191–5, *The Athenian Empire on Stone Revisited*, 16.)

171

Athenian decrees relating to the Sicilian expedition, 415

Eight fragments probably from two marble *stelai* (or one *stele* thicker at the bottom, fr. *g*, than at the top, fr. *c*); found on the Athenian acropolis; now in Epigraphical Museum. The top of *a*, the right of *b*, *f* and *g*, and the left margin of *c* are preserved.

Attic letters, *stoichedon* (length of line unknown). The aspirate is rarely omitted.

M&L 78*; Dover, *HCT* iv. 225–7; *IG* i³ 93. Trans. Fornara 146 (frs. *b*, *c*, *d* and *g* only). See also Samons, *Empire of the Owl*, 167, 239–40; Kallet, *Money and the Corrosion of Power in Thucydides*, 184–93.

First stele *(?)*

Fragment *b*

[- - - - - - - - - - - - - - - -]ν̣αν[. . . .]ν[— 10 —]νι̣[. . . .]ο̣ι̣ο[— 5 —]
[- - - διαχεροτονε̂σαι τὸν δε̂μ]ον αὐτ̣ί̣κ̣α μάλα εἴτε δοκε̂ι hένα στρατ[εγ]-
[ὸν - - - - - - - - - - - - - - - - h]ελέσθαι τύχει ἀγαθε̂ι νυνὶ hοίτινε[ς] α̣-
[- - - - - - - - - - - - - - - -]τ̣ο̣[.] τὸς πολεμίος hος ἂν δύνονται πλει-
[στ- - - - - - - - - - - - - - - - - -]ο̣σθον δὲ καὶ τὸν χσυμμάχον hοποσ̣-
[- π]όλες ἐς τὲμ βολὲν τὲν Ἀθεναίο[ν]
[- h]ε̣χσέκοντα νεο̂ν hόταμπ̣ε̣ρ [. . .]
[- -]αις ἂμ βόλοντ[αι — 9 —]
[- -]λλ̣ο[— 16 —]
- -

Fragment *c*

[. . .] βολὲν καθότι ἄριστα κ̣[- - - - - - - - - - - - ἐά]-
ν τε ἀπὸ το̂ τιμέματος δοκε̂ι [- - - - - - - - - - - - ἐάν]
τε τὲμ πόλιν ἀναλο̂ν hόσον α[- - - - - - - - - - - - - τὰ]-
ς hεχσέκοντα ναῦς ἐὰμ προσ[- - - - - - - - - - - - - - -]
μενον ἐ͂ι ἐσφέρεν hόταν δεε[- - - - - - - - - - - - - ἐκκ]-
λεσίαν ποιεσάντον δέκα hε[μερο̂ν - - - - - - - - - - - π]-
ερὶ ἄλλο μεδενὸς πρότερον [- - - - - - - - - - - - - - -]
ε ἐκκλεσίαν ποιε̂ν τὸς πρυτ[άνες - - - - - - - - - - - - -]
αι τοῖς στρατεγοῖς το̂ν νεο̂ν [- - - - - - - - - - - - - - - -]
οις· περὶ δὲ το̂ ἔκπλο το̂ν νεο̂ν [- - - - - - - - - - - - - ἐ]-
πανορθο̂σθαι ἐν τοῖ δέμοι hο[- - - - - - - - - - - - - - - ἐ]-
κκλεσίαν ποιόντον hόταν κε[- - - - - - - - - - - - - - - - -]
ον καὶ τε̂ς ἄλλες hυπερεσίας [- - - - - - - - - - - - - - - -]
καὶ ἀργύριο ἐς καλλιέρεσιν [- - - - - - - - - - - - - - - - -]
[.] hεχσ̣ακοσίον [καὶ] χιλίον [- - - - - - - - - - - - - - - -]
- -

b. 3 εἴτε πλείος or εἴτε τρε̂ς seems inevitable, M&L.

First stele *(?)*

Fragment *b*

– – – the people are to vote immediately whether they resolve that one general – – – to choose with good fortune now who – – – the enemy who are most capable – – – let also as many of the allies – – – cities to the Athenian council – – – of sixty ships whensoever – – – they may wish – – –

Fragment *c*

– – – the council just as best – – – and if it resolves from the assessment – – – and if the city spend as much as – – – the sixty ships if – – – it has been —ed to levy an *eisphora* whenever it is necessary – – – let them call an assembly within ten days – – – about nothing else prior – – – the *prytaneis* are to make an assembly – – – to the generals of the ships – – – And as for the sailing out of the ships – – – be set straight among the people – – – let them make an assembly whenever – – – and the rest of the ships' officers – – – and money for auspicious sacrifice – – – 1,600 – – –

Second stele *(?)*

Fragment *a*

[ἔδοχσεν τε͂ι βολε͂ι καὶ το͂ι δ]ẹ́μοị [- - - - - - - - - - - - - - - - - -]
[—— 20 —— εἶ]πε· τύχε[ι ἀγαθε͂ι - - - - - - - - - - - - -]
[—— 22 ——]μένας μισ[θ- - - - - - - - - - - - - - - - -]
[—— 21 —— τ]ετταράκον[τα - - - - - - - - - - - - - - -]
[—— 19 —— πελ]ταστᾶις χρ[- - - - - - - - - - - - - - - -]
[—— 22 —— τ]οχσότας π[- - - - - - - - - - - - - - - -]
[—— 23 ——]δεει ἐκ το[- - - - - - - - - - - - - - - - -]
[—— 21 —— τ]έτταρας ὀβο[λὸς - - - - - - - - - - - - - -]
[—— 17 —— κυβε]ρνέτας δὲ καὶ [- - - - - - - - - - - - - -]
[—— 19 —— τ]αμίαν δὲ χσυμπ[- - - - - - - - - - - - - -]
[—— 20 ——] hε βολὲ hόταμ μẹ[- - - - - - - - - - - - - -]
[—— 16 —— τοῖ]ς τριεράρχοις κα[- - - - - - - - - - - - - - - -]
[—— 21 ——] το͂μ πολεμίον λ̣[- - - - - - - - - - - - - - - -]
[—— 21 ——]λ̣λον hότι αν[- - - - - - - - - - - - - - - - - -]
- -

Fragments *d* and *g*

[- -]ιọ[— 5 —]
[- -]σοτοντ[.]
[- - - - - - - - - - -]α̣ι̣ ἒ φρορο͂σι τὲ[μ πόλιν ἒ τὲ]ν χόραν τ-
[- - - - - - - - - - -]ν hὸς ἂν μὲ περιπο[λε͂ι μεδὲ μ]ισθοφορε͂-
[ι - - - - - - - - - - -]το πλὲν hοπόσοις [— 7 — h]ε βολὲ καὶ
[- - - - - - - - - - - ἔ]νοχον ε͂ναι ζεμία[ι — 6 —]αι μέτε τον
[- - - - - - - - - - -πρ]υτάνες· λῦσαι δὲ [— 7 —]αι τὸ φσέφι-
[σμα - - - - - - - - - τ]ο͂ ἔκπλο το͂ν ἐχσέ[κοντα νεο͂]ν hέος ἂν ḥ-
[- - - - - - - - - - - ἐ]π' ἄλλο ἔργον με[δ' ἐπ' ἄλλεν σ]τρατιὰν
[- - - - - - - - - - -τ]ρισχιλίον· ἐ[ὰν δέ τιν εἴπει] ἒ ἐπιφσ-
[εφίσει - - - - - - - - - -]ς ἐχσαιρ[—— 14 ——]ον μ̣[.]
[- - - - - - - - - - - - - -]ογ̣ι̣ṭ [—— 20 ——]
- -

Unknown stele

Fragment *e*

]ΙΙΙΟΣ[
]ṭε͂ι Ἀθενᾶι κ[
στρα]τιόταις διανε[μ
]ẹναι το͂ν νεο͂ν [
]ρχ̣σοσι[
- - - - - - - - - - - -

Second stele (?)

Fragment *a*

Resolved by the council and people – – – proposed: with good fortune – – – pay – – – forty – – – light-armed troops – – – archers – – – from the – – – four obols – – – steersmen – – – and the treasurer all – – – the council whenever – – – to the trierarchs – – – the enemy – – – that – – –

Fragments *d* and *g*

– – – or guard the city or the countryside – – – whoever does not serve on patrol or for pay – – – except for as many as – – – the council and – – – be liable for punishment – – – nor of the – – – *prytaneis*. And to repeal – – – the decree – – – of the sailing out of the sixty ships until – – – for any other task nor for another campaign – – – three thousand. If someone proposes or puts to the vote – – –

Either stele

Fragment *e*

– – – to Athena – – – distribute to the soldiers – – – of the ships – – – officers – – –

Fragment *f*

]τ̣εν̣κ̣[—7—]
hεκ]ατὸν τριέρε̣[ς .]
] πολέμιοι hότι
]α̣στέσασθαι το
ἐπιτ]έδιον ἐ̑ναι h-
]αμ ποι χρεσ-
]ς ναυσὶν
πρυ]τανε-
]ντ-
- - - - - - - -

Fragment *h*

]αν[
]ι̣τοι[
]ος χσυμμάχος α[
]ς κ[αὶ] τομ φορον [
]σθαι τ[
]ο̣ε̣[
- - - - - - - -

Not every decision of the Athenian people was inscribed. Normally those inscribed were decisions whose effect was ongoing—a treaty, a regulation, a decision about worship of the gods. Decisions which led to immediate action were not normally inscribed, though those actions might result in records elsewhere if they occasioned financial outlay. We therefore have no inscribed record of decisions to go to war, and major debates in Thucydides, such as that about how to punish the Mytilenaeans when their revolt had been suppressed, leave no epigraphic trace.

These fragments, however, clearly relate to a decision to appoint generals and institute military activity. So why were they inscribed? The military activity is substantial, raising the issue of whether one or more generals should be in charge and involving the allies, a large fleet (sixty ships are mentioned and then 100), light-armed troops and archers. Special financial arrangements are also in question—an *eisphora* (exceptional property tax: see **144** and Thuc. III. 19. i) and something to do with the tribute. Sacrifices are ordained. Furthermore the earlier part of the decree appears to refer forward from the assembly meeting at which it was passed to a further assembly meeting within ten days. None of these factors individually will have dictated inscription, but together with them there may have been political motives too (see below).

The decision to launch a military expedition on this scale during the Peloponnesian war cannot have escaped the attention of Thucydides (for expeditions involving sixty ships during the Peloponnesian War see III. 80. ii, IV. 53. i), and so we would expect to be able to match the expedition described here to an expedition described

Fragment *f*

– – – hundred triremes – – – enemy that – – –
establish – – – to be necessary – – – to the ships
– – – *prytaneis* – – –

Fragment *h*

– – – allies – – – and the tribute – – –

---

by Thucydides. One expedition offers itself: the expedition against Sicily launched in 415. Thucydides tells us that after several previous discussions of the requests of Egesta's envoys (VI. 6. iii), two meetings of the assembly were needed to finalise the decision (meetings four days apart, VI. 8. iii, which is consonant with the 'within ten days' prescribed on the stone). Further, it is clear from his account that there was indeed an issue over who should be put in command (implied by Alcibiades' speech, VI. 17. i), that first sixty (VI. 8. ii) and then 100 ships (VI. 25) were voted, that the allies were summoned (VI. 25–6), that light-armed troops were included (VI. 25) and that there were elaborate religious rituals before the expedition departed (VI. 32). The fit between these fragments and Thucydides' text is substantial.

Despite this, some scholars have been doubtful, worried about points at which Thucydides seems to imply a rather different picture (especially Kallet, 184–93). Thucydides' brief description of the first assembly says nothing about the Athenians seeking help from their allies (as seems to be in question in *a.* 5–6), and the only financial matter that he mentions is the Athenian satisfaction that Egesta has significant monetary resources. But the description that he gives of the vote to have three named generals, and to make the aim of the expedition not simply to help Egesta against Selinus but also to restore Leontini and settle matters in Sicily generally, implies that there was a detailed discussion covering potential activity which the Athenians could not expect to have been bankrolled by Egesta. It is therefore not surprising to find possible sources of finance being considered, and there seems no significant conflict here between prudent financial planning (*eisphora* 'if needed') and Thucydides' indication that the city had just recovered from plague and the long war and that manpower and capital were again accumulating (VI. 26. ii). Certainly Nicias is able to present that recovery as precarious: 'we must remember that it is only recently that we have gained a little respite from the great plague and war, so as to be increased in funds and manpower' (VI. 12. i: βραχύ τι λελωφήκαμεν is misrepresented by some translators, with Mynott talking of being 'sufficiently recovered', as well as being ignored by Thucydides in his VI. 26. ii restatement). There is nothing in fragments *b* and *c* that is seriously surprising for a decree resulting from the assembly meeting related at VI. 8. ii.

Fragments *a*, *d* and *g*, and *f* seem to relate well to the second assembly, from which the two (effectively three) speeches of Nicias and speech of Alcibiades are recorded (VI. 8. iii–26. i). It is here that light troops, as demanded by Nicias (VI. 25. ii), appear, along with reference back to prior decisions about the sending out of sixty ships and the mention of 100 ships (again as Nicias demanded and as were sent, VI. 43). That a great deal of detail is specified here does not conflict with the generals being left to decide the final size of the army (VI. 26. i), and Thucydides' claim that the popular enthusiasm for the expedition was not dampened by the fact that the preparation for it was troublesome (which is what ὀχλῶδης means at VI. 24. ii) implies that the people were prepared to spend time on the detail, rather than that they were not.

It is not clear that anything in the fragments relating to the second assembly concerns finance. Fragment *c*, we believe, relates to the first assembly, and the unplaced fragment *h*, which mentions tribute, might well relate to fragment *b*. The mention of 'three thousand' in *d/g*. 10, often taken as a reference to 3,000 talents supposedly set aside for the expedition, is more likely to relate to troop numbers (cf. Kallet, 190–1; for the number finally sent see VI. 43).

172

Confiscated property of the Hermocopidae, 414

A

Excerpt from two fragments from a *stele* of yellowish-grey marble, of which fifteen fragments survive, found in various places in Athens; now in the Epigraphical Museum and the Agora Museum. Phot. *Hesperia* xxii 1953, pls. 67–9, 72; Tracy, *Athenian Lettering of the Fifth Century BC*, 58–9.

The text was laid out in four columns (we give col. i only). There was no general heading, and the text must have been continued from another *stele*. Attic letters, partly *stoichedon*.

W. K. Pritchett, *Hesperia* xxii 1953, 225–99, xxv 1956, 276-81, xxx 1961, 23–9 (three new fragments); M&L 79. A; *IG* i³ 421*. See also Pritchett, *Hesperia* xxv 1956, 178–317; D. A. Amyx, *Hesperia* xxvii 1958, 163–310; D. M. Lewis, in *Ancient Society and Institutions . . . V. Ehrenberg*, 177–91 = his *Selected Papers in Greek and Near Eastern History*, 158–72.

One unexpected aspect of the decree stemming, as we believe, from the second assembly is the mention of garrisons for the city and countryside and service as a *peripolos*. *Peripoloi* were responsible for patrolling the frontiers, performing much the role later performed by ephebes (cf. Hornblower, *Comm. Thuc.*, on IV. 67. ii), and were based in forts close to the Attic frontier. Nothing in Thucydides leads us to expect that there was any discussion of the protection of the Athenian countryside at the second assembly, but the question may have been raised about what would happen if Athens' enemies took advantage of the absence of so large a fleet in order to attack Attica, and the provisions here will have been intended to guarantee Athenian security.

The inscription of these decisions might be best interpreted in the light of Nicias' later decision to write a letter to the Athenians, rather than trusting messengers (VII. 8. ii–iii, 10–15), because he wanted to make sure that the full force of his words was not lost in transmission. The decisions recorded here were clearly unusually contentious, and it would not be surprising if either those pressing for the expedition in the first place or those who shared Nicias' doubts wanted to get all the detail recorded and displayed so as to ensure both that there was no backsliding and, in the face of those who thought the decision hasty, that the care with which the expedition was designed was manifest. Despite claims that the content of the inscription conflicts with the tone of Thucydides, the unusual and detailed publication here might be held to support Thucydides' picture of an exceptionally involved political background.

For the assembly being asked to decide between different options compare **152**.

IG i^3 291, which lists contingents from Sicilian cities, has sometimes been associated with the Sicilian expedition, but the presence there of Rhegium, alongside Naxos and either Catane or Camarina, argues rather for an association with Athenian interventions in Sicily in 427–424, since Rhegium remained neutral in 415–413 (C. Ampolo, *PP* ccxxxii 1987, 5–11).

a			*column i*
			6 *lines lost*
	--	---	[— 6 —]ς
	--	---	[— 5 —]ε
	--	---	[παῖς Π]ẹισίστρατος Κάρ
			[κεφάλαιο]ν Ἑφαιστοδόρο
			[— 8 —]ͰͰIIIIC
			[Ἀλκιβιάδο τ]ô Κλεινίο
			[Σκαμβονίδ]ο σκεύε τάδε ἐπρά[θ]ε
	--	---	[. . . .]τια
	--	---	[χύτ]ρα χαλκε̂
	--	---	[χύτ]ρα χαλκε̂
	--	---	[χύτρ]ạ χαλκε̂
	--	---	[— 5 —]ς χαλκôς
			lacuna
b	--	[.]Δ--	[.]I---
	[I]II	ΔΓͰͰͰ	ἐπικαρπ̣ί̣[α]
			Θρίαι
	[I]II	ΔΔ	ἐπικαρπία
			Ἀθμονοῖ
			κεφάλαιον σὺν ἐπονίο[ις]
			ΧΧΧΧ𐅅ΗΗΔΔͰͰͰIIIII
			Πολυστράτο τô Διο[δόρο]
			Ἀγκυλε̂θεν
	ͰͰI	ΗΗͰͰ	Πίστος
	[Ͱ]	ΔΔΔͰͰ	ἐπικαρπία Ἀγ-
			κυλε̂σι
			κεφάλαιον σὺν ἐπονίο[ις]
			ΗΗΔΔΔΔΓͰͰI
			Κεφισοδόρο μετοίκο ἐμ Περα[ιεῖ οἰκôντος]
	ͰͰ	Η𐅄ΔΓ	Θρᾶιττα
	ͰIII	ΗΔΔΔΓ	Θρᾶιττα
	[Ͱ]Ͱ	Η𐅄ΔΔ	Θρᾶιχς
	ͰͰIII	ΗΗΔΔΔΔ	Σύρος
	[Ͱ]III	ΗΓ	Κάρ
	ͰͰ	Η𐅄ΔͰ	hιλλυριός
	ͰͰIII	ΗΗΔΔ	Θρᾶιττα
	ͰIỊ	ΗΔΓ	Θρᾶιχς
	ͰIII	ΗΔΔΔΔͰͰͰͰ	Σκύθες
	ͰIII	ΗΔΔͰ	hιλλυριός
	ͰͰ	Η𐅄ͰͰͰ	Κόλχος

29 the sales-tax figure is certain, but is an overcharge (Pritchett, *Hesperia* xxii 1953, 229, 246).

column i

6 *lines lost*

– –	– – –	– – –
– –	– – –	– – –
		Slave boy, Pisistratus, Carian.
		Total of Hephaestodorus:
		>2 dr. 4½ ob.
		Of Alcibiades son of Cleinias
		of Scambonidae these items of equipment were sold:
		– – –
		bronze pot
		bronze pot
		bronze pot
		bronze —
		lacuna
– –	>10 dr.	– – –
3 ob.	18 dr.	crops
		at Thria
3 ob.	20 dr.	crops
		at Athmonum
		Total, with sales tax:
		4,723 dr. 5 ob.
		Of Polystratus son of Diodorus
		from Ancyle
2 dr. 1 ob	202 dr.	Pistus
1 dr.	42 dr.	crops at
		Ancyle
		Total with sales tax:
		247 dr. 1 ob.
		Of Cephisodorus, metic living in Piraeus
2 dr.	165 dr.	Thracian woman
1 dr. 3 ob.	135 dr.	Thracian woman
2 dr.	170 dr.	Thracian man
2 dr. 3 ob.	240 dr.	Syrian man
1 dr. 3 ob.	105 dr.	Carian man
2 dr.	161 dr.	Illyrian man
2 dr. 3 ob.	220 dr.	Thracian woman
1 dr. 3 ob.	115 dr.	Thracian man
1 dr. 3 ob.	144 dr.	Scythian man
1 dr. 3 ob.	121 dr.	Illyrian man
2 dr.	153 dr.	Colchian man

ⱵⱵ Η𐅄ΔΔⱵⱵⱵⱵ Κὰρ παῖς
Ⱶ 𐅄ΔΔⱵⱵ Καρικὸν παιδίον
[Ⱶ]ⱵⱵΙ ΗΗΗⱵ Σύρος
[Ⱶ] Η𐅄̣Ⱶ Μελιττ[ενός *or* ενέ]
Ⱶ 𐅄ΔΔΔΓ[. .]Ι̣ Λυδέ
– –

B

One of four fragments of white marble found in the Athenian agora. Phot. *Hesperia* xxii 1953, 77; Tracy, *Athenian Lettering of the Fifth Century BC*, 65 fig. 10.

The text was laid out in three columns (we give part of col. ii only). Attic letters. Not *stoichedon*.

W. K. Pritchett, *Hesperia* xxii 1953, 264–8 (*SEG* xiii 16); *IG* i³ 425*.

– – – – – – – – – –
– – – – – σι̣π̣[ύε]
– – – – – ἐπίκ̣[λιντρον]
– – – – – κλῖναι ΙΙΙΙ
– – –ΔⱵ κιβοτὸς θυριδοτέ
– – – – – κριθôν φορμοί ΔΓΙ
– – –ⱵⱵⱵ κριθôν φορμοί ΔΓ
– – – – – φλιαί ΓΙ
– – – –ν δέμαρχος ἀπ̣έγραφε
– – – –κ̣ον· κριθôν φιδάκνι[α – – –]
– – – – – ἕτερα ΔΙ ἐμίσε{ι}α
[Ἀθμονέ]ο̣ν δέμαρχος ἀπ̣[έγραφε]
[ἐν τôι χ]ορίοι τôι Ἀθμον[οῖ]·
[– – – χά]ρακες ὑπὸ ταῖς ἀ[μπέλοις]
– – – – – φιδάκναι Ι̣– – –
[Κεραμέο]ν δέμαρχο[ς ἀπέγραφε]
– – – ἐν Κεραμ̣[έον – – –]
[. . .]ν Ι⁄⁄
[– – – – –]ι̋ο
– – – – – [λε]ν̣οὶ λίθιναι Ι[– – –]
– – – – – [τρ]ιπτε͂<ρ>ε κε<ρ>αμεί̣[ο ΙΙ]
– – – – – [β]αθρόθυμα
– – – – – φιδάκνε(ς) στόμα
– – – – – [μ]ύκε χô μολυβδόδετος
– – – – – [π]λίνθοι σταφυλοβόλοι
– – – – – φάτνε
– – – – – – – – δέμαρχος ἀπέγραφε
[ἐν – – – – – –]ον· κλισιάδες
– – – – – [κ]επαία ἐπὶ τôι βο<ô>νι

2 dr.	174 dr.	Carian child
1 dr.	72 dr.	Little Carian child
3 dr. 1 ob.	301 dr.	Syrian man
2 dr.	151 dr.	Maltese man (or woman)
1 dr.	85+ 1 ob.	Lydian woman

– –

– –   – – –   – – – – –

		pot for barley meal
		head-rest for couch
		4 couches
>11 dr.		chest with doors
		baskets of barley 16
>3 dr.		baskets of barley 15
		door-jambs 6

The demarch of —— registered for sale
– – – small *pithoi* of barley – – –
another 11 half-sized
The demarch of Athmonum registered for sale
in the land at Athmonum
– – – stakes under the vines
small *pithoi* >1
The demarch of Cerameis registered for sale
at Cerameis

– – –

– – –

stone wine vats >1
ceramic basins 2
censer pedestal
lid for a small *pithos*
mushroom-shaped pot, sealed with lead, capacity one *chous*
bricks for a treading-floor
manger
The demarch of —— registered for sale
in the land of —— double doors
gate to the cow-shed

		[- - - - - - - δ]έμαρχος ἀπέγραφε
		- - - - - - - - -νος τε̂ς μέζονος
		- - - - - - - - - ΗΗΗΗΔΓΙ
--	---	[. . .]νος κεραμείας
--	---	[στά]μνοι Γ
--	---	[στά]μνοι Γ
--	---	[στάμ]νοι Γ
--	---	[στάμ]νοι Γ
--	---	[στάμ]ν̣οι Γ
--	---	[στάμν]οι Γ
--	---	[στάμν]οι Γ
--	---	[στάμν]ο̣ι̣ Γ
- - - - - - - - - - - - - - - - - -		

C

Excerpt from eight joining fragments of white marble, part of a total of seventeen fragments belonging to the same *stele* found at various places in Athens and now in the Epigraphical Museum and the Agora Museum. Phot. *Hesperia* viii 1939, 71, xxii, pl. 78; *AJA* lvi 1952, pl. 5; Tracy, *Athenian Lettering of the Fifth Century BC*, 66.

Attic letters. Generally *stoichedon*, with considerable variations in spacing.

W. K. Pritchett, *Hesperia* xxii 1953, 268–79, xxx 1961, 28 (another fragment); M&L 79. B; *IG* i[3] 426*.

column ii

---	---	[. . . .] καὶ ἔ[γγονα τούτον]
		vacat
		vacat
	[Ἀδειμάν]το τô Λε[υκ]ολοφίδο Σκα[μβονίδο]·	
---	[. .]	ἀνὲρ [Ἀρ]ιστόμαχος
		ἀγρὸς [ἐν] Θάσοι ἐν Ἰ̣[- - -]
		καὶ οἰκ[ία]·
---	[. . .]ΗΗ𐅅	ἔπεστιν [πίθ]οι ἐνν̣[- - -]
		hυγιε̂ς ΔΔ̣[. . σ]αθρο̣[ὶ - - -]
		ἐπιθέμα[τα ἔχοντες].
---	[. .]Η𐅄ΔΔΔ	οἴνο ἀμφο[ρε̂]ς [- - -]
		𐅅𐅄𐅅̣ΔΔΔΔ τρ[ε̂]ς χόε[ς].
		vacat
	[Π]αναιτίο·	
---	[.]ΔΔ	οἴνο ἀμφορ[ε̂]ς Ἀττι[κô]
		καθαρô ΗΙΙΙΙ ἑ[π]τὰ χὸ[ες]
[ͰͰͰ]	[Η]Η𐅄Δ	σμένε ἐν τôι [ἀ]γρ[ôι]
		τôι ἐν Ἰσ[—6—]ΔΓ̣[- - -]
[ͰΙ]	[Η]	βόε ἐρ[γάτα δ]ύο ἐν Ἀρ[- - -]
[Ͱ]	[𐅄]ΔΔ	βόε [δύο]

50–4 On wine prices see Pritchett, *Hesperia* xxv 1956, 199–203; [𐅅]ΔΔ is very probable in l. 54.

The demarch of —— registered for sale
– – – – – – – – – of the larger
– – – – – – – – – >416

– –	– – –	ceramic – – –
– –	– – –	jars 5
– –	– – –	jars 5
– –	– – –	jars 5
– –	– – –	jars 5
– –	– – –	jars 5
– –	– – –	jars 5
– –	– – –	jars 5
– –	– – –	jars 5

– – – – – – – – – – – – – – – – –

---

column ii

– – – and their young.
2 *lines empty*

Of Adeimantus son of Leucolophides of Scambonidae.

– – –	– – –	A man Aristomachus
		A field in Thasos in ——
		and a house.
– – –	>250 dr.	Includes jars nine – – –
		sound: 20; broken – – –
		with lids;
	>180 dr.	Amphoras of wine
		590, and three *choes*
		1 *line empty*

Of Panaetius

– – –	>20 dr.	Amphoras of pure Attic
		wine 104, and seven *choes*
3 dr.	260 dr.	Beehives in the field
		in Is— >15
1 dr. 1 ob.	100 dr.	Two working oxen in Ar—
1 dr.	70 dr.	Two oxen

---	---	β[όε]ς τέτταρες καὶ μό[σχοι - - -]
		πρόβατα 𐅄ΔΔΔIIII
---	---	καὶ ἔκγονα τούτον
[Γ⊢⊢III]	[𐅅HH]Δ	αἶγες 𐅄ΔΓII καὶ ἔγγον[α τούτον].
		vacat
	[Πολυστρά]το τô Διοδόρο Ἀγκυλέος·	
		οἰκία ἐγ Κυδαθεναίο[ι, ἕ͂ι πρόθυρον]
		τὸ δίκιον, ἕ͂ι γεῖτόν ἐ[στι τὸ hιερὸν]
---	[....]𐅄	Ἀρτέμιδος τε͂ς Ἀθμον[όθεν]
		Ἀμαρυσίας
		χόριον Ἀγκυλε͂σι νο[τόθεν]
	---	τὸ λόφο hίνα τὸ hιẹ[ρὸν - - -]
		3 *lines vacant*
Νικίδ[ο τô] Φοινικ̣ί[δο Μ]ελιτ[έος]·		
⊢	𐅄⊢⊢	ἐκχαλ̣[- - -]
		vacat
	Εὐφιλέτο τô Τ[ιμοθέο Κυδαθεναιέος]·	
	περὶ ἀμφότερα· οἰκ[ία - - -]	
ΔΓ	X𐅅	ἀπ[- - -]
		2 *lines vacant*
	Φερεκλέος τô Φẹ[ρεν]ικα[ίο Θεμακ]έο[ς]·	
	περὶ ἀμφότερα· οἰκ[ία ἐ]μ Βατε͂ι [καὶ] χορίον	
		vacat
		hέτ[ερον] χορίον [...]α̣λαν[- - -]
		ετρ̣[....] *vacat*
		χορί[ον π]αρὰ τὸ Πύθ[ιον .]ΙΟ[- - -]
		vacat
Δ⊢⊢	XHH	ο]ἰκό[πε]δ̣ον [ἐ]λὺ [κ]αὶ χέρ̣[ρον]
		παρ[ὰ τὸ Π]ύθιον
		hέτε[ρον] χορίον παρὰ τ̣[ὸ]
		hερά[κλε]ιον
		ὀργά[δος] τὸ hέμισυ τε͂ς ἐ[ντὸς τô]
		Πυθ[ίο ᵛ κ]αὶ διανόμο τô ἀπὸ [τô hιερô]
		[τὸ δὲ ἄλλ]ο hέμισυ ἐγ Κυκάλει·
		τα̣[ῦτα ἐπ]ράθε συνλέβδεν hάπαν[τα].
		2 *lines vacant*
	μισθόσες hαίδε κ̣[ατε]βλέθεσαν	
	τôν ἀσεβεσάντο[ν περὶ] τὸ θεό·	
	Φ̣α̣ίδρο τô Πυθο[κλέος] Μυρρινοσίο	

76 ἐκ Χαλ[κίδος ἐπικαρπία *vel sim.* Lewis, 191 n. 56 = 169 n. 56. 79, 84 περὶ ἀμφότερα was added later in both these lines.

---	---	Four oxen and --- calves
---	---	Sheep 84
		and their young
7 dr. 3 ob.	710 dr.	Goats 67 and their young
		1 line empty
	Of Polystratus son of Diodorus of Ancyle	
		House in Cydathenaeum, whose porch
		has two columns, which is next to the temple
---	>50 dr.	of Artemis Amarousia
		from Athmonum
	---	Land at Ancyle, on the south
		of the hill where there is the temple ---
		3 lines empty
	Of Nicides son of Phoenicides of Melite	
1 dr.	52 dr.	---
		1 line empty
	Of Euphiletus son of Timotheus of Cydathenaeum,	
	on both matters. House ---	
15 dr.	1,500 dr.	---
		2 lines empty
	Of Pherecles son of Pherenicaeus of Themacus	
	on both matters. House at Bate and land	
		1 line empty
		another piece of land ---
		---
		land by the Pythion ---
		1 line empty
12 dr.	1,200 dr.	Building plot, swampy and a wasteland,
		by the Pythion
		Another piece of land by the
		Heracleion
		Half the sacred land inside the
		Pythion and canal from the temple
		and the other half in Cycale.
		These were all sold as a single lot.
		2 lines empty
	These rents were deposited	
	from those guilty of impiety concerning the Two Goddesses	
	Of Phaedrus son of Pythocles of Myrrhinous	

𐅄 o[ἰκίας μ]ίσθοσις κατεβλέθε
[γε̂ς Μυρρ]ινο̂ντι μίσθοσις
ΗΗΗ𐅄 [κατεβλέ]θε
Ṇ ἐκ το̂ν Ἀδειμ[άντο το̂ Λ]ευκολοφίδο Σκαμβονίδο
Ι ΧΗ𐅄...

106–7 Traces of another column to the left.

While the Athenians were preparing their expedition to Sicily an incident occurred. The pillars of Hermes ('Herms') that stood in public and private doorways all over the city were vandalised: Thucydides says that their faces were mutilated, Aristophanes implies that their genitals were broken off (Thuc. vi. 27; Ar. *Lys.* 1093–4). In the investigation that followed, a second incident came to light: 'the profanation of the Mysteries', a parodying, in a private house, of the initiatory rituals of Demeter and Kore at Eleusis. Alcibiades (for whose earlier career see 165, 171; for his later career see 184, 185, 192) was implicated in both incidents (for modern scholarship on both incidents see Hornblower, *Com. Thuc.* iii. 367–71). Despite his request to be tried before the expedition departed, the expedition was dispatched, and only later in the summer was a state trireme sent to Sicily to summon Alcibiades to Athens (but not arrest him) (Thuc. vi. 53, 60–1). He returned only as far as Thurii, where he jumped ship. Thucydides records simply that 'The Athenians condemned Alcibiades and those with him to death *in absentia*' (Thuc. vi. 61. vii). The Atthidographer Philochorus recorded that those guilty of mutilating the herms 'were in the archonship of Chabrias [= Charias, archon in 415/4] condemned to death and their names were written on a *stele*, their property confiscated, and a reward of a talent per head advertised for any who killed them' (*FGrH* 328 F 134). The lexicographer Pollux, who perhaps saw them (C. Theodoridis, *ZPE* xxiii 1976, 63–73), recorded that 'on the Attic *stelai* which are set up at Eleusis, the sale of the confiscated property of those who committed impiety concerning the two goddesses is recorded' (x. 97). Fragments of ten *stelai* recording property sales, written up by more than ten hands (Tracy, *Athenian Lettering of the Fifth Century BC*, 55–73), have been recovered, mainly from the south-east corner of the agora where the Eleusinium was located. Either there were duplicates at Eleusis, of which no trace has been found, or Pollux' text has corrupted 'in the Eleusinium' into 'at Eleusis'. The decision to display the lists in the Eleusinium was an indication to the gods as well as to the Athenian public that appropriate action had indeed been taken against the impious.

60 dr. Rent of a house was deposited
Rent of land at Myrrhinous
350 dr. was deposited
From the property of Adeimantus son of Leucolophides of Scambonidae
1,632 dr. 3 ob. – – –
From the property of Axiochos son of Alcibiades of Scambonidae
1,633 dr. 2½ ob. – – –
250 dr.
162 dr. 4 ob.
From the – – –
– –

The lists, published or republished with useful commentary by W. K. Pritchett and others in *Hesperia* xxii, xxv, xxvii and xxx, shed fascinating light on Athenian institutional, political, social and economic history, giving us our richest glimpse into the households of wealthy Athenians. For the complete texts see *IG* i^3 421–30, which are cited below without specification of *IG* i^3.

The investigation of the mutilation of the Herms and profanation of the Mysteries was an extremely unusual affair. Athens had no investigative police force, relying rather on injured parties bringing prosecutions themselves and on volunteer prosecutors. In this case an appeal was made for information and informants were offered immunity and rewards. As seems only to have occurred in religious cases (cf. Osborne, in Edmonson & Hunter (edd.), *Law and Social Status in Classical Athens*, 75–92) slaves too were offered rewards for informing (Thuc. vi. 27. ii, 28. i, 53. ii). Investigators (*zetetai*) were appointed (Andoc. i. *Mysteries* 14, 40) and the politically ambitious Peisander was among those (Andoc. i. 27, 36). These measures led to information being laid against large numbers of individuals: according to Andocides (i. 12–13) ten were denounced over the Mysteries by a slave of Alcibiades named Andromachus, eleven more (plus himself) by a Megarian named Teucrus, who subsequently denounced eighteen men over the mutilation of the Herms, three more by Agariste the wife of Alcmaeonides, and more by Lydus slave of Pherecles of Themacus, while one Dioclides denounced forty-two men (not listed by Andocides) over the mutilation of the Herms but said that 300 men had been involved. Andocides himself denounced four men as mutilators (i. 67).

The sale of just how many individuals' confiscated property was recorded on these *stelai* cannot be reconstructed. Twelve of the thirty-three names recorded by Andocides as denounced over the Mysteries and four of the twenty-two names that he gives of mutilators of the Herms appear, along with one further name; some men appear in the inscriptions as denounced 'on both matters' (e.g. *C.* 79, 84). This high degree of correspondence strongly confirms the accuracy of Andocides' lists. We tabulate the details (see table 1).

Table 1. Denunciations over Mysteries and/or Herms

Name	Denounced by	Denounced for	Andocides 1	*IG* i³ 421–30
Adeimantus son of Leucolophides of Scambonidae	Agariste	Mysteries	16	422. 191; 426. 10, 43, 106, 141, 185, 190; 430. 3, 10, 27
Alcibiades son of Cleinias of Scambonidae (*APF* 600)	Andromachus (his own slave) and Agariste	Mysteries	11, 16	[421. 12]; 424. 27
Alcibiades of Phegous (*APF* 600 VI [C])	Diocleides	Persuading Diocleides to give false information	65	428. 3
Axiochus son of Alcibiades of Scambonidae (*APF* 600 VI [B])	Agariste	Mysteries	16	422. [193], 202; [424. 10]; 426. 108, 125; 427. 46, 63, [82, 85]; 430. 6, 8, 25, 33
Cephisodorus, metic living in Piraeus	Teucrus	Mysteries	15	421. 33
Chaeredemus son of Elpias of Ach—	Andocides	Herms	52, 67	428. 7
Euphiletus son of Timotheus of Cydathenaeum	Teucrus and Andocides	Herms (?also Mysteries)	35, 56, 61 cf.17?	426. 788; 430. 14
Eurymachus son of Eu—	Teucrus	Herms	35	422. 223
Hephaestodorus	Teucrus	Mysteries	15	421. 10
Nicides son of Phoenicides of Melite	Andromachus	Mysteries	13	422. 212, 216; 424. 17, 426. 75, 178
Oeonias son of Oeonochares of Atene (*APF* 11370)	Andromachus	Mysteries	13	422. 217, 219, 375; [428. 8], 430. 36
Panaetius (1)	Andromachus	Mysteries	13	—
Panaetius son of Philochares of Aphidna	Andocides	Herms	52, 67	422. 204, 210; 426. 52

Name	Denounced by	Denounced for	Andocides I	*IG* i³ 421–30
Phaedrus son of Pythocles of Myrrhinous (*APF* 13960/5951)	Teucrus	Mysteries	—	422. 229; 426. 102
Pherecles son of Pherenicaeus of Themacus	Lydus and Teucrus	Mysteries and Herms	17, 35	426. 83
Polystratus son of Diodorus of Ancyle	Andromachus	Mysteries	13	421. 26; 422. 220; [424. 5]; [426. 65]

One of those listed on the *stelai* was certainly executed (Polystratus, Andoc. I. 13); some others had simply fled. Two features of the names on this list are to be noted. One, relevant to Athenian attitudes to Socrates, is that, along with Alcibiades himself, Phaedrus and Axiochus were both part of the Socratic circle and feature in Platonic dialogues. The other is that the spread of demes from which these people come—revealed by the *stelai* since they, unlike Andocides, regularly give demotics—is very narrow. Of those whose property is sold on the *stelai*, three come from Scambonidae, one from Cydathenaeum and one from Melite: that is five from within the Themistoclean wall. Two further individuals come from demes certainly or probably just outside the walls, Ancyle and Themacus, and one is a metic living in Piraeus. Only three of those whose names are completely preserved come from demes at any distance from Athens: Myrrhinous, Aphidna and Atene; in two further names where the demotic survives but not the personal name, the demes are Eitea (near Aphidna), and Anagyrous (modern Vari). We know the demes of just three of the other accused, Andocides himself from Cydathenaeum (*APF* 828), Eucrates of Cydantidae (in the Mesogaia) (*APF* 5757/10808) and Theodorus of Phegous (location unknown). The urban bias here contrasts with the patterns of participation in even elected public office in the fifth century (for which see C. Taylor, *Hesperia* lxxvi 2007, 323–45).

The operation to acquire information about who was responsible for the mutilation of the Herms and the profanation of the Mysteries was only a small part of what was required to enable property confiscation on this scale. Not only was there a complex interplay between assembly and courts in bringing those accused to trial (cf. e.g. the *graphe paranomon*, the first such prosecution known, brought by Andocides' father Leogoras against Speusippus, Andoc. I. 17, 22), but once men had been condemned the process of tracing their property cannot have been easy. Whether all of those accused were rich is not clear, but the wealth of those whose property is listed on the *stelai* is palpable, and, as the lists reveal, it was held in a very wide variety of forms: real estate, both in Attica and elsewhere, stores of agricultural produce, slaves, and furnishings of all sorts. The *stelai* reveal something of the labour of bringing together a man's property portfolio and getting it into a state to be sold: even in the fragments that we have, property of Axiochus and of Adeimantus is sold on nine separate occasions (on all this see Lewis).

The sale of confiscated property in the fourth century was in the hands of the *poletai* (*Ath. Pol.* 47. iii; cf. R&O 36; *Agora* xix). They were probably responsible in this case, but are never named. The *poletai* simply conducted the sale by auction; the listing of property for confiscation (*apographe*) was normally done by individual Athenians or by demarchs. Demarchs were certainly involved on this occasion (*B.* 23, 26, 30, 41, 44), but property outside Attica cannot have come under the purview of any demarch. It is unclear whether the role of the investigators extended to assembling the property portfolios for sale or whether the Athenians relied on private individuals (by contrast to the fourth-century lists, no private individual is recorded in that capacity here). The different form of these sales accounts may derive from their being primarily accounts for the gods; this also makes it hard to use these documents to audit the sales. The presence of a sales tax (*eponion*) here, however, parallels that found in fourth-century *poletai* records. It is calculated not on a fixed percentage but on a scale where sums from 1 ob. to 4 dr. 5 ob. pay 1 ob. tax, sums ≥ 5 dr. but < 50 dr. pay 3 ob. tax, sums ≥ 50 dr but < 100 dr. pay 1 dr. tax, sums ≥ 100 dr. but < 105 dr. pay 1 dr. 1 ob. tax, and so on up to 1,200 dr., at which the anomalous payment for sums ≥ 1200 but < 1205 dr. is dropped. This is a scale where the minimum tax was 1 per cent. In the sales of the property confiscated from the Thirty and others the sales tax seems to be exactly double this (cf. esp. *Agora* xix P 2. *g.* 7, 12 with *CP* li 1956, 100–2).

Something of the cumbersome process of assembling the property for sale emerges in the lists. The first list has a heavy focus on movable goods and on the city, with standing crops sold off but not land itself, and the second is similar, with a great deal of kitchen equipment and only one land sale—the sale of the largest single property known from Attica, the land of Oeonias in Euboea (see further below). By contrast the fourth *stele* is primarily a land sale, and there is much further land sold in *stele* 6. But although there is a broad pattern, it is clear that property of any sort might be sold at almost any stage, presumably because further property had been identified and brought to the attention of the *poletai* (crops abroad are still being sold off in the last of the *stelai*, where the addition of dates shows the slow pace of the sales). Because of the length of the process the *poletai* had, unusually, to deal with income other than from sales, in particular rent from land (*IG* i^3 422. 200, 213; 426. 100–5) and possibly items of cash and precious metal that went straight into the treasury (422. 222; 426. 183).

At various points (*A.* 10, 24, 31; 422. 191, 202, 210, 216, 219, 367; 424. 13, 426. 138, 159; 427. 37, 38, 42, 82, 84, 86; 430. 4, 12, 19, 20, 30) the figures in the lists are totalled, but this random selection of totals cannot be used to give anything more than an impression of the total value of the property sold. Lewis estimated the total sale to have realised between 500 and 1,000 tal. This makes an interesting comparison with the 6,000 tal. that was the total assessment of the value of Athenian real estate in the 370s (Polyb. II. 62 vii, Dem. XIV. 19). It also indicates the sorts of sums of money that wealthy Athenians could find to purchase real estate and slaves even in the middle of the Peloponnesian War and at a time when *eisphorai* were being at least contemplated (cf. **171**)—although we should perhaps allow for the possibility of non-Athenian purchasers of land outside Attica.

If the total value realised by the sales can only be guessed at, they do give us firm figures for a wide variety of items that Athenians regularly bought and sold (although we cannot be certain that the prices are typical: see below), and some of the best evidence that we have for the whole property portfolio of individuals. Particularly striking is the distribution of landed property. Polystratus, for instance, has land in his own deme of Ancyle but also a house, picked out for its two-column porch, in Cydathenaeum and another in Piraeus (*A.* 26–30, *C.* 75–81, 424. 5–8). Pherecles, known from Andocides (I. 17) to have had a house in his own deme of Themacus, also has property in the urban deme of Bate (*C.* 83 sqq.) and various other places which we cannot locate; Euphiletus of Cydathenaeum has a house in Semachidae, land at Gargettus, land at Myrrhinoutta with a house and garden, and land at Aphidna (430. 14–18); the prices for these are the lowest on the *stele*—no other preserved price for real estate of any description is less than 1,200 dr.—but the reason for this (small size? arrival of the Spartans at Decelea?) is opaque. Land holdings consisting of many different properties are well attested in all our Athenian sources, sometimes strongly locally focused and sometimes well scattered (Osborne, *Demos*, ch. iii). Fragmented land-holdings may have been in part the result of Athenian partible inheritance rules, but they also both enabled and bore witness to the market in land. That there were limits to what would sell, however, seems indicated by the failure of the land at issue in Lysias VII. *Olive Stump* to sell for three years after it was confiscated from Peisander because of his role in the Four Hundred (Lys. VII. 6).

The biggest revelation made by these *stelai* is of the scale to which wealthy Athenians invested in property in the Athenian empire. How they had acquired these properties is unclear, although the prospectus of the Second Athenian League (R&O 22. 35–41) shows that such acquisition was unpopular. On the second and tenth *stelai* there seem to have been headings 'land abroad' ([χορία ὑ]περόρια, 422. 15, hυπερορία γε φσιλ[έ], 430. 42) and across the *stelai* we hear of property at various locations on Euboea, on Thasos and at Abydus as well as at Oropus (not a tributary member of the Athenian empire but under Athenian control until 411 (Thuc. VIII. 60), cf. R&O 27). Literary texts alert us to Athenian cleruchies and colonies, but not to independent individual holdings, and not at all to the potential scale of those holdings. The stand-out case is the holding of Oeonias. We first meet income in excess of 650 dr. from standing crops on his property in the Lelantine plain (422. 217–8). Then, perhaps at the end of that same list (the position of the fragment is not certain), we have an entry selling off his property in the Lelantine plain, in Dirus and in Geraestus, apparently as a single lot, for the extraordinary sum of 81 tal. 2,000 dr. (422. 375–8). This evidently did not exhaust his property, since his name appears twice in later *stelai*. This sum is vastly in excess of any other sum in the *stelai*: the next-largest sum is 1 tal. 10 dr. for various pieces of land sold together (427. 76). It is also vast in relation to the sums for landed property mentioned in the orators (where the largest sum is 2 tal. 3,000 dr. for land at Thria (part of Stratocles' total fortune worth 8 tal.: Isae. XI. *Hagnias* 41–2) or in the *hekatostai* inscriptions from Lycurgan Athens, where the highest price is 4 tal. for two pieces of land at Halae Aexonides and two other properties at Rhamnous fetch over 3 tal. (Lambert, *Rationes Centesimarum*, 128, 134 and 229–33). The vastly different scale of Oeonias' holdings from anything else we know of gives pause for thought—not least if it is the case, as it appears to be, that another Athenian could *purchase* this property for that price, something which indicates astonishing liquidity. Lewis (188 = 171) commented on this 'one 81 talents entry which happens to survive' that 'I do not suppose this was unique'; on the contrary, it seems rather unlikely that this was not unique. Only two further prices for property abroad survive in the *stelai*: the property of Adeimantos on Thasos sold for a minimum of 950 dr. at *C*. 45–9, and a property of Axiochus at Abydus sold for 310 dr. (427. 78). This is part of a number of houses and pieces of land belonging to Axiochus that are sold in total for 2 tal. 192 dr., and all of these may well be abroad.

Besides real estate the most valuable property sold in the *stelai* consists of slaves. The *stelai* record some forty-four slave sales, including at least sixteen from the property of the metic Cephisodorus (*A*. 33–49; as a metic he could not own land in Attica), at least nine from Adeimantus (426. 10–16, 44 [= *C*. 44]; 430. 3, 27–8) and at least six from Axiochus (422. 193–9; 430. 7, 9). Some of the slaves have names, which range from names regularly borne by Athenians (cf. Pisistratus, *A*. 9; Polyxena, 422. 79; Aristarchus, 426. 14) to names particularly suitable for slaves (cf. Pistos ('Trusty'), *A*. 28; Arete ('Virtue') and Habrosyne ('Pretty'), 422. 195, 197), or characteristic of their origin (cf. Carion for a Carian, 427. 8–9) (for patterns among slave names see K. Vlassopoulos, *ZPE* clxxv 2010, 113–44 and below, 181, 190). In most cases as well as or instead of a name we have an indication of their origin; the thirty-two origins given divide between twelve Thracians, seven Carians, three Scythians, two Syrians, two Illyrians and one each from Colchis, Lydia, Macedonia, Phrygia, Messenia and Melitene (?); in addition three are identified as home-bred (*oikogenes*). In one case where three slaves, a man and two women, all Thracians, are sold off for a single price it looks as if we might have a family group (422. 195–9). Twenty-seven prices are preserved (for twenty-nine slaves). There is no obvious pattern of higher prices for men than women or for those of one origin over another, though the two Syrian men sold from the property of Cephisodorus fetch unusually high prices of 240 and 301 dr. Only a small number of slaves have their profession identified: as well as the goldsmith we have a bronze-smith, a spit-maker, table-maker, leather-workers, donkey-driver. Too few prices are preserved in these cases to offer any general link between profession and price. The highest price is 360 dr. for a male Carian goldsmith, the lowest 72 dr. for a Carian boy (where the low price seems to guarantee that *paidion* indicates youth, not just slave status), the mean price 169 dr. and the median 155 dr. (dividing the single price for three slaves equally between the three). This run of prices compares with prices in the fourth-century orators ranging from 125 dr. ([Dem.] LIII. *Nicostratus* 1) to 600 dr. (Dem. XXVII. *Aphobus i.* 9 for slaves working in a sword-factory; discounting the 3,000 dr. for a prostitute in [Dem.] LIX. *Neaera* 29), with several figures of 200 dr. (Dem. XXVII. *Aphobus i.* 9, 18; XXXVII. *Pantaenetus* 18; XLI. *Spoudias* 8). Allowing for the different nature of the sources, and evidence of general inflation between fifth and fourth centuries, this does not suggest that the prices in the Attic *stelai* are particularly depressed.

These *stelai* provide our best glimpse of what a wealthy Athenian might have owned. A wide range of ceramics are recorded: particularly storage vessels (*pithoi*, amphoras, etc.) and cooking-wares. Fine pottery in general, however, is not strongly represented: sympotic vessels are relatively scarce—the term *kylix* does not occur, there are only two mentions of craters and only two uses of the generic term *poterion* (drinking vessel); nor are there many perfume vessels—no *aryballoi* or *lekythoi* are mentioned and the only *alabastra* (here *alabastoi*) come in a single lot of six vessels sold together. There are also bronze vessels, particularly vessels for heating water, and some basins known as *kardopoi* occur in both stone and clay (422. 4, 11, 272–3 [stone]; 422. 9–10, 118–19, 270–71; cf. also 422. 32–7, two basin bases, one broken). There are some items of basketwork, for instance a basketwork lunchbox (*kiste oisuine*, 422. 38). Household furniture of various sorts is found: chairs of various forms (*anaklisis*, 421. 209; *thronoi*, 422. 108, 160, 237), benches (*bathra*, 422. 160; 423. 11; 425. 14; *thranidion*, 421. 140), stools (*diphroi*, 421. 208; 422. 107, 161, 264, 268, 283), along with couches, some of them specified as of Milesian workmanship (*klinai*, 421. 202, 206; 422. 7, 104, 278, 281, 282, 284, 285, 286, 292, 295, 296; 423. 6; 425. 18, 107; 426. 33, 34; *klinidion*, 423. 7; *klinter*, 422. 165), a head-rest for a couch (*epiklintron*, 422. 286, 425. 17), beds (*skimpous*, 423. 8; 425. 11 [broken], 426. 31; *chameuna*, 421. 204) and household chests (*kibotoi*, 421. 201; 422. 106, 277, 279; 425. 19; *kibotia*, 421. 188, 189; *koitai*, 421. 184, 186). The sale of tiles and doors reminds us that these were thought of as movable items (tiles, 422. 136–8, 427. 94–9; doors, 422. 13–16; 425. 4–5, 8, 22, 42–3; cf. *Hell. Oxy.* 20. iv Chambers). We also get an idea of how houses were furnished; we find tables (*trapezai*, 421. 110. 203; 422. 105, 164, 262, 263, 293; 425. 109; 426. 35), lampstands (*lychneia*, 422. 109 [iron], 240 [wooden]), rugs of different kinds and colours (*amphitapai*, 422. 164–72 [white, except for one described as 'Orchomenian']; *dapis/tapis*, 421. 175), reed and rush mats (*kanna*, 421. 211; *psiathos*, 421. 108; 422. 261), cushions (*knephalla*, 421. 190, 191; 422. 259, 260), bedspreads (*epibletia*, 421. 192–6), curtains (*parapetasmata*, 421. 173, 174, 205) and pictures (*pinakes*, 427. 59, 60, 62). The pictures are found together in a list of items sold off immediately before the sale of land belonging to Axiochus (some of it, at least, abroad); all three entries are qualified, as 'drawn' or 'painted' (*gegrammenos*), as small, or as coloured. The small picture fetches 6 dr. 4 ob.; the unknown number of 'drawn/painted pictures' fetch 60 dr.

A number of personal effects are also sold, in particular clothes. The item most frequently found is the cloak (*himatia*, 421. 182, 183, 222–49; 427. 101–6), but we also meet mantles (*ampechonon*, 421. 160; *tribones*, 422. 120–6), tunics (*exomides*, 427. 107–11). A pair of sandals is sold (*krepidion*, 422. 246) as are shoes of various kinds (*amyklaidia*, 422. 244, with a note that they are old; *askera*, 422. 163). There is no armour and just two weapons, a short spear and a spear lacking its butt-spike (422. 266, 267).

A great many farm animals are sold off: pairs of oxen (*C.* 58–60), sixty-seven goats and their young (*C.* 63), eighty-four sheep and their young (*C.* 61–2). A hive at a given location is sold, presumably, given the high price it fetches (260 dr.), complete with its bees as a going concern. Agricultural products are extensively mentioned: along with the 'Mediterranean triad' of cereals (barley, millet, wheat; cf. chaff), wine (grapes, wine and vinegar) and olives (which are present both as olives and as oil), we find figs, pulses (bitter vetch, lentils), nuts (almonds), seeds (sesame) and herbs (coriander). A number of agricultural tools are sold in a group on the second *stele* (422. 134–146), including a mattock (*dikella*), a pruning-hook (*drepanon*), a fork (*thrinax*), two sorts of hoe (*skalis*, *sminye*), a harrow (*okistion*), a millstone, an axe (*pelekys*), a winnowing-shovel (*pteon*), even a weasel trap (*galeagra*), together with various bits and pieces one can imagine lying around on a farm (an axle, a sheaf-band, tongs,

---

173

Oligarchic Athens honours Pythophanes, 411

A fragment of a marble *stele*, with the left-hand edge preserved, found on the south slope of the Athenian acropolis, now in the Epigraphical Museum. Phot. Kirchner rev. Klaffenbach, *Imagines Inscriptionum Atticarum*, Taf. 20 Nr. 44; Walbank, *Athenian Proxenies*, pl. 49.

Ionic lettering. *Stoichedon* 30; ll. 29 sqq. inscribed by a different cutter (Lewis *ap.* de Ste. Croix, below).

IG ii² 12; *IG* i² p. 297; M&L 80; Walbank, *Athenian Proxenies*, 75; *IG* i³ 98*. Trans. Fornara 149. See also A. Wilhelm, *JŒAI* xxi–xxii 1922–4, 147–52 = his *Abhandlungen und Beiträge*, i., 611–6; W. S. Ferguson, *CP* xxi 1926, 72–5; E. Weston, *AJP* lxi 1940, 345–6, 356–7; U. Kahrstedt, *Klio* xxxiii 1940, 11–12; T. Lenschau, *RM*² xc 1941, 26–8; G. E. M. de Ste. Croix, *Historia* v 1956, 17–19; E. M. Harris, *HSCP* xciii 1990, 257–8; Shear, *Polis and Revolution*, 55–8.

§i

[—8—]ην[—20—]
[—6—]ηι ην τε[—18—]
[—6—]άτης Ἰκα[ριεὺς ἐγραμμάτευεν·]
[βολῆ]ς ἐπεστάτε [—17—]
[. . . κ]αὶ μετ' αὐτô π[—16—]
[. Ξυ]πεταιών, Διωπ[—16—]

2 τ|ῆι γνώμ]ηι ἣν Τε[ισάμενος εἶπεν *vac.* 5 Wilhelm, ἔδόξεν | τῆι βολ]ῆι. ἣν τε[τάρτη τῆς πρυτανείας D. M. Lewis *ap.* de Ste. Croix, but 'probably wrong' M&L, and cf. on **162**. 4. 4 Wilhelm. 5 π[ρόδρευον *vel sim.* Wilhelm, π[ρυτάνες *vel sim.* Kahrstedt.

a meat-hook, a drill, a pulley, stakes, a beam of wood, planks of wood, brushwood and firewood). Household supplies other than food appear rarely. Some soap is sold (*litron*, 422. 150) and some form of salve (*kerote*, 421 163, restored on the basis of Poll. x. 150).

Although prices and the items to which they refer are too infrequently preserved for us to get a full picture of the cost of living in Athens in 414–413, some individual prices are worth noting. Far from a spit (*obelos*) costing an obol, nine little spits (*obeliskoi*) fetch 26 dr. (i.e. just over 17 ob. per *obeliskos*). Various lots of ten Panathenaic amphoras are sold (422. 41–60), fetching between 4 dr. and 6 dr. 1 ob. The short spear fetches 2 dr. 5 ob. Chests (*kibota*) are expensive: 85 dr., 180 dr. Couches by comparison are inexpensive: several at just over 5 dr., but two at less than 2 dr. Even a couch of Milesian work fetches only 7 dr. 3 ob. A table sells for a similar price (6 dr. 2 ob.). When seven couches are sold together for 42 dr. (422. 296: the best-preserved furniture prices are in 422. 277–96) we may suspect that this is a set to equip a room for a symposium.

---

§i

– – –; —ates of Icaria was the secretary (?); the council's (?) chairman was ——, and with him the (*proedroi*? *prytaneis*?) were —— of Xypete, Diop— of ——,

[. .] Κεφαλῆθεν, Καλ[— 16 —]
[. Ἱ]ππομένης εἶπε· [— 16 —]
σ̣τίωι, ἐπειδὴ πρόξ[ενος ἐστι Ἀθηναίω]-
ν καὶ εὐεργέτης κ[αὶ εὖ ποεῖ ὅ τι δύνατ]-
αι τὴν πόλιν τὴν Ἀθ[ηναίων καὶ τὴν . . .]
στίων, τὸ ψήφισμα τ[ὸ πρὀψηφισμένον α]-
ὐτῶι ἀναγράψαι ἐν σ[τήληι λιθίνηι τὸ]-
ν γραμματέα τῆς βολ[ῆς τὸν νῦν γραμμα]-
τεύοντα καὶ κατα̣θε̂ν̣[αι ἐν πόλει. τὰ δὲ]
χρήματα ἅ ἐστιν Πυθοφά[νει Ἀθήνησιν]
ἢ ἄλλοθί πο ὧν Ἀθηναῖοι κ[ρατôσιν, καὶ]
περὶ τῆς νεὼς ἃ λέγει καὶ [περὶ τῶν χρη]-
[μ]άτων, μὴ ἀδικε̂ν μηδένα, κ[αὶ ἀσυλίαν ε̂]-
ναι αὐτῶι καὶ τοῖς χρήμα[σι αὐτô καὶ ἀ]-
νιόντι καὶ ἀπιόντι. ταῦτ[α μὲν ἔστω ἐψ]-
ηφισμένα ὅσης Ἀθηναῖοι [κρατôσι πᾶσ]-
ι τοῖς Πυθοφάνος κατὰ τα[ὐτά. ὅπως δ' ἂν]
ταῦτα γίγνηται, τοὺς στ[ρατηγὸς τὸς α]-
[ἰ]εὶ στρατηγôντας ἐπιμ[έλεσθαι καὶ τ]-
[ὴ]ν βολὴν τὴν αἰεὶ βολεύ[οσαν. προσανα]-
[γ]ράψαι δὲ καὶ τόδε τὸ ψή[φισμα ἐς τὴν α]
[ὐ]τὴν στήλην τὸγ γραμμ[ατέα τῆς βολῆς.]

§ii

vv ἐπὶ Ἀριστοκράτους ἄ[ρχοντος. *va* c.5]
[ἔδ]ο̣ξ̣[εν] τ̣ῆ̣[ι] β[ολ]ῆι. Κεκρ[οπὶς ἐπρυτάνε]-
[υε· — 7 — ἐγρα]μμάτε[υεν· Ἀριστοκρά]-
της ἦρχε· — 7 —]ς ἐπε[στάτε. — 7 —]
- -

8–9 εἶπε· [Πυθοφάνει τῶι Καρυ] | σ̣τίωι Köhler, εἶπε[ν· Πυθοφάνει τῶι Φαι] | σ̣τίωι M&L, εἶπε[ν· Πυθοφάνει τῶι Ση] | σ̣τίωι (one letter too few) Harris. 11–12 Καρυ] | στίων (one letter too many) Köhler, Φαι] | στίων M&L, Ση] | στίων (one letter too few) Harris. 15 Leonardos: πόλει. *vvvv*] Wilhelm. 18–19 M&L: ἐμπολη | μ]άτων Wilamowitz *ap. IG* ii².

---

§i is a decree for one Pythophanes, apparently a merchant, of a city whose name ends -stus (there are various possibilities: see *apparatus*). It is supplementary to a previous decree, not hitherto inscribed, which had made him *proxenos* and benefactor (8–15), and it has presumably been occasioned by the particular concern for his money and ship addressed in ll. 15–21. The instruction to inscribe it 'on the same *stele*' (26–8) suggests that the previous decree was inscribed above this one. In §ii we have the beginning of a decree of 399/8: if Lewis was right to see this as the work of a different cutter from that of §i, §ii did not authorise the republication of a demolished text (as some decrees of soon after 403 did: cf. below) but was added

—— of Cephale, Cal— of ——. Hippomenes proposed:

8 For Pythophanes of —stus, since he is a *proxenos* and benefactor of the Athenians and does what good he can to the city of Athens and that of —stus, the decree previously voted for him shall be written up on a stone *stele* by the current secretary of the council and placed on the acropolis.

15 The money belonging to Pythophanes in Athens or in any other place which the Athenians rule, and what he says about the ship and about the money (?), nobody shall wrong, and he shall have immunity from seizure for himself and his money both coming and going.

21 Let this be decreed, wherever the Athenians rule, for all the family of Pythophanes in the same way.

23 So that this shall come about, the generals in office at any time and the council in office at any time shall take care.

26 This decree also shall be written up on the same *stele* by the secretary of the council.

§ii

29 In the archonship of Aristocrates [399/8].

30 Resolved by the council. Cecropis was the prytany; —— was the secretary; Aristocrates was the archon; —— was the chairman. – – –

---

under a still-standing text. It may have contained further honours for Pythophanes, or it may have been concerned with somebody else, e.g. a member of Pythophanes' family.

§i is typical of the fifth and early fourth centuries in not specifying the honorand's good services (cf. **157**, **162**). What is highly unusual about §i is its prescript, which was significantly different from those of decrees acted under the democracy (cf. Introduction, pp. xxi–xxii). The first two lines cannot be convincingly reconstructed; the placing of the secretary in l. 3 is plausible; and then ll. 5–8 seem to have named a chairman (of the council?) and four colleagues. Wilhelm compared the five presiding officers (without title), one acting as chairman, in the 'future' oligarchic constitution of *Ath. Pol.* 30. v, and assigned the decree to the intermediate régime of 411/0, in which he was generally followed (cf. most recently Harris). However, Lenschau and de Ste. Croix noted that Carystus, then regularly restored as Pythophanes' city, was in revolt at the time of the intermediate regime (Thuc. VIII. 95. vii), and preferred the regime of the Four Hundred in summer 411, whose recruitment was centred on five *proedroi* (Thuc. VIII. 67. iii, not necessarily repeating the word used at the time) and once in office appointed an unknown number of *prytaneis* (Thuc. VIII. 70. i, cf. *Ath. Pol.* 29. v). One other decree of the intermediate regime is known, quoted in [Plut.] *X Or.* 833 E–F. That is a decree of the council, but its prescript is closer to the democratic pattern, with an enactment formula, date within prytany, secretary, chairman, proposer: ἔδοξεν τῇ βουλῇ. μιᾷ καὶ εἰκοστῇ τῆς πρυτανείας· Δημόνικος Ἀλωπεκῆθεν ἐγραμμάτευε· Φιλόστρατος Παλληνεὺς ἐπεστάτει. Ἄνδρων εἶπε. Since we do not believe that the 'future' constitution was ever implemented (cf. Rhodes, *Comm. Ath. Pol.* 387–9), we are not inclined to see our decree's presiding officers as those of *Ath. Pol.* 30. v, and think the regime of the Four Hundred the more likely. Develin, *Athenian Officials*, 191–2 with 194, doubted whether the five men were *proedroi* of the oligarchy, and suggested that the secretary in l. 3

174

Payments from the treasury of Athena, 411

The upper part of the left-hand side of a marble *stele*, found on the Athenian acropolis, now in the Epigraphical Museum; the *stele* has been reconstructed with accounts of 432/1 (*IG* i^3 365) upper front, 431/0 (366) lower front, 414/3 (371) upper back, 413/2 (?) (372) lower back (and the lost 412/1 perhaps below that). Phot. Meritt, *AFD*, 91 fig. 18; facsimile *AFD*, pl. I.

Ionic writing, apart from Attic *lambda* and ἐνάτει for ἐνάτηι in l. 16; non-*stoichedon*.

IG i^2 298; Meritt, *AFD*, 93; M&L 81; *IG* i^3 373*. Trans. Fornara 150.

[Ἀθηναῖοι ἀνήλο[σαν ἐπὶ]
[Μνασιλ]όχου ἄρχοντος.
vacat
[ταμί]αι ἱερῶν χ[ρημάτ]-
[ων τῆ]ς Ἀθηναία[ς [Ἀσω]-
[πόδω]ρος Κυδαθ[ηνα]-
[ιεὺς] καὶ συνάρχο[ντ]-
[ες,] οἷς Εὔανδρος Ἐ[ρ]-
[ι]θαλίωνος Εὐωνυμ-
[ε]ὺς ἐ[γρ]αμμάτευεν,

might be Amphicrates (cf. *IG* i^3 177) and the year might be 415/4, but that is hard to reconcile with the departure of the opening lines from the normal democratic pattern. The previous decree may have been enacted either very slightly earlier, already under the Four Hundred, or under the democracy.

For immunity from seizure (19–21) cf. **117**; for 'wherever the Athenians rule' (22), the phrase which led Wilhelm to identify this as a decree of the fifth century, cf. on **165**. The instructions to the generals and council to see to the implementation of the decree (23–6) are more specific than the general instructions to protect an honorand against injustice found e.g. in **184**.

From §ii we have only the prescript, but that is remarkable for identifying the decree as one of the council, not the council and the people. It is one of a number of such decrees from the early fourth century, all honorific: either the council was allowed to authorise the republication of earlier honours annulled and demolished under the Thirty (for such republication cf. **157**, **161**, **177**. *B*) or for a time some ratified *probouleumata* may have been published with a misleading prescript which omitted to mention the assembly (cf. Rhodes, *Boule*, 82–4, 271). If §ii was added under a still-standing text, republication cannot be the explanation in this case.

The Athenians expended in the archonship of Mnasilochus [first two months of 411/0]:

3 The treasurers of the sacred monies of Athena Asopodorus of Cydathenaeum and his colleagues, for whom Euandrus son of Erithalion of Euonymum was

παρέδοσαν ἐλληνο-
ταμίαις Ἀντισθέν-
ει Ἑρμείωι καὶ συν-
άρχοσιν, ψηφισαμέ-
νης τῆς βολῆς, Ἑκατ-
[ο]μ̣βαιῶνος ἐνάτει
[φθί]νοντος, ἀπὸ τῶν
[χρημάτ]ων Ἀθηναίας
[Πολιά]δος ⁝ Δ̣Δ̣𐅈ΤΤΧΧ
[–c.4/5–]𐅄ΔΔ𐅂𐅂𐅂ΙΙΙΙ· τῆ̣-
[ς Νίκης Ἀ]θηναίας ἀπὸ
[–c.9–]ων 𐅅ΗΔΔΔΔ̣
– – – – – – – – – – – – – –

Reconstructed by Meritt. 22 [τῶν ἐπετεί]ων ? M&L (cf. **180**. 3). 𐅅ΗΔΔΔΔ̣ M&L, *IG* i[3], after Lolling: 𐅅ΗΔΔΔ[.] Meritt.

Mnasilochus was the archon appointed for 411/0 by Athens' oligarchy of the Four Hundred, whose rule spanned the end of 412/1 and the beginning of 411/0, and was replaced for the remainder of that year by Theopompus (*Ath. Pol.* 33. iii). This text shows that, irregular as the regime of the Four Hundred was in many ways (cf. Thuc. VIII. 67. iii, *Ath. Pol.* 29. v), it continued the practice by which the treasurers of Athena handed over money to the *hellenotamiai*. However, the production of this separate record suggests that the treasurers and/or the *hellenotamiai* appointed by the Four Hundred at the beginning of 411/0 (or appointed when they seized power in spring 412/1, and retained in office for 411/0) were, like Mnasilochus, deposed at the fall of the Four Hundred and replaced by new officials, and this separate record for their portion of 411/0 was produced for that reason, and was added to a *stele* which had already been used for other years.[1] (A fragment of two lines, *IG* i[3] 374, perhaps

[1] Cf. Shear, *Polis and Revolution*, 54–5; but on the need to reconsider the distribution of financial records over *stelai* see the end of the commentary on **170**.

secretary, handed over to the *hellenotamiai* Antisthenes of Hermus and his colleagues, under a decree of the council, on the ninth of the waning of Hecatombaeon [21. i or 22. i], from the monies of Athena Polias 27 tal. 2,000 – – + 74 dr. 4 ob.; of Athena Nike from – – – 640 dr. +. – – –

---

inscribed below our text, may belong to a record from the intermediate regime of the remainder of 411/0.) This record differs from the others (e.g. **170**, **180**) in not naming a first secretary, in citing as its authority a decree of the council (i.e. of the Four Hundred) and in dating not by prytany but by the ordinary calendar. Mnasilochus, as the Four Hundred's archon for 411/0, was deposed at their fall, but he survived to become one of the Thirty in 404/3 (Xen. *Hell.* II. iii. 2).

The use of Ionic lettering, with η, ξ (no instance in this text), ψ and ω, and no h, was increasing towards the end of the fifth century (cf. Introduction, p. xxvii): this is the earliest of these financial texts to use it; **180** and *IG* i[3] 376 revert to Attic lettering; 377 is the work of two cutters, one using Attic and one using Ionic (but not ω); 378 (incompletely) and 379 use Ionic. Under a regime which represented itself as returning to tradition (e.g. *Ath. Pol.* 29. iii, 31. i), we doubt if the use of Ionic in this inscription should be seen as a political gesture.

175

Eretria thanks Hegelochus for assistance in its liberation from Athens, 411

A white marble *stele*, found at Eretria; now in the Eretria museum. Phot. *IG* xii. ix, pl. i (part); Knoepfler (below), figs. 11–12.

Ionic writing (for the circular letters, see *BSA* lvii 1962, 3 n. 27). *Stoichedon* 23 (ll. 2–10).

IG xii. ix 187. A; *SIG*^{3} 105; *DGE* 804; Buck 13; M&L 82*. Trans. Fornara 182; Colvin 27; Dillon & Garland^3 13. 29. See also Knoepfler, *Décrets érétriens de proxénie et de citoyenneté*, ii. 77–88, where this text is II.

θεοί.
ἔδοξεν τε̑ι βουλῆι· Ἡγέλοχον
τὸν Ταραντῖνον πρόξενον εἶ-
ναι καὶ εὐεργέτην καὶ αὐτὸν
κ[α]ὶ παῖδας καὶ σίτηριν εἶνα-
ι καὶ αὐτῶι καὶ παιρίν, ὅταν ἐ-
[π]ιδημέωριν, καὶ ἀτελέην καὶ
προεδρίην ἐς τὸς ἀγῶνας, ὡς σ-
υνελευθερώραντι τὴμ πόλιν
ἀπ' Ἀθηνάων.

In the summer of 411, in response to an appeal from the Euboeans, a fleet of forty-two ships under the command of the Spartan Agesandridas son of Agesandrus (Thuc. viii. 91. ii), which the Athenians had feared would attack the Piraeus, sailed instead round Sunium and up to Oropus (Thuc. viii. 95. i). The Athenians sprang into action ('with Attica closed off [by the Spartan occupation of Decelea], Euboea was everything to them', writes Thuc. viii. 95. ii), sending ships to join some already at Eretria, and a naval battle off Eretria followed. The Athenians were slow to get their ships into the sea because the Eretrians had intentionally removed food supplies from the agora; they resisted the Spartan fleet for a short time, but then retreated to Eretria where some of them were killed by the Eretrians and twenty-two of their thirty-six ships were captured and their crews killed or taken alive. The revolt of all Euboea except Oreus (Hestiaea) followed. Thucydides records that for the Athenians this was an even bigger shock than the Sicilian disaster (Thuc. viii. 95–96. i).

The Peloponnesian fleet on this occasion included Italian and Sicilian ships and in particular contingents from Taras and from Locris (Thuc. viii. 91. ii). This decree honouring a Tarantine surely belongs to this occasion. The Tarantine involved has normally been considered to be the commander of the Tarantine ships, and scholars have sometimes wondered (cf. Knoepfler, 83) what greater honour (citizenship? a statue?) the Spartan admiral Agesandridas might have received, when this subordinate commander (and other subordinate commanders from

Gods.

2 The council resolved: that Hegelochus of Taras be a *proxenos* and benefactor, himself and his children, and that he and his children should enjoy maintenance whenever they visit, should pay no taxes and have a front seat at contests, on the grounds that he has helped to liberate the city from the Athenians.

Locris and Sicily?) received proxeny. Hegelochus is not a common name; we know it to have been the name that the seer Teisamenus, who had acquired citizenship at Sparta, gave to his son, whose own son was seer at Aegospotami (Paus. III. 11. v), and so Hornblower has recently suggested that the Hegelochus of this inscription might be Teisamenus' son (Taras was the daughter city of Sparta) and his role here seer rather than commander (*Comm. Thuc.* iii. 1017–8; and in Agocs *et al.* (edd.), *Reading the Victory Ode*, 99–102). Ingenious though this is, it is hard to understand why a man who had dual Spartan-Tarantine citizenship should be recorded here as simply Tarantine.

This decree is issued solely in the name of the council, by contrast to other proxeny decrees at Eretria where the people also are named. It is plausible that the democracy at Eretria had been overthrown in late 412 at the instigation of Athenian oligarchs (Thuc. VIII. 64) and now the council was the organ of government (Rhodes with Lewis, 246, 248–9). For a similar occurrence in contemporary Rhodes, see *SIG*³ 110.

The inscription uses neither Eretrian epichoric letters, nor the Attic letters used in an earlier fifth-century text (*IG* XII Supp. 549 a, Knoepfler, no. 1), which also marks the influence of Athens in its *stoichedon* arrangement. This inscription retains a *stoichedon* arrangement but uses Ionic letters; the particularities of the script (the angular forms of *rho* and *beta* in particular) identify the mason as the same who inscribed the treaty between Eretria and Hestiaea in the last years of the fifth century, and who was probably the only mason employed by Eretria during these years (Lewis, *BSA* lvii 1962, 3 n. 27; Knoepfler, 81–2).

Various characteristics of the Euboean dialect of Ionic are to be observed: rhotacism of intervocalic *sigma* (as in σίτηριν for σίτησιν, l. 5); πρόξενον in l. 3 where Ionic would have πρόξεινον. The retention of ε for ει in εἰς and ο for ου in the article in ἐς τὸς ἀγῶνας in l. 8 is a result of the pre-consonantal treatment of ἐνς and the article in this dialect. τε̂ι βουλῆι in l. 2 nicely demonstrates the

---

176

Rewards for denouncing uprisings at Thasos, 411–409 (?)

A block of white marble with a raised edge round the inscription, found in the agora at Thasos; now in the Thasos museum. Phot. Pouilloux (below), pl. XIII. 1; *LSAG*, pl. 58.

Parian alphabet, but with *xi*, uniquely in this script. The letters of the second law are smaller and more closely spaced, but show no other difference from the first.

Pouilloux, *Recherches sur l'histoire et les cultes de Thasos*, i. 139–62 no. 18; M&L 83*. Trans. Fornara 153; Arnaoutoglou, *Ancient Greek Laws*, 72. See also F. Chamoux, *REG* lxxii 1959, 351–6; H. W. Pleket, *Historia* xii 1963, 75–7; H. C. Avery, *CP* lxxiv 1979, 234–42; A. J. Graham & R. A. Smith, *AJP* cx 1989, 405–12.

§i

ὃς ἂν ἐπανάστασιν βολευομένην ἐπὶ Θάσωι κατείπηι καὶ φανῆι ἐόντα ἀληθέα, χιλίος στατῆρ-
ας ἐκ τῆς πόλεως ἰσχέτω· ἢν δὲ δο̂λος κατείπηι, καὶ ἐλεύθερος ἔστω· ἢμ πλέος ἢ εἷς κατείπωσι,
τριηκόσιοι κρινόντων δίκην δικάσαντες· ἢν δέ τις τῶν μετεχόντων κατείπηι, τό τε ἀργύριον
ἰσχέτω καὶ κατώμοτος κατ' αὐτõ μὴ ἔστω μηδὲ δίκη μηδεμία μήτε ἱρὴ μήτε βεβήλη περὶ τότων
μηδὲ ἐν τῆι ἐπαρῆι ἔστω πλὴν ἑνός, τõ πρώτο βολεύσαντος· ἄρχει εἰνάτη ἀπιόντος Ἀπατορι-
ῶνος, ἐπὶ Ἀκρύπτο, Ἀλεξιμάχο, Δεξιάδεω ἀρχόντων.

§ii

ὃς ἂν ἐν τῆις ἀποικίησιν ἐπανάστασιν βολευομένην κατείπηι, ἢ προδιδόντα τὴν πόλιν Θασίων
τινὰ ἢ τῶν ἀποίκων, καὶ φανῆι ἐόντα ἀληθέα, διηκοσίος στατῆρας ἐκ τῆς πόλεως ἰσχέτω· ἢν δὲ τὰ

way in which, because the article coheres closely with the noun, the long diphthong there, being followed by a consonant, shortens more readily than in the noun ending which is more independent from the next word. Note also the loss of ι in ει and αι before vowels, common to many dialects, in ἀτελέην (l. 7) and Ἀθηνάων (l. 9).

The *stele* was used also for a second proxeny decree for Heracleitus of Taras in the fourth century (perhaps 390–70, Knoepfler, no. III) and for an engraved abacus, on which see Knoepfler, 78.

---

§i

Whoever denounces an uprising that is being plotted on Thasos and is shown to be truthful, let him have 1,000 staters from the city. If a slave makes the denunciation, let him also be free. If more than one man makes the denunciation let three hundred decide after judging the case. If one of those who are part of the plot makes the denunciation, let him have the money and let him not be under oath against himself; let there be no case, either sacred or secular, about these things, and let him not be under the curse except for the one man who is the instigator of the plot. The law comes into effect on 21 Apatourion, under the *archontes* Acryptus, Aleximachus, Dexiades.

§ii

Whoever denounces an uprising that is being plotted in the settlements abroad, or someone betraying the city of the Thasians or of the cities abroad, and is shown to be truthful, let him have 200 staters from the city. If the property of the

χρήματα ἧι τô ἐπανισταμένο πλευνὸς ἄξια διηκοσίων στατήρων, τετρακοσίος στατῆρας ἐκ τῆς πόλεως ἰσχέτω· ἂν δὲ δôλος κατείπηι, τό τε χρῆμα ἰσχέτω καὶ ἐλεύθερος ἔστω· ἢμ πλέος ἢ εἷς κατείπωσι, τριηκόσιοι κρινόντων δίκην δικάσαντες· ἢν δέ τις τῶν μετεχόντων κατείπηι, τό τε ἀργύριον ἰσχέτω καὶ κατώμοτος κατ' αὐτô μὴ ἔστω μηδὲ δίκη μηδεμία μήτε ἱρὴ μήτε βεβήλη περὶ τότων μηδὲ ἐν τῆι ἐπαρῆι ἔστω πλὴν ἑνός, τô πρώτο βολεύσαντος· ἄρχει τῆι ῥήτρηι τρίτη ἱσταμένο Γαλαξιῶνος, ἐπὶ Φανοδίκο, Ἀντιφάνεος, Κτησίλλο ἀρχόντων.

Greek cities commonly both cursed conspirators against the current regime (above, **102**) and encouraged their citizens to resist and kill any who sought to overthrow it. Laws to this effect tended to be passed, or reaffirmed, in the wake of attempts at revolution or other crises thought likely to encourage such attempts. The Aristotelian *Ath. Pol.* thinks that the Athenians had had from an early date a variety of provisions against those who would overthrow the existing regime (*Ath. Pol.* 8. iv, 16. x, with Rhodes, *Comm. Ath. Pol.*, *ad loc.*). Ar. *Av.* 1074–5 alludes to rewards for tyrant-killers, and in the wake of the oligarchic revolution of 411 Demophantus had the Athenians reaffirm this with a universal oath (Andoc. 1. *Mysteries* 96–8; J. L. Shear, in Sommerstein & Fletcher (edd.), *Horkos*, 148–60).[1] Athens would introduce further similar legislation after the crisis of Chaeronea (R&O 79). The Athenians had encouraged informers to denounce anyone who instigated revolt at Chalcis (**131**. 25), and Miletus urged the killing of conspirators in the middle of the fifth century (**123**).

These two laws, most closely paralleled in a fragmentary third-century law from Abdera (*BCH* lxvi–lxvii 1942–3, 189–95 no. 3), conform to this wider pattern. They are notable for the care with which they consider the problems which might affect the informer, both the need to offer slaves freedom if they are to feel they can inform on their owner, and the need to think about the position of the conspirator who turns state's evidence and informs upon himself. In the latter case they have gone as far as to realise that most conspiracies bind conspirators by an oath, and it is therefore necessary to assure conspirators that breaking that oath will not be a problem (for the resolution of the difficult phrase involved, κατώμοτος κατ' αὐτô μὴ ἔστω, see Graham & Smith).

The rewards offered to those denouncing uprisings are not large: 1,000 staters amounts to around 2,600 Attic drachmas, 200 staters to 520 Attic drachmas (sums comparable to those in Miletus, **123**, but in contrast to the rewards of a talent

[1] The authenticity of Demophantus' decree and some other documents in that speech has been challenged by M. Canevaro & E. M. Harris, CQ^2 lxii 2012, 98–129; this decree is defended by A. H. Sommerstein, CQ^2 lxiv 2014, 49–57; Harris replies in *τεκμήρια* xii 2013–4 (publ. 2015), 121–53.

person making the uprising is worth more than 200 staters, let him have 400 staters from the city. If a slave makes the denunciation, let him have the money and let him also be free. If more than one person makes the denunciation, let three hundred decide after judging the case. If one of those who are part of the plot makes the denunciation, let him have the money and let him not be under oath against himself; let there be no case, either sacred or secular, about these things, and let him not be under the curse except for the one man who is the instigator of the plot. The law comes into effect on 3 Galaxion, under the *archontes* Phanodicus, Antiphanes, Ctesillus.

---

offered in third-century Ilium, *OGIS* 218). Such sums were unlikely to influence the behaviour of the wealthy, but it was presumably democratic uprising that was primarily in question here. Whether the difference between the sums in the two laws reflects financial difficulties, as Pouilloux suggested, is doubtful, since there can have been little expectation that denunciations would be frequent; it may rather reflect the lesser threat presented to the Thasians by uprising in settlements abroad.

Two questions have been much discussed. One is the political background to and date of these laws. The other is what 'let three hundred decide after judging the case' means in institutional terms. Answering these questions depends in part on the relation of these texts to **177**. *A*.

The general historical background seems clear, as established by Avery. Thasian democrats running the city as part of the Athenian empire are unlikely to have felt the need for laws such as these. Such laws would most naturally be passed after the democracy had been overthrown in 411. While other late fifth-century inscriptions from Thasos are written in Ionic letters (**177**. *A*), these texts are written in what seems to be a consciously archaising Parian alphabet (i.e. the alphabet which some of the original settlers brought to Thasos, along with their calendar, on which see below). This seems good evidence that they belong to the regime which was in place after pro-Athenians had been expelled in (probably) July 411, and which seems to have remained in place until 407 (Xen. *Hell.* I. iv. 9). The dates given in the two texts can be reasonably securely placed on the basis of our knowledge of the Thasian calendar (F. Salviat, in *Mélanges P. Lévêque*, vi. 261–8). Apatourion was the first month of the Thasian year, and fell in November/December. Galaxion was the fifth month, and fell in March/April. Since the magistrates are different we must be dealing with a gap of sixteen months between these two laws, and the most probable absolute dates are November 411 and March 409, although dates a year later are also possible. The context for the second law is presumably the attempt by the Thasian oligarchs to effect similar anti-Athenian regime change in settlements of Thasian origin on the mainland (for resistance to this by Neapolis see **187**).

The question of who are referred to in the phrase 'three hundred' is discussed in relation to **103** and **177**. *A*. The reference here is clearly to a court, and three hundred specifies the size of the court. That three hundred also appears as the size of a court in much earlier fifth-century Thasian legislation (**103**) suggests either that the court system had been constant during the fifth century or that the new regime

---

177

Thasian supporters of democracy and Athens, after 411

A

A block of grey marble. Seen and copied by Cyriacus of Ancona; found against the west wall of the acropolis of Thasos, *BCH* xlv 1921, 145. Now in the Thasos museum. Phot. Pouilloux (below), pl. XIII. 4.

Ionic letters.

IG xii. viii 263 with *IG* xii Supp., p. 151*; Pilhofer. *Philippi*, ii. 711c. See also Pouilloux, *Recherches sur l'histoire et les cultes de Thasos*, i. 145–6; H. C. Avery, *CP* lxxiv 1979, 234–42.

ἐπὶ θεορῶν
Ἀντιφῶντος τô Κριτοβόλο,
Ἀθηνίππο τô Κλεο<λ>όχο,
Κλεο<λό>χο τô Ἀλκίππο·
τῶνδε ἱρὰ τὰ χρήματα
τô Ἀπόλλωνος κατὰ τὸν
ἅδον τῶν τριηκοσίων·
Ἀπημάντο τô Φ̣ί̣λ̣ωνος,
Ἡροστράτο, *vacat*
Φίλωνος τô Θεογείτονος,
Λύσιος τô [Τί]μωνος,
Διοσκοριάδεω Νεοπολίτεω,
Ἀπημάντο Νεοπολίτεω.

B

Three fragments of a marble *stele* found on the Athenian acropolis, now in the Epigraphical Museum. Phot. Kern, *Inscriptiones Graecae*, pl. 20 (upper image).

Ionic letters. *Stoichedon* 20 (except l. 1).

SIG^3 119; *IG* ii^2 6 (with addenda p. 655)*; Tod 98.

had reinstated early fifth-century institutions. Since it is hard to think that Thasian democrats will have objected to courts of three hundred men, it is probably best to think that the new regime had left the courts untouched.

The inscription is in the Ionic dialect, with consistent use of ο for ου (but not ε for ει). ἰρή (ll. 4, 12) is an alternative Ionic form for ἱερή (see also **177**. *A*. 5).

Under the *theoroi* Antiphon son of Critobulus, Athenippus son of Cleolochus, Cleolochus son of Alcippus:

5 The property of the following is sacred to Apollo according to the decision of the Three Hundred:

8 Apemantus son of Philon, Herostratus, Philon son of Theogeiton, Lysias son of Timon, Dioscurides of Neapolis, Apemantus of Neapolis.

θεοί.
[Ἀμύντο]ρος, Εὐρυπύλο, *vvv*
[Ἀργεί]ο, Λόκρο, Ἀλκίμο. *vvv*
[ἔδοξ]εν τῆι βολῆι· Οἰνηῒς
[ἐπρυ]τάνευε, Δεξίθεος ἐγ-
[ραμ]μάτευε, Δημοκλῆς ἐπε-
[σ]τάτε· Μονιππίδης εἶπε· Ἀ-
μύντορι καὶ Εὐρυπύλωι κ-
αὶ Ἀργείωι καὶ Λόκρωι κα-
ὶ Ἀλκίμωι τοῖς Ἀπημάντο
παισί, ἐπειδὴ καθηιρέθη
ἡ στήλη [ἐ]πὶ τῶν τριάκοντ-
α ἐν ἧι ἦ[ν α]ὐτοῖς ἡ προξεν-
ία, ἀναγράψ[αι] τὴν στήλην
τὸγ γραμμα[τ]έα τῆς βολῆς
τέλεσι τοῖς Εὐρυπύλο· κα-
λέσαι δὲ καὶ ἐπὶ ξένια Εὐ-
ρύπυλον ἐς τὸ πρυτανεῖο-
ν ἐς αὔριον. *vacat*
vacat

We have better data for politics on Thasos at the end of the fifth century than for any other ally of Athens (see **176**), and Thasos has long been seen as a key example in the debate about the popularity of the Athenian empire (so first H. W. Pleket, *Historia* xii 1963, 70–7). When the Athenians planning an oligarchic coup in Athens in 411 decided to replace democracies among their allies by oligarchies, they sent Dieitrephes to Thasos in the summer of 411, and on his arrival he abolished the democracy there (Thuc. VIII. 64. ii). Shortly after his departure, Thucydides tells us (VIII. 64. iii), the Thasians decided that they no longer needed 'aristocracy with the Athenians' (cf. Thuc. III. 82. viii for this use of 'aristocracy') when they were expecting liberation from the Spartans any day, and they set about rebuilding their walls (pulled down, or rather breached, *c.*462, Thuc. I. 101. iii). Thucydides notes the particular role played by exiles in bringing up a squadron of ships to support revolt, and *Hell. Oxy.* 10. iv Chambers tells how Timolaus of Corinth, after earlier anti-Athenian activities in which he defeated an Athenian general and intervened at Amphipolis, sailed to Thasos and caused its revolt. What the epigraphic record shows is the ongoing politics of exile at Thasos and the bitter internal divisions over whether or not to 'atticise'.

That the confiscation of property recorded in *A* belongs to the context of the initial replacement of democracy by oligarchy on Thasos is indicated by its relationship to *B* and to **176**. *B* orders the republication of the award of proxeny, made by the Athenians at some point before 404, to the sons of one Apemantus, the

Gods.
2 Concerning Amyntor, Eurypylus, Argeius, Locrus, Alcimus.
4 Resolved by the council. Oeneis was the prytany; Dexitheus was the secretary; Democles was the chairman. Monippides proposed: since the *stele* was destroyed under the Thirty on which was their proxeny, the secretary of the council is to write up the *stele* for Amyntor and Eurypylus and Argeius and Locrus and Alcimus the sons of Apemantus, at the expense of Eurypylus. And invite Eurypylus also to hospitality at the *prytaneion* tomorrow.

---

original record of which had been destroyed by the Thirty. The destruction of these honours indicates that Apemantus' sons had been honoured for their opposition to oligarchy (we know of the Thirty knocking down other *stelai* that recorded decrees honouring supporters of democracy (**157**, **161**, **191**, cf. *IG* ii^2 9, 52 as restored by Wilhelm) and laws that they regarded as the crucial basis of democratic power, *Ath. Pol.* 35. ii). These honours show that Apemantus' sons were pro-Athenian, which makes it highly plausible that Apemantus son of Philon, who has his property confiscated in *A*, was their father and a pro-Athenian democrat (see further on Amyntor below).

The action against Apemantus and others recorded in *A* is best dated, as Avery has argued, very shortly after Dieitrephes' intervention, perhaps very precisely in June 411, when the division in Thasos was over democracy or oligarchy. This is indicated by the Ionic letters of *A*, which contrast with the Parian letters of **176**. When the Thasian oligarchs decided to turn away from Athens they seem to have chosen to re-emphasise their Parian roots through the choice of script.

The decision to confiscate the property of Apemantus *et al.* has been taken by a body calling themselves 'the Three Hundred' (with a definite article). In **103** (see commentary) those to whom deposits have to be made are 'three hundred' (without the definite article), and in **176** 'three hundred' (without the definite article) are to hear a case and make a judgment. Scholars have been divided over what significance to give the presence or absence of the definite article, and some have thought that 'the Three Hundred' must be a standing body. However, in the other cases reference is to future action, when here action has already taken place; it makes sense of the usage that whereas in prospect what is required is that a court consisting of three hundred jurors should pass judgment, in retrospect the judgments made will have been made by *the* three hundred who formed the court on that day.

Two aspects of the language of the decision are worth noting. One is that there may be some deliberate archaism and an oligarchic overtone to the term used for the decision of the Three Hundred here—ἅδος, a term which otherwise is found only in **132** from Halicarnassus (and cf. M&L 2, from Drerus); this is a term which refers to what it has pleased a body to do, not, as does the regular term *psephisma*, what a majority vote has decided. The second is that there are two ways of describing decisions to confiscate property. One is to talk about the property becoming public (with the verb δημοσιεύω/δημοσιόω, or description of items as δημιόπρατα as in *SEG* xlv 42, for which see below); the other is to talk of property becoming sacred. The latter is normally used in the context of transgressions of sacred laws. The use of the language of 'becoming sacred' here may be both avoidance of any reference to the *demos* and denial that the new regime is enriching itself from these confiscations.

When the Athenians retook Thasos in 407 they insisted on the restoration of exiles (Diod. Sic. XIII. 72. i–ii) and restored democracy (see also **187**). But after the battle of Aegospotami (**192**) Lysander gained control of Thasos and butchered

---

178

Theozotides and the Athenian orphans, *c*.410

A white marble *stele* found in the agora, used as a cover slab for the Great Drain. Now in the Agora Museum. Phot. *Hesperia* xl 1971, pls. 60–1; Matthaiou (below), pl. 12.

Ionic letters. *Stoichedon* 31.

R. S. Stroud, *Hesperia* xl 1971, 280–301 (*SEG* xxviii 46); Matthaiou, *τὰ ἐν τῆι στήληι γεγραμμένα*, 71–81*. See also I. Calabi Limentani, in *Studi ... C. Sanfilippo*, v. 115–28.

front

ἔδοξεν τῆι βολῆ[ι καὶ τῶι δή]μωι. Ἀντιοχ-
[ὶ]ς ἐπρυτάνευε· [— 8 —]ς ẹ̓γραμμάτευ-
εν· Καλλισθένη[ς ἐπ]εστ[άτε. Θεο]ζοτίδης
εἶπεν· ὁπόσοι Ἀθηναίω[ν] ἀ[πέθαν]ον [β]ιαί-
ωι θανάτωι ἐν τῆι ὀλιγ[αρχίαι β]ο̣[ηθ]ôντ-
ες τῆι δημοκρατίαι, τοῖς [παισ]ὶ τότων ε-

5–6 β]ο̣[ηθ]ôντ|ες Stroud: .]ο̣[. .]ôντ|ες Matthaiou.

those sympathetic to Athens (Polyaenus, *Strat.* I. 45. iv, cf. Nep. *Lys.* 1–2). The question of relations between Thasos and Athens remained live into the fourth century. At a date that has been disputed, between shortly after 403 and shortly after 385, the Athenians granted exemption from taxation to at least thirty-four Thasians who had been exiled 'for pro-Athenian behaviour' ([ἐπ' ἀ]ττικισμῶι, *IG* ii^{2} 33.6–7). Those on the list include [Amynto]r son of Apemantus, plausibly the same man given proxeny here. On a separate occasion in the 380s or early 370s the Athenians seem to have had occasion to take a decision involving Thasians after their property had been confiscated (*SEG* xlv 42). Two further Thasians, Archippus and Hipparchus, were given Athenian citizenship for services rendered in the context of Thrasybulus' activities around Thasos at some point in the early 380s (Osborne, *Naturalization*, D 9 with ii. 48–57) and further honours of citizenship were given to another Thasian Archippus in 334 (*IG* ii^{3} 333). As with **157** this case of the sons of Apemantus indicates how successfully the Athenians retained the long-term friendship of some individuals and families by the care they took of them (cf. in this context Dem. xx. *Leptines* 59–62, referring to Ecphantus of Thasos, whose name also appears in *IG* ii^{2} 33).

In *A* ο is used for ου and also for ω in some circumstances (so θεορῶν in l. 1, Θεογείτονος in l. 10 but Τίμωνος in l. 11). Note also the Ionic genitive Νεοπολίτεω in ll. 12 and 13. For ἱρὰ (l. 5) compare **176**. 4, 12.

---

front

Resolved by the council and the people. Antiochis was the prytany; —— was secretary; Callisthenes was chairman. Theozotides proposed:

4 As many Athenians as died in the oligarchy by a violent death while trying to assist the democracy, to grant to the

[ὐ]ε̣ργεσ:ίας ἕν [εκ]α τῶμ πατ[έρων] α[ὐ]τῶν ἐς
[τ]ὸ[ν δῆμ]ον τὸν Ἀθ̣[ην]αίω[ν καὶ ἀνδ]ραγαθ[ί]-
α[ς, διδο]ν̣αι τοῖς π[α]ισὶ α[— 6 —] τ[ότ]ω[ν] ὀ-
[β]ο̣λ̣ὸν [τῆς] ἡ̣μέρας τ[ροφὴν — 7 —]Δ̣Ι̣ το-
ῖς ὀρφανο[ῖς] ἀποδίω[σι — 10 —] το
Πρυτανει[ο . . . .]ο αὐτὸς [— 6 —]η[. . .]ιν
[ἐπιμέ]λ̣ε̣σ̣θ̣[αι — 8 —]ο[— 10 —]Σ
[— 7 —]την ΟΣ[— 19 —]
δ[οκι]μασάτω αὐ[τ]ὸ[ς — 16 —]
διδόναι αὐτ[— 18 — κα]θ-
άπερ [τ]ῶν ἐν τῶι [— 18 — τ]-
[ὸ]ς Ἑλληνοταμίας το[.]α[— 13 —]
[. καθά]περ τὸς ὀρφανὸ[ς — 13 —]
[. . . .]ο Ἀθηναίων ΤΗΜΗ[— 14 —]
[— 5 —]ι καὶ [. . .]ερ[. .] αὐτο[. . .]μοσ[— 5 —]
[. .]αιον ε[. .]ηρι[— 19 —]
[— 5 —]ιανα[— 22 —]

left side

Κλεόβολος
Ἀνδροκλέος
Ἀνδροκλῆς
Ἀνδροκλέος
Ἀφιδναίω
vacat 0.037 m.
Λυσανίας
Ὀλυμπί[χο]
Ἵππων
[Ὀ]λυμπίχο
Κυδαθην[α]-
[ι]εῖς
Ἀθήναιος
Φιλοναύ-
το
Ἀλωπεκ-
ῆθεν
Χαρικλῆ[ς]
Χαιρεδή-
μο
Χαιρέδη-
μος

10 τ[ροφὴν — 7 —] Stroud: τ[— 12 —] Matthaiou. Δ̣Ι̣ Matthaiou: δ̣ε̣ Stroud.

sons of these, because of the well-doing of their fathers towards the people of the Athenians and because of their manly goodness, an obol a day as maintenance – – – give to the orphans – – – the *prytaneion* – – – them – – – look after – – – let him/it conduct the scrutiny of (*dokimazein*) them – – – give – – – just as of those in the – – – the *hellenotamiai* – – – just as the orphans – – – of Athenians – – – and – – – it/him/them – – –

left side

Cleobulus
son of Androcles;
Androcles
son of Androcles
of Aphidna.
empty space
Lysanias
son of Olympichus;
Hippon
son of Olympichus
of Cydathenaeum;
Athenaeus
son of Philonautes
of Alopece;
Charicles
son of Chaeredemus;
Chaeredemus

Χαιρεδή-
μο
Κολ[— c.4 —]
ς

The regulations for Eleusis (**106**) seem to have made provision for orphans to be initiated (*C.* 28–42). These were presumably war orphans, support for whom at Athens is said by Diogenes Laertius (I. 55) to have been instituted by Solon, although Aristotle (*Pol.* II. 1268 A 8–11) ascribed the invention of such support to the fifth-century town-planner and social theorist Hippodamus of Miletus. By the time of the Peloponnesian War war orphans at Athens were certainly supported until they came of age: Thucydides has Pericles allude to that support in the funeral oration (II. 46. i, cf. Pl. *Menex.* 248 E 6–8) and [Xenophon]'s *Constitution of the Athenians* mentions it (iii. 4, cf. *Ath. Pol.* 24. iii). On coming of age they were presented with armour as part of the pre-play ceremonial at the festival of the Dionysia (Isoc. VIII. *Peace* 82, Aeschin. III. *Ctesiphon* 153–5; cf. S. D. Goldhill, *JHS* cvii 1987, 63–4). Outside Athens our best evidence for support of war orphans comes from fourth-century Thasos (*SEG* lvii 820).

Theozotides' decree proposes to extend provision of maintenance to the sons of those who died violent deaths (parallels for the phrase make it clear that this means murder/execution, not death in battle: cf. **157**. 20) 'in the oligarchy'. Although the word identifying the orphans might be translated 'children', rather than 'sons', the preserved names are all of boys and there is no reason to think that the Athenians took any concern for the daughters of those who died, except in as far as the archon was concerned with looking after orphan estates (for which see *Ath. Pol.* 56. vi).[1] The decree assimilates those murdered to other benefactors, using the language of benefaction and of manly goodness (on which see D. Whitehead, in *Greek History and Epigraphy . . . P. J. Rhodes*, 47–58; for the notion of 'helping democracy' see the reference in Lys. XX. *Polystratus* 17 to those who failed to help the people at the time of the Four Hundred).

But what does this decree mean by 'in the oligarchy'? Scholars have debated whether this decree should be related to the Four Hundred in 411 (for which see **173**), or the Thirty in 404–403 (cf. R&O 4). Various considerations tell in favour of the former. The most powerful is the number of orphans listed. We can no longer read the primary list on the lower part of the *stele*, and have only the names written on the left-hand side, in three different hands, implying piecemeal addition. But since the *stele* survives complete it is possible to compute the approximate number of orphans ever listed. Stroud calculated that there was space for 126 lines in six columns. If we assume that, as on the side, each name with patronymic and demotic takes three

[1] On Greek treatment of and attitudes to orphans more generally see den Boer, *Private Morality in Greece and Rome*, 37–56.

son of Chaeredemus
of Col—

---

lines, but that sons of the same father repeat patronymic but not demotic, 126 lines would allow for forty-two single sons (i.e. forty-two dead fathers) or twenty-four pairs of sons and two single sons (i.e. twenty-six dead fathers), and the number who have died violently leaving underage sons recorded on the front is likely to lie between these figures. But the number of victims of the violence of the Thirty is too high to be compatible with this figure, with 1,500 the figure that Athenians repeated in the fourth century (Isoc. vii. *Areop.* 67; Aeschin. iii. *Ctesiphon* 235; *Ath. Pol.* 35. iv). The loss of the full list of names is much to be regretted, since the numbers of surviving sons would potentially provide some unique demographic data.

The phrase 'in the oligarchy' is unparalleled in Athenian inscriptions with reference to either the Four Hundred or the Thirty, though used by *Ath. Pol.* with regard to both (32. ii, 37. i, of the Four Hundred; 34. iii, 38. iv, of the Thirty, cf. 'the oligarchy under the Thirty', 53. i). It may have been used by the Athenians in their honours for the Samians passed in 412/1 with reference to events on Samos (*IG* i^3 96. 3, as restored by Lewis). Otherwise it seems to have been used to refer to hypothetical oligarchic regimes (R&O 41. 26). However, Athenian inscriptions refer to the oligarchy of 404/3 as 'the Thirty' (e.g. **177**. *B.* 12–13), and we would expect that phrase here if the events of 404/3 were at issue.

Property affairs of orphans were in the hands of the archon. Pl. *Menex.* 248 E says that war orphans came under the 'the greatest magistracy', but a scholiast on Dem. xxiv. *Timocrates* 20 (56 Dilts) says they were looked after by the polemarch. The name of a magistrate probably appeared in l. 14, but there is not room there for that to be the polemarch. Who conducts the scrutiny in l. 15 is not clear, but this might be the council or a lawcourt, rather than an individual magistrate.

Although the beginning of his name is lost, there can be no doubt that the proposer of this decree was Theozotides. This is a very rare and distinctive name, and it is likely that all the fifth-century references to a Theozotides are to the same man, Theozotides of Athmonum (Davies, *APF* 6915; *LGPN* ii *s.n.* [2]: the demotic deduced from a great-grandson recorded at *IG* ii^2 1927. 38–9 with *SEG* xxviii 190, of *c.*325). If this is correct then he was born *c.*450, was prominent enough to be attacked by Cratinus before 423 (fr. 489 KA), had two sons who associated with Socrates (Pl. *Apol.* 33 E), was cursed on a doll and on the lead coffin containing it that was found in the Ceramicus (*SEG* xxxviii 31), and *c.*400 proposed a rider to an honorary decree concerned to enhance the care offered to some persons whom the Athenians had honoured (*SEG* xiv 36, revising *IG* ii^2 5). He is also known from a Lysias speech of which substantial fragments survive from a Hibeh papyrus and a mention in Pollux (Lysias frs. lxiv. 128–50 Carey). That speech attacks Theozotides in a *graphe paranomon* case for a proposal that limited support for war orphans to those who were legitimate sons of the dead soldiers, excluding both bastard sons and adopted sons (and also reduced the pay of *hippeis* and *hippotoxotai*).

Both this decree of Theozotides and the decree of Theozotides attacked in court concern orphans, and some scholars (most recently J. H. Blok, *ZPE* cxciii 2015, 95–6) would identify the two. The decree attacked in court concerned war orphans, and it seems to have been intended to reduce Athenian expenditure. Its restriction on support for orphans may have been intended to prevent use of *post-mortem* adoption, itself perfectly legal, to gain financial maintenance for boys who were not actually dependants, and similarly to prevent false claims that boys were illegitimate sons of dead soldiers (cf. N. W. Slater, *Scholia* ii 1993, 81–5). Such a measure would fit into the straitened financial circumstances of the Athenians either in the period between the two oligarchic coups or after the fall of the Thirty. Either of the decrees might have

---

179

Gravestone of the Athenian Myrrhine, *c*.410

A marble *stele* found at Zographo on the western slopes of Hymettus. Phot. Ἀρχ. Ἐφ. 1945–9, 147; *Studies . . . P. H. von Blanckenhagen*, fig. 30. 1; *BSA* lxxxi 1986, fig. 12. c; Connelly, *Portrait of a Priestess*, 228 fig. 8. 1.

Ionic letters with some residual atticisms (ll. 11, 12. cf. 9), *stoichedon* 12.

CEG 93; *IG* i^3 1330*. Trans. Connelly, *Portrait of a Priestess*, 227; Kearns, *Ancient Greek Religion*, 250.

Καλλιμάχο θυγ-
ατρὸς τηλαυγὲ-
ς μνῆμα, / ἣ πρώτη
Νίκης ἀμφεπόλ-
ευσε νεών. / εὐλο-
γίαι δ' ὄνομ' ἔσχ-
ε συνέμπορον, ὡ-
ς ἀπὸ θείας / Μυρ-
ρίν<η ἐ>κλήθη συ-
ντυχίας ἐτύμω-
ς ⁝ / πρώτε Ἀθηναί-
ας Νίκες ἕδος ἀ-
μφεπόλευσεν / ἐ-
κ πάντων κλήρω-

8–9 Μυρ|ρίν<η ἐ>κλήθη *IG*: Μυρ|ρινέη κλήθη Papadimitriou, *CEG*; see Threatte, *The Grammar of Attic Inscriptions*, i. 51.

motivated a curse on Theozotides, but, since his name appears with other names in the curse, that might have been occasioned by quite separate matters. We remain uncertain whether the two decrees are to be identified.

None of the fathers named on the side of the *stele* has a name distinctive enough to allow certain identification, but it is attractive, with Matthaiou, to think that the Androcles whose sons head the list on the left side may be the Androcles whose death at the hands of young supporters of the Four Hundred is recorded by Thucydides (VIII. 65. ii). He was a man who had lodged accusations with the council at the time of the affair of the Herms and the Mysteries (Andoc. I. *Mysteries* 27: see above, **172**). But the name Androcles is very common.

The *stele* shows clear signs that another stone was attached above, which carried a relief and perhaps the name of the archon and the invocation 'Gods', which are otherwise absent from the text (C. Lawton, *Hesperia* lxi 1992, 246).

Callimachus' daughter's memorial, visible far off;
she first served the temple of Nike.
She possessed a name that travelled with her fame,
since by divine fortune in truth she was called Myrrhine.
Myrrhine was the first who served the statue of Athena Nike,

ι, Μυρρίνη εὐτυ-
χίαι.

---

137 records the decision by the Athenians to choose a priestess by lot for Athena Nike 'from all Athenian women'. This late-fifth-century epitaph for one Myrrhine, in three elegiac couplets (scholars supplement the first verse with τόδ' ἐστίν, 'this is', after μνῆμα to create a full hexameter), identifies her as the first both to look after the temple of Athena Nike and the statue (see above, on **156**), and exceptionally makes the manner in which she was chosen a cause of boasting (Connelly, *Portrait of a Priestess*, 49, 227–9). It also draws attention to her name and the appropriateness of its link with the myrtle, from which wreaths were made both for use at symposia (Ar. *Nub.* 1364) and sacrifices (Ar. *Vesp.* 861, *Thesm.* 36–8) and for magistrates and priests, particularly in association with the cult of Demeter (cf. the purchase of myrtles along with incense in the Eleusis accounts of 408/7, *IG* i^3 386. 150; award of a myrtle wreath, *IG* ii^2 949. 18). This memorial raises three questions: was Myrrhine chosen to serve for life? Did her appointment result directly from the passing of **137**, or only from the passing of **156**? And should we connect this Myrrhine with the Myrrhine of Aristophanes' *Lysistrata*?

Although a cult of Athena Nike in the sixth century is certain, separate cults did not always have separate priests; we find sacrifice to Athena Nike closely linked to the Panathenaea in the fourth century (R&O 81. *B.* 21–3), and it is plausible that sacrifices to Athena Nike prior to the creation of the 'democratic' priestess had been the responsibility of the priestess of Athena Polias, who was chosen from the *genos* of the Eteoboutadai. Myrrhine will have been the first priestess specifically chosen for the cult of Athena Nike as well as the first chosen by lot from all Athenian women. Whether she was chosen around 437 or only in 423 it is impossible to be certain: the answer depends entirely on whether we think that the building activity that also followed the passing of **137** meant that the Athenians delayed appointing the new priestess (presumably leaving the old arrangements in place for traditional sacrifices to Athena Nike). It may be that it was only when a significant increase in the scale of sacrificial activity became possible that **156** was passed and the proposal in **137** was put into practice. Subsequent priests and priestesses chosen by lot seem to have been chosen simply for a year (see S. D. Lambert, *Historia* lix 2010, 156–61, on the priests of Asclepius, Meter, and Calliste and Ariste, and the priestess of Aphrodite Pandemos). But was this priestess different? Certainly **156** does not specify that the office is annual, but that is not decisive, and our view of Myrrhine's term of office depends in part on what we make of the link with *Lysistrata*.

The name of Myrrhine is used for one of the major female characters in Aristophanes' *Lysistrata* of 411, the star of a scene in which she plays up to but then abandons her husband Cinesias who desperately wants to make love to her. Lysistrata's own name was the name of a priestess of Demeter at Eleusis in the mid-fifth century (*IG* i^3 953) and recalls that of the long-serving priestess of Athena Polias, Lysimache, who was the very priestess likely to have performed the sacrifices to

chosen by lot from all by good
fortune.

Athena Nike before Myrrhine's priesthood was created. Lysimache is well known from an early fourth-century base for a portrait statue, found on the acropolis (*IG* ii^2 3453), from Pliny *H.N.* xxxiv. 76, and from the base (*IG* ii^2 3464) for a portrait of her own attendant Syeris mentioned by Paus. i. 27. iv (for the date see C. M. Keesling, *Hesperia* lxxxi 2012, 467–505). The possible link between these priestesses and the play is made more emphatic since the play is set on the acropolis (D. M. Lewis, *BSA* l 1955, 1–12 = his *Selected Papers in Greek and Near Eastern History*, 187–202). Although scholars have worried about why Aristophanes should use Myrrhine's (not uncommon) name unchanged but change that of Lysimache, both the greater importance of the priestess of Athena Polias and the possibility of making allusion to the priestess at Eleusis offer plausible explanations. Although the fact that Myrrhine was the first priestess to be elected by lot may well have brought her brief celebrity, it seems unlikely that there would have been any high degree of name recognition from Athenians unless Myrrhine had obtained office not for a year but for life.

The prominence of the name of Myrrhine's father is notable: verse epitaphs which open with a name regularly open with the name of the deceased. Here the use of the patronymic allows attention to be drawn to the appropriateness of the delayed personal name. It also gives a great deal of prominence to the father of the first priestess for whom, unlike for priesthoods that belonged to *gene*, ancestry (other than from an Athenian mother and father) was not important, as if to make the point that Myrrhine's family was not less distinguished because she was chosen by lot from all Athenians. The appropriateness of Myrrhine's name is itself stressed to emphasise (cf. *eutychia* as the last word) the role of the gods in allotment (Pl. *Leg.* vi. 759 b–c), but also because within priestly families appropriate names were given, emphasising that it was in the so-named individual's nature to perform the role (S. D. Lambert, in Horster & Klöckner (edd.), *Civic Priests*, 71 n. 19): here the lot has done exactly what ancestry does in other priesthoods.

The epigram is elegantly constructed, with careful use of repetition and close echoes (πρώτη 3, πρώτε 11; ἀμφεπόλ | ευσε νεών 4–5, ἕδος ἀ | μφεπόλευσεν 12–13; εὐλο | γίαι 5–6, συ | ντυχίας 9–10, εὐτυ | χίαι 15–16). τηλαυγὲς ('visible far off', or 'shining far off'), a poetic term, but not one conventionally used of grave-markers, immediately signals an elevated style, further sustained by the poetic metaphor in συνέμπορον ('companion'), and although the terms used here for being a priestess and for a statue (ἀμφιπολεύω, ἕδος) occur in prose texts they are not the everyday terms (ἕδος in later prose comes to be used for 'temple', but its fifth-century poetic use is for a seated statue: cf. Soph. *El.* 1374). Notions of fate are regularly invoked on grave *stelai* with reference to the circumstances of death (cf. συντυχία so used in *CEG* 469. 3, 591. 8), strengthening the contrasting emphasis on happy fate here.

This inscription can be dated only by letter forms, which place it in the last quarter of the fifth century: Tracy has identified the hand as that of 'The Cutter of *IG* i³ 50', whose work can be traced from the 430s to after 410.[1] The link with Aristophanes' Myrrhine suggests a date of death after 411. A grave-marker consisting of a marble

[1] Tracy, *Athenian Lettering of the Fifth Century BC*, 113–6; Tracy himself thinks that the letters of Myrrhine's epitaph date 'closer to the year 425 than to 400' (115–16).

180

Payments from the treasury of Athena, 410/09

The front of a marble *stele*, the Choiseul Marble, taken from Athens to Paris by the Comte de Choiseul-Gouffier in 1788, now in the Louvre. On the back of the *stele* are the accounts for the end of 408/7 and the beginning of 407/6 (?) (*IG* i³ 377: see S. D. Lambert, *AIO Papers* v 2014, 2–4). Phot. and facsimile Meritt, *AFD*, pls. II–VI. At the top is a relief showing Athena armed, an olive tree and Erechtheus or Demos. Relief Meyer, *Die griechischen Urkundenreliefs*, 270. A 16; Lawton, *Attic Document Reliefs*, 86–7. A 8 with pl. 5; and see K. Hoekstra, in Bourke & Skinner (edd.), *Popular Sovereignty in Historical Perspective*, 32–4 with fig. 1. 1.

Developed Attic writing, inconsistent in the use of h and using the initial χ of χσυνάρχοντες only in l. 2. Non-*stoichedon*.

IG i² 304. *a*; Meritt, *AFD*, 62–3, 94–108; M&L 84; Pritchett, *The Choiseul Marble*, esp. 18–21, 104–16; *IG* i³ 375*. Trans. Fornara 154. See also A. Andrewes, *JHS* lxxiii 1953, 5–6; W. E. Thompson, *C&M* xxviii 1967, 226–31; S. D. Lambert, *AIO Papers* v 2014.

Ἀθεναῖοι ἀνέλοσαν ἐπὶ Γλαυκίππο ἄρχοντος καὶ ἐπὶ τε͂ς βολε͂ς ἓι Κλειγένες hαλαιεὺς προ͂τ[ος]
ἐγραμμάτευε. ταμίαι hιερο͂γ χρεμάτον τε͂ς Ἀθεναίας Καλλίστρατος Μαραθόνιος καὶ χσυνάρχο[ν]-
τες παρέδοσαν ἐκ το͂ν ἐπετείον φσεφισαμένο το͂ δε͂μο ἐπὶ τε͂ς Αἰαντίδος πρότες πρυτανευόσες· hε[λλ]-
[ε]νοταμίαις παρεδόθε ⁝ Καλλιμάχοι hαγνοσίοι ⁝ Φρασιτελίδει Ἰκαριεῖ ⁝ hίπποις σῖτος ἐδόθε ⁝ Ἀθεναίας Πολ[ιά]-
[δ]ος ⁝ ΤΤΤΧΧΧΗΗΔΔΔΓ⊢⊢C ⁝ Νίκες 𐅄ΔΔΔ⊢IIID ⁝ ἐπὶ τε͂ς Αἰγείδος δευτέρας πρυτανευόσες ⁝ ἀθλοθέταις παρεδ[ό]-
θε ἐς Παναθέναια τὰ μεγάλα ⁝ Φίλονι Κυδαθεναιεῖ καὶ συνάρχοσιν, Ἀθεναίας Πολιάδος ⁝ 𐅇 ⁝ hιεροποιοῖς κατ' [ἐ]-

Part has been lost on the left and on the right in ll. 34 sqq., but above that the text is almost complete.

4 Φρ . σιτρ[.]ίδει Pritchett: no other Phrasitelides is known from Athens, and no one whose name would fit Pritchett's reading.

lekythos, found near Syntagma Square in 1873, commemorates a Myrrhine (N.M. 4485, *IG* ii^2 1285). Four figures are shown in relief, but Myrrhine is both the centre of attention and the only figure named. There is nothing about the iconography to identify her as a priestess, but the diadem and bracelet that she wears may point to a public role. The style of lettering and of carving indicate a date around 400 (P. J. Rahn, *BSA* lxxxi 1986, 195–201). The existence of more than one funerary monument for the same person can be paralleled (cf. R&O 7).

The Athenians expended in the archonship of Glaucippus [410/09] and under the council for which Cleigenes of Halae was first secretary:

2 The treasurers of the sacred monies of Athena Callistratus of Marathon and his colleagues handed over out of annual income under a decree of the people, in the prytany of Aiantis, the first prytany; it was handed over to the *hellenotamiai* Callimachus of Hagnus, Phrasitelides of Icaria; it was given as a fodder grant for horses: of Athena Polias 3 tal. 3,237 dr. ½ ob.; of Nike 91 dr. 3¼ ob.

5 In the prytany of Aegeis, the second prytany, was handed over to the *athlothetai* for the Great Panathenaea, Philon of Cydathenaeum and his colleagues, of Athena Polias 5 tal. 1,000 dr.; to the annual *hieropoioi* Diyllus of Erchia and his

νιαυτὸν ⋮ Διύλλοι hερχιεῖ καὶ συνάρχοσιν ἐς τὲν ἑκατόμβεν ⋮ 𐅆ΗΔ⊢⊢⊢⊢ ⋮ ἐπὶ τε̂ς Οἰνείδος τρίτες πρυταν[ε]-
υόσες ⋮ hελλενοταμίαις παρεδόθε ⋮ Περικλεῖ Χολαργεῖ καὶ συνάρχοσιν ⋮ hίπποις σῖτος ἐδόθε ⋮ ΤΤ𐅆ΗΗΗΗΔΔ[⋮]
ἕτερον τοῖς αὐτοῖς hελλενοταμίαις hίπποις σῖτος ἐδόθε ⋮ ΤΤ𐅆ΗΗΗΗ ⋮ ἕτερον τοῖς αὐτοῖς hελλενοταμία[ις]
hέρμονι ἐδόθε ἄρχοντι ἐς Πύλον ⋮ 𐅈Τ ⋮ ἕτερον ⋮ τοῖς αὐτοῖς ἑλλενοταμίαις ἐς τὲν διοβελίαν ⋮ ΤΤ ⋮ ἐπὶ τε̂ς Ἀκ-
αμαντίδος τετάρτες πρυτανευόσες ⋮ hελλενοταμίαις παρεδόθε ⋮ Περικλεῖ Χολαργεῖ καὶ συνάρχοσιν ⋮ σ[ῖ]-
τος <hí>ποις ἐδόθε ⋮ ΤΤΤ ⋮ ἕτερον τοῖς αὐτοῖς hελλενοταμίαις ἐς τὲν διοβελίαν ἐδόθε ⋮ 𐅈ΤΤΤΧΗΗΗ𐅄Γ ⋮ ἐπὶ τ[ε̂]-
ς Κεκροπίδος πέμπτες πρυτανευόσες ⋮ hελλενοταμίαις παρεδόθε ⋮ Περικλεῖ Χολαργεῖ καὶ συνάρχοσιν ἐ[ς]
τὲν διοβελίαν ΤΤΤΤΧΧΗΗ ⋮ ἐπὶ τε̂ς Λεοντίδος hέκτες πρυτανευόσες ⋮ τρίτει ἑμέραι τε̂ς πρυτανείας,
ἑλλενοταμίαις παρεδόθε ⋮ Διονυσίοι Κυδαθεναιεῖ καὶ συνάρχοσιν ⋮ ΧΗΗ𐅄ΔΔΔ⊢⊢⊢⊢ ⋮ ἐνάτει τε̂ς πρυτανε[ί]-
ας, hελλενοταμίαις Θράσονι Βουτάδει καὶ συνάρχοσιν ⋮ ΤΤΤΧ𐅄ΔΔΔ⊢⊢⊢ΙΙ ⋮ hενδεκάτει τε̂ς πρυτανείας, hε-
λλενοταμίαις παρεδόθε ⋮ Προχσένοι Ἀφιδναίοι καὶ συνάρχοσιν στρατεγο̂ι ἐχς Ἐρετρίας ⋮ Εὐκλείδει ἀνομολόγ-
εμα ⋮ ΧΧΧ𐅅ΗΗΔΔΔΔΙƆ ⋮ τρίτει καὶ δεκάτει τε̂ς πρυτανείας, hελλενοταμίαις Περικλεῖ Χολαργεῖ καὶ συνάρχοσιν ⋮ [.]
ΧΧΧΧ𐅅ΗΗΗΗΓ⊢ ⋮ ὀγδόει καὶ εἰκοστε̂ι τε̂ς πρυτανείας ⋮ hελλενοταμίαις ⋮ Σπουδίαι Φλυεῖ καὶ συνάρχοσιν ⋮ ΤΤΧΧ [.]-
Η ⋮ τριακοστε̂ι τε̂ς πρυτανείας, τὰ ἐχσάμο ἀνομολογέθε ⋮ hελλενοταμίαι ⋮ Ἀναιτίοι Σφεττίοι καὶ παρέδροι [Π]-
ολυαράτοι Χολαργεὶ 𐅄𐅈ΤΤΧ ⋮ ἐπὶ τε̂ς Ἀντιοχίδος ἑβδόμες πρυτανευόσες ⋮ πέμπτει τε̂ς πρυτανείας, παρεδ[ό]-
θε Διονυσίοι Κυδαθεναιεῖ καὶ συνάρχοσιν ἐς τὲν διοβελίαν ⋮ Τ ⋮ ἑβδόμει τε̂ς πρυτανείας, hελλενοταμίαις Θρ[ά]-
σονι Βουτάδει καὶ συνάρχοσιν ἐς τὲν διοβελίαν ⋮ ΤΧΗΗΔΔΔ⊢⊢ΙΙƆ ⋮ τε̂ι αὐτε̂ι ἑμέραι, hελλενοταμίαις Φαλάνθοι [Ἀ]-
λοπεκε̂θεν καὶ συνάρχοσιν σῖτος hίπποις ⋮ Ṭ ΤΤΤ ⋮ hέκτει καὶ δεκάτει τε̂ς πρυτανείας, hελλενοταμίαις Προ[χσέ]-
νοι Ἀφιδναίοι καὶ συνάρχοσιν ⋮ Χ𐅅ΔΔΔ⊢⊢⊢ΙΙΙ ⋮ τετάρτει καὶ εἰκοστε̂ι τε̂ς πρυτανείας, hελλενοταμίαις Εὐπόλι[δι Ἀ]-
φιδναίοι καὶ συνάρχοσιν ⋮ 𐅆ΗΗΗΗ ⋮ ἑβδόμει καὶ εἰκοστε̂ι τε̂ς πρυτανείας, hελλενοταμίαις Καλλίαι Εὐονύμ[εῖ κ]-

12 the stone has ΙΗΠΠΟΙΣ. 19 space for [ΧΧ] Pritchett. 24 σῖτον *AFD*, clear on photograph: σῖτος M&L, σῖτοṿ *IG* i³.

colleagues for the hecatomb 5,114 dr.

7 In the prytany of Oeneis, the third prytany, was handed over to the *hellenotamiai* Pericles of Cholargus and his colleagues; it was given as a fodder grant for horses: 2 tal. 5,420 dr.

9 Another grant to the same *hellenotamiai* was given as a fodder grant for horses: 2 tal. 5,400 dr.

9 Another grant was given to the same *hellenotamiai* for Hermon, the officer to Pylos: 6 tal.

10 Another to the same *hellenotamiai* for the *diobelia*: 2 tal.

11 In the prytany of Acamantis, the fourth prytany, was given to the *hellenotamiai* Pericles of Cholargus and his colleagues; it was given as a fodder grant for horses: 3 tal.

12 Another was given to the same *hellenotamiai* for the *diobelia*: 8 tal. 1,355 dr.

12 In the prytany of Cecropis, the fifth prytany, was handed over to the *hellenotamiai* Pericles of Cholargus and his colleagues for the *diobelia*: 4 tal. 2,200 dr.

14 In the prytany of Leontis, the sixth prytany, on the third day of the prytany, was handed over to the *hellenotamiai* Dionysius of Cydathenaeum and his colleagues: 1,284 dr.

15 On the ninth of the prytany, to the *hellenotamiai* Thrason of Butadae and his colleagues: 3 tal. 1,083 dr. 2 ob.

16 On the eleventh of the prytany, was handed over to the *hellenotamiai* Proxenus of Aphidna and his colleagues for the general from Eretria Eucleides, acknowledgement: 3,740 dr. 1 ¼ ob.

18 On the thirteenth of the prytany, to the *hellenotamiai* Pericles of Cholargus and his colleagues: [one digit] + 4,906 dr.

19 On the twenty-eighth of the prytany, to the *hellenotamiai* Spudias of Phlya and his colleagues: 2 tal. 2,000 [one or two digits] + 100 dr.

20 On the thirtieth of the prytany, monies from Samos acknowledged, to the *hellenotamias* Anaetius of Sphettus and the *paredros* Polyaratus of Cholargus: 57 tal. 1,000 dr.

21 In the prytany of Antiochis, the seventh prytany, on the fifth of the prytany, was handed over to Dionysius of Cydathenaeum and his colleagues for the *diobelia*: 1 tal.

22 On the seventh of the prytany, to the *hellenotamiai* Thrason of Butadae and his colleagues for the *diobelia*: 1 tal. 1,232 dr. 3 ¼ ob.

23 On the same day, to the *hellenotamiai* Phalanthus of Alopece and his colleagues, fodder grant for horses: 4 tal.

24 On the sixteenth of the prytany, to the *hellenotamiai* Proxenus of Aphidna and his colleagues: 1,534 dr. 3 ob.

25 On the twenty-fourth of the prytany, to the *hellenotamiai* Eupolis of Aphidna and his colleagues: 5,400 dr.

26 On the twenty-seventh of the prytany, to the *hellenotamiai* Callias of Euonymum

αὶ συνάρχοσιν ⁝ ΤΧΧ𐅅𐅄ΔΓIIIIC ⁝ ἐπὶ τε̂ς hιπποθοντίδος ὀγδόες πρυτανευόσες, δοδεκάτει τε̂ς πρυτανείας ⁝ hελ[λενο]ταμίαις παρεδόθε Προχσένοι Ἀφιδναίοι καὶ συνάρχοσιν ⁝ ΤΤΤ𐅅ΗΔΔΔͰͰͰIIII ⁝ τετάρτει καὶ εἰκοστε̂ι τε̂ς πρ[υτα]νείας, hελλενοταμίαις ἐδόθε Διονυσίοι Κυδαθεναιε̂ι καὶ συνάρχοσιν⁝ ΤΤΤΧΧΧΧΗΗΗΔΓͰͰͰC ⁝ hέκτει καὶ τριακοσ[τε̂ι] τε̂ς πρυτανείας, hελλενοταμίαις ἐδόθε Θράσονι Βουτάδει καὶ συνάρχοσιν ⁝ ΤΧΧΧΗΗΗΔΔΓͰͰͰIII ⁝ ἐπὶ τε̂ς Ἐρεχθείδ[ος] ἐνάτες πρυτανευόσες, δοδεκάτει τε̂ς πρυτανείας ⁝ hελλενοταμίαις ἐδόθε Προχσένοι Ἀφιδναίοι καὶ συνάρχοσιν [⁝] ΧΧΗ𐅄ΔΔΔΓͰͰͰ ⁝ τρίτει καὶ εἰκοστε̂ι τε̂ς πρυτανείας ⁝ hελλενοταμίαις ἐδόθε Διονυσίοι Κυδαθεναιε̂ι καὶ συνάρχοσ[ιν] [.] ΤΤΤ𐅅ΗΗ𐅄ΔΔΔΔͰͰIII ⁝ hέκτει καὶ τριακοστε̂ι τε̂ς πρυτανείας ⁝ hελλενοταμίαις ἐδόθε Θράσονι Βουτάδει καὶ σ[υν][ά]ρχοσιν ΤΤΧΧΧ𐅅ΗΗΗ𐅄IIC ⁝ ἕκτει καὶ τριακοστε̂ι τε̂ς πρυτανείας, τὰ ἐχσάμο ἀνομολογέσα[ντο hοι σύ]μμαχ[οι] [⁝ το]ῖς στρατεγοῖς ⁝ ἐς Σάμοι Δεχσικράτει Αἰγιλιε̂ι ⁝ Δ̣Δ̣ΤΧ ⁝ Πασιφο̂ντι Φρεαρρίοι ⁝ 𐅈Τ ⁝ Ἀριστοκρά[τει —8—]ι ⁝ 𐅈 ⁝ Ε[...][....] Εὐονύμει ⁝ 𐅈ΧΧΧ𐅅ΗΗΗ𐅄ΔΔΔΔΓͰ ⁝ Νικεράτοι Κυδαντίδει τριεράρχοι ΧΧΧ ⁝ Ἀριστοφάνει Ἀνα̣[—5—ίοι τριε]ράρ[χοι] [—6— ⁝] ἐπ[ὶ] τε̂ς Πανδιονίδος δεκάτες πρυτανευόσες ⁝ ἑνδεκάτει τε̂ς πρυτανείας, ἑλλενο[ταμίαις ἐδόθε] Προ[χσ][ένοι Ἀφιδναίοι] καὶ συνάρχοσιν ⁝ 𐅈ΗΗΗΗΔΔΔΔͰͰIIIII ⁝ τρίτει καὶ εἰκοστε̂ι τε̂ς πρυτανείας ⁝ hελλεν[οταμίαις ἐδόθε ....] [—c.14— καὶ συνάρχοσι]ν ⁝ ΤΤ𐅆𐅄ΔΔΔIII ⁝ ἕκτει καὶ τριακοστε̂ι τε̂ς πρυτανείας, hελ[λενοταμίαις ἐδόθε ...] [—c.19— καὶ συνάρχ]οσιν ⁝ 𐅈ΧΧΧΧ𐅅Η𐅄ΓͰIIII ⁝ *vv* κεφάλαιον ἀργυρίο σύμπαν ὃ Κ̣[αλλίστρατος Μαραθόνιος] [και συνάρχοντες παρέδοσαν —c.5—] *vacat*

34 no punctuation after ἄρχοσιν Pritchett. 35 punctuation at beginning of line doubted H. T. Wade-Gery, *JHS* liii 1933, 136, M&L. Ἀριστοκρά[τει Τρινεμεε]ῖ J. K. Davies *ap.* M&L. 35–6 Ε[ὐμ|άχοι] D. W. Bradeen, *Hesperia* xxxiii 1964, 49 n. 65. 36 Ἀν[αγυρασίοι or Ἀν[αφλυστίοι Pritchett; second α reaffirmed *IG* i³, and bottom-left tip visible on photograph. 40 [Καλλίστρατος Pritchett; Κ reaffirmed *IG* i³. Omit Μαραθώνιος to allow more space for numerals? M&L.

As in previous records (cf. **160**, **170**, **174**), there are inconsistencies between entries: in particular here, dates within the prytany are given only from the sixth prytany onwards, while objects of expenditure are usually omitted from the sixth prytany onwards. Thompson, noting that without exact dates interest could not be reckoned, suggested that under the intermediate regime of 411/0 all the monies received by the *hellenotamiai* were handed over to Athena, and could then be withdrawn without attracting interest, and the restored democracy continued that practice for the first

and his colleagues: 1 tal. 2,565 dr. 4½ ob.

27 In the prytany of Hippothontis, the eighth prytany, on the twelfth of the prytany, was handed over to the *hellenotamiai* Proxenus of Aphidna and his colleagues: 3 tal. 634 dr. 4 ob.

28 On the twenty-fourth of the prytany, was given to the *hellenotamiai* Dionysius of Cydathenaeum and his colleagues: 3 tal. 4,318 dr. 1½ ob.

29 On the thirty-sixth of the prytany, was given to the *hellenotamiai* Thrason of Butadae and his colleagues: 1 tal. 3,329 dr. 3 ob.

30 In the prytany of Erechtheis, the ninth prytany, on the twelfth of the prytany, was given to the hellenotamiai Proxenus of Aphidna and his colleagues: 2,188 dr. 1 ob.

32 On the twenty-third of the prytany, was given to the *hellenotamiai* Dionysius of Cydathenaeum and his colleagues [one digit] + 3 tal. 793 dr. 3 ob.

33 On the thirty-sixth of the prytany, was given to the *hellenotamiai* Thrason of Butadae and his colleagues: 2 tal. 3,850 dr. 2½ ob.

34 On the thirty-sixth of the prytany, the allies acknowledged monies from Samos, for the generals at Samos Dexicrates of Aegilia: 21 tal. 1,000 dr.; for Pasiphon of Phrearrhii: 6 tal.; for Aristocrates of (Trinemea?): 5 tal.; for (Eumachus?) of Euonymum: 5 tal. 3,896 dr.; for the trierarch Niceratus of Cydantidae: 3,000 dr.; for the trierarch Aristophanes of (Anagyrus *or* Anaphlystus): – – –

37 In the prytany of Pandionis, the tenth prytany, on the eleventh of the prytany, was given to the *hellenotamiai* Proxenus of Aphidna and his colleagues: 5 tal. 442 dr. 5 ob.

38 On the twenty-third of the prytany, was given to the *hellenotamiai* —— of —— and his colleagues: 2 tal. 5,090 dr. 3 ob.

39 On the thirty-sixth of the prytany, was given to the *hellenotamiai* —— of —— and his colleagues: 5 tal. 4,656 dr. 4 ob.

40 Whole total of the monies which Callistratus (of Marathon?) and his colleagues handed over: – – –

---

half of 410/09; but that depends on the assumption that details absent from the inscribed text were absent from the original records too.

Another change is that from the sixth prytany onwards a different *hellenotamias* is named on different occasions: all the members of the board will have been constitutionally equal (cf. Dover, cited at **148**, p. 280); Andrewes suggested that different sub-groups handled different areas of business, e.g. Dionysius and Thrason the *diobelia*, as in 21–3, but that is a great deal to build on those two entries. Altogether eleven *hellenotamiai* are named, including three from Acamantis (V), Callimachus (4), Pericles (8, etc.) and Anaetius (20), and two from Aiantis (IX), Proxenus (17, etc.) and Eupolis (25–6).

The tribute paid by members of the Delian League was replaced by a 5 per cent harbour tax in 413 (Thuc. VII. 28. iv). Unless the 5 per cent harbour tax was considered to be so directly a replacement for the tribute that the proceeds were given to the *hellenotamiai* for the League's treasury, the original purpose of the *hellenotamiai* will then have disappeared, but they were certainly not abolished (cf. their appearance in **174**. 11–12, of 411). The 'future' constitution of 411 envisaged twenty *hellenotamiai* to handle all secular funds (*Ath. Pol.* 30. ii); after 411 the *kolakretai* (cf. **153**, **167**) are not found again and the *hellenotamiai* pay for inscriptions (e.g. **183**); so it seems to be the case that the *kolakretai* were abolished in or before 411 and thereafter there was a board of twenty *hellenotamiai* whose remit extended beyond the funds of the Delian League. Whether the tribute was reimposed, perhaps in 410, remains uncertain: *IG* i^3 100 is a fragment of an assessment which could but need not belong to this year.

If, as we believe, the *hellenotamiai* served for the Panathenaic year, Callimachus and Phrasitelides will be the outgoing *hellenotamiai* of 411/0, appointed under the intermediate regime (cf. on **174**) and allowed to serve out their term of office. There will then be the awkwardness that Callistratus appears from his mention in l. 2 to be a treasurer for the Panathenaic year 410/09, but the first payment is attributed to him at a time when, on this interpretation, he had not yet entered office: Pritchett's alternative solution was that the first payment fell after the Panathenaea, and that the twenty *hellenotamiai* did not have to be two from each tribe (cf. on **160**: here Callimachus, a recipient of the first payment, Pericles and Anaetius are all from Acamantis).

The first payment was made, by decree of the assembly, from income (3),[1] and editors have assumed that that is true of all this year's payments and (since there is no instance of this in earlier records) that there was no reserve left; from the third prytany of the year we have a decree which seems to order the repayment of accumulated debts (*IG* i^3 99).

On the payment for the Panathenaea (5–7) cf. **170**.[2] *Hieropoioi* were religious functionaries other than priests. *Ath. Pol.* 54. vii mentions a board of annual *hieropoioi* who 'perform some sacrifices and admnister all the quadrennial festivals except the Panathenaea', and R&O 81 has *hieropoioi* who administer the Annual Panathenaea: S. D. Lambert argues that technically the Little or Annual Panathenaea was the festival celebrated every year, not just three years in four, and was administered by the annual *hieropoioi*, and the Great Panathenaea was the additional elements

[1] This will have been derived particularly from rents for landed property: see Papazarkadas, *Sacred and Public Land in Ancient Athens*, 16–98, esp. 18–21.

[2] Meritt, believing that this payment though in the second prytany must precede the festival, supposed that the democracy was restored and a new council entered office early (2 Scirophorion (xii) 411/0 in *PAPS* cxxviii 1978, 289–90) and the council's year 410/09 was of 390 days: that supposition is not incredible, but the basis for it is insecure.

celebrated one year in four, and administered by the *athlothetai*, so that in ll. 5–7 both the payment to the *athlothetai* and the payment to the *hieropoioi* are for the festival of 410 (*ZPE* cliv 2005, 146 = his *Inscribed Athenian Laws and Decrees, 352/1–322/1 BC*, 83–4). Hecatomb (6–7), etymologically a sacrifice of a hundred oxen, could be used more generally of large-scale sacrifices: see on **158**. In the fourth century cows for sacrifice might cost between 70 and 100 drachmas (R&O p. 401); in the last phase of the Peloponnesian War, with the Attic countryside occupied by the Spartans, it might be harder than otherwise to obtain sacrificial animals, so if 'hecatomb' is understood literally (as by Rosivach, *The System of Public Sacrifice in Fourth-Century Athens*, 101–2), a sum of 5,110 dr. is perhaps surprisingly low; but compare 40–50 dr. for a cow in **146**. 28–30, of *c*.430.

Payments in this inscription and in *IG* i^3 377 are summarised and discussed by Lambert, 4–8; the total amount in this year was somewhat over 180 talents. Pylos (9–10) was attacked and recovered by Sparta in 410 or 409, and the Athenian general Anytus, prevented by bad weather from arriving in time, was charged with betrayal but acquitted, in a notorious case of alleged bribery: see Xen. *Hell.* I. ii. 18, Diod. Sic. XIII. 64. v–vii, and *Ath. Pol.* 27. v with Rhodes, *Comm. Ath. Pol.*, 343–4.

The *diobelia* (l. 10, etc.), introduced by Cleophon, was a subsistence grant of some kind: see *Ath. Pol.* 28. iii and Buchanan, *Theorika*, 35–48; Rhodes, *Comm. Ath. Pol.* 355–6; J. H. Blok, *ZPE* cxciii 2015, 87–102. The payments explicitly recorded amount to 16 tal. 4,787 dr. 3¼ ob. (just short of 302,363 payments of 2 ob.). If Andrewes were right about the *hellenotamiai* (cf. above), all the unspecified payments to Dionysius and Thrason could be added, a further 15 tal. 2,659 dr. minimum. The considerable variation in amounts between prytanies perhaps reflects the amounts of money otherwise available.

The only places of campaigning mentioned are Pylos (above), Eretria (ll. 16–18: reflecting an Athenian attempt to recover Euboea after losing it in 411?) and Samos (34–7). Samos was in the last phase of the Peloponnesian War (e.g. Thuc. VIII. 25. i) the Athenians' naval base in the Aegean; Thrasyllus' Aegean campaign, for which his starting-point was Samos, on our reading of Xenophon belongs to 409 (Xen. *Hell.* I. ii. 1–13; Diod. Sic. XIII. 64. i ['Thrasybulus']).[3] Monies from Eretria (16–17) and from Samos (20–1, 34–7) Lambert suggests are rents received from Athena's properties there (5 nn. 14–15); there is no need to think of a still-continuing payment of reparations after the war of 441–440 (cf. **139**, **152**, **160**, **170**). The references to 'acknowledgment' seem to be to direct payments made locally which did not physically pass through the treasury of Athena. The payment of ll. 27–8 seems to be that recorded in **187**. 47 as made to Oenobius in the vicinity of Thasos. There is no mention of, and no substantial payment appropriate to, the Athenian fleet operating in the Hellespont, under Alcibiades and others, in 410: until Alcibiades' return to Athens in 407 that fleet seems to have been semi-autonomous, and if it received any

[3] For the chronological problem see A. Andrewes, in *CAH* v^2, 503–5.

payments from Athens this year (as it perhaps did not) they must have been made in another way.

Of the individuals named, Pericles (l. 8, etc.) is the son of Pericles and Aspasia, one of the generals of 406/5 involved in and executed after the battle of Arginusae (Xen. *Hell.* I. v. 16, vii. 2); Hermon (10) was an officer under the Four Hundred who joined the revolt against them (Thuc, VIII. 92. v); Proxenus (17, etc.) was a descendant

---

181

Erechtheum building accounts, 409/8 and 408/7

A

Seven fragments from a marble *stele*, now in the British Museum and the Epigraphical Museum. Line drawing Paton (below), tab. 47. Phot. Cook, *Greek Inscriptions*, p. 37 fig. 28 (part).

Attic letters.

L. D. Caskey, in Paton (ed.), *The Erechtheum*, 286–99; *IG* i^3 474*. Trans. Caskey, in *The Erechtheum*, 286–99; G. Ferrari, *AJA*^{2} cvi 2002, 20, 31–2 (ll. 1–7, 8–92). See also R. H. Randall, *AJA*^{2} lvii 1953, 199–210; G. Ferrari, *AJA*^{2} cvi 2002, 11–35; Feyel, *Les Artisans dans les sanctuaires greques*, esp. 31–57, 320–5.

We print ll. 1–100 (fr. II) only.

[ἐ]πιστάται τô νεὸ τô ἐμ πόλει ἐν hôι τὸ ἀρχαîον ἄγαλμα, Βροσυν[ί]-
[δ]ες Κεφισιεύς, Χαριάδες Ἀγρυλε̂θεν, Διόδες Κεφισιεύς, ἀρχιτέκτο[ν]
[Φι]λοκλε̂ς Ἀχαρνεύς, γραμματεὺς Ἐτέαρχος Κυδαθεναιεύς,
[τά]δε ἀνέγραφσαν ἔργα τô νεὸ hος κατέλαβον ἔχοντα κατὰ τὸ φσέ-
[φισ]μα τô δέμο hὸ Ἐπιγένες εἶπεν, ἐχσεργασμένα καὶ hεμίεργα, ἐπὶ Διο-
[κ]λέος ἄρχοντος, Κεκροπίδος πρυτανευόσες πρότες, ἐπὶ τε̂ς βολε̂ς
[h]ε̂ι Νικοφάνες Μαραθόνιος πρôτος ἐγραμμάτευσεν.

column i

τô νεὸ τάδε κατελάβομεν hεμίεργα·
ἐπὶ τε̂ι γονίαι τε̂ι πρὸς τô Κεκροπίο·
πλίνθος ἀθέτος με̂κος τετρά-
IIII ποδας, πλάτος δίποδας, πάχος
τριhεμιποδίος.
μασχαλιαίαν με̂κος τετράποδα,
I πλάτος τρίποδα, πάχος τριôν
hεμιποδίον.
ἐπικρανίτιδας με̂κος τετράπο-

of the tyrannicide Harmodius (Isae. v. *Dicaeogenes* 6 with 46–7); Eucleides (17) and Anaetius (20) may be men who were in 404/3 among the Thirty (Xen. *Hell.* II. iii. 2); Aristocrates is probably a man who was a leader of the revolt against the Four Hundred (Thuc. VIII. 89. ii, 92. ii, iv) and another of the generals at Arginusae; Niceratus (36) is a son of the Nicias who was often general until put to death in Sicily in 413, and was himself put to death by the Thirty (Xen. *Hell.* II. iii. 39).

The *epistatai* of the temple on the acropolis in which the ancient statue is, Brosynides of Cephisia, Chariades of Agryle, Diodes of Cephisia, architect Philocles of Acharnae, secretary Etearchus of Cydathenaeum, wrote up these works of the temple in the state they found them in, according to the decree of the people which Epigenes proposed, those that were complete and those half-done, in the archonship of Diocles (409/8), in the first prytany, of Cecropis, in the council for which Nicophanes of Marathon was the first secretary.

column i

8 We found these parts of the temple half done:

10 at the corner towards the Cecropium: four blocks unplaced: length four feet, width two feet, thickness one and a half feet; one *maschaliaia*: length four feet, width three feet, thickness one and a half feet; five blocks for the wall-capital:

Γ δας, πλάτος τρίποδας, πάχος
τριôν hεμιποδίον.
γονιαίαν μêκος hεπτάποδα,
[I] πλάτος τετράποδα, πάχος
τριôν hεμιποδίον.
γογγύλος λίθος ἄθετος, ἀντίμο-
[I] ρος ταῖς ἐπικρανίτισιν, μêκος
δεκάπος, hύφσος τριôν
hεμιποδίον.
ἀντιμόρο τοῖς ἐπιστυλίοις
II μêκος τετράποδε, πλ[άτος πεν]-
τεπαλάστο.
κιόκρανον ἄθετον [ἐπὶ τὸ]
I μέτοπον τὸ ἔσο μêκ[ος τρίπον,]
πλάτος τριôν hεμιποδ[ίον, πάχος]
τριôν hεμιποδίον.
ἐπιστύλια ἄθετα μ[êκος ὀκτ]ό-
Γ ποδα, πλάτος δυοῖν π[οδοῖν]
καὶ παλαστêς, πάχος [δίποδα.]
ἐπιστύλια ἄνο ὄντα [ἔδε]
ἐπεργάσασθαι μêκος ὀκτόπο-
III δα, πλάτος δυοῖν ποδοῖν καὶ πα-
λαστêς, πάχος δίποδα.
τô δὲ λοιπô ἔργο hάπαντος
ἐγ κύκλοι ἄρχει ho Ἐλευσινιακὸς
III λίθος πρὸς hôι τὰ ζôια, καὶ ἐτέθε
ἐπὶ τôν ἐπιστατôν τούτον.
τôν κιόνον τôν ἐπὶ τô τοίχο
τô πρὸς τô Πανδροσείο,
IIII κειμένον κιόνον
ἄτμετα ἐκ τô ἐντὸς ἀνθε-
μίο ἑκάστο τô κίονος τρία
hεμιπόδια.
ἐπιστυλίο ὀκτόποδος
ἐπὶ τô τοίχο τô πρὸς νότον
κυμάτιον ἐς τὸ ἔσο ἔδε
ἐπιθêναι.
τάδε ἀκατάχσεστα καὶ
ἀράβδοτα·
τὸν τοῖχον τὸν πρὸς νότο
ἀνέμο ἀκατάχσεστον
πλὲν τô ἐν τêι προστάσει
τêι πρὸς τôι Κεκροπίοι.

length four feet, width three feet, thickness one and a half feet; one corner block: length seven feet, width four feet, thickness one and a half feet; one moulded block, unplaced, corresponding to the wall-capitals: length ten feet, height one and a half feet; two corresponding to the architrave: length four feet, width one and a quarter feet; one column capital, unplaced, for the interior pilaster: length three feet, width one and a half feet, thickness one and a half feet; five architrave blocks, unplaced: length eight feet, width two and a quarter feet, thickness two feet; three architrave blocks already in place to be finished: length eight feet, width two feet and a quarter, thickness two feet.

40 The course of Eleusinian stone against which will be the figures begins all of the remaining work all round, and three blocks were placed under these *epistatai*.

44 Of the columns on the wall at the Pandroseum, of the four columns in position, one and a half feet of each column was uncut from the inner face of the floral ornament.

50 An eight-foot architrave block on the wall to the south needed to have its *kymation* moulding added on the inside.

54 These were unsmoothed and unchannelled: the wall towards the south wind, unsmoothed except in the porch at the Cecropium; the orthostates unsmoothed on the outside all round except those in the porch at the Cecropium; all the

τὸς ὀρθοστάτας ἀκατα-
χσέστος ἐκ τô ἔχσοθεν ἐγ κύκλ[οι]
πλὲν τôν ἐν τêι προστά-
σει τêι πρὸς τôι Κεκροπίοι.
τὰς σπέρας ἀπάσας
ἀρραβδότος τὰ ἄνοθεν·
τὸς κίονας ἀραβδότος hάπαντας
πλὲν τôν ἐπὶ τô τοίχο· τὲν κρεπîδα ἐγ
κύκλοι hάπασαν ἀκατάχσεστον.
τô τοίχο τô ἐντὸς ἀκατάχσεστα
τô <γο>γγύλο λίθο τετραποδίας ΓΙΙΙ.
τô ἐν τôι Προστομιαί[οι]
τετραποδίας ΔΙΙ.
τêς παραστάδος
τετραποδίας Γ̣Ι̣Ι.
τô πρὸς τô ἀγάλ[μ]ατος
τετραποδίας ΙΙ.
ἐν τêι προστάσει τêι πρὸς
τô θυρόματος
τὸμ βομὸν τô θ[υ]εχô
ἄθετον.
τêς ἐπορoφίας σφεκίσκος
καὶ hιμάντας ἀθέτος.
ἐπὶ τêι προστάσει τêι πρὸς τô[ι]
Κεκροπίοι ἔδει
τὸς λίθος τὸς ὀροφιαίος τὸς
ἐπὶ τôν κορôν ἐπεργάσα-
ΙΙΙ σθαι ἄνοθεν μêκος τριôν
καὶ δέκα ποδôν, πλάτος π[έ]ντε
ποδôν.
τὰς κάλχας τὰς ἐπὶ τοῖς ἐπι-
στυλίοις ἐχσεργάσασθαι
ἔδει.
[λ]ίθινα παντελôς ἐχσεργ[α]σμέ[να]
hὰ χαμαί.
πλίνθοι τετράποδες μêκος,
πλάτος δίποδες, πάχος
ΔΙ τριôν hεμιποδίον, ἀριθμὸ[ς].
μασχαλιαία μêκος τετρά-
Ι πος, πλάτος τρίπος, πάχος
τριôν hεμιποδίον.

lacuna

bases unchannelled on the top; all the columns unchannelled except the ones on the wall; the substructure all around unsmoothed; of the wall inside the unsmoothed parts were eight four-footers of moulded stone; of that in the *prostomiaion* [the western room], twelve four-footers; of the *parastas* [projecting wall] seven four-footers; of that towards the statue, two four-footers.

77 In the porch before the doorway, the altar of the *thyechoos* is unplaced; the rafters and crosspieces of the roof are unplaced.

83 In the porch at the Cecropium three stones for the ceiling over the maidens need to be dressed on the top side: length thirteen feet, width five feet; the rosettes on the architrave blocks needed to be finished.

93 Stones completely worked which are on the ground:

95 Eleven blocks: length four feet, width two feet, thickness one and a half feet; one *maschalaia*: length four feet, width three feet, thickness one and a half feet.

lacuna

B

Fragments from a series of marble plaques affixed to a wall, mostly now in the Epigraphical Museum. Line drawing *The Erechtheum*, pl. 49.

Attic letters but with some use of H for η and Λ for λ. Many incorrect additions of the aspirate.

L. D. Caskey, in *The Erechtheum*, 370–416; *IG* i³ 476*. Trans. Caskey, in *The Erechtheum*, 370–416.

We print only fr. XVII, col. i (ll. 158–248).

[——— 22 ——— τ]-
[ὸν τὸ δ]όρυ hέχοντα, 𐅄Δ. Φυρόμα-
[χος Κ]εφισιεύς, τὸν νεανίσκο-
[ν τὸ]ν παρὰ τὸν θόρακα, 𐅄Δ. Πραχ-
[σίας] ἐμ Μελίτει hοικôν, τὸν h-
[ίππο]ν καὶ τὸν hοπισθοφανε̂ τ-
[ὸν πα]ρακρόοντα, ΗΔΔ. Ἀντιφάν-
[ες hεκ] Κεραμέον, τὸ ἅρμα καὶ τ-
[ὸν νε]ανίσκον καὶ τὸ hίππο τὸ
[ζευγ]νυμένο, ΗΗΔΔΔΔ. Φυρόμαχ-
[ος Κε]φισιεύς, τὸν hάγοντα τὸ-
[ν hί]ππον, 𐅄Δ : Μυννίον hαγρυλε̂-
[σι] hοικôν, τὸν hίππον καὶ τὸν
[hά]νδρα τὸν hεπικρόοντα καὶ
[τὲ]ν στέλεν hύστερον προσέθ-
[εκ]ε : ΗΔΔΓ⊢⊢. Σôκλος hαλοπεκε̂-
[σι] hοικôν, τὸν τὸν χαλινὸν hέ-
[χο]ντα, 𐅄Δ : Φυρόμαχος Κεφισιε-
[ύς], τὸν hάνδρα τὸν hεπὶ τε̂ς βα-
[κτ]ερίας εἱστεκότα τὸν παρὰ
[τὸ]ν βομόν, 𐅄Δ : hίασος Κολλυτε-
[ύς], τὲγ γυναῖκα ε̂ι ἑ παῖς προσ-
[πέ]πτοκε, 𐅄ΔΔΔ ᵛ κεφάλαιον hα-
[γα]λματοποϊκô, ΧΧΧΗΗΗΔΓ ᵛ λε̂-
[μμ]α, <Χ>ΧΧΧΗΗΗ⊢⊢Ι : hανάλομα τὸ α-
[ὐτ]ον.⌋ *vacat* hεπὶ τε̂ς Πανδι-
[ονί]δος ὀγδόες πρυτανευούσ-
[ες] ᵛ λέμματα παρὰ ταμιôν τε̂ς
[θε]ô, Ἀρεσαίχμο hαγρυλε̂θεν κ-
[αὶ] συναρχόντον, ΧΗΗΔΔΔΓ⊢⊢⊢
[⊢Ι ᵛ hα]ναλόματα. hονέματα· σα-
[νί]δες δύο hες ἃς τὸν λόγον hα-
[ν]αγράφο[μ]εν, δραχμε̂ς hεκατέ-
[ρα]ν, ⊢⊢. κεφάλαιον hονεμάτον
[⊢⊢]. λιθοργικô· ῥαβδόσεος τôν
[κι]όνον τôν πρὸς ἔο τôν κατὰ τ-
[ὸν] βομόν· τὸν τρίτον hαπὸ τô β-

– – – the one with the spear, 60 dr.; Phyromachus of Cephisia, the young man next to the breastplate, 60 dr.; Praxias living in Melite, the horse and the man appearing behind it, striking it, 120 dr.; Antiphanes from Cerameis, the chariot and the young man and the two yoked horses, 240 dr.; Phyromachus of Cephisia, the man leading the horse, 60 dr.; Mynnion living in Agryle, the horse and the man whipping it and he added the *stele* afterwards, 127 dr.; Soclus living at Alopece, the man holding the bridle, 60 dr.; Phyromachus of Cephisia, the man leaning on the stick by the altar, 60 dr.; Iasus of Collytus, the woman whom the child has leant against, 80 dr.

180 Total for sculpture 3,315 dr.; receipts 4,302 dr. 1 ob. Expenses: the same.

183 In the eighth prytany, of Pandionis. Received from the treasurers of the goddess, Aresaechmus of Agryle and his colleagues, 1,239 dr. 1 ob.

188 Expenses: purchases: two boards on which we write up the accounts, a drachma for each; 2 dr. Total for purchases, 2 dr.

192 Stonework: for fluting the columns at the east by the altar: the third

[ομ]ô τε̑ς Διόνες, hαμεινιάδες
[ἐν Κ]οίλε<ι> hοικôν, ΔΓͰͰͰ. hαισχ-
[ίνε]ς : ΔΓͰͰͰ. Λυσανίας, Δ ΓͰͰͰ. Σ-
[ομέ]νες hαμεινιάδο : ΔΓͰͰͰ : Τι-
[μοκ]ράτες : ΔΓͰͰͰ : τὸν hεχόμεν-
[ον ἐχσ]ε̑ς, Σιμίας Ἀλοπεκε̑σι h-
[οικôν : Δ]ͰͰͰ. Κέρδον : ΔͰͰΙΙΙΙΙ : Σίν-
[δρον Σιμ]ίο, ΔͰͰΙΙΙΙΙ. Σοκλε̑ς hαχ-
[σιοπείθ]ος, ΔͰͰΙΙΙΙΙ. Σαννίον Σι-
[μί]ο, Δ[ͰͰΙΙ]ΙΙΙ. hεπιείκες [Σ]ιμίο : Δ
[ͰͰΙ]ΙΙΙΙ. Σό[σ]ανδρος Σιμίο, ΔͰͰΙΙΙΙΙ.
[τὸ]ν hεχόμενον ἐχσε̑ς, [h]ονέσι-
[μος] Νικοστρ[ά]το : ΔΓͰ[ΙΙΙ]Ι. hεύδο-
[χσο]ς Ἀλοπεκε̑σι hο[ικô]ν, ΔΓͰΙΙ
[ΙΙ: Κλ]έον : ΔΓͰΙΙΙΙ. Σίμ[ον hαγ]ρυλε̑-
[σι h]οικôν : ΔΓͰΙΙΙΙ. [hαντ]ίδοτος
[Γλαύ]κο, ΔΓͰΙΙΙΙ. hε[ύδι]κος, ΔΓͰΙΙ
[ΙΙ. τὸν] hεχόμενον [hεχ]σε̑ς, Θευγ-
[ένες] Πειραιεύ[ς, ΔΓ]. Κεφισογέ-
[νες Π]ειραιεύ[ς, ΔΓ. Τ]ε[υ̑]κρος ἐν
[Κυδα]θεναίοι [hοικ]ôν, ΔΓ. Κεφι-
[σόδο]ρος ἐ[ν Σκαμβ]ονιδôν hοι-
[κôν], ΔΓ. Νικό[στρατος] : ΔΓ. Θευγε-
[ίτον] Πειραι[εύς], ΔΓ. τὸς ὀρθοσ-
[τάτ]ας καταχ[σô]ντι τὸ παρὰ τὸ-
[ν θ]υεχô βομό[ν], Πολυκλε̑ς [Λ]ακι-
[άδε]ς : ΔΔΔΓ. ῥα[β]δόσεος τôν κιό-
[νον τ]ôν πρὸ[ς ἕ]ο τôν κατὰ τὸν β-
[ομό]ν· τὸν πρὸς τô βομô τε̑ς Διό-
[νες, Λ]άοσσος Ἀλοπεκῆ[θ]εν, ΔΔ. Φ-
[ίλο]ν hερχι[ε]ύς, ΔΔ. Παṛṃένον Λ-
[αόσ]σο, ΔΔ. Κ[αρί]ον Λαόσσο : ΔΔ: hί-
[καρος : Δ] Δ. τὸν hεχόμενον [ἔ]χσε̑-
[ς, Φά]λ̣ακρος Παιανιεὺς : ΔΔ : Φιλ-
[όστρ]ατος Παιανιε, ΔΔ. Θ[α]ργέλ-
[ιος Φ]αλάκρο, [Δ] Δ. Φιλôρ[γο]ς Φαλ-
[άκρ]ο : ΔΔ. Γε̑ρυ[ς] Φαλάκρ[ο], ΔΔ : τὸν
[hεχ]όμενον [ἐχ]σε̑ς, Ἀμ[ει]νιάδε-
[ς ἐ]ν Κοίλε[ι οἰ]κôν : ΔΔ. Αἰσχίνη-
[ς, Δ] Δ. Λυσα[νίας, Δ] Δ. Σο[μ]ένες hαμ-
[ει]νιάδ[ο, ΔΔ. Τ]ιμοκ[ρ]άτες, ΔΔ. τὸ-
[ν h]εχό[μεν]ον ἐχσε̑ς, Σιμίας ⁝ Ἀλ-
[οπ]εκε̑σι hοικôν, ΔͰͰͰͰΙΙ. Κέρδ-

from the altar of Dione, Ameiniades living in Coele, 18 dr.; Aeschines, 18 dr.; Lysanias, 18 dr.; Somenes slave of Ameiniades, 18 dr.; Timocrates, 18 dr.

199 The one next to it in order, Simias living in Alopece, 13 dr.; Cerdon 12 dr. 5 ob.; Sindron, slave of Simias, 12 dr. 5 ob.; Socles slave of Axiopeithes, 12 dr. 5 ob.; Sannion slave of Simias, 12 dr. 5 ob.; Epieices slave of Simias, 12 dr. 5 ob.; Sosandrus slave of Simias, 12 dr. 5 ob.

206 The next to it in order, Onesimus slave of Nicostratus, 16 dr. 4 ob.; Eudoxus living in Alopece, 16 dr. 4 ob.; Cleon, 16 dr. 4 ob.; Simon living in Alopece, 16 dr. 4 ob.; Antidotus slave of Glaucus, 16 dr. 4 ob.; Eudicus, 16 dr. 4 ob.

212 The next to it in order: Theugenes of Piraeus, 15 dr.; Cephisogenes of Piraeus, 15 dr.; Teucrus living in Cydathenaeum, 15 dr.; Cephisodorus living in Scambonidae, 15 dr.; Nicostratus 15 dr.; Theugeiton of Piraeus 15 dr.

218 For the person smoothing the orthostates by the altar of the *thyechoos*, Polycles of Laciadae, 35 dr.

221 For fluting the columns at the east, by the altar, the one by the altar of Dione, Laossus of Alopece, 20 dr.; Philon of Erchia, 20 dr.; Parmenon slave of Laossus, 20 dr.; Carion slave of Laossus, 20 dr.; Icarus, 20 dr.

227 The next to it in order, Phalacrus of Paeania, 20 dr., Philostratus of Paeania, 20 dr.; Thargelius slave of Phalacrus, 20 dr.; Philorgus slave of Phalacrus, 20 dr.; Gerys slave of Phalacrus, 20 dr.

231 The next to it in order: Ameiniades living in Coele, 20 dr.; Aeschines, 20 dr.; Lysanias, 20 dr.; Somenes slave of Ameiniades, 20 dr.; Timocrates, 20 dr.

235 The next to it in order: Simias living in Alopece, 14 dr. 2 ob.; Cerdon, 14

[ον], Δ⊢⊢⊢⊢ΙΙ. Σίνδρο[ν] Σιμίο : Δ⊢⊢
[⊢⊢Ι]Ι. Σοκλε̂ς hαχσ[ιοπ]είθος, [Δ⊢]
[⊢⊢⊢]ΙΙ. Σαννίον Σι[μίο], Δ⊢⊢⊢[⊢ΙΙ. h]-
[επιε]ίκες Σιμίο, [Δ⊢⊢]⊢⊢[Ι. Σόσα]-
[νδρος] : Δ⊢⊢⊢⊢Ι : τ[ὸν hε]χό[μενον]
[ἐχσε̂ς], hονέσιμ[ος Νικοστράτ]-
[ο, ΔΓ⊢⊢]⊢ΙΙΙC. h[ε]ύ[δοχσος Ἀλοπεκ]-
[ε̂σι hοικ]ο̂ν, Δ[Γ⊢⊢⊢. Κλέον, ΔΓ⊢⊢]
[⊢ΙΙ. Σίμον hαγρυλε̂σι hοικο̂ν, Δ]
[Γ⊢⊢⊢ΙC. hαντίδοτος Γλαύκο, ΔΓ]
[⊢⊢⊢ΙC. hεύδικος, ΔΓ⊢⊢⊢ΙC].

lacuna

We do not know for certain when building work began on the Erechtheum, the irregular Ionic temple that came to house the old statue of Athena Polias, and was also home to various other cults (of Poseidon, Hephaestus, the hero Boutes: see Pausanias I. 26. v; see further Hurwit, *The Athenian Acropolis*, 200–2 for the cults, 205–6 for the date). Although the decree ordering the building may partly survive, its date is uncertain and the reference is not certainly to the Erechtheum (*IG* i³ 132). Similarities of conception between the Erechtheum and the Propylaea, which can be firmly dated to the 430s (*IG* i³ 462–6), and the fact that column drums from the sixth-century *propylon* have been found in the foundations of both, have encouraged claims that the Erechtheum was planned and begun before 431 (cf. on **137**). The mention of a future shrine of Erechtheus in the closing lines of Euripides' *Erechtheus* has encouraged the view that the Erechtheum was at least planned by the date of that play (perhaps late 420s, and certainly before 411, when it is quoted in Ar. *Lys.* 1135 and *Thesm.* 120). We know the the Propylaea was left not completely finished when the Archidamian War began (cf. on **144**), but if foundations for the Erechtheum had been laid then one might perhaps have expected more progress to have been made during the years 421–413. Whenever building began, work had stopped before it was completed, most plausibly when the Spartans occupied Decelea in 413.

Given the survival of accounts for other major acropolis buildings in the second half of the fifth century (**145**, cf. **135**), the absence of building accounts for the early work on the Erechtheum is surprising. But from the time when the Athenians took the decision to resume construction extensive records were kept. Substantial parts of the records in Attic letters for 409/8, 408/7 and perhaps 407/6 survive; smaller fragments in Ionic letters survive from perhaps 407/6 and certainly 406/5 and 405/4 (see S. D. Lambert, *ZPE* cxxxii 2000, 157–60). We give extracts here from the earliest account, firmly dated to 409/8, which has the *epistatai* in charge of the project (cf. **145** and commentary on **141**) inspect the building and report on the finished and unfinished work, and from the accounts for 408/7, in which various sculptural and architectural work is being undertaken.

dr. 2 ob.; Sindron slave of Simias, 14 dr. 2 ob.; Socles slave of Ameiniades, 14 dr. 2 ob.; Sannion slave of Simias, 14 dr. 2 ob.; Epieices slave of Simias, 14 dr. 1 ob.; Sosandrus 14 dr. 1 ob.

242 The next to it in order: Onesimus, slave of Nicostratus, 18 dr. 3½ ob.; Eudoxus living in Alopece 18 dr.; Cleon 18 dr. 2 ob.; Simon living in Agryle, 18 dr. 1½ ob.; Antidotus slave of Glaucus, 18 dr. 1½ ob.; Eudicus, 18 dr. 1½ ob.

lacuna

The interest of these accounts lies in the Athenian decision at this time to resume construction of this building, the care taken to assess the task, and the organisation of the work that is carried out.

The task of assessing the state of the abandoned work on the Erechtheum was undertaken at the very beginning (first prytany) of the council's year 409/8—i.e. in about July 409. In 410/09 the Athenians had taken a firm grip on their finances and had introduced the *diobelia* (**180**). After a show of force by the Spartan king Agis, who marched from the fort at Decelea to the walls of Athens, had been repelled, the Athenians seem to have reasserted themselves in their own territory and fortified Thoricus (Xen. *Hell.* I. i. 33–4, I. ii. 1, and perhaps the payment at *IG* i[3] 377. 18–20). In 409 military activity was resumed on a significant scale and Thrasyllus was sent with a fleet to the Aegean (Xen. *Hell.* I. ii. 1–17, **180**). In all these ways the Athenians seem to have been keen to re-establish democratic control both of Athens itself and Attica and also of the empire. The decision to renew building of the Erechtheum belongs to this context.

The assessment of the state of building by the *epistatai* has occasioned some controversy. There is no doubt that from *A.* 40 onwards they are describing the Erechtheum, but Ferrari has argued that the description in *A.* 8–39 related instead to the old temple of Athena Polias, the remains of which were still visible just north of the Parthenon and the north foundation wall of which runs beneath the Caryatid porch of the Erechtheum. Ferrari's argument rests on the description of the *epistatai* as the *epistatai* 'of the temple on the acropolis in which the ancient statue is' and the implausibility that the ancient statue was already in an unfinished building. Ferrari suggests that the *epistatai* were responsible for a range of buildings, including a temporary shelter for the old statue that had been erected on the site of the ruined temple of Athena Polias, and that the opening description here is of that temple, not the Erechtheum. However, this explanation creates as many problems as it solves: reference to 'the ancient statue' is made in l. 75 and again in *IG* i[3] 475. 269–70, where the reference to the Erechtheum is undoubted; the reference in *A.* 40 to 'all the remaining work' is not naturally understood to mean 'all the remaining work, which is on a different building'; and the nature and dimensions of the blocks referred to in *A*. 8–39 point firmly to the Erechtheum. We therefore continue to think that the *epistatai* are in charge of the Erechtheum alone and that it is the Erechtheum that is described throughout *A* here.

The description given by the *epistatai* is sufficiently detailed to give a precise picture of the state in which they found the Erechtheum, and allows us to reconstruct the order in which building activities were carried out (for what follows see Caskey, in *The Erechtheum*, 301–18). The whole of the central building of the Erechtheum had been constructed up to the frieze of Eleusinian limestone (*A*. 41–2) except at the south-west corner where the tomb of Cecrops was. Here work was complete, to above the height of the Caryatid porch, on which only finishing work remained to be done, but the upper blocks of the wall and the wall-capital and architrave blocks remained to be placed. Some, and perhaps all, of the blocks to complete the wall at this corner were ready, and lying on the ground; they had simply not been put in place when the work had stopped (93–100; a gap in the text follows at this point). A puzzle remains, however, over exactly where the backing-stones described for both the wall-capitals and the architrave belonged. Otherwise what remained to be done was finishing work: columns were unfluted, as were column-bases, and the orthostates and walls were not smoothed. We find confirmation of this being the standard order of work in the unsmoothed walls of the Propylaea and the unfluted columns of the temple of Nemesis at Rhamnous, building of which was also interrupted, probably by the Peloponnesian War.

Once their audit of the state of the building was complete the *epistatai* took charge of completing the building (they are already placing some blocks during their audit: see *A*. 42–3). In *B* we give an extract from the accounts for 408/7. At this point the sculptors are making the figures which were fixed (with lead, also purchased in this year) to the frieze-blocks of Eleusinian stone in order to constitute a frieze running around the exterior of the central building, continuous except where it was interrupted by the north porch which had a separate, slightly taller, frieze. The Eleusinian stone, of a blue-grey colour, provided a naturally coloured, fade-free, backdrop for the frieze, avoiding the need to paint the background as was normal practice. As far as we know, this was the first time an architectural frieze had been carved in this way; the technique was used on some statue bases and in the metopes of the temple of Athena Alea at Tegea in the fourth century, but never caught on. More than a hundred fragments from the Erechtheum frieze survive, but it is possible to reconstruct neither their subject nor their original arrangement, though some identifications with groups described in these accounts have been offered (see further on the frieze P. Boulter, *Antike Plastik* x 1970, 7–25; Ridgway, *Fifth Century Styles in Greek Sculpture*, 93–4; M. Brouskari, in *Kanon . . . E. Berger*, 60–8; K. Glowacki, *Hesperia* lxv 1995, 325–31; B. Holtzmann, *BCH* cxxiv 2000, 221–6). The other work undertaken in 408/7 includes fluting columns, constructing the ceiling, putting up and taking down scaffolding, payments to sawyers and joiners, encaustic painting of architectural mouldings, smoothing of orthostates, making of ceiling-coffer lids and models for coffer decoration, purchase of gold leaf, and purchase of sheets of papyrus (χάρται) on which the working accounts can be written down (two sheets are needed, and cost 2 dr. 4 ob.: *IG* i³ 475. 289–91) and from which this inscription is presumably then made.

The Erechtheum accounts offer us the most detailed picture that we have from the fifth century of the labour force working on a building project, and our best evidence for wage rates (see generally Randall; Feyel, 320–5). 'Architects' (whom we might better term 'master-builders' or 'clerks of works', cf. **141**. 11–12) seem to have been appointed, who oversaw the whole project, and these had annual contracts. Philocles of Acharnae (*A*. 3) was architect in 409/8, Archilochus of Agryle architect in 408/7 (*IG* i³ 476. 2–4). The architect and the labourers, both skilled and unskilled, were employed either on a day-wage or on piece-rates that seem often to be computed on the basis of a day-wage (Loomis, *Wages, Welfare Costs and Inflation in Classical Athens*, 105–8, 115–19). The day-wage is regularly 1 dr. a day. That is what the architect is paid (36 or 37 dr. per prytany, *IG* i³ 476. 59–61, 266–8), and it is the rate of pay for sawyers and carpenters. Piece-work rates are calculated on this basis for unskilled work: putting up and taking down scaffolding, placing ceiling beams. But there are some lower pay rates: the under-secretary is paid only 5 ob. a day (*IG* i³ 476. 61–2, 268–9), which is presumably a matter of hierarchy; but so is one carpenter, perhaps because he had worked less than a full day rather than because he was less skilled. Scholars have debated whether there is any premium for skill in these accounts. Sculptors and those fluting columns are paid by the piece or the task, with the costs of sculptural figures being standard (*B*. 158–80: 60 dr. for one figure, 120 dr. for groups of two, 240 dr. for groups of four, with intermediate prices where groups involve smaller figures). Is that in the expectation that one figure took sixty days' labour? If so (but see *contra*, B. Wesenberg, *AA* 1985, 55–65), then the cost of 350 dr. for fluting one column (see Caskey's discussion in *The Erechtheum*, 411–13) presumably implies an expectation that there is one man-year of labour involved in fluting each column. Laying blocks of Eleusinian stone costs 10 dr. per 16 cubic foot block (*IG* i³ 475. 3; *pro rata* at 475. 5, 6), which should perhaps be seen as a day's labour for a ten-man team, though the payment is made to a single individual.

In the case of the fluting of columns (*IG* i³ 476. 72–104, 192–248 (= *B*. 192–248), 304–27) we can reconstruct a sophisticated work organisation (Caskey, in *The Erechtheum*, 411–13; Feyel, 324). Each of the columns on the east façade of the temple was in the hands of a particular group of labourers, and each group was paid the same total for each of a series of four operations carried out in the same order and for which the price paid was 50, 90, 100 and 110 dr. In some cases two of the operations are carried out in the same prytany, and in one case one operation seems to have been split over two prytanies. Three of the columns are worked on by teams of five men, two by teams of six, and one by a team of seven. (Two teams show some variation over the year: the team with Phalacrus working column 2 has its full five members only in prytany 8; Philorgus slave of Phalacrus is absent in prytany 9; the team of seven with Simias working column 4 has a slave of Simias called Epigenes in prytany

7, replaced by a slave of Simias named Epieices in prytanies 8 and 9. In this latter case we might wonder whether the name had been wrongly recorded or wrongly read from the paper record in prytany 7.) In our extract payments to individual labourers are recorded separately, but elsewhere a single payment is sometimes recorded to the whole group. When separate payments are recorded, most of the time the different labourers fluting the same column are each paid the same amount of money, but occasionally there are slight variations: Simias is paid 13 dr. when six others working on the same column are paid 12 dr. 5 ob. (presumably this was because the total sum for the task did not neatly divide by 7); Onesimus, slave of Nicostratus, is paid 18 dr. 3½ ob. when the others working with him are variously paid 18 dr., 18 dr. 2 ob. or, in three cases, 18 dr. 1½ ob. The maximum income per labourer during a single prytany is 38 dr. for the team of five men who accomplish both the 90-dr. and the 100-dr. task on column 3 in prytany 8. That prytany was thirty-six days long, so this comes close to a day rate of 1 dr. a day. It seems that the price for fluting was fixed in advance, that workmen undertook the task in groups that were either pre-formed or established at the very beginning, but that the groups were still regarded as a set of individuals rather than the total price being paid to the group as a whole and the group deciding how to divide that price up among themselves.

The way in which the sculpted frieze is organised is particularly interesting. In total nine sculptors are paid for frieze figures, Agathanor, Antiphanes, Diocles, Iasus, two sculptors named Mynnion (registered in different demes during the same prytany, and hence not plausibly just one person), Phyromachus, Praxias, Soclus; of these Antiphanes of Cerameis, Iasus of Collytus and Phyromachus of Cephisia are citizens, the rest metics living variously in the urban demes of Agryle, Alopece, Collytus and Melite. None of these sculptors can certainly be identified with sculptors otherwise known, although Phyromachus may be the Pyromachus responsible for a sculpture of Alcibiades driving a chariot mentioned by Pliny (*H.N.* xxxiv. 80), and Praxias may be the man mentioned by Pausanias working at Delphi in the fourth century (x. 19. iv). But the sculpted fragments that survive indicate that their workmanship was of high quality. The team assembled to sculpt the Erechtheum frieze was not nearly as large as that required for the Parthenon, but nevertheless someone in Athens had mustered and organised a team to carve a coordinated frieze in a consistent style. Who was responsible for the design and overseeing the execution is unknown.

In the case of the sculptors we might guess that at least some of the metics involved had moved to Athens specifically to take up these commissions (the Mynnion living in Agryle in 408/7 seems to have moved to the deme of Melite by 406/5). We do not know to what extent that was true of metic labour on the Erechtheum more generally, or whether the labour was drawn from normally resident metics. But it is notable that all the metics bar one, who is registered in Semachidae, come from demes within or immediately around the Themistoclean wall (Feyel, 342–8; cf. **107**).

Of the eighty-six workmen on the Erechtheum whose status is known, Randall counted twenty-four citizens, forty-two metics and twenty slaves; Feyel counted twenty-two citizens, fifty-six metics and eighteen slaves; the differences partly depend on whether or not one counts cases where the name is lost but the presence of the formula 'living in' guarantees a metic (but not necessarily one not mentioned elsewhere).[1] On either count, the pattern is clear. Slaves are found in only two professions, as masons or as carpenters. There are no slave sculptors, woodcarvers, painters, gilders or makers of wax models. In most cases the slave works with and at the same profession as his master (except that the architect Philocles has two slaves who are carpenters), suggesting professional specialist teams. All workers are paid the same for the same job, regardless of status (slave-owners presumably took the wages of their slaves). With the exception of the roles of architect and under-secretary, all the roles taken by citizens are also taken by metics, though metics also supply some skills not here represented by citizens. Some individuals work at more than one trade, most commonly swapping between the less skilled trades: both carpenters and masons appear also as general labourers, though no one appears as both carpenter and mason. One sculptor also produces wax models, as does one woodcarver, while another woodcarver, Manis, a metic and, from his name, possibly an ex-slave, appears also as carpenter, joiner and labourer. All the labourers are male, but one female metic, 'Satyra living in Scambonidae', appears in 405/4 as supplying something, probably oil (fr. XXVIII = *IG* ii² 1654. 40 with S. D. Lambert, *ZPE* cxxxii 2000, 159).

Is this mix of citizen, metic and slave typical of building projects? Or typical of the labour force of craftsmen as a whole? Because the bulk of the actual construction work had been done before these accounts start, the specialised trades involved in finishing the work off are over-represented. This is likely to reduce the proportion of citizens and slaves of citizens and increase the number of metics (with their slaves), since the more specialist the trade the more frequent relocation would be needed to find employment (cf. S. Epstein, *ZPE* clxvi 2008, 108–12, *Anc. Soc.* xl 2010, 1–14). Less certain is whether war casualties have reduced the proportion of citizens. Comparison with accounts from fourth-century Epidaurus suggests that the pattern on the Erechtheum needs no special explanation since major building projects generally relied on access to labour from outside the city concerned: Corinthians, Argives, Athenians, Parians and men from Stymphalus and Tegea are all involved in building the temple of Asclepius and the *tholos* at Epidaurus (Burford, *The Greek Temple Builders at Epidauros*, 201–6). In the light of Vlassopoulos' recent work on the distribution of slave names (*ZPE* clxxv 2010, 113–44, and in Taylor & Vlassopoulos (edd.), *Communities and Networks in the Ancient Greek World*, 101–27; see also on **190**), it is worth noting that of the sixteen different complete names of slaves preserved, just three are names never borne by citizens (an ethnic name, Carion; a foreign name borne by two different slaves, Gerys; and a character name, Epieices, 'Reasonable'—but see above for the suggestion that this name is an error); all the others names are certainly or probably

[1] For important suggestions about the crucial fragments XXVII–XXVIII (*IG* ii² 1654) see S. D. Lambert, *ZPE* cxxxii 2000, 157–60.

also carried by citizens (even character names like Sannion ('Zany') and Sindron ('Rascal') or composite names like Philourgos ('Work-lover')). The proportion of citizen-attested names, and of slaves bearing citizen-attested names, is higher here

---

182

Athens honours the assassins of Phrynichus, 410/09

Six fragments, five of them joining, of a *stele* of Hymettian marble, found on the acropolis; now in the Epigraphical Museum.

Developed Attic writing, use of aspirate inconsistent. Raubitschek detected the same mason's hand in *IG* i³ 180. Lines 3–47 *stoichedon* 36.

M&L 85*; Osborne, *Naturalization in Athens*, D 2; *IG* i³ 102. Trans. Fornara 155; Dillon and Garland³ 13. 30. See also P. J. Wilson, *CQ*² lix 2009, 8–29; A. C. Scafuro, in *Ἀττικά Ἐπιγραφικά . . . C. Habicht*, 47–66.

§i

[ἐπὶ Γλαυκί]ππο ἄ[ρ]χον[τ]ος·
[Λόβον ἐκ] Κεδõν ἐγραμμάτευε.
[ἔδοχσεν τε̃ι] βολε̃ι καὶ τõι δέμοι. hιπποθοντὶ-
[ς ἐπρυτάνε]υε· Λόβον ἐγραμμάτευε· Φιλιστίδε-
[ς ἐπεστάτε·] Γλαύκιππος ἐ̃ρχε : Ἐρασινίδες εἶπ-
[ε· ἐπαινέσα]ι Θρασύβολον ὁς ὄντα ἄνδρα ἀγαθὸ-
[ν περὶ τὸν δε̃μ]ον τὸν Ἀθεναίον καὶ πρόθυμον π-
[οιε̃ν hó τι δύνα]ται ἀγαθόν· καὶ ἀντὶ hõν εὖ πεπο-
[ίεκεν τέν τε πόλιν] καὶ τὸν δε̃μ[ο]ν τὸν Ἀθεναίο-
[ν στεφανõσαι αὐτὸν χρυσõι στε]φάνοι, ποιε̃σα-
[ι δὲ τὸν στέφανον ἀπὸ χιλίον δρ]αχμõν· hοι [δὲ h]-
[ελλενοταμίαι δόντον τὸ ἀργύρι]ον. καὶ [ἀνειπ]-
[ε̃ν Διονυσίον τραγοιδõν ἐν τõι] ἀγõνι hõν hέν-
[εκα αὐτὸν hο δε̃μος ἐστεφάνοσ]ε ⁝

§ii

Διοκλε̃ς εἶπε·
[τὰ μὲν ἄλλα καθάπερ τε̃ι βολε̃ι·] εἶναι δὲ Θρασύ-
[βολον Ἀθεναῖον, καὶ φυλε̃ς τε κ]αὶ φρατρίας hõ-
[ν ἂν βόλεται γράφσασθαι αὐτό]ν· καὶ τἆλλα τὰ ἐ-

We have offered full restorations but these are not secure in their details. We list important areas of uncertainty. 9 πόλιν: βολέν is also possible. 13 Διονυσίον τραγοιδõν ἐν τõι] ἀγõνι P. J. Wilson & A. Hartwig, *ZPE* clxix 2009, 21–2: τὸν κέρυκα Διονυσίον ἐν τõι] ἀγõνι M&L.

even than in Vlassopoulos's sample of freedmen. Vlassopoulos's suggestion that the use of citizen-attested names occurred more in more skilled professions gains some support from this sample.

---

§i

In the archonship of Glaucippus; Lobon from Cedoi was secretary.

3 Resolved by the council and people. Hippothontis was the prytany; Lobon was the secretary; Philistides was chairman; Glaucippus was archon. Erasinides proposed:

6 Praise Thrasybulus, who is a man good to the people of the Athenians and keen to do all the good he can. And in return for the good he has done the city and the people of the Athenians, crown him with a gold crown, and make the crown from 1,000 dr. The *hellenotamiai* are to give the money. And announce at the tragedy competition of the Dionysia the reason why the people crowned him.

§ii

14 Diocles proposed: In other respects in accordance with the council, but Thrasybulus is to be an Athenian and he is to be enrolled in whichever tribe and phratry he may want. And the other

[φσεφισμένα τôι δέμοι κύρια ἐ͂]ναι Θρασυβόλο- [ι· ἐ͂ναι δὲ αὐτõι εὑρίσκεσθαι π]αρὰ Ἀθεναίον κ- [αὶ ἄλλο hó τι ἂν δοκε͂ι ἀγαθὸν π]ερὶ hõν εὐεργέ- [τεκεν τ̀ν δε͂μον τὸν Ἀθεναίον.] καὶ ἀναγραφσά- [το ho γραμματεὺς τὰ ἐφσεφισμ]ένα· hελέσθαι δ- [ὲ ἐγ βολε͂ς πέντε ἄνδρας αὐτί]κα μάλα, hοίτινε- [ς] δι[κάσοσι Θρασυβόλοι τὸ μέ]ρος τὸ γιγνόμεν- ον. τὸς [δὲ ἄλλος, hóσοι τότε εὖ ἐ]ποίεσαν τὸν δε͂- μον τὸν Ἀθε[ναίον, — 10 —]ιν καὶ Ἀγόρατο- ν καὶ Κόμονα [καὶ — 6 —]ọ[.]ọ[....] καὶ Σῖμον κα- ὶ Φιλῖνον κα[ὶ — 8 —]α, εὐεργέ[τα]ς [ἀ]ναγράφ- σαι ἐμ πόλε[ι ἐν στέλει λ]ιθίνει τὸν γραμ[μα]τέ- α τε͂ς βολε͂ς. [καὶ ἔγκτεσι]ν εῖναι αὐτοῖς ὅμπερ Ἀθεναίοις, [καὶ γεπέδο]ν καὶ οἰκίας, καὶ οἴκεσ- ιν Ἀθένεσι, [καὶ ἐπιμέλ]εσθαι αὐτõν τὲν βολὲν τὲν αἰεὶ β[ολεύοσαν κα]ὶ τὸς πρυτάνες, hόπος ἂ- ν μὲ ἀδι[κõνται. τὲν δὲ σ]τέλεν ἀπομισθοσάντο- [ν hοι πολεταὶ ἐν τε͂ι βο]λε͂ι· τὸς δὲ hελλενοταμ- [ίας δõναι τὸ ἀργύριον]. ἐὰν δὲ δοκε͂ι αὐτὸς καὶ [ἄλλο εὑρίσκεσθαι, τὲν] βολὲν προβολεύσασαν [ἐχσενεγκε͂ν ἐς τὸν δε͂μ]ον :

§iii

Εὔδικος εῖπε· τὰ μὲν [ἄλλα καθάπερ Διοκλε͂ς· περὶ] δὲ τõν δοροδοκεσ- [άντον ἐπὶ τõι φσεφίσματι], ὃ ἐφσεφ[ί]σθε Ἀπολλ- [οδόροι, τὲν βολὲν βολεῦσ]αι ἐν τε͂ι πρότει hέδ- [ραι ἐν τõι βουλευτερί]οι, καὶ κολάζεν, τõν [δ]ορο- [δοκεσάντον καταφσ]εφιζομένεν καὶ ἐς δικασ- [τέριον αὐτὸς ἐσάγε]ν, καθότι ἂν δοκε͂ι αὐτε͂[ι]· τ- [ὸς δὲ βολευτὰς τὸς] παρόντας ἀποφαίνεν hά[ττ'] [ἂν εἰδõσιν, καὶ ἐάν] τίς τι ἄλλο αἰδε͂ι περὶ τ[ού-] [τον· ἐχσε͂ναι δὲ καὶ] ἰδιότει, ἐάν τις βόλετα[ι. *v*]

vacat

23 [ὲ τὸν δε͂μον τρε͂ς ἄνδρας] Michel. 36 ἐὰν δὲ δοκε͂ι αὐτὸς καὶ | [ἄλλο ἄχσιος ἀγαθõ *IG* i^{2}. 44 αὐτὸς ἐσάγε]ν *IG* i^{2}, Rhodes, *Boule*, 161 n. 4: παραδιδõσα]ν Lipsius, *Das attische Recht und Rechtsvervahren*, 184 n. 23, M&L, *IG*.

Phrynichus comes to our attention as a political figure only in 411, though what the speaker of Lys. xx. *Polystratus* 10–12 says about him implies that he was probably then in his sixties, and he had some previous political prominence (Lys. xxv. *Overthrowing Demos* 9). He had been elected general for 412/1, and was sent with two

things that have been decreed by the people are to be valid for Thrasybulus. And it shall be possible for him to find also from the Athenians whatever else may seem good concerning the benefaction he has bestowed on the people of the Athenians. The secretary is to write up what has been decreed. Let five men be chosen from the council immediately to decide the part due to Thrasybulus. And the secretary of the council is to write up the others who did good to the people of the Athenians then, —is and Agoratus and Comon and —— and Simon and Philinus and —es, as benefactors on the stone *stele* on the acropolis. They are to have the same right to own property that the Athenians have, both a plot of land and houses, and to dwell at Athens, and whatever council and *prytaneis* are in power are to look after them in order that they suffer no wrong. The *poletai* are to put the *stele* out to tender in the council. The *hellenotamiai* are to give the money. And if it resolves that they be found something additional, the council is to make a preliminary proposal and bring it to the people.

§iii

38 Eudicus proposed: In other respects in accordance with Diocles, but concerning those who have given bribes for the decree which was voted for Apollodorus, the council is to take counsel at the first sitting in the council chamber and to punish them, condemning those who have given bribes and bringing them to a court as seems best to it. The councillors present are to reveal what they know, including anything else anyone knows about these men. And it is to be possible also for a private invididual (to give information) if someone wishes to do so.

---

colleagues and forty-eight ships to Samos (Thuc. VIII. 25. i). He caused the Athenians to withdraw to Samos after an incomplete victory at Miletus, because he had intelligence of the arrival of a Peloponnesian fleet, and earned Thucydides' praise for being 'not unintelligent' in this as in other actions (VIII. 27. v). Subsequently he led the opposition to proposals from Alcibiades about securing assistance from Tissaphernes and the Persian King, reckoning that Alcibiades was simply attempting to serve his own personal interests and that the allies wanted freedom rather than a change to oligarchic rule. When it looked as if he would be unsuccessful in this opposition he engaged in a series of intrigues against Alcibiades which secured his own standing with the Athenian troops (VIII. 48–51). However, his conduct was presented in such a way by Peisander that the Athenians dismissed Phrynichus from the generalship (viii. 54. III). He returned to Athens, and was sufficiently reconciled with the other oligarchs to be keenly involved in the coup after they had decided to go ahead without Alcibiades—motivated, Thucydides suggests, by fear of Alcibiades and determination to prevent Alcibiades' return (VIII. 68. iii). Arist. *Pol.* v. 1305 B 27 tells us that Phrynichus' group (οἱ περὶ Φρύνιχον) became dominant among the Four Hundred by demagogy, but we have no details of how the Four Hundred worked, and we meet Phrynichus in action only as one of the Four Hundred sent as an ambassador to Sparta (Thuc. VIII. 90) to make peace on any acceptable terms. It was on his return from Sparta and in the context of public suspicion created by building-work in the Piraeus that Phrynichus was murdered (Thuc. VIII. 92. ii).

This decree, dated to the spring of 409, a year and a half after Phrynichus' murder, attests to the controversy that surrounded that event. In the decree, which never names Phrynichus, honours are given to one Thrasybulus: initially a gold crown, but increased in Diocles' amendment to citizenship. The amendment also records a further set of men as benefactors—a list including Agoratus, Comon, Simon and Philinus and three or four others. In a further amendment reference is made to an earlier decree honouring one Apollodorus and to men who bribed their way onto that *stele*, ordering the council to investigate.

The debate about who was involved and what reward they deserved is revealed also by the varied accounts given in literary sources. According to Thucydides the murder occurred 'in the crowded agora, not far from the council chamber', and the man responsible was 'one of the *peripoloi*' whose accomplice, an Argive, was captured, and tortured, named no names but claimed that many had been in on the plot. Eighty years later, in his speech *Against Leocrates* (§112), Lycurgus claimed that the murder had happened by night 'by the fountain at the osiers', that those responsible had been Apollodorus and Thrasybulus, that they had been arrested and imprisoned, but released by the people who had insisted on an inquiry which had declared Phrynichus a traitor and those who had killed him wrongly arrested; and that Critias had moved a decree which had condemned Phrynichus for treachery *post mortem*, insisted on his body not being buried in Attica, and threatened any who defended him with the same punishment. (Plut. *Alc.* 25. xiv claims the murderer was Hermon, but this is due to Plutarch's confused memory, conflating Thuc. VIII. 92. ii with 92. v.)

The fullest account of the aftermath of the murder comes from Lysias' speech XIII. *Against Agoratus*, dated to the early 390s, in which Lysias tries to show that Agoratus had not been himself involved in the murder (70–2). According to Lysias, Thrasybulus of Calydon and Apollodorus of Megara were responsible for the murder, and Thrasybulus was the one who struck the blow. He quotes a decree which he says names both Thrasybulus and Apollodorus and grants them citizenship but does not make Agoratus a citizen. He then claims that others managed to get themselves listed as 'benefactors' by giving money to the proposer of the decree, and he quotes another decree to this effect.

In some ways Lysias' claims chime well with this decree: Thrasybulus is here made a citizen and Apollodorus has certainly been honoured. Agoratus is among those given some honour, and there is suspicion of individuals having bribed their way onto the list of benefactors. But in other respects the relationship is highly problematic. Agoratus is mentioned in association with the honours for Thrasybulus, but the suspicion of bribery surrounds the honours for Apollodorus. If Thrasybulus was the one who struck the blow, why is Apollodorus the first to be honoured? And if Apollodorus had already been honoured with citizenship, why was granting citizenship to Thrasybulus only an afterthought? That Apollodorus was given citizenship, or at least the right to own land, and that Apollodorus' claims were not impugned, whatever the enquiry about bribery in relation to the decree for him found, seems confirmed by his being given land once owned by Peisander and retaining it till shortly before the installation of the Thirty (Lys. VII. *Olive Stump* 4). Was Lysias giving a very misleading account of the decrees he selectively quoted? Or was this decree followed by a further decree, quoted by Lysias, which reaffirmed the honours for Apollodorus (and Thrasybulus) but also confirmed that others had falsely got themselves lesser honours by bribery? Even in such circumstances, the Thucydidean claim that the deed was done by a *peripolos* (i.e. an Athenian citizen border guard: see Andrewes, *HCT* v. 310, and above on **171**), assisted by an Argive, needs to be borne in mind (whether any Argives hide in the list of names in ll. 26–8 we cannot tell). Thucydides' language, in particular his insistence that the Argive accomplice revealed no names, suggests that he pressed his own version despite knowing that the Athenians had honoured others for this action (cf. Hornblower, *Comm. Thuc.*, on Thuc. VIII. 92. ii).

This decree shows well the working of the Athenian political system. The original proposal by Erasinides, who is plausibly the man who was general at Arginusae in 406 and subsequently executed (Xen. *Hell.* I. vi. 29, vii. 2, 34; Philoch. *FGrH* 328 F 42), to honour Thrasybulus with a crown was made in the council. Whether there was a debate there about the scale of honour is unknown, and we should not exclude the possibility that the council deliberately backed the 'safe' option. One Diocles then tried out on the assembly the proposal to grant citizenship to Thrasybulus and the right to own land and a house at Athens to the seven or eight others involved, and this passed. This effectively treated these foreigners in the way that men like Heracleides of Clazomenae were treated (**157**; cf. *IG* i^3 81. 22, the only other example of an *enktesis* grant in the fifth century), and imposed a duty on the council to look after those honoured. Eudicus then took advantage of Diocles having opened up the subject of discussion beyond Thrasybulus in order to raise the question of bribery in relation to the decree about Apollodorus, and everything was referred back to the council (on Eudicus' amendment see Scafuro).

That so many non-Athenians were involved in the assassination of Phrynichus, or could plausibly claim to be involved, is at first sight surprising. Those whose origins we know of here are from Arcadian Calydon, Megara and Argos—cities within the Peloponnesian League or which had good reason to fear Sparta. That Phrynichus was killed in the immediate aftermath of his mission to Sparta may indicate that what particularly disturbed these men was the prospect that Sparta, and Spartan influence over her allies and the cities of the Peloponnese, was about to become even stronger. One might compare the number of non-Athenians who took part in the restoration of democracy at Athens in 403 (cf. R&O 4). The provision here that the council take care of those honoured, which is parallel to the provisions of protection for those honoured as *proxenoi*, who might be thought to need protecting for championing unpopular Athenian interests in their home cities, may indicate the expectation of a possible backlash from the supporters of oligarchy.

This is an important document in the history of Athenian honours. Athens had long honoured Athenians who were victors in panhellenic games, and it honoured the 'tyrannicides', Harmodius and Aristogeiton, with statues and their descendants with meals in the *prytaneion* (*IG* i^3 131). But the only individual Athenian we know to have been honoured in the fifth century is Cleon, after his victory at Pylos, to whose meals in the *prytaneion* and front seat in the theatre Aristophanes repeatedly alludes (*Eq.* 280–1, 573–6, 702–9, 766, 1404). Fifth-century Athens restricted its inscribed honours to non-Athenians, initially granting them the status of '*proxenos* and benefactor' and judicial rights and tax status equivalent to those possessed by Athenians (e.g. *IG* i^3 19, 24, 27, of *c*.450). In the 420s the right to own land at Athens seems to have been added (see above, and cf. J. Pečírka, in *Geras . . . G. Thomson*, 193–201) in some cases, presumably where there was some expectation that the person honoured might wish to move to Athens. But the honours in this inscription are different, both because this is the first time that we have either a gold crown or

183

Republication of Athenian laws, 410/09–400/399

A (Draco's law on homicide)

The upper part of a marble *stele* (broken but repaired), found during the building of the cathedral at Athens, now in the Epigraphical Museum. Phot. Stroud, *Drakon's Law on Homicide*, pls. 1–3; facsimile *op. cit.*, fig. 1.

Developed Attic writing, using h except in ll. 1–9. *Stoichedon* 50 apart from the headings in ll. 1, 2, 10, 56 (on ll. 28–9 see *apparatus*).

an announcement at the Dionysia (cf. P. J. Wilson & A. Hartwig, *ZPE* clxix 2009, 17–27; Wilson, esp. 20–2), and because the non-Athenians honoured here seem generally expected to remain in Athens (and in the case of Agoratus, at least, did). Although the Athenians had made a mass grant of citizenship to the Plataeans in 427 (cf. **191**), the few individual citizenship grants until this date seem to have been reserved for foreign rulers (Sadocus, Tharyps, perhaps Alexander of Macedon), signal generosity (Menon of Pharsalus) or betraying a foreign city in crucial circumstances (Carystion of Samos; perhaps Eponphes, *IG* XII. iii 1187 = i^3 1505 (a Melian given Athenian citizenship?); cf. Byzantines in Xen. *Hell.* II. ii. 1 with I. iii. 18); the decision to grant citizenship in this case was therefore not trivial.[1] This decree paves the way for the (debates about the) honours for those non-Athenians who helped in the restoration of democracy in 403 (R&O 4). Only in the 390s do the Athenians begin to publish honours for their own citizens, awarding a statue to Conon (cf. R&O 8, 11).

The delay between the fall of the Four Hundred and the passing of these honours may not have been due only to the multiple claims made to involvement in the killing. The announcement of the honours for Thrasybulus at the Dionysia followed the mass oath taken by the Athenians 'before the Dionysia' of 409 (Andoc. I. *Mysteries* 96–8), which itself reiterated the demand that Athenians rally to the defence of democracy and kill tyrants (Wilson; J. L. Shear, in Sommerstein & Fletcher (edd.), *Horkos*, 148–60). This was a highly political festival, and one at which the victorious tragedy was a powerful exploration of the relations between force and persuasion, Sophocles' *Philoctetes*.

[1] The grants to the painter Polygnotus of Thasos and to Pericles' son by Aspasia seem to be unique uses.

IG i^2 115; M&L 86; Stroud, *Drakon's Law on Homicide*; *IG* i^3 104*. Trans. Fornara 15. B; Arnaoutoglou 63; Dillon & Garland[3] 8. 3. See also MacDowell, *Athenian Homicide Law in the Age of the Orators*; Gagarin, *Drakon and Early Athenian Homicide Law*; G. Thür, in *Law, Rhetoric and Comedy in Classical Athens ... D. M. MacDowell*, 37; A. B. Gallia, *CQ*[2] liv 2004, 451–60.

§i

Διόγν[ε]τος Φρεάρριος ἐγραμμάτε[υε·]
Διοκλε͂ς ε͂ρχε.
ἔδοχσεν τε͂ι βουλε͂ι καὶ το͂ι δέμοι. Ἀκα[μ]αντὶ̣ς ἐπ[ρ]υ̣τάνευε· [Δ]ι̣ό[γ]-
νετος ἐγραμμάτευε· Εὐθύδικος [ἐ]πεστάτε. [. .]ε[. . .]άνες εἶπε· τὸ[ν]
Δράκοντος νόμον τὸμ περὶ το͂ φό[ν]ο ἀναγρα[φ]σά[ν]τον οἱ ἀναγραφε͂-
ς το͂ν νόμον παραλαβόντες παρὰ το͂ β[α]σ̣[ι]λ̣έ[ος με[τ[ὰ το͂ γραμμ]ατέο-
ς τε͂ς βουλε͂ς ἐστέλει λιθίνει καὶ κα[τ]α[θ]έντ̲[ον πρόσ]θε[ν] τε͂ς στο-
ᾶς τε͂ς βασιλείας· οἱ δὲ πολεταὶ ἀπ̣ομι[σθο]σ[άντον κατὰ τὸν ν]όμο-
ν· οἱ δὲ ἑλλενοταμίαι δόντον τὸ ἀρ[γ]ύ[ρ]ι[ον.] *vacat*

§ii

προ͂τος ἄχσον.
καὶ ἐὰμ μὲ ᾿κ [π]ρονοί[α]ς̲ [κ]τ̲[ένει τίς τινα, φεύγ]ε[ν. δ]ι-
κάζεν δὲ τὸς βασιλέας αἴτ̣ιο[ν] φόν̣[ο] Ε[——17——]Ε [β]ολ-
εύσαντα· τὸς δὲ ἐφέτας διαγν[ο͂]ν̣[α]ι̣. [αἰδέσασθαι δ' ἐὰμ μὲν πατὲ]ρ ε͂-
ι ε͂ ἀδελφὸ[ς] ε͂ hυε͂ς, hάπαντ[α]ς ε͂ τὸν κ̣ο[λύοντα κρατε͂ν. ἐὰν δὲ μὲ] ḥοῦ-
τοι ο͂σ̣ι, μέχρ' ἀνεφ[σι]ότετος καὶ [ἀνεφσιο͂, ἐὰν hάπαντες αἰδέσ]α̣σ-
θαι ἐθέλοσι, τὸν κο[λύ]οντ̣α [κ]ρα[τε͂ν. ἐὰν δὲ τούτον μεδὲ hε͂ς ε͂ι, κτ]ε-
νει δὲ ἄκο[ν], γνο͂σι δὲ hο̣ι [πε]ντ[έκοντα καὶ hε͂ς hοι ἐφέται ἄκοντ]α̣
κτε͂ναι, ἐσέσ̲θ[ο]ν δὲ ḥ[οι φ]ρ[άτερες ἐὰν ἐθέλοσι δέκα· τούτος δ]ὲ ḥο̣-
ι πεντέκο[ν]τ[α καὶ] hε͂ς ἀρ̲[ι]στ̲[ίνδεν hαιρέσθον. καὶ hοι δὲ πρ]ότε[ρ]-
ον κτέ[ν]α[ντ]ε[ς ἐν] το͂[ιδε το͂ι θεσμο͂ι ἐνεχέσθον. προειπε͂ν δ]ὲ το͂ι κ-
τέν̣α̣ν̣[τι ἐν ἀ]γορ[ᾶι μέχρ' ἀνεφσιότετος καὶ ἀνεφσιο͂· συνδιόκ]εν
δὲ [κ]ἀνεφσ[ιὸς καὶ ἀνεφσιο͂ν παῖδας καὶ γαμβρὸς καὶ πενθερὸ]ς κ-
αὶ φρ[ά]τ[ε]ρ̲[ας ——36——] αἴτι-
ος [ε͂ι] φό[νο ——26—— τὸς πεντέκοντ]α κ̣α̣ὶ
h[ένα ——42——] φόνο
hέλ̣οσ[ι ——35—— ἐὰν δ]έ [τ]ις τ-
ὸ[ν ἀν]δ̣ρ[οφόνον κτένει ε͂ αἴτιος ε͂ι φόνο, ἀπεχόμενον ἀγορᾶ]ς ἐφο-
ρί[α]ς κ̣[α]ὶ [ἄθλον καὶ hιερο͂ν Ἀμφικτυονικο͂ν, hόσπερ τὸν Ἀθεν]αῖον κ̣-
[τένα]ν̣[τα ἐν τοῖς αὐτοῖς ἐνέχεσθαι· διαγιγνόσκεν δὲ τὸς] ἐ[φ]έτα[ς].
after which only a few letters can be read at the beginnings and ends of lines as far as l. 58; most noteworthy are

Letters underlined were seen by earlier scholars but could not be seen by Stroud. 4 [Ἀθ]ε[νοφ]ά̣νες U. Köhler, *Hermes* ii 1867, 27–36, [Χσ]ε[νοφά]νες A. Kirchhoff, *IG* i¹ 61, and there are other possibilities. 10 προ͂τος ἄχσον is in larger letters than the surrounding text, and the line which we number 11 continues from that on a slightly lower level, so that there is a blank space between ll. 9 and 11. 12 ε͂ [τὸν αὐτόχερα ε͂ τὸν βου]λ|εύσαντα H. J. Wolff, *Traditio* iv 1946, 71–8, before Stroud's edition, ε[ἴτε τὸν αὐτόχερα εἴτ]ε *vel sim.* Stroud, ε͂[ναι ε͂ χειρὶ ἀράμενον] ε͂ G. Thür, *JJP* xx 1990, 152 cf. Antiph. vi. *Chor.* 16. 13–23 restored from law *ap.* Dem. xliii. *Macartatus* 57, where the text of 20–3 precedes that of 13–20, and 14–16 is omitted. 18, 23 φράτερες/ας Lambert, *The Phratries of Attica*, 248–9 n. 19: φράτορες/ας editors. 26–9 restored from Dem. xxiii. *Aristocrates* 38–42 with law *ap.* 37 (28 as restored has 52 letters and 29 as restored has 51 letters).

§i

Diognetus of Phrearrhii was the secretary; Diocles [409/8] was the archon.

3 Resolved by the council and the people. Acamantis was the prytany; Diognetus was the secretary; Euthydicus was the chairman. —phanes proposed:

4 Draco's law about homicide shall be written up on a stone *stele* by the *anagrapheis* ['writers-up'] of the laws, taking it over from the *basileus* and the secretary of the council, and placed in front of the Stoa of the *Basileus*. The *poletai* shall make the contract in accordance with the law; the *hellenotamiai* shall provide the money.

§ii

10 First *axon*.

11 And if anybody kills anybody not from forethought, he shall be exiled. The *basileis* shall pronounce responsible for homicide [?the one who himself killed or the one] who planned it; the *ephetai* shall decide it.

13 There shall be reconciliation, if there are a father or brother or sons, to be granted by all, or the objector shall prevail. If these do not exist, then as far as cousinhood and cousin, if they are all willing to grant reconciliation, or the objector shall prevail. If none of these exists but he killed unwillingly and the fifty-one *ephetai* decide that he killed unwillingly, let ten members of the phratry allow him to enter if they are willing: these shall be chosen by the fifty-one on the basis of good birth.

19 And those who killed previously shall be liable to this ordinance.

20 There shall be a proclamation against the killer in the agora by those as far as cousinhood and cousin; there shall join in the prosecution cousins and cousins' sons and brothers-in-law and fathers-in-law and phratry members. – – –

23 – – – is responsible for homicide – – – the fifty-one – – – convict of homicide – – –

26 If anybody kills a killer, or is responsible for his being killed, when he is keeping away from a frontier market and Amphictyonic contests and rites, he shall be liable to the same things as for killing; the *ephetai* shall decide – – –

36 ΕΙΣΕ ἐλεύθ-
ε[ρ]ος ἒ̣ι. κ̣α̣[ὶ ἐὰν φέροντα ἒ ἄγοντα βίαι ἀδίκος εὐθὺς] ἀ̣μυνόμενο-
ς κτέ[ν]ει, ν̣[εποινὲ τεθνάναι.
and
56 [δεύτ]ε̣ρος [ἄχσον.]
which with the text continuing from it seems to have been treated in the same way as ll. 10–11.

36–8 restored from Dem. XXIII. 60 with law.
We learn that a new study of the readings and restorations is to be published by E. M. Harris.

After the legislation of Draco in the late seventh century and of Solon in the early sixth Athens had no further comprehensive act of legislation, but laws were made by decrees of the assembly as and when they were felt necessary. At the end of the fifth century and the beginning of the fourth, perhaps as a result of realising in connection with the oligarchic revolutions of 411 that on many points it was not clear what the currently valid law was, the Athenians embarked on a new publication of the current laws.

We learn from Lys. XXX. *Nicomachus*, esp. 2–5, that Nicomachus was one of a board of *anagrapheis* who were appointed in 410/09 to write up the laws of Solon, that they had still not finished when the Thirty came to power in 404, and that they were reappointed on the restoration of the democracy and worked again, particularly on the religious calendar, from 403/2 to 400/399.[1] Andoc. I. *Myst.* 81–2 with decree of Teisamenus *ap.* 83–4[2] tells us that the restored democracy was to be based on the laws of Solon and the ordinances (*thesmoi*) of Draco. It appears that what was intended, and what led to the work's taking longer than expected, was that the *anagrapheis* should in fact republish all the laws valid under the late fifth-century democracy, and this gave Nicomachus' prosecutor the opportunity to accuse him of departing from his brief by making additions and subtractions. Solon in 594/3 was believed to have replaced all of Draco's laws of 621/0 except that on homicide (*Ath. Pol.* 7. i, Plut. *Sol.* 17. i); it may well be that despite the silence of Lys. XXX Draco was coupled with Solon in 410/09 as in 403/2. This inscription records in §i a specific instruction to the *anagrapheis* in 409/8 to republish Draco's law on homicide (and Gallia considers why there might have been a specific instruction in this case). Payment for the inscription by the *hellenotamiai* reflects the new financial regime in force from 410 (cf. on **180**).

The law is quoted from a 'first *axon*' (10), followed by a 'second *axon*' (56). Solon's laws too were published on *axones* or *kyrbeis* (*Ath. Pol.* 7. i, Plut. *Sol.* 25. i–ii), and there

[1] On the whole project see Shear, *Polis and Revolution*, 70–101, 238–45.

[2] The decree of Teisamenus is rejected as a forgery by M. Canevaro & E. M. Harris, *CQ*[2] lxii 2012, 110–6, but what we state here is stated in Andocides' own text.

36 – – – he is a free man. And if he kills a man by defending immediately when he is forcibly and unjustly taking and removing, that man shall have been killed without penalty – – –

56 Second *axon.*

57 – – –

---

has been much discussion of whether the words denote one set of objects or two different sets, what they were like and how long they survived: Rhodes, *Comm. Ath. Pol.*, 131–5, surveys the evidence and modern bibliography, arguing for one set of four-sided wooden pillars revolving on axles (cf. the drawing in his *Aristotle, The Athenian Constitution*, 123 fig. 1), of which the original text and/or a transcription was accessible in the fourth century, but the questions remain controversial. According to *Ath. Pol.* Solon's *axones* were placed in the Stoa of the *Basileus*, the northernmost building on the west side of the agora; but that was not built until the late sixth century or later (cf. Camp, *The Athenian Agora: Site Guide*[5], 79), so it cannot have been their original home. Some have doubted whether Draco's laws were published on *axones* and what we have is in fact Draco's law (e.g. T. J. Figueira, in *Nomodeiktes . . . M. Ostwald*, 291–5).

The law as quoted begins with the word *kai*, 'and' or perhaps 'even' (11), and proceeds to deal with killing 'not from forethought' (11) or 'unwillingly' (17). Some, including Stroud, 34–40, Gagarin, cf. Osborne, *Greece in the Making*[2], 176, believe that if the word is translated 'even' this can indeed be the beginning of Draco's law; others, including M&L and Rhodes, *Comm. Ath. Pol.*, 111–12, believe that Draco's law cannot have begun so abruptly and the beginning must have been omitted, presumably because a more recent law had supplanted it. In the classical period cases of 'willing' homicide were tried by the Areopagus (*Ath. Pol.* 57. iii), but it seems likely that at least until the time of Solon the Areopagus as a body was involved with major offences against the state but not with homicide (Solon's amnesty law in Plut. *Sol.* 19. iii–iv with Ruschenbusch, *Solon: Das Gesetzeswerk—Fragmente*, 27–8, 137). There is disagreement also whether 'not from forethought' and 'unwillingly' are synonymous (e.g. MacDowell, 59–60, and his *Demosthenes, Against Meidias*, 258–9, Gagarin, 46–7, with which we agree), or the latter is a sub-category within the former (e.g. Stroud, 40–1); on the difference between 'willing' and 'unwilling' homicide see also Rickert, *ἕκων and ἄκων in Early Greek Thought*; E. M. Harris, in Leão *et al.* (edd.), *Nomos*, 245–51. Dem. XXIII. 72 gives more detail about the sentence of exile.

The *basileis* have to *dikazein*, and the *ephetai* have to *diagnonai* (11–13). Most probably this means that the *ephetai* decide the verdict and the *basileis* formally pronounce the outcome (Stroud, 42–5, MacDowell, 38, Gagarin, 47–8), but some have seen it as the *basileis*' task to initiate rather than conclude the process (for instance, G. Thür, e.g. in *Law, Rhetoric and Comedy . . . D. M. MacDowell*, 36–8). *Basileis* (plural) might refer to successive holders of the position of *basileus*, one of the nine archons, in successive years (Stroud, 45–6), but that would be an abnormal usage; the court to try homicide attributed to animals and inanimate objects comprised the *basileus* and the *phylobasileis*, the heads of Athens' four old tribes (*Ath. Pol.* 57. iv), and we agree with M&L and the majority of recent discussions that they are probably what is meant here (MacDowell, 87–8, is agnostic).[3] The *ephetai* (13) number fifty-one (17): it is perhaps more likely than not that they were members of the Areopagus, but this remains uncertain (cf. MacDowell, 48–57, Stroud, 47–9, Rhodes, *Comm. Ath. Pol.*, 646–8). They also tried cases for killing non-citizens, for lawful homicide and for a second homicide alleged against a man already exiled for a first (*Ath. Pol.* 57. iii–iv). *Bouleusis* is planning an act performed by somebody else, in this context presumably an act of unwilling homicide (cf. *Ath. Pol.* 57. iii, MacDowell, 60–9).

Ath. Pol. 57. iii refers to men subject to exile in cases where 'reconciliation (*aidesis*) is possible', and here ll. 13–20 spell out the conditions for granting reconciliation to an unwilling killer, by concentric circles of men related to the victim. If they exist, it must be granted by his father, brother(s) and sons, who must be unanimous. If there are none of them, by the wider family 'as far as cousinhood and cousin', with 'cousinhood' usually interpreted as sons of cousins, i.e. cousins once removed (Dem. XLIII. 63 with

[3] For a very different view of 11–13 see W. Schmitz, *Klio* lxxxiii 2001, 7–38.

B (laws about the council of five hundred)

Four fragments of a marble *stele* (broken but repaired), found on the acropolis, now in the Epigraphical Museum. Phot. *BSA* xxxiii 1932/3, 114–16 figs. 7–9, and pl. 15; drawings 117 fig. 10, pl. 16. (Wade-Gery's fragments *a, b, c, d* = *IG* i³'s fragments *a, b, d, c*; and in *IG* the label *c* should be applied to the right-hand ends of ll. 21–5.)

Developed Attic writing, using h. *Stoichedon* 66.

IG i² 114 + 49. *c*; *IG* i³ 105*. See also H. T. Wade-Gery, *BSA* xxxiii 1932/3, 113–22; D. M. Lewis, *JHS* lxxxvii 1967, 132; Rhodes, *Boule*, 183, 195–9; F. X. Ryan, *JHS* cxiv 1994, 120–34.

A complete text cannot be reconstructed: out of sixty lines from which there are some letters preserved we print 27–52.

[— 11 — οὐκ ἐπιφσ]εφιô ἐμ [β]ολ̣ε̂ι: οὔ[τ'] ἐ̣[ν ἐ]κ̣[λεσίαι] α[— 16 —] ι[.]ι[. .]
[— 9 — ἐὰν δὲ ἐπιφσ]εφίζο τ[. .]μ̣οσ[. . .]ο̣[— 25 —]ο̣σ̣ιον̣[. .]
[— 12 — μέτε δεμ]οσίον μέτε [ἰδ]ίον [— 27 —]ο[.]π[. . .]
[— 19 —] βολεύεν [τ]ὸ[ς] πεντακ[οσί]ο[ς — 21 —] .[. . . .]
[— 17 — πε]ν̣τ̣ακοσι[. .]δραχ̣μ̣[— 6 —]το[— 18 —]Λ[.] . [. . . .]
[— 5 — ?μέχρι πεντακοσί]ον δρ[α]χμ[ôν], πλέον δὲ μ̣ὲ ἒ̣ν̣αι ἐ̣π̣[ιβάλλεν? — 8 —] . [,]
O[— 5 —]
[— 20 —]ον ἐν τôι ·βολευτερίοι τὲν βο[λὲν — 11 —] . . O . [— 5 —]

law *ap.* 62, cf. MacDowell, 18), though I. Kidd, in *Owls to Athens* . . . *K. Dover*, 216–17, argues for 'cousinhood, i.e. cousin'. If there are none of them either, then the killer may be 'allowed to enter [Attica]' by ten members of the phratry, the notional kinship-group, to which the victim belonged, to be chosen by the *ephetai aristinden*: that word normally means 'on the basis of good birth' (e.g. *Ath. Pol.* 3. vi); MacDowell, 124, is agnostic as to what it might mean in practice in this context; Lambert, *The Phratries of Attica*, 249 with n. 23, discusses possible interpretations. Lambert notes that it is assumed, in Draco's law as later, that every citizen will belong to a phratry, and that, as later, it is a responsibility of the phratry to support the immediate family and where that does not exist to take on its role. The clause making these rules retrospective (19–20) will have become redundant after a generation, but Stroud, 50–1, notes that the *anagrapheis* punctiliously retained it.

The law then moves backwards to deal with the procedure to be followed before the trial, beginning with a proclamation in the agora by the victim's family as defined above (20–1), and including also among those to share in the prosecution his brothers-in-law and fathers-in-law (21–3). On the various proclamations in cases of homicide see MacDowell, 23–7. Another clause which can be restored deals with those who kill an exiled killer who is duly avoiding places which he is required to avoid (26–8: Dem. XXIII. 39–40 sees frontier markets as needing explanation in the fourth century): Demosthenes takes 'Amphictyonic' with 'rites' only, but it should perhaps be taken with 'contest' also (K. Latte, *RE* xvi 286–7, cf. MacDowell, 121, Stroud, 53–4). Another clause deals with those who kill in defence against violent seizure of person or property (37–8).

---

27 '– – – I shall not put to the vote in the council or
in the assembly – – – if I do put to the vote – – –
neither public nor individual – – –'
30 – – – the five hundred shall deliberate – – – five
hundred drachmas – – – up to (?) five hundred
drachmas: a larger [fine] it shall not be able to
impose (?) – – – the council in the council house – – –

[— 22 —]ν : τάδε ἔδοχσεν ἐλ Λυκείο τ̣ôι δ̣[έμοι τôι Ἀ]θ̣ε̣[να]ίον [vvv ἄν]-
[ευ τô δέμο τô Ἀθεναίον πλεθ]ύ̣ο̣[ντ]ος μὲ ἐ͂ναι πόλεμον ἄρασθα̣ι̣ [μέτε καταλ]ῦ̣[σ]α[ι] μέτε ε̣-
[. . . . ἄνευ τô δέμο τô Ἀθεναίον πλε]θύοντος μὲ ἐ͂ναι θαν̣[ά]τοι [ζεμι]ο̣͂σαι — 5 —] Ἀθενα[ι]-
[— 22 — ἄνευ τô δ]έμο τô Ἀθεναιον πλεθ[ύο]ν̣τ̣ο̣ς̣ [. . .] . . Ο . . ΙL [.]ΤΙ[.]
[— 17 —]Ν̣\ . . . . . [. . .]\ΟΕΝ̣Β̣Ο[. .] . [. .] . . [.] . ΣΟΙ . [.]Ν ḥόπος ἂ[ν] βόλεται· μὲ ἐ͂ν̣-
[αι — 9 — ἐντ]ὸς τριάκοντα [ἑ]μερõν ἐπειδ[ὰν δόχσει· τὸν δὲ] δε͂μον μὲ ἐ͂ναι α̣μ̣[. . . .]
[— 7 — Ἀθενα]ίον μεδὲ hενὶ : μέ[τε] βολε͂ι μέτε . [— 6 — ἄνευ τô δ]έμο τô Ἀθε̣να[ί]ο[ν] πλε-
[θύο]ν̣τος μὲ ἐ̣͂ν̣α̣ι θοὰν ἐπιβαλε͂ν̣ [Ἀθε]ναίον μεδὲ̣ hενὶ — 25 —]
[. . .] ε͂ βόλεσιν : ἄνευ τô δέμο τô Ἀθ[εν]αίον πλεθύο[ντος — 25 —]
[. . .] hόπος ἂν δοκε͂ι : : : δέμοι τộι Ἀ̣[θεναίον πλε[θύοντι — 23 —]
[. . . .]ον κατὰ ταὐτὰ hαιρε͂σθαι : τὰ χρέματα τὰ δε[μόσια ἀπολογίσασθαι ἐν τε͂ι ἐκκλεσ]-
[ίαι τ]ὸς πεντακοσίος πρὶν π̣α̣ύεσθαι τε͂ς ἀρχε̣͂[ς — 24 — τôι δε]-
[μοι τô]ι Ἀθεναίον πλεθύοντι hó τ̣ι̣ ἂν βόλετα[ι — 25 — τὸν χρ]-
[εμάτο]ν τôν δεμοσίον ἐπάναγκες ἐ͂ν̣[α]ι τ̣[ε͂]ι βολ̣[ε͂ι — 20 — πρôτον μὲ]-
[ν hιερ]ά, δεύτερον πρεσβείαν, τρίτον δεμόσ[ια — 30 —]
[— 6 —]ς πρὸς τὸς πρυτάνες καὶ βολε̣ύ̣ε̣ν̣ [— 34 —]
[— 5 — κ]αὶ τô πολέμο πέρι καὶ τôν ε̣τ̣[— 38 —]
[— 6 —]να τôι δέμοι ἐντὸς hεχσέ[κοντα hεμερôν — 29 —]
[. . . χσυ]μβάλλεσθαι τὲν βολὲν [— 42 —]

Lines 44–5 if correctly restored give us the best indication of the length of the lines; Wade-Gery calculated that the width of this *stele* would have been the same as the width of *A*. 47–8 cf. Aeschin. I. *Timarchus* 48, *Ath. Pol.* 30. v, 43. vi. δεμόσ[ια χρέματα Wade-Gery, *IG* i^3.

In *A* quotations in the Demosthenic corpus enable us to restore much of the text: we are not so fortunate with this product of the process of revising the laws. It seems to contain a collection of laws about the council of five hundred (one of the categories in the law about the making of laws *ap.* Dem. XXIV. *Timocrates* 20). These laws need not all have been originally enacted at the same time. While the inscription should be seen in context as part of the reinscription of all Athens' currently valid laws, it will have been particularly important after the oligarchic regimes of 411–410 to spell out what the council was and was not entitled to do.

34 This was resolved in the Lyceum by the people of Athens: without the people of Athens fully assembled it shall not be permitted to raise war or to end war or – – – without the people of Athens fully assembled it shall not be permitted to punish with death – – – Athen— – – – without the people of Athens fully assembled – – – however it wishes. It shall not be permitted – – – within thirty days after it is decided. It shall not be permitted to the people – – – of the Athenians not one, neither to the council nor – – – without the people of Athens fully assembled it shall not be permitted to impose a fine on any of the Athenians, not one – – – or intention. Without the people of Athens fully assembled – – – however it is decided by <the> people of Athens fully assembled – – – elect in the same way.

44 The five hundred shall give account of their public monies in the assembly before demitting office – – – to the people of Athens fully assembled whatever it wishes – – – of the public monies it shall be obligatory for the council – – – first sacred business, secondly an embassy, thirdly public – – – to the *prytaneis* and deliberate – – – and about war and – – – to the people within sixty days – – – the council shall contribute [its view]

The earlier part, with the negative *ou*, seems to contain the oath of office sworn by the members (instituted when the new council was first appointed, in 501/0, according to *Ath. Pol.* 22. ii, which need not mean that no changes were made subsequently). This part ends with occurrences of the verb *epipsephizein*, 'put to the vote' (27, 28).

From l. 29 onwards the negative is *me*, and we have laws about what the council is or is not to do. There are various references to τô δέμο τô Ἀθεναίον πλεθύοντος (25, 35, 36, 37, 42, 43, 45–6), which probably means simply 'the people of Athens fully assembled', i.e. 'in assembly', rather than something more specialised, such as a meeting which satisfies a quorum requirement (Rhodes). Ostwald suggested that in the judicial contexts the phrase denotes a court, and that the council whose powers were originally restricted was not the five hundred but the Areopagus (*From Popular Sovereignty to the Sovereignty of Law*, 31–40), but was answered by Hansen (*The Athenian Ecclesia, II*, 258–60). Ryan argues that all the items with this formulation are of the same date, and that the reforms of Solon at the beginning of the sixth century provide the best context; but we are not confident that that is right.

In ll. 31 and 32 there are references to 500 drachmas, in 36 one thing which the council may not do without the people is sentence to death, and in 41 it may not inflict a *thoa* (a fine of some kind): the limitation of the council's punitive powers to a fine of five hundred drachmas is mentioned in [Dem.] XLVII. *Evergus & Mnesibulus* 43, and *Ath. Pol.* 45. i has a story about the reduction of the council's powers (though Rhodes suspects that it never had the greater powers of which it is there said to be deprived: *Comm. Ath. Pol.*, 537–8). Another thing which the council may not do without the people is 'to raise war or to end war' (35). This again will have been of particular relevance after 411, when the Four Hundred tried but failed to make peace with Sparta (Thuc. VIII. 70. ii – 71, 86. ix, 90. ii, 91. i, *Ath. Pol.* 32. iii); in 396

184

Athens honours Oeniades of (Palae)Sciathus, 408/7

A marble *stele*, of which the bottom left-hand corner is missing, found on the north slope of the Athenian acropolis, now in the Epigraphical Museum. Phot. Austin, *The Stoichedon Style*, pl. 10; Kirchner rev. Klaffenbach, *Imagines Inscriptionum Atticarum*, Taf. 18 Nr. 41; A. G. Woodhead, *The Study of Greek Inscriptions*, pl. 2; Walbank, *Athenian Proxenies*, pl. 60; our pl. 15.

Ionic writing. *Stoichedon* 23.

IG i^2 118; M&L 90; Walbank, *Athenian Proxenies*, 87; *IG* i^3 110*. Trans. Fornara 160.

θεοί.
ἔδοξεν τῆι βολῆι καὶ τῶι δήμ-
ωι. Ἀντιοχὶς ἐπρυτάνευε· Εὐκ-
λείδης ἐγραμμάτευε· Ἱεροκλ-
ῆς ἐπεστάτε· Εὐκτήμων ἦρχε. *v*
Διειτρέφης εἶπε· ἐπειδὴ ἀνή-
ρ ἐστι ἀγαθὸς Οἰνιάδης ὁ Παλ-
αισκιάθιος περὶ τὴν πόλιν τ-
ὴν Ἀθηναίων καὶ πρόθυμος πο-
ιε͂ν ὅ τι δύναται ἀγαθόν, καὶ ε-

Demaenetus had secret backing from the council when he set out with a ship to join Conon, then serving the Persian satrap Pharnabazus, but when he was discovered the council panicked and pretended to know nothing about it (*Hell. Oxy.* 9, 11 Chambers).

On the Lyceum (34), to the north-east of the acropolis, see Ar. *Peace* 353–6 with Olson, *Aristophanes, Peace, ad loc.*; and for its location *AR* xliii 1996/7, 8–10. We do not know when or why the assembly should have met there: Ryan stresses Solon's interest in Apollo and uses this in his argument for ascribing some of the provisions to Solon; M. H. Jameson, *Ἀρχαιογνωσία* i 1980, 213–36 = his *Cults and Rites in Ancient Greece*, 41–61, discusses the Lyceum as a place of cult, military exercise and private athletics, and (believing in a late sixth-century date for this item) remarks on pp. 226 = 52–3 that 'the link between the exercise ground of the armed forces and their place of assembly as the citizen body may be long-standing and significant'.

Lewis noted that l. 43 has hόπος ἂν δοκε̂ι : : : δέμοι τộι Ἀ̣θεναίον πλε[θύοντι, with three pairs of points between δοκε̂ι and δέμοι, where the definite article, τôι, is obviously required, and he suggested that the cutter could not read the word in the original which he was copying, and did not presume to make this most obvious of restorations.

Gods.

2 Resolved by the council and the people. Antiochis was the prytany; Eucleides was the secretary; Hierocles was the chairman; Euctemon [408/7] was the archon. Dieitrephes proposed:

6 Since Oeniades of Palaesciathus is a good man with regard to the city of Athens and eager to do what good

ὖ ποιεῖ τὸν ἀφικνόμενον Ἀθη-
ναίων ἐσκίαθον, ἐπαινέσαι τ-
ε αὐτῶι καὶ ἀναγράψαι αὐτὸν
πρόξενον καὶ εὐεργέτην Ἀθη-
ναίων καὶ τὸς ἐκγόνος αὐτô· κ-
αὶ ὅπως ἂν μὴ ἀδικῆται ἐπιμε-
λεσθαι τήν τε βολὴν τὴν ἀεὶ β-
ολεύοσαν καὶ τοὺς στρατηγ-
ὸς καὶ τὸν ἄρχοντα τὸν ἐν Σκι-
άθωι ὃς ἂν ἦι ἑκάστοτε. τὸ δὲ ψ-
ήφισμα τόδε ἀναγράψαι τὸγ γ-
ραμματέα τῆς βολῆς ἐν στήλη-
ι λιθίνηι καὶ καταθε͂ναι ἐμ π-
όλει. καλέσαι δὲ αὐτὸν καὶ ἐπ-
ὶ ξένια ἐς τὸ πρυτανεῖον ἐς α-
ὔριον. *v* Ἀντιχάρης εἶπε· τὰ μὲ-
ν̣ ἄλλα καθάπερ τῆι βολῆι, ἐς δ-
[ὲ τ]ὴ̣γ γνώμην μεταγράψαι ἀντ-
[ὶ τô "Σ]κιαθίο" ὅπως ἂν ἦι γεγρα-
[μμένο]ν̣ "Οἰνιάδην τὸν Παλαισ-
[κιάθιον".] *vacat*
vacat

21 τὸγ *IG* i², Walbank, cf. Tracy, *Athenian Lettering of the Fifth Century* BC, 127: τὸν M&L, *IG* i³.

The island of Sciathus is immediately to the east of the south end of the peninsula which forms the east side of the Gulf of Pagasae; for the *polis* see G. Reger in *Inventory*, 773–4 no. 520. A member of the Delian League which had paid 1,000 dr. annually in tribute, it will have been important to Athenians sailing to and from Macedon and Thrace.

Here we have a typical honorific decree: since the formal duty of a *proxenos* was to look after the interests of the other city in, and visitors from the other city to, his own city (cf. on **157**), the fact that Oeniades is already doing the latter makes him well qualified to be a *proxenos*. For instructions to the council and others to protect an honorand against injustice cf. Henry, *Honours and Privileges*, 171–6: *proxenoi* may have been readily suspected in their cities of preferring Athenian to local interests (cf. the

he can, and does good to any Athenian who arrives in Sciathus, praise him and write him up as a *proxenos* and benefactor of Athens, and his descendants; and so that he is not wronged care shall be taken by the council currently in office and the generals and whoever the officer in Sciathus may be on each occasion.

20 This decree shall be written up by the secretary of the council on a stone *stele* and placed on the acropolis.

24 Also invite him for hospitality to the *prytaneion* for tomorrow.

26 Antichares proposed: in other respects in accordance with the council; but correct 'of Sciathus' in the proposal so as to write 'Oeniades of Palaesciathus'.

Athenian *episkopos* in Ar. *Birds* 1021, making his first question, 'Where are the *proxenoi*?'). In this case among those to whom the instructions are addressed is 'whoever the officer in Sciathus may be on each occasion': in some texts *archontes* have been identified as Athenian when they are more probably local officials (cf. on **155**), but in the last phase of the Peloponnesian War Athenian officers in allied states do seem to have become more frequent, and probably an Athenian officer is referred to here.

The text ends with an amendment (26–31), to change 'of Sciathus' to 'of Palaesciathus' and make it clear that Oeniades is from the old town, presumably because Oeniades is particularly proud of his place of origin. In ll. 7–8 that change has been made, but the amendment ordering it to be made is still included in the inscription.

185

Athenian ratification of Alcibiades' treaty with Selymbria, 407

Five fragments of a marble *stele*, with a stump at the bottom for insertion into a base, found on the south slope of the Athenian acropolis, now in the Epigraphical Museum. Phot. Walbank, *Athenian Proxenies*, pl. 59.

Attic writing, with frequent lapses into Ionic. Inaccurate *stoichedon* (cf. Austin, *The Stoichedon Style in Greek Inscriptions*, 51–3), with a basic 36-letter line.

IG i² 116; *SdA* 207; M&L 87; Walbank, *Athenian Proxenies*, 86; *IG* i³ 118*; Cataldi, *Symbolai e relazioni*, 315–48 no. 12. Trans. Fornara 162. See also B. D. Meritt, *Hesp.* x 1941, 327–8; Gauthier, *Symbola*, 162–3.

§i

[—— 31 ——]ẹροσα
[—— 30 ——]ạι Ἀθεν-
[—— 30 ——]ẹχ̣σạγο
[—— 31 ——]νκ[. .]ιε
[—— 34 ——]σẹ
[—— 23 ——]ελλ[. . .] Ἀθεν-
[—— 22 —— κ]ατάλογον κατ[. .]
[—— 21 —— ὁ]μέρος δὲ hὸς ἔχο[σ]-
[ιν Ἀθεναῖοι ἀποδôναι, τὸ δὲ] λοιπὸμ μὲ λαμβάν-
[εν. καταστέσασθαι δὲ Σελυμ]β̣ριανὸς τὲμ πολι-
[τείαν αὐτονόμος τρόποι h]ότοι ἂν ἐπίστοντ-
[αι —— 17 —— ὄφ]ελε τὸ κοινὸν τὸΣη-
[λυμβριανôν ἒ ἰδιοτôν τι]ς Σελ<υ>μβριανôν τοι
[—— 18 ——] ẹἴ το [χ]ρέματα ἐδεδέμε-
[υτο ἒ εἴ τις τôι κοινôι] ὄφελεν ἒ εἴ τις ἐτίμοτ-
[ο —— 20 ——] φεύγοσι Σελυμβριανôν
[—— 15 ——]ος πολεμίος δὲ καὶ φιλίος
[—— 14 ——] ạ̃ δὲ ἀπόλετο ἐν τôι πολέμοι
[χρέματα Ἀθεναί]ον ἒ τôν συμμάχον ἒ εἴ τι ὀφελ-
[όμενον ἒ παρακ]αταθέκεν ἔχοντός το ἔπραχσα-
[ν οἱ ἄρχοντες,] μὴ ἐ̃ναι πρᾶχσιν πλὴγ γε̃ς καὶ οἰ-
[κίας. ὅσα δὲ ἄ]λλα χσυμβόλαια πρὸ τô ἐ̃ν τοῖς ἰ-
[διόταις πρ]ὸς τὸς ἰδιότας ἒ ἰδιώτει πρὸς τὸ κ-
[οινὸν ἒ κο]ινôι πρὸς ἰδιότεν *v* ἒ ἐάν το ἄλλο γίγ-

1 προσα Walbank. 2 ?ἀνα]γραφε̃ν Walbank. 3 εισαγο Walbank. 4 ν κạὶ ε Walbank. 5 ν σε Walbank. 6]γ̣ελλ Walbank. 7 κατạ[.] Walbank. 8 ἔχο[σιν: ο read by M&L, ọ by Walbank, a vertical by E. Erxleben *ap. IG* i³. 13 the stone has ν (Walbank). 13–14 τοῖ | [ς φεύγοσι· μὲ δὲ κύρια ἒ] ẹἴ Cataldi. 16–18 [κάθοδον δ' ἐ̃ναι τοῖς] φεύγοσι Σελυμβριανôν | [ἑγομένοις τὸς αὐτ]ὸς πολεμίος δὲ καὶ φιλίος | [τοῖς ἐν τε̃ι πόλει A. Wilhelm *ap. IG* i², νομίζοσιν better than ἑγομένοις, and δὲ after πολεμίος problematic, M&L, φιλίος | [τὸς αὐτὸς νομίσαι.] Cataldi.

§i

– – –

8 The Athenians shall give back the hostages whom they have, and in future shall not take any.

10 The Selymbrians shall be autonomous and shall establish their constitution in whatever way they know. – – –

12 – – – is owed by the community of the Selymbrians or by any individual among the Selymbrians to – – – if anybody's property has been confiscated or if anybody is in debt to the community or if anybody has been deprived of rights – – – exiles of the Selymbrians – – – enemies and friends – – –

18 Any property of the Athenians or the allies which has been lost in the war, or if anything is owed or deposited and the officials exacted it from the one who had it, there shall be no exaction except for land and house.

22 Whatever other causes of dispute there were heretofore, of individuals against individuals or an individual against the community or the community against an individual, or if there are

[νεται, δια]λ̣ύεμ π[ρ]ὸς ἀλλέλος· ὅ τι δ' ἂν ἀμφισβη-
[τôσι, δίκας] ε̑ναι ἀπὸ χσυμβόλον. τὰς δὲ χσυνθέκ-
[ας ἀναγράφ]σαντας ἐ[ς] στέλεν θε̑ναι ἐς τὸ hιερὸ-
[ν το ——7——]ς. ὤμοσαν Ἀθεναίον οἱ στρατεγοὶ
[καὶ οἱ τριέραρχ]οι καὶ hοι hοπλῖται καὶ εἴ τι-
[ς ἄλλος Ἀθεναίον] παρε̑ν καὶ Σελυμβ[ρ]ιανοὶ π-
[ά]ντε[ς. *v*

§ii

Ἀλ]κιβ[ιάδες] εἶπε· καθὰ χσυνέθεντο Σε-
[λυμ]βρ̣ι̣α̣[ν]οὶ πρὸς Ἀθ]εναίος, κατὰ ταῦτα ποιε̑ν,
κ̣α̣ὶ καταθε̣̑ναι ἐν̣ [πόλ]ει ἀναγράφσαντας τὸστ-
[ρ]ατε<γ>ὸς [τ]ὰ̣ς συνθέ[κ]α̣ς μετὰ τô γραμματέος τ-
[ε̑ς] βολε̑ς [[——18——]] ἐν στέλει λιθί-
[ν]ει τέλεσι τοῖς αὐτôν̣ κ̣αὶ τὸ φσέφισμα τόδε.
[Ἀπο]λλόδορον δὲ τὸν Ἐμπέδο ἐπαινέσαι καὶ ἀφε̑ν-
[α]ι̣ αὐτὸν τε̑ς ὁμερέας, καὶ [ἐ]χσαλεῖφσαι τὰ ὀνόμα-
[τα] τôν ὁμέ̣[ρ]ον τôν Σελυμ[β]ριανôν καὶ τôν ἐγγυε-
[τôν α]ὐτôν [α]ὔριον τὸν γραμ[ματ]έα τε̑ς βολε̑ς [ὅπο
[ἐσὶ ἀν]α̣γεγ[ρ]αμμένο̣ι̣ ἐναντίον τῶμ πρυτάνε-
[ων. . . . .]όμ[α]χον δὲ τὸν Σελυμβ[ρια]νὸν ἀναγρά-
[φσαι ἐν τ]ε̑ι [αὐ]τε̑ι στέλει πρόχσε[νον Ἀθ]εναίον·
[ε̑ναι δὲ καὶ] Ἀπολλοδόροι τὲμ προ[χσε]νίαν κα-
[θάπερ τôι] π̣ατρὶ αὐτô. τὸς δὲ πρέσβ[ες καὶ] Ἀπολ-
[λόδορον κ]αλέσαι ἐς πρυτανεῖον ἐπ̣[ὶ χσέν]ια ἐ-
[ς αὔριον.] *vacat*

28 Ἀπόλλονο]ς (?) A. Kirchhoff, *IG* i^{1} 61*a*, one letter too many. 30 Σελυμβ{ι}ριανοὶ Walbank. 34 -[ρ]ατε<γ>ὸς printed without comment Walbank, *IG* i^{3}. 35 τ||[ε̑ς βολε̑ς καὶ τὸν Σελυμβριανôν] Wilhelm, *Sb. Wien* CCXVII. v 1939, 89 = his *Akademieschriften*, i. 609, not acknowledging the erasure, [[καὶ τὸ φσέφισμα τόδε]] Meritt. 40 γραμ<μ>α[τ]έα Walbank (the second μ omitted on the stone). 40–1 M&L: [ὁ]π̣[ό|σοι εἰσὶ γεγ]ραμμένοι Kirchhoff. 44–6, fr. c, with the underlined letters, is now lost.

Walbank, *Athenian Proxenies*, pp. 443–4, publishes a small fragment which may be from the same *stele*.

Alcibiades went into exile when accused of involvement in the religious scandals of 415 (cf. **172**); his attempt to return to Athens was one factor in the oligarchic revolutions of 411, and from 411 to 408 he was with the Athenian fleet though not formally reinstated in Athens. In 407 he returned to Athens and was welcomed back, and he seems to have proposed a series of decrees to regularise things that had been done in the preceding years (cf. **186** and the small fragment *IG* i^{3} 120; but there is no good reason to restore him as the proposer of **188**).

Selymbria, on the European shore of the Propontis (*Inventory*, 921–2 no. 679; modern Silivri), had been a member of the Delian League, normally paying 5–9

any others, they shall settle them between one another; for what they cannot agree over, the lawsuits shall follow the conventions.

26 The agreement shall be written up on a *stele* and placed in the sanctuary of ——.

28 There swore of the Athenians the generals and the trierarchs and the hoplites and any other Athenian who was present; and all the Selymbrians.

§ii

31 Alcibiades proposed:

31 The agreement made by the Selymbrians with the Athenians shall be acted on; and the generals shall write up the agreement and place it on the acropolis together with the secretary of the council [[*words deleted*]], on a stone *stele* at their own expense, and this decree.

37 Praise Apollodorus son of Empedus, and release him from his position as hostage; and the names of the Selymbrian hostages shall be deleted tomorrow by the secretary of the council wherever they have been written up, in the presence of the *prytaneis*.

42 —machus the Selymbrian shall be written up on the same *stele* as a *proxenos* of the Athenians; and Apollodorus also shall have the position of *proxenos* as his father did.

45 Invite the envoys and Apollodorus to the *prytaneion* for hospitality tomorrow.

---

talents in tribute; it was in revolt from Athens by 410, though Alcibiades was able to obtain money from it (Xen. *Hell.* I. i. 21), and in the course of the successful campaign of 408 he recovered it and treated it mildly, while persuading it to accept a garrison and pay him money (Xen. *Hell.* I. iii. 10, Diod. Sic. XIII. 66. iv, Plut. *Alc.* 30. iii–x). §i is the treaty made then: conscious of the desirability of retaining Selymbria's loyalty, he released hostages, granted Selymbria the freedom to choose its own form of constitution and limited the Athenians' rights to reclaim property. *Archontes*, if correctly restored in l. 21, are probably officials of Selymbria (contrast **184**. 19). For *xymbolaia*, 'causes of dispute' (22), and *dikai apo xymbolon*, lawsuits regulated by a convention between states (26), cf. **120**: presumably for the latter the unresolved disputes which are envisaged are between Selymbrians and others. Athens' swearers include 'the generals' (plural) (28): perhaps Thrasyllus had gone with Alcibiades to Selymbria, and Theramenes had been left to handle the settlement with Calchedon alone (Diod. Sic. XIII. 66. iii, contr. Xen. *Hell.* I. iii. 8).

§ii is a decree proposed by Alcibiades, in Athens after his return there in 407, to ratify the treaty originally made on the spot without consultation of Athens. After

---

186

Ratification of an Athenian treaty with the Clazomenians at Daphnus, 407

The upper left-hand part of a marble *stele*, found on the north slope of the Athenian acropolis, now in the Epigraphical Museum. Phot. *Ἐφ. Ἀρχ.* 1898, πιν. I. A. Wilhelm, *AM* xxviii 1903, 446 = his *Abhandlungen und Beiträge*, iii. 522, assigned the fragmentary *IG* i^3 120, which perhaps mentions Alcibiades, to the same *stele*, but not necessarily correctly.

Ionic writing. *Stoichedon* 34.

IG i^2 117; M&L 88; *IK Erythrai und Klazomenai* 501; *SdA*^{2} (1975) 207a; *IG* i^3 119*. Trans. Fornara 163.

ἔδοξεν τῆι βολῆ[ι καὶ τῶ]ι δήμ[ωι. —6—ὶς ἐ]-
πρυτάνευε· Κράτη[ς] ἐγραμμ[άτευε· Ἐπιγέν]-
ης ἐπεστάτε. Ἀλκιβιάδης εἶπ[ε· τὰς ξυνθήκα]-
ς ἃς ξυνέθεντο οἱ στρατηγοὶ [τοῖς οἰκίσασ]-
ι Δαφνôντα εἶναι αὐτοῖς κατὰ [τὰ ξυγκείμε]-
να, ἐπειδὴ ἄνδρες ἐγένοντο ἀγ[αθοί. καὶ ἀνα]-
γράψαι τὸγ γραμμα̣[τέα τῆς βολῆς ἐν στήληι]
λιθίνηι ἐν̣ [πόλει τάς τε ξυνθήκας καὶ τὸ ψή]-
[φισμα τόδε ——25——]
- -

1 Ἀντιοχὶς or Ἐρεχθεὶς or Κεκροπὶς.

Clazomenae, an island city off the south coast of the Gulf of Smyrna (cf. *Inventory*, 1076–7 no. 847), was a strategically important site, and a long-standing member of the Delian League. In 412 Alcibiades and the Spartan Chalcideus, with whom he was then cooperating, detached it from Athens; later Athens recovered the city and the opponents of Athens moved to Daphnus, perhaps further east (J. M. Cook, *Ἀρχ. Ἐφ.* 1953–4, ii. 157), and a subsequent approach to Clazomenae by the Spartans was

the deletion of some words, the text of ll. 33–6 requires the generals themselves to pay for the inscription: that would be most unusual (but cf. the restoration of **191**. 38–9 for their involvement in publication), and it is possible that originally the Selymbrians were to pay (for payment by the state concerned cf. **120**. 22–7) but they objected. Records were commonly annulled by the physical destruction of the text (cf. *Ath. Pol.* 47. v–48. i): the verb *exaleiphein* (38) was particularly appropriate for 'wiping out' a temporary text written in charcoal on a whitewashed board.

Resolved by the council and the people. —— was the prytany; Crates was the secretary; Epigenes was the chairman. Alcibiades proposed:

3 The agreement which the generals made with those living at Daphnus shall be for them in accordance with what has been established, since they have been good men.

6 Also the secretary of the council shall write up on a stone *stele* on the acropolis the agreement and this decree – – –

---

unsuccessful (Thuc. viii. 14. iii, 23. vi, 31. i–ii). Clazomenae remained pro-Athenian in 410 (Xen. *Hell.* i. i. 10–11), and in 407/6, when it was attacked by exiles (Diod. Sic. xiii. 71. i). Whether the men at Daphnus in this inscription are the anti-Athenians of 412, won back by Athens, or a different set of men (and the anti-Athenians of 412, possibly but not certainly to be identified with the exiles of Diodorus, were now based elsewhere) is not clear, but evidently at some time after 412 men at Daphnus made a treaty with the Athenians on the spot, and after that earned Athens' praise. Like the treaty of 408 with Selymbria in **185**, that treaty was in 407 ratified by the Athenian assembly, on the proposal of Alcibiades after his return to Athens, and we may guess that Alcibiades had been one of the generals involved in making the original treaty.

In common with other early decrees, this one praises the Clazomenians as 'good men' without indicating in what respects they had displayed their goodness; but this is exceptionally laconic, not even going so far as to say that they have been

---

187

Athens honours Neapolis in Thrace, 409–407

Nine fragments (we omit fr. *h*, preserving 1–4 letters in nine lines in which no certain word can be read) of a marble *stele*, found in or on the south slope of the acropolis; previously in the Epigraphical Museum, but now displayed in the Acropolis Museum. A relief is partly preserved above the decree (Lawton no. 7: photo her pl. 4). Phot. *BSA* xlvi, pl. 23.

First decree (ll. 1–47), largely Attic letters (but Ionic H = *eta*, and Λ = *lambda* once in l. 44); not *stoichedon*. Second decree (ll. 48–64) consistently Attic letters; *stoichedon* 73. *ου* used consistently for *ο* in the first decree, occasionally in the second.

B. D. Meritt & A. Andrewes, *BSA* xlvi 1951, 200–9; Pouilloux, *Recherches sur l'histoire et les cultes de Thasos*, i. 155–60; M&L 89; *IG* i^3 101*. Trans. *BSA* xlvi 1951, 207–9; Fornara 156, Dillon & Garland^3 13. 31.

[θε]ο[ί].
[Ν]εο[π]ολιτô [ν]
[τ]ôμ παρὰ Θάσ[ον].

§i

[ἔ]δοχσεν τῆι β[ο]υ[λῆι] καὶ τôι δήμοι· Λεοντὶς ἐπρυτά̣[νευεν],
Σιβυρτιάδη[ς ἐγρα]μμάτευεν, Χα̣ιριμένης ἐπεστ[άτει, Γλ]-
αύκιππος ἦρχ[ε, ...]θ̣εος εἶπεν· [ἐπ]αινέσαι τοῖς Νεοπ[ολίταις] <τοῖς>
παρὰ Θάσον [πρôτον μ]ὲν ⟦[ὅτι ἄποικοι ὄντες Θασίον]⟧ [καὶ πολιο]-
ρκόμενοι ⟦[ὑπ' αὐτôν]⟧ καὶ Πελο[πονν]ησίον οὐκ ἠθ[έλησαν ἀ]-
[πο]στῆνα[ι ἀπ' Ἀθηναί]ον, ἄνδ[ρες δ'] ἀ̣γ̣α̣θ̣ο̣ὶ ἐγένο[ντο ἔς τε τὴ]-
[ν στρα]τ[ιὰν καὶ τὸν δῆ]μον τ[ὸν Ἀθηναίον κα]ὶ το[ὺς χσυμμά]-
[χους —— c.13 ——]˘[—— c.16 ——]Ε[—— c.8 ——]

lacuna (includes fr. *h*, ll. 12–20, which we omit)

7–8 in place of the erased letters, a hand different from those that inscribed the main text of both decrees wrote: ὅ{υ}τι συνδιεπο[λέμεσ]αν τὸν πόλεμον μετὰ Ἀθεναίο[ν καὶ πολιο]|ρκόμενοι ὑπ[ὸ Θασίον].

good men to 'the people/city of Athens' (cf. **161**, **162**). Also its prescript omits mention of the archon, normally included in the late fifth century (cf. Introduction, p. xxii).

In 387/6 Athens praised Clazomenae in a context of continuing *stasis*, and considered whether to install a governor and garrison but decided not to do so (R&O 18); but in the Peace of Antalcidas which followed Clazomenae was claimed by Persia, as an exception to the rule that outside mainland Asia Minor cities and islands were to be autonomous (Xen. *Hell.* v. i. 31).

Gods.

2 Concerning the people of Neapolis by Thasos.

§i

4 Resolved by the council and people. Leontis was the prytany; Sibyrtiades was secretary; Chaerimenes was chairman; Glaucippus was archon. —theus proposed:

6 Praise the people of Neapolis by Thasos, first because although they are Thasian settlers and were besieged by them (*underlined phrase erased and replaced by* because they fought the war alone with the Athenians and when they were besieged by the Thasians) and by the Peloponnesians they were not willing to revolt from the Athenians, but were good men towards the army and people of the Athenians and the allies – – –

lacuna

[— c.26 — Ἀθ]ηνα[ιο — c.13 —]
[— c.27 —] χρήματα̣ [— c.11 —]
[— c.25 —]νηι Ἀθηναίο̣ν [— c.9 —]
[— c.24 —]ι‴ασιν εἶναι Νεοπο[λιτ— c.4 —]
[— c.22 —]ον καὶ χρῆσαι ΤΤΤΤΧΧ[— c.7 —]
[— c.22 —]ον ἐδέοντο ὅπος ἂν ἔχο̣[σιν ἐς]
[τὸν πόλεμον· — c.8 — πο]ι̣ε͂σθαι αὐτοῖς ἐκ το͂γ χρημ[άτον .]
[— c.10 — τῆς Νέας Π]όλεος ἐκ τοῦ λιμένος, τοὺς ἐ̣ν [Θάσοι]
[στρατηγὸς ἑκάστο τô ἐ]νιαυτô ὃς ἀφειληφότας παρὰ [σφο͂ν γρα]-
[φσαμένος ἕος ἂν ἐντελ]ε͂ ἀποδοθῆι· ποιε͂ν δὲ ταῦτα ἕ[ος ἂν αὐ]-
[τοῖς ὁ πόλεμος ἦι ὁ πρὸς] Θασίος· ὃ δὲ διδόασι ν[ῦν Νεοπολῖτ]-
[αι — c.11 —]ς καὶ βου̣λόμενοι καὶ ἐθελοντ[αὶ ἔδοσαν τοῖς]
[ἑλληνοταμ]ίαις ΓΧΧΧΧΡΗΗΗ καὶ πρόθυμοί εἰσ[ι ποιε͂ν ὅ τι δύν]-
[ανται ἀγ]αθὸν αὐτοὶ ἐπαγγειλάμενοι καὶ λ[όγοι καὶ ἔργοι ἐς τ]-
[ὴν πόλ]ιν τὴν Ἀθηναίον, καὶ ἀντὶ τῆς εὐεργε[σίας ταύτης τὸ νῦ]-
[ν εἶν]αι καὶ ἐν τôι λοιπôι χρόνο[ι] παρ' Ἀθηνα[ίον — c.12 — αὐ]-
[τ]ο̣ῖς ὁς ἀνδράσιν οὖσιν ἀγαθο[ῖ]ς καὶ τὴ[ν πρόσοδον εἶναι αὐτ]-
οῖς πρὸς τὴμ βουλὴν καὶ τὸν δῆ[μ]ον π[ρότοις μετὰ τὰ ἱερὰ ὁς]
εὐεργέταις οὖσιν Ἀθηναίον· το[ὺς δὲ πρέσβεις τὰ ὑπομνήμα]-
τα τούτον ἃ οἱ Νεοπολῖται ἔδο[σαν πάντα παραδοῦναι τôι γρ]-
αμματεῖ τῆς βουλῆς, χορὶς μὲν [τὰ νῦν δεδομένα, χορὶς δὲ τἆλ]-
λα, καὶ τὸ φσήφισμα τόδε ἀναγρά[φσας ὁ γραμματεὺς ὁ]
τῆς βουλῆς ἐστήληι λιθίνηι καταθ[έτο ἐμ πόλει τέλεσι τοῖ]-
ς Νεοπολιτôν· ἐν δὲ Νέαι Πόληι αὐτοὶ [ἀναγράφσαντες καταθ]-
έντον ἐν τôι ἱερôι τῆς Παρθένο ἐστήλ[ηι λιθίνηι· καλέσαι δὲ καὶ]
ἐπὶ χσένια τὴμ πρεσβείαν ἐς τὸ πρυτα[νεῖον ἐς αὔριον. vvvv]
Οἰνοβίοι Δεκελεεῖ στρατεγôι ΤΤΤΡΗ[ΔΔΔͰͰͰΙΙΙΙ].

§ii

Ἀχσίοχος εἶπε : ἐπαινέσαι τοῖς Νεοπολίταις τοῖς ἀπὸ [Θράικες hος ο͂σιν ἀνδράσιν ἀγαθοῖς]
ἔς τε τὲν στρατιὰν καὶ τὲμ πόλιν τὲν Ἀθεναίον καὶ hότ[ι ἐς Θάσον ἐστρατεύοντο χσυμπολιορ]-
κέσοντες μετὰ Ἀθεναίον ⁝ καὶ hότι χσυνναυμαχôντ[ες ἐνίκον] καὶ [κατὰ γε͂ν χσυνεμάχον τὸν πά]-
ντα χρόνον καὶ τὰ ἄλλα hότι εὖ ποιôσιν Ἀθεναίο[ις, καὶ ἀντὶ τ]ο̣ύτον [— 16 — παρὰ Ἀ]-
θεναίον εἶναι αὐτοῖς καθhάπερ ἐφσέφισται τ[ôι δέμο]ι ⁝ [κα]ὶ hόπος ἂμ μ̣[ὲ ἀδικôνται μεδὲν μέτ]-
ε ὑπὸ ἰδιότο μέτε ὑπὸ κοινô πόλεος, τός τε σ[τρατεγὸ]ς hοὶ ἂν hεκάστοτε ἄ[ρχοσι πάντας ἐπιμέ]-

25–6 [καθά|περ οἱ στρατηγοὶ οἱ Ἀθηναί]ον ἐδέοντο: Meritt & Andrewes. 27 δάνεια δὲ πο]ι̣ε͂σθαι Meritt & Andrewes. 27–8 [τ|ούτον ἅ ἐστι] Meritt and Andrewes. 31–2 [Νεοπολῖτ|αι οἱ ἀπὸ Θράικη]ς Meritt & Andrewes. 36 παρ' Ἀθηνα[ίον χάριτας εἶναι Meritt & Andrewes. 47 The numeral here is restored on the basis of a sum received by the treasurers of Athena in the eighth prytany of 410/09: *IG* i³ 375. 28. 51 ἀντὶ τ]ο̣ύτον [τôν ἀγαθôν χάριτας Meritt & Andrewes.

21 – – – Athenians – – – money – – – of the Athenians – – – to be for the Neapolitans – – – and use 4 tal. 2,000+ dr. – – – they need in order that they may have resources for the war – – – make it for them from the money – – – of Neapolis from the harbour, the generals on Thasos, writing up each year how they have received the money from them, until it has all been paid. They are to do this while they are at war with the Thasians. And what the people of Neapolis give now – – – and gave voluntarily and willingly to the *hellenotamiai*, 5 tal. 4,800 dr., and they are keen to do whatever good they can to the city of the Athenians, and have announced this both by word and deed, and in return for this benefaction they are to be, both now and in future time, from the Athenians – – – for them, since they are good men, and they are to have access to the council and the people first after the sacred things, on the grounds that they are benefactors of the Athenians.

39 The ambassadors are to hand over to the secretary of the council all the records about what the people of Neapolis gave, keeping separate what has been given and the other things, and the secretary of the council, when he has written up the decree on a stone *stele,* is to set it up on the acropolis at the expense of the people of Neapolis. In Neapolis they are to write it up themselves and place it in the temple of the Parthenos on a stone *stele.* And summon the embassy to hospitality in the *prytaneion* tomorrow.

47 To Oenobius of Decelea, the general, 3 tal., 634 dr. 4 ob.

§ii

48 Axiochus proposed: Praise the people of Neapolis from Thrace for being men good both to the army and the city of the Athenians and because they campaigned against Thasos to besiege it along with the Athenians, and because they were victorious in a sea battle and fought as allies on land for the whole time and because they do good to the Athenians in other ways, and in return for these services – – – is from the Athenians to them just as has been decreed by the people, and in order that they may not be wronged in any way either by an individual or by a *polis* as a community, both all the generals who are in charge

λεσθαι αὐτôν hó τι ἂν δέονται ⁝ καὶ τὸς ἄρχ[ο]ν[τ]ας τοὺς Ἀθεναίον hoὶ ἂν hεκ[άστοτε ——9——]
ον τὲμ πόλιν Νεοπολίτας φυλάττοντα[ς] καὶ προθύμος ὄντας ποιε͂ν hó τι ἂν [——15——]
καὶ νῦν hευρίσκεσθαι αὐτὸς παρὰ τ[ô δ]έμο τô Ἀθεναίον hó τι ἂν δοκε͂ι ἀγαθ[ὸν ——9—— περὶ]
ἐ τε͂ς ἀπαρχε͂ς τε͂ι Παρθένοι h[έπερ κ]αὶ τέος ἐγίγνετο τε͂ι [θε]ôι ἐν τôι δέμο[ι πρᾶχσαι πρὸς αὐ]-
τός· ἐς δὲ τὸ φσέφισμα τὸ πρό[τερον ἐ]πανορθôσαι τὸγ γραμματέα τε͂ς βολε͂ς ⁝ ḳ[αὶ ἐς αὐτὸ μεταγρ]-
[ά]φσαι ἀντὶ τε͂ς ἀποικίạ[ς τε͂ς Θασί]ον hότι συνδιεπολέμεσαν τὸμ πόλεμον μ[ετὰ Ἀθεναίον ⁝ καὶ]
[——8——]ọαι : καὶ Π[——7—— καὶ . . .]οφάντοι : ἐπαινέσαι hάτε νῦν λέγοσιν κ[αὶ πράττοσιν ἀγα]-
[θὸν hυπὲρ Ἀθε]ν[αίον τô δέμο καὶ hότι] πρόθυμοί εἰσι ποιε͂ν hó τι δύνανται ἀ[γαθὸν ἐς τὲν στρα]-
[τιὰν καὶ τὲμ πόλιν ἐς τὸ λοιπὸν καθhά]περ τὸ πρότερον· καλέσαι δὲ καὶ ἐπὶ χ[σένια ἐς αὔριον ᵛ]
[——7—— εἶπε : τὰ μὲν ἄλλα καθhάπερ τε͂ι] βουλε͂ι· τε͂ι δὲ Παρθένοι ἐχσαιρε͂[σθαι τὲν ἀπαρχὲν . .]-
[————32———— hο δ]ε͂μος ε[ὔ]χσεται. *vacat*
vacat

54–5 hεκ[άστοτε hορôσιν σφ|ôν Meritt & Andrewes. 56 ἀγαθ[ον τε͂ι βολε͂ι Meritt & Andrewes; ἀγαθ[ον hο δεôνται Rhodes, *Boule*, 82 n. 2. 63–4 ἐχσαιρε͂[σθαι τὲν ἀπαρχὲν κα|θhάπερ τὸ πρότερον hὲν ἂν Νεοπολιτôν hο δ]ε͂μος ε[ὔ]χσεται Meritt & Andrewes; ἐχσαιρε͂[σθαι τὲν ἀπαρχὲν κα]θhάπερ τὸ πρότερον ——15—— hο δ]ε͂μος ε[ὔ]χσεται M&L.

In 411, after democracy had been replaced by oligarchy at the instigation of Athenian oligarchs, the Thasians had turned against Athens and introduced laws offering rewards to any who denounced plots to change the regime, either on Thasos or in her settlements abroad (above **176** and **177**). But Thasos' relations with what she thought of as 'her' settlements abroad were evidently not entirely friendly. It had been over her relations with and exploitation of the settlements on the mainland opposite that Thasos had revolted in 465 (Thuc. I. 100. ii), and we should not exclude, as is usually done, the possibility that the views of the mainland settlements influenced Athenian action. Athens had taken away Thasos' mainland possessions when she finally put down the revolt (Thuc. I. 101. iii), and although some scholars consider it likely that Thasos took back some control in the 440s when her tribute was raised (see above on **119**), the way in which Oesyme and Galepsus went over to the Spartans in 424 (Thuc. IV. 107. iii; Galepsus was recovered by Athens in 422/1, V. 6. i) suggests considerable independence. This

at any particular time are to take care of all their needs and the Athenian magistrates who – – – on each occasion, guarding the city of the people of Neapolis and being keen to do whatever – – – , and now they are to obtain from the Athenian people whatever seems good – – –.

56 Concerning the firstfruits for the Parthenos which were made until now for the goddess, the matter should be dealt with in the assembly in relation to them.

58 In the earlier decree, the secretary of the council is to make a correction, and write in it instead of 'settlement of the Thasians' that 'they fought the war along with the Athenians'.

59 – – – and – – – —ophantus: praise them because they now say and do good on behalf of the Athenian people and because they are keen to do whatever good they can to the army and the city for the future just as in the past. Summon them to hospitality tomorrow.

63 —— proposed: otherwise as the council proposed, but set apart the firstfruits for the Parthenos, – – – the people vow.

---

inscription confirms that independence for one particular settlement, and reveals just how resented were Thasian claims (as in **176**) that these places were her 'settlements abroad' (*apoikoi*).

Neapolis (cf. *Inventory*, 862–4 no. 634) was one of several places in the Greek world called 'New City' (there were others in the Chalcidice and in Propontic Thrace as well as Neapolis/Naples in southern Italy). It was situated at the strategically key site of the modern city of Kavala. Its Thasian origin is confirmed by the letter forms in sixth-century graffiti and its early coin types, which follow Thasian models. We know nothing of its earlier fifth-century history except that it appears in the tribute lists from 454/3 onwards consistently assessed for tribute at 1,000 dr., initially recorded as 'Neapolis in Thrace' (*IG* i^3 259. vi. 9–10) or 'Neapolis by Antisara' (263. iii. 13–14) or just Neapolis (265. i. 20) but later, from 443/2 on, as Neopolitai (265. ii. 28) or Neopolitai by Antisara (282. ii. 19–20).

The first decree here is firmly dated to 410/09 by the archon. In it the Athenians praise the people of Neapolis for their loyalty and acknowledge financial help given and more general services rendered (this is the first certain occurrence of the abstract noun *euergesia* ('benefaction', l. 35) in Athenian inscriptions; its restoration elsewhere in *IG* i³ 162 and 167 is dubious). The people of Neapolis are given privileged access to the council and people, as some individual benefactors have been (cf. *IG* i³ 65. 17–20, honouring Apollophanes of Colophon in 427/6).

A second hand then records a contribution to Athenian funds which, if correctly identified with a payment recorded in the accounts of the treasurers of Athena, was made later in that same year.

The second decree, beginning at l. 48, has no prescript and must be dated from its content. It is written in a third hand and a significantly smaller script. Both script and language are less influenced by Ionic practice than those of the first decree. It repeats the praise for Neapolis' help, now in the context of the siege of Thasos, and arranges for the Athenian generals and Athenian *archontes* to protect the city. The Athenians had regularly called on their generals, council and *prytaneis* to protect Athenian *proxenoi*, etc. (cf. e.g. *IG* i³ 72. 12), but Athenian *archontes* are not mentioned in this context although they appear in some general imperial decrees (cf. **155**, **184**), and it is likely here that the reference is to Athenian officials at Neapolis itself (cf. *IG* i³ 62. 5). The implication is that the siege of Thasos is concluded, and this implies a date in or after 407 when Thasos was recovered by Thrasybulus, who obliged the Thasians to take back their exiles (Xen. *Hell.* I. iv. 9; Diod. Sic. XIII. 72, i; cf. *SEG* xxxviii 851, an Athenian decree restoring democracy to Thasos, and **177**. *A*). The proposer of the second decree here, Axiochus, is likely to be the uncle of Alcibiades, who had had his property confiscated for his involvement in the profanation of the Mysteries (Andoc. I. *Mysteries* 16, and **172**). We know that Alcibiades returned to Athens in 407, and Axiochus may have returned with him.

The second decree contains two additional provisions. The second of these (ll. 58–9) corrects the language of the original decree, removing the references to Neapolis being a Thasian settlement. Those references were duly removed from the original *stele*, and indeed this piece of Athenian diplomatic insensitivity is known only from the record of it in this decree (cf. **184**). Erasures to correct or update inscriptions are not uncommon (cf. **149**; and S. Bolmarcich, *CQ*² lvii 2007, 480–2,

---

188

Athens honours Archelaus of Macedon, 407/6

Two joining fragments of a marble *stele*, from the acropolis; now in the Epigraphical Museum. Phot. *JŒAI*, xxi–xxii 1922–4, 123.

Attic letters; *stoichedon* 31.

IG i² 105; M&L 91; Walbank, *Athenian Proxenies*, 90*; *IG* i³ 117 + Addenda p. 948; Engen, *Honor and Profit*, no. 6. Trans. Fornara 161; Engen.

485–6), but this is more a matter of erasing to ensure political correctness (for a slightly different version of which see R&O 22. 12–15). On erasures and the reasons for them see Rhodes, in Petrović *et al.* (edd.), *The Materiality of Text*, forthcoming: it shows more perceptiveness than we sometimes find, that the man who made the correction in l. 7 realised that since the Thasians had disappeared there they needed to be specified in l. 8.

The first provision (ll. 56–8) concerns firstfruit offerings to the Parthenos, and is not easy to understand. Parthenos was the poliad deity of Neapolis, and her sanctuary, dating back to the seventh century and with a monumental temple from the sixth century, has been excavated on the Pharos peninsula at Kavala (*BCH* lxxxvi 1962, 830–40, *Ἀρχ. Δελτ.* xvii 1963, χρον. 235–8). She was almost certainly represented in the relief heading this decree, as she is in that heading a fourth-century decree of 356/6 (*IG* ii^2 128; Lawton, *Attic Document Reliefs*, no. 28), in which Athens responds to Neapolis' appeal for help against Macedon, where she takes the form of an archaistic statue standing opposite and clasping the hand of a figure of Athena. The main text of the decree here refers the matter of 'the firstfruits for the Parthenos which were made until now for the goddess' to the decision of the assembly, and the amendment then makes a specific proposal about them, that whatever the people of Neapolis vowed should be set apart just as before. The difficulty of understanding this rests partly on the ambiguity of 'for the goddess' (l. 57) and partly on understanding the constitutional position. In the normal course of events one would not expect Athens to be involved in decisions by the people of Neapolis about firstfruits that they offered to their own goddess. Moreover, in an Athenian decree 'the goddess' should refer to Athena, not to a goddess at Neapolis. But can the Athena at Athens really have been in receipt of firstfruits that were owed to Parthenos at Neapolis? And does the 'setting apart' of those firstfruits (l. 63) simply continue that practice? Given our uncertainty any restoration of l. 64 that supposes that existing practice continued is rash.

Fragments of two copies of a treaty of reconciliation between Thasos and Neapolis, perhaps from shortly after 407, survive from Paros and from Delphi (*SEG* xxxviii 852; *REG* cii 1989 (*Bulletin épigraphique*), 394–6 no. 254).

[——— 23 ———]χ[.]λα[....]
[ἔδοχσεν τε͂ι βολε͂ι καὶ] τ[ο͂]ι δέμοι. Ἀκαμ[α]-
[ντὶς ἐπρυτάνευε· Φελ]λεὺς ἐγραμμάτ[ευ]-
[ε· Ἀντιγένες ἐ͂ρχε· Σι]βύρτιος ἐπεστά[τε].
[— 10 — εἶπε· ἐς τ]ὲν πο[ίε]σιν το͂ν ν[ε]-
[ο͂ν δανεῖσαι τὸς στρα]τεγὸς τὸς μετὰ Πε-
[ρικλέος ἀργύριον παρ]ὰ το͂ν [[τ̣ο͂ν]] ὄντον ἀ-
[ποδεκτο͂ν τοῖς ναυπεγ]οῖς· hὸ δ' ἂν δανεί-
[σοσιν, ἀποδόντον αὐτο]ῖς πάλιν hοι τρι-
[εροποιοί· τὸς δὲ τεταγ]μένος πλε͂ν ἐπὶ τ-
[ὲν πλέροσιν το͂ν νεο͂ν h]ος τάχιστα ἀποσ-
[τελάντον hοι στρατεγ]οί· εἰ δὲ μέ, ἐσαγό-
[σθον προδοσίας ἐς τὸ δ]ικαστέριον· hο[ι]
[δὲ στρατεγοὶ περὶ το͂] μὲ ἐθέλοντος ἀπι-
[έναι ἐσαγόντον· τε͂ς δ]ὲ κομιδε͂ς το͂ν νεο͂-
[ν, hὰς ἂν hοι ναυπεγοὶ] ἐγ Μακεδόνιας στ̣-
[έλλοσι, τὲν βολὲν ἐπι]μελεθε͂ναι, hόπος
[ἂν σταλο͂σιν hος τάχισ]τα Ἀθέναζε καὶ π-
[λεροθο͂σι καὶ ἐπὶ Ἰονί]αν κομίζεται hε
[στρατιὰ φυλάχσοσα φυ]λακὲν τὲν ἀριστ-
[εν· ἐὰν δέ τις μὲ ποέσει] κατὰ ταῦτα, ὀφελ-
[εν . . . ίας δραχμὰς αὐτὸ]ν hιερὰς τε͂ι Ἀθ-
[εναίαι· το͂ι δὲ πρότοι ἐλθ]όντι καὶ κομ[ι]-
[σαμένοι ναῦν δο͂ναι δορεὰν] καθάπε[ρ δο]-
[κε͂ι το͂ι δέμοι · ἐπειδὲ δὲ Ἀρχέ]λα[ς καὶ νῦ]-
[ν καὶ ἐν το͂ι πρόσθεν χρ]ο̣ν̣οι ἐσ[τὶν ἀν]-
[ὲρ ἀγαθὸς περὶ Ἀθεναί]ος τός τε ἐκπλ[εύ]-
[σαντας Ἀθεναίον ἀνέλ]α̣βεν καὶ ἐς τὸ[..]
[——— 18 ———] ἀ̣πέπεμφσεν καὶ
[——— 17 ——— τ]ὸ στρατόπεδον κ-
[αὶ ἔδοκεν αὐτοῖς χσύλ]α καὶ κοπέας καὶ
[ἄλλα hόσον ἐδέοντο παρ'] αὐτο͂ ἀγαθά, ἐπα-
[ινέσαι Ἀρχέλαι hος ὄν]τι ἀνδρὶ ἀγαθο͂ι
[καὶ προθύμοι ποιε͂ν hό]τι δύναται ἀγαθ-
[όν, καὶ ἀνθ' ο͂ν εὐεργέτε]κεν τέν τε πόλιν
[καὶ τὸν δε͂μον τὸν Ἀθενα]ίον ἀναγράφσα-
[ι αὐτὸν καὶ παῖδας προχσένο]ς καὶ εὐερ-
[γέτας ἐμ πόλει ἐστέλεν λιθίνε]ν κ[αὶ ἐπ]-
[ιμέλεσθαι αὐτο͂ν ——— 17 ———]

5 [Ἀλκιβιάδες εἶπε] Meritt. 10–11 Hiller (*IG* i²): τ¦[ὲν τε͂ς Λέσβο φυλακὲν h]ος Kirchhoff; τ¦[ὲν το͂ν κεπέον κομιδὲν] Wilhelm. 13–14 Meritt: ἐσαγό¦[ντον αὐτὸς θανάτο ἐς δ]ικαστέριον Kirchhoff; ἐσαγό¦[ντον hοι ἕνδεκα κτλ.] Mattingly. 21 [χιλίας] Kirchhoff; [μυρίας] Wilhelm. 28–30 καὶ ἐς τὸ [ἐπ|ὶ Πύδνει στρατόπεδον] ἀ̣πέπεμφσεν κα[ὶ | εὖ ἐπόεσεν Ἀθεναίον τ]ὸ στρατόπεδον Meritt.

– – –

2 Resolved by the council and the people. Akamantis was the prytany; Phelleus was the secretary; Antigenes was the archon; Sibyrtius was the chairman. —— proposed:

4 The generals with Pericles are to loan money for the construction of ships from the current *apodektai* to the shipbuilders. Let the *trieropoioi* pay back to them whatever they loan. Let the generals dispatch those appointed to sail in order to fill the ships as quickly as possible. If not, let them be brought before the court on a charge of treachery. The generals are to bring actions concerning anyone not willing to depart.

14 The council is to see to the bringing of whatever ships the ship-builders send from Macedonia, in order that they may send them as quickly as possible to Athens and may man them and the army, keeping the best guard, may be brought to Ionia. If anyone fails to act in this way, he is to owe — drachmas sacred to Athena. A prize is to be given to the first to come and bring a ship, just as the people resolved.

24 Since Archelaus both now and in former times is a man good to the Athenians and received the ship-builders who sailed out and to the – – – sent away and – – – camp, and gave to them wood and oars and other good things, as much as they asked from him, praise Archelaus because he is a good man and keen to do whatever good he is able, and in return for the good that he has done the city and people of Athens write him and his sons up as *proxenoi* and benefactors on a stone *stele* on the acropolis and look after them – – –

Although less than half of each line of this inscription is preserved, the general sense, if not the details of phraseology, can be quite clearly understood. The Athenians are honouring a benefactor whose services include the something to do with oars at the end of a decree which mentions something coming from Macedonia, and which involves the generals, loans of money, potential court action and a need for speed. We are clearly in a context where the Athenians are trying to put together a fleet in a hurry and have reason to be grateful to a Macedonian for helping to supply them with oars and other things.

Macedonia, Thrace, southern Italy, the southern shores of the Black Sea, Mt Olympus in Mysia and Mt Ida in the Troad were, according to Theophrastus (*H.P.* IV. 5. v), the only sources of good ship-timber (see further Meiggs, *Trees and Timber in the Ancient Mediterranean World*, ch. v). Its resources of timber, as well as of silver, were one of the reasons why Macedon was of great strategic importance (cf. Hdt. v. 23. ii). Athenian determination to establish a presence in Thrace (Thuc. I. 100. ii–iii) was at least partly motivated by a desire to have access to timber, as Thucydides makes clear when he explains why Amphipolis was crucial to the Athenians (IV. 108. i). The need for Athens to secure for herself an alternative supply of ship-timber stemmed in part from the fact that in Macedonia timber was a royal monopoly (M. Faraguna, *Athenaeum*^{2} lxxxvi 1998, 367–8; the most direct evidence for this is Livy XLV. 29. xiv, where after defeating Perseus Aemilius Paulus forbids the Macedonians to cut timber for ships). Almost certainly after Athenian problems in Thrace in 424, and probably in the closing years of Perdiccas' reign (when Archelaus was old enough to be among those who swore the oath, l. 60 cf. 38), the Athenians concluded a treaty with Macedon (*IG* i^3 89) in which the Macedonians agreed that they would export oars only to Athens (l. 31).

Athens, whose fleet perhaps reached 400 ships ([Xen.] *Ath. Pol.* iii. 4 with V. Gabrielsen, in Burrer & Müller (edd.), *Kriegskosten und Kriegsfinanzierung in der Antike*, 52–3), regularly had a substantial need for ship-building timber, and this only increased after the loss of her fleet in Sicily in 413. The Athenians immediately decided to rebuild the fleet (Thuc. VIII. 1. iii, cf. 4, 15. i). Andocides claims that in 411 he used his friendship with Archelaus (whose accession occurred in about 413) in order to supply oars to the fleet on Samos (Andoc. II. *Return* 11). It is very likely that an Athenian decree honouring Antiochides and Phanosthenes for supplying oars dates to 410–407, supplying further evidence of Athenian need at this point (*IG* i^3 182 with B. Macdonald, *Hesperia* l 1981, 141–6).

The stress on the supply of oars in all this material is notable. Oars were 9 or 9.5 cubits long (something over 4 m., depending on the precise length of the cubit) and were 'massive affairs shaped from a single piece of timber' (Morrison *et al.*, *The Athenian Trireme*^{2}, 173, cf. 246). They were often broken in the course of combat, and triremes always carried spare oars in addition to the 170 used on each ship (*op. cit.* 111, 136). Access to high-quality oars was the most crucial part of the timber supply for the Athenian navy.

More than the supply of oars, however, is at issue in this text. The restoration of the beginning of the decree to refer to the construction of ships is compelling, and a reference to shipwrights in ll. 8 and 16 seems very likely. If this is correct, then the ship construction for which this decree makes arrangements took place in Macedon (l. 16). Modern scholars debate whether it was normal to transport timber to Athens for fleets to be constructed there or whether ship construction regularly took place at or near the place of origin of the timber. D. J. Blackman (*Second International Symposium on Ship Construction in Antiquity: Proceedings*, 47–8: see *SEG* xl 16) has ingeniously used the evidence of a large group of anchors of Athenian triremes that are made of a dark stone not found in Attica but native to Thessaly and Chalcidice to argue that triremes were regularly made near the source of wood rather than constructed at the Piraeus.

The man honoured in this inscription has a name seven letters long (ll. 25, 33), and, given that export of timber from Macedonia requires royal permission, this must surely be the name of a king. Hence the restoration of the name of Archelaus seems certain. An archon date is entirely restored in this inscription, but although it gives an unusual order of mention for the various Athenian officials, the order is paralleled in **191** and seems secure. The name of the archon in l. 4 is likely to have had nine letters (although it would also be possible to restore the text to allow a name with seven or eight letters), and the only nine-letter names of archons between 413 and the end of the Peloponnesian War are Theopompus, the archon for 411/0, and Antigenes, the archon for 407/6. There was certainly contact between Athens and Archelaus in 411/0, when Theramenes took a fleet to aid the king in his siege of Pydna (Diod. Sic. XIII. 49. i), but this decree was passed with full democratic process, not under the Four Hundred, and the only two prytanies during which Theopompus served as archon after the restoration of democracy were Aiantis and Aegeis, so this decree, passed in the prytany of Acamantis, cannot date to 410. The date of 407/6 seems certain.

What is impossible, however, is to restore the name of the proposer of the decree, since all that we know is that that name had ten letters. B. D. Meritt speculated (in *Classical Studies . . . E. Capps*, 249) that the proposer might have been Alcibiades. Alcibiades returned to Athens in triumph in 407, having restored Athenian fortunes with a series of military successes. Although Alcibiades was responsible in 407 for motions relating to Selymbria and Clazomenae (**185**, **186**), in both cases we know that he had been involved with those communities before his return to Athens. We know of no comparable involvement by Alcibiades in Macedonian affairs, and should therefore resist the temptation to see 'the boldness and originality of Alcibiades' (M&L, p. 279) here. Nevertheless the action taken here confirms Athenian ambition and suggests preparation for emphatic military action.

S. V. Tracy (*Athenian Lettering of the Fifth Century* BC, 149–80) has identified the letter-cutter of this inscription as responsible also for seventy-two other inscriptions, including *IG* i³ 425 (part of **172**) and R&O 4, ranging in date from 414/3 (*IG* i³ 106) to 386/5. In this as in most of his texts down to this date (but not *IG* i³ 339 or 515) this cutter uses Attic letters. From the following year, 406/5 (*IG* i³ 341, 470), he uses Ionic.

If ll. 7–8 are correctly restored, the financial officials named *apodektai* ('receivers') are mentioned here for only the second time in Athenian inscriptions, the first mention being in **167**.

189

An Athenian decree concerning Carthage, 406

Two fragments of a marble *stele*, *a* found in the Nike bastion of the Athenian acropolis, both now in the Epigraphical Museum. Phot. *HSCP* Supp. i 1940, figs. 1 (*a*), 2 (squeeze of *b*).

Developed Attic writing. *Stoichedon* , probably 36.

(*b*) *IG* i² 47; (*a* + *b*) B. D. Meritt, *HSCP* Supp. i 1940, 247–53 (*SEG* x 136); *SdA* 208; M&L 92*; *IG* i³ 123 (Woodhead). Trans. Fornara 165. See also S. Ya. Luria, *VDI* xxi = 1947. iii, 122–5; K. F. Stroheker, *Historia* iii 1954, 163–71; R. Vattuone, *Epigraphica* xxxix 1977, 41–50.

a [ἔδοχσεν τε͂ι βο]λ̣ε͂ι κ[αὶ το͂ι δέμοι. —c.6— ἐπρυ]-
[τάνευε· —c.6—]ς Ἀφιδ[ναῖος ἐγραμμάτευε· . . .]
[—12—]ς ἐπεσ[τάτε. - - - εἶπε· - - -]
[—11—]κανκα[—19—]
[—12—]ονοτα[—19—]
[—11— ἀ]ναγρά[φσαι δὲ Καρχεδονίος εὐ]-
[εργέτας Ἀθενα]ίον τὸγ [γραμματέα τε͂ς βολε͂ς ἐ]-
[μ πόλει ἐστέλ]ει λιθίν[ει. —16—]
[—11—] ἐς Σικελ[ίαν πέμφσαι πρὸς στρα]-
[τεγὸς Ἀννίβα]γ Γέσκον[ος καὶ Ἱμίλκονα Ἄννον]-
[ος —9—]ς αὐτὸς [—20—]
[—13—]τ̣α̣[—21—]

lacuna

b [—c.35— π]-
[ρὸς στρατεγὸς Ἀννίβας Γέσκονος καὶ Ἱμ]ίλκο-
[να Ἄννονος. ἐπαινέσαι δὲ καὶ τὸς κέρυκα]ς τὸς
[Ἀθέναζε ἀφιγμένος ὅτι εἰσὶν ἄνδρες ἀγ]αθοὶ
[περὶ τὸν δε͂μον τὸν Ἀθεναίον. καλέσαι δὲ] καὶ ἐ-
[πὶ χσένια ἐς τὸ πρυτανεῖον ἐς αὔριον. *vv*]*vacat*
[—29— Ἀνν]ίβας
[—34—]υτ
- -

Even the restorations which we print above are speculative, and we note only here the more adventurous restorations of Meritt, which are retained in *IG* i³. 3–6 κέρυ|χσι μὲν ὃς ἀφhε͂]καν Κα[ρχεδόνιοι πρόσοδον ε͂ν|αι πρὸς τὸν δε͂μ]ον ὅτα[μπερ προ͂τον ἐκκλεσία κ|υρία γένεται Meritt. 6 Καρχεδονίος Meritt: τὸς hέκοντας Luria. 8–9 κέρυκας δὲ Ἀθεναίο|ν αὐτίκα μάλα Meritt. 11 αἰτέσοντα]ς αὐτὸς φ[ιλίαν καὶ συμμαχίαν Meritt. After the lacuna [— εἶπε· τὰ μ|ὲν ἄλλα καθάπερ τε͂ι βολε͂ι· πέμφσαι δὲ κέρυκα|ς ὃς ἂν hέλονται οἱ πρυτάνες μετὰ τε͂ς βολε͂ς π|ρὸς στρατεγὸς Meritt. 19 [Καρχεδονίον οἵδε ὄμνυον τὸν ὅρκον· Ἀνν]ίβας | [Γέσκονος, Ἱμίλκον Ἄννονος, —12—]υτ Meritt.

Resolved by the council and the people. —— was the prytany; —— of Aphidna was the secretary; —— of —— was the chairman. —— proposed:

3 – – – the Carthaginians shall be written up as benefactors of Athens by the secretary of the council on the acropolis on a stone *stele.*

8 – – – send to Sicily to the generals Hannibal son of Gescon and Himilco son of Annon – – –

lacuna

13 – – – to the generals Hannibal son of Gescon and Himilco son of Annon.

15 Praise also the heralds (?) who have arrived in Athens because they are good men with regard to the people of Athens. Invite them also for hospitality to the *prytaneion* tomorrow.

19 – – – Hannibal – – –

Meritt's restoration of a decree around two meagre fragments was speculative, and was offered only *exempli gratia*, but the references to Sicily and Gescon in ll. 9–10, Himilco in 14–15 and Hannibal in 19 provide a sufficient indication of the context and subject-matter. Hannibal and Himilco were in Sicily together in the first half of 406, until Hannibal died (Diod. Sic. XIII. 80. i–ii, 86. iii; Vattuone suggests as a more likely date for the decree 408/7, when Alcibiades was in favour in Athens, but Himilco does not appear in Diodorus' narrative until 406); and apart from this decree the earliest appearance of demotics for officials named in a decree prescript is in *IG* i³ 126 of 405/4 (cf. Henry, *Prescripts*, 11–12).

Athenian ambitions extending to Carthage are suggested in Ar. *Eq.* 173–4, 1303–4, and, in connection with Alcibiades, for Athens' Sicilian expedition of 415 (Thuc. VI. 15. ii, 90. ii, cf. 34. ii); but in fact in winter 415/4 the Athenians in Sicily sent a trireme to Carthage 'about friendship' (88. vi)—with what result, we are not told. After the Athenians' defeat, Egesta gave way to Selinus in the dispute which had elicited the Athenian intervention, but when Selinus took more land than Egesta was willing to give Egesta appealed to Carthage, perhaps in 410 (Diod. Sic. XIII. 43). Carthage had not intervened in Sicily since 480, and had not responded to an appeal from Egesta in 416/5 (Diod. Sic. XII. 82. vii), but now it did respond, sending an advance force in 410 and a larger force in 409 (Diod. Sic. XIII. 44, 54. i–59. iv).[1] In a series of wars from

[1] The suggestion that Euripides' Phoenician Women, in 409, seem to have come from Carthage (ll. 202–14) is rejected by E. M. Craik, *Euripides, Phoenician Women*, 183–4, and D. J. Mastronarde, *Euripides, Phoenician Women*, 209–10.

190

List of sailors in Athenian triremes, 412–405

Twelve fragments of fine-grained white marble from a large *stele*, mostly found in and around the Erechtheum on the acropolis. Eleven are now in the Epigraphical Museum, one in the Agora Museum. Phot. *AJA*² xxxi 1927, 467 fig. II (EM 12365), 469 fig. III (EM 12366); *Hesperia* ii 1933, 393 fig. 62 (*j*); *Hesperia* iv 1935. 165 fig. 52 (*k*); *Ἀττικαὶ Ἐπιγραφαί . . . A. Wilhelm*, 149 (*c*, *f*, *j*); our pl. 16 (*c*, *f*, *j*).

Ionic letters.

D. R. Laing, 'A New Interpretation of the Athenian Naval Catalogue *IG* ii² 1951'; *IG* i³ 1032*. See also A. J. Graham, *TAPA* cxxii 1992, 257–70, *TAPA* cxxviii 1998, 89–114; G. Bakewell, in Mackay (ed.), *Orality, Literacy, Memory in the Ancient Greek and Roman World*, 143–62.

We print the best-preserved part of the *stele*, along with a further section of column vii.

then onwards the Carthaginians never gained control of the whole island but were never dislodged from the west end.

Athens was in no position to help the Carthaginians in Sicily, but it would welcome a war there which would hinder the Greek Sicilians from helping Sparta in the Aegean, while Carthage would be glad that the war in the Aegean hindered the Peloponnesians from intervening in Sicily. Selinus was supported by Syracuse and the cities in the south of the island, but not (Stroheker notes) by the more pro-Athenian Naxos and Catana, and the treaty which ended this war achieved one of the Athenians' Sicilian objectives, the refoundation of an independent Leontini (Diod. Sic. XIII. 114. i; cf. Thuc. III. 86, V. 4, v, VI. 8. ii). From what can be recovered of this text, it appears that the Carthaginians in Sicily sent representatives to Athens, the Athenians responded by sending representatives to the Carthaginians in Sicily (but there is nothing to suggest that they sent men actually to Carthage), and it is possible that the Athenians not merely praised the Carthaginians (restoration of ll. 6–8) but made some kind of agreement with them.

Invitations to hospitality commonly come at the end of a decree (cf. **184**. 24–6, **187**. 62, **191**. 37 (but there the publication clause follows)), and the end of l. 18 has been left uninscribed; but here the text continues and includes a further mention of Hannibal, where Meritt, believing in a formal alliance, restored a record of oath-taking.

A

col. vi

\------
\------
---χος
[ξένο]ι
---έκρ̣ατος Κήιο(ς)
---οκράτης Κήι
---τύαλος Κήι
---ά̣νθης Κήι
-----ων Κήι
-----ν Κήι
-----ν [Κ]ήι
----ιος Κήι
---ονικος Κήι
---αντίδης Κήι
-φαντίδης Κήι
Διόδωρος Ἀφυ(ταῖος)
Σάτυρος Σαμό(θραιξ)
Ἀρχέδημος Πεπ(αρήθιος)
Φίλτων Πεπαρ(ήθιος)
Ν̣ίκων Κιμων
[Φ]ανόστρατος Κύ(θνιος)
-χέδημος Κύθ(νιος)
-γων Νάξι(ος)
--υμαρτος Νά
---τος Νάξι
-----ης Ῥ̣όδι(ος)
--- ᵛ -ς Ῥόδι
-----Κυθ
-------η̣ι
-----τος Χῖο
-----ς Χῖο
------ς Ἀφυτ
------ες
\--------

col. vii

Μνησιτέλης Φ--
Πυρράκος Ἀχ
Πεισίλεως Σ̣υπ
Λυσίστρατος Π[-?-]
Εὔδρομος Πειρ
Πολύχαρμος Π̣ε̣
Μάλιχος Εὐων
Ἀρίτιος ἐξ Οἴο
Σωσιγένης Ἐλευ
Εὔδικος Μαραθ
Σάτυρος Λακιά
Δημοχάρης Θορί
Μύρμηξ Συπαλή
Ἐπιγένης Ὀῆθ
Πελάγων Ἀθην
Δημαρχίδης Ἀγν
Ἀπατόριος Περγ
Σωιναύτης Ἀναγ
Νίκανδρος *vac.*
Ἑλίκων Ἀναφλ
Ἀμφίας Ἀγρυλ
Εὐφημίδης Κηφ
Αἰσχύλος Δε[κ-?-]
Λύκων Φρεά[-?-]
Τρόχιλος Ο̣[?-]
Ἀριστοφαν— —
Κυθήρριο[ς]
Ἀνθεμίω[ν --]
Λύσιππο[ς --]
Μελήσιπ[π--]
Σιμίας ᵛ---
Πολυχ---
Ἀριστο---
Μυρρ---
Σωσ----
Σω-----
Δ̣η-----
lacuna

col. viii

---χείδης Ἀμει
[Γ]ῆρυς Ἀπολλω[-?-]
Κτίτας Ἐπικράτ
Εὔφρων Ἀρχεδή
Ἀπολλώνιος
Ἀριστομένος
Ἡρακλέδης
Φιλωνιχίδο
Στρομβιχίδης
Χαριδήμο
Φοῖνιξ Εὐχέρο
Ναύσων Θεοφίλο
τριηράρχω
Πρωτόμαχος Κηφι
Π̣αυσίστρατος Στε
[ἐ]πιβάται
[Χ]αιρήμων Ἀγρυλ
[Μ]νησίας Ἀγρυλῆ
[Φρ]ούραρχος Ἀγρυ
[Ἀμ]φικλῆς Ἀγρυ
[Ἱππ]οδάμας Ἀγρυ
[Ἰάσ]ων Ἀγρυλῆ
--στρατος Ἀγρυ
--ος Κηφισι
----Λαμ
[--- Τρ]ικο
[ναυπηγός]
-----ης Στερ
[κυβερνή]της
-----ης
Χερρ(ονησίτης)
[πρωιράτ]ης
-----δ̣ης ἐκ Κε
[κελευστ]ής
-----νης Πτε(λεάς)
[αὐλητής]
-----ν Πρι
[πεντηκό]νταρχ
-----λ̣ης Παι
[τοξόται]
----- Οἰναῖ
-----ς
[ναῦται ἀσ]τοί

col. ix

Συ̣--------
Πύρρος Τ----
Ἀρτέμω̣[ν ---]
Ἡρακλείδ[ης ---]
Εὑρεσ-------
Σαρπη[δὼν]
Παυσιστράτ[ο]
Ἀριστόδημ[ος]
Λυσιστράτ[-?-]
Καρίων Κηφ---
Ἑρμάφιλος
Κτησικλε---
Ἐπιμέλης
Παυσιστρ[άτο]
Μάρων Με---
Ἀρτίμας
Διονυσί[ο]
Ἀγάθων ---
Λάκων Ο---
Εὐ̣ξε------
Δεξίθε[ος --]
Ἕρμων ---ο
Δημήτ[ριος]
Κτησι[φῶντ]ος
Ἑρμαῖ̣[ς] Φιλοκλέ
Σάτυρ[ο]ς Πειθαγό
Θρᾶιξ [Π]ειθαγό
Πα[ρμ]ένων
Ἀ[γαθ]οκλέος
----νιος Εὐκλείδ
-----ς Κτησικλ
---ων Μνησίο
[Ν]ο̣μήνιος Φρουρά
Θρᾶιξ Ἀμφικλ
Θρᾶιξ Ἱπποδάμα
Καλλίστρατος
Ἰάσονος

69 Graham, *TAPA* cxxviii 1998, 94: --- vv *IG*. 87 Κιμώ(λιος)? Kirchner (*IG* ii^2 1951). 100 ες preceded by upward-sloping horizontal stroke, *IG*; [θεράπον]τες Laing; see Graham, *TAPA* cxxviii 1998, 99. 374–5 Graham *TAPA* cxxviii 1998, 96: Ἀγάθων | Λάκωνο[ς] *IG*.

A

col. vi

– – – – – –
– – – – – –
– – – – – –
– – –
—chus
FOREIGNERS
—ecratus of Ceos
—ocrates of Ceos
—tyalus of Ceos
—anthes of Ceos
—on of Ceos
—n of Ceos
—n of Ceos
—ius of Ceos
—onicus of Ceos
—antides of Ceos
—phantides of Ceos
Diodorus of
Aphy(tis)
Satyrus of
Samo(thrace)
Archedemus of
Pep(arethus)
Philton of
Pepar(ethus)
Nicon of Cimon
[Cimolus?].
Phanostratus of
Cy(thnos)
—chedemus of
Cyth(nos)
—gon of Nax(os)
—ymartus of
Na(xos)
—tus of Nax(os)
—es of Rhod(es)
—s of Rhodes
—— of Cythnos
—— of Ceos
—tus of Chios
—s of Chios
—s of Aphytis
– – – – – – –
– – – – – – –
– – – – – – –
– – – – – – –

col. vii

– – – – – –
—omerus
Mnesiteles of Ph—
Pyrrhacus of
Ach(arnae)
Peisileos of Sy(palettus)
Lysistratos of ——
Eudromus of Pir(aeus)
Polycharmus of
Pe(raeus)
Malichus of
Euon(ymum)
Aritius from Oion
Sosigenes of Eleu(sis)
Eudicus of Marath(on)
Satyrus of Lacia(dae)
Demochares of
Thori(cus)
Myrmex of
Sypale(ttus)
Epigenes from Oe
Pelagon of Athen
Demochares of
Hagn(ous)
Apatourius of Per(gase)
Sonautes of
Anag(yrous)
Nicandrus
Helicon of
Anaphl(ystus)
Amphias of Agryle
Euphemides of
Ceph(isia)
Aeschylus of De—
Lycon of Phrea(rrhii)
Trochilus of O—
Aristophan—
of Cytherrus
Anthemio—
Lysippu—
Melesip—
Simias ——
Polych—
Aristo—
Myrrh—
Sos—
So—
De—
lacuna

col. viii

– – – – – –
—cheides of Amei.
Gerys of Apollo—
Ctitas of Epicrat.
Euphron of Archede.
Apollonios
of Aristomenes
Heracleides
of Philonichides
Strombichides of
of Charidemus
Phoenix of Eucheirus
Nauson of Theophilos
TWO TRIERARCHS
Protomachus of
Cephi(sia)
Pausistratus of Ste(iria)
MARINES
Chaeremon of Agryle
Mnesias of Agryle
Phrurarchus of
Agry(le)
Amphicles of Agry(le)
Hippodamus of
Agry(le)
Iason of Agryle
—stratus of Agry(le)
—us of Kephisi(a)
—— of Lam(ptrae)
—— of Trico(rynthus)
SHIPWRIGHT
—es of Ster.
HELMSMAN
—es of Cherr.
BOW OFFICER
—des from Ce(rameis)
BOATSWAIN
—nes of Ptelea
PIPER
—n of Pri.
OFFICER OF THE 50
—les of Paeania
ARCHERS
—— of Oinae
—— of —s
CITIZEN SAILORS

col. ix

Sy—
Pyrrhus of T—
Artemon ——
Heracleides ——
Eures—
Sarpedon
of Pausistratus
Aristodemus
of Lysistratus
Carion of Ceph—
Hermaphilus
of Ctesicles
Epimeles
of Pausistratus
Maron of Me—
Artimas
of Dionysius
Agathon of ——
Lacon of O—
Euxe—
Dexitheus ——
Hermon of ——
Demetrius
of Ctesiphon
Hermaeus of
Philocle—
Satyrus of
Peithago—
Thraix of Peithago
Parmenon
of Agathocles
—nius of Eucleides
—— of Ctesicles
—on of Mnesius
Noumenius of
Phroura—
Thraix of Amphicl—
Thraix of
Hippodamus
Callistratus
of Iason
Callias of Hippos—

- - - - - Κηφ[-?-]
- - - - - Κηφι
[- - - - - - Κη]φι
[- - - - - - Κ]ηφι
- - - - - - -ς Κηφ
- - - - - - - Κηφι
- - - - - -σ̣ης Κηφ
- - - - - -ος Κολλ
- - - - - -λης Κολλ
- - - - -ωρος Παλ
- - - - - -ης Ἀγκυλ
- - - - -λος Ἀγρυ
- - - - - -ο̣ς ἐκ Κερ
[- - - - - - Φ]λ̣υε

Καλλίας Ἱπποσ
Θρᾶιξ Μίκο
Ἀπολλώνιος
Ναυ<κρ>
Αἴσωπος Λυσιμαχ
Ἡραῖος Ὀνησίμο
Σύρος Χαιρήμο
Ἕρμων Θεοφράσ
Ἡρακλείδης Καλ
Ἀρτίμας Ἀρχεσ
Καρίων Εὐάρχο
Γῆρυς Εὐάρχο
Μάνης Ἀρχίο
Θρᾶιξ Ἀρχίο
τριηράρχω
Ποσείδιππος Περγ
[Μ]όρυχος Θριάσι
[ἐπιβ]ά̣ται
- - - -ς Ἀχαρν

B

a lower part of col. vii

θεράποντες
Ἡρακλείδης
Ἱερομνήμονος
Ἡρακλείδης δεύτε
Μῦς Πολέμωνος
Λάκων Φυλίππο
Ἀρκέσας Καλλίο
Δᾶος Φάνο
Ἡρακλείδης
Μελησάνδρο
Παντάρκης
Δημοφίλο
Ἕρμαιος Μικυλίω
Εὐβολίδης Μνησίπ
Μύρμηξ Εὐξ<ι>θέο
Εὔαινος Εὐξιθέο
Ἀλύπητος Ἀριστάρ
Εὔφρων Εὐφρονίο
Ἱερόμβροτος
Ἀρίστωνος

—— of Cephi(sia)
——of Cephi(sia)
—— of Cephi(sia)
—— of Cephi(sia)
—s of Ceph(isia)
—— of Cephi(sia)
—ses of Ceph(isia)
—us of Coll(ytus)
—les of Coll(ytus)
—orus of Pal(lene)
—es of Ancyle
—lus of Agry(le)
—us from Cer(ameis)
—— from Phlya
lacuna

Thraix of Mikon
Apollonius of Nau—
Aesop of
Lysimachus
Heraeus of
Onesimus
Syrus of
Chaeremon
Hermon of
Theophrastus
Heracleides of Call—
Artimas of Arches—
Carion of Euarchus
Gerys of Euarchus
Manes of Archias
Thraix of Archias
TWO TRIERARCHS
Poseidippus of
Perg(ase)
Morychus of Thria
MARINES
—— of Acharn(ae)

B

a lower part of col. vii

SERVANTS
Heracleides
of Hieromnemon
Heracleides 2nd
Mys of Polemon
Lacon of Phylippus
Arcesas of Callias
Daus of Phano.
Heracleides
of Melesander
Pantarces of
Demophilus
Hermaeus of Micylio—
Euboulides of Mnesip—
Myrmex of Euxitheus
Euaenus of Euxitheus
Alypetus of Aristar—
Euphron of Euphronius
Hierombrotus
of Ariston

Ἀριστόβολος Ἀριστά
Θρᾶιξ Νικοβόλο
Εὐαρχίδης Κηφισοκ
Ἀπολλωνίδης
Ἀντιφάτος
Ἡγίας Ἀντιφάτος
Ἀρτίμας Ἀντιφάτ
Νομήνιος Πυθέο
Τίβειος Πυθέο
Σύρος Χαριδήμο
Γέλων Χαριδή
Ἀντιφάνης Ἀριστοτ
Σιμία[ς Κ]λ̣έω̣νος
Πατι ⁞ [.]ς Δ[ιφ]ί̣λ[ο]
Γῆρυς Ἀμυνάν[–?–]
Γλαυκία[ς] Ἀ ⁞ ολ̣[–?–]

There is no difficulty working out what this document is. Although the heading is lost, it is clear that we have a list of crews of triremes, each headed by the name of the trierarch, followed by the marines, the ship's officers, the citizen sailors, the non-citizen free sailors and the slaves. The difficulty lies in assessing when and why these lists were inscribed. But they have much interest regardless of their date and occasion, since they give us by far our best information about the composition of the crews of Athenian triremes.

Careful epigraphic work by Laing (followed by Lewis in *IG* and checked by Graham 1998) established the relationship of the surviving fragments of this *stele*. Originally there were ten columns of around 204 lines listing the trierarchs, marines, officers and other specialists, and the rowing crew of eight triremes (each trireme took up about 240 lines because of headings and two-line entries). The surviving fragments list the complement (of 200) of four triremes (which we refer to as triremes I, II, III and IV; the names of trierarchs preserved in ll. 21, 141, 276 and 407). The trierarchs and marines are listed first, the archers and rowers last, but the officers, etc. seem to have been named in varying order (for trireme IV we have no list and for triremes I and III some titles have to be completely restored, but enough survives to make some difference in order certain), and the proportion of citizens, foreigners and slaves differs from trireme to trireme.

Trireme I: The citizen rowers on trireme I were listed between ll. 50 and 70. Sixteen names are wholly or partially preserved but about nineteen lines have been lost; some citizen names spread over two lines so the maximum number of citizens is just over thirty.[1] The free foreign rowers were listed from l. 71 to (at least) l. 99; these

[1] For the problems with the text of l. 70, and the possibility that the number of citizens was not much greater than sixteen, see Graham, *TAPA* cxxviii 1998, 94–6.

Aristobulus of Arista—
Thraix of Nicoboulus
Euarchides of Cephisoc—
Apollonides
of Antiphates
Hegias of Antiphates
Artimas of Antiphat—.
Noumenius of Pytheas
Tibeius of Pytheas
Syrus of Charidemus
Gelon of Charide—
Antiphanes of Aristot—
Simias of Cleon
Pati – s of Diphilus
Gerys of Amynan—
Glaucias of A – ol—

---

are all single-line entries, giving a foreign complement of twenty-eight. Of these eleven, listed together, come from Ceos (as may one other, listed separately), three from Naxos, three (probably) from Cythnos, and two each from Aphytis, Peparethus, Rhodes and Chios, with one each from Samos and Cimolus (if the entry in l. 87 that reads 'Cimon' is a stone-cutter's error for 'Cimol.'). Line 100 may read 'Servants', in which case the list of slave rowers began there and continued to l. 140—given lacunas, an extent of about 134 lines. Allowing for some possible two-line entries this would nevertheless certainly yield more than 120 names. But the doubts about the reading of l. 100 are real.

Trireme II: The list of citizens on trireme II began at l. 172 and continued at least to l. 211. The names in ll. 212–20 might be of citizens or foreigners; those in ll. 221–6 are certainly foreigners. There were therefore at least thirty-nine citizens. Unfortunately, beyond knowing that there were some foreigners we cannot estimate their number: unlike the foreigners in trireme I, who were listed by ethnic, the foreigners here seem to have been listed by the deme in which they were registered as metics (cf. l. 226, 'Euphronius living in Sunium'). The list of slaves on trireme II begins at l. 227 and ends at l. 276 (with a small gap between two fragments of the stone). Forty slaves names are preserved and the total number would have been slightly greater than this.

Trireme III: The citizens rowing on trireme III were listed between ll. 305 and 319 (fourteen names, seven from Cephisia). The end of the list of citizens, and the list of any foreign rowers, are lost in the long lacuna between ll. 319 and 320. The names of about thirty-six slaves on trireme III are listed between ll. 320 and 356 of column viii and a further forty-three between ll. 357 and 406 of column ix. About seventeen lines seem to have been lost between the bottom of column viii as preserved and the top of column ix as preserved, and we do not know how many lines before ll. 320 the list of slaves rowers began. The list of slaves must have originally covered at least ninety-six lines.

Trireme IV: The beginning of the list of citizens rowing in trireme IV is lost in the lacuna between ll. 412 and 413; this lacuna can be calculated at about eighty-five lines, sixty of which will have been filled with names of citizen rowers; four citizen names are then preserved before the list of foreigners begins at l. 417, again listed by the deme in which they were registered as metics (with the exception of 'Simus of Thasos' in l. 431), not by ethnic. At least thirty-three names are preserved. About sixteen lines are lost at the bottom of column ix, and the list of slave rowers began in that lacuna. The arrangement of column x was peculiar, with a space left at the top of the column and at the bottom. At least thirty-five slave names are preserved between ll. 449 and 483, but there must originally have been about ninety-three lines in column x. Allowing for two-line entries, which occur mostly with slaves and citizens, the 180 names of the rowers (including ten non-rowing slaves who served the helmsman and bow-officer, for whom see Morrison *et al.*, *The Athenian Trireme*², 113) are likely to have been divided into about fifty-five citizens, eighty-five slaves and forty foreigners.

The four triremes therefore vary between *c.* thirty (trireme I) and *c.* fifty-five (trireme IV) citizens, twenty-eight (trireme I) and forty (trireme IV) foreigners (but trireme II, where the number of foreigners cannot be reconstructed, is likely to have had in excess of forty), and *c.* forty-five (trireme II) and 120 (possibly trireme I) slaves, but with three of the four triremes certainly or probably having half their rowers slaves. Among the non-rowing personnel who are specifically identified, the marines are always Athenians; on trireme III seven out of ten marines come from the deme of Agryle, and on trireme I perhaps four out of the ten from Lamptrae. The helmsmen appear to be consistently non-Athenian (—nd– [from Myndus?] on trireme I, Diphilus of Elaeus on trireme II, —— from Chersonesus on trireme III), as do the pipers (—— of Chios on trireme I, Sogenes of Siphnos on trireme I, —n from Priene on trireme III) and the shipwrights (—— of Chalcis on trireme I and Amynandrus metic on trireme II (the only use of the term metic in the text), —es Ste– on trireme III) but at least five archers were Athenian (—— of Erchia on trireme I, —— of Oenoe on trireme III) and only —ly– [from Ialysus?] on trireme I seems certainly to be non-Athenian (but note that Philonichus on trireme II comes from Oropus, which was never an Athenian deme).

The different proportions of slaves in each case may reflect different recruitment practices among trierarchs. As Bakewell has pointed out, it is notable that on trireme III seven out of ten marines come from a single deme, Agryle in Erechtheis, and that the citizen sailors on trireme III also occur in deme clusters; by contrast on trireme II the marines come from nine different demes in six different tribes and there is no deme clustering among the citizen rowers. Overall the lists are strongly biased towards the tribe of Erechtheis, with one of each of the pairs of trierarchs being from that tribe and overall thirty-two of the 106 demotics in this inscription being from demes in Erechtheis (and no more than ten from any other tribe); the find-spot of many fragments of the inscription in or near the Erechtheum further encourages the thought that these crews had a particularly close connection to that tribe (three decrees of Erechtheis were also found on the acropolis: see N. F. Jones, *Hesperia* lxiv 1995, 507). The strong influence of tribal organisation, formally important in the organisation of the Athenian infantry and cavalry (cf. above **109**, **129**, R&O 88, 89), is apparent here. Whether the different approaches to listing non-citizens (by their ethnic or the deme in which they were registered as metics) is simply a matter of different trierarchs conceiving of those they recruited differently, or whether some recruited metics and others recruited directly from outside Athens is not clear, but the fact that the non-Athenians listed by ethnic come from a relatively small number of places, most of them Aegean islands, may suggest that the trierarch in question had travelled round collecting men.

The lists of slaves are headed '*therapontes*', rather than *douloi*. This seems to have been the regular term for slaves serving in the army or navy. It is the term used on the only casualty list on which slaves are identified by a heading (*IG* i^3 1144. 139, the only other use of the term in an Athenian inscription before 403), and is used by Thucydides in relation to slaves serving in Sicily (VII. 13. ii; cf. IV. 16 of slaves in the Spartan army). By contrast it is *doulos* or *andrapodon* that is used in the Attic *stelai* (**172** at *IG* i^3 422. 194, 205, 427. 2, 430. 3).

The slave names in this inscription give a good picture of the full range of slave-naming practices (see more generally B. Robertson, in *Epigraphy and the Greek Historian* < . . . *P. E. Harding*> 79–116; K. Vlassopoulos, *ZPE* clxxv 2010, 113–44; Vlassopoulos, in Taylor & Vlassopoulos (edd.), *Communities and Networks in the Ancient Greek World*, 101–27; cf. **172**, **181**). At one end are those simply called by their place of origin: in particular there are no fewer than six slaves called 'Thraix', 'Thracian', another six called 'Syrian', and six with the name 'Carion'—just a minor variant on 'Carian'. There are then slave names characteristic of the place of origin (Manes, occurring eight times here, or Tibeius, occurring twice, both Phrygian names) or that refer to physical features (Simus, snub-nosed, occurring three times, or Pyrrhus, red-head, occurring once). Some slaves have names that refer to domestic animals ('Mys', mouse, 'Myrmex', ant) or to grotesque figures or archetypal slaves (we have a Satyrus, satyr, and an Aesopus, Aesop), others to heroic figures, presumably to point up the incongruity (such as Sarpedon). Some slaves have 'theophoric' names that are formed from those of gods and goddesses, like Artemidorus, Hermaeus, Hermon, Demetrius, Apollonius, Heraeus or Heracleides (of which there are seven cases here); indeed it is to be noted that this form of name is much more common among the slaves than among the free in this inscription (R. C. T. Parker, in Hornblower & Matthews (edd.), *Greek Personal Names*, 65). Some owners seem to have named their slaves in the hope that they would live up to their name: Ergophilus ('Work-lover'), Ophelion ('profitable'), Alypetus ('No-trouble') or Euarchus ('easy to command'). Euarchus is, however, a name also borne by a slave-owner here, and Ergophilus and Alypetus are also names found in the Athenian citizen body and so come into the majority of slaves who have names regularly (47 per cent) or occasionally (10 per cent) found among Athenians: Callistratus, Callias, Lysanias, Iatrocles, Xanthippus, etc.

(Vlassopoulos, *ZPE*, 127 Table 16). Other names, while not known among Athenian citizens, are known among non-citizens, and only 11 per cent of the slaves here have names found only among slaves. Some unusual names shared by slaves and citizens (e.g. Strombichides) may indicate that these were slaves born in the household of the citizen in question (but see Vlassopoulos, in Taylor & Vlassopoulos, 111–12).

Because slaves are listed with their master's name, in the formula 'S of M', it is possible to trace links between the slaves and others among the trireme's complement. Because of the preservation of the *stele*, this can best be seen on trireme II, where the names of the officers are best preserved. Here the trierarchs, Pytheas of Cephisia and Charidemus of Xypete, have two and three slaves, respectively, rowing for them (ll. 142–3, 254–7, 272–3); five of the marines, Aristotle of Coele, Epicrates of Lamptrae, Aristomenes of Crioa, Archedemus of Oion and Cleon of Lamptrae have slaves with them (147–9, 151, 153, 258–9, 266–9), Antiphates of Cytherrus the *pentekontarchos* has three slaves among the rowers (161, 250–3), the archers Ameinias of Cydathenaeum and Philonichus of Oropus each have slaves among the rowers (169–70, 264, 270–1), and the foreign helmsman Diphilus of Elaeus and the metic shipwright Amynandrus each have a slave rower (157, 165, 260, 261). In all, twenty-two of the thirty-two trierarchs and officers whose names are preserved are found to own slaves who also serve. Two foreigners among the rowers also have slaves rowing on the same trireme: Archedemus of Peparethus and his slave Timagenes on trireme I (85, 134); Euphronius living at Salamis and his slave Euphron on trireme II (226, 244). Various matches between the names of citizens or foreigners serving in one trireme and the owners of slaves on another trireme can be found, but we cannot be certain that more than a coincidence of names is involved in these cases.

Employment of slaves, as well as of free non-Athenians, in Athenian triremes was regular, and, as Graham (1992) has shown, is well illustrated by Nicias' letter to the Athenians as given by Thucydides, which describes how the Athenian forces are evaporating as slaves desert and their masters take leave to try to recover them (Thuc. VII. 13. ii: see generally Hunt, *Slaves, Warfare, and Ideology in the Greek Historians*, 83–101; Welwei, *Unfreie im antiken Kriegsdienst*, i. 65–104). We now have another fragmentary inscription listing of the crew of a trireme, perhaps from *c.*400 (*SEG* liv 226, where the trireme is identified as of the Erechtheid tribe, with trierarch and marines all from that tribe but with non-Athenian helmsman and boatswain), and *Hesperia* xli 1972, 427–8 no. 59 might be from a similar list, but listing the complement of a trireme was certainly not regular.[2] So when and why were the full crews of eight triremes inscribed in this way?

[2] The exclusivity of the tribal emphasis in *SEG* liv 226 raises the possibility that this lists the crew of a trireme that won the tribal race to Sunium (for which see Lys. XXI. *Bribery* 5, Hdt. VI. 87).

Since the full complement of each of the triremes is listed, this cannot be from a casualty list. Even in the case of the notorious battle of Arginusae, where Athenian loss of life caused so much grief, Xenophon explicitly notes that there were survivors from each ship (*Hell.* I. vi. 34), and in any case when there were joint trierarchs each served for only half the year (cf. [Dem.] L. *Polycles* 68), so both trierarchs could not have been casualties. Nor is it clear that listing crews in this way would serve any administrative purpose (for which, in any case, whitened boards would have been more appropriate given the time-limited use; see further Bakewell, 146–56). As the find-spot of most of the fragments (in and around the Erechtheum) further argues, this must be a commemorative monument. These eight crews must be being honoured for some distinctive naval achievement. But what?

The only epigraphic indication of date is provided by the Ionic letters and the possible identification of this stonemason's hand in the Erechtheum accounts for 408/7 (**181**) and as the third hand in **187**. This suggests a date towards the end of the fifth or early in the fourth century, but cannot offer any more precision. It has sometimes been thought that the occurrence of the Rhodian ethnic points to a date after Rhodian synoecism in 408, but in fact Thucydides (III. 8. i) is happy to use that ethnic in connection with events in 428. Similarly the occurrence of joint trierarchs is known certainly to have been possible from 409 (Lys. XXXII. *Diogeiton* 24), but joint trierarchies may have occurred earlier. Scholars have been tempted by the thought that the crews listed here are those who escaped after the battle of Aegospotami, but that hardly seems something that would have earned monumental celebration. Graham (1998, 103–8) suggested that these were the eight triremes sent under Strombichides to Samos in 412 (Thuc. VIII. 15. i–16. i), the first expedition by the Athenians to Ionia after the defeat of the Sicilian expedition. But Strombichides signally failed to prevent the revolt of various allies in Ionia, and this expedition can surely not have been celebrated in this unprecedented manner. No particular occasion can reliably be identified. As Bakewell has pointed (147) out, the crew of a trireme was not static, with sickness, accidents or desertion liable to cause substitutions: these lists, in particular with their listing of both trierarchs, present an ideal rather than an actual trireme complement. This might encourage us to see in these triremes not battle-hardened survivors of some campaign but those who presented themselves first for service. We know the Athenians to have awarded prizes to the triremes that got ready first (cf. **171**; R&O 100. 190–204): might this list have commemorated a particular proud moment for Erechtheis when all the most-ready trierarchs turned out to come from that tribe?

191

Athens honours the Samians, 405/4

Two contiguous fragments of the upper part of a marble *stele* (complete to l. 18), of which the lower part, with two further fragments, contains R&O 2; at the top of the *stele* is a relief showing Athens and Samian Hera clasping hands; *a*, the first fragment, found on the acropolis, *b* with the others found between the theatre of Dionysus and the odeum of Herodes Atticus; previously in the Epigraphical Museum but now displayed in the Acropolis Museum. Phot. Kern, *Inscriptiones Graecae*, tab. 19; Kirchner rev. Klaffenbach, *Imagines Inscriptionum Atticarum*, Taf. 19 Nr. 43; Meyer, *Die griechischen Urkundenreliefs*, Taf. 10. 1 (no. 26); Lawton, *Attic Document Reliefs*, pl. 7 (no. 12) (the last three, top of *stele*, with relief, only); R&O pl. 1.

Ionic lettering. (1–2) large letters; (3–4) intermediate-size letters; (5–40) *stoichedon* 57–61, often ending a line with the end of a word or syllable.

IG ii^{2} 1; *SIG*^{3} 116; M&L 94; *IG* i^{3} 127; Osborne, *Naturalization*, D5*. Trans. Fornara 166; Dillon & Garland^{3} 13. 34. See also R. Merkelbach, *ZPE* iii 1968, 124–5; A. L. Boegehold, *AJA*^{2} lxxvi 1972, 23–5; D. Whitehead, *ZPE* lii 1983, 113–14; J. L. Cargill, *GRBS* xxiv 1983, 321–32; Whitehead, in *Nomodeiktes . . . M. Ostwald*, 321–9; C. Koch, *Tyche* viii 1993, 63–75; A. Blanshard, in Newby & Leader-Newby (edd.), *Art and Inscriptions in the Ancient World*, 19–37; J. Elsner, *CSCA* xxxiv 2015, 33–73.

Κηφισοφῶν Παιανιεὺς
vac. ἐγραμμάτευε. *vacat*
Σαμίοις ὅσοι μετὰ τô δήμο τô Ἀθηναί-
ων ἐγένοντο. *vacat*
ἔδοξεν τῆι βολῆι καὶ τῶι δήμωι. Κεκροπὶς ἐπρυτάνευε· Πόλυμνις Εὐωνυμεὺς
ἐγραμμάτευε· Ἀλεξίας ἦρχε· Νικοφῶν Ἀθμονεὺς ἐπεστάτει. γνώμη Κλεσόφο
και συνπρυτάνεων· ἐπαινέσαι τοῖς πρέσβεσι τοῖς Σαμίοις τοῖς τε προτέρο-
ις ἥκοσι καὶ τοῖς νῦν καὶ τῆι βολῆι καὶ τοῖς στρατηγοῖς καὶ τοῖς ἄλλοις
Σαμίοις, ὅτι ἐσὶν ἄνδρες ἀγαθοὶ καὶ πρόθυμοι ποιεν̂ ὅ τι δύνανται ἀγαθόν,
καὶ τὰ πεπραγμένα αὐτοῖς ὅτι δοκôσιν ὀρθῶς ποιῆσαι Ἀθηναίοις καὶ Σαμί-
οις. καὶ ἀντὶ ὧν εὖ πεποιήκασιν Ἀθηναίοις καὶ νῦν περὶ πολλô ποιôνται καὶ
ἐσηγôνται ἀγαθά, δεδόχθαι τῆι βολῆι καὶ τῶι δήμωι Σαμίος Ἀθηναίος ἐ̂ναι,
πολιτευομένος ὅπως ἂν αὐτοὶ βόλωνται· καὶ ὅπως ταῦτα ἔσται ὡς ἐπιτηδειό-
τατα ἀμφοτέροις, καθάπερ αὐτοὶ λέγοσιν, ἐπειδὰν ἐρήνη γένηται, τότε περὶ
τῶν ἄλλων κοινῆι βολεύεσθαι. τοῖς δὲ νόμοις χρῆσθαι τοῖς σφετέροις αὐτῶν
αὐτονόμος ὄντας, καὶ τἆλλα ποιεν̂ κατὰ τὸς ὅρκος καὶ τὰς συνθήκας καθάπερ
ξύνκειται Ἀθηναίοις καὶ Σαμίοις. καὶ περὶ τῶν ἐνκλημάτων ἃ ἄγ γίγνηται
πρὸς ἀλλήλος διδόναι καὶ δέχεσθαι τὰς δίκας κατὰ τὰς συμβόλας τὰς ὄσας.
[ἐ]ὰν δέ τι ἀναγκαῖογ γίγνηται διὰ τὸν πόλεμον καὶ πρότερον περὶ τῆς πολι-
[τ]είας, ὥσπερ αὐτοὶ λέγοσιν οἱ πρέσβες, πρὸς τὰ πάροντα βολευομένος ποιεν̂
[ἧ]ι ἂν δοκῆι βέλτιστον ἐ̂ναι. περὶ δὲ τῆς ἐρήνης, ἐὰγ γίγνηται, ἐ̂ναι κατὰ ταὐτὰ
[κ]αθάπερ Ἀθηναίοις καὶ τοῖς νῦν οἰκôσιν Σάμον· ἐὰν δὲ πολεμεν̂ δέηι, παρασκ-
[ε]υάζεσθαι αὐτὸς ὡς ἂν δύνωνται ἄριστα πράττοντας μετὰ τῶν στρατηγῶν·
[ἐὰ]ν δὲ πρεσβείαν ποι πέμπωσιν Ἀθηναῖοι, συνπέμπεν καὶ τὸς ἐξ Σάμο παρόντας,
[ἐά]ν τινα βόλωνται, καὶ συνβολεύεν ὅ τι ἂν ἔχωσιν ἀγαθόν. ταῖς δὲ τριήρεσι
[ταῖς] ὅσαις ἐς Σάμωι χρῆσθαι αὐτοῖς δôναι ἐπισκευασαμένοις καθότι ἂν αὐ-

Cephisophon of Paeania was the secretary.

3 For the Samians who joined with the people of Athens.

5 Resolved by the council and the people. Cecropis was the prytany; Polymnis of Euonymum was the secretary; Alexias (405/4) was the archon; Nicophon of Athmonum was the chairman. Proposal of Cleisophus and his fellow *prytaneis*:

7 Praise the Samian envoys, both those who came previously and those who have come now, and their council and their generals and the other Samians, because they are good men and eager to do what good they can, and the actions which they have performed are judged to have been performed rightly for the Athenians and the Samians.

11 And in return for the good which they have done for the Athenians, and because they now attach importance to the Athenians and propose good things for them, be it resolved by the council and the people that the Samians shall be Athenians, living under whatever constitution they wish; and, as they themselves suggest, so that this shall be as advantageous as possible for both parties, when peace has been made, then we shall deliberate jointly about the other matters. They shall be autonomous, using their own laws, and in other respects act in accordance with the oaths and the agreements as agreed by the Athenians and Samians.

17 Concerning any complaints which the two parties may have against each other, they shall give and receive justice in accordance with the existing convention.

19 If any emergency arises about the constitution because of the war and before [*sc.* the peace], as the envoys themselves suggest, the [*sc.* Samians] shall deliberate in the light of the circumstances and do what they judge best.

21 Concerning the peace, if it is made, it shall be also for those now living in Samos on the same terms as for the Athenians; if it is necessary to make war, they shall prepare as best they can, acting together with the [*sc.* Athenian] generals; if the Athenians send an embassy anywhere, those present from Samos shall send jointly if they wish to send anybody, and shall give what good advice they can.

25 The triremes which are at Samos shall be given to [*sc.* the Samians] to use, after

[τοῖς δ]οκῆι· τὰ δὲ ὀνόματα τῶν τριηράρχων ὧν ἦσαν αὗται αἱ νῆες ἀπογράψαι
[τὸς πρέσ]βες τῶι γραμματεῖ τῆς βολῆς καὶ τοῖς στρατηγοῖς, καὶ τούτων εἴ πο-
[θέν τί ἐστιν ἀ]ναγεγραμμένον ἐν τωι δημοσίωι ὡς παρεληφότων τὰς τριήρες,
[ἅπαντα ἐξαλειψά]ντων οἱ νεωροὶ ἁπανταχόθεν, τὰ δὲ σκεύη τῶι δημοσίωι ἐσ-
[πραξάντων ὡς τάχιστα κα]ὶ ἐπαναγκασάντων ἀποδôναι τὸς ἔχοντας τούτων
[τι ἐντελῆ. γνώμη Κλεσόφο καὶ] συνπρυτάνεων· τὰ μὲν ἄλλα καθάπερ τῆι βολῆι·
[κυρίαν δὲ ἐ̂ναι δὲ τὴν δωρειὰν τοῖς ἥ]κοσιν, καθάπερ αὐτοὶ αἰτôνται, καὶ νε̂μαι
[αὐτὸς αὐτίκα μάλα τὸς ἄρχοντας ἐς τ]ạ̀ς φυλὰς δέκαχα. καὶ τὴν πορείαν παρα-
[σκευάσαι τοῖς πρέσβεσι τὸς στρατηγὸς ὡ]ς τάχιστα. καὶ Εὐμάχωι καὶ τοῖς
[ἄλλοις Σαμίοις πᾶσι τοῖς μετὰ Εὐμάχο ἥκοσ]ι ἐπαινέσαι ὡς ὄ̂σιν ἄνδρασιν
[ἀγαθοῖς περὶ τὸς Ἀθηναίος. καλέσαι δ' Εὔμ]αχον ἐπ̣[ὶ δ]εῖπνον ἐς τὸ πρυτανέον
[ἐς αὔριον. ἀναγράψαι δὲ τὰ ἐψηφισμένα τ]ὸγ γραμμ[ατέα τῆς] β̣[ο]λῆς μετὰ τῶν
[στρατηγῶν ἐστήληι λιθίνηι καὶ κατα]θε̂ναι ἐς πόλι[ν, τὸς δὲ ἑλλην]οταμίας
[δôναι τὸ ἀργύριον· ἀναγράψαι δ' ἐς Σά]μωι κατὰ ταὐτὰ τέ[λε]σι [τοῖς ἐκέ]νων.

Several letters are in several places incompletely inscribed.

29 Boegehold: [τι ὑπάρχει ἀ]ναγεγραμμένον Lolling, [τί ἐστι ὄφλημ]α γεγραμμένον Köhler (*IG* II. v 1b). 31 μηχανῆι οὐδεμιᾶ]ι (?) Merkelbach, ἀπολολότα κα]ὶ Cataldi. 32 [τι ἐντελῆ doubted Merkelbach, Boegehold, accepted Osborne. The calculation of Cargill, *Athenian Settlements of the Fourth Century BC*, 208, that the standard restoration has one letter too many is mistaken. 33 M. Feyel, *RPh*[3] xix 1945, 124–8 (suggesting [κυρίαν δ' ἐ̂ναι τὴν πολιτείαν τοῖς as another possibility): [ἐ̂ναι δὲ τὴν δωρειὰν Σαμίων τοῖς Kirchner (*IG* ii[2]): [εἶναι δὲ πολιτείαν Σαμίων τοῖς Wilhelm (*IG* ii[2] *addenda*), Osborne (but Osborne himself shows that the Athenians did not use the language of giving πολιτεία until *c.*229: *Naturalization*, i. 15–17). 34 Wilhelm, Osborne (ạ), Whitehead: ἐς τὸς δήμος καὶ τὰ]ς Lolling, but δέκαχα is inappropriate to the demes. 37 π̣ Osborne. 38 β̣ Osborne.

Samos (*Inventory*, 1094–8 no. 864) was the Athenians' main base in the Aegean from 412 (Thuc. VIII. 16. i) to the end of the Peloponnesian War. Whether or not it was oligarchically ruled throughout or towards the end of 439–412 (cf. on **139**), it declared for democracy in 412 (Thuc. VIII. 21, cf. *IG* i[3] 96), and an oligarchic movement was defeated in 411 (Thuc. VIII. 63. iii, 73). It then remained loyal to democratic Athens until the end of the war; the reference to a slaughter of the aristocrats in Xen. *Hell.* II. ii. 6 is probably to that of 412 (but possibly to a further episode in 405). After the battle of Aegospotami in 405, while Athens was blockaded, the Spartan Lysander besieged Samos, eventually capturing it and imposing a decarchy, rule by a clique of ten men (Xen. *Hell.* II. iii. 6–9 cf. II. ii. 16, Diod. Sic. XIII. 106. viii, XIV. 3. iv, Lys. XII. *Eratosthenes* 71, P. Michigan 5982. 38–43 (the 'Theramenes papyrus': *ZPE* ii 1968, 161–9), Plut. *Lys.* 14. ii: we need not discuss here the timetable of Lysander's movements). A story in Plut. *Apophth. Lac.* 233 D and elsewhere suggests that in the peace negotiations the Athenians tried unsuccessfully to lay claim to Samos. This decree belongs to a time in the earlier part of 405/4, when neither Athens nor Samos had yet capitulated to Sparta, and peace was under consideration but not yet certain (19–25).

On the significance of the relief see especially Blanshard; and on the multiple questions arising in the interpretation of the whole monument, which combines the

they have repaired them in accordance with their own judgment; the names of the trierarchs to whom the ships were assigned shall be reported by the envoys for the secretary of the council and the generals; and, if for any of these anything is written up anywhere in the public realm from when they took over the triremes, all of this everywhere shall be deleted by the *neoroi*, but the equipment shall be exacted for the state as soon as possible, and those who have any of it shall be compelled to give it back intact.

32 Proposal of Cleisophus and his fellow *prytaneis*: In other respects in accordance with the council; but the grant shall be valid for those who have come, as they themselves ask, and they shall be distributed immediately by the archons on the basis of ten among the tribes.

34 Travelling expenses shall be provided for the envoys by the generals as soon as possible.

35 Praise Eumachus and all the other Samians who have come with Eumachus, bcause they are good men with regard to the Athenians.

37 Invite Eumachus to dinner in the *prytaneion* tomorrow.

38 What has been decreed shall be written up on a stone *stele* by the secretary of the council together with the generals and placed on the acropolis, and the *hellenotamiai* shall provide the money; it shall be written up at Samos in the same way at their own expense.

---

relief with the (re)publication of this decree and further decrees of 403/2 (R&O 2), yet does not mention that the regime of the Thirty has intervened, see Elsner.

Lines 1–2 provide a heading for the whole inscription, dated by Cephisophon, secretary in 403/2 when the last of the decrees on the *stele* was enacted (R&O 2. 56–7); but 3–4 may have been the heading for this decree when it was first published. If this decree was set up on the acropolis (38–40), it was presumably demolished by the Thirty, and for that reason reinscribed with the later decrees in 403/2 (cf. on **157**, **177**).

The secretary (5–6) is the only Athenian Polymnis in *LGPN*, so the funerary urn and juror's *pinakion* recovered from a grave in a cemetery of the deme Euonymum (*SEG* xlvii 238: noted at <www.seangb.org>) presumably belong to him or a homonymous relative. This decree was proposed not by a single individual, whose official position if any would not be stated (as was the case for all but a handful of surviving decrees: for another exception see **141**), but, uniquely, by the whole board of *prytaneis* (6–7), and the amendment beginning in 32 is likewise proposed by the whole of that board. In l. 12 we have the earliest surviving instance of the motion formula, 'be it resolved by the council and the people', which from the fourth century onwards is increasingly included in inscribed decrees instead of or in addition to the enactment formula at the beginning. In what became the standard Athenian practice it was preceded by a motivation clause (cf. R&O, p. xx). Here there is an approach to that: the substance of the decree begins (7) 'Praise the Samian envoys . . . because they are good men . . .', and then continues (11) 'And in return for . . . be it resolved . . .'.

Athens had made a mass grant of citizenship to the Plataeans, perhaps in 519 or 480 (Thuc. III. 55. iii), and that was activated after the destruction of Plataea in 427 by the surviving Plataeans in Athens ([Dem.] LIX. *Neaer.* 104–6, cf. Lys. XXIII. *Pancleon*, Isoc. XII. *Panath.* 94). Here a mass grant is made to the Samians (11–17), but the references to their constitution and autonomy, and the judicial convention, indicate that that is not expected to be activated. Koch stresses that this should be seen as an exceptional arrangement in exceptional circumstances, rather than as an anticipation of *isopoliteia* grants between cities which were to be made later. For freedom to choose their own constitution cf. Alcibiades' treaty with Selymbria, **185**. 10–12. Samos' autonomy is likely to have been guaranteed, and a judicial convention (18, cf. on **120**) made, in 411 if not earlier (cf. Thuc. VIII. 75. iii: on the significance of 'autonomy' here see Whitehead). 'Those now living in Samos' are specified to distinguish them from exiles who would be supported by Lysander.

In 25–32 Athenian triremes at Samos (presumably the twenty left by Conon and Philocles before Aegospotami: Diod. Sic. XIII. 104. ii) are to be given to the Samians; anything 'written up' (whatever the precise text which is to be restored) will refer to the obligations which their trierarchs had incurred; but the Samians are to have any

---

192

Thank-offering for victory at Aegospotami, shortly after 405

Twelve blocks of grey limestone from a base for multiple bronze statues. Ten blocks were found at the south-east entrance to the sacred precinct at Delphi, one at the north-east corner of the temple terrace and one has no recorded find-spot. Reconstruction Pouilloux & Roux, *Énigmes à Delphes*, 57. Facsimiles *F. Delphes* III. i, pp. 30 ff. Photos *F. Delphes* III. i, pl. ii. 1–2 (*b* and *c*); *BCH* lxxxiii 1959, 176 fig. 22 (*a*); *BCH* lxxxv 1961, 73 fig. 4 (*a*); *BCH* xc 1966, 432 figs. 2–3 (*b*), 438 fig. 4 (top. of *j*).

front row

(*a*) [– – – . . . .]ι̣ . . Ν̣ . Ω̣Ι̣ [—c.8—]
[– – – . . . Τ]υνδαριδ[—c.8—]
[– – – . . . .] . Λύσανδ[ρ]ος [. . .] . . [–?–]
[– – –]ε̣ον θεῶν ἱερὸν δάπεδον. *vacat*

necessary repairs made, and any movable equipment which the trierarchs had taken from the Athenian stores for their ships is to be returned to Athens. The *neoroi* (30) appear otherwise only in the fragmentary *IG* i[3] 154, which is concerned with ships, dockyards and equipment: the principal fourth-century dockyard officials were the *epimeletai ton neorion*, curators of the dockyards (e.g. R&O 100. 178–9), and they appear already in another fragmentary naval inscription, *IG* i[3] 236, of *c.*410–404.

The amendment (32–40), with the same proposers as the original decree, presumably results from realisation in the assembly's debate that not everything which was needed had been included in the original proposal. It begins with confirmation of the citizenship grant for 'those who have come' (33–4), and their distribution among the tribes: these will be the envoys and presumably a significant number of others (cf. 35–6, and Shipley, *A History of Samos, 800–188* BC, 130–1, Cargill) who, while Samos is being besieged by Lysander, may be unable or unwilling to return, and who therefore want their grant to be activated. Cargill suggests that a number of Samians who took up their citizenship in Athens may have returned as participants in the Athenian cleruchy of 365. Similarly, since Samos will not be able to refund its envoys' travelling expenses, Athens undertakes to do that (34–5). Since by this decree Eumachus becomes an Athenian citizen, he is invited not to 'hospitality' but to 'dinner' (37–8: cf. on **166**).

Involvement of the generals with the secretary in the publication of the decree (38–40) is unusual (but cf. **185**. 33–5), but these were unusual circumstances.

Ionic writing. Roughly *stoichedon*, except *c* (see Austin, *The Stoichedon Style in Greek Inscriptions*, 78).

F. Delphes III. i. 50–68; *SIG*[3] 115; M&L 95 (* except *a*); J. Bousquet, *BCH* lxxxv 1961, 71–4 (* *a*); *CEG* 819; *Choix Delphes* 25 (*c* only). See also E. Bourguet, *F. Delphes* III. i, pp. 24–40; P. de la Coste-Messelière, *BCH* lxxvii 1953, 182–9; Pouilloux & Roux, *Énigmes à Delphes*, 55–60; J. Bousquet, *BCH* xc 1966, 428–40; J.-F. Bommelaer, *BCH* xcv 1971, 43–64; Bommelaer, *Lysandre de Sparta*, 14–16, 18; Bommelaer & Laroche, *Guide de Delphes: le site*, 108–10; Jacquemin, *Offrandes Monumentales à Delphes*, 191–2; Scott, *Delphi and Olympia*, 105–7.

front row

(*a*) – – – Tyndaridae – – – Lysander – – – sacred ground of the gods.

(*b*) [παῖ Διός, ὦ] Πολύδẹṿ[κ]ες, Ἴωṿ [καὶ τοῖσ]δ' ἐλεγείοι[ς]
[λαϊνέαν] ḳρηπῖδ' ἐστεφάνωσ[ε τεά]ν,
[ἀρχὸς ἐπ]ẹὶ πρῶτος, πρότερο[ς δ' ἔ]τι τοῦδε ναυάρ[χου],
[ἔστας ἁγ]εμόνων Ἑλλάδος εὐρ[υχ]όρου.

(*c*) εἰκόνα ἑὰν ἀνέθηκεν [ἐπ] ἔργωι τῶιδε ὅτε νικῶν
ναυσὶ θοαῖς πέρσεν Κε[κ]ροπιδᾶν δύναμιν
Λύσανδρος, Λακεδαίμονα ἀπόρθητον στεφανώσα[ς]
Ἑλλάδος ἀκρόπολ[ιν, κ]αλλίχορομ πατρίδα.
ἐξάμο ἀμφιρύτ[ου] τεῦξε ἐλεγεῖον ⁝ Ἴων.

back row

(*d*) [. . . .]θιος
[Λυσι]μαχίδαο
[Βοιω]τῶν.

(*e*), (*f*) (adjoining blocks)

Κ[ιμμ]έριος	Αἰαντίδης	Θεόπομπος
Πελάσγο	Παρθενίου	Λαπόμπου
Ἐφέσιος.	Μιλήσιος.	Μάλιος.
		Ἄλυπος ἐποίει.

on the top of block (*f*)

Αἰαντίδης
Παρθενίου
Μιλήσιος.
Τείσανδρος ἐποί[ησ]ε.

(*g*), (*h*) (adjoining blocks)

Α[ὐτ]όνομος	Ἀπολλόδωρος
Σαμίου	Καλλιφῶνος
Ἐρετριεύς	Τροζάνιος.

[Κώμ]ων
[. . .]ωνδα
[Μεγα]ρεύς

(*j*)

[Πυθόδοτος]
[. . . .]ρε[– –]
Κορίνθιος

c. 5 ἐξάμο *F. Delphes*, Bommelaer, *BCH* xcv 1971, 63 n. 34 (*a*): ἐχσάμο M&L. *d.* 3 J.Bousquet, *RA* 1970, 342: Βοιω]τῶν ṿ[αύαρχος] M&L following *F. Delphes*. *j* and *k* are not adjoining blocks: Bommelaer, *BCH* xcv 1971, 62 n. 27. *j* [Πυθόδοτος] de la Coste-Messelière, *BCH* lxxvii 1953, 184 n. 5, Bousquet, *BCH* xc 1966, 440, restored from Pausanias on the basis of the order in which he gives the names.

(*b*) O Polydeuces [Pollux] son of Zeus, Ion crowned
  your stony base even with these verses
when you stood as the first leader, even before this admiral,
of the leaders of Greece with its broad dancing-floors.

(*c*) Lysander set up his statue on this monument when, victorious
  with swift ships he destroyed the power of the children of Cecrops
Crowning Sparta, the never-sacked acropolis of
  Greece, fatherland of fine dancing.
  Ion from sea-girt Samos constructed the verse.

(*d*) —thius, son of Lysimachides, of the Boeotians.

(*e*), (*f*)

Cimmerius son of Pelasgus Ephesian.	Aiantides son of Parthenius Milesian.	Theopompus son of Lapompus Melian. Alypus made it.

(top of *f*) Aeantides son of Parthenius, Milesian. Teisander made it.

(*g*), (*h*)

Autonomus son of Samius Eretrian.	Apollodorus son of Calliphon Troezenian.

(*i*)

Comon
son of —ondas
Megarian.

(*j*)

Pythodotus
. . . . re – – –
Corinthian.

(*k*) ——– – –

——– – –

Z[– – –]

(*l*) κᾶρυξ

When the Spartans defeated the Athenian fleet at Aegospotami in 405 they effectively won the Peloponnesian War, since they could then blockade the Hellespont, command the seas and starve Athens into submission. They celebrated their victory and that of their allies by constructing this massive monument, 18 m. long and 4.5 m. wide, carrying some forty bronze statues, just inside the entrance to the sacred enclosure at Delphi, next to and dwarfing the monument of the Athenian eponymous heroes (see reconstruction drawing in Scott, 104). Because the path beside it was climbing, the end near the entrance will have towered over the visitor: as Bommelaer & Laroche write in their guidebook to the site (109), 'L'offrande était conçue pour faire impression'. We know the monument not simply from the surviving stones but from descriptions by Pausanias and Plutarch.

Plutarch, *On the Pythian Oracles* (395 B), makes it clear that 'the sea captains', as he refers to them, with their fine deep-blue patina, constituted the first monument that visitors to Delphi encountered (cf. *Lys.* 18. i, where he ascribes the initiative for the monument to Lysander). Paus. X . 9. vii–x gives an extremely full description:

> Directly opposite these [a later statue group put up by the Tegeans to celebrate victory over the Spartans] are dedications made by the Spartans from the Athenians: the Dioscuri, Zeus, Apollo and Artemis, and in addition Poseidon and Lysander son of Aristocritus being crowned by Poseidon, Agias who was seer to Lysander on that occasion and Hermon the helmsman of Lysander's flagship. Theocosmus of Megara is likely to have sculpted this statue of Hermon, because he was given citizenship by the Megarians. The Dioscuri are by Antiphanes of Argos, and the seer is the art of Piso from Calaureia near Troezen. Athenodorus and Dameas, the latter made the Artemis and Poseidon and also Lysander, and Athenodorus made the Apollo and the Zeus: they were Arcadians from Cleitor. Behind the statues I have described are dedicated statues of all those who collaborated with Lysander at Aegospotami, whether among the Spartans themselves or their allies. They are as follows: Aracus and Erianthes, the former from Sparta, the latter a Boeotian,[1] <*lacuna likely to have concluded 'Erythrae'*> above Mimas, from there Aristocrates, and the

[1] Pausanias' 'Erianthes' (cf. Plut. *Lys.* 15. iii, 'Erianthus') suggests restoring [Ἀριάν]θιος in *d.* 1, but there is space for only four letters. The scholiast on Dem. XIX. *Embassy* 65 gives the name as 'Euanthus', but whether Euanthius was inscribed in *d* is very uncertain.

(*k*) ----

Z—

(*l*) herald

Chians Cephisocles, Hermophantus and Hicesius, Timarchus and Diagoras of Rhodes, the Cnidian Theodamus, Cimmerius from Ephesus, the Milesian Aeantides. Tisander made these, and Alypus of Sicyon the ones that follow: Theopompus of Melos [corrected from the inscriptions from the 'Midian' or 'Myndian' offered by the MSS], Cleomedes of Samos, and from Euboea Aristocles of Carystus and Autonomus of Eretria, and Aristophantus of Corinth and Apollodorus of Troezen and from Epidaurus in the Argolid Dio. Next to these are Axionicus the Achaean from Pellana, Theares of Hermione, the Phocian Pyrrhias, Comon of Megara and Agesimenes of Sicyon, and from Ambracia and Corinth and Leucas Telycrates and Pythodotus of Corinth, and the Ambraciot Euantidas. Finally there are Epicydidas and Eteonicus the Spartans. They say that these are the work of Patrocles and Canachus.

This description makes apparent not only the size of the monument (three times as many figures as on the Athenian monument to victory at Marathon), with its unprecedented and never imitated double rank of statues, but its binary organisation. At the front (Pausanias probably describes the figures from right to left: Bommelaer, *BCH* xcv 1971, 63) was a scene that put the victory at Aegospotami into a cosmic context (for the role of the Dioscuri at Aegospotami see Plut. *Lys.* 12. i), at the back (where Pausanias goes from left to right) the whole anti-Athenian force arrayed in battle order (Bommelaer, *Lysandre*, 15). Both aspects of this organisation are significant.

Although the epigram ascribes the leading part in the victory to Pollux, the iconography, by having Poseidon crown Lysander as the only action, put all the emphasis on Lysander, singling out a man who in formal terms was only the deputy commander at the time of the battle (Xen. *Hell.* II. i. 7). The presence of the seer and the helmsman makes Lysander here the equivalent of Pelops and Oenomaus with the seer and their charioteers on the east pediment at Olympia. This promotion of Lysander is entirely in accordance with the dedication by Lysander of statues of Victory at Sparta (Paus. III. 17. iv) and of a gold-and-ivory trireme, given him by Cyrus, and gold stars, symbols of the Dioscuri, at Delphi (Plut. *Lys.* 18. i–ii). There is no doubt that Lysander was indeed much fêted by Greek states (cf. the statues of him at Olympia dedicated by the Samians and the Ephesians: Paus. VI. 3. xiv–xvi) and the naming of the festival of Hera at Samos after Lysander, where a later writer, Duris, claimed that sacrifices were made to Lysander as to a god (Plut. *Lys.* 18. v–vi).

The array of commanders of the fleet is no less notable. Its effect was to set out the breadth of support which the Spartans had had, both from their traditional Peloponnesian League allies (Boeotia, Corinth, Megara, the cities of the Argolid and of Achaea) and from the former members of the Athenian empire (Chios, Rhodes, Cnidus, Miletus, Ephesus, Samos, Carystus, Eretria). From this image of Spartan power one element is strikingly lacking: the Spartan kings. Although this is in a sense a necessary consequence of the celebration of a naval battle, given that Spartan kings did not take command by sea, it also fits with Lysander's own political disposition to do away with hereditary kingship at Sparta (Arist. *Pol.* v. 1301 B 19–20; Nep. *Lys.* 3; Cic. *Div.* I. 43; Plut. *Ages.* 8. iii, *Lys.* 24. iii–26. vi).

The size of the monument brought some practical problems. For the front row five sculptors (at least) were involved, and four for the back, where the very wide range of individuals commemorated and the role of individual cities in making arrangements for particular figures must have made the organisation quite complex (statues by different sculptors were erected on the same block). Something of the complexity of this, and also of the sense in which the individual cities felt that they 'owned' the statue of their particular commander, comes out from the detailed epigraphy.

In addition to the inscriptions given above there is a further set of inscriptions on the top face of the stones, often running perpendicular to the inscribed face. So on the top face of the block bearing *a* an inscription reads [Πολυ]δεύκης (Bommelaer, *BCH* xcv 1971, 63 n. 34 (*c*), correcting Bousquet, *BCH* xc 1966, 437); as well as the repeat version of the text on the front, the top of the block with *f* is also inscribed simply Μιλήσιος (Milesian), the top of *g* Ἐρετρι[εύς] (Eretrian), the top of *h* Τροζάνιος (Troezenian). These inscriptions seem best interpreted as indications to the sculptors of which figure needed to be placed where.

Two of the inscriptions on the top face have caused difficulty. On top of *j* (not aligned with the name of the Corinthian on the front face, but far to the left, beside another set of footprints) is an inscription [Χα]λκιδεύ[ς]. Pausanias, however, mentions no Chalcidian. It has been pointed out (by Psoma, *Olynthe et les Chalcidiens de Thrace*, 195–7) that Chalcideus is also attested as a personal name — although the absence from Pausanias remains an issue. That is also the issue with block with the inscription κᾶρυξ (herald) on its top. This block has four footprints, three of them modest in size, but one of them large (the footprints must always have been smaller than the actual feet of the statues: Bommelaer, *BCH* xcv 1971, 53–5); the figures in the back rank were life-size, those in the front slightly over life-size. This shows that it belongs not with the bases at the rear but with those at the front (so de la Coste-Messelière, *BCH* lxxvii 1953, 187). Since the figure of the herald himself was evidently smaller than the other figures in this rank it is not hard to imagine Pausanias overlooking him.

The top face of the base came in time to be used for further inscriptions, with individual figures attracting relevant later honours. On the top face of block *e* (Cimmerius son of Pelasgus of Ephesus) was recorded, perhaps in the late third century, a grant of proxeny to Alcidamas descendant of Pelasgus of Ephesus. Another proxeny grant was inscribed on the top of block *f*, aligned with the name of Theopompus of Melos on the front face; this grant honoured another Theopompus of Melos, the son of Euphorbus. On the front face between the name of Theopompus and the name of Aeantides a third proxeny grant was inscribed, unfortunately for a man whose name is lost.

The most interesting of these later inscriptions appears on the front face of block *k*, to the left of the letter Z which is all that survives of a three-line label. This inscription records a dedication by a Spartan village of Tyritae. On the assumption that this later inscription has been placed, like the others, in relation to a relevant name, the person whose name is lost should be a Spartan, indeed presumably one of the two Spartans with whom Pausanias ends his description, Epicydidas and Eteonicus. Whether this Spartan actually came from Tyritae or from e.g. Zarax depends upon how securely Z can be read, and scholars have disputed this (see *BCH* lxxvii 1953, 184–6; G. Roux, in *Énigmes à Delphes*, 59, *BCH* xc 1966, 285, 428).

We might expect that Pausanias' account derived from his own reading of the inscriptions (although he makes no mention of the epigrams). But, curiously, it appears to be the case that not every figure in the second row was identified by an inscription (see Bousquet, *BCH* xc 1966, 440), and apart from the signature of Teisandrus in the anomalous repeat inscription identifying Aiantides (*f*) there do not seem to have been signatures that would have enabled Pausanias to attribute each of the statues. As often, the precise source of Pausanias' knowledge is unclear.

The monument must have been put up very shortly after the victory at Aegospotami while the diverse cities involved were happy to celebrate together, and the names of the figures on the back row must belong to the completion of the monument. But what about the epigrams? Two of these identify themselves as by Ion of Samos (for self-identification on stone by a poet see R&O 13. *A*. ii; for ἐξάμο compare the Attic equivalent, ἐχσάμο, at **170**. 18–19, **180**. 20, 34), and it is likely that he was responsible for all three. Unfortunately we know nothing further of Ion of Samos, although scholars have speculatively attributed to him some verses attributed to Ion of Chios that fall outside Ion of Chios's lifetime (see Page, *Further Greek Epigrams*, 157–8). The poems are too poorly preserved to be dated by style, and the only dating criteria are therefore the forms of the letters. Epigraphists long convinced themselves that the letter forms were those of the second half of the fourth century, and debated whether the inscriptions had been re-engraved then or had been added for the first time at that point. However, Bousquet (*BCH* lxxx 1956, 581) insisted that the letter forms were not impossible *c*.400. In the absence of any sign of re-engraving or any motivation for adding these inscriptions two or three generations after the monument was erected it seems most sensible to think that the epigrams were part of the original monument, a hypothesis which suits well their promotion of Lysander (cf. *Choix Delphes*, p. 52).

193

Monument of the Lycian dynast Gergis, late fifth century

On the middle part of the northern face (*c*) of a limestone shaft at Xanthus, still *in situ*—the 'Xanthus *stele*' or 'inscribed pillar', which supported a tomb chamber with an elaborate frieze, and a seated statue above it (P. Demargne, in *F. Xanthos*, i, 79–105 with pls. xxvi–xliv). Phot. our pl. 17 (part of *c*, including Greek text). Facsimile: *TAM* i, pp. 40–1.

Ionic writing. *Stoichedon*, except at the ends of the longer lines, and with *iota* often combined with an adjacent letter in one *stoichos* (indicated below by underlining).

TAM i 44; König, *Die Stele von Xanthos*, i (Vienna: Gerold, 1936), 79–81; M&L 93; J. Bousquet, *CRAI* 1975, 138–41*; *CEG* 177. See also Bryce & Zahle, *The Lycians*, i. 97–8, 107–10; I. Savalli, *AC* lvii 1988, 103–23; J. Bousquet, in *F. Xanthos*, ix. 159–66, 172–3; A. G. Keen, *AS* xlii 1992, 53–63; P. Ceccarelli, in *Vir Bonus Dicendi Peritus . . . G. Garuti*, 47–69; Keen, *Dynastic Lycia*, 9–10, 129–47; P. Thonemann, in Ma *et al.* (edd.), *Interpreting the Athenian Empire*, 167–94.

[ἐ]ξ οὗ τ' Εὐρώπην [Ἀ]σίας δίχα πόν[τ]ος ἔνεμ[ε]ν,
[ο]ὐδές πω Λυκίων στήλην τοιάνδε ἀνέθηκ<ε>ν
[δ]ώδεκα θεοῖς ἀ ν ν γορᾶς ἐν καθαρῶι τεμένει,
[ἔρ]γων καὶ πολέμου μνῆμα τόδε ἀθάν<α>τον.
[Γέ]ρ[γ]ις ὅδε Ἀρπάγο υἱὸς ἀριστεύσας τὰ ἅπαντα
[χε]ρσὶ πάλην Λυκίων τῶν τότ' ἐν ἡλικίαι,
[πο]λλὰς δὲ ἀκροπόλες σὺν Ἀθηναίαι πτολιπόρθωι
[π]έρσας συγγενέσιν δῶκε μέρος βασιλέας.
ὧν χάριν ἀθανατοί οἱ ἀπεμν<ή>σαντο δικαίαν.
ἑπτὰ δὲ ὁπλίτας κτεῖνεν ἐν ἡμέραι Ἀρκάδας ἄνδρας,
Ζηνὶ δὲ π<λ>ε͂στα τροπαῖα β<ρ>οτῶν ἔ[στ]ησεν ἁπάν<τ>ων,
καλλίστοις δ' ἔργοις Κα[ρ]ίκα γένος ἐστεφάνωσεν.

The letters enclosed in <angle brackets> in ll. 2, 4, 9, 11 are missing on the stone. 3 The cutter avoided a fault in the stone. 4 [ἔρ]γων Bousquet: [νικ]έων previous editors. 5 [Γέ]ρ[γ]ις Bousquet from R&O 13, cf. the emendation Γέργις ὁ Ἀρπάγου suggested by W. Deecke in Hdt. vii. 82: various other restorations were proposed. 12 Κα[σ]ίκα or Κα[ζ]ίκα also possible Bousquet.

On this monument faces *a*, *b* (south and east respectively) and the upper part of *c* (north) contain a prose text in Lycian (A), giving a detailed chronicle; then follows our Greek text; and then the bottom of *c* and the whole of *d* (west) contain a verse text in a Lycian dialect known as Lycian B. For an interpretation of the whole *stele*, including the Lycian texts, see Thonemann.

Lycia, to the east of Caria in south-western Asia Minor, was on the edge of the Greek world in the fifth century, but easily accessible, and sometimes, though not regularly, penetrated by the Athenians; in the late fifth and early fourth centuries, when Caria was under Persian control, it managed to remain effectively independent

And since the sea divided Europe from Asia, none of the Lycians has ever set up a *stele* such as this to the Twelve Gods in the pure precinct of the agora. This is an undying memorial of deeds and war.

5 This Gergis, son of Harpagus, on all occasions in wrestling with his hands surpassed the Lycians who were then in their prime, he sacked many *akropoleis* with the help of Athena Sacker of Cities, and he gave a share in his kingdom to his kindred.

9 For this the immortals rendered him righteous gratitude. He killed seven Arcadian men who were hoplites in a day, and he of all mortals set up the most trophies to Zeus, and crowned the line of Kheriga (?) with the finest deeds.

---

of both Athens and Persia. Lycia and its city of Telmessus appear in Delian League tribute lists in the middle of the century (*IG* i^3 261. i. 29–30, probably 262. v. 32–3, and 266. iii. 33–4) but not subsequently. In winter 430/29 Thuc. II. 69 records an Athenian expedition of six ships under Melesandrus to Caria and Lycia, 'to raise money there and to prevent raiders from the Peloponnese from using the region as a base to interfere with merchant shipping'. Melesandrus took soldiers into the interior of Lycia, but they were defeated and he was among those killed. A similar Athenian expedition in 428 under Lysicles was similarly unsuccessful in Caria (Thuc. III. 19). The Lycian chronicle of this inscription mentions victory over Melesandrus, and then, Thonemann argues, on Mycale opposite Samos, the defeat of Lysicles' army by an army commanded by Amorges, son of Pissuthnes the satrap of Sardis.[1]

The family with which we are concerned used some Iranian names (Harpagus, Arbinas), but absorbed a good deal of Greek cultural influence: here we see it employing a Greek poet to advertise its achievements, including a victory over Greeks, to a Greek-speaking audience. Sculpture influenced by Greek works is known from Xanthus from the middle of the sixth century, and contact with the east Greek world seems to have increased during the period when Lycia was controlled by Persia. The earliest sculpture comes from tombs, but during the fifth century sculpture appears also on buildings which may have had cult purposes, and is increasingly hellenised in iconography as well as form.

The most striking of the hellenising monuments, the so-called Nereid Monument, dated *c.*380 (now in the British Museum), is perhaps a monument to Arbinas: he was son of the Gergis = Kheriga and therefore grandson of the Harpagus = Arppakhu of our text (and great-grandson of Cybernis = Kuprlli, mentioned in the Lycian prose text), and Gergis reigned between *c.*440 and *c.*410. For other monuments of Arbinas see R&O 13. This monument (one of a number of Lycian pillar tombs, six known from Xanthus: see Keen 1992) is Gergis' tomb and memorial of his achievements. Despite their claims, these dynasts seem to have controlled only the western part of Lycia, adjacent to Caria, and towards the end of Gergis' reign or at the beginning of his own Arbinas had to conquer Xanthus, Pinara and Telmessus (R&O 13. *A*. i. 5–7). Gergis' original capital seems to have been at Phellus, south-east of Xanthus, where most of his coins were minted.

[1] Thonemann follows a series of articles on the *stele* by D. Schürr, in *Kadmos*: Amorges as victor, xxxvii 1998, 153, xlviii 2009, 168–70. For Thonemann's identification in the text of Mt Thorax, north-east of Mycale, cf. J. Burgin, *Kadmos* xlix 2010, 181–6.

194

Funeral law from Iulis on Ceos, late fifth century

A white marble *stele* broken at the bottom, inscribed on the front (*A*), back (*C*) and one side (*B*). Found built into the church of St Basil on Kea; now in the Epigraphical Museum, Athens. Phot. *IG* XII. v, p. 155 (part of *A*. 13–21); Frisone (below), figs. 4–6.

Ionic letters. *Stoichedon* (*A* 31, except l. 17; and *B* 10).

IG XII. v 593 with Addenda p. 332; *SGDI* 5398; *SIG*[3] 1218 (*A* and *B*); Buck 8 (*A*); *LSCG* 97 (*A* and *B**), Koerner 60 (*A*), Frisone, *Leggi e regolamenti funerari nel mondo Greco*, i. 57–102 (*C**); Colvin 24 (*A*. 1–30 only). Trans. Arnaoutoglou 109 (*A* and *B*); Colvin 24 (*A*. 1–30 only); Kearns, *Ancient Greek Religion*, 110–1 (*A* and *B*). See also Parker, *Miasma*, 34–41; R. Garland, *BICS* xxxvi 1989, 11–13; Engels, *Funerum sepulcrorumque magnificentia*, 60–4.

The Greek text of this monument is in a mixture of somewhat forced hexameters and (3, 4, 6, 8) pentameters (e.g. trisyllabic βασιλέας for βασιλείας, 8); Ceccarelli analyses it as four quatrains—two hexameters + two pentameters, two elegiac couplets, four hexameters — and we have reflected that analysis in the paragraphs of our translation. Line 1 is a direct quotation of the first line of an epigram commemorating an Athenian success in Cyprus, probably that of *c.*449 (Diod. Sic. XI. 62. iii, associating it with the battle of the Eurymedon, and later texts = Simonides fr. 103 Diehl = 'Simonides' xlv in Page, *Further Greek Epigrams*, 266–8). In this context the τ' is at first sight meaningless, but Ceccarelli defends its retention as a deliberate choice by the poet, advertising this epigram and the success which it commemorates as a sequel to what has gone before, and she sees further echoes in what follows. This epigram 'annexes the Greek conception of the separation of Europe and Asia, and turns it into an expression of Asiatic national identity' (Thonemann, 181).

On the agora of the Twelve Gods at Xanthus (2–3) see F. J. Tritsch, *JHS* lxii 1942, 41–2; C. Picard, *BSA* xlvi 1951, 137–8. τόδε (4) refers to the monument as a whole, ὅδε (5) to the statue. Surpassing with his hands (5–6) echoes Soph. *Trach.* 488, where the phrase is used of Heracles. Athena (7) was depicted on most of the coins issued by Gergis (O. Mørkholm & J. Zahle, *A. Arch.* xlvii 1976, 47–90). Giving a share of the kingdom to his kindred (8) is perhaps a reminiscence of the division of the Lycian kingdom in Hom. *Il.* VI. 193 (cf. M. Wörrle, *Chiron* xxi 1991, 208–9), and, if Kherẽi (mentioned in the Lycian prose text) and Arbinas ruled in some places while Gergis was still alive, that will be the fact alluded to. Line 9 is an echo of Hes. *Theog.* 503, where the being to whom gratitude is given is Zeus. For killing seven men (10, reflected in the frieze) cf. **130**. 2–3; the Arcadians may have been mercenaries fighting for the Spartans or (cf. Thuc. VIII. 28. iv) for Amorges when he rebelled against Persia.

A

οἵδε νό[μ]οι περὶ τῶγ καταφθιμ[έ]νω[ν· κατὰ]
[τά]δε θά[π]ṭεν τὸν θανόντα· ἐν ἐμ[α]τίο[ις τρ]-
[ι]σὶ λευκοῖς, στρώματι καὶ ἐνδύματι [καὶ]
[ἐ]πιβλέματι. ἐξεῖναι δὲ καὶ ἐν ἐλάσ[σ]οσ[ι μ]-
[ὲ] πλέονος ἀξίοις τοῖς τρισὶ ἑκατὸν δρ[α]-
[χ]μέων· ἐχφέρεν δὲ ἐγ κλίνηι σφηνόπο[δ]ι [κ]-
[α]ὶ μὲ καλύπτεν τὰ δολ[ο]σχερ[έα] τοῖ[ς ἑματ]-
ίοις· φέρεν δὲ οἶνον ἐπὶ τὸ σῆμα μ̣ὲ π̣[λέον]
τριῶν χῶν καὶ ἔλαιον μὲ πλέο[ν] ἑ̣ν̣ό[ς, τὰ δὲ]
[ἀ]γγεῖ[α] ἀποφέρεσθαι. τὸν θανό[ν]τα [φέρεν]
[κ]ατακεκαλυμμένον σιωπῆι μέχρι [ἐπὶ τὸ]
[σ]ῆμα. προσφαγίωι [χ]ρεσθαι κ̣ατὰ ṭὰ π[άτρι]-
[α. τ]ὴγ κλίνην ἀπὸ το[ῦ] σή[μ]ατο[ς] καὶ τὰ σ[τρώ]-
ματα ἐσφέρεν ἐνδόσε, τῆι δὲ ὑστεραί[ηι δι]-
αρραίνεν τὴν οἰκίην ἐλεύθερον θαλά[σσηι]-
[ι] πρῶτον, ἔπειτα δ̣ὲ̣ ὕ[δ]ατι λούεν γῆ[ι] χ[ρίσ]-
αντα· ἐπὴν δὲ διαρανθῆι, καθαρὴν ἐ͂ναι τὴν οἰκίην καὶ θύη θύεν ἐφ[ίστι]-
[α]. τὰς γυναῖκας τὰς [ἰ]ούσας [ἐ]πὶ τὸ κήδ[εον]
ἀπιέναι προτέρας τῶν {αν} ἀνδρῶν ἀπὸ [τοῦ]
[σ]ήματος. ἐπὶ τῶι θανόντι τριηκόσṭ[ια μὲ]
[π]οιεν̃. μὲ ὑποτιθέναι κύλικα ὑπὸ τὴγ [κλί]-
[ν]ην, μεδὲ τὸ ὕδωρ ἐκχεν̃ μεδὲ τὰ καλλύ[σμα]-
τα φέρεν ἐπὶ τὸ σῆμα. ὅπου ἂν [θ]άνηι, ἐπὴ[ν ἐ]-
ξενιχθε̃ι, μὲ ἰέναι γυναῖκας π[ρὸ]ς τ[ὴν οἰ]-
κίην ἄλλας ἒ τὰς μιαινομένας· μια[ίνεσθ]-
αι δὲ μητέρα καὶ γυναῖκα καὶ ἀδε[λφεὰς κ]-
αὶ θυγατέρας· πρὸς δὲ ταύταις μὲ π[λέον π]-
[έ]ντε γυναικῶν· παῖδας δὲ [δύο θ]υγ[ατέρας]
[ἀ]νεψιῶν· ἄλλον [δ]ὲ μ[ε]δέν[α]. τοὺς μι[αινομέ]-
[νους] λουσαμένο[υς] π[ε]ρ̣ὶ κ̣α̣[ὶ κατακέ]φ[αλα]
[ὕδατ]ος [χ]ύσι κα[θαρ]οὺς ἐ͂ναι εωι [—7—]
[—7—]η . νυ[—20—]
- -

A. 2 ἑμ̣α̣τίο[ις O&R following *IG majuscule*: ἑμα[τ]ίο[ις *LSCG*; ἑμ[α]τίο[ις *IG minuscule*. 7–8 *IG*: καλύπτεν, τὰ δ' ὀλ[ο]σχερ[έα] τοῖ[ς ὀθον]|ίοις Solmsen, *LSCG*. 11 *IG*: μέ[χ]ρι *LSCG*. 16–17 Klaffenbach, *LSCG*: ἔπειτα δ̣ὲ̣ ὑ[σ]ώπωι ο[ἰκη]τή[ρια ἅπ|α]ντα *IG*; ἔπειτα δ̣ὲ̣ ὑ[σ]ώπωι ο[ἰκ]έτη[ν τὰ π|άντα Schwyzer; ἔπειτα δ̣ὲ̣ ὑ[σ]ώπωι ο[ἰκ]έτη[ν ἐμβ|άντα Bechtel (in *apparatus*). 17 The original text of this whole line was erased and the longer text given here inserted in smaller letters. 18 Cauer in *IG* (but κήδεον is not otherwise attested: [ἐ]πὶ τὸ κῆδ[ος μὲ] *IG* (but this gives one letter too many). 28–9 Dittenberger: παῖδας δὲ [οἳ ἂν] ὑ[πάρχωσι | ἀ]νεψιῶν Roehl; παῖδας δὲ τ[ῶν θ]υγ[ατρῶν κ|ἀ]νεψιῶν *LSCG*, Hoffmann; although widely adopted and fitting Hiller's reading of a T after ΔΕ (Koehler, *AM* i 1876, facing p. 140, had read nothing in this *stoichos*) Hoffmann's suggestion is, as Bechtel pointed out (*SGDI*) implausible because the article (τ[ῶν θ]υγ[ατρῶν) and the crasis (κ|ἀ]νεψιῶν) are inappropriate.

A

The following are the laws about the deceased. Bury the dead person according to these instructions: in three white cloths, under-blanket, top sheet and cover—they may be wrapped in fewer—the three together not worth more than 100 drachmas; carry the corpse on a bier with wedge-shaped feet, and do not cover the handles of the bier with the cloths; take not more than three *choes* of wine to the tomb and not more than one of oil, and take away the vessels again; carry the dead person covered up, in silence, as far as the tomb; conduct a pre-sacrifice in accord with ancestral practices; bring the bier from the tomb and the coverings inside; on the day afterwards, a free man is to sprinkle the house with sea-water first, and then smear it with earth and wash it with water; and when it has been sprinkled the house is pure and sacrifices may be sacrificed at the hearth.

18 The women who go to the funeral are to leave the tomb before the men. Do not perform thirty-day rites for the dead. Do not put a drinking-cup under the bier, nor pour out the water, nor bring the sweepings to the tomb. Wherever a person dies, once the body has been carried out, no women are to go to the house other than those who are polluted. The mother is polluted, and the wife and the sisters and the daughters, but in addition to these not more than five women, two children, daughters of cousins, but no other person. The polluted, once they have washed themselves all over from head to foot by pouring water, are to be pure.

– – – – – –

B

[ἔδο]ξεν τῆι ᵛ
[β]ουλῆι καὶ ᵛ
[τ]ῶι δήμωι· ᵛᵛ
[τ]ῆι τρίτηι ᵛ
[κα]ὶ τοῖς ἐνι-
[αυ]σίοις κα- ᵛ
[θ]αροὺς εἶ- ᵛᵛ
[ν]αι τοὺς ποι-
[οῦ]ντας· ἐς ἱ- ᵛ
[ε]ρὸν δὲ μὴ ἰ- ᵛ
[έ]ναι καὶ τὴν
[ο]ἰ[κ]ίαν καθα-
[ρ]ὴν εἶναι, μẹ́-
[χρι] ἂν ἐκ τοῦ
[σ]ήματος ἔλθ-
[ωσιν]. *vacat*

C

[ἔδ]οξεν τῆι βουλῆι καὶ τῆι ἐκκλẹ[σίαι].
[– – –]Ι[. . .]ΝΤ[.] ẹἶπεν̣· τοὺς ΕΔΕ[—c.7—]
[. . .]ΝΤΟ̣[.] τέσσα̣[ρ]α̣ [.]α̣μφ[—c.5—] Ι[.]ΩΝ[. .]Ι[.]Τ[.]Ν
[. . . .]ΝΩ[.]ΙΕΟΝΤΑΙΙΝΛ̣Ẹ̣Ι[.]ΙΔΩ̣ΣΙΔΟ[. . .]Ι[.]
[– – – – – – – – –]Ι[– – – – – – – – – –]Γ[– – – – – –]
[– –]
[– – – – – – –]ΔΕΥ[– – – – –]Ο[– – –]Λ[– – – – – –]
[– – – –]Κ̣[.]ΛΑ̣ΣΙΑΜ̣Τ[. . .]Μ[.]ηι ἔξω τῶ[ν]
[. . .] δẹδόχθ̣αι [– – – –] ἔχειν, ẹἰσφέρειν εἰς τὰς
[. . .]ΙΤΑ̣ΣẸΜ[– –]
ll. 11–18 have been erased
[– – – – – – – – – – – – – – – – – –]ΙΕ[– – – – – – – – –]
[– – – – – – – – – – – – – – – –]ẸΡΛΙΤ[. . .]ΝΟ̣ περιφέ-
[ρειν. – – – – – – – – – – – το]ὺ̣ς ποιοῦντ[α]ς πρωτ[. . .]
[– – – – – – – – – – – – – – –]Ο[.]ΣΙΙΙΟΠΑΣ[. . .]
[– – – – – – – – – – – – – – – – – –]ἀ̣ργύριον ΠΛ
[– – – – – – – – – – – – – – – –]ΣΠ[.]οντας ΙΕ
[– – – –]ΙΛΥΛ[– – – – – – –] θυγατ̣ẹ́ρα̣ς ΙΑ
[– – – – – – – – – –]ΟΥΣ[.]ΔΙΑΛ[.]ΛΣΚΛ[. . .]
[– – –]Λ[– – – – – –]ΙΤ[.]ẸΛΙ[. . . .]ΔΕΜΗΔ[.]
[– – – – – – – – – – – – – – –]ΙẸΣ[.] ἀπ' ἄρχον[τος]
[. . .]ΙΜΙ[.]ΙΙΜ[– – – – – –]Υ[.]π̣έμπτης ἐπ[ὶ]
[δέκα – –] *vacat*

B. 13–14 Dittenberger: μẹ́ | [ἕως] ἂν *LSCG.*
C. 8 [ἀ]κ[ο]λα̣σία̣ν W. Bannier, *RM*[2] lxxiv 1925, 291.

B

Resolved by the council and people. Those who perform the rites on the third day and at the year's end are pure, but are not to go to a sanctuary—and the house is pure—until they return from the tomb.

C

Resolved by the council and assembly: – – – proposed: those – – – four – – – outside – – – has been resolved – – – to have, to bring into the – – –

ll. 11–18 have been erased

19 – – –carry around – – –those who perform the first – – –silver – – – daughters – – –from when the archon – – – on the fifteenth.

[ἔδοξεν τῆι] βουλ[ῆ]ι καὶ τῶι δ̣[ήμωι]·
[- - - τ]οῦ θανόντος E[- - - - - -]
[- - - -]ON[- - - - - -]

Funerals are moments when strong emotion is felt, and this makes them potentially volatile occasions. The loss of a member undermines group solidarity, and both the ritualised and the non-ritualised behaviour around funerals seek to restore that solidarity (cf. Seaford, *Reciprocity and Ritual*, 86–92). Formal regulation of behaviour at funerals is first known from Athens, where Solon's legislation is variously cited by Demosthenes (XLIII. *Macartatus* 62), Cicero (*Leg.* II. 59) and Plutarch (*Sol.* 21). Solon regulated how the corpse was treated (it could be buried in no more than three cloths), what could be brought to and done at the tomb (food and drink brought to the tomb was limited, the size of the offering basket used was restricted, no ox could be sacrificed on the grave) and how the mourners should behave (female mourners could not wear more than three cloaks, mourners could not travel in darkness except in the funerary cart and with a light, could not lacerate themselves, or sing prepared dirges, and could not visit the tombs of or lament for anyone other than the dead person being buried. The point of this legislation seems to have been to prevent burials being excessively showy or extravagant on the one hand, or secret on the other, and to ensure that they did not become mass occasions at which opportunity was taken to associate the death commemorated with other past deaths.

The law on face *A* of this stone from the city of Iulis on Ceos shares much with the Solonian laws, by which it may have been influenced, and with funerary legislation from other cities (notably the law of the Labyadai from Delphi, R&O 1) and indeed Plato's ideal legislation in *Laws* (XII. 959 E–960 B). Here too the number, expense and indeed colour (cf. Artem. *Oneirocritica* II. 3, Paus. IV. 13. iii, Plut. *Quaest. Rom.* 270 F for burial in white) of clothes used to wrap the corpse is restricted (though 100 dr. would surely purchase a very elaborate garment or piece of cloth), as is the quantity of wine and oil to be taken to the grave (one *chous* = 3.283 litres, if Cean measures equate to Athenian), where the sacrificial rites have to conform to ancestral practice (the use of the term *prosphagion*, a *hapax legomenon*, seems to imply that the slaughter of the animal was not followed by dining: see Ekroth, *The Sacrificial Rituals of Greek Hero-Cults*, 229–30). As at Delphi, the funeral procession is to take place in silence. But whereas both the Solonian and the Delphic legislation are concerned with the extravagance of the mourning at the tomb, both in terms of laceration and wailing, and with extending mourning activity to other tombs, the Iulis law as extant is concerned with neither aspect. It is concerned rather with restricting the pollution associated with the death, both the pollution of the house and the pollution of the mourners—concerns which are completely absent from Solonian and Delphic laws, and present in the third-century law from Gambreion (*LSAM* 16) only in as far as those who disobey the law are to be held to be polluted and those who obey it pure.

31 Resolved by the council and people
– – –of the dead person – – –

Limits imposed on what the corpse can be dressed in and what can be done at the tomb suggest a need to restrict excessive display, and the banning of 'thirty-day' rites, which seem to have been normal in Attica (cf. Photius κ 24 Theodoridis καθέδρα), points in a similar direction, and chimes with the claim in Heraclides Lembus' excerpts from the Aristotelian *Constitutions* (Arist. fr. 611. 28 in the Teubner edition of V. Rose = fr. 28 in Dilts, *Heraclidis Lembi Excerpta Politiarum*) that Ceos was notable for men there not cutting their hair or wearing different clothes to show that they were in mourning, and for women mourning for a year when a newborn died. But the concerns here to restrict the possibilities of becoming polluted or exploiting pollution suggest that local tensions also revolved around attempts to claim to be, or claim that others were, polluted, and therefore unable to take part in public life. The purification ceremonies for the house are probably extremely straightforward: they can be performed by a free man and, on the text preferred here, simply involve use first of sea-water (for which see Eur. *I.T.* 1192–3, Paus. IX. 20. iv) and then, after smearing with earth, of fresh water. The smearing with earth is unexpected (the verb χρίω normally means 'anoint') but the act of smearing with earth can be paralleled in a ritual context by the rubbing of initiates with clay and bran (Dem. XVIII. *Crown* 259; cf. **115** for sprinkling followed by anointing; and for the use of χρίω cf. Poll. VII. 124). We should see heavy symbolism here: salt water and earth are cleared away by pure water—i.e. all dirty liquids and solids are removed by pure water—and the normal sequence of anointing following washing is here reversed. An earlier reading (see *apparatus*) had the second stage involve hyssop and be performed by a slave, but this would be significantly the earliest mention of hyssop in a Greek text, and hyssop belongs much more to Judaeo-Christian ritual than to Greek.

The text is particularly concerned with women and pollution: there are instructions about their leaving the tomb (before the men on the text we prefer; but it is also possible to restore the sentence with a negative). Only women closely related to the deceased (mother, wife, sisters and daughters—in normal circumstances hardly more than half a dozen people, presumably—along with up to five others who must also be related) are polluted by the death, and washing with water brings an end to pollution. There is a strange slippage of genders, where all those specified as polluted are women, but both the stipulation that 'no one else' is polluted and the note about washing with water (*A*. 30) use masculine forms. Most plausibly these are 'generalising masculines', serving to show that the non-mention of polluted men is not an oversight, but in that case the absence of polluted men is striking. The instruction to bring back wine- and oil-containers from the grave may be not simply to keep Iulis tidy but to prevent any claim of pollution by contact with vessels used in connection with the dead, and the strange prohibitions on putting a cup under the bier and on pouring out water and taking sweepings to the tomb may be similar. As Parker (*Miasma*, 36) comments, 'it is remarkable to find the Ceans legislating against practices that are, it seems, socially objectionable only in being superstitious'.[1]

Texts *B* and *C* seem to be later additions to the law. Whereas the law on face *A* cites no authority, those on *B* and *C* are explicitly decrees of the city. *B* seems to be further responding to those who want to extend pollution. *C* contains two decrees, the first strangely (and uniquely for a decree from Ceos) claiming to be a decree of the 'council and assembly' rather than of the 'council and people' (the second decree has the regular heading). The second of these decrees is certainly about the dead, and it is likely that the first is also. If, with Bannier, we read *akolasia* ('wanton behaviour') in *C*. 8, behaviour in the context of funerals would be further regulated here. For this community what to do about the dead was evidently an ongoing concern.

The matter-of-fact treatment of the dead which these laws promote accords with a strong ancient tradition that the people of Ceos were proponents of euthanasia. This was referred to in the Aristotelian *Constitution*, to judge from Heraclides Lembus (Arist. fr. 611. 29 Rose = Heraclides fr. 29 Dilts), where the hemlock is taken simply to anticipate the ravages of illness, Menander (fr. 879 KA, *ap.* Strabo 486 / x. v. 6), who claims compulsory hemlock-drinking by those over 60, and later authors (esp. Ael. *V.H.* III . 37).

This text is not easy to read (as is nicely shown by the way in which scholars have read both ὕ[δ]ατι λούεν γῆ[ι] and ὑ[σ]ώπωι ο[ἰκη]τή[ρια in *A*. 16: see

[1] For the importance of this law as evidence for the nature of pollution see further Osborne, *The History Written on the Classical Greek Body*, 164–5.

195

Monetary pact between Mytilene and Phocaea, late fifth century (?)

The lower part of a *stele* of grey marble found built into a house on the slopes of the acropolis at Mytilene. Now in the museum at Mytilene.

Stoichedon (with final iota supplementary to the grid in l. 17).

IG XII. ii 1; Tod 112; Buck 25; Bodenstedt, *Die Elektronmünzen von Phokaia und Mytilene*, 29–33; A. J. Heisserer, *ZPE* lv 1984, 115–32*; Melville-Jones, *Testimonia Numaria*, no. 348; Labarre, *Les Cités de Lesbos*, no. 90; Colvin 17. Trans. Heisserer, *ZPE* lv 1984, 116; Melville-Jones, no. 348; Colvin 17. See also J. F. Healy, *JHS* lxxvii 1957, 267–8; R. Hodot, *AION (filol)* xix 1997, 387, 392–3, 398–9; E. Mackil & P. G. van Alfen, in *Agoranomia . . . J. H. Kroll*, 210–8.

G. Klaffenbach, *Philologus* xcvii 1948, 372–3). The difficulty is compounded by use of vocabulary not met elsewhere. We have seen one example in *prosphagion* (*A.* 12); and see *apparatus* on κήδεον (*A.* 18). In *A.* 6 the reading σφηνόπο[δ]ι seems secure, but σφηνόπους (which should mean 'with wedge-shaped feet') occurs nowhere else. Why insist on wedge-shaped feet? We suspect that the answer lies not in the particular desirability of feet of this shape, but the undesirability of e.g. lion-foot biers: this is another attempt to forbid elaboration. The most difficult term occurs in *A.* 7 and also seems to relate to the bier. Koehler's original transcription suggests the following sequence of letters (where the stops represent letters that cannot be read): ΤΑΔΟΛ . ΣΧẸΡ . . Ṭ ΟΙ. . We need a direct object for the command 'do not cover' with which the line begins. This suggests reading here τὰ ΔΟΛ . ΣΧΕΡ . . τοῖς, where the article in the dative introduces what the object is not to be covered with. But no known Greek word fits those traces. Scholars have therefore wondered whether one might understand the bier as the object for 'do not cover' and have a new phrase here beginning τὰ δ' but the traces that follow (ΟΛ . ΣΧΕΡ . .) also correspond to no known word. We have printed what we regard as the most plausible reading, a direct object for the prohibition on covering, but the word δολ[ο]σχερ[έα] (referring to part of the bier) is neither known nor of transparent etymology (but NB Hesychius δ 2164 Latte δόλος· πάσσαλος ['peg']).

The text is written in Ionic letters and Ionic dialect. In *A*, long *e* is generally represented by ε rather than η, as is the diphthong ει in the infinitive (θάπτεν for θάπτειν, etc.) but η is used for long *a* and in contractions (e.g. θύη < θύϝεα). Complete consistency is not observed, however (e.g. σφηνόποδι should have been σφενόποδι). *B* and *C* show greater influence from Attic (e.g. εἶναι, μή).

[—7—]ε[—18— ὄττι]
[δὲ κε αἰ] πόλις [ἀ]μ̣φότ[εραι διὰ συνθήκα]-
[ς προσ]γράφωισι εἰς ταὶ̣[ς στάλλαις ἢ ἐ]-
[κκόπ]τωισι, κύ[ρ]ιον ἔστω. τ̣[ὸν δὲ κέρναν]-
[τα τὸ] χρύσιον ὑπόδικον ἔμ̣[μεναι ἀμφο]-
[τέρ]αισι ταῖς πολίεσσι· δικ̣[ά]σ̣[ταις δὲ]
[ἔμ]μεναι τῶι μὲν ἐμ Μυτιλήναι κ̣[έρναν]-
[τι] ταῖς ἄρχαις παίσαις ταὶς ἐμ Μ[υτιλ]-
ήναι πλέας τῶν αἰμίσεων, ἐμ Φῶκαι δ[ὲ τ]-
αὶς ἄρχαις παίσαις ταῖς ἐμ Φώκαι πλ[έ]-
ας τῶν αἰμίσεω[ν]· τὰν δὲ δίκαν ἔμμεναι
ἐπεί κε ὠνίαυτος ἐξέλθηι ἐν ἒξ μήννε<σ>-
σι· αἰ δὲ κε καταγ[ρέ]θηι τὸ χρύσιον κέρ-
ναν ὐδαρέστερο[ν] θέλων θανάτωι ζαμι-
ώσθω· αἰ δὲ κε ἀπυ̣φύ̣γηι μ[ὴ] θέλων̣ ἀμβρό-
την, τιμάτω τὸ̣ δικαστήριον ὄττι χρὴ α-
ὔτ<ο>ν πάθην ἤ κατθέ[μ]εναι· ἀ δὲ πόλις ἀναί-
τιος καὶ ἀζάμιος [ἔσ]τω. ἔλαχον Μυτιλή-
ναοι πρόσθε κόπτην. ἄρχει πρότανις ὀ
πεδὰ Κόλωνον, ἐ[μ Φ]ώκαι δὲ ὀ πεδὰ Ἀρίστ̣-
αρχον.

2–3 Heisserer's speculative restoration, which is based on epigraphic parallels (e.g. *IG* xii. ii 645. 50–1) and treaties quoted in literary texts (e.g. Diod. Sic. xii. 75. ii). 15 Hodot: ἀπυφ[ύ]γηι Heisserer. 17 Our punctuation follows Hodot.

Mytilene, on the island of Lesbos, and Phocaea, almost due south on the mainland coast, were effectively neighbouring cities forty or so miles apart, and for many ships moving north or south along the Ionian coast to or from the Hellespont they will have been successive ports of call. Phocaea had begun to mint coinage to her own standard in the later part of the seventh century, minting electrum (an alloy of gold and silver) and silver (for cities with electrum issues, silver served as 'small change' and tended to be minted in small denominations). The obverses of Phocaea's electrum coinage included the image of a seal, whose Greek name *phoke* both punned on the name of the city and appropriately alluded to Phocaean maritime activity. Mytilene began to mint electrum coinage on the Phocaic standard towards the end of the sixth century (she also minted billon, an alloy of silver and copper, in the fifth century, and silver). Both Mytilene and Phocaea minted electrum in the denomination known as *hektai* (sixths), to produce coins comparable in value to Athenian tetradrachms.

Naturally occurring electrum contains varying proportions of gold. Herodotus implies that naturally occurring electrum might have 70 per cent gold (i. 50. ii with Healy, 268 n. 12; cf. also Plin. *H.N.* xxxiii. 80, Isid. *Etym.* xvi. 24); investigation of electrum sources suggests variation from 85 to 65 per cent gold; see K. Konuk, in Metcalf (ed.), *The Oxford Handbook of Greek and Roman Coinage*, 43–9. Variable gold

– – – Whatever both cities add to the inscription or delete from it by agreement is to be valid.

4 Whoever dilutes the gold is to be subject to the jurisdiction of both cities. For whoever dilutes in Mytilene more than half the jurors are to come from all the magistrates at Mytilene, and in Phocaea more than half are to be from all the magistrates in Phocaea. The trial is to happen within six months whenever the year [of office] ends. If he is convicted of deliberately diluting the gold to a weaker mix he is to be punished by death. But if he is acquitted of deliberately doing wrong, let the court assess what he should suffer or pay. The city is to be free from responsibility and from punishment.

18 The Mytilenaeans gained by lot the right to mint first. The *prytanis* after Colonus begins the agreement, and the one after Aristarchus at Phocaea.

---

content was a problem for use in coinage, and the proportions of the two metals had to be regularised. This seems to have been done by separating the gold and silver and then producing an artificial alloy (with some addition of copper to affect the colour). Phocaea's earliest electrum coins were about 55 per cent gold; during the period 520–480 they were 46 per cent gold; from then until the end of minting electrum in the 320s the proportion of gold was 40 per cent. In the light of this, 'gold' here (l. 5) must, as Healy (267) maintained, mean not electrum but 'pure gold'. The proportion of gold in the electrum coinage of Mytilene maps the proportion of gold in Phocaea's electrum coinage in a way that suggests that the two coinages were linked from the beginning (Bodenstedt, Anhang 4; his *Phokäisches Elektron-Geld von 600–326 v. Chr.*; C. M. Kraay, *Gnomon* liv 1982, 499), and it appears that some die-cutters worked for both cities as early as the early fifth century (Bodenstedt, *Die Elektronmünzen*, 38–45).

This text is the conclusion of a longer agreement between Mytilene and Phocaea: how long is unclear—the current stele measures 56 × 52 cm., and we might expect it to have been at least twice as high as it is wide; Heisserer (119) speculated that fifty to eighty lines might have been lost, but that is probably excessive. Whether the entire text concerned coinage we cannot surely tell, but the agreement was probably more wide-ranging. Part of the agreement will have been to accept the other's electrum coinage on the same basis as the local electrum coinage. The advantage of this emerges from an anecdote from Callisthenes, preserved in Poll. XI. 93, where a poet remarks that his Phocaean electrum is 'sweeter' (= worth more) at Mytilene than at nearby Atarneus—presumably because at Atarneus there were fees for changing it to local coin.

What is new about this agreement? We cannot tell whether the decision that the two cities should alternate in their minting electrum is new, but the precise dating of the point from which this agreement begins might imply that it is. Alternatively the novelty lies in the decision that quality control over the metal content of the coinage should be exercised by a joint judicial panel, whether the official accused of producing coins with too much silver is a Mytilenian or a Phocaean. We might speculate, on the basis of the explicit declaration (ll. 17–18) that the city itself shall be blameless, that this agreement follows an incident in which 'watered-down' coinage had provoked a diplomatic incident between the two cities. Alternating minting may be less to prevent both cities minting at the same time than to ensure that it was always the case that one of the cities was minting electrum: the popularity of the coinage depended upon there being always coinage available to meet demand, and the use of the coinage as a store of wealth (as in hoards; for Cyzicene electrum similarly used at Athens see Lys. XII. *Eratosthenes* 11) meant that all sorts of local crisis among those using the coinage might produce peaks in demand.

Maintaining a fixed ratio of gold to silver was important because this electrum coinage was intended for circulation outside as well as within the city in which it was minted (contrast the billon coinage of Mytilene). Just how important is shown by the death penalty for the official who deliberately reduces the gold coinage, and the punishment of the official who allows this to happen inadvertently. Negligence is no defence. The whole procedure is set up on the assumption that any dilution will be the fault of the magistrate in charge, and the trial is to confirm this or commute the sentence because the problem was inadvertence. Confidence in their product was vital for Mytilene and Phocaea: they had no sources of electrum in their own territories, and depended on their ability to exchange their electrum coinage at a favourable rate by comparison with the bullion that they bought in (cf. Mackil & van Alfen, 217). The popularity of the electrum coinage of Phocaea and Mytilene is shown by coin-hoard evidence: there are a number of hoards dating to the fifth and fourth centuries which consist entirely of these coins, and hoards containing them have been found both locally (at Erythrae, Chios, Pergamum, Abydus, Atramyttium and Thyateira) and as far away as Myrlea on the Propontis; Phocaean electrum is also recorded in Athenian accounts (Mackil & van Alfen, 213; E. Kosmetatou, *RBN* cxlvii 2001, 11–37). The presence in hoards is good evidence for the confidence people had in this coinage, but it never achieved the popularity of the electrum coinage of Cyzicus, which was the coinage of preference for Black Sea trade.

Mytilene and Phocaea cooperated in the issuing of electrum coins for almost two centuries, and it is therefore very hard to date this particular agreement. Scholars have variously placed it in the last third of the fifth or early in the fourth century, arguing partly from letter forms (but very little comparative evidence is available). Since this text cannot date as early as the origin of the agreement between the cities, it is necessary to seek a point at which there has been some sort of rupture. Although we cannot exclude the possibility that the rupture was produced by some local incident purely related to the minting of the electrum coinage, it is likely that we are dealing with some more general crisis, given the existence of further text before the lines which are preserved. The revolt of Mytilene against Athens in 428–427 provides a plausible context for this rupture, since while Phocaea, which lent no support to the revolt, will have carried on minting as usual the Athenians are not likely to have been happy for Mytilene to do so. But what of the date of this agreement when minting was restarted? Heisserer suggested that the agreement came shortly after the revolt. Part of his argument turned on the identification of the sole surviving Mytilene electrum stater with the production of an emergency coinage for the revolt. However, recent work has suggested that that stater is minted on the Chian weight standard, popularised in Ionia by Lysander, and therefore should be dated *c.*405 and associated with the broader phenomenon of converting Persian *sigloi*, coming in from Cyrus' bank-rolling of the Spartan war effort, into large-denomination coins to pay troops. Bodenstedt (10, 62–4) believed that there was a hiatus in the minting of electrum *hektai* at Mytilene between 427 and 412, and although his grounds for this assertion are not strong, some hiatus seems likely. Mytilene revolted from Athens in 412, but it was immediately brought back into the Athenian empire (Thuc. VIII. 22. ii, 23. ii, 100. iii) and remained loyal until taken by Lysander in 405 (Xen. *Hell.* I. vi. 35, 38; II. ii. 5; Diod. Sic. XIII. 73. v). If Mytilene was sufficiently trusted following 412, it is possible that this agreement dates to the period between 412 and 405; if not, it is likely to date to 404 or shortly afterwards, when normal life began to be restored in the region under Spartan overlordship.

Although there was an Aristotelian *Constitution of the Phocaeans* we know nothing of the internal organization of the city. The mention of a *prytanis* at Phocaea (ll. 19–20) is our only detail of classical Phocaean government. *Prytaneis* are however met in other evidence from Mytilene (R&O 85. 18) and at the Lesbian cities of Methymna and Eresus and the Aeolic city of Nasos.

The language here displays various features of the Lesbian dialect. Heisserer & Hodot have argued that in ll. 13–14 κέρναν should be understood as a participle rather than as an infinitive, i.e. of actually mixing the gold in a more watery way rather than of intending to mix the gold in a more watery way. Other dialect features include α for η and the doubling of consonants, both seen in στάλλαις for στήλαις (l. 3); ἔμμεναι for εἶναι (5, 7, 11); πολίεσσι for πολέσι (6); παίσαις for πάσαις (8, 10); αἰμίσεων for ἡμίσεων (9, 11); Φώκαι contraction for Φωκαίαι (9, 10, 20); ὠνίαυτος for ὁ ἐνίαυτος and the doubling of the ν and σ in μήνεσσι (12); καταγρέθηι for καθαιρηθηι (13); ἀπυφύγηι for ἀποφύγηι, ἀμβρότην for ἁμαρτάνειν (15; cf. κόπτην in 19); ὄττι for ὅτι (16); πρότανις for πρύτανις (19); πεδὰ for μετὰ (20).

ATHENIAN ARCHONS, 478/7–404/3

All the archons for this period are recorded by Diod. Sic. at the beginning of his account of the year in question; for further references see Develin, *AO*.

478/7	Timosthenes
477/6	Adeimantus
476/5	Phaedon
475/4	Dromocleides
474/3	Acestorides
473/2	Menon
472/1	Chares
471/0	Praxiergus
470/69	Demotion
469/8	Apsephion (Phaedon Diod. Sic.)
468/7	Theagenides
467/6	Lysistratus
466/5	Lysanias
465/4	Lysitheus
464/3	Archedemides
463/2	Tlempolemus
462/1	Conon
461/0	Euthippus
460/59	Phrasicles
459/8	Philocles
458/7	Habron
457/6	Mnesitheides
456/5	Callias
455/4	Sosistratus
454/3	Aristion
453/2	Lysicrates
452/1	Chaerephanes
451/0	Antidotus
450/49	Euthydemus
449/8	Pedieus
448/7	Philicscus
447/6	Timarchides
446/5	Callimachus
445/4	Lysimachides
444/3	Praxiteles
443/2	Lysanias
442/1	Diphilus
441/0	Timocles
440/39	Morychides
439/8	Glaucinus
438/7	Theodorus
437/6	Euthymenes
436/5	Lysimachus
435/4	Antiochides
434/3	Crates
433/2	Apseudes
432/1	Pythodorus
431/0	Euthydemus
430/29	Apollodorus
429/8	Epameinon
428/7	Diotimus
427/6	Eucles
426/5	Euthynus
425/4	Stratocles
424/3	Isarchus
423/2	Ameinias
422/1	Alcaeus
421/0	Aristion
420/19	Astyphilus
419/8	Archias
418/7	Antiphon
417/6	Euphemus
416/5	Arimnestus
415/4	Charias
414/3	Teisandrus
413/2	Cleocritus
412/1	Callias of Scambonidae
411/0	Mnasilochus *2 months*
	Theopompus *10 months*
410/09	Glaucippus
409/8	Diocles
408/7	Euctemon
407/6	Antigenes
406/5	Callias of Angele
405/4	Alexias
404/3	Pythodorus (*anarchia* Diod. Sic.)

CONCORDANCE OF STANDARD EDITIONS

Under *IG* the reference is to volume i³ except where otherwise stated, and where a text appears both in i³ and in another volume we give the reference to i³ only. Under 'other' we have been highly selective, and it should not be assumed, for instance, that where no reference to *SEG* is given no text has been published in *SEG*. With those exceptions, we have aimed at completeness for the editions which we cite. We have not distinguished here instances in which an edition includes only part of the text. Other editions of our texts can be found through the online concordance CLAROS (see Bibliography).

O&R	*IG*	*SIG*³	M&L	other	Fornara
101		35. *B. a*	29	*I. Olympia* 249	64. A
102. *A+B*		37+38	30	Buck 3, *SEG* xxxi 984, *Nomima* i 104	63
102. *C*				*SEG* xxxi 985, *Nomima* i 105	
103. *A*				*SEG* xviii 347, *Nomima* ii 96	
103. *B*	XII Supp. 347				169
104				*SEG* xlii 785, *Nomima* ii 95	
105				*I. Olympia* 267–9	
106	6	42		*LSS* 3, *I. Eleusis* 19	75 (B and C)
107	244			*LSCG* 10	
108	7			*LSCG* 15	
109	1147	43	33		78
110. *A*	XII. vi. 1 279		34	*CEG* 421	77
110. *B*	XII. i. 1 468		34 (*add.*)		
111	1149		35	*Agora* xvii 4; *CEG* 135	
112			36	*I. Olympia* 253, *CEG* 351	
113	1503			*CEG* 80	
114	xiv 268	1122	38	Buck 98	91
115				*SEG* xliii 630, Colvin 44	
116	9			Tod 39, *SdA* 142	82
117. *A*				*SEG* xvii 243	
117. *B*				*SEG* xxxiv 560, *CEG* 637	
118	IX. ii 257	55		Buck 35, *Nomima* i 33	
119	259–80		39, 50		85, 95. M
120	10		31	*SdA* 149	68
121	14	41	40	*ATL* ii D 10, *SdA* 134	71

O&R	*IG*	*SIG*³	M&L	other	Fornara
122				*IK Erythrai und Klazomenai* 2, *Nomima* i 106	
123		58	43	*Milet* I. vi 187	66
124				*SEG* xli 778–95	
125			41	Buck 117, *IC* iv 72, *Nomima* ii 30–6, 40, 45, 48–9, 51, 53–4, 66	88
126		55 (*B*)	42	*I. Creticae* I. xxx 1 + I. viii 4, Buck 85, *SdA* 147–8, *Nomima* i. 54, Colvin 38	89
127				*SEG* li 532	
128			(*add.*) 67 *bis*	*Nomima* i 55	
129	1162		48	*CEG* 6	
130	1353		51	*CEG* 83	101
131	40	64	52	*ATL* ii D 17	103
132		45	32	Buck 2, *Nomima* i 19	70
133				Buck 4	
134	248		53	*I. Rhamnous* 182	90. B
135	458–60		54		114
136	1454	129		Tod 110	
137	35	63. *a*	44		93
138	363 + 454		55		113
139	48		56	*ATL* ii D 18, *SdA* 159	115
140		61	57	*I. Olympia* 254 (cf. 255–6)	112
141	78	83	73	*I. Eleusis* 28a	140
142	46	67	49	*Agora* xvi 7	100
143				*Milet* VI. iii 1218	
144	52	91	58	*ATL* ii D 1–2	119
145	449		59		120
146	256 *bis*				
147	402		62	*I. Délos* 89	141
148	364	72	61		126
149. *A*	53	71	63	*SdA* 162	124
149. *B*	54	70	64	*SdA* 163	125
150	61	75	65	*ATL* ii D 3–6	128
151	V. i 1	84	67		132
152	68		68	*ATL* ii D 8	133
153	71		69	*ATL* ii A 9	136
154	34		46	*ATL* ii D 7	98
155	1453	87	45	*ATL* ii D 14	97
156	36	63. *b*	71		139
157	227+ *add.*	118	70 + *add.*	*SdA* 123	138
158				Buck 7, *LSS* 38, *C. Delphes* i 7	

O&R	*IG*	*SIG*³	M&L	other	Fornara
159	258				
160	369		72		134
161	227 *bis*			*SEG* l 45	
162	92	132			
163				*SEG* li 642	
164	ix. i² 656	80	74	*I. Olympia* 259	135
165	83			Tod 72, *SdA* 193	
166 §§i–ii	11		37	*SdA* 139	81
166 §iii	12			*SdA* 174	
167	84	93		*LSCG* 14	
168	287		75	*ATL* ii list 33	
169	329		76		
170	370	94	77		144
171	93		78		146
172	421–30	96–103	79		147. D
173	98		80		149
174	373		81		150
175	xii. ix 187	105	82	Buck 13, Colvin 27	182
176			83		153
177. *A*	xii. viii 263				
177. *B*	ii² 6	119		Tod 98	
178				*SEG* xxviii 46	
179	1330			*CEG* 93	
180	375	109. *a*	84		154
181	474				
182	102	108	85	Osborne *Naturalization* D 2	155
183. *A*	104	111	86		15. B
183. *B*	105				
184	110	114	90	Walbank *Proxenies* 87	160
185	118	112	87	*SdA* 207, Walbank *Proxenies* 86	162
186	119	113	88	*IK Erythrai und Klazomenai* 501, *SdA*² (1975) 207a	163
187	101	107	89		156
188	117	104	91	Walbank *Proxenies* 90	161
189	123		92	*SdA* 208	165
190	1032				
191	127	116	94	Osborne *Naturalization* D 5	166
192		115	95	*CEG* 819, *Choix Delphes* 25	
193			93	*TAM* i 44, *CEG* 177	
194	xii. v 593	1218		Buck 8, *LSCG* 97	
195	xii. ii 1			Tod 112, Buck 25, Colvin 17	

BIBLIOGRAPHY

Articles in periodicals are cited in sufficient detail in the course of this book. Here we give details in §1 of collections of inscriptions, and in §2 of other books cited (entered under title or author/editor according to the abbreviation used, with a cross-reference under the abbreviation when that is far distant in alphabetical sequence from the main entry; where necessary, we give in square brackets at the right-hand margin the abbreviations by which we cite the books). In §2, *Festschriften* are listed under the names of the honorands, after books by them; except in a few special cases other collective volumes are listed under the names of the editors. Some books could have been cited in either section: if a book is not found in one section, look in the other.

1. COLLECTIONS OF INSCRIPTIONS

Arena, R. *Iscrizioni greche arcaiche di Sicilia e Magna Grecia.* Italy: various publishers, 1989–98.

Arnaoutoglou, I. *Ancient Greek Laws: A Sourcebook.* London: Routledge, 1998. [Arnaoutoglou]

The Athenian Agora, xvi, xvii, xix. Princeton: A.S.C.S.A., 1997/74/91. [*Agora*]

The Athenian Tribute Lists, ed. Meritt, B. D., Wade-Gery, H. T., & McGregor, M. F. Harvard U.P. for A.S.C.S.A. → Princeton: A.S.C.S.A., 1939–53. [*ATL*]

Buck, C. D. *The Greek Dialects.* U. of Chicago P., 1955. [Buck]

Carmina Epigraphica Graeca, ed. Hansen, P. A. Berlin: De Gruyter, 1983–9. [*CEG*]

Cataldi, S. *Symbolai e relazioni tra le città greche nel V sec. a.C.* Pisa: Scuola Normale Superiore, 1983.

Choix d'inscriptions de Delphes, traduites et commentées, ed. Jacquemin, A., Mulliez, D., & Rougemont, G. Athens: École Française d'Athènes, 2012. [*Choix Delphes*]

Claros (online concordance) <http://www.dge.filol.csic.es/claros/2claros.htm>.

Clinton. K. *Eleusis: The Inscriptions on Stone: Documents of the Sanctuary of the Two Goddesses and Public Documents of the Deme.* Athens: Archaeological Society, 2005–8. [*I. Eleusis*]

Colvin, S. *A Historical Greek Reader: Mycenaean to the Koiné.* O.U.P., 2007. [Colvin]

Cordano, F. *Le tessere pubbliche dal tempio di Atena a Camarina.* Rome: Istiututo Italiano per la Storia Antica, 1992.

Corpus des inscriptions de Delphes. Paris: De Boccard for École Française d'Athènes, 1977– . [*C. Delphes*]

Corpus Inscriptionum Graecarum, ed. Boeckh, A. Berlin: Officina Academica, 1825–77. [*CIG*]

Dedications from the Athenian Acropolis: A Catalogue of the Inscriptions of the Sixth and Fifth Centuries BC, ed. RAUBITSCHEK, A. E., with JEFFERY, L. H. Cambridge, MA: Archaeological Institute of America, 1949. [*DAA*]

Dialectorum Graecarum Exempla Epigraphica Potiora, ed. SCHWYZER, E. Leipzig: Hirzel, 1923. [*DGE*]

Didyma, ii. *Die Inschriften*, ed. REHM, A., & HARDER, R. Berlin: Mann for Deutsches Archäologisches Institut, 1958. [*I. Didyma*]

DILLON, M., & GARLAND, L. *Ancient Greece: Social and Historical Documents from Archaic Times to the Death of Socrates (c. 800–399 BC)*. London: Routledge, ³2010. [Dillon & Garland³]

DUBOIS, L. *Inscriptions grecques dialectales de Grande Grèce*, i. Geneva: Droz, 1995.

—— *Inscriptions grecques dialectales de Sicile: contribution à l'étude du vocabulaire grec colonial.* Rome: École Française de Rome, 1989.

DUCHÊNE, H. *La Stèle du port: Fouilles du port*, 1: *Recherches sur une nouvelle inscription thasienne.* Paris: De Boccard for École Française d'Athènes, 1992.

οι επιγραφές τού Ωρωπού, ed. PETRAKOS, B. Ch. Athens: Archaeological Society, 1997. [*I. Oropos*]

FORNARA, C. W. *Translated Documents of Greece and Rome*, i. *Archaic Times to the End of the Peloponnesian War.* C.U.P., ²1983. [Fornara]

Fouilles de Delphes, vol. iii. Paris: Fontemoing → De Boccard for École Française d'Athènes, 1909–85. [*F. Delphes*]

Fouilles de Xanthos. Volumes cited Paris: Klincksieck, 1958– . [*F. Xanthos*]

FRISONE, F. *Leggi e regolamenti funerari nel mondo Greco*, i. *Le fonte epigrafiche.* Galatina: Congedo, 2000.

GAGARIN, M., & PERLMAN, P. *The Laws of Ancient Crete, c. 650–400 BCE.* O.U.P., 2015.

(*The Collection of Ancient*) *Greek Inscriptions in the British Museum.* O.U.P., 1874–1916. [*GIBM*]

Greek Sacred Law : A Collection of New Documents, ed. LUPU, E. Leiden: Brill, 2004. [*NGSL*]

HELLMANN, M.-C. *Choix d'inscriptions architecturales grecques, traduites et commentées.* Lyon : Maison de l'Orient méditerranéen. 1999.

I. Didyma. See *Didyma.*

I. Eleusis. See Clinton.

Inschriften griechischer Städte von Kleinasien. Bonn: Habelt, 1972– . [*IK Placename*]

Die Inschriften von Olympia (*Olympia: Die Ergebnisse der . . . Ausgrabung*, v), edd. DITTENBERGER, W., & PURGOLD, K. Berlin: Ascher, 1896. [*I. Olympia*]

Inscriptiones Creticae, ed. HALBHERR, F., & GUARDUCCI, M. Rome: Libreria dello Stato, 1935–50. [*I. Creticae*]

Inscriptiones Graecae. Berlin: Reimer → De Gruyter for Berlin Academy under its various titles, 1873– . [*IG*]

Les Inscriptions de Thespies, 1–483, ed. Roesch, P., put in electronic form by Argoud, G., *et al.* Lyon: Maison de l'Orient et de la Méditerranée, 2007–9. [*I. Thespies*]

I. Oropos. See οι επιγραφές τού Ωρωπού.

I. Rhamnous. See Petrakos.

Iscrizioni storiche ellenistiche, ed. Moretti, L., & Canali De Rossi, F. Florence: La Nuova Italia, 1967 → Rome: Herder, 2006. [*ISE*]

Koerner, R., ed. Hallof, K. *Inschriftliche Gesetzestexte der frühen griechischen Polis aus dem Nachlass von R. Koerner.* (*AGR* ix.) Cologne: Böhlau, 1993. [Koerner]

Lois sacrées d'Asie Mineure, ed. Sokolowski, F. Paris: De Boccard for École Française d'Athènes, 1955. [*LSAM*]

Lois sacrées des cités grecques, ed. Sokolowski, F. Paris: De Boccard for École Française d'Athènes, 1969. [*LSCG*]

Lois sacrées des cités grecques: Supplément, ed. Sokolowski, F. Paris: De Boccard for École Française d'Athènes, 1962. [*LSS*]

Meiggs, R., & Lewis, D. M. *A Selection of Greek Historical Inscriptions to the End of the Fifth Century* BC. O.U.P., ²1988. [M&L]

Milet: Ergebniise der Ausgrabungen, i. i–ix, ed. Wiegand, T. Berlin: Reimer for Königliche Museen, 1906–28. [*Milet*]

——vi. i–iii, ed. Herrmann, P., *et al.* Berlin: De Gruyter, 1997–2006. [*Milet*]

Monumenta Asiae Minoris Antiquae. Manchester U.P. for A. Soc. for Arch. Research in Asia Minor → Society for Promotion of Roman Studies, 1928– . [*MAMA*]

NGSL. See *Greek Sacred Law*

Nomima: Recueil d' inscriptions politiques et juridiques de l' archaïsme grec, ed. van Effenterre, H., & Ruzé, F. Rome: École Française de Rome, 1994–5. [*Nomima*]

Osborne. M. J. *Naturalization in Athens.* Brussels: Royal Academy, 1981–3. [Osborne, *Naturalization*]

Osborne, R. G. *The Athenian Empire.* LACTOR i ⁴2000.

Peek, W. *Griechische Vers-Inschriften*, i. Berlin: Akademie-Verlag, 1955–7. [Peek, *GVI*]

Petrakos, B. Ch. *ο δήμος τού Ραμνούντος· συνόψη τών ανασκαφών καί τών ερεύνων (1813–1998)*, i. τοπογραφία; ii. οι επιγραφές. Athens: Archaeological Society, 1999. [*I. Rhamnous*]

Pfohl, G. *Geschichte und Epigramm: Ein kleines Quellenlesebuch griechischer Inschriften zum Studium der Geschichte und der Literatur.* Stuttgart: Klett, 1964.

Pilhofer, P. *Philippi*, ii. *Katalog der Inschriften von Philippi.* Tübingen: Mohr Siebeck, 2000.

Pleket, H. W. *Epigraphica*, i. Leiden: Brill, 1964.

Rhodes, P. J., & Osborne, R. G. *Greek Historical Inscriptions, 404–323* BC. O.U.P., 2003. [R&O]

Sammlung der griechischen Dialekt-Inschriften, ed. Collitz, H., & Bechtel, F. Göttingen: Vandenhoeck & Ruprecht, 1885–1915. [*SGDI*]

SORDI, M. *La lega tessala fino ad Alessandro Magno.* Rome: Istituto Italiano per la Storia Antica, 1958.

Die Staatsverträge des Altertums, vol. ii, ed. BENGTSON, H. Munich: Beck, 1962, rev. 1975. [*SdA*]

Supplementum Epigraphicum Graecum. Leiden: Sijthoff → Brill, 1923– . [*SEG*]

Sylloge Inscriptionum Graecarum, first ed. DITTENBERGER, W. Leipzig: Hirzel, ^{3}1915–24. [*SIG*]

Tituli Asiae Minoris. Vienna: Hölder for Kaiserliche Akademie der Wissenschaften in Wien → Österreichisch Akademie der Wissenschaften, 1901– . [*TAM*]

TOD, M. N. *A Selection of Greek Historical Inscriptions.* O.U.P., ^{2}1946, 1948.

WALBANK, M. B. *Athenian Proxenies of the Fifth Century* BC. Toronto & Sarasota; Stevens, 1978. [Walbank, *Athenian Proxenies*]

2. OTHER BOOKS

Acta of the Fifth International Congress of Greek and Latin Epigraphy, Cambridge, 1967. Oxford: Blackwell, 1971.

AGOCS, P. *et al.* (edd.), *Reading the Victory Ode.* C.U.P., 2012.

ALLEN, T. W., HALLIDAY, W. R., & SIKES, E. E. *The Homeric Hymns.* O.U.P., ^{2}1936.

ANTONETTI, C., & DE VIDO, S. (edd.), *Temi selinuntini.* Pisa: E.T.S., 2009.

ARCHONTIDOU, P., *et al.* *Ἀρχαιολογικὸ Μουσεῖο Χίου.* Mytilene: Ὑπουγεῖο Πολιτισμοῦ, 1999.

ARRINGTON, N. *Ashes, Images and Memories: the Presence of the War Dead in Fifth-Century Athens.* O.U.P., 2015.

AUSTIN, R. P. *The Stoichedon Style in Greek Inscriptions.* O.U.P., 1938.

BALCER, J. M. *The Athenian Regulations for Chalkis. Historia* Einz. xxxiii 1978.

BALTRUSCH, E. A. *Symmachie und Spondai: Untersuchungen zum griechischen Völkerrecht der archaischen und klassischen Zeit (8.–5. Jahrhundert v. Chr.).* Berlin: de Gruyter, 1994.

BARRON, J. P. *The Silver Coins of Samos.* London: Athlone P., 1966.

BEAZLEY, J. D. *Attic Red-Figure Vase-Painters.* O.U.P., ^{2}1963. [Beazley, *ARV*^{2}]

BECK, H., & FUNKE, P. *Federalism in Greek Antiquity.* C.U.P., 2015.

BEHREND, D. *Attische Pachturkunden: Ein Beitrag zur Beschreibung der misthōsis nach den griechischen Inschriften.* Munich: Beck, 1970.

BELOCH, K. J. *Griechische Geschichte.* Strassburg: Trübner → Berlin & Leipzig: de Gruyter, ^{2}1912–27. [Beloch, *GG*^{2}]

BÉRARD, F., *et al.* *Guide de l'épigraphiste: Bibliographie choisie des épigraphies antiques et médiévales.* Paris: Éditions Rue d'Ulm/Presses de l'École Normale Supérieure, ^{4}2010; kept up to date online at <http://www.antiquite.ens.fr/publications/guide_fr.htm>.

BERGER, E. *Kanon: Festschrift Ernst Berger zum 60. Geburstag . . . gewidmet.* Basel: Vereinigung der Freunde Antiker Kunst, 1988.

BERVE, H. *Das neue Bild der Antike*. Leipzig: Koehler & Amelang, 1942.

BILABEL, F. *Die ionische Kolonisation*. Leipzig: Dieterich, 1920.

BINGEN, J. *Pages d'épigraphie grecque*, i. *Attique–Égypte (1952–82)*. Brussels: Epigraphica Bruxellensia, 1991.

BLANCKENHAGEN, P. H. VON. *Studies in Classical Art and Archaeology: A Tribute to Peter Heinrich von Blanckenhagen*. Locust Valley, N.Y.: Augustin, 1979.

BLOK, J. H., EIJNDE, F. VAN DER, & STROOTMAN, R. (edd.), *Feasting and Polis Institutions*. Leiden: Brill, forthcoming.

BOARDMAN, J., & VAPHOPOULOU-RICHARDSON, C. E. (edd.), *Chios: A Conference at the Homereion of Chios, 1984*. O.U.P., 1986.

BODEL, J. (ed.), *Epigraphic Evidence: Ancient History from Inscriptions*. London: Routledge, 2001.

BODENSTEDT, F. *Die Elektronmünzen von Phokaia und Mytilene*. Tübingen: Wasmuth, 1981.

—— *Phokäisches Elektron-Geld von 600–326 v. Chr.: Studien zur Bedeutung und zu den Wandlungen einer antiken Goldwährung*. Mainz: von Zabern, 1976.

BOECKH, A. *Die Staatshaushaltung der Athener*, rev. FRAENKEL, M. Berlin: Reimer, ³1886.

BOEGEHOLD, A. L. *The Athenian Agora*, xxviii. *The Lawcourts at Athens*. Princeton: A.S.C.S.A., 1995.

—— *Gestures: Essays in Ancient History, Literature and Philosophy Presented to A. L. Boegehold*. Oxford: Oxbow, 2003.

BOER, W. DEN. *Private Morality in Greece and Rome: Some Historical Aspects*. Leiden: Brill, 1979.

BOMMELAER, J.-F. *Lysandre de Sparta: histoire et traditions*. Athens: École Française d'Athènes, 1981.

BOMMELAER, J.-F., & LAROCHE, D. *Guide de Delphes: le site*. Athens: École Française d'Athènes, 1991.

BONDESSON, B. *De Sonis et Formis Titulorum Milesiorum Didymaeorumque*. Diss. Lund 1946.

BOURKE, R., & SKINNER, Q. (edd.), *Popular Sovereignty in Historical Perspective*. Cambridge U.P., 2016.

BOWDEN, H. *Classical Athens and the Delphic Oracle: Divination and Democracy*. C.U.P., 2005.

BRADEEN, D. W., & MCGREGOR, M. F. *Studies in Fifth-Century Attic Epigraphy*. U. of Oklahoma P. for U. of Cincinnati, 1973.

BRAUND, D. (ed.), *Scythians and Greeks: Cultural Interactions in Scythia, Athens and the Early Roman Empire (Sixth Century BC–First Century AD)*. U. of Exeter P., 2005.

BRESSON, A. & ROUILLARD, P. (edd.), *L'Emporion*. Paris: De Boccard, 1993.

BRUMFIELD, A. C. *The Attic Festivals of Demeter and their Relation to the Agricultural Year*. New York: Arno, 1981.

BRUNT, P. A. *Studies in Greek History and Thought*. O.U.P., 1993.

BRYCE, T. R., & ZAHLE, J. *The Lycians*, i. Copenhagen: Museum Tusculanum P., 1986.

BUCHANAN, J. J. *Theorika*. Locust Valley, N.Y.: Augustin, 1962.

BURFORD, A. *The Greek Temple Builders at Epidauros: A Social and Economic Study of Building in the Asklepian Sanctuary, During the Fourth and Early Third Centuries BC*. Liverpool U.P., 1969.

BURRER, F., & MÜLLER, H. (edd.), *Kriegskosten und Kriegsfinanzierung in der Antike*. Darmstadt: Wissenschaftliche Buchgesellschaft, 2008.

BUXTON, R. (ed.), *Oxford Readings in Greek Religion*. O.U.P., 2000.

CALDER, W. M., III. *The Inscription from Temple G at Selinus*. GRBMon. iv 1963.

CALERO SECALL. I. *Leyes de Gortina*. Madrid: Ediciones Clásicas, 1997.

CAMP, J. McK. II, *The Athenian Agora: Site Guide*. Princeton: A.S.C.S.A., [5]2010.

CAPPS, E. *Classical Studies Presented to Edward Capps*. Princeton U.P., 1936.

CARGILL, J. L. *Athenian Settlements of the Fourth Century BC*. Leiden: Brill, 1995.

CARPENTER, R. *The Architects of the Parthenon*. Harmondsworth: Penguin, 1970.

CARRADICE, I. (ed.), *Coinage and Administration in the Athenian and Persian Empires*. BAR Int. Ser. cccxliii 1987.

CASTRIOTA, D. *Myth, Ethos, and Actuality: Official Art in Fifth-Century BC Athens*. U. of Wisconsin P., 1992.

CAVAIGNAC, E. *Études sur l'histoire financière d'Athènes au Ve siècle: le trésor d'Athènes de 480 à 404*. Paris; Fontemoing, 1908.

CAVANAUGH, M. B. *Eleusis and Athens: Documents in Finance, Religion and Politics in the Fifth Century BC*. Atlanta, Ga.: Scholars P., 1996.

CHAMBERS, M. H. *Text and Tradition . . . M. Chambers*. Claremont, Calif.: Regina, 1999.

CHANKOWSKI, V. *Athènes et Délos à l'époque classique: recherches sur l'administration du sanctuaire d'Apollon délien*. Athens: École Française d'Athènes, 2008)

CHRYSOSTOMIDES, J. *et al.* (edd.), *The Greek Islands and the Sea*. Camberley: Porphyrogenitus, 2004.

CLAIRMONT, C. *Patrios Nomos: Public Burial in Athens during the Fifth and Fourth Centuries BC: The Archaeological, Epigraphic–Literary and Historical Evidence*. BAR Int. Ser. clxi 1983.

CLINTON, K. *Myth and Cult: The Iconography of the Eleusinian Mysteries*. Stockholm: Swedish Institute at Athens, 1992.

—— *The Sacred Officials of the Eleusinian Mysteries*. Philadelphia: American Philosophical Society, 1974.

COHEN, D. J. *Law, Sexuality and Society: The Enforcement of Morals in Classical Athens*. C.U.P., 1991.

COHEN, E. E. *Ancient Athenian Maritime Courts*, Princeton U.P., 1973.

CONNELLY, J. B. *Portrait of a Priestess: Women and Ritual in Ancient Greece*. Princeton U.P., 2007.

CONSTANTAKOPOULOU, C. *The Dance of the Islands*. O.U.P., 2007.

CONZE, A. *Die attischen Grabreliefs*. Berlin: Spemann, 1890–1922.

COOK, B. F. *Greek Inscriptions*. London: British Museum Publications, 1987.

Cooper, C. (ed.), *Politics of Orality*. Leiden: Brill, 2007.

Cosmopoulos, M. B. (ed.), *Greek Mysteries: The Archaeology and Ritual of Ancient Greek Secret Cults*. London: Routledge, 2003.

Coulson, W. D. E., *et al.* (edd.), *The Archaeology of Athens and Attica under the Democracy*. Oxford: Oxbow, 1994.

Craik, E. M. *Euripides, Phoenician Women*. Warminster: Aris & Phillips, 1988.

Culasso Gastaldi, E. *Le prossenie ateniesi del IV secolo a.C.: Gli onorati asiatici*. Alessandria: Edizioni dell'Orso, 2004.

Daverio Rocchi, G. *Frontiera e confini nella Grecia antica*. Rome: 'L'Erma di Brestschneider, 1988.

Davies, J. K. *Athenian Propertied Families, 600–300 BC*. O.U.P., 1971. [Davies, *APF*]

—— *Democracy and Classical Greece*. London: Fontana, [2]1993.

Davison, C. C., with Lundgreen, B., ed. Waywell, G. B. *Pheidias: The Sculptures and Ancient Sources*. *BICS* Supp. cv 2009.

De Ste. Croix, G. E. M. *Athenian Democratic Origins and Other Essays*. O.U.P., 2004 (but essays written much earlier).

—— *The Origins of the Peloponnesian War*. London: Duckworth, 1972.

—— *Crux: Essays in Greek History Presented to G. E. M. de Ste. Croix*. *History of Political Thought* vi. i–ii 1985 = London: Duckworth, 1985.

Develin, R. *Athenian Officials, 684–321 BC*. C.U.P., 1989. [Develin, *AO*]

Dilts, M. R. *Heraclidis Lembi Excerpta Politiarum*. GRBMon. v 1971.

Dover, K. J. *Greek Popular Morality in the Time of Plato and Aristotle*. Oxford: Blackwell, 1974.

—— *The Greeks and Their Legacy* (*Collected Papers*, ii). Oxford: Blackwell, 1988.

—— *Owls to Athens: Essays on Classical Subjects Presented to Sir K. Dover*. O.U.P., 1990.

Dow, S. *Studies Presented to S. Dow*. GRBMon. x 1984.

Eckstein, F. *ἀναθήματα: Studien zu den Weihgeschenken strengen Stils im Heiligtum von Olympia*. Berlin: Mann, 1969.

Edmonson, J., & Hunter, V. (edd.), *Law and Social Status in Classical Athens*. O.U.P., 2000.

Ehrenberg, V. *Ancient Society and Institutions: Studies Presented to V. Ehrenberg*. Oxford: Blackwell, 1966.

Eidinow, E. *Oracles, Curses and Risk among the Ancient Greeks*. O.U.P., 2007.

Ekroth, G. *The Sacrificial Rituals of Greek Hero-Cults in the Archaic to the Early Hellenistic Periods*. Liège: Centre International d'Étude de la Religion Grecque Antique, 2002.

Engels, J. *Funerum sepulcrorumque magnificentia: Begräbnis- und Grabluxusgesetze in der griechisch-römischen Welt, mit einigen Ausblicken auf Einschränkungen des funeralen und sepulkralen Luxus im Mittelalter und in der Neuzeit*. *Hermes* Einz. lxxviii 1998.

Engen, D. T. *Honor and Profit: Athenian Trade Policy and the Economy and Society of Greece, 415–307 BCE*. U. of Mochigan P., 2010.

Études Delphiques. *BCH* Supp. iv 1977.

Fama, M. L., & Tusa, V. *Le stele del Meilichios di Selinunte*. Padua: Bottega d'Erasmo, 2000.

Ferguson, W. S. *The Treasurers of Athena*. Harvard U.P., 1932.

Ferlauto, F. *Il testo di Tucidide in traduzione latina di Lorenzo Valla*. U. di Palermo, Ist. di Fil. Greca, 1979.

Ferrario, S. B. *Historical Agency and the 'Great Man' in Classical Greece*. C.U.P., 2014.

Feyel, C. *Les Artisans dans les sanctuaires greques aux époques classique et hellénistique, à travers la documentation financière en Grèce*. Athens: École Française d'Athènes, 2006.

Figueira, T. J. *Athens and Aigina in the Age of Imperial Colonization*. Johns Hopkins U.P., 1991.

—— *Excursions in Epichoric History: Aiginetan Essays*. Lanham, Md.: Rowman & Littlefield, 1993.

—— *The Power of Money: Coinage and Politics in the Athenian Empire*. U. of Pennsylvania P., 1998.

Finley, M. I. *Studies in Land and Credit in Ancient Athens, 500–200 BC: The Horos-Inscriptions*. Rutgers U. P., 1952.

Fisher, N. R. E. *Sociable Man: Essays on Ancient Greek Sociable Behaviour, in Honour of Nick Fisher*. Swansea: Classical P. of Wales, 2011.

Flower, M. A. *The Seer in Ancient Greece*. U. of California P., 2008.

Foley, H. (ed.), *The Homeric 'Hymn to Demeter'*. Princeton U.P., 1994.

Fornara, C. W., & Samons, L. J., II, *Athens from Cleisthenes to Pericles*. U. of California P., 1991.

Forrest, W. G. *Herodotus and his World: Essays from a Conference in Memory of George Forrest*. O.U.P., 2003.

Foxhall, L. *Olive Cultivation in Ancient Greece: Seeking the Ancient Economy*. O.U.P., 2007.

Foxhall, L., & Lewis, A. (edd.), *Greek Law in its Political Setting: Justification Not Justice*. O.U.P., 1996.

Fraser, P. M., & Matthews, E. (edd.), *Lexicon of Greek Personal Names*. O.U.P., 1987– . Updated and searchable version <www.lgpn.ox.ac.uk>; updated version of vol. ii <www.seangb.org>. [*LGPN*]

Gabrielsen, V. *Financing the Athenian Fleet*. Johns Hopkins U.P., 1994.

Gagarin, M. *Drakon and Early Athenian Homicide Law*. Yale U.P., 1981.

—— *Writing Greek Law*. C.U.P., 2008.

Gagarin, M., & Cohen, D. (edd.), *The Cambridge Companion to Ancient Greek Law*. C.U.P., 2005.

Gager, J. *Curse Tablets and Binding Spells from Antiquity and the Ancient World*. O.U.P., 1992.

Gaifman, M. *Aniconomism in Greek Antiquity*. O.U.P., 2012.

Garlan, Y. *Amphores et timbres amphoriques grecs: entre erudition et idéologie*. Paris: De Boccard, 2000.

—— *Esclavage, guerre, économie en Grèce ancienne: Hommages à Yvon Garlan.* Rennes: Presses Universitaires de Rennes, 1997.

Garland, R. *Introducing New Gods: The Politics of Athenian Religion.* London: Duckworth, 1992.

Garnsey, P. D. A. *Cities, Peasants and Food in Classical Antiquity: Essays in Social and Economic History.* C.U.P., 1998.

—— *Famine and Food Supply in the Graeco-Roman World.* C.U.P., 1988.

Garuti, G. *Vir Bonus Dicendi Peritus: Omaggio dell' Università dell' Aquila a G. Garuti* (San Severo: Gerni, 1996)

Gauthier, P. *Symbola: Les Étrangers et la justice dans les cités grecques.* Nancy: Annales de l'Est, Mém. xlii 1972.

Gehrke, H.-J. *Stasis: Untersuchungen zu den inneren Kriegen in den griechischen Staaten des 5. und 4. Jahrhunderts v. Chr.* Munich: Beck, 1985.

Gell, W. *et al.* *The Unedited Antiquities of Attica, Comprising the Architectural Remains of Eleusis, Rhammus, Sunium and Thoricus.* London: Longman *et al.*, 1817.

Giornate Internazionali di Studi sull' area Elima, 19–22.ix.1991. Pisa: Scuola Normale Superiore & Comune di Gibellina, 1992.

Goldhill, S. D., & Osborne, R. G. (edd.), *Art and Text in Ancient Greek Culture.* C.U.P., 1994.

—— *Performance Culture and Athenian Democracy.* C.U.P., 1999.

Gomme, A. W., Andrewes, A., & Dover, K. J. *A Historical Commentary on Thucydides.* O.U.P., 1945–81. [Author, *HCT*]

Gorman, V. B. *Miletos: The Ornament of Ionia.* U. of Michigan P., 2001.

Graef, B., & Langlotz, E. *Die antiken Vasen von der Akropolis zu Athen.* Berlin: de Gruyter, 1925–33.

Graham, A. J. *Colony and Mother City in Ancient Greece.* Manchester U.P., 1964.

—— *Oikistes: Studies in Constitutions, Colonies, and Military Power in the Ancient World Offered in Honor of A J. Graham.* Leiden: Brill, 2002.

Greece, i (Geographical Handbook Series). Naval Intelligence Division, 1944.

Greco, E., & Lombardo, M. (edd.) *La Grande Iscrizione di Gortyna, Centoventi anni dopo la scoperta . . . 25-28.v.2004.* Athens: Scuola Archeologica Italiana di Atene, 2005.

Grotta, C. *Zeus Meilichios a Selinunte.* Rome: Bretschneider, 2009.

Gschnitzer, F. *Ein neuer spartanischer Staatsvertrag und die Verfassung des Peloponnesischen Bundes* (Beitr. kl. Phil. xciii). Meisenheim an der Glan: Hain, 1978.

Guarducci, M. *Epigrafia greca.* Rome: Istituto Poligrafico dello Stato, 1967–78.

Guido, M. *Sicily: An Archaeological Guide.* London: Faber, 1967.

Habicht, C. *Pausanias' Guide to Ancient Greece* (Sather Lectures l). U. of California P., 1985.

—— *Ἀττικά Ἐπιγραφικά· μελέτες πρός τιμήν τού C. Habicht.* Athens: Greek Epigraphic Society, 2009.

HÄGG, R., & ALROTH, B. (edd.), *Greek Sacrificial Ritual, Olympian and Chthonian: Proceedings of the Sixth International Seminar on Ancient Greek Cult . . . 25–27 April 1997*. Stockholm: Åström for Swedish Institute at Athens, 2005.

HAMMOND, N. G. L. *Studies in Greek History*. O.U.P., 1973.

HAMMOND, N. G. L., & GRIFFITH, G. T. *A History of Macedonia*, ii. O.U.P., 1979 [cited with the author *not* responsible for the passage in question bracketed].

HANSEN, M. H. (ed.) *The Athenian Ecclesia*. Copenhagen: Museum Tusculanum P., 1983.

—— *The Athenian Ecclesia, II*. Copenhagen: Museum Tusculanum P., 1989.

—— *The Polis as an Urban Centre and as a Political Community* (C.P.C. Acts iv.) Copenhagen: Munksgaard for Royal Danish Academy, 1997.

—— *The Shotgun Method: The Demography of the Ancient Greek City-State Culture*. U. of Missouri P., 2006.

—— *Polis and Politics: Studies in Ancient Greek History Presented to M. H. Hansen*. Copenhagen: Museum Tusculanum P., 2000.

HANSON, V. D. (ed.), *Hoplites: The Classical Greek Battle Experience*. London: Routledge, 1991.

HARDER, R. *Kleine Schriften*. Munich: Beck, 1960.

HARDING, P. E. *Epigraphy and the Greek Historian* <*. . . P. E. Harding*>. *Phoenix* Supp. xlvii 2008.

HARRIS, D. *The Treasures of the Parthenon and Erechtheion*. O.U.P., 1995.

HARRIS, E. M. *Democracy and the Rule of Law in Classical Athens*. New York: C.U.P., 2006.

HARRIS, E. M., & RUBINSTEIN, L. (edd.), *Law and the Courts in Ancient Greece*. London: Duckworth, 2004.

HARRISON, A. R. W. *The Law of Athens*, ii. O.U.P., 1971.

HATZOPOULOS, M. B., with PSILAKAKOU, B. (edd.), *Φωνῆς Χαρακτήρ Ἐθνικός* (Μελετήματα lii). Athens: Centre for Greek & Roman Antiquity, 2007.

HELLY, B. *L'État thessalien: Aleuas le Roux, les tétrades et les tagoi*. Lyon: Maison de l'Orient, 1995.

HENRY, A. S. *Honours and Privileges in Athenian Decrees*. Hildesheim: Olms, 1983.

—— *The Prescripts of Athenian Decrees*. *Mnemosyne* Supp. xlix 1977. [Henry, *Prescripts*]

HERMAN, G. *Morality and Behaviour in Classical Athens: A Social History*. C.U.P., 2006.

HIGBIE, C. *The Lindian Chronicle and the Greek Creation of their Past*. O.U.P., 2003.

HIGHBY, L. I. *The Erythrae Decree: Contribution to the Early History of the Delian League and the Peloponnesian Confederacy*. *Klio* Bhft. xxxvi 1936.

HIGNETT, C. *A History of the Athenian Constitution to the End of the Fifth Century BC*. O.U.P., 1952.

HILL, G. F., rev. MEIGGS, R., & ANDREWES, A. *Sources for Greek History between the Persian and Peloponnesian Wars*. O.U.P., 1951.

HODKINSON, S., & POWELL, A. (edd.), *Sparta: New Perspectives*. London: Duckworth with Classical P. of Wales, 1999.

HOOKER, G. W. (ed.), *Parthenos and Parthenon. G&R* Supp. to vol. ²x 1963.

HORNBLOWER, S. *A Commentary on Thucydides.* O.U.P., 1991–2008. [Hornblower, *Comm. Thuc.*]

—— *Mausolos.* O.U.P., 1982.

HORNBLOWER, S., & MATTHEWS, E. (edd),. *Greek Personal Names: Their Value as Evidence. PBA* civ 2000.

HORSTER, M., & KLÖCKNER, A. (edd)., *Civic Priests.* Berlin: de Gruyter, 2011.

HUMPHREYS, S. C. *The Strangeness of Gods.* O.U.P., 2004.

HUNT, P. *Slaves, Warfare, and Ideology in the Greek Historians.* C.U.P., 1998.

HURWIT, J. M. *The Athenian Acropolis: History, Mythology, and Archaeology from the Neolithic Era to the Present.* C.U.P., 1999.

IMMERWAHR, H. R. *Attic Script: A Survey.* O.U.P., 1990.

An Inventory of Archaic and Classical Poleis, ed. HANSEN, M. H., & NIELSEN, T. H. O.U.P., 2004. [*Inventory*]

ISAAC, B. *The Greek Settlements in Thrace, until the Macedonian Conquest.* Leiden: Brill, 1986.

ISAGER, S., & PEDERSEN, P. (edd.), *The Salmakis Inscription and Hellenistic Halikarnassos.* U.P. of Southern Denmark, 2004.

JACQUEMIN, A. *Offrandes monumentales à Delphes.* Athens: École Française d'Athènes, 1999.

JAMESON, M. H. *Cults and Rites in Ancient Greece : Essays on Religion and Society.* C.U.P., 2014.

JAMESON, M. H., JORDAN, D. R., & KOTANSKI, R. D. *A Lex Sacra from Selinous.* GRBMon. xi 1993.

JAMESON, M. H., RUNNELS, C. N., & VAN ANDEL, T. H. *A Greek Countryside: The Southern Argolid from Prehistory to the Present Day.* Stanford U.P., 1994.

JEFFERY, L. H. rev. JOHNSTON, A. W. *The Local Scripts of Archaic Greece.* O.U.P., 1990. [*LSAG*]

JOHNSTON, S. I., & STRUCK, P. T. (edd.), *Mantike: Studies in Ancient Divination.* Leiden: Brill, 2005.

JOHNSTONE, S. *A History of Trust in Ancient Greece.* U. of Chicago P., 2011.

JONES, N. F. *Public Organization in Ancient Greece.* Philadelphia: Am. Philos. Ass., 1987.

KALLET, L. *Money and the Corrosion of Power in Thucydides.* U. of California P., 2001.

KALLET-MARX, L. *Money, Expense and Naval Power in Thucydides' History, I–V. 24.* U. of California P., 1993.

KEARNS, E. *Ancient Greek Religion: A Sourcebook.* Chichester: Wiley–Blackwell, 2010.

—— *The Heroes of Attica. BICS* Supp. lvii 1989.

KEEN, A. G. *Dynastic Lycia. Mnemosyne* Supp. clxxviii 1998.

KEESLING, C. M. *The Votive Statues of the Athenian Acropolis.* C.U.P., 2005.

KERN, O. *Inscriptiones Graecae.* Bonn: Marcus & Weber, 1913.

KIRCHNER, J., rev. KLAFFENBACH, G. *Imagines Inscriptionum Atticarum*. Berlin: Mann, 1948.

—— *Prosopographia Attica*. Berlin: Reimer, 1901 [Kirchner, *PA*]

KLAFFENBACH, G. *Griechische Epigraphik*. Göttingen: Vandenhoeck & Ruprecht, ²1966.

KNOEPFLER, D. *Décrets érétriens de proxénie et de citoyenneté* (*Eretria: Fouilles et recherches*, xi). Lausanne: Payot, 2001.

KÖNIG, F. W. *Die Stele von Xanthos*, i (all published). Vienna: Gerold, 1936.

KOLBE, W. *Thukydides im Lichte der Urkunden*. Stuttgart: Kohlhammer, 1930.

KORRES, M. *From Pentelicon to the Parthenon: The Ancient Quarries and the Story of a Half-Worked Column Capital of the First Marble Parthenon*. Athens: Melissa, 1995.

KROLL, J. H. *Agoranomia: Studies in Money and Exchange Presented to John H. Kroll*. New York: American Numismatic Society, 2006.

KUNZE, E. *V Bericht über die Ausgrabungen in Olympia*. Berlin: De Gruyter, 1956.

KYRIELIS, H. (ed.), *Olympia, 1875–2000: 125 Jahre Deutsche Ausgrabungen . . . 9–11.xi.2000*. Mainz: von Zabern for Deutsches Archäologisches Institut, 2002.

LABARBE, J. *Thorikos: les testimonia*. (*Fouilles de Thorikos*, i.) Gent: Comité des Fouilles Belges en Grèce, 1977.

—— *Stemmata: Mélanges de philologie, d'histoire et d'archéologie grecques offertes à Jules Labarbe*. Liège & Louvain-la-Neuve: *L'Antiquité Classique*, 1987.

LABARRE, G. *Les Cités de Lesbos aux époques hellénistique et imperial*. Paris: De Boccard, 1996.

LAING, D. R. 'A New Interpretation of the Athenian Naval Catalogue *IG* ii² 1951.' U. of Cincinnati thesis, 1965.

LAMBERT, S. D. *Inscribed Athenian Laws and Decrees, 352/1–322/1 BC*. Leiden: Brill, 2012.

—— *Rationes Centesimarum: Sales of Public Land in Lycurgan Athens*. Amsterdam: Gieben, 1997.

——*The Phratries of Attica*. U. of Michigan P., 1993.

LAPATIN, K. D. S. *Chryselephantine Statuary in the Ancient Mediterranean World*. O.U.P., 2001.

LARSEN, J. A. O. *Greek Federal States: Their Institutions and History*. O.U.P., 1968.

—— *Representative Government in Greek and Roman History* (Sather Lectures xxviii). U. of California P., 1955.

LARSON, J. L. *Greek Heroine Cults*. U. of Wisconsin. P., 1995.

LAWTON, C. *Attic Document Reliefs*. O.U.P., 1995.

LEAKE, W. M. *Travels in Northern Greece*. London: Rodwell, 1835.

LEÃO, D. F., *et al.* (edd.), *Nomos: Direito e sociedade na Antiguidade Clássica*. U. of Coimbra P. & Madrid: Ediciones Clásicas, 2004.

LEFÈVRE, F. *L'Amphictionie pyléo-delphique: histoire et institutions* (BEFAR cclxxxviii). Paris: De Boccard for École Française d' Athènes, 1998.

LÉVEQUE, P. *Mélanges Pierre Lévêque*. Paris: Les Belles Lettres, 1988–95.

LÉVY, E. (ed.), *La Codification des lois dans l'Antiquité . . . 27–29.xi.1997* (Paris: De Boccard for U. de Strasbourg, 2000.

LEWIS, D. M. (1928–94), *Selected Papers in Greek and Near Eastern History*. C.U.P., 1997.

—— *Ritual, Finance, Politics: Athenian Democratic Accounts Presented to David Lewis.* O.U.P., 1994.

LEWIS, D. M. (b. 1985), *Greek Slave Systems and their Eastern Neighbours: A Comparative Study.*

Lexcon Iconographicum Mythologiae Classicae, edd. ACKERMANN, H. C., & GISLER, J.-R. Zurich: Artemis, 1981– . [*LIMC*]

LGPN. See Fraser & Matthews.

LINDERS, T. *The Treasurers of the Other Gods in Athens and their Functions*. Meisenheim an Glan: Hain, 1975.

LINDERS, T., & NORDQUIST, G. (edd.), *Gifts for the Gods*. Stockholm: Almqvist & Wiksell International for Uppsala U., 1987.

LIPSIUS, J. H. *Das Attische Recht und Rechtsverfahren*. Leipzig: Reisland, 1905–15.

LÖHR, C. *Griechische Familienweihungen: Untersuchungen einer Repräsentationsform von ihren Anfängen bis zum Ende des 4. Jhs. v. Chr.* Rahden (Westf.): Leidorf, 2000.

LOOMIS, W. T. *The Spartan War Fund. Historia* Einz. lxxiv 1992.

—— *Wages, Welfare Costs and Inflation in Classical Athens*. U. of Michigan P., 1998.

LORAUX, N. *L'Invention d'Athènes: histoire de l'oraison funèbre dans la 'cité classique'*. Paris: Mouton, 1981.

LOW, P. A. *Interstate Relations in Classical Greece*. C.U.P., 2007.

LSAG. See Jeffery.

LURAGHI, N. *The Ancient Messenians*. C.U.P., 2008.

MA, J., PAPAZARKADAS, N., & PARKER, R. C. T. (edd.), *Interpreting the Athenian Empire*. London: Duckworth, 2009.

MACDOWELL, D. M. *Athenian Homicide Law in the Age of the Orators*. Manchester U.P., 1963.

—— *Demosthenes, Against Meidias*. O.U.P., 1990.

—— *The Law in Classical Athens*. London: Thames & Hudson, 1978.

—— *Law, Rhetoric and Comedy in Classical Athens: Essays in Honour of D. M. MacDowell.* Swansea: Classical Press of Wales, 2004.

MACKAY, E. A. (ed.), *Orality, Literacy, Memory in the Ancient Greek and Roman World. Mnemosyne* Supp. ccxcviii 2008.

MAFFI, A. *Il diritto di famiglia nel Codice di Gortina*. Milan: C.U.E.M., 1997.

—— *L'iscrizione di Ligdamis*. Trieste: Bernardi, 1988.

MARGINESU, G. *Gli Epistati dell'Acropoli: Edilizia sacra nella città di Pericle, 447/6–433/2 a.C.* Paestum: Pandemos, 2010.

MARINCOLA, J. (ed.), *A Companion to Greek and Roman Historiography*. Oxford: Blackwell, 2007.

MARK, I. *The Sanctuary of Athena Nike in Athens: Architectural Stages and Chronology.* (AIA Monographs² ii.) *Hesperia* Supp. xxvi 1993.

MASTRONARDE, D. J. *Euripides, Phoenician Women.* C.U.P., 1994.

MATTHAIOU, A. P. *"καττάδε ἔδοξε τοῖς Λακεδαιμονίοις": ἐπιγραφὲς δημοσίου χαρακτῆρα ἀπὸ τὴν Σπάρτη τοῦ 5ου αἰῶνα π.Χ.* Athens: Greek Epigraphic Society, 2006.

—— 'Studies in Attic Inscriptions and the History of the Fifth Century BC' La Trobe U. thesis, 2009.

—— *τὰ ἐν τῆι στήληι γεγραμμένα: Six Fifth-Century Greek Historical Inscriptions.* Athens; Greek Epigraphic Society, 2011.

—— *The Athenian Empire on Stone Revisited.* Athens: Greek Epigraphic Society, 2010.

MATTINGLY, D. J., & SALMON, J. B. (edd.), *Economies beyond Agriculture in the Classical World.* London: Routledge, 2001.

MATTINGLY, H. B. *The Athenian Empire Restored.* U. of Michigan P., 1996. [Mattingly, *AER*]

—— *Ἀθηναίων ἐπίσκοπος: Studies in Honour of H. B. Mattingly.* Athens: Greek Epigraphic Society, 2014.

MAURER, K. *Interpolation in Thucydides. Mnemosyne* Supp. cl 1995.

MEADOWS, A., & SHIPTON, K. (edd.), *Money and its Uses in the Ancient Greek World.* O.U.P., 2001.

MEIGGS, R. *The Athenian Empire.* O.U.P., 1972.

—— *Trees and Timber in the Ancient Mediterranean World.* O.U.P., 1982.

MELVILLE-JONES, J. R. *Testimonia Numaria.* London: Spink. 1993–2007.

MERITT, B. D. *Athenian Financial Documents of the Fifth Century.* U. of Michigan P., 1932. [Meritt, *AFD*]

—— *Documents on Athenian Tribute.* Harvard U.P., 1937.

—— *The Athenian Calendar in the Fifth Century.* Harvard U.P. for A.S.C.S.A., 1928.

—— *The Athenian Year* (Sather Lectures xxxii). U. of California P., 1961.

—— *Φόρος: Tribute to B. D. Meritt.* Locust Valley, N.Y.: Augustin, 1974.

MERITT, B. D., & WEST, A. B. *The Athenian Assessment of 425 BC.* U. of Michigan P., 1934.

METCALF, W. E. (ed.), *The Oxford Handbook of Greek and Roman Coinage.* O.U.P., 2012.

MEYER, E. *Forschungen zur alten Geschichte.* Halle: Niemeyer, 1892–9.

MEYER, M. *Die griechischen Urkundenreliefs. AM Beiheft* xiii 1989.

MILES, M. M. (ed.), *Autopsy in Athens: Recent Archaeological Research on Athens and Attica.* Oxford: Oxbow, 2015.

—— *The Athenian Agora*, xxxi. *The City Eleusinion.* Princeton: A.S.C.S.A., 1998.

MILLETT, P. C. *Lending and Borrowing in Ancient Athens.* C.U.P., 1991.

MITCHELL, L. G., & RHODES, P. J. (edd.), *The Development of the Polis in Archaic Greece.* London: Routledge, 1997.

Morrison, J. S., *et al. The Athenian Trireme: The History and Reconstruction of an Ancient Greek Warship.* C.U.P., ²2000.

Muller-Dufeu, M. *La Sculpture grecque: Sources littéraires et épigraphiques.* Paris: École Nationale Supérieure des Beaux-Arts, 2002.

Müller-Strübing, H. *Aristophanes und die historische Kritik.* Leipzig: Teubner, 1873.

Murray, O. & Price, S. R. F. (edd.), *The Greek City from Homer to Alexander.* O.U.P., 1990.

Mussche, H. F. *Thorikos: A Mining Town in Ancient Attika.* (*Fouilles de Thorikos*, ii.) Gent: École Archéologique Belge en Grèce, 1998.

Mylonas, G. E. *Φίλια ἔπη εἰς Γεώργιον Ε. Μυλωνᾶν δια τα 60 ἔτη τοῦ ἀνασκαφικοῦ του ἔργου.* Athens: Greek Archaeological Society, 1986–90.

Newby, Z., & Leader-Newby, R. (edd.), *Art and Inscriptions in the Ancient World.* C.U.P., 2007.

Nielsen, T. H. *Arkadia and its Poleis in the Archaic and Classical Periods* (Hypomnemata cxl). Göttingen: Vandenhoeck & Ruprecht, 2002.

Ogden, D. (ed.), *Companion to Greek Religion.* Malden, Mass.: Blackwell, 2007.

—— *Magic, Witchcraft, and Ghosts in the Greek and Roman Worlds.* O.U.P., 2002.

Olson, S. D. *Aristophanes, Peace.* O.U.P., 1998.

Olympische Forschungen. Berlin: de Gruyter, 1844– .

Osborne, M. J. *Φιλαθήναιος: Studies in Honour of M. J. Osborne.* Athens: Greek Epigraphic Society, 2010.

Osborne, R. G. *Athens and Athenian Democracy.* C.U.P., 2010.

—— *Demos: The Discovery of Classical Attika.* C.U.P., 1985.

—— *Greece in the Making.* London: Routledge, ²2009.

—— *The History Written on the Classical Greek Body.* C.U.P., 2011.

Ostwald, M. *From Popular Sovereignty to the Sovereignty of Law.* U. of California P., 1986.

—— *Language and History in Ancient Greek Culture.* U. of Pennsylvania P., 2009.

—— *Nomos and the Beginnings of the Athenian Democracy.* O.U.P., 1969.

—— *Nomodeiktes: Greek Studies in Honor of M. Ostwald.* U. of Michigan P., 1993.

Page, D. L. *Further Greek Epigrams.* C.U.P., 1981.

Palagia, O. (ed.), *Art in Athens during the Peloponnesian War.* C.U.P., 2009.

Papazarkadas, N. *Sacred and Public Land in Ancient Athens.* O.U.P., 2011.

Parlama, L., & Stampolidis, N. Ch. (edd.), *Athens: The City beneath the City: Antiquities from the Metropolitan Railway Excavations.* Athens: Greek Ministry of Culture: Museum of Cycladic Art, 2000.

Parker, R. C. T. *Athenian Religion: A History.* O.U.P., 1996.

—— *Miasma.* O.U.P., 1983.

—— *On Greek Religion.* Cornell U.P., 2011.

—— *Polytheism and Society at Athens*. O.U.P., 2005.

Paton, J. M (ed.), *The Erechtheum*. Harvard U.P., 1927.

Pečírka, J. *The Formula for the Grant of Enktesis in Attic Inscriptions*. Prague: Charles University, 1966.

Peppas-Delmousou, D. *The Institution of Public Accountants in Ancient Greece*. Athens: Institute of Certified Public Accountants of Greece, 1963.

Perlman, P. *City and Sanctuary in Ancient Greece: The Theorodokia in the Peloponnese* (Hypomnemata cxxi). Göttingen: Vandenhoeck & Ruprecht, 2000.

Petrović, A., Petrović, I., & Thomas, E. V. (edd.), *The Materiality of Text: Placements, Presences and Perceptions of Inscribed Text in Classical Antiquity*. Leiden: Brill, forthcoming.

Piccirilli, L. *Gli arbitrati interstatali greci*. Pisa: Marlin, 1973.

Pistorius, T. *Hegemoniestreben und Autonomiesicherung in der griechischen Vertragspolitik klassischer und hellenistischer Zeit*. Frankfurt: Lang, 1985.

Platt, V. J. *Facing the Gods: Epiphany and Representation in Graeco-Roman Art, Literature and Religion*. C.U.P., 2011.

Poccetti, P. (ed.), *L'onomastica dell'Italia antica: aspetti linguistici, storici, culturali, tipologici e classificatori*. Rome: École Française de Rome, 2009.

Poralla, P., rev. Bradford, A. S. *Prosopographie der Lakedaimonier bis auf die Zeit Alexanders des Grossen/A Prosopography of Lacedaemonians from the Earliest Times to the Death of Alexander the Great*. Chicago: Ares, 1985.

Pouilloux, J. *La Forteresse de Rhamnonte (étude de topographie et d'histoire)*. Paris: De Boccard, 1954.

—— *Recherches sur l'histoire et les cultes de Thasos*, i. Paris: De Boccard, 1954.

Pouilloux, J., & Roux, G. *Énigmes à Delphes*. Paris: De Boccard, 1963.

Πρακτικά Ά Διεθνούς Σιφναϊκού Συμποσίου, Σίφνος, 25–8.vi.1998. Athens: Society of Siphnian Studies, 2000,

Πρακτικά τού Η΄ Διεθνούς Συνεδρίου Ἑλληνικῆς καί Λατινικῆς Ἐπιγραφικῆς, 1982, i (Athens: Ὑπουργείο Πολιτισμού καί Ἐπιστημών, 1984).

Price, S. R. F. (1999), *Religions of the Ancient Greeks*. C.U.P., 1999.

Pritchett, W. K. *Ancient Athenian Calendars on Stone*. U. Calif. Pub. Cl. Arch. iv. iv 1963.

—— *Athenian Calendars and Ecclesias*. Amsterdam: Gieben, 2001.

—— *Marathon*. U. Calif. Pub. Cl. Arch. iv. ii 1960.

—— *The Choiseul Marble*. U. Calif. Pub. Cl. Stud. v 1970.

—— *The Greek State at War*. U. of California P., 1974–91 (vol. i originally published as *Ancient Greek Military Practices*, i: U. Calif. Pub. Cl. Stud. vii 1971).

——*Thucydides' Pentekontaetia and Other Essays*. Amsterdam: Gieben, 1995.

Pritchett, W. K., & Neugebauer, O. *The Calendars of Athens*. Harvard U.P. for A.S.C.S.A., 1947.

PSOMA, S. *Olynthe et les Chalcidiens de Thrace: études de numismatique et d'histoire*. Stuttgart: Steiner, 2001.

PULLEYN, S. D. *Prayer in Greek Religion*. O.U.P., 1997.

REDEN, S. VON, *Money in Classical Antiquity*. C.U.P., 2010.

RHODES, P. J. *Aristotle, The Athenian Constitution* (Penguin Classics). Harmondsworth: Penguin, 1984.

—— *The Athenian Boule*. O.U.P., 1972. [Rhodes, *Boule*]

—— *The Athenian Empire*. *G&R* New Surveys xvii, rev. 1993.

—— *A Commentary on the Aristotelian Athenaion Politeia*. O.U.P., 1981. [Rhodes, *Comm. Ath. Pol.*]

—— *A History of the Classical Greek World, 478–323 BC*. Chichester: Wiley-Blackwell, ²2010.

—— *Greek History and Epigraphy: Essays in Honour of P. J. Rhodes*, Swansea: Classical P. of Wales, 2009.

RHODES, P. J., with LEWIS, D. M. *The Decrees of the Greek States*. O.U.P., 1997. [Rhodes with Lewis]

RICHARDSON, N. J. *The Homeric Hymn to Demeter*. O.U.P., 1974.

RICKERT, G. A. *ἕκων and ἄκων in Early Greek Thought*. Atlanta, Ga.: Scholars P., 1989.

RIDGWAY, B. S. *Fifth Century Styles in Greek Sculpture*. Princeton U.P., 1981.

ROBERT, J. & L. *Fouilles d'Amyzon en Carie*, i. Paris: De Boccard, 1983.

ROBERT, L. *Collection Froehner*, i. *Inscriptions grecques*. Paris: Éditions des Bibliothèques Nationales, 1936.

—— *Opera Minora Selecta*. Amsterdam: Hakkert, 1969–90.

—— trans. Engelmann, H. *Die Epigraphik der klassischen Welt*. Bonn: Habelt, 1970.

ROBERTSON, N. *Religion and Reconciliation in Greek Cities: The Sacred Laws of Selinus and Cyrene*. O.U.P., 2010.

ROBINSON, E. S. G. *Essays in Greek Coinage Presented to Stanley Robinson*. O.U.P., 1968.

ROEHL, H. *Imagines Inscriptionum Graecarum Antiquissimarum, in Usum Scholarum*. Berlin: Reimer, ³1907.

ROSENMEYER, T. G. *Cabinet of the Muses: Essays on Classical and Comparative literature in Honor of Thomas G. Rosenmeyer*. Atlanta, Ga.: Scholars Press, 1990.

ROUX, G. *L'Amphictionie, Delphes et le temple d'Apollon au IVᵉ siècle*. Paris: De Boccard for Lyon: Maison de l' Orient, 1979.

ROSIVACH, V. J. *The System of Public Sacrifice in Fourth-Century Athens*. Atlanta, Ga.: Scholars P., 1994.

RUSCHENBUSCH, E. *Solon: Das Gesetzeswerk—Fragmente*, ed. BRINGMANN, K. *Historia* Einz. ccxv 2010.

RUTHERFORD, I. *State Pilgrims and Sacred Observers in Ancient Greece*. C.U.P., 2013.

SAGE, M. M. *Warfare in Ancient Greece: A Sourcebook*. London: Routledge, 1996.

SALMON, P. *La Politique égyptienne d'Athènes (VIe et Ve siècles avant J.-C.)*. Brussels: Palais des Académies, 1981.

SAMARAN, C. M. D. (ed.), *L'Historie et ses méthodes*. Paris: Gallimard, 1961.

SANFILIPPO, C. *Studi in onore di Cesare Sanfilippo*. Milan: Giuffrè, 1982–91.

SAMONS, L. J., II. *Empire of the Owl: Athenian Imperial Finance*. *Historia* Einz. cxlii 2000.

SAMUEL, A. E. *Greek and Roman Chronology* (HdA I. vii). Munich: Beck, 1972.

SÁNCHEZ, P. *L'Amphictionie des Pyles et de Delphes*. *Historia* Einz. cxlviii 2001.

SAUPPE, H. *Satura Philologica. Hermanno Sauppio Obtulit Amicorum Conlegarum Decas*. Berlin: Weidmann, 1879.

SCOTT, M. C. *Delphi and Olympia: The Spatial Politics of Panhellenism in the Archaic and Classical Periods*. C.U.P., 2010.

SEAFORD, R. A. S. *Reciprocity and Ritual: Homer and Tragedy in the Developing City-State*. O.U.P., 1994.

Second International Symposium on Ship Construction in Antiquity: Proceedings. Athens: Hellenic Institute for the Preservation of Nautical Tradition, 1990.

SHEAR, J. L. *Polis and Revolution: Responding to Oligarchy in Classical Athens*. C.U.P., 2011.

SHEAR, T. L., JR. *Trophies of Victory: Public Buildings in Periklean Athens*. Princeton U.P. for Princeton University Department of Art and Archaeology, 2016.

SHIPLEY, D. G. J. *A History of Samos, 800–188 BC*. O.U.P., 1987.

Sicilia Epigraphica: Atti del convegno internazionale Erice, 15–18.x.1998. *Ann.Pisa*[4]*: Quaderni* i–ii 1999.

SICKINGER, J. P. *Public Records and Archives in Classical Athens*. U. of North Carolina P., 1999.

SMARCZYK, B. *Untersuchungen zur Religionspolitik und politischen Propaganda Athens im Delisch-Attischen Seebund*. Munich: tuduv, 1990.

SOMMERSTEIN, A. H. *Aeschylus, Eumenides*. C.U.P., 1989.

—— & BAYLISS, A. J. *Oath and State in Ancient Greece*. Berlin: de Gruyter, 2013.

—— & FLETCHER, J. (edd.), *Horkos: The Oath in Greek Society*. Exeter: Bristol Phoenix P., 2007.

—— & TORRANCE, I. C. (edd.), *Oaths and Swearing in Ancient Greece*. Berlin: de Gruyter, 2014.

SOURVINOU-INWOOD, C. *Athenian Myths and Festivals: Aglauros, Erechtheus, Plynteria, Panathenaia, Dionysia*. O.U.P., 2011.

—— *'Reading' Greek Death, to the End of the Classical Period*. O.U.P., 1995.

STEWART, A. *Greek Sculpture: An Exploration*. Yale U.P., 1990.

STROUD, R. S. *Drakon's Law on Homicide*. U. Calif. Pub. Cl. Stud. iii 1968.

—— *The Athenian Empire on Stone*. Athens: Greek Epigraphic Society, 2006.

—— *ἄξων: Studies in Honor of Ronald S. Stroud*. Athens: Greek Epigraphic Society, 2015.

Stupperich, R. *Staatsbegräbnis und Privatgrabmal im klassischen Athen.* Münster U. thesis, 1977.

Suter, A. *The Narcissus and the Pomegranate: An Archaeology of the Homeric Hymn to Demeter.* U. of Michigan P., 2002.

Symposion 1995. AGR xi 1997.

Symposion 2005. AGR xix 2007.

Taylor, C., & Vlassopoulos, K. (edd.), *Communities and Networks in the Ancient Greek World.* O.U.P., 2015.

Thesaurus Cultus et Rituum Antiquorum. Los Angeles: Getty Publications for Basel: Fondation pour le Lexicon Iconographicum Mythologiae Classicae, 2004–14. [*ThesCRA*]

Thompson, E. M., *et al. Facsimiles of Ancient Manuscripts, etc.: Second Series.* London: New Palaeographical Society, 1913–30.

Thomson, G. D. *Geras: Studies Presented to George Thomson.* Prague: Charles U., 1963.

Threatte, L. *The Grammar of Attic Inscriptions.* Berlin: de Gruyter, 1980–96.

Tomlinson, R. A. *Argos and the Argolid.* London: Routledge, 1972.

Tracy, S. V. *Athenian Democracy in Transition: Attic Letter-Cutters of 340–290 BC.* U. of California P., 1995.

—— *Athenian Lettering of the Fifth Century BC: The Rise of the Professional Letter Cutter.* Berlin: De Gruyter, 2016.

—— *Studies in Greek Epigraphy and History in Honor of S. V. Tracy* (Ausonius Éditions, Études xxvi). Paris: De Boccard for U. de Bordeaux III, 2010.

Traill, J. S. *Persons of Ancient Athens.* Toronto: Athenians, 1994–2012. The website <www.chass.utoronto.ca/attica> contains *addenda* and *corrigenda*, and allows searches for names beginning Β, Γ or Δ.

Travlos, J. *Pictorial Dictionary of Ancient Athens.* London: Thames & Hudson for Deutsches Archäologisches Institut, 1971.

Tréheux, J. *Comptes et inventaires dans la cité grecque: Actes du colloque international d'épigraphie tenu à Neuchâtel 1986 en l'honneur de J. Tréheux.* Geneva: Droz for U. de Neuchâtel, Faculté des Lettres, 1988.

Treves, P. *Xenia: Scritti in onore di P. Treves.* Rome; L'Erma di Bretschneider, 1985.

Trümpy, C. *Untersuchungen zu den altgriechischen Monatsnamen und Monatsfolgen.* Heidelberg: Winter, 1997.

Virgilio, B. *Epigrafia e storiografia.* Pisa: Giardini, 1988.

Vlachopoulos, A. G. (ed.), trans. Doumas, A. *Archaeology: Euboea and Central Greece.* Athens: Melissa, 2009.

Vollgraff, C. W. *Le Décret d'Argos relatif à un pacte entre Knossos et Tylissos.* Amsterdam: Noord-Hollandsche Uitgevers Maatschapij for Kon. Ned. Akad., 1948.

Wackernagel, J., ed. Langslow, D. R. *Lectures on Syntax, with Special Reference to Greek, Latin and Germanic.* O.U.P., 2009.

Wade-Gery, H. T. *Essays in Greek History*. Oxford: Blackwell, 1958.

Welwei, K.-W. *Unfreie im antiken Kriegsdienst*. Stuttgart: Steiner, 1974–88.

Westermark, U., & Jenkins, G. K. *The Coinage of Kamarina*. London: Royal Numismatic Society, 1980.

Whitehead, D. *The Demes of Attica*. Princeton U.P., 1986.

—— *The Ideology of the Athenian Metic*. *PCPS* Supp. iv 1971.

Wijma, S. M. *Embracing the Immigrant: The Participation of Metics in Athenian Polis Religion (5th–4th century BC)* *Historia* Einz. ccxxxiii 2014.

Wilamowitz-Moellendorff, U. von. *Aus Kydathen*. Berlin: Weidmann, 1880.

Wilhelm, A. *Abhandlungen und Beiträge zur griechischen Inschriftenkunde*. Leipzig: Zentralantiquariat der D.D.R. → Vienna: Verlag der Österreichischen Akademie der Wissenschaften, 1984–2003.

—— *Akademieschriften zur griechischen Inschriftenkunde*. Leipzig: Zentralantiquariat der D.D.R., 1974.

—— *Ἀττικαὶ Ἐπιγραφαί· πρακτικὰ συμποσίου εἰς μνήμην A. Wilhelm*. Athens: Greek Epigraphic Society, 2004.

Willetts, R. F. *The Law Code of Gortyn*. Berlin: de Gruyter, 1967.

Wilson, P. J. *The Athenian Institution of the Khoregia*. C.U.P., 2000.

Woodhead, A. G. *The Study of Greek Inscriptions*. C.U.P., 1959; [2]1981.

Yalouris, A. & N. *Olympia: The Museum and Sanctuary*. Athens: Ἐκδοτικὴ Ἀθηνῶν, 1991.

Zizza, C. *Le iscrizioni nella Periegesi di Pausania: Commento ai testi epigrafici*. Pisa: E.T.S., 2006.

INDEX I

PERSONS AND PLACES

(Figures in ordinary type refer to pages;
figures in **bold** type refer by number to inscriptions.)

INDEX II
SUBJECTS

(Figures in ordinary type refer to pages;
figures in **bold** type refer by number to inscriptions.)

INDEX III

SIGNIFICANT GREEK WORDS

The manufacturer's authorised representative in the EU for product safety is Oxford University Press España S.A. of El Parque Empresarial San Fernando de Henares, Avenida de Castilla, 2 - 28830 Madrid (www.oup.es/en or product.safety@oup.com). OUP España S.A. also acts as importer into Spain of products made by the manufacturer.
Printed and bound by CPI Group (UK) Ltd, Croydon, CR0 4YY
30/01/2026
02045254-0003